1810	Initial success of Latin-American independence movement
1815	Battle of Waterloo (June 20) Vienna settlement reshaping Europe after Napoleonic wars
1823	Monroe Doctrine set forth: U.S. opposed to fresh intervention by European powers in New World
1830	Revolutions in France, Belgium, Poland
1832	First Reform Bill in Britain: initial step toward British political democracy
1846	Repeal of Corn Laws in Britain: victory of new industrial classes
1848	*Communist Manifesto,* by Marx and Engels Wave of liberal and nationalistic revolutions in Europe
1851	(December 2) *Coup d'état* in France by Louis Napoleon, soon to be Emperor Napoleon III
1853	U. S. Commodore Perry's visit to Japan: prelude to rapid Japanese emergence as important power
1859	Darwin's *Origin of Species:* landmark in nineteenth-century scientific and intellectual revolution
1861	Outbreak of Civil War in U.S. Emancipation of Russian serfs by Tsar Alexander II
1866	Austro-Prussian War: Bismarck unifying Germany under Prussia
1867	British North America Act (Canada a dominion): start of transformation of British Empire into the Commonwealth *Ausgleich* (compromise): Habsburg Empire reorganized as dual monarchy

A
HISTORY
OF
CIVILIZATION

CRANE BRINTON

McLean Professor of Ancient and Modern History, Harvard University

JOHN B. CHRISTOPHER

University of Rochester

ROBERT LEE WOLFF

Harvard University

A HISTORY OF CIVILIZATION

VOLUME II: 1715 to the Present

PRENTICE-HALL, INC.   *Englewood Cliffs*

PRENTICE-HALL HISTORY SERIES
Donald C. McKay, Editor
Harvard University

Grateful acknowledgment is made to the following publishers for granting permission to use the material quoted on the pages indicated: *George Allen & Unwin Ltd.,* 366; *Ernest Benn Limited,* 572; *Christy & Moore Ltd.,* 639; *Duell, Sloan & Pearce, Inc.,* 643; *E. P. Dutton & Co., Inc.,* 17, 21, 48, 56, 57, 61, 62, 84, 85, 122, 148, 149, 150, 157, 159, 209, 215; *Hafner Publishing Company,* 59, 60; *Harcourt, Brace and Company, Inc.,* 456; *Harper & Brothers,* 19, 404; *Harvard University Press,* 478, 619; *William Hodge & Co. Ltd.,* 393; *Houghton Mifflin Company,* 129, 138, 526; *Alfred A. Knopf, Inc.,* 623; *The Macmillan Co.,* 204, 217, 431, 447, 461; *Methuen & Co. Ltd.,* 573; *Oxford University Press (London),* 349, 626; *Oxford University Press (New York),* 493; *Princeton University Press,* 581; *Random House, Inc.,* 222, 226; *Charles Scribner's Sons,* 341; *University of California Press,* 48; *Yale University Press,* 338.

"The White Man's Burden" on page 403 is from "The Five Nations" by Rudyard Kipling. Copyright 1903 by Rudyard Kipling, reprinted by permission of Mrs. George Bambridge, Doubleday & Company, Inc., and Methuen & Co. Ltd. "The Rowers" on page 427 and "For All We Have and Are" on page 449 are from "The Years Between" by Rudyard Kipling. Copyright 1919 by Rudyard Kipling, reprinted by permission of Mrs. George Bambridge, Doubleday & Company, Inc., and Methuen & Co. Ltd.

Fourth printing....April, 1956

Printed in the United States of America
38983

Acknowledgments

IN A BOOK of this magnitude it would be quite impossible to make adequate acknowledgment of all our collaborators. They begin, of course, with all those who have written, or made, history in the past. On a far more modest scale, it would be very difficult even to assemble the names of all those who have contributed in a very immediate way, through suggestion or criticism. The following, however, have read all or part of the two volumes and have made extensive and helpful suggestions, resulting in many cases in significant improvement. To these gentlemen go our very warm thanks: Professors Richard V. Burks, Wayne University; Leland H. Carlson, Northwestern University; Myron P. Gilmore, Harvard University; E. H. Harbison, Princeton University; Harry Kimber, Michigan State College; Harry R. Rudin, Yale University; Kenneth Setton, Columbia University; Robert A. Spiller, University of Pennsylvania; and Henry R. Winkler, Rutgers University. We are also grateful to Donald C. McKay, of Harvard University, who has contributed both guidance and enthusiasm ever since the project was in the early planning stages. Finally, we are grateful to the members of the Prentice-Hall staff, who have given their skills and energies without stint in seeing this book through all its complicated processes.

Crane Brinton
John B. Christopher
Robert Lee Wolff

Maps   *by Vaughn Gray*

Contents

Freudianism.   V: POLITICAL AND SOCIAL THOUGHT. Mosca and
Pareto. Political Thought in Review.

XXVI: Communist Russia 1917-1941

I: INTRODUCTION. II: THE RUSSIAN REVOLUTION OF 1917. The Immediate Background. The March Revolution. The Provisional Government. Lenin and Bolshevism. The Coming of the November Revolution. The Constituent Assembly. III: WAR COMMUNISM AND NEP, 1917-1928. War Communism. Civil War. Why the Counter-Revolution Failed. NEP ("The New Economic Policy"). The Struggle for Power: Stalin versus Trotsky. The Struggle for Power: Stalin's Victory. IV: STALIN'S SUPREMACY: RUSSIAN INTERNAL AFFAIRS, 1928-1941. Collectivized Agriculture. Industrialization. The Social Impact. The Purge Trials. The Authoritarian State. The Russian Thermidor? V: SOVIET FOREIGN POLICY, 1918-1941. Foreign Office and Comintern, 1918-1928. Stalin and the West, 1929-1939. Stalin and the Second World War. VI: CONCLUSION.

XXVII: The Rise of Fascism 1918-1939

I: INTRODUCTION. II: ITALY AND FASCISM. The Setting. Mussolini: Early Career. Mussolini: Rise to Power. The "March" on Rome. The Fascist Dictatorship. The Corporative State. Other Fascist Domestic Policies. Fascist Foreign Policy and Its Consequences. The Forerunners of Fascism. III: GERMANY AND THE WEIMAR REPUBLIC, 1918-1933. The Impact of Defeat. Postwar Political Alignments and Activities. The Weimar Constitution, 1919. Right and Left Extremism, 1920-1922. Hitler: Early Career. Beginnings of the Nazi Party. The Inflation, 1922-1923. The Consequences of Inflation. The End of Inflation, 1923-1924. Recovery at Home, 1924-1929. "Fulfillment" Abroad, 1925-1930. The Impact of the Depression, 1929-1931. The Republic in Danger, 1931-1932. Hitler: Rise to Power, 1932-1933. IV: GERMANY UNDER HITLER, 1933-1939. The Nazi Dictatorship. The "Blood Purge" of 1934. Racism. Legal and Economic Policies. Religion and Culture. The Bases of Foreign Policy. V: THE FAILURE OF PARLIAMENTARISM IN SPAIN AND EASTERN EUROPE, 1918-1939. Spain: The Background. Birth of the Spanish Republic. Crisis of the Spanish Republic, 1933-1936. The Spanish Civil War, 1936-1939. Eastern Europe. Austria. Hungary. Yugoslavia. Other Authoritarian Regimes. Fascism in Review.

CONTENTS

XXVIII: The Atlantic Democracies
During the Twenty Years' Truce   567

I: INTRODUCTION.   II. GREAT BRITAIN. The Postwar Depression. Textiles and Coal. The Conservative Program. The Labor Program. Postwar Politics. Settlement of the Irish Question. The British Commonwealth of Nations. The Abdication Episode. III: FRANCE. The Impact of the War. Social and Political Tensions. The Stavisky Case and the Popular Front. Divided France. IV: THE UNITED STATES. The Impact of the War. Isolationism. The Road to International Leadership. Boom—and Bust. The New Deal. The New Deal in Perspective. Confident America. V: INTERNATIONAL POLITICS, 1919-1932. The "Era of Fulfillment." The League of Nations. Attempts at Disarmament, 1922-1932. Why "Fulfillment" Faded. The Halting Partnership of France and Britain. The Aggressors.   VI: THE ROAD TO WAR, 1931-1939. The First Step: Manchuria, 1931. The Second Step: German Rearmament, 1935-1936. The Third Step: Ethiopia, 1935. The Fourth Step: The Spanish Civil War, 1936-1939. The Fifth Step: "Anschluss," 1938. The Sixth Step: Czechoslovakia Dismembered, 1938-1939. The Final Step: Poland, 1939. Democratic Policy in Review.

XXIX: The Loosening of Imperial Ties   609

I: INTRODUCTION.   II: THE FAR EAST. The Chinese Revolution of 1911. Japan's Attempted Aggression, 1915-1922. Main Elements of Recent Chinese History. Japan's Aggressions, 1931-1945. Nationalists and Communists. The Road to Communist Success in China. The Communist Victory in China. The Political Development of Japan, 1919-1941. Japanese Imperialism, 1931-1945. Occupied Japan, 1945-1954. Southeast Asia.   III: THE INDIAN SUBCONTINENT. Hindu-Moslem Tensions. The Hindu Way of Life. The Population Problem. Self-Government—and Partition. IV: THE NEAR EAST. Political Changes Since 1918. Oil and Communism. Differences among the Arabs. Israel.   V: AFRICA AND ELSEWHERE. Other Non-western Peoples. "Black" Africa. "White" Africa. Kenya. South Africa: Racial and National Tensions. South

A
HISTORY
OF
CIVILIZATION

The Eighteenth Century:

The International Balance

CHAPTER XVI

Madame de Pompadour, by Boucher, 1758.

I: Introduction: The Prospect in 1715

LONG YEARS of peace and quiet appeared to be in prospect for Europe in 1715. Although fighting was still going on in Turkey and the Baltic, the possibility of a new general war seemed remote. The Peace of Utrecht, signed in 1713, had restored the balance of power in the West and had ended Louis XIV's attempt to extend French dominance. The death of the "Sun King" himself in 1715 gave fresh promise of international stability. For the crown of France passed to his great-grandson, Louis XV, a boy of five. A long regency was necessary, which meant that France would probably be too preoccupied with internal problems to play the aggressor. Moreover, the great conflicts of Louis XIV had exhausted his own nation and had brought even his victorious opponents to the edge of bankruptcy. Government debts had mounted alarmingly.

In 1715, the forms of government in Europe ranged from absolute monarchy, as in France and Russia, to the constitutional monarchy of Britain and the republics of the Swiss and the Dutch. The differences among these forms are important, but they should not conceal the fact that all gov-

EUROPE IN 1715

Brandenburg – Prussia
Austrian Habsburg Lands
Swedish possessions
Venetian possessions
Ottoman Empire
Boundary of the Holy Roman Empire
× Battle sites

NORWAY

Oslo

Stockholm

North Sea

DENMARK

Copenhagen

Baltic

SCOTLAND

Edinburgh
Berwick

ULSTER
IRELAND
Limerick
Drogheda
Dublin
Boyne

ENGLAND

KINGDOM OF GREAT BRITAIN

London

Hamburg

Bremen

BRANDENBURG
Fehrbellin
Berlin

Elbe

THE

SAXONY

EMPIRE

Prague
BOHEMIA

SILESIA

Atlantic Ocean

Tor Bay
C. La Hogue

UNITED NETHERLANDS
Ryswick
Utrecht
Nimwegen

Dover

Oudenarde
Ramillies
Aachen
WEST PHALIA

AUSTRIAN NETHERLANDS

Mal-plaquet

Seine R.

Paris
Versailles

Orleans
Blois

Verdun
Metz
Toul

Rhine R.

LORRAINE

ALSACE

Rastadt

Strasbourg

Blenheim

Augsburg

MORAVIA

AUSTRIA

FRANCE

Nantes

Loire R.

FRANCHE COMTE

Geneva

SWITZERLAND

BAVARIA

Vienna

STYRIA

CARINTHIA

HUN

Bordeaux

Rhône R.

SAVOY

MILAN

TYROL

VENETIAN
Venice

CARNIOLA

REPUBLIC

Adriatic

Avignon
(to the papacy)

Genoa

PORTUGAL

Burgos

Ebro R.

Madrid

Marseilles

Florence

PAPAL STATES

Rome

NAPLES

Ragu

Lisbon

Tagus R.

SPAIN

Barcelona

CORSICA
(to Genoa)

Valencia

Guadalquivir R.

Seville

Granada

Gibraltar
(Br.)

BALEARIC IS.

MINORCA
(Br.)

SARDINIA
(to Austria, 1714;
to Savoy, 1720)

Naples

Mediterranean

Palermo

SICILY

(to Savoy, 1
to Austria

ALGERIA

TUNIS

MALTA

G.-

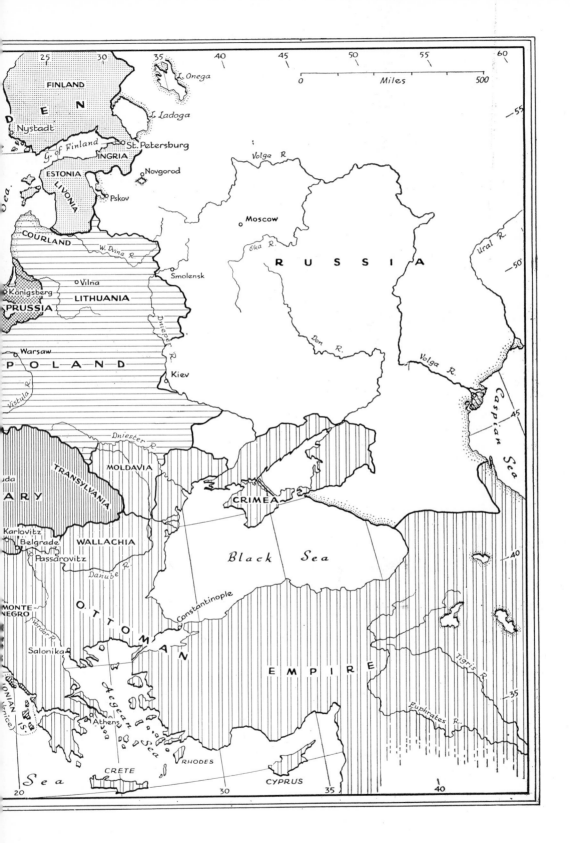

ernments then represented the interests of the privileged few. In Britain, titled nobles, country squires, and rich merchants virtually monopolized the right to vote and to hold high office. Wealthy businessmen controlled the Dutch Republic. And the so-called absolute monarchs often wielded powers less absolute, in fact, than the theory of divine right suggested. As we shall see, Peter the Great of Russia, the most ruthless absolutist of the age, met bitter though ineffectual opposition, especially from the nobility; his weaker successors made sweeping concessions to the nobles. Louis XIV, though he had allowed the nobles and prelates of France little say in affairs of state, had never dared to deprive them of their financial and social privileges. As soon as Louis died, the nobles set about trying to regain their lost political influence. Indeed, it may be convincingly argued that almost every state in Europe showed some of the characteristics of oligarchy.

Historians use the term "Old Régime" to describe the oligarchical institutions of western Europe, especially France. It was the Old Régime of the eighteenth century in contrast to the "new" régime issuing from the French Revolution of 1789. The Old Régime departed sharply in some respects from the older traditions of medieval civilization. The French concept of classical balance had largely replaced the Christian ideals of the Middle Ages, and religion no longer held first claim on the loyalties of statesmen. In western Europe, the peasants had long ago cast off the bonds of serfdom, and the bourgeoisie had overcome the medieval prejudice against amassing private wealth with a finality that would have astonished a great personage of the thirteenth century like St. Louis or St. Thomas Aquinas.

In the East, however, particularly in Russia, serfdom was steadily deepened and extended, and even the Old Régime of western

Europe was often closer to the Middle Ages than to the twentieth century. Most Europeans of the eighteenth century lived in farming villages and retained their traditional parochial outlook; only a few had a real sense of nationalism, a sense of belonging to a larger entity transcending the merely local. The feudal concept of caste still underlay the Old Régime. Peasants, merchants, and craftsmen had improved their lot since the Middle Ages, but most of them remained within the great majority of the underprivileged. Only the wealthier bourgeois families enjoyed a voice in politics or a share in the prerogatives of the first two estates. Europe had always been in the main agrarian, parochial, and oligarchical; in 1715, it seemed likely to remain so forever.

The Old Régime, however, did not last forever. Its apparent stability was deceptive, and by the middle of the eighteenth century its foundations were beginning to crumble in the West under the pressure of revolutionary economic changes. At the same time, the leaders of the great cultural and intellectual movement called the Enlightenment (see Chapter XVII) were voicing the demands for reform that culminated in the great French Revolution of 1789. The international stability promised by the Utrecht settlement also proved illusory. The defeat of Louis XIV in the War of the Spanish Succession had not ended the world-wide rivalry of France and Britain, which again broke into war in 1740. Meanwhile, Russia was emerging from semi-isolation to participate actively, often aggressively, in the European system of states. And, in the decades following 1713, Prussia became a first-rate power, intent on expansion even at the cost of provoking a general European war. The balance of power that was established in 1713 survived uneasily for a generation and then dissolved.

CHAPTER XVI

II: The Economic Revolutions in the West

Three great sets of economic changes —in commerce, in agriculture, and in industry—helped to undermine the Old Régime and to alter the European balance. These were in fact economic revolutions, slower and less dramatic than political revolutions, but in the long run every bit as revolutionary in their effects upon human history. All three, of course, continued after the close of the eighteenth century, and we shall return to examine them again in the nineteenth century (see Chapter XX). Between 1715 and 1789 the commercial revolution was the most mature of the three. It extended to almost every European country, and it profoundly influenced war, politics, and society. In comparison, the agricultural and industrial revolutions were still in their infancy. Yet they were lusty infants, already providing farms and workshops with new techniques and lending new strength to Britain, France, and Prussia.

The Commercial Revolution

The basic institutions of the commercial revolution had developed before 1715. Banking and insurance houses dated back to the Renaissance and beyond, and chartered trading companies dated back to the sixteenth century. Mercantilism, the philosophy underlying the policies of government toward commerce, had matured in the Spain of Philip II and the France of Louis XIV and Colbert. The steady growth of trade in the eighteenth century, however, quickened the pace of the commercial revolution. Old aids to business and transport were extended and improved; new ones were perfected.

The record-breaking volume of trade, for example, increased the demand for insurance on ships and cargoes. The insurance brokers of eighteenth-century London, like many other businessmen, often gathered in coffee houses to discuss business, news, and politics. Specialists in marine insurance gravitated to Edward Lloyd's coffee house in Lombard Street and continued to meet there after Lloyd himself died in 1713. Thus was born Lloyd's of London. The name stuck, even after the firm moved from the coffee house to more dignified quarters in the Royal Exchange in 1774. Lloyd's developed the standard form of policy for marine insurance and published *Lloyd's List,* the first detailed and accurate shipping newspaper. It also achieved a certain melancholy fame by ringing a ship's bell whenever it got news of a marine disaster.

The informal atmosphere of the coffee house nurtured a second great London institution, the stock exchange. As the buying and selling of shares in joint-stock companies increased, traders began to gather at Jonathan's. In 1773, they changed the name of Jonathan's to the Stock Exchange Coffee House; thirty years later, they dropped "Coffee House" from the title and incorporated their business.

Meantime, other aids to commerce were appearing. The improvement of charts and the installation of lighthouses and buoys made navigation safer. At sea, captains learned to determine their geographical position by using two new instruments, the sextant and the chronometer. The sextant, an elaboration of the telescope, showed the altitude of the sun at noon and thus indicated the ship's latitude. Whereas ordinary clocks behaved erratically because of the motion of the ship, the chronometer ran very accurately. It was kept on Greenwich

Restoration of the interior of the coffee-house where Lloyd's of London started.

Mean Time (the time at the meridian running through Greenwich near London). The two new instruments made it possible to calculate the ship's longitude, which represented the difference between Greenwich Mean Time and the local time aboard ship, calculated at noon with the sextant.

On land, the improvements in communication and transport came much more slowly than they did at sea. Except for the good highways of France, European roads were scarcely better than paths or trails. The shipment of goods overland remained slow, unsafe, and expensive until after 1750, when the construction of turnpikes and canals gradually eased the situation. The pioneer English canal, built in 1759-1761 by the Duke of Bridgewater, cut in half the cost of moving coal from the mines on his estate to the new factory town of Manchester. Soon the Duke extended his canal from Manchester to the port of Liverpool, and other canals were started. These were the beginnings of the revolution in transport, which culminated after 1800 in the hard-surfaced highway and the railroad.

Businessmen also faced the handicaps resulting from restrictive guild regulations and from the inconvenience and profusion of local weights, measures, coins, and tolls. Sweden, for example, used copper for coins of all denominations, including a monstrosity weighing 43 pounds. Baden, one of the smaller German states, had 112 separate measures for length, 65 for dry goods, 123 for liquids, and 163 for cereals, not to mention 80 different pound weights. A German merchant who contracted to ship timber down the Elbe from Dresden in Saxony to Hamburg had to pay so many tolls to the towns and principalities along the way that of 60 planks floated at Dresden only six would reach Hamburg. The boat trip over the same distance, which should have taken only a week, required a month because of the innumerable stops for toll collection. Even in France, where Louis XIV had expected all things to be uniform and centralized, barriers to internal trade persisted. Local French levies were so numerous and so intricate that a French financial expert declared, "Scarcely one or two men in a generation are able to attain a perfect knowledge of them."

Economic reformers attacked most of these anachronisms before 1789, but they won only an occasional victory, notably in standardizing and simplifying money. This

CHAPTER XVI

was an important matter, for a state's success or failure in attacking the vested interests of guilds and local tax authorities directly affected its prosperity. In England, which had long been a unified national state, economic localism was dying, and trade thrived. In disunited Germany, on the other hand, commerce languished; few merchants had the patience to master the weights and measures of Baden or to attempt shipments on the Elbe.

The survival of local vested economic interests throughout the eighteenth century showed the limitations of the power of the mercantilist state. Mercantilism meant that trade should be regulated on the national, rather than the local, level. But no eighteenth-century government, not even the English, possessed the staff of officials needed to make national regulation effective. States had to rely heavily on private companies and individuals to execute most of their policies. Thus the English East India Company enjoyed virtually sovereign powers over its colonial preserve. Inventors worked on their own, for there were no government laboratories. Occasionally, under the pressure of business groups, the state did offer prizes on matters of critical importance. The English Parliament promised £20,000 for the discovery of a northwest passage from the Atlantic to the Far East, and another £20,000 for the invention of a reliable "sea-going" clock. At that, the inventor of the chronometer had to wait twenty-five years to collect his prize money.

The Mississippi and South Sea Bubbles

This contrast between private enterprise and governmental sluggishness is best illustrated by two speculative booms of the early eighteenth century—the "Mississippi Bubble" in France and the "South Sea Bubble" in England. In 1715, hardly a state in Europe could manage the large debts that had piled up during the recent wars. Yet every state had to find some way of meeting at least a part of the large annual interest on its bonds and other debts, or else go bankrupt. The governments of France and England chose the way of experiment. They shifted responsibility for the management of state debts to joint-stock companies, which they rewarded with trading concessions. The commerce of the companies, it was hoped, would prove so lucrative that their profits would easily cover the interest charges on government bonds.

John Law (1671-1729), a Scottish mathematical wizard, presided over the experiment in France. Exiled from Britain for killing a dueling opponent, Law amassed a large fortune at continental gaming tables and cultivated the friendship of the mighty, among them the Duke of Orléans. He also studied monetary problems and banking methods, especially in Amsterdam, then the commercial capital of Europe. Law was a mercantilist, but with a difference. He agreed with the doctrine that the strength of a state depended upon the quantity of money it possessed. But, he asserted, silver and gold coins were not necessarily the most desirable form of money. The limited supply of the precious metals made it difficult to increase the amount of specie circulating in any country and therefore difficult to promote business. Paper money, Law concluded, was the solution—paper money backed by a nation's wealth in land and in trade. The quantity of paper money in circulation could easily be raised or lowered in accordance with the needs of business. Trading companies would prosper as never before, the whole country would prosper, and, in the midst of the general prosperity, government debts would be paid off.

For years before 1715, Law vainly sought a chance to try out his "system." Finally, with the death of Louis XIV, he secured his opportunity. His gambling crony, the Duke of Orléans, now Regent of France (1715-1723), permitted Law to set up a central bank in Paris. The value of French money had been sinking steadily because the government continually debased the coinage. Law's bank, following the practice of the Bank of Amsterdam, issued paper notes of stable value; business activity was at once stimulated. Next, Law set up the Mississippi Company, which received a monopoly of commerce with the Louisiana colony and soon absorbed the other French colonial trading companies.

Law's system now reached to almost every corner of the French economy, and Law himself, appointed controller-general of France, became the economic dictator of the kingdom. His company took over the government debt, agreeing to accept government bonds in partial payment for shares of Mississippi stock. Many bondholders responded enthusiastically to Law's offer, for the government's credit was so poor that its bonds had depreciated to 20 per cent or less of their face value. Law, however, had to sell additional shares of Mississippi stock in order to obtain sufficient working capital for the enlarged operations of his company. To attract cash purchasers, he painted the company's prospects in brightest colors; in short, Law deliberately promoted a boom in Mississippi stock. Investors, large and small, caught the fever of speculation, which resembled the Wall Street boom of the late 1920's. By the close of 1719, Mississippi stock was selling at forty times its par value.

The Mississippi Bubble soon burst, for Law's paper money could not stand the strain imposed upon it. These banknotes could be redeemed in metal coins at any time. Ordinarily, there were few demands for redemption, since the notes commanded wide confidence. But, as the price of Mississippi shares rose higher and higher, cautious investors became convinced that the boom could not last and decided to cash in. They sold their shares, received payment in banknotes, then took the notes to Law's bank and demanded their redemption. The bank exhausted its reserves of gold and silver and suspended specie payments in February, 1720. Law was forced to relinquish the post of controller-general in May, 1720; he fled France shortly thereafter.

The Mississippi Bubble had international repercussions, for within a few weeks of Law's resignation the South Sea Bubble burst in London. It might have been expected that management of the English government's debt would devolve upon the Bank of England. Founded in 1694 as a private institution (it was fully nationalized only after World War II), the Bank of England had already made a secure place for itself in the national economy by issuing stable banknotes and by performing many other valuable services during the last two wars against Louis XIV. The debt, however, was taken over not by the Bank but by the new South Sea Company, which paid the government the exorbitant sum of more than seven and a half million pounds. The resources of the South Sea Company were slim; they consisted largely of the right to exploit the trading concessions that Britain obtained under the Asiento agreement at the end of the War of the Spanish Succession. These privileges were limited to furnishing Spain's American colonies with 4800 slaves annually and to sending one ship a year to Panama for general trade.

The South Sea Company, like the Mississippi, invited government creditors to transfer their bonds into company stock. To push up the price of the stock and thus attract fresh capital, its directors took a series of ingenious moves. They bought and sold shares secretly to create a more lively market, encouraged purchasers to buy stock with a down payment of only 10 per cent in cash, and spread false reports of forthcoming sailings by the company's ships on voyages of unparalleled promise.

The cycle of "boom and bust" soon ran its full course. South Sea shares, with a par value of £100, sold for £129 in January of 1720, and for £1050 in June. Dozens of other promoters sprang into action, advertising schemes for wheels of perpetual motion, for making salt water fresh, for artillery to fire square cannon-balls, "for carrying on an undertaking of great advantage, but nobody to know what it is"—for everything and anything, including the fabrication of gold bricks, or at least turning copper into gold. The gullibility of the investing public was remarkable, but it was not inexhaustible. South Sea shares slipped to £880 in August, 1720, and skidded to £150 in September. Parliament now ordered an investigation of the company and, to protect the company's creditors, seized the estates of the South Sea directors. The latter, having destroyed the company's books, left England in considerable haste.

The Consequences of the Bubbles

The two bubbles produced some unfortunate results. The collapse of the Mississippi scheme left the fiscal policies of France in worse condition than ever. It ruined Law, whose talents, if used more discreetly, might have arrested the financial paralysis creeping over the French government. In England, the South Sea fiasco long impeded the development of new stock companies, which were henceforth required to buy costly charters. It tarnished the reputations of many in high places. The mistresses of George I and the King himself had been "let in on the ground floor" and had endorsed the venture too enthusiastically. More than a hundred members of Parliament had borrowed money from the company in order to buy its shares on the installment plan. The holders of government bonds, after the estates of the directors were confiscated, lost half their original investment.

The bubbles, however, were not unmitigated misfortunes. They were the growing pains of the European economy, of states groping for solutions to new and baffling financial problems. As Voltaire later declared, Law's "imaginary system gave birth to a real commerce," and "the nation as a whole became more prosperous." Law released French business from the torpor induced by the defeats of Louis XIV. The Mississippi Company, reorganized after 1720, consistently made a handsome profit.

In England, the South Sea Bubble scarcely affected the strongest institutions. The English East India Company went right on paying an annual dividend of 5 to 10 per cent. The Bank of England, no longer competing with the South Sea Company for government favors, became more than ever the financial mainstay of the realm. In the political shake-up following the Bubble, Robert Walpole (see p. 17) came to power with a program of honoring the debt as a *national* debt. This was a novel concept and a great step forward in fiscal morality in an age when most other states still treated their debts as the monarch's personal obligation, to be recognized or repudiated as he saw fit.

The Improving Landlords

The agricultural revolution, the second of the great series of changes transforming the economy of the modern world, has centered on improvements that enable fewer farmers to produce more crops. In our own day, these innovations derive largely from advances in technology and science; farmers use machinery and such products of chemical and biological research as inorganic fertilizers and the selective breeding of everything from beef cattle to apple trees. The application of scientific discoveries to agriculture is actually an old story, as old as the irrigation ditches of ancient Egypt and the improved plows and the horse-collars of the Middle Ages. In the eighteenth century, the tempo of the advance in farming techniques began to move for the first time at an almost revolutionary pace. The leaders of the movement were the improving landlords of England, notably Jethro Tull, Viscount Townshend, Robert Bakewell, and Arthur Young.

Jethro Tull (1674-1741) studied the painstaking methods used in French truck-gardens and vineyards. French gardeners obtained a big yield from small plots by planting seeds individually and by carefully hoeing the soil around each plant and vine. Tull adapted French methods to the much larger grain fields of England. In place of the inefficient custom of scattering seed broadcast, he planted it deeply in regular rows with a horse-drawn "drilling" machine, and he cultivated his crops with a horse-drawn hoe. The outstanding production record of Tull's test farm quickly justified his innovations.

Viscount Townshend (1674-1738) used his Norfolk estate to experiment with two valuable new crops brought in from Holland—turnips and clover. By storing sufficient turnips to feed all the livestock until the arrival of the spring pasturing season, Townshend avoided the customary slaughter of stock at the onset of winter. Clover, by fixing nitrogen in the soil, increased the fertility of the land and curtailed the wasteful practice of letting fields lie fallow every third year. "Turnip" Townshend's four-year rotation—planting the same field to turnips, barley, clover, and wheat, in successive years—soon became the standard procedure on many English estates.

Robert Bakewell (1725-1795) applied scientific principles to raising livestock. Before Bakewell's time, most farm animals were gaunt and spindly creatures, almost too tough to be eaten, and useful chiefly as draft animals or for their manure, skins, or wool. Bakewell carefully inbred selected strains of sheep, doubled the average weight of his stock, and marketed lamb and mutton of really appetizing quality. Although a critic complained that Bakewell's meat was "too expensive to buy and too fat to eat," his methods were widely copied.

Arthur Young (1741-1820) became the great publicist of the new agriculture. Gifted with a rare capacity for traveling, observing, and reporting, he began to make systematic trips through the farming districts of the British Isles and the Continent. In one five-year period, during the late 1760's and early '70's, he produced more than a dozen volumes on agrarian practices and economic problems. Campaigning for the innovations of Tull and Townshend, Young put his arguments so persuasively and entertainingly that he soon gained an international reputation. George Washington, Lafayette, and Catherine the Great corresponded with him; George III and Napoleon read his books.

The Spread of the Agricultural Revolution

Before 1789 the agricultural revolution made very uneven progress. It enlisted the support of only the most enterprising farmers and gained a secure foothold in only a few countries. On the Continent, Prussia took the lead, and King Frederick the Great directed his subjects to breed livestock, grow fodder crops, and rotate plant-

12

Turner's shop with various forms of lathes, as illustrated in the great French Encyclopédie (see Chapter XVII).

ings, all in the advanced English manner. In Britain itself, the new farming found favor chiefly among the holders of large estates, with King George III, "Farmer George," at their head.

Essentially, the agricultural revolution was an important stage in the evolution from the partly self-sufficient medieval manor to the modern capitalist farm producing specialized crops for the market. The techniques recommended by the improving landlords of the eighteenth century were capitalistic because they required a large investment of money. They also required large fields unencumbered by the traditional practices of manorialism—by the subdivision into individual strips, for instance. But many English villages were still surrounded by common fields subdivided into strips. The improving landlords therefore demanded that the common fields be "enclosed," fenced off as the private land of an individual proprietor.

The enclosure movement of Tudor days had aimed to extend privately owned sheep pastures. This new movement was directed chiefly at increasing the land available for planting and growing crops. Enclosures

reached their peak in the last decades of the eighteenth century and the first decades of the nineteenth, when Parliament passed hundreds of separate enclosure acts affecting several million acres. Rural England was assuming its modern aspect of large fields fenced by hedgerows.

From the standpoint of social welfare, enclosures brought unhappy results. In eighteenth-century England, as in ancient Greece and Rome, the development of large estates, capitalistically run, tended to ruin the small farmers. The "little fellows" of English agriculture usually could not afford to install fences, buy tools, and assemble large fields—in short, they could not afford to become enclosing, improving landlords. Enclosures forced some of the small farmers to become hired hands on larger farms, and others to seek work in the towns.

From the standpoint of agrarian productivity, however, enclosures marked a great step forward. They promoted the creation of large farms well suited to the application of drill-planting, horse-hoeing, and crop rotation. Britain, in consequence, as yet experienced no difficulty in feeding her growing population. Moreover, by in-

Hargreaves' spinning jenny, 1764.

creasing farm output yet releasing part of the labor force for jobs off the farm, the agricultural revolution was assisting the industrial revolution. It made available both the food and the men required by the industrial towns.

The Beginnings of the Industrial Revolution

The industrial revolution, further, required raw materials for its factories, markets for its manufactures, and capital to finance the building of factories and to equip them with machines. The raw materials and the markets were supplied in part by the colonies overseas, and the capital in part by merchants. Thus the commercial revolution, too, assisted the industrial revolution. But we may postpone more detailed discussion of these interactions until later chapters dealing with the full flowering of nineteenth-century industrialism and imperialism (see Chapters XX and XXIV). Here we shall emphasize the de-velopments that marked the beginning of the great industrial change.

In the industrial revolution, machines superseded simple hand tools, and water or steam replaced human muscles and animal energy as the source of power. Because the power-driven machines were often big, complicated, and costly, large factories were needed to house them. The factory system thus supplanted production in small workshops or by small craftsmen at home. By 1789, these revolutionary changes had affected only a few industries; but those involved were in fact key industries—mining, metallurgy, munitions, and textiles.

Coal-mining was becoming a big business in the eighteenth century. Arthur Young found "all the activity and industry" of Britain "fast concentrating where there are coal pits," and reported in 1770 that at Newcastle, in the north of England, the number of coal-miners was "prodigiously numerous, amounting to many thousands." The increased demand for coal resulted partly from the needs of iron smelters. For centuries, the smelters had used charcoal to make iron from the raw ore, and they continued to do so in countries like Sweden that had abundant wood for charcoal. But in England, where almost all the great forests had been cut down, the price of charcoal rose so high that it constituted 80 per cent of the cost of producing iron. By 1750, consequently, despite the abundant native supply of ore, the output of English smelters was declining rapidly, and the country was relying more and more on imported iron. Ordinary coal could not replace charcoal as smelter fuel because the chemicals in coal made the iron too brittle. Here necessity mothered invention. The Darby family of Coalbrookdale in Shropshire discovered how to remove the chemical impurities from coal by converting it into coke through an oven process. Since coke was almost pure carbon, it produced iron of high quality.

In England, the Darbys and other private firms were the pioneers in metallurgy. On the Continent, governments took the lead—a significant exception to the general rule about the inability of states to solve economic problems. Warfare required weapons and munitions in unprecedented quantities; France and Prussia met the demand by setting up state-financed and state-operated foundries and arms factories.

The revolution in textiles centered on the cheaper production of cotton cloth. The "flying shuttle," a technical device first applied to the hand loom in England (1733), enabled a single weaver to do work that had previously required the services of two. The looms equipped with the flying shuttle used up the supply of thread so rapidly that the London Society for the Encouragement of Arts, Manufactures, and Commerce offered a prize for improvement of the tedious process of spinning cotton thread by hand. James Hargreaves won the prize in 1764 with his "spinning jenny," a series of spinning wheels geared together which made eight threads simultaneously. Soon the jenny was adapted to water power, and its output was increased to a hundred or more threads at once. Moreover, in the 1760's the Scotsman, James Watt, introduced the steam engine, which would eventually free industry from dependence on unreliable water power.

Although Britain had nearly 150 cotton mills by 1789, woolens and dozens of other basic commodities continued to be made by hand. In England, and even more on the Continent, individual craftsmen and small enterprises greatly outnumbered mill-hands and large factories. The full sweep of industrial development could not come until the canal and the railroad provided cheap transport of heavy freight. The shortage of capital and the paucity of skilled labor sometimes retarded the advance of industry. A Swedish inventor of the early 1700's designed excellent machines for cutting wheels and files but could not raise the money to put them into operation. And in Britain the difficulty of making precisely fitting parts for Watt's engine held back its production on a large scale. The eighteenth century had taken many of the initial steps in the industrial revolution; it remained for the nineteenth century to apply them on a truly revolutionary scale.

III: The Western Powers

Britain's Assets

The leadership of Britain in the economic revolutions made her the wealthiest nation in the world. British bankers, buttressed by the Bank of England and by the careful management of the national debt, extended credit to business enterprises at the relatively low interest rate of 5 per cent. The City, the square mile comprising the City of London proper and including the financial district, recovered quickly from the South Sea Bubble and was soon challenging Amsterdam's position as the international capital of trade and finance. In the course of the eighteenth century, British merchants outdistanced their old trading rivals, the Dutch, and gradually took the lead over their new competitors, the French. Judged by the three touchstones of mercantilism—commerce, colonies, and sea power—Britain was the strongest state in Europe.

Supervision of British colonies rested with a government department, the Board of Trade, which followed an easygoing policy of "salutary neglect" in contrast to the rigid mercantilistic controls exerted by other imperial states over their possessions. Only the colonies of Britain enjoyed considerable rights of self-government. In the long run, as the American Revolution was to show, these rights did not satisfy the colonists. But in the short run "salutary neglect" worked reasonably well, and the British Empire surpassed all others in prosperity and self-reliance.

The Royal Navy surpassed all others by virtue of its superior officer corps and its greater size. Future captains went to sea at the age of sixteen, or even younger, and passed through a long course of practical training before receiving commissions. The ships they commanded in the wars of the mid-eighteenth century were inferior in design to those of Britain's enemies, France and Spain; they were less seaworthy and less heavily armed. But there were more of them. Britain had a 2 to 1 advantage over France in number of warships, a 6 to 1 lead in merchant ships, and a 10 to 1 lead in total number of experienced seamen, merchant and naval. In wartime, the fleet could draw on the merchant marine for additional sailors and for transports and other auxiliary vessels.

Service on His Majesty's ships two hundred years ago was not exactly pleasant. The food doled out to the sailors was monotonous, wormy, and unhealthful. Captains frequently ordered the punishments of flogging and of keel-hauling, in which the offender was dragged along the barnacle-encrusted keel from bow to stern. Tobias Smollett, who sailed as a surgeon's mate on a British warship in the 1740's, exposed these brutalities in *Roderick Random*, one of the first English novels. Roderick Random recounts the manner in which he was "recruited" by the press gang:

. . . As I crossed Tower Wharf, a squat tawny fellow, with a hanger by his side, and a cudgel in his hand, came up to me, calling, 'Yo, ho! brother, you must come along with me.' As I did not like his appearance, instead of answering his salutation, I quickened my pace, in hope of ridding myself of his company; upon which he whistled aloud, and immediately another sailor appeared before me, who laid hold of me by the collar and began to drag me along. Not being of a humour to relish such treatment, I disengaged myself of the assailant, and with one blow of my cudgel, laid him motionless on the ground; and perceiving myself surrounded in a trice by ten or a dozen more, exerted myself with such dexterity and success, that some of my opponents were fain to attack me with drawn cutlasses; and, after an obstinate engagement, in which I received a large wound on my head, and another on my left cheek, I was disarmed, taken prisoner, and carried on board a pressing tender, where, after being pinioned like a malefactor, I was thrust down into the hold among a parcel of miserable wretches, the sight of whom well-nigh distracted me.*

Impressment, keel-hauling, malnutrition, and disease, however, were the common afflictions of all sailors in the eighteenth century; they did not put the British navy at a comparative disadvantage.

The army, on the other hand, constituted Britain's chief liability. Its officers were reputed to be the poorest in Europe, and its soldiers were in part mediocre mercenaries from the German state of Hesse-Cassel, the Hessians of the American Revolutionary War. The British avoided a large army because it would have been both expensive and, since the British Isles were relatively safe from invasion, unnecessary. Moreover, they feared a standing army as an instrument of potential absolutism, for they remembered the use that Cromwell and James II had made of this weapon.

The Cabinet

The Glorious Revolution, which had done so much to confirm distrust of the army, had also confirmed Britain's unique and greatest asset—the supremacy of Parliament over the king. Parliament had replaced James II with William and Mary; when Anne, the last Stuart monarch, died in 1714, Parliament had already arranged for the succession of the House of Hanover. Under the first two Hanoverians, the cabinet, which was the instrument for the everyday assertion of parliamentary supremacy, underwent a rapid development. George I (1714-1727) and George II (1727-

* Everyman ed. (New York, 1927), 143.

1760) did not abdicate all their royal powers. They took a direct interest in the South Sea Bubble and other financial matters; they sometimes intervened personally in the conduct of diplomacy and war. George II was the last English monarch to command troops in person on the battle-field—in 1743 during the War of the Austrian Succession. But the first two Georges did not enjoy the crown that had been thrust upon them. They never mastered the English language, and they took long holidays back in Hanover, where there was no Parliament to limit their authority. Homesick for Hanover, ill at ease in England, they gladly shifted the responsibility for many executive decisions to the cabinet.

George I and George II chose their cabinet ministers from the Whig party. They did so, not because Parliament forced them, but because it suited their convenience, and, even more, because they really had no other choice. They thoroughly distrusted the other party, the Tories, who were generally identified with the royal policies that had been discredited by the Glorious Revolution. Some Tories were involved in futile Jacobite activities, plots to restore to the English throne the descendants of James II (Jacobite from Jacobus, Latin for James). The Whigs, in contrast, had engineered the Glorious Revolution and had arranged the Hanoverian succession; they now controlled the House of Commons.

For twenty-one years following the collapse of the South Sea Bubble, from 1721 to 1742, Robert Walpole, who led the Whigs in the House of Commons, headed the ministry. Walpole increased the power and prestige of the cabinet. Although the title was not yet official, he was in fact prime minister, the foremost political figure in the realm. And in 1733, when he forced the resignation of some ministers who opposed his plan for a drastic reduction of customs duties, he took a major step toward establishing the important principle of cabinet unanimity on a critical issue.

Thus, by the death of George II in 1760, it was *customary* for the king to select his ministers from the majority party, but it was not yet *obligatory*. George III then tried to change the custom, battled the issue out with Commons, and lost (see Chapter XVII). The critical years in the growth of the English cabinet began in 1760. But the formative years preceding 1760 had already begun to shape the great instrument that would eventually assure the control of the executive branch by Parliament and thus by the people who elected the members of the House of Commons.

The Whig Oligarchy

Disraeli, the great nineteenth-century Tory, dubbed the Whig cabinets of the first two Georges a "Venetian oligarchy." As in Renaissance Venice, he claimed, wealthy merchant and banking families controlled both legislature and executive. Whig rule, though emphatically oligarchical, was not so Venetian as Disraeli supposed. The Whig party was a coalition of landed gentry and "funded" gentry, of land-owning nobles and squires and of businessmen from London and other towns. In the Whig party the political leaders of town and country renewed an alliance that had first appeared in the later Middle Ages when the knights of the shire had joined the burgesses to form the House of Commons.

In the Whig Parliaments the country gentlemen predominated by sheer numbers. In 1754, for instance, they outnumbered the merchants and lawyers by 5 to 1 in the House of Commons. Family ties, common political aims, and a common reverence for property bound together the senior and junior partners of the Whig party. To con-

Sir Robert Walpole, 1676-1745.

solidate the gains of the Glorious Revolution, the Whigs opposed Jacobite schemes and supported the unprepossessing Hanoverians. To protect their lands and other investments, they passed legislation making death the penalty for stealing livestock, for cutting down cherry trees, and for other relatively minor violations of the sanctity of property.

Robert Walpole himself exemplified the fusion of landed and funded elements in the party. He inherited his manners and his tastes from his father, a country squire. He fixed the English politician's tradition of the long country weekend in order to indulge his passion for hunting. Devoid of any hint of delicacy, he drank heavily and habitually told bawdy stories at mixed dinner parties. Like many Whig squires, Walpole married into the aristocracy of trade; his wife was the daughter of a well-to-do timber merchant and former Lord Mayor of London. As prime minister, Walpole, the

18

country gentleman, promoted the interests of the City. His basic policy coincided with the City's program: financial stability through the gradual retirement of the national debt, political stability through the cabinet system and the new Hanoverian dynasty.

Democracy, both in the sense of the career open to talents and of rule by the many, scarcely existed in Walpole's England. In the professions, a social minority, the "gentlemen," alone could hope to become army and navy officers, lawyers, teachers, clergymen, and physicians. In politics, though the aristocracy of commerce gained admission to the Whig oligarchy, the millions of ordinary people were excluded. The landed gentry alone supplied the justices of the peace, who ran the local courts, fixed wage scales, superintended the relief of the poor, provided for the maintenance of bridges and highways, and were in general the despots of the English countryside. Fanatic defenders of the propertied classes, the justices of the peace represented the most unattractive side of oligarchy. As magistrates, they often ignored the rights of the defendant and readily sentenced petty thieves to death. The saying that "You may as well be hanged for [stealing] a sheep as a lamb" is a bitter reminder of their standards of justice.

In the main, only gentlemen had the right to vote for members of Parliament. The small number of voters in many constituencies encouraged corruption, particularly in the "rotten" or "pocket boroughs," boroughs with such a tiny electorate that control of their parliamentary representatives reposed in the pocket of some wealthy lord. The politicians took full advantage of their opportunities by bribing the voters outright or by promising them places on the government payroll. An immensely rich Whig, the Duke of Newcastle, controlled the outcome of elections in four counties and in seven pocket boroughs. Families with influential connections often obtained an immense amount of government patronage. Witness the harvest of spoils recorded on one tombstone:

> Here rest all that was mortal of Mrs. Elizabeth Bate,
> Relict of the Reverend Richard Bate,
> A woman of unaffected piety
>   And exemplary virtue.
> She was honourably descended
> And by means of her Alliance to
> The illustrious family of Stanhope
> She had the merit to obtain
> for her husband and children
> Twelve separate employments
> In Church and State.
> She died June 9, 1751, in the 75th year of her age.*

In Britain, as on the Continent, the ruling classes governed the voteless masses. But there was an all-important difference between the island kingdom and the continental countries. The British ruling classes, selfish and narrow-minded though they often were, had at their best a sense of *noblesse oblige*—that is, of public spirit and civic-mindedness. Within the aristocracy of land and trade there were fewer social barriers than on the Continent, and the gentry as a whole were more responsive than their continental counterparts to the need for economic changes and, eventually, for political and social reforms as well. The British parliamentary system, for all its oligarchy and corruption, provided the most enlightened and flexible government in Europe.

The Liabilities of France

Where Britain was strong, France was weak. The France of Louis XV (1715-1774) suffered from the rigidity of its co-

---

* Quoted by G. M. Trevelyan, *England under Queen Anne* (New York, 1930-1934), III, 317.

lonial system, the inferiority of its navy, and the very mediocre abilities of most of its statesmen. The Ministry of the Navy, which ruled the overseas empire, regarded these possessions as so many warships permanently at anchor. In contrast to the British Board of Trade, it refused to sanction any steps toward self-government. It applied the same detailed regulations to colonies as different as the sugar islands of the West Indies and the wilderness outposts of Canada.

Under this regime, the mother country prospered and the colonies languished. Commercial activity doubled in Nantes, Bordeaux, and other French Atlantic ports. New refineries grew up to process the raw sugar imported from the plantations of Guadeloupe and Martinique. Overseas, however, the plethora of regulations, many of them ill-conceived, stifled the initiative of the colonists. The French imperial system lacked the elasticity and the energy to meet the test of war successfully.

The French navy needed greater resources and better leadership. Its warships, though admirably designed, were inadequate in number. Since Dutch and British vessels carried much of France's expanding commerce, the French merchant marine was too small to supplement the fleet in wartime. French naval officers, though rigorously trained in the classroom, lacked the experience gained by British captains in a lifetime at sea. In the best (or worst) manner of the Old Régime, aristocratic officers devoted much of their energies to thwarting the rise of officers from the middle class. In fairness, it must be added that French rulers were almost bound to neglect the navy in order to concentrate on the army. France was above all a land power, and its vulnerable northeastern frontier, lying across the Flemish plain, invited invasion.

Except in size, however, the army of Louis XV scarcely lived up to the great traditions of Louis XIV. The troops were poorly trained. The military organization was top-heavy with superfluous officers; there was one officer to fifteen men in the French army, compared with one to thirty-five in the more efficient Prussian army. As in the navy, aristocratic officers despised their bourgeois colleagues, and many of them regarded a commission simply as a convenient way of increasing their personal wealth. In the midst of an eighteenth-century war, a French marshal complained:

The lieutenant and the captain do not know how to command their companies, and colonels, brigadiers, and lieutenant-generals are similarly incapable of leading their regiments, brigades and divisions. . . . All our officers individually have as much courage as the officers of our enemies, and more talent and intelligence. But they err on a very essential matter. There are few among them who do not devise their own campaign projects, and who do not criticize the generals. And almost none of them but regards his own rank as beneath him.*

Both the navy and the army underwent important reforms after 1763 and the defeats suffered by France in the Seven Years' War (see p. 42). The number of warships was increased, the officer corps of the army was cleared of much dead wood, and a new and more aggressive school of military tactics was introduced. These improvements accounted in part for the excellent showing made by France in the American Revolutionary War and in the military campaigns resulting from her own revolution. They came too late, however, to save the vanishing prestige of the Old Régime.

The Old Régime was weakest, not in its fighting arms or colonial appendages, but at its very head, the monarchy itself. Successful divine-right monarchy required a perpetual series of able kings, ably assisted by men like Colbert and Richelieu. There were

---

* Quoted in Albert Sorel, *L'Europe et la Révolution Française* (Paris, 1895), I, 201. Our translation.

CHAPTER XVI

no "sun kings" in France after the death of Louis XIV, and few ministers of the caliber of their illustrious predecessors.

The Duke of Orléans, the Regent from 1715 to 1723, was a gambler, drunkard, and pervert, who popularized the word "roué" by remarking that his friends deserved to be broken on the wheel (*roue* is French for wheel). The Regent, however, did attempt two important administrative experiments. He allowed John Law to try out his "system," and, in place of Louis XIV's method of ruling through individual bourgeois ministers, he set up ministerial councils staffed by men from the most distinguished noble families of the realm. Although the first experiment, as we have seen, produced some beneficial results, the second failed so completely that the Regent abandoned it after a three-year trial. It was impossible to reform the French government by restoring the nobles to their old feudal role of counselors. The French second estate had outlived its usefulness. The Regency proved that the nobles were unable to govern, the mid-century wars that they were unable to lead French armies to victory.

Fortunately, power soon passed to one of the few true statesmen of pre-revolutionary France, Cardinal Fleury, the tutor of Louis XV and the chief minister from 1726 until his death in 1743 in his ninetieth year. Without attempting basic reforms, the aged Cardinal gave France a breathing spell, in the words of Voltaire "treating the state as a powerful and robust body which could cure itself." Fleury did not remedy the chronic and deep-seated injustice and inefficiency of French fiscal methods. But he did stabilize the coinage, and he put the farming of taxes on a more businesslike basis by allowing the tax-farmers the comparatively modest profit of 7½ per cent. To make loans more readily available, he established state pawnshops in the chief cities of France. The success of Fleury's policies greatly impressed Lady Mary Montagu, the wife of an English diplomat and one of the shrewdest observers of the century. Lady Mary wrote in 1739:

France is so much improved, it is not . . . the same country we passed through twenty years ago. Everything I see speaks in praise of Cardinal Fleury; the roads are all mended . . . and such good care taken against robbers, that you may cross the country with your purse in your hand. . . . The French are more changed than their roads; instead of pale, yellow faces, wrapped up in blankets, as we saw them, the villages are filled with fresh-coloured lusty peasants, in good cloth and clean linen. It is incredible the air of plenty and content that is over the whole country.*

The air of "plenty and content" remained after Louis XV began his personal rule in 1743, but the administrative stability achieved by Fleury soon vanished. Intelligent but timid and debauched, Louis XV did not have the interest or the patience to supervise the details of government. He appointed and dismissed ministers on a personal whim or at the bidding of his mistresses and favorites. Key ministers, like the controller-general or the foreign secretary, remained in office but two or three years on the average. Each change in personnel meant a shift in policy, and Louis aggravated the instability by conspiring against his own appointees. France had two conflicting foreign policies: the official policy of the diplomatic corps; and the "King's Secret," conducted by royal agents who operated at cross purposes with the regular diplomats. Louis XV allowed the reins of government to go slack, yet refused to give them over to firmer hands.

Nevertheless, in spite of the deluge that Louis XV predicted would come after him, France remained a great power. French tastes, French thought, and the French lan-

---

* *Letters,* Everyman ed. (New York, 1906), 271-272.

guage retained their international pre-eminence. The misgovernment and the other weaknesses of the Old Régime were relative rather than absolute. They did not alter the fact that France was still the most populous country in Europe and possessed almost inexhaustible reserves of strength. Her army, though enfeebled, was the largest in the world, and her navy was the second largest. The French led the world in overseas trade until the British forged ahead of them in the last quarter of the eighteenth century.

The Other Western States

Spain was the only other state in western Europe with a claim to great-power status. Weakness had ended the major international roles that Sweden and Holland had played during the seventeenth century. The campaigns of Charles XII (1697-1718) killed off the flower of Swedish manhood and dissolved Sweden's Baltic empire (see p. 34). After the death of Charles, two factions, derisively nicknamed "Hats" and "Caps," competed for political control and nearly wrecked the government. Holland had been exhausted by the wars against Louis XIV. The Dutch were losing their commercial leadership, and they could no longer afford a large navy or an independent foreign policy. Eighteenth-century Holland, in the phrase of Frederick the Great, was often a "cockboat in the tow of the English frigate."

Spain, however, suffered little real damage as a result of the great war over the succession to her throne. The loss of Belgium and parts of Italy at the Utrecht settlement of 1713 reduced the unwieldy Spanish domains to more manageable size. The new Bourbon kings were a marked improvement over the last Spanish Habsburgs. Philip V (1700-1746), the first of the Spanish Bour-

bons, infused fresh life into the country's fossilized institutions by importing French advisers schooled in the system of Louis XIV. He also enlisted the aid of two able cosmopolitan adventurers, Alberoni and Ripperdá, whose fantastic careers almost outdid John Law's. Alberoni, the son of an Italian gardener, was successively a cook, an Italian diplomat at Madrid, the chief minister of Spain, and a cardinal. Ripperdá, a Dutch business expert and diplomat, ultimately lost the favor of Philip, entered the service of the Sultan of Morocco, and, after a lifelong alternation between the Protestant and Catholic faiths, died a Moslem. Philip and his remarkable advisers cut down the excessive formalities and endless delays of Spanish administration. They reduced the powers of the noble-dominated councils that had been the real locus of authority in seventeenth-century Spain. They improved the tax system, encouraged textiles and other new industries, built up the navy, and fortified strategic points in the Spanish empire in America.

The new dispensation, however, did not strike at the root causes of Spanish decline. The greed of governors and the restrictions of mercantilism still checked the progress of the colonies. The mother country remained impoverished, burdened with reactionary noble and clerical castes, and hampered by inadequate resources and by the apathy of the population. Philip V himself was neurotic, refusing, for instance, to cut his toenails, which grew so long that he limped. He was dominated by his strong-willed second wife, Elizabeth Farnese, the patroness of Alberoni. Since Philip's son by his first marriage would inherit Spain, a single ambition possessed Elizabeth: to provide thrones for *her* two sons, the issue of Philip's second marriage. Elizabeth's persistent attempts to secure the succession of Italian states for them repeatedly threatened the peace of Europe.

CHAPTER XVI

IV: Italy and Germany

In this twentieth-century world we are likely to assume that Italy and Germany have been significant powers for a very long time. In fact, however, both countries are relative newcomers to the family of nation-states; both completed their political unification less than a century ago. In 1715, Italy and Germany were still, in the old phrase, "geographical expressions."

Disunited Italy

In the sixteenth and seventeenth centuries, the Italian states had lost much of the political and economic power they had enjoyed during the great Renaissance. It is not hard to see why. The opening of new worlds overseas and the rise of Spain, England, and the other Atlantic powers naturally diminished the importance of the Mediterranean. In the Mediterranean itself, the Ottoman Turks and their satellites in North Africa long menaced Italian shipping and trade. Moreover, beginning with the French invasion of 1494, Italy was threatened with direct conquest by the rising new powers.

The Spanish Habsburgs made the conquest. For almost two centuries before 1715, Spain ruled Milan, Naples, and Sicily directly and dominated the rest of the peninsula. Then, in the readjustment of the European balance following the War of the Spanish Succession, the Italians exchanged one foreign master for another. The Austrian Habsburgs took over the Italian possessions and the Italian hegemony of their Spanish cousins. The political map of the peninsula in the early 1700's shows Austria established in Lombardy. Flanking Lombardy are the two decaying commercial republics of Venice and Genoa, and in the mountainous northwest the small but rising state of Piedmont-Savoy (technically the Kingdom of Sardinia after its acquisition of that Mediterranean island in 1720). Further down the peninsula are the Grand Duchy of Tuscany (formerly the Republic of Florence), the Papal States, and the Austrian Two Sicilies. None of these states was more than a minor power. In institutions, the Two Sicilies and the Papal States had scarcely emerged from the Middle Ages.

Yet, Italy must not be written off as a negligible quantity in eighteenth-century Europe. Rome remained the capital of the Catholic world. Venice still produced great painters, and Naples was the schoolmaster of European musicians. Piedmont, Lombardy, and Tuscany, and even Naples, contributed to the economic and intellectual advances of the century. Above all, Italy continued to be a big stake in balance-of-power politics, a perennial source of dissension and spoils for the stronger European states. In 1720, to counter the ambitions of the Spanish queen, Elizabeth Farnese, the Austrian Habsburgs took over the island of Sicily, which had gone to Piedmont in the Utrecht settlement of 1713; in return, Piedmont secured Sardinia, originally assigned to Austria. In the 1730's, a complicated series of exchanges gave the Two Sicilies to Elizabeth's elder son, "Baby Carlos," while the Austrians gained some minor bits of territory and the succession of Tuscany. In 1768, Genoa ceded the island of Corsica to France. Defenseless Italy was the natural victim of ambitious dynasts and empire-builders.

Divided Germany: The Habsburg Domains

Germany, too, was divided, split into some three hundred states—large, small, and minute. The Peace of Westphalia in 1648 had added to the sovereign rights of the individual states and had reduced almost to zero the authority of their nominal overlord, the Holy Roman Emperor. Germany also suffered from the blighting effects of the Thirty Years' War and the campaigns of Louis XIV and from its medieval confusion of taxes and standards of measure. But Germany, unlike Italy, was not defenseless: it contained two considerable powers, Austria and Prussia.

The Austrian Habsburgs won a series of military and diplomatic victories in the early eighteenth century. They were pressing their own *Drang nach Osten* against the Turks (see p. 34), and in the last war against Louis XIV they had obtained Belgium and parts of Italy. Yet the acquisitions of 1713 were removed from the central bloc of Habsburg lands in Austria, Hungary, Bohemia, and Silesia. The Emperor Charles VI (1711-1740) scarcely made a beginning at consolidating his rule over this large but disconnected empire. Charles spent much of his reign persuading his own noble subjects to ratify the Pragmatic Sanction, a constitutional agreement whereby, in the absence of sons, his daughter Maria Theresa would succeed him in all his territories. The empire thus carefully preserved was a dynastic creation, an assemblage of lands largely devoid of common interests or real unity. Except in the case of the Pragmatic Sanction, Charles VI made little headway against the Austrian, Bohemian, and Hungarian nobles who preserved most of their medieval prerogatives and who, by controlling local estates and diets, controlled the grant of taxes and the appointment of officials.

Finance and the army were the chief practical weaknesses of the Habsburg regime. Although Charles ruled a population more than twice as large as Britain's, the revenues of his government were less than half as large as Britain's. In 1740, when he died, the pay of the civil service and the army was more than two years in arrears. Small wonder that the army itself fell short of its paper strength of 100,000 men and was ill prepared for the great test of strength with Prussia which came in the 1740's.

The Rise of Prussia

Whereas Austria enjoyed the appearances rather than the realities of great-power status, Prussia possessed few of the appearances but a great many of the realities. In 1715, Prussia looked to be little more than just another German state. Its territories were scattered across North Germany from the Rhine on the west to the Vistula and beyond on the east. Consisting largely of half-deserted tracts of sand and swamp, these lands had meager natural resources and carried on relatively little trade. With less than three million inhabitants, Prussia ranked only twelfth among the European states in population. Even her capital city, Berlin, located on the unimportant River Spree, had scarcely any of the obvious geographical advantages enjoyed by Rome, Constantinople, Paris, London, and the other great capitals.

A wise prophet might well have foreseen that Catholic Austria would never unite a Germany in which Protestantism was so strong. But he would probably have predicted that a new Germany would center in Frankfurt in the heart of the Rhine country, or in Saxon Leipzig or Dresden; he would hardly have chosen the unpromising town of Berlin and the minor house of Hohenzollern. Prussian greatness came in large measure from the energetic policies of a long line of very able Hohenzollern rulers, beginning with the seventeenth-century Great Elector.

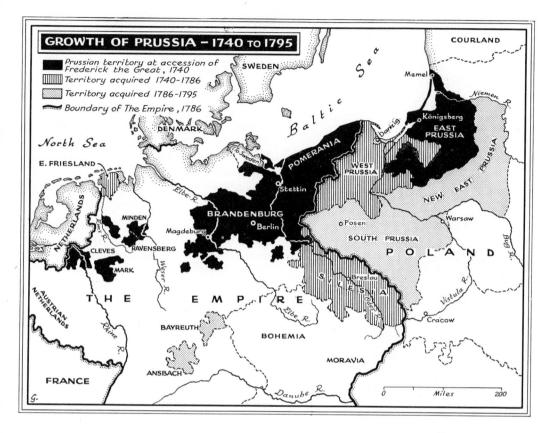

GROWTH OF PRUSSIA – 1740 to 1795

■ Prussian territory at accession of Frederick the Great, 1740
▦ Territory acquired 1740-1786
▒ Territory acquired 1786-1795
‑‑‑ Boundary of The Empire, 1786

COURLAND

North Sea

Baltic Sea

SWEDEN

Memel

DENMARK

Königsberg
EAST
PRUSSIA

Niemen R.

E. FRIESLAND

Danzig

POMERANIA

To Sweden

Stettin

WEST
PRUSSIA

NEW EAST PRUSSIA

NETHERLANDS

MINDEN

Magdeburg

BRANDENBURG

Berlin

Posen

Warsaw

CLEVES

RAVENSBERG

SOUTH PRUSSIA

Bug R.

MARK

Weser R.

Elbe R.

P O L A N D

AUSTRIAN NETHERLANDS

T H E   E M P I R E

SILESIA

Breslau

Oder R.

Vistula R.

Elbe R.

Cracow

Rhine R.

BAYREUTH

BOHEMIA

FRANCE

ANSBACH

MORAVIA

Danube R.

0   Miles   200

G.

The Hohenzollern house had been established since the fifteenth century as Electors of Brandenburg, which lay between the Elbe and Oder rivers and had been an outpost of the *Drang nach Osten* in the Middle Ages. A Hohenzollern had been the last Master of the Teutonic Knights. In the late Middle Ages, the Teutonic Knights had pushed the Germanic frontier east of the Vistula to a land called Prussia at the southeast corner of the Baltic Sea. In 1525, when this Prussian area fell to Brandenburg, it was separated from the center of Hohenzollern power by lands belonging to Poland. In western Germany, the Hohenzollerns acquired parcels of land in the lower Rhine Valley (Cleves and Mark) early in the seventeenth century. A network of other states separated these Rhenish lands from Brandenburg.

Thus, when Frederick William, the Great Elector (1640-1688), succeeded to the Hohenzollern inheritance as the Thirty Years' War was drawing to a close, his lands consisted of a nucleus in Brandenburg with separate outlying regions to east and west. With extraordinary persistence, the rulers of Brandenburg-Prussia for the next two hundred years devoted themselves to the task of making a solid block of territory out of these scattered bits, a task they finished triumphantly in 1866. Unlike most of their major rivals among the princely German houses—the Habsburgs with their vast non-German lands, the Wettins of Saxony with their Polish crown, the Guelfs of Hanover with their English crown—they seldom let themselves be tempted to acquire commitments outside Germanic lands. When later they did share in the partitions

One of the giant soldiers of Frederick William I of Prussia.

of Poland, they settled German landlords on these Polish lands.

The Great Elector directed his foreign policy toward the expulsion of the Swedes from the Pomeranian territories, between Brandenburg and the Baltic, which they had acquired in 1648. Hence his alliance with the French against the Swedes in the 1670's during the Dutch War of Louis XIV, and hence his bitter disappointment that, despite his victory over the Swedes at Fehrbellin in 1675, Prussia got nothing when peace was made in 1679. Under the Great Elector's son, the mediocre Frederick I (1688-1713), Prussia played but a minor part in the great wars that humbled Louis XIV, and she got but minor territorial gains at Utrecht.

The Hohenzollerns did, however, secure a useful gain in prestige. In 1701, as the price for entering the War of the Spanish Succession, Frederick assumed the title, "King in Prussia," and his new status was confirmed at Utrecht. Though technically Frederick was king only in Prussia proper, which lay outside the boundaries of the Holy Roman Empire, even a partial royal title conferred new dignity on the dynasty. According to Frederick the Great, the grandson of the first Hohenzollern king:

> What originally was rooted in vanity turned out to be a masterpiece of statesmanship. The royal crown was a bait that Frederick flung before all his posterity, and by which he seemed to say to them: 'I have procured you a title, therefore show yourself worthy of it.' *

The Great Elector himself had thoroughly prepared the ground for his successors' assumption of royal responsibilities. He had found his lands largely ruined by the Thirty Years' War, the farms wasted, the population cut in half, the army reduced to a disorderly rabble of a few thousand men. He repaired the damage systematically. He encouraged the immigration of Polish Jews and other refugees from religious persecution, notably 20,000 French Huguenots to whom he gave partial exemption from taxation. The Great Elector built a small but efficient standing army that enabled Prussia to command large foreign subsidies for participating in the coalitions against Louis XIV. In peacetime, he had soldiers construct such public works as a canal between the Elbe and the Oder and Berlin's famous park and boulevard, the Tiergarten and Unter den Linden.

Finally, and most important, the Great Elector's administrative policies set the Hohenzollern pattern of centralized absolutism. He began to curb the independence

* Quoted in Robert Ergang, *The Potsdam Führer* (New York, 1941), 20.

CHAPTER XVI

of the *Junkers,* as the landed gentry of the eastern Hohenzollern lands were called. He did not reduce them to the do-nothing status of the French nobility of the sword, and he confirmed their power over the serfs on their own estates. But he pared down the authority of the Junker-controlled provincial diets and made Berlin the real political capital of the Prussian state. He gradually gathered in his own hands the crucial power of levying taxes, which he collected through his own appointees, the nucleus of the famous Prussian civil service. The money thus secured went to the army, officered largely by Junkers. By the eighteenth century, a Junker could hardly have a career except in the royal service. The Great Elector was aided by a Lutheran state church that taught the virtues of obedience and discipline, and by an educational system that did the same.

The Great Elector's son, Frederick I, like many German princes, was a victim of the continent-wide mania for imitating the splendors of Louis XIV. Frederick thought that a suggestion of marital infidelity enhanced sovereign majesty, and so, though happily married, he maintained an official mistress with whom he took decorous afternoon promenades. In futile attempts to copy the other luxuries of Versailles, he nearly bankrupted his state. But he did become King Frederick I, and he and his talented queen attracted artists and intellectuals to the Hohenzollern court.

Frederick William I

The second Hohenzollern king, Frederick William I (1713-1740), resumed the policies of the Great Elector. Frederick the Great summed up the change in an epigram: "Under Frederick I Berlin was the Athens of the north; under Frederick William it became the Sparta." Economy, absolutism, and the army preoccupied this Spartan king. As soon as Frederick William I had given his father a lavish funeral, he ruthlessly dismissed the supernumeraries of the court and reduced government expenses to a fraction of what they had been. He reiterated the order *"Ein Plus Machen"* (show a surplus) and bequeathed a full treasury to his son. But his frugality did not extend to projects that he thought really worth while. He financed the immigration of 12,000 South German Protestants who opened up new farmlands in East Prussia.

To increase centralization, Frederick William I set up a small board of experts to administer his provinces and the departments of his government. This had the explicit and resounding title of *Generalober-finanzkriegsunddomänendirektorium* (General Superior Finance War and Domain Directory—General Directory, for short). The King insisted on hard work and punctuality. He treated the counselors of the General Directory as he treated lesser officials, paying them meanly and belaboring them with his cane for slovenly performance of their duties. A late arrival at one of the daily sessions of the General Directory paid a severe fine; an unexcused absentee faced six months in jail.

Frederick William I doubled the size of the standing army, but he maintained the strength of the laboring force of his underpopulated state by furloughing troops for nine months a year to work on farms. To secure guns and uniforms, he established state factories. The army also prompted his sole extravagance—a regiment of tall grenadiers, all six feet or over, who wore special caps more than a foot high to increase the impression of size. In recruiting his beloved "giants," the king threw economy to the winds, employing scores of scouts in other German states, paying exorbitant prices, and even trading royal musicians and prize stallions for especially tall specimens. Frederick William hoped to found a race of supermen by marrying his grenadiers to "giantesses," but the offspring of this experiment in eugenics were of discouragingly average size.

Eighteenth-century observers rightly called the Prussia of Frederick William an "armed camp" and berated its army for being a "gigantic penal institution" in which death punished minor infractions of the regulations. Like the ancient Spartans, Frederick William devoted himself exclusively to preparation for war. He showed scant appreciation for culture, despised everything French, and neglected the education of his subjects. With typical parsi-mony and short-sightedness, he refused to raise the inadequate fees of judges and lawyers, so that corruption and lethargy obstructed the course of justice in Prussia.

Yet this regime worked and, in terms of power, worked extremely well. The Junkers, for all their old-fashioned feudal outlook, were intensely loyal to the Hohenzollerns and made some of the best army officers of the century. The army itself, though smaller than those of France, Russia, and Austria, was far and away the best drilled and the most rigidly disciplined in Europe. When Frederick William I died in 1740, the Prussian David was ready to fight the Austrian Goliath.

V: The Eastern Powers

Russia under Peter the Great

In the early eighteenth century, Russia, like Prussia, became for the first time a major element in the European balance. The man responsible for the new importance of Russia was Tsar Peter the Great (1689-1725). An enormous man, six feet six inches tall, Peter would have made a capital giant for Frederick William. His enthusiasms, passions, and appetites matched his size. When enraged by revolts, he personally beheaded the culprits, and it took weeks to pick up the pieces after one of his drinking bouts. Peter's orgies threatened the lives of his courtiers, who were expected to keep pace with him, and they finally damaged the iron constitution of the Tsar himself.

In his youth, Peter came under the spell of the West. He hobnobbed with the German, Dutch, and British merchants and adventurers in the "German" quarter of Moscow and with the crews of the Dutch ships putting into Archangel in the far north. His fascination with western military prowess and technological achievements prompted his grand tour of Europe, 1697-98, the first time in more than six hundred years that a Russian monarch had left home except on a military campaign. Peter worked as an apprentice in a Dutch shipyard and studied at first hand the operations of English naval arsenals. He wanted, above all else, to learn how to strengthen the Russian army and build a fleet in the western style. He hoped thereby to extend Russian territories in the Baltic at the expense of Sweden and in the south at the expense of Turkey. He crushed Sweden in the Great Northern War (for details, see p. 34) and, though unable to defeat the Turks decisively, prepared the way for later Russian successes against them.

Peter's ambitions for conquest inspired almost all his innovations in domestic policy.

To provide increased revenues for warfare, he instituted a head tax, a tax on every "soul," as the Russians put it. To staff his enlarged army and administration, he rigorously enforced the rule by which landowners owed service to the state. He decreed "civil death" for those who failed to register, which meant that they were outside the protection of the law and could be attacked without fear of consequences. Universal service was made compulsory for life. The noble was required to leave his estate intact to one of his sons, to avoid its being divided up every generation. At the age of fifteen, every male child of this service class was assigned to his post, in the army or civil service, or at the court. Peter often required his noble servants to do jobs they considered beneath them; he filled their ranks with outsiders and newcomers, to whom he gave rank and title. But these humiliations were not so important as the fact that the entire class of service nobility was brought into a position of complete dependence upon the Tsar. In the administration, Peter borrowed official titles from Germany and Holland, and he copied the central organs of the Swedish government, notably the "colleges," whereby each ministry was directed not by a single minister but by a kind of board of directors. This collegiate system was cumbersome, but it made corruption difficult because any one member of a college could be checked on by all his colleagues.

In a move symbolizing his whole outlook, Peter the Great transferred his capital from Moscow, in central Russia, to Saint Petersburg on an arm of the Baltic in the northwestern corner of his realm. He built the new capital from the ground up on land taken from the Swedes, forced his nobles to build splendid mansions there, and called it his "window to the west." Commercially and strategically, St. Petersburg was indeed a window, for the new city had promise as

a port. But, as a French visitor remarked, it was "a city of palaces in the midst of solitude." The low-lying site was damp, menaced by floods, and far removed from the productive farmlands of the Russian interior. As a place to live, Petersburg was terribly expensive and downright dangerous. Hundreds of workmen lost their lives in constructing the city; wolves roamed its streets, and a pack devoured a woman one afternoon in front of the great house of the Tsar's personal favorite. These handicaps, however, meant nothing to Peter; in fact he rather enjoyed them.

Tsar Peter the Great of Russia. (Wedgwood medallion.)

Even though the Orthodox Church was already generally subservient to the Russian State, Peter determined to disarm possible clerical opposition. Thus, when the Patriarch died in 1700, the Tsar simply failed to appoint a successor. Eventually he extended the collegiate system to the Church. He created a governing agency first called the spiritual college, and later the Holy Directing Synod, and headed by a Procurator, who was always a layman. Peter stated his reasons for abolishing the patriarchate with remarkable frankness:

From the collegiate government of the church there is not so much danger to the country of disturbances and troubles as may be produced by one spiritual ruler. For the common people do not understand the difference between the spiritual power and that of the autocrat; but, dazzled by the splendor and glory of the highest pastor, they think that he is a second sovereign of like power with the autocrat or with even more, and that the spiritual power is that of another and better realm. If then there should be any difference of opinion between the Patriarch and the Tsar, it might easily happen that the people, perhaps misled by designing persons, should take the part of the Patriarch, in the mistaken belief that they were fighting for God's cause.*

Peter made fun of old religious ceremonies and taboos. He ordered the numbering of years from the birth of Christ in the western fashion rather than from the Creation, as had been the Russian custom. He ended the clerical monopoly of education by setting up professional and technical schools under the aegis of the state. With remarkable autocratic impatience, Peter tried to convert Russia to western ways in the course of a single generation. He ordered the printing of foreign scientific books in Russian translation and commanded his subjects to shave, take up smoking, and wear western dress in place of their usual flowing robes. Government agents at city gates collected a tax from every bearded man and delivered a special metal receipt engraved: "A beard is a useless burden."

But the Orthodox Church had long taught that man was made in the image of a bearded God. The majority of Russians regarded Peter's views on shaving as sacrilege and deplored almost all his other innovations. The more devout regarded the Tsar as Antichrist or the herald of the end of

RUSSIA'S WINDOWS TO THE WEST
IN THE EIGHTEENTH CENTURY

Acquired by Peter the Great, 1689-1725
Acquired between 1730-1740
Acquired by Elizabeth, 1741-1762
Acquired by Catherine, 1762-1796

the world. All classes groaned under Peter's tyranny. The hopes of the noble and clerical opposition rested on Alexis, his estranged son and heir, until Peter had the young Alexis put to death by torture. Meanwhile, foreign books, ineptly translated, went unsold and unread, and were finally used as covers for Orthodox devotional volumes. The conservative reaction against Peter could scarcely have been shown more picturesquely.

Peter the Great intensified the influences of the West upon Russian civilization and thus aroused the defenders of Russia's peculiarly Slavic character and her old Byzantine heritage. He came to embody the eternal conflict between the new and the old in Russia. Both those who have hailed his achievements and those who have

---

* Quoted by E. Schuyler, *Peter the Great* (New York, 1884), II, 389.

CHAPTER XVI

denounced him have felt that he was somehow a revolutionary figure.

But was Peter actually a revolutionary? He did not greatly alter, but rather simply intensified, the chief characteristics of Russia—an absolute autocracy, depending for its administration on a class of service nobility, with its economy rooted in the system of serfdom. The position of tsar was more absolute than ever at the end of Peter's reign. Universal service was more rigidly enforced upon the nobles. And serfdom was both deepened and extended, largely as a result of the new system of taxation. When the landlord was made responsible for the collection of the new "soul-tax" on his serfs, he tended to include everybody possible on the lists of those who must pay. Accordingly, thousands of humble men whose status had not previously been servile found themselves, and their descendants, enrolled on the tax lists as serfs. Even the foreign influences in the army, in commerce, and in culture, which Peter the Great is often credited with introducing, had begun well before his accession, and were only increased by him. And the Church, which he weakened as an institution, had already experienced the weakening of the schism of the Old Believers, itself the result of western influences.

Peter is still often regarded as a revolutionary innovator because of the violence with which he pressed his will. He was so large physically, so boisterous, so overflowing with energy, that he seemed always to be at the center of an upheaval. Moreover, the field in which he did make radical innovations—everyday manners and behavior—affected people strongly. When he suddenly ordered a timid gentlewoman, who had been brought up in the sheltered way of the old Russian nobility, to put on a low-cut western dress, to give a mixed party, to dance, and to drink (and, if she refused, Peter was quite capable of holding her nose

and pouring the wine down her throat), this seemed a revolutionary change to her, even though it did not influence Russian history very deeply. Here was a tsar who loved manual labor, who pulled his subjects' teeth for the fun of it, who detested ceremony, who smoked and drank and swore. No wonder the reign of Peter the Great has always appeared to involve more drastic changes than it actually accomplished. Perhaps the most significant change was the new power status gained by Russia as a result of Peter's conquests; no western European government could now afford to ignore either her capabilities or her intentions.

Russia after Peter

In the thirty-seven years after Peter died (1725-1762), there were no fewer than seven nominal Russian autocrats, most of them incapable women or sickly youths brought to the throne through palace revolutions engineered by the Guards' regiments, and occasionally sponsored by intriguing foreign diplomats. None of these sovereigns had the commanding personality of such great Russian rulers as Peter. The temporary weakening of the autocracy permitted other forces to make a bid for power, notably the nobles who were able to secure the gradual relaxation of the rigid rules by which Peter had bound them. Bit by bit, their obligations were relaxed, until in 1762 they were entirely exempted from compulsory service. Yet the service that had been hated when it was compulsory became fashionable now that it was optional. Since there was really little else for a noble to do except serve the state, most Russian nobles continued to do so; but the nobility had now become a privileged order without legal obligations.

Serfdom had originated in large measure to assure the tsar's military-service men of a labor supply to till their estates. Morally speaking, therefore, serfdom should have been abolished as soon as the service-men freed themselves from service. Politically, however, this was impossible, for nobles who could wring concessions from the tsar did not propose to be deprived of the serfs who made possible their lives of ease. Indeed, along with the measures emancipating the nobility came measures extending the nobles' power of punishment and other rights over their serfs. Moreover, the number of serfs increased all the time, as the Crown continued to reward loyal nobles by gifts of land and of the people living on it.

The generation after Peter is also notable for the deeper and deeper involvement of Russia in western European wars and diplomacy. The old Russian isolation was disappearing rapidly. In these decades, too, a deep wave of French cultural influence engulfed the Russian nobility, who became madly enamored of French wines, French manners, and French literature. Scorning their native tongue and their native ways, they spoke French by preference and aped the French every moment of the waking day. This had a marked effect on Russian social life, since French influence affected only the nobility. The lower classes, meanwhile, remained steeped in ignorance and deeply devoted to the ancient Muscovite ways. A cleavage thus opened up between the "Frenchified" nobles and the Russian people, a gap so deep and wide that members of both groups were finding it less and less possible to communicate with each other. This deep rift between classes was to prove of critical importance for later Russian history.

Poland and Turkey

In the eighteenth century, Russia was the only great power in eastern Europe. Poland and Turkey bulked large on the map and still included extensive territories that they were subsequently to lose. Both states, however, suffered from incompetent government and a backward population. These two decaying empires, containing large racial and religious minorities, aroused the aggressive instincts of their stronger neighbors. Poland, consequently, was doomed to disappear before the end of the century, the victim of partition by Russia, Prussia, and Austria. Turkey held on, but only just, and acquired the dangerous status of the "Sick Man of Europe."

An oligarchy of selfish nobles ran eighteenth-century Poland and ruined it. Unlike the English gentry, the Polish nobles ignored economic progress; unlike the Prussian Junkers, they had no concept of service to the Crown, or indeed to anything except their own narrow class interests. They destroyed the middle class and the once-flourishing towns by persecuting Jewish shopkeepers and foreign merchants and by arbitrarily forbidding all imports and exports for long periods of time. They exploited their estates so harshly that they gave Poland the reputation of being the "peasants' hell."

The Polish government was a political curiosity shop. The diet of nobles elected the king, usually the foreign candidate who offered the highest bribes to its members. It may be wondered why anyone should have paid good money to become King of Poland, for each new monarch solemnly contracted to transfer most of his prerogatives to the diet. The diet in turn was corrupted by foreign money and sometimes paralyzed by an extraordinary practice known as the liberum veto that gave a single nobleman the right to block any measure indefinitely. To impose this early Polish improvement on the filibuster, all the minority of one had to do was shout "I do not wish it!" and then gallop off before his colleagues could catch up with him and

CHAPTER XVI

make him change his mind. The weakness resulting from this confusion may be summed up in the fact that eighteenth-century Poland maintained neither a diplomatic service nor a regular army.

Compared with Poland, the Ottoman Empire was at least a functioning state. It was backward, of course, especially in economic and technological matters. It had no Peter the Great to jar it out of isolation, for the sultans of the eighteenth century were the captives of the arrogant caste of janissaries, who had abandoned most of their soldierly duties. Yet this retrograde and corrupt government did at least govern and showed considerable staying power in war. So the "Sick Man" was to linger on through the century, kept alive partly because the would-be heirs of Ottoman territory, Russia and Austria, were bitter rivals.

VI: War and Diplomacy in the Eighteenth Century

From the survey just concluded of the European states in the early 1700's, it is evident that the balance of power was at best rather precarious. Should the strong states prey upon the weak, the balance was almost certain to be threatened. The two rapidly rising powers, Russia and Prussia, did in fact expand at the expense of their neighbors. Here, then, were two of the great issues involved in the wars and diplomacy of the eighteenth century—the aggression of Russia against Sweden, Poland, and Turkey, and the aggression of Prussia against Austria and Poland. The third great international issue concerned the Atlantic powers—the colonial and commercial rivalry between Britain and the Bourbon monarchies of France and Spain. International tensions were increased by all manner of secondary issues. The old competition between French Bourbons and Austrian Habsburgs was still in very lively condition, as was the Habsburgs' traditional aim of advancing down the Danube Valley toward the Black Sea. The family ambitions of Elizabeth Farnese added another disruptive element.

The Great Northern War and Its Aftermath

The first major shifts in the balance of power occurred in northern and eastern Europe. The Great Northern War, 1700-1721, settled a contest for control of the Baltic; the loser was Charles XII of Sweden, and the chief victor was Peter the Great of Russia. Peter had taken the offensive first against the Turks in the hope of ousting them and their satellites from the northern shore of the Black Sea. In 1696, he had acquired the port of Azov, on a northern arm of the Black Sea. Then, in 1697, the fifteen-year old Charles XII succeeded to the Swedish throne. The mere fact of his youth opened up the Baltic question; the states along the eastern and southern rim of the Baltic apparently had a perfect opportunity to break up the Swedish empire established by Gustavus Adolphus in the early seventeenth century. Accordingly, in 1699 Peter of Russia concluded an anti-Swedish alliance with the King of Denmark and with Augustus the Strong, the Elector of Saxony, who had also been elected to the Polish throne.

The opening round of the Great Northern War quickly showed that the allies had miscalculated badly in counting on the youth and presumed ineffectiveness of their opponent. Charles XII was a born fighter, an amazingly warlike young man whose favorite pastime was cutting off the heads of live sheep as they were driven through the corridors of his palace. He beat all his enemies in turn during 1700, forcing Denmark out of the war and humiliating Peter at Narva, on the southern shore of the Gulf of Finland.

After Narva, however, Charles committed a series of fatal blunders. He spent years in the attempt to take the Polish crown from Augustus of Saxony and give it to a mediocre Polish nobleman, Stanislas Leszczynski. Charles finally got the Polish crown for his puppet, but only briefly, and only at the cost of giving Peter time to regroup the Russian forces and seize the bit of Swedish territory on which to build St. Petersburg. When Charles again turned to Russia, he risked all his scanty resources in an invasion of central Russia that ended disastrously at the battle of Poltava (1709), where Peter's army wiped out the stain of Narva. Charles took refuge with the Turks, whom he prodded into war against Peter. In 1711, surrounded by a larger Turkish force, Peter was forced to hand back Azov; Charles however, gained nothing. Returned to Sweden, the perennially belligerent king was shot to death in 1718 during a war with Norway.

The doom of Sweden's Baltic empire was now sealed. The Treaty of Nystadt in 1721 confirmed Russia's acquisition of the former Swedish lands along the eastern and southern shores of the Gulf of Finland. The other beneficiary of Sweden's collapse was Prussia. Peter, after much persuading, had finally convinced the reluctant and economy-minded Frederick William I to take part in the last stages of the war. Prussia thereby secured some of Sweden's Pomeranian lands and the important Baltic port of Stettin.

The Great Northern War affected the balance of power not only by strengthening Russia and Prussia but also by involving Turkey and Poland. For a time it looked as if Turkey's Balkan and Black Sea empire might go the way of Sweden's Baltic one. Although the Ottoman forces had held Peter at bay in 1711, they soon suffered a bad defeat in a war with the Habsburg Emperor Charles VI. This first Turkish war (1716-1718) ended at the Treaty of Passarowitz (1718), which enabled Austria to recover the piece of Hungary still under Ottoman rule and also gave her parts of present-day Rumania and Yugoslavia. A second Turkish war, 1735-1739, revealed the infirmity of the Austrian army, the Turks' capacity for muddling through, and the inevitable frictions between the would-be heirs of the "Sick Man." In this second war, Russia and Austria were allied, but they soon fell to quarreling over the division of the prospective spoils. In the end, Austria lost the gains she had made at Passarowitz, and Russia, though hoping to get the Crimean Peninsula jutting into the Black Sea, merely recovered Azov.

In Poland, meantime, the defeat suffered by Charles XII at Poltava had enabled Augustus the Strong to recover his crown from Stanislas Leszczynski. The Swedish puppet, however, had by no means completed his historical role, for he presently married his daughter, Marie Leszczynska, to Louis XV of France. When Augustus died in 1733, French diplomats engineered the election of Stanislas to succeed him by distributing lavish bribes to the Polish diet. This election provoked a serious international crisis, since both Austria and Russia disliked the prospect of having France control the Polish king. Russia sent 30,000

CHAPTER XVI

troops into Poland and convoked a rump session of the diet which elected a rival king, Augustus III, the son of Augustus the Strong. The stage was set for the War of the Polish Succession (1733-1735)—Stanislas, France, and Spain versus Augustus III, Russia, and Austria.

The war was brief, for none of the participants wanted a real, hard fight. French and Austrian armies fired away at each other for a while in the Rhine Valley and in northern Italy, hundreds of miles from Poland. The diplomats then worked out a compromise settlement that was pleasing to almost all parties. To the satisfaction of Austria and Russia, Augustus III secured the Polish throne. From the French standpoint, Stanislas Leszczynski was well compensated for his loss. He became the Duke of Lorraine, a principality on the northeastern border of France, with the provision that when he died Lorraine would go to his daughter, Marie, and thence to the French Crown. France would thus move one step closer toward filling out her "natural" frontiers. To be sure, Lorraine already had a duke, Francis, husband of the Habsburg heiress, Maria Theresa; the awkwardness was neatly resolved by transferring Francis to the Italian Grand Duchy of Tuscany, where the old line of rulers conveniently died out in 1737. Finally, as a by-product of the settlement, Elizabeth Farnese of Spain capped twenty years of maternal perseverance against Austrian opposition by procuring the Kingdom of Naples for "Baby Carlos," her elder and now grown-up son.

Early Eighteenth-Century Diplomacy in Review

The War of the Polish Succession may well seem futile and trivial, much ado about a kingship possessing no real power. And the postwar settlement, which affected chiefly Italy and Lorraine, may seem to be a striking case of diplomatic irrelevance. Yet the whole Polish crisis is a most instructive example of the workings of dynastic politics and of the constant shifts in the balance of power. Certainly no great national issues were at stake, except for the rather nebulous but nevertheless significant ones of French, Russian, and Austrian national prestige. The statesmen regarded thrones as the pawns of diplomacy, to be assigned without reference to the wishes of the populations involved. None of them contemplated canvassing Neapolitan sentiment on Carlos or conducting a referendum to see whether the Poles preferred Stanislas or Augustus. None of them, of course, gave a thought to the welfare of Poland, which came out of the crisis weaker than ever.

Yet the complicated arrangements of the 1730's did preserve the balance of power by giving something to almost everybody involved. Although the diplomats could not prevent a little war over Poland, they did keep it from becoming a big one. Indeed, throughout the period from 1713 to 1739 the force of diplomacy operated to avoid or at least to localize wars. Britain and France took the lead in the campaign to keep any one power from upsetting the international apple-cart. They both joined with Austria in thwarting Elizabeth Farnese's early attempts to grab part of Italy by force, and "Baby Carlos" had to wait twenty years to get his Neapolitan kingdom. The British dispatched a squadron to the Baltic during the last part of the Great Northern War so that Tsar Peter's gains would not be too great. To prolong the life of the "Sick Man," the British chaperoned the negotiations between Turkey and Austria at Passarowitz in 1718, and the French revived the old Ottoman alliance of Francis I. French aid accounted in part for the favorable terms that Turkey secured from Austria in 1739.

Friction between Britain and the Bourbon Monarchies

Walpole of Britain and Fleury of France both worked for peace in the 1720's and the 1730's because stability abroad would promote economic recovery at home. The informal diplomatic partnership of the two great Atlantic powers did not last very long, for it ran afoul of their growing competition for commerce and empire. Neither Walpole nor Fleury could prevent the world-wide war between Britain and France that broke out in 1739 and 1740 and that lasted, with many intervals of peace, until the final defeat of Napoleon in 1815.

This "Second Hundred Years' War" had already begun half a century before 1739, back in the days of Louis XIV. The Utrecht settlement of 1713 had not fully settled the rivalry between Britain and France (and France's Bourbon partner, Spain). Thus the war of 1739 was as much the renewal of an old struggle as the onset of a new one. The specific issue behind the crisis of 1739 was the comparatively minor question of British chagrin at the disappointing results of the Asiento privilege. As the South Sea Company discovered, the Asiento gave Britain little more than a token share in the trade of the Spanish American colonies. What British captains could not get legitimately they got by smuggling. Spain retaliated by establishing a coast-guard patrol in American waters to ward off smugglers. British merchants complained bitterly of the rough treatment handed out by the Spanish guards, and in 1738 they exhibited to Parliament Captain Jenkins, who claimed that Spanish brutality had cost him an ear. Jenkins duly produced his severed ear, preserved in salt and cotton batting. Asked to state his reaction on losing the ear, he replied, "I commended my soul to God and my cause to my country." Walpole retorted that the protection of British smugglers against legitimate Spanish patrols did not give the government a very strong case. But Walpole could restrain neither the anti-Spanish fever sweeping the country to which Jenkins had commended his cause, nor the bellicose faction of "Boy Patriots" that had arisen within Walpole's own Whig party.

In October, 1739, to the joyful pealing of church bells, Britain began the War of Jenkins' Ear against Spain. "They are ringing their bells now," Walpole observed tartly. "They will be wringing their hands soon." As if to vindicate his prophecy, the British fleet promptly made a mess of the opening campaign in the Caribbean, and France showed every sign of coming to Spain's assistance. Dynastic ties had already brought the two Bourbon monarchies into alliance during the Polish war. Now French economic interests were at stake, for France supplied the bulk of the wares which Spanish galleons carried to America, and which cheaper British contraband was driving out of the Spanish colonial market.

The War of the Austrian Succession, 1740-1748

In 1740, a chain of events occurred that soon bound the colonial war to a great continental conflict over the Austrian succession. On the death of the Emperor Charles VI in 1740, the Habsburg domains fell to his daughter, Maria Theresa, who was only twenty-three years old. Expecting to outwit Maria Theresa because she was young, politically inexperienced, and a woman, the German princes chose to ignore the Pragmatic Sanction guaranteeing her succession. They looked forward to yet another victory in their already successful contest against Habsburg domination; the Elector of Bavaria, for one, hoped to become Holy Roman Emperor. The first to

The Battle of Culloden, showing the rigid battle formations used in the eighteenth century.

strike, however, was Frederick the Great (1740-1786), who had just inherited the Prussian throne from Frederick William I. In December, 1740, Frederick suddenly invaded Silesia, a Habsburg province in the upper Oder Valley to the southeast of Brandenburg. He heated up some discredited old family claims to parts of Silesia and assured his uncle, George II of England, that he aimed at "the preservation and the real benefit of the House of Austria." All this was hypocrisy. Frederick really aimed at the aggrandizement of Prussia and the House of Hohenzollern.

In the War of the Austrian Succession, England and Austria were ranged against France, Spain, Prussia, and some lesser German states. Frederick won an emphatic victory in the campaigns on the Continent.

Though suffering an occasional setback, the Prussian army tenaciously defended its Silesian conquest and astounded Europe by its long night marches, sudden flank attacks, and other tactics of surprise quite different from the usual deliberate warfare of sieges. Frederick, however, deeply antagonized his allies by repeatedly deserting them to make secret peace arrangements with Austria. And he did little to support the imperial aspirations of the Bavarian Elector, who enjoyed only a brief tenure as "Emperor Charles VII."

The Anglo-Austrian alliance worked no better than the Franco-Prussian one. Many Englishmen felt that George II was betraying their true interests overseas by entangling them in German politics and the defense of Hanover. Nevertheless, the British nation still preferred the Hanoverians to the Stuarts. In 1745, "Bonnie Prince Charles," the grandson of the deposed James II, secured French backing and landed in Britain. He won significant recruits only among the chronically discontented Scottish highlanders, and in 1746 he was thoroughly defeated at Culloden. Jacobitism, never a very important political threat, was dead.

Outside Europe, the fighting of the 1740's was quite indecisive. The New England colonists took Louisburg, the French naval base on Cape Breton Island that commanded the approach to the St. Lawrence; on the other side of the world, the French took the port of Madras from the English East India Company. The British fleet did not win a real victory until 1747, and by then British merchant ships had suffered numerous attacks from French privateering expeditions. Although French privateers did comparatively little damage to British commerce, they were most humiliating to patriotic Englishmen. The humiliation increased when retaliatory British raids on French commerce often failed—and for the simple reason that French cargoes were insured in London, where rates were lower than in France, and London insurers kept their French customers informed of the movements of British ships.

The peace settlement ending the War of the Austrian Succession faithfully reflected the outcome of the actual fighting. Overseas, the Treaty of Aix-la-Chapelle (1748) restored both Louisburg and Madras to their former owners, and Britain later agreed to give up the troublesome Asiento privilege. In Central Europe, the war made Prussia a first-rate power and brought international fame to Frederick's army. The peace increased the population of Prussia by half through the permanent cession of Silesia, which had an important textile industry and extensive deposits of coal and iron in addition to a large population. Maria Theresa got scant compensation for this serious loss. Though her husband, Francis, won recognition as Holy Roman Emperor, she surrendered Parma and some other territorial crumbs in northern Italy to Philip, the second son of Elizabeth Farnese.

The Uneasy Peace, 1748-1756

The peace made in 1748 lasted only eight years. Then another and greater conflict, the Seven Years' War (1756-1763), broke out, caused partly by old issues left unsettled at Aix-la-Chapelle and partly by new grievances arising from the Austrian war. The world struggle between Britain and the Bourbons, in which the old war had been an indecisive preliminary engagement, kept right on in the form of an undeclared war during the nominal years of peace.

In Africa, Britain and France tried to exclude one another from the best supplies of slaves, in constant demand to man the sugar, rice, and tobacco plantations of the New World. In Asia, the English and French East India companies fought each other once removed, so to speak, by taking sides in the rivalries of native princes in southern India. By 1751, the energetic French administrator, Dupleix, had won the initial round of this indirect fight. Then the English, led by the equally energetic Clive, seized the initiative, and in 1754 Dupleix was called back home by the directors of the French company, who were unwilling to supply the money needed to continue his aggressive policy.

In North America, the two powers collided head on. English colonists from the Atlantic seaboard had already staked out claims to the rich wilderness between the Appalachians and the Mississippi. But the French, equally intent on appropriating the same area, stole a march on them and established a string of forts in western

CHAPTER XVI

Pennsylvania from Presqu'Isle (later Erie) south to Fort Duquesne (later Pittsburgh) at the head of the Ohio River. In 1754, a force of Virginians under the youthful George Washington tried unsuccessfully to dislodge the French from their strategic position at Fort Duquesne. In 1755, a second attempt, by a British expedition under General Braddock, likewise failed.

Colonists and mother country did not always see eye to eye on matters of basic policy. French recall of Dupleix is one example of such divergence. Another example is provided by the curious situation prevailing in the West Indies, then regarded as the greatest prizes of empire because they produced most of the world's sugar. New England traders could obtain sugar and its by-products (molasses and rum) more cheaply from the French plantations of Santo Domingo (Haiti), Guadeloupe, and Martinique than from Jamaica and other British sugar islands. French sugar made New England rum; New England rum besotted African Negroes; and, to complete this notorious "triangle trade," the sale of African slaves to French planters lined Yankee pockets—all in open violation of the mercantilist regulations that theoretically applied to both the French and British empires, and all to the immense disgust of the influential sugar interests of Britain and slave interests of Nantes in France. "Business as usual" complicated the Anglo-French struggle for world domination.

In Europe, there now occurred the dramatic shift of alliances called the Diplomatic Revolution. In the new war the fundamental conflicts were the same as in the old—Britain versus France, Prussia versus Austria—but the four powers reversed their alliances. Britain, which had joined Austria *against* Prussia in the 1740's, now paired off *with* Frederick the Great. And, in the most revolutionary move of the Diplomatic Revolution, France, which had sided *with* Frederick before, now not only stood *against* him but also joined with her hereditary enemy, Habsburg Austria.

The Diplomatic Revolution of 1756 expressed the resentment of the powers at the disloyal behavior of their old partners during the Austrian war. The French, in particular, had bitter memories of Frederick's repeated desertions and secret peace arrangements. Britain deplored Austrian reluctance to give first priority to the defense of English continental interests, which included maintaining the territorial integrity of Hanover and excluding the French from the Austrian Netherlands. Austria, in turn, regarded Hanover and Belgium as peripheral to her main concern, the recovery of Silesia. In 1755, therefore, Britain concluded a subsidy treaty with Russia to preserve the status quo in Hanover and the rest of North Germany. This British action almost unwittingly touched off the Diplomatic Revolution.

The Anglo-Russian treaty alarmed Frederick the Great, for he feared an eventual conflict with Russia for control of the Baltic and Poland. In January, 1756, accordingly, the Prussian king concluded an alliance with Britain which detached her from Russia. The alliance between England and Prussia isolated France and gave the Austrian chancellor, Kaunitz, exactly the opportunity he had been waiting for. What Austria needed in order to avenge herself on Frederick and to regain Silesia was an ally with a large army; what Austria needed was the alliance of France, not Britain. Using the Anglo-Prussian alliance as an argument, Kaunitz convinced Louis XV and his mistress, Madame de Pompadour, to drop the traditional Bourbon-Habsburg feud in favor of a working partnership. The last act of the Diplomatic Revolution occurred when the Empress Elizabeth of Russia joined the Franco-Austrian alliance. Russia had taken a minor part in the War of the Austrian Succession as a belated ally of Austria and England; Elizabeth now agreed to a larger role because she hated Frederick the Great and feared his aggression all the more now that he had deprived her of her English ally.

The Seven Years' War

The great coalition against Prussia was still incomplete when the war itself began. In May, 1756, Britain and France made official the state of hostilities already existing between them in North America. Three months later, Frederick the Great opened the war season in Europe by taking the offensive against the coalition menacing him. Once more the powers were engaged in a war that was really two separate wars —one continental, the other naval and colonial.

In the European campaigns of the Seven Years' War, both Frederick the Great and the Hohenzollern system faced a most formidable test. Prussia confronted the forces of Austria, France, and Russia, whose combined population was more than fifteen times larger than her own. She had almost no allies except for the British, who supplied financial subsidies but little actual military assistance. The traditions established by the Great Elector and developed by Frederick William I and Frederick the Great enabled the nation to survive. The submissive population of the "armed camp" patriotically applied every ounce of energy to the war effort. The King himself set a commanding example. In 1757, he wrote to one of his French friends:

I am assaulted from every side. Domestic trials, secret afflictions, public misfortunes, approaching calamities—such is my daily bread. But do not imagine I am weakening. If everything collapses I should calmly bury myself beneath the ruins. In these disastrous times one must fortify oneself with iron resolutions and

a heart of brass. It is a time for stoicism: the disciples of Epicurus would find nothing to say. . . .*

The Stoic king was the ablest military leader in the Seven Years' War and, despite his personal horror at the sufferings of the dying and wounded on the battlefield, he was the only one of the European monarchs to share the hardships of campaigning with the soldiers.

Frederick's "iron resolution" and "heart of brass" led him to adopt any expedient, fair or unfair, to gain his ends. To fill up the depleted ranks of his army, he ruthlessly violated international law by impressing soldiers from Prussia's smaller neighbors, Mecklenburg and Saxony. Since British subsidies covered only a fraction of his war expenses, he seized Saxon, Polish, and Russian coins. Then he melted them down, kept for Prussian use a large part of their precious metallic content, recast them with baser metals, and returned them to circulation. Although Frederick eventually had to submit Prussia's own coins to debasement, he made the whole operation the more scandalous by employing Jewish agents to perform it and then sitting back to welcome the anti-Semitic reaction that inevitably followed.

A final factor, perhaps the most important one of all, in saving Prussia was the inadequacy of the coalition arrayed against her. Most fortunately for Frederick, his enemies were never capable of exploiting their military successes to deliver a knock-out blow. Russia's generals were timid, and those of France and Austria were sometimes downright incompetent. Moreover, the French, the strongest of the allies, had to fight a two-front war, in Europe and overseas, and did not possess the financial resources to do justice to both. The grand alliance created by

---

* Quoted in G. P. Gooch, *Frederick the Great* (London, 1947), 41.

CHAPTER XVI

Kaunitz suffered particularly from the friction, mistrust, and cross-purposes that always threaten wartime coalitions. Indeed, his coalition did not last out the war. When the Empress Elizabeth of Russia died in January, 1762, she was succeeded by Peter III, a passionate admirer of Frederick the Great. The new tsar at once deserted Elizabeth's allies and placed Russia's forces at Frederick's disposal; no wonder that the grateful Prussian king called him "a divine ruler to whom I ought to erect altars!" Early in 1763, Frederick won his war. Austria thereupon agreed to the Peace of Hubertusburg, which permitted Prussia to retain Silesia.

While Frederick was having a close shave, his British partners were gaining a smashing victory in the Seven Years' War. Actually the British made a very lame start, suffering a series of setbacks on almost every front during the first year and a half of the fighting. On the Continent, the Duke of Cumberland, a son of King George II, signed a capitulation immobilizing his army and allowing the French to occupy the Electorate of Hanover. At sea, the British lost the important Mediterranean base of Minorca in the Balearic Islands, a disaster to which the home government contributed by sending (too late) reinforcements (too few) under Admiral Byng (a poor choice). Byng was unfairly saddled with the whole blame and was executed—"in order to encourage the others," Voltaire observed ironically. In North America, the British compounded Braddock's earlier failure against Fort Duquesne by losing the outpost of Oswego on Lake Ontario and fumbling an attack on Louisburg, the key to French Canada.

The most dramatic of Britain's misfortunes occurred in India. In June, 1756, the Nawab of Bengal, a native ally of the French, crowded 146 British prisoners into one small room with only two windows. The result was the atrocious "Black Hole" of Calcutta,

thus described by an officer of the English East India Company:

It was the hottest season of the year, and the night uncommonly sultry. . . . The excessive pressure of their bodies against one another, and the intolerable heat which prevailed as soon as the door was shut, convinced the prisoners that it was impossible to live through the night in this horrible confinement; and violent attempts were immediately made to force the door, but without effect, for it opened inward. . . .

The . . . effect of their confinement was a profuse and continued sweat, which soon produced intolerable thirst, succeeded by excruciating pains in the breast, with difficulty of breathing little short of suffocation.

• • •

At two o'clock not more than fifty remained alive. But even this number were too many to partake of the saving air, the contest for which and for life continued until the morn. . . .

An officer, sent by the nawab, came . . . with an order to open the prison. The dead were so thronged, and the survivors had so little strength remaining, that they were employed near half an hour in removing the bodies which lay against the door before they could clear a passage to go out one at a time; when of one hundred and forty-six who went in no more than twenty-three came out alive,—the ghastliest forms that were ever seen alive.*

William Pitt turned the tide in favor of Britain. The "Great Commoner" (so named because of his long and able service in the House of Commons) was the most famous representative of the Whig oligarchy. In Parliament he sat for Old Sarum, a notorious "rotten" borough (see above, p. 19). The grandson of "Diamond" Pitt, a merchant prince who had made a fortune in India, Pitt consistently supported the interests of the City. In the late 1730's he had led the Whig rebels against Walpole's pacifistic policy, the "Boy Patriots" who forced Britain into the War of Jenkins' Ear. Now Pitt's great war ministry (1757-1761) organized

* R. Orme, A History of the Transactions of the British Nation in Indostan (London, 1778), II, sec. 1, 74 ff.

victory from defeat. It ended the shilly-shallying policies of the colorless cabinets that had held office since Walpole's downfall in 1742. For the first time since 1713, British resources were applied in full strength to the prosecution of a war. The government surmounted the financial obstacle with ease. Budget deficits rose higher and higher, but Pitt used his personal and business connections to assist the successful placement of government loans. He gave the Anglo-Prussian alliance meaning by sending Frederick substantial subsidies, repudiating the Duke of Cumberland's Hanoverian capitulation, and placing English forces in Hanover under an able Prussian commander.

Pitt transformed the naval and colonial war by his energetic measures. He replaced the blundering generals and admirals involved in the early fiascoes. Now the French, almost in desperation, were planning a cross-channel invasion aimed at the heart of England. But they could not keep their preparations secret, nor did they have sufficient shipping to transport the immense force needed. In any case, the project collapsed in 1759 when the Royal Navy defeated both the Atlantic and Mediterranean squadrons of the French fleet.

Britain's overwhelming command of the seas had results far more momentous than the protection of the island from a possible French invasion. It enabled Britain to continue trading abroad at a prosperous pace, while French overseas trade rapidly sank to one-sixth of its pre-war rate. And it prevented the French colonies abroad from receiving even the modest amount of money and meager reinforcements available for them at home. Cut off from significant aid and faced by generally superior British forces, the French outposts of empire fell in quick succession.

In Africa, Britain's capture of the chief French slaving station ruined the slavers of Nantes in the mother country. In India, Clive and others avenged the "Black Hole" by punishing the Nawab of Bengal and capturing the key French posts. In the West Indies, the French lost all their sugar islands, except for Santo Domingo. In North America, the 65,000 French, poorly supplied and poorly led, were helpless against the million British colonists, fully supported by their mother country. Fort Duquesne was taken at last, and very appropriately renamed after Pitt, and the British went on to other triumphs in the war that the colonists called "French and Indian." The fate of Canada was certain after the great victories of the English General Wolfe, at Louisburg, which he took in 1758, and on the Plains of Abraham outside Quebec in September, 1759, where he lost his life. Montreal fell in 1760.

NORTH AMERICA AND THE CARIBBEAN, 1763

SITUATION AFTER THE SEVEN YEARS' WAR

BRITISH TERRITORY:
Held before 1763
Acquired From France
Acquired From Spain
Proclamation Line of 1763

CHAPTER XVI

The Peace of Paris

This positive rain of victories aroused the British public to exultation and expectation. The exultation was soon dampened, and the expectation was disappointed. Pitt had won the war, but he did not make the peace: the accession of the strong-minded George III in 1760 resulted in the dismissal of the even more strong-minded minister. In the Peace of Paris, 1763, which ended hostilities between Britain and France, the successors of Pitt allowed France to retain stations in India and on the African slave coast and, above all, to recover her islands in the West Indies. The restoration of the old order in the Caribbean was a great relief to British planters, whose markets had been flooded by sugar from the captured French island of Guadeloupe during the war. But to outraged patriots it seemed as though Britain had let the grand prize slip through her fingers.

The British in their indignation tended to overlook the all-important fact that the Seven Years' War and the Peace of Paris had virtually finished France's career of empire-building, at least for the immediate future. British gained a real ascendancy in India. France, though retaining trading posts there, was not allowed to fortify them or to continue her old policy of supporting claimants to native states. Moreover, France lost all her possessions on the mainland of North America. The British secured both Canada and the disputed territories between the Appalachians and the Mississippi. And they also obtained Florida from Spain, which had committed the folly of joining France in 1762 when the war was already lost. In compensation, Spain received the French colony of Louisiana.

VII: Conclusion:
The International Balance in Review

The peace settlements of Hubertusburg and Paris ended the greatest international crisis between the death of Louis XIV and the outbreak of the French Revolution. New crises were to arise soon after 1763, as the next chapter will show in detail—in 1768, a Russo-Turkish war; in 1772, the first partition of Poland; and, in 1776, the American War of Independence. But the two crises in the East did not greatly change the balance, and the American Revolution, though it cost Britain the thirteen colonies, otherwise did not seriously affect the maritime supremacy that she had secured in 1763. The international balance established in 1763 remained largely unaltered down to 1789. In the incessant struggle for power, the strongest states—Britain, Prussia, Russia—had generally been victorious; the less fit—France, Spain, Austria, Turkey—had survived; and the weakest—Poland and Italy—as Alberoni observed early in the century, had been "pared and sliced up like so many Dutch cheeses."

The Duke of Choiseul, the minister of Louis XV during the Seven Years' War, remarked that the "true balance of power resides in commerce." Choiseul's remark held a large measure of truth, but it did not contain the whole truth. The world struggle between Britain and the Bourbon empires did indeed justify the mercantilist view which conceived of international relations in terms of incessant competition and strife. According to the mercantilist doctrine of the fixed amount of trade, a state could enlarge its share of the existing supply only if it reduced the shares held by rival states, either by war or, in time of peace, by smuggling and retaliatory legislation. All this was borne out by the War of Jenkins' Ear and by British success, and French failure, in maintaining overseas trade during the course of the Seven Years' War.

In the warfare of the eighteenth century, then, economic motives and economic resources played a more decisive role than they had generally played in the past. Yet they by no means fully explain all the shifts in the international balance during the century. The central issues involved in the conquests of Peter the Great, or in the aggressions of Frederick, or in the strife over Poland, were not commercial. The stakes were the aggrandizement of Romanovs, Hohenzollerns, and Habsburgs, and of the nobles and Junkers supporting these dynasties. The victories of Frederick the Great depended in part on his efficient utilization of Prussia's economic resources; but they depended still more on factors that had little to do with economics—the discipline of Prussian society, and the brilliant and ruthless leadership of Frederick himself. Even Britain, the best argument to support Choiseul's contention, owed much of her success to her social and political system, which allowed Pitt to come forward, the right man at the right time. War, in sum, mirrors not only the economy but the many other institutions of the society that wages it.

In the eighteenth century, society did little to prevent wars or to reduce their frequency. Yet the wars of the century did often have the quality of measure and control that we have noted in the aggressions of Louis XIV. This gives some substance to the interpretation of the eighteenth century as a period of relative stability, even with all its fighting— a period of comparative calm between the age of religious strife that had preceded it and the storms of liberalism and nationalism that were to be loosed upon the world by the French Revolution. For example, the Seven Years' War of the eighteenth century did not begin to equal in destructive force the Thirty Years' War of the seventeenth century. Much more was involved here than the relative shortness of the Seven Years' War. Few of the combatants now had the feeling of fighting for a great cause, like Catholicism or Protestantism or national independence. The fighting itself was conducted in a more orderly fashion than it had been a hundred years before; soldiers were better disciplined and armies were better supplied. Troops in the field lived off the land less often and no longer constituted such a menace to the lives and the property of civilians. Even warfare showed indications that this was the century of order and reason, the Age of the Enlightenment.

Reading Suggestions
on the International Balance

The following three volumes in the "Rise of Modern Europe" series (New York: Harper and Brothers) provide a good analysis of eighteenth-century Europe and very full bibliographies: P. Roberts, *The Quest for Security, 1715-1740* (1947). W. L. Dorn, *Competition for Empire, 1740-1763* (1940). L. Gershoy, *From Despotism to Revolution, 1763-1789* (1944).

CHAPTER XVI

A. Sorel, *Europe under the Old Regime* (Los Angeles: W. Ritchie Press, 1947). Translation of the first volume of a major French work on diplomatic history; a classic survey of the international balance in the eighteenth century.

R. R. Palmer, *A History of the Modern World* (New York: Alfred A. Knopf, Inc., 1950). An excellent textbook, especially good on the topics treated in this chapter.

Special Studies

W. E. H. Lecky, *A History of England in the Eighteenth Century*, 8 vols. (London: Longmans, Green & Co., 1883-1890). A famous and detailed old account.

B. Williams, *The Whig Supremacy, 1714-1760* (Oxford: The Clarendon Press, 1939). A competent modern survey; a volume in the "Oxford History of England."

C. G. Robertson, *Chatham and the British Empire* (New York: The Macmillan Company, 1948. Teach Yourself History Library). A good introduction to the elder William Pitt.

H. Dodwell, *Duplex and Clive* (London: Methuen & Co., Ltd., 1920). A balanced treatment of the imperial antagonists in India.

L. Kronenberger, *Kings and Desperate Men* (New York: Alfred A. Knopf, Inc., 1942). An entertaining chronicle of eighteenth-century England; good on social and literary developments.

A. M. Wilson, *French Foreign Policy during the Administration of Cardinal Fleury, 1726-1743* (Cambridge, Mass.: Harvard University Press, 1936). A sound monograph, and one of the few good books in English on the France of Louis XV.

S. B. Fay, *The Rise of Brandenburg-Prussia to 1786* (New York: Henry Holt & Co., 1937. A Berkshire study). An admirable little volume, packed with information.

R. R. Ergang, *The Potsdam Führer* (New York: Columbia University Press, 1941). A splendid book on Frederick William I, both lively and detached.

B. H. Sumner, *Peter the Great and the Emergence of Russia* (New York: The Macmillan Company, 1951. Teach Yourself History Library.) A very good introductory manual.

J. A. Marriott, *The Eastern Question: An Historical Study in European Diplomacy,* 4th ed. (Oxford: The Clarendon Press, 1940). A standard survey.

Sources and Historical Fiction

Lady Mary W. Montagu, *Letters* (New York: E. P. Dutton & Co., 1906. Everyman ed.). By perhaps the best of the many excellent letter-writers of the eighteenth century; particularly valuable for first-hand impressions of the Ottoman Empire.

H. Fielding, *Tom Jones* (many editions). The greatest of eighteenth-century English social novels.

T. G. Smollett, *The Adventures of Roderick Random* (New York: Oxford University Press, 1952. World's Classics). Contains a good contemporary account of life in His Majesty's Navy.

D. Merejkowski, *Peter and Alexis* (New York: G. P. Putnam's Sons, 1905). Good imaginative treatment of the conflict between the great tsar and his son, who opposed Peter's westernizing policies.

The Eighteenth Century:

The Enlightenment

CHAPTER XVII

Thirty-three glimpses of Voltaire (from drawings by Hubert).

I: Basic Principles and Traits

REASON, NATURAL LAW, PROGRESS—these were the key words in the vocabulary of the eighteenth century, the Age of the Enlightenment. This was the age when many believed that human reason could free men of all their ills and lead them infallibly to perpetual peace, utopian government, and a perfect society. *Reason* would discover the *natural laws* regulating existence, thereby insuring the *progress* of the human race.

The prophets of this optimistic creed were known by the French name of *philosophes,* though they were not all French and few of them were philosophers in the strict sense. The *philosophes* were publicists, economists, political scientists, and social reformers. They derived their basic principles from their great predecessors of the seventeenth century, especially from English thinkers and scientists. Their belief in the powers of human reason came from John Locke, their faith in natural law from Sir Isaac Newton.

The Inheritance from Locke and Newton

John Locke was the great defender of the Glorious Revolution of 1688-89, the author of the *Two Treatises of Government*. To strengthen his case against absolute monarchy, Locke outlined a new psychology. Defenders of political and religious absolutism contended that divine-right monarchy was an inevitable human inheritance and that the inclination to submit to absolute authority was an innate idea, present in men's minds when they were born. In the *Essay concerning Human Understanding* (1690), Locke denied the existence of innate ideas. He called the new-born mind a *tabula rasa*, a blank slate:

Let us then suppose the mind to be ... white paper, void of all characters, without any ideas. How comes it to be furnished? ... To this I answer, in one word, from EXPERIENCE. ... Our observation employed either about *external sensible objects, or about the internal operations of our minds perceived and reflected on by ourselves, is that which supplies our understandings with all the materials of thinking.* These two are the fountains of knowledge, from whence all the ideas we have, or can naturally have, do spring.*

In other words, the two "fountains of knowledge" were environment, rather than heredity, and reason, rather than faith. Locke's matter-of-fact outlook and his empiricism (reliance on experience) place him among the rationalists. He believed that human reason, though unable to account for everything in the universe, explains all that men need to know. "The candle that is set up in us," he wrote, "shines bright enough for all our purposes."

Locke pointed the way to a critical examination of the Old Régime. The *philosophes* read and admired both his *Treatises of Government* and his *Essay concerning Human Understanding*. They applied Locke's test of common sense to existing social and economic institutions and found them complex and absurd. Locke's psychology suggested that teachers could make human institutions over by remolding the thinking of the rising generation. The *philosophes* sought the right kind of chalk to use on the "blank slates" of impressionable young minds. They found it in the concept of the Newtonian world-machine.

Newton enunciated in his *Principia* (1687) "Four Rules of Reasoning in Philosophy":

Rule I. *We are to admit no more causes of natural things than such as are both true and sufficient to explain their appearances.*

To this purpose the philosophers say that Nature does nothing in vain, and more is in vain when less will serve; for Nature is pleased with simplicity, and affects not the pomp of superfluous causes.

Rule II. *Therefore to the same natural effects we must, as far as possible, assign the same causes.*

As to respiration in a man and in a beast; ... the light of our culinary fire and of the sun; the reflection of light in the earth, and in the planets.

Rule III. *The qualities of bodies, ... which are found to belong to all bodies within the reach of our experiments, are to be esteemed the universal qualities of all bodies whatsoever.*

... If it universally appears, by experiments and astronomical observations, that all bodies about the earth gravitate towards the earth; that the moon likewise gravitates towards the earth; that, on the other hand, our sea gravitates towards the moon; and all the planets one towards the other; and the comets in like manner towards the sun; we must, in consequence of this rule, universally allow that all bodies whatsoever are endowed with a principle of mutual gravitation. ...

Rule IV. *In experimental philosophy we are to look upon propositions collected by general induction from phenomena as accurately or very nearly true, notwithstanding any contrary hypotheses that may be imagined, till such time as other phenomena occur, by which they may be made more accurate, or liable to exceptions.*

This rule must follow, that the argument of induction may not be evaded by hypotheses.*

---

* *Essay* (New York, 1947), Bk. II, Ch. I.

* *Sir Isaac Newton's Mathematical Principles*, revised translation by Florian Cajori (Berkeley, Calif., 1934), 398-400.

CHAPTER XVII

The laws governing the physical world, then, were simple (Rule I), and they were consistent (Rule II). They could be established by a combination of the inductive and deductive methods (Rules III-IV)—by reasoning from observable particular instances to a general rule (induction), and then by applying this rule to other instances that could not be observed at first hand (deduction).

The *philosophes* seized on Newton's rules of reason and on his scientific discoveries as revelations of ultimate truth. Those who could follow Newton's mathematical calculations read him in the original Latin or in translation; those who could not, turned to *Newtonianism for Ladies* or one of the dozen other popularizations of the *Principia*. In the principle of gravitation, Newton had disclosed the natural force that held the universe together; he made the universe make sense. The eighteenth century believed that other Newtons would find comparable laws governing and explaining all phases of human activity. The *philosophes* pictured themselves as the Newtons of statecraft, justice, and economics who would reduce the most intricate institutions to formulas as neat as Sir Isaac's own mathematical laws and principles.

The world and everything in it, the *philosophes* concluded, resembled a giant machine. Hitherto, men had hampered its operations because they did not understand the machinery. Once they grasped the basic laws by which it ran, they would at last permit the "world-machine" to function smoothly and beneficently. The optimism of the age was summed up in a book aptly entitled *The Progress of the Human Mind* (1794), written by the *philosophe* Condorcet when he was in prison awaiting death during the French revolutionary Reign of Terror. Condorcet asked:

If men can predict, with almost complete assurance, the phenomena whose laws are known to them . . . , why should it be regarded as a vain enterprise to chart, with some degree of probability, the course of the future destiny of mankind by studying the results of human history? Since the only basis of belief in the natural sciences is the idea that the general laws, known or unknown, regulating the phenomena of the universe are regular and constant, why should this principle be any less true for the development of the intellectual and moral faculties of man than for the other operations of nature? *

"Nature has placed no bounds on the perfecting of the human faculties," Condorcet concluded, "and the progress of this perfectibility is limited only by the duration of the globe on which nature has placed us." †

Eighteenth-century Science

The technological and scientific advances of the eighteenth century further strengthened the faith in natural law and progress. The *philosophes* hailed both the practical achievements in industry and agriculture (see Chapter XVI) and the rapidly expanding frontiers of the pure sciences. Biology and chemistry were now starting to acquire a modern look. Linnaeus (1707-1778), a Swede, demonstrated the natural laws of family relationships in biology. He took every known plant and animal, classified it by species, then bracketed several species together in a genus—and so on up the hierarchy of classification from genus through order to class. Thus arose a practice that biologists still follow in assigning every specimen two Latin names, that of its genus and that of its species. The lectures of Linnaeus at the University of Upsala, near Stockholm, attracted such throngs of students that the university's enrollment tripled. His enthusiasm for classification stimulated

---

* Condorcet, *Esquisse d'un Tableau Historique des Progrès de l'Esprit Humain* (Paris, n.d.), 203. Our translation.
† *Ibid.*, 5.

amateur botanizing and led generations of professional botanists and zoologists to discover new species.

The modern science of chemical analysis began with Black and Lavoisier. Joseph Black (1728-1799), a Scottish professor, exploded the old theory that air was composed of a single element. He proved the existence of several air-like substances or gases. Lavoisier (1743-1794), a French chemist and physicist, continued Black's study of gases, invented the name "oxygen," and demonstrated that water was made up of oxygen and hydrogen. He asserted that all substances were composed of a relatively few basic chemical elements, of which he identified twenty-three.

Meanwhile, astronomy and physics were consolidating the great advances they had made in the seventeenth century—the century of genius. Laplace (1749-1827), the "Newton of France," rounded out the great Isaac's investigation of celestial mechanics. In the 1770's and 1780's, Laplace explained the movement of the solar system in a series of mathematical formulas and theorems. The versatile American, Benjamin Franklin (1706-1790), showed that electricity and lightning were really the same thing. By flying a kite during a thunderstorm at Philadelphia, Franklin obtained an electrical charge in a key attached to the kite-string. This experiment aroused a lively interest across the Atlantic, and was repeated at Versailles for the instruction of the French royal family.

Indeed, almost everybody who was anybody attempted experiments or at least dabbled in science. Voltaire made chemistry his hobby; Montesquieu studied physics; and a noble French lady reportedly kept a corpse in her carriage, so that she might employ her travels profitably in dissection and the study of anatomy. Almost every state in Europe had its *philosophes* and its royal society or learned society to promote the progress of knowledge. Newton and Franklin were international celebrities. The Swede Linnaeus enjoyed the patronage of wealthy Dutchmen, studied at the University of Leyden in Holland, and received offers to work at Oxford and at the court of Spain. Scientists and *philosophes* paid scant attention to national frontiers. Even when their countries were at war, they often kept on visiting and corresponding—a striking example of the eighteenth century's cosmopolitanism and its disposition toward "business as usual."

French Leadership

With roots reaching back into seventeenth-century England and with branches extending to Scotland, Germany, Italy, Spain, and the New World, the Enlightenment fully exhibited the cosmopolitan qualities of its century. Yet many, though by no means all, of the *philosophes* were French, and French leadership set an indelible stamp upon the whole Enlightenment. The Age of Reason marked the high point of French cultural hegemony, and it was a great American *philosophe*, Thomas Jefferson, who maintained that every man had two homelands, "his own and France." The French language endowed the Enlightenment with its medium of communication; the *salons* of Paris set the style of enlightened writing; the great *Encyclopédie*, edited and published in France, provided the vehicle for enlightened thought.

By the eighteenth century, French was the accepted international language. Louis XIV had raised it to supremacy in diplomacy; Racine and the other classicists had made it pre-eminent in literature. There was much justice in the claim that "a dangerous work written in French is a declaration of war on the whole of Europe." Almost everywhere, and as far as distant Russia,

CHAPTER XVII

rulers, aristocrats, and intellectuals preferred French to their native tongues. Frederick William I of Prussia, in spite of his vociferous contempt for French culture, knew so little German that he wrote in a jargon composed of French words with German endings tacked on. His son, Frederick the Great, seldom deigned to use German. In 1783, it was the Academy of Berlin that conducted a competition for the best reply to the question, "What has made the French language universal?" The prize-winning essay furnished the answer in a single sentence: "Precise, popular, and reasonable, it is no longer just French; it is the language of humanity."

The Parisian *salons* taught writers precision, reasonableness, and the popular touch. The *salon* was the reception room of a large private home where guests assembled for a long afternoon or evening of conversation under the guidance of the hostess, usually a wealthy woman from the nobility or the upper bourgeoisie. Here is a contemporary report of the way in which Julie de Lespinasse conducted her *salon:*

... This circle was formed of people who were not linked together. She had taken them from here and there, but chosen so well that when they were together they harmonised like the strings of an instrument tuned by a cunning hand. ... She played on this instrument with an art that was almost genius; she seemed to know what sound the string she was going to touch would give: I mean that so well were our characters and minds known to her, that she had only to say one word to bring them into play. Nowhere was conversation livelier, or more brilliant, or better controlled. ... The minds she worked upon were neither shallow nor weak; Condillac and Turgot were amongst them; and near her, d'Alembert was like a simple and obedient child. Her gift for throwing out an idea, and giving it to men of this type to discuss; her gift for discussing it herself, like them, with precision, and sometimes with eloquence; her gift for bringing in new ideas and varying the conversation ... ; these gifts, I say, are not those of an ordinary woman.

Headdresses of the eighteenth century.

It was not with fashionable trifles or self-conceit that, every day for four hours' conversation without weariness or emptiness, she knew how to make herself interesting to these brilliant minds.*

Although the *salons* often suffered from snobbery and superficiality, they did practice a kind of democracy. They welcomed and, if the need arose, protected new men and new ideas. They afforded young *philosophes* the opportunity to obtain a square meal and to receive a hearing. Their pressure determined the outcome of elections to the French Academy, which came under the

* *Memoirs of Marmontel,* Brigit Patmore, trans. (London, 1930), 270.

THE ENLIGHTENMENT

51

Metal-planing and metal-cutting factory in the eighteenth century, as illustrated in the Encyclopédie.

control of the *philosophes* in the 1760's. Finally, the hostesses of the *salons* trained the *philosophes* in mental dexterity and literary facility.

The great organ of the *philosophes* was the *Encyclopédie*, which published the first of its many volumes in 1751. Though neither the earliest nor the most accurate of the great encyclopedias, this famous publication was by all odds the most influential. The roster of 160 contributors amounted to a Who's Who of the Enlightenment; it included Voltaire, Montesquieu, Rousseau, Condorcet, Quesnay, and Turgot. For years the editor-in-chief, Denis Diderot (1713-1784), put in a fourteen-hour working day,

every hour devoted to his crusade for reason and progress.

Diderot and his associates had no intention of issuing a neutral compendium of factual information. As Diderot explained in the article on the word, "encyclopedia," they aimed to assemble knowledge

... in order that the labors of past centuries should not prove useless for succeeding centuries; that our descendants, by becoming better informed, will at the same time *become happier and more virtuous. . . .*

The purpose of the *Encyclopédie* was didactic: to expose the vices of the existing

---

* Our italics. Our translation.

CHAPTER XVII

order, especially religious superstition and intolerance, and to instruct the public in the virtues of natural law and in the wonders of science. Diderot, for instance, learned to manipulate the new industrial machines and commissioned the drawing of superb plates showing the details of their construction and operation. Significantly, the article on the stocking-knitting machine was ten times longer than the article on cathedrals.

In the face of formidable opposition, the *Encyclopédie* accomplished its purpose. The Church condemned its materialism and its highly critical and skeptical articles on religious issues. Louis XV tried to keep it from being printed and circulated. The publishers, without consulting Diderot, reduced some of the controversial articles to a meaningless hash by ordering the printers to cut out all passages likely to cause offense. The indignation of Diderot, the ridicule leveled by the *philosophes* at their detractors, the intense curiosity of the subscribers to the *Encyclopédie*, and the help extended to the editors by Choiseul, the foreign minister, and by Madame de Pompadour, herself an "enlightened" spirit—all frustrated the censors and facilitated the completion of publication. In the small provincial city of Dijon alone there were sixty copies of the *Encyclopédie* in 1768.

II: The Reform Program of the *Philosophes*

Laissez-Faire Economics

The articles written for the *Encyclopédie* by François Quesnay (1694-1774) announced the economic program of the Enlightenment. The versatile Quesnay, biologist, surgeon, and personal physician to Louis XV and Madame de Pompadour, headed a group of thinkers and publicists called the *philosophes économistes*. These economic philosophers later adopted the significant name of Physiocrats, believers in the rule of nature. The new title revealed the basic outlook of the school. The Physiocrats felt with absolute certainty that they were the Newtons of economics and would, as Quesnay claimed, discover natural economic laws "susceptible of a demonstration as severe and incontestable as those of geometry and algebra."

"The sovereign and the nation should never lose sight of the fact that the land is the only source of wealth, and that agricul-ture increases wealth." [*] Thus Quesnay introduced the new Physiocratic concept of natural wealth and consigned almost the whole of mercantilism to limbo. He belittled the significance of money: "The riches which men need for their livelihood do not consist of money; they are rather the goods necessary both for life and for the annual production of these goods." Mercantilist states, Quesnay argued, committed a whole series of errors by placing excessive emphasis on specie. They tried to regulate commerce, when they should have allowed it free play. They made goods more expensive by levying tariffs and other indirect taxes, whereas they should have collected only a single, direct tax on the net income from land.

"Laissez faire, laissez passer," the Physio-

[*] Quesnay, "Maximes Générales du Gouvernement Economique d'Un Royaume Agricole," in E. Daire, ed., *Physiocrates* (Paris, 1846), I, 82. Our translation.

crats urged—live and let live, let nature take its course. They repudiated the controlled economy of mercantilism and enunciated the "classical" or "liberal" doctrine of the free economy. The state ought not interrupt the free play of natural economic forces. Most of all, it ought not threaten private property, so necessary for the production of agricultural wealth.

The classic formulation of laissez-faire was made by the Scotsman, Adam Smith (1727-1790), in his famous *Inquiry into the Nature and Causes of the Wealth of Nations* (1776). Adam Smith carried to vigorous completion the Physiocrats' attack on the theoretical structure of mercantilism. It was both unnatural and uneconomic to restrict imports by tariffs for the protection of home industries:

It is the maxim of every prudent master of a family never to attempt to make at home what it will cost him more to make than to buy. The tailor does not attempt to make his own shoes, but buys them of the shoemaker. The shoemaker does not attempt to make his own clothes, but employs a tailor. . . .
What is prudence in the conduct of every private family, can scarce be folly in that of a great kingdom. If a foreign country can supply us with a commodity cheaper than we ourselves can make it, better buy it of them with some part of the produce of our industry. . . .*

Smith, too, toppled money from the pedestal on which the mercantilists had placed it:

It would be too ridiculous to go about seriously to prove that wealth does not consist in money, or in gold and silver, but in what money purchases, and is valuable only for purchasing. . . . It is not by the importation of gold and silver that the discovery of America has enriched Europe. . . . By opening a new and inexhaustible market to all the commodities of Europe, it gave occasion to new divisions of labour and improvements of art, which, in the narrow circle of the ancient commerce, could never have taken place for want of a

market to take off the greater part of their produce.*

Note here the emphasis on the division of labor. Like the Physiocrats, Adam Smith attributed the wealth of nations to the production of goods; but, as befitted a citizen of Britain, the leading commercial and industrial state of the day, he took a less agrarian view of the matter. For Adam Smith, production depended less on the *soil* (the Physiocratic view) than on the *labor* of farmers, craftsmen, and mill-hands. Finally, in the most famous sentence of *The Wealth of Nations*, Adam Smith reduced government to the status of a passive policeman:

According to the system of natural liberty, the sovereign has only three duties to attend to; . . . first, the duty of protecting the society from the violence and invasion of other independent societies; secondly, the duty of protecting, as far as possible, every member of the society from the injustice and oppression of every other member of it, or the duty of establishing an exact administration of justice; and thirdly, the duty of erecting and maintaining certain public works and certain public institutions, which it can never be for the interest of any individual, or small number of individuals, to erect and maintain.†

The mercantilists had exalted the state over the individual and had declared a ceaseless trade warfare among nations. Adam Smith and the Physiocrats, reversing the emphasis, proclaimed both the economic liberty of the individual and free trade among nations to be natural laws. This laissez-faire program of the Enlightenment marked a revolutionary change in economic thought and foreshadowed the individualism of the industrial revolution in the nineteenth century (see Chapter XX). It did not, however, revolutionize the economic policies of the great powers. In Europe, only

---

* *Wealth of Nations*, Bk. IV, Ch. 2.

* *Ibid.*, Bk. IV, Ch. 1.
† *Ibid.*, Bk. IV, Ch. 9.

CHAPTER XVII

Britain was ever to give laissez-faire a full trial; on the Continent, mercantilism retained much vitality, as we shall shortly see. Turgot, the chief practical exponent of Physiocratic doctrine, tried vainly to emancipate French agriculture and French business during his brief tenure as chief minister in the 1770's (see Chapter XVIII).

The Physiocrats forgot what so many *philosophes* forgot. They overlooked the difficulty of adjusting the complexities of politics and the realities of human nature to the simple and reasonable dictates of natural law. On this point, Adam Smith saw further and more clearly than did his French contemporaries. With all the proverbial canniness of the Scots, he predicted:

To expect, indeed, that the freedom of trade should ever be entirely restored in Great Britain, is as absurd as to expect that an Oceana or Utopia should ever be established in it. Not only the prejudices of the public, but what is much more unconquerable, the private interests of many individuals, irresistibly oppose it.*

Justice

The attitude of letting nature take its course, so evident in laissez-faire economics, also characterized the outlook of the Enlightenment toward problems of justice and education. The *philosophes* believed in giving every man his due, even the avowed enemy of the Enlightenment. They believed, however, that man-made legislation prevented the application of the natural laws of justice. The unjust and antiquated statutes and the cumbersome judicial procedures of the Old Régime horrified the *philosophes*. A new Justinian was needed to humanize and simplify the law codes. A new science was needed to make the punishment of crime both humane and effective.

---

* *Ibid.*, Bk. IV, Ch. 2.

The new science, which anticipated much of modern sociology, was promoted by Cesare Beccaria (1738-1794), an Italian *philosophe* and the author of the *Essay on Crimes and Punishments* (1764). Beccaria formulated three natural laws of justice. First, punishments should aim to

...prevent the criminal from doing further injury to society, and to prevent others from committing the like offence. Such punishments, therefore, ... ought to be chosen, as will make the strongest and most lasting impressions on the minds of others, with the least torment to the body of the criminal.*

Second, justice should act speedily:

...Because the smaller the interval of time between the punishment and the crime, the stronger and more lasting will be the association of the two ideas of *Crime* and *Punishment*. †

And last:

Crimes are more effectively prevented by the *certainty* than by the *severity* of the punishment.... The certainty of a small punishment will make a stronger impression than the fear of one more severe....

If punishments be very severe, men are naturally led to the perpetration of other crimes, to avoid the punishment due to the first....**

Beccaria attacked both torture and capital punishment because they diverged so sharply from these natural laws. Torture, he claimed, falsely assumed that "pain should be the test of truth, as if truth resided in the muscles and fibres of a wretch in torture." Jail sentences, not execution, should be imposed:

The death of a criminal is a terrible but momentary spectacle, and therefore a less efficacious method of deterring others than the continued example of a man deprived of his liberty, condemned, as a beast of burden, to

---

* *Essay on Crimes and Punishments*, Ch. 12.
† *Ibid.*, Ch. 19.
** *Ibid.*, Ch. 27.

repair, by his labour, the injury he had done to society.[*]

Beccaria asserted, however, that punishment alone was not enough. The best method of preventing crime was to "let liberty be attended with knowledge," to "perfect the system of education."

Education

In education, too, the Old Régime failed to pass the tests of reason and natural law. The *philosophes* deplored both the almost universal ecclesiastical control of education and the heavy emphasis placed upon theology, Greek and Latin, and ancient history. They called this version of the humanities "savage" and demanded more consideration of science, modern languages, and modern history. Diderot declared:

Under the name of rhetoric, is taught the art of speaking before teaching the art of thinking; and that of good expression before the students have any ideas to express.

· · ·

Under the name of physics, are wearisome disputations about the elements of matter and the terrestrial systems; but not a word about natural history nor good chemistry, very little about the motion and fall of bodies, very few experiments, still less anatomy and no geography.[†]

Jean-Jacques Rousseau (1712-1778) proposed the most drastic reform of education. Rousseau was a rebel. He rebelled against the strict and disciplined society of his birthplace, Calvinist Geneva. He rebelled against the intensive bookish studies he had been forced to pursue as a young boy, and against the polite conventions he later en-

countered in the Paris *salons*. The result of Rousseau's rebellion was *Emile* (1762), half treatise and half romance, a long and fervent plea for progressive education.

Emile had two heroes—Emile, the student, and Rousseau himself, the teacher. The training that Rousseau prescribed for his pupil departed in every particular from eighteenth-century practice:

Life is the trade I would teach him. When he leaves me, I grant you, he will be neither a magistrate, a soldier, nor a priest; he will be a man.[*]

Rousseau followed a policy of laissez-faire toward his pupil. He did not argue with Emile, or discipline him, or force him to learn reading at any early age. Emile observed the world of nature from first-hand experience, not in books. He learned geography by finding his own way in the woods, and agriculture by working in the fields. And when in his teens he was finally taught to read, his first assignment was Defoe's *Robinson Crusoe,* "the best treatise on an education according to nature."

Rousseau's educational program had many faults. In *Emile,* he was vehement in denouncing conventional schools, yet vague in proposing substitutes; he was impractical, for he assumed that every child should have the undivided attention of a tutor twenty-four hours a day; and he fostered the total and apparently permanent dependence of pupil upon teacher. When Emile married and became a father, he implored his tutor to remain at his post: "I need you more than ever now that I am taking up the duties of manhood."

And yet *Emile* was a great book. Rousseau revived the Renaissance concept of the "universal man" and the Greek ideal of the sound mind in the sound body. Through the work of Pestalozzi (1746-1827), a Swiss educator and humanitarian, the ideal pro-

---

[*] *Ibid.,* Ch. 28.
[†] Diderot, "Plan of a University for the Russian Government," quoted in F. de la Fontainerie, *French Liberalism and Education in the Eighteenth Century* (New York, 1932), 208-209.

[*] *Emile,* Everyman ed. (New York, 1911), 9.

gram of *Emile* was adapted to the practical requirements of the classroom. Pestalozzi set a powerful example by teaching geography, drawing, and other useful novelties in his experimental school. Still more influential was the reaction of Pestalozzi against the barracks tradition of drilling lessons into the student through a combination of endless repetition and bodily punishment. Pupils of the twentieth century may thank the educational reformers of the eighteenth for having discovered the natural law that children should be treated as children, not as miniature adults.

Attitudes toward Religion

The attacks on clerical teaching methods formed part of a vigorous and growing body of criticism aimed at the role of the clergy in the Old Régime. "*Ecrasez l'infâme!*" shouted the *philosophes*—crush the infamous thing, stamp out religious fanaticism and intolerance. They particularly assailed the Jesuit Order, the symbol and instrument of militant Catholicism. The pressure for the dissolution of the Jesuits was so great that Pope Clement XIV yielded. In 1773, he dissolved the Society of Jesus, which was not to be revived until half a century later (see Chapter XIX).

Most *philosophes* not only championed tolerance but also adopted the religious attitude known as *deism*. Deist doctrines arose in seventeenth-century England, the England of the Civil Wars and Newtonian science. The example of the Civil Wars impelled the deists to seek settlement of religious strife by the use of reason rather than by resort to arms. All men, they asserted, could agree on a few broad religious principles. Since the Newtonian world-machine implied the existence of a mechanic, the deists accepted God as the creator of the universe and as the ultimate judge of human conduct. But they denied, or at least doubted, that God answered prayer or extended grace. The world-machine seemed to operate smoothly without God's direct intervention. For the deists, the role of God lay in the dim past and the distant future, not the immediate present.

John Locke stated the case for deism in the *Essay concerning Human Understanding*. Faith, Locke argued, was concerned only with those things "beyond the discovery of our natural faculties and *above reason*." It could not run counter to common sense: "Nothing that is contrary to, and inconsistent with, the clear and self-evident dictates of reason, has a right to be urged or assented to as a matter of faith." *

Voltaire (1694-1778) was the chief exponent of deism in France and the coiner of the anti-clerical watchword, "*Ecrasez l'infâme!*" Voltaire, indeed, was a one-man Enlightenment. A professional writer, he devoted his prodigious energy and versatile talents to the propagation of new ideas. Plays, tales, epic poems, histories, essays, and letters poured from his pen. Clear, witty, and often bitingly satirical, they were immensely popular, not least when they had to be printed outside France or under an assumed name in order to evade the censorship. Voltaire made Frenchmen aware of Newton, Locke, and Shakespeare. He set a new style in history-writing by discussing economics and culture as well as the usual politics and wars, thus foreshadowing the "new history" and the "surveys of civilization" of the twentieth century.

Voltaire experienced intolerance at first hand. As a young man he spent a year in the Bastille and three years of exile in England because he had criticized the French government and had offended a member of the privileged nobility. The relative religious and political freedom of Britain

---

* *Essay,* Bk. IV, Ch. 18.

made an immense impression on the refugee:

If there were just one religion in England, despotism would threaten; if there were two religions, they would cut each other's throats; but there are thirty religions, and they live together peacefully and happily.*

Back in France, Voltaire carried on a lifelong crusade for toleration. In 1762, a Protestant merchant, Jean Calas, was accused of having murdered his son to prevent his conversion to Catholicism. Calas died in agony, his body broken on the wheel. Voltaire discovered that the accusation against Calas was based solely on rumor, and that the court that condemned him had acted under the pressure of a fanatical Catholic mob. Voltaire campaigned for three years until the original verdict was reversed, and the name of Calas was cleared.

The existence of evil—of injustices like that which crushed Calas—confronted the Age of Reason with a major problem. Few of the *philosophes* accepted the traditional Christian teaching that evil arose from original sin, from the fall of Adam and Eve. If God were purely benevolent, they asked, why then had he created a world in which evil so often prevailed? Could a perfect God produce an imperfect creation? Alexander Pope, Voltaire's great English contemporary, answered that this was the best of all possible worlds:

All Nature is but Art, unknown to thee;
All chance, direction which thou canst not
    see;
All discord, harmony not understood;
All partial evil, universal good:
And, spite of Pride, in erring Reason's spite,
One truth is clear, *Whatever is, is right.*

But Pope was a hunchback, and Voltaire asked: How could Pope accept this deformity as evidence of universal good? In his most famous story, *Candide*, Voltaire ridi-

culed the optimists and commented with bitter sarcasm on the disasters that abounded in the best of all possible worlds. A real disaster inspired the writing of *Candide*—the great earthquake and tidal wave that engulfed the city of Lisbon on November 1, 1755, and killed upwards of 30,000 people.

Deism enabled Voltaire to effect a kind of reconciliation between a perfect God and the imperfect world. As a deist, Voltaire believed that God was indeed the Creator:

When I see a watch . . . , I conclude that an intelligent being arranged the springs of this mechanism so that the hand should tell the time. Similarly, when I see the springs of the human body, I conclude that an intelligent being has arranged these organs to be kept and nourished in the womb for nine months; that the eyes have been given for seeing, the hands for grasping, etc.*

But, Voltaire concluded, there was no way to determine whether or not God would attempt to perfect his creation. On one point Voltaire had no doubts: he never questioned the social usefulness of religion. "Man," he stated, "has always needed a brake." For the masses of people almost any religion, no matter how primitive, was better than atheism.

Baron d'Holbach (1723-1789), however, the most outspoken atheist of the Enlightenment, turned the argument based on utility against religion. Religion was not the brake that man needed, he contended, and God was simply a "phantom of the imagination," whose existence was denied by the evil in the world. Simple self-interest, Holbach asserted, would suffice to make men behave morally. If only organized religions could be rooted out, and reason and natural law allowed to hold sway, then this would become the best of all possible worlds.

A wealthy man, Holbach extended the

---

* *Lettres Philosophiques*, Letter No. 6. Our translation.

* *Le Traité de Métaphysique*, Ch. II. Our translation.

CHAPTER XVII

hospitality of his *salon* to all comers, including Jesuit refugees from anticlerical persecution. His tolerance impressed his contemporaries more than his atheism did. Most of the *philosophes* continued to prefer deism, that halfway house between belief and disbelief. The ambiguities and uncertainties of deism clouded the whole religious attitude of the Enlightenment. The *philosophes* were *against* bigotry and persecution; but what they stood *for*, apart from the important principle of toleration, was not so clear.

Political Program: Montesquieu

"In politics as in religion toleration is a necessity," decreed Voltaire; to him, therefore, Britain seemed close to utopia. Voltaire paid the British constitution the most flattering compliment at the command of his age when he claimed that it "might have been invented by Locke, Newton, or Archimedes." Voltaire praised, but did not explain. Montesquieu undertook to analyze and account for the political virtues of Britain.

Montesquieu (1689-1755), a French lawyer and *philosophe,* aspired to be a Newton of political science. His major work, *The Spirit of the Laws* (1748), defined the principles underlying both the British constitution and governments in general. Montesquieu began with the very sensible premise that no one system of government suited all countries. Laws, he wrote,

... should be in relation to the climate of each country, to the quality of its soil, to its situation and extent, to the principal occupation of the natives, whether husbandmen, huntsmen, or shepherds: they should have relation to the degree of liberty which the constitution will bear; to the religion of the inhabitants, to their inclinations, riches, numbers, commerce, manners, and customs.*

* *The Spirit of the Laws,* Thomas Nugent, trans. (New York, 1949), Bk. I, Ch. 3.

Montesquieu cautioned against supposing that old customs and traditions could simply be legislated out of existence and replaced by simpler natural laws. He cited the very telling example of Peter the Great's failure to decree the establishment of western ways in Russia. In specifying the influence of heredity and environment upon forms of government, he explained that republics were best suited to the small and barren countries, limited monarchies to the middle-sized and more prosperous, and despotisms to vast empires.

Britain, being middle-sized and prosperous, was quite properly a monarchy limited by aristocracy. The hereditary nobility sat in the upper House of Parliament; a sort of nobility of talent, the elected representatives, composed the Commons. All this was admirable in Montesquieu's view, for he distrusted democracy and pronounced the mass of people "extremely unfit" for government. If only France had let her aristocrats retain their old political functions, she would never have sunk to her present low state.

Montesquieu found one key to the political superiority of Britain in the preponderance of the aristocracy. Another key he found in the famous concept of checks and balances. In Parliament, Lords and Commons checked each other. In the government as a whole, the balance was maintained by means of *the separation of powers:*

When the legislative and executive powers are united in the same person, or in the same body of magistrates, there can be no liberty; because apprehensions may arise, lest the same monarch or senate should enact tyrannical laws, to execute them in a tyrannical manner.

Again, there is no liberty, if the judiciary power be not separated from the legislative and executive. Were it joined with the legislative the life and liberty of the subject would be exposed to arbitrary control; for the judge would be then the legislator. Were it joined to the executive power, the judge might behave with violence and oppression.*

Montesquieu, however, did not see that the British constitution was moving, not toward the separation of powers, but toward their concentration in the hands of Parliament, and of the Commons in particular. The cabinet was becoming the instrument for the assertion of legislative supremacy over the executive (see Chapter XVI). In fairness, it must be added that these developments were far from obvious in 1748 when *The Spirit of the Laws* appeared.

Montesquieu likewise ran into trouble when he tried to derive specific corollaries from his general theorem about the influence of climate and geography on human institutions. Autocracy and Catholicism, he asserted, flourish in the Mediterranean states because they are endowed with a warm climate and rich natural resources. Moderate government and Protestantism, conversely, are at home in the colder and harsher environment of northern Europe. The facts of history, of course, did not always confirm this rule about North and South. Freedom-loving Protestant Britain and Holland behaved in good northern fashion. But if Montesquieu were correct, Prussia—barren, northern, Protestant Prussia —should have been the greatest citadel of liberty on the Continent, not the stronghold of Hohenzollern absolutism.

By jumping to conclusions from insufficient evidence, Montesquieu committed a fault common in the Enlightenment. But he avoided another fault common to the age. He had too firm a grasp on political realities to assume that governments either were or should be the same everywhere. His mistaken corollaries about North and South did not invalidate his great proposition that a nation's heredity and environment went far toward determining its institutions.

---

* *The Spirit of the Laws*, Bk. XXI, Ch. 6.

Later political thinkers made good use of the comparative methods introduced by *The Spirit of the Laws* and refined Montesquieu's judgments on the interrelationship of geography, religion, and politics. And the American "Founding Fathers" incorporated Montesquieu's concept of the separation of powers into the Constitution of the United States.

Political Program: Rousseau

From the standpoint of contributions to American history, Montesquieu and Locke are the most important political thinkers of the Enlightenment. From the European standpoint, the most important is Jean-Jacques Rousseau, whose ideals inspired the radicals of the French Revolution. Rousseau started with one of those sweeping generalizations so typical of the Enlightenment. Whereas nature dignifies man, he contended, civilization corrupts him; man would be corrupted less if civilized institutions followed nature more closely. This was the theme that ran through many of Rousseau's principal writings. In *Emile*, he placed it at the heart of his program for educational reform; in the *Discourse on the Moral Effects of the Arts and Sciences* (1750), he used it to win a competition set by the Academy of Dijon. The Academy asked: Has the restoration of the arts and sciences had a purifying effect upon morals? Certainly not, the prize-winner answered; it has nearly ruined them.

In a second discourse, *On the Origin of the Inequality of Mankind* (1755), Rousseau blamed the vices of civilization on private property:

The first man who, having enclosed a piece of ground, bethought himself of saying, 'This is mine,' and found people simple enough to believe him, was the real founder of civil society. From how many crimes, wars, and murders, from how many horrors and mis-

CHAPTER XVII

fortunes might not any one have saved mankind, by pulling up the stakes, or filling up the ditch, and crying to his fellows: 'Beware of listening to this imposter; you are undone if you once forget that the fruits of the earth belong to us all, and the earth itself to nobody.' *

Men accepted laws and governors in order to protect their property:

> ... They had too many disputes among themselves to do without arbitrators, and too much ambition and avarice to go long without masters. All ran headlong to their chains, in hopes of securing their liberty; for they had just wit enough to perceive the advantages of political institutions, without experience enough to enable them to foresee their danger. †

Government was evil, Rousseau concluded, but a necessary evil. "What, then, is to be done? Must societies be totally abolished? ... Must we return again to the forest to live among bears?" No, civilized men could not return to a remote and primitive existence, could "no longer subsist on plants or acorns, or live without laws and magistrates." **

Rousseau attempted a positive answer in his major political work, *The Social Contract* (1762), in which he strove to reconcile the liberty of the individual and the institution of government through a new and revolutionary version of the contract theory of government. Earlier theories of contract, from the Middle Ages to John Locke, had hinged on the agreement between the people to be governed, on the one hand, and a single governor or small group of governors on the other. Earlier theories postulated a political contract. Rousseau's contract, as the title of the book suggested, was social. A whole society agreed to be ruled by its *general will:*

Each of us puts his person and all his power in common under the supreme direction of the general will, and, in our corporate capacity, we receive each member as an indivisible part of the whole.*

"Each individual," Rousseau continued, "may have a particular will contrary or dissimilar to the general will which he has as a citizen." If the individual insisted on putting self-interest above community interest, he should be obliged to observe the general will. "This means nothing less than that he will be forced to be free." †

The general will was the central concept of *The Social Contract*. It was ethical as well as political in nature, for it represented what was best for the whole community, what the community ought to do. It was the instrument for expressing the virtuous social instincts of man and for curbing his vicious selfish impulses.

Formulating the general will, Rousseau believed, was the business of everybody. The power of legislation, he contended, could never be properly transferred from the people to an institution like the British Parliament:

> The deputies of the people ... are not and cannot be its representatives; they are merely its stewards, and can carry through no definitive acts. Every law the people has not ratified in person is null and void—is, in fact, not a law. The people of England regards itself as free; but it is grossly mistaken; it is free only during the election of members of Parliament. As soon as they are elected, slavery overtakes it, and it is nothing.**

Executing the general will, however, could legitimately be the business of a smaller group. Like Montesquieu, Rousseau believed that the number of governors should vary inversely with the size and resources of the state:

---

* "Discourse on the Origin of Inequality," in *The Social Contract and Discourses,* Everyman ed. (New York, 1913), 192.
  † *Ibid.,* 205.
  ** *Ibid.,* 228.

---

* *The Social Contract,* Everyman ed. (New York, 1913), 13.
  † *Ibid.,* p. 15.
  ** *Ibid.,* p. 78.

Monarchy . . . suits only wealthy nations; aristocracy, States of middling size and wealth; and democracy, States that are small and poor.*

Rousseau doubted, however, that any state was ready for the extreme sort of democracy in which the many actually execute the laws. "Were there a people of gods, their government would be democratic. So perfect a government is not for men." † Rousseau was quite aware that *The Social Contract* was not a manual of practical politics. At another time, when he made suggestions for the reform of the Polish government, his counsels were moderate, almost conservative. While favoring the abolition of the liberum veto, he advocated only gradual changes in other Polish institutions. The elective monarchy was to be retained; the nobles were to keep many of their old privileges and were to acquire a new sense of duty through education; the serfs might be liberated, but only after they had been taught their responsibilities.

The influence of Rousseau, however, has come from *The Social Contract;* it has not been exerted on the side of moderation and conservatism. Almost every radical political doctrine in the past two centuries has owed something to Rousseau. Patriots and nationalists hail him as an early prophet of the creed that nations do—and should—differ. Throughout his writings he referred again and again to "the dear love of country." In admonishing the Poles, he put great stress on the renewal of their national spirit through education and through patriotic festivals. *The Social Contract* concluded with a plea for the establishment of a "civil religion." The moral code of early Christianity might be retained, Rousseau allowed, but the State should no longer have to compete with the Church for the allegiance of citizens.

* *The Social Contract*, p. 65.
† *Ibid.*, p. 56.

Rousseau may thus be interpreted as worshipping the State and exalting the national welfare over particular individual interests. Socialists find a justification for collectivism in his attacks on the evils of private property and in his insistence that "the fruits of the earth belong to us all." Dictators have used the doctrine of the general will to sanction the methods of the police state. Without bothering about the niceties of ascertaining the general will, the dictator simply assumes that he has a special knowledge of it, as in the case of Hitler's celebrated "intuition." In forcing his subjects to obey his dictates, he is merely "forcing them to be free," in accordance with the precept of Rousseau.

But Rousseau was also the prophet of democracy and individualism. The authoritarian interpretation overlooks both his personal career of rebellion against the Old Régime and the strong idealistic tone of his writings. "Were there a people of gods, their government would be democratic." This declaration has seemed neither cynical nor pessimistic to the democratic disciples of Rousseau. From the French Revolution on down to the present, they have argued that Rousseau shared the optimism of the Enlightenment, implied that human beings might one day become a "people of gods." *Emile* showed how education might help bring this about; *The Social Contract* suggested that men might one day become so virtuous that they would always follow the general will freely and would no longer be "forced to be free."

Enlightened Despotism

Neither the ideal democracy of Rousseau nor the checked and balanced paradise of Montesquieu promised a swift end to the abuses of the Old Régime. Many *philosophes* sought a short cut to utopia, a method

62

practicable and sympathetic to the institution of monarchy. They found it in the magic formula of enlightened despotism.

The Physiocrats, the chief proponents of enlightened despotism, found Montesquieu and Rousseau to be wasting words in arguments over the status of the legislative power. God was the legislator, nature preserved the divine legislation, and the sole duty of government lay in administering these natural laws. Democracy and aristocracy alike had the fatal weakness of delegating administrative authority to individuals whose passing selfish aims clashed with the permanent welfare of the nation. By contrast, the Physiocrats explained, the personal interests of hereditary monarchs coincided with national interests through their "co-ownership" of the territories under their rule. Hence kings should be despots, not in any sinister sense but on the model of the tyrants of ancient Greece or the best of the Renaissance despots. Like a new

Solon, the enlightened despot should unearth the natural laws decreed by God and clear away the accumulation of artificial, man-made law that was choking progress. Then mercantilism would vanish, agriculture would come into its own again, and the law would be codified anew. Europe would be transformed suddenly, miraculously.

Enlightened despotism won an immediate and enthusiastic response from European monarchs. And no wonder: it afforded them the chance to pose as the champions of reason and progress while pressing their age-old fight to make royal authority more absolute. In the late eighteenth century, self-styled "enlightened despots" occupied many European thrones—Frederick the Great in Prussia, Catherine in Russia, Joseph II in Austria, to name only the three chief figures. Their lands were proving grounds for the economic, social, and religious programs of the Age of Reason.

III: The Enlightened Despots

Prussia:
Frederick the Great

Of all the monarchs of eighteenth-century Europe, Frederick II, the Great, of Prussia (1740-1786), appeared best attuned to the Enlightenment. As a youth, he rebelled against the Philistine outlook and drill-sergeant methods of his father, the redoubtable Frederick William I (see Chapter XVI). He delighted in music, played the flute, which he took with him everywhere, even on military campaigns, and composed more than a hundred sonatas for that difficult instrument. An attentive reader of the *philosophes,* he exchanged letters with them and brought

Voltaire to live as his pensioner at Potsdam near Berlin. He wrote a pamphlet, *Anti-Machiavel,* denouncing the immorality of *The Prince.* And he himself laid down the fundamental requirements for an enlightened despot:

Princes, sovereigns, kings are not clothed with supreme authority to plunge with impunity into debauchery and luxury.... [The prince] should often remind himself that he is a man just as the least of his subjects. If he is the first judge, the first general, the first financier, the first minister of the nation, ... it is in order to fulfill the duties which these titles impose upon him. He is only the first servant of the state, obligated to act with fairness, wisdom, and unselfishness, as if at every instant he would have to render an account of his administration to his citizens.*

In many respects, Frederick fully measured up to his own requirements. He shunned "debauchery and luxury," his clothing was stained and shabby, and he was indeed "the first servant of the state," toiling long and hard at his desk or on the battlefield. But did he also act with "fairness, wisdom, and unselfishness"? Here his record was uneven. Despite his *Anti-Machiavel*, Frederick conducted foreign and military affairs in true Machiavellian style; his invasion of Silesia (see Chapter XVI) would have aroused the envy of Caesar Borgia. At home, closeted in his Potsdam palace where he conducted the business of state by correspondence, he drove his subordinates like slaves. Viewed as a general, a diplomat, and the master mechanic of Prussian administration, Frederick the Great was efficient and successful, but he was scarcely an enlightened despot. His reputation for enlightenment must rise or fall on the basis of his social and economic reforms.

No Physiocrat could have done more than Frederick to improve Prussian agriculture. From England he imported clover, crop rotation, and the iron plow, which turned up the soil more effectively than the old wooden share. He drained the swamps of the lower Oder Valley, opened up farms in Silesia and elsewhere, and brought in 300,000 immigrants to populate the new lands. After the ravages of the Seven Years' War, he gave the peasants tools, stock, and seed to repair their ruined farms. He nursed along the admirable German tradition of scientific forestry, then in its infancy.

Yet Frederick was a mercantilist, quite hostile to the Physiocratic doctrine of laissez-faire. He cut imports to the bone in order to save money for support of the army.

His mercantilism stimulated the growth of Prussian industry, particularly the textiles and metals needed by the army. But it also placed a staggering burden of taxation on his subjects and produced several economic absurdities. Frederick attempted to create a native silk industry, an attempt that failed; he tried to make Prussia grow its own tobacco, for which the climate was not suited. And, since the German taste for coffee required a large outlay of money abroad, he urged the consumption of native "beer-soup," laid a heavy duty on imported coffee beans, and established a special corps of French "coffee-smellers" to trap smugglers.

The religious and social policies of Frederick the Great likewise combined the Age of Reason at its most reasonable with the Old Régime at its least enlightened. A deist, Frederick prided himself on religious tolerance. He protected the minority of Catholics in his predominantly Protestant kingdom, urging them to build their church steeples as high as they liked. He invited Jesuits persecuted in Catholic countries to seek refuge in Prussia because he admired their intellectual ability. He even boasted that he would build a mosque in Berlin if Mohammedans wished to settle there. Yet the same Frederick consistently practiced anti-Semitism. He not only employed Jewish agents in the unpopular work of debasing the coinage but also levied special heavy taxes on his Jewish subjects and tried to exclude them from the professions and from the civil service. Jews, he alleged, were "useless to the state."

Frederick the Great rendered Prussians a great service by his judicial reforms. When he came to the throne, the courts were notoriously cruel, expensive, and capricious. He reduced the use of torture; he put an end to the curious custom of taking appeals from the ordinary courts to university faculties and instituted a regular system of appellate courts. He mitigated the venal

---

* "Essai sur les Formes de Gouvernement et sur les Devoirs des Souverains," *Oeuvres Posthumes* (Berlin, 1788), VI, 64, 83-84. Our translation.

CHAPTER XVII

practice of bribing judges by insisting that "tips" received from litigants be placed in a common pool from which each judge should draw only his fair share.

Yet the same Frederick took a positively medieval view of the merits of social caste. He did nothing to loosen the bonds of serfdom that still shackled much of the Prussian peasantry. When he gave the peasants material assistance and urged them to learn the "three r's," his aims were severely utilitarian. Peasants were to learn nothing beyond the rudiments of reading and writing; otherwise, they might become discontented with their station in life. Regarding the middle class, too, with disdain, Frederick respected only the landed nobility and gentry. And even the favored Junkers did not escape Frederick's penny-pinching. Although he appointed only Junkers as army officers, he discouraged their marriage because every officer's wife represented a potential widow to whom the state would owe a pension it could ill afford.

It is easy to see why an English diplomat who knew Frederick well should have been struck by his "motley composition of barbarity and humanity":

I have seen him weep at tragedy, known him to pay as much care to a sick greyhound as a fond mother to a favourite child; yet the next day he has given orders for the devastation of a province or by a wanton increase of taxes made a whole district miserable. He is so far from being sanguinary that he scarce ever suffers a criminal to be punished capitally; yet in the last war he gave secret orders to . . . his army surgeons rather to run the risk of a wounded soldier dying than by the amputation of a limb increase the number and expense of his invalids.*

Frederick seemed constitutionally incapable of getting along with other people. He quarreled with his friends, notably Voltaire; the

Frederick the Great of Prussia playing the flute at his Potsdam palace.

great French champion of toleration could not tolerate the strain of daily association with Frederick. When the King requested Voltaire to edit his indifferent French poetry, Voltaire made a cutting remark about washing the dirty linen of royalty; Frederick retorted by comparing his guest to an orange, to be sucked dry and thrown away. The two men eventually renewed their friendship through the less demanding medium of correspondence. Frederick despised and neglected his wife. His subjects sighed with relief at the news of his death, and his will directed that he be buried beside his pet dogs. "Such," remarked a French observer, "is the last mark of contempt which he thought proper to cast upon mankind."

This harsh judgment should not distort

---

* Sir James Harris, quoted in G. P. Gooch, *Frederick the Great* (New York, 1947), 142.

our final appraisal of Frederick. Actually, Frederick embodied two often conflicting political philosophies—the humane principles of the Enlightenment and the Spartan traditions of the Hohenzollerns. In the long run, he was probably first of all a Hohenzollern, and an enlightened despot only when the precepts of the Age of Reason could be reconciled to the realities of Hohenzollern kingship.

Russia:
Catherine the Great

Foremost among the admirers of Frederick the Great stood the Grand Duke Peter of Russia, the eccentric nephew and heir of the Empress Elizabeth (1741-1762). A perennial child, Peter passed most of his time playing with toy soldiers and drilling live ones. He had been reared in Germany, and he remained thoroughly German in outlook, idolizing the King of Prussia even when Russia was fighting against him in the Seven Years' War. After Elizabeth's death (January, 1762) he reigned for a bare six months as Tsar Peter III. He concluded a peace highly favorable to Frederick, imposed the harsh Prussian discipline on the Russian army, and projected the reform of the Orthodox Church along German Lutheran lines. A conspiracy, engineered by favorites of Catherine, his wife, culminated in July, 1762, with the assassination of Peter III and the proclamation of Catherine as empress.

The new empress, the daughter of an insignificant German prince, possessed all the talent and vitality denied to her weak-minded husband. Catherine paraded her enlightenment. She read voluminously and wrote dramas, satires, and essays. Flouting the widespread suspicion of the new method of inoculation against smallpox, she imported an English physician especially to

Empress Catherine II of Russia.

inoculate herself and her family. She laughed at Frederick the Great's prejudice against coffee; every morning she drank off quantities of it, brewed according to her own heroic recipe of a pound of coffee to five cups of water. When she became empress, her instinct for favorable publicity led her to enlist the *philosophes* as her champions. Wholesale flattery, a becoming modesty about her own ability, and on occasion the judicious grant of pensions were her lures. The *philosophes* rose to the bait magnificently, pronouncing Catherine a new Minerva, a new Juno, a new Ceres. Superlatives gushed from Voltaire:

> ... All eyes must now be turned toward the north star. Your Imperial Majesty has discovered a road to glory hitherto unknown to all other sovereigns. ... You have truly become the benefactress of Europe; and you have acquired more subjects by the greatness of your soul than others have conquered by force of arms.[*]

Catherine was hardly a great soul; courageous, ambitious, and unscrupulous, she was a natural autocrat, a born politician. From the moment she married, political mo-

---

[*] Letter of June 21, 1776, in *Documents of Catherine the Great*, W. F. Reddaway, ed. (Cambridge, England, 1936), 10. Our translation.

CHAPTER XVII

tives had colored her actions. In contrast to Peter, she ostentatiously transformed herself from a German into a Russian, in order to win public favor. She tried to master the Russian language and chose many of her friends and numerous lovers from the influential noble families of Russia. She made a great show of devotion to the Orthodox Church, though she privately called her abandonment of Lutheranism a purely political move comparable to Henry of Navarre's famous conversion to Catholicism. St. Petersburg, too, no doubt was worth a Mass.

Catherine never could safely forget that she was a usurper who owed her crown to the plotting of aristocratic friends. Her anxiety to protect her own position, combined with the immense difficulties in the way of change in Russia, kept her from attempting the sweeping reforms implicit in the theory of enlightened despotism. Caution, conservatism, and absolutism characterized the internal policies of Catherine the Great.

As her first major act of domestic statesmanship, Catherine convoked a commission to codify the laws. Nobles, officials, townspeople, free peasants—every important social group in Russia except the clergy and the serfs—sent delegates to the commission. For their benefit the Empress herself labored three years compiling a detailed *Instruction* that embodied many of the advanced precepts of Montesquieu and Beccaria. The ministers of Louis XV did Catherine the honor of banning the importation of the *Instruction* into France. Yet in the *Instruction* Catherine indicated her own firm belief in autocracy and discreetly avoided committing herself on the great Russian social problem, the tens of millions of serfs. And the legislative commission, when it met, proved to be far from revolutionary.

The delegates to the commission were paid by the treasury, and were exempted from capital punishment. Each one was charged to bring with him a collection of written documents from his neighbors presenting their grievances and demands for change. Study of these documents shows that there was very little dissatisfaction with the autocracy in Russia as such. People sought more rights and duties for local government and a strict definition of their obligations, so that they would know where they stood. The deliberations of the commission show that each class of representatives wanted to extend the rights of its class; the free peasants, for example, wanted to be allowed to own serfs. After a year and a half of discussion and debate, Catherine put an end to the commission in 1768. It had not codified the laws, but it had been a success from her point of view, for it had demonstrated the essential support for the autocracy by all classes of Russians. It is important to remember that, with all its imperfections as a deliberative body, the commission was the last effort by the tsardom to consult the people as a whole for 138 years—until revolution summoned the first Duma (parliament) into existence in 1906 (see Chapter XXII).

Catherine turned the spadework of the legislative commission to good advantage in her later reforms. These reforms resulted from the great rebellion of the Cossacks under the leadership of Pugachev, 1773-1775. Pugachev roused the frontiersmen to revolt against Catherine's cancellation of their special privileges. Pretending to be Tsar Peter III, and promising liberty and land to the serfs who joined his forces, Pugachev swept over a wide area of southeastern Russia and finally marched toward Moscow. Like the disturbances of the seventeenth century, Pugachev's revolt revealed the existence of bitter discontent in Russia, a discontent directed not at the supreme autocrat but at the landlords and local officials. In Russia, peasants identified as their enemy those agents of the system whom they could actually see, and they often rose in rebellion in the name of their sovereign, who was, they felt, far away and kept in ignorance of the truth by the wicked landowners and officials. Like many of his predecessors, Pugachev thus pretended to be a tsar in order to rally support.

The ramshackle structure of provincial administration almost collapsed under the strain of Pugachev's rebellion. Orders filtered down slowly to local officials, and the soldiers defending the government moved almost as slowly. When the rebels were finally suppressed, and Pugachev was traveling northward in an iron cage preliminary to being drawn and quartered, Catherine took action. Her reorganization of local government (1775) created fifty provinces where there had been twenty before. She thus replaced a small number of unwieldy units with a larger number of small provinces, each containing roughly 300,000 to 400,000 inhabitants. The reform of 1775 gave the nobles the lion's share of provincial offices but subjected them to the close direction of the central government, which had its own administrative, financial, and legal representatives in each province.

Ten years later, Catherine made fresh concessions to the nobility. In the charter of 1785 the nobles received exemption from military service and taxation and secured absolute mastery over the fate of their serfs and their estates. In each province they formed a corporate body with its own organization under an elected "Marshal of the Nobility." A charter to the towns in the same year (1785) disclosed Catherine's sympathy with the tiny but growing middle class. It established the principle of municipal self-government, a principle, however, which remained a dead letter because of the rigorous class distinctions maintained in the backward urban centers of Russia. Small towns populated mainly by illiterate miners and laborers who still bore the yoke of serfdom were scarcely ripe for democracy.

For the serfs, of course, there was no charter. Indeed, Catherine gave away to private proprietors, to whom she was obligated for political assistance, crown lands with more than 800,000 peasant inhabitants. These peasants thus became serfs. As serfdom spread into portions of Russia previously very little affected by it, regulations shackled the serfs still more tightly. In 1767, for example, a serf was forbidden to file a complaint against his master; this deprived him of the possibility of redress. So serfdom both widened and deepened in Catherine's Russia at a time when some enlightened despots were alleviating or abolishing it. As yet, there was no strong public sentiment in opposition to serfdom as an institution. In a country where peasants who were free wanted above all else to become proprietors over peasants who were serfs, it would take a long period of education and westernization to create a firm public sentiment for abolition of serfdom. When such sentiment did appear, it would show itself first among the landlords themselves.

The foreign policy of Catherine the Great supports the conclusion that enlightened despotism meant little in the conduct of diplomacy. Catherine sought, and achieved, the expansion of Russia westward against Poland and southward against Turkey. A year after she became empress, the Polish throne fell vacant, and she secured the election of a pro-Russian king, Stanislas Poniatowski, a Polish noble and a former lover of hers. Frederick the Great now joined with Catherine in a campaign to win rights for the persecuted Lutheran and Orthodox minorities in Catholic Poland. No doubt both rulers wanted to further the great principle of toleration, but they also procured a useful cloak for their designs on Polish independence. The Polish nobles, offended both in their ardent Catholicism and in their feudal patriotism, resisted, and secured the aid of France and Austria. The latter powers

CHAPTER XVII

PARTITIONS OF POLAND, 1772-1793-1795

	1772	1793	1795
To Prussia			
To Russia			
To Austria			

0   Miles   200

adopted the stratagem of pressing Turkey into war with Russia to distract Catherine from Poland.

The stratagem backfired badly. Catherine won a string of victories in the Russo-Turkish War, 1768-1774. Poland, in consequence, not only failed to get a breathing spell; her demise as an independent state was actually brought closer. Even before Catherine made peace with Turkey in 1774 her successes alarmed her partner in Polish intrigue, Fred-

erick the Great. Fearing that a victorious Russia would take the lion's share of Poland if he did not act quickly, and fearing also that Austria and Russia might come to blows over the dismemberment of Poland and Turkey, Frederick arranged the first partition of Poland in 1772. Poland lost almost one-third of her territory and one-half of her population to Prussia, Austria, and Russia in this shameless act of international highway robbery. Frederick's share of the loot—

West Prussia—was the smallest but the most strategic, for it comprised the Polish lands that had previously separated East Prussia from Brandenburg. Maria Theresa, the Habsburg monarch, rather reluctantly abandoned both her Turkish and Polish allies to take part in the grab for Polish lands. "She wept," Frederick the Great observed caustically, "but she kept on taking."

The operation of 1772 proved to be habit-forming. The disaster did shock the Polish nobles into a belated strengthening of their country's feudal constitution. But reform came too late to prevent the two subsequent partitions, in 1793 and 1795, which wiped the Polish state off the map.

Catherine's first Turkish war ended with the Treaty of Kutchuk-Kainardji, 1774, which marked a significant shift in the Near Eastern balance of power. She gained part of Turkey's possessions on the northern shores of the Black Sea, trade and navigation rights on that sea, and a vaguely worded permission to protect the Orthodox Christians living under Ottoman rule. This last clause offered Russia a convenient excuse for intervening in Turkish affairs later on. Now Catherine dreamt of reviving the Byzantine Empire as a Russian puppet. She christened one of her grandsons Constantine and, to prepare him properly for a Byzantine inheritance, imported his nurses from Constantinople itself. She invited Austria to share in this "grand design," because she would have aroused bitter Habsburg opposition if she had attempted the single-handed Russian dismantling of the Ottoman Empire.

In 1783, Catherine annexed the Crimean Peninsula, which had been set up as a supposedly independent state in 1774. There she built the important new base and port of Sevastopol. The Turks resisted these encroachments in a new war, 1787-1792, in which Austria and Russia were allied against them. The two partners once more quarreled, as they had already done in the Turkish war of the 1730's (see Chapter XVI), and Turkey again escaped annihilation. Austria pulled out before the war was over, and Catherine, though securing more Turkish lands along the Black Sea, did not accomplish her "grand design."

Catherine's spoliation of Turkey and Poland went a long way toward satisfying the ambitious policies of expansion initiated by Peter the Great. Indeed, in many of her policies Catherine was the true successor of Peter. She continued his efforts to bring the country under the enlightening influence of western culture while avoiding his blunder of trying to cram too many innovations down the Russian throat. She had the very good sense to realize that she could not transplant to Russia the English social and political institutions so much admired by the *philosophes*. Peter would probably have applauded many of her reforms in local government, but he would hardly have approved of her catering to the nobility, however much circumstances forced this upon her. A true enlightened despot, moreover, would have had the intelligence to foresee the subsequent baleful effects of Catherine's alliance between Crown and nobility.

Austria:
Maria Theresa and Joseph II

In the Austrian lands, by contrast, the Crown attacked the feudal rights of the nobles as part of a great program to weld the disparate Habsburg dominions into a single political unit. When the War of the Austrian Succession in the 1740's showed up the basic weakness of Habsburg power (see Chapter XVI), the Empress Maria Theresa (1740-1780) at once began reforms. She took as her model the institutions of her hated but successful rival, Frederick of

Prussia. She increased taxes, especially on the nobility, strengthened the central government at the expense of local aristocratic assemblies, and obliged the non-German provinces to accept the hegemony of the German officials and the German language of Vienna. Maria Theresa employed both force and charm to get her way. The nobles of Hungary momentarily forgot their anti-German tradition when the beautiful and spirited empress, her infant son in her arms, personally appealed to their chivalry in the crisis of the War of the Austrian Succession.

The Empress was the first housewife of the realm as well as the first servant of the state. She was the mother of sixteen children, and she adored Francis, her grasping, fickle husband. Francis' will provided a large bequest for his mistress; his widow executed its terms to the letter. Maria Theresa, however, was no enlightened despot, but a devout Catholic and fundamentally out of sympathy with the Age of Reason. "Lady Prayerful," as Catherine the Great called her, banned the works of Rousseau and Voltaire and even forbade the circulation of the Catholic *Index*, lest that list of forbidden books pique the curiosity of her subjects.

The Habsburg representative of enlightened despotism was Joseph II, the eldest son of Maria Theresa, named by her to be emperor and co-regent on the death of Francis in 1765. Frederick the Great wrote Voltaire an estimate of the new emperor:

Born in a bigoted court, he has cast off its superstition; raised in magnificence, he has assumed simple manners; nourished on incense, he is modest; burning with a thirst for glory, he sacrifices his ambition to the filial duty which he executes scrupulously; and, having had only pedantic teachers, he still has enough taste to read Voltaire and to appreciate his merits.*

* "Correspondance avec les Souverains," *Oeuvres Complètes de Voltaire* (Paris, 1828), LXXIV, 37. Our translation.

Frederick exaggerated only a little. Though Joseph lacked the artistic taste of Frederick (he complained that there were "too many notes" in Mozart's operas), he was a true disciple of the Age of Reason. Earnest and industrious in the highest degree, he promised to make "philosophy the legislator of my empire." Maria Theresa thwarted Joseph until her death in 1780. For fifteen years, mother and son clashed, particularly over Joseph's anticlericalism. As a loving son Joseph mourned the passing of Maria Theresa, but as a *philosophe* he welcomed the release from her tutelage. The impatient emperor, now the sole ruler of Austria, plunged into activity; during his ten-year reign (1780-1790), eleven thousand laws and six thousand decrees issued from Vienna.

Joseph at once reversed his mother's religious policy. "Fanaticism," he wrote to his Dutch physician, "shall in future be known in my states only by the contempt I have for it." Calvinist, Lutheran, and Orthodox gained full toleration for the first time in the history of Catholic Austria. And, with a generosity unparalleled in Habsburg annals, the Emperor took measures to end the ghetto existence of the Jews. He exempted Jews from paying special taxes and from wearing the yellow patch as a badge of inferiority.

Joseph brought the Catholic Church under strict state control, making himself rather than the pope the arbiter of church activities in Austria. He encouraged what he considered socially useful in Catholicism and dealt ruthlessly with what he judged superfluous and harmful. Thus he established hundreds of new churches and at the same time made religious holidays less frequent. Monasticism was the subject of repeated imperial tirades. He called monks "the most dangerous and useless subjects in every state," and he promised to convert "the monk of mere show into a useful

Emperor Joseph II of Austria, working a plow.

citizen." He cut in half the number of monks and nuns and, of 2100 monasteries and nunneries, he suppressed 700, chiefly those run by the contemplative orders. Houses actively engaged in educational or charitable work were generally spared. The government sold or leased the lands of the suppressed establishments, applying the revenue to the support of the hospitals that were beginning to earn Vienna its reputation as the greatest medical center in Europe.

Unlike Frederick and Catherine, Joseph really believed in social equality and popular education. His government provided the teachers and textbooks for primary schools. More than a quarter of the school-age children in Austria actually attended school— the best record of any country in late eighteenth-century Europe. Everyone in Vienna, high and low, was invited to visit the Prater, the great public park of the capital, the entrance to which bore the inscription, "A place of pleasure for all men, prepared for them by their friend." An aristocratic lady committed the blunder of seeking Joseph's help to secure her son a commission in the army. The Emperor's devastating reply pro-

vided a good summary of his social outlook:

Madame,—I do not conceive that a monarch is bound to give any one of his subjects an appointment, merely because he is by birth a nobleman.... Do you not say, that your late husband was a meritorious General, and a Cavalier, of a distinguished house? and that from my generous disposition towards your family, you flatter yourself that you shall obtain a company of infantry for your second son, who has just returned from his travels?

Madame! a man may be the son of a general, without possessing the least qualification for an officer;—a man may be a Cavalier of good family, without having any other merit, than that of being a nobleman merely by the effect of chance.

I know your son, and I know the qualifications requisite for an officer. From this knowledge I am convinced that your son has not the character of a military man, and that he is too much occupied with his birth, for me to expect from him such services, as might one day be the boast of his country.

What I pity you for, Madame, is this, that your son is fit neither for an officer, a statesman, nor for a priest. In short, he is nothing but a nobleman, and this he is from the bottom of his heart.

Thank your good fortune, which, while it denied your son all talents, put him in posses-

CHAPTER XVII

sion of considerable estates, which sufficiently indemnify him, and, at the same time, render my services very superfluous.*

To the insult of words Joseph added the injury of legislation. The new Austrian legal code followed Beccaria in abolishing capital punishment and most tortures and in prescribing equality before the law. Aristocratic offenders, like commoners, were sentenced to stand in the pillory and to sweep the streets of Vienna. Joseph's peasant policy marked the climax of his equalitarianism. He freed the serfs, abolished most of their obligations to the manorial lords, and deprived the latter of their medieval function of administering justice to the peasantry.

Joseph's economic policies incorporated both the new doctrines of the Physiocrats and the old practices of mercantilism. He levied high tariffs on imports, yet experimented with the collection of a single tax on land as recommended by Quesnay. In politics, however, Joseph adhered to his mother's Germanizing program. He customarily spoke German, patronized German writers, and made the French playhouse in Vienna a German-language theater. He rode roughshod over the autonomous rights of Bohemia, Belgium, and Hungary. The protests of an indignant Hungarian nobleman met an icy reception:

The German language is the universal language of my empire; why should the laws be administered, and public affairs transacted in a single province in its own language? I am Emperor of the German Empire; consequently the other states which I possess are provinces, which, together with the whole state, form one body, of which I am the head. If the kingdom of Hungary was the most important and the chief of my possessions, I would make its language the principal language of my dominions; but it is otherwise.†

Pamphleteer, XIX (1822), 286-287.
† *Ibid.*, 282.

More than a sharply worded letter was needed to deal with the increasing opposition aroused by Joseph's reforms. The devout peasants, almost oblivious of his well-meaning attempts to improve their social and economic status, keenly resented his meddling with old religious customs. The nobility clamored against his equalitarian legislation; in the case of the single-tax experiment, their opposition was so violent that he had to revoke the decree a month after it was issued. Hungary and Belgium rose in open rebellion against his centralizing efforts and forced him to confirm their autonomous liberties.

In foreign policy, too, the ambitious—and in this instance unenlightened—plans of Joseph II miscarried. By participating in Catherine's "grand design" for Ottoman dismemberment and in the subsequent Turkish war of the late 1780's (see above, p. 70), Austria gained only a narrow strip of Balkan territory. Meantime, Joseph twice attempted to annex lands belonging to the important South German state of Bavaria, where the death of the ruling family opened another of those succession quarrels so common in the eighteenth century. On both occasions, Joseph was thwarted by Frederick the Great, who was determined to check any advance of Habsburg power in Germany. In the late 1770's, Austria and Prussia fought a war—or, more exactly, glared at each other in the mismanaged "Potato War," in which the troops spent most of their time scrounging for food. Joseph secured only a tiny fragment of the Bavarian inheritance. Then in 1785 he sought the whole inheritance by proposing that the heir to Bavaria take the Austrian Netherlands in exchange. Frederick the Great scored the last diplomatic victory of his career when he organized a league of German princes to block the exchange.

Joseph II worked himself to death, as one of his friends observed, by "governing too much and reigning too little." The Emperor defended his habit of interfering personally in the details of government:

What else can I do in this country devoid of mind, without soul, without zeal, without heart in the work? I am killing myself because I cannot rouse up those whom I want to make work; but I hope I shall not die until I have so wound up the machine that others cannot put it out of order, even if they try to do so.°

Joseph never got the machine properly wound up. He could not implant in the unenlightened Austrian bureaucracy the almost inhuman Prussian discipline that it needed; he could not make Vienna a second Berlin.

Joseph II died unshaken in the conviction that he had pursued the proper course, yet believing that he had accomplished nothing. Posterity has reversed the emphasis. Joseph, it is now clear, was the most truly enlightened despot. In ten years he attempted more than Frederick or Catherine attempted in thrice the time. Though some of his major reforms, like the abolition of serfdom, were repealed soon after his death, others survived him, helping to transform the Habsburg lands into a more modern, centralized state. Yet the Austria of Joseph II was the victim of a program too radically enlightened and of methods too stubbornly despotic.

Sweden and Spain

Among the lesser enlightened despots, Gustavus III of Sweden and Charles III of Spain ranked high. Both retrieved their countries temporarily from the lengthening shadows of obscurity. Gustavus III (1771-1792) was the most theatrical monarch of the century. While he distracted

King Charles III of Spain in hunting costume, by Goya.

Swedish party leaders at the opera one evening, his soldiers staged a *coup* that enabled him to revive the almost extinct royal authority and to dissolve the powerful factions of Hats and Caps (see Chapter XVI). The triumphant Gustavus thus ended the party strife that had wrecked the foreign policy of Sweden and was threatening to make her the Poland of Scandinavia. Trained in the ideas of the Parisian *salons*, Gustavus announced in ringing speeches his devotion to the Age of Reason. In economics and religion, his enlightenment outdistanced that of his uncle, Frederick the Great. He followed laissez-faire to the extent of removing obstacles to both domestic

---

° Quoted in Prince de Ligne, *His Memoirs, Letters, and Miscellaneous Papers* (Boston, 1902), II, 132.

74

and foreign trade, and he extended toleration to Jews as well as to the various Christian sects. Success, however, turned the head of Gustavus III. As he became more arbitrary, the nobles increased their determination to recover their old power. In 1792, Gustavus was assassinated at a masquerade in Stockholm, and the brief candle of Swedish enlightened despotism flickered out.

Charles III (1759-1788), Elizabeth Farnese's "Baby Carlos," inherited the Spanish crown on the death of his older brother. He was a remarkably homely and unregal-looking monarch, but he had already been seasoned in the struggle against feudal and clerical conservatism by a long apprenticeship as King of Naples. In Spain, Charles III energetically renewed the progressive policies begun by his father, Philip VI (see Chapter XVI). Though a pious Catholic, he objected strongly to the political influence of the Church and expelled the Jesuits from the native country of their founder. He further consolidated the authority of the Crown and reduced that of the aristocracy. He curbed the privileges of the great sheep-ranchers, whose almost unlimited grazing rights blighted Spanish agriculture and deprived poor peasants of needed farmland. Reclamation and irrigation projects were undertaken, and new roads, canals, banks, and textile mills were established to enliven the torpid Spanish economy. The results were astonishing: Spain's foreign commerce increased fivefold during the reign of Charles III. Unfortunately, however, the successors of Charles III abandoned his forward-looking policies.

The Limitations of Enlightened Despotism

The problem of succession, in fact, constituted a most glaring defect in the whole structure of enlightened despotism. In Prussia, the great Frederick was followed by his nephew, Frederick William II (1786-1797), a royal nincompoop. In Russia, Catherine the Great's son, Paul I (1796-1801), showed little of his mother's statesmanship but a great deal of Peter III's eccentricity. Oligarchy resumed its feeble course in Sweden after the removal of Gustavus III. The principal exception occurred in Austria, where the enlightened Leopold II (1790-1792), fresh from a long and successful apprenticeship in Tuscany, salvaged some of the reforms of his brother, Joseph II.

Although even the poorest of the enlightened despots improved at least a few of the bad features of the Old Régime, not even the best of them struck a happy balance between enlightenment and despotism. Joseph II was too doctrinaire, too inflexible in his determination to apply the full reform program of the Age of Reason. Catherine and Frederick, on the other hand, obsessed with the desire to strengthen the Crown, leaned too heavily on nobles and Junkers, thereby helping to entrench the power of elements often hostile to the whole Enlightenment.

IV: George III and the American Revolution

George III

The melancholy career of King George III (1760-1820) of Great Britain provided still further evidence of the perils of enlightened despotism. The first Hanoverian born and bred in England, the first of that stolid dynasty to take a real interest in the kingdom, George III proposed to reassert some of the royal prerogatives that had lapsed under the first two Georges. He attempted a policy that may, with some exaggeration, be termed a highly modified form of enlightened despotism. Now the actual enlightenment of "Farmer George" did not go much beyond writing articles on turnips for Arthur Young's *Annals of Agriculture.* He was no tyrant, but he did try to wrest control of the House of Commons from the long-dominant Whig oligarchy and retain it by the Whig devices of patronage and bribery. He endeavored to beat the Whigs at their own parliamentary game.

Virtuous as a person, devoted as a family man, George as a monarch was stubborn, short-sighted, and in the long run unsuccessful. It was easy for him at first to exploit the factional strife among the Whigs, maneuver Pitt out of office in 1761, and make his friend and tutor, Lord Bute, the head of the cabinet. Bute and the King, however, found it hard to justify their failure to deprive France of the sugar-rich West Indies in the Peace of Paris (see Chapter XVI). The Commons ratified the treaty, but George dismissed Bute in 1763 in order to appease the critics of British diplomacy.

The harshest criticism came from John Wilkes, a member of the House of Commons, who dubbed the Peace of Paris "the peace of God, for it passeth all understanding." Wilkes' bitter attack on the treaty in his paper, the *North Briton,* infuriated the King. Bowing to the royal anger, the Commons ordered the offending issue of the *North Briton* to be burnt. Wilkes, who first fled to France, later ran for Parliament three separate times, and three times the Commons, under royal pressure, threw out his election. When Wilkes finally took his seat again in 1774, he was a popular hero, and riots defending "Wilkes and Liberty" had become commonplace. A wise king would have trimmed his sails, but George III did not permit the Wilkes affair to weaken his determination to manage both Parliament and cabinet. After seven years of short-lived, unstable ministries (1763-1770), George had finally cast Lord North in Bute's old role. During North's ministry (1770-1782) the royal chickens came home to roost. Abroad, the King lost the thirteen North American colonies; at home, he unwittingly prepared the way for the increase of parliamentary authority.

Background of the Revolution

The American Declaration of Independence claimed:

The history of the present King of Great Britain is a history of repeated injuries and usurpations, all having in direct object the establishment of an absolute Tyranny over these States.

The Declaration exaggerated. George III's refusal to make concessions to the Americans in the 1770's and his determination to use force against them were merely the last of many events widening the breach between colonies and mother country. The breach first became serious at the close of the Seven Years' War when Britain began

76

to modify the old policy of "salutary neglect" (see Chapter XVI). By 1763, the colonies had acquired the habit of regulating their own affairs, though the acts of their assemblies remained subject to the veto of royally appointed governors or of the King himself. The vast territories in Canada and west of the Alleghenies acquired in 1763 brought Britain added opportunities for profitable exploitation and added responsibilities for government and defense. In 1763, an uprising of the Indians under Pontiac captured or threatened almost every frontier post in the area of the Ohio Valley and the Great Lakes. In the absence of effective concerted action by colonial militias, British regulars were brought in to crush Pontiac. The continuing threat from the Indians prompted the royal proclamation of October, 1763, forbidding "all our loving subjects" to settle west of a line running along the summit of the Alleghenies. To His Majesty's "loving subjects" in the colonies, however, the proclamation seemed deliberately designed to exclude them from the rich trading possibilities of the West.

The colonists resented still more keenly the attempt by Parliament to raise more revenue in North America. The British government had very strong arguments for increasing colonial taxes. The national debt had almost doubled during the Seven Years' War; the colonies' reluctance to recruit soldiers and raise taxes themselves had increased the cost of the war to British taxpayers; now the mother country faced continued expense in protecting the frontier. Surely the Americans would admit the reasonableness of the case for higher taxes.

That, however, was precisely what the Americans did *not* admit. The first of the new revenue measures, the Sugar Act of 1764, alarmed the merchants of the eastern seaboard because the customs officers actually undertook to collect duties on molasses, sugar, and other imports and to prosecute smugglers. Here was a departure from the comfortable laxity of salutary neglect. And here was a threat to the colonial economy, for the import duties had to be paid out of the colonies' meager supply of specie (metal coin). The second revenue measure, the Stamp Act of 1765, imposed a duty on a wide variety of items, including legal and commercial papers, liquor licenses, playing cards, dice, newspapers, calendars, and academic degrees. These duties, too, threatened to drain the supply of specie, which was now so low that some merchants faced bankruptcy.

The revenue measures touched off a major controversy. Indignant merchants in the New World boycotted all imports rather than pay the duties, and in October, 1765, delegates from nine of the thirteen colonies met in New York City as the "Stamp Act Congress." The Congress complained that the new duties had "a manifest tendency to subvert the rights and liberties of the colonists." The Congress resolved:

That His Majesty's liege subjects in these colonies are entitled to all the inherent rights and liberties of his natural born subjects within the kingdom of Great Britain.
That it is inseparably essential to the freedom of a people, and the undoubted right of Englishmen, that no taxes be imposed on them but with their own consent, given personally or by their own representatives.
That the people of these colonies are not, and from their local circumstances cannot be, represented in the House of Commons in Great Britain.
That the only representatives of these colonies are persons chosen therein by themselves, and that no taxes ever have been, or can be constitutionally imposed on them, but by their respective legislatures.*

The Stamp Act Congress thus enunciated the principle of no taxation without representation. Britain surrendered on the prac-

* *Documents of American History*, H. S. Commager, ed. (New York, 1940), 58.

An English commentary on the Boston Tea Party and the tarring and feathering of a royal tax collector, who is forced to drink under a liberty tree.

tical issue, but did not yield on the principle. The appeals of London merchants, near ruin because of the American boycott against British goods, brought the repeal of the Stamp Act in 1765. Nevertheless, in the next year Parliament passed the Declaratory Act asserting that the

...Colonies and plantations in *America* have been, are, and of right ought to be, subordinate unto, and dependent upon the imperial crown and parliament of *Great Britain;* and that the King's majesty, by and with the advice and consent of the lords spiritual and temporal, and commons of *Great Britain,* in parliament assembled, had, hath, and of right ought to have, full power and authority to make laws and statutes of sufficient force and validity to

bind the colonies and people of *America,* subjects of the crown of *Great Britain,* in all cases whatsoever.[*]

For the next decade, Britain adhered firmly to the principles of the Declaratory Act, and colonial radicals just as firmly repeated their opposition to taxation without representation. Parliament again tried to raise revenue, this time by the Townshend duties (1767) on colonial imports of tea, paper, paint, and lead. Again the merchants of Philadelphia, New York, and Boston organized boycotts. In 1770, Lord North's cabinet withdrew the Townshend duties except for the three-penny tariff on a pound of tea, retained as a symbol of parliamentary authority over the colonies. Three years later, the English East India Company, reduced almost to bankruptcy by its own corrupt officials, secured Lord North's permission to take a calculated risk and attempt the sale of its surplus tea in North America. It hoped to overcome American opposition to the hated duty of three-pence per pound by making the retail price of East India tea, duty included, far cheaper than that of Dutch tea smuggled by the colonists. The result was the Boston Tea Party. On December 16, 1773, to the cheers of spectators lining the waterfront, a group of Bostonians, who had a large financial stake in smuggled tea, disguised themselves as redskins, boarded the three East India ships, and dumped into the harbor hundreds of tea chests worth thousands of pounds.

Britain answered defiance with coercion, and the colonists met coercion with resistance. The Quebec Act (1774), incorporating the lands beyond the Alleghenies into Canada, bolted the door to the westward expansion of colonial frontiers. The "Intolerable Acts" (1774) closed the port of Boston to trade and suspended elections in Massachusetts. At Lexington and Concord

[*] *Ibid.,* 60-61.

CHAPTER XVII

in April, 1775, the "embattled farmers" of Massachusetts fired the opening shots of the War of Independence. At Philadelphia on July 4, 1776, the delegates to the Continental Congress formally declared America independent of Great Britain.

Implications
of the Revolution: Britain

For the mother country, the American Revolution implied more than the secession of thirteen colonies. It involved Britain in a minor world war that jeopardized her dominance abroad and weakened the power and prestige of King George III at home. The most crucial battle in North America came early in the war—Burgoyne's surrender of his British forces at Saratoga in 1777. Burgoyne had been marching south from Montreal with the aim of moving down the Hudson Valley and driving a wedge between New England and the other rebellious colonies. Not only did he

Louis XVI and Benjamin Franklin. In commemoration of the Franco-American treaty of 1778.

fail completely, but his surrender convinced the French that support of the American colonists would give them an excellent chance to renew their world-wide struggle with Britain and avenge the humiliation of 1763. Entering the war in 1778, France soon gained the alliance of Spain and eventually secured the help, or at least the friendly neutrality, of most other European states.

In North America, the intervention of the French, particularly a French fleet, prepared the way for the victory of George Washington's forces and the final British surrender at Yorktown in 1781. At sea, the British lost 3,000 merchant vessels before the Royal Navy finally rallied to avert a major disaster to British power. In the peace signed at Paris in 1783, Britain, of course, recognized the independence of her former colonies. To Spain she handed back Florida, which she had taken in 1763, and the strategic Mediterranean island of Minorca. But she kept Gibraltar, which the Spanish had also hoped to recover, and she ceded only minor territories to France.

During the early years of the war, the British public had generally been inclined to agree with Dr. Samuel Johnson's strictures on the Americans: "Sir, they are a race of convicts and ought to be thankful for anything we allow them short of hanging." * But the temper of opinion changed as the strength of American resistance became evident, as instances of British mismanagement piled up, and as most of Europe rallied to the rebellious colonies. By 1780, George III and his policy were so unpopular that the House of Commons passed a resolution declaring that "the influence of the crown has increased, is increasing, and ought to be diminished."

The influence of the Crown *was* dimin-

_____

* *Boswell's Life of Johnson,* G. B. Hill, ed. (Oxford, 1934), II, 312.

ished. In 1782, Lord North, who had been imploring the King to accept his resignation for three years, finally abandoned his increasingly impossible role as George's political mouthpiece. In the next year, the post of prime minister fell to William Pitt the Younger, son of the heroic Pitt of the Seven Years' War. The new minister, though only twenty-five years old, was already a seasoned parliamentarian and was to head the cabinet for the next eighteen years. With the advent of Pitt, control of British politics shifted away from the King and back to the professional politicians. George III briefly contemplated abdication and then gradually resigned himself to the rather colorless role of constitutional monarch. In 1788, he suffered the first serious attack of the insanity that clouded the second half of his long reign. The British flirtation (it was really no more than that) with enlightened despotism had come to an end.

Implications of the Revolution: America

In the rebelling colonies public opinion was far from unanimous in support of the Revolution. Many colonists, including southern planters and well-to-do Pennsylvania Quakers, either backed the mother country or took a neutral position in the struggle. New York supplied more recruits to George III than to George Washington. Some of these "Loyalists" or "Tories" were to flee to Canada when independence became a fact. It has been estimated that perhaps only one-third of the colonists actively backed the Revolution.

The revolutionary minority came in part from social groups who had the habit of questioning established authority—the pioneers living on the frontier, and the numerous Presbyterians, Congregationalists, and other strong-minded Protestant sects. Like adolescents everywhere, the colonists resented parental tutelage yet appealed to family precedent. The Stamp Act Congress had resolved that His Majesty's subjects in the colonies were entitled to "all the inherent rights and liberties of his *natural born subjects within the kingdom of Great Britain.*" * American revolutionaries claimed that they were only following the example set by Englishmen in 1688 and defended by John Locke.

The ideas of Locke and Newton were as well known and as much respected in North America as they were in Europe. They underlay the Declaration of Independence:

When in the Course of human events, it becomes necessary for one people to dissolve the political bands which have connected them with another, and to assume among the Powers of the earth, the separate and equal station to which the Laws of Nature and Nature's God entitle them, a decent respect to the opinions of mankind requires that they should declare the causes which impel them to the separation.

The opening paragraph of the Declaration thus expressed the concept of a world-machine ruled by the "Laws of Nature and Nature's God." The next paragraph applied to the colonies Locke's theory of contract and his justification of revolution:

We hold these truths to be self-evident, that all men are created equal, that they are endowed by their Creator with certain unalienable Rights, that among these are Life, Liberty and the pursuit of Happiness. That to secure these rights, Governments are instituted among Men, deriving their just power from the consent of the governed. That whenever any Form of Government becomes destructive of these ends, it is the Right of the People to alter or to abolish it, and to institute new Government. . . .

The Declaration of Independence revealed the debt of the American Revolution

---

* Italics ours.

to the English prophets of the Enlightenment. The Constitution of the new republic was to show its indebtedness to the French *philosophes,* particularly Montesquieu. The delegates to the Constitutional Convention at Philadelphia in 1787 borrowed from *The Spirit of the Laws* the idea of separating the executive, legislative, and judicial powers. The president's check on the Congress through his veto power, the congressional check on the executive and judiciary through impeachment and the right of confirming appointments, and the check imposed on each house of Congress by the requirement that both houses consent to legislation—all these familiar balancing devices of the American Constitution were derived from Montesquieu. The recurrent tensions between president and Congress thus originated in the American adaptation of an eighteenth-century French misreading of British constitutional practice. The "Founding Fathers" also copied from the constitutions of the thirteen original states and from English precedents. The first ten amendments to the Constitution (1791), guaranteeing freedom of religion, freedom of the press, and other basic liberties, were largely taken from the English Bill of Rights of 1689.

The Constitution abounded in compromises. It attempted a balance between states' rights and the central power of the federal government, and between the democratic principle of a directly elected House of Representatives and the aristocratic principle of an indirectly elected and conservative Senate.

James Madison, a chief architect of the Constitution, made the classic defense of its compromises. He rested his defense on the existence of two forces—property and the spirit of faction or party—which he attributed to human nature:

. . . As long as the reason of man continues fallible, and he is at liberty to exercise it, different opinions will be formed. ... The diversity in the faculties of men, from which the rights of property originate, is not less an insuperable obstacle to an uniformity of interests. The protection of these faculties is the first object of government. From the protection of different and unequal faculties of acquiring property, the possession of different degrees and kinds of property immediately results; and from the influence of these on the sentiments and views of the respective proprietors, ensues a division of the society into different interests and parties.

. . .

A landed interest, a manufacturing interest, a mercantile interest, a moneyed interest, and many lesser interests, grow up of necessity in civilized nations, and divide them into different classes, actuated by different sentiments and views. The regulation of these various and interfering interests forms the principal task of modern legislation, and involves the spirit of party and faction in the necessary and ordinary operations of government.*

The American Constitution, then, was a compromise designed to win support from both rich and poor and from both the aristocratic opponents and the democratic supporters of the recent revolution. Like any compromise, it did not at first please all parties, but it worked well enough to make the new American republic a going concern. The "Founding Fathers" had succeeded in adjusting the ideals of the *philosophes* to the realities of practical politics.

---

* *The Federalist*, No. 10, Max Beloff, ed. (New York, 1948), 42-43.

V: The Culture of the Enlightenment

The Enlightenment, however, seldom produced such happy political results as it did in the case of the United States. On the whole, the *philosophes* expected men to see reason when it was pointed out to them, to abandon the habits of centuries, and to revise their behavior in accordance with natural law. But men would not always see reason; as Joseph II discovered to his sorrow, they *would* cling perversely to irrational customs and unnatural traditions. The rationalism of the Enlightenment tended to omit the complexities of human nature from its calculation.

Responsibility for this major shortcoming lay partly with the "classical spirit" of the seventeenth century, inherited by the Enlightenment of the eighteenth. The writers of the Age of Louis XIV had found in their classical models, not a confirmation of existing standards, but a better, simpler set of standards that the eighteenth-century *philosophes* easily adapted to the concept of "nature's simple plan." The seventeenth-century dramatist Molière, for instance, when he created his character Harpagon in *L'Avare* ("The Miser"), was painting not a unique individual but a miser, the type-miser. The great writers do indeed achieve the miracle of giving life to abstractions, of reconciling the universal and the particular. But the lesser ones make only bloodless types, and encourage in their hearers and readers—the men and women who finally do work out social change—the belief that these easy mental images are somehow more real, and certainly more desirable, than the bewildering complexity of their concrete experiences. Like the "classical spirit," the spirit of natural science went too far when it was applied uncritically to problems of human relations. It gave men the illusion that what was going on in their minds would shortly go on in reality.

A minor *philosophe*, the Abbé Mably, got at this central problem by putting it in the form of a question: "Is society, then, a branch of physics?" Most of the *philosophes* and their followers believed that it was. They applied to the unpredictable activities of man the exact mathematical methods used in the physical sciences. The Physiocrats tried to reduce economic complexities to simple agricultural laws; Montesquieu tried to simplify the intricacies of government in terms of a climatic formula. Like the stars in their courses, human beings were thought to fit neatly into the Newtonian world-machine.

Philosophy

A few eighteenth-century minds disagreed. David Hume (1711-1776), a brilliant Scottish philosopher, doubted the wisdom of assuming that society was a branch of physics, indeed doubted everything. His skeptical mind insisted on submitting principles to the test of factual observation. The errors and illusions of the *philosophes*, he said, resulted from their failure to do this. They deduced untested conclusions from two great abstract principles—faith in natural law, belief in reason.

Hume made short work of the *philosophes'* appeals to nature. The laws of justice, he argued, were not the absolute and inflexible "Laws of Nature and Nature's God":

... Suppose a society to fall into such want of all common necessaries, that the utmost frugality and industry cannot preserve the greater number from perishing, and the whole from extreme misery; it will readily, I believe, be admitted, that the strict laws of justice are suspended, in such a pressing emergence, and give place to the stronger motives of necessity and self-preservation. Is it any crime, after a

shipwreck, to seize whatever means or instrument of safety one can lay hold of, without regard to former limitations of property? Or if a city besieged were perishing with hunger; can we imagine, that men will see any means of preservation before them, and lose their lives, from a scrupulous regard to what, in other situations, would be the rules of equity and justice? *

Nor could human conduct be analyzed "in the same manner that we discover by reason the truths of geometry or algebra."

It appears evident that the ultimate ends of human actions can never, in any case, be accounted for by *reason*, but recommend themselves entirely to the sentiments and affections of mankind, without any dependance [sic] on the intellectual faculties. Ask a man *why he uses exercise:* he will answer, *because he desires to keep his health.* If you then enquire, *why he desires health,* he will readily reply, *because sickness is painful.* If you push your enquiries farther, and desire a reason *why he hates pain,* it is impossible he can ever give any. ...

Perhaps to your second question, *why he desires health,* he may also reply, that *it is necessary for the exercise of his calling.* If you ask, *why he is anxious on that head,* he will answer, *because he desires to get money.* If you demand Why? *It is the instrument of pleasure,* says he. And beyond this it is an absurdity to ask for a reason.†

Hume anticipated the later school of Utilitarians (see Chapter XX), who judged actions in accordance with their utility in arousing pleasure and dispelling pain. Along with Holbach, he found it hard to explain the existence of evil in a world ruled by an omnipotent benevolent deity. For Holbach, atheism was the solution, since he could not reconcile evil on earth and God in heaven. Hume was not so certain; although he could not prove that God existed, neither could he prove that there was no God. To the skeptical mind only one thing was sure. The "mere reason" of the deists was no

* *An Enquiry concerning the Principles of Morals,* L. A. Selby-Bigge, ed. (Oxford, 1902), 186.
† *Ibid.,* 293.

guide to religious truth; "none but mystics" could penetrate the riddle of the universe:

A person, seasoned with a just sense of the imperfections of natural reason, will fly to revealed truth with the greatest avidity.*

David Hume was among the first and most profound critics of the Age of Reason. The Romantics of the next generation would repeat his warnings against the "imperfections of reason" and his pleas on behalf of the "sentiments and affections of mankind" (see Chapter XX). In his own day, Hume won scant appreciation, but he was not quite a voice crying in the wilderness. Rousseau and Kant were also worried by rather similar problems.

Rousseau both represented the Enlightenment and foreshadowed the revolt against it. No *philosophe* defended natural law more ardently, yet no Romantic argued more convincingly in support of emotion and faith. "Too often does reason deceive us," Rousseau wrote in *Emile*. "We have only too good a right to doubt her; but conscience never deceives us; she is the true guide of man; ... he who obeys his conscience is following nature and he need not fear that he will go astray." †

Immanuel Kant (1724-1804), who taught philosophy at the University of Königsberg in East Prussia, raised Rousseau's argument to the level of metaphysics. Kant believed in a higher reality reaching ultimately to God, a realm rather like Plato's world of Ideas. Kant called the eternal verities of the higher world "noumena," in contrast to the phenomena of the material world. Knowledge of the noumenal realm, Kant believed, reached men through reason— reason, however, not as the Enlightenment used the term, not as common sense, but as

intuition, almost as mysticism. The highest expression of the Kantian reason was the "categorical imperative." This was the moral law within, the conscience implanted in man by God. It was the inescapable realization welling up in the individual that, when confronted with an ethical choice, he must choose the good and avoid the evil.

Kant's redefinition of reason and his rehabilitation of conscience shaped the whole subsequent history of philosophy. But his immediate influence was limited, for the understanding of his intricate arguments required immense patience and learning. The intellectual reaction against the dominant rationalism of the Enlightenment reached its highest point with Kant. The popular reaction took the form of the evangelical revival, which began with the German Pietists of the eighteenth century.

The Evangelical Revival

The Pietists were the spiritual descendants of the sixteenth-century Anabaptists. Deploring alike the growing Lutheran concern with the formal aspects of religion and the deists' emphasis on natural law, the Pietists asserted that religion came from the heart, not the head. The God of the Pietists was more than the remote inventor of a world. The chief leader of Pietism was a German nobleman, Count Zinzendorf (1700-1760), founder of the Moravian Brethren. The Moravians set up a model community based on Christian principles, and Moravian emigrants to America planted a colony at Bethlehem, Pennsylvania, founding the "Pennsylvania Dutch" traditions of thrift, hard work, and strict living. In England, meanwhile, the example of Zinzendorf and other Pietists inspired John Wesley.

Ordained a priest of the Church of England, John Wesley (1703-1791) at first

---

* *Dialogues concerning Natural Religion*, N. K. Smith, ed. (Oxford, 1935), 282.
  † *Emile*, Everyman ed. (New York, 1911), 249-250.

CHAPTER XVII

stressed the formal side of religion. But the failure of his two-year ministry to the backward colony of Georgia (1736-1737) convinced him of the weakness of religious formalism. Disillusioned, Wesley felt his own faith evaporating: "I went to America, to convert the Indians: but Oh! who shall convert me! Who, what is he that will deliver me from this evil heart of unbelief?" * Pietism converted Wesley. Following the teachings of the Moravian Brethren, whom he met in England and America, he found faith through inner emotional conviction.

For more than fifty years, Wesley labored tirelessly to share his discovery, traveling throughout the British Isles, and preaching in churches, in the fields, at the pitheads of coal mines, and even in jails. Angry crowds came to scoff but remained to pray. Wesley described a typical scene:

As I returned home in the evening, I had no sooner stepped out of the coach than the mob, who were gathered in great numbers about my door, quite closed me in. I rejoiced, and blessed God, knowing this was the time I had long been looking for; and immediately spake to those that were next me of 'righteousness and judgment to come.' At first not many heard, the noise round about us being exceedingly great; but the silence spread farther and farther, till I had a quiet, attentive congregation; and when I left them, they showed much love, and dismissed me with many blessings.†

When Wesley died in 1791, his movement had already attracted more than a hundred thousand adherents. They were called Methodists, because of their methodical devotion to piety and to the Puritan customs of plain dressing and plain living. Though Wesley always considered himself a good Anglican, the Methodists eventually set up a separate organization—their nonconformist "Chapel" in contrast to the established Church of England. The new sect won its

* John Wesley, *Journal*, Everyman ed. (New York, 1907), I, 74.
† *Ibid.*, I, 287.

following almost entirely among the lower and middle classes, from people who sought the religious excitement and consolation that were denied them by deism and by the austere formalism of the Church of England.

Methodism clashed with enlightened rationalism. Where the *philosophes* advised public reform, the Methodists favored private charity. And where the *philosophes* recommended attacking the *causes* of social evils, the Methodists accepted these evils as part of God's inscrutable plan and sought to mitigate their *symptoms*. They began agitation against drunkenness, the trade in slaves, and the barbarous treatment suffered by prisoners, the insane, and the sick. To launch a program of popular education, John Wesley established schools for coalminers' children. He inveighed against the callousness of some doctors toward poor patients and opened dispensaries for the slum-dwellers of London and Bristol. He wrote, and his preachers distributed, a popular home medical manual: *Primitive Physic, or An Easy and Natural Method of Curing Most Diseases*. The Methodists had in full measure the Puritan conscience of the nonconformists.

Part of their success rested on their social program, and part on the magnetism of John Wesley and of his talented associates. Charles Wesley, John's brother, composed 6500 hymns. George Whitefield, preacher extraordinary, could pronounce "Mesopotamia" so eloquently that he moved the actor Garrick to tears. The Methodist missionaries in America came under the dynamic leadership of Francis Asbury, remembered in the name of Asbury Park, New Jersey, which was once a Methodist camp-meeting site. The number of colleges called Wesleyan and the number of churches and streets called Asbury testify to the importance of Methodism in American history.

Literature

The middle-class public so strongly attracted to Methodism welcomed the novels of the English writer, Samuel Richardson (1689-1761). A printer by trade, he turned to writing late in life and produced three gigantic novels in the form of letters by the chief characters. *Clarissa Harlowe* (1748), the best of them, bore the subtitle: "The History of a Young Lady: Comprehending the Most Important Concerns of Private Life. And particularly Shewing, the Distresses that may attend the Misconduct Both of Parents and Children, in Relation to Marriage." Richardson proceeded in 2400 pages of small print to recount the distresses of Clarissa, whose lover was a scoundrel, and whose relatives were a greedy pack, scheming to secure her considerable property. Drugged and betrayed, Clarissa soon lost almost everything, including her life. But to the end she preserved the capacity to pour out her distresses on paper. If anyone missed the point of *Clarissa Harlowe*, he had only to turn to Richardson's preface:

> What will be found to be more particularly aimed at in the following work is—to warn the inconsiderate and thoughtless of one sex, against the base arts and designs of specious contrivers of the other—to caution parents against the undue exercise of their natural authority over their children in the great article of marriage—to warn against preferring a man of pleasure to a man of probity upon that dangerous but too-commonly-received notion, *that a reformed rake makes the best husband* —but above all, to investigate the highest and most important doctrines not only of morality, but of christianity, by showing them thrown into action in the conduct of the *worthy* characters; while the *unworthy*, who set these doctrines at defiance, are condignly, and, as may be said, consequentially punished.

Modern readers are likely to find *Clarissa Harlowe* tedious and sentimental. But the eighteenth century was entranced. *Clarissa* was read aloud at family gatherings, the story runs, and whenever some new distress overwhelmed her, the members of the family retired to their separate rooms for a good solitary cry. In spite of sentimental exaggerations, Richardson's vivid descriptions of the struggles of passion and conscience nevertheless carried emotional and psychological conviction. Rousseau showed the same qualities in *La Nouvelle Héloïse* (1761), which he modeled on Clarissa. Rousseau's heroine followed his dictum that conscience was the "true guide" of humanity. More fortunate than Clarissa, she renounced illicit love for the happiness of marriage and motherhood.

The novel as a literary form really came into its own during the eighteenth century, particularly in England. By no means all the masters of English fiction were sentimentalists. In *Roderick Random* (1748), as we saw in the last chapter, Tobias Smollett gave an authentic report on life in the navy, with all its cruelty and misery. Henry Fielding introduced a strong leaven of satire and burlesqued the absurdities of Richardson. In his masterpiece, *Tom Jones* (1749), Fielding covered the whole English social scene and depicted both the hard-riding country squires and the low characters of the city slums. Richardson gave the English novel emotional and moral earnestness; Smollett and Fielding added a vigorous realism.

The Enlightenment, in sum, was an age of prose. With a few exceptions, notably Alexander Pope (1688-1744), it produced no poets of great consequence. The literary monuments of the age were the great English novels, the tales and essays of Voltaire, and the letters and miscellaneous writing of the *philosophes*. Last, but not least, came Gibbon's *History of the Decline and Fall of the Roman Empire* (1788). Edward Gibbon used history for a sustained Voltairean attack on Christian fanaticism and perfected a Ciceronian prose style which, by its balance and discipline, perfectly suited the classical temper of the Age of Reason. Enlightened scholarship likewise produced in France the great *Encyclopédie* and in England Dr. Johnson's *Dictionary* (1755).

The autocratic Dr. Samuel Johnson set out to be the Newton of the English language. He declared in the preface to his dictionary:

When I took the first survey of my undertaking, I found our speech copious without order and energetick [*sic*] without rules: wherever I turned my view, there was perplexity to be disentangled, and confusion to be regulated; choice was to be made out of a boundless variety, without any established principle of selection; adulterations were to be detected, without a settled test of purity; and modes of expression to be rejected or received, without the suffrages of any writers of classical reputation or acknowledged authority.

For the most part, Dr. Johnson ably resolved the difficulties thus described, though pedantry and prejudice sometimes got the upper hand. His definition of a cough—"a convulsion of the longs, vellicated by some sharp serosity"—was a horrible lesson in the dangers of using little-known Latin polysyllables. The good Tory doctor brushed aside the Whig as "one of our unhappy terms of disunion," but praised the Tory as "one who adheres to the ancient constitution of the state." And, whenever he could, he aimed a volley at his favorite target, the Scots. Thus he defined oats as "a grain, which in England is generally given to horses, but in Scotland supports the people."

Art

The classicism of the Enlightenment strongly affected its art. Gibbon's great history, the researches of scholars and archaeologists, and the discovery in 1748 of the well-preserved ruins of ancient Roman Pom-

Dr. Samuel Johnson, by Sir Joshua Reynolds.

peii, buried under lava from Vesuvius, kept the interest in classical antiquity at a high pitch. To the Enlightenment, the balance and symmetry of Greek and Roman temples represented, in effect, the "natural laws" of building. Architects retreated somewhat from the theatrical extravagance of the Baroque style and adapted classical models with great skill and variety. They produced the elegance of the London town house, the monumental magnificence of the buildings flanking the Place de la Concorde in Paris, and the pastoral charm of George Washington's house at Mount Vernon. The popularity of the "colonial" and "Georgian" styles in the twentieth century testifies to the lasting influence of eighteenth-century neoclassicism.

Another lasting achievement of the century was its creation of simple, graceful, yet sturdy house furnishings. French cabinetmakers created the styles known as "Louis XV" and "Louis XVI," and Hepplewhite and Sheraton designed neoclassical furniture for English homes. Josiah Wedgwood (1730-1795) made fine china available at a modest price. Wedgwood showed both reverence toward antique models and resourcefulness in employing the new techniques of the infant industrial revolution. He utilized the steam engine and specialization of labor, yet decorated his china with Greek and Roman patterns and called his modern factory "Etruria," after the site of old Roman potteries.

English painting came under the neoclassical influence. The artistic tsar of Georgian England was Sir Joshua Reynolds (1723-1792), the first president of the Royal Academy. Beauty, he told the academy, rested "on the uniform, eternal, and immutable laws of nature," which could be "investigated by reason, and known by study." Sir Joshua pronounced all pictures lacking in proportion to be "false":

Disproportionate ordonnance of parts is not right; because it cannot be true, until it ceases to be a contradiction to assert that the parts have no relation to the whole. Colouring is true, when it is naturally adapted to the eye, from brightness, from softness, from harmony, from resemblance; ... as true as mathematical demonstration; but known to be true only to those who study these things.*

Sir Joshua and his contemporaries, though preaching this coldly reasoned aesthetic, applied warmth and vitality to the actual portraits that they painted of wealthy English aristocrats. This was the age of Reynolds, Lawrence, Gainsborough, Romney, and many others—the golden age of English portraiture.

---

* *Reynolds' Discourses* (Oxford, 1907), 97.

It was also the age of William Hogarth (1697-1764), who cast aside the academic restraints of neoclassicism to do in art what Fielding did in the novel. Instead of catering to a few wealthy patrons, Hogarth sought a mass market for the engravings that he turned out in thousands of copies. Instead of seeking proportion and harmony, he sketched with brutal frankness the vices of London. *Marriage à la Mode, The Rake's Progress, The Harlot's Progress, Beer Street,* and *Gin Lane* were his satires and sermons on a particularly licentious and drunken society.

The realism of Hogarth was far from being the only exception to the prevailing neoclassical bent of art. The fashions for the oriental, the natural, and the Gothic, which were to be such important elements in the Romanticism of the early nineteenth century, were already beginning to catch on. The taste for the exotic produced Chinese wallpaper, the "Chinese" furniture of Thomas Chippendale, and the familiar Chinese pattern of "willow-ware" plates. Gardens were bestrewn with pagodas, minarets, and miniature mosques. Gardeners abandoned the geometrical pattern and tortured shrubs of Louis XIV's landscaping for the wild English garden—the wilder and more natural the effect, the better it was liked.

Even the dominance of neoclassical architecture was threatened. At Strawberry Hill near London, Horace Walpole, the son of the great Robert, concocted a house that anticipated the worst features of the coming Gothic revival. According to Horace himself, Strawberry Hill had an abundance of Gothic "gloomth"—battlements in the medieval style, "lean windows fattened with rich saints in painted glass," and two more windows "the top of each glutted with the richest painted glass of the arms of England, crimson roses, and twenty other pieces of green, purple, and historic bits."

CHAPTER XVII

Hogarth, "The March to Finchley." A commentary on the state of discipline in the British army.

The Great Musicians

The crowning glory of eighteenth-century culture was its music. The first half of the century was the age of Bach and Handel, and the second half was the age of Haydn and Mozart. Johann Sebastian Bach (1685-1750) brought to perfection the Baroque techniques of seventeenth-century composers. He mastered the difficult art of the fugue, an intricate version of the round in which each voice begins the theme in turn while the other voices simultaneously repeat and elaborate it. He resolved a complicated problem in musical mathematics by creating a six-part fugue for his *Musical Offering*, based on a theme by Frederick the Great and offered to the Prussian monarch. Bach also composed a wealth of material for the organ, the most Baroque and the most religious of instruments. Sacred themes inspired many of his cantatas, the Mass in B minor, and the two gigantic choral settings of the Passion of Christ according to St. John and to St. Matthew. The religious music of Bach, dramatic and deeply felt, was a world apart

from the anticlerical temper of the Enlightenment.

Bach led the placid life of a German organist and choir-master. George Frederick Handel (1685-1759), in contrast, had a stormy international career. Born in Germany, Handel studied in Italy, then spent most of his adult years in England trying desperately to run an opera company. The intrigues, the clashes of temperament, and the fiscal headaches inevitable in artistic enterprise nearly ruined him. Yet Handel wrote more than forty operas, including *Xerxes*, famous for "Handel's Largo." He took epic themes from the Bible and used them for *The Messiah* and other vigorous oratorios directed at a mass audience and arranged for large choruses. These massive performances differed greatly from the original oratorios of seventeenth-century Italy, small-scale works written for the tiny prayer chapels called oratories.

Although Bach and Handel composed many instrumental suites and concertos, it was not until the second half of the century that orchestral music really came to the fore. New instruments then appeared, headed by the piano, which greatly extended the limited range of the older keyboard instrument, the harpsichord. New forms also appeared, the sonata and the symphony, developed largely by Joseph Haydn (1732-1809). Haydn wrote more than fifty piano pieces in the form of the sonata, in which two contrasting themes are stated in turn, developed, interwoven, repeated, and finally resolved in a *coda* (the Italian for "tail"). Haydn then applied the sonata to the orchestra, grafting it on the Italian operatic overture, and enlarging it into the first movement of the symphony. He composed 104 symphonies, volume after volume of chamber music, and, for good measure, two masterly oratorios, *The Creation* and *The Seasons*.

The operatic landmark of the early century was John Gay's *Beggar's Opera* (1728). This tuneful work, "popular" in the highest sense of the term, caricatured English society and politics in Hogarthian vein. Christoph Gluck (1714-1787) revolutionized the technique of the tragic opera. "I have striven," he said,

to restrict music to its true office of serving poetry by means of expression and by following the situations of the story, without interrupting the action or stifling it with a useless superfluity of ornaments. . . . I did not wish to arrest an actor in the greatest heat of dialogue . . . to hold him up in the middle of a word on a vowel favorable to his voice, nor to make display of the agility of his fine voice in some long-drawn passage, nor to wait while the orchestra gives him time to recover his breath for a cadenza.*

Gluck executed this declaration of operatic independence. His operas were well-constructed dramas in music, not casual vehicles for the display of the vocal pyrotechnics so long favored in Italian opera. Gluck ad-

hered to the old custom of taking heroes and heroines from classical mythology, but he invested shadowy figures like Orpheus, Eurydice, and Iphigenia with new vitality and character.

Opera, symphony, and chamber works all reached a climax in Wolfgang Amadeus Mozart (1756-1791). As a boy, Mozart was cruelly exploited by his father, who carted "Wolfgangerl" all over Europe to show off his virtuosity on the harpsichord and his amazing talent for composition. Overworked throughout his life, and in his later years overburdened with debts, Mozart died a pauper at the age of thirty-five. Unlike most child prodigies, Mozart was never spoiled. His talent ripened steadily into mature genius, and his facility and versatility grew ever more prodigious. He tossed off the sprightly overture to *The Marriage of Figaro* in the course of an evening. In two months during the summer of 1788, he produced the three great symphonies familiar to concert audiences as No. 39 (E flat major), No. 40 (G minor), and No. 41 ("The Jupiter"). Mozart's orchestral works also included a long list of concertos, with the solo parts sometimes for piano or violin and sometimes, just to show that it could be done, for bassoon or French horn. In chamber music, Mozart experimented with almost every possible combination of instruments, and for the human voice he wrote tender songs, a solemn *Requiem*, and, above all else, operas.

Three of Mozart's great operas were in the comic Italian vein known as *opera buffa*. In *Così Fan Tutte* ("As the Girls Go") he combined pure farce with enchantingly melodic duets. Still more enchanting music graces *The Marriage of Figaro*, based on Beaumarchais' lampoon of the Old Régime caste system (see Chapter XVIII), in which Figaro the valet outwits and outsings his noble employers. Tragic overtones appear in *Don Giovanni*, depicting the

---

* Preface to *Alcestis*, as translated by Eric Blom and quoted in Curt Sachs, *Our Musical Heritage* (New York, 1948), 287.

CHAPTER XVII

havoc wrought by Don Juan on earth before his eventual punishment in hell. Mozart composed with equal skill mournful and romantic arias for the Don's victims, elegantly seductive ballads for the Don himself, and a ribald catalog of the Don's conquests for his valet ("A thousand and three in Spain alone"). The instruments in the pit dotted the "i's" and crossed the "t's" of the plot—scurrying violins to accompany characters dashing about the stage, portentous trombones to announce the entrance of the Devil. For the ballroom scene of *Don Giovanni*, Mozart accomplished the remarkable feat of employing three orchestras, playing simultaneously three different tunes for three different dances—a minuet for the aristocracy, a country dance for the middle class, a waltz for the lower orders. In his last opera, *The Magic Flute*, Mozart abandoned the usual Italian libretto and tried to create a consciously German work. The music, as always, was lovely, but only the vaguest political significance emerged from the confused and fantastic libretto, which apparently sought to vindicate the enlightened ideas of Joseph II and to decry the conservatism of Maria Theresa.

The Magic Flute was a rare exception to the generally cosmopolitan character of eighteenth-century music. The great composers with the German names had very little national feeling. Almost all of them felt equally at home in Vienna, Prague, Milan, Paris, and London, and they gratefully accepted patrons in whatever country they found them. Bach sought the favor of Frederick the Great, and Handel that of the English court. The fortunate Haydn moved from the princely estate of the Hungarian Ezterhazys to score an equal success with the ordinary paying public of the London concert-halls. Italian music was never totally eclipsed, nor was German dominance complete. Bach patterned his concertos on Italian models, Haydn borrowed Italian operatic overtures for his symphonies, and every operatic composer of the century profited from the labors of his Italian predecessors. The fugues of Bach and the sonatas of Haydn brilliantly exemplified classical symmetry and balance, while Mozart's operas added a dash of social criticism in the manner of the *philosophes*.

The great composers also had the human touch so often lacking in the Age of Reason. They borrowed freely from folk-tunes and ballads, the popular music of their day, and were rewarded by having their themes whistled in the streets. Mozart's operas, Haydn's symphonies, and the great choral works of Bach and Handel have never lost this popular appeal. They have always retained the capacity to appeal to the listener's emotions. In this sense, music probably came closest to resolving harmoniously the great conflict in eighteenth-century civilization, the conflict between reason and emotion, between the abstractions of the Enlightenment and the realities of human existence.

In other realms, however, as the century drew toward its close, the lines were drawn for the vigorous prosecution of the conflict. In thought, the ideas of Kant and Hume were challenging the rationalism of the *philosophes*. Romantic artists and Romantic writers were preparing to hurl defiance at the defenders of classicism. And in politics, as the century ended, the powers sought to check the French Revolution, the greatest effort to realize on earth the Enlightenment's dream of reason, natural law, and progress.

Reading Suggestions
on the Enlightenment

General Accounts

The three volumes by Roberts, Dorn, and Gershoy in the "Rise of Modern Europe" series listed in the reading suggestions for Chapter XVI provide succinct coverage of the aspects of eighteenth-century history covered in this chapter. Dorn's volume is particularly helpful on the Enlightenment, and Gershoy's on the Enlightened Despots.

G. Bruun, *The Enlightened Despots* (New York: Henry Holt & Co., 1929. A Berkshire Study). A first-rate brief introduction to the Enlightenment.

R. B. Mowat, *The Age of Reason* (Boston: Houghton Mifflin Company, 1934). A readable general treatment.

Special Studies: The Enlightenment

P. Smith, *The History of Modern Culture,* Vol. II (New York: Henry Holt & Co., 1934). Notable for its painstaking amassing of relevant details.

E. Cassirer, *The Philosophy of the Enlightenment* (Princeton: Princeton University Press, 1951). An important and rather difficult philosophical study.

P. Hazard, *European Thought in the Eighteenth Century* (London: Hollis and Carter, 1954). A significant re-evaluation of the Enlightenment.

C. Becker, *The Heavenly City of the Eighteenth-Century Philosophers* (New Haven: Yale University Press, 1932). A charming series of essays, stressing the similarities between the eighteenth-century Age of Reason and the medieval Age of Faith.

K. Martin, *The Rise of French Liberal Thought,* J. P. Mayer, ed. (New York: New York University Press, 1954). A revised edition of Martin's brilliant and opinionated *French Liberal Thought in the Eighteenth Century.*

J. Morley, *Diderot and the Encyclopaedists,* rev. ed. (London: Macmillan & Co., Ltd., 1923). An old but perceptive account by a noted Victorian Liberal. Morley also wrote useful studies of Voltaire and Rousseau.

N. L. Torrey, *The Spirit of Voltaire* (New York: Columbia University Press, 1938). A thoughtful estimate by a modern scholar.

A. Cobban, *Rousseau and the Modern State* (London: George Allen and Unwin, Ltd., 1934). A good introduction to the implications of Rousseau's thought.

Special Studies: The Enlightened Despots

G. P. Gooch, *Frederick the Great, the Ruler, the Writer, the Man* (New York: Alfred A. Knopf, Inc., 1947), and F. J. P. Veale, *Frederick the Great* (London: Hamish Hamilton, 1935). Two modern and reasonably balanced evaluations of the famous Hohenzollern.

CHAPTER XVII

G. Scott Thomson, *Catherine the Great and the Expansion of Russia* (New York: The Macmillan Company, 1950. Teach Yourself History Series). A sound brief introduction. There are many full-dress biographies of Catherine, of which the best is perhaps still the old K. Walizewski, *The Romance of an Empress* (New York: Appleton, 1894).

C. L. Morris, *Maria Theresa, The Last Conservative* (New York: Alfred A. Knopf, Inc., 1937). A sympathetic biography.

S. K. Padover, *The Revolutionary Emperor, Joseph II* (New York: Ballou, 1934). Warmly favorable to its subject, and rather chill toward Maria Theresa.

Special Studies: The American Revolution

L. H. Gipson, *The Coming of the Revolution, 1763-1775,* and J. R. Alden, *The American Revolution, 1775-1783,* both in the "New American Nation" series (New York: Harper and Brothers, 1954). Full and up-to-date treatments.

C. Becker, *The Declaration of Independence* (New York: Alfred A. Knopf, Inc., 1948). A most instructive monograph, particularly valuable for tracing the European roots of the Declaration.

M. Beloff, *Thomas Jefferson and American Democracy* (New York: The Macmillan Company, 1949. Teach Yourself History Series). A good introduction to one of the most versatile and attractive of the Founding Fathers.

Sources

Note: The chief figures of the Enlightenment generally wrote such clear and readable prose that it is more profitable to read directly from them rather than to read about them in works of historical fiction.

B. R. Redman, ed., *The Portable Voltaire* (New York: Viking Press, 1949). A good selection from Voltaire's writings, prefaced by an informative introduction.

Montesquieu, *The Spirit of the Laws,* F. Neumann, ed. (New York: Hafner, 1949). A well-presented edition of this rather rambling classic.

Rousseau, *The Social Contract and Discourses,* Everyman ed. (New York: E. P. Dutton & Co., 1913). A convenient edition.

Beccaria, *Essay on Crimes and Punishments* (Stanford, Calif.: Academic Reprints, 1953). Short and pungent, this is a good introduction to the writing of the *philosophes.*

A. Smith, *Selections from "The Wealth of Nations"* (Chicago: Henry Regnery, no date). A convenient abridgement of this famous and lengthy work.

M. Beloff, ed., *The Debate on the American Revolution, 1761-1783* (London: N. Kaye, 1949). A useful compilation from writings and speeches pro and con the American revolt.

B. Dobrée, ed., *The Letters of King George III* (London: Cassell, 1935). A very readable collection, giving much of the flavor of late eighteenth-century English politics.

The French Revolution and Napoleon

CHAPTER XVIII

Execution of Louis XVI, January 21, 1793.

I: Causes of the Revolution

THE *immediate* cause of the great French Revolution of 1789 was financial. A rapidly mounting deficit, swollen by the expense of French aid to the American Revolution, drove the monarchy steadily toward bankruptcy. King Louis XVI vainly tried one expedient after another and finally summoned the Estates General, the central French representative assembly that had last met 175 years earlier. Once assembled, the deputies of the nation initiated reforms that were to destroy the Old Régime in France.

The *basic* causes of the French Revolution reached deep into the society and economy of France and into the country's political and intellectual history. Behind the financial crisis of the 1780's lay decades, indeed centuries, of fiscal mismanagement. The government had been courting bankruptcy at least since the reign of Louis XIV. The nobles and clergy, jealously guarding the remnants of their medieval privileges, refused to pay a fair share of the tax burden. Resentment against inequitable taxation and inefficient government built up among the unprivileged—the peasantry, the workers, and, above all, the bourgeoisie. The ideas

Marie Antoinette, 1788.

of the Enlightenment, advanced by the *philosophes,* translated bourgeois resentment into a program of active reform.

The Monarchy

France, the home of the Enlightenment, was never ruled by an enlightened despot until the advent of Napoleon. Louis XV had refused to take decisive steps to remedy the abuses of the Old Régime (see Chapter XVI). What Louis XV would not do, his grandson and successor could not do. Louis XVI (1774-1792), unlike his grandfather, was earnest and pious. Though fat and clumsy, he developed real skill at his favorite pastimes of hunting and locksmithing. But he had a slow mind and was both irresolute and stubborn. Louis labored under the additional handicap of a politically unfortunate marriage. Marie Antoinette, his wife, was frivolous and ignorant; worse still, she was a Habsburg, the daughter of Maria Theresa, a constant reminder to

French patriots of the Franco-Austrian alliance that had led so quickly to the humiliations of the Seven Years' War.

For want of a bold mechanic, the machinery of centralized royal absolutism was gradually falling apart. The fact that it functioned at all could be credited to a relatively few capable administrators, notably the *intendants* who ran so much of provincial France. The best of the *intendants*, like the Physiocrat Turgot at Limoges, provided a welcome touch of enlightened despotism, but they could do little to stay the slow disintegration of the central government.

The whole legal and judicial system required reform. The law needed to be modernized and codified to eliminate useless medieval survivals and to end the overlapping and conflict of the two legal systems—Roman and feudal—that prevailed in France. The courts needed a thorough overhaul to make them swift, fair, and inexpensive. Many judges and lawyers purchased or inherited their offices and regarded them not as a public trust but as a means to private enrichment. Louis XV, in one of his rare awakenings from political inertia, had permitted his ministers to attack the Paris Parlement, the stronghold of these vested interests and the highest court in France. One of the last acts of his reign had been the cancellation of its privileges; one of the first moves taken by Louis XVI was the restoration of the Parlement's full authority.

The First and Second Estates

Like the monarchy itself, the social and economic foundations of the Old Régime were beginning to crumble and slip. An estimate of the numbers and lands of the three estates in 1789 is given in the table at the foot of this page.

The first estate occupied a position of conspicuous importance in eighteenth-century France. The clergy possessed extensive and lucrative lands, kept records of vital statistics, dispensed relief to the poor, and ran the educational system, such as it was. The Gallican Church, however, was a house divided. The lower clergy came almost entirely from the third estate and shared many of its aspirations and its hatreds. Humble, poorly paid, and generally hard-working, the priests resented the wealth and the arrogance of their ecclesiastical superiors. The bishops and abbots maintained the aristocratic outlook of the noble class into which they had been born. Although some of them took their duties seriously, others regarded church office as a convenient means of securing a comfortable income. Dozens of prelates turned the administration of their bishoprics or monasteries over to subordinates, pocketed the revenue for themselves, and took up residence in Paris or Versailles.

The wealth and the lax discipline of the Church invited criticism. Good Catholics deplored the dwindling numbers of monks and

THE THREE ESTATES IN 1789

	Number	Percentage of Total Population	Percentage of Land Held
First Estate (Clergy)	100,000 to 200,000	Less than 1	10
Second Estate (Nobles)	400,000	Less than 2	25
Third Estate	24,000,000	97	—
Peasants more than	20,000,000	—	30
Bourgeoisie less than	2,000,000	—	25

Note: These are rough estimates based chiefly on the calculations of G. Lefebvre, *The Coming of the French Revolution* (Princeton, 1947), 7, 132. The French Crown presumably held much of the 10 per cent of the land not accounted for above.

nuns in France and the growing tendency of monastic establishments to concentrate on exploiting their properties. Well-to-do peasants and townspeople coveted the rich ecclesiastical estates. Taxpayers grumbled at the tithes levied by the Church, even though the full 10 per cent implied by the word "tithe" was seldom taken. They complained again at the Church's exemption from taxation and at the meager size of the "free gift" voted by the clergy to the government in lieu of taxes.

The peasants on the whole remained moderately faithful Catholics and regarded the village priest, if not the bishop, with esteem and affection. The bourgeoisie, however, more and more accepted the anticlerical views of the *philosophes*. The French middle class interpreted Voltaire's plea to "crush the infamous thing" as a mandate to reduce the power of the Church and strip it of its wealth.

The nobles of the Old Régime, like the higher clergy, enjoyed wealth, privilege— and unpopularity. They had virtual exemption from taxation; they monopolized army commissions and appointments to high ecclesiastical office. The French aristocracy, however, comprised not a single social unit but a series of differing groups. At the top were the hereditary nobles, a few of them descended from royalty or from feudal lords of the Middle Ages, but more from families ennobled within the past two or three centuries. These "nobles of the sword" tended to view their countrymen, including the lesser nobility, as vulgar upstarts. In spite of their dismal failure during the regency of Orléans (see Chapter XVI), they dreamed of the day when they might rule France again, as the feudal nobles had ruled in the Middle Ages. If they read at all, they read Montesquieu's *Spirit of the Laws,* because it praised hereditary aristocracy. Clustered at Versailles, they neglected their duties as the first landlords of the realm. Arthur

Young, the observant English economist who made a tour of France in the late 1780's, commented acidly on the uncultivated aristocratic lands in the southwest:

Much of these wastes belonged to the Prince de Soubise, who would not sell any part of them. Thus it is whenever you stumble on a Grand Seigneur, even one that was worth millions, you are sure to find his property desert. The Duke of Bouillon's and this prince's are two of the greatest properties in France; and all the signs I have yet seen of their greatness, are wastes, . . . deserts, fern, ling. . . . Oh! if I was the legislator of France for a day, I would make such great lords skip again! °

Below the nobility of the sword ranked the "nobility of the robe," including the robed justices of the Paris Parlement and other high courts and a host of other officials. The nobles of the robe, or their ancestors, had originally secured aristocratic status by buying their offices. But, since these dignities were then handed down from father to son, the mercenary origins of their status had become somewhat obscured with the passage of time. By the late eighteenth century there was often little practical distinction between the gentry of the robe and their brethren of the sword; intermarriage of the two groups was common. Moreover, whatever the nobles of the robe may have lacked by way of family tree, they more than made up by their accumulation of wealth and office. As a group, they were richer than the nobles of the sword and almost everywhere, except at Versailles itself, they exerted more power and influence by virtue of their firm hold on key governmental positions. The ablest and most tenacious defenders of special privilege in the dying years of the Old Régime were the rich judges of Parlement, not the elegant but ineffectual courtiers of Versailles.

° *Travels in France,* Constantia Maxwell, ed. (Cambridge, England, 1929), 62.

CHAPTER XVIII

Many noblemen, however, possessed little wealth, power, or glamor. They belonged to the lowest, and numerically the largest, category of French aristocracy—the *hobereaux*, the "little falcons" or "sparrow-hawks." They were the eighteenth-century counterparts of the plain medieval knights who had been at the bottom of the feudal pyramid. They vegetated on their country estates, since they could afford neither the purchase of a government office nor the expensive pleasures of the court. Some of them lived in such poverty that they actually ploughed their own fields. In the effort to conserve at least a part of their traditional status, almost all the *hobereaux* insisted on the meticulous collection of the surviving feudal and manorial dues from the peasantry. Their exhumation of old documents to justify levies sometimes long forgotten earned them the abiding hatred of the peasants and prepared the way for the document-burning of the Revolution.

Not every noble was a snobbish courtier or a selfish defender of the status quo. A few *hobereaux* calmly drifted down the social ladder to become simple farmers. Some nobles of the robe, attracted by the opportunities for wealth, took part in business enterprises. Even the loftiest noble families produced enlightened spirits, future supporters of revolution. The Count de Ségur reported on the fashion for advanced ideas among the younger nobles at the court of Louis XVI:

Outwardly we showed respect for the old remains of an antiquated system. . . . Though the forms of the edifice remained intact, we did not realise that it was being undermined from within. We made fun of the serious alarm shown by the old Court and clergy, who were loud in their denunciations of the spirit of innovation. We clapped our hands at the republican scenes in our theaters and applauded the philosophical discourses of our academicians, and the bold writings of our men of letters. Liberty, whatever its language, appealed to us by its courage, as Equality did by its convenience. There is a pleasure in stooping so long as one is certain of being able to raise oneself again at will. Thus with no foresight for the future, we enjoyed both the advantages of aristocracy and the sweets of a plebeian philosophy.*

These were the young bloods who applauded the ingenious valet, Figaro, when he outwitted his social superiors in Beaumarchais' satire on aristocracy, *The Marriage of Figaro*, first staged in 1784.

The Third Estate

The first two estates included only a small fraction of the French nation; at least 95 per cent of Frenchmen fell within the third estate in 1789. The great majority of these commoners were peasants. In some respects, the status of the peasantry was more favorable in France than it was anywhere else in Europe. Serfdom, which was still so prevalent in central and eastern Europe, had disappeared almost entirely except in Lorraine and the Franche Comté (County of Burgundy). While enclosures were gradually pushing small farmers off the land in England, small peasant holdings existed by the millions in France. Three out of every four adult peasants, it is estimated, held some land.

Nevertheless, the observant eye of Arthur Young noted many signs of rural misery in 1787 and 1788. In southwestern France, for example:

Pass Payrac, and meet many beggars, which we had not done before. All the country, girls and women, are without shoes or stockings; and the ploughmen at their work have neither sabots nor feet to their stockings. This is a poverty, that strikes at the root of national prosperity. . . . It reminded me of the misery of Ireland.†

---

* *The Memoirs and Anecdotes of the Count de Ségur,* Gerard Shelley, trans. (New York, 1928), 18.
† *Travels in France,* 23-24.

Young of course also found prosperous regions. But, although the degree of agrarian distress varied greatly from province to province, the total picture was far from bright. The trouble came chiefly from three factors—backward methods of farming, the shortage of land, and overpopulation.

The efficient techniques of the agricultural revolution made little headway in France before 1789. Vast areas were not cultivated at all or lay fallow every second or third year in accordance with medieval manorial practice. The crowded and constantly increasing rural population simply could not find full employment or a decent livelihood. Primitive farming required large tracts of land, but, as a glance at the table on p. 97 will show, the property-holding three-quarters of the French peasantry controlled less than one-third of the land. The average holding was so small that even a propertied peasant might face starvation in poor crop years. The peasant who owned no land turned to begging and sometimes to theft.

Rising prices and heavy taxes also oppressed the peasants. The upward trend of prices in France throughout the eighteenth century brought prosperity to many towns, but to the backward rural economy it meant the new hardship of inflation. Since the price of farm products rose less swiftly than that of the goods which the farmers had to buy, the real income of the peasants shrank. They were the victims of the high cost of living. To the Church the peasants paid the tithe, and to the nobility they paid the obsolete dues that the impecunious *hobereaux* were pressing for. To the state they owed a land tax, an income tax, a poll tax, and a variety of other duties, of which the most widely detested was the *gabelle,* the obligatory purchase of salt from government agents, usually at an exorbitant price. The government made matters worse by assessing the tax on land held by noble tenure at one-quarter the rate levied on that held by plebeian tenure.

France had a long history of agrarian unrest, going right back to the *jacquerie* of the fourteenth century. By 1789, unemployment and poverty had created a revolutionary temper among the peasants. They did not want a change in the form of government; they ignored the reform program of the Enlightenment. But they most emphatically wanted more land, if need be at the expense of the clergy and the nobility. They wanted an end to manorial dues, and, finally, they wanted relief from a system of taxation that bore hardest upon those who could least afford to pay.

The other members of the third estate, the urban workers and the bourgeois, had little reason to cherish the Old Régime. "Labor," in our modern sense of a large, self-conscious body of factory workers, hardly existed in pre-revolutionary France. Yet almost every sizable town had its wage-earners, employed chiefly in small businesses or workshops. These urban laborers felt with particular sharpness the pinch of rising prices. They were not, however, to take the commanding role in the Revolution itself; geographically scattered, lacking in class cohesiveness, they were ready to follow the lead of the bourgeoisie.

The bourgeoisie included Frenchmen of very divergent resources and interests—rich merchants and bankers in the cities, storekeepers and lawyers in country villages and towns, doctors and other professional men, and thousands upon thousands of craftsmen running their own little businesses. Implacable hostility to the privileged estates and warm receptiveness to the propaganda of the *philosophes* cemented this sprawling middle class into a political force. The bourgeois suffered fewer hardships than the peasants and workers did, but they resented the abuses of the Old Régime even more keenly. Though they paid a smaller proportion of their incomes in taxes, they violently denounced the unequal assessments. While profiting by the rise in prices, the wealthier and more enterprising businessmen complained of guild regulations and other obsolete restrictions on free commercial activity. They found it galling to be snubbed by the nobility, treated as second-class subjects by the monarchy, and excluded from the better posts in government, Church, and army.

In sum, the men of the middle class fully realized their own growing economic importance, and they wanted social and political rights to match. Because they were wealthier, better educated, and more articulate than the peasants and wage-earners, they took the preponderant part in formulating the grievances of the entire third estate. These grievances were compiled in statements called *cahiers* and submitted to the Estates-General in 1789.

The *cahier* of the third estate of the Longuyon district in Lorraine provides a good sample of the bourgeois reform program.* Sizable portions of this *cahier* dealt exclusively with local problems, like the destruction of the district's woods to supply fuel for iron-smelters. Other portions, however, showed a sharp awareness of the great issues of the day. The *cahier* pronounced the freedom of the press "the stoutest rampart against abuses" and the "surest means of maintaining the freedom of the nation." It deplored the harshness of the criminal laws; they should conform to "the customs and the character of the French nation, the kindest people in the universe." It recommended "a social contract or act between the sovereign and his people," to safeguard "the personal freedom of all citizens" and "prevent the recurrence of those

disastrous events which at present oppress the king and the nation." There followed a spirited assertion of the sanctity of private property; a rebuke to Rousseau's economic principles thus accompanied the appeal to his political philosophy. The third estate of Longuyon, however, believed in a large measure of equality. It proposed that "all Frenchmen have the right and the hope of securing any State office, of whatever grade, and all military and ecclesiastical dignities." Existing taxes should be swept away, to be replaced by levies on "all property without distinction as to owners, and on all persons without distinction or order and rank."

The Financial Crisis

The chronic financial difficulties of the French monarchy strengthened the hand of the middle-class reformers. The government debt, already large at the accession of Louis XVI, tripled between 1774 and 1789; about half the increase resulted from French participation in the American War of Independence. In 1789, the debt stood at 4,500,000,000 *livres* (roughly approximating in value a similar number of United States dollars after World War II). The budget for 1788, the only one computed for the Old Régime, made alarming reading:

ON THE ROAD TO BANKRUPTCY, 1788 *

Estimated Expenses	(In *livres*)
For debt service	318,000,000
For the court	35,000,000
For other purposes	276,000,000
Total	629,000,000
Estimated Revenues	503,000,000
Estimated Deficit	126,000,000

Note here the relatively modest cost of the court and the very high proportion of rev-

---

* The full text of this *cahier* is printed in B. F. Hyslop, *A Guide to the General Cahiers of 1789* (New York, 1936), 318-326. The quotations that follow are in our translation.

* Based on the figures in G. Lefebvre, *The Coming of the French Revolution* (Princeton, 1947), 21-22.

enues consumed by interest payments on the debt.

Louis XVI, in his feeble way, tried to cope with the growing emergency. On coming to the throne in 1774, he named as chief minister Turgot, a leading Physiocrat with a brilliant record as *intendant* of Limoges. Turgot temporarily reduced the deficit by imposing strict economies, particularly on the expenditures of the court. To increase prosperity and to propitiate the third estate, he curtailed the ancient guild monopolies, lifted restrictions on the internal shipments of grain, and replaced the *corvée*, the work on highways demanded of peasants, with a tax affecting nobles and commoners alike. At this the vested interests rebelled and, seconded by Marie Antoinette, secured Turgot's dismissal in 1776. The ousted minister admonished Louis XVI: "Remember, sire, that it was weakness which brought the head of Charles I to the block."

Louis ignored Turgot's warning. The government continued to raise new loans—653,000,000 *livres* between 1783 and 1786 alone. Then in 1786 the bankers refused to make new advances. The French government was caught between the irresistible force of the third estate's demands for tax relief and the immovable object of the other estates' refusal to yield their fiscal exemptions. The monarchy had temporized and borrowed until it could afford neither fresh delays nor new loans. Calonne, the finance minister in 1786, proposed to meet the crisis by reviving Turgot's reforms. In the hope of persuading the first two estates to consent to heavier taxation, he convoked the Assembly of Notables, the chief aristocratic and ecclesiastical dignitaries of the kingdom. But the Notables declined to be persuaded.

Louis XVI dissolved the Notables and dismissed Calonne. Then, with unaccustomed firmness, he decided to levy a uniform tax on all landed property without regard to the social status of the holder. The clergy replied by reducing their "free gift" for 1788 to one-sixth of what it had previously been. The Parlements in Paris and the provinces declared the new tax law illegal and asserted that only the nation as a whole assembled in the Estates General could institute so sweeping an innovation. The King retreated and in the summer of 1788 announced that the Estates General would meet the following spring.

The Election of the Estates General

Louis XVI thus revived a half-forgotten institution which had represented the nation, after a fashion, but which scarcely seemed likely to enact drastic social and economic reforms. The three estates, despite their immense variation in size, had customarily received equal representation, so that the two privileged orders could outvote the commoners. The Estates General of 1789, however, met under unique circumstances.

In the first place, its election and subsequent meeting took place during a sharp economic crisis that heightened the chronic social and financial tensions. In 1786, a trade treaty between France and Britain lowered French tariffs on British manufactures and allowed cheaper British textiles and metals to invade the French market. By 1789, thousands of French craftsmen were out of work; nor was this all. Hail and drought ruined the harvest of 1788, and the winter of 1788-89 was so bitter that the Seine froze over at Paris, blocking shipments of grain by water. Half-starved and half-frozen, Parisians huddled around bonfires provided by the municipal government. In the spring of 1789, the price of grain rose to double the normal, and in some localities to quadruple.

France had survived depressions, bad weather, and poor harvests many times in the past without experiencing revolution. This time, however, the added economic hardships were in effect the last straw. Starving peasants begged, borrowed, and stole, poaching on the hunting preserves of the great lords and attacking their game wardens. The turbulence in Paris boiled over in a riot (April, 1789), witnessed by Thomas Jefferson, then the American minister to France:

> ... The Fauxbourg St. Antoine is a quarter of the city inhabited entirely by the class of day-laborers and journeymen in every line. A rumor was spread among them that a great paper manufacturer ... had proposed ... that their wages should be lowered to 15 sous a day [three-quarters of a *livre*, roughly 75 cents]. ... They flew to his house in vast numbers, destroyed everything in it, and in his magazines and work shops, without secreting however a pin's worth to themselves, and were continuing this work of devastation when the regular troops were called in. Admonitions being disregarded, they were of necessity fired on, and a regular action ensued, in which about 100 of them were killed, before the rest would disperse.[*]

These disturbances impressed a sense of urgency on the deputies to the Estates General.

In the second place, the methods followed in electing the deputies aided the champions of reform. Contrary to precedent, and against the violent opposition of the Parlements, the third estate secured double representation, thus gaining as many seats as the clergy and the nobility combined. In each district of France, moreover, the third estate chose its deputy not by secret ballot but in a public meeting. Since this procedure greatly favored bourgeois orators over inarticulate farmers or workers, middle-class lawyers won control of the commoners'

deputation. Finally, the radicals of the third estate found a few sympathizers in the second estate and many more in the deputation of the first estate, where the discontented lower clergy had a large delegation:

THE ESTATES GENERAL, 1789

Estate	No. of Deputies
First:	
Higher Clergy	94
Lower Clergy	More than 200
Second	270
Third	578

A majority of the deputies were prepared to make drastic changes in the Old Régime.

But would they succeed in doing so? In all past meetings of the Estates General each estate, or order, had deliberated separately, with the consent of two estates and of the Crown required for the passage of a measure. In 1789, the King and the privileged orders favored retaining this "vote by order." The third estate, on the contrary, demanded "vote by head," with the deputies from all the orders forming a single unit. Pamphleteers invoked Rousseau's concept of the general will. "What is the third estate?" wrote Abbe Siéyès in an influential broadside of the same name. "Everything."

> ... If votes are taken by order, five million citizens will not be able to decide anything for the general interest, because it will not please a couple of hundred thousand privileged individuals. The will of a single individual will veto and destroy the will of more than a hundred people.[*]

The Birth of the National Assembly (June, 1789)

This crucial question of procedure came to a head soon after the Estates General convened on May 5, 1789, at Versailles.

---

[*] *Autobiography of Thomas Jefferson*, P. L. Ford, ed. (New York, 1914), 133-134.

[*] Emmanuel Siéyès, *Qu'est-ce Que le Tiers Etat?*, E. Champion, ed. (Paris, 1888), 82. Our translation.

Siéyès and Mirabeau, a renegade nobleman, led the campaign for vote by head. On June 17, the third estate cut the Gordian knot of procedure by accepting Siéyès' invitation to proclaim itself the "National Assembly." It completed its revolutionary repudiation of the Old Régime by inviting the deputies of other estates to join its sessions.

A majority of the clerical deputies, chiefly parish priests, accepted; the nobility refused. The King barred the commoners from their meeting place, whereupon they assembled at an indoor tennis court on June 20 and solemnly swore never to disband until they had given France a constitution. To the "Tennis-Court Oath" Louis replied by commanding each estate to resume its separate deliberations. The third estate and some deputies of the first disobeyed. Louis, vacillating as ever, now gave in and on June 27 directed the noble and clerical deputies to join the National Assembly. The nation, through its representatives, had successfully challenged the King and the vested interests. The Estates General was dead, and in its place sat the National Assembly, pledged to reform the society and the constitution of France. The revolution was under way.

In France, then, as in the thirteen North American colonies, a financial crisis produced a revolution. There was not only a parallel but also a direct connection between the two revolutions. French assistance in the American War of Independence added more than 1,500,000,000 *livres* to the government debt, and the example of America fired the imagination of discontented Frenchmen. To them Benjamin Franklin, the immensely popular American envoy to France, was the very embodiment of the Enlightenment, and the new republic overseas promised to become the utopia of the *philosophes*. At most, however, the American precedent only speeded up developments in France. The basic factors causing 1789 were almost fully matured in 1776. And, just as the reasons for revolution were more deeply rooted and more complicated in France than in America, so the Revolution itself was to be more violent and sweeping.

II: The Dissolution of the Monarchy

Popular Uprisings (*July, 1789*)

The National Assembly had barely settled down to work when a new wave of rioting swept over France, undermining further the position of the King. The economic depression grew more severe during the summer of 1789. Unemployment increased, and bread threatened to be scarce and expensive at least until completion of the new harvest in the autumn. Meanwhile, the commoners feared that the King and the privileged orders might attempt a counter-revolution. Large concentrations of troops appeared in the Paris area early in July—to preserve order and protect the National Assembly, the King asserted. But the Parisians suspected that Louis was planning the forcible dissolution of the Assembly. Suspicion deepened into conviction after Louis dismissed Necker, the popular financier who had been serving as the chief royal adviser.

The reaction to Necker's dismissal was

The Bastille, July 14, 1789.

immediate and revolutionary. On July 12 and 13, the men who had elected the Paris deputies of the third estate formed a new municipal government and a new militia, both loyal to the National Assembly. Paris was forging the weapons that made it the leader of the Revolution. Mobs were roaming the streets, demanding cheaper bread, parading busts of Necker draped in mourning, and breaking into government buildings to obtain arms. On July 14, the armed mob stormed the Bastille, a fortress in the eastern part of the city, and massacred its garrison.

The fall of the Bastille had little practical significance, but its symbolic value was immense. The gloomy pile frowned like a monster sentry over a teeming and restless working-class quarter of Paris. Its capture and subsequent demolition symbolized the loosening of the shackles of the Old Régime. Further, the public imagined the Bastille to be crowded with innocent victims of royal tyranny. Actually, there were only seven prisoners to be liberated at the time of its capture—five criminals (mostly forgers) and two mental cases. But the anticlimactic facts have never destroyed the legend. Ever since 1789 the Fourteenth of July has been the great national holiday of Frenchmen, the equivalent of the American Fourth of July.

Rioting spread over much of France late in July, as the provincial population responded to the news from Paris or acted on its own. In town after town, mobs attacked the local counterpart of the Bastille. Arthur Young, who was surveying the agriculture of Alsace, witnessed the scene at Strasbourg:

> ... The Parisian spirit of commotion spreads quickly; it is here; the troops ... are employed to keep an eye on the people who shew signs of an intended revolt. They have broken the windows of some magistrates that are no favourites; and a great mob of them is at this moment assembled, demanding clamourously to have meat at 5 *sous* a pound.[*]

The countryside, in the meantime, was experiencing the "Great Fear," one of the most extraordinary attacks of mass delusion on record. From village to village word spread that "brigands" were coming, aristocratic hirelings who would destroy crops and villages and force the National Assembly to preserve the status quo. There were in fact no brigands, only an occasional starving farmhand trying to steal food. But the peasants in many districts went berserk, clutching hoes and pitchforks, anything resembling a weapon. When the brigands did not materialize, they bethought themselves of the food shortage and their long-standing economic grievances. They attacked chateaux and broke into any building that might house a hoard of grain or the hated documents justifying collection of manorial dues. The wiser nobles voluntarily gave the peasants what they wanted; the others saw their barns and archives burnt. The Great Fear, beginning as a psychological aberration, ended in an uprising of the peasantry against its traditional oppressors.

The Early Revolution in Review

By the end of July, 1789, four distinct sets of revolutionary events had taken place in France: (1) the constitutional revolution of June, resulting in the creation of the National Assembly; (2) the Paris revolution and the taking of the Bastille; (3) the comparable outbreaks in provincial cities and towns; and (4) the Great Fear. Each of the four drove another nail into the coffin of the Old Régime. The transformation of the Estates General into the National Assembly and the creation of new local governments destroyed the political superiority of the first two estates. The Great Fear began the destruction of the social and economic privileges of the clergy and nobility. Everywhere, legally constituted officials were turned out, taxes went unpaid, and valuable records were destroyed. In the summer of 1789 the edifice of government was no longer slowly crumbling; it was rapidly crashing to the ground.

March of the women to Versailles, October 5, 1789.

---

[*] *Travels in France,* 181.

The "October Days," the last crisis of a momentous year, demonstrated anew the impotence of Louis XVI and the power of his aroused subjects. As the autumn of 1789 drew on, Parisians still queued for bread and still looked suspiciously at the royal troops stationed in the neighborhood of their city. Rumors of the Queen's behavior further incensed them. Marie Antoinette made a dramatic appearance at a banquet of royal officers, clutching the Dauphin in her arms, striking the very pose that her mother, Maria Theresa, had employed so effectively to win the support of the Hungarians in the 1740's. And, on hearing that the people had no bread, she was said to have remarked callously: "Let them eat cake." This story was false, but it echoed and re-echoed in the lively new Paris papers that delighted in denouncing the "Austrian bitch."

On October 5, 1789, an array of determined Paris housewives marched the dozen miles from Paris to Versailles in the rain. They disrupted the National Assembly and succeeded in extracting a kiss from a baffled Louis XVI. This bizarre demonstration had very significant consequences. On October 6, the women marched back to Paris, escorting "the baker, the baker's wife, and the baker's son"—in other words, the royal family, who took up residence in the Tuileries Palace. The National Assembly, too, moved to Paris. The most revolutionary place in France had captured both the symbol of the Old Régime and the herald of the new.

Accomplishments of the National Assembly (1789-1791)

(1) *Abolition of Caste.* The outlines of the new regime were already starting to take shape before the October Days. The Great Fear prompted the National Assem-

bly to abolish in law what the peasants were destroying in fact. On the evening of August 4, 1789, the Viscount de Noailles, a liberal nobleman, addressed the deputies:

[The countryside] has seen fit to take arms in self-protection and no longer recognizes any brake. Consequently, the kingdom at this moment hangs between the alternative of the destruction of society, and that of a government which will be the admiration and the exemplar of Europe.

How is this government to be established? By public tranquillity.... And to secure this necessary tranquillity, I propose:

(1)... That taxation will be paid by all the individuals of the kingdom, in proportion to their revenues;

(2) That all public expenses will in the future be borne equally by all.[*]

The deputies voted the proposals of Noailles. In addition, the clergy gave up its tithes, and the liberal minority of the second estate surrendered the nobility's game preserves, manorial dues, and other medieval rights. The assembly made it a clean sweep by abolishing serfdom, forbidding the sale of justice or of judicial office, and decreeing that "all citizens, without distinction of birth, can be admitted to all ecclesiastical, civil, and military posts and dignities." When the memorable session inaugurated by Noailles' speech ended at two o'clock on the morning of August 5, the Old Régime was dead.

(2) *Declaration of the Rights of Man.* Three weeks later, on August 26, 1789, the National Assembly formulated the Declaration of the Rights of Man. "Men are born free and equal in rights," it asserted (Art. 1). "These rights are liberty, property, security and resistance to oppression" (Art. 2). Property it called "an inviolable and sacred right" (Art. 17), and liberty "the exercise of the natural rights of each man" within the limits "determined by law" (Art.

---

[*] *Archives Parlementaires,* Series 1, VIII, 343. Our translation.

4). "Law," the Declaration stated, "is the expression of the general will. All citizens have the right to take part, in person or by their representatives, in its formation" (Art. 6). "Any society in which the guarantee of rights is not assured or the separation of powers not determined has no constitution" (Art. 16).*

The Declaration of the Rights of Man mirrored the political and economic attitudes of the middle class. It insisted on the sacredness of property. It committed the French to the creed of constitutional liberalism already affirmed by the English in 1688-89 and by the Americans in 1776, and it incorporated the key phrases of the *philosophes:* natural rights, general will, and separation of powers. The National Assembly made a resounding statement of the ideals of the Enlightenment. Yet, as the subsequent history of the Revolution soon demonstrated, the Assembly found no magic formula by which to translate these ideals into practice.

(3) *Economic Measures.* The economic legislation of the National Assembly provided a case in point. Belief in the theory of the equal taxation of all Frenchmen did not solve urgent practical problems of finance. The new and just land tax imposed by the deputies simply could not be collected. Tax-collectors had vanished in the general liquidation of the Old Régime, and naive peasants thought that they owed nothing to a government turned revolutionary. Once again, the French state borrowed until its credit was exhausted, and then, in desperation, the National Assembly ordered the confiscation of church lands (November, 1789). "The wealth of the clergy is at the disposition of the nation," it declared, explaining that ecclesiastical lands fell outside the bounds of "inviolable" property as

* All passages from the Declaration are as translated in the Appendix to G. Lefebvre, *The Coming of the French Revolution* (Princeton, 1947).

defined in the Declaration of the Rights of Man because they belonged to an institution and not to private individuals.

The government thus acquired an asset worth at least 2,000,000,000 *livres.* On the basis of this collateral it issued *assignats,* paper notes used to pay the government's debts. So far, so good, from the fiscal standpoint at any rate. The *assignats* had adequate security behind them and temporarily eased the financial crisis. Unfortunately, the Revolution repeated the mistake of John Law (see Chapter XVI): it did not know when to stop. As the state sold parcels of confiscated land—that is, as it reduced the collateral securing its paper money—it should have destroyed *assignats* to the same amount. The temptation not to reduce the number of *assignats* proved too great to resist. Inflation resulted. The *assignats,* progressively losing their solid backing, depreciated until in 1795 they were worth less than 5 per cent of their face value.

This economic experiment resulted in the redistribution of some of the best farmland in France. Many peasants enlarged their holdings by buying former ecclesiastical property. But the bourgeoisie also invested heavily in these lands, while the poor and landless peasants gained nothing, since they did not have the money to buy. Following the doctrine of laissez-faire, the National Assembly made no move to help the marginal farmers. Indeed, there was almost no hint of socialism or paternalism in the economic policies of the Assembly. It abolished the guilds and the irksome internal tariffs and tolls. And, deeming the few primitive organizations of labor unnatural restraints on economic freedom, it abolished them too. In June, 1791, following an outbreak of strikes, it passed the Le Chapelier Law banning both strikes and labor unions.

(4) *The Civil Constitution of the Clergy.* Since the suppression of tithes and the seizure of ecclesiastical property deprived the

CHAPTER XVIII

Church of its revenue, the National Assembly agreed to finance ecclesiastical salaries. The new arrangement virtually nationalized the Gallican Church and made it subject to constant government regulation. The Assembly's decision to suppress monasteries and convents caused little difficulty; many of these establishments were already far gone in decay. But an uproar arose over the legislation altering the status of the secular hierarchy.

The Civil Constitution of the Clergy (June, 1790) redrew the ecclesiastical map of France. It reduced the number of bishoprics by more than one-third, making the remaining dioceses correspond to the new civil administrative units known as departments (see below). It transformed bishops and priests into civil officials, paid by the state and elected by the population of the diocese or parish; both Catholics and non-Catholics (the latter usually a small minority) could vote in these elections. Although a new bishop was required to take an oath of loyalty to the state, the Civil Constitution stipulated that he

... may not apply to the Pope for confirmation, but shall write to him as the Visible Head of the Universal Church, in testimony of the unity of faith and communion which he is to maintain therewith.*

These provisions stripped the "Visible Head of the Universal Church" of his effective authority over the Gallican clergy and ran counter to the whole tradition of the Roman Church as an independent ecclesiastical monarchy. Naturally the Pope denounced the Civil Constitution. The National Assembly, after vain attempts at compromise, then required that every member of the French clergy take a special oath supporting the Civil Constitution. Only seven bishops and fewer than half of the

_____
* Title II, Art. 19. J. H. Stewart, *A Documentary Survey of the French Revolution* (New York, 1951), 176.

An assignat *for fifty* livres (*francs*).

priests complied. The National Assembly thus opened a breach between the Revolution and a large segment of the population. Good Catholics, from Louis XVI down to humble peasants, rallied to the non-juring clergy, those who refused the special oath. The Civil Constitution of the Clergy, supplying an issue for rebellion and civil war, was the first great blunder of the Revolution.

(5) *The Constitution of 1791.* The major undertaking of the National Assembly was its effort to put limited monarchy on a permanent footing, culminating in the Constitution of 1791. The Assembly devised a neat and orderly system of local government to replace the bewildering complex of provincial units that had accumulated under the Old Régime. It divided the territory of France into eighty-three departments of approximately equal size. Each department was small enough for its chief town to be within a day's journey of the outlying villages. Each bore the name of a river, a mountain range, or some other natural landmark. The departments were subdivided into *arrondissements* or districts, and the districts into communes—that is, municipalities. The commune-district-department arrangement resembled, on a reduced scale, the American pattern of town-

county-state. In the communes and departments, elected councils and officials enjoyed considerable rights of self-government. The administration of the new France, on paper anyhow, was to be far more decentralized than that of the Old Régime.

Separation of powers was the guiding principle in the reconstruction of the central government. The Constitution of 1791 established an independent hierarchy of courts staffed by elected judges. It vested legislative authority in a single elected chamber. Although the king still headed the executive branch, his actions now required approval by his ministers. He had the power of veto, a suspensive veto that could block legislation for four years. Louis XVI, no longer the absolute "King of France," acquired the new constitutional title, "King of the French."

The new constitution subscribed to many principles issuing straight from the Enlightenment. It promised to give France a new law code, and it declared marriage a civil contract, not a sacrament. The state took over the old ecclesiastical functions of keeping records of vital statistics and providing charity and education. Indeed, the Constitution promised a system of "public instruction for all citizens, free of charge in those branches of education which are indispensable to all men." * Foreshadowing the intense nationalism of the later phases of the Revolution, the constitution-makers announced that

National festivals shall be instituted to preserve the memory of the French Revolution, to maintain fraternity among the citizens, and to bind them to the Constitution, the *Patrie*, and the laws.†

In foreign policy, however, revolutionary France would be more virtuous and less aggressive than autocratic France:

The French nation renounces the undertaking of any war with a view of making conquests, and it will never use its forces against the liberty of any people. *

The Constitution of 1791 went a long way toward instituting popular government, but it stopped well short of full democracy. Restricting the political equality promised by the Declaration of the Rights of Man, it divided Frenchmen into two classes of citizens, "active" and "passive." It limited the right of voting to "active" citizens, who paid annually in taxes an amount equal to at least three days' wages for labor in the locality. The "passive" citizens, numbering about one-third of the male population, enjoyed the full protection of the law but did not receive the franchise. Moreover, the new legislature was chosen by a process of indirect election, in which the electors, chosen by ordinary "active" citizens, were required to be men of substantial wealth. The French middle class assumed that a certain minimum of worldly goods was necessary for political wisdom.

The decentralized and limited monarchy established by the Constitution of 1791 was doomed to fail. It was too radical to suit the King and most of the aristocracy, and not radical enough for the goodly number of bourgeois who were veering toward republicanism. The majority in the National Assembly supporting the Constitution suffered the fate commonly experienced by the politically moderate in a revolution. The middle-of-the-roaders were squeezed out by the extremists. Despite their moderate intentions, they were driven to enact some drastic legislation, notably the Civil Constitution of the Clergy, which weakened their own position. And they failed to develop an effective party organization at a

* Title I. *Documentary Survey of the French Revolution*, 232.
† *Ibid.*

* Title VI. *Documentary Survey*, 260.

CHAPTER XVIII

time when the radical minority of deputies was consolidating its strength.

These radicals were the Jacobins, so named because they belonged to the "Society of the Friends of the Constitution," which maintained its Paris headquarters in a former Jacobin monastery. The Jacobins were no true friends of the Constitution of 1791. They accepted it only as a stopgap until they might end the monarchy and set up a republic based on universal suffrage. To prepare for the republican millennium, the Jacobins used all the techniques of a political pressure group. They planted rabble-rousing articles in the popular press and manipulated the crowds of noisy and volatile spectators at the sessions of the National Assembly. Their network of political clubs extended throughout the provinces, providing the only nation-wide party organization in France. Almost everywhere, Jacobins captured control of the new department and commune councils. In local elections, as in the elections to the Estates General, an able and determined minority prevailed over a largely illiterate and politically inexperienced majority.

The defenders of the Old Régime played right into the hands of the Jacobins. From the summer of 1789 on, alarmed nobles and prelates fled France in a steady stream, leaving behind more rich estates to be confiscated and giving Jacobin orators and editors a splendid opportunity to denounce them as rats leaving a supposedly sinking ship. Many of these aristocratic émigrés gathered in the German Rhineland to intrigue for Austrian and Russian support of a counter-revolution. The King's well-known preference for an absolute rather than a suspensive veto over legislation inspired the Jacobin press to christen Louis and Marie Antoinette "Monsieur and Madame Veto." The King's grave misgivings about the Civil Constitution of the Clergy prompted his disastrous attempt to join the émigrés on the Franco-German frontier. In June, 1791, disguised as a valet and governess, Louis and Marie Antoinette left the Tuileries. But Louis unwisely showed his face in public, and a local official along the route recognized the royal profile from the portrait on the assignats. The alarm was sent ahead, and at Varennes in northeastern France a detachment of troops forced the royal party to return to Paris. After the abortive flight to Varennes, the revolutionaries viewed Louis XVI as a potential traitor and kept him closely guarded in the Tuileries. The experiment in constitutional monarchy began under most unfavorable auspices.

The Legislative Assembly (October, 1791–September, 1792)

On October 1, 1791, the first and the only legislative assembly elected under the new constitution commenced its deliberations. No one faction commanded a numerical majority in the new assembly:

POLITICAL COMPLEXION OF THE
LEGISLATIVE ASSEMBLY, 1791

	Approximate No. of Seats
Right (Constitutional Monarchists)	265
Center (Plain)	345
Left (Jacobins, Girondins)	130

(Here, as is still the practice in most continental European assemblies, the Right sat to the right of the presiding officer as he faced the assembly, the Left to his left, and the Center in between.)

The balance of political power rested with the timid and irresolute deputies of the Center. They were neither strong defenders of the Constitution nor yet convinced republicans. Since they occupied the lowest seats in the assembly hall, they received the derogatory nickname of the Plain or Marsh. The capable politicians of the Left soon captured the votes of the Plain, to demonstrate anew the power of a determined minority.

Leadership of this minority came from a small contingent of Jacobins known as Girondins because they clustered around the deputies from Bordeaux, in the Gironde department. The Girondins specialized in patriotic oratory. They pictured revolutionary France as the intended victim of a great reactionary conspiracy, engineered by the *émigrés*, aided at home by the non-juring clergy and the royal family, and abetted abroad by a league of monarchs under Leopold II, the Austrian emperor. "An open war is less dangerous than this undeclared war," the Girondin leader Brissot informed the assembly in January, 1792. "It is better for a free people to insure their independence by military victory than by diplomatic finesse." * But Louis XVI, despite the flight to Varennes, was no traitor, and Leopold II cautiously limited his aid to the *émigrés.*

The sudden death of Leopold in March, 1792, and the accession of his less cautious and inexperienced son, Francis II, at once increased the Austrian threat. At the same time, belligerent Girondins secured control of French diplomacy. On April 20, 1792, the Legislative Assembly declared war on Austria. In the eyes of Frenchmen the war was defensive, not the sort of aggression that the nation had forsworn in the fine phrases of its constitution.

The war went badly for France at the outset. Prussia soon joined Austria, and on July 25, 1792, the Prussian commander, the Duke of Brunswick, issued a manifesto drafted by an *émigré.* The manifesto stated the war aims of the allies:

... To put a stop to the anarchy within France, to check the attacks delivered against throne and altar, to re-establish legal authority, to restore to the king the security and freedom of which he has been deprived, and to place him in a position where he may exercise the legitimate authority which is his due. *

A threat followed. "If the Tuileries is attacked, by deed or word, if the slightest outrage or violence is perpetrated against the royal family, and if immediate measures are not taken for their safety, maintenance and liberty"—then Paris would witness "a model vengeance, never to be forgotten," and the persons responsible for the disorders would be handed over to the "tortures which they have richly deserved." †

The Duke of Brunswick's manifesto did not frighten the French, as it was intended to do. On the contrary, it stiffened the already firm determination of republicans to do away with the monarchy. All through the early summer of 1792 the Jacobins of Paris had been plotting an insurrection. They won the support of a formidable following—patriotic army recruits, provincial radicals who had come to the capital to celebrate the third anniversary of the Bastille's taking, Paris workingmen angered by the depreciated value of the *assignats*, by a new food shortage, and by the government's failure to take decisive action against these economic hardships. One by one, the forty-eight *sections* or wards into which the city was divided came under the political control of the Jacobins. The process came to a climax on the night of August 9-10, 1792, when the leaders of the *sections* ousted the regularly constituted authorities of the Paris municipal administration and installed a new and illegal Jacobin commune.

The municipal revolution in Paris at once produced decisive results. On the morning of August 10, the forces of the new commune attacked the Tuileries and massacred

---

* *Archives Parlementaires*, Series 1, XXXVII, 464, 466. Our translation.

* *Le Moniteur Universel*, August 3, 1792. Our translation.
  † *Ibid.*

CHAPTER XVIII

the King's Swiss guards. Though Louis XVI and the royal family found temporary safety with the Legislative Assembly, the uprising of August 10 sealed the doom of the monarchy. It demoralized the Assembly, thereafter little more than the errand boy of the illegal Paris commune. With most of the deputies of the Right and the Plain absent, the Assembly soon voted to suspend the King from office, to imprison the royal family, and to order the election of a constitutional convention. Until this new representative body should meet, a temporary Jacobin committee was to run the government. The birth of the First French Republic was at hand.

III: The First Republic

The September Massacres (1792)

The weeks between August 10 and the meeting of the Convention on September 21 were weeks of crisis and tension. The value of the *assignats* depreciated by 40 per cent during August alone. Rabble-rousing Jacobins continually excited the populace of Paris, already stirred by the economic difficulties and by the capture of the Tuileries. Excitement mounted still higher when the news arrived that Prussian troops had invaded northeastern France. In the emergency, Danton, the Jacobin minister of justice, won immortality by urging that the way to beat the enemy was *"de l'audace, encore de l'audace, toujours de l'audace"*—boldness, more boldness, always boldness.

In Paris, audacity took the form of the "September massacres," lynchings of supposed traitors and enemy agents. For five days, beginning on September 2, bloodthirsty mobs directed by Jacobin agents moved from prison to prison. At each stop they tried prisoners before impromptu courts and then executed them. The number of victims exceeded one thousand and included ordinary criminals as well as aristocrats and non-juring priests who were often quite innocent of the treason charged against them. The crowning horror was the mutilation of the Princesse de Lamballe, the Queen's maid of honor. The mob paraded her severed head on a pike before the window of the royal prison so that Marie Antoinette might see "how the people take vengeance on their tyrants."

The September massacres foreshadowed the terror in store for France. During the next two years the revolutionary fever was to mount higher and higher until at length it burned itself out. And through it all France remained at war. A French victory at Valmy (September 20, 1792) turned the Duke of Brunswick and the Prussians back from the road to Paris; more solid French successes followed later in 1792. Then the tide turned again, washing away the conquests of the autumn. By the summer of 1793 half-defeated France faced a hostile coalition including almost every major power in Europe. No wonder an atmosphere of perpetual emergency surrounded the Convention.

Gironde and Mountain

In theory, the election of the National Convention (August-September, 1792) marked the beginning of true political democracy in France. Both "active" and "passive" citizens were invited to the polls. In practice, however, only 10 per cent of the potential electorate of 7,000,000 actually voted. The others abstained or were turned away from the polls by the watchdogs of the Jacobin clubs, ever on the alert against "counter-revolutionaries." The result was a landslide for the republicans:

POLITICAL COMPLEXION OF THE CONVENTION, SEPTEMBER, 1792

	Approximate No. of Deputies
The Right (Gironde)	165
The Center (Plain)	435
The Left (Mountain)	150

The radicalism of the Convention was underlined by the Jacobin antecedents of both its Right and its Left. Many ties in common existed between the Gironde and the Mountain (so named because these left-wing deputies sat high up in the meeting hall). Both factions came from the middle class, both were steeped in the ideas of the *philosophes,* and both united to declare France a republic (September 21, 1792).

Bitter hostility and rivalry, however, soon arose between the Gironde and the Mountain. The Girondin deputies represented provincial interests. As one of them told the Convention:

I fear the despotism of Paris. . . . I do not want a Paris guided by intriguers to become to the French Empire what Rome was to the Roman Empire. Paris must be reduced to its proper one-eighty-third of influence, like the other departments.°

The Girondins deplored the September massacres and favored a breathing spell in revolutionary legislation. Their political program was outlined in the draft constitution completed early in 1793 by one of their most distinguished deputies, Condorcet, the prophet of human progress (see Chapter XVII). Condorcet's draft proposed a large measure of decentralization ("federalism" was the revolutionary term). The legislature and the executive would be independent of each other and separately elected. As further checks and balances, election results would be determined by proportional representation, projected laws would be submitted to a popular referendum, and voters would have the right to recall unworthy elected officials.

The leaders of the Mountain, in contrast, favored an all-powerful central government over federalism. Instead of Girondin laissez-faire, they demanded state intervention in economic affairs to appease their urban supporters. The greatest leader of the Mountain was Maximilien Robespierre (1758-1794). This earnest young lawyer did not look like a revolutionary: he powdered his hair neatly and wore the light-blue coat and knee-breeches of the Old Régime. Yet Robespierre was a political fanatic whose speeches were lay sermons couched in the solemn language of a new revelation. He put his creed most forcefully in a discourse delivered in February, 1794:

What is the goal toward which we are striving? The peaceful enjoyment of liberty and equality: the rule of that eternal justice whose laws have been engraved . . . upon the hearts of men, even upon the heart of the slave who ignores them and of the tyrant who denies them.

We desire an order of things . . . where our country assures the welfare of each individual and where each individual enjoys with pride the prosperity and the glory of our country; where the souls of all grow through the constant expression of republican sentiments; where the arts are the ornament of the freedom which in turn ennobles them; and where commerce is the source of public wealth, not just of the monstrous opulence of a few houses.°

Robespierre sincerely believed that he could realize the ideals of the *Social Con-*

° Lasource, September 25, 1792. *Archives Parlementaires,* Series 1, LII, 130. Our translation.

° *Le Moniteur Universel,* February 7, 1794. Our translation.

CHAPTER XVIII

tract; like Rousseau, he had faith in the natural goodness of humanity, in "the laws of justice engraved upon the hearts of men." For him democracy was not only the best form of government but also a religion, the finest expression of human virtue. Robespierre was sure that he knew the general will, and that the general will demanded a Republic of Virtue. If Frenchmen would not be free and virtuous voluntarily, then he would force them to be free and cram virtue down their throats.

Robespierre and the Republic of Virtue triumphed. The Mountain beat the Gironde in the competition for the votes of the neutral Plain, which held the balance in the Convention (see table above, p. 114). The Girondins met a significant defeat when, after one hundred hours of continuous voting, starting on January 15, 1793, the Convention declared "Citizen Louis Capet" guilty of treason and by a narrow margin sentenced him to the guillotine without delay. Louis XVI died bravely on January 21, 1793. Although the majority of the French population disapproved of the King's execution, the majority did not control the Convention. There some of the Girondin deputies had asserted that Louis did not deserve to die. They took a courageous stand in defense of the humanitarian principles of the Enlightenment, but they also exposed themselves to the charge of being "counter-revolutionaries."

The march of events soon destroyed the Girondins. In February, 1793, the Convention rejected Condorcet's constitutional draft. In March, the army under Dumouriez, a Girondin general, suffered a series of defeats in the Low Countries, and in April Dumouriez deserted to the enemy. Meanwhile, in February, 1793, the Convention declared war on Britain, Spain, and Holland, and France faced a formidable number of enemies. At home, in the face of unemployment, high prices, and food short-

ages, the Gironde had nothing to offer except its hands-off policy of the breathing spell. The leaders of the Mountain urged price controls and food requisitioning and pressed for the expulsion of Girondins from the Jacobin clubs. Finally, on June 2, 1793, the Jacobin *sections* of Paris invaded the Convention and forced it to arrest twenty-nine Girondin deputies. Backed by these armed Parisians, the Mountain intimidated the Plain, and the Convention consigned the arrested Girondins to the guillotine. The Reign of Terror had begun.

The Reign of Terror
(June, 1793–July, 1794)

How was it that the advocates of democracy now imposed a ruthless dictatorship upon France? Here is Robespierre's explanation:

. . . To establish and consolidate democracy, to achieve the peaceful rule of constitutional laws, we must first finish the war of liberty against tyranny. . . . We must annihilate the enemies of the republic at home and abroad, or else we shall perish. . . .

If virtue is the mainstay of a democratic government in time of peace, then in time of revolution a democratic government must rely on *virtue* and *terror*. . . . Terror is nothing but justice, swift, severe and inflexible; it is an emanation of virtue. . . . It has been said that terror is the mainstay of a despotic government. . . . The government of the revolution is the despotism of liberty against tyranny.[*]

The Convention duly voted a democratic constitution, drawn up by the Mountain, granting universal manhood suffrage, and giving supreme power, unhampered by Girondin checks and balances, to a single legislative chamber. When the instrument was submitted to a referendum, less than 2,000,000 of the 7,000,000 qualified Frenchmen voted, and the ballots cast went almost

---

[*] *Le Moniteur Universel*, February 7, 1794. Our translation.

unanimously for ratification. The Convention then postponed indefinitely the operation of this Constitution of 1793, which always remained a dead letter. As Robespierre had explained, "To establish and consolidate democracy, we must first finish the war of liberty against tyranny."

The real government of the Terror centered on a twelve-man Committee of Public Safety, composed of Robespierre and other stalwarts from the Mountain. Though nominally responsible to the Convention, the Committee of Public Safety enjoyed a large measure of independent authority and acted as a kind of war cabinet. A second group of deputies, the Committee of General Security, supervised police activities and turned suspected enemies of the Republic over to the new Revolutionary Tribunal, whose sixteen judges and sixty jurors were divided into several courts to speed the work of repression. At the local level, the Mountain scrapped much of the self-government inaugurated under the Constitution of 1791. Local Jacobin clubs purged department and commune administrations of political unreliables, while special local courts supplemented the grim labors of the Revolutionary Tribunal. To make sure that provincial France toed the line, the Mountain sent out trusted members of the Convention as its agents, the "deputies on mission." From the standpoint of administration, the Terror marked both an anticipation of twentieth-century dictatorship and a return to the age-old French principle of centralization. The deputies on mission were the successors of the *intendants* of Richelieu, the *enquêteurs* of St. Louis, and the *missi dominici* of Charlemagne.

The Record of the Terror

(1) *Victims.* The "swift, severe, and inflexible justice" promised by Robespierre took the lives of 20,000 Frenchmen, ranging from Marie Antoinette down to inoffensive little men and women guilty of nothing more than an inadequate understanding of Rousseau. Some of the victims came from the Vendée, a strongly Catholic and royalist area in western France which had revolted against the Republic's attempts to recruit soldiers. Although the total number of victims may seem unimpressive in our world of total wars, concentration camps, and death-ridden highways, the record was bloody indeed by eighteenth-century standards. And by any standard the Terror perpetrated some grisly deeds. The *noyades* at Nantes drowned more than 2,000 suspects set adrift on the River Loire in leaky boats.

(2) *The War.* The wartime hysteria that helped to account for the excesses of the Terror also inspired a remarkably practical kind of patriotism. On August 23, 1793, the Convention issued a decree epitomizing the democratic nationalism of the Jacobins:

From this moment, until the time when the enemy shall have been driven from the territory of the Republic, all Frenchmen are permanently requisitioned for the service of the armies.

Young men will go into combat, married men will manufacture arms and transport supplies; women will make tents and uniforms and will serve in the hospitals; children will make old linen into bandages; old men will be carried into the public squares to arouse the courage of the soldiers, excite hatred for kings and inspire the unity of the Republic.*

The Committee of Public Safety promptly put these principles into operation. The army drafted all bachelors and widowers from eighteen to twenty-five. Hundreds of open-air forges were installed in Paris to manufacture weapons. Since the war prevented the importation of the saltpeter needed for gunpowder, the government sponsored a great campaign to scrape patches of saltpeter from cellars and stables.

---

* *Le Moniteur Universel*, August 24, 1793. Our translation.

CHAPTER XVIII

Sketch of Marie Antoinette on her way to the guillotine, by David (see p. 153).

By the close of 1793, the forces of the Republic had driven foreign troops off French soil. Credit for this new shift in the tide of battle did not rest solely with the Jacobins. The military successes of the Republic reflected in part the improvements made in the army during the dying years of the Old Régime; they resulted still more from the weaknesses of the coalition aligned against France (see below, p. 122). Yet they could scarcely have been achieved without the new democratic spirit that allowed men of the third estate to become officers, or without the crusading Jacobin fervor that made the French army the most determined and the most enterprising in Europe. In so far as soldiers ever fight for ideals, the French army fought for liberty and equality in 1793 and 1794.

(3) *Economics.* Total mobilization demanded an approximate, if not total, equality of economic sacrifice. To exorcise the twin devils of inflation and food shortage, the Terror issued the *"maximum"* legislation, placing ceilings on prices and wages. Wages were pegged at a point 50 per cent over the 1790 wage-rate; prices at 33 per cent above the 1790 price level. The government rationed scarce commodities, forbade the use of white flour, and directed all patriots to eat *pain d'égalité*—"equality bread," a loaf utilizing almost the whole of the wheat. Finally, early in 1794, the Convention passed the "Laws of Ventôse," named for a month in the revolutionary calendar. These laws authorized seizure of the remaining properties of the *émigrés* and other opponents of the Republic and recommended their distribution to landless Frenchmen.

Socialist historians have often found in the *maximum* and the Laws of Ventôse evidence that the Terror was moving from political to social democracy, that the Republic of Virtue was indeed beginning the socialist revolution. The *maximum,* however, resembled nothing so much as the economic controls employed in the non-socialist United States during World War II, right down to the provision permitting wages to rise proportionately more than prices. Though the *maximum* temporarily checked the depreciation of the *assignats,* black markets flourished during the Terror; even the government patronized them.

Although the redistribution of property foreseen by the Laws of Ventôse did anticipate socialism, the provision was never enforced. Furthermore, the Convention was assured that the Mountain did not intend a general assault on property:

The revolution leads us to recognize the principle that he who has shown himself the enemy of his country cannot own property. The properties of patriots are sacred, but the goods of conspirators are there for the unfortunate.[*]

[*] Saint-Just, February 26, 1794, in *Le Moniteur Universel,* February 27, 1794. Our translation.

To the thorough-going socialist not even the properties of patriots are sacred. The middle-class leaders of the Terror were not genuine socialists; only the emergencies of the Revolution forced them to abandon laissez-faire. They had to make food cheaper for townspeople—whence the *maximum;* and they had to promise men some hope of future well-being—whence the Laws of Ventôse.

(4) *Society and Culture.* The Terror presented its most revolutionary aspect in its drastic social and cultural reforms. "In our land," Robespierre announced, "we desire to substitute all the virtues and all the miracles of the Republic for all the vices and all the nonsense of monarchy." When Robespierre said "all," he meant "all"—clothing, the arts, amusements, the calendar, religion. The Republic of Virtue could tolerate nothing that smacked of the Old Régime. Even the traditional forms of address, "Monsieur" and "Madame," gave way to the newly orthodox "Citoyen" (citizen) and "Citoyenne."

Ever since 1789, revolutionaries had discarded elaborate gowns and knee-breeches (*culottes*) as symbols of idleness and privilege. With the solitary exception of Robespierre, good republican men were *sans-culottes* (literally, without knee-breeches), attired in the long, baggy trousers of the humble peasant or workman. Women affected simple, high-waisted dresses, copied from the costumes of the ancient Romans. Rome became the model for behavior—the virtuous Rome of the Republic, of course, not the sordid Empire. Women strove to emulate Roman matrons in conduct as well as in dress, and parents named their children Brutus or Cato or Gracchus. The theater shelved the masterpieces of Racine and Corneille for stilted dramas glorifying Roman heroes. Cabinet-makers, deserting the graceful style of Louis XVI, produced sturdy neoclassical furniture decorated with

Roman symbols. "The arts," said Robespierre, "are the ornament of the freedom which in turn ennobles them." Playwrights, authors, and editors who failed to ornament freedom properly, experienced censorship or even the guillotine. The Jacobins reduced the many lively newspapers of the early revolution to a few dull semi-official organs.

The sweeping reform of the calendar (October, 1793) was a high point in Jacobin meddling. September 22, 1792, the first day of the Republic, was designated as the initial day of Year I. Roman numerals were used for the years, and the traditional mythological names of the months were abandoned:

THE MONTHS OF THE REVOLUTIONARY CALENDAR

Fall:	Vendémiaire (Grape-Harvest)
	Brumaire (Misty)
	Frimaire (Frosty)
Winter:	Nivôse (Snowy)
	Pluviôse (Rainy)
	Ventôse (Windy)
Spring:	Germinal (Seed)
	Floréal (Flowering)
	Prairial (Meadow)
Summer:	Messidor (Wheat-Harvest)
	Thermidor (Heat)
	Fructidor (Ripening)

Each month had thirty days, divided into three weeks of ten days. Every tenth day was set aside for rest and for the celebration of one of the virtues so cherished by Robespierre—for example, Hatred of Tyrants and Traitors, Heroism, Frugality, Stoicism, not to mention two anticipations of Mother's Day, Filial Piety and Maternal Tenderness. The five days left over at the end of the year became special holidays dedicated to Genius, Labor, Noble Actions, Awards, and Opinion. The new calendar, for all its sanctimonious touches, was a worthy product of the Enlightenment. Yet it naturally antagonized workmen, who disliked laboring nine days out of ten, instead of six out of seven. It never really took root, and Napoleon scrapped it a decade later.

The Convention had much better luck with another reform close to the spirit of the Age of Reason—the metric system. A special committee, including Condorcet, Laplace, Lavoisier, and other distinguished intellectuals, devised new weights and measures based on the uniform use of the decimal system rather than on confused and illogical custom. In August, 1793, a decree made the meter the standard unit of length, and supplementary legislation in 1795 established the liter as the measure of volume and the gram as the unit of weight. The Anglo-Saxon countries have been the chief nations clinging to older and less rational weights and measures, and even in them scientists have adopted the obviously simpler metric system developed in revolutionary France.

By and large, however, the force of tradition proved too strong for the Terror. Nowhere was this more evident than in the attempts to legislate a new religion. Many churches of the old religion were forcibly closed and turned into barracks or administrative offices, and their medieval glass and sculpture were destroyed. Some of the Jacobins launched a "de-Christianization" campaign to make Catholics into *philosophes* and their churches into "temples of Reason." Robespierre, however, disliked this worship of Reason; even the Republic of Virtue, he believed, should acknowledge an ultimate author and judge of morality. The Convention therefore decreed (May, 1794) that "the French people recognize the existence of the Supreme Being and the immortality of the soul." At the festival of the Supreme Being, June 8, 1794, Robespierre set fire to three figures representing Vice, Folly, and Atheism. From the embers the statue of Wisdom emerged, but smudged with smoke because of a mechanical slip-up. The audience laughed. The

"Government of Robespierre." The executioner—having beheaded (from left to right) the clergy, the Parlement, the nobility, the Constituent Assembly, the Legislative Assembly, the Convention, and the people —guillotines himself.

deistic concept of the Supreme Being was too artificial and remote to appeal to the religious emotions of Frenchmen.

The Thermidorean Reaction

The whole Republic of Virtue was too abstract in ideals, and too violent in practice, to retain popular support. Like the Geneva of Calvin, the France of Robespierre demanded superhuman devotion to duty and inhuman indifference to bloodshed. During the first half of 1794, Robespierre pressed the Terror relentlessly; even the members of the Committees of Public Safety and General Security began to feel that they might be the next victims. Fearful deputies of the Mountain joined with the remnants of the Plain to deprive Robespierre of his backing in the Convention. Shouts of "Down with the tyrant!" drowned out his attempts to address the deputies on the ninth of Thermidor, Year II (July 27, 1794). The Convention ordered Robespierre's arrest, and on the next day the great fanatic went to the guillotine. The Reign of Terror was over.

The leaders of the Thermidorean Reaction, many of them former Jacobins, soon dismantled the machinery of the Terror. They disbanded the Revolutionary Tribunal, recalled the deputies on mission, and deprived the Committees of Public Safety and General Security of their independent authority. They closed the Paris Jacobin Club and invited the surviving Girondin deputies to resume their old seats in the Convention. They took the first step toward the restoration of Catholicism by permitting priests to celebrate Mass, though under state supervision and without state financial support. The press and the theater recovered their freedom. Pleasure-seekers again flocked to Paris, liberated from the somberness of the Republic of Virtue. France was resuming a normal existence.

Normality, however, exacted its price. In southern and western France a counterrevolutionary "White Terror," equaling the great Terror in fury, took the lives of many, not only supporters of the Mountain but also purchasers of former church and noble lands. The men of Thermidor precipitated the most acute inflation of the whole revolution by canceling the economic legislation of the Terror. No longer checked by the *maximum*, the prices of some foods rose to a hundred times the level of 1790, and

the *assignats* sank so low in value that businessmen refused to accept them. Impoverished Parisians staged several demonstrations against the Thermidoreans in the course of 1795. Sometimes the rioters voiced their support of the discredited Mountain and its democratic Constitution of 1793 and sometimes they let themselves be used by royalist agents; but always they clamored for bread and lower prices.

The Thermidorean Reaction concluded with the passage of the Constitution of 1795, the last great act of the Convention. The men of Thermidor wanted both to retain the Republic and to assure the dominance of the propertied classes. The Constitution of 1795 therefore denied the vote to the poorest quarter of the nation and required that candidates for public office possess a considerable amount of property. It established a two-house legislature: a lower Council of Five Hundred, and an upper Council of Elders, both to be elected piecemeal after the American practice of renewing one-third of the Senate every two years. Since age and marriage were thought to provide further guarantees of political stability, the members of the lower council were required to be at least thirty years old and the Elders to be forty and either married or widowed. The Council of Five Hundred nominated, and the Elders chose, five directors who headed the executive. Otherwise the Directory was almost totally independent of the legislative councils.

The Constitution of 1795 marked the third great effort of the Revolution to provide France with an enduring government. It followed in part the American precedent of 1787, in part the French precedent of 1791, and, most of all, the precepts of Montesquieu. It embodied the separation of powers and deferred to the aristocracy of wealth, though not to that of birth. By abandoning the political democracy of the

CHAPTER XVIII

still-born Constitution of 1793 and by reverting to the restricted suffrage of 1791, it demonstrated that the most radical phase of the Revolution had passed.

The Directory
(October, 1795–November, 1799)

The new regime dealt harshly with the recurrent plots of royalists or Jacobin extremists. It suppressed with ease the "Conspiracy of the Equals" (1796-97), engineered by Gracchus Babeuf, the one undoubted socialist of the Revolution. Yet, in spite of these successes, political instability plagued the Directory. The directors and the legislative councils clashed repeatedly, each side seeking to turn the political balance in its own favor, and each, in consequence, violating the Constitution. The councils sacked directors before their terms were finished; the directors refused to seat duly elected councilors in the legislature.

The Directory made a vigorous attack on economic problems. It levied high protective tariffs, both as a measure of war against England and as a concession to French businessmen. Again responding to business pressure, it destroyed the plates used to print the now almost worthless *assignats* and in 1797 withdrew paper money from circulation. The return to hard money required stringent governmental economies. The Directory instituted these economies, and it eased the crushing burden of the national debt by simply repudiating two-thirds of it. In short, the Directory brought at least a semblance of order out of the chronic financial chaos.

But it did not bring peace, and therein lay its downfall. The continuing war dominated all the other activities of the Directory; soon all French factions were maneuvering for the political support of the army. The result was the *coup d'état* of Brumaire in 1799 and the dictatorship of a general, Napoleon Bonaparte.

IV: Napoleon and France

Edmund Burke, the British political philosopher, foresaw very early the whole long process that culminated in Napoleon's dominance of France and Europe. Burke warned in his *Reflections on the Revolution in France* (1790):

Everything depends on the army in such a government as yours; for you have industriously destroyed all the opinions, . . . all the instincts which support government. Therefore the moment any difference arises between your National Assembly and any part of the nation, you must have recourse to force. Nothing else is left to you. . . .

• • •

It is besides to be considered, whether an assembly like yours . . . is fit for promoting the discipline and obedience of an army. It is known, that armies have hitherto yielded a very precarious and uncertain obedience to any senate, or popular authority. . . . The officers must totally lose the characteristic disposition of military men, if they see with perfect submission and due admiration, the dominion of pleaders; especially when they find that they have a new court to pay to an endless succession of those pleaders. . . . In the weakness of one kind of authority, and in the fluctuation of all, the officers of an army will remain for some time mutinous and full of faction, until some popular general who understands the art of conciliating the soldiery, and who possesses the true spirit of command, shall draw the eyes of all men upon himself. Armies will obey him on his personal account. There is no other way of securing military obedience in this state of things. But the moment in which that event shall happen, the person who really commands the army is your master; the master . . . of your king, the master of your assembly, the master of your whole republic.*

In 1790, Burke was a solitary prophet; no one else paid much heed to the French army. Sovereigns and statesmen outside France deplored the revolutionary assault on the Old Régime but believed that the very intensity of domestic problems made France incapable of a vigorous foreign policy. The Russian Empress Catherine the Great predicted as late as 1792 that ten thousand soldiers would be sufficient to conquer a France immobilized by revolution. *Philosophes* and liberals outside France hailed the glorious and peaceful promise of the Revolution. The capture of the Bastille delighted Charles James Fox, a leading English Whig: "How much the greatest event it is that ever happened in the world! and how much the best!"

The War Against the First Coalition (1792-1795)

The war that broke out in the spring of 1792 ultimately shattered the illusions of French military weakness and French liberal purity. France soon faced the first of the several coalitions that were to confront the aggressor during the revolutionary and Napoleonic epochs. By the time the war was a year old Austria and Prussia, the charter members of the First Coalition, had been joined by Holland, Spain, and, most significantly, Great Britain. Both ideological and strategic factors brought Britain into the conflict. She regarded the attack on the

Tuileries, the September massacres, and the execution of Louis XVI as outrages against human decency in general and the institution of monarchy in particular. And the French invasion of the Austrian Netherlands in the fall of 1792 raised the unpleasant prospect of a French-controlled Belgium. War between Britain and the French Republic was already inescapable when the Convention made it official on February 1, 1793.

Two years later, however, the First Coalition was on the point of disintegration. At first, the fortunes of war had seesawed. Late in 1792 the French followed up their success at Valmy by the invasion of Belgium, only to lose ground again in 1793 after the defeat and desertion of Dumouriez (see above, p. 115). Then in 1794 the French definitely gained the advantage, and by 1795 French troops had occupied Belgium, Holland, and Germany west of the Rhine.

One reason for French success we have already seen—the Convention's energetic mobilization of national resources. Another reason, equally important yet easy to overlook, was the weakness of the First Coalition. The allies had no first-rate commander, nor did they achieve the effective coordination of the various partners. The Duke of Brunswick's failure to take Paris in 1792, a failure resulting as much from his own deficient generalship as from the battle at Valmy, was characteristic of the bungling, lethargic leadership of the coalition. Moreover, the partitions of Poland in 1793 and 1795 greatly assisted the French. The Polish question kept Catherine the Great from supplying the mere 10,000 troops she deemed sufficient to crush France. It diverted the pick of the Prussian army to occupation duty in the newly annexed Polish provinces and created fresh difficulties between Prussia and Austria. By 1795, things had come to such a pass that the Prussians dared not attack the French for

---

* Everyman ed. (New York, 1910), 217, 215-216.

fear of being assaulted from the rear by their nominal Austrian ally!

Prussia was the first member of the coalition to make peace. In the Treaty of Basel (1795) she ceded to France the scattered Prussian holdings west of the Rhine on the understanding that she might seek compensation elsewhere in Germany. Spain and Holland likewise deserted the coalition in 1795, the former yielding to France the eastern half of the West Indian island of Santo Domingo.

Thus in 1795 France at last secured her "natural frontiers." Besides Belgium and the Rhineland she had also annexed Savoy and Nice, thereby extending her southeastern border to the crest of the Alps. These conquests, however, belied the ideals of the Revolution. In declaring war on Austria in 1792 the Legislative Assembly had sworn to uphold the promise of the Constitution of 1791 about never undertaking a war of conquest. This was to be "not a war of nation against nation, but the righteous defense of a free people against the unjust aggression of a king." But the conquering armies of the First Republic brought closer the day when nation would fight nation—when, hurling the words of the Legislative Assembly back at France, the non-French nations would invoke "the righteous defense of a free people against the unjust aggression" not of a king, but of revolutionary France.

French aggressiveness was already alienating the United States in 1795. The Americans might well have been expected to take a friendly interest in the republican experiment of the country that had done so much to make their own republic possible. France, however, attempted to force and bribe Americans to observe the French blockade against British exports. French meddling provoked an unofficial war of privateers between the two republics lasting through the late 1790's.

The Rise of Napoleon

At the close of 1795, only Britain and Austria remained officially at war with France. The Directory picked Austria as the first target and assigned Napoleon Bonaparte to lead the attack against the Habsburg forces in northern Italy. The youthful commander was at once a *philosophe*, a revolutionary, an inspired general, and a ruthlessly ambitious adventurer. He was born in Corsica in 1769, at a time when France acquired that Mediterranean island from the decadent Republic of Genoa. Napoleon retained throughout his life the strong family loyalty characteristic of Corsican society. From his hands the members of the Bonaparte clan were to receive all the spoils of conquest, even thrones.

As a youth, Napoleon attended military school in France. Largely cut off from his fellow students because he was a "foreigner," he devoted himself to his studies, read widely, especially in Rousseau, and dreamed of the day when he might liberate his native island from French control. Later, however, his zeal for Corsican independence faded. When the Revolution broke out, Napoleon helped to overthrow the Old Régime in Corsica but soon went back to France to resume his military career.

The young army officer defended the Convention, but more from expediency than from political conviction. He commanded the artillery when the forces of the Jacobin Convention recaptured the rebellious Mediterranean seaport of Toulon in December, 1793. In October, 1795, he delivered the famous "whiff of grapeshot" that saved the Thermidorean Convention from a rising of discontented Parisians. Next he advanced his fortunes by marrying Josephine de Beauharnais, a widow six years his senior and an intimate of the ruling clique of the Directory. Josephine's connections and Napoleon's own demonstrated talent as an artillery officer gained him the Italian command in 1796.

In the space of a year, Napoleon cleared the Austrians out of Italy and made them sue for peace. In this famous Italian campaign he showed his remarkable ability to strike quickly and surprise the enemy before they could consolidate their defenses. He also demonstrated his almost unerring sense of what would now be called propaganda and public relations. Witness the proclamation that he issued on April 26, 1796:

> Soldiers! In two weeks you have won six victories; you have made 15,000 prisoners; you have killed or wounded more than 10,000 men.
> Deprived of everything, you have accomplished everything. You have won battles without cannon, negotiated rivers without bridges, made forced marches without shoes, encamped without brandy, and often without bread. Only the phalanxes of the Republic, only the soldiers of Liberty, would have been capable of suffering the things that you have suffered.
> You all burn to carry the glory of the French people; to humiliate the proud kings who dared to contemplate shackling us; to go back to your villages, to say proudly: 'I was of the conquering army of Italy!'
> Friends, I promise you that conquest; but there is a condition you must swear to fulfill: to respect the people whom you are delivering; to repress horrible pillaging.
> Peoples of Italy, the French army comes to break your chains; greet it with confidence; your property, religion and customs will be respected.*

Here was Napoleon's characteristic policy of promising all things to all men. He encouraged the nationalism of underpaid and underfed French soldiers and whetted their appetite for booty. Yet he appealed also to the nationalism of the Italians, promising them liberation from Austria and guaranteeing the orderly conduct of the French army.

---

* Abridged from *Le Moniteur Universel*, May 17, 1796. Our translation.

He did not, of course, tell the Italians that they might perhaps be exchanging one master for another, nor did he publicize the money that he seized from Italian governments and the art treasures that he took from Italian galleries and shipped back to France.

In the Treaty of Campoformio (1797) terminating the Italian campaign, Austria acknowledged the loss of Belgium and Lombardy and recognized the two puppet states that Napoleon set up in northwestern Italy, the Ligurian Republic of Genoa and the Cisalpine Republic of Lombardy. In return, the Habsburgs received the Italian possessions of the once splendid Venetian Republic and a secret French assurance that, despite the specific promise made to Prussia at Basel in 1795, Prussia would not be permitted to compensate for her losses in the Rhineland by lands elsewhere in Germany. Throughout the negotiations at Campoformio Napoleon behaved like an old hand at the devious business of international horse-trading. There seemed to be nothing that this astonishing general could not do—nothing, that is, except accomplish the formidable task of knocking Britain out of the war.

To this task Napoleon now turned. He decided not to attack Britain directly, but rather to hit at her indirectly through Egypt, then a dependency of Turkey. This would-be Alexander the Great, seeking new worlds to conquer, talked grandly of digging a canal at Suez, giving French merchants the monopoly of a new short trade-route to India, and exacting belated retribution from Britain for Clive's victory in the Seven Years' War. Since Napoleon shared the passion of the Enlightenment for science and antiquity, he invited archaeologists and other experts to accompany his army and thereby helped to found the study known as Egyptology. One of his experts, Champollion, deciphered the Rosetta Stone, the first

124

key to the translation of ancient Egyptian hieroglyphics. Napoleon's scholars established in Egypt an outpost of French cultural imperialism that lasted until the twentieth century.

From the military standpoint, however, the campaign failed totally. Having eluded the British Mediterranean fleet commanded by Nelson, Napoleon landed in Egypt in July, 1798, and quickly routed the Mamelukes, the ruling oligarchy. Then disaster struck. On August 1, 1798, Nelson discovered the French fleet anchored at Abukir Bay along the Egyptian coast and destroyed it before its captains had time to weigh anchor. Nelson's victory deprived the French of supplies, of reinforcements, and even of news from home. After a year of futile campaigning in the Near East, Napoleon suddenly left Egypt in August, 1799, and returned home to France. The soldiers whom he thus deserted were not so fortunate; they remained in Egypt until 1801, when arrangements were completed for their withdrawal.

Brumaire

Apparently quite unmoved by his failure in Egypt, Napoleon found the situation back in France ripe for a decisive political stroke. During his absence Jacobinism had experienced a significant revival; several hundred members of the legislative councils belonged to the old Jacobin Club, now resurrected as the "Society of the Friends of Liberty and Equality." Abroad, the Directory had established four new satellite republics with classical names—the Roman, the Parthenopean in Naples, the Batavian in Holland, and the Helvetian in Switzerland. But this new success of French imperialism upset the European balance and provoked a renewal of war on the Continent. The Habsburgs resented the exten-

sion of French influence in their former Italian preserve, and Tsar Paul I (1796-1801) feared that Napoleon would harm Russian interests in the eastern Mediterranean. In December, 1798, therefore, Austria and Russia joined Britain in the Second Coalition. By August, 1799, Austrian and Russian armies had succeeded in expelling the French from Italy and had dismantled the Cisalpine, Roman, and Parthenopean republics.

In these circumstances, patriotic Frenchmen were ready to welcome any military hero, and conservative Frenchmen were ready to welcome a champion of order against the new Jacobin threat. Naturally, Napoleon got a rousing reception on his return from Egypt. Soon he was engaged in a plot to overthrow the Directory, with the complicity of two of the five directors themselves, Roger-Ducos and Siéyès, the champion of the third estate. On November 9 and 10, 1799 (18 and 19 Brumaire by the revolutionary calendar) the plot was executed. First, Napoleon forced the resignation of the three directors not in the plot; next, to win over the consent of the two legislative councils, he hinted at the danger of a Jacobin conspiracy. He gained the approval of the Elders, but in the Council of Five Hundred he lost his self-possession, ranted incoherently, and fainted. His brother, Lucien, the presiding officer of the Council, saved the situation until Napoleon had recovered and a detachment of troops had expelled a majority of the Five Hundred.

This almost comic coup d'état of Brumaire ended the Directory. The Bonapartist minority of the councilors entrusted both the government and the preparation of a new constitution to the victorious triumvirate of Roger-Ducos, Siéyès, and Napoleon, of whom only Napoleon really counted in the long run. One-man rule, apparently destroyed in 1789, rose again from the ashes of the Old Régime. It all happened just as Edmund Burke had predicted:

> In the weakness of authority, . . . some popular general shall draw the eyes of all men upon himself. Armies will obey him on his personal account. . . . The person who really commands the army is your master. . . .

Napoleonic Government

Immediately after Brumaire, Siéyès drew up a constitutional draft based on the autocratic maxim, "Confidence from below, authority from above." Bonaparte amended it according to his own view that constitutions ought to be "short and obscure." This Constitution of the Year VIII erected a very strong executive, somewhat disguised by Roman terminology and other bits of republican window-dressing. Three consuls shared the executive authority—or rather, Napoleon as First Consul took the lion's share, leaving his two colleagues only nominal power. Four separate bodies had a hand in legislation: (1) the Council of State proposed laws; (2) the Tribunate debated them but did not vote; (3) the Legislative Corps voted them but did not debate; (4) the Senate had the right to veto legislation. In all four cases the members were either appointed by the First Consul or elected indirectly by a process so complex that Bonaparte had ample opportunity to manipulate candidates.

The core of this system was the Council of State, staffed by Bonaparte's hand-picked choices, and functioning both as a sort of cabinet and as the highest administrative court in the land. The three remaining bodies were intended merely to go through the motions of enacting whatever the First Consul decreed. Even so, the debates of the Tribunate sometimes got in his way. He periodically cut down its authority and in 1807 abolished the Tribunate altogether. By

then the legislative deliberations had become, in the apt phrase of a contemporary, "echoes in a desert of silence."

Napoleon soon cast off the few restrictions imposed on his own authority by the Constitution of the Year VIII. In 1802, he persuaded the legislators to drop the original ten-year limitation on his term of office and make him First Consul for life, with the power to designate his successor and amend the Constitution at will. In 1804, he took the next logical move and declared himself hereditary Emperor of the French. A magnificent coronation took place at Notre Dame in Paris on December 2. The Pope consecrated the Emperor, but Napoleon placed the crown on his own head in imitation of Charlemagne at Rome a thousand years before.

Each time Napoleon revised the Constitution in a non-republican direction he made the republican gesture of submitting the change to the electorate. Each time, the results of the plebiscite were overwhelmingly favorable: in 1799-1800, the vote was 3,011,107 for Napoleon and the Constitution of the Year VIII, and 1,562 against; in 1802, it was 3,568,885 for Napoleon and the life consulate, and 8,374 against; in 1804, it was 3,572,329 for Napoleon and the Empire, and 2,579 against. Although the voters were exposed to considerable official pressure and the announced results were perhaps rigged a bit, the vast majority of Frenchmen undoubtedly supported Napoleon. His military triumphs appealed to their growing nationalism, and his policy of stability at home insured them against further revolutionary changes. For the time being at any rate Siéyès' maxim applied. Confidence increased from below as authority increased from above.

If by any chance confidence failed to materialize below, Napoleon had the authority to deal with the recalcitrant. He wiped out the local self-government remaining from the early days of the Revolution. In place of locally elected officials he substituted those appointed by himself—prefects in departments, sub-prefects in *arrondissements*, mayors in communes—and all were instructed to enforce compliance with the Emperor's dictates. Napoleon, far more than the Jacobins, made France a highly centralized police state.

Men of every political background staffed the imperial administration. With first-rate political talent hard to find, Napoleon cared little whether his subordinates were returned *émigrés* or ex-Jacobins. Besides, their varied antecedents reinforced the impression that narrow factionalism was dead and that the Empire rested on a broad political base. Napoleon paid officials well and offered the additional bait of high titles. With the establishment of the Empire he created dukes by the dozen and counts and barons by the hundred. He rewarded outstanding generals with the rank of Marshal and lesser civilian officials with the Legion of Honor. "Aristocracy always exists," Napoleon remarked. "Destroy it in the nobility, it removes itself to the rich and powerful houses of the middle class." * The imperial aristocracy gave the leaders of the middle class the social distinction that they felt to be rightfully theirs.

Law and Justice

Napoleon revived some of the aristocratic glamor of the Old Régime, but not its glaring inequalities. His series of law codes, the celebrated *Code Napoléon* (1804-1810), declared all men equal before the law without regard to their rank and wealth. It extended to all the right to follow the occupation, and embrace the religion, of their choosing. The new Justinian ended

* Quoted in H. A. L. Fisher, *Napoleon* (New York, 1913), Appendix I.

the conflict between the Roman and feudal legal systems and gave France the single coherent system of law which the *philosophes* had demanded and which the revolutionary governments had been too busy to formulate.

The *Code Napoléon* did not, however, embody the full judicial reform program of the Enlightenment; it incorporated some of the absolutist features of the Roman law. Though Napoleon confirmed the revolutionary legislation permitting divorce by mutual consent, and though he himself divorced Josephine, he generally preserved the absolute legal superiority of the man of the family. The code canceled revolutionary legislation protecting the interests of wives, minors, and illegitimate children. In trial procedure, the code permitted some use of torture. It favored the prosecution over the defense and the interests of the state over the rights of the individual. Disdaining the separation of powers, Napoleon appointed judges himself and empowered the prefects to select jurors. Now confirming the principles of 1789, and now betraying them, Napoleonic justice offered a fair summary of the fate of the Revolution under the Empire.

A similar ambiguity clouded Napoleon's attitude toward civil liberties. On the one hand, he provoked no Reign of Terror. He practiced religious toleration of a sort and welcomed former political heretics into his administration. On the other hand, Napoleonic generosity stemmed always from expediency, never from any fundamental belief in liberty. If conciliation failed, then he used force. In the western departments, where royalist uprisings had become chronic since the revolt in the Vendée, he massacred the rebels who declined his offer of amnesty in 1800. In 1804, he kidnapped the Duke of Enghien from the neutral German state of Baden because the Duke was believed to be the choice of monarchist

Napoleon, sketched at the theater.

And so on through "bills, posters, advertisements, institutes, literary meetings, sermons and fashionable trials." No segment of public opinion escaped Napoleon's manipulation. He reduced by five-sixths the number of Paris newspapers and pestered theater managers with suggestions for improving the patriotic tone of plays. When he wanted to arouse French opinion, he simply started a press campaign, as in this instance from 1807:

A great hue and cry is to be raised against the persecutions experienced by the Catholics of Ireland at the hands of the Anglican Church. . . . Bishops will be approached so that prayers will be offered entreating an end to the persecutions of the Anglican Church against the Irish Catholics. But the administration must move very delicately and make use of the newspapers without their realizing what the government is driving at. . . . And the term 'Anglican Church' must always be used in place of 'Protestants,' for we have Protestants in France, but no Anglican Church.*

Religion

Political considerations colored all Napoleon's decisions on religion. "I do not see in religion the mystery of the incarnation," he said, "but the mystery of the social order. It attaches to heaven an idea of equality which prevents the rich man from being massacred by the poor." † Moreover, French Catholics still loathed the anticlericalism of the Revolution. Therefore, Napoleon reasoned, he had everything to gain by working out a reconciliation with Rome. If he succeeded in enlisting the support of the Church, he could then recruit what he termed a "spiritual police force."

conspirators for the throne of France. Napoleon immediately discovered the Duke's innocence, but he had him executed none the less.

Even more damaging to Napoleon's reputation in democratic eyes was his repression of the freedom of speech. In July, 1801, for instance, he directed his librarian to read all the newspapers carefully and

. . . make an abstract of everything they contain likely to affect the public point of view, especially with regard to religion, philosophy, and political opinion. He will send me this abstract between 5 and 6 o'clock every day.

Once every ten days he will send me an analysis of all the books or pamphlets which have appeared . . . , calling attention to any passages that might bear on moral questions, or interest me in a political or moral connexion.

He will take pains to procure copies of all the plays which are produced, and to analyse them for me, with observations of the same character as those above mentioned. This analysis must be made, at latest, within 48 hours of the production of the plays.*

---

* Quoted in J. M. Thompson, *Napoleon Self-Revealed* (Boston, 1934), 81.

* *Lettres Inédites de Napoléon* (Paris, 1897), I, 93-94. Our translation.
† Quoted in H. A. L. Fisher, *Napoleon* (New York, 1913), Appendix I.

CHAPTER XVIII

The Concordat that was negotiated in 1801 by Napoleon and Pope Pius VII (1800-1823) accomplished the reconciliation. The French state agreed to pay clerical salaries and to suppress the popular election of bishops and priests. The bishops were to be nominated by the government, and then consecrated by the pope; the priests were to be appointed by the bishops. At this point Napoleon's concessions stopped. By declaring that Catholicism was only the faith of the "majority of Frenchmen," rather than the state religion, the Concordat implicitly admitted the toleration of Protestants and Jews. Furthermore, it granted to the French government vague but extensive powers to regulate church activities. The Concordat of 1801 was a diplomatic victory for Napoleon and a resounding confirmation of the principles of 1789. It canceled only the most extreme provisions of the Civil Constitution of the Clergy. Pius VII accepted the abolition of the tithe and the confiscation of ecclesiastical lands and, by granting Napoleon regulatory powers, allowed the Gallican Church to become in effect the ward of the French state.

So far as France was concerned, the Concordat worked reasonably well. It conciliated large numbers of Catholics, alienated only the relatively small group of determined anticlericals, and remained in force until 1905. The Concordat, however, did not bring complete peace between France and the Vatican. Napoleon insisted that the pope should render to Caesar the things that were Caesar's. When Pius VII objected to Napoleon's turning the Papal States into a French satellite, the new Caesar, like the medieval emperors, lectured him on the proper authority of the spiritual and the temporal powers. Pius VII passed the last years of the Napoleonic regime as Bonaparte's prisoner, first in northern Italy, then in France.

Education

The Revolution and Napoleon cost the Church its monopoly over education. The Constitution of 1791 had promised France a system of state schools.. The Convention, while doing little to apply this principle to primary education, did set up a series of institutions for specialized training, like the famous Paris engineering school, the *Ecole Polytechnique*. In each department it established a "central school" to provide secondary education of high quality at relatively low cost. Napoleon abolished these flourishing central schools in 1802 and replaced them with a smaller number of *lycées* open only to the relatively few pupils who could afford the tuition or who received state scholarships. The change had a political motive. The *lycée* students wore uniforms and marched to military drums, and the curriculum, too, served the ends of patriotic indoctrination. The Emperor, for instance, laid down the following rules for revising and modernizing textbooks on French history:

> The work must be entrusted not merely to authors of real ability, but also—and this is even more important—to adherents of the Government, who will present the facts from their right angle and lay the foundations of healthy education. . . .*

To provide for the general supervision of the school system Napoleon founded in 1808 a body with the misleading name of the "University"; actually it was more like a powerful American school committee or board of regents.

Napoleon, then, scarcely had our modern democratic belief that schools should provide free and, politically speaking, reasonably neutral training. He neglected primary schooling almost completely. Yet,

---

* Quoted in J. M. Thompson, *Napoleon Self-Revealed* (Boston, 1934), 216.

building on the revolutionary base, he did advance the construction of the modern secular French school system. The educational competition of Church and State, so often a bitter issue in modern French life, dates back to the Revolution and Napoleon.

Economics

Political aims likewise determined the economic program of an emperor determined to promote national unity. The French peasants wanted to be left alone to enjoy the new freedom acquired in 1789; Napoleon did not disturb them, except to raise army recruits. The middle class wanted a balanced national budget and the end of revolutionary experiments with paper currency and a controlled economy. Napoleon continued the sound money of the Directory and, unlike the Directory, balanced the budget, thanks to the immense plunder that he gained in war. He greatly improved the efficiency and probity of tax-collectors and established the semi-official Bank of France (1800) to act as the government's financial agent. He strengthened the curbs placed on labor by the Le Chapelier Law of 1791 (see above, p. 108) and obliged every workman to carry a written record of his jobs and his general reputation. Rich

war contracts and subsidies kept employment and profits high. As the war went on and on, however, Napoleon found it particularly difficult to appease the peasantry and the bourgeoisie. Despite the levies on conquered countries, he had to draft soldiers from the peasantry and increase the already unpopular taxes on salt, liquor, and tobacco.

In summary, the domestic policies of Napoleon I had something in common with the methods of all the celebrated one-man rulers, from Caesar through Louis XIV down to the modern dictator. Like Caesar, Napoleon rendered lip-service to the Republic while subverting republican institutions; he used prefects to impose centralized authority as Louis XIV had used *intendants;* and, like Hitler and Stalin, he had only contempt for free speech. Yet Napoleon was also a genuine enlightened despot. His law code and his educational reforms, in particular, would have delighted the *philosophes.* And he ended civil strife without sacrificing the redistribution of land and the equality before the law gained in 1789 and after. Abandoning some revolutionary innovations, modifying others, and completing still others, Napoleon regimented the Revolution, but he did not wholly destroy it.

V: Napoleon and Europe

To many Frenchmen, Napoleon was the Man of Destiny, the most brilliant ruler in their country's long history. To most Europeans, on the other hand, Napoleon was the sinister Man on Horseback, the relentless enemy of individual freedom and national independence. As French conquests accumulated, as French frontiers moved

steadily outward, and as nominally independent countries became nothing more than French puppets, Europe grew to hate the insatiable imperialism of Napoleon. Napoleonic France succeeded in building up a vast empire, but only at the cost of arousing the implacable enmity of the other European nations.

The War (1800-1805)

Napoleon had barely launched the Consulate when he took to the field again. The Second Coalition, which had reached the peak of its success in August, 1799, was now falling to pieces. The unpredictable Russian tsar, Paul I, had deserted his British and Austrian allies in the fall of 1799. In the spring of 1800, Napoleon attacked the Austrians in Italy, eked out a victory in June, and, steadily gathering momentum thereafter, forced the Austrian to sue for peace. The Treaty of Lunéville (1801) extended the gains that Napoleon had secured from Austria four years before at Campoformio. This time Austria had to agree that the German states which had lost territory to France west of the Rhine should be compensated to the east of the Rhine, and that France should have a voice in allotting these compensations. The Lunéville treaty gave Napoleon the right to superintend the reshaping of Germany.

After Lunéville, as after Campoformio, Britain alone remained at war with France. In 1797, the younger Pitt had kept Britain in the war; in 1801, however, the belligerent Pitt was no longer prime minister. British taxpayers wanted relief from the heavy burden of war taxes; British merchants longed to resume trading with continental markets partially closed to them since 1793. Though Britain had been unable to check Napoleon's expansion in Europe, she had very nearly won the colonial and naval war by 1801. She had captured former Dutch and Spanish colonies, and Nelson's fleet had expelled the French from Egypt and the strategic mid-Mediterranean island of Malta. The British cabinet was confident that it held a strong bargaining position and could obtain favorable terms from Napoleon. The French, however, outsmarted the inept British negotiators. In the Peace of Amiens (1802) the British promised to surrender almost all their colonial conquests and got nothing in return. The French refused either to reopen the Continent to British exports or to relinquish Belgium, which remained, in Napoleon's phrase, "a loaded pistol aimed at the heart of Britain."

The one-sided Peace of Amiens provided only a brief truce in the world-wide struggle of Britain and France. Napoleon had no intention of giving up the struggle permanently until he had destroyed British commercial and colonial supremacy and in effect had reversed the direction of the Second Hundred Years' War. Meanwhile, he was alarming Austria and Prussia by using the right granted by Lunéville to revise the map of Germany. In 1803, more than a hundred German states were abolished, chiefly city-states and small ecclesiastical principalities. The chief beneficiaries of this territorial readjustment were the south German states of Bavaria, Württemberg, and Baden, which Napoleon clearly intended to make a "third" Germany dominated by France and independent of Austria and Prussia.

Britain he aroused by a new tariff law (1803) highly unfavorable to British exporters and by a grandiose project for an American colonial empire centering on the island of Haiti (Santo Domingo) and on the vast Louisiana territory that Spain had handed back to France in 1801. French soldiers wrested Haiti from the able Negro chieftain, Toussaint L'Ouverture. But the continued resistance of the Haitians and a virulent outbreak of yellow fever took a fearful toll of the French troops and forced Napoleon to abandon the American project. In 1803, therefore, he sold the whole of Louisiana to the United States for the bargain price of $11,000,000.

By the time the Louisiana Purchase was completed, Britain and France were again at war. From 1803 through 1805, Napoleon actively prepared to invade England. He

assembled more than a hundred thousand troops and a thousand landing barges on the French side of the Straits of Dover. In 1805, he sent Admiral Villeneuve and the French fleet to the West Indies to lure the British fleet away from Europe. Then Villeneuve was to return post-haste to convoy the French invasion force across the Channel while Nelson was still vainly combing the Caribbean.

Villeneuve failed to give Nelson the slip either in the West Indies or on the return voyage; back in European waters, he cautiously put in at a friendly Spanish port instead of heading directly for the Channel as Napoleon had ordered. Nelson engaged the combined French and Spanish fleets off Cape Trafalgar at the southwest corner of Spain (October, 1805). He lost his own life but not before he had destroyed half of his adversaries' ships without sacrificing a single one of his own. Trafalgar gave the British undisputed control of the seas for the balance of the war and blasted forever French hopes of staging a successful cross-Channel invasion.

The Third Coalition (1805-1807)

By this time, Austria and Russia had joined with Britain in the Third Coalition. Bonaparte routed his continental opponents in the most dazzling campaign of his career. At Ulm, on the upper Danube (October, 1805), he captured 30,000 Austrians who had moved westward without waiting for their Russian allies. He met the main Russian force and the balance of the Austrian army near the Moravian village of Austerlitz. The ensuing battle (December 2, 1805) fittingly celebrated the first anniversary of Napoleon's coronation as emperor. Bringing up reinforcements secretly and with great speed, Napoleon completely surprised his opponents; their casualties were three times greater than his own. Within the month he forced the Habsburg emperor, Francis II, to sign the humiliating Treaty of Pressburg. This treaty gave the Austrian Tyrol to Bavaria and gave Venetia to the Napoleonic puppet kingdom of Italy.

A still harsher fate awaited the Prussians,

CHAPTER XVIII

"The Battle of Trafalgar." Painting by Turner.

brought back into the war for the first time since 1795 by Napoleon's repeated interventions in German affairs. The inadequacy of their army, which had not kept up with the military improvements introduced since the campaigns of Frederick the Great, soon forced them out again. In October, 1806, the French pulverized the main Prussian contingents in the twin battles of Jena and Auerstädt, and occupied Berlin. Napoleon paid a respectful visit to the quarters of Frederick the Great at Potsdam and then sent the great Hohenzollern's battle trophies to Paris. He decided to postpone a final settlement with Prussia until he had beaten his only remaining continental opponent.

Russia went down at Friedland (June, 1807).

Napoleon's great string of victories against the Third Coalition resulted partly from the blunders of his enemies. The miscalculations of Austrian and Prussian generals contributed substantially to French successes at Austerlitz and at Jena. Further, the French army was the most seasoned force in Europe, its soldiers of every rank were well trained, and the quality of its officers was improved by the practice of basing promotion on ability rather than on seniority or influence. Finally, Bonaparte seldom risked an engagement unless his forces were the numerical equal of the enemy's;

NAPOLEONIC EUROPE, 1812

Empire of France
States under French control
Allied with France
X Battle sites

Miles
0   500

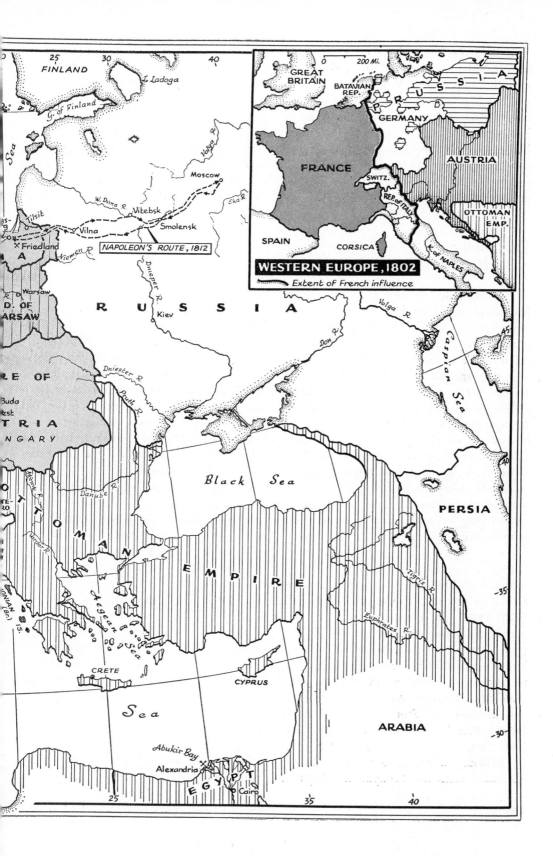

FINLAND

25   30   40

L. Ladoga

G. of Finland

Sea

Volga R.

Moscow

W. Dina R.   Vitebsk

Oka R.

Tilsit

Vilna   Smolensk

X Friedland   Niemen R.

NAPOLEON'S ROUTE, 1812

Dnieper R.

R U S S I A

D. OF
ARSAW

Warsaw

Kiev

Dniester R.

RE OF

Pruth R.

Buda
est

TRIA

NGARY

Don R.

Volga R.

45

Caspian Sea

40

O
T
T
O
M
A
N

Black   Sea

Danube R.

Maritza R.

Vardar R.

E M P I R E

PERSIA

Tigris R.

35

Euphrates R.

Aegean Sea

IONIAN Is.
(Br.)

CRETE

CYPRUS

S e a

ARABIA

30

Abukir Bay

Alexandria   X

Sea

EGYPT   Cairo

25   35   40

GREAT
BRITAIN   0   200 Mi.

BATAVIAN
REP.   P R U S S I A

GERMANY

FRANCE   AUSTRIA

SWITZ.

REP. of ITALY   OTTOMAN
EMP.

SPAIN   CORSICA   K. of NAPLES

WESTERN EUROPE, 1802

Extent of French influence

then he staked everything on a dramatic surprise maneuver, as at Austerlitz. Yet even the French army had defects. The pay was low and irregular, the medical services were a disgrace, and the supplies were so badly managed that French soldiers usually had to live off the land. Eventually these shortcomings were to weaken French striking power; in 1807, however, they did not prevent the ascendancy of Napoleon.

The Empire
at Its Height (1807-1812)

Napoleon reached the pinnacle of his career when he met his Russian adversary, Tsar Alexander I (1801-1825), on a raft anchored in the Niemen River at Tilsit in East Prussia. There, in July, 1807, the two emperors drew up a treaty dividing Europe between them. Alexander acknowledged France's hegemony over central and western Europe and secured in return the recognition of eastern Europe as the Russian sphere. Napoleon pledged Russia a share in the spoils if the Ottoman Empire should be dismembered. He demanded no territory from the defeated Tsar; he required only a commitment to cease trade with Britain and to join the war against her.

Prussia was the chief victim of the Tilsit settlement. While the two emperors negotiated on the raft, Frederick William III (1797-1840), the Prussian king, nervously paced the banks of the Niemen. He had good cause to be nervous, for Tilsit cost him almost half his territory. Prussia's Polish provinces formed a new puppet state, the Grand Duchy of Warsaw, which Napoleon assigned to a French ally, the King of Saxony. Prussian territory west of the Elbe River went to Napoleon to dispose of as he wished. To complete the humiliation, Napoleon stationed occupation troops in

Prussia and fixed the maximum size of its army at 42,000.

This latter-day Caesar was now dividing almost all of Europe into three parts. First came the French Empire, including France proper and the territories annexed since 1789. Second were the satellites, ruled in many cases by relatives of Napoleon. Last, and least subject to Napoleonic control were Austria, Prussia, and Russia, forced by defeat to become the allies of France. Only Britain, Sweden, and Turkey remained outside the Napoleonic system.

The frontiers of the French Empire at their most extensive enclosed Belgium and Holland; the sections of Germany west of the Rhine and along the North Sea; the Italian territories of Piedmont, Genoa, Tuscany, and Rome; and finally, physically detached from the rest, the "Illyrian Provinces," stretching along the Dalmatian coast of the Adriatic, taken from Austria in 1809, and named after a province of the old Roman Empire. These annexations were usually subdivided into departments and ruled by prefects, just like the home departments of France.

The satellites flanked the French Empire. The Kingdom of Italy, an enlarged version of the Cisalpine Republic, included the northern and central Italian lands not directly annexed by France. Napoleon was the king, and his stepson, Eugene de Beauharnais, was viceroy. In southern Italy, Napoleon deposed the Bourbon king of Naples in 1805 and gave the crown first to his brother Joseph and then to his brother-in-law, Joachim Murat, the husband of his sister Caroline. Brother Joseph moved from Naples to Madrid in 1808 when Napoleon deposed the Spanish Bourbons in order to force the unwilling Spaniards to remain in the war against Britain.

In Central Europe, Napoleon energetically pursued his project of a "third" Germany. He decreed a further reduction in

Gillray, "Tiddy-Dolly, the great French Gingerbread-Baker, drawing out a new Batch of Kings—his Man, Hopping-Talley, mixing up the Dough" —a British comment on Napoleon's imperialism.

the number of German states and in 1806 finally dissolved that useless museum piece, the Holy Roman Empire. In its place he created the Confederation of the Rhine, extending farther than its name suggested to include almost every German state except Austria and Prussia. At the heart of this confederation Napoleon carved out for his brother Jerome the Kingdom of Westphalia, which incorporated the Prussian holdings west of the Elbe seized at Tilsit. Two states outside the Confederation of the Rhine— Switzerland and the Grand-Duchy of Warsaw—completed the roster of French satellites. Europe had not seen such an empire since the heyday of imperial Rome.

Napoleon longed to give dignity and permanence to his creation. It was not enough that his brothers and his in-laws should sit on half the thrones of Europe; he himself must found a dynasty, must have the heir so far denied him in fifteen years of childless marriage. He divorced Josephine, therefore, and in 1810 married into one of Europe's most celebrated dynasties by choosing Marie-Louise, the daughter of the Habsburg Francis II. In due time, Marie-Louise bore a son, whom his father

grandiloquently called "The King of Rome."

"Napoleon II," however, was never to rule in Rome or anywhere else. Bonaparte gave his non-French subjects and dependents all things except those they prized most highly. Everywhere he curbed the power of the Church, abolished serfdom, built roads, and introduced the new French law codes. Everywhere, however, he exacted a heavy toll of tribute and subjection. Year after year he increased his demands upon the manpower and material resources of the satellites. In the Kingdom of Italy, for instance, he doubled the tax rate previously levied by the Austrians; half his Italian revenues went to defray the expenses of the French army and the French government.

Napoleon flooded his relatives with instructions on the government of their domains and brought them abruptly to heel whenever they showed signs of putting local interests above those of France. When Louis Bonaparte in Holland dared to disobey the imperial orders, his brother delivered a crushing rebuke:

In ascending the throne of Holland, Your Majesty has forgotten that he is French and has stretched all the springs of his reason and tormented his conscience in order to persuade himself that he is Dutch. Dutchmen inclining toward France have been ignored and persecuted; those serving England have been promoted. . . . I have experienced the sorrow of seeing the name of France exposed to shame in a Holland ruled by a prince of my blood.*

Louis' boldness cost him his throne and the Dutch their last vestige of independence. The kingdom was annexed to France in 1810.

The Continental System

Nowhere was Napoleon's imperialism more evident than in his attempt to regulate the economy of the whole Continent. The Continental System had a double aim: to build up the export trade of France and to cripple that of Britain. Revolutionary France had already levied heavy tariffs on British goods to discourage their importation into France. The collapse of Napoleon's cross-Channel invasion plans led him to expand these measures into a great campaign to bankrupt the nation of shopkeepers. The defeat of the Third Coalition gave him the opportunity to experiment with economic warfare on a continental scale and to carry to a logical extreme the warlike implications of mercantilism.

The Berlin Decree, issued by Napoleon in November, 1806, forbade all trade with the British Isles and all commerce in British merchandise. It ordered the arrest of all Britons on the Continent and the confiscation of their property. Britain replied by requiring that neutral vessels wishing to trade with France put in first at a British port and pay duties. This regulation enabled Britain to share in the profits of neutral shipping to France. Napoleon retaliated with the Milan Decree (December, 1807),

ordering the seizure of all neutral ships that complied with the new British policy. The neutrals, in effect, were damned if they did and damned if they didn't.

Napoleon's vassals and allies had to support the Continental System or suffer the consequences. Of all the "un-French" activities countenanced by Louis Bonaparte, the worst, in Napoleon's view, was his toleration of Dutch smuggling of English contraband. The Emperor likewise expected the satellites to contribute to French industrial prosperity. When the Italians objected to the regulation of their silk exports, Napoleon lectured his viceroy, Eugene, on the facts of economic life:

All the raw silk from the Kingdom of Italy goes to England. . . . It is therefore quite natural that I should wish to divert it from this route to the advantage of my French manufacturers: otherwise my silk factories, one of the chief supports of French commerce, would suffer substantial losses. . . . My principle is *France first.*

. . .

It is no use for Italy to make plans that leave French prosperity out of account; she must face the fact that the interests of the two countries hang together.*

The gigantic attempt to make "France first" failed dismally. Only a few French industries benefited from the Continental System. The cessation of sugar imports from the West Indies promoted the cultivation of native sugar-beets, and the protection of French textiles against British competition brought a temporary boom to the silk industry of Lyons and the cotton mills of northern France and Alsace. But the decline of overseas trade greatly depressed Bordeaux and other French Atlantic ports. The increasing difficulty and expense of procuring raw cotton ended the textile boom, caused widespread unemployment,

---

* *Lettres Inédites de Napoléon,* L. Lecestre, ed. (Paris, 1897), I, 382-383. Our translation.

* Quoted in Thompson, *Napoleon Self-Revealed,* 274-275.

CHAPTER XVIII

and produced a rash of bankruptcies despite Napoleon's financial help to the stricken industry. The new French markets on the Continent did not compensate for the loss of older markets overseas. The value of French exports declined by more than one-third between 1805 and 1813.

The Continental System did not ruin Britain. Fortified by their leadership in the economic revolutions and by the overwhelming superiority of their navy and merchant marine, the British rode out the storm, though they encountered very serious difficulties with agricultural production and high food prices. British commerce and industry remained, from Napoleon's standpoint, maddeningly prosperous. Exporters not only developed lucrative new markets in the Americas but also continued to supply old customers on the Continent. They smuggled their goods in neutral ships and with spurious "Made in France" labels. Napoleon lacked the vast naval force to apprehend smugglers at sea, and he lacked the large staff of incorruptible customs inspectors to control contraband in the ports. The best he could do was to confess his failure by confiscating and re-selling contraband *after* it had already been sold. Moreover, since the French army simply could not do without some items produced only in British factories, Napoleon violated his own decrees by authorizing secret purchases of British cloth and leather for uniforms.

The Continental System antagonized both the neutral powers and Napoleon's allies. French seizure of American vessels in European ports under the terms of the Milan Decree put a dangerous strain on Franco-American relations. A renewal of the undeclared war of a decade earlier was prevented largely because British restrictions likewise bore heavily on the Americans. British impressment of American seamen on the pretext that they were deserters

from the Royal Navy, combined with the designs of American expansionists on Canada, produced the indecisive Anglo-American War of 1812, which actually lasted until 1814.

Insurgent Nationalism: Spain

In Europe, the political and military consequences of the Continental System formed a decisive and disastrous chapter in Napoleonic history. The chapter opened in 1807, when the master of Europe declined to tolerate Portugal's economic ties with Britain. To impose the Continental System on Portugal, he suggested that France and Spain partition the country. The Spanish rulers agreed, not suspecting that Napoleon planned to use the Portuguese expedition as an excuse for French military occupation of Spain itself. Portugal was occupied in 1807, and in the next year Napoleon lured the Spanish royal family away from Madrid and made his brother Joseph King of Spain. But every measure taken by Napoleon—the removal of the incompetent Bourbons, the installation of a foreign monarch, the attempted enforcement of the Continental System, and, not least, the suppression of the Inquisition and the curtailment of noble and clerical privileges—violated Spanish tradition and offended Spanish nationalism. The irreconcilable Spaniards began fighting Napoleon in 1808.

This Peninsular War, named after the Iberian Peninsula, swiftly grew from a minor irritation to a deadly cancer on the body of the Napoleonic Empire. The Spaniards employed ambushes, poisoned wells, and other guerilla devices. The expedition that Britain sent to assist them upset all the rules about British military inferiority. It was ably commanded by Sir Arthur Wellesley (later the Duke of Wellington), generously supplied from home, and firmly based on Portugal and on Britain's unshakable command of the seas. Napoleon poured more than 300,000 troops into the Peninsular campaign, but he never managed to inflict an Austerlitz or a Jena on the Anglo-Spanish forces. His opponents quickly gained the upper hand in 1812, when Napoleon took part of his army for the invasion of Russia. In 1813, King Joseph left Madrid forever, and Wellington, having liberated Spain, crossed into southern France.

Insurgent Nationalism: Germany

Napoleonic imperialism also aroused a national spirit among the traditionally disunited Germans. The leaders of German Romanticism (see Chapter XIX for details) laid the cultural foundations of the new nationalism by praising the literature of medieval Germany and by glorifying the old German heroes like Frederick the Great, Charlemagne, and Arminius—Arminius, above all, for just as the historical Arminius had driven the legions of Augustus back across the Rhine, so a new Arminius would arise to expel the new Caesar. Men of letters launched a campaign against the hegemony that the French language and French culture exerted over Germany during the Enlightenment. Johann Grimm and his brother Wilhelm contributed not only their very popular—and very German—*Fairy Tales* (1812) but also philological researches designed to prove the innate superiority of the German language. The philosopher Fichte delivered at Berlin the highly patriotic *Addresses to the German Nation* (1807-08), claiming that German was the *Ursprache*, the fountainhead, the Platonic Idea of language. And the Germans themselves, Fichte continued, were the *Urvolk*, the oldest and greatest of nations, the true Chosen People.

Napoleon began to feel the impact of German nationalism when Austria re-entered the war in 1809. For the first time in its history, the Habsburg monarchy attempted a total mobilization comparable to that decreed by the French Convention in 1793. It called all young men to military service, and anti-French concerts programmed such pieces as Haydn's "Military" Symphony and "The Militiaman's Farewell to His Parents." In spite of the new spirit, however, the Austrians lost the campaign and for the fourth time in a dozen years submitted to a peace dictated by Napoleon. The Treaty of Schönbrunn (1809) stripped them of the Illyrian Provinces and assigned their Polish territory of Galicia to the Grand Duchy of Warsaw. Francis II gave his daughter to Napoleon in marriage, and his defeated land became the unwilling ally of France. Leadership in the German revival passed to Prussia.

The shock of Jena and Tilsit jarred Prussia out of the lethargy that had overtaken her since the death of Frederick the Great in 1786. The new University of Berlin, founded in 1810, attracted Fichte and other prophets of German nationalism. King Frederick William III, though a colorless monarch, brought to power able generals and statesmen. General Scharnhorst headed a group of officers who improved the efficiency and morale of the army. They abolished its inhuman discipline and made all social classes liable to military service, even the previously exempted educated and well-to-do. The top limit of 42,000 soldiers imposed upon Prussia by Napoleon was evaded by the simple device of assigning recruits to the reserve after a fairly brief period of intensive training and then inducting another group of recruits. By 1813, Prussia had more than 150,000 trained men available for combat duty.

The social and administrative reorganization of the Prussian state was inspired by the energetic Stein—Baron vom und zum

CHAPTER XVIII

"And they are like wild-cats." Etching by Goya (see p. 154) from his series on the disasters of the Peninsular War.

Stein, an enlightened aristocrat. Stein conciliated the middle class by granting towns and cities some self-government, although the state retained control over justice and police. To improve the status of the peasantry, he promoted the great edict of October, 1807, at long last abolishing serfdom in Prussia. The edict, however, did not resolve the agrarian problem. It neither broke up the large Junker estates nor provided land for the liberated serf; nor did it terminate the feudal rights of justice exercised by the Junker over his peasants. Stein and the others eliminated only the worst abuses of the Old Régime and left authority where it had traditionally rested—with the king, the army, and the Junkers. The Hohenzollern state was not so much reformed as restored to the tradition of Frederick William I and Frederick the Great.

1812 and Its Aftermath

The event that finally allowed an aroused German nationalism to turn its full force against Napoleon was the French debacle in Russia in 1812. French actions after 1807 soon convinced Tsar Alexander that Napoleon was not keeping the Tilsit bargain and was in fact moving in on Russia's sphere in eastern Europe. French acquisition of the Illyrian Provinces from Austria in 1809 raised the unpleasant prospect of French domination over the Balkans. The simultaneous transfer of Galicia from Austria to the Grand Duchy of Warsaw suggested that this Napoleonic vassal might next absorb the Polish territories of Russia. Meanwhile, Napoleon's insistent efforts to make Russia enforce the Continental System increasingly incensed Alexander. French annexations in northwest Germany completed the disillusionment of the Tsar, for they wiped out the state of Oldenburg, where his uncle was the reigning duke.

For the invasion of Russia, Napoleon assembled the Grand Army of nearly 500,000 men. A large proportion of the soldiers, however, were not Frenchmen but unwilling conscripts in the service of a foreign master. The supply system of the Grand Army broke down almost immediately, and the Russian scorched-earth policy made it very hard to live off the land. As the Grand Army marched eastward, one of Napoleon's aides reported:

There were no inhabitants to be found, no prisoners to be taken, not a single straggler to be picked up. We were in the heart of inhabited Russia and yet we were like a vessel without a compass in the midst of a vast ocean, knowing nothing of what was happening around us.*

Napoleon marched all the way to Moscow without ever managing to strike a knockout blow. He remained in the burning city for five weeks (September-October, 1812) in the vain hope of bringing Tsar Alexander to terms. Russian obduracy and the shortage of supplies forced him to begin the retreat that became a nightmare. Ill-fed and inadequately clothed and sheltered, the retreating soldiers suffered horribly from Russian attacks on stragglers and from the deadly onslaught of "General Winter." Less than a quarter of the Grand Army survived the retreat from Moscow; the rest had been taken prisoner or had died of wounds, starvation, disease, or the cold.

The British had been the first to resist Napoleon successfully, at Trafalgar and on the economic battlefields of the Continental System. Then had come Spanish resistance, then Russian. Now in 1813 almost every nation in Europe joined the final coalition against the French. Napoleon raised a new army, 400,000 strong, but he could not replace so easily the equipment squandered in Russia. In October, 1813, he lost the "Battle of the Nations," fought at Leipzig in Saxony, and by April, 1814, the forces of the coalition occupied Paris. The Emperor abdicated, to begin an honorable exile as ruler of the minute island of Elba not far from the Italian coast.

The statesmen of the victorious coalition gathered in the Congress of Vienna to draw up the terms of peace (see Chapter XIX). The Bourbons returned to France in the person of Louis XVIII, a younger brother of Louis XVI. Realizing that he could not revive the Old Régime intact, the new king issued the Charter of 1814 establishing a constitutional monarchy. The returned émigrés, however, showed no such good sense. They unleashed a new "White Terror" against the Revolution and all its works. Then, on March 1, 1815, Bonaparte pulled his last surprise: he landed on the Mediterranean coast of France.

For a hundred days, from March 20, 1815, when Napoleon re-entered Paris, the French Empire was reborn. Once again the Emperor rallied the French people, this time by promising a truly liberal regime. He never had time, however, to show the sincerity of his promise, for on June 18, 1815, the British under Wellington and the Prussians under Blücher delivered the final blow at Waterloo, near Brussels. Again Napoleon went into exile, to the remote British island of St. Helena in the South Atlantic. There, in 1821, he died of cancer.

---

* A. A. L. de Caulaincourt, *With Napoleon in Russia* (New York, 1935), 62.

CHAPTER XVIII

VI: The Legacy of the Revolution and Napoleon

Bonapartism did not die in 1815 or 1821, any more than the Caesarism of ancient Rome had died on the Ides of March. A Napoleonic legend arose, glossing over the faults and failures of its hero, depicting him as the paladin of liberalism and patriotism, and paving the way for the advent of another Napoleon in 1848. This legend, with all its implications of hero-worship and belligerent nationalism, was one element in the legacy bequeathed by revolutionary and Napoleonic France. A second, and still more powerful, element was the great revolutionary motto—*Liberté, Egalité, Fraternité*. The motto lived on, to inspire later generations of Jacobins in France and elsewhere. And behind the motto was the undeniable fact that the French enjoyed a larger measure of liberty, equality, and fraternity in 1815 than they had ever known before 1789.

True, the Mountain's deputies on mission and Napoleon's censors and prefects gave new force to the old traditions of absolutism and centralization. But the Revolution founded a potent new tradition of liberty. The middle class had won its freedom from obsolete restraints, and Protestants, Jews, and free-thinkers had gained toleration both in France and in French-dominated countries. French institutions in 1815 by no means measured up to the liberal ideals expressed in the Declaration of the Rights of Man. But the ideals had been stated, and the campaign for their further implementation was to form the main theme of French domestic history in the nineteenth century.

"Men are born free and equal in rights," stated Article 1 of the Declaration of the Rights of Man. Realization of the political equality promised here did not begin until the first experiment with universal manhood suffrage in the France of 1848 (see Chapter XIX). From other standpoints, however, the revolutionary and Napoleonic regimes introduced a large measure of equality. They established the principle of equal liability to taxation. They provided a greater degree of economic opportunity for large numbers of the third estate by breaking up the large land holdings of the clergy and nobility and by removing obstacles to the activity of businessmen, big and little. The *Code Napoléon* buried beyond all hope of exhumation the worst legal and social inequalities of the Old Régime. There was a good deal of truth in Napoleon's boast:

Whether as First Consul or as Emperor, I have been the people's king; I have governed for the nation and in its interests, without allowing myself to be turned aside by the outcries or the private interests of certain people.

• • •

The notions of equality that made the Revolution are today an integral part of the government's strength. It is because no one anticipates or suspects any preferential treatment and because it has no interest in showing favouritism that the government inspires no distrust. Public confidence in the justice of its dealings gives it as much authority as the exercise of its power. That is the secret of my success.[*]

The Revolution and Napoleon promoted fraternity in the legal sense by making all Frenchmen equal in the eyes of the law. They advanced fraternity in a broader sense by encouraging nationalism, the feeling of belonging to the great corporate body of Frenchmen who were superior to all other nations. French nationalism had

[*] Quoted in Caulaincourt, *With Napoleon in Russia*, 364, 367-368.

existed long before 1789; Joan of Arc, Henry IV, and Colbert had all been good nationalists in their diverse ways. But it remained for the Convention to formulate a new hyper-nationalistic creed in its decree of August 23, 1793, providing for the total mobilization of the French nation. The Napoleonic Empire then demonstrated how easily nationalism on an unprecedented scale could lead to imperialism of unprecedented magnitude. Revolutionary and Napoleonic France seldom conceived of fraternity in the still broader sense of the brotherhood of all men regardless of their nationality. All men were brothers only so long as they followed the lead of Frenchmen.

Alexis de Tocqueville, the great French student of democracy, wrote a hundred years ago:

The French Revolution was . . . a political revolution, which in its operation and its aspect resembled a religious one. It had every peculiar and characteristic feature of a religious movement; it not only spread to foreign countries, but it was carried thither by preaching and by propaganda.

•   •   •

It roused passions such as the most violent political revolutions had never before excited. . . . This gave to it that aspect of a religious revolution which so terrified its contemporaries, or rather . . . it became a kind of new religion in itself—a religion, imperfect it is true, without a God, without a worship, without a future life, but which nevertheless, like Islam, poured forth its soldiers, its apostles, and its martyrs over the face of the earth.*

Its early adherents were fanatics—Robespierre and the Jacobins. Its later exponents —the men of Thermidor and Brumaire— modified the creed in the interests of practicality and moderation. Even in the hands of Napoleon, however, the Revolution remained a secular religion, demanding observance of political orthodoxy and punishing heretics, as Napoleon punished King Louis Bonaparte of Holland, by the political equivalent of excommunication. And after 1815, as we shall see in the next chapter, the French Revolution continued to pour forth "its soldiers, its apostles, and its martyrs."

-----

* A. de Tocqueville, *The State of Society in France Before the Revolution of 1789*, 3rd ed. (London, 1888), 9-11.

Reading Suggestions
on the French Revolution and Napoleon

General Accounts

C. Brinton, *A Decade of Revolution, 1789-1799* (New York: Harper and Brothers, 1934); and G. Bruun, *Europe and the French Imperium, 1799-1814.* Two of the best volumes in the indispensable "Rise of Modern Europe" series; notable for interpretations and for bibliographies.

L. Gershoy, *The French Revolution and Napoleon* (New York: Appleton-Century-Crofts, 1933). A first-rate textbook.

Special Studies

G. Lefebvre, *The Coming of the French Revolution* (Princeton: Princeton University Press, 1947). The best short study of the causes and early course of the revolution.

A. de Tocqueville, *The Old Régime and the Revolution* (New York, 1856). A famous old account and one still worth reading.

CHAPTER XVIII

J. H. Stewart, *A Documentary Survey of the French Revolution* (New York: The Macmillan Company, 1951). An ably edited collection of constitutional texts and other source materials.

H. A. Taine, *The Ancient Régime* (New York: Henry Holt & Co., 1876) and *The French Revolution* (New York: Henry Holt & Co., 1878-1887); F. V. A. Aulard, *The French Revolution, A Political History* (New York: Charles Scribner's Sons, 1910); A. Mathiez, *The French Revolution* (New York: Alfred A. Knopf, Inc., 1928) and *After Robespierre: The Thermidorean Reaction* (New York: Alfred A. Knopf, Inc., 1931). These are all classic accounts—Taine from the conservative standpoint, Aulard from the middle of the road, and Mathiez from the Left.

G. Salvemini, *The French Revolution, 1788-1792* (New York: Henry Holt & Co., 1954). A detailed and perceptive account of the early revolution.

C. Brinton, *The Jacobins* (New York: The Macmillan Company, 1930). An instructive description and analysis.

R. R. Palmer, *Twelve Who Ruled* (Princeton: Princeton University Press, 1941). Good brief studies of the members of the Committee of Public Safety.

J. M. Thompson, *Robespierre and the French Revolution* (New York: The Macmillan Company, 1953. Teach Yourself History Series). Good short account by a leading English writer on the revolution.

H. A. L. Fisher, *Napoleon* (New York: Oxford University Press, 1945. Home University Library); and F. M. Kircheisen, *Napoleon* (New York: Harcourt, Brace & Co., 1932). Two standard biographies, the one (Fisher) brief; the other, more detailed.

R. M. Johnston, ed., *The Corsican* (Boston: Houghton Mifflin Company, 1910); and J. M. Thompson, ed., *Napoleon Self-Revealed* (Boston: Houghton Mifflin Company, 1934). Two fascinating attempts to reveal Napoleon's career and character through his own words.

F. M. H. Markham, *Napoleon and the Awakening of Europe* (New York: The Macmillan Company, 1954. Teach Yourself History Series). An introductory manual.

A. A. L. de Caulaincourt, *With Napoleon in Russia* (New York: William Morrow & Co., 1935). Vivid eye-witness account by one of Bonaparte's chief aides.

J. Seeley, *The Life and Times of Stein: Germany and Prussia in the Napoleonic Age* (Boston: Roberts, 1879). Old and still worth reading.

Historical Fiction

A. France, *The Gods Are Athirst* (New York: Roy, 1953). Far and away the best fictional treatment of the French Revolution.

V. Hugo, *'93* (Boston: H. L. Page, no date). The struggles of revolutionary and counter-revolutionary forces in 1793, as seen by the great French Romantic writer.

L. Tolstoy, *War and Peace* (many editions). The justly famous long novel about Napoleon's Russian campaign.

Revolution and Counter-Revolution 1815-1850

CHAPTER XIX

Romantic painting. Delacroix, "The Massacre at Scio," 1824.

I: Introduction

THE HISTORY of the western world during the half-century or so after Napoleon's downfall is crammed with major events. In the period between 1815 and 1870 the industrial revolution came of age, modern doctrines of socialism were born, Darwin initiated his great scientific revolution, and realistic authors and artists worked a great change in culture. In politics, during the same period, Great Britain and the United States pushed steadily ahead toward the practical establishment of democracy, and Italy and Germany achieved their national unification. All these major developments, however, though they were well under way by the middle years of the nineteenth century, reached a climax around 1870 or soon thereafter. For this chronological reason, and also for clarity of presentation, we shall postpone detailed treatment of these developments to later chapters—the impact of industrialism to Chapter XX, the growth of the Atlantic democracies to Chapter XXI, the unification of Italy and Germany to Chapters XXI and XXII, and the intellectual revolution of Darwin and the realists to Chapter XXIII. In this chapter, we shall concentrate on the inter-

147

action of culture and politics, particularly in continental Europe, during the generation immediately following 1815.

One great thread through this period of European history is suggested by the terms "reaction" and "counter-revolution." By 1815, Europe was reacting strongly both against the French Revolution, which had made Napoleon possible, and against the Enlightenment, which had made the Revolution possible. The reaction against the Enlightenment took the form of the Romantic movement. Romantic writers and artists protested against the omnipotent reason of the eighteenth century and on behalf of faith, emotion, tradition, and the other values that the Age of Reason had spurned. The political counter-revolution was very evident at the Congress of Vienna in 1814-1815, where the leaders of the last coalition against Napoleon re-established the European balance of power and repudiated the revolutionary principles that had shattered the eighteenth-century balance. Reason and natural law, in the judgment both of political leaders and of many Romantics, had led not to progress but to the Reign of Terror and to Napoleonic war and imperialism.

But the spirit of 1789 also persisted after 1815. The second great thread through the post-Napoleonic period is the persistence of revolution. Despite the ascendancy of counter-revolutionary forces in 1815, and despite the Romantic appeal to tradition, liberal and nationalistic ideas still flourished. They were to produce new outbreaks of revolution—in the 1820's, in 1830, and in 1848. None of these outbreaks was as formidable as the great upheaval of 1789, but all of them disturbed the status quo to some degree.

II: The Romantic Protest

The Romantic protest against reason reached its full force in the early decades of the nineteenth century; the period 1800-1830 is usually tagged "Romantic." Actually, as we have seen in Chapter XVII, the reaction against the Enlightenment, the reaction that would produce the Romantic movement, had set in soon after 1750. In religion, Wesley and the Pietists were challenging the deism of the *philosophes;* Rousseau proclaimed conscience, not reason, the "true guide of man"; Hume appealed to the "sentiments and affections" of men, not to their reason; and Kant exalted idealism and the eternal verities. Then in 1790 Edmund Burke, the great conservative political philosopher of Romanticism, neatly turned against the *philosophes* their favorite appeal to the simple mathematical laws of Newtonian science. Natural rights, he explained,

... entering into common life, like rays of light which pierce into a dense medium, are, by the laws of nature, refracted from their straight line. Indeed in the gross and complicated mass of human passions and concerns, the primitive rights of men undergo such a variety of refractions and reflections, that it becomes absurd to talk of them as if they continued in the simplicity of their original direction. The nature of man is intricate; the objects of society are of the greatest possible complexity. . . .*

---

* *Reflections on the Revolution in France,* Everyman ed. (New York, 1910), 59.

148

CHAPTER XIX

Literature:
The Revolt against Reason

The Romantic protest may be followed most readily in literature. By the mid-eighteenth century, the novel of sentiment and duty was coming into its own in England and France, with Richardson's *Clarissa* and Rousseau's *Nouvelle Héloïse*. In the 1770's, the German literary world experienced a movement called *Sturm und Drang* ("Storm and Stress") after a minor play by an obscure dramatist. The hero of the play, totally incapable of settling down, flees Europe to fight in the American Revolution:

Have been everything. Became a day-labourer to be something. Lived on the Alps, pastured goats, lay day and night under the boundless vault of the heavens, cooled by the winds, burning with an inner fire. Nowhere rest, nowhere repose. See, thus I am glutted by impulse and power, and work it out of me. I am going to take part in this campaign as a volunteer; there I can expand my soul, and if they do me the favour to shoot me down,—all the better.[*]

The restlessness and self-pity of the *Sturm und Drang* were particularly evident in the *Sorrows of Young Werther*, an immensely popular and lugubrious short novel by the youthful Goethe. No less a realist than Napoleon claimed to have read it seven times, weeping copiously each time at the hero's suicide.

Goethe himself (1749-1832), whose long and productive career extended right through the Romantic era, cannot be labeled simply Romantic. In some respects, Goethe was a thoroughly eighteenth-century sort of intellectual, seriously interested in natural science, happily settled in Weimar at the enlightened court of a small German

state, and almost always rather aloof from such burning issues of the day as the French Revolution and Napoleon. Yet Romantic values lie at the very heart of his greatest work—many would say the greatest work in the German language—*Faust*. Begun when Goethe was in his twenties, and finished only when he was eighty, this long poetic drama was less a play in the conventional sense than a philosophical commentary on the main currents of European thought. According to the traditional legend, the aged Faust, weary of book learning and pining for eternal youth, sold his soul to the Devil, received back the enjoyment of his youth for an allotted time, and then, terror-stricken, went to the everlasting fires. Goethe transformed the legend. Faust does indeed find intellectual pursuits disillusioning and profitless:

> . . . Grey is all theory,
> The golden tree of life is green![*]

Faust makes his infernal compact, but is ultimately saved through his realization that he must sacrifice selfish concerns to the welfare of others. After draining swamps for the benefit of humanity, he dies repentant and assured of salvation. A drama of man's sinning, striving, and redemption, Goethe's *Faust* has been called "the last great poem of the Middle Ages."

This return to the Middle Ages is a striking feature of the whole Romantic movement, as we shall see; for the moment, though, we shall continue to observe the Romantic protest against reason. All over Europe in the early 1800's Romantic writers caught the mood of the *Sturm und Drang* and rebelled against the "classical spirit." They decried what seemed to them the stilted and artificial verses of Racine and Pope. They praised the color and the vigor of the Bible, Homer, and Shakespeare, and

---

[*] Klinger, *Sturm und Drang*, quoted in Kuno Francke, *A History of German Literature as Determined by Social Forces*, 4th ed. (New York, 1931), 309.

[*] *Faust*, Everyman ed. (New York, 1925), 61.

issued impassioned declarations of literary independence, calls for a new literary renaissance. In France, the home of the "classical spirit," the revolt gathered momentum slowly and finally reached full force in the preface that Victor Hugo (1802-1885) wrote for his historical drama, *Cromwell*, in 1827. Hugo believed ardently in the Romantic doctrine of the variety and intricacy of man and nature. The perceptive writer, he asserted,

... will realize that not everything in creation ... is beautiful, that the ugly exists alongside the beautiful, the deformed next to the graceful, the grotesque behind the sublime, the evil with the good, the shadow with the light. [He] will wonder if it is proper for man to correct the work of God, if a mutilated nature will be more beautiful. ... [He] will try to follow nature, to mingle in his writings the shadow and the light, the grotesque and the sublime —in other words, the body and the soul, the animal and the spirit.*

The grotesque, ugly, and deformed are all present in Hugo's vivid novel of fifteenth-century life, *Notre Dame de Paris* (1831), for this is the story of Quasimodo, "the hunchback of Notre Dame."

In England, the Romantic protest had sounded loudly forth a generation earlier in *Lyrical Ballads* (1798), by Wordsworth and his friend Coleridge. There were of course other great Romantic poets in England— Shelley, Keats, Byron—but Wordsworth (1770-1850) and Coleridge (1772-1834) pressed farthest in their reaction against classicism and rationalism. *Lyrical Ballads* sought to reach an audience far larger than the usual rather high-brow readers of verse. As Wordsworth declared in his preface to the volume, *Lyrical Ballads* were an experiment, couched in "the language of conversation in the middle and lower classes of society," and aiming at "a natural delinea-

tion of human passions, human characters, and human incidents." Coleridge later elaborated on the purpose of *Lyrical Ballads:*

In the present age the poet ... seems to propose to himself as his main object ... new and striking images; with incidents that interest the affections or excite the curiosity. Both his characters and his descriptions he renders, as much as possible, specific and individual, even to a degree of portraiture. In his diction and metre, on the other hand, he is comparatively careless.*

The two poets accomplished their purpose. To *Lyrical Ballads* Coleridge contributed *The Rime of the Ancient Mariner*, a supernatural tale of the curse afflicting a sailor who slays an albatross. Still more famous are the lines beginning another poem by Coleridge:

In Xanadu did Kubla Khan
    A stately pleasure-dome decree;
Where Alph, the sacred river ran,
    Through caverns measureless to man
        Down to a sunless sea.†

Among ancient mariners and sunless seas we are far indeed from the optimistic universe of the *philosophes*.

Wordsworth was less concerned than Coleridge with the exotic and the supernatural, but he, too, rejected the Enlightenment. At times he was downright anti-intellectual:

Up! up! my Friend, and quit your books;
Or surely you'll grow double:
Up! up! my Friend, and clear your looks;
Why all this toil and trouble?

. . .

Come forth into the light of things,
Let Nature be you teacher.

She has a world of ready wealth,
Our minds and hearts to bless—
Spontaneous wisdom breathed by health,
Truth breathed by cheerfulness.

---

* *Préface de Cromwell*, M. Souriau, ed. (Paris, n.d.), 191. Our translation.

* S. T. Coleridge, *Biographia Literaria*, Everyman ed. (New York, 1908), 173.
    † *Kubla Khan*, lines 1-5.

One impulse from a vernal wood
May teach you more of man,
Of moral evil and of good,
Than all the sages can.

Sweet is the lore which Nature brings;
Our meddling intellect
Mis-shapes the beauteous forms of things:—
We murder to dissect.

Enough of Science and of Art;
Close up those barren leaves;
Come forth, and bring with you a heart
That watches and receives.*

These verses make Wordsworth's point quite clear, but they scarcely do full justice to the quality of his poetic talent or to the depth of his mystical feeling about Nature. To experience Wordsworth at his best, one should read the long autobiographical poem, *The Prelude*. Here is a brief passage from it that suggests his essential attitude toward the mystery of existence:

Dust as we are, the immortal spirit grows
Like harmony in music; there is a dark
Inscrutable workmanship that reconciles
Discordant elements, makes them cling
    together
In one society.†

So, in place of the light shed by Newton's laws Wordsworth found "a dark inscrutable workmanship," and in place of the *philosophes'* belief in the perfectibility of man through mortal reason he put his faith in the "immortal spirit" of the individual.

Literature:
The Return to the Past

It may seem a very long leap indeed from the un-Newtonian universe of Wordsworth to the Romantics' enthusiasm for the Middle Ages in general and for the earlier history of their own nations in particular.

* *The Tables Turned,* from *Lyrical Ballads,* lines 1-4, 15-32.
† *The Prelude,* Bk. I, lines 340-344.

And yet nationalism at bottom is an irrational, almost mystical, force that in effect "reconciles discordant elements, makes them cling together in one society." But to return to historical facts: the heightened sense of nationalism evident almost everywhere in Europe by 1815 was in part a matter of simple political self-preservation. The preceding chapter has shown how the various nations rallied against the aggressive nationalism of France. In the crisis of the Napoleonic wars the Spaniards naturally became more aware of their Spanish heritage, the Germans of their Germanic one, and so on. Actually, however, the Romantic return to the past, though intensified by the French Revolution and Napoleon, had begun before 1789 as part of the general retreat from the Enlightenment. The *philosophes* hated the Middle Ages, especially the medieval preoccupation with religion. Naturally the forerunners of the Romantic movement tended to cherish what the *philosophes* so detested.

A good case history of these developments is provided by the German writer, Herder (1744-1803), and his disciples. Herder advanced a theory of cultural nationalism. Each separate nation, he argued, like any individual organism, had its own distinct personality and its own pattern of growth. The surest measure of a nation's growth was its literature—poetry in the nation's youth, prose in its maturity. Stimulated by Herder, students of medieval German literature collected popular ballads, and the Grimms compiled their *Fairy Tales*. In 1782, the first complete text of the *Nibelungenlied* was published. This was a heroic saga of the nation's youth that had been much admired in the later Middle Ages only to be forgotten in succeeding centuries.

By putting a new value on the German literature of the past, Herder helped to free the German literature of his own day from its bondage to French culture. Herder, however, was no narrow nationalist; indeed he called excessive national pride "the greatest folly" and asserted that the cultivated man should know cultures other than his own. So Herder also helped to loose the flood of translations that poured over Germany about 1800—translations of Shakespeare, of *Don Quixote*, of Spanish and Portuguese poetry, even of works in Sanskrit.

Some German Romantics, stirred by the patriotic revival after Jena and Tilsit, carried national enthusiasm to an extreme that Herder would have deplored. Thus Fichte and the Grimms claimed pre-eminence for the German language (see Chapter XVIII). The dramatist Kleist (1777-1811), in his *Battle of Arminius*, made the most of his chance to boast of the prowess of the ancient Germans in defeating the Roman legions in 9 A.D. For the Romantic extremists the mere fact of being German appeared to be a cardinal virtue. These extremists, however, were the exceptions. Many German writers struck Herder's happy balance between national and cosmopolitan interests. Goethe, for example, turned to the German Middle Ages for his *Faust*, yet he also admired other cultures and prided himself on being a good European, not simply a German.

Many nations experienced a notable revival of older literature during the Romantic period. In Britain, Sir Walter Scott (1771-1832) assisted in collecting the vigorous folk ballads of the Middle Ages and went on to write more than thirty widely popular historical novels, of which *Ivanhoe*, set in the days of Richard the Lionhearted, is a good sample. France had Victor Hugo and *Notre Dame de Paris*. And Russia had her great poet, Pushkin (1799-1837), who found literary subjects in the "Time of Troubles," two hundred years back in Russia's history. Pushkin virtually created modern Russian literature. Abandoning the custom of borrowing from the western tongues and from the archaic Slavonic of the Orthodox Church, he wrote the first classic works in the national language.

Music

Musicians, too, exploited the popular ballads and legends of the national past. To achieve color and drama, composers of operas and songs turned frequently to Shakespeare's plays, Scott's novels, and the poems of Goethe and Pushkin. In short, literature and music often followed parallel paths of development during the Romantic era. But the parallel was never complete. Romantic musicians scarcely revolted against their great eighteenth-century predecessors in the sense that Romantic poets were revolting against the *philosophes*. Rather, Romantic music evolved peacefully out of the older classical school.

The composer who played the commanding part in this evolution was Beethoven (1770-1827), a Fleming by ancestry and a Viennese by adoption. Whereas Coleridge had said that the Romantic artist might be careless in matters of diction and meter, Beethoven showed a classical concern for the forms and techniques that were the musical counterparts of diction and meter. Yet he also reshaped the great tradition that he inherited from Bach, Haydn, and Mozart. For example, where Mozart and Haydn had used the courtly minuet for the third movement in a symphony, Beethoven introduced the more plebeian and rollicking *scherzo*. Where earlier composers had indicated the tempo with a simple *allegro* (fast) or *andante* (slow), Beethoven added such Romantic designations as *appassionato* and even "Strife between Head and Heart." His compositions sometimes suggest vigorous conflicts and emotions: witness the dramatic opening notes of the famous Fifth Symphony, often compared to the rappings of fate. In good Romantic fashion, Beethoven drew inspiration from nature, as in the "Pastoral Symphony," with its musical thunderstorm and peaceful forest, complete with bird songs. Finally, Beethoven was quick to exploit the enormous range and versatility of the great instrument first perfected during his lifetime, the piano.

To the literature of instrumental music Beethoven himself contributed many sonatas, string trios and quartets, concertos, and symphonies. By the time of his death in 1827, composers of instrumental music were exploring several significant avenues of development. One avenue led to miniature, often delicate, pieces for the piano. Such were the appropriately named impromptus and *moments musicaux* of Beethoven's Viennese contemporary, Franz Schubert (1797-1826); and such were the innumerable waltzes, nocturnes, préludes, mazurkas, and études of the half-French, half-Polish Chopin (1810-1849).

In striking contrast, another, and historically more important, avenue of development led to ambitious orchestral works of heroic dimensions. The pioneer was the Frenchman Berlioz (1803-1869), who seemed to share Victor Hugo's delight in the grotesque. Berlioz actually projected a utopian orchestra of 465 pieces, including 120 violins, 37 double-basses, and 30 each of pianos and harps. Although this gargantuan scheme remained on paper, Berlioz was virtually the first composer to utilize the full complement of instruments, especially winds and percussion, that constitute the modern orchestra. His experiments with the theatrical possibilities of the orchestra culminated in one of the great landmarks in musical history, the aptly titled "Fantastic Symphony" (1830).

Music for the human voice reflected both the increased enthusiasm for instruments and the general Romantic nostalgia for the past. In composing songs and arias, Romantic musicians devoted as much skill to the piano or orchestral accompaniment as to the voice part itself. Franz Schubert made a fine art of blending voice and piano in more than six hundred exquisite *Lieder* (songs), seventy of them musical settings of poems by Goethe. Meantime, in Germany Von Weber (1786-1826) was striving to create a truly national opera. He took an old German legend as the libretto for his opera, *Der Freischütz* ("The Freeshooter," 1820), which ran the good Romantic gamut of an enchanted forest, a magic bullet, and an innocent maiden outwitting the Devil. For the choruses and marches of *Der Freischütz* he employed many folk-like melodies. Weber was by no means the only serious composer to utilize national folk tunes. The Russian Glinka (1804-1857) cast aside the Italian influences that had previously dominated the secular music of his country. He based his opera, *Russlan and Ludmilla* (1842), on a poem by Pushkin and embellished it with dances and choruses derived from the native music of Russia's Asiatic provinces.

The Arts

In the fine arts, the forces of Romanticism gained no such triumph as they won in literature and music. The virtual dictator of European painting during the first two decades of the nineteenth century was the French neoclassicist, David (1748-1825). The official painter of the French Jacobins, David depicted dramatic contemporary events like the Tennis-Court Oath. He generally used traditional techniques: in the "Tennis-Court Oath," for example, he first drew the deputies naked, as if they were ancient athletes, and later painted in their clothes.

Romantic painting. Constable, "Dedham Mill," 1820.

More direct and powerful—and much closer to the Romantic temper—were the works of the great Spanish painter, Goya (1746-1828). No one could have any illusions about Spanish royalty after looking at Goya's revealing portraits of the enlightened Charles III (see p. 74) and his worthless successors. After viewing Goya's "Disasters of War," no one could doubt that Napoleon's forces perpetrated horrors in the Peninsular War (see p. 141). Goya is said to have made the sketches for these etchings in the very blood of the executed Spanish patriots whose agonies he was portraying. The outraged patriotism and frightening immediacy of Goya, however, attracted few imitators. Here is one person to whom the trite phrase "inimitable genius" may be justly applied.

The two men responsible for establishing a Romantic school of painting were Constable and Delacroix. The lovely paintings of the English landscape by Constable (1776-1837) made nature artistically respectable once more. Delacroix (1799-1863), a Frenchman, insisted that color and light mattered more than classical purity of line; young painters, therefore, should study the flamboyant canvases of Rubens, whom David had excommunicated from the ranks of orthodox artists. The purpose of art was "not to imitate nature but to strike the imagination." Delacroix proceeded to strike the imagination of his contemporaries by painting "The Massacre of Scio" (1824) (see p. 146), a bloody episode in the Greek War of Independence (see below, p. 169). Today the picture seems more conventional and less moving

CHAPTER XIX

Neoclassical architecture. Girard College, Philadelphia, 1833-1847.

than Goya's etchings of the Peninsular War. At the time, however, it was denounced as "barbarous, drunken, delirious"—the "massacre of painting." French painters were now divided into opposing schools: the Romantic followers of Delacroix, and the still powerful disciples of David.

In early nineteenth-century architecture, the contrasting schools were the neoclassical and the neo-Gothic. As the century opened, the vogue for Roman buildings introduced by the French Revolution reached its height in Napoleon's *Arc de Triomphe* and in the monumental Paris Church of the Madeleine. The latter was actually copied from a Roman temple, the *Maison Carrée* ("square house") at Nîmes in France. In America, Thomas Jefferson pronounced the *Maison Carrée* the perfect example of "cubical" architecture and adapted it to secular purposes for the Virginia Capitol at Richmond. The versatile Jefferson was a gifted neoclassical architect. Near Charlottesville, he built himself a handsome country residence and in good American style equipped it with all manner

of ingenious gadgets. At Charlottesville, he designed for the University of Virginia a distinguished group of academic buildings centered around a circular library, which Jefferson patterned after the Roman Pantheon (the perfect example of "spherical" architecture). From the library he extended two rows of smaller buildings, each recalling a different Roman temple, and interconnected by colonnades.

In Britain, neoclassical architecture still flourished, but it met competition from the Gothic revival, stimulated partly by the wealth of medieval architectural lore in Scott's novels, partly by the revival of religion, and partly by buildings like Fonthill Abbey. Fonthill Abbey was begun in 1797 at the order of an eccentric millionaire. It consisted largely of immensely high and immensely long corridors and, though it cost £500,000, it was so shoddily built that the central tower collapsed after twenty-five years. Undeterred, British architects applied the Gothic manner to every kind of building after 1820, not only to churches and the Houses of Parliament, but also to

Gothic revival in architecture. The Houses of Parliament, London.

railway stations, elaborate villas, and modest cottages. The high vaulting, arched windows, and general "gloomth" of Gothic were singularly inappropriate to residential construction. And the fad for "medieval" furniture, bristling with spikes and ornamentation, prompted one critic to warn that the occupant of a neo-Gothic room would be lucky if he were not "wounded by some of its minutiae."

The Gothic revival was not an unmitigated artistic calamity. It fostered the preservation and restoration of medieval masterpieces half ruined by centuries of neglect. The British Houses of Parliament

demonstrated a century ago—and college buildings sometimes demonstrate today—that a skilled architect could adapt the old style to new demands successfully and tastefully. The Gothic revival, finally, was a really spectacular victory of Romantic longing over the practical outlook that dominated so much of nineteenth-century life.

Religion and Philosophy

Neo-Gothic architecture was one sign of the religious revival that accompanied the Romantic enthusiasm for the

156

Middle Ages. Another sign appeared in 1814 with the pope's re-establishment of the Jesuits, that symbol of everything the Enlightenment had opposed. Both the materialism of Holbach and the milder anti-clericalism of Voltaire horrified most Romantics. An outspoken atheist like Shelley was an isolated exception to the general rule. In Germany, Catholicism gained many converts among Romantic writers, and in England Wordsworth and Coleridge vigorously defended the established Church. Everything impels us to religious belief, Coleridge declared:

Nature excites and recalls it, as by a perpetual revelation. Our feelings almost necessitate it; and the law of conscience peremptorily commands it.*

Nature, feelings, and conscience were the mainsprings of Romantic religious thought. They led Coleridge to state

... that the scheme of Christianity, as taught in the liturgy and homilies of our Church, though not discoverable by human reason, is yet in accordance with it; that link follows link by necessary consequence; that Religion passes out of the ken of Reason only where the eye of Reason has reached its own horizon; and that Faith is then but its continuation. . . .†

This credo reads almost as though it were restating Kant's moral philosophy; and indeed Coleridge had studied the writings of Kant and his disciples.

The greatest of Kant's disciples, and the most characteristically Romantic philosopher, was Hegel (1770-1831), a professor at the University of Berlin. Like his master, Hegel attacked the tendency of the Enlightenment to see in human nature and human history only what first met the eye. He exalted the moral and ethical faculties of man:

This is the seal of the absolute and sublime destiny of man—that he knows what is good and

* *Biographia Literaria,* Everyman ed., 106.
† *Ibid.,* 334.

what is evil; that his Destiny *is* his every ability to will either good or evil. . . .*

According to Hegel, the history of mankind, properly understood, was the history of human efforts to will good, and this in turn was the unfolding of God's plan for the world. Good, he stated,

. . . is God. God governs the world; the actual working of his government—the carrying out of his plan—is the History of the World.†

For Hegel, history was a *dialectical* process, that is, a series of conflicts. The two elements in the conflict were the *thesis,* the established order of life, and the *antithesis,* the challenge to the old order. Out of the struggle of thesis and antithesis emerged the *synthesis,* no mere compromise between the two but a new and better way, another step forward in man's slow progression toward the best of all possible worlds. The synthesis, in turn, broke down; a new thesis and antithesis became locked in conflict; the dialectic produced another synthesis—and so on.

The death throes of the Roman Republic gave Hegel an illustration of the dialectic at work. The thesis was represented by the decadent republic, the antithesis by oriental despotism, and the synthesis by the Caesarism of the early Roman Empire. Hegel explained that "This important change must not be regarded as a thing of chance; it was *necessary*," a part of God's grand design. Julius Caesar himself Hegel called a "hero," one of the few "world-historical individuals" who "had an insight into the requirements of the time" and who knew "what was ripe for development." **

This dialectical philosophy of history was the most original and influential element in Hegel's thought, the antecedent of the dia-

* *The Philosophy of History,* J. Sibree, trans. (New York, 1944), 34.
† *Ibid,* 36.
** *Ibid.,* 311, 30.

lectical materialism of Karl Marx (see Chapter XX). It is difficult for citizens of a twentieth-century democracy to appreciate that Hegel was once even more famous as a liberal idealist. His emphasis on duty, his choice of Alexander the Great, Caesar, and Napoleon as "world-historical" heroes, his assertion that the state "existed for its own sake"—all this suggests a direct link between Hegel and authoritarianism. In fairness, however, it should be pointed out that Hegel himself seems to have foreseen the final political synthesis not in a brutal police state but in a liberalized Prussian monarchy.

Romanticism Evaluated

Thus Hegel, too, believed in the perfectibility of man, though he suggested that the process would be more laborious than a *philosophe* like Condorcet had ever im-
agined. The Romantics by no means disowned all the favorite beliefs of the Enlightenment. Not only a modified doctrine of progress but also eighteenth-century cosmopolitanism lived on in the Romantic era. Homer, Cervantes, Shakespeare, and Scott all won wide and appreciative audiences in many countries. The very greatest figures of the age, Beethoven and Goethe, deserve to be called citizens of the world.

On balance however, the disparities between Romanticism and the Enlightenment clearly outnumber the similarities. By the early 1800's the Newtonian world-machine had faded out of sight. In its place stood the neo-Gothic world of religious mystery, the Hegelian world of dialectic, and the Wordsworthian world of impulses from the vernal wood. The greatest legacy of Romanticism was its insistence that society was more than a branch of physics and the individual man more than a cog in a world-machine.

III: The Conservative Outlook and the Vienna Settlement

Romanticism exerted a decidedly complex influence upon the course of politics. Its individualism ultimately renewed the strength of liberalism, and its nationalism ultimately grew into a revolutionary force. The immediate political impact of Romanticism, however, was not so much liberal and nationalistic as conservative and counter-revolutionary. Of the English Romantics only Byron and Shelley adhered to the radical political doctrines of the Enlightenment. Wordsworth and Coleridge, for example, soon lost their youthful zeal for Liberty, Equality, and Fraternity.

Burke and Metternich

The new conservative political outlook owed much to the writing of Edmund Burke (1729-1797). As the passage quoted earlier in this chapter shows, Burke could not stomach the simple and optimistic view of human nature taken by the *philosophes*: "The nature of man is intricate; the objects of society are of the greatest possible complexity." Burke, therefore, revered the institutions that had grown up over the long course of human history. He did not, however, believe that these institutions were petrified or changeless; they had developed gradually in the past, they would develop gradually in the future. Political change was possible but difficult, Burke concluded. Reforms had to be introduced so that "the useful parts of the old establishment" might be preserved; they had to be managed slowly and "with circumspection and caution"—in a word, conservatively.

Burke approved of the American Revolution. In his view, it was not so much a revolution as a reaffirmation of the glorious tradition of 1688 and at heart a conservative undertaking. The same reasoning drove Burke to violent condemnation in his *Reflections on the Revolution in France* (1790). The men of 1789 destroyed everything, good, bad, and indifferent. Rage and frenzy, he predicted, "will pull down more in half an hour, than prudence, deliberation and foresight can build up in a hundred years." [*] Thereby the social contract itself is jeopardized. "Society is indeed a contract," Burke stated, but he did not mean quite what Rousseau had meant:

The state ought not to be considered as nothing better than a partnership agreement in a trade of pepper and coffee, calico or tobacco, or some such other low concern, to be taken up for a little temporary interest, and to be dissolved by the fancy of the parties. It is to be looked on with other reverence; because it is not a partnership in things subservient only to the gross animal existence of a temporary and perishable nature. It is a partnership in all science; a partnership in all art; a partnership in every virtue, and in all perfection. As the ends of such a partnership cannot be obtained in many generations, it becomes a partnership not only between those who are living, but between those who are living, those who are dead, and those who are to be born.[†]

The force of tradition bore heavily upon the politics of post-Napoleonic Europe. For this was the Age of Metternich—Prince

Clement Wenceslas Lothair Népomucène Metternich (1773-1859), Austrian foreign minister from 1809 to 1848, and the chief figure in European diplomacy during most of his long career. Handsome and dashing, an aristocrat through and through, Metternich possessed immense self-confidence. "Error," he observed in the twilight of his career, "has never approached my mind."

Metternich shared Burke's reverence for the past:

Man cannot make a constitution properly speaking: that is made only by time.... Let people write as much as they like—and the less will always be the better—and yet you will have nothing in your hand but a sheet of paper. England alone has a Constitution, of which the Magna Carta is but a subordinate element. The English Constitution is the work of centuries. ... Social order ever progresses in this way; it cannot be otherwise, since it is the law of nature.[*]

Metternich's conservatism also proceeded from his own political experiences. His family, living in the German Rhineland, had suffered directly from the French Revolution. He served a state which had felt the disruptive effects of Joseph II's over-ambitious enlightenment and which had undergone many humiliations at the hands of French armies. These misfortunes convinced Metternich that the Austrian Empire was particularly susceptible to injury by the liberal and nationalistic energies released by the Enlightenment and the Revolution. Tradition was the cement that held together the differing parts of the Habsburg realm.

The Congress of Vienna

In 1814 and 1815, Metternich was host to the Congress of Vienna, which ap-

---

[*] *Reflections*, Everyman ed., 164.
[†] *Ibid.*, 93.

[*] *Memoirs of Prince Metternich, 1815-1829*, Prince Richard Metternich, ed. (New York, 1881), III, 366.

The statesmen of Europe at the Congress of Vienna, 1814-1815. Metternich is standing prominently at left front, Wellington at extreme left. Talleyrand is seated at right with his arm resting on the table.

proached the great task of rebuilding Europe with truly conservative deliberateness. For the larger part of a year, the diplomats indulged to the full in balls and banquets, concerts and hunting parties. "Congress dances," remarked an observer, "but it does not march." Actually, the brilliant social life served the very businesslike purpose of distracting the lesser fry while the important diplomats settled things in small, private conferences.

Four men made most of the major decisions at Vienna—Metternich, Castlereagh, Talleyrand, and Tsar Alexander I. Viscount Castlereagh, the British foreign minister, shared the conservative outlook of Metternich. He was less concerned with punishing the French for their past sins than with preventing the appearance of new Robespierres and Bonapartes. Castlereagh announced that he went to Vienna "not to collect tro-

phies, but to bring the world back to peaceful habits."

Talleyrand, the foreign minister of Louis XVIII of France, scored at Vienna the greatest success of his long career. Originally a money-minded bishop of the Old Régime, he had in succession rallied to the Revolution in 1789, supported the Civil Constitution of the Clergy (one of the very few bishops to do so), served as Napoleon's foreign minister, and intrigued against the Emperor during the years after Tilsit. Now he was serving the restored Bourbon king, and in his old age he was later to take an important part in the Revolution of 1830. This supremely adaptable diplomat soon maneuvered himself into the inner circle at Vienna, and the representatives of the victorious powers accepted the emissary of defeated France as their equal. Talleyrand was particularly adept in exploiting his

CHAPTER XIX

nuisance value—acting as the spokesman of lesser diplomats who resented being shoved aside, and making the most of the differences that inevitably appeared among the victors.

To these differences Alexander I contributed greatly. Metternich actually called the Tsar a Jacobin, for he had the reputation of being very enlightened and had already attempted liberal reforms in Russia (for details, see p. 170). By 1814, however, the liberalism of Alexander was giving way to a thoroughly Romantic enthusiasm for religion. For hours on end, the Tsar prayed and read the Bible in the company of Baroness von Krüdener, an ardent disciple of the pietistic Moravian Brethren (see Chapter XVII), who informed him that he was the "living preface of the sacred history which is to regenerate the world." The Tsar and the Baroness jointly prepared a "Holy Alliance" whereby all states would regenerate their policies by following literally the teachings of Christ.

In the first months at Vienna it was not Alexander's Romantic scheme of a Holy Alliance but rather his Polish policy that nearly disrupted the Congress. He proposed a partial restoration of pre-partition Poland, with himself as its monarch. Austria and Prussia would lose the Polish lands they had grabbed late in the preceding century. Alexander won the support of Prussia by backing her demands for the annexation of Saxony, whose king had remained loyal to Napoleon. Metternich, however, did not want Austria's traditional Prussian rival to make such a substantial gain. Moreover, both Metternich and Castlereagh disliked the prospect of a large, Russian-dominated Poland.

The dispute over Saxony and Poland gave Talleyrand a magnificent chance to fish in troubled waters. Thus it was that in January, 1815, the representative of defeated France joined Metternich and Castlereagh in threatening both Prussia and Russia with war unless they moderated their demands. The threat produced an immediate settlement of the controversy. Alexander obtained Poland but agreed to reduce its size and allow Prussia and Austria to keep part of their loot from the partitions. Prussia took about half of Saxony; the King of Saxony retained the balance.

Once the Saxon-Polish question was out of the way, the Congress achieved a fairly amicable resolution of the other important dynastic and territorial questions. According to the doctrine that Talleyrand christened "the sacred principle of legitimacy," thrones and frontiers were to be re-established as they had existed in 1789. In practice, however, legitimacy was ignored almost as often as it was enforced. The diplomats at Vienna were statesmen enough to realize that they could not undo all the changes worked by the Revolution and Napoleon. Hence, although they restored Bourbon dynasties to the thrones of France, Spain, and Naples in the name of legitimacy, they did not attempt to revive all the hundreds of German states that had vanished since 1789.

In Germany, the Congress provided for thirty-nine states, loosely grouped together in a confederation. The German Confederation came close to reincarnating the impotent Holy Roman Empire; its chief organ, the diet, was to be a council of diplomats from sovereign states rather than a representative national assembly. Prussia and Austria obtained important new territories at Vienna. Prussia, in addition to her Saxon annexation, expanded the old scattered Hohenzollern lands in western Germany into the imposing new Rhine Province. Austria lost Belgium, which was incorporated into the Kingdom of the Netherlands. But she recovered the old Habsburg territory of Lombardy, to which Venetia was now joined, and she also got Napoleon's

EUROPE AFTER 1815

Boundary of the German Confederation

KINGDOM OF NORWAY & SWEDEN

UNITED KINGDOM OF GREAT BRITAIN AND IRELAND

North Sea

DENMARK

Atlantic Ocean

IRELAND

SCOTLAND

WALES

ENGLAND

London

The Hague

Brussels

K. OF NETHERLANDS

Aachen

LUX.

P R U S S I A

Berlin

Elbe R.

Weser R.

Oder R.

GERMAN

Wartburg

Frankfurt

Carlsbad

Prag

BOHEMIA

Paris

Meuse R.

Seine R.

CONFEDERATION

Hambach

Danube R.

AUSTRIA

Vienna

FRANCE

Loire R.

Garonne R.

Rhône R.

SWITZERLAND

PIED- MONT

Milan

Turin

LOMBARDY

TYROL

VENETIA

OF

PORTUGAL

SPAIN

Madrid

Ebro R.

Tagus R.

Guadalquivir R.

Lisbon

Barcelona

Par.

Mod.

Venice

Florence

TUSCANY

PAPAL STATES

Rome

Adria

BALEARIC IS.

CORSICA (to France)

KINGDOM OF SARDINIA

Naples

K. OF

THE

TWO

SICILIES

Cadiz

Mediterranean

SARDINIA

SICILY

MALTA (Br.)

Miles

0   500

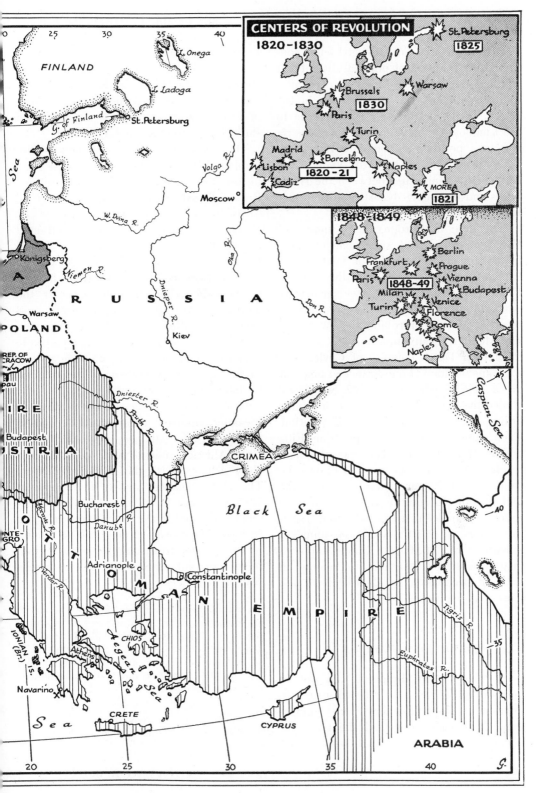

FINLAND

L. Onega

L. Ladoga

Sea

G. of Finland   St. Petersburg

Volga R.

Moscow

W. Dvina R.

Königsberg

A

Niemen R.

R U S S I A

Warsaw

POLAND

Dnieper R.

Oka R.

Don R.

Kiev

REP. OF
CRACOW

Dniester R.

IRE

Prut R.

Budapest

USTRIA

CRIMEA

Caspian Sea

Bucharest

Morava R.

Danube R.

Black   Sea

40

NTE-
GRO

Vardar R.

O T T O M A N   E M P I R E

Tigris R.

Adrianople

Constantinople

35

IONIAN
(Br.) IS.

CHIOS

Athens

Aegean Sea

Euphrates R.

Navarino   X

CRETE

CYPRUS

S e a

ARABIA

20   25   30   35   40   G.

CENTERS OF REVOLUTION
1820-1830   St. Petersburg
                                    1825
                          Brussels   Warsaw
                            1830
                        Paris
                            Turin
                Madrid
                        Barcelona
                Lisbon   Naples
                    1820-21
                Cadiz
                                    MOREA
                                    1821

1848-1849
                            Berlin
            Frankfurt   Prague
    Paris   Vienna
            1848-49
                Milan   Budapest
            Turin   Venice
                        Florence
                        Rome

                        Naples

Illyrian Provinces along the eastern shore of the Adriatic.

In Italy, too, the Congress of Vienna confirmed the tradition of political disunity. It restored the Bourbon Kingdom of Naples in the south and the Papal States in the center. In the northwest it gave Genoa to the Kingdom of Piedmont-Sardinia. Austria was in a position to dominate Italy both by her possession of Lombardy-Venetia and by the close family ties between the Habsburgs and the ruling dynasties in the other Italian states.

Elsewhere in Europe, the Congress of Vienna restored and somewhat enlarged the independent Republic of Switzerland. It transferred Norway from the rule of Denmark to that of Sweden; Sweden, in turn, handed Finland over to Russia. Great Britain received Malta, controlling the "waist" of the Mediterranean, and, outside Europe, the former Dutch colonies of Ceylon and the Cape of Good Hope. France at first was given her boundaries of 1792, which included the minor territorial additions made during the early days of the Revolution. Then came Napoleon's escape from Elba and the Hundred Days. The final settlement reached after Waterloo assigned France the frontiers of 1790, substantially those of the Old Régime. In addition, the French were to return Napoleon's art plunder to its rightful owners, to pay the victorious allies an indemnity of 700,000,000 francs (approximately $140,000,000), and to finance an army of occupation on their soil for not more than five years.

The Quarantine of France

The Vienna diplomats did not so much punish France as take measures to quarantine any possible new French aggression. Castlereagh conceived the policy of strengthening France's neighbors so that they would be able to restrain the troublemaker in the future. Thus to the north the French faced the power of the Belgians and the Dutch combined in the single Kingdom of the Netherlands. On the northeast they encountered the Rhine Province of Prussia, and on the east the expanded states of Switzerland and Piedmont.

The Quadruple Alliance, signed in November, 1815, constituted the second great measure of quarantine. The four allies—Britain, Prussia, Austria, and Russia—agreed to use force, if necessary, to preserve the Vienna settlement. Each party contracted to put 60,000 troops in the field should France make a warlike move. At Castlereagh's insistence, the allies further decided on periodic conferences to consider the measures "most salutary for the repose and prosperity of Nations, and the maintenance of the Peace of Europe." The Quadruple Alliance was to be both a watchdog against France and an experiment in government by international conference.

Public opinion, especially in the English-speaking countries, unfortunately confused the Quadruple Alliance with Alexander's Holy Alliance scheme and identified the Holy Alliance with the blackest reaction. The Holy Alliance, signed in September, 1815, was actually a fairly harmless document dedicated to the proposition that "the policy of the powers . . . ought to be guided by the sublime truths taught by the eternal religion of God our Saviour." The monarchs who signed

. . . will continue united by the bonds of a true and indissoluble fraternity and, regarding themselves as compatriots, they shall lend aid and assistance to each other on all occasions and in all places, viewing themselves, in their relations to their subjects and to their armies, as fathers of families. . . .*

* University of Pennsylvania, *Translations and Reprints from the Original Sources of European History* (Philadelphia, 1897), Vol. I, No. 3, p. 9.

Although most of the major European rulers signed the Holy Alliance, only Tsar Alexander seems to have taken it seriously. Castlereagh called it "a piece of sublime mysticism and nonsense," and the Pope, refusing an invitation to join, remarked that the Vatican could very well dispense with interpretations of Christian doctrine by the laity.

The Vienna Settlement Evaluated

Together with Westphalia (1648), Utrecht (1713), and Versailles (1919), the Vienna settlement of 1814-15 marked one of those rare attempts at the massive political reconstruction of Europe. Of the four, Vienna in many respects succeeded best. There was to be no major European war until the Crimean conflict of the 1850's, and none embroiling the whole of Europe until 1914. Most of the leading diplomats at Vienna could have said with Castlereagh that they acted "to bring the world back to peaceful habits." Seldom have victors treated the defeated aggressor more generously. Castlereagh, above all, deserves credit for his project of pacifying international disputes through conferences of the Quadruple Alliance.

In operation, however, the Quadruple Alliance never fulfilled the noble aims of Castlereagh. Within five years of the Congress of Vienna, revolution broke out again in Europe, causing serious dissension within the Quadruple Alliance. And for these outbreaks the Congress of Vienna was itself partly responsible, because it attempted to stifle liberal and national aspirations.

IV: The Persistence of Revolution

The revolutionary leaders of the early nineteenth century despised as useless barriers to progress the traditions so revered by conservatives. Opposing the counter-revolutionary alliance of throne and altar, they stood for Liberty, Equality, and Fraternity. The connotations of the great revolutionary motto changed little after 1815. Liberty and Equality still meant constitutionalism in politics, the abolition of feudal and clerical privileges in society, and, with few exceptions, laissez-faire in economics. Under the influence of the Romantic movement, Fraternity continued to crystallize into the formidable doctrine of nationalism. Mazzini, the great Italian liberal and nationalist, proclaimed:

Every people has its special mission, which will co-operate towards the fulfilment of the general mission of humanity. That mission constitutes its *nationality*. Nationality is sacred.[*]

The nationalists of the post-1815 generation pictured a utopia where each nation would be free of domination by any other, and where all would live together harmoniously. In terms of practical politics, this signified movements toward national independence and national unification—the struggle of Belgians against Dutch, of Poles against Russians, of Greeks against Turks, and of Italians, Germans, Czechs, Yugoslavs, and Hungarians against the Austrian Habsburg government in Vienna.

---

[*] *Life and Writings of Joseph Mazzini* (London, 1905), III, 33.

The Revolutions of 1820

The first conflicts broke out in Spain, Portugal, and Naples. In all three states the return to legitimacy had restored the Old Régime at its most unenlightened. The great majority of the population responded calmly, even enthusiastically. The aristocracy were delighted to recover ancient privileges; the poor and ignorant peasants welcomed the return of familiar traditions. But a small minority, drawn chiefly from the middle class, the intellectuals, and the army, regretted bitterly the disappearance of the enlightened reforms introduced by Napoleon. The discontent of this liberal minority resulted in the revolutionary movement of 1820.

Trouble first arose in Spain. During the Peninsular War, representatives from Cadiz and other commercial towns had framed the Constitution of 1812. This document, providing for universal suffrage and a severely limited monarchy, was very liberal —too liberal, indeed, to be entirely practical. The Bourbon King Ferdinand VII, who resumed his crown in 1814, soon suspended the constitution. He also persecuted its supporters, restored the social inequalities of the Old Régime, and re-established the twin instruments of Spanish clericalism, the Jesuits and the Inquisition. Finally, Ferdinand determined to recapture the Spanish colonies in the New World.

The colonial independence movement had won its initial success at Buenos Aires in 1810 and then had spread rapidly to Spain's other American possessions. The revolt was caused directly by the refusal of the colonial populations either to recognize Napoleon's brother Joseph as their king or to accept the closer ties between colonies and mother country proposed by patriots in Spain. Behind the Spanish-American independence movement lay several other factors: the powerful examples of the American and

French revolutions; the sympathetic interest of Great Britain, always anxious to release lucrative markets from Spanish mercantilist restrictions; and the accumulated resentment over the centuries of indifferent rule by Spanish governors. Ferdinand VII threatened to crush the rebels by force; to transport troops he augmented the small Spanish fleet with three leaky hulks purchased from Russia. At the end of 1819, this motley new armada, carrying 20,000 men, was about to sail from Cadiz.

It never sailed. On January 1, 1820, a mutiny broke out at Cadiz led by the liberal Colonel Riego. Uprisings soon followed in Madrid, in Barcelona, and in other Spanish cities. The revolutionaries sang "Riego's Hymn" with the refrain, "Swallow it, you dog." The "it" referred to the Constitution of 1812. Ferdinand surrendered.

The liberal minorities in Portugal and Italy followed the Spanish lead. An army faction seized control of the Portuguese government in 1820, abolished the Inquisition, and set up a constitution on the Spanish model of 1812. In Naples, the revolution was the work of the *Carbonari* (charcoalburners), a secret society with a vaguely liberal program and a membership of more than 50,000. Formed originally to combat the French, the Carbonari now opposed King Ferdinand I of the Two Sicilies, who was the uncle of the Spanish Ferdinand VII. Like his Spanish nephew, the Neapolitan Ferdinand gave in at the first sign of opposition in 1820 and accepted a constitution of the Spanish type.

The strength of the revolutionary movement of 1820 ebbed as quickly as it had risen. The Spanish Constitution of 1812 did not work in states where the population had next to no experience in the difficult art of self-government. The new liberal politicians, furthermore, were as inept in their own way as the two Ferdinands were in theirs. The reforms introduced precipitately

CHAPTER XIX

in Spain and Naples soon alienated the bulk of the population at home and alarmed the conservative leaders of the great powers.

The Counter-Revolution of 1821-1823

The revolutions of 1820 tested both the stability of the Vienna settlement and the solidarity of the Quadruple Alliance. The former emerged almost unscathed, but at the cost of destroying the latter. In other words, although legitimacy was restored in Spain and Italy, the process of restoration split the Quadruple Alliance in two. Britain increasingly moved toward a policy of nonintervention in the domestic affairs of other states; Austria, Russia, and Prussia increasingly favored armed intervention to suppress revolution.

The split became evident at the conference of the Quadruple Alliance which met at Troppau in Silesia late in 1820. Castlereagh, knowing that the Neapolitan revolution threatened the Habsburg hegemony in Italy, was willing that Austria should intervene in Naples, but without the backing of the Alliance. The Alliance, Castlereagh declared, was never designed

. . . as an Union for the Government of the World, or for the Superintendence of the Internal Affairs of other States.

We shall be found in our Place when actual danger menaces the System of Europe; but this Country cannot, and will not, act upon abstract and Speculative Principles of Precaution.*

Metternich, on the other hand, was determined to secure from the alliance the very sort of blanket commitment to which Castlereagh was so opposed. He wanted full moral backing for Austrian intervention in Naples. In spite of the protests of Britain,

the Troppau Protocol (November, 1820) was signed by Austria, Prussia, and Russia:

States which have undergone a change of Government, due to revolution, the results of which threaten other states, *ipso facto* cease to be members of the European Alliance, and remain excluded from it until their situation gives guarantees for legal order and stability. If, owing to such alterations, immediate danger threatens other states, the Powers bind themselves, by peaceful means, or if need be by arms, to bring back the guilty state into the bosom of the Great Alliance.*

Under the terms of the Troppau Protocol, an Austrian army duly toppled the revolutionary government of Naples in 1821, and in 1823 a French army crossed the Pyrenees and restored the absolute authority of Ferdinand VII. Hundreds of Spanish liberals were executed at Ferdinand's order, and the body of Colonel Riego was cut into five pieces for public exhibition in the cities that had been the centers of the Spanish constitutional movement. The French intervention in Spain provoked the strong opposition of Great Britain and ended the Quadruple Alliance.

Canning, who had succeeded Castlereagh as British Foreign Minister in 1822, suspected that the continental powers might now aid Spain to recover her former American colonies. So also did the United States, which had recognized the independence of the Latin American republics. But America also feared both a possible Russian move southward from Alaska along the Pacific coast and an attempt by Britain to extend her sphere of control in the Caribbean. Therefore, when Canning proposed a joint Anglo-American statement to ward off any European interference in Latin America, the government of President Monroe refused the invitation.

---

* *British Foreign and State Papers* (London, 1850), X, 73-74.

* Quoted in W. A. Phillips, *The Confederation of Europe* (New York, 1920), 208-209.

In a message to the American Congress in December, 1823, however, President Monroe included the statement that is known to history as the Monroe Doctrine. Here are the key passages of the President's statement:

In the wars of the European powers, in matters relating to themselves, we have never taken any part, nor does it comport with our policy to do so. It is only when our rights are invaded, or seriously menaced, that we resent injuries or make preparation for our defence. With the movements in this hemisphere, we are, of necessity, more immediately connected, and by causes which must be obvious to all enlightened and impartial observers. The political system of the allied powers is essentially different, in this respect, from that of America. ...We owe it, therefore, to candor, and to the amicable relations existing between the United States and those powers, to declare, that we should consider any attempt on their part to extend their system to any portion of this hemisphere, as dangerous to our peace and safety. With the existing colonies or dependencies of any European power, we have not interfered, and shall not interfere. But with the governments who have declared their independence, and maintained it, and whose independence we have, on great consideration, and on just principles, acknowledged, we could not view any interposition for the purpose of oppressing them, or controlling, in any other manner, their destiny, by an European power, in any other light than as the manifestation of an unfriendly disposition towards the United States.

This famous document marks an important assertion of policy and self-confident power on the part of the youthful American republic. But it had little immediate international significance. The European powers were not fully committed to the project of restoring Spain's American empire. And, so far as they were deterred from undertaking that venture, they were deterred less by the Monroe Doctrine than by the opposition of Canning and the British government and the potential opposition of the British fleet.

The Greek War of Independence, 1821-1829

The British fleet was soon to take an important part in assuring the success of another bid for national independence, the Greek revolt against the Ottoman Empire. Leadership in this revolution came from the group known as the "Island" Greeks. These merchants from the islands and ports of the Aegean Sea dominated the commerce of the Near East and had established flourishing business outposts at Vienna, Marseilles, London, and Russia's Black Sea port of Odessa. The "Island" Greeks revived not only the old Greek trading tradition but also some of the old Greek zeal for self-government. From their home islands and from their merchant colonies abroad they poured forth a stream of patriotic exhortation. A typical plea urged the modern Greeks

... to recall the ancient honours of your race. Remember that you are the representatives of the Homers, and the Aristotles, of the Platos ... and Sophocles, whose labours achieved the greatness of Greece; whose names were revered when living, and whose memory has survived decay. You are now the instructors and teachers of your country, but the time is fast approaching when you will be called on to act as lawgivers.*

In cultural matters, Greek nationalism took the form of a campaign to purge the modern Greek language of its Turkish and Slavic words and to return it to the classical tongue of the Age of Pericles. In the political realm, it resulted in a secret society patterned after the *Carbonari* of Italy, and the Freemasons.

Early in 1821 the conspirators fomented a revolt among the peasants of the Morea (the ancient Peloponnesus). The ensuing

---

* J. E. Tennent, *History of Modern Greece* (London, 1845), II, 528, quoted in F. B. Artz, *Reaction and Revolution* (New York, 1934), 252.

CHAPTER XIX

war for independence was from its onset a ferocious conflict. The Morean peasants slaughtered every Turk they could lay their hands on; the Ottoman government retaliated by killing or selling into slavery thirty thousand Greeks from the prosperous Aegean island of Chios (Scio), an atrocity that inspired Delacroix's famous painting. In the work of repression the Ottoman emperor enlisted the aid of his powerful Egyptian vassal, Mehemet Ali. By 1827, it appeared likely that the punitive expedition organized by Mehemet Ali would recapture the last rebel strongholds. Then Britain, France, and Russia intervened to save the Greek independence movement at its darkest hour.

The three-power action resulted from the combined pressures of public opinion and strategic interests. In Britain and France, and also in Germany and the United States, the Philhellenic (pro-Greek) movement had won legions of supporters. "We are all Greeks," Shelley declared in 1821:

Our laws, our literature, our religion, our arts, have their roots in Greece. But for Greece, Rome . . . would have spread no illumination with her arms, and we might still have been savages and idolaters.*

Philhellenic committees sent supplies and money and demanded that civilized governments intervene openly. Intervention hinged on the action of Russia. Catherine the Great had appointed Russia the heir apparent of the Turkish "Sick Man" and the champion of the Christians under Turkish rule (see Chapter XVII). Greek patriots had formed their secret society at Odessa, on Russian soil and with Russian backing. For a time, Metternich was able to restrain Russia; ultimately, Russia rallied openly to the Greek cause. The British and French governments, already bombarded by Philhellenic propaganda, now feared to let

---
* Preface to *Hellas*.

Russia act alone lest she gain mastery over the whole Near East by precipitating the death of the "Sick Man." A three-power intervention seemed the only course that would both rescue the Greeks and check the Russians.

Both aims were partially, but not fully, achieved. In October, 1827, Russian, British, and French squadrons sank the Turkish and Egyptian vessels anchored at Navarino in western Greece and thereby destroyed the chief Ottoman base. The subsequent Treaty of Adrianople, 1829, allowed Russia to annex outright only a little Turkish territory. But it did arrange that the Ottoman Danubian provinces of Moldavia and Wallachia, the core of present-day Rumania, should become a virtual Russian protectorate. After considerable wrangling, the European powers accorded formal recognition to an independent Greek state of very modest size, which left many Greeks still within the Ottoman Empire. And, after an exhaustive search, they finally discovered in the reactionary Otto of Bavaria a prince willing to ascend the shaky new Greek throne.

Neither nationalism nor liberalism had won a complete victory in the Greek war. Greek patriots schemed for the day when they might enlarge the boundaries of their new kingdom. And Greek politicians were to threaten its stability and disillusion Philhellenists abroad by challenging King Otto and continuing the endless feuds that had divided them even in their desperate struggle for independence.

The Decembrist Revolt in Russia

Russia, who did so much to determine the outcome of revolutions elsewhere, herself felt the revolutionary wave, but with diminished force. A brief uprising took place in December, 1825, and in January,

1826, on the death of Tsar Alexander I. Its leaders, the "Decembrists," vainly attempted to apply and extend the program of liberal reforms which the Tsar himself had barely begun.

In his early days, Alexander had indeed given promise of making sweeping changes in Russia. He had been educated in the advanced ideas of the Enlightenment, at the instance of his grandmother, Catherine the Great. He had welcomed the news of the fall of the Bastille and had generally sympathized with the aims of the early revolutionaries in France. In 1801, he had been implicated in the conspiracy that resulted in the strangling of his father, Paul I. Once on the throne, Alexander soon gathered around him a circle of enlightened young nobles and other liberals who dreamed of improving the lot of the serfs and of instituting all manner of other changes. One of these liberals, Speransky, drew up a constitutional draft that would have installed representative assemblies with limited powers at the local, provincial, and national levels.

These ambitious projects produced very little in the way of practical achievement. Alexander did empower private landholders to emancipate their serfs if they wished, but less than 1 per cent of the serf population benefited by the measure. And he did abolish the cumbersome collegial system of administration (see Chapter XVI) and introduce the normal bureaucratic practice of individual responsibility in the various departments of government. This change, though certainly enlightened, actually strengthened the autocracy by improving its efficiency. From the first, the Tsar's liberalism was thwarted by the determined opposition of most nobles. Soon it was submerged in the overriding emergency of 1812 and the final campaigns against Napoleon.

With the return of peace, Alexander again raised liberal hopes. He granted constitutions to the Polish and Finnish lands he acquired by the Vienna settlement, but he granted Russia nothing. Fascinated by the diplomatic game played at Vienna, Troppau, and elsewhere, Alexander spent two-thirds of his time outside Russia. At home, he brought education under rigorous control and even directed professors of mathematics to expatiate on the triangle as a

Tsar Alexander I of Russia.

symbol of the Trinity. In order to provide a constant flow of army recruits, yet reduce the swollen cost of government, he devised a scheme of "military colonies," whereby soldiers were forced to settle on the land, marry peasant women, and raise their children for military service. More than half a million of Alexander's unwilling subjects were actually dragooned into these colonies. The whole scheme was made the more

CHAPTER XIX

odious because it was supervised by an unreconstructed officer, Arakcheev, who had once disciplined a soldier by biting off his ear and who obliged the peasant women on his own estates to produce a male child annually or else pay a fine.

While superstition and reaction colored the policies of the Tsar, liberal ideas continued to penetrate his country. The contrast between the relatively enlightened West and backward Russia made a painfully sharp impression on officers who had served in the campaigns against Napoleon. One of the future Decembrist leaders reported:

From France we returned to Russia by sea. The First Division of the Guard landed at Oranienbaum and listened to the *Te Deum*. . . . During the prayer the police were mercilessly beating the people who attempted to draw nearer to the lined-up troops. . . . Finally the Emperor appeared, accompanied by the Guard, on a fine sorrel horse, with an unsheathed sword, which he was ready to lower before the Empress. But at that very moment, almost under his horse, a peasant crossed the street. The Emperor spurred his horse and rushed with the unsheathed sword toward the running peasant. The police attacked him with their clubs. We did not believe our own eyes and turned away, ashamed for our beloved Tsar.*

High-ranking officers at St. Petersburg secretly formed the Northern Society, which aimed to make Russia a limited, decentralized monarchy, with the various provinces enjoying rights somewhat like those of the states in the American republic. The serfs would receive their freedom but no land, and the whole series of reforms would be achieved by peaceful means. A second secret organization, the Southern Society, acquired a more radical character. Its

leader was Colonel Pestel, an officer of Jacobin sympathies, and its membership included many relatively impoverished officers. On every main issue the program of the Southern Society went beyond that of the Petersburg group. It advocated a highly centralized republic, the granting of land to liberated serfs, and the use of violence to gain its ends.

Both the Northern Society and the Southern Society tried to profit by the political confusion immediately following the death of Alexander I. Since Alexander left no son, the crown would normally have passed to his younger brother, Constantine, his viceroy in Poland. Constantine, however, had relinquished his rights to a still younger brother, Nicholas, but in a document so secret that Nicholas never saw it. When Alexander died, therefore, Constantine declared that Nicholas was the legal tsar, and Nicholas declared that Constantine was. While the two brothers were clarifying their status, the Northern Society summoned the Petersburg garrison to revolt against Nicholas. Throughout the day of December 26, 1825, the rebels stood their ground in the Senate Square of Russia's capital city until Nicholas finally subdued them. Two weeks later, the Southern Society launched a movement that was doomed from the start because its leader, Pestel, had already been arrested.

The Decembrist revolt, for all its seeming triviality, was an important episode. It thoroughly alarmed Tsar Nicholas I (1825-1855), who now resolved to follow a severely autocratic policy. Although he dismissed the highly unpopular Arakcheev and put an end to the military colonies, he also had five of the Decembrists executed and exiled more than a hundred others to Siberia. The Decembrists were the first in the long line of modern Russia's political martyrs.

* Quoted in Anatole G. Mazour, *The First Russian Revolution* (Berkeley, Calif., 1937), 55.

V: The Revolutions of 1830

France: The July Revolution

The revolutionary wave of 1830 originated in the traditional center of unrest, France. Louis XVIII (1814-1824) had given the Bourbon restoration a promising beginning. Aging, fat, and gouty, Louis was in his own lethargic way a good deal of a statesman. From the first, he followed a middle-of-the-road policy, exemplified by the Charter that he granted in 1814. The preamble of the Charter asserted the royal prerogative: "The authority in France resides in the person of the king." * But the document then proceeded to establish a constitutional monarchy. The legislature was to be composed of a Chamber of Peers appointed by the king, and a Chamber of Deputies elected on a very restricted suffrage that allowed fewer than 100,000 of France's thirty millions the right to vote. "In the King alone is vested the executive power," the Charter stated, but in practice Louis usually followed the custom of limited monarchies by appointing ministers who were backed by a majority of the legislature. Most significantly, the Charter confirmed many of the decisive changes instituted in France since 1789. It guaranteed religious toleration, equality before the law, and equal eligibility to civil and military office; it likewise accepted the revolutionary property settlement and the *Code Napoléon.*

The Charter, however, greatly irritated the ultra-royalist faction, drawn from the noble and clerical *émigrés,* who had returned to France after their revolutionary exile. These reactionary "Ultras," grouped around the King's brother, the Count of Artois, were determined to recover both the privileges and the property they had lost during the Revolution. Louis XVIII held the Ultras at bay for five years. When the election of 1815 gave them control of the Chamber of Deputies, he dismissed the Chamber and held a new election, which returned a less fanatical majority. He chose moderate ministers who worked to pay off the indemnity to the victorious allies and, in general, to put French finances in good order. Then France suffered an attack of anti-revolutionary fear, aroused by the revolutions in Spain and Italy and by the assassination of the Duke of Berri, the King's nephew, early in 1820. The Ultras gained enough strength to oblige Louis XVIII to appoint a reactionary ministry, which restricted the freedom of the press and sent French troops to aid Ferdinand VII in Spain.

The tempo of the reaction quickened when Louis XVIII died and the Ultra leader, Artois, became King Charles X (1824-1830). Charles actually attempted to turn back the clock and become a divine-right monarch. He allowed the Church greater influence by encouraging the activities of the Jesuits, who were still legally banned from France, and by appointing clerics as principals and administrators in the state school system. To compensate the former *émigrés* for their loss of property, he granted them state annuities; to finance the annuities, he lowered the interest on government bonds from 5 to 3 per cent. The indemnification of the *émigrés* could be defended both as an act of simple justice and as a sensible political move that lifted the last threat of confiscation from those who had acquired property during the Revolution. But the reduction of interest on government obligations infuriated many in-

---

* University of Pennsylvania, *Translations and Reprints from the Original Sources of European History* (Philadelphia, 1897), Vol. I, No. 3.

fluential Parisian bourgeois and other bond-holders.

Opposition to Charles X grew rapidly, aided to no small extent by two young historians who were destined to play an important part in French politics. Adolphe Thiers (1797-1877) published a popular and sympathetic *History of the French Revolution* and edited a liberal Paris newspaper. François Guizot (1787-1874) wrote a *History of Civilization*, an enthusiastic account of the rise and triumph of those wealthy bourgeois who so detested the Ultras. Guizot also headed a nation-wide organization, *"Aide-toi, le ciel t'aidera!"* ("The Lord helps those who help themselves"), which urged Frenchmen to defend their legal rights against the encroachments of Charles X.

In 1829, Charles X increased the political tension by appointing as his chief minister the Prince of Polignac, an Ultra of Ultras and a religious zealot who claimed to be vouchsafed visions in which the Virgin Mary repeatedly promised him success. Polignac hoped to bolster the waning prestige of his monarch by scoring a resounding diplomatic victory. He therefore attacked the Dey of Algiers, a largely independent vassal of the Ottoman emperor, and notorious for his collusion with the hated Barbary Pirates. The capture of Algiers (June, 1830) laid the foundation of the French empire in North Africa. Meanwhile, the liberal opposition in the Chamber of Deputies had pronounced Polignac's ministry unconstitutional because it had never received the approval of the legislature. In the hope of securing a more tractable chamber, Charles X staged a new election in May, 1830, but the opposition won. On July 25, 1830, without securing the legislature's approval, Charles and Polignac issued ordinances muzzling the press, dissolving the newly elected Chamber, ordering a fresh election, and introducing new voting qualifications that would have dis-

franchised the bourgeois who were the mainstay of the opposition. The King and his chief minister believed that public opinion, mollified by the recent victory at Algiers, would accept these July Ordinances calmly. They miscalculated utterly.

Aroused by the protests of Thiers and other liberal journalists, and encouraged by the fine summer weather and the weakness of the government troops, the workers and students of Paris staged a riot. They threw up barricades and on July 28 captured the Paris City Hall. There they proclaimed their intention of making France a democratic republic with the Marquis de Lafayette, that aged symbol of revolution, as its president. The liberal leaders of the Chamber of Deputies, on the other hand, wanted a safe and sane constitutional monarchy. They wanted to make France's 1830 the counterpart of England's 1688. Headed by Thiers, the wealthy banker Laffitte, and the perennial king-maker Talleyrand, the liberals won handily. They had the money, they had the brains, and they had the perfect candidate for the throne—Louis Philippe, the Duke of Orléans.

Louis Philippe's father had helped to engineer the revolutionary disturbances in Paris during the summer of 1789 and had won the nickname of "Philip Equality" before dying under the guillotine. Louis Philippe himself had fought in the revolutionary army at Valmy in 1792 but had emigrated in 1793 before the worst excesses of the Terror. He had no use either for the extremes of Jacobinism or for the pomp of royalty. He dressed and acted like the sober and well-to-do businessman he was. At the close of July, 1830, the astute Louis Philippe persuaded the gullible Lafayette of his admiration for republicanism. Having won the support of the titular republican leader by this deception, the liberal deputies named Louis Philippe king in place of Charles X, who abdicated and fled to England. They kept most of the central provisions of the Charter of 1814, though they deleted its references to the absolute authority of the king and substituted the tricolor of the Revolution for the white flag of the Bourbons. The suffrage, though enlarged, was still so restricted that only slightly more than 200,000 Frenchmen had the right to vote.

The almost bloodless July Revolution left France a long way from democracy. It was a very moderately liberal movement, based on a narrow interpretation of the ideals of the great revolution. The true standard-bearers of "Liberty, Equality, Fraternity" in 1830 were the defeated republicans of the Paris City Hall.

Belgium

Within a month of the July uprising in Paris, a nationalistic and liberal revolution began in Belgium. The union of Belgium and Holland, decreed by the peacemakers of 1815, worked reasonably well only in economics. The commerce and colonies of Holland supplied raw materials and markets for the expanding manufactures of Belgium, at that time the most advanced industrial area of the Continent. In politics and religion, however, King William I of the Netherlands exerted arbitrary power where he might better have made tactful concessions. He made Dutch the official language throughout his realm and refused to grant special privileges to the Catholic Church in Belgium. He denied the pleas of Belgians for larger representation in the legislature, where the Belgian provinces, though they had almost twice the population of the Dutch, received only half the seats. A common loyalty to the Catholic Church and a common concern for local rights and customs formed the foundation of Belgian nationalism. They welded together two different linguistic groups, the Flemish in the provinces north of Brussels and the French-speaking Walloons of the southern provinces.

The revolution broke out in Brussels on August 25, 1830, at a performance of a Romantic opera which depicted a revolt in Naples. Headed by students, inspired by the example of Paris—and perhaps incited by French agents—the audience rioted against Dutch rule. By the end of September, Dutch troops had been driven out of Brussels, and Dutch rule was collapsing almost everywhere in Belgium. The insurgents recruited their fighters chiefly from the industrial workers, many of whom were the wretched and discontented victims of low pay and frequent unemployment. The Belgian workers, however, like the Parisian workers, lacked good leadership and a concrete political program. The better-organized middle-class liberals soon captured control of the revolutionary movement and predominated in the national Belgian congress that convened in November, 1830.

This congress proclaimed Belgium independent and made it a constitutional monarchy. The new constitution provided for real local self-government, put rigorous limits on the king's authority, and subordinated the executive to the legislature. Although it did not establish universal suffrage, the financial qualifications for voting were markedly lower in Belgium than they were in Britain or France, and the electorate was proportionately larger.

The congress first chose as king the Duke of Nemours, a son of Louis Philippe. Britain protested violently, for this would have brought Belgium within the orbit of France. The congress then picked Leopold of Saxe-Coburg, a German princeling, and the widowed son-in-law of George IV of Britain. Leopold was admirably fitted for the exacting role of a constitutional monarch in

174

a brand-new kingdom. He had already shown his political shrewdness by refusing the throne of Greece; he now demonstrated it by marrying a daughter of Louis Philippe, thus mitigating French disappointment over the aborted candidacy of the Duke of Nemours.

The Belgian revolution made the first permanent breach in the Vienna settlement. It aroused little enthusiasm among the great powers, but they all accepted it. Representatives of Britain, France, Prussia, Austria, and Russia met in London late in 1830 and guaranteed both the independence and the neutrality of Belgium. King William, stubborn as the proverbial Dutchman, tried to retake Belgium by force in 1831-32. A French army and a British fleet successfully defended the Belgians, and prolonged negotiations finally resulted in Dutch recognition of Belgium's new status in 1839.

Poland

Revolution did not always succeed in 1830; the case of Poland contrasted tragically with that of Belgium. In 1815, the Kingdom of Poland enjoyed the most liberal constitution on the Continent; twenty years later, it had become a mere colony of the Russian Empire. The constitution of Alexander I preserved the *Code Napoléon* and the other enlightened measures introduced by the French into the Grand Duchy of Warsaw. A hundred thousand Poles received the ballot, more than the total number of voters in the France of Louis XVIII, which had a population ten times larger. The elective diet was to enjoy large authority in legislation, Poles were to staff the administration and the army, and Alexander was to play the part of a benign constitutional monarch.

The advent of the highly conservative Nicholas I in 1825 soon increased political friction, already stimulated by the popularity of Romantic doctrines of nationalism. Polish nationalists demanded not only the strict observance of the constitution but also the transfer from Russia to Poland of provinces that had belonged to the pre-partition Polish state—Lithuania, White Russia, and the Ukraine. Secret societies on the *Carbonari* model arose in these provinces and in the Kingdom of Poland.

The secret society of army cadets in Warsaw launched a revolution in November, 1830. The rebels were doomed from the start. They split into the two hostile camps of "Whites" and "Reds," the former representing the great feudal aristocrats, the latter the gentry. Neither "Whites" nor "Reds" gained the support of the peasants, whom both factions had long oppressed. The misery of the Poles increased with a terrible epidemic of cholera, the first outbreak of that dreadful scourge in Europe. Russian forces, at first taken off-guard, gradually rallied and by 1833 were masters of the situation. Nicholas I then scrapped Alexander's constitution, imposed a regime of permanent martial law, and closed the Universities of Warsaw and Vilna (in Lithuania), the chief centers of Polish nationalist propaganda. To escape the vengeance of Nicholas, Polish intellectuals fled the country by the tens of thousands. Only the Spain of Ferdinand VII had experienced a reaction comparable in severity to that undergone by Poland.

Italy and Germany

The liberals and nationalists of Italy and Germany likewise suffered defeat in the early 1830's. Italian insurgents briefly controlled the little duchies of Parma and Modena and a sizable part of the Papal States. They counted on French assistance, but the new government of Louis Philippe had no intention of risking war with Austria by poaching on the Habsburg preserve. Again, as in 1821, Metternich sent troops to restore legitimacy in Italy.

Metternich did not require soldiers to preserve legitimacy in Germany; whenever a crisis arose, the Diet of the German Confederation obediently followed the Austrian lead. The poet Heine claimed to hear Germany snoring:

She slept peacefully under the protection of her thirty-six monarchs. In those days, crowns sat firmly on the princes' heads, and at night they just drew their night caps over them, while the people slept peacefully at their feet.[*]

Royal absolutism, Old-Régime style, still dominated German politics. In Prussia, King Frederick William III (1797-1840) had promised to grant a constitution but never made good on his pledge. Mildly liberal constitutions, on the order of the French Charter of 1814, appeared only in Weimar and a few south German states where French influence remained considerable.

Liberalism and nationalism did not as yet stir the great mass of the German people, sleeping peacefully at their sovereigns' feet, as Heine aptly remarked. Political agitation came almost entirely from the small minority of intellectuals—journalists, Romantic writers, university professors, and students. After 1815, German university students formed a new organization, the *Burschenschaft* ("Students' Union"). In October, 1817, during a great rally celebrating the three-hundredth anniversary of Luther's Ninety-Five Theses, the *Burschenschaft* burned a wig, a Prussian officer's corset, and various other symbols of reaction. In March, 1819, a demented theological student, perhaps influenced by *Burschenschaft* extremists, assassinated Kotze-

bue, a reactionary writer and a Russian agent.

Metternich, already alarmed by the rather harmless student prank of 1817, now took vigorous action. At his direction, the Diet of the German Confederation approved the Carlsbad Decrees (September, 1819), which stiffened press censorship and dissolved the *Burschenschaft*. Academic freedom experienced severe restrictions:

The confederated governments mutually pledge themselves to remove from the universities or other public educational institutions all teachers who, by obvious deviation from their duty or by exceeding the limits of their functions, or by the abuse of their legitimate influence over the youthful minds, or by propagating harmful doctrines hostile to public order or subversive of existing governmental institutions, shall have unmistakably proved their unfitness for the important office intrusted to them.[*]

Despite the Carlsbad Decrees, political ferment continued among the German intellectuals. In May, 1832, twenty-five thousand revolutionary sympathizers gathered at Hambach near the Rhine to toast Lafayette and demand the union of the German states under a republic. Next, the revolutionaries made an extremely feeble attempt to seize Frankfurt, the seat of the Diet and the capital of the German Confederation, and then relapsed into inactivity.

The Lessons of 1830

The European revolutionary movement of 1830 emphasized two great facts of political life. First, it widened the split between the West and the East. Britain and France were committed to support mild liberalism both at home and in neighboring

---

[*] Quoted by F. B. Artz, *Reaction and Revolution* (New York, 1934), 137.

[*] University of Pennsylvania, *Translations and Reprints from the Original Sources of European History* (Philadelphia, 1897), Vol. I, No. 3.

CHAPTER XIX

Belgium. On the other hand, Russia, Austria, and Prussia were more firmly committed than ever to the counter-revolutionary principles of the Troppau Protocol. In 1833, Nicholas I, Metternich, and Frederick William III formally pledged their joint assistance to any sovereign threatened by revolution.

Second, revolution succeeded in 1830 only in France and Belgium, only where it enlisted the support of a large segment of the population. It failed in every country where the revolutionaries represented only a fraction of the people. In agrarian Poland, the great bulk of the peasantry viewed both "Whites" and "Reds" as oppressors. The Italian revolutionaries still relied on their Romantic *Carbonari* tradition and on flimsy hopes of foreign aid. In Germany, revolution was a matter of student outbursts, toasts to Lafayette, and other gestures by a small minority. Liberal and nationalist intellectuals needed to make their doctrines penetrate to the grass roots of society, or at least to the lower levels of the middle class. They needed to develop able political leaders and to mature well-laid plans for political reform. These were the tasks they undertook after 1830; their success was to be tested in the most formidable and widespread political uprising in nineteenth-century Europe—the Revolutions of 1848.

VI: The Revolutions of 1848

Common Denominators

In surveying a complex international phenomenon like the Revolutions of 1848, it is essential not to lose sight of the forest for the trees; we must always keep in mind that common elements underlay the various uprisings in 1848. One such common denominator was the force of nationalism, which prompted German and Italian attempts to gain political unification and also inspired the subject peoples of the Habsburg Empire to seek political and cultural autonomy. The Romantic movement had stimulated a nationalistic renaissance not only among Poles and Greeks, as we have already seen, but also among most other peoples in central and eastern Europe. For example, the Czech language was on the verge of extinction in the later eighteenth century, as the Bohemian population increasingly used the German speech of their Austrian rulers. By 1848, however, a Czech linguistic and literary revival was in full swing. Philologists studied the roots of the language and its relation to other Slavic tongues. Patriotic histories of Bohemia and collections of Czech folk-poetry kindled a lively interest in the national past and fostered dreams of a Pan-Slavic awakening in which the Czechs would lead their brother Slavs.

Some nationalists in 1848 preached with Mazzini that each nation's "special mission" fulfilled the "general mission of humanity." Others, however, advanced a more aggressive program that stressed the conflicts, rather than the harmonies, among nations. John Stuart Mill, the great English liberal, deplored the nationalists who ignored the welfare

... of any portion of the human species, save that which is called by the same name and speaks the same language as themselves. . . . In the backward parts of Europe and even (where better things might have been expected) in

Germany, the sentiment of nationality so far outweighs the love of liberty that the people are willing to abet their rulers in crushing the liberty and independence of any people not of their race and language.*

Liberalism, the second common denominator of the revolutions, also encompassed a wide range of programs. In central and eastern Europe, where some of the Old Régime still survived, liberals demanded constitutions to limit absolute monarchy and to liquidate the last vestiges of feudal rights and manorial dues. In France, on the other hand, many liberals sought to replace the constitutional monarchy of Louis Philippe with a democratic republic based on universal male suffrage. French liberalism, in fact, shaded into socialism. The Paris radicals of 1848 organized a concerted campaign not only for political democracy but also for social and economic democracy. They demanded the guarantee of the right

* "The French Revolution and Its Assailants," *Westminster Review*, II (April, 1849), 17.

to work and other measures that still seem rather socialistic today, a century later.

Finally, in the Europe of 1848, as in the France of 1789, an immediate economic crisis helped to catalyze discontent into revolution. A disastrous blight ruined the Irish potato crop in 1845 and soon spread to the Continent. The grain harvest of 1846 failed in western Europe, resulting in a sharp rise in the price of bread and, despite heavy imports from Russia and the United States, in bread riots and actual starvation. The agrarian crisis, in turn, aggravated the misery caused by a severe industrial depression in western Europe. The railroad-building boom of the early 1840's had collapsed by 1847, and produced a crop of business failures.

France

The economic crisis hit France with particular severity. Railroad construction almost ceased, throwing more than half a million laborers out of work; coal mines and

Daumier, "The Legislative Belly" (1834). (Caricature of the rich and selfish French legislators under the July Monarchy.)

CHAPTER XIX

iron foundries, in turn, laid men off. Widespread unemployment increased discontent among French workers already embittered by their low wages and by the still lower esteem in which they were held by the government of Louis Philippe. The July Monarchy, as this regime was termed, encouraged the rapid expansion of industry and trade. The population of factory towns multiplied rapidly; that of Roubaix, for instance, a northern textile center, rose from 8,000 to 34,000 between 1831 and 1841. But the government largely ignored the social misery that accompanied the new prosperity. In its eighteen years of existence, it took only two steps for the welfare of the industrial working class: an extension of the primary school system in 1833, and a laxly enforced law in 1841 limiting the labor of children. There was a great deal of truth in the famous judgment passed by De Tocqueville, an acute political observer— that "Government in those days resembled an industrial company whose every operation is undertaken for the profits which the stockholders may gain thereby."

The 200,000 landowners, investors, and businessmen who had the right to vote formed the stockholders of the July Monarchy. "Get rich!" was the reply made by Guizot, a leading politician, to those who demanded extension of the suffrage. Anyone who wanted to vote could do so, provided he first made himself rich enough to meet the stiff property qualifications for the ballot. The government banned labor organizations and punished rioters after workmen rose in Paris and Lyons during the early 1830's to demand a republic and increased wages. It imposed a censorship when the free press established by the July Revolution mercilessly caricatured the pear-shaped head and the familiar unbrella of the businessman-king.

The opposition, though stifled in the 1830's, revived rapidly during the 1840's. It

Daumier, "The Greatest Tight-Rope Walker of Europe" (caricature of Louis Philippe, with pear-shaped torso and umbrella).

was not a united opposition—a fact that goes far to explain the hectic course of the revolution it set off. Heading one group was Adolphe Thiers, a principal architect of the July Monarchy, who was shelved by Louis Philippe in 1840 in favor of Guizot, the chief minister from then until 1848. Thiers continued to support the principle of constitutional monarchy; the chief difference between him and Guizot was the fact that he was out of office while Guizot was in. The disappointed republicans of 1830 formed a second opposition group. The third, and smallest, group took in various socialists, who were to gain recruits from the economic depression of the late 1840's. Potentially more formidable than any of these, but as yet representing only a vague, unorganized sentiment, were the Bonapartists. The return of the Emperor's ashes from St. Helena to Paris in 1840 revived the legend of a glorious and warlike Napoleon, so different from the inglorious, peace-loving Louis Philippe.

Democracy in the Second French Republic, 1848. The man explains that the gun is to be used against foreign enemies and universal suffrage against domestic enemies.

sian working class, by students, and by the more radical republican leaders, the demonstration of February 22 turned into a riot on the 23rd. Soldiers killed or wounded more than fifty of the mob that attacked the residence of Guizot. Louis Philippe, alarmed by the turn of events, abdicated on February 24.

As in July, 1830, so in February, 1848, working-class radicals and bourgeois moderates competed to fill the political vacuum created by the King's abdication. The radicals demanded a republic that would institute the social and economic changes summed up in the formula, the right to work. Thoroughly revolutionary in spirit, these radicals still lacked the organization necessary to prosecute revolution successfully; their new leaders were almost as gullible as Lafayette had been in 1830. The middle-class moderates were ready to grant universal suffrage but were determined to protect the rights of property and to keep social and economic concessions to a minimum.

The moderates secured the direction of the provisional government formed on February 25. As a sop to the aroused Parisians, they promised to guarantee the right to work and authorized the establishment in Paris of National Workshops, apparently inspired by the socialist, Louis Blanc (1811-1882). Louis Blanc had long advocated what he termed "social workshops," which the workers themselves would own and run with the financial assistance of the state. The National Workshops of 1848, however, did not follow this socialistic blueprint. They were simply a relief project organized along semi-military lines, and enrolling more than 100,000 unemployed from Paris and the provinces. About 10,000 of the recruits received two francs (40 cents) a day for working on municipal improvements like repairing the Paris fortifications and leveling the parade ground of the Champs

In the summer of 1847, constitutional monarchists of the Thiers faction joined with republicans to stage a series of political banquets throughout France calling for reform and for the resignation of Guizot. This campaign appeared comparatively harmless until a particularly large banquet was announced for February 22, 1848, to be held in a radical quarter of Paris. When the Guizot ministry forbade the Paris banquet, the Parisians substituted a large demonstration. On February 23, Louis Philippe dismissed Guizot and prepared to summon Thiers to the ministry. His concessions came too late. Supported by the Pari-

CHAPTER XIX

de Mars. The rest received a dole of one franc a day.

The moderates commanding the provisional government gained new strength as a result of the election of April, 1848—the first election in European history in which almost the entire adult male population of a country exercised the right to vote. Eight million Frenchmen went to the polls to select members of the National Assembly that was to draw up a new constitution. The conservative peasants, who still made up the bulk of the French population, approved the fall of the July Monarchy but dreaded anything resembling an attack on private property. Of the almost 900 deputies elected, therefore, the great majority came from the middle class; only a hundred or so sympathized with the Paris radicals.

The latter, however, refused to accept the decision of the country. On May 15, a noisy but largely unarmed mob invaded the meeting hall of the National Assembly and proposed the dissolution of the Assembly and the formation of a new provisional government at the Paris City Hall. The moderates, now thoroughly alarmed, decided that the National Workshops threatened law and order because they concentrated so many economically desperate men in Paris. The Assembly therefore dissolved the Workshops and gave the recruits the alternative of enlistment in the army or accepting work in the provinces. The workers of Paris resisted. From June 23 to June 26, 1848, the working-class districts of the capital rose in insurrection until they were finally subdued by the troops brought in by General Cavaignac, the energetic Minister of War.

These "June Days" were a landmark in modern history, the first large-scale outbreak of genuine class warfare, with both sides demonstrating a very strong class feeling. The specter of social revolution, for the moment a grim reality, terrified the propertied classes throughout France and through-

out Europe. The panic accounted for the severe repression of the insurgents: at least 1,500 were killed during the fighting, and 4,000 more were subsequently deported, chiefly to Algeria. All socialist clubs and newspapers were padlocked, and Louis Blanc fled to England. France became a virtual military dictatorship under General Cavaignac.

The fears of the moderates were evident in the formal constitution of the Second French Republic which the National Assembly completed in November, 1848. The Assembly declared property inviolable and rejected a motion to list the right to work among the fundamental rights of French citizens. The constitution assigned legislative power to a single chamber, which was to be elected by universal male suffrage every three years. It gave executive authority to a President of the Republic, to be chosen by popular election every four years. The French Constitution of November, 1848, thus inaugurated a regime based partly on Montesquieu's doctrine of the separation of powers and on the American type of presidential government. It abandoned the attempts to imitate the British parliamentary system first made in the Constitution of 1791 and repeated in the Charter of 1814. Its concern for property notwithstanding, it represented a daring venture in political democracy.

France, however, was ill prepared to undertake political democracy. The military rule exercised by Cavaignac while the Assembly was drafting the constitution was one ominous sign. Another was the outcome of the first, and only, presidential election (December, 1848) held under the Second Republic. Fewer than half a million votes were polled by the three genuinely republican candidates; a million and a half were cast for General Cavaignac; some five and a half million votes and the Presidency of the Republic went to Louis Napoleon

Bonaparte, the nephew of Napoleon. President Bonaparte was to subvert the constitution in 1851 and then to proclaim himself Emperor Napoleon III (see Chapter XXI). The French Revolution of 1848, like that of 1789, had produced a republic that ended in a Napoleonic empire.

Italy

In 1849, President Bonaparte sent French troops to Rome to defend the Pope against Italian radicals. By then the Italian revolutions were waning fast. The revolutionary movement was ambitious, but weak and divided. It attempted to cast off the Austrian hegemony with only the slender military resources of the separate Italian states. Piedmont rejected the offer of assistance from revolutionary France in 1848 with the proud statement, *Italia farà da se* —Italy will do it alone.

Throughout the 1840's three schools of liberalism, none of them commanding really wide popular support, competed for leadership. Two of them were only very moderately liberal and agreed that political power in emancipated Italy should be limited to the nobility and the bourgeoisie. But they disagreed on the issue of leadership for united Italy. One group of moderates, centered in the north, favored the single leadership of Piedmont. The other group of moderates called themselves the "Neo-Guelfs" because, like the Guelfs of the Middle Ages, they expected the Pope to free Italy from the control of a German emperor. The Neo-Guelf leader, the priest Gioberti (1801-1852), declared that the fate of Italy depended on "the union of Rome and Turin" (the Piedmontese capital). The Pope would head and the army of Piedmont would defend a federation of Italian states, each with a cautiously liberal constitution.

The third group, "Young Italy," asserted that Italy should be unified as a single state and that that state should be a democratic republic. The founder of "Young Italy" was Mazzini (1805-1872), the great democratic idealist of modern Italian history. Here is a statement of Mazzini's political credo:

We believe, therefore, in the Holy Alliance of the Peoples as being the vastest formula of association possible in our epoch;—in the *liberty* and *equality* of the peoples, without which no true association can exist;—in *nationality*, which is the *conscience* of the peoples, and which, by assigning to them their part in the work of association, . . . constitutes their mission upon earth, that is to say, their *individuality*, without which neither liberty nor equality are possible; —in the sacred *Fatherland*, cradle of nationality; altar and workshop of the individuals of which each nation is composed.*

A good European as well as an ardent Italian nationalist, Mazzini inspired the formation of Young Germany, Young Poland, and still other movements, all joined together in a federation called "Young Europe." He prophesied that Young Italy would lead Europe to political salvation; the events of 1848 proved him a very poor prophet.

Revolution struck first (January, 1848) in the Kingdom of the Two Sicilies, where the King was obliged to grant a moderately liberal constitution along the lines of the French Charter of 1814. During the next two months, King Charles Albert of Piedmont, Pope Pius IX, and the Grand Duke of Tuscany all had to follow suit. The news of the revolution in Vienna (see below, p. 188) provoked a successful insurrection in Milan, the capital of Austrian Lombardy (March 18-22). At the same time, Venice, the capital of the other Austrian province, proclaimed itself the independent Republic of St. Mark. The swift collapse of Habsburg rule in Lombardy-Venetia inspired a national crusade against the Austrians. Charles

---

* "Faith and the Future," in *Life and Writings of Joseph Mazzini* (London, 1905), III, 129.

Albert of Piedmont assumed command; Naples, Tuscany, and the Pope sent soldiers; and volunteers joined up from every section of the peninsula. For the moment, it seemed likely that both nationalism and liberalism would win in Italy.

But only for the moment. During the spring and early summer of 1848, Piedmont annexed Lombardy-Venetia and the two small duchies of Parma and Modena. The populations of the other Italian states, jealous of their particularist traditions, commenced to fear the imperialism of Piedmont more than they desired the unification of Italy. On April 29, 1848, Pope Pius IX announced that his "equal affection" for all peoples obliged him to adopt a neutral position in the war with Austria and to recall his soldiers. The Pope could not be both an Italian patriot and an international spiritual leader. Moreover, Pius was alarmed by the increasingly radical political temper of the Roman population and by the threats of German bishops to create an anti-pope. The Neo-Guelf cause had received a fatal blow. In May, 1848, the King of Naples withdrew his contingents from the war, and the Austrians, taking the offensive, crushed the forces of Charles Albert at Custozza (July, 1848). *Italia farà da se* was an empty boast; Italy had not been able to do it alone.

A few months later, the revolutionary movement got a brief second wind. Roman radicals, dissatisfied with the mildly liberal constitution of March, rose up in November, 1848. After Pius IX had fled to Neopolitan territory, they transformed the Papal States into the democratic Roman Republic, headed by Mazzini himself. In March, 1849, radicals in Piedmont forced a reluctant Charles Albert to renew the war with Austria, but at the battle of Novara (March 22) Austria again overwhelmed Piedmont. This new disaster thoroughly wrecked the Italian revolutions. In August, 1849, the Austrians put an end to the Republic of St.

Mark after a prolonged siege and bombardment of the city of Venice. Meanwhile, besieged by French troops, Mazzini's Roman Republic had surrendered (July, 1849).

Again subdivided into many sovereign states, again dominated by the Habsburgs, Italy returned almost completely to its pre-revolutionary status. The only bright spot in the picture was the emergence of Piedmont

Mazzini.

as the natural leader of Italian nationalism and liberalism. Despite the defeats at Custozza and Novara, despite the loss of the territories momentarily annexed in 1848, Piedmont enjoyed the prestige of having twice defied the hated Austrians.

Germany

The course of the German revolutions in 1848 roughly paralleled that of the

Italian. In Germany, too, liberalism and nationalism won initial victories and then collapsed in the face of internal dissension and Austrian resistance. The failure in Germany was the more surprising—and ominous—since the revolutionary movement had begun to recruit support among peasants who wished to abolish the relics of manorialism and among laborers who were victimized by the industrial revolution. Liberal and nationalist agitation, however, centered in the well-to-do bourgeoisie and in the professional classes, especially university professors, who enjoyed more influence and respect in Germany than anywhere else in Europe. Except for a few republicans and socialists, the German liberals were moderates. They wanted constitutional monarchy in the various German states, an end to the repressive hegemony of Metternich, and the strengthening of the German Confederation.

The hero of German liberals was King Frederick William IV of Prussia (1840-1861). Attractive and cultivated, the Prussian king was also infatuated with divine-right concepts of kingship. He promised much but delivered little, and that little after endless hesitation. He promised to carry out his father's unhonored pledge to give Prussia a constitution and a representative assembly. But the diet that he convoked at last in 1847 was neither popularly elected nor allowed the initiative in legislation.

Not this royal knight-errant, but rather the *Zollverein* (customs union) constituted Prussia's most solid contribution to German unification before 1848. In 1818, Prussia had abolished internal tariffs within its scattered territories and had applied a uniform tariff schedule to imports. This reasonable innovation so stimulated commerce that by 1844 first Prussia's immediate neighbors and then almost all the German states, except for Austria, had joined the customs union. The *Zollverein* liberated Germany from the oppressive burden of local tolls and taxes and cleared the way for her phenomenal economic development later in the century. Although it did not exercise a decisive influence on politics, it suggested that the state which had achieved the economic unification of the Germans might naturally take the initiative in political unification.

Political unification seemed almost a certainty in 1848. Stimulated by the example of Paris, the revolutionaries scored their first successes in the western German states at the end of February, 1848. From there, the demands for constitutions, civil liberties, and a strengthened German Confederation fanned out rapidly. By mid-March, demonstrators were throwing up barricades in Berlin. Frederick William IV faced the unpleasant alternatives of surrendering some of his cherished royal prerogatives or of ordering his soldiers to fire on his "beloved Berliners." At first, he tried to evade the issue by accepting some of the liberals' demands and by appealing for calm among "ye inhabitants of my true and beautiful Berlin." His appeal came too late. Before it could be fully publicized, rioting broke out with redoubled violence, and more than two hundred rioters, chiefly working men, were killed. The mob broke into the royal palace and forced the King to go through a grotesque ceremony of saluting the corpses of the victims. Overwrought by the humiliation to himself and by the death of his subjects, Frederick William accepted all the demands of liberals and nationalists. He summoned a constitutional convention for Prussia, declared Prussia "merged in Germany," and proclaimed himself "King of the free regenerated German nation."

Drastic reform of the German Confederation now began. In May, 1848, a great constitutional convention held its first session in the Church of St. Paul at Frankfurt, the capital of the Confederation. Its members,

CHAPTER XIX

Barricades in Berlin during the revolution of March, 1848.

popularly elected throughout Germany, represented the flower of the German intelligentsia: 18 doctors, 33 clergymen, 49 university professors, 57 schoolteachers, 223 lawyers and judges—but only one dirt farmer, and not a single laboring man.

The Frankfurt Assembly had to decide the geographical limits of Germany. The Confederation, like the Holy Roman Empire before it, included Austria proper but excluded most of the non-German Habsburg territories. Neither did it include the eastern provinces of Prussia, notably those acquired in the partitions of Poland. The Austrian issue divided the assembly into two camps: the "Big Germans" who favored, and the "Little Germans" who opposed, the inclusion of Austria and Bohemia in the projected German state. Austrian opposition to a "Big Germany" insured the Assembly's adoption of the "Little Germany" proposal.

On the question of Prussian Poland, the nationalism of the Frankfurt Assembly overcame its liberalism. By a large majority it voted to include some Prussian areas in which the Poles formed the majority of the population. The arguments advanced against the Poles in the assembly debates revealed German nationalism at its most superheated. One orator declared that the minority of Germans had a natural right to rule the Poles, who had "less cultural content":

It is high time for us . . . to wake to a wholesome national egotism, to say the word right out for once, which in every question places the welfare and honour of the fatherland uppermost. . . . Our right is none other than the right of the stronger, the right of conquest.*

In contrast, the national constitution promulgated by the Frankfurt Assembly in March, 1849, was a decidedly liberal document, a combination of principles drawn from the American federal system and British parliamentary practice. The individual states were to surrender many of their powers to the German federal goverment. The federal legislature would consist of a

---

* Quoted in J. G. Legge, *Rhyme and Revolution in Germany* (London, 1918), 397.

lower house, elected by universal male suffrage, and an upper house, chosen by the governments and the legislatures of the constituent states. Ministers responsible to the legislature would form the federal executive. Over all would preside a constitutional monarch, the German emperor.

The Frankfurt Constitution died a-borning. The Assembly elected the King of Prussia to be emperor, but Frederick William, ignoring his fine promises of March, 1848, and alarmed by Austrian opposition, rejected the offer. He called the Frankfurt Constitution a "bastard" product:

The crown is no crown. The crown which a Hohenzollern could accept . . . is not one created by an Assembly born of revolutionary seed. . . . No it must be a crown set with the seal of the Almighty, one which makes him who assumes it . . . Sovereign 'by the Grace of God.' . . .*

Since the only serious candiate for the imperial office had balked, the Frankfurt Assembly soon came to an end. It had never secured recognition from foreign governments, had never raised a penny in taxes, had never exerted real sovereignty over Germany. Its solitary concrete achievement was to collect funds by popular subscription for the purchase of two second-hand ships at Hamburg as the nucleus of a German navy. It had demonstrated that the national unity of Germany could not be achieved through moral suasion.

German liberalism, too, suffered a major defeat. After the initial shock of the revolutions, the German princes either revoked or abridged the constitutions that they had granted in 1848. In Prussia, Frederick William and his conservative advisers repeatedly doctored the work of the constitutional convention summoned in 1848. The end product, the Prussian Constitution of 1850, made Prussia relatively safe for autocracy

---

* *Ibid.*, 516-517.

and aristocracy down to World War I (for details, see Chapter XXII).

The Habsburg Domains

The fate of German and Italian nationalism in 1848 rested partly with the outcome of the revolutions in the Habsburg Empire. If these revolutions had immobilized the Habsburg government for a long period, then Italian and German unification might have been realized. But Austria, though buffeted by wave after wave of revolution, rode out the storm. The success of the counter-revolution in the Habsburg Empire assured its victory in Italy and Germany.

The nature and the outcome of the Habsburg revolutions depended in turn on the complex structure of nationalities within the Austrian Empire:

NATIONALITIES UNDER HABSBURG
RULE, 1848

Nationality	Percentage of Total Population
German	23
Magyar (Hungarian)	14
Czech and Slovak	19
South (Yugo-) Slav	
Slovene	4
Croat	4
Serb	5
Pole	7
Ruthenian (Little Russian)	8
Rumanian	8
Italian	8

These percentages are drawn from L. B. Namier, "1848: The Revolution of the Intellectuals," *Proceedings of the British Academy, 1944* (London, 1947), 259.

Complexity was further complicated because these national groups were not always neatly segregated geographically, each in its own compartment. For instance, in the Hungarian part of the Empire the Magyars dominated but nevertheless fell slightly short of forming a numerical majority of the population. Geographical

Hungary contained important minorities of Slovaks, in the north; of Rumanians, in the east (Transylvania); of Croats and Serbs, in the south; and of Germans, scattered throughout.

Nationalism developed particular force not only among Italians and Czechs but also among Magyars and Croats. Magyar nationalism won its first victory in 1844, when it secured the substitution of the Hungarian language for the traditional Latin as the official language of the Hungarian sections of the Empire. Now Hungary was largely a rural country, still dominated by nobles and country squires who controlled its political life by their monopoly of seats in the county assemblies and the central diet. One school of Magyar nationalists aimed at the gradual modernization of Hungary's culture and economy along English lines. The less moderate nationalists, however, whose spokesman was the spellbinding orator, Louis Kossuth (1802-1894), hoped to revolutionize the political status of their land. For these extremists the linguistic reform of 1844 was but the first in a series of projected reforms cutting the ties with the Vienna government. Naturally, Magyar nationalists bitterly opposed the political awakening of their Slavic subjects, particularly the Croats, who were enjoying a nationalistic renaissance begun when their homeland was exposed to French revolutionary influences as the Illyrian Provinces of Napoleon's empire.

This antagonism between Croats and Magyars revealed an all-important fact about the nationalistic movements within the Habsburg Empire. Some nationality groups—Italians, Magyars, Czechs, Poles—resented the German-dominated government in Vienna. Others, notably the Croats and Rumanians, were not so much anti-German as anti-Hungarian, since they were concerned most with their Magyar masters. Here was a situation where the central government might apply to advantage the policy of "divide and conquer," pitting the anti-Magyar elements against the anti-German Magyars, and conquering both. This was substantially what happened in 1848. Indeed, a similar policy had already been used in 1846 to suppress a revolt in Galicia, the province that Austria acquired in the partitions of Poland. When the Polish landlords revolted, their exploited Ruthenian peasants rose against them and got the backing of Vienna.

Liberalism also played a significant part in the Habsburg revolutions. Austria proper was the center of liberal discontent. The expanding middle class desired guarantees of civil liberties, a voice in the government, and the lifting of the old-fashioned mercantilist restrictions that hampered business activity. In Vienna, as in Paris and Berlin, the workers went further and demanded radical democratic reforms.

From 1815 to 1848, the Habsburg government virtually ignored the grumblings and protests that arose in almost every quarter of the Empire. If Prince Metternich had had his way, he would probably have granted a constitution, a conservative constitution to be sure, but one that would have made concessions to liberal and nationalist aspirations. But Metternich, though he enjoyed a nearly free hand in foreign affairs, did not have his way in domestic policy. He was blocked by the emperors—the bureaucratic Francis I (1792-1835) and the feeble-minded, epileptic Ferdinand I (1835-1848) —and by the vested interests of the aristocrats. The Habsburg government was an inefficient autocracy, supported by an army of censors and spies, yet made somewhat tolerable by its own slackness. Austria, Metternich accurately stated, was "administered, but not ruled."

The news of the February revolution in Paris shook the Empire to its foundations. Four separate revolutions broke out almost simultaneously in March, 1848. (1) In Italy, Lombardy and Venetia revolted. (2) In Hungary, Kossuth and his ardent Magyar supporters forced Emperor Ferdinand to accept the "March Laws," which gave Hungary political autonomy within the empire. The March Laws instituted parliamentary government and substituted an elected legislature for the feudal Hungarian diet. They abolished serfdom and ended the immunity of nobles and gentry from taxation. But the new constitution rode roughshod over the rights of non-Magyars in Hungary by making use of the Hungarian language a requirement for election as a deputy to the legislature.

(3) Aroused by the Hungarian revolt, the workers and university students of Vienna rose on March 12. On the next day, Prince Metternich resigned from the post he had held for thirty-nine years and fled to Britain disguised as an English gentleman. Although the imperial government repeatedly promised reforms, rioting continued in Vienna, and by May the political atmosphere was so charged that Emperor Ferdinand and his family left the capital. Pending the meeting of a constituent assembly in July, the effective government in Vienna was entrusted to a revolutionary council, the Committee of Safety.

(4) Meanwhile, in Prague, the Bohemian capital, Czech nationalists were demanding rights similar to those granted the Magyars in the March Laws. Discontent mounted with the news that the "Big German" faction at Frankfurt was contemplating the inclusion of Bohemia in a German federation. In June, 1848, the Czechs organized a Pan-Slav Congress to promote a solid front of Slavic peoples against "Big German" encroachments. The Pan-Slav Congress set off new street demonstrations, in the course of which Princess Windischgrätz, the wife of the commander of the Austrian garrison at Prague, was accidentally killed (June 12,

1848). Five days later, Prince Windischgrätz, after bombarding Prague, dispersed the Czech revolutionaries and established a military dictatorship in Bohemia. The counter-revolution was beginning.

A month later, the Austrian army in Italy defeated Piedmont at Custozza. In September, 1848, the Vienna Constituent Assembly, which represented all the provinces of the Empire except the Italian and Hungarian, passed a great reform measure that actually strengthened the counter-revolution. It emancipated the peasantry from the last remaining servile obligations, notably the requirement to work for their landlords. The peasants, the great core of the Habsburg population, had secured their main ambitions; they therefore tended to withdraw their support from further revolutionary activities.

The time was ripe for the policy of "divide and conquer." In the Hungarian provinces, the Germans, Slovaks, Rumanians, Serbs, and Croats, all outraged by the discrimination against them in the March Laws, had risen up against the Magyars. In September, 1848, the imperial government authorized Jellachich, the governor of Croatia, to invade central Hungary. While the hard-fighting Magyars still held off the forces of Jellachich, the radicals of Vienna revolted again, proclaiming their support of the Magyars and declaring Austria a democratic republic. The armies of Jellachich and Windischgrätz crushed the Vienna revolution (October 31, 1848) and executed the radical leaders.

The counter-revolution was hitting its full stride. In November, 1848, the energetic and unscrupulous Prince Felix Schwarzenberg (1800-1852), the brother-in-law of Windischgrätz, became chief minister of the Habsburg government. Schwarzenberg engineered the abdication of the incapable Ferdinand I in December and the accession of Ferdinand's eighteen-year-old nephew,

CHAPTER XIX

Metternich.

Russian Poland unless it was checked. Schwarzenberg accepted the Tsar's offer, and in August, 1849, Russian troops helped to subjugate the Hungarian republic.

The Lessons of 1848

Tsar Nicholas I boasted in 1850 that Providence had assigned him "the mission of delivering Europe from constitutional governments." By 1850, almost the whole Continent was in the process of being delivered from the constitutional governments established in 1848. In France President Bonaparte, in Prussia Frederick William IV, and in Austria and Italy Prince Schwarzenberg guided the triumphant course of the absolutist revival. Kossuth, Mazzini, and other revolutionaries went into exile. In the early months of 1848, enthusiastic liberals had hailed the arrival of the "peoples' springtime." It had been a false spring.

Mazzini himself undertook to explain why counter-revolution had cut short the peoples' springtime. In 1850, he wrote from London:

Why, then, has *reaction* triumphed?
Yes: the cause is in ourselves; in our want of organisation;... in our ceaseless distrust, in our miserable little vanities, in our absolute want of that spirit of discipline which alone can achieve great results; in the scattering and dispersing of our forces in a multitude of small centres and sects, powerful to dissolve, impotent to found.
The cause is in the gradual substitution of the worship of material interests ... for the grand problem of education, which alone can legitimatise our efforts. .... It is in the narrow spirit of *Nationalism* substituted for the spirit of Nationality; in the stupid presumption on the part of each people that they are capable of solving the political, social, and economical problem alone; in their forgetfulness of the great truths that the cause of the peoples is one; that the cause of the Fatherland must lean upon Humanity. .... The language of narrow nationalism held at Frankfort destroyed

the Emperor Francis Joseph (1848-1916), who was at least neither feeble-minded nor epileptic. Schwarzenberg declared that the promises made by the old emperor could not legally bind his successor and therefore shelved the constitutional projects of the Austrian Constituent Assembly.

Schwarzenberg's reassertion of the dominance of Vienna infuriated the Magyars, who fought on like tigers. In April, 1849, the parliament of Hungary declared the country an independent republic and named Kossuth its chief executive. Russia now providentially offered Austria military assistance, for Tsar Nicholas I feared that the revolutionary contagion might spread to

the German Revolution; as the fatal idea of aggrandisement of the House of Savoy [Piedmont] destroyed the Italian Revolution.*

The revolutionaries of 1848 had not fully learned the lessons of 1830. They relied too heavily on spontaneous mass uprisings. They expended too much energy on factional arguments, so that the strength of their movement was sapped by the disputes between working-class radicals and bourgeois moderates, between the followers of Gioberti and those of Mazzini, between "Big" and "Little" Germans, and between Magyars and Slavs. "The worship of material interests" noted by Mazzini helped to explain why the French bourgeoisie and peasantry feared the Paris socialists' threat to private property and why the Habsburg peasants lost interest in the revolution after they had secured the abolition of manorialism.

"The narrow spirit of nationalism" was

_____

* Preface to "Faith and the Future," written fifteen years after the essay. *Life and Writings of Joseph Mazzini* (London, 1905), III, 76-77.

by no means dispelled after 1848. It was to haunt the Habsburg Empire for the rest of its days and eventually to destroy it. The failure of the liberals to unify Italy and Germany in 1848 transferred the leadership of the nationalist movements from the amateur revolutionaries to the professional politicians of Piedmont and Prussia. In the case of Italy, the transfer augured well, for Piedmont, alone among the Italian states, retained the moderately liberal constitution it had secured in 1848. In the case of Germany, however, the anti-liberal Bismarck was to achieve through "blood and iron" what the Frankfurt Assembly had not accomplished by peaceful means.

Equally prophetic was the class warfare of the June Days in Paris. New demands for social and economic rights and privileges were arising alongside the older demands for political liberties and constitutions. Europe was beginning to feel the challenge of the forces released by industrialism. The year 1848 saw not only revolutions but also the first publication of *The Communist Manifesto* by Marx and Engels.

Reading Suggestions
on Revolution and Counter-Revolution

General Accounts

F. B. Artz, *Reaction and Revolution, 1814-1832* (New York: Harper and Brothers, 1950). This volume in the "Rise of Modern Europe" series presents a painstaking survey of all aspects of European history during the period indicated.

A. J. May, *The Age of Metternich, 1814-1848* (New York: Henry Holt & Co., 1933. A Berkshire Study). Handy brief introduction.

Special Studies

A. N. Whitehead, *Science and the Modern World* (New York: New American Library. A Mentor Book). Contains a most significant chapter appraising the meaning of the Romantic protest.

G. Brandes, *Main Currents in Nineteenth-Century Literature*, 6 vols. (London: Wm. Heinemann, Ltd., 1901-1905). An important, detailed study.

C. Brinton, *Political Ideas of the English Romanticists* (London: Oxford University Press, 1926). A useful study.

A. Cobban, ed., *The Debate on the French Revolution, 1789-1800* (London:

Nicholas Kaye, 1950). The selections here illuminate the contrasts between the revolutionary and counter-revolutionary creeds.

G. Boas, *French Philosophies of the Romantic Period* (Baltimore: Johns Hopkins University Press, 1934). A perceptive study.

K. Francke, *A History of German Literature as Determined by Social Forces* (New York: Henry Holt & Co., 1907). Lives up to its title.

Maurice Raynal, *The Nineteenth Century: Goya to Gauguin* (Geneva, Switzerland: Editions Albert Skira, 1951). A superbly illustrated introduction to nineteenth-century painting.

K. Clark, *The Gothic Revival* (London: Constable & Co., Ltd., 1950). An instructive and entertaining commentary on English architecture.

A. Einstein, *Music in the Romantic Era* (New York: W. W. Norton and Co., 1947). A good survey.

C. K. Webster, *The Congress of Vienna, 1814-1815* (London: George Bell & Sons, Ltd., 1934). A technical manual, but very sound history.

C. Brinton, *The Lives of Talleyrand* (New York: W. W. Norton and Co., 1936). A spirited defense of the great French opportunist.

P. Viereck, *Conservatism Revisited* (New York: Charles Scribner's Sons, 1949). A judicious, brief re-evaluation of Metternich.

E. L. Woodward, *Three Studies in European Conservatism* (London: Constable and Co., Ltd., 1929). Thoughtful essays on Metternich, Guizot, and the Catholic Church in the nineteenth century.

H. Treitschke, *History of Germany in the Nineteenth Century*, 7 vols. (New York: McBride, Nast, 1915-1919). Well-written and strongly nationalistic.

J. C. Legge, *Rhyme and Revolution in Germany: a Study in German History, Life, Literature, and Character, 1813-1850* (London: Constable & Co., Ltd., 1918). Meets the specifications of its full title; an engaging book.

A. G. Mazour, *The First Russian Revolution, 1825* (Berkeley: University of California Press, 1937). Valuable also for the reign of Alexander I.

A. J. Whyte, *The Evolution of Modern Italy* (Oxford: B. Blackwell, 1944). A good introduction.

I. Silone, *The Living Thoughts of Mazzini* (New York: Longmans, Green & Co., 1939). A useful selection from the writings of the great Italian liberal nationalist.

P. Robertson, *Revolutions of 1848: A Social History* (Princeton: Princeton University Press, 1952). Detailed, colorful, and reasonably well balanced.

L. B. Namier, *1848: The Revolution of the Intellectuals* (London: British Academy, 1947). An important essay, castigating some of the "liberals" of 1848.

Historical Fiction and Sources

The best way to study this period through imaginative literature lies through the writings of the great men of the period. The following are particularly recommended (almost all are available in several editions): the Waverley novels of Sir Walter Scott; the two great novels of Victor Hugo (*Notre Dame*, and *Les Misérables*); the novels of the French Romantic realist, Stendhal, particularly *The Red and the Black;* and the poems of Coleridge and of Wordsworth.

The Impact of the Economic Revolutions

CHAPTER XX

I: Introduction

ON MAY 1, 1851, in London, Queen Victoria opened the "Great Exhibition of the Works of Industry of All Nations." The first of many "world's fairs," this international exposition displayed the latest mechanical marvels in a setting that was itself a marvel of engineering—the Crystal Palace, a structure of iron and glass stretching like a mammoth greenhouse for more than a third of a mile in Hyde Park. To the visitors who thronged the Crystal Palace it was evident that Britain was the workshop of the world. The industrial revolution had come of age.

The London exhibition, of course, marked neither the beginning nor the end of the industrial revolution. Machines and factories had already begun to change the face of Britain in the late eighteenth century (see Chapter XVI), and in the century since 1851 they have altered profoundly not only Britain and other western nations but also many of the other countries on the globe. In the mid-nineteenth century it was plain that revolutionary changes in technology and business organization were bringing revolutionary consequences for society and politics.

London slums.
Woodcut after Doré.

Industrial marvels on display at the Great Exhibition, London, 1851.

Industrialism bound nations closer together by stimulating international exchange and by lowering the barriers of distance through improvements in transport and communication. Yet it heightened international tensions by fortifying nationalism with economic ambition and by inspiring a bloodless war for markets and raw materials. Businessmen demanded national policies that would foster swift and profitable economic development, and they sought the political rights that would give them a voice in determining those policies. The industrial revolution raised standards of living and enabled increasing numbers of men to enjoy the decencies and comforts of existence. It also aggravated problems of unemployment, low wages, and bad living and working conditions. Industrial workers clamored for the right to work, to organize, to strike, and to vote.

The rise of industry and labor called forth divergent schools of social and political thought. One school believed in the kind of liberalism preached by the exponents of laissez-faire and practiced by the July Monarchy in France. What was good for business was necessarily good for labor, too. If a worker wanted economic security and political status, he should win them through his own efforts, by becoming rich enough to obtain them. Another school of liberals, however, believed that the state should occasionally undertake benevolent reforms to assist the workers. These moderate reformers satisfied some workingmen, but

CHAPTER XX

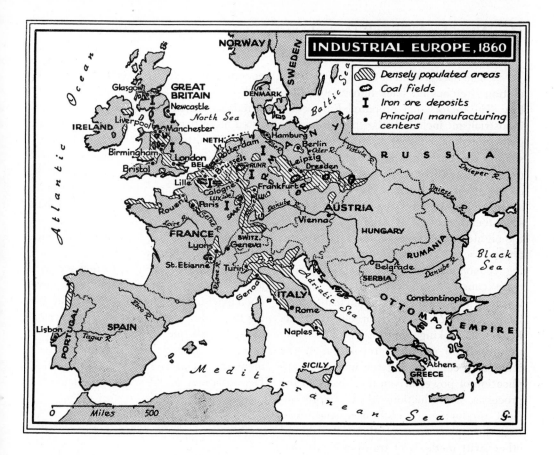

other workers turned to the more drastic but still peaceful changes of the type recommended by Louis Blanc (see Chapter XIX) and his fellow advocates of Utopian socialism. Still others accepted revolutionary socialism, the violent and inevitable class war predicted by Marx and Engels in *The Communist Manifesto*.

In short, many of the great economic and political issues that are still very much with us today came to the fore a century ago. Industrialism created a new labor problem and intensified the older farm problem. It sharpened the differences between the

champions of relatively free international trade and the economic nationalists who demanded protective tariffs. It divided liberals between the opponents and the defenders of the benevolent or welfare state. It created a radical wing of the working class, soon to be split between the rival schools of Utopian and Marxian socialism. It altered the course of human history even more radically than did a great political upheaval like the French Revolution of 1789. This great development fully deserves to be recognized by history as the industrial revolution.

II: The Industrial Revolution

The background of the industrial revolution stretches far back into western history. The factors that prepared Europe for industrialism included the political, religious, scientific, and intellectual forces that shaped the early modern world. The rise of the competitive state system, the Protestant stress on hard work, the brushing aside of tradition by the scientists of the seventeenth century and the *philosophes* of the eighteenth—all played their part in creating a society and culture ready for sweeping economic changes. Although the ultimate causes of the industrial revolution involved a wide range of human institutions, its immediate causes were largely economic. Four interlocking developments directly produced the industrial revolution of the nineteenth century: (1) the increasing application of power-driven machinery to the processes of production; (2) the more efficient production of coal, iron, and steel; (3) the appearance of the railroad and other swift methods of transport and communication; and (4) the expansion of banking and credit facilities.

The Machine

A hundred years ago, cotton was the king of mechanized industries. Beginning with the spinning jenny in the 1760's, the use of machinery gradually spread to many phases of cotton manufacturing. In 1793, the American Eli Whitney devised the cotton "gin," an engine that separated the fibers of the raw cotton from the seeds and enabled a single slave to do what had previously required the hand labor of fifty slaves. Meanwhile, British inventors perfected a power-driven loom for weaving cotton thread into cloth. By 1830, Britain

operated more than 50,000 power looms, and cotton goods accounted for half of Britain's exports. The British census of 1851 listed more than half a million workers employed in cotton manufacturing alone.

Advances in mechanical engineering made this rapid expansion possible. Earlier, the difficulty of getting exactly fitting parts had greatly limited the usefulness of machines like Watt's steam engine. Then British engineers studied the precision techniques used by the makers of watches and clocks. They devised a lathe that turned screws of almost perfect regularity, and they developed machines for sawing, boring, and turning the pulley blocks used by British vessels in the Napoleonic Wars. Eli Whitney, meantime, was undertaking important experiments at his arms factory in Connecticut. He explained in 1798 that he planned to

An early Singer sewing machine, 1854.

"make the same parts of different guns, as the locks, for example, as much like each other as the successive impressions of a copper-plate engraving." In other words, Whitney was discovering the concept of standardized and interchangeable parts, one of the basic principles of our assembly-line methods today.

For half a century, however, many American and British manufacturers ignored the revolutionary implications of Whitney's experiments. The tempo of mechanization, though quickening, was still slow, held back by the survival of handicraft techniques, and dependent on the appearance of new inventions. For example the mechanization of the woolen and clothing industries did not come until the 1850's, when Britain produced a machine for wool-combing and the American, Isaac Singer, popularized the sewing-machine.

Coal and Iron

Coal ranked with cotton as an industry that pioneered in the solution of urgent technical problems. Steam engines pumped water from the mines; ventilating shafts and power fans supplied them with fresh air; and safety lamps gave miners protection against dangerous underground gases. Miners were thus able to work seams more than a thousand feet below the surface. The coal output of Britain, then the world's leading producer, rose steadily from about 16,000,000 tons in 1816, to 30,000,000 in 1836, and 65,000,000 in 1856.

The increased consumption of coal resulted chiefly from the steady expansion of the iron industry, which used large quantities of coal to make the coke needed in smelting. The efficiency of smelting advanced rapidly after the development of the blast furnace (1828), in which fans provided a blast of hot air to intensify the action of the hot coke on the iron. Thanks to the blast furnace, Britain produced iron strong enough for use in bridges and in factory buildings. Yet the best grade of iron lacked the tremendous strength of steel, which is iron purified of all but a minute fraction of carbon through a process of prolonged, intensive heating. Steel could be made in the early 1800's, but only by methods so costly that the expense of producing a ton of steel was five times that of making a ton of iron. Then in 1856 Bessemer, an Englishman of French extraction, invented the converter, which accelerated the removal of impurities by shooting jets of compressed air into the molten metal. A decade later, Siemens, a German living in England, devised the "open-hearth" process, which utilized scrap as well as new iron, and which handled larger amounts of metal at one time than the converter could. The inventions of Bessemer and Siemens lowered the cost of making steel so substantially that the world output increased tenfold between 1865 and 1880.

Transport and Communication

A great consumer of iron and steel was the railroad, which marked the culmination of the revolution in transport. During the first three decades of the nineteenth century, many hundreds of miles of canal were dug in Europe and in North America. Highway construction was improved by the Scot, Macadam, who devised the durable road-surfacing material of broken stones that still bears his name. Canals and improved roads, however, did not provide a means for overland shipment of heavy bulky items like coal and iron. The answer was found, of course, in the railroad. By the 1820's, Britain had several hundred miles of short, horse-drawn rail lines. Methods of rolling rails and constructing solid roadbeds were already known; only mechanization remained to be accomplished. In 1827, George Stephenson and others put the steam engine on wheels and created the locomotive. Two years later, Stephenson's "Rocket" demonstrated the power of the locomotive by running twelve miles in fifty-three minutes on the new Liverpool and Manchester Railway, the first line to be operated entirely by steam. The railroad building boom was soon in full swing: Britain had 500 miles of track in 1838, 6,600 miles in 1850, and 15,500 in 1870.

Steam also revolutionized water transport. Fulton's steamboat, the "Clermont," made a successful trip on the Hudson River in 1807, and soon steamers plied the inland waterways of the United States and Europe. Ocean-going steamships, by contrast, long proved uneconomical to operate because of the inefficiency of the marine engine. When the Scot, Samuel Cunard, inaugurated the first regular transatlantic steamer service (between Liverpool and Boston in 1840), the coal required for the voyage took up almost half of the space on his vessels. Consequently, only passengers and mails went by steamship; most freight was still handled by the more efficient sailing ships like the beautiful American clippers. Finally, in the 1860's, the development of better marine engines and the substitution of the screw propeller for the cumbersome paddle wheel forecast the eventual doom of the commercial sailing vessel.

Meanwhile, communications were experiencing radical improvements. A rather mild beginning was made in 1840, when the government of Great Britain inaugurated the penny post. To send a letter from London to Edinburgh, for instance, now cost only a penny, less than one-tenth of the old rate. Other countries soon followed Britain's lead in providing cheap, efficient postal service. More dramatic was the utilization of electricity for ultra-swift communications. An impressive series of "firsts" started with the first telegraph message, from Baltimore to Washington in 1844. Then came the first submarine cable, under the English Channel in 1851; the first transatlantic cable, 1866; and the first telephone, 1876.

Banking and Capital

The exploitation of all these new inventions and discoveries required a constant flow of fresh capital. Here the older and richer commercial community supported the young industrial community. Tobacco merchants of Glasgow provided the funds that made their city the foremost industrial center of Scotland, and tea merchants in London and Bristol financed the ironmasters of South Wales. Bankers played such an important role that Disraeli, the British politician, listed the Barings of London and the international house of Rothschild among the great powers of Europe.

In the early nineteenth century each of the five Rothschild brothers, sons of a German Jewish banker, established himself in an important economic center—London, Paris, Frankfurt, Naples, and Vienna. The Austrian government gave all five the title of baron in return for their financial services and made the London and Paris Rothschilds its consular representatives. The Rothschilds prospered because they sought only a relatively modest profit and because, in an age of frequent speculation, they avoided investment in unduly risky undertakings. Moreover, the international ramifications of the house facilitated investment by residents of one state in the projects of other states. The Paris Rothschild, for instance, secured British capital for the construction of French railroads in the 1840's.

Banks further assisted economic expansion by promoting the use of checks and banknotes in place of specie. During the

198

Napoleonic War the shortage of coins forced British mill-owners to pay their workers in goods or in scrip of unstable value; the British government empowered local banks to issue paper notes supplementing the meager supply of coins. But, whenever financial crises occurred—and they came frequently before 1850—dozens of local banks failed, and their notes became valueless. Parliament gradually devised more permanent remedies. It encouraged the absorption of small shaky banks by the larger and solider institutions, and in 1844 it gave the Bank of England a virtual monopoly of the issuing of banknotes, thus providing a very reliable paper currency. It also applied, first to railroads and then to other companies, the principle of limited liability, indicated by the familiar "Ltd." after the names of British firms. In the early industrial revolution the shareholders in most British companies had unlimited liability: they might find their personal fortunes appropriated to satisfy the creditors of an unsuccessful company. The practice of limiting each shareholder's liability to the value of his shares encouraged wider public investment by diminishing its risks.

British Leadership

Fiscal legislation was only one factor among many accounting for the industrial leadership of Britain in the nineteenth century. She possessed large and easily available deposits of coal and iron; the geographical compactness of the British Isles made shipments from mine to smelter and from mill to seaport short and cheap. The large population furnished a reservoir of laborers ready to learn industrial skills and to work for relatively low pay in the new mills. Two particularly important sources of workers were the marginal farmers, driven off the land by the enclosure move-

ment (see Chapter XVI), and the Irish, seeking to escape from their poverty-ridden and overcrowded island.

The commercial and naval leadership gained by Britain in the eighteenth century and fortified by the Napoleonic Wars paved the way for her industrial leadership. It facilitated the search for raw materials and markets, and the profits from overseas trade and the empire swelled the capital available for investment in industry. The Napoleonic Wars themselves stimulated demand for metal goods and the invention of new machines. And the construction of great docks along the lower Thames during the wars entrenched London in its position as the greatest economic center in Europe.

The tangible signs of Britain's economic predominance were evident on every hand about 1850—in the teeming London docks, in the thriving financial houses of the City, in the exhibits at the Crystal Palace, in the mushrooming industrial cities of the Midlands and the North of England, and in other quarters of the globe. British capital and thousands of skilled British workers participated in the construction of French railroads. American trains ran on rails rolled in British mills. Cotton goods made in Lancashire clothed a sizable part of the world's population. In the mid-nineteenth century, Britain accounted for about half the world output of finished iron, and in textiles she possessed 18,000,000 power spindles, as compared with the 5,500,000 of the United States and the 4,000,000 of France, her two closest competitors.

The Timetable of Industrialization

Yet Britain, even in the heyday of her leadership, did not monopolize inventive skill. France, for example, devised the chlorine process of bleaching cloth and the

Early American reaping machine, invented by McCormick.

Jacquard loom for weaving intricate patterns. Germany led the world in agricultural chemistry and in the utilization of the valuable by-products of coal. In Belgium, Solvay discovered how to made industrial soda and its compounds. And from the United States came Eli Whitney, Morse and the telegraph, Singer and the sewing-machine, and Cyrus McCormick, whose reaper (1831) was the first of many agricultural machines developed in America.

But the timetable of industrialization depended on much besides inventions; factories required raw materials, large amounts of capital and skilled labor, and a favorable political climate. The presence of all these elements made Britain the workshop of the world in the nineteenth century. But when other countries, notably the United States and Germany, began to enjoy a favorable combination of industrial requisites, Britain lost the advantage of her head start. Although the textiles of New England had been flourishing since the early 1800's, the exploitation of rich agricultural resources dominated the American economy until the time of the Civil War. Germany's indus-

trialization awaited the stimulus provided by the successful completion of political unification in 1871. During the last third of the nineteenth century, both America and Germany began to hit their stride industrially; by 1900, they were formidable rivals of Great Britain.

Since 1900, the industrial revolution has marched steadily on, ever intensifying and ever widening. Oil and electricity have ended the dominance of coal; aluminum and the alloys have challenged that of steel; rayon and other synthetic fibers have partly displaced cotton and wool; automobiles, trucks, and airplanes have partly superseded the railroad. Even in the oldest of mechanized industries, cotton, the revolution still goes on today with the introduction of a mechanical cotton-picker. Among the older industrialized countries, the United States in particular has witnessed wave after wave of fresh technological advance. And Russia has become a major industrial power for the first time within the past quarter-century as a result of her Five-Year Plans.

Industry has indeed revolutionized our world and our lives. To name but a few of its most obvious consequences, it has created great corporations, which are virtually powers in their own right; it has made possible the newspaper, the radio, and other media of mass communication; it has devised assembly-line methods of mass production applicable to many fields of human endeavor. The full nature and the full consequences of the industrial revolution, especially since 1900, will become more evident in later chapters of this book, as we examine the history of the leading countries during the past century. In this chapter, we shall stress the economic and social consequences of industrialism in the nineteenth century.

III: Economic and Social Consequences of Industrialization

The Agricultural Revolution

Improvements in industry brought improvements in farming, thus accelerating the agricultural revolution that had begun in the eighteenth century (see Chapter XVI). Factory-made implements like the reaper and the steel plow aided the cultivation of the North American prairie, and drainage pipes made of inexpensive tile converted useless marshes into fertile fields. The mechanical cream-separator raised the dairy industry to a big business. Railroads and steamships sped the transport of produce from farm to market. The processes of canning, refrigeration, and freezing, all industrial in origin and all first applied on a wide scale during the last third of the nineteenth century, permitted the almost indefinite preservation of many perishable commodities.

Farmers found a steadily expanding market in both the raw materials consumed by the mills of industry and the food required by teeming new factory towns. International trade in farm products increased rapidly during the second half of the nineteenth century. The annual export of wheat from the fertile prairies of the United States and Canada rose from 22,000,000 bushels in the 1850's to 150,000,000 in 1880. Imported flour, chiefly from North America, accounted for one-quarter of the bread consumed in Britain during the 1850's and for one-half in the 1870's. Denmark and the Netherlands increasingly furnished the British table with bacon, butter, eggs, and cheese; Australia supplied its mutton and Argentina its beef.

Germany now partly assumed Britain's old role as the pioneer of scientific agriculture. German experimenters, shortly after 1800, extracted sugar from beets in commercially important quantities, thus ending Europe's dependence on the cane sugar of the West Indies. In the 1840's the German chemist, Liebig, published a series of influential works on the agricultural applications of organic chemistry. Plant growth, Liebig argued, depended on three basic elements—nitrogen, potassium, and phosphorus. But the production of crops and fodder leached these elements from the soil; unless they could be returned to it, formerly fertile lands might go the way of "the once prolific soil of Virginia, now in many parts no longer able to grow its former staple productions—wheat and tobacco." Liebig's gloomy predictions did not generally come true, for his teachings promoted the wide use of fertilizers—guano from the nesting islands of sea-birds off the west coast of South America, nitrate from Chile, and potassium from European potash mines.

Farming progressed, expanded, and prospered in the nineteenth century as never before. Yet the agricultural revolution exacted a price, sometimes a very high price. Faced with the competition of beet sugar, the sugar-cane islands of the West Indies went into a prolonged slump from which they have not fully recovered to this day. In the most industrialized countries the social and political importance of agricultural interests began to decline. Farming was no longer the principal occupation of Englishmen in the nineteenth century, and land was no longer the almost universal yardstick of wealth and political power. The manufacturers and merchants of Britain scored a decisive victory over the landed gentry in the campaign to repeal the Corn Laws, the tariffs on the importation of the wheat and other cereals which the English term collectively "corn." The Corn Laws protected British farmers at the expense of British workers and industrialists. The latter, organized in the powerful Anti-Corn Law League, protested that the tariffs "artificially enhance the price of food in this country," and "prevent the exchange of the products of . . . industry for the food of other countries." Free trade was the remedy prescribed by the Anti-Corn Law League, and free trade came when Parliament repealed the Corn Laws in 1846. The decisive factor was the disastrous attack of black rot that ruined the Irish potato crop two years running and made the importation of cheap grain essential to avert widespread starvation in Ireland. Industrial Britain had abandoned the attempt to be self-sustaining in food.

Population

As a matter of fact, the population of the British Isles was growing so rapidly that self-sufficiency was virtually impossible. The number of inhabitants in England and Wales more than tripled during the course of the nineteenth century, from about 9,000,000 in 1800 to 32,500,000 in 1900. Yet in some predominantly agricultural countries the rate of increase almost matched that of industrial Britain. For example, the Russian population, still rural in the great majority during the nineteenth century, rose from about 36,000,000 in 1800 to about 100,000,000 in 1900.

The most important social change flow-

British demonstration against the Corn Laws.

ing from the industrial revolution was not the increase in the population but the alteration in its structure and balance. Wherever mills, mines, and factories were opened, towns and cities appeared. Large areas of once-rural England became urban England, and a similar transformation was beginning in the lowlands of Scotland around Glasgow, in the northern French plain around Lille, in the German Rhineland, and along the rivers of the northeastern United States. The growth of an urban population caused a rise in the numbers and influence of the two social classes that form the backbone of an industrial society. These are the businessmen and the workingmen. Industrialists, bankers, managers, and promoters of every sort joined the already established capitalists to form the modern middle class or bourgeoisie. Millhands, railwaymen, miners, clerks, and a host of other recruits swelled the ranks of wage-earning laborers.

The impact of capital and labor upon the life of industrial nations was becoming increasingly evident by the middle of the nineteenth century. Some of the signs pointed to steady material progress—the wonders of the Crystal Palace, or the conquest of the barriers of space by the railroad, the steamship, and the telegraph. Other signs, however, portended serious dislocation and violent change. The repeal of the Corn Laws buried an old agrarian way of life in Britain. The industrial depression of the late 1840's suggested an alarming pattern for economic slumps. By throwing hundreds of thousands out of work it aggravated social discontent and in Paris led to the outbreak of genuine class warfare in the violent "June Days" of 1848 (see Chapter XIX).

Now it is essential for the student of history to fix his attention on *both* the peaceful and the disruptive social effects of the industrial revolution. Unemployment and the other miseries of industrial labor have produced some of the most dramatic pages of modern history, but they do not tell the whole story. The slums of the ugly new factory towns a hundred years ago were often horrible indeed, yet even these horrors were relative. The urban slums sometimes represented a positive improvement over the rural slums in which the grandparents of the millhands had lived. Too often, whitewashed or vine-covered country cottages concealed behind their picturesque exteriors a contaminated water supply, a total lack of sanitary facilities, and an appalling incidence of infant mortality and tuberculosis. In the cities, infant mortality dropped because of improvements in medicine and sanitation. Adults lived longer because they had better hospital facilities, ate a more balanced and nourishing diet, and observed a higher standard of personal cleanliness. The industrial revolution played its part by increasing the supply of fresh food and by permitting the use of cheap and washable cotton clothing in place of woolens which were seldom, if ever, laundered.

The Aspirations of the Middle Class

A famous parable, first published in France in 1819, furnishes a revealing view of middle-class aspirations. The author, Saint-Simon, supposed that France suddenly lost "fifty of her best mechanical engineers, civil and military engineers, architects, doctors, surgeons, apothecaries, seamen, clockmakers; fifty of her best bankers, two hundred of her best business men"—and so on through a long list comprising the three thousand leading men in industry, science, and the arts. These men, Saint-Simon stated, are "in the most real sense the flower of French society," "the most useful to their country." "The nation would become a lifeless corpse as soon as it lost them."

Let us pass on to another assumption. Suppose that France preserves all the men of genius that she possesses in the sciences, fine arts and professions, but has the misfortune to lose in the same day Monsieur the King's brother [and many other members of the royal family]. Suppose that France loses at the same time all the great officers of the royal household, all the ministers (with or without portfolio), all the councillors of state, all the chief magistrates, marshals, cardinals, archbishops, bishops, vicars-general, judges, and, in addition, ten thousand of the richest proprietors who live in the style of nobles.

This mischance would certainly distress the French, because they are kind-hearted, and could not see with indifference the sudden disappearance of such a large number of their compatriots. But this loss of thirty-thousand individuals, considered to be the most important in the State, would only grieve them for purely sentimental reasons and would result in no political evil for the State.

These suppositions underline the most important fact of present politics: . . . that our social organization is seriously defective. . . .

The scientists, artists, and artisans, the only men whose work is of positive utility to society, and cost it practically nothing, are kept down by the princes and other rulers who are simply more or less incapable bureaucrats. Those who control honours and other national awards owe, in general, the supremacy they enjoy, to the accident of birth, to flattery, intrigue and other dubious methods. . . .

These suppositions show that society is a world which is upside down.*

To the men of the middle class, the state indeed seemed upside down. In the Britain of the 1820's the new industrialists had small opportunity to mold national policy. Few of them had the right to vote for members of Parliament; booming industrial cities like Manchester and Birmingham sent not a single representative to the House of Commons. A high proportion of businessmen belonged not to the Church of England but to non-Anglican Protestant chapels. Nonconformists, as these dissenters were now

termed, could not hold public office or send their sons to Oxford or Cambridge; such privileges were reserved for Anglicans. Even in France, despite the gains made in 1789, the bourgeois enjoyed as yet only the second-class citizenship sketched by Saint-Simon.

The middle class very soon won the place in the sun which they felt they deserved. In Britain, the gradual process of reform gave them substantially all they wanted. The high spot, higher even than the repeal of the Corn Laws, was the Reform Bill of 1832, which extended the suffrage to the middle class (for details, see Chapter XXI). In France, as we have already seen, the bourgeois had their revolution in 1830 and got their July Monarchy and their citizen-king. The wealthier bourgeois won the vote in 1830, and the rest of the male population got it in 1848. In Belgium, the revolution of 1830 marked a very great advance in the power of the middle class. Elsewhere the movements of 1830 and 1848 had less favorable results, yet even at their most disappointing they represented a step forward in the political evolution of the middle class.

The Grievances of the Working Class

The grievances of workingmen were more numerous than those of their masters, and they were more difficult to satisfy. The right of laborers to vote and their right to organize and carry on union activities may serve as examples. In Britain, substantial numbers of workers first secured the vote in 1867, a generation after the enfranchisement of the wealthier middle class. France adopted universal male suffrage in 1848, eighteen years after the upper bourgeois had gained a political voice.

During most of the nineteenth century,

* Saint-Simon, *Selected Writings*, F. M. H. Markham, ed. (New York, 1952), 72-74.

labor unions and strikes were regarded as improper restraints on the free operation of natural economic laws. Hence the specific ban on such combinations, as they were termed, imposed by the British Combination Acts at the close of the eighteenth century. The Act of 1799 declared "illegal, null, and void"

all contracts, covenants, and agreements whatsoever, in writing or not in writing, at any time or times heretofore made or entered into by any journeymen manufacturers or other workmen, or other persons within this kingdom, for obtaining an advance of wages . . . or for lessening or altering their . . . usual hours or time of working or for decreasing the quantity of work. . . .*

Continental governments imposed similar restrictions, as in the Le Chapelier Law passed by the French National Assembly in 1791 (see Chapter XVIII). It took labor a long time to win legal recognition of union activities—until 1890 in Germany, for instance, 1867 in Austria, and 1872 in the Netherlands. In France, the July Monarchy repressed strikes with great brutality; the Le Chapelier Law was at length relaxed in the 1860's and repealed outright in 1884. In Britain, Parliament modified the Combination Acts early, in the 1820's, but did not repeal them until 1876. For three-quarters of the nineteenth century British workmen had at most a very limited right to strike.

Labor's drive for political and legal rights, however, was only a side issue during the early days of the industrial revolution. Workmen faced more immediate and pressing problems. They had to find jobs and to make ends meet on inadequate wages. The modern western world has always experienced the business cycle, with its alternations of full employment and unemploy-

ment. The industrial revolution intensified the cycle. Boom periods became more hectic and more prosperous, and general depressions, like that of the late 1840's, became more frequent and more severe. Moreover, factories at first made little attempt to provide a fairly steady level of employment in both boom times and slack times. When a batch of orders came in, machines were worked to capacity and men were worked to the limit of their endurance until the orders were filled. Then the factory simply shut down to await the next flurry of orders. This practice resulted in the seasonal unemployment still sometimes encountered today in exceptionally seasonal industries like clothing. A hundred years ago it was rather the rule than the exception.

A century and more ago labor sometimes got such low wages that only a single man could maintain himself on his earnings. The French or British textile worker who was a family man might have to put both his children and his wife to work as a matter of sheer economic necessity. Humanitarian tradition probably exaggerates the extent to which industry exploited and degraded women and children, probably tends to view the exceptional instance of extreme hardship as the average situation. Still, exploitation and degradation unquestionably did occur. Just as one lynching is a shocking thing, so it is a shocking thing to encounter one instance of the kind here recorded in the testimony of a factory worker, Samuel Coulson, before a British parliamentary committee in 1831-32:

At what time in the morning, in the brisk time, did those girls go to the mills?
In the brisk time, for about six weeks, they have gone at 3 o'clock in the morning, and ended at 10, or nearly half-past, at night.

What intervals were allowed for rest or refreshment during those nineteen hours of labour?
Breakfast a quarter of an hour, and dinner half an hour, and drinking a quarter of an hour.

---

* Quoted in A. E. Bland, P. A. Brown, R. H. Tawney, *English Economic History: Select Documents* (London, 1915), 626-627.

Child labor in a United States shoe factory, about 1840.

Was any of that time taken up in cleaning the machinery?

They generally had to do what they call dry down; sometimes this took the whole of the time at breakfast or drinking, and they were to get their dinner or breakfast as they could; if not, it was brought home.

Had you not great difficulty in awakening your children to this excessive labour?

Yes, in the early time we had them to take up asleep and shake them when we got them on the floor to dress them, before we could get them off to their work; but not so in the common hours.

What was the length of time they could be in bed during those long hours?

It was near 11 o'clock before we could get them into bed after getting a little victuals, and then at morning my mistress used to stop up all night, for fear that we could not get them ready for the time. . . .

So that they had not above four hours' sleep at this time?

No, they had not.

For how long together was it?

About six weeks it held; it was only done when the throng was very much on; it was not often that.

The common hours of labour were from 6 in the morning till half-past eight at night?

Yes.

With the same intervals for food?

Yes, just the same.

Were the children excessively fatigued by this labour?

Many times; we have cried often when we have given them the little victualling we had to give them; we had to shake them, and they have fallen to sleep with the victuals in their mouths many a time.

Did this excessive term of labour occasion much cruelty also?

Yes, with being so very much fatigued the strap was very frequently used.

Have any of your children been strapped?

Yes, every one; the eldest daughter; I was up in Lancashire a fortnight and when I got home I saw her shoulders, and I said, 'Ann, what is the matter?' She said, 'The over-looker has strapped me; but,' she said, 'do not go to the overlooker, for if you do we shall lose our work.' I said I would not if she would tell me the truth as to what caused it. 'Well,' she said, 'I was fettling the waste, and the girl I had learned had got so perfect she could keep the side up till I could fettle the waste; the overlooker came round, and said, "What are you doing?" I said, "I am fettling while the other girl keeps the upper end up"; he said, "Drop it this minute"; she said, "No, I must go on with this"'; and because she did not do it,

CHAPTER XX

Industrial landscape. Steel works at Pittsburgh, 1876.

he took a strap, and beat her between the shoulders. . . .

What was the wages in the short hours?
Three shillings a week each.

When they wrought those very long hours what did they get?
Three shillings and sevenpence halfpenny.

For all that additional labour they had only sevenpence halfpenny a week additional?
No more.*

Excessively long hours, low pay, and sub-human working conditions were the most general grievances of early industrial workers. Many plants tolerated conditions hazardous to their employees. Few had safety devices to guard dangerous machinery, and cotton mills maintained both the heat and the humidity at a high level because threads broke less often in a hot, damp atmosphere. Here is another case history, probably not typical of a whole industry, but nasty enough in itself. In 1823, the laborers at an English spinning plant near Manchester worked a 14-hour day in a temperature of 80° to 84°. If they opened a window for

* Bland, Brown, and Tawney, *English Economic History: Select Documents*, 510-513.

fresh air, they were fined a shilling, and a long list of other offenses brought fines—being dirty during working hours (a shilling) and washing during working hours (the same); turning on the gaslights too early in the evening (a shilling) and keeping them on too late in the morning (two shillings); even whistling while they worked (one shilling). Most seriously affected was the laborer absent because of sickness; if he did not provide a competent substitute, he paid the exorbitant fine of six shillings.

Many workers could not afford decent housing, and if they could afford it, they could not always find it. Some of the new factory towns were reasonably well planned, with wide streets and space for yards and parks. Some even had a copious supply of good water and arrangements for disposing of sewage. But in rapidly growing London the Thames soon became an open sewer that stank so foully that riverside dwellers were reluctant to open their windows. Windows themselves were at a premium in England because of an old regulation, not repealed until 1851, taxing every window in excess of eight, even in multi-family dwellings. Fantastic numbers of human beings were jammed into the overcrowded slums of Lille in France and of Liverpool and Manchester in England. A parliamentary committee reported on the state of Manchester in the depression year of 1840:

Manchester has no Building Act, and hence . . . each proprietor builds as he pleases. . . . A cottage row may be badly drained, the streets may be full of pits, brimful of stagnant water, the receptacle of dead cats and dogs, yet no one may find fault.

So long as this and other great manufacturing towns were . . . prosperous, every fresh addition of operatives found employment, good wages, and plenty of food; and so long as the families of working people are well fed, . . . they maintain their health in a surprising manner, even in cellars and other close dwellings. Now, however, the case is different. Food is dear, labour scarce, and wages in many branches very low; consequently, . . . disease and death are making unusual havoc. . . . It is in such a depressed state of the manufacturing districts as at present exists that unpaved and badly sewered streets, narrow alleys, close, unventilated courts and cellars, exhibit their malign influence. . . . Manchester has no public park or other grounds where the population can walk and breathe the fresh air. . . . In this respect Manchester is disgracefully defective; more so, perhaps, than any other town in the empire. Every advantage of this nature has been sacrificed to the getting of money in the shape of ground-rents.*

When a man sweated all day in a dirty, overheated factory, when he returned to cold, damp lodgings with no bathing facilities, when he ate chiefly bread and potatoes—his health was bound to suffer. Lord Shaftesbury, an English reformer of the 1840's, predicted that, unless conditions were improved, Lancashire would soon be-

*Bland, Brown, and Tawney, *English Economic History: Select Documents*, 520-521.

come "a province of pigmies." The industrial nations also threatened to remain nations of semi-literates. Until they finally made provisions for free public schools, during the last third of the nineteenth century, educational facilities were grossly inadequate. In England, as often as not, only the Sunday school gave the millhand's child a chance to learn his abc's. The millhand himself, if he had great ambition and fortitude, might get a bit of knowledge by spending his rare free hours attending one of the adult schools known as "mechanics' institutes." No wonder that in the 1840's one-third of the men and one-half of the women married in England could not sign their names on the marriage register and simply made their mark. And no wonder that Disraeli, the Tory reformer, had the characters in his social novel, *Sybil* (1845), speculate on the two nations into which Britain was divided:

'Well, society may be in its infancy,' said Egremont, slightly smiling; 'but, say what you like, our Queen reigns over the greatest nation that ever existed.'

'Which nation?' asked the younger stranger, 'for she reigns over two.'

The stranger paused; Egremont was silent, but looked inquiringly.

'Yes,' resumed the younger stranger after a moment's interval. 'Two nations; between whom there is no intercourse and no sympathy; who are as ignorant of each other's habits, thoughts, and feelings, as if they were dwellers in different zones, or inhabitants of different planets; who are formed by a different breeding, are fed by a different food, are ordered by different manners, and are not governed by the same laws.'

'You speak of—' said Egremont, hesitatingly. 'THE RICH AND THE POOR.' *

*B. Disraeli, *Sybil* (London, 1900), 76-77.

CHAPTER XX

IV: The Responses of Liberalism

Suffering and evil are nature's admonitions; they cannot be got rid of; and the impatient attempts of benevolence to banish them from the world by legislation . . . have always been productive of more evil than good.*

Such was the argument advanced by laissez-faire liberals in the British Parliament against the first piece of legislation to safeguard public health. It sums up the initial response of liberalism to the grave social problems created by the industrial revolution. Human interference with the processes of nature would only make things worse; nature would have to take her course—*laissez faire, laissez passer.*

The Classical Economists

The thinkers who advanced these ideas in the early nineteenth century were followers of Adam Smith (see Chapter XVII). They are known to history as the classical economists; to their enemies they were the architects of the "dismal science." The most famous of them were two Englishmen, Thomas Malthus (1766-1834) and David Ricardo (1772-1823). "Dismal science" is hardly too strong a term for the theories of Malthus. Though educated for the ministry, he became perhaps the very first professional economist in history and spent his mature years teaching at a college, near London, which trained young men for service with the East India Company. In 1798, he published the famous *Essay on the Principles of Population,* a dramatic warning that the human species would always breed itself into starvation.

In the *Essay,* Malthus formulated a series of natural laws:

---

* *The Economist,* May 13, 1848.

The power of population is indefinitely greater than the power in earth to produce subsistence for man.

Population, when unchecked, increases in a geometrical ratio. Subsistence only increases in an arithmetical ratio. . . . Through the animal and vegetable kingdoms, nature has scattered the seeds of life abroad with the most profuse and liberal hands. She has been comparatively sparing in the room and the nourishment necessary to rear them. . . . Necessity, that imperious, all-pervading law of nature, restrains them within the prescribed bounds. Among plants and animals its effects are waste of seed, sickness, and premature death. Among mankind, misery and vice.*

Misery and vice would spread, Malthus believed, because the unchecked increase in human numbers would lower the demand for labor and therefore lower the wages of labor.

When the wages of labour are hardly sufficient to maintain two children, a man marries and has five or six. He of course finds himself miserably distressed. He accuses the insufficiency of the price of labour to maintain a family. . . . He accuses the avarice of the rich, who suffer him to want what they can so well spare. He accuses the partial and unjust institutions of society, which have awarded him an inadequate share of the produce of the earth. He accuses perhaps the dispensations of Providence, which have assigned to him a place in society so beset with unavoidable distress and dependence. In searching for objects of accusation, he never adverts to the quarter from which his misfortunes originate. The last person that he would think of accusing is himself, on whom in fact the whole of the blame lies. . . .†

The reduction of the human birth rate was the only hope that this prophet of gloom held out to suffering humanity. It was to be achieved by "moral restraint," specifically

---

* *Essay on the Principles of Population,* Bk. I, Ch. 1.
† *Ibid.,* Bk. IV, Ch. 3.

by late marriage and by "chastity till that period arrives."

Ricardo, too, was a prophet of gloom. He was a landowner and a speculator, so successful in business that he bought his way into the House of Commons by paying £20,000 for the seat of a "rotten borough" in Ireland. His classic work, *On the Principles of Political Economy and Taxation,* attributed economic activity to three main forces. There was rent, paid to the owners of great natural resources like farmland and mines; there was profit, accruing to the enterprising individuals who exploited these resources; and there were wages, paid to the workers who performed the actual labor of exploitation. Of the three, rent was in the long run the most important. As a follower of Malthus, Ricardo believed that the human element would outgrow the natural element. Farms and mines would become depleted and exhausted, but their produce would continue in great demand. Rent, accordingly, would consume an ever larger share of the economic pie, leaving smaller and smaller portions for profit-making capitalists and wage-earning workers.

Ricardo tempered his pessimistic forecasts with many qualifications and reservations. He did not, for instance, believe that the size of the economic pie was altogether fixed, in other words, that the total wealth of mankind was irrevocably "frozen." Still, the *Principles of Political Economy* did sketch a picture of eventual stagnation, of man as the exploiter, the depleter, the wastrel. Where Adam Smith had placed the division of labor and the increase of wages at the center of economic life, Ricardo brought labor and wages under the Malthusian formula:

Labour, like all other things which are purchased and sold . . . , has its natural and its market price. The natural price of labour is that price which is necessary to enable the labourers, one with another, to subsist and to

perpetuate their race, without either increase or diminution.

. . .

The market price of labour is the price which is really paid for it, from the natural operation of the proportion of the supply to the demand; labour is dear when it is scarce, and cheap when it is plentiful. . . . It is when the market price of labour exceeds its natural price, that the condition of the labourer is flourishing and happy, that he has it in his power to command a greater proportion of the necessaries and enjoyments of life, and therefore to rear a healthy and numerous family. When, however, by the encouragement which high wages give to the increase of population, the number of labourers is increased, wages again fall to their natural price, and indeed . . . sometimes fall below it.*

Ricardo's disciples hardened this principle into the "Iron Law of Wages," which bound workmen to an everlasting cycle of high wages and large families, followed by an increase in the labor supply, a corresponding increase in the competition for jobs, and an inevitable slump in wages. In the long run, the worker was doomed to an endless economic treadmill. Ricardo himself, however, regarded the cycle not as an "iron law" but simply as a probability. Unforeseen factors might in the future modify its course and might even permit a gradual improvement of the worker's lot. But Ricardo seemed certain of one thing. Unforeseen factors would be the work of nature alone:

Like all other contracts, wages should be left to the free competition of the market, and should never be controlled by the interference of the legislature.†

---

* *On the Principles of Political Economy,* Ch. V, in *The Works and Correspondence of David Ricardo,* P. Sraffa, ed. (Cambridge, England, 1951), I, 93-94.

† *Ibid.,* 105.

CHAPTER XX

Laissez-Faire
Liberalism Appraised

It is easy to see why Malthus and Ricardo were regarded as great exponents of laissez-faire. It is more difficult for the twentieth-century observer to understand why they were also ranked among liberals. Yet the classical economists were indeed liberals in a sense; like the eighteenth-century *philosophes,* they did not doubt that natural laws were superior to man-made laws. Ricardo steadfastly believed in free trade, even though it would damage his own pocketbook. He supported the movement against the Corn Laws long before their actual repeal, though as a grain-growing landholder he stood to profit by the maintenance of tariffs on imported foodstuffs.

The thing that distinguished the classical economists from their predecessors of the Enlightenment was, of course, their pessimism. Adherents of the "dismal science" no longer viewed nature as the creation of the beneficent God of the deists; she was at best a neutral force and at worst a sinister one. Man himself—wasteful, careless, improvident—seemed once more afflicted with a kind of original sin. It is significant that Malthus, who passed such bleak judgments on man, was trained in the doctrines of Christianity, with their emphasis on the human propensity toward sin. Certainly the classical economists put a new emphasis on the realities of the human predicament and supplied a needed corrective to the naive optimism of the *philosophes.*

Yet the classical economists, too, had their naive faith. They mapped the economic world in terms of a world-machine governed by a few simple, almost unalterable laws—Malthusian laws of population, Ricardian laws of rent and wages. The history of the last century has demonstrated the inadequacy of their map. Malthus simply did not foresee that scientific advances would make the output of agriculture expand at a positively geometrical ratio. He did not foresee that the perils of increasing birthrates would sometimes be averted by the use of contraceptives, first popularized during the nineteenth century, or by recourse to emigration. Many millions of people moved from crowded Europe to lightly populated America during the nineteenth century. The exodus from overcrowded Ireland, in particular, continued so steadily after the famine of the 1840's that by 1900 the Irish population was little more than half what it had been fifty years earlier.

Famine still haunts the world today, and neo-Malthusian writers still view with alarm each new report of higher birthrates or of droughts, dust storms, and other agrarian disasters. Yet shortages of food have not so far prevented a simultaneous increase in human numbers and in the standard of human existence. The size of the economic pie has expanded far beyond the expectations of Ricardo, and so have the portions that are allotted to rent, to profit and to wages.

The classical economists did not take sufficient account of the immense changes being worked by the agricultural and industrial revolutions. Nevertheless, the laissez-faire liberalism that they championed won particular approval from the new industrial magnates. The captains of industry were perhaps disturbed by Ricardo's prediction that lower profits were inevitably coming; but they could take immense comfort from the theory that "suffering and evil" were "nature's admonitions." It was consoling to the rich to be told, in effect, that the poor deserved to be poor because they had indulged their appetites to excess. In the world of laissez-faire economics whatever was, was right, or at any rate ordained by nature.

To the working class, however, the

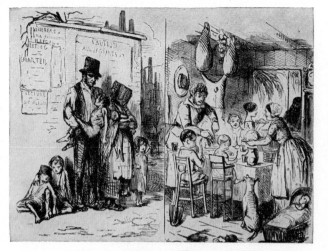

Here or There—a British comment on emigration as a remedy for industrial misery.

vauted freedom of laissez-faire often meant freedom to be undernourished, ill-housed, and alternately overworked and unemployed. It meant, too, the exchange of one set of masters for another, as the middle class tended to take over the privileges formerly reserved for the aristocracy of the Old Régime. Naturally the poor did not like to hear that they deserved to be poor. Naturally they sometimes felt that whatever was, was wrong and needed to be remedied, if necessary by interference with supposedly sacred natural laws.

To sum up: in the face of positive social evils, the classical economists offered only the essentially negative policy of laissez-faire. They were often very earnest men, honestly convinced that letting Nature take her course was the only thing to do. Yet they were open to the accusation of acting without heart and without conscience, and of advancing economic theories that were only rationalizations of their economic interests. It is not surprising that, as a practical and social political philosophy, strict laissez-faire liberalism today is almost extinct.

Utilitarianism: Bentham

The retreat from laissez-faire originated, rather paradoxically, with a man who was himself the friend and patron of the classical economists—Jeremy Bentham (1748-1832). Bentham was a child prodigy, who had read a history of England at the age of three and had taken an Oxford degree by the time he was sixteen. A rich bachelor, he behaved precisely as popular opinion expects an eccentric philosopher to behave. He amazed his guests by trotting and bobbing about the garden before dinner, or, as he put it, performing his "anteprandial circumgyrations." In death, he directed that his body be mummified and kept at the University College of London, which he had helped to found. In life, he projected dozens of schemes for the improvement of the human race, among them a model prison and reformatory which he called the "Panopticon," because guards stationed in a central block could survey the activities of all the inmates. He coined new words by the dozen, too, some of them happily forgotten but others valuable contributions to the language, like "minimize," "codify," "international," and the term most closely identified with his own thought, "utility."

Bentham submitted all human institutions and principles to the great test of utility, and denounced those which failed to measure up. The French revolutionaries' Declaration of the Rights of Man moved him to a characteristic outburst: "*Natural rights* is simple nonsense: natural and imprescriptible rights, rhetorical nonsense,—nonsense upon stilts." It was nonsense because Bentham did not believe in any such organism as society, did not believe in any case that natural laws determined morality:

Nature has placed mankind under the governance of two sovereign masters, *pain* and *pleasure*. It is for them alone to point out what we ought to do. . . . They govern us in all we can do, in all we say, in all we think: every effort we can make to throw off our subjection, will serve but to demonstrate and confirm it. In words a man may pretend to abjure their empire: but in reality he will remain subject to it all the while. The *principle of utility* recognizes this subjection, and assumes it for the foundation of that system, the object of which is to rear the fabric of felicity by the hands of reason and of law.

. . .

The interest of the community is one of the most general expressions that can occur in the phraseology of morals: no wonder that the meaning of it is often lost. When it has a meaning, it is this. The community is a fictitious *body,* composed of the individual persons who are considered as constituting as it were its *members.* The interest of the community then is, what?—the sum of the interests of the several members who compose it.

It is in vain to talk of the interest of the community without understanding what is the interest of the individual. A thing is said to promote the interest, or to be *for* the interest of an individual, when it tends to add to the sum total of his pleasures: or, what comes to the same thing, to diminish the sum total of his pains.*

The concept of utility advanced by Bentham had a long history reaching back through Hume and Holbach all the way to the Epicureans of the ancient world. Bentham, however, was the first to develop a system of utilitarianism. He listed a dozen or so simple pleasures and pains—the pleasures of the senses and the corresponding pains, the pleasure of wealth and the pain of privation, the pleasure of skill and the pain of awkwardness, and so on. Each category was subdivided, the pleasures of the senses, for instance, into those of taste, intoxication, smelling, touch, hearing, see-

ing, sex, health, and novelty. And each pleasure or pain could be evaluated according to its intensity, its duration, its certainty or uncertainty, its propinquity or remoteness, its fecundity, and its purity. This "felicific calculus," as Bentham termed it, was a good example of the eighteenth century's attempts to measure the immeasurable and to apply the exact methods of natural science to the subtleties of human behavior.

Nevertheless, Bentham was no doctrinaire *philosophe.* He dismissed the eighteenth-century theory of political contracts as a mere fiction. Ordinarily, he believed, governments could best safeguard the security of their subjects by following a hands-off policy. In social and economic matters, they should generally act as "passive policemen." Hence the close and sympathetic relationship between Bentham and the classical economists. Yet Bentham realized that occasions might arise when the state would have to become a more active policeman and go beyond the limited functions assigned to it by laissez-faire liberalism. The pursuit of self-interest by individuals might not always work to the best interest of all individuals. If the pains endured by the many exceeded the pleasures enjoyed by the few, then the state would have to step in and do something about it. In such a situation Bentham believed the state to be, in a word of his own devising, "omnicompetent," fit to undertake anything for the general welfare. Twentieth-century theories of the welfare state owe a good deal to this aspect of Bentham's utilitarianism.

By the time of his death, Bentham was gaining an international reputation. He had advised reformers in Portugal, Russia, Greece, and Egypt, and his writings were to exert a broad influence, particularly in France, Spain, and the Spanish-American republics. As late as 1920, his "Panopticon" provided the plan for an American prison

------

* *An Introduction to the Principles of Morals and Legislation,* Ch. I, Wilfrid Harrison, ed. (New York, 1948), 125-127.

(in Joliet, Illinois). His most important disciples, however, were English. The next chapter will show how a group of them, the Philosophic Radicals, pressed for reforms by parliamentary legislation. Here we shall see how his most important English follower, Mill, broadened and deepened utilitarianism into a doctrine of democratic liberalism.

Democratic Liberalism: Mill

John Stuart Mill (1806-1873) grew up in an atmosphere dense with the teachings of utilitarianism and classical economics. From his father, who worked closely with Bentham and was a good friend of Ricardo, he received an education almost without parallel for intensity and speed. He began the study of Greek at three, was writing history at twelve, and at sixteen organized an active "Utilitarian Society." It is scarcely remarkable that at the age of twenty this bright but overworked youth suffered a nervous breakdown. As Mill relates in his *Autobiography,* he had become "a mere reasoning machine" and undervalued the significance of emotions. So Mill turned to music and to the poetry of Wordsworth and Coleridge; presently he fell in love with Mrs. Taylor, a woman of warm personality, to whom he assigned the major credit for his later writings. The two maintained a close but Platonic friendship for twenty years until the death of Mr. Taylor at length enabled them to marry. Mill's personal history is important, for it goes far to explain why he endowed the liberal creed with the qualities which it so markedly lacked in the hands of the classical economists. He gave it new warmth and compassion.

Mill's humane liberalism stands forth most clearly in his essay *On Liberty* (1859) and his *Autobiography* (1873). But it is

evident, too, in his more technical works, notably *The Principles of Political Economy.* He first published this enormously successful textbook in 1848 and later revised it several times, each revision departing more and more from the "dismal science" of Ricardo and Malthus. Even the first edition of the *Principles* rejected the gloomy implications of the "iron law" of wages:

By what means, then, is poverty to be contended against? How is the evil of low wages to be remedied? If the expedients usually recommended for the purpose are not adapted to it, can no others be thought of? Is the problem incapable of solution? Can political economy do nothing, but only object to everything, and demonstrate that nothing can be done? *

Of course something could be done, and Mill proceeded to outline schemes for curbing overpopulation by promoting emigration to the colonies and by "elevating the habits of the labouring people through education," if need be through education by state compulsion and at state expense.

This one example is typical of the way in which Mill's quest for positive remedies led him to modify the laissez-faire attitude so long associated with liberalism. He sympathized with the French "National Workshops" of 1848 (see Chapter XIX) and with some of the moderate socialistic projects that we shall examine later in this chapter. Although Mill did not accept the socialistic solution of abolishing private property, his views on wealth gave little comfort to the propertied classes:

The social arrangements of modern Europe commenced from a distribution of property which was the result, not of just partition, or acquisition by industry, but of conquest and violence; and notwithstanding what industry has been doing for many centuries to modify the work of force, the system still retains many

---

* J. S. Mill, *Principles of Political Economy,* Bk. II, Ch. xiii (Boston, 1848).

traces of its origin. The laws of property have never yet conformed to the principles on which the justification of private property rests. . . . They have not held the balance fairly between human beings, but have heaped impediments upon some, to give advantages to others; they have purposely fostered inequalities, and prevented all from starting fair in the race.*

Mill asserted that the laws of property would operate more fairly if the workers could organize trade unions, form co-operatives, obtain higher wages, and even receive a share of profits. These changes could best be secured by private enterprise, he believed, and not by public intervention. But he also believed that there were some matters so pressing that the state would have to step in. He read the reports of the parliamentary investigating committees already cited in this chapter, and he was shocked by their accounts of human exploitation and degradation. So he recommended legislation to protect child laborers and to improve intolerable living and working conditions.

Where Bentham had accepted the sanctity of private property, Mill questioned it. Where Bentham had accepted universal suffrage and universal education only as ultimate goals for the distant future, Mill made them immediate objectives. All men, he believed, should have the right to vote; all should be prepared for it by receiving a basic minimum of schooling. Moreover, women should have the same rights—for Mill was a pioneer in the movement for feminine emancipation. He also proposed the introduction of proportional representation in the House of Commons, so that

political minorities might be sure of a voice and might not be overwhelmed by the tyranny of the majority.

The scheme of proportional representation and the fears that actuated it are particularly characteristic of Mill. He made protection of the individual's rights the basis of his famous essay On Liberty:

A government cannot have too much of the kind of activity which does not impede, but aids and stimulates, individual exertion and development. The mischief begins when, instead of calling forth the activity and powers of individuals and bodies, it substitutes its own activity for theirs; when, instead of informing, advising, and, upon occasion, denouncing, it makes them work in fetters, or bids them stand aside and does their work instead of them. The worth of a State, in the long run, is the worth of the individuals composing it; . . . a State which dwarfs its men, in order that they may be more docile instruments in its hands even for beneficial purposes—will find that with small men no great thing can really be accomplished. . . .*

Mill, then, did not so much reject, as modify and broaden, the liberalism of the classical economists. He, too, believed that laissez-faire was generally the best policy—except when the complete freedom of some individuals would harm other individuals. Perhaps Mill had a more tender conscience than did Adam Smith or Ricardo or even Bentham; certainly he lived at a later time, when the vices of industrialism were plainer. At any rate, he found the exceptions to the rule of laissez-faire more numerous and more urgent than his predecessors had ever imagined them to be.

* Ibid., Bk. II, Ch. ii.

* Utilitarianism, Liberty, and Representative Government, Everyman ed. (New York, 1910), 169-170.

V: The Socialist Response—the Utopians

Socialism Defined

In his later years, Mill referred to himself as a "socialist." By his standard, however, most of us are at least passive socialists today. Universal suffrage for men (and women), universal free education, the curbing of laissez-faire in the interests of the general welfare, the use of the taxing power to limit the accumulation of masses of private property—all these major reforms foreseen by Mill are widely accepted policies in the twentieth-century democracies. But they are not authentically socialistic. The authentic socialist does not stop, as Mill did, with changes in the *distribution* of wealth; he goes on to propose a radical change in arrangements for the *production* of goods. The means of production are to be transferred from the control of individuals to the control of the community as a whole.

Socialism—like fascism, liberalism, democracy—is one of those key words in the vocabulary of politics so heavily loaded with moral connotations that they are bound to be controversial. Everyone uses the word, yet mostly to indicate emphatic approval or disapproval of a given policy. The historian, however, attempts to use the word neutrally, for purposes of description and not of passing judgment. Historically, then, socialism denotes any political or economic philosophy that advocates the vesting of production in the hands of society and not those of private individuals. In practice, it usually means that the state, acting as the trustee of the community, owns major industries like coal, railroads, and steel. Socialism in its most complete form involves public ownership of almost all the instruments of production right down to the land itself with its farms and its mineral deposits.

Today we tend to term this complete form "communism"; a century ago, however, the terms "socialism" and "communism" were used almost interchangeably. A hundred years of history have gone into making the distinction now usually drawn between the two. The distinction is not simply one between incomplete and more complete versions of the same thing. Both present-day "socialists" and "communists" promote the collectivization of property—nationalization or, at the local level, "municipalization." But today the socialists believe this should be achieved gradually and peacefully through normal political methods and with at least some compensation for private owners. The communists believe that it should be achieved swiftly and violently, by revolution and outright seizure. Though the ends have their similarities, the means are worlds apart. This highly significant difference reflects the development of two divergent schools of socialist thought in the nineteenth century, the Utopian and the Marxian. Broadly speaking, such contemporary socialists as the British Laborites are in part the heirs of the nineteenth-century Utopians; the Russian communists, of course, are the heirs of Marx.

The Utopian socialists were essentially good sons of the Enlightenment. If only men would apply their reason to solving the problems of an industrial economy, if only they would wipe out man-made inequalities by letting the great natural law of brotherhood operate freely—then utopia would be within their grasp, and social and economic progress would come about almost automatically. This is the common belief linking together the four chief Utopians of the early nineteenth century—Saint-Simon, Fourier, Robert Owen, and Louis Blanc.

Saint-Simon

Henri, Count of Saint-Simon (1760-1825), belonged to a French noble family so old and aristocratic that it claimed direct descent from Charlemagne. Educated by *philosophes,* Saint-Simon fought with the French army in the American War of Independence. During the French Revolution he won a large fortune by speculating in lands expropriated from the Church and the *émigrés,* then lost most of it through the trickery of an unscrupulous partner. Despite his own reverses, he never lost his admiration for the businessmen and workmen elevated to prominence by industrialism. His enthusiasm reached a high pitch in his parable of the old and the new leaders of France, quoted earlier in this chapter (see above, p. 204).

Saint-Simon would have given supreme political power to the great leaders of industry, science, and art. But he reminded them: "Christianity commands you to use all your powers to increase as rapidly as possible the social welfare of the poor!" * Saint-Simon had all the Enlightenment's respect for science, yet he proclaimed the one science transcending all others to be the quest for the application of the Golden Rule. The only thing wrong with Christianity was that it had never really been tried: Saint-Simon accepted this view so often taken by social reformers.

Reform should come peacefully, through "persuasion and demonstration," and it should affect particularly the idlers, the rich drones of existing society. Since all men were brothers, even men of different nations, Saint-Simon envisaged a federation of European states. It would start with a union of the most advanced countries, France and Britain, and would culminate in the estab-

lishment of a European parliament when all states had been "organized" to the point where they merited popular representation. "Organization" was Saint-Simon's favorite word, but he seldom attempted to spell out precisely what he meant by it.

Fourier

By contrast, his compatriot and contemporary, Fourier (1772-1837), evolved an elaborate socialist plan, carried down to the last detail. At the French textile center of Lyons, Fourier was shocked by the extremes of wealth and poverty that he observed. At Paris, he was shocked when he found that a single apple cost a sum that would have bought a hundred apples in the countryside. Clearly, he concluded, something was amiss in a society and economy that permitted such fantastic divergences. He compared the historical importance of his apple with that of Newton. He was not joking, for he believed himself to be, quite literally, the Newton of the social sciences. Just as Newton had found the force holding the heavenly bodies in a state of mutual attraction, so Fourier proclaimed his own discovery of the force holding the individuals of human society in a state of mutual attraction or, as he put it, "association."

According to Fourier, human beings are attracted one to another by their passions. And he drew up a roster of passions, rather like the list of pleasures in Bentham's "felicific calculus"—sex, companionship, food, luxury, variety, and so on. It seemed obvious to Fourier that existing society frustrated the satisfaction of these instincts. Society, therefore, needed remodeling, needed to be rearranged into units that he called *phalanges,* "phalanxes." Some 1800 volunteers would compose each phalanx; they would form a kind of community com-

---

* Saint-Simon, *Selected Writings,* F. M. H. Markham, ed. (New York, 1952), 116.

pany, agreeing to split its profits three ways —five-twelfths to those who did the work, four-twelfths to those who undertook the management, and three-twelfths to those who supplied the capital.

Fourier's phalanx, with its relatively generous rewards to managers and capitalists, fell short of complete equality. However, it gave labor the largest share of the profits, and it foreshadowed many other features of socialist planning. Adult workers who did the most dangerous or unpleasant tasks would receive the highest remuneration. The inhabitants of the phalanx were to live in one large building, a sort of apartment hotel, which Fourier called a *phalanstère*. The *phalanstère* would provide the maximum opportunity for the satisfaction of man's sociable instincts, and it would also make the routine of daily living more efficient by substituting one central kitchen for hundreds of separate ones. The sordid features of housekeeping could be left to the children, who loved dirt anyhow and could form special squads to dispose of garbage and refuse.

From start to finish, the phalanx bore witness to Fourier's reaction against the monotony of the ordinary worker's existence. Places of work would be made as pleasant as possible by frequent, colorful redecoration. Members of the phalanx would change their jobs eight times a day because "enthusiasm cannot be sustained for more than an hour and a half or two hours in the performance of one particular operation." The phalanxes would be largely self-sufficient units, raising and making most of the things they required. And their inhabitants would be transformed, working from four or five in the morning to eight or nine at night, needing only five hours of sleep, since the delightful variety of work would not tire them and the days would not be long enough to permit them to taste the pleasures of existence.

Hopefully expecting some millionaire to finance his phalanxes, Fourier announced that he would be in his office every day at noon. For ten years he kept his daily office hour; naturally, no rich philanthropist ever appeared. Yet Fourier cannot be dismissed as a mere ineffectual crackpot. He undoubtedly had many wild and radical notions and carried the principle of uninhibited human association to the extreme of advocating sexual promiscuity in the *phalanstères,* thereby making "free love" and Utopian socialism synonymous. But he also made substantial contributions to socialist theory and to social psychology. Some of his recommendations, like higher pay for dangerous jobs and devices for relieving the tedium of work, have become common practice in the world of modern business.

Owen

One of the greatest Utopians was a self-made businessman, Robert Owen (1772-1858), a prosperous manufacturer of Manchester, England. When he was still in his twenties, Owen took over the large cotton mills at New Lanark in Scotland, a day's ride from Glasgow. Although the former owner of the mills had been accounted benevolent by the standards of the day, conditions there shook Owen to the core. A large part of the working force consisted of children who had been recruited from charitable institutions in Edinburgh when they were between six and eight years old. These youngsters did get a little schooling after hours, but Owen found many of them "dwarfs in body and mind." Adult laborers at New Lanark fared little better.

Theft and the receipt of stolen goods was their trade, idleness and drunkenness their habit, falsehood and deception their garb, dissentions [sic] civil and religious their daily practice; they united only in a zealous systematic opposition to their employers.*

Owen set out to show that he could increase his profits and increase the welfare of his laborers at the same time. He soon made New Lanark over into a model industrial village. For the adults he provided better working conditions, a ten-and-a-half-hour day, higher pay, and cleaner and roomier housing. He restrained the traditional Scottish Saturday night drunk by closing down the worst resorts, making good liquor available at cheap prices, and punishing offenders who made themselves a public nuisance. Even Robert Owen could not overcome another Scottish tradition—a sabbatarianism so strict that even outdoor exercise on Sunday was considered sinful. But he did at least encourage his millhands to cultivate their gardens after work on weekdays. Toward children he took no such brutish attitude as that of Fourier. He raised the minimum age of employment to ten, hoping ultimately to put it at twelve, and he gave his child laborers time for some real schooling. Owen's educational practices were very much in the manner of Rousseau; advanced bookish subjects were avoided, while crafts, nature study, and other "practical" subjects received much attention.

Education was Owen's great cure for the ailments of industrial Britain. He agreed with Locke that the infant mind was a *tabula rasa*, capable of almost indefinite perfectibility through the proper training. The right education could wipe out old and vicious customs, could raise human beings to a high plane of equality, and in general could promote unparalleled human progress. A really well-trained nation, for example, would make short work of the gloomy predictions of Malthus:

All men may, by judicious and proper laws and training, readily acquire knowledge and habits which will enable them, if they be permitted, to produce far more than they need for their support and enjoyment. . . .

Mr. Malthus is however correct, when he says that the population of the world is ever adapting itself to the quantity of food raised for its support; but he has not told us how much more food an intelligent and industrious people will create from the same soil, than will be produced by one ignorant and ill-governed. It is however as one, to infinity.

For man knows not the limit to his power of creating food. How much has this power been latterly increased in these islands! And in them such knowledge is in its infancy.*

Owen inherited much of the optimism of the *philosophes;* he also inherited some of their failures and disappointments. Despite his own success as a philanthropic capitalist, few businessmen followed his example. Disappointed but not disheartened, Owen drew up plans for an idealized version of New Lanark, very much like Fourier's phalanx, and found a few financial supporters, among them Ricardo. He called his utopia a "parallelogram," for the buildings were to be arranged in that geometrical pattern. It was to be a voluntary organization, relatively small in size, neatly balanced between farming and industry, decidedly advanced in Owen's recommendation for the abandonment of most conventional ties of marriage and the family.

In the 1820's, Owen financed an abortive effort to set up a parallelogram at New Harmony, Indiana. This venture almost ruined him financially, but it did not dampen his enthusiasm. He spent the rest of his long and fruitful career publishing and supporting projects for social reform. He advocated the association of all labor in one big union—an experiment that failed; and he sought to reduce the expenditures of workingmen by promoting the formation

---

* Robert Owen, *A New View of Society* (1817 ed., reprinted by Free Press, Glencoe, Ill.), 50.

* *Ibid.,* 174-175.

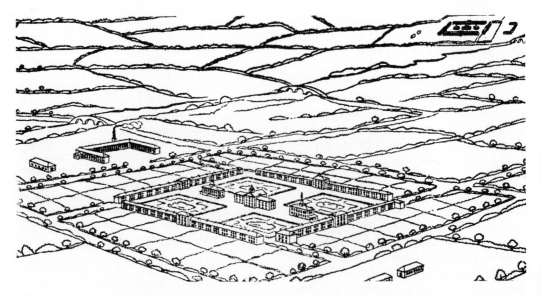

Sketch of an "Agricultural and Manufacturing Village of Unity and Mutual Co-operation," projected by the British Utopian socialist, Robert Owen, 1817.

of consumers' co-operatives—an experiment that succeeded. Throughout, he offended many of his contemporaries by his advocacy of sexual freedom, by his Voltairean attacks on established religion, and, in his old age, by his interest in spiritualism.

The Early Utopians Appraised

Owen and Fourier both attracted a fair number of followers not only in their native lands but also in the United States, where various religious sects were already launching ventures in communal living. The American Fourierists included many intellectuals, among them the crusading editor, Horace Greeley, and the poet, John Greenleaf Whittier. They sponsored more than thirty attempts to set up actual *phalanstères;* two of the most celebrated were Brook Farm, near Boston, and Phalanx, in New Jersey. America also witnessed more than half a dozen Owenite experiments in addition to New Harmony. Like New Harmony itself, however, most of the attempted

"phalanxes" and "parallelograms" did not prosper or last very long. And the few that got firmly established soon returned to conventional ways of individual profit-taking and family life.

Owen and Fourier relied on private initiative to build from their blueprints the model communities that they so hopefully expected to become widely copied examples for the reconstruction of society. Saint-Simon, too, believed in the power of example, but with his stress on "organization" he presumably meant to give government a larger role. The early followers of Saint-Simon in France developed the strain of social Christianity in the master's teaching and formed a fantastic religious cult; later some of the Saint-Simonians did achieve notable feats of practical "organization," like De Lesseps, the builder of the Suez Canal. But it remained for another student of Saint-Simon, Louis Blanc, to recommend "organization" on a large scale by the state.

Implacable critic of the bourgeois policies

CHAPTER XX

of the July Monarchy, Louis Blanc (1813-1882) devised the scheme that helped to produce the controversial workshops of the Paris revolution in 1848 (see Chapter XIX). He first outlined his plan in a pamphlet, *The Organization of Labor* (1839). "What proletarians need," he wrote, "is the instruments of labor; it is the function of government to supply these. If we were to define our conception of the state, our answer would be, that the state is the banker of the poor." * The government would finance and supervise the purchase of productive equipment and the formation of "social workshops." Naturally, it was to be a dem-

* "L'Organisation du Travail," in *The French Revolution of 1848*, J. A. R. Marriott, ed. (Oxford, 1913), I, 14. Our translation.

ocratic government, and it would withdraw its support and supervision once the workshops were on their feet. As the workshops gradually spread throughout France, socialistic enterprise would replace private enterprise, profits as such would vanish, and labor would be the only class in society. All workers would receive the same pay, and the equality promised in 1789 would at long last become a reality.

Much of Louis Blanc's socialism is conventionally Utopian; he, too, for instance, relies on the workers' voluntary participation in arrangements for communal living. The real novelty of his plan lies in the role, however brief, assigned to the state. With Blanc, socialism is beginning to move away from the realm of private philanthropy.

VI: The Socialist Response—Marx

With Karl Marx (1818-1883), the "Red Prussian," socialism assumed its most radical form—revolutionary communism. Where the early socialists had anticipated a gradual and peaceful evolution toward utopia, Marx forecast a sudden and violent proletarian revolution. Where they had mistrusted governments by and large, Marx urged the workers to capture the governments and make them the instruments for securing proletarian welfare. Of all the socialists, Marx was the most dogmatic and the most cocksure. He was sure that he alone knew the answers and that the future of mankind would develop inevitably according to the pattern which he found in human history.

Basic Principles

Marx found three laws in the pattern of history. First, *economic determinism:* he

believed that economic conditions largely determined all other human institutions— society and government, religion and art. Second, the *class struggle:* he believed that history was a dialectical process, a series of conflicts between antagonistic economic groups, between "haves" and "have-nots." Third, the *inevitability of communism:* he believed that the class struggle was bound to produce one final upheaval that would raise the victorious proletariat over the prostrate bourgeoisie in eternal triumph.

The Marxian philosophy of history derived from many older schools of thought. Marx himself was born and died in the nineteenth century; yet he belonged in spirit partly to the eighteenth. Though both his grandfathers were rabbis, his father was a deist and a skeptic who trained him in the rationalism of the Enlightenment. Marx early acquired the kind of faith in natural law that had characterized the *philosophes;* in his case it was faith in the natural laws of economic determinism and the class struggle. From this followed the boast of Marx and his disciples that their socialism alone was "scientific," as opposed to the dreamy and unrealistic doctrines of the Utopians.

The philosophy of Hegel (see Chapter XIX) provided the intellectual scaffolding for Marxism. Although Hegel had died in 1831, his influence permeated the University of Berlin during the time that Marx was a student there (1836-1841). Marx translated the Hegelian dialectic into the language of the class struggle. He made the thesis the bourgeoisie, and the antithesis the proletariat; the synthesis was to be a classless utopia issuing from the communist revolution. In his later years, Marx explained his relation to Hegel:

My dialectic method is not only different from the Hegelian but is its direct opposite. To Hegel, the life-process of the human brain, . . . which, under the name of 'the Idea,' he even transforms into an independent subject, is the demiurgos of the real world, and the real world is only the external, phenomenal form of 'the Idea.' With me, on the contrary, the ideal is nothing else than the material world reflected by the human mind, and translated into forms of thought.*

But Marx also declared:

The mystification which dialectic suffers in Hegel's hands, by no means prevents him from being the first to present its general form of working in a comprehensive and conscious manner. *With him it is standing on its head. It must be turned right again,* if you would discover the rational kernel within the mystical shell.†

By the time Marx was thirty, he had completed the outlines of his theory of scientific, revolutionary socialism. He had also be-

come a permanent exile from his native Germany. On leaving the University of Berlin, he worked for a newspaper at Cologne in the Prussian Rhineland, then moved to Paris in 1843 after his atheistic articles had aroused the authorities against him. Exiled again, because the government of Louis Philippe feared his anti-bourgeois propaganda, he went to Brussels in 1845. Wherever he happened to be, he read widely in the economists of the past and talked long and hard with the socialists and other radicals of his own generation.

Everything Marx read and everyone he met strengthened his conviction that the capitalistic order was unjust, rotten, doomed to fall. From Adam Smith's labor theory of value he concluded that only the worker should receive the profits from the sale of a commodity, since the value of the commodity should be determined by the labor of the man who produced it. The "iron law of wages," however, confirmed Marx's belief that capitalism would never permit the worker to receive this just reward. And from reading other economists and observing the depression of the late 1840's (see Chapter XIX), he concluded that economic crises were bound to occur again and again under a system that allowed labor to consume too little and capital to produce too much.

Meanwhile, Marx began his long friendship and collaboration with Friedrich Engels (1820-1895). In many ways, the two men made a striking contrast. Marx was poor and quarrelsome, a man of few friends; except for his devotion to his wife and children, he was utterly preoccupied by his economic studies. Engels, on the other hand, was the son of a well-to-do German manufacturer and represented the family textile business in Liverpool and Manchester. He loved sports, women, and high living in general. But he also hated the iniquities of industrialism and, when he met Marx, had

---

* Preface to the second edition of *Capital,* Modern Library ed. (New York, n.d.), 25.
† *Ibid.* Italics ours.

already written a bitter study, *The Condition of the Working Class in England.* Both Engels and Marx took an interest in the Communist League, a small international organization of radical workingmen. In 1847, the London office of the Communist League requested them to draw up a program. Engels wrote the first draft, which Marx revised from start to finish, and the result, published in January, 1848, was *The Manifesto of the Communist Party.*

The Communist Manifesto

Today, more than a century after its original publication, the *Manifesto* remains the classic statement of Marxian socialism. It opens with the dramatic announcement that "A spectre is haunting Europe—the spectre of Communism." It closes with a supremely confident appeal:

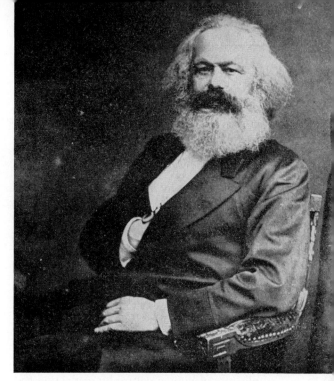

Karl Marx.

Let the ruling classes tremble at a Communist revolution. The proletarians have nothing to lose but their chains. They have a world to win.

Workingmen of all countries, unite!

In the few dozen pages of the *Manifesto,* Marx and Engels rapidly block in the main outlines of their theory. "The history of all hitherto existing society," they affirm, "is the history of class struggle." Changing economic conditions determine that the struggle should develop successively between "freeman and slave, patrician and plebeian, lord and serf, guild-master and journeyman." The guild system gave way first to manufacture by large numbers of small capitalists, and then to "the giant, modern industry."

Modern industry is a Frankenstein monster that will inevitably destroy bourgeois society. It creates a mounting economic pressure by producing more goods than it can sell. It creates a mounting social pres-sure by narrowing the circle of capitalists to fewer and fewer individuals and by forcing more and more people down to the property-less status of proletarians. These pressures increase to the point where a revolutionary explosion occurs, a massive assault on private property. Landed property will be abolished outright; other forms of property are to be liquidated more gradually through the imposition of severe income taxes and the denial of the right of inheritance. Eventually, social classes and tensions will vanish, and "we shall have an association in which the free development of each is the condition for the free development of all."

"The free development of each is the condition for the free development of all"— the *Manifesto* provides only this vague description of the society that would exist after the revolution. Since Marx defined political authority as "the organized power of one class for oppressing another," he apparently expected the state to disappear once it had created a classless regime. He also apparently assumed that the great dialectical process of history, having achieved in the classless society its final synthesis, would then cease to operate in its traditional form and might be resumed in the realm of art and philosophy. But, readers of the *Manifesto* may inquire, is it possible for the process to be so transformed? Would not the dialectic continue forever creating economic and political theses and antitheses? Will not the state always be with us? To these questions Marx offered no satisfactory answer beyond the implication that somehow the liquidation of bourgeois capitalism would radically alter the course of human history and bring the human race close to perfection.

Certainly Marx oversimplified the complexities of human nature by neglecting the non-material interests and motives of men. The history of the century since the publication of the *Communist Manifesto* has demonstrated that neither proletarians nor bourgeois have proved to be the simple economic stereotypes of Marx. Labor has often behaved in scandalously un-Marxian fashion by assuming a markedly bourgeois outlook and mentality. It is a truism that almost all Americans consider themselves middle-class. And capitalism has put its own house in better order by eliminating the worst injustices of the factory system. No more than Malthus did Marx foresee the notable rise in the standard of living that would take place between the mid-nineteenth and mid-twentieth centuries.

Marx never made a greater mistake than when he failed to observe the growing strength of nationalism. The *Manifesto* confidently expected the class struggle to transcend national boundaries. In social and economic warfare, nation would not be pitted against nation, nor state against state; the proletariat everywhere would fight the bourgeoisie. "Workingmen have no country" —except, one is tempted to add, Proletaria— and "national differences and antagonisms are vanishing gradually from day to day." In Marx's own lifetime, however, national differences and antagonisms were increasing rapidly from day to day. Within a few months of the publication of the *Manifesto*, the Revolutions of 1848 were revealing the antagonism between Italians and Austrians, Austrians and Hungarians, Hungarians and Slavs, Slavs and Germans. Nationalism awakened not only the bourgeois but also the laborers themselves, who responded with increasing fervor to its powerful emotional appeal.

The *Communist Manifesto* thus revealed the greatest blind spots of Marxian socialism. The communist movement in its subsequent history has often shown a comparable failure to appreciate the significance of nationalism and a comparable attempt to squeeze human nature into the rigid mold of economic determinism. It must never be forgotten, however, that the *Manifesto* was also one of the half-dozen most influential works written during the whole sweep of human history. Just as it foreshadowed some of the weaknesses of international communism, so also it anticipated its strengths.

First, it anticipated the remarkable character of communist propaganda. It supplied the first of those effective catch-phrases that have become the mark of the communist movement—the constant sneering at bourgeois morality, bourgeois law, bourgeois property, and the dramatic references to the "spectre haunting Europe" and to the proletarians who "have nothing to lose but their chains." Second, the *Manifesto* anticipated the emphasis later to be placed on the party's role in forging the proletarian revolution. The communists, Marx declared in 1848, were a spearhead, "the most advanced section of the working class parties

CHAPTER XX

of every country." In matters of theory, "they have over the great mass of the proletariat the advantage of clearly understanding the line of march, the conditions, and the ultimate general results of the proletarian movement."

Third, the *Manifesto* anticipated the equally great role to be played by the state in the revolution. Among the policies recommended by Marx were "centralization of credit *in the hands of the state*," and "extension of factories and instruments of production *owned by the state*." * The *Manifesto* thus faintly but unmistakably foreshadowed the totalitarian state of the Soviet Union. And, finally, it clearly established the line dividing communism from the other forms of socialism. Marx's dogmatism, his philosophy of history, and his belief in the necessity for a "total" revolution, sweeping and violent, made his brand of socialism a thing apart. Like a religious prophet granted a full revelation of the universe and its meaning, Marx expected his gospel to supplant all others. He scorned and pitied the Utopian socialists. They were about as futile, he wrote, as "organizers of charity, members of societies for the prevention of cruelty to animals, temperance fanatics, hole-and-corner reformers of every kind." Their schemes and projects were "small experiments doomed to failure," "castles in the air," "pocket editions of the New Jerusalem."

The Later Career of Marx

Age neither mellowed Marx nor greatly altered his views. From 1849 until his death in 1883, he lived in London. There, partly because of his own financial mismanagement, the Marx family experienced at first hand the misery of a pro-

---

* Italics ours.

letarian existence in the slums of Soho; poverty and near-starvation caused the death of three of the Marx children. Eventually, Marx obtained a modest income from the generosity of Engels and from his own writings.

Marx wrote and studied constantly. He produced a series of pamphlets, of which the most famous was *The Eighteenth Brumaire of Louis Napoleon*, a study of the fall of the short-lived Second French Republic. Throughout the 1850's he contributed a weekly article on British politics or international affairs to Horace Greeley's radical paper, *The New York Tribune*. Meantime, he spent his days in the British Museum, reading the reports of parliamentary investigating committees like those already quoted in this chapter, and piling up evidence of the conditions of miners and factory hands. Thus Marx accumulated the material for his full-dress economic study, *Das Kapital*. The first volume of this massive analysis of capitalism appeared in 1867; two further volumes, pieced together from his voluminous notes, were published after his death.

In *Das Kapital*, Marx elaborated, but did not substantially revise, the doctrines of the *Communist Manifesto*. For example, he spelled out his labor theory of value. According to Marx, the worker created the total value of the commodity that he produced yet received in the form of wages only a part of the price for which the item was sold; the difference between the sale price and the worker's wages constituted *surplus value*. This celebrated Marxian concept of surplus value represented something actually created by labor but appropriated by capital as profit.

Das Kapital goes on to relate surplus value to the ultimate doom of capitalism. It is the nature of capitalism, Marx insists, to diminish its own profits by replacing human labor with machines and thus gradually choking off the source of surplus value. Hence will come the mounting crises of overproduction and underconsumption predicted by the *Manifesto*. In a famous passage toward the close of Volume I of *Das Kapital*, Marx compared capitalism to an integument, a skin or shell, increasingly stretched and strained from within. One day these internal pressures would prove irresistible:

This integument is burst asunder. The knell of capitalist private property sounds. The expropriators are expropriated.*

In 1864, three years before the first volume of *Das Kapital* was published, Marx joined in the formation of the First International Workingmen's Association. This was an ambitious attempt to organize workers of every country and of every variety of radical belief. But the First International resembled a loose federation of trade unions rather than a coherent political party. It soon began to disintegrate, and it expired in 1876. Increasing persecution by hostile governments helped to bring on its end; but so, too, did the internal quarrels that repeatedly engaged both its leaders and the rank and file of its members. Marx himself set the example by his intolerance of disagreement and his utter incapacity for practical politics.

In 1889, the Second International was organized; it lasted down to the time of World War I and the Bolshevik revolution in Russia. The Second International was

* *Capital*, Modern Library ed., 837.

more coherently organized and more political in character than the First International had been. It represented the Marxian socialist parties which, as we shall see in later chapters, were becoming important forces in the political life of the major countries of continental Europe. Among its leaders were men more adept than Marx himself at the political game. Yet the old spirit of factionalism continued to weaken the International. Some of its leaders tenaciously defended what they considered the spirit of the laws handed down by the master and forbade any co-operation between socialists and the "bourgeois" political parties; these were the "orthodox" communists. Other leaders of the Second International, however, were from the orthodox standpoint "heretics." They, too, called themselves disciples of Marx; yet they also believed in co-operation between classes rather than in a struggle to the death, and they trusted that human decency and intelligence could avert the horrors of class war.

Though the precise connotations of the terms vary with the turnings of the party line, "orthodox" and "heretical" communists are still with us today. Witness the break between Moscow and Tito of Yugoslavia, and the repeated purges within the Soviet ruling class. The factionalism that had split the First International lived on to plague the Second International and its later twentieth-century successors, the Comintern and the Cominform.

VII: Other Responses

Socialism, both Marxian and Utopian, and liberalism, both bourgeois and democratic, were the most important responses to the economic and social problems

of the nineteenth century. But they were not the only responses. Nationalists revived the old economic philosophy of mercantilism, not only advocating tariffs to protect the economy at home but also demanding empires abroad to provide new markets for surplus products and new settlements for surplus citizens. Analysis of this neo-mercantilism is best postponed to later chapters (see, particularly, Chapters, XXI, XXII, XXIV). Here we shall deal with two other sets of responses—anarchism, and the reform program known as "Christian socialism" or "Christian democracy."

The Anarchists

An anarchist believes that the best government is no government at all. Most of the recipes for socialism contained at least a dash of anarchism. The Utopians, by and large, mistrusted governments, and Marx anticipated that his longed-for revolution would eventually produce a classless society where, in the famous phrase, "the state would wither away." For a few of Marx's contemporaries, however, it was not enough that the state should wither at some distant time; this instrument of oppression should be annihilated here and now. The means to this end was terrorism, especially assassination of heads of state.

The anarchistic terrorists provided the stereotype of the bearded, wild-eyed, bomb-carrying radicals we have all seen in the comic strips. Half a century and more ago, their assassinations took an impressive toll —the French President Carnot in 1894, King Humbert of Italy in 1900, and the American President McKinley in 1901. Otherwise terrorism accomplished little directly except to drive the governments that it hated to more vigorous measures of defense and retaliation. Yet, negative and destructive though it was, the doctrine did leave its mark on the proletarian movement.

A famous exponent of anarchism was the Russian Bakunin (1814-1876), who helped to shape the revolutionary movement in his native country (see Chapter XXII) and, by his participation in the First International, won the attention of workers from many countries. An idealist, Bakunin wanted to replace the state with a loose confederation of autonomous units that would both end the injustices of private property and assure individuals complete freedom. The millennium was to be achieved through an international rebellion set off by small groups of anarchist conspirators.

Bakunin contributed to the formation of the program known as *anarcho-syndicalism.* "Anarcho" connotes its distrust of political action; "syndicalism" comes from the French *syndicat,* an economic grouping, particularly a trade union. The anarcho-syndicalists disbelieved in political parties, even Marxist ones; they believed in direct action by the workers. Direct action was to culminate in a spontaneous general strike that would free labor from the capitalistic yoke. Meantime, workers could rehearse for the great day by forming unions and by engaging in acts of anti-capitalist sabotage.

Proudhon

The writer most frequently cited by the anarcho-syndicalists was Proudhon (1809-1865). This prolific French publicist began his writings with what seemed to be a straightaway socialist attack on the evils of capitalism. "What is property?" he asked in a famous pamphlet of 1840; "property is theft." Karl Marx praised him for his "scientific" socialism and predicted that Proudhon's pamphlet would be to the coming social revolution what Siéyès famous tract about the third estate had been to 1789. Within a few years, however, Marx's praise had turned to contempt. A second pamphlet by Proudhon, *The Philosophy of Poverty,* elicited a Marxian rebuttal tartly entitled *The Poverty of Philosophy.* Part of the trouble was that Proudhon did not share Marx's views on the best procedure for improving the social and economic order.

Moreover, the property that Proudhon called "theft" was not all property but unearned income, the revenues that men gained from investing their wealth rather than from the sweat of their brows. Of all the forms of unearned income, the worst, in Proudhon's view, was the "leprosy of interest"; and the most diabolical of capitalist villains was the money-lender. Under existing conditions only those who were already rich could afford to borrow, but in the utopia envisaged by Proudhon all men would be able to secure credit. Instead of private banks and the Bank of France, there would be only a "People's Bank," lending to all without interest and issuing notes that would soon replace ordinary money. What Proudhon had in mind was a sort of barter economy, in which an individual would exchange the commodities he produced for the commodities produced by others. The credit provided by the People's Bank would enable each man to become a producer on his own.

Thus, where Marx foresaw a revolution in ownership of the means of production, Proudhon foresaw a "revolution of credit," a revolution in financing production. Where Marx proposed to have the proletariat liquidate the bourgeoisie, Proudhon proposed to raise the proletarians to the level of the bourgeois by making every worker an owner. Proudhon's utopia was not collectivized or socialized; it was a weakly organized association of middle-class individualists. Because Proudhon dreaded restraints upon the individual, he opposed the social workshops of Louis Blanc and the phalanxes of Fourier; they were too restrictive. He projected, instead, a society founded upon "mutualism." Economically, mutualism would take the form of associations of producers, rather like the producers' co-operatives sometimes found in dairy farming today. Politically, it would take the form of a loose federation of these associations, which would replace the sovereign, centralized state.

Proudhon's doctrines exerted a strong appeal in a country like France, with its devotion to individualism and its large quotient of "little business." France had tens of thousands of small businessmen on the lower fringes of the middle class, often on the edge of being pushed down into the proletariat, often denied financial credit by the bankers whom Proudhon attacked so bitterly. "Mutualism" and "federalism," furthermore, were part of the revolutionary tradition, inherited from the Constitution of 1791 and the platform of the Girondins (see Chapter XVIII). Proudhon naturally fed the anarchist strain in anarcho-syndicalism.

Yet much of Proudhon's teaching contradicted the syndicalist strain. Not only did he dislike trade unions as unnatural restrictions on individual liberty; he deplored all activities suggesting class strife, including the very strikes so beloved by the syndicalists. At times Proudhon, despite his anarchism, seemed to favor the methods of the police state; indeed he has been called a "herald of fascism." If rival classes would not co-operate voluntarily, then he was willing to have co-operation forced upon them by a chosen few. His hatred of bankers made him an anti-Semite, because of the number of Jews engaged in finance. It is difficult to decide whether Proudhon should be assigned a place at the extreme Left of the political spectrum, or at its extreme Right.

The Christian Socialists

By contrast, the Christian socialists occupy a position close to the political Center. Historically, the Christian socialists were a small group of English reformers, drawn from the clergy of the established Church and active in the mid-nineteenth century. Their church, they believed, needed to put theological problems to one side and direct its efforts to the remedying of social abuses. One of their best known leaders was Charles Kingsley (1819-1875), the novelist, author of *The Water Babies* and *Westward Ho!* In his own day, Kingsley won fame by writing earnest social novels and a stream of pamphlets against the wickedness of laissez-faire. He delivered particularly telling blows at one of the unhealthiest of industries, tailoring. His didactic novel, *Alton Locke,* and his bitter tract, *Cheap Clothes and Nasty,* both published in 1850, exposed the "show-shops" and "slop-shops" which forced tailors and seamstresses to labor hard and long for meager pay, often in appallingly crowded and unsanitary surroundings.

Kingsley proposed the following remedies for these sweatshops:

First—this can be done. That no man who calls himself a Christian—no man who calls himself a man—shall ever disgrace himself by dealing at any show-shop or slop-shop. It is easy enough to know them. The ticketed garments, the impudent puffs, the trumpery decorations, proclaim them. . . . Let no man enter them—they are the temples of Moloch—their thresholds are rank with human blood.

. . .

But let, secondly, a dozen, or fifty, or a hundred journeymen say to one another: 'It is competition that is ruining us, and competition is division, disunion, every man to himself, every man against his brother. The remedy must be in association, co-operation, self-sacrifice for the sake of one another. . . . Why should we not work and live together in our own workshops, or our own homes, for our own profit?'

. . .

And, again, let one man, or half-a-dozen men arise who believe that the world is not the devil's world at all but God's: that the multitude of the people is not, as Malthusians aver,

the ruin, but as Solomon believed, 'the strength of the ruler.' . . . Let a few men who have money, and believe that, arise to play the man.

Let them help and foster the growth of association by all means. Let them advise the honourable tailors, while it is time, to save themselves from being degraded into slop-sellers by admitting their journeymen to a share in the profits. . . . Let them, as soon as an association is formed, provide for them a properly ventilated workshop, and let it out to the associate tailors at a low fair rent. I believe that they will not lose by it—because it is right. God will take care of their money. The world, it comes out now, is so well ordered by Him, that model lodging-houses, public baths, washhouses, insurance offices, all pay a reasonable profit to those who invest money in them—perhaps associate workshops may do the same. . . .

But above all, so soon as these men are found working together for common profit, in the spirit of mutual self-sacrifice, let every gentleman and every Christian . . . make it a point of honour and conscience to deal with the associated workmen, and get others to do the like. *It is by securing custom, far more than by gifts or loans of money, that we can help the operatives.*[*]

This passage summarizes the positive doctrine of the Christian socialists. It is notable for its attack on materialism and its stress on brotherly love as against un-brotherly strife, on association and co-operation as against exploitation and competition. It is notable also for its optimism: if men would only act as Christians, they might solve their social problems. Indeed the Christian socialists were more Christian than socialistic; they relied more on private philanthropy than on state intervention. Kingsley himself hoped to accomplish much by exhortation and by pointing out the gap between professed Christian ideals and actual economic practice. He set an example for concrete improvement when he helped to launch the Working Men's College in Lon-

[*] C. Kingsley, "Cheap Clothes and Nasty," in *Alton Locke,* Eversley ed. (London, 1893), I, 103-107.

don and promoted other activities of the type that the Y.M.C.A. has made familiar to us.

The Catholic Response

Catholics, too, reacted against the evils of industrialism. Essentially, their program resembled that of the Anglican Christian socialists, but they called it by the more accurate name of "Christian democracy" or "social Christianity." Christian democracy formed a central part of the Catholic response to the problems of the modern world. As we shall see in later chapters, these problems bore heavily upon the Church. Anticlerical legislation threatened its position in France, Germany, Italy, and elsewhere. The Papal States and then Rome herself, after more than a thousand years of papal rule, passed to the control of the newly unified Kingdom of Italy. Science, nationalism, and the materialistic doctrines issuing from the industrial revolution were all competing for the loyalties of men. In Catholic countries the working classes especially were drifting away from the Church.

The Church first tried to meet these problems by taking refuge in the past. Pope Pius IX (1846-1878) took an uncompromising stand in the *Syllabus of Errors*, which he issued in 1864. He made a blanket condemnation of all theories and institutions that were not consecrated by centuries of tradition. He assailed the labor unions and democratic governments for which workingmen were striving, and made it an error to suppose that the pope "can and ought to reconcile and harmonize himself with progress, liberalism, and modern civilization."

The Catholic Church, however, has not endured all these centuries by turning its back on progress, liberalism, and modernity. Pius IX was followed in the See of Peter by

Leo XIII (1878-1903), the outstanding pope of modern times. Leo fully recognized the rapid changes being worked by science and technology. As a papal nuncio, he had witnessed them at first hand in the industrial regions of Belgium, France, and Germany. He knew that Catholicism was flourishing in the supposedly hostile climate of the democratic United States. Moreover, his studies of St. Thomas Aquinas convinced him that the Church had much to gain and little to lose by following the middle-of-the-road social and economic policies recommended by that great medieval Schoolman. Leo XIII came to terms with the modern world through a series of famous documents, the most celebrated of which was the encyclical letter, *Rerum Novarum* ("concerning new things," 1891).

In *Rerum Novarum*, Leo XIII exposed the defects of capitalism with as much vigor as any socialist. Then he attacked with equal vigor the socialistic view of property and the socialistic doctrine of class war. He pronounced it a "great mistake" to believe

... that class is naturally hostile to class, and that the wealthy and the workingmen are intended by nature to live in mutual conflict. . . . Each needs the other: Capital cannot do without Labor, nor Labor without Capital. . . . Perpetual conflict necessarily produces confusion and simple barbarity.*

Leo therefore urged the economic man to act as a Christian man of good will:

Religion teaches the laboring man . . . to carry out honestly and fairly all equitable agreements freely entered into; never to injure the property, nor to outrage the person, of an employer; never to resort to violence . . . nor to engage in riot or disorder; and to have nothing to do with men of evil principles, who work upon the people with artful promises, and excite foolish hopes which usually end in useless regrets, followed by insolvency. Religion

* *The Great Encyclical Letters of Pope Leo XIII* (New York, 1903), 218.

CHAPTER XX

teaches the wealthy owner and the employer that their work-people are not to be accounted their bondsmen; that in every man they must respect his dignity and worth as a man and as a Christian; that labor is not a thing to be ashamed of, if we lend ear to right reason and to Christian philosophy, but is an honorable calling, enabling a man to sustain his life in a way upright and creditable; and that it is shameful and inhuman to treat men like chattels to make money by, or to look upon them merely as so much muscle or physical power.*

The state must always remain subordinate to the interests of the individuals who compose it. But this did not mean that government should adopt an attitude of laissez-faire. On the contrary, Leo repeatedly cited St. Thomas to prove that the state should indeed take measures for the general welfare. On behalf of capital, it should discourage agitators and protect property from violence. On behalf of labor, it should work to remove "the causes which lead to conflict between employer and em-

ployed." For example, it should curb exploitation by regulating child labor, limiting the hours of work, and insisting that Sundays be free for religion and rest. Leo also believed that the workers must help themselves, and *Rerum Novarum* concludes with a fervent appeal for the formation and spread of specifically Catholic trade unions.

These Catholic unions do exist today, but they are only a minority force in the realm of organized labor. Neither the Christian democracy of Leo XIII nor Christian socialism has achieved all that the founders hoped. Nevertheless, both have attracted many followers. There is a large element of Christian socialism, larger than most Americans would suspect, in the British Labor party. And the Christian democrats, though some of them are at best half-hearted democrats, have played a very important role in the politics of many Catholic states since World War II. At the very least, the Anglican and Catholic reformers have enriched the liberal response to industrialism and have broadened the liberal appeal.

---

* *Ibid.*, 219.

Reading Suggestions
on the Economic Revolutions

General Accounts

W. Bowden, M. Karpovich, A. P. Usher, *An Economic History of Europe Since 1750* (New York: American Book Co., 1937); S. B. Clough and C. W. Cole, *Economic History of Europe*, rev. ed. (Boston: D. C. Heath and Co., 1946); and H. Heaton, *Economic History of Europe*, rev. ed. (New York: Harper and Brothers, 1948). Three useful general economic histories.

J. Clapham, *An Economic History of Modern Britain*, 3 vols., 2nd ed. (Cambridge, England: The University Press, 1930-1938). A major scholarly work on the key country in the economic revolution.

L. Mumford, *Technics and Civilization* (New York: Harcourt, Brace & Co., 1934). A sweeping survey, often very stimulating, of technology and its impact.

T. S. Ashton, *The Industrial Revolution, 1760-1830* (New York: Oxford University Press, 1948. Home University Library). A clear and sound introductory account.

Special Studies

P. Mantoux, *The Industrial Revolution in the 18th Century,* rev. ed. (New York: Harcourt, Brace & Co., 1929). A standard survey of the beginnings of industrialism.

A. E. Bland, P. A. Brown, R. H. Tawney, eds., *English Economic History: Select Documents* (London: G. Bell and Sons, Ltd., 1915). A convenient collection of source materials often hard to locate.

J. L. and B. Hammond, *The Bleak Age,* rev. ed. (Harmondsworth, Middlesex: Penguin Books, 1947). An exposé, aimed at the general reader, of the social results of industrialism, which the authors view with unrelieved horror. The Hammonds have written other detailed volumes in the same vein.

M. C. Buer, *Health, Wealth, and Population in the Early Days of the Industrial Revolution* (London: G. Routledge and Sons, Ltd., 1926). Takes a decidedly more cheerful view of the social results of industrialism than do the Hammonds.

C. Brinton, *English Political Thought in the Nineteenth Century,* new ed. (Cambridge, Mass.: Harvard University Press, 1949). Includes essays on Bentham, Owen, Mill, and Kingsley.

J. S. Schapiro, *Liberalism and the Challenge of Fascism: Social Forces in England and France (1815-1870)* (New York: McGraw-Hill Book Co., 1949). Suggestive essays on major thinkers, better balanced when dealing with liberalism than when dealing with the "challenge of fascism" in the mid-nineteenth century.

P. C. Newman, *The Development of Economic Thought* (New York: Prentice-Hall, Inc., 1952). An elementary manual.

J. S. Mill, *Autobiography* (New York: Oxford University Press, 1924. In World's Classics) and *Utilitarianism, Liberty, and Representative Government* (New York: E. P. Dutton & Co., 1910. Everyman ed.). The essential writings of the most important nineteenth-century English liberal thinkers.

E. Halévy, *The Growth of Philosophic Radicalism* (New York: The Macmillan Company, 1928). The standard study of Bentham and Utilitarianism.

H. W. Laidler, *Social-Economic Movements: An Historical and Comparative Survey of Socialism, Communism, Coöperation, Utopianism* (New York: Thomas Y. Crowell Co., 1949). A handy survey of the subjects listed.

E. Wilson, *To the Finland Station* (Garden City, N. Y.: Anchor Books, 1953). Inexpensive reprint of a sympathetic yet balanced survey of socialism, Utopian and Marxian.

C. H. de Saint-Simon, *Selected Writings,* F. M. H. Markham, ed. (New York: The Macmillan Company, 1952). A useful compilation from the works of the early French Utopian.

The Life of Robert Owen, by Himself (New York: Alfred A. Knopf, Inc., 1920). Autobiography of the famous British Utopian socialist.

F. Podmore, *Robert Owen, A Biography* (New York: D. Appleton, 1924). One of many useful studies of Owen.

CHAPTER XX

E. Burns, ed., *A Handbook of Marxism* (New York: Random House, 1935). Very useful compilation from the writings of Marx himself and the later prophets of his doctrine.

I. Berlin, *Karl Marx: His Life and Environment,* 2nd ed. (New York: Oxford University Press, 1948. Home University Library.) A short and extremely good biography.

L. Schwarzchild, *The Red Prussian: The Life and Legend of Karl Marx* (New York: Charles Scribner's Sons, 1947). A hostile interpretation.

The Great Encyclical Letters of Pope Leo XIII (New York: Benziger Brothers, 1903). The best introduction to modern Catholic social philosophy.

R. Fülöp-Miller, *Leo XIII and Our Times* (New York: Longmans, Green & Co., 1937). A very sympathetic study.

Historical Fiction

C. Dickens, *Hard Times* (New York: E. P. Dutton & Co., 1907. Everyman ed.). Short and relatively little known, this is one of Dickens' best social novels; excellent descriptions of "Coketown" and of middle-class attitudes.

E. Gaskell, *North and South* (New York: E. P. Dutton & Co., 1914. Everyman ed.) and *Mary Barton* (New York: E. P. Dutton & Co., 1912. Everyman ed.). Two very sound social novels by Mrs. Gaskell, better known as the author of the genteel *Cranford*.

B. Disraeli (Lord Beaconsfield), *Sybil* (New York: Oxford University Press, 1925. World's Classics). An important fictional presentation of the "two nations," rich and poor, by a leading politician and reformer of Victorian Britain.

C. Kingsley, *Alton Locke* (New York: Harper and Brothers, 1850). Not a very good novel, but a useful delineation of Kingsley's Christian program for social reform.

E. Zola, *Germinal* (many editions). The best French novel on industrial problems; markedly more realistic and less sentimental than its English counterparts.

E. Bellamy, *Looking Backward, 2000-1887* (New York: Modern Library, 1951). An interesting American adaptation of Utopian socialist views.

The Western Democracies in the Nineteenth Century

CHAPTER XXI

The First Reform Bill passed by the British House of Commons, 1831.

I: Background of the North Atlantic Community

Historians in any generation tend to organize their material in the light of the great political facts of their own day. In our day, the great political fact has been the cleavage and the conflict between the democracies of the West and the totalitarian states, both fascist and communist. In this book, therefore, we shall use the concept of the North Atlantic community, the mid-twentieth century grouping of states opposed to the Soviet Union. The North Atlantic community has as its core Great Britain, France, and the United States; Italy is in some ways one of its core states, though Italy is geographically a Mediterranean power and was in the recent past one of the fascist countries.

All these core states experienced the influence of the industrial revolution, of the political revolutions against absolute monarchy, and of the intellectual revolution of the eighteenth-century Enlightenment. No such value-charged term as "liberalism" or "democracy" can be laid like a blanket over the last century or two of the history of these core states. Neither liberalism nor democracy meant quite the same thing in all of them. Moreover, all of them have pro-

235

duced discordant and recalcitrant men and movements not in any sense to be fairly termed liberal or democratic—the plotting Ulster Unionists of 1914, many a British or French imperial proconsul, a Louis Napoleon, a Mussolini, or a Huey Long.

Yet the core states of the North Atlantic community of today have shared in the immediate past a certain minimum of democratic political institutions and ideas. In all of them, first, a majority of citizens has been able to put through or block major political measures, despite the delays imposed by constitutional "checks and balances." Second, all of them have developed in law and in practice effective ways of protecting the individual citizen from arbitrary arrest, arbitrary confiscation of property, arbitrary exclusion from following his own ideas and ideals—in short, of protecting civil liberties or civil rights. Americans often assume that they have from the start been the really good democrats of the North Atlantic community, that the other states have always been more tempted to backsliding. Actually, throughout the nineteenth century Britain was commonly regarded in the world as the center of these liberal and democratic ideals.

The smaller nations of western and northern Europe—the Netherlands, Belgium, Switzerland, the Scandinavian countries—are also part of the North Atlantic community. All these smaller states have worked out their own national variants of liberalism and democracy. In particular, the Scandinavian countries, with their homogeneous populations, their common Lutheran religion, their common traditions, and their very high rate of literacy, have sometimes surpassed the larger states in making democracy function effectively. Visitors to Copenhagen or Stockholm are impressed not only by their tidiness but also by the absence of slums and other signs of poverty. And the co-operatives of Denmark and Sweden have received much praise as the "middle way" between socialism and uncontrolled individualism.

The separate histories of these smaller states must inevitably be slighted in a general survey like this. But it must not be forgotten that they have helped to establish the balance of international politics and that in many fields their citizens have contributed proportionately more heavily to our modern western culture than their numbers would suggest. Switzerland supplied the great historian of the Renaissance, Burckhardt, and Belgium the poet and playwright Maeterlinck. From Finland came the composer Sibelius; from Norway, Ibsen and his modern social dramas; from Holland, the physicist Lorentz, winner of the Nobel prize in 1902; and from Sweden, Nobel himself, the munitions king who endowed the Nobel prizes for peaceful achievement.

By the end of the nineteenth century, the *forms* at least of modern parliamentary or congressional democracy had spread far beyond the nucleus of the North Atlantic community. As we shall see in later chapters, even tsarist Russia had its local assemblies or *zemstvos*, and after 1905 its national Duma. The Balkan states, too, had representative assemblies. The two great Central European states, Austria-Hungary and Germany, had their legislatures elected by a wide popular electorate. At the turn of the century, many Germans felt that the Hohenzollern monarchy was, in spite of the mouthings of the new Emperor William II, in fact a limited monarchy. But in two world wars Germany set herself in action against the West, and developed her own anti-democratic philosophy and institutions, and remains today torn between these ways and the attraction of the West, to which she has been so closely linked since Charlemagne. Communist Russia has quite definitely developed a culture which, though it has borrowed the magic word "democ-

CHAPTER XXI

racy," has in fact set itself even more firmly than Germany ever did against the liberal democracy of the West.

The North Atlantic community itself remains the heir of the Enlightenment. The nation-states that make it up are united in much—in common interest against totalitarian threats, in the common cultural inheritance that we have traced in these pages. But they are divided also by many phases of that inheritance, and especially by those phases which have headed up into the complex we call nationalism. The English philosopher of history, Arnold Toynbee, is justified in calling the totality of North Atlantic states a "society," or "western civilization," and its constituent units in some senses mere "parochial nation-states" inextricably bound one to another in this world. Nevertheless, one cannot understand the basic problems now facing these western states except by tracing their separate internal histories in the last hundred years or so. To this task we now turn.

II: Britain, 1815-1914

The Process of Reform

Great Britain emerged from the world war of 1792-1815 victorious over her rival France. The British economy had been able to support the costs of the war and indeed to increase its financial and industrial capabilities. British society was certainly divided by class interests, but—save for the native Irish—it was fundamentally united in patriotic loyalty. The British political system was no democracy, yet its king was already a very limited monarch, and its Parliament was by no means without roots in public opinion. In normal times, the British subject enjoyed the full protection of civil rights.

In the years immediately after Waterloo, Britain went through a typical postwar economic crisis. Unsold goods accumulated, and the working classes experienced widespread unemployment and suffering. Although trade unions were forbidden by the Combination Acts, the workers none the less asserted themselves in strikes and in popular agitation that helped prepare the way for the parliamentary Reform Bill of 1832. But by the 1820's economic conditions had improved, and Britain had embarked on the first stage of those political reforms that were to make of her a democratic state.

Into this process, of course, there went economic and social drives, and the Britain of our mid-twentieth century was to be not only a very complete political democracy but also in part an economic and a social democracy. But the process of reform focused always on concrete political action. It is a process of which the British are very proud, for it was achieved without revolution and almost without violence or indeed any serious civil disturbance. The fruits of discussion, education, and propaganda were consolidated in a specific "reform bill," followed by another stage of preparatory work and another reform bill.

Parliamentary Reform

The process is most clearly marked in the great milestones of parliamentary reform that transformed the government of Britain from an oligarchy into a democracy.

Britain emerged from the Napoleonic Wars with its executive, a cabinet of ministers presided over by a prime minister, wholly under the control of Parliament. The Crown was now, as the nineteenth-century political writer Bagehot was to put it, largely "decorative." On that decorative post, held for most of the century (1837-1901) by Queen Victoria, who has given her name to an age and a culture, were centered the patriotic emotions of loyal British subjects. Victoria probably never quite thought of herself as a mere figurehead; she was a determined, sensible, emotional, conventional, and intellectually unsophisticated Victorian lady.

Real power lay in the legislative branch, by no means directly representative of the masses. The House of Lords, which for all save money bills had equal power with the lower house, was drawn from the small, privileged class of peers. The House of Commons, its members unpaid, was recruited wholly from the gentry, the professional classes, and very successful businessmen, and was chosen by less than one-sixth of the adult male population. We cannot go into the details of the suffrage qualifications and the electoral districts ("parliamentary constituencies") of the unreformed Parliaments; they were varied, the result of the piling up of concrete acts since the Middle Ages, a sort of crazy quilt of social classes and geographical distribution. The big fact is that in 1815 both the working classes in town and country and the run of prosperous but not spectacularly successful middle-class people were excluded from the franchise. Moreover, the largely rural South, once the most populous area of the kingdom, now had more representatives than it deserved, including a large contingent from the "rotten boroughs." The teeming new industrial centers of the North were grossly under-represented.

Projects to begin modernizing the structure of representation came close to being adopted in the late eighteenth century. But the wars with Revolutionary and Napoleonic France made reform impossible; in wartime and in the immediate postwar years, even moderate reformers were denounced as Jacobins. In 1819, a nervous Tory government permitted the soldiery to break up a large and peaceful mass meeting assembled at St. Peter's Field near Manchester to hear speeches on parliamentary reform. This "Peterloo" massacre resulted in several deaths, the wounding of hundreds, and the temporary curtailment of free speech and the free press. Suppression, however, was not the British way, and soon after Peterloo the great campaign of agitation was resumed which produced the parliamentary reform of 1832.

In this campaign the middle class did not hesitate to appeal to the lower classes for aid by using freely the language of popular rights, and even of universal suffrage. Many popular leaders talked as if the Reform Bill would bring political democracy to England at once. Yet much of the preparation for reform was actually the work, not of liberal agitators, but of conservatives. Guided by enlightened individuals such as Canning and Robert Peel, the Tory governments of the 1820's lifted the various restrictions on civil rights imposed during the war period and the postwar crisis. They partially repealed the Combination Acts against trade unions, reformed the antiquated criminal code, and began the reduction in protective tariffs that was to lead to free trade. The seventeenth-century Test Act, which, though not observed, legally excluded nonconformists from public life, was repealed. So, under the name of "Catholic emancipation," were the laws that really did exclude Catholics from public life. In international politics, Canning lined Britain up as a "liberal" power against the conservative monarchies of central and eastern Europe (see Chapter XIX).

CHAPTER XXI

The Reform Bill itself was enacted under the leadership of the Whig Lord Grey, backed by a full apparatus of agitation and pressure groups. Tory opponents of parliamentary reform were won over—even the very Tory Duke of Wellington was converted at the last moment—until only the Tory House of Lords blocked the measure. At this climax, Lord Grey persuaded King William IV (1830-1837) to threaten the creation by royal prerogative of enough new Whig peers to put the reform through the Lords. This threat, combined with the real danger of popular violence, put the bill through on June 4, 1832.

This First Reform Bill did not bring political democracy to England. It did diminish the great irregularities of electoral districts, wiping out more than fifty rotten boroughs and giving seats in the Commons to more than forty hitherto unrepresented industrial towns. The franchise was made more uniform; the number of voters was increased by about 50 per cent so that virtually all the middle class got the vote. The bill by no means enfranchised the working classes; it actually excluded some working-class voters in a few boroughs that had had wide popular franchises.

From the new ground of the partly reformed Parliament, the agitation for a still wider suffrage went on. The middle class had won its gains, not in the name of its own admission to an oligarchy, but in the name of the right of all competent men to have the vote. With the gradual spread of literacy to the lower classes, with their gradual political awakening, the middle classes could not find very good arguments for refusing to extend the franchise; moreover, a good many of the British middle classes sincerely believed in a gradual widening of the franchise.

The Second Reform Bill came in 1867 in no such dramatic series of crises as those which had won over Wellington and William IV in 1832; the bill was indeed, by one of the ironies of history, put through by that Tory party that traditionally stood for resistance to the widening of the suffrage. But the three decades after 1832 had produced a ground swell of agitation for more parliamentary reform, a ground swell with many cross-currents from downright radical republicanism to a resigned belief that democracy was irresistibly the wave of the future. Disraeli (1804-1881), the Tory leader in the Commons, almost certainly thought that if one party did not put through reform the other one would. With a politician's sense of reality, he decided his party might as well get the credit, and therefore, as he himself once put it, "caught the Whigs bathing and walked away with their clothes." Disraeli also thought that the newly enfranchised urban working class, hostile to their middle-class employers, would vote for the Tories, who were country gentlemen, good responsible caretakers of the lower classes, not exploiters like the middle-class businessmen. Astute though he was, Disraeli's guess was not in the immediate instance correct. The first election after the reform saw the voters turn the Tories out of office in 1868.

The Second Reform Bill by no means introduced full manhood suffrage. Like the first, it was a piecemeal change that brought the electoral districts into more uniformity and equality, but left them still divided into boroughs and shires as in the Middle Ages. It about doubled the number of voters in Britain by giving the vote to householders —that is, settled men owning or paying rent on their dwellings—in the boroughs (urban). Such people in the shires (rural), as well as lodgers, bachelors without their own domestic establishments, servants, and of course women, were still without the vote. None the less, the bill of 1867 is really the crucial one, for it gave the vote to some million of the working and lower white-

The British two-party system. London crowds outside a newspaper office watching returns from the Conservative-Liberal competition in the election of 1892.

collar classes, men without the "stake" of property.

The next reforms in the series were, more logically, put through by the Liberal party, the former Whigs, under the leadership of Gladstone (1809-1898). Even these reforms of 1884 and 1885 did not introduce the kind of neat democratic uniformity the French had already established. They still tinkered with medieval forms, which were now pretty completely modernized. Lodgers and a few floaters, and women, were still without the vote; districts were not quite equalized; a few thousand voters with business property in one district and a home in another could vote twice; and graduates of Oxford and Cambridge could vote a second time for special university members. Still, by 1885 Britain was clearly a political democracy, in which the majority of the people, through their representatives in the House of Commons, were politically "sovereign." Perhaps not quite, for the hereditary House of Lords had still a veto power over legislation that did not specifically appro-

priate money. This last limitation was in fact removed in 1911, in a kind of codicil to the reforms of the nineteenth century, when the Parliament Act of that year left the Lords with no more than a delaying or suspensive veto.

The Two-Party System: Liberals and Conservatives

We have outlined above the legislative landmarks in the nineteenth-century democratization of the British constitution. Now the dynamics of that process are certainly in part explicable in terms of the "class struggle." Broadly speaking, over the century the "have nots"—perhaps better, the "have littles"—gained a voice in the politics of Britain they did not have in 1815. But the central human institution of the dynamics, the *party*, clearly does not present a neat alignment of the "have littles" against the "have much." That should be clear even from the very summary account of the

CHAPTER XXI

reform bills we have given. The Disraeli who took the "leap in the dark" of 1867 was a conservative, not a radical leader, and he hoped that the newly enfranchised workingmen would vote conservative, not radical. He was wrong in 1868, but in the longer run not wholly wrong, for after his death his party was returned to power triumphantly under the even wider franchise of 1885 for a ten-year tenure of power, 1895-1905. Some British poor and middling men obviously voted for the party of their "betters."

The fact is that the British party system was not clearly based on an opposition between a possessing class and a non-possessing class. The eighteenth-century oligarchic factions of Whigs and Tories were transformed in the course of the nineteenth century into the modern mass parties of Liberals and Conservatives, both organized on a national basis, with local committees at the bottom, and making full use of party machinery for getting out the vote. The Whigs, in broadening into the Liberals, sought an electoral base ranging from the old great families, still represented in the early part of the century by men like Grey and Palmerston, to the little and big businessmen, the nonconformists, the radical white-collar men. The Tories, in broadening into Conservatives, sought a base, first under Peel and then under Disraeli, from the country gentlemen and Anglican clergymen to the agricultural laborers, the small townspeople, and even some of the urban white-collar and working classes. Both parties frankly appealed to the "people"; and the Conservatives, with their "Primrose League" in memory of Disraeli's favorite flower, their appeal to love of Queen and country, their record of social legislation against the worst evils of the new factory system, did at least as good a job in building a party machine as did the Liberals. In the Victorian heyday, the librettist

Gilbert was quite justified in having his guardsman sing in the operetta "Iolanthe":

> That every boy and every gal
> That's born into the world alive
> Is either a little Liberal
> Or else a little Conservative.

Now this does not mean that each party was a monolithic block with all members in complete agreement on political matters. Each was in fact a coalition of diverse groups that somehow managed to hold together for elections, and even, with some straying, for votes in Parliament. Moreover, the essential dynamics of change take the form of a splinter group within a major party which splits off on some critical issue and becomes a "third" party. But the inertia of the two-party system is so great in Britain that this third party is relatively quickly merged for the most part into the originally opposing party, to which it imparts a slightly different direction, and the two-party equilibrium is restored. This happened, for instance, to the "Peelites" who seceded from the Conservatives in 1846 under conditions we shall shortly describe, and who became mostly good Liberals.

The Two-Party System: An Explanation

The two-party system is almost wholly confined to the English-speaking lands, to Britain, the United States, and the British Commonwealth countries. On the Continent, not only in France, Italy, and pre-Hitler Germany, but also in the little democracies of Scandinavia, Switzerland, Holland, and Belgium, the multi-party system has prevailed, and governments are generally coalitions of parties with separate organizations. English-speaking opinion probably exaggerates the defects and dangers of multi-party democracy. At least under good economic conditions and in the absence of great danger from war, even the politically divided Third French Republic was a going concern. But it is clear that a two-party democracy does have distinct advantages in the way of stability and continuity of policy, if only because a given group can enjoy a longer, more assured tenure of power. The historian must attempt somehow to explain why the English-speaking peoples have developed this unique institution. He must seek somewhat different explanations for Britain and for the United States, for though both have two-party systems, their whole political situations are far from alike.

In terms of political psychology, the two-party system means that the millions of individual voters who make up each party are in greater agreement than disagreement over what the party stands for; or at least that when they vote for a candidate they feel he stands more for what they want than for what they don't want. Each voter makes some kind of compromise *within himself,* takes something less in practice than he would ideally like. This sort of compromise the French voter of the 1880's for instance did not need to make, at any rate not to anything like the same degree as the British voter. The Frenchman could choose, from among a dozen or more platforms and candidates, the one tailored closest to his desires.

We must still ask why Englishmen made these compromises, why they agreed more than they disagreed. The answer must be sought in the long working out of British history. One part of it lies in the relative security of the islands from external foes, in the long years in which British political habits of moderation and compromise could mature without the constant pressure of foreign wars. The immediate crisis of war may indeed promote a temporary unity in a threatened nation, like the France of 1792-94. But long, steady exposure to war danger—and all continental states were so

exposed—seems in fact to encourage party divisions in the threatened country, seems to promote psychological tendencies to seek final and extreme solutions.

This same relative isolation of Britain also contributed to the relatively mild form that the universal western struggle between feudalism and the new-model centralized state took there. In France, and on the Continent generally, the new-model triumphed only in the seventeenth century, and in the form of divine-right monarchy. Continental states in the nineteenth century had only just gone through—or were still going through—the popular revolutionary modification of absolutism, and were still torn by major class antagonisms between a noble privileged class, backed usually by orthodox religion, and a middle class. In England, as we have seen in earlier chapters, that struggle had taken place a full century and a half earlier and had never been quite as bitter as on the Continent. It had left England in charge of a ruling class that was itself the product of a compromise between the old landed gentry and the new commercial classes, a ruling class that could develop within itself habits of moderation and compromise. The deep abyss the French Revolution had dug between nineteenth-century royalists and republicans on the Continent did not exist in nineteenth-century England.

Thus, even more important than the fact that the Liberals and Conservatives each held together as parties whose members could sink differences in a common party action is the fact that both parties had a wide area of mutual agreement above and beyond party. To put it quite baldly, there wasn't much difference between the Conservatives and the Liberals. When one went out of power and the other came in, the ship of state tacked a bit, but it did not change direction. The Conservative Disraeli and the Liberal Gladstone were perhaps not quite shadow-boxing in their heated parliamentary exchanges, but they clearly were not fighting to kill, nor perhaps even for the knockout. The contemporary writer, Walter Bagehot, who understood and expressed his own age very well, wrote in a passage that throws much light on Victorian politics:

... It may seem odd to say so, just after inculcating that party organisation is the vital principle of representative government, but that organisation is permanently efficient, because it is not composed of warm partisans. The body is eager, but the atoms are cool. If it were otherwise, parliamentary government would become the worst of governments—a sectarian government. The party in power would go all the lengths their orators proposed —all that their formulae enjoined, as far as they had ever said they would go. But the partisans of the English Parliament are not of such a temper.... They are not eager to press the tenets of their party to impossible conclusions. On the contrary, the way to lead them—the best and acknowledged way—is to affect a studied and illogical moderation. ... Most men of business love a sort of twilight. They have lived all their lives in an atmosphere of probabilities and of doubt, where nothing is very clear, where there are some chances for many events, where there is much to be said for several courses, where nevertheless one course must be determinedly chosen and fixedly adhered to. They like to hear arguments suited to this intellectual haze. So far from caution or hesitation in the statement of the argument striking them as an indication of imbecility, it seems to them a sign of practicality. They got rich themselves by transactions of which they could not have stated the argumentative ground—and all they ask for is a distinct though moderate conclusion, that they can repeat when asked; something which they feel *not* to be abstract argument, but abstract argument diluted and dissolved in real life. 'There seem to me,' an impatient young man once said, 'to be no stays in Peel's arguments.' And that was why Sir Robert Peel was the best leader of the Commons in our time; we like to have the rigidity taken out of an argument, and the substance left.*

---

* Walter Bagehot, *The English Constitution* (London, 1922), 143-144.

To sum up, government by discussion, Her Majesty's Government and Her Majesty's Opposition equally loyal to established ways, under the shelter of the English Channel and the British navy, in a prosperous land without deep-seated class antagonisms or insuperable class barriers and rigidities—all this had developed in the British people habits of compromise, of law-abidingness, a sort of political sportsmanship. And these habits survive even in the mid-twentieth century, when Victorian geographical security has gone with the airplane and Victorian prosperity has gone with the rise of competing industrial nations.

Reforms of the Utilitarians

The Reform Bill of 1832 was followed by a series of major reforms that helped make over, not merely British political life, but British economic and social life as well. The inspiration of these reforms came in large part from a small but influential middle-class group, the "Philosophic Radicals" or Utilitarians (see Chapter XX). These disciples of Bentham and of the Enlightenment believed that men are, if once educated, impelled by rational self-interest and thus automatically do what is best for all their fellows. Under the influence of the Philosophic Radicals, English local government and the English legal system were made simpler, and were cleansed of some of the impediments to efficient government action left by the long accumulation of traditional stopgaps. These middle-class radicals, however, believed firmly that that government governs best which governs least, and they sought rather to expedite that minimum of government than to add to its tasks. They believed firmly in education, but not in compulsory public education; private initiative would in their opinion do well what the government would do poorly and tyrannically. Large-scale government reform of British popular education had therefore to wait until 1870. Meanwhile, the private initiative preached by the Utilitarians sponsored mechanics' institutes and other means of adult education. It also sponsored all sorts of private schools, and universities in London, Manchester, and some other British cities.

The typical Utilitarian reform, the one that stirred up public opinion most thoroughly, was the New Poor Law of 1834. This bill codified, centralized, and made more coherent a complicated system of public relief that had originated in the Elizabethan Poor Law of 1601 and earlier Tudor legislation. But it did more: it shifted the base of this relief. The old methods of poor relief, "outdoor relief," had gradually come to permit supplementary payments from the parishes to able-bodied poor working on low wages, supplements for children, and in general by no means generous but still easy-going "doles" direct to families in their homes. The new system would have none of this laxness, this encouragement of men in what the Utilitarian, in spite of his belief in human rationality, rather feared was their "natural" laziness. Poor Law Unions united parishes for greater efficiency, and supplied in the workhouses the "indoor relief" by which able-bodied paupers were made as uncomfortable as decency would allow. This discomfort would then encourage them to become self-supporting outside. The New Poor Law offended humanitarians in the upper classes, and was a hard blow to democrats who had backed the First Reform Bill in the hope of improving conditions of the working classes. Nevertheless, from the point of view of middle-class business interests, it had the decided merit of making poor relief both more efficient and more economical.

Free Trade

Greatest of these Utilitarian reforms in its long-run consequences was the repeal of the Corn Laws in 1846, after a long campaign headed by the Anti-Corn-Law League. This effective pressure group worked, as did the American Anti-Saloon League much later, on both political parties. The movement against tariffs on grains was led by Richard Cobden, an agitator so respectable, so high-minded, so Victorian, that he no longer seems much like an agitator. What the Free Traders wanted, and ultimately got, was a political economy in which food and other raw materials were imported from abroad without tariffs, and manufactures were exported to pay for the imports. In the long run—in another century—the difficulty for Britain would lie in the fact that other parts of the world too would become industrial workshops. In the short run, in the early nineteenth century, the difficulty was that protective tariffs in favor of English agriculture made importation of the cheapest possible foodstuffs from abroad impossible. To this difficulty the English industrialists addressed themselves in the campaign against the Corn Laws. Their victory was achieved in 1846 by the conversion of the Conservative leader Peel to their cause, and by the alliance of Peelites and Liberals that put the bill through. Britain was now a free-trade nation, the only major free-trade nation in a world that never quite lost its mercantilist preconceptions and habits.

The Improvement of Labor

Still another series of reforms helped make the prosperous England of Gladstone and Disraeli. These were the Factory Acts, begun in 1802 and 1819 with bills sponsored by Peel's father. Addicts of the economic interpretation of history hold that middle-class people put through reforms like those of the Poor Law and the repeal of the Corn Laws, but that the landed gentry and upper-class intellectuals, jealous of the new city wealth and outraged by the ugliness of the new industrial towns, put through reforms like those of the Factory Acts regulating hours of labor, sanitation, and the labor of women and children. It is true that many leaders of the movement to use the power of the state to regulate some part of economic life were not themselves business-men or industrialists. They were either members of the old Tory ruling class or intellectuals, like Disraeli, Carlyle, Ruskin, and Matthew Arnold, who preached against the horrors of working-class life in prosperous Victorian England. And it is true that the formal philosophy of the British business class was laissez-faire. But the practice was a different matter: none of the Factory Acts and similar reforms of the nineteenth century could really have gone through Parliament successfully without some support from both political parties. Moreover, neither landed gentry nor industrialists and businessmen were mutually exclusive "classes" in a neat Marxist sense. Rather, they were thoroughly mingled in education, marriage, and even in economic interests, since the gentry invested in stocks and bonds and the industrialists invested in landed estates. The elder Peel, father of the Factory Acts, was a self-made industrialist.

The Factory Acts followed a sequence not unlike the sequence of acts that reformed the suffrage. The first acts were very modest indeed; they underlined the frightful conditions they were designed to remedy. That of 1819, for instance, applied only to the cotton industry, forbade night work for children, and limited day work to twelve hours. Even so, it provided for no really effective inspection, and was violated with impunity by many employers. The Act of 1833, forbidding child labor entirely be-low the age of nine, and restricting it to nine hours for those below thirteen, and twelve for those below eighteen, marked an important stage by setting up salaried inspectors to enforce the law.

By the end of the nineteenth century, there was on the books a whole code of labor legislation, regulating hours of labor for everyone, giving special protection to women and children, and including provisions that made the employer responsible for workmen's compensation in industrial accidents. Then in 1911 came the great National Insurance Act, which provided through combined payments from the state, from employers, and from employees compulsory health and unemployment insurance. The "welfare state" was firmly established in Britain well before the Labor party had come to power.

Education

The same story of piecemeal but cumulative reform holds true in education. The idea that education is not properly a function of the state held back a general education act until 1870. The issue was complicated by the wrangling of Anglicans and nonconformists, for many existing schools were controlled by a society that made instruction compulsory in the doctrines of the Church of England. But even before 1870 a Privy Council committee had been supplementing local education boards by making grants from the national treasury (in 1860 these grants reached nearly a million pounds), by providing an inspection service, and by helping to organize teacher training. School attendance, however, was not compulsory, and the average age for leaving school was eleven years. After workingmen got the vote in 1867, worried Tories —and Liberals—began to urge the slogan, "Educate your masters." The bill of 1870, put through under Gladstone's Minister of

Education, William Forster, did not quite set up compulsory national education at the elementary level. It did permit the local boards to compel attendance, and it did extend national aid and supervision. The religious difficulty was solved by the provision that religious instruction in tax-supported schools should be nonsectarian and not required of the pupils. Church schools were allowed public aid, a feature that continued on into our own time.

Still, the basis for widespread compulsory education was firmly laid, and by the end of the century illiteracy in Britain had pretty generally been eliminated. Beginnings were made in publicly supported schools at the secondary level, though the British "public school," which in American terms is a "private school," continued until our own day to maintain a privileged position in the British social system. In comparison with public school systems in Germany, France, and the United States, British education on the eve of World War I was administratively complex and full of anomalies. On the whole, though, it got the job done, and the general level of popular education in the British Isles was at least as high as in the other liberal democracies.

Chartism

Only one of the major reform movements of the nineteenth century seems to have failed completely. This was Chartism, which played a major role in the political excitements of the 1830's and 1840's, and greatly alarmed the conservative classes. The Chartists were the closest (but still not very close) English equivalent of the radical parties which on the Continent carried on the Jacobin tradition of the French Revolution, mingled with the elements of nascent socialism. The Chartists had a formal program drawn up in a "People's Charter," calling for universal manhood suffrage, the secret ballot, abolition of property requirements for members of Parliament, payment of members, equal electoral districts, and annually elected Parliaments. Their strength lay in the new urban industrial proletariat, and especially in the more active and radical members of the proletariat, men who clearly believed that if they got the political democracy they wanted the masses would vote themselves, if not full socialism, at least a considerable degree of leveling of incomes, probably by graduated income taxes. Their leaders were often doctrinaire radicals prone to quarreling among themselves over ideas, and unsparing of bourgeois sensibilities in such matters as religion. They frightened the majority of Englishmen, who felt that the Chartists wanted to lead England in the same paths that had led the French to the Reign of Terror. The movement petered out in a monster petition to Parliament which was never even considered, and in the rising prosperity of the 1850's and 1860's it was effectively stifled. Yet of the original Chartist program all but the demand for annual Parliaments, which soon seemed pointless even to radicals, was achieved by the outbreak of war in 1914.

Foreign Policy

Nowhere does the basic unity that underlies the party strife of nineteenth-century Britain come out more clearly than in foreign relations. The strife is real enough on hundreds of concrete matters of detail; but so is the unity in the broad lines of British policy. Almost all Britishers were agreed on the fundamental position of Britain: maintain the European state-system in balance, preferably by diplomatic rather than military action, but seek no new territories in Europe; police the seas with the

British navy; open world markets to British goods; maintain—and in Africa extend—the vast network of the British Empire, made up of self-governing, English-speaking lands and colonial "possessions" in lands inhabited by the darker-skinned peoples. It is certainly true that the Liberals verbally and emotionally sided in Europe with the liberal nationalist movements, that they sympathized with the struggling Italians, Greeks, and Poles, and that they disliked the old Metternichian powers, especially Russia. It is even true that a Liberal—or better, a belated Whig—foreign minister like Palmerston in mid-century pursued an active policy of near-intervention in behalf of oppressed nationalities, and that British benevolence was a factor in the attainment of Italian unity.

Yet the only European war in which Britain became involved between 1815 and 1914 was the Crimean War of 1854-56, in which France and England went to war as allies against Russia to protect Turkey and their own Near Eastern interests from Russian aggression (see Chapter XXII). This was a somewhat blundering war on both sides. But it at least checked Russian advance for a time and made the ultimate disposition of the Balkan regions of the decaying Turkish Empire a matter of European concern. It was, in fact, a typical balance-of-power war in which Britain played its traditional role of taking arms against a major power that seemed about to add unduly to its lands or its "spheres of influence."

Imperial Policy

On imperial policy it seems at first glance as though British public opinion really was deeply divided. Disraeli and Gladstone were never so gladiatorially fierce as when the Conservative defended the greatness of the Empire and the Liberal attacked imperialism at home and abroad as un-Christian and unwise. And it would be absurd to maintain that in action there was no real difference between the two. Disraeli, on the one side, triumphantly made his royal mistress, Queen Victoria, even more than royal as Empress of India (1876), and bought up the financially embarrassed Khedive of Egypt's shares in the French-built Suez Canal, thus initiating the modern British control of Egypt. On the other side, Gladstone withdrew British troops from Afghanistan, neglected the British General Gordon surrounded by rebels in the Sudan, and conceded independence to the Boer Republics in South Africa. Yet Gladstone kept British armies on the northwest frontier of India. It was under his administration in 1882 that the British actually bombarded Alexandria and monopolized control of Egypt. Gladstone did send troops to rescue Gordon, though they arrived too late, and even in South Africa the Boer Republics were freed only under the "suzerainty" of Britain. In short, Gladstone regretted and no doubt even neglected the Empire; but he kept it (for details, see Chapter XXIV).

In the long view, both parties made possible the most significant development in relations between Britain at home and Britain overseas. This was the growth of the idea and practice of responsible self-government in the colonies of settlement, Canada, Australia, New Zealand, and South Africa. The initiative here was taken by the Liberals, indeed by the Whigs before they were christened Liberals; and in this instance it appears as though men had actually learned from history. For a while in the 1830's it looked as if Canada might go the way the thirteen colonies had gone in 1776. Colonial assemblies in both Lower (French) and Upper (English, or Scots-English) Canada were quarreling with governors and councils appointed by and responsible to the

Crown in Britain. In 1837, these quarrels broke out into open revolt in both colonies. A great Whig lord, Durham, was sent out, and in 1839 after the revolt had been quelled he made his famous report recommending the union of Upper and Lower Canada with responsible government. Final political decisions were to be made by popularly elected assemblies and their executive cabinets, leaving the British governor-general as the symbolic representative of the Crown, no more powerful there than Queen Victoria was at home.

The Durham Report was but a beginning. The British Parliament by the Union Act of 1840 united Upper and Lower Canada. Responsible government came in characteristically British fashion not by formal enactment but by practice under the governorship of Lord Elgin in 1849. In 1867 the British North American Act divided Canada into Quebec and Ontario, and added to them the Maritime Provinces to form a new Canada, with the vast lands of the west open for settlement and the founding of new provinces much as the American West was open to settlement and the founding of new states. The process was not as easy as it sounds in outline. The special difficulties of the French-speaking province of Quebec required patient handling, and are perhaps responsible for the fact that in practice at least Canadian provinces have somewhat more "states' rights" than have American states.

The same process went on, again not without difficulties, in the other colonies of British settlement. The separate Australian colonies were given home rule in 1850, and the federal union was achieved in 1901 with the formation of the Commonwealth of Australia. New Zealand attained full dominion status in 1907, and—thorniest problem of all—South Africa was federated into the Union of South Africa in 1910. This union was achieved only with the greatest difficulty, and under such conditions of national and racial tension that the region remains in mid-twentieth century but incompletely integrated into the British Commonwealth of Nations (for details, see Chapter XXIV).

The Irish Problem

Much nearer home, a nationality problem grew more acute as the nineteenth century came to a close, and did draw something more than a verbal line between Conservatives and Liberals. This was the Irish problem, a problem that had beset the English in one form or another, now acute and now mild, ever since the Norman-English conquest of Ireland in the twelfth century. The English, and the Scots who came to settle in the Irish province of Ulster in the sixteenth and seventeenth centuries, had remained as a privileged land-owning group in the midst of a subject population of native Irish peasants. As the nineteenth century opened, the English attempted to solve the problem by a formal union of the two kingdoms, with Irish members admitted to the British Parliament, in which they were of course a minority. In the prevailing temper of nineteenth-century Britain, it was quite impossible to deny the Irish natives all political rights; and indeed, beginning with the Catholic Emancipation Act of 1829, the various suffrage reforms we have outlined above were extended to Ireland. The Irish, led by Daniel O'Connell, the "Great Emancipator," organized politically to press for reforms and, eventually, for home rule of the kind the dominions were gradually achieving. They sought not only for political home rule, but also for land reforms, and for disestablishment of the Anglican Church in Ireland.

Irish hatred for the English was fanned by the disastrous potato famine of the

1840's, when blight ruined a crop essential to the Irish food supply. Although the beginnings of modern transportation by railway and steamship existed, the British government was not organized for prompt and efficient relief measures, nor was the kind of international organization for such relief afforded nowadays by the Red Cross yet in existence. The result was a medieval famine in the heart of modern western civilization, in which tens of thousands died of starvation, and other tens of thousands were forced to migrate, mostly to the United States. The immigrants added to British difficulties, for they carried their rancors with them, and formed pressure groups, like the Fenian Brotherhood organized in New York in 1858 to raise funds to aid Irish resistance and to make trouble generally for the British wherever they could.

British governments made piecemeal reforms. The Anglican Church in Ireland was disestablished in 1869 and in the next year an Irish Land Act began a series of agrarian reforms that were designed to protect the tenant from "rack-renting"—the extraction by the landlord, often an absentee member of the British "garrison," of as high a rent as the tenants, forced by overpopulation into intense competition, could pay. The reforms were neither far-reaching nor rapid enough to satisfy the Irish. Moreover, the emotional strength of Irish nationalism grew with the spread of elementary education and the usual literary and cultural forms of national self-consciousness. The Irish question was not just a matter of land, or of religion, but also of a peculiarly intense form of underdog awareness of cultural differences and of nationality. Then in the 1870's a brilliant Irish leader arose, Charles Parnell, himself a Protestant descendant of the "garrison," but a firm Irish patriot. Under the leadership of Parnell in the British Parliament, the Irish nationalists were welded into a firm, well-disciplined party which, though it held less than a hundred seats, could swing the balance between Liberals and Conservatives.

The critical step came when Gladstone, converted to Home Rule, introduced in 1886 his first Home Rule Bill. This bill provided for a separate Irish parliament with some restrictions on its sovereignty, and of course under the Crown. Gladstone's decision split his own Liberal party in something like the way Peel's conversion to Free Trade had split the Conservatives in 1846. A group led by Joseph Chamberlain, who had begun political life as the reform leader of the great city of Birmingham, seceded under the name of "Liberal Unionists." In effect, they joined the Conservative party, which is often known in the next few decades, so great were the passions aroused in Great Britain by this proposed cutting loose of Ireland, simply as the "Unionist" party. Gladstone lost the election brought on by the split, and Home Rule was dropped for the moment.

Agitation continued in Ireland. It became more bitter when Parnell, involved in a divorce scandal, was dropped by the virtuous Gladstone and by some of his own Irish followers. In 1892, however, Gladstone won a close election on the Irish issue —or, rather, he obtained enough English seats to get a Second Home Rule Bill through the Commons with the aid of eighty-one Irish nationalists. It was defeated, however, in the Conservative House of Lords, and was dropped once more. The Conservatives, when they came in for their ten-year reign in 1895, sought to "kill Home Rule by kindness," carrying several land reform bills that furthered the process of making Ireland a land of small peasant proprietors.

But Ireland was now beyond the reach of kindness, and Irish problems were no longer—if they ever had been—largely economic and administrative. Irish nationalism was now a full cult, nourished by a remarkable literary revival in English and in Gaelic. Even W. B. Yeats, a cloistered intellectual known to our time as a difficult and very modern poet, went down to preach to the people. The scene of his one-act play, *Cathleen ni Hoolihan,* is set in Ireland in 1798 when the French revolutionaries were about to land. Cathleen is the traditional symbol of Ireland, and she appears as The Poor Old Woman. She talks with Michael, an Irish lad, to whom she is simply a poor old woman who has wandered into his village.

MICHAEL. Have you no man of your own, ma'am?

THE POOR OLD WOMAN. I have not. With all the lovers that brought me their love, I never set out the bed for any.

MICHAEL. Are you lonely going the roads, ma'am?

THE POOR OLD WOMAN. I have my thoughts and I have my hopes.

MICHAEL. What hopes have you to hold to?

THE POOR OLD WOMAN. The hope of getting my beautiful fields back again; the hope of putting the strangers out of my house.

MICHAEL. What way will you do that, ma'am?

THE POOR OLD WOMAN. I have good friends that will help me. They are gathering to help me now. I am not afraid. If they are put down today, they will get the upper hand tomorrow. [*She gets up.*] I must be going to meet my friends. They are coming to help me, and I must be there to welcome them. I must call the neighbours together to welcome them.[*]

Michael, though about to marry, breaks away from his fiancée and sets off to help Cathleen ni Hoolihan. The play ends as the disappointed mother-in-law asks:

Did you see an old woman going down the path?

PATRICK. I did not, but I saw a young girl and she had the walk of a queen.

---

[*] W. B. Yeats, *The Hour-Glass and Other Plays* (New York, 1904), 70-72.

The Liberals, back in power after 1905, found they needed the votes of the Irish nationalists to carry through their proposal for ending the veto power of the Lords. After some soul-searching, the Liberals struck the bargain: Home Rule in return for the Parliament Act. They introduced in 1912 a Home Rule Bill which—the Parliament Act in 1911 having destroyed the veto power of the Lords—was placed on the books as a law. It never went into force, however, for as Home Rule seemed about to become a fact the predominantly Protestant North of Ireland, the province of Ulster, bitterly opposed to separation from Great Britain, was organized to resist by force of arms. The Home Rule Bill as passed carried the rider that it was not to go into effect until the Ulster question was settled. The outbreak of war in 1914 made such a settlement out of the question, and the stage was set for the Irish Revolution of our own day (see Chapter XXVIII).

Gladstone's action in espousing Home Rule was politically courageous, and was hailed at the time by liberal opinion at home and abroad as dictated by liberal principles. But it is possible now to defend the thesis that it was not a wise act, that it was premature, that its destruction of Liberal party unity made impossible a slow, quiet working out of Irish social, religious, and economic problems in the course of which Protestant Ulster opinion might gradually have been won over to dominion status for the whole island.

The Threat to Free Trade

As Great Britain approached the twentieth century, then, new problems arose to disturb the underlying serenity and assurance of the Victorian Age. The Boer and Irish troubles, the rising international tensions that were to lead to World War I (see Chapter XXV), and the difficulties of adjusting the new distribution of national income made necessary by the rise of the "welfare state," confronted the British people all at once. Though here as always in history we must avoid the temptation to seek a single underlying cause, there was undoubtedly one major factor at work. The long lead Britain had gained in the industrial revolution was being lost as other nations acquired the technical skills of large-scale production. Germany, the Low Countries, the United States, and in a measure all the West, were competing on the world market.

Under such conditions, it was natural that some Britishers should come to doubt the wisdom of the Free Trade policies that had won the day in 1846. For the Germans and others were not only underselling the British abroad; they were actually invading the British home market. Why not protect that market by a tariff system? Few Britishers were foolish enough to believe that the home islands, already by the 1880's too densely populated to feed themselves and constitute a self-sufficient economy, could surround themselves with a simple tariff wall. But the Empire was world-wide, with abundant resources, with thousands of square miles of agricultural lands. Within it the classical mercantilist interchange of manufactures for raw materials could still provide a balanced economic system. Britain could still be, if not the workshop of the world, at least the workshop of a quarter of the world, the British Commonwealth and Empire.

The same Joseph Chamberlain who led the secession from the Liberals on the question of Home Rule for Ireland also led a secession on an issue of much more fundamental importance. He advocated protective tariffs, a policy which early in the next century his Tory successors focused on a system of imperial preferences through which the whole complex of lands under the Crown would be knit together in a tariff union. The Conservatives, never wholly reconciled to Free Trade, welcomed the recruits, and the new Unionist party made protection a major plank in its program. Liberal opposition, however, was still much too strong, and there was opposition even in Conservative ranks. Chamberlain, reversing the aims but imitating the methods of Cobden and the Anti-Corn Law League of the 1840's, organized a Tariff Reform League. In 1903, he introduced a sweeping measure that would have restored moderate duties on foodstuffs and raw materials (largely to give a basis for negotiating with the dominions, which already had tariff systems of their own) and on foreign manufactured goods. But the Conservative leader, Balfour, did not dare go so far, and Chamberlain resigned with his bill unpassed. The new Liberal government of 1905 continued the policy of Free Trade.

The Welfare State

The Liberals were, however, committed to another policy not as consciously planned to enable Britain to compete directly with her industrial rivals, but quite as contrary to the classical philosophy of laissez-faire as was protectionism. This was the welfare state—social security through compulsory insurance managed by the state, and in part financed by the state, minimum-wage laws, progressive taxation on incomes and inheritances, compulsory public education, public works and services of all kinds. The dramatic point in the working out of the program was the "People's Budget" of 1909, introduced by a new figure on the political stage, the Liberal Chancellor of the Exchequer, Lloyd George (1863-1944). This budget, which frankly proposed to tax the rich to finance the new welfare measures, and also the rising naval costs brought on by the armament race with Germany (see Chapter XXV), was clearly no ordinary tax measure. It was a means of altering the social and economic structure of Britain. Its opponents rightly called it "not a budget, but a revolution." It passed the Commons, but was thrown out by the Lords, even though it was a "money bill." The Liberals went to the country, and after an exciting election in which the Liberals gained but two seats, they were able to put through the Parliament Act of 1911, which took away from the Lords all power to alter a money bill, and left them with no more than a three-year delaying power over all other legislation. The Liberal program of social legislation was saved.

But was it a *Liberal* program? The dissenting Liberals who had followed Joseph Chamberlain out of the party in the 1880's thought not, and it was normal enough for Chamberlain's two sons, Austen and Neville, who played an important part in twentieth-century politics, to think of themselves as Conservatives. For what happened in the generation after 1880 was a major change in the political orientation of British parties. The Liberals, who had believed that that government governs best which governs least, and least expensively, had come to believe that the state must interfere in economic life to help the underdog, had come to adopt Lloyd George's plan for redistributing the national wealth by social insurance financed by taxation of the rich and well-to-do. And the Conservatives, who in the mid-nineteenth century had stood for factory acts and at least mild forms of the welfare state, were now in large part committed to a program astonishingly like that of the Liberals of 1850.

The Labor Party

One factor in this change had been the growth of the British Labor party, which originated in a number of groups formed in the late nineteenth century. One group was based on straightforward labor-unionist aims to secure better working conditions. Another, the Fabians, intellectuals like Sydney and Beatrice Webb, George Bernard Shaw, and H. G. Wells, was bent on the *gradual* introduction of socialism (hence, from the Roman general Fabius, who believed in delay, the "Fabians"). A third, led by Keir Hardie, one of the very first Labor members of Parliament, acted on the Puritan nonconformist conscience and believed socialism to be the only Christian solution for social problems. Finally, there was a small but determined group of Marxists.

Labor, though never perfectly unified (and always troubled by cleavages between its left and right wings), had developed by 1905 into a party able to command fifty-three seats in the Commons. It wanted the welfare state, and indeed some Laborites wanted a socialist state in which at least the major industries were nationalized. Part of the motivation for the Liberal program of social legislation was a desire to forestall Labor. Just as in 1867 the Tories had "walked away with the Whigs' clothes" and had given the workingman the vote, so in 1911 the Liberals stole Labor's clothes and gave the workingman social security. But these tactics worked no better in the twentieth century than in the nineteenth, and the workingmen on the whole stuck by the Labor party, leaving the Liberals to die on the branch.

Not all the motivation of the Liberals in these early years of the twentieth century was, however, mere fear of Labor. In part, their conversion from laissez-faire to social security was a positive one, a sincere belief that the logic of their democratic assumptions must drive them to raise the general standard of living in Britain by state action. Something broadly analogous was happening throughout the democratic

West—in France, in the smaller democracies, and, a few decades later, in the United States. An important part of the bourgeoisie in all these countries swung over, not to doctrinaire socialism, but to programs of social legislation put through by the usual machinery of change under a wide democratic suffrage. The English Chartists who back in the early nineteenth century had had the apparently naive belief that universal suffrage would pave the way to greater economic equality. In the long run, events were to prove that the Chartists were far from being entirely wrong.

III: France—Second Empire and Third Republic

The Coup d'Etat of 1851

One hundred years ago France seemed to many English-speaking critics, as she seems to many today, a rather uncertain member of the community of nations ruled by the democratic decencies—that is, government by discussion, peaceful alternation of "ins" and "outs" through the working of the party system, and the usual freedoms of the "rights of man." The democratic revolution, so optimistically begun in 1848 (see Chapter XIX), had by 1852 brought still another Bonaparte to the throne of France in Napoleon III, nephew of the first Napoleon. As President of the Second Republic, Prince Louis Napoleon had soon quarreled with the National Assembly, which refused to amend the Constitution of 1848 to allow him a second term of office. Fearful of radicals and socialists, the Assembly also whittled down the universal male suffrage of 1848 and thus enabled the Prince-President to pose as the champion of persecuted popular democracy.

The coup d'état of December 2, 1851, artfully timed for the sacred Napoleonic day of the first coronation (December 2, 1804) and Austerlitz (December 2, 1805), was a stereotyped affair. Controlling the army, Louis Napoleon and his fellow conspirators found it easy to purge the Assembly and make way for a popular vote on a new constitution. Even the expected street fighting on the barricades of Paris, which broke out on December 3, proved to be no wholesale bloodletting. It left victims enough as martyrs, however, and, politically more important, it enabled the President to pose as the champion of order against a largely imaginary socialist plot. Napoleon quickly got himself approved by a plebiscite, which by 7,500,000 votes to 640,000 gave him the right to draw up a new constitution.

The plebiscite was accompanied by skillful propaganda, but it was not crudely a work of force. Though many opponents of Napoleon simply did not vote, it seems that a majority of Frenchmen over twenty-one really were willing to try another dictator. There were many reasons why men voted "yes." Almost all were weary of the struggles of the last three years. Many were frightened by the specter of socialism, now for the first time under that name a definite factor in western politics. For nearly three decades the full force of fashionable French literature had been at work making the Napoleonic legend, and identifying the name of Napoleon with the "pooled self-esteem" of French patriotism. Many a man voted "yes" not to Louis Napoleon, but to the music of the "Marseillaise," the cannon of Austerlitz, to all the glories of France.

Indeed, the Napoleonic legend is a classic example in a complex modern society of the growth of a major cluster of ideas centered on a person. The legend was not "invented" by any one man or group; it was not "put across" like the kind of planned advertising campaign for a given product that our generation knows so well. But many groups, often using quite deliberate propaganda techniques, helped a growth that found favorable natural conditions in nineteenth-century France. By the 1840's, the first Napoleon was a hero, a saint of nationalism. The "people's poet," Béranger, could write "A People's Memories," in which children ask their aged grandmother about Him.

> 'But when poor Champagne, invaded,
> Shook beneath the stranger's tread,
> He alone, it seem'd, made head
> Against our country's foes, unaided.
> Once (to-night as it might be)
> Came a knock: the door was barr'd:
> Swift I opened—gods! 'twas he!
> Follow'd by a scanty guard.
> Down he sat, in yonder chair,
> From his lips a cry there burst,
> "Oh, war accurst!" '
> 'Grandam, was he seated there?
> Was he seated there?' *

Here Napoleon has already been transformed into a hater of war!

The Second Empire, 1852-1870: Domestic Developments

The new constitution set up a lightly veiled dictatorship very much like that of

* Béranger's Songs of the Empire, the Peace, and the Restoration, Robert B. Brough, trans. (London, 1856), 50-51.

Napoleon I. The "chief of state" (he became formally "emperor" again on the sacred date, December 2, in 1852) had full authority; he was responsible only to the nation. He governed through ministers, judges, and a whole bureaucracy, in the appointment of which he had the final voice. The popularly elected assembly, the *Corps Législatif*, was filled with "official" candidates sent up by influence of the efficient appointed officials in the provinces. It had no power to initiate or amend legislation; it had only a veto, which in the first few years it rarely used. Yet Napoleon III insisted that he was no mere tool of the possessing classes, no conservative, but an agent of real reform, an emperor of the masses, a kind of continental equivalent of the "Tory democrat" that Disraeli was claiming to be. This claim indeed has been made by almost all our recent dictators, from Stalin to the Perons; they all claim to be *real* democrats, really protectors of ordinary men who in the classical western democracies, they insist, are actually victims of capitalist exploitation. Napoleon III has sometimes been seen as the first of these modern dictators, as a "proto-fascist"; and the careful student of his career can learn much that throws light on our own problems today.

Certainly by comparison with later social legislation in Germany, Britain, or Scandinavia, Napoleon's concrete achievements in direct benefit of the workers were slight. He did carry through a great program of public works, notably in Paris, where his prefect Haussmann cut through the medieval mazes of streets those broad straight avenues which all the world knows so well, and which, incidentally, can be easily swept by gunfire and make street fighting that much more difficult. And he did help with housing and encourage workers' mutual aid societies. But the legal code of labor in France in 1860 was less "modern" than that of England. The standard of living of French labor in the growing cities was well behind that of Britain, and behind that of Germany and the smaller democracies. French labor did indeed benefit from the general prosperity that came to France in the 1850's as it came to Great Britain, but the gains in wages were at least counterbalanced by rising prices.

It was the bourgeoisie that made most out of the Second Empire. Napoleon's government encouraged improvement in banking facilities, helped the great growth of French railways by state guaranties, and in general furthered the rise of industry in the two decades after 1850. That rise was, especially in large-scale heavy industries, definitely inferior to that of the British and to the already growing basic German industry. But it was in absolute terms a very real rise. Paris grew into a major metropolitan area, and centers like Lyons and Rouen in textiles, Clermont-Ferrand and St. Etienne in metallurgy, and many other cities came to have genuine industrial economies, with all the problems of slums, trade unions, and other signs of modernity. Yet there remained then as under later French governments an adhesion to older methods of doing business, to small firms often under family control, to luxury trades in which handicraft skills remained important in spite of the machine, to a kind of conservatism which meant that in quantitative terms of actual production France fell behind the industrial West. Statistics of national productivity, which though imperfect can be reconstructed after a fashion for early modern times, would show that, whereas the France of Colbert was up near the leaders, in the nineteenth and twentieth centuries France was no longer at the level of her major western rivals. Her growth in population, too, fell well behind that of the others. At the end of the nineteenth century, she was not much more than 50 per cent more populous than at the beginning— and this with almost no emigration. Britain, in spite of a large emigration, had about tripled her population, and Germany, too, was growing rapidly. Even Italy, with slender natural resources and less industry than France, was growing in population faster than France, and was to outstrip her in our own times.

The Second Empire: Foreign Policy

Yet the France of the Second Empire was still a very great power, and the extent of her comparative decline was by no means clear to contemporaries. Although the French gained little from the Crimean War, they did at least have the satisfaction of playing host to the postwar congress at Paris in 1856. And the Paris Exposition of 1855, a counterpart of the famous London exhibition of 1851, was a great success that showed Napoleon III at the height of his power. He had pledged himself to use that power for peace, but he allowed himself, partly through a romantic interest in "oppressed nationalities," partly from age-old motives of prestige, to become involved in a war against Austria for the liberation of Italy. French armies won victories in this war of 1859; but then the Italians took things into their own hands and set about organizing the whole peninsula, including papal Rome, into an Italian kingdom. Napoleon depended too much on Catholic support at home to be able to permit the extinction of papal power; moreover, the too great success of his plans was threatening the European balance of power. He therefore temporized, permitting the union of most of Italy under the house of Savoy, but protecting the Pope's temporal power with a French garrison in Rome, leaving Venetia still in Austrian hands, and taking

BOW-WOW !!

British reaction to saber-rattling by Napoleon III, 1859.

from Italian Piedmont Nice and the French-speaking part of Alpine Savoy as a reward for his services. He thus managed to offend most Italians, as well as most of his own Catholic supporters at home.

To make matters worse, Napoleon began in 1861 a wild adventure in Mexico, supporting there with French arms and men an expedition to put the Austrian prince Maximilian on an imperial throne. The United States, engaged in the Civil War, could do nothing at the time against what Americans were bound to regard as an infraction of the Monroe Doctrine. But after peace had been restored in the United States, the American government protested strongly, and Napoleon, faced also with Mexican opposition, withdrew his support. Maximilian faced a firing squad in 1867.

The "Liberal Empire"

Napoleon had come to power, as we have seen, on a platform of national unity against the extreme demands of the social revolutionists of 1848. But in spite of the plebiscite, it became more and more clear that if France had a national unity, it was not of the monolithic, totalitarian sort, but a unity that had to be worked out in the open competition of modern western political life—with parties, parliamentary debate, newspapers, in short, with government by discussion. Napoleon could not in fact be a symbolic head of state, above the struggle, nor even a final umpire. He could not be a republican, though much of France was republican; he could not be a legitimate monarchist, though much of France, and particularly the conservative France which held authoritarian views, was loyal to the legitimacy of the Bourbons, or the somewhat dubious legitimacy of the Orléanists. He could not even be a good devout Catholic, in spite of the orthodoxy of his wife, the Empress Eugénie, for his Bonapartist background was heavily tinged with the anticlericalism of the eighteenth century, and his bungling of the Italian problem had deeply offended clericals. He could only head an "official" party, relying on the manipulative skills of his bureaucrats to work the cumbersome machinery of a parliamentary system designed, like that of Napoleon I, as a disguise for dictatorship.

As the pressure of genuine party differences rose, Napoleon slowly abandoned the measures of repression he had begun with, and sought to establish himself in something like the position of a constitutional monarch. An act of 1860 gave the Legislative Assembly power to discuss freely a reply to the address from the throne, and throughout the 1860's these powers were extended in the name of the "Liberal Empire." Gradually, political life in France took on a pattern of parliamentary government, with a Right, Left, and Center. As a result of the general election of 1869, the government was faced with a strong legal opposition, thirty of whom were declared republicans. On July 12, 1869, Napoleon

CHAPTER XXI

The Paris Commune, 1871. Destruction of the Vendôme column commemorating Napoleon I.

capitulated, and granted the Legislative Assembly the right to propose laws, and to criticize and vote the budget. Partial ministerial responsibility seemed just around the corner as Napoleon entrusted the government to the head of the moderates, Emile Ollivier. A plebiscite in May, 1870, overwhelmingly ratified these changes.

It is at least possible that the Second Empire might thus have been converted into a constitutional monarchy. The changes had indeed been wrung from the Emperor by popular agitation, not merely political but also economic in the form of strikes. It is quite as possible that the radical republican ground swell would have gone on to submerge the Empire in any case. But the disastrous defeats of the French armies in the Franco-Prussian War into which Napoleon was maneuvered by the skill of Bismarck (see Chapter XXII) put an end to the experiment of the Liberal Empire. On September 4, 1870, after the humiliating capitulation of Sedan, a Parisian mob forced a rump Legislative Assembly to decree the fall of the Empire, and at the classic center of French republicanism, the Paris City Hall, the Republic was proclaimed.

The Birth of the Third Republic

The new republic was too good a child of 1792 to give up the war against the national enemy. A government of national defense tried to continue the struggle, but the miracle of Valmy (see Chapter XVIII) was not to be repeated. In October, General Bazaine surrendered a large French force at Metz, and the disorganized elements of other French armies were helpless before the powerful German forces. An exhausted nation, sick of the war, chose in February a National Assembly that met at Bordeaux and sued for peace. The special circumstances of that election, however, placed on the new Republic an additional handicap. For meanwhile Paris, besieged by the Germans, had resisted desperately until starvation forced its surrender in January, 1871. Even under pressure of the siege, Parisian radicals tried to seize power and revive the old Paris Commune, or city government, of 1792. These radicals could not stomach the capitulation that the rest of the country seemed to be preparing. In the elections to the National Assembly, their intransigence helped to turn the provincial voters toward conservative candidates pledged to make peace—and to restore, not the Republic, but the old monarchy.

This new Assembly, on March 1, 1871, voted to accept a peace ceding Alsace-Lorraine to Germany and paying an indemnity of five billion francs (about $1,000,000,000). Then the Paris National Guard, which had not been disarmed by the Germans, went over to the radicals, and the Paris Commune was set up. Marxist legend has consecrated the Commune of 1871 as the first major socialist government. The Communards were in fact rather Jacobins, radical and highly patriotic republicans who wanted a society of small independent shopkeepers and artisans, not the abolition of private property. In any case, they had no chance in the besieged city to introduce sweeping social reforms. But they alarmed the rest of France, and their refusal to accept the peace was a challenge the National Assembly had to meet. To the horrors of the first siege by the Germans were added the horrors of a new siege by the government of the National Assembly, which gathered its troops at Versailles and in the "Bloody Week" of May 21-28 advanced through the barricades to clear the city.

The Third French Republic was thus born in foreign and in civil war, and began with a heritage of unresolved cleavages. Indeed, it was not at all clear in 1871 that there was a Third Republic. More than half the members of the new National Assembly were monarchists, anxious to undo the formal declaration of a republic made in Paris right after Sedan. But now we encounter one of those concrete events that are the despair of those who seek the clue to history in vast impersonal forces beyond the play of human personality. About half the monarchist deputies were pledged to the elder "legitimate" Bourbon line represented by the Count of Chambord, grandson of

Charles X, and the other half to the younger Orléanist line that had come to the throne in 1830, represented by the Count of Paris, grandson of Louis Philippe. Chambord might have become in fact what he was to his supporters, King Henry V, had he been willing to make the slightest concession to Orléanist sentiments and accept the revolutionary blue, white, and red tricolor flag that Louis Philippe had himself accepted as the flag of France. But he insisted on the white flag and gold lilies of Bourbon, which for millions of Frenchmen meant complete repudiation of all that had happened since 1789. He meant to be king, not just a Victorian symbol; but no one could be that sort of king in France any longer.

In the resulting stalemate, the republican minority was able to maintain itself, and slowly gather strength. Thiers, the elder statesman of the Orléanist monarchy, who had been a leader in the opposition to Napoleon III, was recognized as "President of the Republic" and carried through the final settlement with Germany. He was succeeded in 1873 by Marshal MacMahon, a soldier and a monarchist, who was elected to hold the government together while the monarchist majority made peace between Bourbons and Orléanists. That peace was never made, as Chambord continued to insist on the white flag, and in 1875 a series of constitutional measures formally established the Third Republic.

The Constitution of 1875

These laws, known collectively as the Constitution of 1875, provided for a president elected by an absolute majority of Senate and Chamber of Deputies sitting together as a National Assembly, the usual ministers, and a bicameral legislature elected by universal manhood suffrage. The

258

Senate was chosen by indirect election, the Chamber of Deputies by direct election; all legislation had to pass both houses, though only the lower could initiate finance bills. The critical point was that of the responsibility of the ministers. Had the president been able to dismiss them, a new Napoleon III might easily have arisen to destroy the Republic. MacMahon attempted to exercise this power when on May 16, 1877, he dismissed the anticlerical premier, Jules Simon. But this crisis of the *Seize Mai* (May 16) forced a national election, and the new Chamber upheld the principle of parliamentary supremacy. MacMahon was forced to resign in 1879, and was succeeded by the orthodox republican, Jules Grévy. Nine years after its establishment in name, the Third Republic had at long last become a fact.

It was in form a kind of republican transposition of constitutional monarchy, with an ornamental president instead of an ornamental king. In the letter of the Constitution, the president might dissolve the Chamber and appeal to the country in a new election; but the fate of MacMahon after the *Seize Mai* had been decisive, and the procedure of dissolution was so discredited that it was never tried again. The real executive, as in England, was the ministry, in effect a committee responsible to the legislature—indeed to the Chamber of Deputies, which soon became the focus of political action, leaving the Senate little more than a dignified republican refuge for elder statesmen. The Chamber, reflecting the political habits of the country, was composed not of two, but of a dozen or more parties, so that any ministry had to be supported by a coalition subject to constant shifting in the play of personalities and principles. The result was a marked instability of ministries. The "life expectancy" of a ministry under the Third Republic was hardly a year.

Yet such a figure is misleading. A French ministry under the Third Republic—and indeed under the present Fourth Republic—does not usually resign and give way to a totally different ministry with totally different policies. Instead, its personnel is shifted a bit, a compromise or so is made with certain parliamentary groups, and the new ministry carries on much as did the old. For instance, Briand, the great champion of collective security, headed ten different cabinets at various times between 1909 and 1926; Delcassé, the architect of France's entente with England, served as foreign minister continuously through several cabinets and seven years (1898-1905). And in our own day two individuals from the same party, Schuman and Bidault, alternated in the foreign ministry through a dozen cabinets of the Fourth Republic. Moreover, the day-to-day task of governing is carried on by a civil service, by experts in the law courts and in the educational system as well as in the executive department. This permanent personnel, subject only to broad policy control from above, preserves a basic continuity in French political action.

The system is highly democratic, for it can work only by means of constant and subtle compromises. These, the essence of democratic government, are made in France —and in most of the democratic world outside the English-speaking countries—by the several parties in the legislature *after* an election. In the English-speaking countries, these compromises are made *before* an election, *within* each of the two major parties. Probably the English-speaking method both conceals antagonisms and encourages the habit of willing compromise more effectively than does the continental method. But neither method will work if the underlying antagonisms are really intense, beyond compromise. For example, the American two-party system obviously failed to work in 1861.

Boulanger and Panama

Bitter antagonisms did indeed threaten the Third French Republic between 1879 and 1914, but they did not destroy it. For one thing, the Republic's opponents on the Right and on the Left could never get together. On the Right, although the royalists eventually patched up their quarrels between Bourbon and Orléanist, and although they had some support in literary circles, they could not recover the strength they had dissipated in the 1870's. Nor could the Bonapartists make serious gains in public opinion, though they survived as a political group into the twentieth century. The Catholics, though they feared the anticlerical orientation of many republicans, were after the accession of Pope Leo XIII in 1878 encouraged to develop their way of life by frank acceptance of the freedom of worship that the Constitution of the Republic offered them. The out-and-out Rightist enemies of the Republic were forced to do violence to their own conservative and legitimist principles and to seek some new man who would win over the floating discontent always present in a modern industrial state and set up a dictatorship.

In the 1880's, they hoped that they had found such a man in General Boulanger, an ambitious soldier who had as minister of war catered to French desire for revenge on Germany. But the Boulangist movement was founded on a man of straw. The General cut an impressive figure in public appearances, and in by-elections to fill vacancies in the Chamber he showed he could command a popular following. But from the point of view of conservatives he had compromising origins and radical friends, and, as it became clear that Boulanger in power might rush the country into war, his following threatened to desert him. In January, 1889, he swept a by-election in Paris,

General Boulanger.

but his nerve failed when he was faced with the need to resort to the classic technique of the *coup d'état.* Instead of seizing power by force of arms, he sought refuge with his mistress. The government now took courage and threatened to try him for treason; Boulanger fled to Brussels and committed suicide on the grave of his beloved in 1891. The Republic had surmounted its first great crisis.

Boulanger's cause had gained strength from a scandal in republican ranks. Daniel Wilson, President Grévy's son-in-law, was implicated in the selling of posts in the Legion of Honor. The opposition press made out that the government was riddled with graft. More fuel went on the fire in the early 1890's, when there burst into publicity one of those crises of corruption, graft, and racketeering that seem endemic

CHAPTER XXI

in modern western societies. This was the Panama scandal which was brought on by the failure of De Lesseps' attempt to duplicate in Panama his success in building the Suez Canal. It involved accusations of criminal corruption ministers, deputies, financiers, and an unfortunate Jewish banker, Reinach, who either committed suicide or was murdered just before his trial. Bad as it was, the Panama scandal was to pale before the Dreyfus affair.

The Dreyfus Case

Dreyfus, a Jew and a captain in the French army, was the almost accidental victim of an espionage intrigue and of the anti-Semitism then prevalent in France, especially in military and Catholic circles. Accused of selling military secrets to the Germans, he was railroaded into trial as a scapegoat and was convicted of treason in 1894. Colonel Picquart, an intelligence officer, became convinced that the document on which Dreyfus had been convicted was a forgery, and that the real traitor was a disreputable adventurer of Hungarian blood but of French birth, Major Esterhazy. Picquart was quietly shipped off to Africa by his superiors, who wished to let sleeping dogs lie. But the Dreyfus family independently arrived by investigation at the conclusion that Esterhazy was the traitor, and sought to reopen the case. Esterhazy was tried and acquitted, but the affair was now too public for such silencing. In 1898, the famous novelist Zola brought matters to a crisis by publishing his open letter, "J'Accuse." Zola accused the military leaders, one by one, of sacrificing an innocent man deliberately in order to save the reputation of the army. His letter ended with an affirmation of his passion for truth:

As for the men I accuse, I do not know them, I have never seen them, I bear no rancor or hatred against them. For me they are only entities, forces of social malevolence. And the deed which I perform here is only a revolutionary way of precipitating the explosion of truth and justice.

I have only one passion, that of enlightenment, in the name of humanity, which has suffered so much and has a right to happiness. My flaming protest is only the cry of my soul. . . .[*]

France was now divided into Dreyfusards and Anti-Dreyfusards; the former defended in Dreyfus the Republic, the latter attacked it. All the far Left, which had hitherto held aloof from the affair as just one more example of the rottenness of the bourgeois state, now rallied to the Third Republic. Dreyfus was brought back from his prison on Devil's Island in French Guiana, and was retried in the midst of a frenzied campaign in the press and on the platform. The military court, faced with new evidence brought out by the suicide of Colonel Henry, the real forger of the most incriminating of the original documents used to convict Dreyfus, again found Dreyfus guilty of treason, but with the almost incredible qualification—in a treason case—of "extenuating circumstances." This attempt at face-saving saved nothing. Dreyfus was pardoned by the President of the Republic in 1899, and in 1906, after the tensions had abated, he was acquitted and restored to the army with the rank of major.

The Dreyfus affair presents a remarkably well-documented case study in social psychology. The simple juridical issue—was this man guilty or not guilty of treason—never wholly disappeared in the mass hysteria. Many Frenchmen who did not like Dreyfus or Jews or who did revere the Church, Army, and the whole apparatus of the Right, none the less sought to make up their minds solely on the basis of the facts. Yet many on both sides worked themselves up to a

---

[*] Quoted by A. Zévaès, *Histoire de la Troisième République* (Paris, 1938), 227. Our translation.

point where the question of Dreyfus' guilt was wholly submerged in this great confronting of the "two Frances." For the ordinary person, the open admission of forgery by Colonel Henry and his subsequent suicide were enough; he now thought Dreyfus innocent. But for the violent Anti-Dreyfusard, Henry's act made him a hero and a martyr; he had died for his country! A paper was circulated in Paris asking for a memorial to Henry:

Colonel Henry's Devotion to his Country.
Public subscription for a monument to be raised to him.
When an officer is reduced to committing a pretended forgery in order to restore peace to his country and rid it of a traitor, that soldier is to be mourned.
If he pays for his attempt with his life, he is a martyr.
If he voluntarily takes his life,
HE IS A HERO.*

A provincial paper declared:

When Iscariot had taken the thirty pence, the price of the Just One's blood, he went and hung himself in a field, his belly burst asunder, and his bowels gushed forth upon the ground.
It was the Immanent Justice of things which thus manifested itself. . . .
Justice Immanent!
And yesterday, Dreyfus, grandson of Judas, after taking German marks in payment for the strips of flesh which he tore from off our country in order to sell, was seen condemned, degraded; button by button, galloon by galloon were torn from the noble uniform of the French officer. And now he is choking, the death-rattle in his throat, in a cage, too small to contain his offence, yet too large in proportion to the punishment his crime deserves.
Justice Immanent!

· · ·

To think that this monstrous Israelite should come forward and threaten the General Staff of the French army, which is made of the blood and bone of our country, threaten its members with revelations such that they all ought to flee and hide themselves like the most abject criminals! *

The Republic after Dreyfus

With the victory of the Dreyfusards, the Republic moved to the Left and punished the Church for its support of the army and the Anti-Dreyfusards. The triumphant republicans in a series of measures between 1901 and 1905 destroyed the Concordat of 1801 between Napoleon I and the Pope which had established the Roman Catholic Church in a privileged position in the French state (see Chapter XVIII). The Catholic teaching orders were forced to dissolve, and some 12,000 Catholic schools, which had been formidable rivals of the state school system, had to close down. The state was no longer to pay the clergy, and private corporations organized by the faithful were to take over the expenses of worship and the ownership and maintenance of the churches. The Catholics refused to accept this settlement, and the churches remained technically government property.

But, though the separation had been carried out amid great bitterness, though the debates had revived the ferocious language of the 1790's, there was no recourse to the violence of the past. Catholicism was not proscribed, and somehow or other worship continued in churches that were not the legal property of the faithful. Catholic education was indeed severely hindered, but there was no formal persecution. The separation did not really alter the fundamental social position of the Church in France. The upper classes, and the peasantry of the north and west, remained loyal Catholics; many of the townspeople, and the country folk in the southwest and center

---

* F. C. Conybeare, *The Dreyfus Case* (London, 1898), 298.

* *Journal du Centre*, Châteauroux, June 28, 1898. Our translation.

especially, remained what they had become over the last few centuries, indifferent Catholics or outright and determined secularists.

The indifferent and the anticlerical formed the backbone of the central supporting party of the Republic, the Radical Socialists, who were not socialists at all but petty bourgeois, French Jeffersonians. Indeed, the French Republic of the early twentieth century was a typically bourgeois state. It made certain concessions to demands from the workers for social security and better living conditions, but not nearly so many as the British constitutional monarchy was then making, nor indeed so many as the only partly constitutional German monarchy had made already. Trade unions in France were legal, but they had hard sledding against the reluctance of French workers to pay dues and accept union discipline. France remained in the twentieth century what she had been since the great revolution of 1789, a land of small, independent, farm-owning peasants, very conservative in their farming methods, and of relatively small, family-controlled industries, very conservative in their business ways. Some great industry there was, and with it a numerically small industrial proletariat already socialist in allegiance. But they were not typical of France—a land backward by the standard of great industry, well-balanced by the old-fashioned standard of a self-sufficient economy.

The Third Republic had weathered the storms of domestic differences at bottom because, though some Frenchmen disliked it intensely, and though many Frenchmen felt toward it that distrust of the "government" not unknown in the American democracy, most Frenchmen felt it somehow to be the embodiment of *la patrie,* the fatherland. Differences did arise among them, notably on questions of imperial policy. The great expansion of French power in Africa, Indo-China, and Oceania which made the world empire of France second only to Britain's was the work of a determined minority (see Chapter XXIV). Many Frenchmen viewed their colonies with antagonism or apathy.

France since 1870 had often seemed dangerously divided on matters of domestic and imperial concern; yet on foreign policy the Third Republic was essentially united. Disagreement on the big questions of foreign policy concerned details of timing, not ultimate aims. France wanted revenge for 1870; France wanted Alsace-Lorraine back. In the complex workings of international politics from 1870 to 1914 (see Chapter XXV), the foreign ministries of the Third Republic, shifting though their personnel was through the workings of the multi-party system, none the less brought France to a position in which revenge on Germany became possible. Democracies are sometimes held to be at a disadvantage in the conduct of foreign relations in comparison with states under strong monarchic or dictatorial control. Yet in 1870 democratic France was isolated, and imperial Germany was the center of a marvelous system of alliances; in 1914, democratic France was firmly allied with a powerful Britain and a Russia powerful at least for the moment, and imperial Germany, save for a weak Austro-Hungarian ally, was essentially isolated.

IV: Italy, 1848-1914

Italian national unity, which seemed after the events of 1848-49 (see Chapter XIX) as far away as ever, was triumphantly achieved between 1859 and 1870. The Kingdom of Italy that began to emerge after 1860 had a constitution very much like that of the Third French Republic, with an ornamental king instead of an ornamental president. The ministry was responsible to a lower house which in practice developed a multi-party system rather like that of France. At first, a property qualification severely limited the suffrage; after 1881, this qualification was low enough—a direct tax of 19 lire, or about $4.00—so that the electorate numbered over 2,000,000. What amounted to full universal manhood suffrage was not, however, introduced until 1912.

Cavour and the Completion of Unification

The architect of Italian unification was Cavour (1810-1861), who became the chief minister of Piedmont in 1852. Though of aristocratic origin himself, and trained for the highly conservative career of an army officer, Cavour enthusiastically supported the economic revolutions and the aspirations of the business classes. He visited France and England as a young man and was deeply influenced by their economic accomplishments and ideas. Back in Piedmont, he applied the newest agricultural methods to his family estates and promoted the introduction of steamboats, railroads, industries, and banks in order to prepare Piedmont for leadership in unified Italy. Cavour was a good, moderate, mid-nineteenth-century liberal.

But Cavour was also a superlatively adept practitioner of the realistic diplomacy often called *Realpolitik*. As the chief minister of Piedmont, he set about cultivating French and English support, bringing Piedmont into the Crimean War on their side against Russia. He got no immediate award, for England was unwilling to take steps that would offend Austria. But, though bitterly disappointed, he put a good face on his defeat, and finally persuaded Napoleon III that the Austrian hold in northern Italy was an anachronism, a flying in the face of the principle of nationality. In 1859, France and Piedmont went to war with Austria, and won bloody victories at Magenta and Solferino in June. Sympathetic nationalist risings broke out in Tuscany and the Papal States. But the threat of Prussian help to Austria alarmed Napoleon, who held a conference with the Emperor of Austria, Francis Joseph, at Villafranca (July, 1859) and arranged a compromise by which Lombardy was to go to Piedmont but Venetia to remain Austrian, and the rest of the peninsula to remain divided. Cavour resigned in bitter protest.

He had, however, already really won. A wave of popular agitation in the smaller states of northern and central Italy brought almost bloodless revolutions, and plebiscites demanding annexation to Piedmont. Cavour came back into office to accept the annexations, and to take advantage of the promising situation developing in the Papal States in the South. For in May, 1860, one of the most successful filibustering expeditions in history had set out for Naples and Sicily under the command of a radical, indeed republican, nationalist agitator, Garibaldi. Cavour, though a monarchist, was too much a realist to deny himself this aid in a pinch, and secretly supported the expedition. Garibaldi and his thousand "red-

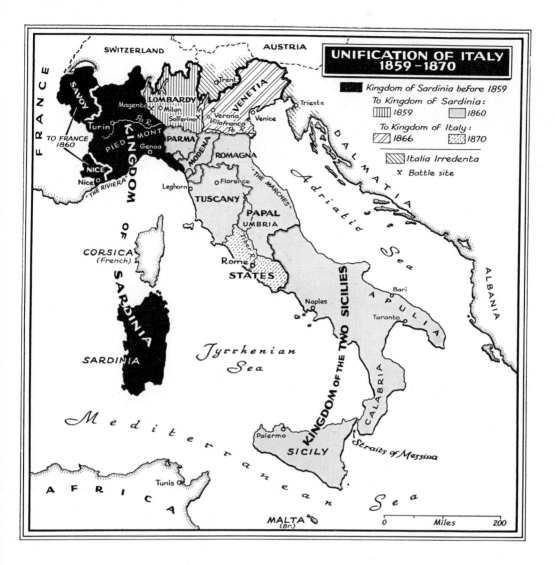

UNIFICATION OF ITALY
1859 – 1870

■ Kingdom of Sardinia before 1859

To Kingdom of Sardinia:
▥ 1859   ▦ 1860

To Kingdom of Italy:
▨ 1866   ▩ 1870

▨ Italia Irredenta

X Battle site

shirts" had no trouble overcoming the feeble opposition of the Bourbon Francis II in Sicily. Recruits swarmed to his flag. Popular opinion throughout the West, even in cautious England, was overwhelmingly on the side of this romantic adventurer. Garibaldi, who had announced his loyalty to the King of Piedmont, Victor Emmanuel, now crossed the Straits of Messina with the approval of the British minister, Lord Palmerston, and continued his victorious march on the mainland. Cavour, afraid that Garibaldi might bring on a crisis with Napoleon by taking Rome, sent Piedmontese troops into the Papal States. They disposed of the papal forces easily, and occupied all save the area about Rome itself. Meanwhile, by a plebiscite, Naples and Sicily voted for union with the North.

The upshot of all these rapidly unrolling events was the proclamation of the Kingdom of Italy with Victor Emmanuel of Savoy at its head in March, 1861. Cavour died in June, but what had seemed impos-

Meeting of Garibaldi (left) and King Victor Emmanuel (right).

sible only two short years ago at Villafranca had now been realized. Rome, under French occupation, and Venetia, still held by Austria, kept the new kingdom from the territorial completion the patriots wanted. Garibaldi made an attempt in 1862 to take Rome in a filibustering expedition, but the troops of the new kingdom were too much for him. He was beaten and captured, but soon amnestied. He returned to make still another attempt on Rome in 1867 after the French had withdrawn, but was defeated by French troops who now once more returned to occupy the city.

Venetia and Rome soon came easily into the kingdom in the play of international politics, and cost Italy little in bloodshed. Venetia came as a reward for Italy's siding with Prussia in the brief war of 1866 that saw Prussia defeat Austria; Rome came when the war of 1870 with Prussia forced Napoleon III to withdraw from papal territory (see Chapter XXII). On October 2, 1870, Rome was annexed to the Kingdom of Italy and became its capital. All the peninsula, save for Trieste and Trent in the north, was now under one rule. These two small bits of *Italia Irredenta* (Italy unredeemed) are of no small importance, for Italian patriots remained unreconciled to

Austrian possession of them, and went to war against Austria and her German ally in 1915 largely to obtain them.

Assets and Liabilities of United Italy

The new kingdom started out with the asset of favorable public opinion throughout the non-Catholic segments of the western world. Italian national unity seemed a natural and desirable thing, and it had been achieved without too much bloodshed, with a mixture of Garibaldian romance and Cavourian realism. Within the Kingdom the enthusiasm that had brought the *Risorgimento* (resurrection) to fruition was now in the service of united Italy. Italians were a frugal, hard-working people, and in the north they made promising beginnings in the new industry of the machine age.

Yet striking liabilities impeded the new Italy. The deep gulf between clericals and anticlericals—better, between Christians and "free-thinkers"—dug by the French Revolution was essentially as profound in Italy as in France. In Italy it was deepened by the circumstances of the final drive for

CHAPTER XXI

union, the annexation of the Papal States without the Pope's consent, the "Roman question." Italy lacked coal and iron; in terms of modern international economic competition, she was a "have-not" country. Much of mountainous central Italy and all southern Italy were really marginal to nineteenth-century western civilization, with a poverty-stricken, illiterate peasantry rooted in age-old local ways utterly different from those of modern urban life, and with a small feudalistic aristocracy to whom a man like Cavour was really quite incomprehensible. Neapolitans and Sicilians resented the new political preponderance of northern Italians in the unified kingdom, much as American Southerners resented Yankee "carpetbaggers" after the Civil War. Moreover, at least half of Italy lacked experience in self-government. It had no tradition of government by discussion, of law-abidingness, of comfortable middle-class compromise. Italy was not indeed the land of mixed stereotypes—sunny gaiety, dark passions, music, and *banditti*—which northern

Rivalry of the powers in Italian unification.

Europeans and Americans believed it to be. It was a land of deep-seated class antagonisms, regional variations, fervent localism, a whole inheritance from the past which made democratic government very difficult.

The Roman quesion became a chronic rather than a critical one. The Pope, who refused to accept the legality of the new kingdom, simply stayed in the Vatican Palace as a "prisoner." The Vatican remained the center of the world-wide organization of the Roman Catholic Church, and in no important sense was the Pope impeded in the exercise of his powers over the faithful throughout the world. Within Italy, the Church forbade Catholics to participate in politics and urged a Catholic boycott of the new state. Gradually, in fact, Catholics did take an increasing part in politics, but the Roman question itself remained unsettled until 1929, when Mussolini and Pope Pius XI agreed to set up the Vatican City as a sovereign state of 108 acres.

The new kingdom made appreciable economic progress. Railroads, built and managed by the state, were pushed rapidly into the backward south, a brand-new merchant marine brought the new Italian flag into the seven seas, and an army and navy gave it standing as a power. Even the national finances seemed for a time under conservative leadership to be sound. But the 1880's brought a letdown, the growth of parliamentary corruption and laxness. Moreover, Italy was now launching itself on a career of imperial aspiration which seems a good example of the desire to keep up with the Joneses. Since France—the envied Latin sister—and Britain had empires, since a great power had to have an empire, and since Italy, or rather the guiding groups in Italy, wanted to be a great power, some way of territorial expansion had to be found. The conventional economic explanations of the imperialist drive hardly make sense for the Italy of the 1880's and 1890's, a nation with no important exportable capital, with no need for colonial markets, and with plenty of domestic difficulties. True, Italy had a rapidly expanding population that found relatively few economic opportunities at home, especially in the south. But, since other countries had such a head start in empire-building, what was left open to Italian seizure was very little indeed. And it was not territory suitable for colonial settlement by Europeans. It was only the poorer parts of Africa, which were hardly worth the difficulty of exploitation.

Even so, the effort to take Ethiopia (then called Abyssinia) drained the resources of the government, and was halted by the disastrous military defeat inflicted by the Abyssinians on the Italian expeditionary force at Adowa in 1896. The general depression of the 1890's, a bank scandal, and the Adowa failure cast a shadow on the last years of the century. Grave bread riots broke out in Milan in May, 1898, the *fatti di Maggio* (deeds of May), and in 1900 King Humbert was assassinated by an anarchist. The accession of a new king, Victor Emmanuel III, who was believed to have liberal leanings, gave new heart to many, and the years just before the outbreak of World War I were on the whole years of comparative quiet and prosperity, of partial reconciliation with the Church,

and of the final establishment of universal suffrage. Giolitti, the political leader from 1901 to 1914, though as corrupt a manipulator of the electorate as his predecessors, was also an intelligent moderate who did much to end social tensions and to promote the growth of western-style political parties. Parliamentary democracy seemed at last to be sending down solid roots. And in the years 1890-1914 the vast emigration to North and South America—the number of emigrants exceeded half a million in the peak year of 1913—almost canceled out the serious economic difficulties attendant on the high Italian birth rate.

Yet the men who ran Italy could never quite content themselves with a position, say like that of a Mediterranean Sweden, quite outside the competition for empire and quite outside the "great powers." Italy was not a great power, but her leaders, and their millions of followers, wanted very much to make her one. Pushed out of Abyssinia, and forced by the increasing tensions of international politics to yield to the French in Tunisia, Italy finally got from the other great powers a free hand in poverty-stricken and parched Tripoli, a fragment of the old Turkish Empire in North Africa. In 1911, she went to war with Turkey over Tripoli, thus stimulating the cycle of Balkan wars that were to ripen into World War I.

V: The United States

World War I was also to mark the full participation in the international balance of another relative newcomer to the family of nations, the United States. The simplest and in many ways the most important fact of her brief national history is that in a little over a century she secured

in terms of actual power a position like that of the great states that have filled these pages for many chapters—Austria, France, England, and the rest. The United States came to be a "great power," despite words and even sentiments that placed her outside international competition, in "isola-

268

tion." Two simple sets of statistics point up this fact. In 1790, the United States comprised 892,000 square miles, and in 1910 3,754,000 square miles; even more important, the population of the United States was 3,929,000 in 1790, and 91,972,000 in 1910. The 1910 population was greater than that of either of the most powerful European states, Germany and Great Britain, indeed second only to that of Russia. And, still more important, American industrial and agricultural capacities were already greater than those of any other single country.

The Federal Union

The land that had become so powerful in a brief century was in the late eighteenth century almost empty beyond the Alleghenies, save for a few Indians of Stone Age culture; yet millions of square miles were as suited to intensive human use as any in Europe. Most interested observers knew this in 1781, and they expected the central parts of the North American continent to fill up eventually. But most of them, including Americans like Jefferson, did not believe that the process would be as rapid as it in fact was. Moreover, all but the most optimistic felt that the developed and fully peopled continent could not possibly come under one political rule. They felt that it must be divided—as indeed the South American continent came to be—into a number of independent nations on essentially the European model. The most pessimistic or merely hostile observers did not believe that the thirteen Atlantic seaboard colonies gathered together to fight the British could possibly maintain their own union. Here is a sample prediction:

As to the future grandeur of America, and its being a rising empire under one head, whether republican or monarchical, it is one of the idlest and most visionary notions that ever was conceived even by writers of romance. The mutual antipathies and clashing interests of the Americans, their difference of governments, habitudes, and manners, indicate that they will have no centre of union and no common interest. They never can be united into one compact empire under any species of government whatever; a disunited people till the end of time, suspicious and distrustful of each other, they will be divided and subdivided into little commonwealths or principalities, according to natural boundaries, by great bays of the sea, and by vast rivers, lakes, and ridges of mountains.*

Yet hold together the former colonies did. Though the union was often sorely tested, once in the greatest war Americans have fought, it is a central fact of history that the United States did not go the way of the Latin American states. Why the United States held together cannot be explained by any single factor. Geography was certainly kinder to her than to the Latin Americans, for the Appalachians were no barrier at all even in the eighteenth century; the Rockies were not the barrier the Andes are; and the Mississippi Valley, unlike that of the Amazon, was a help rather than a hindrance to settlement and communications. The railroad and the telegraph arrived just in time to enable goods and ideas to move fast and far enough to hold Americans together. The communications and transportation network already developed by 1860 enabled the North to count on the West in the decisive struggle of the Civil War. The sheer size of the new republic after the decisive acquisition of the Mississippi-Missouri Valley by purchase from Napoleon in 1803 seemed historically compatible with a loosely held empire of many tongues and peoples, like those of ancient Persia or Rome, but not with a unified nation-state. The achievements of modern technology in

---

* Josiah Tucker, Dean of Gloucester, quoted in John Fiske, *The Critical Period of American History, 1783-1789* (Boston, 1888), 57-58.

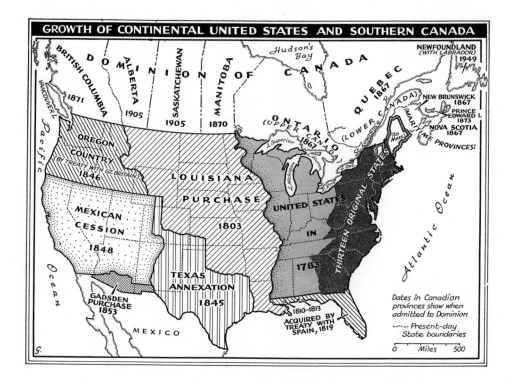

GROWTH OF CONTINENTAL UNITED STATES AND SOUTHERN CANADA

effect reduced sheer size to manageable proportions. After the first transcontinental railway was completed in 1869, Californians could get to the federal capital more quickly than New Yorkers could have in 1800.

Yet it will not do to emphasize purely material factors in the holding together of the United States. The resistance to Britain had helped forge a genuine national patriotism. The colonists, in spite of contrasts between "Puritan" New England and "Cavalier" tidewater South, in spite of Dutch and German elements in the middle colonies, brought with them one language and one law, one basic culture. Almost all the colonies had "frontiers," areas on their western edges where a lively population was winning new lands from the wilderness. This frontier population was a powerful force for unity, for it had little attachment to the older centers of colonial (now state) group-

consciousness, and it had great confidence in its own "manifest destiny" to keep pushing westward with the blessing and patronage, and without more than the remote control, of the new federal government.

Americans gained their independence from Britain in a civil war and a social revolution that were rather mild affairs compared, say, with the French Reign of Terror. And, after the more committed Loyalists had left for Canada or Britain, Americans took up national life without any seriously alienated minorities. They achieved at the Philadelphia convention of 1787 and in the campaign for adoption during the next two years a federal constitution that set up a central government with the essential attributes of all governments—the ability to tax individuals (not just to obtain monies as contributions from constituent states), to control armed forces, and to maintain a monopoly of foreign relations.

270

The new constitution, in short, set up a sovereign federal state, not a mere league of sovereign states. On the whole, this result was achieved under conservative groups anxious to preserve their economic and social privileges, afraid that democracy in separate, quasi-independent states would go too far. But this conservative conclusion to the American Revolution gave the infant federal state a safer start. Finally, the threat that British control of Canada seemed to offer put a limit on domestic divisions. The United States grew up in its earliest years aware of the need for union against a possible foreign danger.

The new republic entered the world war of the Napoleonic period in 1812. Neither the French nor the British really tried to observe the freedom of commerce that the United States claimed as the right of a neutral, but the British, who were by 1812 masters of the sea, seemed to be infringing neutral rights more seriously than the French. Moreover, American expansionists, the "war hawks," saw a possible prize in Canada to be wrested from England, and no such prize to be got from France. The American attempt to invade Canada failed, not only from ineptness, but from the determined resistance of the Canadians. In isolated combats on the seas, the United States won victories that made up for her failures on land, and helped bolster national pride. The war on the whole was a stalemate, in which the United States experienced no important gains or losses.

Civil War and Reconstruction

The great test of the new republic was called the "Civil War" by the Northerners and the "War between the States" by the Southerners. War broke out in 1861 after long years of sectional strife within the union between North and South. The Civil War was really an abortive nationalist revolution, the attempt of the Confederate states to set up a separate sovereign nation. The South was predominantly agricultural, with a society based on plantation slavery and on a single major crop, cotton, much of which was exported abroad. The North was increasingly industrial, with a society based on free labor and on independent farm owners.

To the conflict of economic interest was added, as almost always in human affairs, a conflict of ideals, of ways of life. That conflict was not as deep-seated, as irreconcilable, as it seemed to be to the generation that went to war in 1861—or the South, like Ireland or Poland, would presumably have tried again to free itself. But the fires of conflict were fanned especially by the question of slavery, which seemed immoral to many in the North and which seemed the order of nature to many in the South. They were fanned also by writers and preachers on both sides, the Northerners thinking of themselves as heirs of the Puritans, the Southerners as heirs of the Cavaliers. With the secession of South Carolina and its sister states, antagonism reached the point of open war.

In retrospect, the victory of the North has an air of inevitability, especially since by 1861 the middle and upper Mississippi was bound firmly to the North by economic and cultural ties. In population—especially since the South could not, did not dare, use the Negroes as soldiers—and in industrial resources above all, the North was greatly superior. Yet, aided by a very able corps of officers, by the advantages in morale that accrue to determined underdogs, and by the disastrous early overconfidence of the North, the South won initial victories that gave its cause great momentum. But the North thwarted the efforts of Confederate diplomats to secure British intervention and was able to improvise a

Military Railroad of the Union forces in Virginia during the Civil War.

naval force that gradually established a blockade shutting off the South from importation of necessary war materials. In the long run, Northern strength in men and materials wore the Southern armies down.

The striking thing about the Civil War is not that the North won it finally in the field, but that the South accepted the verdict of battle as final, that the Union in which Americans today have grown up should be so firm and final. The "Road to Reunion" after 1865 was indeed no easy one, and in the first years of the Reconstruction period after the war it appeared to many an almost impossible one. With the assassination of Lincoln by the fanatical Booth in 1865, the one great moderate who might have lessened the vengefulness of the Northern radicals was lost. The South was occupied by Northern soldiers, the illiterate Negroes were enfranchised, and Northern "carpetbaggers" and Southern "scalawags"—and many sincere idealists who believed they could bring liberty and equality to a "misguided" South—combined to bring what seemed a reign of terror to old Confederates.

Yet even in these early days the Civil War did not end, as such wars have often ended, in wholesale reprisals, executions, and exile. Very few even of the Confederate leaders went into exile. The soldiers of the South returned, often to devastated homes and lost fortunes, but they returned home under amnesty. Gradually the crusading fervor of the North wore off, and the Southerners, reinforced by new men, some of them immigrant Northerners, took over control in their states. Slavery, abolished by Lincoln's proclamation in 1863, was never restored, but the Negroes were in effect disenfranchised, "white supremacy" was restored, and the race question in the New South took on its familiar forms.

And it was a "New South," which is one of the basic reasons why the region has come to accept the Civil War as ended, with due sentimental compensations in wistful feeling for the past. Slowly in the late nineteenth century, more rapidly in the twentieth, it has built up its own industries, taken steps to free itself from cotton monoculture and to integrate its economy and its society with the rest of the country. The South remained throughout this period a relatively backward area, with its own

272   **CHAPTER XXI**

Ruins at Charleston, South Carolina, at the close of the Civil War.

special problems of poverty, illiteracy, and race difficulties, but it was not an alien land, not an oppressed nationality eager to revolt.

The end of Reconstruction, usually assigned to the year 1876, left the Democratic party in control of what came to be called the "solid South." This was a natural development, for it was the Republican party that had guided the North during the war, and that had tried to carry through Reconstruction. This fact has worked to strengthen the American two-party system, since with so solid a block secure for the Democrats, the Republicans have been forced either to make compromises among themselves to preserve their own party unity, or to lose power; and the Northern Democrats have been forced to make compromises with their Southern wing. The fact that the presidency, the great prize of political action, could be obtained only by securing a majority of the Electoral College meant also that a careful balancing of regional interests had to be maintained; a minority party could get nowhere in American politics.

This is not, of course, the whole explanation for the fact that the United States, like Britain, has long maintained a two-party system. It is striking that the two-party system has endured so firmly in both countries despite the great differences between the American political machinery of checks and balances among executive, legislative, and judiciary and the British political machinery centered in an omnipotent Parliament. It is tempting to see in both an underlying habit of political compromise with common roots in a long past of government by discussion.

Economic and Social Development

In 1865, the American economy was still in many senses "colonial"—that is, it produced foods and other raw materials to be exchanged abroad for manufactured goods and, in financial terms, it was dependent on foreign money markets (chiefly London). By 1914, the United States had been transformed into a great industrial nation, with its agriculture already to a high degree mechanized, and with financial resources so great that after the World War I New York was to take over in part the place of London as a world financial center. This transformation could not have taken place, certainly not at the rate it did, without the existence of abundant manpower, of great

The American two-party system. "Twenty Years After" (1902). "The Republican party is trying to do today what the Democratic party did in 1882."

and still almost untouched natural resources, and of the traditions of individual initiative and freedom of enterprise—which in part were certainly a product of the "frontier." Europe played a significant role in American economic growth by furnishing investment capital and, above all, by sending forth a steady flow of emigrants.

This great expansion in national wealth was achieved in a climate of opinion that supported overwhelmingly the view that the federal government should not interfere directly with business enterprise beyond maintaining public order, enforcing contracts, exercising some control over the actual coinage of money—and maintaining a protective tariff. Nor, of course, were the state and local governments to go beyond such appropriate limits. This view we have already met in the classical economists who followed Adam Smith in Britain and in some of the continental states. It is a view that in the West has generally accompanied the first stages of the industrial revolution. But this revolution came relatively late to the United States, and for this if for no other reason a belief in free enterprise, in a minimum of government interference in

economic activities, maintained itself more firmly in the twentieth century there than in the other parts of the western world.

This belief was reinforced by the Fourteenth Amendment to the Constitution, passed in 1866 and aimed to protect the freed Negroes in the South from state action to deprive them of civil rights. The Amendment contained the famous "due process" clause: "nor shall any state deprive any person of life, liberty, or property without due process of law." In the great era of free enterprise that followed the Civil War, the Supreme Court of the United States interpreted the celebrated clause to mean that state governments should not deprive businessmen—including corporations as "persons"—of property by regulating wages, prices, conditions of labor, and the like.

Immigration since the 1890's had brought in millions of aliens from eastern and southern Europe, men and women ignorant of American ways, and readily exploited by unscrupulous or merely conventional employers. These immigrants were hard to organize in labor unions; moreover, they and their children, uprooted, scorned though they might be, readily absorbed the

CHAPTER XXI

American belief that no man is a proletarian by nature. Yet even at the height of this "Gilded Age" or "Age of the Robber Barons" there was a movement toward the welfare state. Apparently there never was a time when laissez-faire was a universally accepted principle (except for the tariff), and wistful businessmen who look back to the nineteenth century in America as free from the curse of government interference are simply inventing a myth.

Many of the same forces that had produced the Factory Acts in Britain gradually brought to the United States minimum-wage acts, limitation of child labor and women's labor, sanitary regulation, control of hours of labor, and workman's compensation. Characteristically, and in spite of the Fourteenth Amendment, these measures were taken at the state rather than at the national level, and they varied greatly in the different states. The state of Wisconsin early established a reputation for advanced social legislation, but many of the older northeastern states played an important part in the movement. By the early twentieth century, public opinion was ready for increased participation of the national government in the regulation of economic life.

Theodore Roosevelt, president from 1901 to 1909, promised to give labor a "square deal" and to proceed vigorously with "trust-busting," attacks on the great trusts or combinations that had come to monopolize important sectors of the American economy. Although Theodore Roosevelt did not always fulfill his promises, his administration did assail the trusts in railroads and tobacco and did press the federal regulation of great corporations. During the first administration of Woodrow Wilson (1913-1917), the process gained momentum. More regulatory legislation was passed, notably the Federal Reserve Act of 1913, which gave federal officials more control over banking, credit, and currency.

Approval of these measures was not, of course, unanimous, since Americans differ loudly and widely about almost everything from metaphysics to sports. But, save for the Civil War, they have usually been willing in the end to differ no more than vocally, to accept varieties of belief and action where they appeared harmless or avoidable, to conform to the law with no more than occasional violence. To outsiders, and to many native critics, American life in the decades between the Civil War and 1917 often seemed one great brawl, a more-than-Darwinian struggle for wealth and power. Yet this apparently anarchistic society achieved extraordinary material things—bridges, dams, railroads, great cities—which required the co-operation of millions of men and women disciplined to a common task. This paradox of the co-existence in the United States of "rugged individualism" and social cohesion still disturbs many commentators on the American scene.

In spite of the more than usual dose of distrust of "government" common in western—perhaps in human—tradition, government has in the United States come to play a larger and larger part in the lives of all. Although this is true of local and state governments too, it holds more especially of the federal government. The gradually increasing importance of the federal government, and the gradually decreasing initiative of state governments, are as objectively clear in the period 1789-1917 as is the material growth of the United States in population and wealth.

The Myth of Isolation

Quite as objectively clear, though still the subject of infinite debate among Americans, is the emergence of the United States as a great international power. The United States was never literally "isolated." From the very beginning, she had a Department of State and the proper apparatus of ministers, consuls, and ambassadors. She was involved in the world war of the Napoleonic era, and by the Monroe Doctrine of the 1820's she took the firm position that European powers were not to extend their existing territories in the Western Hemisphere. This was no mere negation, but an active extension of American claims to a far wider sphere of influence than the continental United States. Although Americans took no part in the complex balance-of-power politics in Europe, they showed an increasing concern with a balance of power in the Far East, where they had long traded. After the brief war of 1898 with Spain, a war that broke out in Cuba, always a close concern of the United States, Americans found themselves directly involved with the newly annexed territories of the Philippine Islands, Hawaii, Puerto Rico—in short, with an American empire.

Theodore Roosevelt was a vigorous imperialist who built the Panama Canal, pressed the Far Eastern interests of the United States, and advocated a larger navy. This new "navalism," which also had assertive spokesmen in Britain and Germany, derived many of its doctrines from the writings of an American officer, Captain Alfred T. Mahan. Mahan's book, *The Influence of Sea Power upon History* (1890), and his later works assigned navies a place of pre-eminent importance in determining power status and found an influential audience both at home and abroad.

Furthermore, over these many decades of expanding wealth and trade, the United States had come to take full part in international commercial relations. In these relations she had, save when the federal government was blockading the Confederacy, stood out firmly for rights to trade even though there was a war on somewhere, stood out for the "rights of neutrals." This fact alone would probably have brought the United States into the world war of 1914-1918, as it had brought her eventually into the world war of 1792-1815. But in 1917 America was, as she had not been in 1812, a great and active participant in the world state-system.

Reading Suggestions
on the Western Democracies

Note: See also the reading suggestions for Chapters XIX and XX.

E. Halévy, *A History of the English People in the Nineteenth Century,* 2nd rev. ed., 5 vols. (New York: P. Smith, 1949-1951). The classic detailed study.

E. L. Woodward, *The Age of Reform* (Oxford: The Clarendon Press, 1938), and R. C. K. Ensor, *England, 1870-1914* (Oxford: The Clarendon Press, 1936). Two very useful volumes in the "Oxford History of England."

D. Thomson, *England in the Nineteenth Century* (Harmondsworth, Middlesex: Penguin Books, 1950). An excellent short account.

P. Magnus, *Gladstone: A Biography* (New York: E. P. Dutton & Co., 1955). A sound study of the great Victorian Liberal.

F. A. Simpson, *The Rise of Louis Napoleon,* 3rd ed. (London: Longmans, Green, 1950) and *Louis Napoleon and the Recovery of France,* 3rd ed. (London: Longmans, Green, 1951). The most detailed study in English; stops in 1856.

J. M. Thompson, *Louis Napoleon and the Second Empire* (Oxford: Basil Blackwell, 1954). A useful synthesis, based on detailed scholarly works.

CHAPTER XXI

A. Guérard, *Napoleon III* (Cambridge, Mass.: Harvard University Press, 1943). A spirited attempt to see the Emperor as a "Caesarean democrat."

D. W. Brogan, *France under the Republic* (New York: Harper and Brothers, 1940). A witty, perceptive, but allusive history of the Third Republic.

D. Thomson, *Democracy in France: The Third and Fourth Republics*, 2nd ed. (London: Oxford University Press, 1952). A brilliant essay.

R. Soltau, *French Political Thought in the Nineteenth Century* (New Haven: Yale University Press, 1931). A good survey, though harsh to conservatives.

S. B. Clough, *France, A History of National Economics, 1789-1939* (New York: Charles Scribner's Sons, 1939). Particularly valuable for its informative notes.

G. Bruun, *Clemenceau* (Cambridge, Mass.: Harvard University Press, 1943). An excellent brief biography of the redoubtable politician of the Third Republic.

A. J. B. Whyte, *The Making of Modern Italy* (Oxford: Basil Blackwell, 1944). One of the very few good accounts in English.

G. M. Trevelyan, *Garibaldi and the Making of Italy* (New York: Longmans, Green & Co., 1912) and *Garibaldi and the Thousand* (London: T. Nelson and Sons, Ltd., 1924). Vivid re-creations of the most colorful figure of the Risorgimento.

A. J. B. Whyte, *The Political Life and Letters of Cavour, 1848-1861* (London: Oxford University Press, 1930). The best introduction to Cavour.

B. Croce, *A History of Italy, 1871-1915* (Oxford: The Clarendon Press, 1929). By a distinguished philosopher of history; thoughtful, but has been criticized for being too severe on Italy's parliamentary leaders.

R. B. Morris, *Encyclopaedia of American History* (New York: Harper and Brothers, 1953). A standard reference work.

S. E. Morison and H. S. Commager, *The Growth of the American Republic*, 4th ed., 2 vols. (New York: Oxford University Press, 1950-1951). One of the best textbooks.

C. A. and M. A. Beard, *The Rise of American Civilization* (New York: The Macmillan Company, 1936). A famous popular account, written from the standpoint of the economic interpretation.

R. Hofstadter, *The American Political Tradition and the Men Who Made It* (New York: Alfred A. Knopf, Inc., 1948). An excellent study.

Historical Fiction

B. Disraeli, *Coningsby* (New York: E. P. Dutton and Co., 1911. Everyman ed.). Significant for its statement of the enlightened Conservative political position.

A. Trollope, *The Prime Minister* (London: Oxford University Press, 1951. World's Classics ed.). Probably the best novel on Victorian politics.

E. Zola, *The Downfall* ("La Débacle") (New York: D. Appleton, 1902). Good novel of the French defeat in 1870; by the famous naturalistic writer.

R. Martin du Gard, *Jean Barois* (New York: The Viking Press, 1949). Sound novel about the crisis of the French conscience over the Dreyfus affair.

W. D. Howells, *The Rise of Silas Lapham* (many editions). One of the best fictional introductions to American middle-class life in the late 19th century.

U. Sinclair, *The Jungle* (New York: The Viking Press, 1946). A famous exposé of the bad conditions in the meat-packing industry of Chicago about 1900.

Central and Eastern Europe:

To the Outbreak of World War I

CHAPTER XXII

I: Introduction

IN THIS CHAPTER, we shall deal with Germany (1850-1914), the Habsburg Monarchy (1850-1914), and Russia (1825-1914). These three empires were partners in crime in the partitions of Poland of the late eighteenth century, and firm allies in the Metternich system of European balance after 1815. After 1850, they passed through periods of mutual affection and hatred. In 1914 all went to war, with Germany and Austria-Hungary as allies against Russia. Internally they had much in common, although each followed its own peculiar development. In contrast with the countries of western Europe, these were the lands of autocratic monarchy and relatively powerless parliaments appearing on the scene relatively late. In 1914, all three were "empires," a title that only the tottering Ottoman state also claimed in Europe. This title had become a symbol of pretensions that could no longer be made good.

II: Germany, 1850-1914

In 1914, the blatantly militarist and nationalist German Empire was a powerful, unified industrial state with a highly edu-

Bismarck.

cated, obedient, and competent population. By supporting the Balkan policies of its ally, Austria-Hungary, it helped to plunge the entire world into the first of the twentieth century's wars of mass slaughter. Germany had emerged as a great continental power only after 1850, although for more than 1400 years millions of Germans had been living in the heart of Europe under a variety of political regimes. The militarism, the authoritarianism, the whole social and cultural tone of the Germany of 1914 were determined by the fact that it was the Kingdom of Prussia that had achieved German unification. Characteristic Prussian attitudes had overcome other German ways of looking at society, and had imposed themselves on non-Prussians. The Prussian triumph was complete by 1871.

Prussia, Bismarck, and the Junkers

Between 1850 and 1871, and especially after 1862, Prussia moved with ever-accelerating speed from triumph to triumph. Doubters and protesters were silenced or dazzled by the glitter of each new achievement; moral objections were regarded as unpatriotic. Bismarck, who directed policy, spoke of respect for legality and decency as "humanitarian twaddle" and proclaimed an era when "blood and iron" alone would decide. The ends seemed so desirable and were being gained so rapidly that even stern moralists could tell themselves that this time they need not examine the means. They shook their heads and voted the government new subsidies.

The creation of imperial Germany was above all the work of Otto von Bismarck (1815-1898). Brilliant, unscrupulous, ruthless, a genius at maneuver and at concealing his real intentions, Bismarck was often bewilderingly inconsistent in his policies. Sometimes he pursued two apparently con-

tradictory policies at the same time, until the moment came when he had to make a final decision on which policy to follow. His intense loyalty to the Prussian Crown, however, did not falter during his long years in office, although after his dismissal by William II in 1890 he felt that his work was being undone and he often tried to embarrass the Emperor and his own successors in the government. He could not endure criticism of himself. He loathed liberals, Catholics, and socialists at different periods, and despised his intellectual inferiors even when they belonged to his own class, the Prussian landed nobility: the Junkers.

As a class, the Junkers had never developed a sense of *noblesse oblige* or the enlightened attitudes of Whigs and Tories in England. The Junkers believed firmly in their own privileges, governed the peasants on their estates, monopolized commissions in the Prussian army, and dominated the administrative services of the Prussian state. On their behalf, on behalf of the monarchy, and on behalf of his own career, Bismarck was willing to do literally anything, even to co-operate temporarily for tactical ends with domestic opponents and foreign enemies, whom he would first use and then try to destroy. Whatever his policy of the moment, force lay at its roots. Influential before 1862, he towered over Prussia from 1862 to 1871, and over the German Empire thereafter until 1890. Yet his efforts could not have succeeded had they not met with general approval from the German people, who had hungered for unity since before 1848.

Prussia and the German Confederation, 1850-1859

The first major question facing the statesmen of Central Europe after the Revolutions of 1848 was whether Prussia or Austria would dominate the German Con-

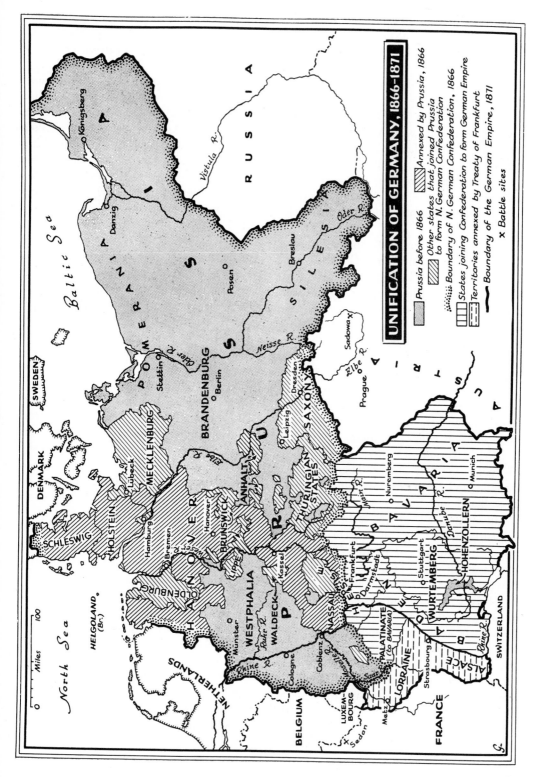

UNIFICATION OF GERMANY, 1866-1871

Prussia before 1866

Annexed by Prussia, 1866

Other states that joined Prussia
to form N. German Confederation

Boundary of N. German Confederation, 1866

States joining Confederation to form German Empire

Territories annexed by Treaty of Frankfurt

Boundary of the German Empire, 1871

x Battle sites

RUSSIA

Baltic Sea

SWEDEN

DENMARK

SCHLESWIG

HOLSTEIN

HELGOLAND
(Br.)

North Sea

NETHERLANDS

BELGIUM

LUXEM-
BOURG

FRANCE

SWITZERLAND

Königsberg

Danzig

POMERANIA

Stettin

Oder R.

MECKLENBURG

Lübeck

Hamburg

Bremen

Weser R.

OLDENBURG

HANOVER

Münster

WESTPHALIA

WALDECK

Cologne

Ruhr R.

Coblenz

Rhine R.

Moselle R.

Metz

Sedan

LORRAINE

Strasbourg

ALSACE

Rhine R.

PALATINATE
(to BAVARIA)

Hanover

BRUNSWICK

ANHALT

Elbe R.

P R U S S I A

BRANDENBURG

Berlin

Posen

Vistula R.

SILESIA

Breslau

Oder R.

Neisse R.

Elbe R.

SAXONY

Leipzig

Dresden

THURINGIAN
STATES

HESSE

Frankfurt

Darmstadt

Kassel

NASSAU

Main R.

Nuremberg

B A V A R I A

Stuttgart

WÜRTEMBERG

HOHENZOLLERN

Munich

Danube R.

Sadowa x

Elbe R.

Prague

A U S T R I A

Miles
0   100

G.

281

federation. Indeed, in a broader sense, this was a question of what form the Confederation would now take. A creation of the Congress of Vienna (see Chapter XIX), it had been temporarily shaken and split by the developments of 1848, and now needed to be rebuilt. The "Big German" solution favored federation with Austria; the "Small German" solution favored separation from Austria or even from South Germany. The "Small German" program meant Prussian domination of the non-Austrian German states, and therefore became Bismarck's goal.

The period after 1848 opened with a defeat for a Prussian "Small German" solution. King Frederick William IV, who had refused to accept the imperial crown "from the gutter" when it was offered by the Frankfurt Assembly (see Chapter XIX), none the less cherished the hope that the German princes might offer it to him. Taking advantage of Austria's pre-occupation with the remnants of the revolution of 1848, and overriding his own Prussian conservatives, who wished simply to strengthen their own state, Frederick William IV formed the Erfurt Union of Princes, an agreement to pool military resources. This union was designed to lead to Prussian political as well as military dominance.

The Austrians managed to bring Russian pressure to bear on Prussia. The Tsar opposed the unification of the Germans no matter under whose auspices. At Olmütz, in November, 1850, the Prussians renounced the Erfurt Union, and reluctantly agreed to the revival of the Confederation. This episode is known as the "humiliation" of Olmütz, a term that shows how bitterly many Prussians resented it. Yet Bismarck himself defended the treaty, and as a result was sent as Prussian representative to the Diet of the Confederation.

Although Bismarck made a speech approving Olmütz, he took every occasion at the Diet to work against Austria, and to thwart Austrian designs. As one facet of his policy, he strove to keep Prussia neutral in the Crimean War (1854-56), in which England and France fought with Turkey against Russia, and Austria harassed rather than helped the Russians (see below, p. 295). Realizing that Austrian behavior was alienating Russia, and that Russian friendship would be valuable later when Prussia came to grips with Austria, Bismarck frustrated the more liberal Prussians who hoped that Prussia would enter the war against Russia and thus line up with the West. He was counting on a military showdown with Austria, and on pushing Austria out of Germany, which he felt was too small for both powers. With this purpose in mind, he also wooed the French Emperor Napoleon III, despite the horror that many Prussians felt over dealings with a Bonaparte, whom they regarded as the heir of the French Revolution. Early in 1859, after Frederick William IV had become insane and his younger brother William had become regent, Bismarck was recalled from the Diet and was sent as ambassador to Russia. But in his eight years at Frankfurt as Prussian representative, Bismarck had demonstrated his extraordinary intelligence, persistence, and skill, and had helped check the Austrian bid for German leadership.

Simultaneously, during the 1850's, both the constitutional and the economic foundations of future Prussian development were laid. The Prussian Constitution of 1850 lasted down to the end of World War I. It provided for a bicameral legislature: a hereditary upper house including the nobles and royal appointees, and an elected lower house. But the method of electing this lower house made it certain that the popular will would be frustrated. Electors were divided into three classes, according to the size of the taxes they paid. Although there were fewer rich men who paid high taxes than

CHAPTER XXII

poor men who paid low taxes, the rich had as many representatives as the poor. The 4 per cent of the electorate who paid high taxes selected one-third of the representatives. The 14 per cent of middle taxpayers selected another third, and the remaining 82 per cent of low taxpayers selected the last third.

Even so, the lower house had very little to do beyond approving the budget. Policy questions were decided in the upper house, or still more often by the king and his personal circle of military and political advisers. The king appointed his ministers, could veto any bill he disapproved, and had a fixed sum of money at his disposal for expenses. He had a special "military cabinet" for army affairs that reported neither to the ministers nor to the legislature. Practically speaking, the king and the Junkers ran Prussia.

With its possessions in western Germany, including the Ruhr, Prussia had the richest coal deposits in Europe. She now began to build the iron and steel industry without which her future political and military triumphs would have been impossible. Alone among the continental nations, the Prussians turned over the planning of their new railway system to the army general staff, which laid out the lines with an eye to rapid and efficient mobilization and transportation of troops in time of war. The new railway net bound Prussia together. When Napoleon III went to war against Austria in 1859 in order to liberate Italy, the Prussians mobilized. Bismarck hoped that Prussia would go to war on the side of the French, whereas the more traditionally minded thought that Prussia should help Austria. Although the Prussians in the end helped neither side, the new railroads had been given a trial. The general staff had learned practical lessons, which they turned to good account only seven years later.

Bismarck Comes to Power

Indeed these military lessons led directly to the beginning of Bismarck's undisputed domination of Prussian policies. The regent William, who became King William I in 1861, was above all a soldier. His minister of war, Roon, a friend of Bismarck's, easily persuaded the King that an army reorganization was necessary. He wanted to increase the number of conscripts called in each year from 40,000 to 63,000, and to lengthen the term of their service from two to three years. Behind Roon's military projects lay a political motive: to keep the army as conservative as possible, and to make it as big as possible, so that it might serve as counterweight to any liberal or revolutionary tendencies in the state. A prolonged political crisis arose over these aims in 1861 and 1862, when the Prussian parliament refused to vote the budget. At the very height of the crisis, Roon summoned Bismarck back to Berlin, and the King, convinced that here was a man who did not care about parliaments, appointed Bismarck prime minister of Prussia and minister of foreign affairs.

On the fallacious principle that there was a "gap" in the constitution that permitted the government to collect taxes even when the budget had not been approved by parliament, Bismarck now collected and spent revenue quite illegally. Again and again he dissolved the parliament, called new elections, faced another hostile house, and then repeated the process. As he said: "If a compromise cannot be arrived at and a conflict arises, then the conflict becomes a question of power. Whoever has the power, then acts according to his opinion." * Bismarck had the power. He suppressed hostile newspapers in defiance of a constitutional proviso

---

* Quoted in E. Eyck, *Bismarck and the German Empire* (London, 1950), 61.

that the press should be free. He indicted an opposition deputy, himself a judge and a loyal Prussian, in spite of the constitutional provision that deputies could not be indicted for anything they said on the floor of the house. Yet after four years (1862-1866) of this unconstitutional behavior he got away with everything in the end, because of the glittering successes he scored in foreign policy.

Since Bismarck intended to overthrow the German Confederation as it was then constituted, he opposed Austrian efforts to reform it. Austria wished to create an assembly of delegates chosen by the parliaments of the member states, in addition to those named by the princes, and a directorate of six monarchs. Bismarck prevented William I from attending a congress of princes called by Austria to discuss these proposals, and thus wrecked the congress (1862). In 1863, he kept Austria out of the Zollverein, the German Customs Union (see above, p. 184). Because he wanted to be on good terms with Napoleon III, in 1862 he supported a trade treaty with France, although as a member of the Zollverein Prussia did not have legal authority to conclude such a treaty. In 1863, he consolidated his good relations with Russia during the Polish revolt (see below, p. 320) by concluding the Alvensleben convention, which allowed the Russians to pursue fleeing Poles onto Prussian territory and capture them there. Thus Bismarck wooed the Russians a second time, as he had during the Crimean War.

The Schleswig-Holstein Question, 1863-1865

When the King of Denmark died in late 1863, the celebrated Schleswig-Holstein question gave Bismarck further opportunities. The Prime Minister of England once remarked that only three men had ever understood this complex problem, and that one was dead and one insane, while he himself, the third, had forgotten all about it. In brief, the duchies of Schleswig and Holstein at the southern base of the Danish peninsula had been ruled by the King of Denmark, but not as part of Denmark. A fifteenth-century guarantee assured the duchies that they could never be separated from each other. Yet Holstein to the south was a member of the German Confederation; Schleswig to the north was not. Holstein was mostly German in population; Schleswig was mixed German and Danish. In 1852, Prussia had agreed in an international conference on an heir who would succeed both to the Danish throne and to the duchies. At the same time, Prussia had joined the other powers in recommending that Denmark and the duchies should be united by a constitution. But, when the constitutional union of Denmark and the duchies was attempted, the duchies resisted, and the Danes tried to incorporate Schleswig. German patriots objected. The Prussians and Austrians wanted the duchies to have special representation inside the Danish parliament, and insisted that Schleswig should *not* be incorporated into Denmark. None the less, the King of Denmark in 1863 followed a policy that supported annexation.

Into this situation Bismarck now moved to win the duchies for Prussia. He wanted both the prestige that Prussia would gain and the valuable commercial port of Kiel in Holstein. First he maneuvered Prussia and Austria together into a victorious war against Denmark (1864), although Austria had no real interest in the duchies. Then he quarreled with the Austrians over the administration of the duchies. At the Convention of Gastein, 1865, it was decided that Prussia was to administer Schleswig and that Austria was to administer Holstein.

But this arrangement provided only a temporary halt in Bismarck's drive against Austria.

War with Austria, 1866

Bismarck kept nagging Vienna about Austrian behavior in Holstein. He tried and failed to tempt France into an alliance. But he did succeed in lining up the Italians, who secretly obliged themselves to go to war on the side of Prussia if Prussia fought Austria within three months. This was contrary to the constitution of the German Confederation, which forbade members to ally themselves with a foreign power against other members. So distressed was William I at this illegality that he lied flatly when the Austrian Emperor asked him if such a treaty existed. Finally, Bismarck suddenly proposed that the German Confederation be reformed, and that an all-German parliament be elected by universal suffrage, which everybody knew he hated.

Bismarck probably advanced this proposal for universal suffrage in order to make it appear that his quarrel with Austria rested on a less sordid ground than the mere Schleswig-Holstein question. Yet the proposal also reflected his calculation that enfranchisement of all Germans would weaken the Progressive party, heir to the liberalism of 1848, and would produce many conservative and royalist votes from the peasantry. He had seen how Napoleon III had risen to imperial power in France on the strength of universal suffrage. And he had been influenced by conversations with Ferdinand Lassalle, a German socialist, who argued that universal suffrage would weaken the middle classes. Bismarck had hoped that the Austrians might try to throw his plan out, but the other members of the Confederation asked Prussia to propose a full plan of reform. Austria now laid the Schleswig-Holstein question before the Diet of the Confederation. Bismarck ordered Prussian troops into Holstein, and declared that Austrian motions in the Diet were unconstitutional. He had succeeded in provoking war with Austria. It was an all-German civil war, since Bavaria, Würtemberg, Saxony, and Hanover (the four other German kingdoms) and most of the lesser German states sided with Austria.

The war lasted seven weeks, and was virtually decided in less than three. The Austrians had to commit a substantial part of their forces against Italy. Skillfully using their railway network, the telegraph, and superior armaments, the Prussians quickly overran northern Germany, invaded Bohemia, and defeated the Austrians at König-gratz (Sadowa). This battle has been referred to as a Gettysburg won by the secessionist Prussians. As the rapid German civil war continued, the Prussians defeated the Bavarians and entered Frankfurt, seat of the German Confederation. The states of Hanover, Hesse-Cassel, and Nassau were all annexed to Prussia and their dynasties were expelled. Schleswig-Holstein and the free city of Frankfurt were also taken over.

Bismarck successfully opposed the generals, and even his king, who wished to punish Austria severely. Except for the cession of Venetia to Italy, Austria suffered no territorial losses as a result of the Peace of Prague (1866), but she did pay a small indemnity. Most important from Bismarck's point of view, Austria had to withdraw forever from the German Confederation, which now ceased to exist. Germany north of the Main River was to join a new North German Confederation to be organized by Prussia. However, it was stipulated that the German states south of the Main were to be free to form an independent union of their own. But Bismarck had previously concluded secret treaties of alliance with the most important South German states—

Bavaria, Württemberg, and Baden—who promised to put their armies at the disposal of the King of Prussia in case of war. So the proposed South German union could never come into existence. Bismarck thus broke the Peace of Prague before it had been concluded, a real piece of diplomatic skill. Bismarck's gentle treatment of Austria was not just a matter of generosity. He was convinced that Prussia would need Austrian help in the future. Now that he had expelled Austria from Germany, imposed a "Small German" solution, and elevated Prussia to the position of dominance, he had scored his point.

Now Bismarck was free to turn to the Prussian parliament, with which he had been feuding for four years. He asked for an "indemnity," that is, a certification that all the revenue he had illegally collected and illegally spent, ever since the parliament had refused to pass the budget in 1861, had in fact been legally collected and legally spent. The deputies were so dazzled by the feats of arms against Denmark and Austria, and by the enormous new acquisitions of power and territory, that they voted the indemnity, and awarded Bismarck personally a cash gift of roughly $300,000. The indemnity marked an important defeat for parliamentary government.

The North German Confederation

An assembly elected by universal manhood suffrage now debated and adopted a constitution for the new North German Confederation, of which the Prussian king was president. The draft that Bismarck submitted is eloquent testimony to his determination to "kill parliamentarism through parliament." The future parliament (Reichstag) was to have no power over the budget, and the ministers were not to be responsible to it. Instead, a Federal Council (Bundesrat), consisting of delegates from the member states and voting according to instructions from their sovereigns, would reach all key policy decisions in secret, and would have veto power over any enactment of the Reichstag. A chancellor would preside over the Bundesrat but would not have to explain or defend its decisions before the Reichstag. Since Prussia now had not only its own votes in the Bundesrat, but those of the newly annexed states, Bismarck's plan in effect made it possible for the king of Prussia to run Germany.

This plan was only slightly modified so that the future chancellor would have to sign every act undertaken by the king of of Prussia as president of the Confederation. But the executive was in no way made "responsible" to the Reichstag. Bismarck's plan also specified that, beginning five years later in 1872, the size of the army would be fixed by law, and that the Reichstag would have a vote on the budget. However, Bismarck, who became chancellor, saw to it that the debate on the military budget did not take place every year, but that sums were appropriated for long periods in advance. The constitution did little more than sanction Prussian military domination over Germany.

Showdown with France

During the next four years, the power of the new Prussian-dominated German state created by Bismarck's destruction of the Vienna system began to make itself felt. Increasing uneasiness reigned in Europe. As long as Bismarck needed the benevolent neutrality of Napoleon III, he had hinted that he might not object if Napoleon took Belgium. Now the gullible Napoleon

A Prussian battery before Paris during the Franco-Prussian War.

found that Bismarck no longer remembered the matter. Hoping to be compensated for his assistance in making peace between Prussia and Austria, Napoleon III made unscrupulous attempts to acquire Luxemburg by purchase from the King of Holland. Again he was frustrated by Bismarck. Suddenly confronted with the new Germany, many members of the French public and press hoped to get "revenge for Sadowa," and became strongly anti-German. The German press responded in kind. Napoleon III strove to create an alliance with Austria and Italy in order to thwart further Prussian expansion. But the Austrians shied away from a true commitment, and the Italians were unable to reach an agreement with the French because of the Roman question (see above, p. 267).

When the Spaniards ousted their queen in 1868, one of the candidates for the throne was a Hohenzollern prince whom Bismarck secretly backed by discreetly bribing influential Spaniards. Because of family dynastic practice, it was necessary to secure the consent of the reluctant King William I of Prussia, and this Bismarck

finally extracted without hinting that war with France might result. Napoleon, also deep in Spanish intrigue, feared that a Hohenzollern on the Spanish throne would expose France to a two-front attack. French diplomatic pressure was exerted directly on King William, and the Hohenzollern candidate withdrew. At this moment, Bismarck seemed to be defeated.

But the French, overstimulated by their success, now demanded that William publicly endorse the withdrawal of the candidacy and promise never to allow it to be renewed. William, who was at Ems, courteously refused, and sent a telegram to Bismarck describing his interchange with the French ambassador. Bismarck then abridged this famous Ems telegram and released it to the press and all the European chanceries. He made it seem that William had thoroughly snubbed the French ambassador, and that the ambassador had been "provocative" to the King. Public opinion was inflamed, and the result was precisely what Bismarck hoped it would be: the French declared war on July 19, 1870.

Within six weeks the Germans had advanced into France, bottled up one French army inside the fortress of Metz, defeated another at Sedan, and captured Napoleon III himself. The protracted siege of Paris followed, ending in surrender early in 1871. A new French government had to make peace. Bismarck forced the French to pay a billion-dollar indemnity, to cede the rich provinces of Alsace and Lorraine (which the German military wanted as a defense against possible future French attack), and to support German occupying forces until the indemnity had been paid.

The German Empire

Even before this peace had been imposed, King William of Prussia was proclaimed Emperor of Germany in the great Hall of Mirrors in Louis XIV's palace at Versailles. Bismarck had to make a few unimportant concessions to the rulers of the South German states to secure their entry into the new empire, but he never had to consult the Reichstag, which simply hastened to send its own deputation begging the King to accept the crown. The proclamation took place in a ceremony of princes and soldiers. When a constitution for the new empire was adopted, it was simply an extension of the constitution of the North German Confederation of 1867. Although the German Empire was brought into being by Bismarck's trickery and brutality, it certainly answered the popular demand of masses of Germans, and made them feel that their national destiny had at last been triumphantly realized. Bismarck himself became a prince and received a million dollars as a gift.

As Chancellor of the German Empire from 1871 to 1890, Bismarck became the leading statesman in all Europe. He felt that Germany had no further need for territory or for war. As a nineteenth-century realist with no dream of world-empire, he felt that his limited goals had been attained. As diplomat, he henceforth worked for the preservation of Germany's gains against threats from abroad, especially the threat that haunted him most: foreign coalition against Germany (see Chapter XXV). As politician, he worked for the preservation of the Prussian system against all opposing currents.

Bismarck's chancellorship falls naturally into two periods: (1) a period of free trade, co-operation with the Liberals, and opposition to the Catholics (1871-1878); and (2) a period of protective tariffs, co-operation with the Catholics, and opposition to the socialists (1878-1890).

Domestic Developments, 1871-1878

At home, a multitude of economic and legal questions arose as a result of the creation of the new empire. Working with the moderate Liberal party in the Reichstag, Bismarck put through a common coinage and a central bank, co-ordinated and unified the railroads and postal systems, and regularized the legal and judicial systems. In 1871, the Reichstag voted to maintain 1 per cent of the population under arms for three years. In 1874, Bismarck, simply by threatening to resign, forced the Reichstag to fix the size of the army at 401,000 for a seven-year period, until 1881. In 1880, a year before the period expired, he forced an increase to 427,000 for another seven years, to 1888. The privileged position of the army made a military career ever more attractive, and served as a constant spur to German militarism.

But the great drama of the 1870's in Germany was furnished by Bismarck's attack on the Roman Catholic Church, the *Kulturkampf* ("battle for civilization"). The "Syllabus of Errors," published by the Vatican in 1864 (see Chapter XX), denounced the toleration of other religions, secular education, and state participation in church affairs. Then in 1870 the first general council of the Church to meet since the Council of Trent in the Reformation period adopted the dogma of papal infallibility. This dogma asserted that the judgments of the pope on faith and morals were infallible. To many non-Catholics this seemed to say that no state could count on the absolute loyalty of its Catholic citizens.

In Germany, the Catholics were a large minority of the population. They had formed a political party, the Center, that quickly became the second strongest party in the Empire. The Center defended papal infallibility and wished to restore the pope's temporal power, which had been ended by the unification of Italy. The Center not only had many sympathizers in the Catholic Polish provinces of Germany but also sponsored a labor movement of its own, which seemed to pose a social threat. Catholic peasant and workman, priest and nobleman, all opposed the Protestant urban middle class and the Prussian military predominance in the state. Bismarck identified his clerical opponents with France and Austria, the two nations he had defeated in making the new Germany.

In collaboration with the Liberals, Bismarck put through laws expelling the Jesuits from Germany, forbidding the clergy to criticize the government, and closing the schools of religious orders. In Prussia, civil marriage was now required, appropriations for the Catholic Church were stopped, and priests were forced to study at secular universities. The Pope declared these laws null and void, and summoned all good Catholics to disobey them. Catholic services stopped in towns and villages, and many Catholics were deprived of their sacraments.

Bismarck never appreciated that the Church thrives on persecution. By declaring that he would not "go to Canossa," he summoned up for Protestant Germans the picture of the German Emperor Henry IV humbling himself before the Pope in 1077. But a young Catholic tried to assassinate Bismarck, and great excitement resulted from the rigorous enforcement of the anti-Catholic laws. Bismarck in the end had to go to Canossa, and repealed in the eighties most of the anti-Catholic measures he had passed in the seventies. By then he needed the support of the Center party against his former allies the Liberals, whose demands for power he found exorbitant, and against the growing menace of the Social Democrats. Moreover, the Protestant church itself and many of the conservative Prussian nobility had grown alarmed over the excesses of the anti-Catholic campaign.

Domestic Developments, 1878-1890

Indeed, in 1877 and 1878 Bismarck had begun a gradual shift in policy, dictated in the first place by the need for more revenue. The Empire got its money in part from indirect taxes imposed by the Reichstag on tobacco, alcohol, sugar, and the like. The rest came from the individual states, which controlled all direct taxation and made contributions to the imperial budget. As military costs mounted, the government's income became insufficient, and Bismarck did not want to increase the Empire's dependence on the states by repeatedly asking them to increase their contributions. He wanted the Reichstag to vote higher indirect taxes, but its Liberal members naturally suspected that if they acceded he might do to them what he had formerly done to the Prussian parliament. They suspected that he might govern without them if a dispute arose, and depend on the money he would collect from the higher taxes they had granted him. Therefore they wanted some sort of guarantee before they untied Bismarck's hands.

Basically, German tariff policy had been one of free trade, with little protection for German goods. But after a financial panic in 1873, the iron and textile industries put pressure on Bismarck to shift to a policy of protection that would help them compete with England. Moreover, an agricultural crisis led conservatives to abandon their previous support of free trade, and to demand protection against cheap grain from eastern Europe. In 1879, Bismarck put through a general protective tariff on all imports, a move on which his former allies, the Liberals, were split.

In order to avoid granting the constitutional guarantees demanded by the Liberals, Bismarck gradually abandoned the *Kulturkampf*. The Catholic Center favored his protectionist policy; moreover, the lessening of the clerical threat in France and the conclusion of a firm German alliance with Austria in 1879 (see Chapter XXV) removed the foreign causes for the attack on the Church. Bismarck therefore secured the support of the Center as well as that of the conservatives. Thus he was able to avoid making concessions to the Reichstag, and thus he launched Germany on an era of protection. The protectionist policy spurred still further the rapid and efficient growth of industry, especially heavy industry. Politically, the conservative Protestant agrarian forces now grew stronger, and gained many urban votes. But Bismarck never entirely trusted the Center, and strove successfully to remodel the Liberals into a stanchly conservative industrialist group.

While he was easing the *Kulturkampf* and swinging to protection in 1878-1879, Bismarck also began to proceed against the Social Democratic party. The Marxists Liebknecht and Bebel had founded this small party in 1869; in 1875, they enlarged it, much to Marx's own disgust, by accepting the followers of Lassalle, an apostle of non-violence. The German Social Democrats were not nearly so revolutionary as their own Marxist phraseology suggested, and had no doubt inherited some of Lassalle's willingness to make a deal with the existing regime. They did not threaten the state, as Bismarck pretended to think, but they had many supporters among intellectuals and former liberals, and a substantial trade-union following. They polled half a million votes in 1877, about 10 per cent of the total electorate. The Social Democrats were prepared to concentrate their efforts on improving working conditions rather than on revolution. But Bismarck always needed an enemy against whom he could unify his supporters; besides, he had been deeply impressed by the Paris Commune (see Chapter XXI), and believed that something similar might occur in Germany.

Using as a pretext two attempts by alleged Social Democrats to assassinate William I, Bismarck called a general election in 1878 and rammed through the Reichstag a bill making the Social Democratic party illegal, forbidding its meetings, and suppressing its newspapers. Individual socialists could even be expelled from their domiciles by the police. Abandoning their alleged principles, the Liberals supported this law, but they would not allow Bismarck to make it a permanent statute. He had to apply to the Reichstag for its renewal every two or three years; it was renewed each time, until just before Bismarck's own downfall in 1890. An average of a few more than one hundred people a year were imprisoned under the law. Interestingly enough, Social Democrats were still allowed to run for the Reichstag, and their votes increased during the years when they were suffering legal disabilities. What appeared by the standards of its own time to be a savage piece of repressive legislation seems tame enough in comparison with twentieth-century fascist, Nazi, and communist attacks on political opponents.

But Bismarck felt that "a remedy cannot be sought merely in repression of Socialist excesses—there must be simultaneously a positive advancement of the welfare of the working classes." As a result, all during the 1880's, the government put forward a series of bills in favor of the workers: in 1882 compulsory insurance against illness, and in 1884 against accidents. The sickness insurance funds were raised by contributions from both workers and employers; the accident insurance funds were contributed altogether by the employers. In 1889, old-age and invalidism insurance followed, with employers and employees contributing equally, and with an additional subsidy from the state. Thereafter, benefits were increased, were opened to farm laborers, and were extended to include free medical and hospital services. The German system of social security as developed initially under Bismarck did not reduce the Social Democratic vote, but it did provide much that the worker desired. Bismarck put through these measures with the assistance of his old enemies, the Catholic Center, and against the opposition of his old allies, the Liberals, who were becoming the party of big business and feared all interference with "free enterprise."

William II

Bismarck's faithful William I died at the age of ninety in 1888, and his son, Frederick III, already mortally ill, ruled for only about three months. The next emperor was Frederick's son, William II, a young man of twenty-nine whose advent his father had greatly feared because of his immaturity, impulsiveness, and conceit. The entire Bismarckian system had been built to support an autocratic King of Prussia as Emperor of the Germans. William I allowed Bismarck to act for him, but William II was determined to act for himself. This determination underlay the subsequent controversy between him and Bismarck. The cult of the House of Hohenzollern, which had been taught by thousands of schoolteachers and university professors to hundreds of thousands of school boys and students, created an atmosphere of adulation that went to William's head. William, though intelligent and quick, was bored by detail, and would not give affairs of state the attention they needed. He listened to the voices of those who urged him to go it alone. Chief among these advisers was Stöcker, the Lutheran court chaplain, a violent anti-Semite and leader of the right-wing conservatives.

On his accession, William loudly proclaimed his sympathy with the workingman. When the anti-socialist law came up for renewal, the Emperor supported a modified version that would have taken away the power of the police to expel Social Democrats from their residences. Bismarck opposed the measure, hoping that the Socialist Democrats would indulge in excesses which would give him the excuse to suppress them by armed force. As a result, there was no anti-socialist law after 1890. Other differences arose between the Chancellor and the Emperor over relations with Russia and over procedure in reaching policy decisions. Finally, in March, 1890, William commanded Bismarck to resign.

Although four chancellors succeeded him during the years before the outbreak of war in 1914, none of them can be compared with Bismarck in ability and influence. The years 1890-1914 are truly the years of William II. Energetic but unsteady, pompous and menacing but without the intention or

"Dropping the Pilot." Punch comments on *William II's dismissal of Bismarck, 1890.*

the courage to back up his threats, emotional and vacillating, William was ill-suited to govern any country, much less the militaristic, highly industrialized, imperial Germany with its social tensions and its lack of political balance.

Domestic Tensions, 1890-1914

Party structure reflected the strains in German society. The Liberals, a party of big business, usually had little strength in the Reichstag, although many industrialists were on intimate terms with the Emperor

personally. The great landowners banded together in protest against a reduction in agricultural duties which was included in a series of trade treaties concluded between Germany and other continental European countries between 1892 and 1894. In 1894, they organized the Agrarian League, which spearheaded all conservative measures and became enormously powerful in German politics. In 1902, they forced a return to protection. Middle-class city-dwellers, especially the merchants, disliked the Junkers' power and hoped to reform the imperial constitution to make it more like that of Britain. Since they had almost no representatives in the Reichstag, they often collaborated with the Social Democrats.

The electoral strength of the Social Democrats increased during William's reign from 1,500,000 to 4,250,000, and embraced one-third of the voting population by 1914. Freed from interference by the removal of the anti-socialist law, they organized trade unions, circulated newspapers, and successfully brought pressure on the regime for more social legislation. The party had no immediate plan for a revolution, although its radical wing expected, especially after the Russian revolution of 1905 (see below, p. 324), that a revolution would come. The moderate or "revisionist" wing, which expected no open conflict between capital and labor, felt that by allying with the middle class to attain a majority in the Reichstag the Social Democrats might eventually overthrow the militarist regime. This the radical wing scornfully dismissed as mere temporizing. The Emperor, furious over the failure of the new social measures to weaken the Social Democrats, told new army recruits as early as 1891 that some day he might have to order them to shoot down their own brothers and parents.

As the Social Democrats became more powerful, the government allied itself more closely with the Catholic Center. Between

CHAPTER XXII

1895 and 1906, and again between 1909 and 1914, a coalition of conservatives and the Center formed the majority group in the Reichstag. The coalition did not wish to see any increase in the powers of parliament. Yet left-wingers within the Center party occasionally called for a liberalization of the system and for tactical purposes would even ally with the Social Democrats.

Meanwhile, issues of military, colonial, and foreign policy began to complicate the internal politics of Germany. The size of the army rose from 479,000 in 1892 to 870,000 in 1913. And for the first time Germany sought a big navy after Admiral Tirpitz became minister of the navy in 1897. The Emperor issued a series of warlike and grandiose statements hailing Germany's "future on the waters," and he and Tirpitz planned a high-seas fleet to supersede the naval forces that had been designed for coastal defense and for the defense of commerce. The navy boom was at least partly intended to supply a market for the expanding steel industry. A Navy League, ostensibly a private organization but constantly hand in glove with the regime, spread propaganda on behalf of the new fleet. The first rather modest naval law of 1898 provided for a navy that was doubled by the second law of 1900.

But the army and navy were only the most obvious weapons of world power. Bismarck's saturated country seemed saturated no longer. The Colonial Society thrived as Germany seized lands in the Far East and in Africa (see Chapter XXIV), despite the drain on the budget (for the colonies were never profitable), and despite scandal after scandal (for the Germans were often brutal colonial administrators). "Pan-Germans" planned the great Berlin-Bagdad railway to the Near East and cried shrilly for more and more adventure and conquest.

William's naval and colonial policies embittered Germany's relations with Great Britain. In 1896, the Emperor himself sent the Boer President Kruger a telegram congratulating him on his having repelled the Jameson Raid (see below, p. 385), and hinting that Germany would have been willing to intervene on the side of the Boers against Britain. Again in 1908, he gave an interview to a London newspaper, the *Daily Telegraph*, in which, with monumental indiscretion, he protested his friendship for Britain, yet at the same time declared that the English had been ungrateful to him in not acknowledging that his own military plans, sent to them in secrecy, had enabled them to win the Boer War. Of course there was nothing in his claim. Moreover, William actually declared that Germany's new navy was directed against the Japanese.

The *Daily Telegraph* affair aroused a storm of protest against William in Germany itself, and the Emperor had to apologize and promise to do better in the future. This episode illustrates the dangerous instability of the man who was all-powerful in a mighty military state. Moreover, it also reveals the general uneasiness that underlay the apparently smooth and prosperous surface of William's Germany. The protest against the anachronistic system under which Germans lived and labored, and against the external bombast and internal insecurity of the regime, was expressed in the enormous vote of the Social Democrats in 1912.

In 1913-1914, a German army officer in the Alsatian town of Saverne (Zabern) wounded a lame shoemaker with his sword, and the commanding officer of the German garrison illegally arrested and jailed townspeople who protested against German arrogance and brutality. The bitter resentment of the Alsatians was echoed by a tremendous number of Germans who had become resentful over the outrageous and unrestrained behavior of their military. By a vote of 293 to 54, the Reichstag passed a resolution of censure against the government in which the Center joined with the Social Democrats and the Liberals. Even more interesting is the sequel, for William decorated the guilty officer, who was acquitted by a court-martial. The Saverne affair proved that the German public was still capable of feeling discomfort over the excesses of their Prussian masters, but it also proved that even a public expression of disapproval had little effect on these masters—the Emperor, the Junkers, and the military.

III: The Habsburg Monarchy, 1850-1914

Character of the Empire

The extraordinary empire of the Habsburgs has been called ramshackle, heterogeneous, and anachronistic. And much scorn has been poured upon it for its incompetence, its smugness, its stupidity, and its failure to keep up with modern times. No doubt these charges are largely justified. But in recent years voices have been raised mourning the Empire's disappearance, and regretfully echoing a nineteenth-century Czech patriot's celebrated remark that if the Empire did not exist it would be necessary to invent it. These expressions of longing come not only from reactionaries, monarchists, and clericals lamenting a past hopelessly beyond recovery. They can be heard from the lips of old men in Tito's Yugoslavia and in the "people's republics" of Rumania, Poland, and Hungary. These old men remember with longing a regime which they felt in their youth to be oppressive and unfair.

Perhaps these sentiments are not so much praise for the Habsburgs as blame for the communists who now rule much of the former Habsburg territory, and for the extreme nationalist or fascist regimes that preceded the communist triumph. In any case, it comes as a shock to realize that the ancient collection of real estate governed by the Habsburg dynasty was dispersed only a generation ago. It is even more depressing to reflect that the problem of the national hatreds and rivalries that haunted and finally destroyed the Habsburgs is with us still in modified form today, and that this same problem still causes suffering and threatens war.

During the entire period from 1850 to 1914, the Emperor Francis Joseph sat on the Habsburg throne. Simple in his personal life and immensely conscientious, he worked hard at his desk, reading and signing state papers for hours every day. But he was without fire or imagination, uninterested in books dealing with current problems, or even in newspapers, devoted to the rigid court etiquette prescribed for Habsburgs, inflexibly old-fashioned and conservative, and selfish in the old Habsburg way, always ready to dismiss a minister of whose further usefulness he was not convinced. He was intensely pious. He loved to hunt. His mere longevity inspired loyalty, but it must be admitted that he was a dull fellow, in every sense of the term. Except for Prince Schwarzenberg between 1849 and 1852, Francis Joseph never had a prime minister. He was his own prime minister, and had to make decisions on policy himself. His decisions usually came too late, and conceded too little.

Political Experiments, 1850-1867

The period of Habsburg history from 1850 to 1914 may be divided into unequal portions, with the dividing line coming in 1867 when the Empire became the dual monarchy of Austria-Hungary. Before 1867, there was a decade of reaction which ended in 1859 with the war against Piedmont and France (see Chapter XXI); then came eight years of political experimentation from 1859 to 1867, punctuated by the war of 1866 with Prussia. The ten years following the repression of the revolutionary movements of 1848-1849 are usually called the "Bach period," from the name of a repressive minister of the interior. All parts of the Empire were now for the first time unified and directly ruled from Vienna by German-speaking officials. Not only the Magyars, Czechs, and Italians, who had revolted against the system, but the Croats and Rumanians, who out of dislike for the Magyars had assisted Vienna in putting down the revolutions, were subjected to the same authoritarian regime. As a Croatian remarked to a Magyar, "What you got as a punishment, we got as a reward."

In 1855, the state signed a concordat with the Catholic Church giving clerics a greater influence in education and in other fields than they had enjoyed since the reforms of Joseph II. Because the repressive domestic policies of the Bach system required expensive armies and policemen, the state went into debt. Instead of investing in railroads and industry, Austria spent its money on enforcing the Bach system. These expenditures left it at a disadvantage compared with Prussia. Then, during the Crimean War, instead of repaying Tsar Nicholas I for Russia's aid in subduing the Hungarian revolution, Austria "astonished the world by her ingratitude." Not only did Francis Joseph fail to assist the Russians,

he actually kept them in fear of an attack by occupying the Danubian principalities (modern Rumania). In 1857, Austria experienced a severe financial crisis partly as a result of this long mobilization.

The defeat of 1859 at the hands of the French and Italians, and the loss of Lombardy with its great city of Milan, brought about the end of the Bach system. War continued to threaten, and the nationalities inside the Empire, especially the Magyars, could not be kept in a state of smoldering discontent which would render their troops unreliable. Several solutions were now tried in an effort to create a structure that would withstand the domestic and foreign strains, but which would not jeopardize the Emperor's position. Francis Joseph made no effort to consult the people. Instead, he listened first to the nobles, who favored a loose federalism, and then to the bureaucrats, who favored a tight centralism.

First, a constitutional change in 1860, the "October Diploma," set up a central legislature to which the aristocratic provincial assemblies throughout the Empire were to send delegates, and which would deal with economic and military questions. All other problems were to be left to the provinces. This, however, did not satisfy the most important non-German province in the empire—Hungary. Except for the great magnates, the Magyars were still discontented and continued to press the demands for autonomy that they had made in 1848. They refused to vote taxes or recruits. But Francis Joseph, who hated the thought of abandoning the uniformity of the Bach system even though he was ready to soften its rigor, opposed the Magyar wishes for special treatment. He was leaning on the aristocracy in the hope that they could hold off liberalism.

On the other hand, the German liberals and bureaucrats of Austria felt that the October Diploma went too far and gave the

Emperor Francis Joseph.

for all members of the last two classes. As in the Prussian constitution of 1850, the class or "curial" system was highly discriminatory, and worked to disfranchise the peasants. Moreover, in regions like Bohemia, where the town population was heavily German and the countryside population heavily Czech, it worked to benefit the rich and the Germans. Yet it continued until 1907, favoring the Germans and hurting the Czechs.

Naturally, the Magyars objected to this second solution even more than to the first, and flatly refused to participate. To the applause of the Germans in Vienna, including the liberals, Hungary was returned to authoritarian rule. Czechs and Poles also eventually withdrew from the central parliament and left only a German rump. Disturbed, the Emperor suspended the February Patent; he began to negotiate with the Magyars, who were represented by the intelligent and moderate Francis Deák, but the negotiations were interrupted by the war with Prussia in 1866. The Austrian defeat at Sadowa (see above), the expulsion of Austria from Germany, and the loss of Venetia seemed to threaten the entire Habsburg system. Francis Joseph resumed negotiations with the Magyars, with the help of the great Magyar noble, Andrassy, and of Beust, who had become Austrian foreign minister. Beust regarded himself as an "official washerwoman," cleaning out the accumulation of centuries of dirty wash. In 1867, a formula was found which was to govern and preserve the Habsburg domains down to the World War of 1914-1918.

Magyars too much. To them it seemed that the Empire was being dismembered on behalf of the nobility, who dominated the provincial assemblies. The "February Patent" of 1861 was actually a new constitution in line with their views. It proclaimed a more centralized scheme. Now the Emperor leaned on the liberals, in line with their "Big German" ideas, which were thwarted by Bismarck. The imperial legislature took over most of the powers the October Diploma had reserved for the provincial assemblies or diets; the legislative functions of the diets were reduced to little more than the naming of delegates to the imperial parliament, although the diets later came to have many local administrative duties.

Great landowners, town chambers of commerce, townsmen, and peasants formed the four classes of electors to these provincial diets, and there were tax qualifications

The Dual Monarchy, 1867

This was the famous *Ausgleich*, or "compromise," which created the "dual monarchy" of Austria-Hungary. The Hun-

CHAPTER XXII

garian constitution of 1848 was restored, and the entire Empire was reorganized on a strict partnership basis. Austria and Hungary were united in the person of the emperor, who was always to be a Catholic legitimate Habsburg, and who was to be crowned King of Hungary in a special ceremony in Budapest. For foreign policy, military affairs, and finance, the two states had common ministers appointed by the emperor. A customs union subject to renewal every ten years also united them. Every ten years the quota of common expenditure to be borne by each partner was to be settled. A unique body, the "delegations," made up of sixty members from the Austrian and sixty members from the Hungarian parliament, meeting alternately in Vienna and in Budapest, was to decide on the common budget. After the budget had been approved, it had to be ratified by the full parliaments of both countries, and signed by the emperor-king. The delegations also had supervisory authority over the three joint ministers, and might summon them to give an account of their activities. In practice, the delegations seldom met, and were almost never consulted on questions of policy. The system favored Hungary, which had 40 per cent of the population but never paid more than one-third of the expenses. Every ten years, when the quota of expenses and the customs union needed joint consideration, a new crisis arose.

Otherwise, Hungary and Austria were separate states. As King of Hungary, Francis Joseph appointed cabinet ministers, professors, bishops, civil servants, and other officials. He was obliged at least once a year to summon the Hungarian legislature, which had an upper house of hereditary peers and a lower house elected by an elaborate system with more than fifty types of voters. However, qualifications regarding economic status and nationality made the Hungarian lower house entirely undemocratic; the voters never totaled more than 6 per cent of the population. For its part, Austria retained the parliament and the seventeen provincial assemblies provided by the February Patent of 1861. According to the new Austrian constitution of 1867, the authority of the emperor somewhat resembled that of other constitutional monarchs, with the fundamental exception that he could legislate by himself when parliament was not in session. Since he could dissolve parliament at will, he enjoyed a very large discretion.

The dual structure of Austria-Hungary was unique in Europe, and indeed in history. Because of it, many domestic developments in the two parts of the monarchy may be considered quite separately. Yet one overwhelmingly important and complicated problem remained common to both halves of the monarchy: the problem of the national minorities that had not received their autonomy. Some of these minorities (Czechs, Poles, Ruthenes) were largely in Austria; others (Slovaks, Rumanians) were largely in Hungary; the rest (Croats, Serbs, Slovenes, all of them south Slavs) were in both states. These nationalities were at different stages of development and of national self-consciousness. Some of them were subject to pressures from fellow-nationals living in states outside the dual monarchy.

The Austrian constitution of 1867 provided that all nationalities enjoy equal rights, and guaranteed that each might use its own language in education, administration, and public life. Even the Hungarians in 1868 abandoned on paper the fierce Magyar chauvinism of Kossuth and the superpatriots of 1848 (see above, p. 188), and put on the statute books a law that allowed the minorities to conduct local government in their own language, to hold the chief posts in their counties, and to have their own schools. But in practice, neither the Austrian nor the Hungarian statute was respected. The nationalities suffered varying degrees of discrimination and even persecution. Since the nationality problem was common to Austria and to Hungary, and since it brought down the entire dual monarchy in the end, we must examine it in some detail.

The Czechs

After 1867, the highly nationalistic Czechs felt that they were entitled to an *Ausgleich* on the model which the Magyars had obtained. They talked of the lands of the Crown of St. Wenceslaus (who died in 929), by which they meant the provinces of Bohemia, Moravia, and Austrian Silesia, as possessing rights comparable to those that the Magyars had successfully claimed for the lands of the Crown of St. Stephen (997-1038). Not only was this argument historically unsound, but the Czechs never had the power or the opportunity that the Magyars had to bring pressure on the Austrians. After the *Ausgleich*, some Czech leaders visited Russia, and hailed Russian publicists' pleas for the unanimity and union of the Slavic peoples. This "Pan-Slavism" they tried to use as an instrument of pressure on the Vienna government. Czech deputies also boycotted the Austrian parliament in the hope that Francis Joseph would consent to become King of Bohemia in Prague as he had become King of Hungary in Budapest.

In 1871, the Emperor did indeed offer to be crowned as King of Bohemia. The Bohemian diet, from which all the Germans had withdrawn in a fury, drew up proposals that would have produced a triple instead of a dual monarchy, with arrangements quite parallel to those enjoyed by the Magyars. The rage of Austrian and Bohemian Germans, the opposition of Mag-

yar politicians, who predicted chaos, and a Slavic uprising in southern Austria forced Francis Joseph to change his mind. He discharged the ministers who had sponsored the advances to the Czechs, and the episode came to an end. Deeply disappointed, the Czech nationalist leaders returned to passive resistance.

By 1879, when the Czech deputies returned to the Vienna parliament, they were divided into "old Czechs" and "young Czechs." The moderate "old Czechs" sought autonomy, but under aristocratic and clerical auspices; the more impetuous and radical "young Czechs" held democratic and liberal views and favored a pro-French and pro-Russian foreign policy. Against German opposition, the Czechs secured cultural and political gains, including a statute that required all government officials and judges in Czech lands to render decisions and conduct trials in the language of the petitioner. This meant that many German civil servants would have to learn Czech; most Czech civil servants knew German already. The natural result was an increase of Czechs in the civil service, and the development of an experienced body of Czech officials.

During the 1880's, fierce Czech-German strife broke out in Bohemia, and for a time the angry Germans boycotted the Bohemian diet. In 1890, the Vienna ministry and the "old Czechs" temporarily reached a compromise on an administrative division of Bohemia along national Czech and German lines. But the militant "young Czechs" swept the next elections and, when the administrative partition bill was presented, simply rioted on the floor of their diet. The government's answer was repression: Prague was placed under a state of siege.

The siege was not lifted until 1897, when a new ministry in Vienna needed the support of Czech votes. The language enactments were broadened to require that all

civil servants in Czech lands after 1901 be bilingual. These new concessions to the Czechs produced German filibusterings, rowdyism, duels, press blasts, throwing of inkwells, and blowing of whistles in parliament. Government in Vienna became bedlam, and the ministry resigned. Martial law was clamped down on Prague once more, and Czech extremists began to make pro-Russian and pan-Slav gestures, even calling for a general Slav showdown with the Ger-

mans. Alarmed German extremists called Prague the "western Moscow." All compromise plans failed and at the turn of the twentieth century the moderates on both sides of the Czech question were disappearing in the waves of noise and hatred emanating from German and Czech extremists. No parliament could stay in session, and the Austrian government had to be conducted by imperial decree.

Under the stress of prolonged agitation,

and influenced by the apparent triumph of constitutionalism in Russia (see below, p. 326), Francis Joseph finally decided to reform the franchise. In 1907, the "curial" system came to an end. All male citizens of the Austrian lands were now enfranchised and could vote for deputies of their own nationality. Of the 516 deputies in the new parliament, 233 would be German and 107 Czech, a figure almost proportional to the census figures. The first elections under the new system weakened the "young Czechs" and in general showed that the public at large cared as much for the social as for the national problem.

Yet in 1913 the Bohemian diet was dissolved by a *coup*, and in 1914 Czech deputies in the Austrian parliament refused to allow national business to proceed. Thus war began with both parliament and the Bohemian diet dissolved, and with the Emperor and ministers ruling by themselves. Perhaps chief among the many causes for this general parliamentary breakdown was the failure to give the Czech provinces the self-government they had vainly sought since 1867. Most Czechs did not wish to cut loose from the Empire and establish a separate state of their own. Even Beneš, later one of the founders of the Czechoslovak Republic, still believed that Czech demands could and should somehow be satisfied inside the framework of the Habsburg Monarchy. Amounting to about 23 per cent of the Austrian population, the Czechs formed a hard core of discontent.

Yet, political considerations apart, the Czechs had prospered in the Empire. From the economic and cultural points of view, they were by far the most advanced of the Slavic peoples in either part of the dual monarchy. By 1900, the famous Skoda armament works had become the largest in the Empire and the rival of Krupps in Germany. Porcelain and glassware, lace and beer, sugar and the tourist trade, made the Czech middle class rich and Czech craftsmen famous. Laboring conditions were bad, however, and the Czech Social Democrats were weakened by their refusal to work with their German opposite numbers. Many Czechs emigrated to the United States; others flocked to the towns and transformed them from predominantly German into predominantly Czech settlements.

Czech nationalism was fostered by an active Czech-language press, by patriotic societies, by Czech schools, and by the famous *sokols* ("hawks"), a physical-training society with strong nationalist leanings. At the ancient Prague University learned Czech scholars taught, of whom Thomas Masaryk, married to an American, became the most famous. Professor of philosophy and student of Slavic culture, but a lover of the West, Masaryk deeply influenced generations of students, and boldly upheld democratic ideals in politics. Historians studied and revived the heroic past of the Czechs, and poets, novelists, and musicians glorified it for the popular audience. Deprived of their national autonomy and exposed to German bias though the Czechs were, they can hardly be regarded as a persecuted minority. They had their language and their freedom to develop under Austrian domination.

Poles and Ruthenians

Of all the minorities in Austria, the Poles were the most satisfied. Most of them lived in Galicia, where they formed the landlord class and generally oppressed their peasants, especially the backward Ruthenians (Ukrainians). Although the Galician Poles, like the Czechs, asked for provincial self-government on the Magyar model, and although, like the Czechs, they were denied this request, they did enjoy privileges that made them the only contented Poles in

Europe. They had their own schools, and Polish was the language of administration and the courts. The Poles enjoyed favorable financial arrangements, and after 1871 there was a special ministry for Galicia in Vienna.

The contrast between this generous treatment and the brutality suffered by the Poles living in Prussian and Russian Poland led Poles everywhere to look to Austrian Galicia as the center of national life and culture. Polish refugees from tyranny elsewhere took refuge in the cities of Cracow and Lemberg. Here were splendid Polish universities, noble families living grandly as they always had in Poland, and political opportunities to serve the Crown in the provincial administration. The universities trained generations of Poles who were available later for service in independent Poland. Polish literature and the study of Polish history flourished. Though slowly, industrialization began, and a promising petroleum industry was launched. Only the Ruthenians and the Jews suffered discrimination and hardship.

The Poles eliminated Ruthenians from the Galician diet and long kept them from the imperial parliament. The Ruthenians themselves were divided into an older pro-Russian generation, and a younger generation of Ukrainian nationalists, often fanatical, who hated Poles and Russians alike and who hoped for their own autonomous status within the monarchy. Under the new suffrage laws of 1907, 27 Ruthenians were returned to parliament in Vienna. All 27 inveighed against the Poles, and 22 of them inveighed against the other five, who were pro-Russian. In 1908, a Ukrainian assassinated the Polish governor of Galicia after a horrible instance of Polish police brutality. Thus the large Polish minority, about 18 per cent of the Austrian population, lived in contentment and loyalty, persecuting their Ruthenian tenants. Since they hated Russia, Pan-Slavism never tempted them as

it did the Czechs; they were not even very much interested in a future independent Poland.

Other Minorities in Austria

The other minorities in Austria, the Italians and south Slavs, were far less numerous. Less than 3 per cent of the population was Italian in 1910; about 4½ per cent was Slovene; and less than 3 per cent was Serb and Croat. The Italians of the south Tyrol and Istria, where their center was the seaport of Trieste, were far more important than their numbers warranted, however, because of the existence of the Kingdom of Italy across the monarchy's frontier. Almost all of them wanted to belong to Italy, and Italy regarded their lands as *Italia Irredenta* (see Chapter XXI). Although the Italian government tried to quiet the agitation, relations between Rome and Vienna were strained until formation of the Triple Alliance of 1882 (see Chapter XXV). Even thereafter Irredentism always existed as a source of friction between Austria and Italy. Italians were barred from public service, and martial law and strict censorship governed the Italian regions at the time of the outbreak of war in 1914. Of all the Austrian minorities, the Italian steadily proved itself the most anxious to get out of the Habsburg Monarchy altogether.

Among the south Slavs in Austria proper, the Slovenes were the most contented. Scattered in six provinces, and often living at odds with their German or Italian neighbors, they usually made only local demands, like that for lecture courses in Slovene at Graz University. The Croats in Austria (mostly in Dalmatia) were fewer and less disaffected than those in Hungary, and the Serbs in Austria were far fewer and less disaffected than the Serbs in Hungary and in the separate province of Bosnia. Yet both

Serbs and Croats in Austria were divided into groups that preferred autonomy within the Empire and groups that looked long ahead to a future independent south Slav state (Yugoslavia), of which they would some day be a part.

Minorities in Hungary: Slovaks, Rumanians, South Slavs

In Hungary, minority problems were even more acute. Chauvinist and unintelligent, Magyar behavior toward other national groups grew increasingly outrageous as moderate counsels vanished in the face of short-sighted demagoguery. The Slovaks, the Rumanians, and the Serbs and Croats living in Hungary proper were the worst victims of a deliberate policy of Magyarization, but even the Croatians of Croatia, whose province had its own constitutional special status, suffered. The Magyar aim was actually to destroy the national identity of the minorities and to transform them into Magyars. The weapon they used was language.

It is perhaps difficult to understand the passionate attachment felt by the backward peasant peoples of southeastern Europe for their own languages. Yet, deprived of economic opportunity and sometimes of complete religious freedom, these peoples in the nineteenth century came to feel that their language was their "dearest treasure," as a representative of the Rumanian population in Hungarian Transylvania once said. The Magyars too, who made up only 55 per cent of the population of their own country exclusive of Croatia, had a fanatical devotion to their own language, an Asiatic tongue quite unrelated to the German, Slavic, or Rumanian languages of the minorities. They tried to force it into every aspect of the daily lives of the subject peoples, but particularly into education. All state-supported schools had to give instruction in Magyar, from kindergartens to universities. The state postal, telegraph, and railroad services used only Magyar.

The Slovaks, numbering about 11 per cent of the population of Hungary, were perhaps the most Magyarized. Poor peasants for the most part, the more ambitious of them often became Magyars simply by adopting the Magyar language as their own. Kossuth himself was a Slovak by birth, and yielded to nobody in his insistence on Magyarization. In 1875, the Magyars suppressed the Slovak cultural society founded before the *Ausgleich,* and permitted no chair of Slovak in the University of Budapest. As time passed, a few Slovaks came to feel a sense of unity with the closely related but far more advanced Czechs across the border in Austria, and Masaryk, himself part Slovak, drew Slovak students to Prague. The pro-Czechs among the Slovaks were usually liberals and Protestants. Catholic and conservative Slovaks toward the end of the century found their leader in a priest, Father Hlinka, who wanted Slovak autonomy without Czechs. After Czechoslovakia had been formed in 1918, the Hlinka movement continued to be anti-Czech, and became pro-Hitler in the 1930's. Although many Slovaks had learned Magyar and had become Magyars to all intents and purposes, the rest cherished Slovak national aspirations. But they quarreled among themselves over what these were and how they should be attained.

The Rumanians, who lived in Transylvania, amounted in 1910 to 16½ per cent of the population of Hungary, and possessed a majority in Transylvania itself. For centuries they had been downtrodden by the Magyars, and had had to fight to achieve recognition of their Orthodox religion. Indeed, largely in the hope of receiving better treatment, many of them had become Uniates, accepting the supremacy of Rome but otherwise preserving their own liturgy. Despite a fantastic series of laws designed to eliminate the use of the Rumanian language, and a great deal of petty persecution, the Rumanians stoutly resisted assimilation. For redress of grievances, many looked to Vienna, which before the *Ausgleich* had often been a source of assistance against the Magyars, but which was now committed to give the Magyars a free hand. These Rumanians hoped that Transylvania might again be made autonomous, as it had once been in the past. They pressed for the enforcement of the liberal Hungarian nationalities law of 1868. They wanted their language and their church to have equal standing with other languages and other churches.

But when in 1892 the Rumanians petitioned Vienna on these points, and commented that they were worse treated than a conquered people, their petition was returned unopened and unread. When they translated the petition and circulated it widely abroad, their leaders were tried and jailed. It was little wonder that many Transylvanian Rumanians ceased to look west to Vienna for help that never came and began to look south and east across the Carpathians to Rumania, where their fellow-nationals had a kingdom of their own and a strong wish to annex Transylvania. Rumanians of Rumania proper thus felt about Transylvania as Italians of Italy proper felt about *Italia Irredenta*.

Under Magyar rule, some Serbs and Croats lived in Hungary proper and others in Croatia. In 1910, those in Hungary totaled about 600,000, of whom two-thirds were Serbs. Living in a compact mass in the southern and western frontier regions, these were the inhabitants of the old Habsburg military frontier against the Turks. They were transferred to Magyar rule in 1869, and they resented it. The Serbs especially disliked Hungarian administration,

and looked to the independent kingdom of Serbia to the south. Less harassed by Magyarization policies than Slovaks or Rumanians, the Serbs of Hungary had their own patriotic press and secret society in the 1880's. But a far greater menace to Hungarian unity was provided by Croatia proper.

Croatia

The Croats, though connected since the eleventh century with the Crown of Hungary, had become strongly nationalistic under the impact of the Napoleonic occupation, and had fought on the side of the monarchy against the Magyar revolutionaries of 1848. None the less, Francis Joseph, as part of the *Ausgleich* settlement, handed them back to the Magyars. Croatian nationalists were deeply disappointed. Led by the famous Roman Catholic Bishop Strossmayer, a man of deep intelligence, high culture, and liberal views, they had hoped for an autonomous Croatia and Dalmatia inside the Empire, which would serve as a nucleus to attract in the future all the other southern Slavs. But instead, the Magyar moderates, led by Deák, worked out in 1868 an *Ausgleich* of their own between Hungary and Croatia.

All military and economic affairs were to be handled in Budapest by a special cabinet minister for Croatian affairs. Representatives from the Croatian parliament at the Croatian capital of Zagreb would sit in Budapest whenever Croatian affairs were under discussion. Croatian delegates would be part of the Hungarian "delegation" of the dual monarchy. The Croatian language could be spoken by Croat representatives at the sessions of any body they attended, and the language of command in the Croatian territorial army would be Croatian. The Croats would control their own educational system, their church, their courts and police, but all taxes would be voted by Budapest and collected by agents of Budapest. Although the Croats were far better off than any national minority in Hungary, this "compromise" did not satisfy them.

The "Party of the Right," the ancestor of Croat extremism in our own day, wanted a completely autonomous Croatia, and scorned as inferior the Serbs and other non-Catholic south Slavs, whom Strossmayer had hoped to attract. Another source of dissension was provided by the seaport of Fiume, which the Hungarians simply took from the Croats by pasting a false version of the agreement over the true one. Fiume subsequently became a Magyar seaport that rivaled its Austrian neighbor, Trieste, but it was always regarded by the Croats as lost territory belonging to them.

Further problems were created in Catholic Croatia by the existence of a Serb Orthodox minority (more than a quarter of the population), which spoke the same language as the Croats, and which was racially indistinguishable from them. But the Orthodox minority worshiped in different churches, and was therefore subject to religious discrimination.

For twenty years at the close of the nineteenth century the Hungarian-appointed governor cleverly fostered this Serb-Croat antagonism by using the Serbs for local offices. He received the support only of those Croats who had become Magyar-speaking, usually great landowners or government officials. Leaders of the extreme Croatian nationalists, on the other hand, were imprisoned, and Croat-Serb rioting produced repeated disorders. About 1900, Stepan Radich founded the peasant party, which favored a patriotic program for severing the ties with Hungary, the social emancipation of the peasantry, and the end of the prevailing landlordism of the Magyar type.

By 1903, Serbs and Croats were beginning to co-operate against Hungarian rule, and to spread pro-Slav propaganda in Dalmatia. Prague helped to inspire the south Slav movement, since many Serbs and Croats went to Prague as students and returned home imbued with Masaryk's democratic and nationalist views. In the Fiume Resolutions of 1905, Croats asked Vienna for Dalmatia and for electoral reforms, but professed that they wanted to observe faithfully the arrangement of 1868 with Hungary. Serbians endorsed these Croatian demands, though some Serbs hoped for union with independent Serbia, and some Croats still hoped for complete independence.

The hopes of the moderates were dashed by the fearfully unpopular Railway Servants Act (1907), which forced all railroad workers to speak Magyar. Croats began to boycott Hungarian-made goods; the Croatian diet refused to collaborate with the new governor, who ruled (1908-1910) in arbitrary fashion. In 1909, he arrested fifty-odd Croats and Serbs and charged them with plotting to unite Croatia and Bosnia with Serbia. The evidence was ridiculously inadequate, and the defendants, though condemned, obtained a reversal of the sentences on appeal to a higher court. But these Zagreb trials gave the Slavic press a splendid opportunity to denounce the policy of the dual monarchy.

In the same year, 1909, a celebrated Austrian historian, Friedjung, charged in the Vienna press that the Croatian and Serbian politicians in Croatia were plotting with Serbians in Serbia. Friedjung was eventually forced to admit that his documentary sources, which in all probability had been fed to him by the Vienna foreign office, were forgeries. The Zagreb trials and the Friedjung case, coming only five years before the assassination of Francis Ferdinand by a Bosnian Serb and the outbreak of war,

CHAPTER XXII

demonstrate the incompetence of the dual monarchy in dealing with its own loyal south Slav inhabitants.

Indeed, the Railway Servants Act was not repealed despite promises in 1910 that it would be. In 1912, a Bosnian student studying at Zagreb tried to assassinate the Hungarian governor of Croatia. The assassin was a member of a secret society organized in Belgrade, capital of independent Serbia, and dedicated to the creation of a "greater Serbia," which would include Bosnia and Croatia. The Serbian press openly hailed him. A new liberal governor was shot at in 1913 and again in 1914, once by a Bosnian. These were ominous rehearsals for the crime of June 28, 1914: a Bosnian student with a gun, a Habsburg administrator as the target, and south Slav nationalism as the motivating force. The 1914 crime was to take place in Bosnia instead of Croatia, the target was to be hit rather than missed, and the victim was to be a person of much greater importance—the heir to the imperial throne. As a result, the crime led to world war and not merely to internal crisis.

Bosnia-Herzegovina

We must complete our examination of the national minorities in the dual monarchy with a brief discussion of the region of Bosnia-Herzegovina, which had a special status. In the 1870's, these two provinces had been part of the Ottoman Empire for about four centuries. Although entirely south Slav from the ethnic point of view, the population included in 1879 about half a million Moslems, half a million members of the Orthodox Church, and perhaps 150,000 Catholics, as well as a few Jews. Under Turkish rule, those who accepted Islam enjoyed economic advantages. By the nineteenth century, most of the Ortho-

dox Christian population consisted of peasants working on the estates of Moslem landlords and looking across the frontiers to Serbia in hope of liberation. Some of the Catholics were educated in Strossmayer's seminary, and leaned toward eventual absorption in his south-Slav state, but almost nobody wanted to join the Habsburg Monarchy as it was then constituted.

The Herzegovinian uprising of 1875 precipitated first a general Balkan Slavic attack on the Turks, and then a Russo-Turkish War (see below, p. 320). Before Russia went to war against the Turks, the Austrian and Russian foreign ministers reached an agreement on the future status of the two provinces. But they later disagreed on what the agreement had been. At the Congress of Berlin in 1878 (see below, p. 320), the Austrians obtained the right to occupy the provinces, but not to annex them.

From 1878 to 1908, the forces of the monarchy occupied Bosnia and Herzegovina, which at first furiously resisted the entry of the Habsburg troops, and forced them to fight a little war to establish themselves. The sovereignty of the Turkish sultan was recognized throughout this period, but in fact the provinces were ruled from Vienna, though not as part of either Austria or Hungary. Instead, they were put under the common Austro-Hungarian minister of finance, one of the three ministers whom the two halves of the monarchy had in common. The emperor alone could legislate for the provinces, which were given a local military governor with a civilian associate. After a new uprising in 1881, Baron Kallay, an able Magyar joint minister of finance, ruled Bosnia-Herzegovina until 1903. He is remembered especially for the roads, railroads, and aqueducts built under his direction, for his sponsorship of native crafts, for the good system of education that he instituted, for his improvement of agriculture and medicine, and for the efficient administration of his bureaucrats. Yet Kallay was a hated foreigner, and the monarchy never could have held on to the provinces if it had not maintained a large garrison. Nor did the occupiers tamper with the hated social system of rapacious Moslem landlords and resentful Orthodox Christian share-croppers, who still worked the land under primitive conditions.

The discontent of the Orthodox Serbs of Bosnia was fanned by propaganda from Serbia itself. Patriotic Serbs considered that the first logical step toward creating a greater Serbia would be to incorporate these provinces inside their own frontiers, and they resented the decision of the Congress of Berlin that had allowed Habsburg occupation. However, so long as the occupation was not turned into annexation, the Serbs preserved the hope that the provinces might some day become theirs, and meanwhile flooded them with agents and plotters. The Moslems, though favored by the Habsburg authorities, never reconciled themselves to the ending of Turkish rule, and the Catholics hoped to join Croatia.

Thus these provinces perpetually threatened to create an explosion that would rock the monarchy. The more intelligent observers in Vienna pressed for some sort of an all-south-Slav solution, not unlike that of Strossmayer. This would have put Dalmatia, Croatia, and Bosnia-Herzegovina together into a south-Slav kingdom under Francis Joseph, with the same status as Hungary—a triple rather than a dual monarchy. The advocates of this solution, known as "trialists," met the fiercest kind of hatred from the Magyars.

However, the Young Turk Revolution of 1908 caused the adventurous Austrian foreign minister Aehrenthal to fear that the status of the provinces might be changed. Fortified by a previous secret agreement with Russia, Aehrenthal simply annexed the two provinces in October, 1908, and announced that they would be given a diet of their own. This move precipitated a major European crisis (see below, p. 429), which threatened world war, but eventually blew over, leaving its deepest scars in Serbia. Serbian ambition to acquire the provinces now seemed permanently checked. The humiliation of Serbia, the disappointment of Russia, the solidarity of Germany with Austria-Hungary as revealed by the crisis, helped set the stage for the catastrophe of 1914. The discontent of the population of Bosnia, when added to the discontent of the Czechs and Italians in Austria, and of the Slovaks, Rumanians, Croats, and other south Slavs in Hungary, is the best single clue to the wartime weaknesses and postwar disintegration of the dual monarchy.

Yet the minority question, critical though it was, does not provide the entire answer. We must now briefly consider the Austrian-German and Hungarian majorities, both in their separate development and in their critical relationship to each other. Only then can we see that even the two ruling groups were subject to divisive forces that crippled them individually and together.

Austrian Society and Politics, 1867-1914

From the earliest days of the *Ausgleich*, the Austrian liberals fought the clerical conservatives. They legalized civil marriages, secularized all but religious instruction, canceled the concordat of 1855 after the proclamation of papal infallibility in 1870, and taxed church property (1873). These measures were the Austrian counterpart of the German *Kulturkampf*, but they were much milder, since Austria was 90 per cent Catholic and did not share the Protestant Prussian suspicion of the Vatican. The liberals were discredited by the financial crash of 1873, during which it was revealed that some of them had accepted bribes in return for voting in favor of charters for shady and unstable new companies. From this period dates the earliest political anti-Semitism in Austria, since some Jewish liberals were involved in the scandals and served as convenient scapegoats. Economic advance during the early years of the monarchy had brought the usual increase in the working class, which after the crash turned toward socialism in both its Marxist and its milder forms.

The Austrian aristocrats, who often owned great estates which they ruled almost like independent potentates, were on the whole frivolous in their tastes, and took little interest in the problems of the nineteenth and twentieth centuries. They squandered their incomes on high living and gambling, never realizing that their privileges brought them responsibilities. Yet they supplied almost all the political leadership that the nation got. The large size of their estates was one fundamental reason for the small size of the average peasant holding, and made it necessary even for landowning peasants to try to obtain part-time employment on a noble's property. The peasants' standard of living and level of literacy were extremely low, yet the influence of the clergy kept them subservient to their masters, loyal to the dynasty, and almost contented with their lot.

The middle class of town-dwellers and men of business, so familiar in western Europe, came later and was smaller in number in Austria. The wealthier tried to imitate the aristocracy's mode of life and to buy their way into the charmed circle. Others joined the professions, which they found overcrowded and badly paid. The unemployment of the intellectual is an extremely dangerous matter politically.

Among the bourgeoisie there were many

Jews. Numbering 5 per cent of the total population of Austria, the Jews (except for very few) could not be aristocrats, peasants, members of the clergy, bureaucrats, or army officers. So they were forced to enter trade, the professions, and the arts, where they often prospered and distinguished themselves. What we mean when we refer loosely to pre-war "Viennese" life, with its charm and gaiety, its cultivation, its music, its cafés, its high reputation in medicine and science, was the life of a society very largely Jewish or part-Jewish. Conversion, intermarriage, and assimilation were not uncommon among the upper-middle-class Jews.

Anti-Semitism, fanned by the continued migration of poorer Jews from regions of eastern Europe where oppression had rendered them squalid and uncouth, was general among the non-Jews of Austria. But we must distinguish between the social anti-Semitism of most aristocrats, which was often simply a form of snobbery, and the serious political anti-Semitism of the lower middle classes, often the unsuccessful competitors of the Jews in the world of small shop-keeping. Partly out of religious prejudice, partly out of distaste for the liberal politics usually preferred by the middle-class Jews, the clericals inveighed against them. The lower clergy, the demagogues among the lower middle classes, took the lead. One response among the Jews to the swelling chorus of anti-Semitism was Zionism (sponsorship of a Jewish state in Palestine), which originated in the dual monarchy.

The stresses and strains inherent in this social structure, aggravated by the problems of the national minorities, produced in the late nineteenth century two important new political movements among the Germans of Austria: Pan-Germanism and Christian Socialism. In the early 1880's, even moderate Austrian Germans wanted to hand over the Slavic lands of Austria to the Hungarians to rule, and then, stripped to the German core, to unite economically with Germany. The Pan-Germans were more radical and more violent. They opposed the Habsburg dynasty. They opposed the Catholic Church, and led a noisy movement called "Away from Rome" (*Los von Rom*). They demanded that Austria become Protestant and unite politically with Germany. They were furiously anti-Slav and anti-Semitic. They adored Bismarck and Wotan, but Bismarck did not encourage them. Their leader, Schönerer, himself a convert to Protestantism, was elected to the Austrian parliament in 1873 from the same district that later gave birth to Adolf Hitler. His followers always led the opposition to any attempt by the Austrian government to make concessions to the Czechs. But the pan-Germans never managed to become more than an extreme vocal minority.

The Christian Socialists, on the other hand, became the most important Austrian political party. Strongly Catholic and loyal to the Habsburgs, they appealed at the same time to the peasant and the small businessman by favoring social legislation and by opposing big business. They too were violently anti-Semitic. At first skeptical of the value of Christian Socialism, the clergy later made the movement its own, and especially in the country prevailed on the people to vote for its candidates. The most famous single Christian Socialist was the perennial Mayor of Vienna after 1895, Karl Lueger, the idol of the lower middle classes of the capital. For years he sponsored public ownership of city utilities, parks, playgrounds, free milk for schoolchildren, and other welfare services. Lueger always catered to his followers' hatred of Jews, Marxian socialists, and Magyars. Hitler, who saw Lueger's funeral procession in 1910, hailed him in *Mein Kampf* as the greatest statesman of his times. It is impossible to understand the doctrines of German Nazism in this century without understanding the social and racial structure of the Habsburg Monarchy in which Hitler grew up, and especially the doctrines and the appeal of Pan-Germanism and Christian Socialism.

To the Pan-Germans and the Christian Socialists, the Austrian Social Democrats, founded in 1888, responded with a Marxist program calling for government ownership of the means of production and for political action organized by class rather than by nationality. But the Austrian Social Democrats were not revolutionaries, and set as their goals such political and social gains as universal suffrage, secular education, welfare legislation, and the eight-hour day. They were usually led by intellectuals, many of them Jewish, but they were followed by an ever-increasing number of workers. Their pressure contributed to the broadening of the franchise in 1907 (see above, p. 300), and immediately afterward they raised their number of seats in parliament from 11 to 87.

On the nationality question, Social Democratic leaders strongly urged a reform in the direction of democratic federalism. Each nationality should have control of its own affairs in its own territory; in mixed territories, minorities should be protected; and a central parliament should decide matters of common interest. Cultural autonomy for the nationalities of a multi-national state was by no means an impractical or doctrinaire Marxist idea. Its practicality was later attested by the Soviet Russians, faced as they were with a similar problem and much influenced by the thinking of Austrian Social Democrats on the question. Otto Bauer, a doctrinaire Marxist, tried to explain away national antagonisms in the Empire as a manifestation of class warfare. But the program of another Social Demo-

CHAPTER XXII

crat, Karl Renner, who lived to be chancellor of the Austrian Republic when it was founded in 1919 and again when it was re-created in 1945, might have averted the necessity for the foundation of any republic at all. A believer in the dual monarchy, Renner advocated treating the nationalities as if they were churches, and allowing each citizen to belong to whatever one he chose. Each of these "national associations" would have its own schools, and disagreements among them would be settled by a high court of arbitration. Who is to say that if these reasonable and totally undoctrinaire views had been adopted, the monarchy might not have been preserved? As it was, the political tensions among the ruling German group in Austria only helped create intolerable weakness.

Hungarian Society and Politics, 1867-1914

In Hungary, the social structure was somewhat different. The great landed gentry, owning half of Hungary in estates of hundreds of thousands of acres apiece, were of course a small class numerically. Loyal to the dynasty, sometimes kind to their tenants, and socially contemptuous of all beneath them, they were often intelligent and discriminating, yet more often just as frivolous and empty-headed as their Austrian counterparts. But Hungary had a far larger class of country gentlemen, the squirearchy, whose holdings were far smaller and whose social position was lower, but whose political influence as a group was even greater. After the emancipation of the serfs in 1848, and during subsequent periods of uncertain agricultural conditions, many members of the gentry became civil servants or entered the professions. The peasantry suffered from small holdings, insufficient education, primitive methods of farming, and a low standard of living.

The Magyars were country folk, and the towns for centuries had been centers for Germans and Jews. But during the nineteenth century, the towns became steadily more Magyar, as members of the gentry and peasantry moved into them. The Jewish population grew enormously during the same period, mostly by immigration from the north and east. In Hungary, many Jews were converted and assimilated and became strongly Magyar in sentiment and behavior. When they grew rich enough, they bought land and titles, and became gentry. But here too they were greatly disliked, especially among the poorer city population, and in the countryside, where they were associated with money-lending and tavern-keeping, two professions that kept the peasant in their debt. Yet though anti-Semitism existed in Hungary, it never gained as many followers or became as important a political movement as in Austria.

At the bottom of the social pyramid was a small class (never more than 20 per cent of the population) of industrial workers in the cities, mostly in the textile and flour-milling industries. Wages were low, and living and working conditions were abominable, like those in Russia rather than those in the West. Yet more and more welfare measures were passed toward the end of the century. Because of its feebleness and lack of self-consciousness, this class could not be organized into an effective socialist party.

Although the Catholic Church was immensely powerful and rich in Hungary as in Austria, Catholicism was the faith only of about 60 instead of 90 per cent of the population. Some Hungarian magnate families and many of the gentry had never returned to Catholicism after the Reformation. They remained Calvinists. Several hundred thousand Germans, chiefly in Transylvania, were Lutheran. And in Transylvania also there were Magyar Unitarians. Clericalism could never become in Hungary the dominant force it was in Austria, and consequently the Catholic Church could not exert so great a political influence in Hungary.

Thus, because of its differing social and religious structure, Hungary could not produce strong parties like the Austrian Social Democrats and Christian Socialists. Austria had a relatively liberal franchise before 1907 and universal manhood suffrage thereafter. Hungary, in contrast, never really changed its law of 1874, by which only about 6 per cent of the population could vote. Moreover, Magyars of all shades were pretty well united in their determination to subjugate the national minorities in Hungary. Internal political or social issues, therefore, did little to determine Hungarian political alignments. The only real issue, and the chief source of Magyar political differences, was the question of Hungary's position in the dual monarchy.

Hungarian opponents of the *Ausgleich* were in the early days organized into two groups. The Kossuthists favored complete independence; a slightly more moderate party called the "Tigers" wished to improve the position of Hungary inside the monarchy by securing for the Hungarians control over their own army, over diplomatic service, and over finances, and by limiting the tie with Austria to the person of the monarch. When the great Deák passed from public life, one of the Tigers, Coloman Tisza, abandoned his opposition to the *Ausgleich,* joined the pro-*Ausgleich* Deákists, and came to power in 1875, to govern as prime minister for the next fifteen years. Thereafter, this merger of the Tigers and Deákists dominated Hungary except for the period from 1905 to 1910, and stayed in power largely by electoral manipulation.

Called the Liberals, this group resisted any reform of the franchise and agrarian conditions, or of the treatment of the minorities. Kossuthists maintained their opposition to the *Ausgleich.*

Toward 1890, angered by an incident in which an Austrian general put wreaths on the graves of Austrian officers killed during the Hungarian revolution of 1848, the Kossuthists began to press ever more violently for a purely national army. They did so even though Hungarian troops were now commonly kept together and put under the command of Hungarian officers. Specifically, the Kossuthists demanded that the language of command for all Hungarian troops in the imperial armies be Magyar—a typical piece of chauvinism of the sort to which Magyar extremists were addicted. Tisza refused to endorse this demand, and soon afterwards retired over the immediate issue whether to grant honorary Hungarian citizenship to the 88-year-old Kossuth, who was still in exile.

The Kossuthists grew in power after their sainted leader died and his son came back to head the party. He took a formal oath to the Crown, but still pressed for independence (1894). The one-thousandth anniversary of the arrival of the Magyars in Hungary (1896) and the discussions on the economic arrangements for the next decade with Austria (1897-8) both stimulated the Kossuthists. They began to boycott Austrian goods, and continued to use every excuse, no matter how trivial, for anti-Austrian agitation. In 1902, the provision that Hungary's contribution to the common army should be increased proportionally with the increase in population led the Kossuthists and other nationalists to demand once more that the Magyar language be used to command Hungarian troops, and that they be allowed to carry the Hungarian flag. When the ministry refused to make these demands its own, the Kossuthists be-

CHAPTER XXII

gan to filibuster, and effectively paralyzed the Hungarian parliament.

Since the Emperor refused to yield to pressure, the crisis between Magyar separatists and the government grew ever more acute. Coloman Tisza's son, Stephen, became premier in 1903, and worked through the increasing storm to preserve the *Ausgleich*. When he tried to limit debate in order to permit the accomplishment of official business, his opponents wrecked the parliament chamber. He called an election in 1905, but he was defeated by an opposition coalition including the Kossuthists, who now won a majority. When Francis Joseph refused to meet the demands of the new majority and appointed a loyal general as premier, the Kossuthists screamed military dictatorship, cheered in parliament for Norway, which had recently separated itself from Sweden, and urged patriots not to pay taxes or perform military service.

Actually, the entire struggle between the partisans of dualism and those of independence moved only the ruling caste of Magyars, and bore no relation whatever to the sentiments and needs of the larger part of the population. To mitigate the struggle, Francis Joseph had only to threaten to decree universal suffrage for Hungary, as he intended to do in Austria. This would open the gates to the discontented minorities, and would encourage social and economic change. Under this threat, the opposition coalition eventually yielded (1906) and voted the necessary economic and military laws. They obtained the right to revise the franchise themselves, a task they had every interest in putting off. Yet a new crisis arose in 1908-1910 over the establishment of a separate Hungarian bank, which Francis Joseph would not permit until the franchise had been revised.

In 1910, the younger Tisza, who had refurbished the Liberal party and now called it the Party of National Work, won a victory in the elections by the time-honored methods of corruption and intimidation. Worried about war with Russia and convinced that Austria and Germany were necessary allies for Hungary, Tisza dropped the separatists' demands, which had been convulsing the country for more than a decade. Hungary got no bank, no separate army, and no substantial franchise reform. Kossuthists had to be removed by force from parliament, and gag-rule had to be imposed. Tisza was kept busy fighting sabre duels with the Kossuthist leaders. In this atmosphere, Hungary received the news that the heir to the throne had been assassinated.

IV: Russia, 1825-1914

Character of the Empire

The third and largest of the great eastern European empires, Russia, took far longer, as was its way, to catch up with the political and social developments elsewhere in Europe. Thus there was no parliament in Russia until after the revolution of 1905, and even then the tsardom was able to weaken and eventually to dominate the new representative body. Serfdom did not disappear until 1861, and agrarian problems were in some ways intensified by the liberation of the peasants. Each time reform came, in the 1860's and in 1905 and 1906, it came as a direct result of military defeat abroad, which rendered reform absolutely essential. Thus the reforms of Alexander II (1855-1881) were inspired by Russia's defeat in the Crimean War (1854-56), and the revolution of 1905 was made possible by Russia's failure in the Russo-Japanese War (1904-1905). During most of the nineteenth and early twentieth centuries, even after the reforms, the Russian tsars claimed for themselves the same autocratic rights that Peter the Great and his Muscovite predecessors had exercised. Thus the Russian people experienced long periods of reaction: the entire reign of Nicholas I (1825-1855), and a protracted period from 1866 through 1904, including the last fifteen years of Alexander II's reign (1866-1881), the whole of Alexander III's (1881-1894), and the first ten years of Nicholas II's (1894-1917), the last of the tsars.

The failure to adjust willingly to the currents of the times and the attempt to preserve autocratic rule produced unparalleled discontent in Russia. Disillusioned and angry intellectuals in the 1830's and 1840's gave way to proponents of social change in the 1850's and early 1860's, and then to determined revolutionaries and terrorists in the late 1860's and the years that followed. Although Marxist literature was known early in Russia, and Marxist political groupings existed after 1896, the Marxists were by no means either the most numerous or the most effective of Russian revolutionaries. Native non-Marxist revolutionary parties long performed the killings and other acts of violence that convulsed the regime and won the support of large groups of Russians. It was only Lenin's transformation of the Marxist doctrines and his adaptation of Marx to the Russian scene that made it possible for his Bolsheviks to emerge as an important threat. And it was only Lenin's supreme tactical skill and boldness that enabled him to bring his Bolsheviks, still a minority, to power during

the revolution of 1917, a movement that was itself made possible by Russian losses in still another war. There was nothing inevitable about the triumph of the Bolsheviks (see Chapter XXVI).

Despite censorship and an atmosphere of repression, Russia experienced during the nineteenth century an amazing literary flowering. Poets, novelists, and playwrights produced works that rank with the greatest of all time. Like a sudden blossoming of orchids on an iceberg, the Russian literary renaissance cannot easily be explained. The literary talents of the Russian people had long lain dormant, and now awoke in an expression of unparalleled vigor and beauty.

Amid the official attempts to preserve sixteenth-century patterns, Russia experienced the impact of nineteenth- and twentieth-century industrialization. New resources were developed, thousands of miles of railroads were built, and factories sprang up, engaged in both heavy and light industry. A new laboring class thronged the cities, as elsewhere in Europe, but it lived and worked under conditions far worse than those in any other country. The native Russian revolutionaries looked to the peasants, in traditional Russian fashion, to provide them with their base, and they considered peasant problems paramount. The Marxists, on the other hand, true to the teachings of their master, recruited their following among this new proletariat, and focused their attention on its problems. But they deliberately relied for their tightly organized leadership almost exclusively on a little body of intellectuals and theorists.

Nicholas I (1825-1855)

Coming to the throne amid the disorders of the Decembrist Revolution (see above, Chapter XIX), Nicholas I (1825-1855) remarked sardonically that this was a *nice* beginning for his reign. Deeply curious about the motives of the noble revolutionaries, the Tsar himself personally presided over the investigation into their movement and prescribed their punishment. He used their confessions as a source of information on the state of Russian opinion. Nicholas I has been more resoundingly damned by liberals, both Russian and foreign, than has any other tsar. They have portrayed him as a kind of scarecrow of an autocrat. Reactionary and autocratic though he was, literal-minded and devoted to military pursuits, he was perhaps not such an inflexible tyrant as he has been made out.

Nicholas I worked hard at the business of the state, and firmly believed that the imperial word was sacred. Although he despised all constitutions, he honored the liberal constitution which his elder brother Alexander had granted to the Poles (see above, p. 175) until the Poles themselves revolted. He believed that his own autocratic power had been ordained by God; the autocrat could not, even if he wished, limit his own authority. Naturally such a man loathed the thought of revolution anywhere, and was perfectly prepared to cooperate abroad with the Metternich system. At home, he was prepared to make changes and improvements, but not to touch the fundamental institution of the autocracy. Though he was uneasy over the dangers inherent in serfdom, he was afraid to reform it in any serious way, because he feared that concessions would stimulate revolution among the peasants. Nicholas leaned heavily on the nobility as a class, referring to its members as his "benevolent police-chiefs."

So personal was Nicholas' rule that his own chancery or secretariat became the most important organ of Russian government. He enlarged it by creating several sections, including a notorious "third section" for political police activity, which spread rapidly and kept Russian political life under surveillance. This enormous expansion of the Tsar's own secretariat did not result in the abolition of any of the older organs of government. Consequently, bureaucratic confusion became very great, paper work was multiplied, and much injustice was done through sheer incompetence. Although the Russian laws were collected for the first time since 1649, the collection was not a true codification or modernization.

In the field of education, Nicholas favored the improvement of technical schools, but was deeply worried about the possibility that subversive foreign ideas might penetrate into the universities. After the Revolutions of 1848 in Europe, his reactionary minister of education, Uvarov, abolished the study of philosophy in the University of St. Petersburg, because, as he said, the usefulness of the subject had not been proved, and it might do harm. Uvarov formulated Nicholas' policies under the three heads of Autocracy, Orthodoxy, and Nationality: the unlimited power of the monarch, the sanctity of the Russian Church, and the adoption of policies in accordance with the "Russian national character." The result was a police-state, complete with censorship and terror, yet not nearly so efficient as a twentieth-century despotism.

We have already seen Nicholas putting down the Polish revolution of 1830 and intervening in 1849 to restore Hungary to the Habsburgs (see Chapter XIX). He believed in dynastic friendships, and counted on the alliance with Prussia and Austria without realizing that conflicting national interests were more important than friendships between monarchs. Thus he failed to see that Prussia would combat his own efforts to thwart the unification of Germany, and that Austria's interests conflicted with his own in southeastern Europe. It was partly Nicholas' failure to see the weaknesses of his own system of alliances that led him into the disastrous Crimean War.

The Crimean War

Like other Russian leaders before him, Nicholas confidently expected the collapse of the Ottoman Empire. Russia wished to protect the Orthodox subjects of the sultan, and also had important economic interests at stake. The great Russian wheat-producing areas in the south were being developed in earnest, and Odessa on the Black Sea had become a great commercial port for the grain trade. Nicholas hoped to establish a Russian sphere of influence in the Balkans, and even to take possession of Istanbul itself. We have already witnessed his intervention in the Greek War of the 1820's (see Chapter XIX). When the governor of Egypt, Mehemet Ali, revolted against the Ottoman Sultan in 1832 and threatened Istanbul, Nicholas landed a Russian army and got credit for saving the sultan's capital.

In 1833, the Turks paid the bill for these services by signing the Treaty of Unkiar Skelessi with Russia. Nicholas took the Ottoman Empire under his protection, and the Turks agreed to close the Straits (the Bosporus and Dardanelles) to the warships of any nation. Alarmed at the preponderance that the treaty gave to Russia in an area of the world vital to British imperial and commercial interests, British diplomacy turned its efforts to undoing it. The next time Mehemet Ali revolted, in 1839, the British were able to put him down with their fleet before he came within distance of a Russian land force. In 1841, all the other important powers joined Russia in guaranteeing the integrity of Turkey, thus putting an end to the exclusive position obtained by Russia at Unkiar Skelessi.

During the next twelve years (1841-1853), Nicholas tried to reach an agreement with Britain on what should be done with Ottoman territory if Turkey collapsed. The British did not believe that such collapse was imminent, and they hoped to prevent Russia from doing anything to hasten it. The two parties misunderstood each other. By 1853, the Tsar mistakenly felt that Britain was not opposed to Russian domination of Turkey, and Britain mistakenly believed that the Tsar would not act in Turkey without consulting her.

Then a dispute arose over whether the Roman Catholics, backed by Napoleon III, or the Orthodox clergy, backed by the Tsar, should have the right to perform certain functions in the Christian "Holy Places" in Palestine, which was still part of the Ottoman dominions. This trivial dispute was the immediate cause of the Crimean War. But the underlying cause was the Tsar's wish to re-establish the exclusive Russian position of the Unkiar Skelessi, and the British unwillingness to permit him to do so. Nicholas coupled a demand for this exclusive position with the demand that the Turks settle the dispute over the Holy Places amicably. The latter demand was possible; the former was not. When Nicholas occupied the Danubian principalities to enforce his demands, the situation became even tenser. And so, after many months of elaborate diplomatic negotiations in which all the powers strove to work out a suitable formula to avoid war, the drift toward war proved too strong to be checked.

Famous as the occasion of the charge of the Light Brigade, and of Florence Nightingale's pioneer efforts to save the lives of sick and wounded soldiers, the Crimean War consisted mostly of the siege of the great Russian naval base at Sebastopol in the Crimea. Military operations on both sides were inefficiently conducted, but eventually the Russians were compelled to surrender. In the Peace of Paris of 1856,

Russia was forbidden to fortify the Black Sea coast or to maintain a fleet there. This made it impossible for the Russians to defend their own shores or to conduct their shipping in security. It now became the paramount object of Russian foreign policy to alter the Black Sea clauses of the treaty. Not only had Russia lost the war, but Prussia had not helped her, and Austria had been positively hostile (see above, p. 295). Nicholas did not live to see the total failure of his policy. He died during the war, and was succeeded in 1855 by his son Alexander II (1855-1881).

Alexander II and Reform

By this time a very substantial segment of Russian public opinion favored reforms, in reaction to the long period of repression at home and failure abroad. Moreover, the economic developments of the early nineteenth century had rendered the system of serfdom less and less profitable. In the south, where land was fertile and crops were produced for sale as well as for use, the serf tilled his master's land usually three days a week, but sometimes more. In the north, where the land was less fertile and could not produce a surplus, the serfs often had a special arrangement with their masters called "quit-rent." This meant that the serf paid the master annually in cash instead of in work, and usually had to labor at home as a craftsman or go to a nearby town and work as a factory hand or small shopkeeper to raise the money. It is probable that about a quarter of the serfs of all Russia paid quit-rent by 1855. Neither in the south nor in the north was serfdom efficient in agriculture. As industries grew, it became clearer and clearer to factory owners who experimented with both serf and free labor that serf labor was not productive. Yet free labor was scarce, and the growing population needed to be fed. Many estates were mortgaged to state credit institutions, because of inefficient management and the extravagance of the landlords. Serfdom had become uneconomic.

But this fact was not widely realized among Russian landowners, who knew only that something had gone wrong somewhere. They wished to keep things as they were, but they did not as a class feel that emancipation was the answer. Yet the serfs showed increasing unrest, and cases of revolt rose in number. Abolitionist sentiment had now spread widely among intellectuals. Conscious of the unrest, Alexander II, though almost as conservative as his father, determined to embark on reforms, preferring, as he put it, that the abolition of serfdom come from above rather than from below. Through a cumbersome arrangement in which local commissions made studies and reported their findings to members of the government, an emancipation law was eventually formulated and proclaimed early in 1861.

A general statute declared that the serfs were now free, laid down the principles of the new administrative organization of the peasantry, and prescribed the rules for the purchase of land. A whole series of local statutes governed the particular procedure to be followed in the different provinces. Without going into details of the widely varying local practices, we may say that all peasants, crown and private, were freed, and that each peasant household received its homestead and a certain amount of land, usually the amount the peasant family had cultivated for its own use in the past. The land usually became the property of the village commune, which had the power to redistribute it periodically among the households. The government bought the land from the proprietors, but the peasants had to redeem it by payments extending

Ceremony during emancipation of Russian serfs.

over a period of 49 years. The proprietor retained only the portion of his estate that had been farmed for his own purposes.

This statute, liberating more than 40 million human beings, has been called the greatest single legislative act in history. There can be no doubt that it acted as an immense moral stimulus to peasant self-respect. Yet there were grave difficulties. The peasant had to accept the allotment, and since his household became collectively responsible for the taxes and redemption payments, his mobility was not greatly increased. The commune took the place of the proprietor, and differing local conditions caused great difficulty in administering the law. Moreover, the peasants in general got too little land, and had to pay too much for it. They did not get important forest and pasture lands. The settlement, however, was on the whole surprisingly liberal, despite the problems it failed to solve and despite the agrarian crises that developed in part as a result of its inadequacies.

The end of the landlords' rights of justice and police on their estates made it necessary to reform the entire local administration. By statute, in 1864, provincial and district assemblies, or *zemstvos*, were created. Chosen by an elaborate electoral system that divided the voters into categories by class, the assemblies none the less gave substantial representation to the peasants. The assemblies dealt with local finances, education, medical care, scientific agriculture, maintenance of the roads, and similar economic and social questions. Starting from scratch in many cases, the *zemstvos* made great advances in the founding of primary schools and the improvement of public health. They brought together peasant and proprietor to work out local problems. They served as schools of citizenship for all classes, and led tens of thousands of Russians to hope that this progressive step would be crowned by the creation of a central parliament, or *duma*. Despite the pressure that such men tried to bring on the government, the duma was not granted, partly because after the first attempt on the life of the Tsar in 1866 the regime swung away from reform and toward reaction.

But before this happened, other advances had been made. The populations of the cities were given municipal assemblies, with duties much like those of the *zemstvos* in the countryside. The Russian judicial

CHAPTER XXII

system and legal procedure, which were riddled with inequities, were reformed. For the first time, juries were introduced, cases were argued publicly and orally, all classes were made equal before the law, and the system of courts was completely overhauled. Censorship was relaxed, new schools were encouraged, the universities were freed from the restraints that Nicholas had imposed on them, and the antiquated and often brutal system of military service was modernized and rendered less severe.

Yet, despite all these remarkable advances accomplished in a relatively few years, Alexander II became the target for revolutionaries in 1866, and terrorist activity continued throughout the seventies until the assassins finally killed the Tsar in 1881. It is impossible to understand these developments without taking a brief look at Russian intellectual life under Nicholas and Alexander.

Russian Intellectual Life

Early in Nicholas' reign, Russian professors and students, influenced by German philosophers, were devoting themselves to passionate discussions on art, philosophy, and religion. Many intellectuals outside the universities followed suit. These were the first groups known as the "intelligentsia," a peculiarly Russian class. By the 1830's, they were beginning to discuss Russia's place in the world, and especially its true historical relationship to the West and the proper course for it to follow in the future. Out of their debates there arose two important opposing schools of thought: the "Westerners" and the "Slavophiles" (friends of the Slavs).

The Westerners stated their case in a famous document called the "Philosophical Letter," published in 1836, though written earlier. Its author, Chaadaev, lamented the damaging effect of Byzantine Christianity and the Tartar invasions upon Russian development, and declared that Russia had made no contribution to the world. He hailed Peter the Great's efforts at westernizing Russia as a step in the right direction. He regarded the Roman Church as the source of much that was fruitful in the West of which Russia had been deprived. Nicholas I had Chaadaev certified as insane, and commanded that he be put under house arrest with a physician visiting him every day. Yet, despite scorn and censorship, the Westerners could not be silenced. They continued to declare that Russia was a society fundamentally like the West, but that history had delayed its full development. Russia should now catch up. The implication was that the time had come for Russia to emerge from a period of absolutism and to enter upon the paths of parliamentary government and constitutional monarchy already trodden by the West.

In response, the opponents of the Westerners, the Slavophiles, vigorously argued that Russia had its own national spirit, like the *Volksgeist* that Herder (see Chapter XIX) had discovered in the Germans. Russia was, they maintained, essentially different from the West. The Orthodox religion of the Slavs was not legalistic, rationalistic, and narrow like the Roman Catholicism of the West, but substantial, emotional, and broad. The Slavophiles violently attacked Peter the Great for embarking Russia on a false course. The West ought not to be imitated but opposed. The Russian upper classes should turn away from their Europeanized manners, and look for inspiration to the simple Russian peasant who lived in the truly Russian institution of the village commune. Western Europe was urban and bourgeois; Russia was rural and agrarian. Western Europe was materialistic; Russia was deeply spiritual. Like the Westerners, the Slavophiles attached fundamental importance to the national religion, and made it the center of their arguments; but they praised where the Westerners damned. The Westerners' views had democratic and constitutional political implications; the Slavophiles' views had anti-constitutional and anti-democratic implications.

It is very important, however, to realize that this does not mean that the Slavophiles embraced the "nationality" doctrine of Nicholas I, or that they approved of his regime. These were not the chauvinist nationalists who appeared later. They opposed the tyranny and the bureaucratic machine of Nicholas I as bitterly as did the Westerners. But they wanted a patriarchal, benevolent monarchy of the kind they fancied had existed before Peter the Great, instead of a constitutional regime on the western pattern. Instead of a central parliament, they looked back with longing to the feudal Muscovite assembly, the *zemski sobor,* and to other institutions of the tsardom before Peter. Extremists among them went about the streets dressed in the old boyars' robes that Peter had made illegal. Many intellectuals shifted back and forth between the hotly debating camps, and few ever adopted in full the ideas of either side.

Alexander Herzen (1812-1870), for example, began his intellectual career as a Westerner and a devotee of French culture. The illegitimate son of a nobleman brought up in his father's house, he was charming, engaging, and highly intelligent. Like most Russians, he was not a good interpreter of western society, however, and was deeply fascinated with the thought that its structure might be rotten and doomed. The failure of the Paris revolution of 1848, which he saw as an eye-witness, convinced him that this was true, and he now became a revolutionary socialist. At the same time, he became convinced that the Westerners'

thesis must be wrong: how could Russia in a short time pass through the stages of development which the West had taken centuries to experience but which Russia had missed? So Herzen became a Slavophile. As a revolutionary, he preached the destruction of existing institutions, and as a Slavophile he looked to Russia, with its peculiar institution of the peasant commune, the *mir,* to provide an inspiration for all Europe. Herzen became an influential publicist and issued a Russian-language paper in London which was widely read by Russian intellectuals. His memoirs provide perhaps the best picture preserved to us of the intellectual ferment of the age of Nicholas.

Michael Bakunin (1814-1876) reached roughly the same conclusions as Herzen at roughly the same time. But he was a practical anarchist tactician who loved violence, not a peaceful man of letters (see also Chapter XX). He enjoyed participating in revolutions, and had a long career in and out of jail in most of the countries of Europe. He looked forward to a great revolution spreading perhaps from Prague to Moscow and thence to the rest of Europe, followed by a tight dictatorship; beyond this he was entirely vague about the future. Atheism was a fundamental part of his program—not a casual part, as it always was to the Marxists. In his long career, Bakunin was to exert from abroad a considerable influence on Russian radicals.

Nihilism, Populism, Terrorism

In the 1860's, and especially after the emancipation in Russia, the Russian "intelligentsia," like intellectuals elsewhere in Europe, reacted against the romanticism of their predecessors. Suspecting idealism, religion, and metaphysics, they turned now to a narrowly utilitarian view of art and society. As one of these young men said, a pair of shoes to him was worth more than all the madonnas of a great Renaissance painter. All art must have a social purpose, and the bonds holding the individual tightly to society must be smashed. Away with parental authority, with the marriage tie, with the tyranny of custom. For these people the name "nihilist" (a man who believes in nothing) quickly became fashionable. The portrait of a nihilist was drawn by the great novelist Turgenev in Bazarov, the hero of his novel *Fathers and Sons*. Rude and scornful, obstinate and arrogant, Bazarov was actually accepted as a model by intellectual leaders of youth in revolt against established ways of behavior. Yet nihilism as such was not a political movement, and many of the nihilists cared nothing for politics. They enjoyed shocking their parents by calling for an end to the old moral system, advocating, for instance, the extermination of everybody in Russia over the age of 25.

In the 1860's, many of these young Russian intellectuals went to Switzerland, where the proper Swiss bourgeoisie were scandalized at the men with their hair cut long and the girls with their hair cut short, at their loud voices and insolent behavior. The standard cartoonist's picture of a Russian revolutionary dates from the first startled glimpse which the Swiss had of the nihilists, who at the time had not even begun to be interested in political revolution. Herzen himself was shocked by their behavior. He died in 1870, his intellectual leadership forfeit. But Bakunin understood them, and influenced many of them during their stay in Switzerland. Bakunin urged them to go back to Russia and preach an immediate revolution to the peasants.

Also present in Switzerland were two other important Russian revolutionary thinkers: Lavrov and Tkachev. Lavrov (1823-1900) taught his followers that as intellectuals they owed a great debt to the Russian peasant, whose labor for many generations had enabled their ancestors to enjoy leisure and had made their own education possible. More gradual in his approach and more realistic in his estimates of the Russian peasant than Bakunin, Lavrov advised the nihilist students first to complete their education and then to return to Russia and go among the peasants, educating them and spreading among them propaganda for an eventual, not an immediate, revolution of the masses. On the other hand, Tkachev (1844-1886) taught that no revolution could ever be expected from the peasant masses, but that it would have to come from a tightly controlled small revolutionary elite, a little knot of conspirators who would seize power. Though not very influential at the time, Tkachev was important in Lenin's later thinking.

Under the impact of these teachers, especially Bakunin and Lavrov, Russian nihilism turned to a new kind of movement, which is called "populism." Young men and women, swept by idealistic fervor, decided to return to Russia and live among the peasants. When a government decree in 1872 actually summoned them back, they found that a parallel movement had already begun at home. About three thousand young people now took posts as teachers, innkeepers, or store-managers in the villages. Some tried to spread revolutionary ideas, others simply to render social service. Their romantic views of the peasantry were soon dispelled. The young populists did not know how to dress like peasants or how to talk to peasants. Suspicious of their talk, the peasants often betrayed them. The populists became conspicuous, and were easily traced by the police, who arrested them in droves. Two famous mass trials were held in the 1870's, at which the general public for the first time learned about the populist movement. After the trials, the populists who remained at large decided that they needed a determined revolutionary organization. With the formation of the "Land and Liberty" society in 1876, the childhood of the Russian revolutionary movement was over.

The revolutionaries had been stimulated by Alexander II's grant of reforms. So great had the discontent become that it is doubtful whether any Russian government could have proceeded fast enough to suit the radicals, who had come to believe in violent overturn of the regime and were not satisfied with piecemeal and gradual reform. Stemming from John Stuart Mill and from western Utopian socialists like Fourier and Robert Owen (see Chapter XX), Russian socialism was not yet greatly influenced by Marx. In some ways it was almost Slavophile, not urban but rural, not evolutionary but revolutionary, not a mass political party but a conspiracy. Its members lived underground and developed a conspiratorial psychology. They proposed to overthrow a bourgeois society before one ever got started. The movement became more and more radical, and in 1879 those who believed in the use of terror as a weapon separated from the others and founded the group called the *People's Will;* the anti-terrorists called themselves the *Black Partition.*

The members of the People's Will now went on a hunt for Tsar Alexander II himself. They shot at him and missed. They mined the track on which his train was traveling, and blew up the wrong train. They put dynamite under the dining room of the palace, and exploded it. But the Tsar was late for dinner that night, and eleven servants were killed instead. They rented a cheese-shop on one of the streets along which he drove, and tunneled under it. Finally they killed him (March, 1881) with a crude hand-made grenade, which blew

up the assassin too. The supreme irony was that Alexander II had that day signed a document designed to summon a consultative assembly, which everybody expected to lead to further constitutional reform. His successor, the reactionary Alexander III (1881-1894) refused to confirm the document, and Russia was left to stagnate in a renewed repression. The terrorists were rounded up and punished, and their organization was smashed. Despite their occasional high-flown claims to enormous popular support, they had never numbered more than a mere handful of people, and their movement had been a failure.

Foreign Policy under Alexander II

In foreign policy, Alexander II made an uneven record. In Europe, the Russians successfully repressed the Polish uprising of 1863. They seized the opportunity provided by the Franco-Prussian War of 1870, and simply tore up the Black Sea provisions of the Treaty of Paris, declaring unilaterally that they would no longer be bound by them. This was an illegal act, to which the powers later reluctantly gave their assent. It was another illustration of the immorality in international affairs that Bismarck had made fashionable.

In 1877, the Russians went to war against Turkey on behalf of the rebellious Balkan Christians of Bosnia, Herzegovina, and Bulgaria. By the peace of San Stefano, dictated early in 1878 to the defeated Turks, Russia obtained, contrary to her previous agreements, a large independent Bulgarian state, which Russian policy-makers hoped to turn into a useful Balkan satellite. But the powers at the Congress of Berlin later in the same year reversed the judgment of San Stefano. They permitted only about one-third of the planned Bulgaria to come into existence as an autonomous state, while another third obtained autonomy separately, and the rest went back to Turkey. Russian public opinion resented the powers' depriving Russia of the gains scored in the Russo-Turkish War. Bitterness ran particularly high among those who hoped to unite all Slavs in a kind of federation, the Pan-Slavs (not to be confused with the Slavophiles).

Meanwhile, in Asia, encroachments begun under Nicholas I against the Chinese territory in the Amur River valley were regularized by treaty in 1860. Russian settlements in the "maritime province" on the Pacific Ocean continued to flourish. In Central Asia, a series of campaigns conquered the Turkish khanates, and added much productive land to the crown. Here, however, the advance toward the northwest frontier of India brought Russia into a region of great interest to Britain, and fanned hostile public opinion in Britain.

The Reaction, 1881-1904

The reign of Alexander III and the first ten years of the reign of his son, Nicholas II, formed a quarter-century of consistent policies (1881-1904). Both tsars loathed liberalism as expressed in the earlier reforms, and were determined that there would never be any more of it. Yet a peasant bank set up under Alexander III made the redemption payments easier for the peasants to pay. And a few pieces of labor legislation enacted under the influence of Bismarck's example made working conditions a bit more tolerable—for example, hours were shortened for women workers. Offsetting these measures were the establishment of a special bank that extended credit to the impoverished nobility, the re-institution of rigorous censorship, and the institution in the countryside of so-called "rural leaders" or "land captains" in place of the elected justices of the peace of Alexander II. Election procedure for the *zemstvos* and for the city assemblies was made far less democratic. Now there began a vigorous persecution of the minority nationalities, a policy called "Russification," and quite in line with the "nationality" of Nicholas I's formula. The Finns, Poles, Ukrainians, Armenians, and Jews all suffered discrimination, varying from loss of their own institutions, which the Finns had enjoyed, to outright government-sponsored massacres in the case of the Jews. On his accession, Nicholas II referred to all hopes for a change as "senseless dreams."

These years were notable also for the steady growth of the Russian railroad network, largely built and owned by the state. The Donets coal basin was exploited for the first time; the Baku oil fields came into production; steel and cotton output soared. In 1892, there came to the Ministry of Finance a self-made railroad man, Witte, who for the next twelve years was personally responsible for the ever-mounting economic progress. Witte began the Trans-Siberian railroad, put Russia on the gold standard, attracted much foreign capital, especially French, for investment, and balanced the budget, in part through government monopoly of the sale of vodka. The railroad network doubled in length between 1894 and 1904, and the need for rails stimulated the steel industry. Correspondingly, the number of urban workers multiplied, and strikes called in protest against wretched working conditions mounted in number. In 1897, the working day was fixed by the state at eleven hours for adults, and other provisions were adopted to improve and regularize conditions. These, however, were difficult to enforce.

Under the circumstances, many of the young generation of revolutionaries now turned to Marxist scientific socialism, preaching the class struggle and predicting the inevitable downfall of capitalism. A small clandestine group of "intelligentsia," formed in 1894-1895 at St. Petersburg, proposed to overthrow the regime, working with all opponents of the class system. The members of the group included Lenin, a vigorous young intellectual of upper-middle-class origin, whose brother had been executed for an attempt on the life of Alexander III. In 1898, this group and others formed the Social Democratic party, which in 1900 began to publish its own newspaper. Within party ranks, grave dissension sprang up over the question of organization. Should the party operate under a strongly centralized directorate, or should each local group of Social Democrats be free to agitate for its own ends? In the tradition of Bakunin and Tkachev, Lenin insisted on the tightly knit little group of directors at the center. At the party congress of Brussels and London in 1903, the majority voted with him. Lenin's faction thereafter was called by the name Bolshevik, meaning majority, as against the Menshevik (minority) group, which favored a loose democratic organization for the party. Both groups remained Social Democrats, or SDs, as they were often called.

Meanwhile, the non-Marxist revolutionaries, who were the direct heirs of the People's Will tradition, also organized a political party. They were the Social Revolutionaries, or SRs, with their own clandestine newspaper. Where the SDs as Marxists were interested almost exclusively in the urban workers, the SRs as populists were interested in the peasantry. Their chief aim was to redistribute the land, but they continued in their terrorist ways. They assassinated several cabinet ministers, using as their slogan the cry, *We don't want reforms, we want reform.*

A third political grouping was that of the moderates and liberals, not SD or SR in orientation, but mostly veterans of the *zemstvos* and intellectuals indignant over the government's policies of repression who favored only such measures as compulsory free private education and agrarian reform. The regime stupidly made no distinction between these men and the die-hard terrorists or the rabid Marxists. Thus the moderates also gradually organized and had their own clandestine paper favoring a constitution and a national parliament for Russia. In 1905, they took the name Constitutional Democrats, and were thereafter usually referred to as Kadets, from the Russian initials KD. Faced by this political activity among its radical and moderate opponents, the government only tightened the reins, and by 1904 had adopted the view that a short victorious war was all that would be necessary to unite the country.

The Russo-Japanese War

Trans-Siberian railway construction made it desirable for the Russians to obtain a right of way across Chinese territory in Manchuria. They took the initiative in preventing Japan from establishing herself on the Chinese mainland after her defeat of China in 1895, and then required the Chinese in exchange to allow the building of the new railroad. In 1897, they seized Port Arthur, the very port they had earlier kept out of Japanese hands. Further friction with the Japanese took place in Korea, where both powers had interests. Then, after the Boxer Rebellion of 1900 in China (see Chapter XXIV), the Russians kept their troops in Manchuria after the other nations had withdrawn theirs. Although the Russians promised to withdraw their forces by stages, they failed to do so, largely because Russian foreign policy fell into the hands of shady adventurers, some of whom had a lumber concession in Korea and wanted war with Japan. After it became apparent that the war party had got control in Russia, the Japanese without warning attacked units of the Russian fleet anchored at Port Arthur in February, 1904. The Russo-Japanese War had begun.

Far from their bases and taken by surprise, the Russians none the less stabilized a front on land. But their fleet, which had steamed all the way around Europe and across the Indian Ocean into the Pacific, was decisively defeated by the Japanese in the battle of Tsushima (May 27, 1904). To the Russian people, the war was a mysterious, distant political adventure of which they wanted no part. Many intellectuals opposed it, and the SRs and SDs openly hoped for a Russian defeat, which they expected would shake the government's position. Alarmed at the growing unrest at home, the Russian government was per-

suaded by President Theodore Roosevelt to accept his mediation, which the Japanese also actively wished.

Witte, the go-getting businessman who had opposed the war from the first, was sent to Portsmouth, New Hampshire, as Russian representative. Here he not only secured excellent terms for Russia, but also won a favorable verdict from American public opinion, which had previously been strongly pro-Japanese and had thought of Russians as either brutal aristocrats or bomb-throwing revolutionaries. By the Treaty of Portsmouth (1905), Russia recognized the Japanese protectorate over Korea, ceded Port Arthur and the northern half of Sakhalin Island, together with fishing rights in the North Pacific, and promised to evacuate Manchuria. Russian prestige as a Far Eastern power was not deeply wounded or permanently impaired by the

Building the Trans-Siberian Railroad.

Sinking of a Russian warship during the battle of Tsushima, May 27, 1904.

reactionary minister of the interior, was assassinated by an SR bomb in July, 1904. His successor was a moderate. The *zemstvo* liberals, the future Kadets, were encouraged, and held banquets throughout Russia to adopt a series of resolutions for presentation to a kind of national congress of *zemstvo* representatives. Although the congress was not allowed to meet publicly, its program—a constitution, basic civil liberties, class and minority equality, and extension of *zemstvo* responsibilities—became widely known and approved. The Tsar temporized, issued so vague a statement that all hope for change was dimmed, and took measures to limit free discussion.

Ironically, it was a police agent of the government itself who struck the fatal spark. He had been planted in the St. Petersburg factories to combat SD efforts to organize the workers and to substitute his own union. He organized a parade of workers to demonstrate peacefully and to petition the Tsar directly for an eight-hour day, a national assembly, civil liberties, the right to strike, and a number of other moderate demands. When the workers tried to deliver the petition, Nicholas left town and ordered the troops to fire on the peaceful demonstrators, some of whom were carrying his portrait to demonstrate their loyalty. About a thousand workers were killed on "Red Sunday" (January 22, 1905). This massacre made revolutionaries out of the urban workers. Strikes multiplied, the moderate opposition joined with the radical opposition, and university students and professors demanded the same reforms as wild-eyed bomb-hurlers.

Amid mounting excitement, the government at first seemed to favor the calling of a *zemski sobor*, consultative, not legislative, in the old Russian pattern rather than the western parliamentary one, but still a national assembly of sorts. But then even this project was whittled away, as the timid,

defeat or by the treaty. Yet the effect of the defeat in Asia was to transfer Russian attention back to Europe, where the tempo of diplomacy and crisis now quickened and helped move the world toward war (see Chapter XXV.)

The Revolution of 1905

The most important immediate result of the Russo-Japanese War was its impact on Russian domestic developments. While it was still going on, Plehve, the

Workers fighting on the barricades in Moscow, 1905.

vacillating, and unintelligent Nicholas II listened to his reactionary advisers. Under the impact of delays and disappointments, demonstrations and outbreaks occurred during the summer of 1905. In October, the printers struck. No newspapers appeared, and the printers, with SD aid, formed the first "soviet" or workers' council. When the railroad workers joined the strike, communications were cut off between Moscow and St. Petersburg. Soviets now multiplied. Of the one formed in St. Petersburg, Lenin declared that it was "not a workers' parliament, nor an organization of proletarian autonomy, but a combat organization pursuing definite ends."

This reflects the Bolsheviks' view of the soviet as an instrument for the pursuit of their program of armed revolt, for the establishment of a provisional government, for the proclamation of a democratic republic, and for the summoning of a constituent assembly. This program, put forth by the most "extreme" of the revolutionaries of 1905, differed relatively little from the program of the most moderate liberals, who would, however, have kept the monarchy, and striven to obtain their ends by persuasion and pressure rather than by violence. At the time, and for years to come, the Bolsheviks, like other Marxists, accepted the view that it was necessary for Russia to pass through a stage of bourgeois democracy before the time for the proletarian revolution could come. They were therefore eager to help along the bourgeois revolution.

Nicholas was faced, as Witte told him, with the alternatives of imposing a military dictatorship and putting down the opposition by force, or of summoning a truly legislative assembly with veto-power over the laws. The Tsar finally chose the latter course, and in October, 1905, issued a manifesto that promised full civil liberties at once, and a legislative assembly or *duma* to be elected by universal suffrage. In effect, this famous October Manifesto put an end to the autocracy, since the duma was to be superior to the tsar in legislation.

Yet the issuance of the October Manifesto did not meet with universal approval or even end the revolution at once. On the Right, a government-sponsored party called the "Union of the Russian people" demonstrated against the manifesto, proclaimed its undying loyalty to the autocrat, and organized its own storm troops, or "Black Hundreds," which killed more than 3,000 Jews in the first week after the issuance of the manifesto. The armies returned from the Far East, and proved to be still loyal to the government. Thus the soviets of 1905, unlike those of 1917 (see Chapter XXVI), included only workers, and no soldiers. On the Left, the dissatisfied Bolsheviks and SRs made several attempts to launch their violent revolution, but failed, and the government was able to arrest their leaders and eventually to put them down after several days of street fighting in Moscow in December, 1905. In the Center, one group of liberals, pleased with the manifesto, urged that it be used as a rallying point for a moderate program. These were the Octobrists, so called after the month in which the manifesto had been issued. The other groups, the Kadets, wished to continue to agitate by legal means for further immediate reforms. But the real fires of revolution had burned out by the opening of the year 1906.

The Dumas, 1906-1914

Suffrage for the Duma was universal, but voters chose an electoral college who then selected the 412 deputies. Although SRs and SDs boycotted the elec-

tions out of discontent over the indirect election system, many of their number were elected. The Kadets were the strongest single party. Quite against the expectation of the government, the peasants' vote was not conservative, but highly liberal. But even before the first Duma had met, Witte was able to reduce its powers. He secured a large French loan, which made the government financially independent of the Duma, and issued a set of "fundamental laws," which the Duma was not to be competent to alter. The Crown was to continue to control war and foreign policy; the minister of finance was to control loans and currency. The tsar's council of state was transformed by adding members from the clergy, nobility, the *zemstvos*, the universities, and chambers of commerce. It became a kind of upper house, which had equal legislative rights with the Duma, and could therefore submit a rival budget, for example, which the government could then adopt in preference to that of the Duma. Finally, the tsar could dissolve the Duma at will, provided he set a date for new elections. When it was not in session he could legislate by himself, although his enactments had later to be approved by the Duma.

The first Duma, the "Duma of Popular Indignation," met between May and July, 1906. It addressed a list of grievances to the Tsar, asking for a radical land reform that would give the peasants all state and church land, and part of the land still in private hands. The government flatly refused to accept this attack on property, and after some parliamentary skirmishing the Duma was dissolved. The Kadet membership, maintaining incorrectly that the dissolution was unconstitutional, crossed the frontier into Finland, and there issued a manifesto urging the Russian people not to pay taxes or report for military service unless the Duma was recalled. Its authors were soon tried and declared ineligible for office; so future Dumas were deprived of the services of this capable Kadet group of moderates.

With the dissolution of the first Duma there came to power as chief minister the highly intelligent and conservative Peter Stolypin, who stayed in office until 1911, when he was assassinated. Together with Witte, he was the leading statesman of the last period of tsarist Russia. Stolypin put through a series of agricultural laws which enabled the peasants to free themselves from the commune. A peasant wishing to detach his property could demand that he be given a single tract, which meant that the scattered strips assigned to other families would also be consolidated so that each would obtain a single plot. This program Stolypin called the "wager on the strong and sober"; he was encouraging the initiative and enterprise of individual Russian peasants who had the will to operate on their own as successful small farmers. Stolypin hoped to create a responsible and conservative class of yeomen in Russia. His program accomplished much of what he hoped for. It is estimated that about a quarter of the peasant households of European Russia (almost 9,000,000) emancipated themselves from the communes during the years between 1906 and 1917. Only war and revolution kept the process from going still further. Lenin and others who hoped for revolution were deeply suspicious and afraid of Stolypin's agrarian reforms. They rightly feared that the peasant grievances would be removed, and understood that no revolution in Russia could in the end succeed without the peasants.

Simultaneously with his agrarian program, Stolypin carried on unremitting war against terrorists and other revolutionaries. He showed no hesitation in acting in the most unconstitutional fashion when it suited him. He did everything he could to interfere with the elections to the second Duma, but the SRs and SDs were well represented, and the Duma itself (March-June, 1907) would not work with the government. It was dissolved because it refused to suspend the parliamentary immunity of the SD deputies, whom Stolypin wanted to arrest.

After the dissolution of the second Duma, the government quite illegally altered the election laws, cutting the number of delegates from the peasants and national minorities, and increasing the number from the gentry. By this means the government got a majority, and the third Duma (1907-1912) and the fourth (1912-1917) lived out their constitutional lives of five years apiece. Unrepresentative and limited in their powers though they were, they were still national assemblies. In their sessions the left-wingers could be heard, and could question ministers like any other member. The Dumas improved the conditions of peasant and worker, and helped strengthen national defense as the World War drew closer. Their commissions, working with individual ministers, proved extremely useful in increasing the efficiency of government departments. The period of the third Duma, however, was also notable for the continuation of "Russification," and the Finns in particular lost their remaining rights (1910).

Under the fourth Duma, the government, with Stolypin dead, tended more toward reaction. The Leftists organized busily for another revolution, working in unions, cooperatives, evening classes for workmen, and a whole network of other labor organizations. A vast web of police spies challenged them at every turn. Meanwhile, the imperial family drifted into a very dangerous situation, as the fanatically religious and autocratically minded empress fell more and more under the sway of a half-mad, wholly evil, dirty, ignorant, and power-hungry monk from Siberia. This man, Rasputin, had the mysterious ability, possibly hypnotic, to stop the bleeding of the young heir to the throne, who suffered from hemophilia. Since the Empress had enormous influence on her beloved husband, Nicholas II, Rasputin became in a real sense the ruler of Russia, much to the horror of a great many loyal supporters of the imperial house, and greatly to the detriment of the rational conduct of affairs in an enormous twentieth-century state. At the moment when the World War began, Russia was in the throes of a major crisis precipitated by the government's reactionary policies, the scandal of Rasputin's influence, and the indignation of the loyal Duma.

V: Conclusion

Parliamentary government was, as we have seen, a comparative stranger to the three eastern European empires. The King of Prussia, with Bismarck's help, used his extraordinary military system to conquer and unify Germany. He imposed on all non-Austrian Germans the Prussian system of autocracy almost undiluted by a weak and subservient parliament, and backed by the army and the Junkers. The Habsburg emperor, though faced after 1907 with an Austrian parliament elected by universal suffrage, in 1914 still made virtually all policy decisions by himself. The Hungarian parliament was never genuinely representative, and the emperor successfully used universal suffrage as a threat to quell Magyar separation. The tsars, forced at last by defeat in wars to grant a modified constitution in 1905, were still able to hamstring their own central legislative body, and to wield a preponderant personal influence in politics.

In all three countries, none the less, for the first time in their history, modern political parties during this period coalesced around principles. As in the West, the governments collaborated with parties or coalitions of parties, but always faced an opposition. What a party stood for was determined largely by the peculiar circumstances of the country that gave it birth. Yet certain parallels reached across national boundaries. Although no group in Russia can be compared with the German Catholic Center, the Austrian Christian Socialists do resemble it in many ways. No group in either Germany or Austria is comparable with the Russian populists (Social Revolutionaries). Yet German Liberals, Austrian Liberals, and Russian Kadets or Octobrists can perhaps be roughly equated. So can the Pan-Germans with the Pan-Slavs. The Social Democrats were Marxist in all three countries, but increasingly less revolutionary in Germany and Austria-Hungary, and increasingly more so in Russia.

All three countries during this period experienced a striking economic boom and an occasional depression; the industrial revolution struck them late, but with terrific impact. By the turn of the twentieth century, Germany had made such advances that its steel production surpassed that of England, and was second in the world only to that of the United States. Though far behind Germany both in resources and in technology, Austria-Hungary too was becoming rapidly industrialized. In Russia, transport and industry boomed.

Yet in all three countries, the landed nobility continued to exercise political influence quite out of proportion to their numbers. Everywhere the existence of a new and underprivileged class of urban workers stimulated intellectual leaders to form Marxist political groups, to preach the class struggle, and, except in Russia, to strive for immediate improvements in conditions rather than for the violent overthrow of the regime. Last of all the European countries, Russia emancipated her serfs in 1861, and began a new era of agrarian experiment and unrest. In Germany, protection was the great agrarian issue after the late 1870's. In Austria-Hungary, the peasants suffered with docility.

All three countries had minority problems of varying seriousness. Germany persecuted the Poles and, after 1871 and less severely, she persecuted the Alsatians and Lorrainers. More and more, Russia persecuted the Finns, Poles, Ukrainians, and Armenians. In Austria-Hungary alone, however, the minority problem proved fatal. German anti-Slav sentiment in Austria, and Magyar mistreatment of all non-Magyars in Hungary, alienated potentially loyal subjects, and finally helped explode the state from inside. In all three countries the Jews created a special problem and suffered different degrees of discrimination and persecution.

In Germany, a combination of circumstances led first to an assault by the government on the Catholic Church and then to an alliance between the government and the Catholic political party. In the Habsburg Monarchy, a milder anticlericalism had its day, but the Church retained its hold on the population and continued to exercise enormous political influence. In Russia, the Orthodox Church as usual played almost no role in the cultural development of the people. But one group of influential intellectuals attacked it as the source of Russia's troubles, while another group hailed the Church as the true source of Russia's strength and the fountainhead of all national virtue.

So it was that the main currents of the time flowed with uneven force over the Germans, Austrians, and Russians. Nationalism, materialism, militarism, imperialism, clericalism, constitutionalism, landlordism, and socialism were all experienced to a varying degree by all the countries. What determined each country's answer to social pressure, however, was its own peculiar past and its own peculiar character.

Reading Suggestions
on Central and Eastern Europe

General Accounts

R. C. Binkley, *Realism and Nationalism, 1852-1871* (New York: Harper and Brothers, 1935). Though this volume, in the "Rise of Modern Europe" series, develops a somewhat implausible thesis about the possibilities of "federative polity," it provides an often illuminating discussion of the period indicated.

C. J. H. Hayes, *A Generation of Materialism, 1871-1900* (New York: Harper and Brothers, 1941). Another volume in the "Rise of Modern Europe" series, this does some penetrating probing beneath the surface of an apparently successful era, particularly in Germany.

A. J. P. Taylor, *The Struggle for Mastery in Europe, 1848-1918* (Oxford: The Clarendon Press, 1954). The first volume to be published in "The Oxford History of Modern Europe"; crisp and provocative.

Special Studies: Germany

R. Flenley, *Modern German History* (New York: E. P. Dutton & Co., 1953) and K. S. Pinson, *Modern Germany, Its History and Civilization* (New York: The Macmillan Company, 1954). Two textbooks, of which Pinson's is the longer and Flenley's perhaps the more useful.

A. J. P. Taylor, *The Course of German History* (New York: Coward-McCann, 1946). A lively essay on the period since 1815, with strong, but not unreasonable, anti-German overtones.

F. Meinecke, *The German Catastrophe* (Cambridge, Mass.: Harvard University Press, 1950). A useful antidote to Taylor, by a very great German historian.

T. Veblen, *Imperial Germany and the Industrial Revolution*, new ed. (New York: Viking Press, 1954). An old, brilliant, and still very important analysis by a great American sociologist.

J. H. Clapham, *The Economic Development of France and Germany, 1815-1914*, 3rd ed. (Cambridge, Eng.: The University Press, 1928). A somewhat out-of-date but still instructive introduction to the subject.

F. Darmstaedter, *Bismarck and the Creation of the Second Reich* (London: Methuen & Co., 1948). A valuable study.

E. Eyck, *Bismarck and the German Empire* (London: George Allen and Unwin, 1950). Translation and condensation of a large standard work in German.

Special Studies: The Habsburg Monarchy

A. J. May, *The Hapsburg Monarchy, 1867-1914* (Cambridge, Mass.: Harvard University Press, 1951). Concise general account.

A. J. P. Taylor, *The Habsburg Monarchy, 1809-1918*, 2nd ed. (London: Hamish Hamilton, 1948). A spirited brief treatment.

R. A. Kann, *The Multinational Empire*, 2 vols. (New York: Columbia University Press, 1950). A monograph, arranged nationality by nationality, and discussing national sentiments and the government's efforts to deal with them.

O. Jászi, *The Dissolution of the Habsburg Monarchy* (Chicago: University of Chicago Press, 1929). From a rare point of view, that of the liberal Magyar.

R. W. Seton-Watson, *German, Slav, and Magyar* (London: Williams and Norgate, 1916). By the greatest British authority on southeast Europe, the author of many other valuable studies of the area.

E. Wiskemann, *Czechs and Germans* (London: Oxford University Press, 1938). A good case history of national antagonisms.

Special Studies: Russia

H. Seton-Watson, *The Decline of Imperial Russia, 1855-1914* (New York: Praeger, 1952). The only sound work in English covering virtually all the period dealt with in this chapter.

G. T. Robinson, *Rural Russia under the Old Regime*, 2nd ed. (New York: The Macmillan Company, 1949). A splendid monograph on the peasant question.

R. Hare, *Pioneers of Russian Social Thought* (New York: Oxford University Press, 1951). Chapters, varying in value, on the chief non-Marxist thinkers of nineteenth-century Russia.

CHAPTER XXII

N. V. Riasanovsky, *Russia and the West in the Teaching of the Slavophiles* (Cambridge, Mass.: Harvard University Press, 1953). A useful study of one side of the chief intellectual controversy of the period.

D. Footman, *Red Prelude* (New Haven: Yale University Press, 1945). A good biography of Zhelyabov, *narodnik* and terrorist.

B. Pares, *The Fall of the Russian Monarchy* (London: Jonathan Cape, 1939). An excellent study of the period between 1905 and 1917; by an authority who was frequently on the spot.

A. Herzen, *My Past and Thoughts,* 6 vols. (London: Chatto and Windus, 1924-1927). The classic picture of nineteenth-century Russia, by its most distinguished rebel.

S. Witte, *Memoirs* (New York: Doubleday & Co., 1921). The somewhat apologetic memoirs of the man who did most to industrialize imperial Russia.

B. D. Wolfe, *Three Who Made a Revolution* (New York: Dial Press, 1948). A fine triple study of Lenin, Trotsky, and Stalin; with emphasis on the period before 1914.

A. Lobanov-Rostovsky, *Russia and Asia,* rev. ed. (Ann Arbor, Mich.: G. Wahr, 1951). A useful introductory survey.

B. H. Sumner, *Russia and the Balkans, 1870-1880* (Oxford: The Clarendon Press, 1937). A monograph including a helpful discussion of Panslavism.

Historical Fiction

T. Mann, *Buddenbrooks* (New York: Pocket Books, Inc.). Inexpensive reprint of a long novel about a family in imperial Germany.

G. Hauptmann, *The Weavers, Hannele, The Beaver Coat* (New York: Rinehart & Co., 1951). Three plays that convey some of the flavor of nineteenth-century Germany.

R. Musil, *The Man without Qualities* (New York: Coward-McCann, 1953). A novel steeped in the atmosphere of pre-1914 Vienna.

M. Jókai, *Eyes Like the Sea* (New York: G. P. Putnam's Sons, 1901). Fictionalized autobiography of a romantic Hungarian novelist, the author of many novels that give insights into Magyar nationalism.

I. Turgenev, *Fathers and Sons* (sometimes called *Fathers and Children*—many editions) and *Smoke* (New York: E. P. Dutton & Co., 1949. Everyman ed.). Superb contemporary realistic fiction reflecting Russian intellectual and political life.

F. Dostoevsky, *The Brothers Karamazov* (New York: Modern Library, 1937) and *Crime and Punishment* (New York: Modern Library, 1932). Famous novels depicting the turbulent life of Russian intellectuals in the mid-nineteenth century; more romantic in tone than Turgenev's works.

The Portable Chekhov (New York: Viking Press, 1947). A selection from the short stories and plays of A. Chekhov, a skillful portraitist of the upper classes in tsarist Russia.

L. Tolstoy, *Anna Karenina* (New York: Modern Library, 1935). A celebrated novel set in late nineteenth-century St. Petersburg and the countryside.

The Intellectual Revolution

CHAPTER XXIII

I: Darwinism

IN 1859 there was published in London a volume on natural history that began with the true scientist's caution:

When on board H.M.S. 'Beagle,' as naturalist, I was much struck with certain facts in the distribution of the organic beings inhabiting South America, and in the geological relations of the present to the past inhabitants of that continent. These facts, as will be seen in the latter chapters of this volume, seemed to throw some light on the origin of species—that mystery of mysteries, as it has been called by one of our greatest philosophers. On my return home, it occurred to me, in 1837, that something might perhaps be made out on this question by patiently accumulating and reflecting on all sorts of facts which could possibly have any bearing on it. After five years' work I allowed myself to speculate on the subject, and drew up some short notes; these I enlarged in 1844 into a sketch of the conclusions, which then seemed to me probable: from that period to the present day I have steadily pursued the same object. I hope that I may be excused for entering on these personal details, as I give them to show that I have not been hasty in coming to a decision.*

Darwin's *On the Origin of Species by Means of Natural Selection,* thus modestly

---

* Charles Darwin, *The Origin of Species,* Introduction.

and cautiously introduced to the public, is one of the books that mark a revolution in intellectual history. Like all important revolutions, the Darwinian was no bolt from the blue. Into Darwin's work had gone long years of preparation, not merely those of Darwin's own life, but those of his predecessors and colleagues in the scientific study of what was then called natural history and is now called biology. From his work flowed consequences that were to be important far beyond the field of biology. Indeed the term revolution, accurate though it is in many ways, is perhaps not the best one to describe the work of Darwin. It may better be seen as a kind of focusing lens into which are gathered a wide range of rays.

Darwin himself was a biologist, and he thought always of his work as a study aimed at understanding how living individual organisms came to be what they were. He lived to see his ideas expanded, adapted, indeed often exaggerated, as they were applied to politics, economics, religion, to the whole complex fabric of human activities. He realized the implications of his scientific work for man's whole attitude toward the universe. But he stuck to his last, which was biology, leaving to men like T. H. Huxley and Herbert Spencer the task of making Darwinism into a creed for living. Karl Marx once said, "I am not a Marxist." Darwin might also have said, "I am not a Darwinist."

We must then begin with Darwin's own ideas in biology. He was a careful and conscientious observer, with a great fund of facts; but his mind was always searching for the law, the theory, that would tie the facts together. The set of facts before him was the long record of the hundreds of thousands of years of organic life on earth. Already well established by geologists like Sir Charles Lyell and by paleontologists, this record told of the rise, development,

sometimes of the disappearance, of thousands of different forms of plant and animal organisms, or *species*. It contradicted an important part of the commonly accepted theory men of the West had about the past of organic life. The Bible in the Book of Genesis described all forms of life as begun in the space of a single week by a Creator about 6,000 years ago. And this same religious account furthermore stated explicitly that all existing men and animals were descended from single pairs of each species preserved in Noah's ark during a great universal flood that took place some time after the Creation.

Now Darwin was by no means the first to find a discrepancy between the historical and scientific record and the accepted Biblical explanation. The men of the Enlightenment had felt compelled by the facts of the record to give up the Biblical explanation. Some of them had gone so far as to conceive the record as a very long evolutionary process in which no God, at least no personal, Christian God, had a hand, but only the impersonal forces of Nature or the deist's "watchmaker God" (see Chapter XVII). But they had arrived at no satisfactory explanation of how Nature or the watchmaker God had done the job; they had no theory of how organisms had evolved. This Darwin gave the world.

Darwin's Theories

One of his clues he found in the work of the economist Malthus (see Chapter XX). In his *Essay on Population*, Malthus had pointed out that organisms— including man—tended to multiply to a point where there simply was not food enough for them all. In the intense competition for food, some of these organisms did not get enough, and died. This was the germ of the conception Darwin phrased as the *struggle for existence.* He next asked himself what determined that certain individuals would survive and that others would die. Obviously the surviving ones got more food, better shelter, better living conditions of all sorts. If they were all identical, the only explanation—apart from the intervention of a supernatural being—would have to be mere chance. But it was clear from observation that individuals of a given species are not identical. Their variations appear even at birth. Thus in a single litter of pigs there may be sturdy, aggressive piglets and a runt. The runt, even if a sentimental farmer tries to protect it, is likely to get shoved aside in suckling by his sturdier brothers, and starve. In the wild state, in free competition, the runt is almost certain to die. In the struggle for existence, the runt is proved unfit.

Here is the second of Darwin's key phrases, the *survival of the fittest.* The organism best endowed in its variations to get food and shelter lives to procreate young that will tend to inherit these favorable variations. The variations are slight indeed, but over generation after generation they are cumulative; finally an organism so different from the long-distant ancestor is produced that we can speak of a new species. This new species has *evolved.* It has evolved by the working of *natural selection.* Man as a plant and animal breeder has long made a common-sense use of this process, and has vastly hastened and indeed guided it for his own purposes by "artificial selection," by breeding only the best strains. But man has been doing this in the case of domesticated plants and animals for but a tiny period of geological time, and for but relatively few species. Over the aeons, natural selection has been the working force; and for man himself, as an organism, natural selection alone has been at work, since man has yet to breed his own kind as he breeds his domestic plants and animals.

Darwin held that the variations in individuals of the same species at birth are accidental, and that they are generally transmitted through inheritance. He did not—and this is a very important point—believe that the evidence showed that variations produced in an individual organism in the course of its life could be transmitted to its offspring. Thus, Darwinism denies the inheritance of "acquired characteristics." Obviously, a man with an amputated leg will not produce one-legged children. Experimenters have docked the tails of generations of laboratory rats, but the rats are still born with long tails.

Today, nearly a century after the publication of the *Origin of Species,* Darwin's work as a biologist is still accepted in most of its larger outlines. Later work, however, has found that variations of importance in the evolutionary process are probably not so much the numerous tiny ones Darwin emphasized, but rather bigger and much rarer ones now known as "mutations." Darwin believed that what he called "sexual selection"—that is, the ability of the fittest individual to attract and mate with fittest individuals of the opposite sex and thus produce the fittest offspring—was a very important factor in natural selection. Although sexual selection is by no means wholly discarded by geneticists today, many of them do not accept Darwin's version of it. The actual mechanism of heredity we know much better than Darwin did, thanks to the work of an Austrian monk, Gregor Mendel, in the late nineteenth century.

Before we turn to the effect of Darwin's work and that of his school on fields outside biology proper, we must note that even as plain biology Darwin's work does contain overtones that give the word "evolution" something of a purposive, or at any rate evaluative, cast. For Darwin and his followers find in a long course of evolution as recorded in geological time a tendency toward development from the "lower" to the "higher," from simple one-celled organisms to the complex many-celled mammals and to man himself, who appears as a kind of apex. They recognize the fact, however, that many organisms seem to have evolved into overelaborate forms unsuited to the environment, and that such species have failed and have become extinct, like the dinosaur and dodo. They recognize that there has been degeneration as well as progress, that evolution has been no simple process. As scientists, they are trained to distrust notions of purposiveness, or *teleology*. But, when their ideas begin to be applied outside biology, they provide an element in several quite different teleological views of the universe. The fittest appear to be the best by the mere fact of their survival.

The Effect on Religion

The first edition of the *Origin of Species,* though of only a few thousand copies, was sold out the day of its publication. What Darwin himself considered a book of interest only to students of "natural history" became a best seller, reviewed in newspapers and magazines all over the world. The major reason for this attention was almost certainly the challenge that orthodox Christians found in the book. Darwinism was a phase of what President Andrew D. White of Cornell University called the "warfare of science with theology." Yet Darwin's book was no new denial of the fundamentalists' belief in the accuracy of the account of Creation in the Book of Genesis. Natural scientists had for over a century been publishing work that frankly denied the possibility that the earth could be only 6,000 years old. The doctrine of God's special creation of each species had

been challenged before Darwin. But the work of Darwin by its very success focused the attention of fundamentalists.

Darwin also got attention because he seemed to provide for the secularist a process (Evolution) and a causal agent (Natural Selection) where before there had been only vague "materialistic" notions. Above all, Darwin seemed to have struck a final blow against the argument, still very popular in Victorian times, that the organic world was full of incontrovertible evidence of God the great designer. The human eye, for instance, the theologians said, was inconceivable except as the design of a God; and now Darwin said it is the result of millions of years of natural selection working on certain nerve ends "accidentally" more sensitive to light than others.

These reactions come out well in one of the first American reviews of the *Origin of Species,* by the Harvard economist and philosopher, Francis Bowen:

Mr. Darwin openly and almost scornfully repudiates the whole doctrine of Final Causes. He finds no indication of design or purpose anywhere in the animate or organic world. . . . The nicest and most complex adaptations do not to him prove design. The eye was not made to see with, or the ear to hear. The fact that these organs respectively do see and hear is accounted for, on this theory, by supposing that, through an accidental and purposeless variation, some one zoöphyte or other animal very low down in the scale happened to be born with a faint glimmering of vision—with the poor rudiment of an eye,—'an optic nerve merely coated with pigment, and without any other mechanism'; that this 'slight accidental variation' passed down by inheritance, giving to the possessors of it a great advantage over their fellows,—even so great that the former were preserved, while the latter died out; that in the lapse of years, another and yet another 'slight accidental variation' successively supervened, and, if an improvement, was retained, while those not having it, and those variations which were not improvements, perished.°

°*North American Review,* XC (1860), 475.

CHAPTER XXIII

Bowen also offers the criticism, so often and so unfairly advanced since, that Darwin makes the monkey man's brother. Later, in the *Descent of Man*, Darwin carefully points out that *homo sapiens* is descended not from any existing ape or monkey, but from a very distant common primate ancestor and by lines we cannot quite fill in.

Yet the *Origin of Species* did stir up a heated theological controversy. Especially in Protestant countries, scholarly historical criticism of the Bible stirred up further heat (see Vol. I, pp. 39 and 132). *Essays and Reviews*, by seven British theological liberals, was published in 1860, only a year after the *Origin of Species*. Fundamentalists, both Protestant and Catholic, simply stuck by Genesis and damned Darwin and the higher critics. But the Catholic Church and many Protestant bodies eventually took at least a neutral attitude toward Darwinism, which they viewed as a biological, not theological, hypothesis. The higher criticism by 1900 seemed acceptable to all but fundamentalists. The great majority of Christians tacitly or openly accepted sufficient modification of Genesis to accommodate the scientist's time-scale, and adjusted the classic theological arguments from first cause, design, and the like to a God who worked his will in accordance with organic evolution. For it was quite clear to reflective men that nothing Darwin or any other scientist could produce would give ultimate answers to the kind of problem set by the existence of God. It was quite clear that since God's eye is now on the sparrow, it must once have been on the dinosaur. Christians can be Darwinians: millions of them are.

The Effect on Social and Economic Attitudes

The theological conflict had pretty well run its course by the beginning of the twentieth century. More important in the long run was the use men made of some of Darwin's basic concepts—or at least, of his more smoothly coined phrases—in debates on matters moral, economic, and political. The blanket term, "Social Darwinism," which covers all these transfers of ideas from biology to the social sciences and human relations, takes in a very wide range of persons and ideas.

The central idea that social and political thinkers took over from Darwin was that of competition. It was of course already central in their thinking, but Darwin buttressed it with the great prestige of the natural sciences. Men, too, take part in the struggle for existence. They struggle against other organisms; but that struggle they have already won, thanks in part to science and technology. At least they were increasingly well equipped to master other organisms, even those micro-organisms or "germs" the Frenchman Louis Pasteur and his fellow scientists were beginning to discover. More important for the Social Darwinists was the struggle for existence among individual human beings. The great majority of these late nineteenth-century thinkers interpreted the human struggle as a struggle for the means of livelihood—for money. The variations that counted here were the variations that brought success in economic competition—the variations that produce inventors, business organizers, even perhaps the political, artistic, and professional leaders. Darwin's work in natural history came to confirm the economist's doctrine of laissez-faire individualism (see Chapter XX).

Formal economics did not indeed make much use of, or have much need for, Darwin. The classical economists had already brought the arguments for laissez-faire to their height. On the whole, for the rest of the century, the economists were to temper somewhat the rigor of the doctrine of competition among individuals. But the average successful middle-class person in the West took Darwin to heart. Here was scientific confirmation of the middle-class notions that the universe was designed to reward hard work, thrift, intelligence, and self-help and to punish laziness, waste, stupidity, and reliance on charity. Above all, the middle-class person of the time took Darwin to confirm the notion that the poor were poor because they were unfit, badly designed for living. The work of Darwin confirmed the complementary notion that attempts by private charity or by state action to take from the rich and moderately well-to-do and give to the poor were useless and quite contrary to nature, shocking efforts to reverse the course of evolution. If a man cannot earn enough to feed himself, it was argued, he had better die; lowlier organisms too incompetent to feed themselves certainly die off, to the greater good of the species. Herbert Spencer (1820-1903), an ardent British evolutionist, summed it up neatly:

Of man, as of all inferior creatures, the law by conformity to which the species is preserved, is that among adults the individuals best adapted to the conditions of their existence shall prosper most, and the individuals least adapted to the conditions of their existence shall prosper least. . . . Pervading all Nature we may see at work a stern discipline which is often a little cruel that it may be very kind. . . . The ultimate result of shielding men from folly is to fill the world with fools.*

The American sociologist, W. G. Sumner (1840-1910) of Yale, linked Darwinism and private property, quite in accordance with the feelings of men of property everywhere in the West:

Private property, also, which we have seen to be a feature of society organized in accordance with the natural conditions of the

* Herbert Spencer, *Principles of Ethics* (London, 1879-1893), section 257; *Social Statics* (London, 1851), p. 149; *Autobiography* (London, 1904), II, 5.

struggle for existence produces inequalities between men. The struggle for existence is aimed against nature. It is from her niggardly hand that we have to wrest the satisfactions for our needs, but our fellow-men are our competitors for the meager supply. Competition, therefore, is a law of nature. Nature is entirely neutral; she submits to him who most energetically and resolutely assails her. She grants her rewards to the fittest, therefore, without regard to other considerations of any kind. If, then, there be liberty, men get from her just in proportion to their works, and their having and enjoying are just in proportion to their being and their doing. Such is the system of nature. If we do not like it, and if we try to amend it, there is only one way in which we can do it. We can take from the better and give to the worse. We can deflect the penalties of those who have done ill and throw them on those who have done better. We can take the rewards from those who have done better and give them to those who have done worse. We shall thus lessen the inequalities. We shall favor the survival of the unfittest, and we shall accomplish this by destroying liberty. Let it be understood that we cannot go outside of this alternative: liberty, inequality, survival of the fittest; not-liberty, equality, survival of the unfittest. The former carries society forward and favors all its best members; the latter carries society downwards and favors all its worst members.*

Herbert Spencer himself, if it came to that, could not have stood by while the unemployed and their families starved to death. He had an almost maniacal hatred of the state, of local government as well as national; he held out even against compulsory sewage in cities. But even Spencer could not transfer to the struggle for existence among human beings the fine ruthless freedom of the jungle, of what Tennyson called "Nature red in tooth and claw." He was against all forms of government provision for what we now call "social security." But what government may not do the ethically sound individual will do as charity.

* *Sumner Today,* Maurice R. Davie, ed. (New Haven, 1940), 72-73.

CHAPTER XXIII

The rich and well-to-do will take care of the poor voluntarily—not enough to spoil them, not enough to frustrate the designs of evolution by letting them prosper and propagate their kind, but enough to prevent their starving or freezing to death.

In his *Principles of Ethics*, Spencer discovers that the softer emotions promoted by Christianity and the other higher religions—kindness, dislike of cruelty, love—were also in accord with the intentions of the laws of the universe as summed up in evolution. Mutual extermination might be the law for tigers, but not for human beings. Indeed, Spencer and many other Social Darwinists held that altruistic moral sentiments that impel us toward charity are the highest achievement of the evolutionary process, and that a society with many altruists is thereby shown to be the fittest for survival.

Eugenics

The Social Darwinists were, then, faced with this primary difficulty. Darwin seemed to have shown that the unmitigated struggle for life within a given species, and among rival species, was the law of the universe; but human history, and human feelings, showed that men could not in practice look on with indifference while their fellow men starved to death. One way out of the dilemma was that of Spencer, a sort of humanized and mitigated struggle in which the incompetent were shelved but not destroyed. Many who held this view accompanied it with a faith in what came to be called eugenics. For them the question was not so much the elimination of the unfit but the deliberate encouragement of the production of the fit. Darwin had begun his *Origin of Species* with a consideration of the extraordinary success men had had with artificial selection in the breeding of plants and animals. Why not do the same thing with human beings? Since, according to strict Darwinian theory, acquired characteristics were not transmitted by heredity, no amount of manipulation of the social environment, no amount of wise planning of institutions, would alter human beings. Therefore, the only way to secure permanent improvement of the race was by deliberate mating of the fit with the fit.

The eugenicists, however, ran at once against the fact that man, though he domesticates plants and animals, is still himself a "wild" animal. The individual human being in choosing a mate is no doubt influenced by a great variety of motives, which the social scientist still understands only imperfectly. But no master human breeder decides who shall mate with whom. So far, the eugenicists have had little success with the positive side of their program. On the negative side, they have urged that the obviously unfit, the idiots, the feeble-minded, the insane, be prevented, even if necessary by compulsory sterilization, from having children. Some few American states have passed laws for such compulsory sterilization, but only a tiny handful of human beings, not enough to affect in the slightest the course of human physical evolution, have undergone this treatment. Moreover, the eugenicists have aroused the opposition of many Christians, who believe that it is wrong to tamper with God's human creations.

"Racism"

By far the commonest way out of the dilemma facing the Social Darwinists lay in the obvious notion that it is not so much among individual human beings that the struggle for existence really goes on, as it is among human beings organized in groups, as tribes, "races," territorial states.

The struggle that counts is not the struggle, say, among individual Englishmen to survive, but the struggle between the entity England—or Great Britain—and its rivals. The struggle for existence among men is now lifted from the biology of the individual to the politics of the group. And for the nineteenth century the group had to be the nation-state, perhaps kindred nation-states that could be organized for the struggle as one bloc of states, such as the "Nordic" or the "Latin," or perhaps at the very widest the Caucasian or white peoples in competition with the colored peoples, yellow, brown, or black. This struggle had an ultimate form: war. The group that defeated another group in war had thereby shown itself to be fitter than the beaten group, and it had a right—indeed in evolutionary terms a duty—to eliminate the beaten group, seize its lands, and people them with its own fitter human beings. The English imperialist Cecil Rhodes held that a world wholly and exclusively peopled with Anglo-Saxons would be the best possible world.

The idea of a Chosen People was of course not a new one in Darwin's time. But there is no doubt that Darwin's work, however little he may have meant it to be, was a most important element in the special forms that competition among organized states took in the latter half of the nineteenth century, and right on to our own day. Darwinism came too late to do more than prop up the philosophy of laissez-faire, the concept of the struggle for existence among men as basically an economic struggle within the state. But Darwinism came at just the right time to bolster the struggle among the organized human groups we call states.

The particular groups that were to benefit as the elect of evolution in this special political sense varied with the aims, sympathies, and actual citizenship of the individual who was seeking to promote an ultimate evolutionary victory. Britain, Germany, the United States, the Latins, the Slavs, the Nordics, the whites, even indeed the Christians, were all defended as the true elect of evolution. Most of the writers who preached this kind of political evolution proceeded from the assumption that at bottom the men of a given group had certain physical traits in common, traits that gave them their superiority, and that could not possibly be transmitted to men of another group. Most of these writers, in short, were "racists" who believed that in fact *homo sapiens* had already evolved into what were really separate species. A black skin, for instance, was for them a sign of innate inferiority. The blacks would simply have to go the way of the dinosaurs, into extinction. Evolution had spoken.

There were indeed all sorts of half-way stations proposed by these writers. Few of them quite dared to preach what has in our own day been christened genocide—that is, the actual wholesale murder of "inferior" and beaten "races." We had to wait for Hitler for this. Most of them, though perhaps they held that in the long run the inferior peoples would in fact die out, were willing to see the inferiors duly subjected to the superiors, to have the less fit peoples serve as hewers of wood and drawers of water for their masters. Indeed, some Social Darwinists applied their theories to a new form of caste organization, which came to be known as "élitism." For them, the distinction between superior and inferior was not always one of race or even of existing state organizations, but one that applied to a cross section of the whole human race. The fit were not limited to any one race, but they were still marked out by the rigid hand of biological inheritance. They were the master group, the élite, the "supermen"; and they should everywhere band together against the dull average men. The Ger-

CHAPTER XXIII

man, Friedrich Nietzsche, who gave currency to the phrase "superman," was a subtle and difficult thinker, who disliked Darwin as a grubbing Englishman. Still Nietzsche's influence among the half-educated who admired him in the late nineteenth and early twentieth centuries was to further racist and élitist causes. (For details, see below, Chapter XXVII.)

Theories of the evolution-guided superiority of certain groups were not limited to Europe. In the United States, the innate, unchangeable superiority of whites to blacks was an article of faith among many whites in the North and almost universally in the South. This faith was greatly bolstered by Darwinian anthropologists and biologists. The notion that the degree of blondness, and other readily visible traits, such as long-headedness and tallness, measured suitableness for citizenship in a great democracy helped dictate the American immigration act of 1924, which encouraged immigrants from northwestern Europe, and very seriously discouraged those from southern and eastern Europe. The American, Madison Grant, in his *The Passing of the Great Race*, published in 1916, asserted that the Nordics—the tall, long-headed, light-haired peoples of northern Europe—were "a race of soldiers, sailors, adventurers and explorers, but above all, of rulers, organizers and aristocrats." Grant continued:

Before leaving this interesting subject of the correlation of spiritual and moral traits with physical characters we may note that these influences are so deeply rooted in everyday consciousness that the modern novelist or playwright does not fail to make his hero a tall, blond, honest and somewhat stupid youth and his villain a small, dark and exceptionally intelligent individual of warped moral character. So in Celtic legend as in the Græco-Roman and mediæval romances, prince and princess are always fair, a fact rather indicating that the mass of the people were brunet at the time when the legends were taking shape. In fact, 'fair' is a synonym for beauty. Most ancient tapestries show a blond earl on horseback and a dark haired churl holding the bridle.

The gods of Olympus were almost all described as blond, and it would be difficult to imagine a Greek artist painting a brunet Venus. In church pictures all angels are blond, while the denizens of the lower regions revel in deep brunetness. 'Non Angli sed angeli,' remarked Pope Gregory when he first saw Saxon children exposed for sale in the Roman slavemart.

In depicting the crucifixion no artist hesitates to make the two thieves brunet in contrast to the blond Saviour. This is something more than a convention, as such quasi-authentic traditions as we have of our Lord strongly suggest his Nordic, possibly Greek, physical and moral attributes.*

The title of Madison Grant's book, however, betrays an anxiety that is never far from the surface even in the most confident of these Social Darwinists. Grant feared that his "great race," gifted summit of evolution though it was, was paradoxically not going to survive. The lower races were breeding faster; democratic equalitarianism was lopping off the best and encouraging the worst. Somehow evolution was going wrong. Degeneration, not progress, was the mark of the times. Like those other "scientific" determinists, the Marxists, the Social Darwinists believed that men of good will had to set to work with pen and tongue to help along the predetermined process and keep it on the right track.

A New Historical Determinism

Darwinian science no more than Newtonian science really answered the great questions about good and evil, about the ends of human life, that men have been asking and answering ever since we have had historical records. Darwinian science, and indeed the physics, chemistry, and other

---

* Madison Grant, *The Passing of the Great Race*, 4th rev. ed. (New York, 1921), 229-230.

sciences that flourished in the nineteenth century, recast for many the whole frame of reference in which these questions were asked. Do not mistake. Traditional Christianity, as well as many other supernatural faiths, survived Darwin as they had survived Newton. Many men continued to believe that a God, or gods, not bound by the laws men discovered in laboratory experiments and in other systematic observations, guided their steps and gave meaning to their lives in this world and in the other world after death. But with the spread of popular education, especially in the West, great numbers came to believe that no such God or gods existed, that the material universe of science and common sense went on its regular ways in accordance with laws or uniformities which men might eventually understand completely, and which they were already beginning to understand quite well. And in its turn, this materialist view of the universe had repercussions on all but the most determined and fundamentalist of the supernatural faiths; at the very least, they pared down the scope of divine action, cribbing and confining it.

Darwin's work and that of many other scientists, in combination with the work of historians and philosophers and men of letters, worked a major change in the way men looked at their universe. It is an undue simplification to say that the Newtonian universe was static, the Darwinian dynamic, but the generalization is a good rough working approximation. The eighteenth-century Enlightenment (see Chapter XVII) was certainly feeling its way far more than its later Romantic critics admitted toward a view of the universe as developing, progressing, evolving. But, as one can see from the work of so typical a *philosophe* as Condorcet, the eighteenth century had no good explanation of the way change came about. This explanation Darwin provided for natural history, and the Romantic historians

and their fellow workers in other fields provided it for human history.

Today we are still in the climate of opinion set for us in the late nineteenth century. We still believe, to a greater or less degree, in what has been labeled "historicism"—that is, in the doctrine that the course of history in the widest sense shows a regular, if bewildering, unfolding that has "determined" everything now existing and that will determine everything in the future. The wildest believer in this doctrine had to admit that since he could not in fact understand the whole process in the past, he could not wholly understand the present or wholly predict the future. Still, the clue lay in the past, out of which the present has developed as the oak has developed from the acorn.

The Christian and Hebraic calendar made the earth 6,000 years old, but the Darwinian calendar envisaged millions of years for organic life alone. It might seem, therefore, that historicism, especially when reinforced by the emphasis Darwin put on the immense reaches of time, would confirm conservative opposition to rapid change, or at least breed in men a certain resignation in the face of this slow-moving universe. And so it did for some men. Darwin's grandson, Sir Charles Galton Darwin, published in 1953 a book entitled *The Next Million Years*. He concludes that, since it is now held that it takes about a million years for a species to evolve, it will be a million years before evolution produces a creature any better than man; and that therefore for the next million years we shall have a history much like that of the last few thousand, with wars, revolutions, pestilence, the rise and fall of thousands of Egypts, Romes, Britains, and Americas.

But historicism in the nineteenth and twentieth centuries has had for most people a rather different consequence. It has served to convince impatient and hopeful men that they had really mastered the secrets of the universe, that they understood as misguided predecessors had not just where the forces of history were leading. They could, then, help the process instead of hindering it. Marxism is the classic example of this faith in historical determinism, but nationalism, racism, and a host of others all drew nourishment from it. The extraordinary speeding-up of technological improvements lent strength to this view that moral and political improvement could also be speeded up. Evolution, then, though logically it should have lessened the force of evangelical and utopian faiths, did in fact increase them.

II: Literature and the Arts

The Victorian Age

It is risky to generalize about the literature and the art of the later nineteenth century. But these years do largely deserve to be called the "Victorian Age." This age has not the neatness of style we can find in Periclean Athens or Renaissance Italy or Elizabethan England. We can evoke a Victorian drawing room, where Maud or Mélanie in ringlets and crinolines, surrounded by what-nots, bric-a-brac, plush hangings, and Landseer engravings, reads Tennyson, Longfellow, or Heine, or plays Liszt on the pianoforte. But so much went on outside that drawing room!—not only in the lives of peasants, workers, and businessmen, but even in art and letters. Maud or Mélanie might indeed have been reading Dickens or Balzac, but these writers hardly fitted the drawing room. Nor would Thoreau and Melville, Zola and Dostoevski. It is quite certain that the girls would not have been reading Marx.

For the safest thing we can say about the formal culture of the second half of the nineteenth century is that it has wide variety, that indeed it is very *eclectic*. We may also add that a great deal of this formal culture was now, more clearly than ever before in western history, produced and cultivated by men and women in conscious revolt against the tastes of the politically and economically dominant class of their time—that is, the middle class. Unless Maud and Mélanie were very advanced young women indeed, they did not like much of what a hundred years later we single out as important in Victorian art and literature. If they were ordinary middle-class young women, they read sentimental novels now forgotten save by the social historian, and they lived in a culture to which the derogatory overtones that the word "Victorian" still often has apply well enough.

Their fathers and brothers, indeed, were often so concerned with industry and trade that they had no time for literature and the arts, which they tended to leave to their women folk. Or if they did have wider concerns, these concerns were rather with political and social problems, with the material betterment of their class, and—to be fair—with that of the working class too. But most of these middle-class men felt that the most that could be done for the workers was to raise their standard of living slowly under existing capitalist laissez-faire. They held that Church and State should join to restrain by law and by religion of an essentially puritanical cast the lack of self-restraint these middle-class men found too characteristic of their inferiors. For with these Victorians laissez-faire was a strictly economic matter; in morals they believed firmly that organized institutions should interfere to restrain the populace from the drunkenness, idleness, and loose living they were supposedly inclined to.

The Realistic Novel

We may, then, leave these middle-class leaders of the West, whom the English critic Matthew Arnold rather harshly called the "Philistines," and proceed to some of the complex currents of formal culture of the time. In literature, the later nineteenth century was a great period for the novel. Here the accepted label for the novel of the time is "realism," in contrast with the Romanticism of the earlier part of the century (see Chapter XIX). Yet as one usually finds in examining these sharp contrasts between the cultural attitudes of succeeding generations in the modern West, the realists are quite obviously children of the Romanticists. The Romantic of 1830, fleeing this ugly world for an idealized Middle Ages, when knighthood was in flower and there were no sooty factories, or writing of the idyllic Indian tribes of America, can indeed look very different from the realist of 1860, analyzing with fascination and disgust the men and women of the mill towns, the slums of the great cities, the unidyllic countryside of peasant labor. Yet in the sense of close attention to authentic detail, of effort to picture men and women as they really were, there is much realism even in the work of a Romantic novelist like Victor Hugo. Certainly no sharp break occurred about 1850.

Dickens and Balzac were both writing in the period we label "Romantic." Both revel in exaggerations, both pour themselves out freely in undisciplined torrents of words,

both achieve an effect of unreal intensity—Romantic traits, surely. Yet both are thoroughly immersed in the world of their time, both are in many ways realists. On the other hand, the leading French realist of the later nineteenth century, Flaubert (1821-1880), wrote one of his novels, *Salammbô,* about an ancient and, in spite of his great efforts at historical accuracy, not very real Carthage. And in his masterpiece, *Madame Bovary,* which satirizes the romantic longings of a small-town doctor's wife, Flaubert betrays a most ambivalent feeling toward his heroine. Indeed, he once said, "*I am Madame Bovary.*" Flaubert hated the bourgeois world he wrote about quite as much as did the escapist writers of an earlier generation.

Nevertheless, there remains a difference between the writing of the second half of the century and that of the first. The realists did abandon the Romantic pursuit of the ideal and the remote and chose subjects close to their own lives. They did generally avoid tempestuous extremes and concentrate on the quieter ordinary folk. They did pay great attention to choosing the right word, the word that should stand exactly for the experience, the emotion depicted, and not rouse all sorts of irrelevant overtones. We may take as good realists the Englishman Trollope and the Russian Turgenev. Trollope (1815-1882) wrote dozens of novels about Victorian clergymen and politicians and country gentlemen, carefully observing the English decencies, never raising his voice or his style, but imparting understanding, sympathy, and a suitable, modest irony. Turgenev (1818-1883) wrote about his fellows with classic restraint, skirting delicately the depths of the Slavic soul. Or we may take William Dean Howells (1837-1920), who in the *Rise of Silas Lapham* and other novels sought to apply realism to the American scene.

CHAPTER XXIII

The Naturalistic Novel: Zola

Howells seemed to later critics a representative of what they called the "genteel tradition." They accused him of omitting the more unpleasant facts of life, of softening the crudities of the new industrial civilization. For as the twentieth century drew near the realists were confronted with a rebel generation that found them not "realistic" enough. This school rose first in France, where they took for themselves the name of "naturalists." Their leader, Emile Zola (1840-1902), shows clearly the influence of the scientific revolution centered about the work of Darwin. For Zola was not content with the realist's aim to reflect the life around him with simple accuracy; he sought to exercise the traditional moral and aesthetic selectivity of the artist.

The novel was to Zola an instrument of scientific generalization. He would do for society, for men in their relations with other men, what Darwin had done for natural history. He would show what men are like, of course, but he would also show how they came to be what they are, and even what they were going to be. He called his great series of novels about a family under the Second Empire, the Rougon-Macquart, the "natural history" of a family. In a famous manifesto he championed the "experimental novel":

> . . . The experimental novel is a consequence of the scientific evolution of the century; it continues and completes physiology, which itself leans for support on chemistry and medicine; it substitutes for the study of the abstract and the metaphysical man the study of the natural man, governed by physical and chemical laws, and modified by the influences of his surroundings; it is in one word the literature of our scientific age, as the classical and romantic literature corresponded to a scholastic and theological age.*

---

* Zola, *The Experimental Novel*, Belle M. Sherman, trans. (New York, 1893), 23.

From our perspective, it does not look as if Zola's novels achieved the goal he set for himself. They do not explain the France of Louis Napoleon, let alone the France of today. They do not show how social environment works on heredity to make men behave as they do. Of course they were not experimental, not the products of a laboratory. They were, if you like, case histories based at least in part on Zola's own scarcely rigorous medical training. They reflect his own moral and political position, that of a good French republican—he was later to figure as an important defender of Dreyfus (see Chapter XXI)—an anticlerical materialist and radical. They concentrate on the seamier side of life. Indeed, Zola's work scandalized the conventional Victorians, who found the secret of his success in sheer pornography. And it is difficult to avoid agreeing with critics who found that he called a spade by no means a spade, but rather a bloody shovel.

Zola's work points up one of the tendencies not only of the late nineteenth-century novel, in those days the spearhead of literature, but of other forms of literature as well. The literature of the time, and to a great extent of the twentieth century too, is overwhelmingly a literature of discontent, of protest against things-as-they-are. Now it is quite true that from Socrates on great thinkers have held that their times were peculiarly out of joint. They had to protest against the abuses of their age, had to stir their fellows into bettering their ways. But there are certainly periods when the intellectuals are *relatively* conformist—the great age of Latin literature from Livy to Vergil or the age of Louis XIV, for example. And there are ages when the intellectuals, even though they are bitterly against things-as-they-are, write with hope and confidence of what is to come—as in the eighteenth-century Enlightenment. We have already noted that the Romantic movement has its pessimistic side. With the second half of the nineteenth century there sets in a strain of pessimism—at least among many leading writers—that has continued to this day. It is by no means the only strain in modern western literature, and it is by no means a strain of unrelieved pessimism. Writers on the Left, notably the socialists, are obliged by their creed to hold that somehow mankind will win through to a better society.

The Literature of Pessimism and Protest

The pessimists reacted against the eighteenth-century doctrine of the natural goodness of man. Certainly "nature" and "natural" as they figure in the work of a Zola carry very different connotations from these words as the eighteenth, and even the early nineteenth, centuries used them. Nature by the late nineteenth century apparently made men greedy, selfish, combative, not very bright, and extremely addicted to a variety of irregular sexual relations which brought out to the full their other bad traits. Sometimes, as with the English novelist Thomas Hardy (1840-1928), this pessimism is built up from a series of incidents in private lives into a grand cosmic irony not without its consoling side. But for the most part these writers are concerned directly with the cruelties, stupidities, the downright insanities of ordinary people.

In France, De Maupassant (1850-1893), a master of the short story, wrote sparely and simply, after the manner of his master Flaubert, about the tragedies and comedies of ordinary life; but the tragedies, or at least the ironies, prevail. In Russia, Chekhov (1860-1904), a medical man by training, used the prose drama and the short story to show how life harasses us all. Ibsen (1828-1906) in Norway, Brieux (1858-

Caricature of George Bernard Shaw by Max Beerbohm.

1932) in France, and George Bernard Shaw (1856-1950) in England all helped to develop the characteristically late-nineteenth-century form of the drama, the "problem play." The problem was sometimes one of wide moral and political concern, as in Ibsen's *Enemy of the People* or Shaw's *Man and Superman,* but it was very often concerned mainly with the stupid tangles of men's private, and in particular their sex, lives. Ibsen shocked his contemporaries in his *Doll's House* by having his heroine rebel against the "doll-house" atmosphere that her husband had created for her. His *Ghosts* scandalized his contemporaries by bringing to the stage the problem of syphilis.

Bernard Shaw did much to defend the

CHAPTER XXIII

problem play as the suitable form of the drama for his time, a time when, Shaw apparently hoped, men were almost willing to face reality. Here is a characteristic bit from Shaw's introduction to an English translation of the French playwright Brieux, who also brought syphilis onto the stage with his *Damaged Goods:*

Not only is the tradition of the catastrophe unsuitable to modern studies of life: the tradition of an ending, happy or the reverse, is equally unworkable. The moment the dramatist gives up accidents and catastrophes, and takes 'slices of life' as his material, he finds himself committed to plays that have no endings. The curtain no longer comes down on a hero slain or married: it comes down when the audience has seen enough of the life presented to it to draw the moral, and must either leave the theatre or miss its last train.

The man who faced France with a drama fulfilling all these conditions was Brieux. He was as scientific, as conscientious, as unflinching as Zola without being in the least morbid. He was no more dependent on horrors than Molière, and as sane in his temper. He threw over the traditional forced catastrophe uncompromisingly. You do not go away from a Brieux play with the feeling that the affair is finished or the problem solved for you by the dramatist. Still less do you go away in 'that happy, easy, ironically indulgent frame of mind that is the true test of comedy,' as Mr. Walkley put it in *The Times* of the 1st October, 1909. You come away with a very disquieting sense that you are involved in the affair, and must find the way out of it for yourself and everybody else if civilization is to be tolerable to your sense of honor.[*]

The problem play, the problem novel, the problem short story spread through all the literatures of the West. They spread with the usual speed to the United States, where by the end of the nineteenth century the "genteel tradition" was already scorned by the bright young men, and the novelists Stephen Crane and Theodore Dreiser were bringing out the harsh realities of war,

[*] *Three Plays by Brieux* (New York, 1913), xv-xvi.

business, and love. It took a while for the extremes of "naturalism" to gain the United States, and it was not until our own day, and then of all places in the South of magnolia and roses, that Faulkner, Caldwell, and their many followers really plumbed the depths behind the Anglo-Saxon four-letter words they used so freely.

Most of this realistic or naturalistic writing, even when it is by no means of Marxist inspiration, is hostile to the middle classes. The bourgeois is no longer just the Philistine the Romantic disliked, the puritanical conformist, the stuffy enemy of sweetness and light. He is still that, but he is also the rapacious titan of industry, the jingoistic nationalist, authoritarian browbeater of his children, the tasteless addict of "conspicuous consumption" (a phrase of the American economist, Thorstein Veblen), the hypocritical practitioner of a "double standard" of sexual morality, and worse. Flaubert, who began so much, may be said to have begun this with his unfinished *Bouvard et Pécuchet*, in which he makes his two bourgeois "heroes" run the gamut of human futility, failing ludicrously in their effort to educate themselves. In England, Samuel Butler (1835-1902) in *The Way of All Flesh* set the pattern, since followed freely, for the novel in which the writer-son blames all on the tyrannical male parent. Shaw found a great simple phrase to sum up what was wrong—"middle class morality." Ibsen's *Enemy of the People* is ironically named; the real enemy of the people is the people themselves, not the misunderstood leader who would bring them better things.

Even where the writers are not embittered, even where their main concern is to balance good and evil as, one suspects, they are balanced in life, the middle class does not often come out well. English novelists like H. G. Wells, Galsworthy, and Arnold Bennett, French novelists like Anatole France, and most writers of tsarist Russia find something wrong with the middle classes. An epitome of this relatively kindly and relatively objective attack on the middle classes is afforded by an American, who wrote in the 1920's, chronologically rather later than the period with which we are here concerned. Sinclair Lewis' *Main Street* and *Babbitt* are realistic rather than naturalistic novels, and George Babbitt is almost a hero without ironic quotation marks. Still, Babbitt came to sum up for thousands of American intellectuals what was wrong with a naive materialistic civilization. The novels of Sinclair Lewis sold by the hundred thousands, so that it is clear that George Babbitt himself must have relished, or at least read, these satires on his way of life. Indeed, since many of the writers we have been dealing with were able to sell their works in a mass market, one is forced to conclude that a good portion of the middle classes in the West were in revolt against their own shortcomings, although some of them were doubtless quite unable to see themselves as others saw them.

Not all that was written between 1850 and the outbreak of war in 1914 was a literature of scorn or protest. The daughters of the Maud or Mélanie with whom we began could about 1900 read the standard conventional fare, historical novels, novels of escape, novels of true love. They could even find in writers like Kipling men who, if not exactly convinced that this was the best of possible worlds, were at least convinced that the English middle classes were the best of the lot. They could, in short, read for pleasure and edification, and go on with the serious business of life.

Poetry

Few writers tried to make poetry "naturalistic" in Zola's sense. Nor, on the other hand, was the late nineteenth century a period in which the epic or the grand philosophical poem, like Wordsworth's *Prelude*, flourished. Poets did attempt the drama in verse, but these dramas remained poetry to be read in the study, not plays for the boards. Tennyson, who can stand very well for the more conventional Victorian poets, tried the epic in his *Idyls of the King*, based on the legends about King Arthur's court, and he tried the philosophical poem, such as *In Memoriam*, and several "closet" dramas. But he perhaps succeeded best in his shorter lyrics.

In England Tennyson, in America Longfellow and his New England colleagues, in France Victor Hugo, wrote the staple poetry the late nineteenth century liked and read a great deal. These poets deserve the tag, "household words." In form, their work differs little from the norms set by the earlier Romantic movement, and their subjects are love, death, nature, patriotism, and longing, the eternal lyric repertory. And they sometimes came down into the arena to deal with politics, as in Whittier's anti-slavery poems, and in James Russell Lowell's "Biglow Papers," poems in Yankee dialect on the crisis of the Civil War. The spiritual crisis brought on by loss of Christian faith in a scientific age is evident in many poems of Matthew Arnold and Arthur Hugh Clough, as well as Tennyson. Even the horrors of the industrial revolution are apparent in Thomas Hood's "Song of the Shirt":

With fingers weary and worn,
  With eyelids heavy and red,
A woman sat in unwomanly rags,
  Plying her needle and thread—
    Stitch! stitch! stitch!
In poverty, hunger, and dirt,
  And still with the voice of dolorous pitch
She sang the 'Song of the Shirt!'

  Work! work! work!
While the cock is crowing aloof!
  And work—work—work,
Till the stars shine through the roof!

It's O! to be a slave
  Along with the barbarous Turk,
Where woman has never a soul to save,
  If this is Christian work!

              .   .   .

'Work—work—work!
  My labor never flags;
And what are its wages? A bed of straw,
  A crust of bread—and rags.
That shattered roof—and this naked floor—
  A table—a broken chair—
And a wall so blank, my shadow I thank
  For sometimes falling there!' *

Yet in these same years poetry went far along the road that brought it to our times, when the poet often writes difficult, private, experimental verse for a handful of initiates. Poetry for the Romanticist was indeed the reflection of his own inner world, but he hoped it would not prove a quite private world. In the second half of the nineteenth century, the French Parnassians deliberately sought the seclusion of perfect form, of polished verse fit for but few, of "art for art's sake." Still later, with Symbolists like Mallarmé, they went on to very difficult verse indeed, in which the meaning had to be wrung with effort from symbols nested one within another, in which the harmonies, like those of modern music, are by no means at once apparent to the untrained listener. Significantly, when twentieth-century poets went back for their predecessors they did not go to Tennyson, Hugo, Longfellow, or Kipling, but to late Victorian poets hardly known to their contemporaries, like the English Gerard Manley Hopkins and the American Emily Dickinson. Here is a passage from Hopkins:

  Across my foundering deck shone
A beacon, an eternal beam. | Flesh fade,
  and mortal trash
Fall to the residuary worm; | world's wild-
  fire, leave but ash:

In a flash, at a trumpet crash,
I am all at once what Christ is, | since he
  was what I am, and
This Jack, joke, poor potsherd, | patch,
  matchwood, immortal diamond,
  Is immortal diamond.*

Painting

In Victorian literature, then, there was a popular and conventional, but not vulgar, level of writing represented by men like Hugo and Tennyson. In painting, there was a similar level, represented by artists whose work now fills many galleries—the Fontainebleau school in France; Watts, Burne-Jones, and Rossetti in England; George Inness, and later Winslow Homer and John Singer Sargent in the United States; and many, many others throughout the West. The *avant garde*, the advanced innovators in art, gave the paintings of these men the derogatory label "academic." Actually, the academic painters were technically very skillful, for they had the advantage of the long tradition of western painting since the Renaissance. They could mirror man and nature faithfully, more faithfully than the camera. They were perhaps realists, but they were not naturalists in Zola's sense. They rather avoided the shambles of the industrial revolution, and to their *avant garde* opponents they seemed too much concerned with the pretty in nature and with the aristocratic or striking in portraiture.

The first great innovators in later nineteenth-century painting were the French impressionists. This school once had to content itself with separate salons, for the academics would have none of it. But it is now safely enshrined as "classic." The impressionists, too, show one of the cross-

---

* Thomas Hood, *Poetical Works*, Epes Sargent, ed. (Boston, 1854), 147-148.

* Gerard Manley Hopkins, *Poems*, 3rd ed. (New York, 1948), 112.

An impressionist painting by Claude Monet ("La Grenouillière").

fertilizations between science and art, but in a rather subtler way than does the naturalist movement in fiction. One of the things science does is to show us that the "real" world is not what the hasty eye finds, that things are not what they seem. The impressionists were not content with the camera eye of the academics. Light, they learned from the physicists, was not a simple thing, but a complex that the eye puts together from the prismatic reflections of nature. So they proposed to break up light themselves, and put it together on their canvases. They painted landscapes for the most part, and they built up their trees and flowers and buildings and skies from thousands of little dabs or points of color, so that the result, when seen from a few feet away, is hardly more than a formless mesh of color, but seen from an adequate distance does indeed take the form of a landscape, a landscape flooded in light.

The great master of the impressionist school, Claude Monet (1840-1926) was a prolific painter, whose work is well represented in public museums. Monet repeatedly painted the same subjects, notably Rouen Cathedral and the lily pond in his own garden, to show how they varied in appearance at different times of day and under changing conditions of light. Light interested many other painters, like Turner in England, who specialized in marine pictures (see illustration on p. 133), and the Anglicized American, Whistler, who did misty scenes in London and, incidentally, was very ashamed of the fact that he had been born in Lowell, Massachusetts.

Realism of a less technically experimental kind, realism more like that of the novel, is to be found in a nineteenth-century school of painting represented by the Frenchman Edouard Manet (1832-1883). This realism is in part one of subject. One of Manet's masterpieces is the execution of Emperor Maximilian of Mexico, the un-

CHAPTER XXIII

Edouard Manet, "The Death of Maximilian."

happy victim of the imperial ambitions of Napoleon III, and he has left many portraits of ordinary people. But it is also a realism of sharp, sometimes almost harsh color, of simple but effective drawing. Some of the best work of the middle of the century was done in drawing and engraving, where new methods of reproduction made prints available to all. Here again the French are at their best, severe moralists in the Voltairean tradition, as in the caricatures of Daumier (see illustrations on pp. 178 and 356) and Forain.

Toward the end of the century the *avant garde* turned to another technique, somewhat more difficult than impressionism to describe. The great figure here is another Frenchman, Cézanne (1839-1906). This painter, too, wanted to go beyond the smooth techniques of the academics, but he found impressionism too fuzzy, too obsessed with light. The impressionists had to him lost the sense of shape, lost the three dimensions of the real world. He proposed to put them back, not with the classic, flowing perspective inherited by the academics from the Italians, but with blocks, chunks of color blended into a result that is after all realistic. From Cézanne there stemmed in a sense much of twentieth-century painting. Cubism, which is the exaggeration of Cézanne's insistence on hard three-dimensionality, is most obviously in his debt, but so too are Abstractionism and even Surrealism. Cézanne's work and that of two of his contemporaries, the Dutchman Van Gogh and the Frenchman Gauguin, were once thought wild, private, and unprofitably experimental. But they are now popular in museums and in countless inexpensive reproductions.

The Other Arts

The nineteenth century was not a great period for sculpture. An age that had mastered the industrial arts so well pro-

A landscape by Cézanne (near Aix-en-Provence, with Mont Sainte Victoire in background).

duced monumental statues aplenty. The most famous for Americans is the Statue of Liberty in New York harbor, the work of the French sculptor Bartholdi, a gift from the Third French Republic to the American Republic. But the statues of statesmen and warriors that adorn public places everywhere in the West are so conventionally realistic that we hardly recognize them as human beings. Sculpture in the large at least would appear to be an aristocratic art, designed for the palace and the formal garden. Its nineteenth-century civic use seems at its best—or least bad—in Paris, in the decoration of the great Arc de Triomphe, a delayed memorial to the Grand Army of Napoleon I, and in the new Opera and many other buildings. Toward the end of the century, Frenchmen like Rodin and Maillol began a break with the formal statuary of their time, simplifying and strengthening the contours of their men and women. It should be noted that inex-

pensive, small-scale copies of the great sculpture of antiquity and the Renaissance now became common, and many a Victorian drawing room in Europe and in Europe overseas boasted a plaster Venus or a bronze Mercury. Museums, too, could all afford large plaster casts. Some direct acquaintance with the great artistic achievements of the past was now available to a very wide public.

Indeed the nineteenth century knew almost too much of the past of the arts and was too eclectic and derivative in its tastes. Certainly this eclecticism weighed heavily on the architect. Somewhere on earth in these years someone built something in almost every style that had ever been used. Men built Chinese pagodas, Egyptian pyramids, Greek temples, and, especially in America, Gothic universities. In the United States buildings were typed for style: banks, those solid institutions, went back to Greece and Rome, at least for their

CHAPTER XXIII

fronts; churches and universities relied on Gothic; public buildings went in for the Renaissance, duly modified by the reigning taste in the Paris Ecole des Beaux-Arts (School of Fine Arts); private citizens went in for anything that pleased them for their own houses, modified by the traditions of their region. Individual architects worked on a historic style that they adapted in their own way. Thus the American Richardson revived the Romanesque, with its round arches and its solidarity, achieving certainly a style of his own, which can be seen in Trinity Church in Boston.

Two broad styles may be found in the confusion of nineteenth-century architecture. One style, for public buildings, was basically Renaissance, with pediments, balconies, sometimes with domes, and with friezes and other decorations. This style varied somewhat from nation to nation. French public buildings, under the influence of the Beaux-Arts, looked at least vaguely like a chateau in Touraine; German buildings kept a touch of the huddled Middle Ages; and British buildings, much imitated in Boston and New York, were simpler, more in the manner of Palladio. The other style, for private homes, was represented in Europe by the "villa," and in America by the residence, often a "mansion," that the successful businessman built for himself on Elm Street. In the United States this style was at its most flaunting in the mansions of the 1870's, the "era of General Grant." These were big houses, for families were large, domestic servants were plentiful and cheap, and building costs were relatively low. They ran to high ceilings, for the bourgeois wanted nothing to remind him of the low rooms of his peasant past. Today they look too tall for their width, and their lines seem much too broken by little towers, porches, scroll work, all sorts of decorative devices. But they had the latest comforts, if they

Maillol, "La Méditerranée."

were in a town large enough—gas light, bath and water closet, and central heating, though western Europeans came rather slowly to the latter innovation.

In architecture, as in sculpture, true innovation began toward the end of the century. In structural steel, men now had a way of emancipating themselves from the limitations that had so taxed the Gothic builders; they could now go as high as they pleased. They began to do so in the United States, where the first "skyscraper," the Home Insurance Building in Chicago, was put up in 1885. Although some later skyscrapers ended up in Gothic towers, abundantly decorated, the general tendency imposed by the materials was toward simplicity of line. This taste for simplicity began to spread, and with the twentieth century the way was open for modern "functional" architecture. Structural steel

Architecture of the industrial age. The Firth of Forth Bridge in Scotland.

should remind us that some of the most satisfying work of the late nineteenth century was not primarily meant for beauty, but very often achieved it. The great bridges of the time, for example, the Firth of Forth Bridge in Scotland, and Brooklyn Bridge, are still impressive and still useful.

In the minor arts of furniture, household decoration, and clothing, the Victorian Age seems to us now most characteristic and most ugly. Although it is hard to believe that men will ever collect "antiques" of the 1870's as they now collect the work of earlier periods, horsehair sofas and marble-topped tables are nowadays coming into the trade in antiques. So, we return to the Victorian drawing room with which we began. It was an incredibly heavy and incredibly dark room, for the height of the windows was canceled by the dark carpets, upholstery, and hangings, and by the mahogany or walnut furniture. And it was cluttered with what were known as *objets d'art*. Our taste in interior decoration today is different from that of the Victorians in part because in our society domestic labor is scarce and expensive; the mere job of dusting the bric-a-brac of a nineteenth-century house would be too much for the modern housewife.

Music

One great art remains to be discussed—music. The place of leadership that France has occupied for most of nineteenth-century art goes in music clearly to Germany. From Richard Wagner through Brahms to Richard Strauss the great names of music are to an extraordinary degree German. Theirs was indeed no monopoly. The Russians with Moussorgsky, Rimsky-Korsakov, Tschaikovsky, and their colleagues wrote music that is now part of our inheritance. Verdi and other Italians wrote operas a little too conventional for the highbrow, but still played all over the world. And toward the end of the century Frenchmen like Claude Debussy began the shift from Wagnerian grandiloquence to the subtleties

The first skyscraper: the Home Insurance Building in Chicago.

Nineteenth-century interior decoration. The library of Richard Wagner's villa.

and understatements of modern harmony. Still, the most representative composer of the nineteenth century clearly remains Wagner (1813-1883).

Wagner set out to make the opera the supreme manifestation of the drama. He gave up the routine récitatif, interlarded with arias in which the singer or singers dropped what action there had been and advanced boldly to the front of the stage to launch into song. He sought rather to combine music and action in a realistic and dramatic whole. His characteristic device was the *Leitmotiv,* a definite and recognizable melodic theme associated with a given character or symbolizing an element in the drama. These themes he wove together for both voices and orchestra into a continuous flow of music. He chose epic subjects: the four operas of the *Ring of the Nibelungen,* in which he drew on the Teutonic myths, by no means without thought for Teutonic greatness; *Parsifal,* on the theme of the Holy Grail; *Tristan and Isolde,* a drama of fatal love taken from the Arthurian legends. Wagner's operas call for robust voices, which in turn call for barrel-chested tenors and huge sopranos ill-suited to concepts of

romantic love or indeed of heroism. From time to time Wagner's popularity has suffered because of his Victorian heaviness, his inordinate lengths, and the great noise he makes. Nietzsche once wrote aptly that Wagner's music *sweats.*

In concert music, the Wagnerian desire to marry music to the rest of life shows itself in the vogue of program music, that is, music that suggests something definite—birdcalls, thunderstorms, a battle, death and transfiguration. The tone poem, of which Richard Strauss (1864-1949) was master, takes a theme and develops it orchestrally without regard for the classic form of the symphony. Strauss wrote tone poems on Don Quixote, on Nietzsche's *Zarathustra,* even, in his "Domestic Symphony," on the cares and humors of family life. But the older forms of "absolute" music, the symphony and the various kinds of chamber music, survived the vogue for programs. Light music flourished, in the tuneful operettas of Offenbach, like *La Belle Hélène,* based on the legend of Helen of Troy, in the waltzes of Johann Strauss and Waldteufel, and for Anglo-Saxons in the satirical operas of Gilbert and Sullivan.

Daumier caricature. How the public feels after listening to the music of the future by Wagner.

The Arts in Review

To sum up, the literature and the art of the late nineteenth century had all sorts of cross-currents, which were set in motion by the differences between countries, as we have seen, and also by the differences between social classes. There was a popular culture, an art of the simple age-old story and of the picture that tells a similar story. This popular art was perhaps more sentimental, more hopeful of human happiness, and less satirical and earthy than the popular art of an earlier period like the Middle Ages. There was also a more formal culture, which on the whole deserved to be called "realistic" and "materialistic," though it was not devoid of Romantic attempts to flee this harsh world for a better one. Formal art and literature were above all eclectic, borrowing freely from the past, and therefore they are very hard to pin down in terms of "style."

Perhaps we may call this culture "middle class," for much of it deals with bourgeois lives, and reflects the seriousness, the devotion to hard work, the concern with earning a living, the conventional morality, the puritanical streak we associate with the middle classes. But it also produced an art and literature of protest against things-as-they-are, which ranged from the gentle satire of a Trollope to the great disgust of a Nietzsche, through all the moral and political shades of Marxism, socialism, the Single Tax, free love, the rights of women, a revived Christianity, and a refurbished eighteenth-century rationalism. Its span can be neatly summarized in two utopian tales, both very popular in their time, with quite opposite ideas of the perfect life. In *Looking Backward* (1888), by the American Edward Bellamy, the machine has made life perfect for all; Bellamy vaguely anticipates radio, for his hero can push a button in his room and hear sweet music. In *News from Nowhere* (1891), by the Englishman William Morris, men have broken up all their horrid machines and have gone back to what Morris considered the real comforts of the Middle Ages.

CHAPTER XXIII

III: Philosophy

Idealism and Realism

The art and literature of the later nineteenth century furnish samples of almost the full range of human attitudes toward the world. The formal philosophy and the less formal view of life taken by ordinary educated people varied quite as widely, and we can find as many different schools in metaphysics and ethics as we can find in literature and art. The philosophical school of idealism was born in its modern form in the Germany of Kant and Hegel (see Chapters XVII, XIX). In the later nineteenth century it continued to thrive in the land of its birth; it made converts in the Oxford School of T. H. Green, Bradley, and Bosanquet, and in the American philosopher, Josiah Royce; and it even penetrated into the Latin countries. The philosophical opposite of idealism, now christened "realism," was at least as widespread. This modern realism was, of course, very different from the Platonic sort of realism adopted by some of the Scholastic philosophers of the Middle Ages. Modern realism had its roots in the scientific rationalism of the eighteenth-century *philosophes*.

The American philosopher, William James (1842-1910), found two terms to sum up this polar antithesis of idealism and realism that runs through western philosophical tradition. Men are, wrote James, by disposition either "tender-minded" or "tough-minded." They are either tough-mindedly convinced that the world of sense-experience is the *real* world or tender-mindedly convinced that the world of sense-experience is somehow an illusion, or at any rate an imperfect, changing, and therefore unreal copy or reflection of the *real* world which is in our minds—and in God's mind.

One might conclude that, since the later nineteenth century was a period of great material progress, deeply concerned with this world of the senses, then on the whole the "tough-minded" would prevail over the "tender-minded." Yet this was by no means true in formal philosophy, where the tender-minded were quite numerous and articulate. Perhaps the ordinary unreflective man leans toward the tough-minded side, if only because common sense urges upon him the presence of the world of sense-experience, the world of matter. But there are no reliable statistics on this point, and we must remember that to the extent that Christianity forms an inescapable underpinning for the world-view of western men, not even common sense can altogether dispose of the world of the tender-minded, of concepts like "soul," "spirit," the "other world."

Certain common denominators, however, underlay the formal thought of the later nineteenth century. Here, too, Darwinism left its mark. The thought of the period had a historical and evolutionary cast that not even the tender-minded could avoid. The idealist, following Hegel, believed that above the whirl and change of this world of the senses there was an unchanging, perfect world of the Absolute. But he also believed that this imperfect world was being slowly drawn toward that other world, developing by ways he could only incompletely understand, but developing, growing, evolving. On the other hand, the nineteenth-century realist no longer held that his reason could give him a neat mathematical formula for the good life; he too thought that everything grows, that even what is made according to human plans must take account of nature's mysterious ways of growth.

The Cult of the Will

A second and related note in the thought of the period is an emphasis on will, often capitalized into Will, the life-force that makes the "struggle for existence." The word appears everywhere, even as a title—Schopenhauer's *World as Will and Idea*, Nietzsche's *Will to Power*, William James' *Will to Believe*. It appears but slightly disguised in the French philosopher Henri Bergson's "creative evolution" and "élan vital" and in Bernard Shaw's "life-force." It lies behind the use of the word "myth" by the French anarcho-syndicalist, Georges Sorel, and the German Hans Vaihinger's phrase, the "philosophy of the as-if." For both these latter thinkers, the great ideas, the great abstractions of Right and Wrong, are not mere attempts of the mind to understand the world; indeed they are quite false if taken as analytically descriptive of this world. But they are, rather, the guides our desires, our wills, set up for our action. They are fictions, myths, "as-if," but all the more *real* for being such.

The pragmatism of William James, somewhat unfairly described by its critics as the philosophy that nothing succeeds like success, is clearly one of these philosophies of the will. To James, himself "tough-minded," reality is no Absolute as in the idealist tradition; indeed, reality is nothing fixed and certain. Reality is what works for us human beings; truth is what we want to believe. James thought he had saved himself from the obvious danger of this line of thought—that is, making reality and truth purely subjective, purely individual—by granting that not everything we want is practical, that not all our desires "work." If my will to believe tells me I can make a broad jump of three hundred feet, experience, the "pragmatic" test, will prove that I cannot. But to many of James' critics, he had by no means saved himself from sub-

jectivism. Pragmatism remained to these critics a doctrine dangerously erosive of traditional values, leading either to an exaltation of mere vulgar success, or to a silly belief in believing for the sake of believing.

James belongs on the whole to those who distrust the instrument of thought, at least in the sense of reasoning and conventional logic, in the sense of a closed system open only to the duly—and usually academically —licensed. Here is a very typical passage from one of his later works:

All philosophies are hypotheses, to which all our faculties emotional as well as logical, help us, and the truest of which will at the final integration of things be found in possession of the men whose faculties on the whole had the best divining power.[*]

The Revolt against Reason

The cult of the will brings us to a major current in the broad stream of later nineteenth-century thought. This was an intensification of the revolt against reason already initiated by the Romantics earlier in the century; it may be called "anti-intellectualism," "irrationalism," or, more exactly, "anti-rationalism." Even this last term is somewhat misleading, for it stresses negation, whereas the attitude it describes is also an affirmation. There seems, however, to be no better term for the attitude than anti-rationalism.

One further caution. This anti-rationalism is one of the "roots" of contemporary totalitarianism, and especially of fascist and Nazi totalitarianism (see Chapter XXVII). But it is by no means a simple synonym for totalitarianism. It is a much broader and more inclusive term. It is quite possible to

---

[*] William James, *Essays in Radical Empiricism* (New York, 1912), 279.

have been influenced by anti-rational currents and remain a good, if not altogether orthodox, democrat and individualist. It is quite possible to be a Marxist totalitarian and reject a great deal, especially in its psychological core, of modern anti-rationalism.

The basic position of anti-rationalism, and one for which it is heavily indebted to the Romantic movement, is a rejection of the eighteenth-century Enlightenment's belief that the ordinary human being is naturally reasonable. To the extent that it rejects the Enlightenment, anti-rationalism is indeed a negation, as the "anti" implies. But it has its positive side—the belief that if men can accept and understand their true, complex nature, their irrationality, and their dependence on forces beyond their immediate control, they can win their way to a richer life than the rationalists ever planned for them. Yet anti-intellectualism is part of the intellectual revolution; the anti-rationalist himself has to use his mind to communicate with his fellows. He is tied to the ultimate rationality of grammar, of words, and of thinking.

The Chastened Rationalists

Broadly speaking, there are two kinds of anti-rationalism, which shade into one another: the moderate and the extreme. Moderate anti-rationalism at bottom is trying to salvage as much as possible of the eighteenth-century belief in human rationality. Such on the whole is the attitude of modern psychology from Freud and William James on. It seeks to aid human reason by pointing out the difficulties under which it must work. Reason is limited by men's instincts or "drives," by their biological inheritance of animality, so much emphasized by the evolutionists, and by their sociological inheritance of custom and tradition, so much emphasized by historians and by the school of Edmund Burke (see Chapter XIX).

To use a metaphor from John Locke, moderate anti-rationalists regard human reason as a flickering candle, not as the great white universal light it appeared to be to *philosophes* like Condorcet. *But they do not wish to extinguish this candle.* On the contrary, they wish to keep it alive, to nurse it along into greater and greater brightness. This process, in keeping again with the views of the evolutionist, they regard as inevitably long and slow, likely to be hindered rather than helped by ambitious plans to hasten it. These moderate thinkers were not so much anti-rationalists as they were disillusioned or chastened rationalists.

We may take as a clear example of this chastened rationalism the work of an English writer on political and social problems, Graham Wallas (1858-1932). The example is a good one, for Wallas was a member of the English Labor party, a man who shared the hopes the eighteenth-century democrats put in the common man. His book, *Human Nature in Politics* (1908), was based on his experiences in practical politics as a candidate for the London County Council. He had been trained in the belief, characteristic of the eighteenth-century inheritance, that if men are properly educated in political matters they will understand what is the rational course, and will vote for measures and men in accordance with enlightened self-interest, which will also be in accordance with the common interest. Wallas found in actual canvassing for votes that men were in fact influenced by all sorts of irrational words and acts not anticipated by his faith in human reason. He found in effect, that it paid a candidate to kiss babies, to flatter mothers, to gossip cheerfully on matters not directly germane to the governing of London.

Here is a characteristic passage:

Writers on the 'psychology of the crowd' have pointed out the effect of excitement and numbers in substituting non-rational for rational inference. Any cause, however, which prevents a man from giving full attention to his mental processes may produce the phenomena of non-rational inference in an extreme degree. I have often watched in some small sub-committee the method by which either of the two men with a real genius for committee work whom I know could control his colleagues. The process was most successful towards the end of an afternoon, when the members were tired and somewhat dazed with the effort of following a rapid talker through a mass of unfamiliar detail. If at that point the operator slightly quickened the flow of his information, and slightly emphasised the assumption that he was being thoroughly understood, he could put some at least of his colleagues into a sort of waking trance, in which they would have cheerfully assented to the proposition that the best means of securing, e.g., the permanence of private schools was a large and immediate increase in the number of public schools.*

Wallas' book would teach nothing new in the mid-twentieth century to American politicians or advertising men, or even to professors of political science. But half a century ago it was revolutionary in the thinking of good British radicals, nursed in the high rationalist ideals of the Utilitarians and the Fabian socialists. Wallas was a bit shocked by the reception of his book, and feared that it had perhaps encouraged the anti-rationalists of conservative stamp too much. He did not want to help put out the candle of reason, so he wrote another book, *The Great Society* (1914), in which he came to the defense of "thought":

The whole of our analysis up to this point goes to prove that, as the scale of social organisation extends, the merely instinctive guidance of Fear, or Love, or Pleasure, or Habit becomes more and more unsafe; and that not only is a

clearer consciousness of his actions and a stronger habit of forecasting their result needed by the ordinary man, but Thought in the great sense, the long-continued concentration of the professed thinker in which new knowledge is made available for the guidance of human life, is required as it has never been required before.*

The Extreme Anti-rationalists

By contrast, the second kind of anti-rationalism would actually put out the candle of human reason. For the extreme anti-rationalists reason is not just feeble; it is bad. It is for them, so to speak, a mistake evolution has made, a wrong turning, from which the human race must somehow retrace its steps to a sounder life of instinct, emotion, and faith. Thomas Hardy, the English novelist, put the position clearly in the remark, "Thought is a disease of the flesh." There was a strong dose of this extreme anti-rationalism in the Nazi movement. Hitler himself distrusted reason as a degenerate French invention. Good Germans, he hoped, would come to think with their blood, with their German folk inheritance. Extreme anti-rationalism may also be found at the bottom of some of the wilder movements in modern art, which want to do away with all the rules of grammar or harmony or perspective, and write or compose music or paint from the heart—or the guts—without regard for "meaningless forms."

The position of these extremists is strongly rooted in the Romantic movement, with its emphasis on the heart as against the head, on fresh instinct as against stale logic, on "the desire of the moth for the star." These anti-rationalists are direct descendants of the Goethe who wrote:

---

* Graham Wallas, *Human Nature in Politics* (Boston, 1916), 110.

* Graham Wallas, *The Great Society* (New York, 1914), 182.

CHAPTER XXIII

```
... Grey is all theory,                          Of moral evil and of good,
The golden tree of life is green!                Than all the sages can.

They descend from the Wordsworth who                        .    .    .
wrote:
                                                 Enough of science and of art;
    One impulse from a vernal wood               Close up these barren leaves;
    May teach you more of man,                   Come forth, and bring with you a heart
                                                 That watches and receives.
```

IV: Psychology

The historian of modern thought finds it convenient to group together many of the manifestations of the attitude toward life of a given period under the natural science that enjoyed nearly universal prestige at the time. This is the science that finds its way through the channels of popularization to the drawing room, the lecture platform, the press, and the schools. Such for the eighteenth century was Newton; men saw the universe in terms of a huge "Newtonian world-machine" (see Chapter XVII). Such, even before Darwin in the nineteenth century, and for some decades after the publication of the *Origin of Species* in 1859, was natural history, or biology. Men saw the universe not as a machine running automatically in a timeless groove, to which men should fit themselves, but as a vast organism composed of many parts, all growing, all evolving in a pattern never quite fixed. Then toward the end of the nineteenth century there began the great prestige of another science—a science indeed that many exact scientists still regard as no science at all, for it still cannot be put in mathematical terms. This is the science of psychology, into which our contemporary anti-rationalism fits neatly.

This sequence of the radiation of the sciences into general thought may be observed in the smooth coins of conversation and journalism of a given age. The novels, newspapers, and letters of the eighteenth century referred constantly to Newton, to universal attraction and repulsion, to the world-machine. In the early nineteenth century the Frenchman Fourier set up what he called *l'attraction passionnelle*— a sort of political and social gravity, and asserted, "I am the Newton of social science" (see Chapter XX). Similarly, as we have just seen, the Social Darwinists of the late nineteenth century were all talking about the "struggle for existence" and the "survival of the fittest." And of course in the twentieth century phrases like "reflex," "sublimation," "inferiority complex," "Oedipus complex," and many others have gone from the laboratory of the psychologist and the couch of the psychoanalyst into common speech. A more detailed account of anti-rationalism, in both its moderate and extreme forms, may therefore begin with the science of psychology to which both owe so much.

Pavlov

From the Russian psychologist, Pavlov, whose basic work was done toward the end of the nineteenth and the beginning of the twentieth century, we get the now familiar term "conditioned reflex." Pavlov's dogs are as famous as any laboratory animals have ever been. After being repeatedly fed at a certain signal, such as a bell, his dogs came to water at the mouth in anticipation of food at a mere signal. The natural —that is the untrained—response of watering at the mouth would ordinarily come only when the dog had actual food before him; Pavlov got the same response artificially by a signal that certainly did not smell or look like food to the dog. The upshot was clear evidence that training or conditioning could produce automatic responses in the animal that were essentially similar to the kind of automatic responses the animal is born with. Conditioned reflexes, like watering at the mouth at a signal, were the same as natural reflexes, like watering at the mouth when meat is offered the animal.

Pavlov's experiments had important implications for the social scientist. It confirmed eighteenth-century notions about the power of environment, of training and education, in the sense that environment can be manipulated to give organisms new responses. But—and this is a bitter blow to eighteenth-century optimism—once such training has taken hold, the organism has, so to speak, incorporated the results almost as if they had been the product of heredity, not environment, and further change becomes very difficult, in some instances impossible. Pavlov, after having trained some of his dogs, tried mixing his signals, frustrating and confusing the dogs by withholding food at the signal that had always produced food for them. He succeeded in producing symptoms of a kind close to what in human beings would be neurosis.

Now the cautious social scientist does not, of course, take over Pavlov's conditioned reflexes and apply them uncritically to all human behavior. He does not assume, for instance, that the Vermonter voting the

Sigmund Freud.

straight Republican ticket is behaving quite like the dog watering at the mouth as an accustomed bell is rung. Even in Vermont, voting Republican is not quite a conditioned reflex. But the cautious social scientist will hold that concepts like that of the conditioned reflexes do throw light on a great deal of habit-determined human conduct. For the anti-rationalist, Pavlov's work was further demonstration that a very great deal of our behavior is not determined, or even greatly influenced, by what goes on in the cerebral cortex.

Freud

Anti-rationalism also derived much from another great psychologist, Sigmund Freud (1873-1939). Freud was a physician, trained in Vienna in the medical tradition of the late nineteenth century. His interest was early drawn to mental illness, where he soon found cases in which patients exhibited symptoms of very real organic disturbances, but for which no obvious organic causes could be found. He studied for a time in Paris under a French physician, Charcot, who treated such patients by hypnotizing them. Freud himself used hypnosis for a while, but gradually evolved his own method, which is called psychoanalysis. Under analysis the patient, relaxed on a couch, is urged to pour out what he can remember of his earliest childhood, or indeed infancy. After many such treatments, the analyst can hope to find what is disturbing the patient, and by making him aware of what that is, can hope to cure him.

Had Freud merely contented himself with this kind of therapy, few of us would have heard of him. But from all this clinical experience he worked out a system of psychology that has had a very great influence, not only on psychiatry and psychology, but on some of our basic conceptions of human relations. Freud starts with the concept of a set of "drives" with which each person is born. These drives, which he at first called the *libido* and later the *id*, try to get satisfaction, to realize themselves in action. The infant, notably, is "uninhibited"; that is, his drives well up into action from the id without restraint from his conscious mind. But by no means without restraint from his parents or nurse—and there's the difficulty. The infant finds himself frustrated. As he grows, as his mind is formed, he comes to be conscious of the fact that some of the things he wants to do are objectionable to those closest to him, and on whom he is so dependent. He himself therefore begins to repress these drives from his id.

With his dawning consciousness of the world outside himself, he has in fact developed another part of his psyche, which Freud at first called the "censor," and later divided into two phases which he called the "ego" and the "superego." The *ego* is the individual's private censor, his awareness that in accordance with what Freudians call the "reality principle" certain drives from his id simply cannot succeed. The *superego* is something like what common language calls "conscience"; it is the individual's awareness that he is part of a social system in which certain actions are proper and certain actions improper.

Now these drives of the id, and indeed in some of its phases the actions of the ego, are for Freud a sort of great reservoir of which the individual is not normally aware; that is, they are part of his "unconscious." (Pavlov's conditioned reflexes are of course also unconscious.) In a mentally healthy individual, enough of the drives of the id succeed so that he feels contented. But even the healthiest of individuals has of course had to repress a great deal of his drives from the id. This successful repression the Freudians account for in part at least by a process they call "sublimation." That is, they think that the healthy individual somehow finds for a drive suppressed by ego or superego, or by both working together, a new and socially approved outlet or expression. Thus a drive toward sex relations not approved in one's circle might be sublimated into the writing of poetry or music, or into religious devotion, or even into athletics.

With the mentally ill person, however, Freud held that drives, having been suppressed, driven back down into the unconscious, find no suitable other outlet or sublimation, and continue, so to speak, festering in the id, trying to find some outlet. They find all sorts of outlets of an abnormal sort, symptoms of illness in great variety. They display themselves in all sorts of neuroses and phobias, which have in common a failure to conform to the "reality principle." The neurotic individual is "maladjusted." And if the failure to meet the reality principle is really complete, the individual is insane, "psychotic," and lives in an utterly unreal private world of his own.

Freud, especially in his earlier years, did indeed hold that the libido, or the id, is wholly, or almost wholly, sexual in nature. Sexual drives he found—and this is above all what shocked his contemporaries—in the infant. He worked out a time-scheme for this libido, which appears first as "oral eroticism," and is associated with suckling at the breast, then as "anal eroticism," and then, when the child is about six to twelve years old, becomes, he thought, actually quiescent in most individuals. Then, with the onset of puberty, sexuality comes back in its normal form of "genital eroticism." Moreover, the child undergoing this process of growth comes at a certain stage to feel sexual attraction for the parent of the opposite sex, the son for the mother in the famous "Oedipus complex," and the daughter for the father in the less famous "Electra complex."

Now our western society frowns on these earlier manifestations of sexuality. Mothers in Freud's day, for instance, would try hard to prevent the child's sucking its thumb, in Freudian terms an obvious, and harmless, form of oral eroticism. Other forms of infantile sexuality meet with even stronger disapproval. The infant and later the child are therefore obliged to repress their sexuality. In the neurotic person, Freud believed, this repression is the main source of his difficulties. As an adult, he finds it impossible to achieve normal sex relations, but "regresses" to earlier stages of oral or anal eroticism, or takes refuge in masturbation or homosexual relations. Since all these "irregular" manifestations of sexuality are very strongly condemned by our society, the individual driven to them by his unconscious either suppresses them, or if he indulges in them, feels a great sense of guilt. Either way he may end as a neurotic.

Freud's therapy rested on the belief that if the individual neurotic could come to understand why he behaved as he did he could make a proper adjustment and lead a normal life. But here Freud parted company with the rationalist tradition of the eighteenth century. He held that there was no use preaching at the individual, reasoning simply with him, telling him the error of his ways, pointing out what was unreasonable in his behavior. Reason could not get directly at the unconscious, where the source of his trouble lay. Only by the long slow process of psychoanalysis, in which the individual day after day sought in memories of his earliest childhood for concrete details, could the listening analyst pick from this stream of consciousness the significant details that pointed to the hidden repression, the "blocking" that came out in neurotic behavior. Freud gave special importance to the dreams of the patient, which he must patiently describe to the analyst; for in dreams, Freud thought, the unconscious wells up out of control, or but partly controlled, by the ego. Once the patient, however, got beneath the surface of his conscious life, and became aware of what had gone wrong with his hitherto unconscious life, he might then cure himself.

The Implications of Freudianism

What is important for us in the wider implications of Freud's work, his part in the broad current of anti-rationalism, is first this concept of the very great role of the unconscious drives, that is, the unthinking, the non-rational, in our lives. Ordinary reflective thinking is for the Freudian a very small part of our existence. We are back at the metaphor of reason as a flickering candle, or to use another well-worn metaphor, of reason as simply the small part of the iceberg that shows above the water, while submerged down below is the great mass of the unconscious. Much even of our conscious thinking is what psychologists call "rationalization," thinking dictated, not by an awareness of the reality principle, but by the desires of our id. One can get a good measure of the difference between eighteenth-century rationalism and Freudian psychology by contrasting the older belief in the innocence and natural goodness of the child, Wordsworth's "mighty prophet, seer blest," with the Freudian view of the child as a bundle of unsocial or antisocial drives, as in fact a little untamed savage.

But second, and most important, note that the Freudians do not wish to blow out the candle of human reason. They are moderate, not extreme, anti-rationalists; they are chastened rationalists. Their whole therapy is based on the concept, which has Christian as well as eighteenth-century roots, that "ye shall know the truth, and the truth shall make you free." Only, for the Freudian, truth is not easily found, not distillable into a few simple rules of conduct which all men, being reasonable and good, can use as guides to individual and collective happiness. It is on the contrary very hard to establish, and can be reached only by a long and precarious struggle. Many will not reach it, and will have to put up with all sorts of maladjustments and frustrations. The Freudian is at bottom a pessimist in that he does not believe in the perfectibility of man. But he is also something of an idealist; he believes in the struggle to make human life better here on earth, even if it cannot be made perfect.

V: Political and Social Thought

Many psychologists who rejected Freud's system as a whole nevertheless agreed with him on the great part played in human motivation by instinct, impulse, drives, urges, by something non-rational if not irrational. Their anti-rationalism came over in many ways into political and social thought. Here the distinction between moderate and extreme anti-rationalists is most important.

Many of the extreme anti-rationalists turned violently against democracy, which seemed to them to rest on an altogether false estimate of what human beings were really like. The democrat believes at bottom that the ordinary man can be freed from the weight of erroneous traditions, habits, and prejudices. Once he has the real facts before him, he can attain by free discussion among his fellows a series of decisions that will be incorporated in acts and institutions under which all men can live happily. But if you hold that men are by nature incapable of fair, dispassionate thinking and discussion, if you hold that the load of tradition, habit, and prejudice cannot by any system of education be lifted from them, if in short you hold that men are by nature irrational, you will at least have to revise drastically your notions of democracy, or reject them.

The extreme anti-rationalist rejected the notions of democracy. The German philosopher Nietzsche, who did most of his work in the 1880's, will do as a sample of such political thinkers in this period. Nietzsche wrote mostly in short aphoristic passages, which are hard to systematize and are often quite contradictory. But the central line of his thinking led to the concept of a new aristocracy, to the "superman" (in German,

Uebermensch). Nietzsche's followers, who were numerous thoughout the West in the two decades before 1914, insisted that he meant a new *spiritual* aristocracy. The supermen would be above the petty materialism and national patriotism of the middle classes; they would be more than Platonic, more than Christian, in their devotion to the hard heroic life of the beautiful and the good. Nietzsche's opponents, who were also many, held that he was just another preacher of Nordic superiority, that his supermen were, as he put it in one of his famous passages, "the blond beasts" who had so often terrorized Europe. Certainly some of his German followers took him at his word, and held that he meant the real live Germans to be his supermen.

At any rate, Nietzsche was clearly an enemy of democracy, which he held to be second only to its child, socialism, as a society in which the weak unjustly and unnaturally ruled the strong. Here are some of his aphorisms, from which the reader can judge for himself:

Democracy represents the disbelief in all great men and in all élite societies: everybody is everybody else's equal. 'At bottom we are all herd and mob.'
I am opposed to Socialism because it dreams ingenuously of 'goodness, truth, beauty, and equal rights' (anarchy pursues the same ideal, but in a more brutal fashion).
I am opposed to parliamentary government and the power of the press, because they are the means whereby cattle become masters.

. . .

. . . Is it not high time, now that the type 'gregarious animal' is developing ever more and more in Europe, to set about rearing, thoroughly, artificially, and consciously, an opposite type, and to attempt to establish the latter's virtues? And would not the democratic movement itself find for the first time a sort of goal, salvation, and justification, if some one appeared who availed himself of it—so that at last, beside its new and sublime product, slavery (for this must be the end of European

democracy), that higher species of ruling and Cæsarian spirits might also be produced, which would stand upon it, hold to it, and would elevate themselves through it? This new race would climb aloft to new and hitherto impossible things, to a broader vision, and to its task on earth.*

Clearly Nietzsche hoped that the herd, the slaves, the masses would, in spite of their crass materialism, somehow recognize the true masters, the new enlightened despots.

Mosca and Pareto

More down to earth as political thinkers and moralists are the Italian writers, Gaetano Mosca (1858-1941) and Vilfredo Pareto (1848-1923), whose work shows clearly the mark of their countryman Machiavelli. These new Machiavellians devoted themselves to the realistic study of democracy in their time. All were marked by the anti-rationalist trend in the sense that they agreed that democracy was not working out into the government by rational discussion that the eighteenth-century *philosophes* had hoped for. Indeed, the thesis of Mosca's major work, translated into English under the title of *The Ruling Class,* is that even under democracy there is no such thing as the rule of the majority. There is always a relatively small "political class" who make the decisions, and a large class of the governed who do but acquiesce in the decisions of their rulers. The "scientific" study of politics should therefore concern itself with the way the ruling class is formed, how it maintains itself, and how it obtains the acquiescence of the ruled. Mosca delights in pointing out the tricks of practical politics, the ritual and the "myths" by which the ruling class in parliamentary democracy keeps its power. He is disturbed by the increasing tendency in these democ-

---

* Friedrich Nietzsche, *The Will to Power,* A. M. Ludovici, trans. (London, 1910), II, 206, 360-361.

CHAPTER XXIII

racies toward some kind of collectivism, toward a leveling state socialism. He has, however, no clear formula of his own for a new kind of élite and a new kind of government.

Pareto's work well displays the mixed attitude of many late nineteenth-century anti-rationalists toward democracy. At bottom, they share the eighteenth-century rationalist dream of a highly individualistic society. But, like Freud in another field, they are oppressed by the evidence of the irrationality of ordinary men, by the tendency away from the variety, the richness, of individualism. Pareto is in some sense a disillusioned liberal, trying to fight his way out of disillusion, but unwilling to accept any simple élitist formula like Nietzsche's superman or the fascist "leader-principle," and even more unwilling to go back to medieval concepts of an ordered Christian society.

Pareto as a sociologist in his *The Mind and Society* is concerned chiefly with the problem of separating out in human actions the rational from the non-rational. What interests Pareto is the kind of action that is expressed in words, ritual, symbolism of some kind. Buying wool socks for cold weather is one such action. If they are bought deliberately to get good socks at a price the buyer can afford, this is rational action in accord with the doer's interests. If, however, they are bought without regard for price by a sentimental lover of England who buys imported English socks in order to do his bit to help England, then clearly something else, something the economist has to disregard in his price statistics, has come into play. This something else is the substance of Pareto's study.

Pareto distinguishes part of social action as *derivations*, which are close to what most of us know as rationalizations. These are the explanations and accompanying ritualist acts associated with our religion, our patriot-ism, our feelings for groups of all kinds. Prayer, for instance, is for Pareto a derivation; he was, like so many of this period, a materialist, at bottom hostile to Christianity, though he approved of it as a means of social concord. It is irrational, or non-rational, to pray for rain, because we know as meteorologists that rain has purely material causes quite beyond the reach of prayer. These derivations are indeed a factor in human social life, but they do not really move men to social action.

What does move men in society, and keeps them together in society, says Pareto, is the *residues*. These are expressions of relatively permanent, abiding sentiments in men, expressions that usually have to be separated from the part that is actually a derivation, which may change greatly and even quickly. Pagan Greek sailors sacrificed to Poseidon, god of the sea, before setting out on a voyage; Christian Greek sailors a few centuries later prayed, lighted candles, and made vows to the Virgin Mary just before sailing. The *derivations* are the explanations of what Poseidon and the Virgin respectively do. They vary. The believer in the Virgin thinks his pagan predecessor was dead wrong. The *residues* are the needs to secure divine aid and comfort in a difficult undertaking, and to perform certain ritual acts that give the performer assurance of such aid and comfort. The residues are nearly the same for our two sets of sailors. Both the pagans and the Christians have the same social and psychological needs and satisfy them in much the same ways, though with very different explanations of what they are doing.

Two of the major classes of residues Pareto distinguishes stand out, and help form his philosophy of history. These are first the residues of *persistent aggregates*, the sentiments that mark men who like regular ways, solid discipline, tradition and habit, men like the Spartans. Second, there are the residues of the *instinct for combinations,* the sentiments that mark men who like novelty and adventure, who invent new ways of doing things, who like to cut loose from the old and the tried, men not easily shocked, men who hate discipline, men like the Athenians. In societies of many individual members, men influenced largely by one or the other of these major residues tend to predominate, and to characterize that society. Like most philosophers of history, Pareto is far from clear on just how a conservative society where the residues of persistent aggregates predominate changes into another kind of society. But he does have this conception of a pendulum swing, even a struggle of thesis and antithesis.

The nineteenth century in the West was in Pareto's mind a society in which the residues of instinct of combinations played perhaps the greatest role of which they are capable in a human society. The nineteenth century was a century of competition among individuals full of new ideas, inventions, enterprises, convinced that the old ways were bad, that novelty was the great thing to strive for at the expense of everything else. It was a society notably out of equilibrium. It had to turn toward the other kind of residues, toward the persistent aggregates, toward a society with more security and less competition, more discipline and less freedom, more uniformity and less variety. It had to go the way we seem to be going in the twentieth century.

Pareto's final general conception is that of an equilibrium in a society. It is an equilibrium constantly disturbed, at least in western society, but constantly renewed by a sort of natural healing force not to be supplanted by any social physician or planner. Pareto does not entirely rule out the possibility that human beings by taking thought may in little ways here and there change social arrangements in such a way that what they plan turns out to be a

reality. But the overwhelming emphasis of his work is that change in human conduct as a whole must be distinguished from change in human ideas and ideals. Since man is what he is, and, in our western culture, since the residue of instinct of combinations is so widespread, there is bound to be change in many fields of human interest. Fashion and all its commercial dependents can almost be said to be change for change's sake. But for Pareto there was also a level of human conduct where change is very slow indeed, almost as slow as the kind of change the geologist and the evolutionist study.

This level of human conduct where change is very slow indeed is the level of the residues. At most, Pareto held, the skilled political leader can manipulate the derivations in such a way that some residues are made relatively inactive, and others are activated. He cannot possibly produce new residues or destroy old ones. He will get effective governmental inspection of meats, for instance, not just by an appeal to men's sense of civic responsibility, not just by a rational argument of the eighteenth-century sort, but also by propaganda, by literary work like the American Upton Sinclair's exposé of the stockyards in his novel, *The Jungle.* As many people as possible must *feel fear* that they will eat uninspected dirty meat and die of food poisoning unless the government does inspect. Obviously, the men who direct modern advertising are Paretans without knowing it.

The wise leader according to Pareto will read Bacon's famous aphorism, "Nature is not to be commanded save by obeying her," as "*Human* nature is not to be commanded save by obeying it"—or at least by taking it into account. You must not expect human beings to be consistently unselfish, sensible, devoted to the common good, kindly, wise. Above all, you must not expect that any institution, any law, any constitution, any treaty or pact, will make them so. But

Pareto goes a bit beyond this position. Planning, except for limited and always very concrete ends, is dangerous. Not only is it very likely that a big, ambitious, legislated change will not achieve the results the planners planned; it is likely to produce unpredictable and perhaps unfortunate results. Pareto would have gloated a bit, one suspects, over the fate of the Eighteenth Amendment, which did not promote temperance in the United States, but produced the speakeasy instead. Until we know more of social science, Pareto holds, the best thing to do is to trust to what the upstart intellectual arrogantly condemns as the irrational side of human nature. We must believe that the ingrained habits of the human race are, even by evolutionary standards, more useful to survival than the impertinent logic of the reformers.

Political Thought in Review

Pareto is trying to be a chastened rationalist, and in spite of the use fascists have made of his work, deserves to be so classified. He is essentially a nineteenth-century liberal who felt uncomfortable in a world in which the great wars of our own time were clearly brewing, a world in which the Victorian decencies were slowly dissolving. But, as we have seen in Graham Wallas, many thinkers whose sympathies with the democratic system of values were clearer than Pareto's were none the less influenced by the anti-rationalist's doubts about the natural goodness and reasonableness of man. John Stuart Mill in the mid-nineteenth century had worried over the "tyranny of the majority" (see Chapter XX). Walter Bagehot, a good English liberal (see Chapter XXI) much influenced by Darwin, pointed out in his *Physics and Politics* (1872) how strong was the accumulated force of habit and tradition, which he called

the "cake of custom," how hard it was to persuade men to rational action. By the end of the century, liberals throughout the West were facing the problem of revising their attitudes toward life to conform with the new emphasis on the tough network of habit, custom, and prejudice.

Already by 1914 the broad lines of the social attitudes of our own time were being laid out. One line goes toward some kind of revolutionary élitism, toward the seizure of power by a minority that believes itself to have the formula whereby the gifted few can put order into a society threatened with chaos because of attempts to make decisions by counting heads, no matter what is inside them. The variety of these specific formulas is, however, very great, for the late nineteenth century was in its political and ethical ideas at least as eclectic as it was in architecture. Some make race the mark of the élite, and go so far as to preach world rule for their chosen race. Others make class the mark of the élite, and seek to achieve the "dictatorship of the proletariat." Indeed, as Marxian socialism developed in Lenin's hands the élitist implications, which were never very much hidden in the work of that truculent and impatient hater of human beings, Karl Marx, come out openly as the doctrine that the enlightened minority must seize power and rule dictatorially for a while, at least. Others dream of a brand-new élite, such as Nietzsche's supermen, to be created by a kind of new religion. Others look to eugenics to make possible the breeding of such a new élite—though it must be confessed that in spite of their appeal to natural science, these are among the most impractical of the lot.

A second line goes toward a more flexible form of élitism, one that tries to conserve as much as possible of democratic values. On the whole, English Fabianism and continental revisionist socialism deserve this classification. The leaders of these movements want no violent overturns, no seizure of power. They believe in gradualness, even in the basic democratic counting of heads. But there is in all of them a strong touch of doubt as to the political capacity of the ordinary man. They are not for the extension of New England town-meeting democracy to the millions of the modern state. They hope they can persuade the millions to elect legislators who will listen to the wise planners who have studied the social sciences, who can devise the wise new institutions that will make human life so much better. Above all, the planners themselves will by no means disdain what the anti-rationalists have taught them about the irrationality of ordinary men; they will make full use for good ends of what they can learn from the "practical" politician, the advertising man, the skilled professional manipulator of human beings; they will be Machiavellians, but Machiavellians on the side of the angels.

A third line seeks to preserve and protect what they consider a good, or at any rate an existing, élite from democratic drives toward equality, especially in the form of state intervention in economic and social life to promote security for all. This is substantially the line followed by men like Pareto, by the American sociologist William Graham Sumner, by the English philosopher Herbert Spencer, and by many others throughout the West. They are not unfairly labeled conservatives, for they seek to preserve in its broad lines an established order. But they are not simply routine, unphilosophical conservatives who oppose any changes at all. They have a definite philoso-

phy, strongly influenced by the spirit of the times, by the anti-rationalism we have here outlined. Their basic position is a distrust of the instrument of thought applied unsparingly to human society, and in this they go back to Burke and indeed to philosophical conservatives throughout the western tradition.

But they are clearly children of their age, above all in their concrete fears of "socialism." Most of them believe in progress, and most of them prize material plenty, peace, industrial society. They hold, however, that on the whole the existing middle classes, the existing leaders of a business world, the existing network of Victorian habits and morals, are the best insurance that progress will continue. Above all, they fear planners and planning, at least in political positions. They distrust the state. At bottom, they are good Darwinians, who believe that the evolutionary process depends on the struggle for life among competing individuals fettered as little as possible by planned human attempts to "rig" the struggle. They believe that evolution cannot be hastened, and that attempts to hasten it, no matter how well meant, will in fact retard it by limiting actual human variation and initiative. They are by no means altogether without sympathizers among us today, but it must be admitted that theirs has not, so far, been the "wave of the future." The Herbert Spencer who thought compulsory sewage disposal in cities was an interference with the "right" of the individual to conduct his own private struggle against typhoid fever would be even more uncomfortable in the mid-twentieth century than he was in the late nineteenth.

CHAPTER XXIII

Reading Suggestions
on the Intellectual Revolution

General Accounts

C. Brinton, *Ideas and Men* (New York: Prentice-Hall, Inc., 1950). The later chapters of this general survey of intellectual history are also available in an inexpensive reprint: *The Shaping of the Modern Mind* (New York: New American Library, 1953. A Mentor Book).

R. C. Binkley, *Realism and Nationalism, 1852-1871* (New York: Harper and Brothers, 1935) and C. J. H. Hayes, *A Generation of Materalism, 1871-1900* (New York: Harper and Brothers, 1941). These two volumes in the "Rise of Modern Europe" series provide fairly full coverage of the topics treated in this chapter.

Special Studies: Darwinism

C. Darwin, *On the Origin of Species by Natural Selection* (New York: Modern Library, 1936) and *Journal of Researches into the Geology and Natural History of the Various Countries Visited during the Voyage of H.M.S. Beagle round the World* (New York: E. P. Dutton and Co., 1908. Everyman ed.). Respectively, Darwin's classic exposition, and his often fascinating report on the *Beagle* expedition that provided some of the evidence for his theories.

J. Barzun, *Darwin, Marx, Wagner* (Boston: Little, Brown & Co., 1941). An interesting study; finds common denominators in men usually catalogued as quite different.

H. Spencer, *The Man versus the State*, A. J. Nock, ed. (Caldwell, Idaho: Caxton Printers, Ltd., 1940). A representative work by a whole-hearted Social Darwinist.

Sumner Today, M. R. Davie, ed. (New Haven: Yale University Press, 1940). Selected essays by William Graham Sumner, the most famous American Social Darwinist.

W. Bagehot, *Physics and Politics*, new ed. (New York: Alfred A. Knopf, Inc., 1948). An early and suggestive adaptation of Darwinism to the political realm; very good reading, unlike the work of some other Social Darwinists.

Special Studies: Literature and the Arts

G. M. Young, *Victorian England: Portrait of an Age* (Garden City, N. Y.: Doubleday, 1954. An Anchor Book). A brilliant evocation.

E. Wilson, *Axel's Castle, A Study in the Imaginative Literature of 1870-1930* (New York: Charles Scribner's Sons, 1931). A very solid study.

G. Brandes, *Main Currents in Nineteenth-Century Literature*, 6 vols. (London: Wm. Heinemann, Ltd., 1901-1905). A valuable detailed study.

R. E. Fry, *Characteristics of French Art* (London: Chatto and Windus, 1932). Includes brief but highly useful essays on major French painters of the nineteenth century.

M. Raynal, *The Nineteenth Century: Goya to Gauguin* (Geneva, Switzerland: Editions Albert Skira, 1951). A superbly illustrated volume on painting.

S. Giedion, *Mechanization Takes Command* (New York: Oxford University Press, 1948). Interesting account of the effects of industrialism on the arts.

P. H. Láng, *Music in Western Civilization* (New York: W. W. Norton and Co., 1941) and C. Gray, *History of Music*, 2nd ed. (New York: Alfred A. Knopf, Inc., 1947). Two very different and helpful histories of music.

Special Studies: Psychology and Thought

B. P. Babkin, *Pavlov, A Biography* (Chicago: University of Chicago Press, 1949). Good introduction to the work of the famous Russian psychologist; by one of his former students.

S. Freud, *An Outline of Psychoanalysis* (New York: W. W. Norton and Co., 1949). The great psychologist's last word on his craft.

E. Jones, *The Life and Work of Freud* (New York: Basic Books, 1953). Widely considered the best book on Freud.

D. Riesman, *The Lonely Crowd* (Garden City, N. Y.: Doubleday, 1954. An Anchor Book). Temperate application of the findings of social psychology to the American scene.

H. Bergson, *The Two Sources of Morality and Religion* (Garden City, N. Y.: Doubleday, 1954. An Anchor Book). Characteristic work by an important critic of rationalism.

G. Sorel, *Reflections on Violence* (Glencoe, Ill.: Free Press, 1950). A significant and very readable application of the anti-rational view to social and political problems.

R. Humphrey, *Georges Sorel, Prophet without Honor* (Cambridge, Mass.: Harvard University Press, 1951). Good study of Sorel, with a valuable discussion of anti-intellectualism.

G. Wallas, *Human Nature in Politics* (London: A. Constable, 1908). A pioneer study of the non-rational elements in politics.

C. Brinton, *English Political Thought in the Nineteenth Century*, new ed. (Cambridge, Mass., 1949) and E. Barker, *Political Thought in England, 1848-1914* (London: T. Butterworth, Ltd., 1930. Home University Library). Two useful studies.

D. C. Somervell, *English Thought in the Nineteenth Century* (London: Methuen & Co., Ltd., 1929). Valuable work; emphasizing formal thought.

The Philosophy of Nietzsche (New York: Modern Library, 1937). A convenient collection, including *Thus Spake Zarathustra* and other representative works of the controversial German philosopher.

C. Brinton, *Nietzsche* (Cambridge, Mass.: Harvard University Press, 1941) and G. A. Morgan, Jr., *What Nietzsche Means* (Cambridge, Mass.: Harvard University Press, 1941). Two very different interpretations.

G. C. Homans and C. P. Curtis, Jr., *An Introduction to Pareto* (New York: Alfred A. Knopf, Inc., 1934). The handiest approach to a difficult thinker.

Novels and Dramas

G. Flaubert, *Madame Bovary* (many editions). The classic novel of French realism.

E. Zola, *Germinal* (many editions) and *L'Assommoir* (translated under several titles, including *Nana's Mother;* New York: Avon Books, 1950). Two characteristic novels by the great French exponent of naturalism.

S. Butler, *The Way of All Flesh* (many editions). A good example of gloomy naturalism in the novel, English-style.

S. Lewis, *Babbitt* (New York: Harcourt, Brace & Co., 1949) and *Main Street* (New York: Harcourt, Brace & Co., 1950). Novels that are important documents of American social history in the early twentieth century.

E. Bellamy, *Looking Backward, 2000-1887* (New York: Modern Library, 1951); H. G. Wells, *A Modern Utopia* (New York: Charles Scribner's Sons, 1905); and W. Morris, *News from Nowhere* (New York: Longmans, Green & Co., 1901). Three contrasting visions of utopia in the light of science and industrialism.

H. Ibsen, *Ghosts, An Enemy of the People, A Doll's House, The Master Builder* (New York: Modern Library, no date). Four pioneering dramas by a master of late nineteenth-century realism.

E. Brieux, *Damaged Goods,* preface by G. B. Shaw (London: A. C. Fifield, 1914). The famous play about venereal disease.

G. B. Shaw, *Man and Superman* (Harmondsworth, Middlesex: Penguin Books, no date) and *Back to Methuselah* (New York: Oxford University Press, 1947. World's Classics). Two of Shaw's many plays that discuss aspects of the modern intellectual revolution.

Nineteenth-
Century
Imperialism

I: The Movement in General

Iℕ ᴛʜᴇ *Oxford English Diction-ary*, which tries to find the earliest possible example of a definition, the editors can go no further back than 1881 for "imperialism: the principle of the spirit of empire; advocacy of what are held to be imperial interests." The word is new; what it stands for is very old indeed. Ever since the first chapter of this book we have seen organized human groups moving into lands not their own, and driving out, or exterminating, or simply bringing into subjection the former inhabitants. The specific sequence of European—more accurately, western—expansion that reached a culmination in the late nineteenth century began back in the fifteenth century.

CHAPTER XXIV

Imperialism, New and Old

We must not let the term "imperialism" make us lose our sense of proportion. We must not assume, as many modern publicists have, that the movement was something altogether new, unprecedented, and especially virtuous or especially wicked. Yet there were some important new elements in the imperialism of western peoples in the

Chinese painting of the arrival of one of the first English steamers and her passengers at Canton, about 1840.

375

nineteenth century, as the very form of the word suggests. An "ism" is a belief, a set of principles that men hold consciously as a guide to living. In early modern times groups of Europeans went abroad for all sorts of motives, which were seldom neatly correlated into a public policy and seldom debated very widely among the people. Nineteenth-century imperialism, by contrast, was in almost every country a major part of political life, with goals, methods, and advocates known to all who were concerned with politics. And since by 1900 almost all of western and central Europe, the United States, and indeed all the outposts of European culture enjoyed high literacy and widespread public discussion, imperialism took its place with liberalism, conservatism, nationalism, socialism, and a host of other "isms" as a subject of universal debate. To some of the arguments for and against imperialism we shall return later in this chapter.

A second obvious novelty had become clear by the outbreak of World War I in 1914. The process of western imperial expansion had gone territorially about as far as the geography of the planet earth permits. Through a long catalogue of imperial forms, ranging from outright annexation to "spheres of influence," almost all the globe had come under western control or western influence. All that was left at the beginning of the twentieth century was the bleak and uninhabited continent around the South Pole, which the leading nations were engaged in exploring and dividing. In 1908, the British issued letters patent setting up the Falkland Dependency, including, along with certain islands off the southern tip of South America, a wedge-shaped section between 80° and 20° West Longitude running right to the Pole. But the other nations were also staking out claims. The Norwegian Amundsen hoisted the flag of Norway at the South Pole itself on December

16, 1911. A month later the Englishman Scott also reached the Pole, but he and his companions died before they could get back. Australians, French, Germans, Argentinians, and Americans were also making claims, official or unofficial. Antarctica was an unpromising place for human habitation; but it was part of the globe, and it might, after all, contain its share of mineral wealth.

The Economic Aspect

Carefully defined, this third point— the economic aspect—may be said to distinguish nineteenth-century imperialism from early forms of imperialism. No doubt the economic motive runs through all forms of territorial expansion from prehistoric times to the present. It is clear in the earliest days of Spanish and Portuguese expansion in the quest for gold, silver, and profits. But, as the nineteenth century wore on, imperialist nations were responding to economic pressures in a new form. English liberals hostile to imperialism, like J. T. Hobson, whose *Imperialism* was published in 1902, differentiated this form from older ones a bit too sharply. They made it into an over-simple and unique explanation that did violence to the complex of motives behind the movement. The differentiation was put even more sharply for the Marxists by Rosa Luxemburg and, with due variations, by Lenin himself, notably in his *Imperialism as the Latest Stage of Capitalism* (1917).

According to these economic critics of imperialism, capitalists and industrialists in the older countries began to discover in the nineteenth century that they were unable to market at home all they could produce. But, being capitalists, they could not bring themselves to solve their difficulties by paying *less* in interest, dividends, and other payments to their own kind of people, the upper classes, and paying *more* in wages, pensions, bonuses, and the like to their workmen. Instead of sharing the wealth and creating at home the mass purchasing power and the mass market they needed, they preferred to turn to the non-western world, to markets abroad, to the exploitation of dependent peoples. This attempt to bolster the capitalist system meant competition among the great western industrial powers for land and peoples to exploit. Lenin stressed the need to use the finance-capital that was rapidly accumulating, rather than the need for markets. The great bankers, according to Lenin, drove the willing politicians into the search for dependencies, a search that marked what he termed the inevitable "last stage of capitalism."

No one who has studied this great nineteenth-century expansion questions that economic pressures were among the motivations of the men who carried it out. Quite impeccably anti-Marxist Americans sometimes hold that capitalism in the United States has been saved by its higher wages and mass market, and that in Europe capitalism is in shakier condition because European businessmen have been reluctant to give their workingmen a greater portion of the total product of industry. Furthermore, as we have already seen, leading industrial powers in both America and Europe were experiencing an increasing demand for higher tariffs by the late 1800's. In the United States and Germany, and even in free-trading Britain, industrialists wanted protection against foreign competitors. This was an era of neo-mercantilism, reviving and "streamlining" the older mercantilist doctrines of Colbert and others. Colonies as well as tariffs entered into the strategy of the neo-mercantilists, as they had done in the case of the old.

In sum, there is something in the Hobson-Luxemburg-Lenin argument. But by no means everything. The great outpouring of western energies into the rest of the world in the century between the Napoleonic Wars and the War of 1914, like such great bursts of energy as the Renaissance, cannot be explained by any such one-way causation as the economic interpretation sets up. Into this outpouring there went all the pooled self-esteem of nationalist feeling, the desire of rulers and of the majority of the politically conscious among the ruled to "keep up with the Joneses"—that is, to have an empire because the British, or the French, or the Portuguese, had one. There went the cumulative pressures of military and naval rivalries, of "geopolitics," as the earlier rivalries among nation-states widened into a global scale. There went the heady theories of philosophers of progress, the magic of evolution by competition among peoples, in which the fittest were obviously destined to rule over the less fit. There went the honest conviction that the West had the mission of bringing to less fortunate peoples the great moral gift of civilization. This conviction was often blind to facts at home as well as abroad, often singularly obtuse in its attitudes toward natives and toward competing westerners. But it was at its best in many missionaries, Christian and secular—a warm, humane desire to make life better for all on this earth.

Migration

A final general consideration must be faced in this problem of the motivation of the great nineteenth-century expansion of the West. How far was it simply a swarming from an overpopulated area, a movement caused at bottom, as we assume many prehistoric and ancient population movements were, by lack of "room" at home? It was most certainly a swarming. Some 60,000,000 people, it is estimated,

SOUTH AMERICA, 1914

///// Disputed areas, 1914 (Boundaries through these areas as defined by 1942)

◎ Capital cities

Dates here show when territories were acquired by powers concerned

GUIANAS
(Br.) (Dutch) (Fr.)
1781 1667 1626
1803

DEVIL'S ISLAND

VENEZUELA

COLOMBIA

ECUADOR

PERU

BRAZIL

BOLIVIA

PARAGUAY

CHILE

ARGENTINA

URUGUAY

Pacific Ocean

Atlantic Ocean

FALKLAND IS. (Br.)

Str. of Magellan
Punta Arenas (Magallanes)

Cape Horn

0   Miles   800

Cartagena
Caracas
Medellin
Bogotá
Quito
Guayaquil
Georgetown
Paramaribo
Cayenne
Orinoco R.
Negro R.
Manaos
Amazon R.
Belem (Pará)
Natal
Recife (Pernambuco)
Amazon R.
Purus R.
Madeira R.
Tapajos R.
Tocantins R.
São Francisco R.
Callao
Lima
Cuzco
L. Titicaca
La Paz
Arequipa
Sucré
Tacna
Arica
Antofagasta
GRAN CHACO
Paraguay R.
Parana R.
São Paulo
Santos
Rio de Janeiro
Tucuman
Asuncion
Porto Alegre
Cordoba
Valparaiso
Santiago
Mendoza
Buenos Aires
de la Plata
Montevideo
Colorado R.
Bahia Blanca
PANAMA CANAL

Area shown in map of Caribbean America

U.S. OF MEXICO

REPUBLIC OF HAITI

UNITED PROVINCES OF CENTRAL AMERICA

GREAT COLOMBIA

GUIANAS

PERU

EMPIRE OF BRAZIL

BOLIVIA

PARAGUAY

CHILE

URUGUAY

ARGENTINE CONFEDERATION

LATIN AMERICA 1828
After the Wars for Independence

0   Miles   2,000

G.

378

took part in intercontinental migration between 1800 and 1924; of these, 36,000,000 came to the United States. Some of the emigrants moved because they felt oppressed or persecuted at home, because they wanted change or adventure, or simply because they couldn't get on with mother-in-law. Still, the migrations during these years were certainly produced in part by lack of economic opportunities in the home country.

Yet the fact that so many emigrants went to the United States, and were lost to the imperial enterprises of the mother country, suggests that this swarming of the West needs to be distinguished from imperialism, strictly speaking. The emigrants went mainly to "colonies of settlement," which could support a large population of Europeans, in contrast to "colonies of exploitation," like India or tropical Africa, which could not. They went to Canada, parts of South America, Australia and New Zealand, South Africa, Siberia, and the United States. But the great areas white men commonly want to live in were already by the early 1800's, if by no means fully settled, at least under the political control of great powers that could not be dispossessed short of disastrous defeat in war. At stake in the nineteenth-century imperialist scramble were potential "colonies of exploitation." These were tropical and semi-tropical lands sometimes well populated, such as Egypt and Indo-China, or at least moderately populated, such as most of Negro Africa and the Philippines. Here white men did not settle as true colonists; they did not displace the native population as they did in most of the continental United States. They became government administrators, plantation owners, import and export merchants, teachers, missionaries—in short, a ruling class. But the native population remained, and indeed between 1815 and 1914 often increased in numbers.

The Powers Involved

Rivalries among competing empires grew sharper during the decades after 1870. Germany and Italy, newly united and ambitious nations, were added to the list of competitors, and increasing geographical exploration opened the last of the great relatively unknown areas, Africa. The devotees of economic interpretation would add: capitalist competition among the great powers was stepped up as their industrial systems grew more and more complex and more in need of cheap raw materials for import and an outlet for mass-produced cheap goods abroad.

The year 1870 is a convenient dividing line between the more active age of imperialism that was to come and the less active age that had preceded. The period from 1815 to 1870 saw a partial decline in imperial fortunes, as most of Spain's American colonies gained their independence, and as Britain took the first steps leading to the virtual independence of Canada (see below, p. 409). In this same period, however, the French established themselves in Algeria, and the British extended their rule in India. The dividing line of 1870 does not mark a sharp break in the history of imperialism, but rather the acceleration of a movement that had never ceased.

The successful competitors in nineteenth-century imperialism, those who brought new lands under their flags, were Great Britain, which already in 1815 had a great empire, France, Germany, Italy, and the United States. Even little Belgium, itself a "new" nation in 1830, acquired a tremendous piece of tropical Africa, the Congo, 900,000 square miles in area in comparison to the homeland's 11,775 square miles. Russia did not expand overseas, and indeed parted with her vast but thinly inhabited possession in North America when the tsarist government sold Alaska to the United

States in 1867. But she began the effective settlement of the great areas east of the Urals, and began to push into the borderlands of the Middle and Far East, toward Persia, India, and China. One of the old empires, that of Holland, on the whole marked time. Another, that of Portugal, lost Brazil, which became independent in 1822, but the Portuguese pushed far inland from their old colonies on the African coasts. The remnants of the Spanish empire were practically wiped off the map when the Spanish-American War of 1898 brought the loss of the rich islands of Cuba and the Philippines.

In the process of expansion, the expanding nations inevitably rubbed up against one another in all sorts of competition, from the merely economic to actual shooting war. Almost every major international conflict of the nineteenth century, save for the mid-century duels between Prussia and Austria and between Prussia and France, had a direct concern in imperialist rivalries outside Europe. And even the wars for the unification of Germany and Italy were by no means without overtones of reference to the great scramble for overseas lands. Imperial competition is a complicated story, then, woven into the whole fabric of international relations in the nineteenth century. We shall note briefly the major areas of inter-European rivalries and then summarize the growth of the major empires over the century.

The Areas Involved

The Monroe Doctrine (see Chapter XIX), toward which European nations were increasingly respectful as the strength of the United States increased, helped to keep both American continents free from further actual annexation by outside powers. So, too, did the British navy. Toward the fateful year of 1914, the competition between Britain and Germany for markets and for fields of investment in South America grew intense, and was one of the many factors that brought these powers to war. Since no state was strong enough to take from Britain her older colonies, throughout the nineteenth century British problems in both colonies of settlement and colonies of exploitation were limited to the British system itself. However, although these were not international problems, Germany and Russia sometimes threatened to become involved in them during the last decades of the pre-war period.

A major field of imperialist rivalry and penetration was the Near or Middle East, essentially the widespread lands under varying degrees of Turkish control, and Persia. In earlier chapters (XIX and XXII) we saw how the Balkans and the Straits became major issues in nineteenth-century diplomatic history. The whole "Eastern Question," as it is sometimes called, revolved around the problem of what was to be done with these old lands, which were peopled almost wholly by Moslems. They were backward lands by nineteenth-century western standards, mostly with poor rainfall and farm lands exhausted by centuries of primitive agriculture. They were poor also in natural resources (for their great wealth in petroleum was not really known or very important until the twentieth century). England, France, and Russia were in active competition over the Near East early in the nineteenth century, and they were later joined by Italy and Germany.

Africa was the scene of the most spectacular imperial rivalry. In 1815, except for the nominally Turkish lands of North Africa, the little Dutch settlement at the Cape of Good Hope (taken over by the British in 1815), and a string of Portuguese, Spanish, French, and British "factories" or trading posts along the old Portuguese exploration route that went back to the fifteenth century, Africa was untenanted by Europeans and, in the interior, almost unexplored. It was peopled by Negro races, long subjected to the horrors of the slave trade, and often living at the level of primitive tribesmen. The slave trade was pretty well abolished in many areas by mid-century, and exploration was pretty well under way. Then in the latter half of the century the great powers—Britain, France, and Germany—with Portugal, Italy, and Belgium tagging along, succeeded in blocking out in territorial units under their respective flags almost the whole of the continent. The only exceptions were the small Republic of Liberia, which had been set up by American anti-slavery groups as a land for emancipated American Negro slaves (though very few of them went there), and the mountainous and backward inland state of Abyssinia (now known as Ethiopia). And Abyssinia, coveted by Italy, had a very narrow escape. In 1896, the Abyssinians, under their Emperor Menelek and with French help, defeated an Italian army at Adowa and secured a respite in independence until the Italians tried again under Mussolini.

The Far East, too, was a major scene of imperialist rivalries. European powers strengthened their hold on older colonies and acquired new ones in Southeast Asia—the mainland areas of Burma, Indo-China, and Malaya, and the island groups between Australia and the mainland. But the ancient, thickly populated, highly civilized Chinese Empire was never subjected, as was Africa, to actual partition and direct annexation. China was, however, not well enough organized politically or industrially to stand up against European penetration, and was by the end of the century subjected to a rough, *de facto* partitioning among Britain, France, Germany, and Russia. Each power, operating from certain treaty ports as centers, was able to exercise a degree of control—basically economic—over considerable areas. European rivalry, and the rising power of the United States, which was exercised in favor of the "Open Door" policy of permitting as much free trade in China as was possible and of preserving Chinese sovereignty, served to counterbalance Chinese weakness, and kept China on the list of independent nations.

Finally, Japan kept herself isolated from the rest of the world for two centuries, from the mid-seventeenth to the mid-nineteenth. This compact island empire was closed to foreigners during the period when the European powers slowly strengthened their small holds in China. Then in 1853 the American naval officer, Perry, induced Japan to open her ports to outside trade. By adopting some western ways, particularly economic ways, Japan was able not merely to preserve her real independence during the late nineteenth century but actually to begin her own imperial expansion on the mainland of Asia (see p. 401, below).

II: The British Empire

We may now move on through the imperial record, country by country. Nineteenth-century Britain retained and, with the help of emigrants from the mother country, developed the great areas that were suitable to white colonization—Canada, Australia and New Zealand, and South Africa. This section focuses on Britain's im-

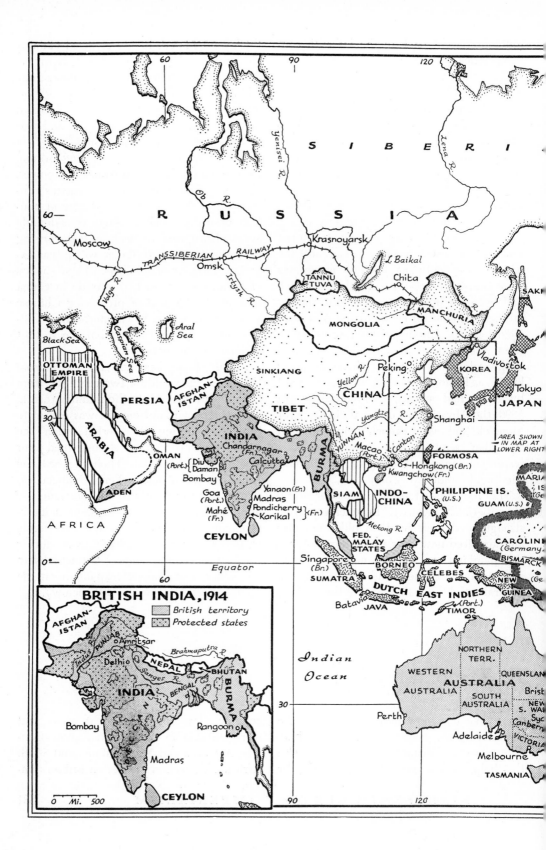

SIBERIA

RUSSIA

Moscow

TRANSSIBERIAN RAILWAY

Omsk

Krasnoyarsk

L. Baikal

Chita

SAKH

TANNU TUVA

MONGOLIA

MANCHURIA

Vladivostok

KOREA

Black Sea

Aral Sea

Caspian Sea

OTTOMAN EMPIRE

PERSIA

AFGHAN-ISTAN

SINKIANG

CHINA

Peking

Tokyo

JAPAN

TIBET

Shanghai

ARABIA

OMAN

INDIA

Chandarnagar (Fr.)

Calcutta

Diu (Port.)

Daman

Bombay

BURMA

YUNNAN

Macao (Port.)

Canton

AREA SHOWN IN MAP AT LOWER RIGHT

FORMOSA

ADEN

AFRICA

Goa (Port.)

Yanaon (Fr.)

Madras

Mahé (Fr.)

Pondicherry

Karikal

(Fr.)

CEYLON

SIAM

INDO-CHINA

Hongkong (Br.)

Kwangchow (Fr.)

PHILIPPINE IS. (U.S.)

GUAM (U.S.)

MARIA

IS. (Ge

CAROLIN (Germany)

BISMARCK

Equator

Singapore (Br.)

FED. MALAY STATES

SUMATRA

Mekong R.

BORNEO

CELEBES

NEW GUINEA

(Ge

DUTCH EAST INDIES

Batavia

JAVA

(Port.)

TIMOR

Indian Ocean

AUSTRALIA

NORTHERN TERR.

WESTERN AUSTRALIA

QUEENSLAN

SOUTH AUSTRALIA

Brist

NEW S. WA

Syc

Canberra

VICTORIA

Perth

Adelaide

Melbourne

TASMANIA

BRITISH INDIA, 1914

British territory

Protected states

AFGHAN-ISTAN

PUNJAB

Amritsar

Indus R.

Delhio

Brahmaputra R.

NEPAL

BHUTAN

Ganges R.

BURMA

INDIA

BENGAL

Bombay

Rangoon o

Madras

0   Mi.   500

CEYLON

ASIA AND THE PACIFIC, 1914

British territory
British protected states
French territory
Japan & Japanese territories
United States & possessions
Dutch territory
German territory

ALASKA

(RUSSIA) (U.S.)

CANADA

ALEUTIAN IS.

Pacific Ocean

UNITED STATES

San Francisco

MEXICO

MIDWAY IS. (U.S.)

HAWAIIAN ISLANDS (U.S.)

WAKE (U.S.)

Honolulu

RSHALL IS. (Germany)

GILBERT IS.

PHOENIX IS.

(Great Britain)

OLOMON IS.

ELLICE IS.

W. SAMOA (Germany)

AMERICAN SAMOA (U.S.)

W IDES & Fr.)

FIJI IS. (Br.)

NEW CALEDONIA (France)

Auckland

NEW ZEALAND

INTERNATIONAL DATE LINE

MANCHURIA

JEHOL

GREAT WALL

Peking (Peiping)

Tientsin

RUSSIA

Vladivostok

Mukden

Port Arthur (Jap.)

KOREA (Japan)

Seoul

Sea of Japan

HOPEI

SHANTUNG

Yellow R.

Wei-hai-wei (Br.)

Kiaochow Bay (Germany)

Pusan

Shimonoseki

TSUSHIMA

Kyoto

CHINA

KIANGSI

R.

Nanking

Yangtze

Nagasaki

JAPAN

Shanghai

Hangchow

CHEKIANG

Wenchow

East China Sea

RYUKYU IS.

Pacific Ocean

OKINAWA

Foochow

FUKIEN

To Canton

Amoy

FORMOSA

0   Miles   400

perial possessions in Africa and Asia. The development of self-government in Canada, Australia, and New Zealand will come more appropriately at the close of this chapter, in our survey of the results of nineteenth-century imperialism.

South Africa

In 1815, Britain had just acquired from the Netherlands Cape Colony at the southern tip of Africa. Cape Colony was inhabited by a few Dutch and French Huguenot colonists and was suited, in spite of a relatively low rainfall, to European living. As Britishers moved in, the older colonists, known in their own Dutch vernacular as Boers, grew more and more discontented. The adoption of English as the sole official language, the abolition of slavery throughout the Empire in 1834, the attempts of the government at London to protect the native blacks, and other measures of Victorian liberalism went against the grain of the patriarchal Boers, who were fundamentalist Christians for whom slavery was ordained of God and for whom liberalism was the work of the devil. Between 1835 and 1837, some ten thousand Boers moved north overland in the "Great Trek," a heroic folk migration that bulks even larger in contemporary nationalist South African feeling than do the comparable sagas of covered-wagon days in American tradition. After some confused three-cornered fighting among Boers, British, and native Zulus, the Boers established two virtually independent South African states—the Transvaal and the Orange Free State. Well inland, on territory suitable for grazing but not for intensive agriculture, these thinly populated states lived on for a time hardly noticed by the outside world.

The British in South Africa noticed them, of course, and many of the British wished to add these lands to the Empire. They worked up from Cape Colony and established another British province to the east, along the Indian Ocean side, known as Natal. In the course of the century, Cape Colony and Natal, which together had a black population heavily outnumbering the British and remaining Boers combined, acquired the self-governing rights that British colonies of settlement in Canada, Australia, and New Zealand were also acquiring. British South African leaders for the most part wanted to bring the Boer Republics under the British flag. But as the London home government swung between Tory and Liberal domination, it also swung between a policy of imperialist expansion and the "Little Englander" policy of leaving the Trekkers alone. In 1852, by the Sand River Convention the British acknowledged the independence of Transvaal. But in 1877 they reversed themselves and annexed it as a step toward the federation of all South Africa under the British Crown. The Boers revolted in 1880 and the Liberal Gladstone, then in power, lived up to his principles by making at Pretoria in 1881 a treaty with the Boers which re-established Transvaal as independent, though under the "suzerainty" of Great Britain.

The British were already filtering up through the semi-desert country to the west of the Boer Republics when the discovery of gold and the development of the diamond industry in these republics undid Gladstone's work. Transvaal was no longer just poor and isolated grazing lands; it offered a great source of wealth that tempted quite a different kind of settler. In the Transvaal the region about Johannesburg, the famous Rand, filled up with adventurers of a dozen nations, all looking to Britain to protect them from the conservative Boers, to whom they were undesirable *Uitlanders* (outlanders, foreigners).

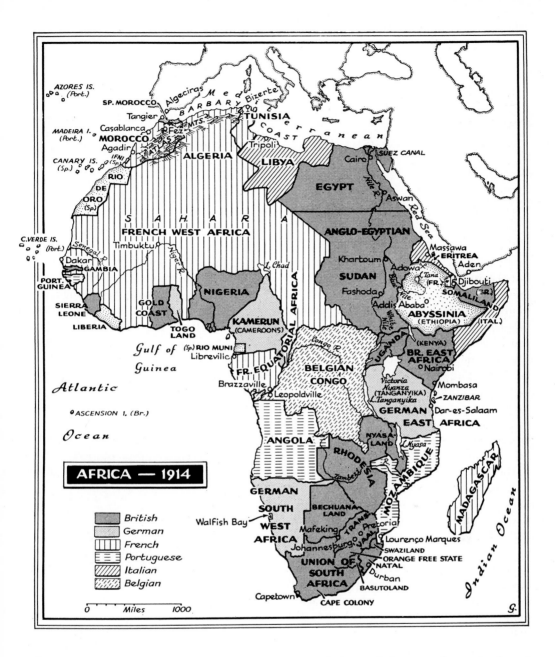

AFRICA — 1914

Legend:
- British
- German
- French
- Portuguese
- Italian
- Belgian

The Boer War and After

The inevitable conflict came to a head with the Jameson Raid of December 29, 1895—midsummer in South Africa. The British in South Africa were now under the leadership of Cecil Rhodes, prime minister of Cape Colony, a determined and articulate imperialist who had made a quick fortune consolidating the chaotic diamond industry. The raid itself, under a follower of Rhodes, Dr. Jameson, was an invasion of Transvaal from British territory to the west, and was planned to coincide

A 6-inch gun in difficulties during the Boer War.

with a rising of Uitlanders in Johannesburg. But the rising did not take place, and the President of Transvaal, Kruger, had no trouble in defeating Jameson's handful of invaders. The famous "Kruger telegram," in which the German Kaiser congratulated the Boer President, was one of the critical steps in sharpening the Anglo-German rivalry that led to world war in 1914 (see Chapter XXV). Its immediate effect in South Africa was to harden Boer resistance and to lead in 1899 to the outbreak of war between Britain and the two Boer Republics.

The war, following the pattern of British wars in modern times, went badly at first for the British, who did not have enough troops immediately available to put down determined men who had been brought up in outdoor life and who were fighting on their own ground. Western opinion generally sided with the underdog Boers, and even in Britain many Liberals and Laborites strongly opposed the war. But in the long run the overwhelming strength of the British prevailed. By the middle of 1900 the British had won in the field, but they needed another eighteen months to subdue the desperate guerrilla bands into which Boer opposition dissolved. In 1902, by the Treaty of Vereeniging, the Boers accepted British rule, with the promise of ultimate self-government. This promise the British

fulfilled speedily. In 1910, there came into being a Union of South Africa, uniting the two former Boer Republics, Cape Colony, and Natal in a state in which the central government was stronger than the provinces. English and Afrikaans, as the South African Dutch dialect had come to be called, were set up as equally official languages.

On the eve of World War I, South Africa was among the self-governing British dominions. British and Boer seemed to be well on the way to composing their long quarrel, and to be ready to collaborate in setting up a new outpost of the West. But there were ominous signs even then. The Boers had by no means been Anglicized, and they were still fundamentally opposed to their partners in empire. And the two European elements together were in a minority of one to four as compared with the non-Europeans—the native blacks, the East Indians (who had come in numbers as immigrants, especially to Natal), and the "colored" peoples of mixed blood. The seeds of the current troubles in South Africa were clearly present even in the hopeful days after the establishment of the Union.

Egypt

At the opposite end of Africa, Britain during the last half of the nineteenth century took over from the French the control of Egypt, nominally a vassal state of the crumbling Ottoman Empire. French influence there, already strong in the eighteenth century, was increased by Napoleon's expedition (see Chapter XVIII); indeed, French cultural influence persists among the Egyptian upper classes and intellectuals to this day. Under French supervision, a private company built between 1859 and 1869 the Suez Canal, which united the Mediterranean with the Red Sea and shortened the

CHAPTER XXIV

sea trip from Europe to India and the Far East by thousands of miles. The British had bitterly opposed the building of this canal under French patronage; but now that it was finished, the canal was clearly an essential part of the "lifeline" of the British Empire.

Accordingly, the British took over Egypt and with it Suez. They carried out this action skillfully and slowly, threatening at crucial moments to use force, but not using it on any large scale. The decisive step in the process was the purchase by the British under Disraeli of 176,000 shares of stock in the Suez Canal Company. These shares had originally been assigned to the ruler of Egypt, the Khedive, as the price of his consent and co-operation in the canal project. The Khedive, a great and unwise spender, was heavily in debt to European financiers by 1875, and he sold his shares for a good price. The largest block of Suez stock was now in British hands.

By the eve of World War I, Britain exercised virtual sovereignty over Egypt. The Khedive and his government remained, and on paper Egypt was still a separate state. But a British Resident was always at hand to exercise firm control, especially over foreign relations. Under this British regime— the word "protectorate" is the usual term —much was done to modernize Egypt. The standard of living of the masses in Egypt was by no means raised to anything like that of the European masses. But the great dam at Aswan on the Nile, finished in 1902, was the first of a series of public works that added to the total productive power of the country, improved public health, lowered the mortality rate, and strengthened the numbers and prosperity of the middle class. Modernization also meant the beginnings of a wider literacy, of an educated middle class, and indeed of an intellectual class that earned its living by the written or spoken word. Most of these people re-

THE LION'S SHARE.

Disraeli purchases the Suez Canal shares held by the Khedive of Egypt.

sponded by hating the British and by nursing a constantly growing nationalism— "Egypt for the Egyptians." We shall encounter this pattern again elsewhere.

The Rest of British Africa

In between South Africa and Egypt the British pieced out their African possessions throughout the century. At its end, they had the lion's share of the continent. They had only 4,000,000 square miles out of over 11,000,000, but they controlled 61,000,000 people out of not much over 100,000,000. A mere listing of these holdings would be a dull and unenlightening catalogue. They can be found, usually colored red, in any good atlas of the turn of the century and on a famous British postage stamp of late Victorian times (see also the maps accompanying this chapter). A good sample of these colonies is Nigeria, in which the great administrator Sir Frederick (later Lord) Lugard worked out the characteristic British method of colonial government in tropical Africa that was known as "indirect rule."

The colony and protectorate of Nigeria was formally put together from earlier West African colonies in 1914. It centers around the great river Niger, which the ancient Greeks knew of vaguely in its northern course at the edge of the Sahara and which they apparently believed flowed into the Nile; it actually flows into the Atlantic at the Gulf of Guinea. Northern Nigeria was ruled by Moslem emirs of the Fulani race whose culture was superior to that of the subject and exploited Negroes; southern Nigeria was inhabited by numerous heathen tribes that had long been harassed by slave raids. The British had first to subject the Fulani by force, a process that was completed late in the nineteenth century.

They then applied, as a French statesman put it, "with method but not with system," what came to be called indirect rule. Emirs and chieftains were confirmed in their separate rules, subject to the banning of internal warfare, the abolition of slavery, and similar measures imposed from above. A British Resident supervised the rule of the leading chiefs, with district Residents (later Commissioners) to supplement the work in the local subdivisions. But native law, native religion, and native traditions, in so far as they did not conflict violently with western standards, were carefully maintained. The British staff was never large; Lugard complained that in 1903 he had only one British administrator on the average for every 400,000 natives. But somehow the handful of imperial officials were able to ensure the peace. Slowly, much too slowly for impatient idealists, railroads, roads, improved agriculture, commerce, and education—the externals at least of western civilization—began to appear in Nigeria. Early in the twentieth century the first African Negro students began to appear in British universities.

In ideal, this method of rule would eventually bring the great material and spiritual benefits of western civilization to the natives without destroying their own centuries-long development, without trying to make them over into Europeans. In practice, although material progress had been marked by 1914, the transition from primitive to modern ways of life had been but spottily achieved. A Negro élite had been developed far beyond the capacity of the great mass of the natives to follow them. But Lugard's achievements were great. The following passages from his book, *The Dual Mandate in British Tropical Africa,* show the spirit with which he approached his work, and notably his defense against the charge of Christian missionaries who held that he unduly restricted their activities:

Bishop Tugwell, whose long and faithful service in West Africa has chiefly lain in the coast area and its immediate hinterland, writes: ' "Indirect rule" is direct rule by indirect means. The Emir's position and salary are secure. His sway, backed by British authority, is rendered absolute, while his people become his serfs, or those of the British Government. Their life is thus robbed of all initiative or desire for progress—intellectual, social, moral, religious, or political.' The Emir, he adds, who is appointed by the Government, is the instrument of the Resident, and 'the name of Christ must not be proclaimed lest this blighting system should be overturned.' ... Bishop Tugwell, unconsciously perhaps, gives imperfect expression to an aspect of the matter on which I have already touched. It was naturally a cause for anxiety and misgiving that the British Government, by supporting native rule, and the authority of the native courts, should accept some measure of responsibility for evils which its meagre staff of British officials was unable to control adequately. ... To overthrow an organisation, however faulty, which has the sanction of long usage, and is acquiesced in by the people, before any system could be created to take its place—before, indeed, we had any precise knowledge of Moslem methods or of native law and custom—would have been an act of folly which no sane administrator could at-

CHAPTER XXIV

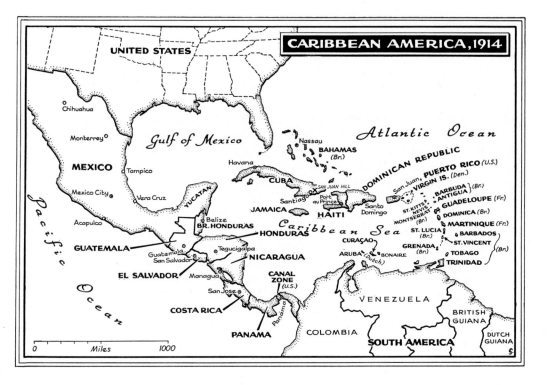

CARIBBEAN AMERICA, 1914

tempt. The very necessity for avoiding pre-
cipitate action, and the knowledge that reform
could only be effective, and enlist native co-
operation, if it was gradual, made the responsibility all the more onerous. To infer that it was
not realised, or was lightly regarded, is to do a
great injustice to the administrative staff of the
early Government of Northern Nigeria. . . .

. . .

The object of substituting for British rule, in
which the chiefs are mere agents of the Government, a system of native rule under the
guidance and control of the British staff,
whether among advanced or backward communities, is primarily educative. Among backward tribes the chiefs have to learn how to
exert and maintain authority, and establish a
chain of responsibility reaching down to the
village head. Among the more advanced their
interest is directed to education, forestry, sanitation, prevention of disease, and public works.
In all alike the endeavour is to prevent dena-
tionalisation, to develop along indigenous lines,
to inculcate the principle that the function of
the ruler is to promote the welfare of his people
and not to exploit them for his own pleasure,

and to afford both to rulers and people the
stimulus of progress and interest in life.*

Other British Spheres

In the Americas, Britain maintained
her colonial dependencies in the Caribbean,
in Bermuda and the Bahamas, and, on the
mainland, in British Honduras and British
Guiana. Self-rule of the seventeenth-century kind, which some of them lost in
the mid-nineteenth century, was granted
them gradually only in the twentieth
century. These were all tropical or semi-
tropical lands, with a relatively small
planter class and with large Negro or
mixed lower classes. These lands suffered
gradual impoverishment as a result of
certain economic developments, notably

* F. D. Lugard, *The Dual Mandate in British
Tropical Africa* (Edinburgh and London, 1923),
223-224, 228-229.

the great competition offered to the staple cane sugar of the region by the growth in temperate climates of the beet-sugar industry, together with an increase in population beyond the limited resources of the region. By 1914, the British West Indies had already become a "problem area."

In the Pacific and in Southeast Asia, Britain in the nineteenth century added some red dots on the map of her empire, and especially in Malaya she developed the great industries of rubber and tin that were to be major factors in her economy after World War I. She took an important part in the process of opening China to western trade by means of treaty-port concessions and spheres of influence. Indeed, Britain took one of the great steps in breaking down Chinese attempts to keep off the foreigner, for in 1841 she waged what has come to be called invidiously but not unjustly the "Opium War." This war was brought on by a Chinese attempt to control the opium trade in which British merchants had an important stake. By the Treaty of Nanking in 1842, Britain acquired Hong-kong and secured the opening of five ports, including Canton and Shanghai. By the end of the century, Britain had a preponderant share in the China trade, with direct possession of Hongkong, a full share in the great international port of Shanghai, and a lease on the naval station of Wei-hai-wei as a balance to the Russian lease on Port Arthur.

India: Political Organization

In China, however, Britain was but one, though the most important, of the Great Powers scrambling for empire in that densely peopled land. In India her victory over France in 1763, confirmed by her victory in 1815, left her in sole control over a subcontinent of Asia, for the remnants of French and Portuguese possessions there hardly counted. India was the richest of Britain's overseas possessions, the center and symbol of empire, as the imaginative Disraeli realized when in 1877 he had Queen Victoria proclaimed Empress of India.

In 1763, India was already a great and well-peopled land, but not, in the European sense, a single *nation*. It was a vast congeries of races and religions, ranging from the most cultivated and philosophic Brahmins to the most primitive tribesmen, still in the Stone Age. As the nineteenth century began, the two main methods of British control had already become clear. The richest and most densely populated regions, centering on the cities of Calcutta, Madras, Bombay, and the Punjab, were under direct British rule. The British government did not annex these lands directly; they were first administered as the property, so to speak, of the English East India Company, a chartered enterprise surviving from the great days of mercantilism in the seventeenth and eighteenth centuries. The company in its heyday, led by empire-makers like Clive and Warren Hastings, had taken on enormous territories, and made treaties like a sovereign power. Hastings was prosecuted for "high crimes and misdemeanors" in a famous trial of the late eighteenth century. But what he acquired the British kept.

In the nineteenth century the company was regarded by most economists and political thinkers as a shocking anomaly, and the India Office of the central government in London gradually took over the real control and administration of British India. The trading monopoly of the company had long since been undermined. In 1857, the company's native army of Sepoys rebelled. As usual in such major uprisings, the rebellion was brought on by a number of causes. But the basic cause was that the soldiers, Hindu, Moslem, and others, all had come to fear that British ways were

Execution of mutineers after the Sepoy Rebellion in India, 1857.

being imposed on them to the destruction of their own ways. And behind it all there was able propaganda of the "whispering campaign" sort. Moslem soldiers were told that the cartridges that had to be torn out with their teeth for the new Enfield rifle were greased with hog fat, which was tabu to them; Hindu soldiers were told that the cartridges were greased with beef fat, which was tabu to them. It seems clear that animal fat of some kind actually was used, good evidence of the insensitiveness of the British rulers. The Sepoy Rebellion was put down, but not before several massacres of Europeans had occurred, and not without a serious military effort by the British. The mutiny meant the end of the English East India Company. In 1858, the British Crown took over the company's lands and obligations, announcing that no further annexations were sought in India.

The rest of India—roughly a third of its area and a fourth or a fifth of its population —came to be known as the "feudal" or "native" states. These were left nominally under the rule of their own princes, who might be the fabulously rich Sultan of Hyderabad or Gaekwar of Baroda, or merely a kind of local chieftain. The "native" states were actually governed by a system of British Residents somewhat like the system we have just seen in Nigeria. The India Office never hesitated to interfere with the succession, or to disallow acts of princes, or even to assume direct rule for a time when it was thought necessary. The "native" states add many pictureque notes to a detailed history of India, but in the long run the distinction between direct and indirect rule in India did not mean very much in practice.

India: "The Meeting of East and West"

The years between 1763 and 1919 in India are a fascinating record of what Arnold Toynbee, the philosopher of history, calls "contacts between civilizations." Indeed, anyone who wants to understand the great contemporary problem of relations between the West and the rest of the world —to use clear terms, between white peoples and colored peoples—will do well to learn all he can of this great meeting of East and West in the subcontinent of India.

In material terms, many phases of the British rule in India are readily measurable. In 1864, the British *Statesman's Year Book* gave the population of India as about 136,000,000, and in 1904 close to 300,000,000. Although the latter figure includes additional territories, in Burma and elsewhere, it is clear that nineteenth-century India saw a significant increase in total population. In 1901, nearly 15,000,000 males out of a total of 150,000,000 were literate in some language; one out of ten could read and write, a low rate of literacy by western standards, but already a high one by contemporary Asian standards. It is characteristic of Indian society that the comparable figures for women in the same census of 1901 show that only one out of one hundred and fifty could read and write.

Such statistics are plentiful, and what they show is an India on the eve of World War I with thousands of miles of railroads, telegraph lines, universities teaching in English to a native minority, hospitals, factories, and great and busy seaports. But, in proportion to the total population, India did not have these advantages to anything like the extent that even the poorest of European countries had them. Statistics show a native ruling class sometimes fantastically rich, and an immense peasant class for the most part living as their ancestors had lived, on the edge of starvation. A middle class was just beginning to form, and, like all the middle classes formed in non-European lands under European penetration, it had proportionately far more aspirants to genteel white-collar professional posts than to posts in commerce, engineering, and industry.

The total wealth of India certainly increased under British rule in this century and a half, and in 1914 it was spread more widely among the Indian populations, save for the most primitive areas, than it had been in 1763. Proportionately less and less wealth went directly from an "exploited" India to an "exploiting" Britain. The familiar Englishman of the seventeenth and eighteenth centuries, the "nabob" who made a fortune in India and retired with it to comfort, and perhaps to a peerage, in England, almost ceased to exist as the nineteenth century wore on. Anglo-Indian economic relations took on more and more the form of trade between a developed industrial and financial society in Britain and a society geared to the production of raw materials in India. In this trade, native Indians took an increasing part if only as middlemen, and toward the end of the century native industries, notably textile manufacturing, financed for the most part with British capital, began to arise in India.

Throughout the century, of course, a large number of British—small in proportion to the total population, but numbering in the hundred thousands—were basically supported by the Indian economy; they "lived off India." Some of them were private businessmen, but the greater number were military and civilian workers, the latter the celebrated Indian Civil Service who "ran" India. Yet natives were gradually working their way into positions of greater responsibility, into both private and public posts at the policy-making level.

Of the British ruling class in India one very important fact is now plain: it did not, like the English and Scots who went to Ireland in early modern times, really take root in India. Britain—one must be careful not to say "England," for the Scots played a conspicuous role in India as they did throughout the Empire—was always "Home," always the place where one hoped to end one's days. Though son not infrequently followed father in the Indian army or civil service, or even in business, these "Sahibs" as a whole never became fully adjusted to life in India. The spiritual climate was perhaps an even greater barrier than the physical climate. Here is a letter from an Englishwoman in Madras in 1837:

It is wonderful how little interested most of the English ladies seem by all the strange habits and ways of the natives; and it is not merely that they have grown used to it all, but that, by their own accounts, they never cared more about what goes on around them than they do now. I can only suppose they have forgotten their first impressions. But this makes me wish to try and see everything that I can while the bloom of my Orientalism is fresh upon me, and before this apathy and listlessness have laid hold on me, as no doubt they will.

I asked one lady what she had seen of the country and the natives since she had been in India. 'Oh, nothing!' said she: 'thank goodness, I know nothing at all about them, nor I don't wish to: really I think the less one sees and knows of them the better!' *

The natives, too, often found the gap between East and West too great to be bridged. Another Englishwoman writes in 1913:

Coming home we saw a native cooking his dinner on a little charcoal fire, and as I passed he threw the contents of the pot away. Sur-

prised, I asked why. 'Because,' I was told, 'your shadow fell on it and defiled it!' *

Yet the work of raising the economic basis of Indian life was in large part the work of the British. They were often overbearing, insensitive, white men at their worst in their dealings with the natives. But they were, more often than the doctrinaire liberal will admit, men devoted to the task of bettering the lot of their charges, men who made a real effort to understand them. Their work is reflected in the following passage from an "Address from the Inhabitants of Dhuboy to the English Collector" on the morning of his final departure:

... All castes who looked up to him obtained redress, without distinction and without price. When he took the poor by the hand he made him rich: under his protection the people were happy, and reposed on the bed of ease. When he superintended the garden, each gardener performed his duty; and all the trees in the garden flourished. So equal was his justice, that the tiger and the kid might drink at the same fountain; and often did he redeem the kid from the tiger's mouth. ... In this country we have not known any government so upright as that of the English:—Alas! if our protector forsakes us we shall be disconsolate as a widow: we shall mourn the loss of a father and weep as for the death of a mother!—ALLA! in thy mercy continue him to us! †

* Hilton Brown, ed., *The Sahibs* (London, 1948), 225.

* *Ibid.,* 230.
† *Ibid.,* 223-224.

III: The Other Empires

The French: North Africa

The British victory in the "Second Hundred Years' War," capped by their defeat of Napoleon in 1815, had stripped France of all but insignificant remnants of her former empire. Yet during the nineteenth century France succeeded in building up a new colonial empire second in area only to that of the British. France, despite her frequent revolutionary changes in government, maintained an imperialist

*French victory near
Algiers, 1830.*

policy that added between 1824 and 1914 close to three and a half million square miles to the lands under the tricolor flag, and some fifty million people, almost all non-European. The figures for area are indeed somewhat misleading, for a million and a half square miles are included in the Sahara Desert, which is almost uninhabited.

Little of this second French colonial empire was suitable for settlement by Europeans. The great exception was French North Africa, including Tunisia, Algeria, and Morocco. As the provinces of Africa and Mauretania, these lands were once flourishing parts of the Roman Empire; since France took them over, they have reached a greater degree of material prosperity than they have enjoyed for nearly eighteen centuries. These lands, which have a typically Mediterranean climate, are inhabited chiefly by Berber and Arab peoples of Moslem faith. Though the total native population has increased greatly under French rule, something over a million European colonists have moved in. In majority French, but with sizable groups of Italians

and Spaniards, these colonists have taken land from the natives, though they have added to the total arable acreage by initiating irrigation projects and other improvements.

Into the narrative history of the growth of French power in North Africa we need not go in detail. The French got a toe-hold in 1824 through a punitive expedition against the Algerian pirates, with whose Tripolitan counterparts, incidentally, the United States had fought a war in 1801. The French stayed on in Algiers, gradually increasing their control over Algeria and adding protectorates over Tunisia to the east in the 1880's and over Morocco to the west in the early twentieth century. Britain gave the French a free hand in Morocco as compensation for their exclusion from Egypt (see above, p. 386).

Especially in Algeria and Tunisia, the French promoted European settlement while trying not to antagonize the natives. They called their policy one of "assimilation," in contrast with the British policy of hands off and indirect rule. They hoped,

CHAPTER XXIV

they explained, to assimilate Africans into French civilization, making them ultimately into good children of the eighteenth-century Enlightenment, good citizens of the Republic founded on the principles of 1789. They hoped to create an empire of "100,-000,000 Frenchmen," more than half of them overseas, and to draw on abundant native manpower to fill up the ranks of the Republic's armies.

In the military sense, the policy of assimilation worked out somewhat as the French had hoped; in the main, however, assimilation was difficult and only partially successful. The French, always desirous of spreading their culture, have indeed assimilated to a surprising degree some of the native ruling classes. Under the Third Republic they made Algeria politically a part of France itself, organizing it into three departments and giving them representatives to the Chamber of Deputies, with a franchise open to the small group of Europeanized natives as well as to colonists. But here, as throughout the non-European colonial world, vigorous native nationalist movements have arisen with complete separation as their goal.

In Morocco, too, native nationalism has appeared, though here the French have taken a somewhat different tack. They have sought, in part successfully, to open the country to French business and to the international tourist trade. And, without quite admitting the fact, they have really abandoned assimilation for something close to the British policy of indirect rule. In 1912, the very able colonial administrator, Marshal Lyautey, began to organize turbulent Morocco, applying the "splash of oil" policy—that is, he pacified certain key centers by establishing firm working relations with the natives and then let pacification spread over the surface of Morocco like a splash of oil on water. The Sultan and his feudal subordinates were maintained in Morocco, relatively free to carry on many of their age-old ways.

The French: Tropical Africa

In 1815, the British had left France her small posts in West Africa at the mouth of the Senegal River, together with the slight foothold France had obtained in the seventeenth century on the great Island of Madagascar off the East African coast. By 1914, the French had been very successful in the partition of Africa, perhaps at bottom because the British preferred French to German aggrandizement, especially after 1870. By 1914, at any rate, France numbered in Africa alone nearly as many inhabitants as in her home territories (about 39,000,000).

Except in North Africa, these people were almost all Negroes who were still essentially at the Stone Age level of material culture, and who were for the most part untouched by either Islam or Christianity. Except in certain coastal towns, where their administration and business were concentrated, the French had not by 1914 achieved very much toward assimilating or westernizing these vast districts. Most of their attempts to hasten the economic development of their African lands by organized joint-stock companies failed miserably.

It is quite possible that France spent more on these African colonies than she gained from them. Indeed, one of the stock arguments of nineteenth-century anti-imperialists was that colonies did not "pay" the mother country, and the French African colonies were one of their favorite exhibits. One economist—an Englishman, to be sure, and presumably unmoved by much that moves Frenchmen—concluded that in 1892 French gains from colonial trade were 16,000,000 francs, whereas net government expenditures for the colonies were 174,-000,000 francs. For 1915, he made an even more discouraging estimate.* Such figures, however, seem not to have discouraged any of the great powers in their imperialist efforts. Obviously the simplest form of the economic interpretation of history, the notion that political entities are moved by simple bookkeeping concepts of economic profit and loss, does not hold true for nineteenth-century imperialism.

Again, though French colonies in tropical Africa had by no means been modernized even in material conditions by 1914, everywhere a beginning had been made. Everywhere the tricolor went, there also went medicine and hygiene, modern methods of communication, industry, and agriculture, and formal education for at least a few natives. In justifying the policy of assimilation, the French claim for themselves, in contrast with the British, a lack of race prejudice, a willingness to accept the blacks as equals. This contrast is underlined by the English author whose figures we have just quoted:

Of course, it is true that the French also attempt to understand the native and in the main to give him freedom to produce as he pleases. The Frenchman actually tends much more to be a 'good fellow' with the natives than does the Briton, who is much more aloof. But this greater democracy does not seem to inspire a greater degree of confidence. Somehow, the Briton is more apt to succeed in instilling in the native confidence in the results of producing by the system that he recommends.†

Although there is some truth in the claim for greater French toleration, the deed is not quite up to the word. The French in Africa do not often marry Negroes—always one of the clearest tests of racial equality;

Negroes, even educated Negroes, very rarely *command* white Frenchmen in military or civilian activity. Both at home and in Africa, on the other hand, once the Negroes seemed firmly under control, the French have gone a long way toward encouraging Negro art and folkways, in keeping with a policy very close to the ideal delineated by Lugard for Nigeria. The British, however, especially in recent years, have been edging toward some kind of assimilation; African Negro undergraduates in British universities take on a lot more of Britishness than just their fine standard English accent. The contrast between British and French African policies is far from complete.

The French: Asia

In Asia, the French took over in the nineteenth century lands that came to be called French Indo-China. These lands included two rich rice-growing deltas (around Hanoi in the north and Saigon in the south), inhabited by peoples culturally and in part racially related to the Chinese. And they also included a number of mountainous and jungle-covered areas with quite primitive populations. French experience here on the whole ran parallel to imperialist experience elsewhere in Southeast Asia, though the Anglo-Saxon fondness for nagging the French has tended to create the impression that the French did far worse in Indo-China than did the Dutch in Java or the British in Malaya. Slow but real material progress was made, though the basic problem of poverty among the masses remained unsolved. Native nationalist movements, nourished by educated natives with jobs of less dignity and authority than they believed should be theirs, rose in strength as the years went on. France also took part, from her base in Indo-China, in

---

* Constant Southworth, *The French Colonial Venture* (London, 1931), 122.
† *Ibid.*, 193.

the struggle for control of China proper. The French sphere of influence was southern China, in particular the province of Yunnan adjoining Indo-China, and in 1898 the French got the usual ninety-nine-year lease, of a port concession, in this case Kwangchou Bay.

The Germans

We can be brief in listing the colonial acquisitions of the other powers. Germany and Italy came late to the imperial scramble, as they came late to national unity. Nevertheless they were "great powers," and they managed to acquire the token colonies, at least, that seemed necessary to that dignified status. Germany in 1914 had three really large pieces of tropical and subtropical Africa—the Kameruns (Cameroons), German Southwest Africa, and German East Africa—and the smaller Togoland, close to a million square miles in all. The German achievement on the whole was not greatly different from that of other European powers in Africa; it was neither morally nor economically much better or much worse. In the Pacific, the Germans picked up some small islands, and a large, primitive territory on the island of New Guinea. Germany took part in the attempted partition of China; *her* ninety-nine-year lease was on Kiaochow Bay.

The German drive for colonies was quite self-conscious; it was well organized in a pressure group with all the fixings of modern propaganda. Bismarck himself, who cared little for the prestige of colonies, was obliged to give way and consent to African ventures. His successors went further, and William II helped Germany to enter one of the most confused and dangerous fields of imperialist expansion, the Near East. On the eve of World War I, the German "Berlin to Bagdad" push was well under way,

and the Germans had supplanted the British as patrons of the Turks.

The Italians and Belgians

Italy, condemned to the role of weakest of the great powers, got very little, even out of the partition of Africa. Tunis, which she coveted, went instead to France. Italy's major imperial effort centered on the African lands at the southern end of the Red Sea, but after her defeat by the Abyssinians under Menelek in 1896 she had to content herself with a few thousand square miles of desert in Eritrea and Somaliland. Italian efforts to add to this inadequate empire by taking Tripoli from its nominal Turkish suzerains succeeded, but these same efforts led to the Italo-Turkish war of 1911, which was in a sense the real beginning of World War I (see Chapter XXV). The Italians had so little to work with it is hard to assess their success or failure.

Little Belgium, largely through the enterprise of her King Leopold II (1865-1909), managed to acquire a large piece of equatorial Africa. This project began as the Congo Free State, with all sorts of noble ideals of co-operative European civilizing missions in Africa; but it ended up in 1908 as simply the Belgian Congo. Nineteenth-century scandal about forced labor and native exploitation in the Congo called Leopold's experiment to the attention of the world and provided liberal anti-imperialists with fresh arguments. But the Belgians, who have long since moderated Leopold's policies, still have the Congo.

The Americans

To the horror and indignation of many Americans, to the delight of others, the United States at the very end of the

President Theodore Roosevelt and Panama.

century joined the great powers and acquired overseas lands. In 1898, she waged a brief and successful war with Spain, for which the immediate cause was the mysterious sinking of the American battleship *Maine* in the harbor of Havana, Cuba. The Spanish-American War left the United States in control of the remnants of the Spanish Empire in America (the Caribbean islands of Cuba and Puerto Rico) and the archipelago of the Philippines off the coast of Asia. Meantime, the United States also acquired Hawaii (1898) and part of the Samoan Islands in the Pacific (1899). Then in 1903 American support of a revolution in Panama, then a part of Colombia, assured the independence of a new republic and direct American control of the zone of the projected Panama Canal.

The Americans withdrew from Cuba, leaving her as an independent republic, though subject under the Platt Amendment of 1901 to what in foreign eyes has always seemed American "protection." The rest of her acquisitions the United States kept for the time, though in the Philippines she had to put down an armed rising by Filipinos who wanted immediate independence. American anti-imperialists attempted to upset the somewhat anomalous arrangement under which their government kept lands without strict authorization from the Ameri-

CHAPTER XXIV

can Constitution. But a Supreme Court decision in the so-called "Insular Cases" (1901) held that territory might be subject to American jurisdiction without being incorporated constitutionally in the United States of America. Under this decision, Americans began the process of training the Filipinos for eventual independence. Meanwhile, the United States, too, had an empire, which on the maps was duly colored as an American possession.

The Japanese

One more empire was being formed during the decades before World War I, the only empire to be created by a people of non-European stock—the Japanese. The way for Japanese imperialism was cleared when a United States naval squadron, commanded by Commodore Matthew Perry, sailed into Tokyo Bay in 1853 and threatened to use force against the Japanese unless they permitted westerners to trade with them. Thus ended Japan's two centuries of isolation, and thus began her rapid rise as a modern power. The results of Perry's action, however, should not be exaggerated. Japan's isolation before 1853 was never absolute, and her adoption of modern, western ways after 1853 was far from complete. Even during their isolation, the Japanese had maintained an interest in western developments, particularly in technology, and had imported western books through the trading station that the Dutch were allowed to maintain at Nagasaki.

More important, in 1853 the basic political and economic structure of Japan had long needed overhauling. An oligarchy of the feudal type ruled, but its ineffective government, its grasping tax-collection, and the economic misery resulting all made it widely unpopular. Discontent was growing, especially among two important social classes. One was the urban middle class

Japanese portrait of the American Commodore Perry, about 1853.

of merchants and craftsmen. Although the industrial revolution had not yet reached Japan, the country already had populous cities, notably Tokyo (then called Yedo or

Edo). The urban middle class, somewhat like the French bourgeoisie on the eve of 1789, wanted political rights to match their increasing economic power. The other discontented class may be compared roughly with the poorer gentry and lesser nobility of Europe under the Old Régime. These were the *samurai* or feudal retainers, a military caste now threatened with impoverishment and political eclipse. The *samurai* dreaded the growth of cities and the subsequent threat to the traditional domination of agriculture and the landlords; many of them also resented the fact that they were largely excluded from positions of power by the prevailing oligarchical regime. These social pressures, more than any outside western influence, forced the modernization of Japan.

Economically, the transformation proceeded rapidly. By 1914, Japan very often resembled an advanced western country. She, too, had railroads, fleets of merchant vessels, a large textile industry, big cities, and big business firms. The industrialization of Japan was the more remarkable in view of her meager supplies of many essential raw materials. But she had many important assets. As a glance at the map will show, her geographical position with respect to Asia is very like that of the British Isles with respect to Europe. Japan, too, found markets for her exports on the continent nearby and used the income to pay for imports. The ambitious Japanese middle class, supplemented by recruits from the *samurai*, furnished aggressive business leadership. A great reservoir of cheap labor existed in the peasantry, a large and submissive class. The peasants, who needed to find jobs away from the overcrowded farms, were inured to a very low standard of living, and were ready to work long and hard in factories for what seemed by western standards indecently low wages.

Politically, Japan appeared to undergo a major revolution in the late nineteenth century and to remodel her government along western lines. Actually, however, the change was by no means so great as it seemed. A revolution did indeed occur, beginning in 1868 when the old feudal oligarchy crumbled under the pressure of the discontented elements. Authority and prestige were restored to the position of emperor, a largely forgotten office whose incumbents had long been mere "do-nothing" kings. In 1889, the emperor bestowed a constitution on his subjects, with a bicameral diet composed of a noble House of Peers and an elected House of Representatives.

The architects of these changes, however, were not democrats. They were aristocrats, ambitious young *samurai,* supported by allies from the business world and determined to make Japan over from above as they wished. The result was to substitute a new oligarchy for the old; a small group of aristocrats dominated the emperor and the state. The constitution of 1889, rather like that of the German Empire, provided only the outward appearances of liberal parliamentary government. The ministry was responsible not to the diet but to the emperor, and hence to the dominant aristocrats. The diet itself was scarcely representative; the right to vote for members of its lower house was limited to a narrow electorate, including the middle class but excluding the peasants and industrial workers. As Sir George Sansom, a British expert on Japan, has observed, she had no trouble in accepting western "things," but a great deal in handling western "ideas."

The Japanese, however, had no difficulty in taking over the western idea of empire. Imperialism naturally appealed to the policy-makers of an ambitious, economically expanding state that also had a large and growing population, little arable land, and sparse natural resources. After the revolution of 1868, the Japanese soon built up a

CHAPTER XXIV

modern army and navy. Their first victim was China, whom they defeated in the Sino-Japanese War of 1894-1895. Japan took as her spoils two outlying Chinese dependencies—the island of Formosa, which she annexed, and the piece of Asiatic mainland closest to Japan, the peninsula of Korea, whose independence China was forced to recognize as a preliminary to eventual Japanese annexation. But Russia, too, had designs on Korea; the results of this rivalry were the Russo-Japanese War of 1904-1905 and a second great Japanese victory (see Chapter XXII). Japan now secured unchallenged preponderance in Korea, which she annexed in 1910, special concessions in the Chinese province of Manchuria, and the cession by Russia of the southern half of the island of Sakhalin, to the north of the main Japanese islands.

By 1914, the Japanese empire was undergoing rapid economic development by emigrants from the home islands. But the harsh treatment of the subject peoples of Formosa and Korea by their new masters was preparing the way for later troubles in the Far East. So, too, were the grandiose projects for taking over China formulated by Japan's rulers, whose heads had been turned by their spectacular string of easy successes.

IV: The Debate Over Imperialism

In the nineteenth century all the western countries, even monarchical states like Germany, had a wide range of free public opinion, and some kind of parliamentary government by discussion. The kind of expansion we call imperialism, therefore, had to be defended articulately, since it was attacked articulately. The defense and attack are both important parts of the intellectual history of our times, for the debate, under greatly changed conditions, still goes on in mid-twentieth century.

Pro: The Argument from Social Darwinism

One central argument for the defense borrowed heavily from the Social Darwinists (see Chapter XXIII). Europeans both in Europe and in their "colonies of settlement," so ran the argument, were able to beat non-Europeans in war. By this very fact they had shown that they were in terms of evolution and progress more fit to survive than were the non-Europeans. Eternal competition is the price of survival. White men, this argument insisted, are simply better specimens of *homo sapiens* than are colored men; Anglo-Saxons (or Germans, or Slavs, or Latins, depending on the writer's origins) are simply better specimens than other white men.

Here is a passage from a British imperialist in 1899, by no means the most extreme that can be found:

Like all living organisms, States are ever struggling against strong outer forces, whether in the way of commercial, colonial, or territorial rivalry, or in actual war. In this struggle weakness means defeat. Now the essential element of all healthy life, power, or influence, is force or strength; either material brute force that crushes resistance, or force of will, character, and intelligence, that creates the impression of definite superiority and asserts itself. History has never revealed a State that was great without at some time showing both these elements of strength. Powerful armed forces and high-souled leadership are indispensable for any State aspiring to a commanding position. . . .

The strong and healthy sentiment of national ambition cannot perhaps be justified by logic except to your own sympathizers, present or future. Probably every one would agree that an Englishman would be right in considering his way of looking at the world and at life better than that of the Maori or Hottentot, and no one will object in the abstract to England doing her best to impose her better and higher view on those savages. But the same idea will carry you much further. In so far as an Englishman differs in essentials from a Swede or Belgian, he believes that he represents a more perfectly developed standard of general excellence. Yes, and even those nations nearest to us in mind and sentiment—German and Scandinavian—we regard on the whole as not so excellent as ourselves, comparing their typical characteristics with ours. Were this not so, our energies would be directed to becoming what they are. Without doing this, however, we may well endeavour to pick out their best qualities and add them to ours, believing that our compound will be superior to the foreign stock.

It is the mark of an independent nation that it should feel thus. How far such a feeling is, in any particular case, justified, history alone decides. But it is essential that each claimant for the first place should put forward his whole energy to prove his right. This is the moral justification for international strife and even of war, and a great change must come over the world and over men's minds before there can be any question of everlasting universal peace or the settlement of all international differences by arbitration. More especially must the difficulty caused by the absence of a generally recognized standard of justice be felt in the case of contact between civilized and uncivilized races. Is there any likelihood of the gulf between the white and the black man being bridged within any period of time that we can foresee? Can there be any doubt that the white man must and will impose his superior civilization on the coloured races? The rivalry of the principal European countries in extending their influence over other continents should lead naturally to the evolution of the highest attainable type of government of subject races by the superior qualities of their rulers.*

* Earl Grey, *Hubert Hervey, Student and Imperialist* (London, 1899), 55-58.

An imperialist like Cecil Rhodes, to judge from much that he wrote and said, very likely dreamed of a world which in the fullness of time and evolution would be peopled entirely by Anglo-Saxons. Their breed would actually be improved over their ancestors of 1900, after the inferior peoples had died out—or had been killed off. But these were very distant views indeed. The prospect of ruddy Kentish farmers actually established in freeholds along the Congo was too unrealistic for the present. At this point, imperialistic doctrine generally held that throughout the tropical world, the superior white men would put order and prosperity into the lives of colored men, would as trustees of civilization give up the comforts of Europe to rule in discomfort in the hot countries. Some imperialists thought that this benevolent rule of white men in the tropics would last indefinitely, since in their opinion non-whites were totally unable to undertake tasks of leadership and to assume moral responsibility.

Pro: The Argument of the "White Man's Burden"

Other European imperialists, however, took the attitude that, though the non-whites cannot run their own affairs now, they can ultimately learn to do so. For the present and for a good many years to come, whites will have to educate them on the spot; someday—the length of time judged necessary varied with the temperament of the judge—these non-whites will have matured sufficiently to take over responsibilities that now must be confined to whites. These are not responsibilities of *ownership*, but rather responsibilities of *trusteeship*. Kipling put the case comfortably enough—for white men—in his famous poem:

CHAPTER XXIV

Take up the White Man's Burden—
  Send forth the best ye breed—
Go bind your sons to exile
  To serve your captives' need;
To wait in heavy harness,
  On fluttered folk and wild—
Your new-caught, sullen peoples,
  Half-devil and half-child.

Take up the White Man's Burden—
  In patience to abide,
To veil the threat of terror
  And check the show of pride;
By open speech and simple,
  An hundred times made plain.
To seek another's profit,
  And work another's gain.

Take up the White Man's Burden—
  The savage wars of peace—
Fill full the mouth of Famine
  And bid the sickness cease;
And when your goal is nearest
  The end for others sought,
Watch Sloth and heathen Folly
  Bring all your hope to nought. *

This argument of trusteeship was by all odds the most popular defense of imperialism, particularly among Anglo-Saxon peoples. Few westerners, even in Germany where racism was already popular, could quite stomach the doctrine of Social Darwinism at its crudest: that the fit prove their fitness by killing off the unfit. To the liberal anti-imperialist, this elevating of the argument to the plane of trusteeship was most irritating. Hobson, for instance, complains that the doctrine of Social Darwinism takes on a large complexity of ethical and religious finery, and we are wafted into an elevated atmosphere of "imperial Christianity," a "mission of civilization," in which we are to teach "the arts of good government" and "the dignity of labour." †

Yet the historian, aware of the complexi-

* "The White Man's Burden," from "The Five Nations," *Rudyard Kipling's Verse, 1885-1932* (London, 1933), 320-321.

† J. A. Hobson, *Imperialism* (London, 1905), 137.

ties of human nature, will be wary of the notion that the ethical arguments of the imperialists were insincere. Many a European both in and out of the colonies of exploitation really believed in the trusteeship theory, and really did his best to live up to it. The Christian missionary is a major factor in the nineteenth-century expansion of the West. Indeed, Kenneth Latourette's long and thorough history of the expansion of Christianity has a final volume entitled *The Great Century* for the nineteenth century. More formal converts to Christianity were made all over the world in this century, so often labeled the century of materialism, than ever before.

How thorough the conversion of the colored peoples was is a difficult problem. In areas of primitive culture, whole tribes accepted Christianity but continued many of the immemorial ways of their heathen past. In India, China, and Japan, old civilized countries with deep-rooted religious faiths of their own, Christianity did not win over anything like a majority of the people. Nevertheless, the missions did succeed in the course of the century in building up devoted native followers, of whom the most intelligent were often sent to Europe or the United States to complete their education. Professor Latourette has modestly but hopefully summarized the nineteenth-century missionary movement:

Among non-European peoples the Christianity thus planted had a much more extensive influence than the size of the churches which were called into being would have led one to expect. . . . Hundreds of languages were for the first time given a written form, the Bible was translated into them in whole or in part, other Christian literature was prepared, and schools of a Western type were opened, often the pioneers of the kind of education which was to prevail as governments, either colonial or indigenous and independent, undertook an educational system for the new day. Orphanages were conducted in which thousands of children were cared for who would otherwise have perished. Famine relief was undertaken and attempts were made to introduce improvements in agriculture and forestry which would reduce or eliminate famine. Hospitals were founded and steps were taken to initiate medical and nursing professions trained in the science and techniques which were making rapid strides in the Occident. Public health education was inaugurated. Efforts were made to raise the status of women. All this, and more, was accomplished through a body of missionaries, men and women, which never numbered more than a quarter of a million and which was usually much less and which was not concentrated in one country but was distributed thinly over more than half the land surface of the globe and among much more than half the earth's population.

In addition the Christian conscience fought the selfish exploitation of non-white peoples by the dominant white race. Sometimes it found expression in missionaries. Even more often it stirred to action Christians who were not missionaries. It brought about the abolition of Negro slavery. It sought to curb the production and sale of opium and opium derivatives. It opposed any form of forced labour. The empire which ruled over the most people and the widest area was that of Great Britain. In the nineteenth century the quality of the British colonial official showed a marked improvement over the eighteenth century. The official might still regard himself as belonging to a superior race and culture and speak contemptuously of those whom he ruled as 'lesser breeds without the law' and as 'half devil and half child,' but towards them he felt an obligation to give devoted and honest service. . . . This improvement seems to have been due, at least in part, to the Evangelical Awakening, the revivals which followed it, and the general rise in the level of Christian living which were their products.[*]

Pro: The Defensive Argument

Finally, the imperialist philosophy of 1900 was by no means based on an unworried sense of white supremacy. Western civilization is one of the most worrying of all civilizations. Many publicists regarded

[*] K. S. Latourette, *A History of Christianity* (New York, 1953), 1135-1136.

imperialism as essentially defensive. The whites, outnumbered in a harsh world, had to organize themselves and hold the non-whites off. There was talk of the "yellow peril" and of white "race suicide." The writings and speeches of such apparently confident imperialists as Rhodes, Kipling, and Theodore Roosevelt sounded this curious note of fear and uncertainty. We are the best, but really we are a little too good for this world; we cannot breed fast enough.

Con: The Arguments of the Anti-Imperialists

Against imperialism, opponents marshaled a great many arguments. To the Social Darwinists the anti-imperialists replied by denying that the struggle for existence applied to human groups in the way it applied to plants and animals. It is precisely by sublimating the crude conflict of kill-or-be-killed into the higher rivalry for cultural excellence that human societies transcend the struggle for life. Each group, each race, has something to contribute to the total of civilization, and the deliberate destruction or suppression of any group lames and lessens the others, prevents the true working out of evolution among human beings as contrasted with mere animals. The anti-imperialists also brought forward very prominently the economic argument we have already noted. They worked hard to show that in fact, especially in Africa, colonies did not "pay," that the imperialist appeal to self-interest in the homeland was a delusion, the dishonest work of propagandists for the privileged minority in the homeland and in the colonies who *did* profit personally from imperialist ventures.

From this point the anti-imperialists went on to maintain that support at home for colonial expansion rested therefore on the ordinary man's vicarious satisfactions from national achievements. The ordinary man

CHAPTER XXIV

liked to see his country figure in the world atlas as an imperial power. He liked to think of Britain's empire on which the sun never set; or, if he was a Frenchman, of the tangible evidence that France was still a great power, still carrying on her *mission civilisatrice;* or, if he was an Italian, that at last Italy too was a nation, and behaving as nations should. The anti-imperialists were on the whole not very successful in their attempts to use ridicule and irony against behavior that they found irrational. But their conviction that human action ought to be rational and devoted to the greatest good of the greatest number placed them firmly in the liberal tradition.

So strong was the anti-imperialists' belief that they were right—in spite of the growth of empires all about them—that in Britain the school of "Little Englanders," much influenced by laissez-faire economics, came to the comforting assurance that imperialism was impossible. The colonies, they held, must inevitably drop away from the mother country—to use their favorite stereotype—like ripe fruit from a tree. Why not

then avoid getting into the futile process further by *not* taking any more of Africa or China? Why not hasten the inevitable by giving up the empire?

What sank into the mind and feelings of the ordinary westerner as a result of the anti-imperialist arguments was an uneasy awareness that somehow the practice of imperial expansion did not square with the best avowed intentions of democracy. Particularly in the United States, the feeling grew that imperialism and colonialism were contrary to the ideas of liberty and equality, even if the imperialists honestly claimed to be following the "trusteeship" principle. America took over an empire in 1898, but not without vigorous protests from numerous groups of anti-imperialists, and not without specific promises from the government that it would "free" dependents the moment they were capable of self-rule. This opposition of Americans to colonialism, especially when practiced by themselves, is one of the important factors in the world situation of the mid-twentieth century, and we shall return to it in later chapters.

V: The Results of Imperialism

The Results in General

The broad general results of this long phase of European expansion down to 1914 may now be summarized. First and most obviously, in the nineteenth century almost the whole planet was affected by the process that had begun with Da Gama and Columbus, and in a sense with the Crusades—the process of the actual spread of westerners in person, of their goods and ideas. By the early twentieth century, as we have seen, the explorer who wanted to do something

big had to work on the bleak continent of Antarctica. There were, however, detailed discoveries still to be made in Central Asia, in the Amazon Basin, even in Labrador and Alaska. And there were still many little inaccessible "islands" of territory where men lived as they had lived for centuries, without benefit of modern western culture. Moreover, the degree to which western ideas and ideals had really penetrated among non-western peoples varied greatly. On the whole, this penetration was much less deep than many nineteenth-century imperialists in the West believed it to be. Still, the white man was almost everywhere by 1914, and white explorers not infrequently found that the tin can, that ubiquitous symbol of the West, had got there ahead of them.

Second, the expansion of Europe was accompanied by a numerical expansion of the whole human race. Population statistics are by 1800 far from perfectly accurate, especially for countries outside the United States and Europe, but they are basically not misleading. Between 1800 and 1900 the population of the world just about doubled, from some 800,000,000 in 1800 to some 1,600,000,000 in 1900. European white stock did indeed account for the most spectacular part of the rise, but non-whites in Asia and elsewhere also increased. We do not sufficiently understand human population growth to say flatly that the expansion of Europe *caused* the growth of population among non-European peoples in the nineteenth century. But it did bring to many areas of the world some increase of law and order, some increase in material production and in health and sanitation—factors that probably contribute to population growth. And, with such exceptions as the native Australian "Blackfellows" and some North American Indians, European expansion did not usually mean the physical extermination of non-European peoples.

Third, we may say with no reservations whatever that by 1914 it was quite clear that "natives" were beginning to reject the claims of white supremacy. Among the more civilized and long-established peoples in the Near East and Asia the educated classes were already developing a sense of nationalism. They took over from the West that particular form of group consciousness that is attached to a territorial political unit and that is shared, in principle at least, by all who live within the unit. This nationalism was a new thing outside Europe, and a very

important one for us today, for it has gone on increasing and developing. In the early twentieth century, it was most evident in Japan and, to some extent, China, and in advanced "colonial" nations like Egypt and India.

This new phenomenon was not the same thing as simple hostility to whites, or to particular nations among the whites. It was an organized political faith—in short, modern "patriotism." Naturally, Egyptian, Indian, and Chinese patriots were first of all concerned with getting rid of their European imperial masters; their attitudes were those of oppressed nationalistic groups everywhere, even in Europe itself. They were touchy, addicted to nursing grievances imaginary as well as real, eager to seize on any national trait that could be glorified, admiring, hating, and envying their masters. Above all, they were organized on a new principle taken from the West, a principle that is ultimately perhaps more destructive of their own traditional cultures than anything else that has come to them from the West. This is the equalitarian and leveling, if not democratic, spirit inherent in the secular religion of nationalism. In theory at least nationality transcends the dividing lines of profession, social class, and even caste. The fellah, the Egyptian peasant whose ancestry reaches back through the centuries, could claim to be as good an Egyptian as the aristocratic pasha—indeed a better one, since he was uncorrupted by European culture.

Fourth, and in spite of the gloomy economic conclusions of anti-imperialists, there seems no doubt that over the century the homelands of Europe gained in total wealth from their expansion overseas. Indeed, raw materials from overseas were necessary to maintain the standard of living in thickly populated countries like Britain, Germany, Belgium, and the Netherlands. Theoretically, these raw materials could have come into European lands in free trade with free countries overseas; actually they came in part from imperial expansion.

Finally, imperialist rivalries, especially after 1870, exacerbated the normal rivalries among the European great powers, and were thus a major factor in the complex of causes that brought on general war in 1914 (see also Chapter XXV). This is particularly true of the Anglo-German rivalry, which, unlike that between France and Germany or between Austria and Russia, had no long background of purely European tradition. One of the chief factors in the growing tension between Britain and Germany after 1870 was the rivalry for actual imperial territories and the accompanying rivalry for markets in semi-colonial regions like South America.

The Colonies of Settlement

Thus far our account of the nineteenth-century expansion of Europe has been limited largely to the "colonies of exploitation," the protectorates, and the spheres of influence held by Europeans. No such account is at all complete, for the most striking thing about this expansion was that it involved an actual transplantation of Europeans to "colonies of settlement" on a scale incomparably greater than in the previous three centuries since Columbus. Before 1800, the two Americas, Australasia, South Africa, and Siberia numbered together but a few millions of European stock. By 1900, they numbered several hundred millions; the United States alone had nearly eighty millions.

The colonies of settlement were originally very thinly inhabited lands. Australia, indeed, was almost empty; and the whole native Indian population of America north of the Rio Grande was almost certainly in 1800 not over a million. The European settlers simply overwhelmed these primitive peoples. In Tasmania, a large island to the south of the Australian mainland, the natives were totally wiped out, and in Australia itself they were very nearly wiped out. In the United States the Red Indians were so far eliminated that many an American grew up in the nineteenth century without ever seeing a redman except in a Wild West show.

In most of Latin America, however, the native Indian stock, far from being wiped out, persisted; the upper class, politically and economically, was drawn from European "creole" stock; and a great many people of mixed European and Indian and Negro blood filled the lower social ranks. In the far south of the continent, in the Argentine and Chile, conditions resembled more clearly those in the United States, and these twentieth-century nations are now almost wholly European in stock. These facts help to explain why some of the states in the Americas appear more westernized and more Europeanized than do others.

The expansion of Europe into the Americas was also an expansion of Africa. By 1850 the leading European powers had pretty generally got the slave trade under control; but the nucleus of Negroes brought in by the trade in the earlier centuries continued to grow. Despite handicaps of race barriers, strongest in the United States, the Negroes multiplied; by 1900, for example, there were some 9,000,000 of them in the United States.

Canada: The Background of Revolt

Apart from the extraordinary growth of the United States, the most important phase of the nineteenth-century movement of Europeans overseas is the growth of what is now called the British Commonwealth of Nations, or, more correctly, simply the Commonwealth. Doubtless it is an oversimplification to claim that the British learned their lesson from the American Revolution, and that consequently in Canada, Australia, and South Africa they were wise enough to abandon the policies of George III and Lord North. But the formula is fundamentally sound. The first laboratory for this experiment in a new kind of "colonialism" was Canada (see map on p. 270).

The rebellious thirteen colonies of North America had wanted a fourteenth, and had tried hard to win Canada. But a complex of causes all contributed to leaving Canada in British hands at the peace in 1783. The French Canadians in Quebec distrusted the new Protestant power growing up to the south; the American rebels had grave difficulties keeping up an army to cope with the British in the United States itself; America's French ally did not wish the new country to be too strong. Later, as we have seen in Chapter XXI, the United States failed in the War of 1812 to reverse the verdict of 1783.

American "loyalists," faithful to the mother country, had begun to filter into Canada before 1783; they settled in great numbers in New Brunswick, which was separated from Nova Scotia in 1784, and in Upper Canada, later called the Province of Ontario. These loyalists and their descendants, organized as the United Empire Loyalists, were in the nineteenth century a major factor in the growth of Canadian nationalism. But their hostility to the United States, though not even today wholly allayed, has not since 1812 been nourished on actual warfare. Upper Canada, which was mainly British in stock, and Lower Canada (Quebec), which was mainly French, and the Maritime Provinces of Nova Scotia, New Brunswick, and Prince Edward Island were at first quite separate British "colonies," as the American thirteen had once been. Each had an apparatus quite like the old American one—a royal governor appointed by the Crown, a council appointed by the governor, and an elected assembly based on a more or less popular franchise. This arrangement continued into the early nineteenth century because of the beginnings of settlement in the Canadian West, because of the need for intensive development in all the provinces, and because of the need to hold together against the United States in the War of 1812. But just as in the thirteen colonies during the preceding century, the arrangement bred conflicts between the assemblies and the royal government. In 1837, revolts broke out in both Lower and Upper Canada, with popular leaders like Mackenzie and Papineau arrayed against the governor and his followers, and with essentially the same kind of constitutional and financial grievances that the thirteen colonies had had sixty years before.

Canada: The Durham Report and Dominion Status

The revolt of 1837 was a military fiasco, and it is probable that public opinion in both provinces was against the rebels; there was probably a fear that too close an imitation of the American Revolution would lead to absorption by the United States. But the British government was alarmed, and sent out as governor-in-chief of all the British North American provinces the Earl of Durham, a young lord of Whig antecedents and Utilitarian leanings. Durham, feeling that he was not properly supported from London, resigned after less than a year in Canada. But the famous report he made to the British Parliament on his return in 1839 became the cornerstone of the new British imperial structure of dominions, a constitutional document that Durham's admirers have sometimes ranked with Magna Carta.

The Durham Report proposed the union of Upper and Lower Canada and the establishment of responsible government—that is, a popularly elected legislature with ultimate authority—for both the union and the separate provinces. The report is still of great interest. Durham had all the average Englishman's insensitivity to things French, and it is an understatement to say that he never understood the Québecois of Lower Canada. But he was true to his principles —even these French Canadian Catholics must have their own responsible government. As he wrote:

The greater part of the plans which have been proposed for the future government of Lower Canada suggest . . . that the Government of that Province should be constituted on an entirely despotic footing, or on one that would vest it entirely in the hands of the British minority. It is proposed either to place the legislative authority in a Governor, with a Council formed of the heads of the British party, or to contrive some scheme of representation by which a minority . . . is to deprive a majority of all voice in the management of its own affairs.

The maintenance of an absolute form of government on any part of the North American Continent can never continue for any long time, without exciting a general feeling in the United States against a power of which the existence is secured by means so odious to the people; and as I rate the preservation of the present general sympathy of the United States with the policy of our Government in Lower Canada as a matter of the greatest importance, I should be sorry that the feeling should be changed for one which, if prevalent among the people, must extend over the surrounding Provinces. The influence of such an opinion would not only act very strongly on the entire French population, and keep up among them a sense of injury and a determination of resistance to the Government, but would lead to just as great discontent among the English. In their present angry state of feeling, they might tolerate, for a while, any arrangement that would give them a triumph over the French; but I have greatly misunderstood their character if they would long bear a Government in which they had no direct voice. Nor would their jealousy be obviated by the selection of a Council from the persons supposed to have their confidence. It is not easy to know who

really possess that confidence; and I suspect that there would be no surer way of depriving a man of influence over them than by treating him as their representative without their consent. . . .

But the great objection to any government of an absolute kind is that it is palpably of a temporary nature; that there is no reason to believe that its influence, during the few years that it would be permitted to last, would leave the people at all more fit to manage themselves; that, on the contrary, being a mere temporary institution, it would be deficient in that stability which is the great requisite of government in times of disorder. There is every reason to believe that a professedly irresponsible government would be the weakest that could be devised. Every one of its acts would be discussed, not in the Colony, but in England, on utterly incomplete and incorrect information, and run the chance of being disallowed without being understood. The most violent outcry that could be raised by persons looking at them through the medium of English and constitutional notions, or by those who might hope thereby to promote the sinister purposes of faction at home, would be constantly directed against them. Such consequences as these are inevitable.*

The actual realization of Durham's recommendations was achieved with due British slowness, piece by piece. The first step, the Union Act of 1840 passed by the British Parliament, though it did unite Upper and Lower Canada was at the very least unspecific on the critical point of responsibility —that is, on whether an administration defeated in the legislature had to resign or not. Nearly a decade later, under the governorship of Lord Elgin, the principle was quietly established in practice, never to be withdrawn. Nor was the next step unduly hurried. The British North America Act of 1867 achieved in principle the union of all the British provinces in North America, except Newfoundland, oldest of all, whose separatist tendencies were so strong it did not join Canada until 1949. The act of 1867

* Sir Reginald Coupland, *The Durham Report* (Oxford, 1945), 155-157.

set up the Dominion of Canada by the union of Ontario, Quebec, and the Maritime Provinces, with provision for the admission of territories in the west as provinces on something like the pattern for admission of the western states in the United States. There were still many survivals of the former "colonial" status of Canada, from the bestowal of titles, especially knighthood with its unrepublican and undemocratic "Sir," to the possibility of judicial appeal from Canadian courts to the Privy Council in Westminster. Above all, the relation of Canada to Britain in terms of international affairs, armed forces, right of secession, and much else was not yet spelled out, and was not to be spelled out formally until the Statute of Westminster in 1931 (see Chapter XXIX).

The Extension of Dominion Status

Yet the nineteenth century saw the essentials of the British Commonwealth of Nations firmly established. The process as worked out first in Canada was worked out for other colonies of settlement, always with attention to particular local problems, but with a firm logical basis in abstract ideas. (That the British do not allow themselves to follow ideas or a logical program is a satisfying but inaccurate myth that they have nursed for some time.) The extension of dominion status was grounded in the Durham Report and its Utilitarian-Liberal ideology.

The individual provinces of Australia had common British origins and had relatively short lives as separate territorial units—the oldest, New South Wales, dates only from 1788. But, in spite of these facts, these provinces developed their local differences and separateness, symbolized by the fact that they used differing gauges for their railroads. They gained the essentials of self-

government in the Australian Colonies Government Act of 1850, but federal union of New South Wales, Victoria, Queensland, and the others was not achieved until the Commonwealth of Australia was formed in 1901. The influence of the American example is clear in the constitution of the Commonwealth, which provides for a senate with equal membership for each of the six states, a house of representatives apportioned on the basis of population, and a supreme court with something close to the American power of judicial review. But in Australia as in the other British dominions, the parliamentary system of an executive (prime minister and cabinet) dismissible by vote of the legislative body was retained; the American "presidential" system was deliberately rejected.

Australia, like Canada, was essentially an empty country in 1800, and like Canada it filled gradually with immigrants, mostly from Britain. Perhaps the head start of the United States, with its great attraction for European immigration, slowed down the growth of these British dominions. But the process, though slow, was steady, and by 1914 all the dominions, including the quiet islands of New Zealand, traditionally most "English" of them all, were prosperous, democratic societies just settling down from the last of the pioneer stage. Their narrative history is most interesting, but we cannot go into it here, nor into the fascinating and illuminating subject—insufficiently pursued—of the likenesses and unlikenesses of the corporate personalities of these new countries and the United States, all offsprings of the "frontier."

Minority Problems in the British Commonwealth

Most of the dominions had some sort of minority problem. The most serious one, as we have seen earlier in this chapter,

410

Australia grows up. Lord John Russell, a British statesman, measures the growth.

as settlers, but the original tiny group had increased to a million and a half by 1901, despite considerable emigration from Quebec to the mill towns of New England. The French Canadians continued to dominate the Province of Quebec and were spreading into Ontario and the new western provinces. They had a considerable measure of self-government within the Dominion, since the original union put their own language on a basis of equality with English and granted them other specific rights, such as that of using public taxation to support Catholic schools employing the French language. On the whole, the Canadian experience with a federal state with two "national" groups divided by language and religion was heartening for those who hoped to transcend nationalism in a world where nationalist feeling was being whipped up to the explosive point of 1914. In Chapter XXIX we shall return to this Canadian experience in our own generation.

Finally, there were in New Zealand a few tens of thousands of Maoris, a tribe akin to the Polynesian inhabitants of the smaller islands of the central Pacific area. The nineteenth-century Polynesians could not resist the inroads of Europeans at all successfully and have died out proportionately to other peoples even in Hawaii. The Maoris, more numerous and with more space, fought the Europeans as the Indians of the Great Plains and Rocky Mountains fought the Americans. Inevitably they lost, and after the close of the Second Maori War in 1870 they settled down in apparent resignation to the loss of their lands and to ultimate extinction. They had, however, gained the right to send four representatives to the New Zealand legislative assembly, and they were on the whole less subject to the humiliating status of being mere wards than were the American reservation Indians at that time. By 1900, it began to be clear that,

affected the Union of South Africa, which achieved dominion status in 1910. Whereas the other dominions were true colonies of settlement, in South Africa the Europeans were heavily outnumbered by non-Europeans. And the European South Africans were themselves divided into a slender majority of Afrikaans-speaking descendants of Dutch and Huguenot settlers and a substantial minority of English-speaking *Uitlanders.*

In Canada, only a few thousand French had ever migrated from Old to New France

alone of the Polynesian groups, the Maoris had probably ceased to lose in numbers. They were in no sense a menacing minority in the New Zealand of the early twentieth century, a land that had begun to attract attention for its very "advanced" social-security legislation.

The British Commonwealth in Review

In the nineteenth century, Americans pushing west and Russians pushing east added millions of square miles to their respective lands as colonies of settlement. Although in both, and especially in America, this process of the "frontier" had important effects on their national character, it did not create great immediate problems concerning the "independence" of the settlers. The British, however, went thousands of miles overseas for their colonies of settlement. They found very soon that these colonies could not be treated as the long tradition since 1450 prescribed—that is, as mere outposts of the mother land with no political self-rule, held in strict mercantilist economic leading strings. Nor could they be, if only because of the separating seas, simply added as a territorial continuation of the mother land, like Siberia or the American West. By 1914, the British at home and the citizens of their overseas colonies of settlement had worked out something new in political configurations, unprecedented in man's brief history. There is perhaps a faint analogy with Greek colonialism of the seventh century B.C. The Greeks who left their mother city took their freedom and their citizenship with them, and set up in the new land a new *polis* (city-state). But the new *polis,* if it kept a patriotic awareness of its origin in the homeland, was from the beginning quite free from its mother *polis* politically and economically.

Canada, Australia, New Zealand were indeed by 1914 wholly self-governing. They could and did even level customs dues on imports from Britain. They had the beginnings of military forces of their own, and of course complete control of that clear attribute of "sovereignty"—their own internal police. Men were even beginning to speculate about whether they were not in possession of that other clear attribute of sovereignty—the right to conduct foreign relations, both diplomatic and military. For example, could Canada be at peace with a country with which Great Britain was at war?

The test came in 1914. All the dominions went to war against Germany and her allies. Even the dubiously loyal Union of South Africa went to war against the sender of the Kruger telegram; we are bound to record that the always land-hungry Boers had their eyes on the German colonies in Africa, and especially on the big empty colony of German Southwest Africa, right adjacent to the Union. The government of each dominion, however, went through the formal process of declaring war, just as "sovereign" countries do. Yet it was clear that in fact the relation between Canada, for instance, and Great Britain was something more than the relation between Greek Massilia (Marseille) or Sicilian Syracuse and their Greek motherland. The dominions had not quite set up wholly for themselves, or, to revert to the favorite cliché of the nineteenth-century Little Englander, they had not dropped off like ripe fruit. The nature of the tie between the dominions and Britain was not clear then, and it must be admitted it is not fully clear now. But it exists, and to it also we shall return in a chapter on imperialism in our own day.

CHAPTER XXIV

Reading Suggestions
on Nineteenth-Century Imperialism

General Accounts

W. L. Langer, *The Diplomacy of Imperialism, 1890-1902,* 2nd ed. (New York: Alfred A. Knopf, Inc., 1951). A detailed study of a particularly hectic period of the imperial scramble; also includes a valuable discussion of the forces making for imperialism.

J. A. Hobson, *Imperialism, A Study* (London: J. Nisbet and Co., 1902). Perhaps the most famous attack on imperialism.

V. I. Lenin, *Imperialism, The Highest Stage of Capitalism* (New York: International Publishers, 1939). The classic expression of the communist interpretation of imperialism.

B. Kidd, *The Control of the Tropics* (New York: The Macmillan Company, 1898). A good example of the serious defenses of imperialism offered at the end of the nineteenth century.

J. A. Schumpeter, *Imperialism and Social Classes* (New York: Noonday Press, 1955). A valuable essay on imperialism from the standpoint of the economist and sociologist.

K. S. Latourette, *A History of the Expansion of Christianity,* 7 vols. (New York: Harper and Brothers, 1937-1945). Volumes 5 and 6 of this major work concern the expansion of Christianity into the non-European world, 1800-1914.

Special Studies: Africa

L. Woolf, *Empire and Commerce in Africa* (London: G. Allen and Unwin, 1919). A detailed and highly critical account from a left-wing point of view.

H. H. Johnston, *The Opening Up of Africa* (New York: Henry Holt & Co., 1911. Home University Library). Sympathetic popular account by the author of many other works on Africa.

H. L. Hoskins, *European Imperialism in Africa* (New York: Henry Holt & Co., 1930. A Berkshire Study). Handy introductory manual.

R. L. Buell, *The Native Problem in Africa* (New York: The Macmillan Company, 1928); and H. A. Wieschoff, *Colonial Policies in Africa* (Philadelphia: University of Pennsylvania Press, 1944). Two solid and helpful studies.

C. W. de Kiewiet, *A History of South Africa, Social and Economic* (Oxford: The Clarendon Press, 1941), and E. A. Walker, *A History of South Africa,* 2nd ed. (New York: Longmans, Green & Co., 1940). Two good studies of the area.

Basil Williams, *Cecil Rhodes* (London: Constable & Co., 1921). Probably the best book on the famous empire-builder.

Basil Williams, *Botha, Smuts, and South Africa* (New York: Macmillan, 1948. Teach Yourself History series). Introduction to the period following the Boer War.

F. D. Lugard, *The Dual Mandate in British Tropical Africa,* 3rd ed. (Edinburgh: W. Blackwood and Sons, 1926). Significant detailed account of British colonial policy in action.

H. R. Rudin, *Germans in the Cameroons, 1884-1914: A Case Study in Imperialism* (New Haven: Yale University Press, 1938). Good study of the topic indicated.

L. de Lichtervelde, *Léopold of the Belgians* (New York: The Century Co., 1929) and L. Bauer, *Leopold the Unloved, King of the Belgians and of Wealth* (Boston: Little, Brown & Co., 1935). Vindicating and attacking, respectively, the great exploiter of the Congo.

Special Studies: Asia

J. T. Pratt, *The Expansion of Europe into the Far East* (London: The Sylvan Press, 1947). Excellent introduction to the subject.

D. E. Owen, *Imperialism and Nationalism in the Far East* (New York: Henry Holt & Co., 1929. A Berkshire Study). Handy brief introductory manual.

K. S. Latourette, *The Development of China*, 6th ed. (New York: The Macmillan Company, 1946). A good survey.

A. C. Lyall, *The Rise and Expansion of British Dominion in India*, 5th ed. (London: John Murray, 1914). Sympathetic account.

R. Coupland, *Britain and India, 1600-1941* (New York: Longmans, Green & Co., 1941). Very brief introduction by an authority on imperial questions.

G. Sansom, *The Western World and Japan, A Study in the Interaction of European and Asiatic Cultures* (New York: Alfred A. Knopf, Inc., 1950) and *Japan, A Short Cultural History*, rev. ed. (New York: Appleton-Century, 1943). Two indispensable works by a great authority on Japan.

E. O. Reischauer, *Japan, Past and Present* (New York: Alfred A. Knopf, Inc., 1946). Helpful and reliable brief introduction.

B. H. Sumner, *Tsardom and Imperialism in the Far East and Middle East, 1880-1914* (London: British Academy, 1944). Good short account.

H. Brown, ed., *The Sahibs: The Life and Ways of the British in India as Recorded by Themselves* (London: W. Hodge, 1948). An illuminating compilation.

Special Studies: The British Empire and Dominions

J. H. Rose and others, eds., *The Cambridge History of the British Empire*, 7 vols. (New York: The Macmillan Company, 1940). This solid work, more useful for facts than for interpretation, has separate volumes on such major areas as India, Canada, and Australia-New Zealand.

P. Knaplund, *The British Empire, 1815-1939* (New York: Harper and Brothers, 1941). A standard, accurate account.

P. McGuire, *Experiment in World Order* (New York: William Morrow and Co., 1948). A hopeful survey of British expansion.

C. E. Carrington, *The British Overseas: Exploits of a Nation of Shopkeepers* (Cambridge, England: The University Press, 1950). A detailed account with good maps and portraits, but some inaccuracies of detail.

D. G. Creighton, *Dominion of the North: A History of Canada* (Boston: Houghton Mifflin Co., 1944). A good account.

R. Coupland, ed., *The Durham Report* (Oxford: The Clarendon Press, 1946). The famous document that in a sense marks the beginning of the development of the British Commonwealth.

Special Studies: Other Subjects

S. H. Roberts, *History of French Colonial Policy, 1870-1925*, 2 vols. (London: P. S. King and Son, Ltd., 1929). Detailed and substantial study.

H. I. Priestley, *France Overseas* (New York: Appleton-Century, 1938). Another useful account.

D. W. Brogan, *France under the Republic* (New York: Harper and Brothers, 1939). Contains a brief and illuminating treatment of French imperialism.

M. E. Townsend, *The Rise and Fall of Germany's Colonial Empire, 1884-1918* (New York: The Macmillan Company, 1930). A useful account.

J. W. Pratt, *America's Colonial Experiment* (New York: Prentice-Hall, Inc., 1950). A valuable survey of the American empire.

D. Perkins, *Hands Off: A History of the Monroe Doctrine* (Boston: Little, Brown & Co., 1941). A useful popular account.

Historical Fiction

R. Kipling, *Kim* (many editions) and *Soldiers Three* (many editions). Famous works by the even more famous champion of imperialism.

N. Coward, *Cavalcade*, in *Play Parade* (Garden City, N. Y.: Garden City Publishing Co., 1933). A patriotic play and a sentimental tribute to old imperial glories.

S. Cloete, *The Turning Wheels* (Boston: Houghton Mifflin Co., 1937). A novel about nineteenth-century Boers.

O. Schreiner, *The Story of a South African Farm* (London: E. Benn, 1930). An older and celebrated novel about South Africa.

A. Gide, *The Immoralist* (New York: Alfred A. Knopf, Inc., 1948). A novel in which the European hero is thoroughly corrupted by North Africa.

E. M. Forster, *A Passage to India* (many editions). A celebrated and astringent novel about the British in India.

L. Hémon, *Maria Chapdelaine* (New York: The Macmillan Company, 1940). The best-known novel about rural French Canada.

H. H. Richardson, *The Fortunes of Richard Mahony* (New York: Readers Club, 1941). A series of novels about modern Australia by an Australian.

H. Rider Haggard, *King Solomon's Mines* (New York: Longmans, Green & Co., 1926). A splendid example of the rousing novel of imperialist adventure.

The First
World War

I: Introduction

CHAPTER XXV

ON JUNE 28, 1914, the Habsburg Archduke Francis Ferdinand, heir to the throne of Austria-Hungary, and his wife were assassinated in the streets of Sarajevo, capital of the recently (1908) annexed province of Bosnia. The assassin, Princip, was a Serbian nationalist. Bosnia had long been coveted by the Serbs, and many Bosnians would have liked to join Serbia. The Austro-Hungarian government, alarmed by the ambitions of Serbian nationalists, took the occasion of the assassination to send a severe ultimatum to Serbia. The Serbian refusal to accept the ultimatum in its entirety led to an Austrian declaration of war on Serbia, on July 28. Within the week, the great states of Europe were engaged in a general war—the Central Powers (Austria-Hungary and Germany) against the Allies (Serbia, Russia, France, and Britain). Princip's revolver was eventually to kill some ten million men.

Wars get named, usually after they have ended, from some feature that has impressed the public mind—from their chief geographical theater, like the Italian Wars; from mere duration, like the Thirty Years' War; from a causal factor, like the War of

French defenders of Verdun.

the Spanish Succession; from a ruler, like the Napoleonic Wars. But professional historians rarely name wars, or the War of 1914-1918 would not be known to us as the First World War or World War I. Readers of this book know that a number of earlier general wars were fought on sea and land in most parts of both the Old and the New Worlds, and were therefore in the most obvious senses "world wars." They may well conclude that one or another of the wars of Louis XIV has perhaps the best claim to be known as World War I. Usage, however, is what counts in these matters. For our generation the war that began in 1914, and that was known to its own participants quite simply as the "Great War," has since the outbreak of another general war in 1939 been known as the First World War.

It was the first general war, the first war to involve most of the members of the world state-system, since the wars of the French Revolution and Napoleon a century earlier. There had indeed been wars enough, foreign and civil, in the century between. They were, however, wars between two parties, like the Franco-Prussian War of 1870, the bloody American war between North and South in 1861-1865, and a whole series of colonial wars against rebellious natives. Even the Crimean War of 1853, between Russia on the one hand and Great Britain, France, Turkey, and Piedmont on the other, was by great diplomatic effort kept from spreading out into a world war, and was confined to relatively minor fighting in the small peninsula of Crimea.

A statistician counting every war from the big duels between great powers and the revolutionary disturbances to the "punitive expeditions" against recalcitrant tribesmen like the American Sioux Indians could certainly make the period from 1815 to 1914 seem far from peaceful. These wars did not, however, strike the public imagination as do the all-out general or world wars. The important thing to note is that in 1914 a great many people in Europe and America felt that this sort of general war was all but impossible. These people, predominantly liberal intellectuals, had been alarmed by the series of crises we shall shortly describe, crises that showed how close a general war might be. But they had followed hopefully the movements for international peace and co-operation—the Red Cross, the international labor movements, and the Hague conferences of 1899 and 1907, which, though they failed to achieve their avowed purpose of armaments limitation, did set up a tribunal for the arbitration of international disputes, the "world court."

The state of mind of liberal intellectuals is well reflected in a famous book of 1910, *The Great Illusion*, by an English publicist, Norman Angell. War, Angell argued, could not possibly benefit even a victor, for the new complex economic life of the world would be so badly disrupted by a general— and necessarily brief—war that victor and vanquished alike would emerge poorer. Angell had enough hope in human reason to hold that if everyone knew that his country was sure to lose in a war, no one would start a war. Even those who disagreed with Angell's thesis and who thought a general war might break out were sure it would so disrupt the complex structure of western society that it would necessarily be a very short war.

World War I, however, was long, bloody, and destructive. The shock of its outbreak, vastly increased by the strains of the war itself, and above all by the failure of the postwar peace settlement, brought on in the 1920's a most extraordinary discussion of the causes of the war. This discussion was by no means limited to professional historians. It was carried on in the press and on the platforms by all the agencies that touch public opinion. Most of it was designed to "revise" the verdict of the Versailles Treaty of 1919, in which the victorious Allies declared Germany and Austria-Hungary solely responsible for precipitating the war of 1914. The beaten Germans, penalized in the peace, had obvious reasons for trying to prove themselves innocent of war guilt. But important currents in public opinion in Great Britain, the United States, and even in France also flowed into this "revisionist" movement. So far did revisionism go in the 1920's that some American historians parceled out varying portions of the guilt among the victors and vanquished alike, with the confidence of schoolmasters handing out merits and demerits.

We cannot be so confident today. From our further perspective, the question of war guilt fades out into a question of historical causation, and into the fact of historical tragedy. We can say with the English writer, George Meredith:

> In tragic life, God wot,
> No villain need be! Passions spin the plot.
> We are betrayed by what is false within.[*]

No one power or group of powers caused the war of 1914. Its causes lie deep in the history of the state-system of western civilization, and, more particularly, in its history since 1870. The dramatic date of the assassination of Francis Ferdinand, June 28, 1914, serves as a dividing line between the ultimate, or long-term, factors and the proximate, or short-term, factors.

[*] *Modern Love,* XLIII.

II: Causes of the War

The Shift
in the Balance of Power

In the long term, an obvious factor that made war more likely was the unification of Germany and Italy. The creation of these two new major states in the 1860's and 1870's altered the always delicate balance of power in the European state-system. The efforts of statesmen during the next forty years to adjust the system and to take account of the two new powers and their claims proved ultimately unsuccessful. The older established powers were by no means willing to give up their own claims. We have seen that ever since the modern European—or, better, the western—state-system developed out of medieval fragmentation the separate units, the states, have tried to grow. They have tried to grow in wealth, in prestige, and, most of all, in territory. In the second half of the nineteenth century, with the principle of national sovereignty well established, with even the smaller states like Switzerland and Sweden generally accepted as not to be swallowed, there was little territory in Europe that could be easily disposed of for the purpose of making adjustments. Unification had closed Germany and Italy, which as recently as the eighteenth century had been classic areas for "compensation." Only southeastern Europe, the Balkan lands of the obviously weakening Turkish Empire, remained as possible pickings for ambitious powers. Even there, the growth of national feeling in states like Rumania, Serbia, Bulgaria, and Greece made sheer annexation difficult. Nevertheless, Russia and Austria-Hungary both had ambitions in the Balkans; behind them, aiming rather at domination of Turkey and the Near East, came Germany and Great Britain.

Outside Europe, territory was available for distribution, even in the last quarter of the nineteenth century. This territory included much of Africa, where the European powers had not completely staked out their claims, and some parts of Asia and Oceania, notably the great and weakened empire of China. In the forty years before 1914, almost all the great powers that waged the war of 1914-1918 took an active part in the competition for what was left to be absorbed in Africa and Asia, either by actual annexation or by establishing protectorates or "spheres of influence."

Meantime, influenced by their rivalries in Europe and abroad, the great powers were also choosing sides in a series of alliances and agreements. By the early years of the twentieth century two camps existed —the Triple Alliance of Germany, Austria-Hungary, and Italy, and the Triple Entente of France, Britain, and Russia. The system, as many people at the time saw clearly, had grown so tightly organized that there was almost no free play left, and with the wisdom of hindsight we can now see that after 1900 almost any crisis might have led to war. Sarajevo was the one that did.

In this "international anarchy," as the English publicist Lowes Dickinson christened it, in concrete instance after concrete instance two or more powers wanted the same piece of land, as a territorial addition or as a sphere of influence. France and Great Britain both wanted Egypt; France and Germany both wanted Morocco; Russia and Austria-Hungary both wanted control over the Balkans; Russia and Japan both wanted Manchuria; and so on around the map. Compromises were made, lands and spheres of influence were shared, but in the long run there simply wasn't enough to go around.

In this scramble a rough distinction can be made between the "haves," or "saturated powers," and the "have-nots," the powers that had not done well in previous competition. Notable among the "have-nots" were Germany and Italy, which had not been united nations when the other great powers were expanding overseas, and which did not yet have in 1870 colonial empires. They had to take the leavings in Africa and Oceania. The "have-nots" were not always aggressors, nor were the "haves" always the defenders of the status quo. The latter, even powerful Britain, wanted some things that others wanted. Yet in these years Germany, newly united, with a rapidly growing population, with an efficient industrial economy, appears as the power with most to gain by disturbing the system radically. Germany appears, to use a morally neutral word, as the main "perturber." And Great Britain, as the old-established leader of the world, rich, powerful, and full of prestige, appears as the main defender of the world-system of states as embodied in international law, or, more cynically, as the defender of things-as-they-are.

The Role of Public Opinion

We have in this outline used the shorthand of names like "Great Britain" or "Germany." But these are mere symbols, as colored blobs on a map are symbols, for millions of human beings whose desires somehow do add up into the actions of states, did add up to the war of 1914. In no state were the millions all in agreement. There were Germans who wanted no bit of Africa or any other piece of land. There were Englishmen who, far from being content with Britain's place in the world, wanted more, wanted Britain to be for the whole round world what Rome had been for the Mediterranean world in the first centuries of the Christian Era, hoped eventually to kill off all but Englishmen in a fine Darwinian struggle. There were everywhere in Europe at least a few absolute pacifists, men who were determined under any conditions to refuse to fight, men who once war broke out became "conscientious objectors." We must not think of the war and the events that led up to it as simply the work of a few men at the top in each nation, the professional soldiers, the villainous diplomats in frock coats and striped trousers. In all the countries, there is a spectrum that runs from the militarist to the pacifist, through all shades of opinion.

But the outbreak of the war saw in each belligerent nation a broad national public opinion in support of the government. In 1914 some men marched to war convinced that war was a beneficial thing. Here is the account of a young German on the last train out of Switzerland in July, 1914:

An elderly gentleman was sitting in our compartment. He began to talk to us at once, as if we were intimate acquaintances. On the back of his hotel bill he had added up the numerical strength of the European armies and balanced them against each other. He compared the two totals and assured my mother that the spiritual qualities of the German troops compensated for the numerical superiority of the Russians. For in this war spiritual qualities alone would decide the day, and Germany's spiritual qualities were the best in Europe. As a university professor he knew that our youth were ready for the fray, and full of ideals. At last the hour had come when our people could enter on its great world mission. He himself had been almost cast into despair by the crass materialism of the last few years—particularly in the lower classes; but at last life had regained an ideal significance. The great virtues of humanity, which had found their last refuge in Germany—fidelity, patriotism, readiness to die for an idea—these were triumphing now over the trading and shopkeeping spirit. This was the providential lightning flash that would clear the air; after it a new German people would arise whose victory would save the world from mediocrity, brutalizing materialism, western democracy and false humanitarianism.

He could see a new world, ruled and directed by a race of aristocrats, who would root out all signs of degeneracy and lead humanity back again to the deserted peaks of the eternal ideals. Those who were too weak must perish by the wayside. The war would cleanse mankind from all its impurities.*

This was a war in which the bands played and the people sang. Out of it came "Tipperary," a conventional vaudeville song that somehow came to lift the hearts of the British everywhere, "Madelon," a lively song honoring in true French fashion the *fille* (literally, "daughter") of the regiment, a whole set of nostalgic songs like "There's a Long, Long Trail A-winding," and the usual wildly bawdy soldiers' favorites like "Mademoiselle from Armentières." Even the deliberately planned patriotic rousers, like George M. Cohan's "Over There," were popular. The war of 1914-1918, though it evoked, as we shall see, a literature of protest from intellectuals, though it came to weigh heavily on ordinary people, was nevertheless for many who fought in it a great adventure, even a crusade. We must therefore try to get beyond the colorless abstractions of balance of power, and see how the people—the ordinary people, the good citizens—felt about the events that had brought them into war.

German Aspirations

Most Germans in 1914 were sincerely convinced that their country had been denied its proper "place in the sun" by the selfish policy of rival powers, and especially by Britain. They were convinced that ever since 1870 these powers had been combining to keep Germany down, to keep her from acquiring colonies, to keep her poor by denying her access to world markets. They knew, indeed, that their country

---

* Ernst Glaeser, *Class of 1902*, Willa and Edwin Muir, trans. (London, 1929), 171-172.

Berlin crowds singing "Deutschland über Alles," 1914.

had in spite of all this managed to acquire two big blocks of land in Africa, German Southwest Africa and German East Africa, and some smaller bits in other parts of Africa and in Oceania. They knew that she, along with the older powers, had a foothold in China and that she was taking Britain's traditional place as the most influential great power in Turkey. They knew, certainly, that Germany was everywhere accepted as a great power.

But it was not enough. The colonial empire, add up its square miles and its population as you would, came out much less than that of Great Britain, much less even than that of France, whom the Germans had soundly beaten in 1870 and whom they regarded as degenerate. And wherever, as in the Near East and in China and North Africa, Germany strove hard to push her way, she met the resistance of France and Britain. So, many Germans joined various pressure groups to help them get their way —a Navy League to raise men and money for a navy that would be almost the equal of England's, a Colonial League to get men out to the colonies and to found new ones,

societies to promote German culture in the outside world and to hold in their German allegiance Germans who had migrated to America or other parts of the world. They believed that they were working to break up what they felt was the isolation, the "encirclement" of Germany by her jealous rivals.

The Germans were led in this by their young Kaiser, William II, who had come to the throne in 1888. In the hectic five weeks after Sarajevo, as we shall see, the "revisionists" showed that the Kaiser, contrary to world opinion at the time, had not worked steadily for war, that indeed he had tried to prevent war. But he cannot be even partially absolved for the long-term, for the ultimate, causes of the war. In the decisive years between 1888 and 1914 he was the posturing, aggressive leader of patriotic expansion, the "White Knight" leading his people to glory (see also Chapter XXII). He was perhaps more of a figurehead, less of an actual maker of policy than the world took him to be, but still a willing and effective figurehead for expansionists.

CHAPTER XXV

German ambitions and German fears produced an intense hatred of Britain, a hatred mixed with envy and a sense of inferiority, a hatred that focused on the English upper classes, perfectly tailored, serene in effortless superiority, the favorite children of fortune. Many a German tourist, perhaps quite accidentally given an Italian hotel room inferior to that given a traveling Englishman, would come home burning with indignation at this personal evidence that Germany was being denied its place in the sun. In the German navy, in the years before the war, there was a simple toast in the officers' mess: *Der Tag* (The Day). Everyone knew that this was the day of the declaration of war between Germany and Britain. These feelings are all condensed in the famous "Hymn of Hate" of the German poet Ernst Lissauer:

> Take you the folk of the earth in pay,
> With bars of gold your ramparts lay,
> Bedeck the ocean with bow on bow,
> Ye reckon well, but not well enough now.
> French and Russian they matter not,
> A blow for a blow, a shot for a shot,
> We fight the battle with bronze and steel,
> And the time that is coming, Peace will seal.
> You will we hate with a lasting hate,
> We will never forego our hate,
> Hate by water and hate by land,
> Hate of the head and hate of the hand,
> Hate of the hammer and hate of the Crown.
> Hate of the seventy millions choking down.
> We love as one, we hate as one,
> We have one foe and one alone:
> England! *

British Aspirations

Few Englishmen returned this hate; the English were still on top. Yet as the years wore on, the expensive race between Britain and Germany in naval armaments continued; in incident after incident Ger-

* Ernst Lissauer, "A Chant of Hate Against England," trans. by Barbara Henderson, in Burton E. Stevenson, comp., *The Home Book of Verse,* 3rd ed. (New York, 1918), II, 2549-2551.

man and British diplomats took opposite sides; and—this seemed especially important to the hard-headed—German wares of all sorts undersold British wares in Europe, in North and South America, and in Asia. Englishmen began to think that someone ought to teach these ill-mannered Germans a lesson. Moreover, they had begun to worry about their own position of prosperity and leadership. In India, the greatest possession of the English, it was clear already that great concessions toward self-government would have to be made to the natives. Close at home the Irish question was in one of its most acute phases, with Ulster in arms against the proposed Home Rule. Englishmen were worried about their obsolescent industrial plant, their apparent inability to produce goods as cheaply and as efficiently as the Germans; they were self-critical about their failures as salesmen abroad, their stodgy self-satisfaction.

A great many Britishers thought of themselves as good liberals and good internationalists, anxious to preserve the peace and the decencies of international life. Many were radicals and Labor party men committed to pacifism. The coming of war in 1914 was to show how thoroughly almost all these men identified Great Britain and righteousness. As for the bulk of the conservatives, they were as nationalist as in any other great country. In Britain, their nationalism attached itself to the Empire, to the "White Man's Burden," to a whole set of symbols that the Germans found intolerable.

The Other Belligerents

In democratic France as in democratic England there was a wide spread of opinion on international politics. A numerous socialist Left was committed to pacifism and to the concept of a kind of international strike of workers at the threat of actual war.

A more moderate group also opposed conventional patriotic aggressiveness toward the foreigner. Both among the men who conducted French foreign relations and among the general public, however, there remained right down to the eve of the Great War the embittered patriotism of the beaten. Frenchmen wanted *revanche,* revenge for the defeat of 1870. They wanted Alsace-Lorraine back. For all these years, the statue representing Strasbourg among the cities of France in the Place de la Concorde in Paris was draped in black. With the warmest patriots, the organizers of patriotic societies, the editors of patriotic journals, this feeling for revenge was obsessive.

By the opening decade of the 1900's many observers thought that the new generation was losing its desire for revenge, that Frenchmen had at last decided to accept the verdict of 1870. But French diplomatists continued to preserve and strengthen the system of alliances against Germany, and in the excited weeks of July, 1914, it was clear that the French were ready for war. When it came, the old scenes of joy in war were repeated:

> Throughout this period, Paris was under pressure. Puissant virtues of patriotism, born deep down beneath the skulls of men, burst through and spilled out over the public squares and boulevards. To Berlin! To Berlin! The word *Berlin* filled Paris. Detachments passed, and every rifle owned the right to a flower, and every soldier owned the right to a kiss. Women softened at sight. Their dresses could no longer contain their hearts. They felt a thousand obligations of love in themselves. They distributed their lips to those young men in arms with the pride of priestesses. A kind of brotherhood like that of flowers, a white sentimental friendship, a universal innocence fell upon every creature. *Le mal,* the notion of evil —and *le mâle,* the male—disappeared. They were all children, angels. For a few days, France was Paradise on earth.[*]

---

[*] Joseph Delteil, *The Poilus,* Jaques Le Clercq, trans. (New York, 1927), 28-29.

In the other major belligerents, too, the ultimate decisions of governments won much popular support. Russians were filled with the "pooled self-esteem" of nationalism, were convinced that God and the right were on their side. Italians saw in war the chance to get *Italia Irredenta* and still more territory from the Habsburg Monarchy. In the dual monarchy, as we have seen (Chapter XXII), the loyalty of subject nationalities could scarcely be counted on; but the dominant Germans of Austria and Magyars of Hungary welcomed the opportunity to put the troublesome Slavs in their place for good and all.

The Era of Bismarck, 1871-1890

The road to Sarajevo starts in 1871, at the Treaty of Frankfurt, where France was obliged to cede Alsace and Lorraine to the new German Empire. It was no straight road, but one of many twists and turnings, and few historians would now maintain that 1871 made 1914 inevitable. We cannot follow the road in detail, but we must map its main course.

For some twenty years Bismarck was its chief engineer. In fairness to the Iron Chancellor, it must be said that during his last twenty years in office he sought peace, and indeed obtained it. Powerful elements in the new empire made it impossible for him to grant to France the same kind of generous peace he had given Austria in 1866. Yet Bismarck did try to salve the wound he knew France had suffered; he encouraged her to expand her empire in North Africa by the acquisition of Tunis in 1881, even though this offended the Italians, who also coveted Tunisia. But he feared a French attempt at revenge, and sought to isolate her diplomatically by building a series of alliances from which she was ex-

CHAPTER XXV

cluded. Germany, he insisted, was now a "saturated" power, and wanted nothing more in Europe. Above all, he sought to keep on good terms with both Austria and Russia, and, what was much more difficult, to keep both these powers on good terms with each other. Since both wanted predominance in the Balkans, Bismarck's task was formidable.

As a result of the Turkish War of 1877-1878, the Russians succeeded briefly in setting up a greater Bulgaria as a kind of client state that brought Russian influence almost to the gates of Constantinople (see Chapter XXII). Since both Britain and Austria-Hungary were unwilling to allow Russia this increase of power, Bismarck played host to a general European diplomatic congress at Berlin (1878), at which Russian gains were considerably pared down. Both Russia and Austria-Hungary were discontented over this compromise. Nevertheless, Bismarck soon laid the cornerstone of his diplomatic system by a defensive alliance with Austria-Hungary in 1879, an alliance that held right down to 1918. And he was able to make a secret treaty, the so-called League of the Three Emperors, which bound Germany, Russia, and Austria together. The three powers agreed to act together in dealings with Turkey, and to maintain friendly neutrality should any one of them be at war with a fourth power other than Turkey. Next, working skillfully on Italian annoyance over the French expansion in Tunis, Bismarck secured an alliance among Germany, Austria-Hungary, and Italy, directed chiefly against France. This was the famous Triple Alliance of 1882, often renewed, which on paper still existed in 1914.

On this series of tight-ropes Bismarck maintained a precarious balance through the 1880's. Chief in his mind was the danger that the Russians, always fearful of Austrian schemes in the Balkans, would desert him and ally themselves with France, still a great power and anxious to escape from the isolation that Bismarck had designed for her. In 1887, Russia did refuse to renew the League of the Three Emperors, but Bismarck was able to repair the breach for the moment by a secret Russo-German agreement known as the Re-insurance Treaty. The two promised each other neutrality in case either was involved in a war against a third power; but this neutrality was not to hold if Germany made an "aggressive" war against France or if Russia made an "aggressive" war against Austria. Since Russian nationalist agitation continued against both Austria and Germany, Bismarck in 1888 made public as a warning to Russia the terms of the Austro-German alliance, and allowed the main terms of the Triple Alliance to be known informally.

Formation of the Triple Entente, 1890-1907

Then in 1890 the young Emperor William II dismissed Bismarck. The Emperor's advisers, headed by Baron von Holstein, persuaded him not to renew the Re-insurance Treaty with Russia, in spite of Russian desire for such renewal. Shortly afterward, what Bismarck had worked so hard to prevent came about. After lengthy negotiations, Russia and France in 1894 came together in an alliance that ended French isolation. It was formally a defensive alliance, in which each was to come to the aid of the other if Germany or Austria made "aggressive" war against either, and it was accompanied by the necessary military agreements between the two general staffs. Against the Triple Alliance there now stood, quite openly, a Dual Alliance of France and Russia. England remained technically uninvolved.

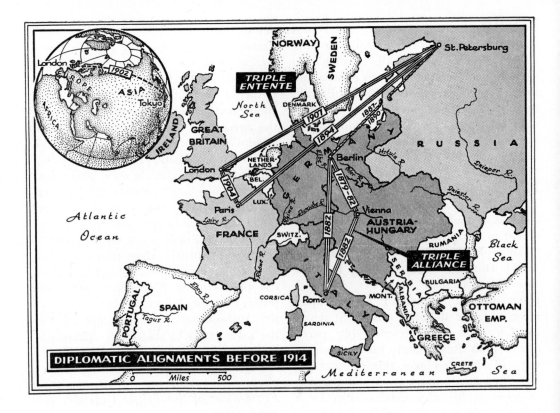

DIPLOMATIC ALIGNMENTS BEFORE 1914

The next great stage in the tightening network of alliances was to bring Great Britain in against the Central Powers. Britain had long kept her hands free on the Continent, refusing formal alliances, but not really outside the diplomatic net. In the 1890's, her prime minister, Lord Salisbury, asserted that hers was a policy of "splendid isolation." But in the two decades after the accession of Kaiser William II Britain was to commit herself to a formal alliance with Japan and to an "understanding" (in French, *entente*) with France and Russia. What chiefly drove Britain to these actions was the naval race with Germany and the rapid worsening of Anglo-German relations, a worsening even more evident perhaps at the level of public opinion than at the level of formal diplomacy.

A good concrete instance of this rising hostility is the Kruger telegram of 1896, in which the Kaiser congratulated President Kruger of the Boer Republic of Transvaal on the defeat of the Jameson raid (see Chapters XXII and XXIV). It may be that the Kaiser and his circle hoped at bottom that this gesture would be taken by the English government as a kind of polite and permissible diplomatic blackmail, an evidence of how great a nuisance the German government could be to the British if it were not on their side. But the British press took the telegram as an unbearable insult, and the German press replied angrily to British anger. Here is a sample from the dignified and conservative London *Saturday Review*, a passage that shows how clear the shape of things to come already was to the knowing:

CHAPTER XXV

It is not only the German Emperor that is in the dark as to the strength of Great Britain. The 'Times' published on Monday a letter from 'A German in England,' declaring that Germany hates England because she cannot win her alliance, and then proceeds, 'Europe is a camp, and if it came to fighting, England, with all her wealth and position, would rank as a second-class Power, because she has not the number of soldiers, nor sufficient armament for a great struggle.' And, therefore, we are told, 'with that growing hatred of England on the Continent a kind of contempt for her has grown.' But this 'German in England' contradicts himself. If England is only a second-class Power, why should Germany get so angry because she cannot secure her as an ally? Germany does not rage against Spain because Spain has not joined the Triple Alliance, nor does the Kaiser write insulting messages about the Portuguese. The truth is that German military pride, combined with the trading German's envy of British commerce and the British Empire, make him try to believe that England is a second-class Power; but in his heart he knows better. He knows that now, even more than at the end of the Napoleonic wars, England is the Arbiter of Europe. Her alliance would make the Triple Alliance invincible, and were her aid given to Russia and France, the German hegemony on the Continent would be doomed.*

Add to this some of Kipling's verse; the occasion was a German proposal (1902) for a joint demonstration of the British and German fleets to collect debts from Venezuela:

'Neath all the flags of all mankind
    That use upon the seas,
Was there no other fleet to find
    That you strike hands with these?

.   .   .

In sight of peace—from the Narrow Seas
    O'er half the world to run—
With a cheated crew, to league anew
    With the Goth and the shameless Hun! †

* "Notes," *Saturday Review of Politics, Literature, Science and Art* (London), LXXXI (Jan. 11, 1896), 27.
† "The Rowers," from "The Years Between," *Rudyard Kipling's Verse, 1885-1932* (London, 1933), 280-281.

As early as 1902 the Germans are already the "Huns," an epithet much used during World War I by Allied propagandists.

It was fear of Russia rather than fear of Germany, however, that inspired Britain to make the first break with formal isolationism, the alliance with Japan in 1902. The outbreak of war between Russia and Japan hastened negotiations between Britain and France. In the Anglo-French Entente of 1904 France gave England a free hand in Egypt, England gave France a free hand in Morocco, and various outstanding difficulties between the two in other parts of the world were ironed out. More important, the base was laid for general collaboration between the two in international affairs. Only six years previously there had been a grave flare-up of the traditional colonial rivalry between France and England when a French column was met by a British column at Fashoda in the disputed Sudan territory of the upper Nile Valley. Fashoda caused quite as big an outbreak of fury in the French and the British press as the Kruger telegram only two years before had caused in the German and the British press. Yet Fashoda left wounds much less deep than the Kruger telegram; the contemporary press is not always a faithful guide to the climate of public opinion.

The final stage in aligning the two camps came in 1907 when Russia, chastened by her defeat at the hand of Japan and encouraged by the French, came to an agreement with Great Britain. Both countries made concessions in regions where they had been imperialist rivals—Persia, Afghanistan, Tibet—and the British at last made some concessions toward the Russian desire to open up the Straits. The agreement was scarcely based on any genuine sympathy between the two peoples, for the British, notably, had been Russophobic for well over a century. Nevertheless, it did round

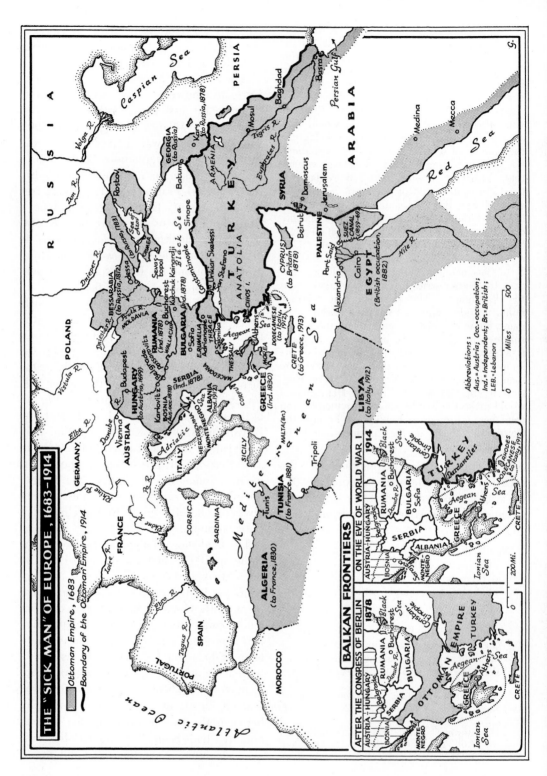

THE "SICK MAN" OF EUROPE, 1683–1914

Ottoman Empire, 1683
Boundary of the Ottoman Empire, 1914

Abbreviations:
Aus.= Austria; Occ.= occupation;
Ind.= independent; Br.= British;
LEB.= Lebanon

0 100 200 300 400 500 Miles

BALKAN FRONTIERS

AFTER THE CONGRESS OF BERLIN
1878

ON THE EVE OF WORLD WAR I
1914

0 100 200 Mi.

out the Triple Entente against the Triple Alliance.

A Decade of Crises, 1905-1914

The last decade before 1914 is a series of crises and local wars, any one of which might have spread into a world war. First came a deliberate theatrical gesture from the Kaiser, when in 1905 he made a ceremonial visit to Tangier in Morocco as a way of telling the world that the Germans would not accept the Anglo-French assignment of Morocco to France. The net effect was to tighten the entente between France and Britain, for the British indicated clearly to the French that they would support them. Although the French Foreign Minister, Delcassé, a partisan of firm policy toward the Germans, was forced out of office, even this partial victory did the Germans no good. French public opinion was infuriated by this intervention in their domestic politics. In the end, a general international conference at Algeciras in Spain (1906) backed up the French, who went ahead with their plans for a protectorate in Morocco. At Algeciras American diplomatic influence was used on the side of France; the United States, too, was beginning to emerge from its own variety of isolationism.

A decisive turn of the road toward Sarajevo came in 1908. For some years the Austrians had been very active in the Balkans, seeking to extend their influence southeastward to the Aegean Sea. They had been involved in complicated negotiations over railroads in European Turkey and over the vexed question of Macedonia, a province of European Turkey with perhaps the most mixed population of all in an area where peoples had been mixing, without full mutual assimilation, for centuries. Greeks, Serbs, and Bulgarians all had fellow nationals in Macedonia, and all therefore had designs on the territory. Then in 1908 Austria formally proclaimed the annexation of the old Turkish provinces of Bosnia-Herzegovina, which she had occupied since 1878 (see Chapter XXII). Austria's decisive act infuriated the Serbs, who wanted to add Bosnia to their state. It also infuriated the Russians, all the more since few Russians knew that their diplomat Izvolski had in fact made an informal agreement with the Austrian minister Aehrental in September, 1908, to accept the annexation of Bosnia-Herzegovina in return for Austrian support of an agreement permitting Russian warships to use the Straits. In the event, Austria did the annexing, but Russia did not get her use of the Straits. This wound to Russian pride was profound.

War now broke out on the edges of Europe. In 1911, the Italians sent troops to Tripoli, the poorest part of North Africa, but at least a part that had not yet been taken from the Turks by other Europeans. Then in 1912 war spread to the Balkans. Nationalist revolutionaries called the "Young Turks" had risen successfully against the Sultan in 1908. Though the Young Turk movement was hardly a "democratic" one, it did aim at arresting the long decline of the "Sick Man of Europe," and it did therefore alarm powers who hoped to benefit from that decline. It began to look as if those who hoped to divide up Turkey had better hurry while the dividing was good. In the hurry, the world got swept into the War of 1914, the preliminary stages of which were the Balkan Wars.

In the first of these wars, in 1912, an alliance of Bulgaria, Serbia, and Greece beat the Turks, and started the process of dividing up most of European Turkey. But here Austria imposed an absolute veto on granting Serbia territories that would give

Turkey Gobblers after their rations.

her access to the Adriatic Sea. Meanwhile, the victors quarreled among themselves, and in the Second Balkan War, of 1913, the Greeks and Serbs, joined by the Rumanians and the all-but-beaten Turks, readily defeated the Bulgarians. Turkey got back some of her territory in Europe. But the Balkans were in a state of unusual uncertainty and bad blood when Francis Ferdinand was assassinated.

430

CHAPTER XXV

The Final Crisis, July–August, 1914

There are millions of words in print about the proximate causes of World War I and the six weeks between the assassination and the general spread of war on August 4, when Britain came in against Germany. Thanks to the end of the Hohenzollern, Habsburg, and Romanov houses as a result of the war, the secret archives were thrown open much sooner than would be normal by the governments that succeeded them. And in the pressure of debate over the question of war guilt in the 1920's, even the victorious countries, Britain, France, and the United States, opened their archives to a surprising extent. These are weeks for which documents, often telegrams, can be dated by the hour and minute. These are weeks in which messages are constantly crossing each other, confusing things hopelessly. These are weeks in which professional diplomatists and statesmen, egged on by an excited—and it must be said usually *irresponsible*—press, nevertheless tried for the most part to master the crisis without recourse to war. They failed; but in justice to them we must at least go as far as the American historian Sidney Fay, whose *Origins of the World War* (1928) is the fairest and best-balanced work of the revisionists:

None of the Powers wanted a European War. Their governing rulers and ministers, with very few exceptions, all foresaw that it must be a frightful struggle, in which the political results were not absolutely certain, but in which the loss of life, suffering, and economic consequences were bound to be terrible. This is true, in a greater or less degree, of Pashitch [of Serbia], Berchtold [of Austria], Bethmann [of Germany], Sazonov [of Russia], Poincaré [of France], San Giuliano [of Italy], and Sir Edward Grey [of Britain]. Yet none of them, not even Sir Edward Grey, could have foreseen that the political results were to be so stupendous, and the other consequences so terrible, as was actually the case.[*]

The diplomats and statesmen were drawn into war because almost all of them believed that they faced an alternative worse than war, a defeat or humiliation for their nation. Austria believed correctly, though positive proof was lacking, that the Serbian government had some foreknowledge of the plot of the assassin Princip and should therefore have given her warning. For this reason, and also because she wished to check the Serb agitation that had long been unsettling the Yugoslav peoples living in the dual monarchy, Austria decided to make stiff demands on Serbia after the assassination of Francis Ferdinand. Before doing so, however, she consulted her German ally, who promised to support whatever policy Aus-

[*] S. B. Fay, *The Origins of the World War* (New York, 1928), II, 547.

Princip, immediately after the assassination at Sarajevo, June 28, 1914.

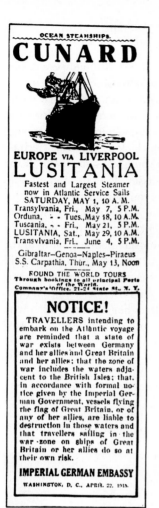

Two advertisements that appeared in New York City newspapers, 1915. The sinking of the British liner, Lusitania, by a German submarine (May, 1915) claimed more than one thousand lives, some of them American.

in principle; but they refused to accept two of them, which would have permitted Austrian police or military men to take an actual part in a Serbian investigation of Princip's plot. Probably Serbia had some assurance that Russia was willing to give her a kind of "blank check," and would assist her if the partial refusal of the ultimatum led to war. The Serbian reply, therefore, was a little less virtuously honest than it seemed to most of the world in July, 1914. Still, the Austrian ultimatum appears to have been couched in terms deliberately unacceptable to the Serbs, and the Serb reply seems to have been a base for more consideration than it got from the Austrians. Because the Serbs had not accepted the whole of the ultimatum, Austria declared war on July 28, after turning down as inconsistent with national honor a European conference proposed by the British foreign minister, Sir Edward Grey.

From now on, the German diplomatists, backed by William II and actually resisting the German military men, tried to hold back their Austrian ally. It is impossible to clear William from responsibility for the German "blank check," which had emboldened Austria and had perhaps been designed by Germany to do just that. Now, however, the Germans certainly tried to revoke the check and made a last effort to stop the spread of the war. Since Russia was beginning the full mobilization of her armies, the Kaiser, on July 29, told Tsar Nicholas II in a personal telegram of the German attempt to get the Austrians to compromise. Apparently this telegram served to get full Russian mobilization modified into partial mobilization and to get direct Austro-Russian talks resumed on July 30. For a brief moment it looked as if the crisis might be overcome.

But mobilization was not easy in Russia, a country of long distances, poor communications, and bureaucratic red tape, and the

tria might adopt toward Serbia. This German response has became famous as a diplomatic "blank check," duly signed by Germany in advance with the precise amount to be filled in later by Austria.

Thus encouraged, the Austrian government, on July 23, sent Serbia an ultimatum to be answered within forty-eight hours. The ultimatum made many separate demands, which added up to an insistence that Serbia and Serb propagandists keep their hands off Habsburg territories and populations, now and in the future. Most of the demands the Serbs accepted, at least

432

Russian military feared that their enemies would get the jump on them. At the last moment Russia made her mobilization general again. Germany at once insisted that all Russian mobilization cease, and, when it continued, ordered her own at 4:00 P.M. on July 31, and declared war on Russia at 7:00 P.M. the same day. France, meantime, had determined to stand by her Russian ally, now evidently about to be attacked, and had mobilized at 3:55 P.M. the same day. Germany declared war on France on August 3.

Britain was still wavering. Although her entente with France did not legally bind the two nations together, it had led to the very close co-ordination of defense plans by the French and British staffs. Perhaps, then, Britain would have come into the war anyway. What made her entry certain was the German violation of the neutrality of Belgium, which both Britain and Prussia had joined with other powers to guarantee in 1839. The German military were determined to take decisive action in the West and to knock France out of the war before the Russians could get their slow-moving armies into action. Accordingly, German plans called for a sweep through a corner of Belgium to avoid the heavily fortified and hilly terrain in northeastern France. On August 2, the Germans had notified Belgium that they intended to march through her territory, though they promised to respect her territorial integrity in the peace to come.

Belgium rejected this demand, and appealed to the other guaranteeing powers. Sir Edward Grey, though opposed in the British cabinet by two pacifists, seized firmly on this ground of action, and on August 4 Britain declared war on Germany. The German chancellor, Bethmann-Hollweg, informed of this action, let slip the phrase that Britain had gone to war just for a "scrap of paper"—the treaty of 1839 that guaranteed Belgium against invasion. This unhappy phrase, seized upon by the press of the world, not only solidified British opinion in favor of the war but was responsible more than any other single factor for the charge of war guilt laid against Germany.

The Entry of Other Powers

By August 6, when Austria declared war on Russia, all the members of the Triple Alliance and the Triple Entente had come to blows, with the exception of Italy, who, however, had never really been a good ally of Austria because of the Irredentist issue. Italy, refusing to consider herself bound by the Triple Alliance, declared her neutrality. The Central Powers of Germany and Austria-Hungary, then, stood against the Allies—Russia, France, Britain, and Serbia. Japan came in on the side of the Allies late in August, and Turkey came in on the Austro-German side in November, 1914. Then the Allies in secret agreements promised Italy a great deal of land (see p. 440); Italy, therefore, joined them in May, 1915.

As the war turned into a stalemate, in the winter of 1916-1917, the Germans made the desperate decision to try to get at Great Britain by the only way that seemed available. They would use their submarines to cut off the food and raw materials that came to the British Isles from overseas, and without which their peoples would have starved. This unrestricted submarine warfare meant sinking American ships that Americans held were quite legally bringing such supplies to England and France, in accord with international law. On April 6, 1917, the United States completed the roster of great powers involved in the conflict by declaring war on Germany. Dissident Americans, then and since, have declared that the United States was enticed into the war by the wicked few —by sentimental lovers of England or

France; by bankers who had lent money to the Allies and wanted to protect their investments; by silly idealists who agreed with President Wilson in wishing to "make the world safe for democracy"; and, of course, by scheming Allied diplomatists, corrupt Europeans who held a strange fascination over American "babes in the wood." Yet it is debatable that the United States would ever have entered the war had there been no unrestricted submarine warfare by the Germans. All told, since many of the South and Central American states followed the lead of the United States, there were from 1914 through 1918 something over sixty separate declarations of war or severances of relations. It was indeed a "world war."

III: The Course of the War

The war proved prophets like Norman Angell wrong in two important respects. It was, as they had predicted, enormously expensive in human lives and in material resources. But it was by no means a short war, and, however great the damage it did in the long run to western society—damage we cannot really assess even now—it did not prove more than that society could bear. Western society at least survived World War I.

Resources of the Belligerents

As the opposing nations lined up in 1914, the Allies had an overwhelming superiority in total population and resources. Germany, Austria-Hungary, and Turkey had in their own continental lands not over 150,000,000 people; Britain, France, Russia, and Italy in their own continental lands had at least 125,000,000 more people than their enemies. Moreover, in their overseas possessions, which included the 315,000,000 people of India, the Allies had many millions more. As for material resources, the Central Powers had, especially in Germany, admirably organized industries and enough coal and iron to fight a long war. But here too the statistics were overwhelmingly in favor of the Allies. Moreover, though German submarines and, in the early days, surface raiders were able to interrupt seriously Allied lines of communication overseas, on the whole the Allies were still able to get from these overseas sources indispensable food and other supplies. And when in 1917 a beaten Russia, in the throes of a revolution, ceased to be of aid, the Allies gained the great resources of the United States.

In the long run, much as in the American Civil War, the side with the most men and materials wore down its enemies and won the war. But it was by no means the uneven struggle that the statistics of total population and material resources would indicate. Again as in the Civil War, the weaker side had initially important advantages, won great victories, seemed indeed at critical moments on the point of final victory. Not until the very last months before the armistice of November, 1918, could the Allies really feel confident of victory.

Geography gave Germany and Austria the advantages of being side by side, and of having interior lines of communication, which enabled them to make rapid transfers of troops from one threatened front to another. Though the Germans and Austrians did not always see eye to eye, they did speak the same language, and had for long been firmly allied; moreover, Germany was the predominant partner, and the ultimate decisions were made by her general staff. Most important of all, Germany in particular was more ready for war than were her enemies. She had an efficiently organized military machine and a good stock of munitions, her industry could be readily geared to war, her plans were complete, her people were united in support of the war, and they enjoyed the great psychological advantage of being on the offensive, of carrying the war to the enemy. Indeed, no important part of the war was ever fought on German soil; it ended, with important results for later history (see Chapter XXVII), with the German army still in being, with the soil of the German Fatherland still uninvaded.

By contrast, geography had separated the western Allies from Russia. German control of the Baltic and Turkish control of the Straits proved throughout the war a serious obstacle to communication between Russia and her allies, who had to take roundabout and difficult routes through Archangel in Arctic waters and even through Vladivostok on the Pacific. For the Allies, transfer of troops between eastern and western fronts was militarily almost impossible, even had it been politically possible. It was not, however, politically possible, and here is one of the greatest weaknesses of the Allies.

Russia, Britain, and France had only recently come together, as friendly powers and not as close allies. Each of them was a strongly marked nationality, having many sources of conflict with the others. They had no long tradition of mutual co-operation, no common language. France and England were democracies, and though the peoples of both rallied firmly to the national cause

in 1914, they were unused to the kind of firm, centralized, political and military control that is necessary in war. As for unified military planning and administration, it was never achieved between Russia and the western Allies. Even among Britain, France, and the United States on the Western Front, it was not achieved until the French General Foch was appointed commander-in-chief in 1918, and then only imperfectly.

Finally, of the three great Allied powers in 1914, only France was ready with a good big land force, and France, with only 39 millions of people as against Germany's 65 millions, was the weakest of the Allies in manpower. Britain was indeed prepared on the sea, and her navy was an invaluable asset; but it could not be of direct use against the German army. Russia had universal military service and an army great in numbers. But she had vast distances to overcome, an inadequate railway system, a relatively undeveloped heavy industry, an army whose morale had been shaken by the recent defeat at the hands of the Japanese, a people whose morale had been shaken by the recent abortive revolution, a military and a political organization riddled with inefficiency and corruption.

The Western Front: German Offensive of 1914

The Germans had a plan, the so-called Schlieffen plan, which they immediately put into execution. It called for a wide sweep toward Paris with great forces, pivoting on a southern anchor in Alsace-Lorraine, where the French frontier was strongly fortified. While this southern or left flank of the Germans held down large French armies, the center would advance slowly and the right very swiftly indeed, somewhat as in the game of snap-the-whip. The

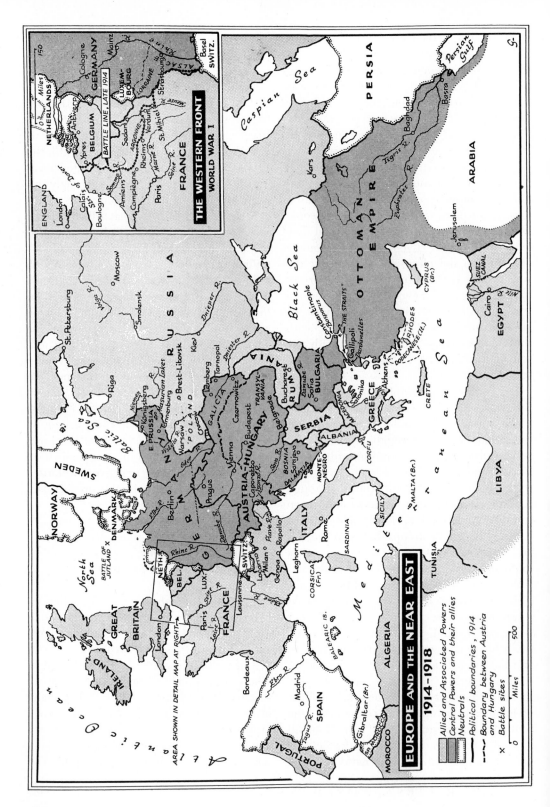

THE WESTERN FRONT
WORLD WAR I

BATTLE LINE, LATE 1914

EUROPE AND THE NEAR EAST
1914–1918

Allied and Associated Powers
Central Powers and their allies
Neutrals
Political boundaries, 1914
Boundary between Austria and Hungary
✕ Battle sites

0 Miles 500

AREA SHOWN IN DETAIL MAP AT RIGHT →

British troops entering Cambrai in France, October, 1918.

German right flank was supposed to move fast because the French had expected a frontal attack from the east, and had not fully expected the sneak through Belgium, so that the French fortifications on the north were less developed and less well-manned than those on the east. While this great enveloping movement in the west swiftly eliminated France, relatively weaker German forces, it was planned, would hold down the slow-moving Russians. With France beaten, the Germans could turn their full force against the Russians and beat them. Then there would be only the British left, and the future would take care of them.

The German plan almost succeeded. It failed for two reasons, to which a great number of separate tactical factors contributed. In the west, the French, with help from the Belgians and the British, stopped the German drive short of its goal, Paris, and its

even more important goal, the destruction of the Allied armies. In the east, the Russians, despite their weaknesses, advanced far enough and quickly enough to frighten the German general staff into withdrawing troops from the west and sending them to the east. It is possible that the German chief of staff, Moltke, who made this fateful decision to send extra troops to fight the Russians, was motivated less by fear of the Russians than by a mistaken belief that the campaign in the west was going so well that it was already won. At any rate, on August 25 Moltke detached six army corps from the west, and actually got two of them all the way to the Russian front. There they arrived too late to be needed in the crisis, for the Russians had already been disastrously beaten.

Moltke's decision did not appear unreasonable in late August. Although Belgian resistance had held the Germans up briefly at Liége, and a small but good British professional army had had time to get in place on the Allied left, on the whole the German advance had gone according to plan, and Paris was so menaced that the French government moved to Bordeaux. Then, in the first week in September, something went wrong for the Germans. The whip had snapped too fast; it had broken apart. On the extreme German right, Von Kluck's 1st Army lost contact with Von Bülow's 2nd Army on the left. Von Kluck, trying to reestablish contact, turned some ninety degrees and, contrary to plan, moved southeast away from Paris instead of keeping southwest to envelope it. Meanwhile, the French commander, Joffre, had hastily organized a new French army around Paris. This army was now squarely on Von Kluck's exposed flank. Here occurred the now legendary incident of the French taxicab army, which was moved in commandeered taxis from suburban Paris to action on the Marne River. The few thousand soldiers who made the trip probably did not decide the battle, but this evidence of resourcefulness immensely cheered the fading Allied morale.

The tactical details of this great battle of early September, 1914, which is known in history as the first Battle of the Marne, are exceedingly complicated. But the upshot is clear. Urged on by Galliéni, military governor of Paris, Joffre issued a general order to attack, and in the confusion of battle the gap between the armies of Von Kluck and Von Bülow was never adequately closed. The German general staff, alarmed by the reports of the situation, decided to withdraw temporarily, and the French and British moved gingerly forward. The German advance, which had been almost continuous since August 2, had been stopped. In the next few weeks the opposing forces engaged in what came to be called the "race for the Channel," with the Germans trying

to outflank the Allies and get the Channel ports, thus shutting the short sea passage to future British reinforcements. They failed here, too, and throughout the war the ports of Calais and Boulogne, and indeed a small southwestern corner of Belgium, were to remain in Allied hands—a valuable military advantage.

By the autumn of 1914 the Western Front was thus stabilized. For over three hundred airline miles between the Channel and the Swiss border near Basel, hundreds of thousands of soldiers faced each other in a continuous line that was full of bends called "salients." Both sides "dug in" and formed a series of rough fortifications. The central feature of these fortifications was a series of parallel trenches deep enough to conceal a man standing upright. As time went on, these trenches were greatly improved; they were supplied with parapets, machine-gun nests, and an elaborate network of approach trenches and strong points, until the whole front became one immense fortification. Thousands of local actions in the four years of trench warfare shifted the lines here and there, and a series of partial break-throughs occurred on both sides. But on the whole the lines held, and the actual fighting in the west was confined to an extraordinarily narrow, though very long, field.

On this Western Front the ultimate decision was reached; but there were many other fronts. Some of them were disparagingly called "the side-shows" by those who advocated concentrating in the west. Yet in perspective we can now see that they all played a part in determining the final result. Since, over the long pull, the Germans had fewer men and resources, the dispersal of energies that these "side-shows" called for, and the continuous need to bolster their Austrian and Turkish and Balkan allies, were major factors in their defeat. For the sake of clarity, we shall here take up these other fronts separately and briefly, but the reader must never forget that for the belligerents the war was a whole; its wide-flung theaters were mutually dependent, with each one influencing the others.

The Eastern Front

The Eastern Front, where the Russians faced both the Germans and the Austrians, was no mere side-show. Millions of men were involved on both sides, and had the Russians not held out, as they did, until the end of 1917 the Allies in the west could never have withstood the reinforcements that the Germans and Austrians would have been able to send to France and Italy. The war in the east was more a war of movement than the war in the west. But even in the east there were long periods of stalemate, especially during the winters, periods when the opposing armies faced each other in long lines of improvised fortifications.

The Russians began well. Against the exposed Austrian salient of Galicia (Austria's share of the eighteenth-century partitions of Poland), the Russians threw in vast masses of men. They pushed the Austrians out of the oil-rich lands around Lemberg, and by the end of September, 1914, they had reached the northern ends of some of the passes leading into Hungary through the Carpathian Mountains. Against the Germans, who also had to defend in East Prussia a salient surrounded on the east and south by Russian territory, the Russians won the Battle of Gumbinnen, in August, 1914, and so alarmed the German general staff that the Germans felt obliged to reorganize their eastern command. General von Ludendorff, under the nominal command of his senior, Von Hindenburg, and aided by a brilliant junior, Von Hoffmann, turned successively against the two

Russian armies, which were attempting a pincers movement. Late in August, at Tannenberg, the Germans decisively defeated a Russian army under Samsonov, who committed suicide. And early in September they won another decisive victory against the Russians at the Masurian lakes, thus clearing East Prussia of Russians.

The Germans' hard-pressed Austrian allies to the south were by now clamoring for help, and the Western Front was still demanding men. Hindenburg and his aides had to do their best with what they had. In a series of hard-fought battles in Poland they succeeded in relieving the pressure on the Austrians. The end of the year 1914 found the Austrians still hanging on in Galicia, and found the Germans in a good position to push eastward from East Prussian and Polish bases. In two great joint offensives in May and July, 1915, the Central Powers won substantial successes; they inflicted severe losses on the Russians from which the Russians never really recovered. At the end of the year 1915 the battle line ran roughly from near Riga, deep in the Baltic provinces of Russia, to the eastern edge of Galicia at Tarnopol and Czernowitz.

In 1916, the Russians, with a new commander, General Brusilov, undertook a great new offensive against the Austrians in the south. The Russian need to bolster their failing morale would probably have made some action necessary, but the Russians were also being pressed by the Allies to do something to help the Italians, who were threatened by the Austrians in the region of Trent. It seems likely that the Brusilov offensive was begun too soon, without adequate preparation. It scored a striking success at first; in places, the Russians drove the Austrians back some eighty miles, and they took large numbers of prisoners. But once more the Germans came to the rescue; with fresh troops transferred from the west, they halted Brusilov before he had won a decisive success.

It was from the backwash of this defeat that the Russian Revolution, which began early in March, 1917, was born. In the moderate phase of that uprising, before the Bolshevik revolution of November, 1917, Brusilov undertook one last desperate offensive. But he was soon checked, and the way was open for the Bolsheviks to carry out their promise to make peace. By the end of 1917, Russia was out of the war. She was forced by the Central Powers to sign the extraordinarily punitive Peace of Brest-Litovsk (March, 1918), by which she lost her Polish territories, her Baltic provinces, the entire Ukraine, Finland, and some lands in the Caucasus. The Caucasian lands went to Turkey; most of the others came under the temporary domination of Austria and Germany.

The Italian Front

In April, 1915, Italy concluded with Britain, France, and Russia the secret Treaty of London. The Italians were promised the long-sought-for Irredenta around Trent and Trieste, and, what was to prove much more embarrassing in the final peace settlements, important lands on the eastern side of the Adriatic in what we now know as Yugoslavia. Since Serbia, also one of the Allies, had been promised these same Adriatic lands, the transaction was certainly a shady one. It brought the Allies little good, for Italy proved on the whole a military liability rather than an asset. Yet in our modern state-system, in the stress of war, men are tempted to pay almost any price for a new ally against a powerful enemy.

In May, 1915, the Italians formally declared war on Austria-Hungary (they did not declare war on Germany until August, 1916), and a new front was added along the Austro-Italian frontier at the head of the Adriatic. Much of this front was too mountainous for effective action, and it was pretty much confined to some sixty miles along the Isonzo River. For two years there was a series of bloody but indecisive actions along this river that at least pinned down several hundred thousand Austrian troops. Then in the late autumn of 1917, with Russia already beaten, came the blow that very nearly knocked Italy out. Once again the Germans supplied the propulsive force. Ludendorff, now in supreme command, sent six German divisions to the Isonzo. The Germans and Austrians broke through at Caporetto, and sent the Italians into a retreat across the Venetian plains, a retreat that was really a rout. French and British reinforcements were hastily rushed across the Alps, but what did most to stop the Austro-Germans was probably the grave difficulty, under modern conditions of warfare, of supplying mass armies in rapid advance. The Italians were able to hold along the line of the Piave River, almost at the Po.

Balkan and Turkish Fronts

Serbia's part in the outbreak of the war had insured that there would be a Balkan front from the start. The Austrians failed here also, and although in December, 1914, they did manage to take the Serbian capital, Belgrade, they were driven out again. Bulgaria, wooed by both sides, finally came in with the Central Powers in the autumn of 1915. The Germans sent troops and a general, Von Mackensen, under whom the Serbs were finally beaten. The remnant of their armies was driven to take refuge on the island of Corfu in neutral Greece. To counter this blow in the Balkans, the Allies had already landed a few divisions in the Greek town of Saloniki, and had established a front in Macedonia. The Greeks them-

CHAPTER XXV

selves were divided into two groups. One was headed by King Constantine, who at bottom was sympathetic with the Central Powers, but who for the moment was seeking only to maintain Greek neutrality. The other was a pro-Ally group headed by the able old politician Venizelos. Although the Allies rode roughshod over formal notions of Greek neutrality, Venizelos did not get firmly into the saddle until June, 1917, when Allied pressure compelled King Constantine to abdicate in favor of his second son, Alexander.

Meanwhile Rumania, whom the Russians had been trying to lure into the war, finally yielded to promises of great territorial gains at the expense of Austria-Hungary and came in on the Allied side late in August, 1916, a most inopportune time. Stiffened by German help, the Austrians swept through Rumania and by January, 1917, held most of this oil-rich country. When the Russians made the separate Peace of Brest-Litovsk with the Germans in March, 1918, the Rumanians were obliged to make cessions of territory to Bulgaria, and to grant a ninety-year lease of oil lands to Germany.

In spite of the formal accession of Greece, the Macedonian front remained in a stalemate until the summer of 1918, when, with American troops pouring rapidly into France, the Allied military leaders decided they could afford to build up their forces in Saloniki. The investment paid well, for under the leadership of the French general, Franchet d'Esperey, the Allied armies on this front were the first to break the enemy completely. The French, British, Serbs, and Greeks began a great advance on September 15, 1918, all along the line from the Adriatic to the Bulgarian frontier. They forced the Bulgarians to conclude an armistice on September 30, and by early November they had crossed the Danube in several places. The armistice in the west on November 11 found the tricolor of France, with the flags of many allies, well on its way to Vienna. This hark-back to Napoleon helped inspire in the French a somewhat unfounded confidence that they were once more the dominant nation on the continent of Europe.

The most interesting of the "side-shows" was one that had important repercussions in World War II. With the entry of Turkey into the war in November, 1914, and with the Western Front capable of being held against the Germans by the French alone, a group of British military and political leaders advanced the idea that British strength should be put into amphibious operations somewhere in the Aegean area. A steady drive could also be made overland toward Vienna and Berlin through territory where the Central Powers were not expecting an attack in force. The great exponent of this "Eastern Plan," was Winston Churchill, First Lord of the Admiralty. The British decided to try the plan. The point of attack chosen was the Dardanelles, the more westerly of the two straits that separate the Black Sea from the Aegean. Here Allied victory would have had the additional advantage of opening communication with Russia via the Black Sea.

In March, 1915, the British and French fleets tried to force the Straits, but they abandoned the attempt somewhat prematurely when several ships struck mines. Later landings of British, Australian, New Zealand, and French troops at various points on both Asian and European shores of the Dardanelles were poorly co-ordinated and badly backed up. They met with fierce and effective resistance from the Turks—a junior officer named Mustapha Kemal greatly distinguishing himself—and in the end they had to be abandoned. Russia remained sealed in by the Straits all during the war. But Churchill continued to believe that the Dardanelles plan had failed, not because it was a bad plan, but because it had not been carried out with determination. And in the Second World War he was to revive, against American military opinion, something of his old plan, which became known as the plan to strike at the "soft underbelly" of the Axis.

The Near East and the Colonies

A whole series of fronts throughout the world was involved in what we may call the colonial "clean-up," the subduing of the German overseas empire and of the outlying parts of the Turkish Empire. The Turks, trained and in part officered by German experts, often resisted effectively. In Mesopotamia, in April, 1916, they forced the surrender of the British general, Townshend, who had landed at Basra from India in 1915 and had marched up the Tigris-Euphrates Valley. But the Turks were never able to take the Suez Canal, nor to advance far into Russian Armenia. Moreover, the British were able to play on the Arabs' dislike for their Turkish suzerains. In a series of desert campaigns the romantic Colonel T. E. Lawrence, an Englishman who knew the Arabs intimately, played a leading part. By the end of 1917, the British held Bagdad and Jerusalem. In September, 1918, a great British offensive in Palestine was so successful that on September 30 the Turks concluded an armistice which took them out of the war.

These campaigns, fought in the lands that had been the cradles of western civilization, were of great importance in making the world we live in today. For from them came not only the independent Arab nations (Syria, Lebanon, Iraq, Jordan, Saudi Arabia, Egypt) but also the Jewish national state of Israel, to which these Arab states are so hostile. In November, 1917, in the Balfour Declaration, the British promised "the establishment in Palestine of a national home for the Jewish people." This promise bore fruit in the mandate of 1922, by which such a state was set up under British protection.

In the colonies the Germans, though cut off from the homeland by the British navy, fought well. In German East Africa they actually managed to hold out to the bitter end in a series of skillful campaigns, so that they still had forces in the field in East Africa on Armistice Day, 1918. But elsewhere they were fighting with inadequate bases and with inadequate forces, so that by the end of 1914 the British, Australians, South Africans, French, and Japanese had pretty well taken over the German overseas possessions.

The War at Sea

This brings us to a most important front—the war at sea. In the long pull, British sea power, reinforced by the French and later by the Italian and the American navies, once more proved decisive. The Allied command of the sea made it possible to draw on the resources of the rest of the world, and in particular to transfer with surprisingly few losses large numbers of British and American troops to the crucial Western Front. Quite as important, sea power enabled the Allies to shut Germany and her allies off from overseas resources. The Allied blockade slowly but surely constricted Germany, limiting not merely military supplies for her armies, but food supplies for her civilian population. At the end of 1918, Germans were suffering from malnutrition, an important factor in their willingness to surrender without fighting to the bitter end.

Yet the war at sea was not easy for the Allies. The submarine, which the Germans had invested in heavily, proved every bit as dangerous as British alarmists before the war had feared. When the Germans launched their unrestricted submarine warfare, they made dangerous inroads on the merchant ships that were essential to the very life of Britain. By the end of 1917, some 8,000,000 tons of shipping had been sunk by the Germans, most of it by submarines. And at one point in 1917 the British had barely enough food reserves to last a month. The submarine menace was eventually overcome by a series of measures co-ordinated between the Allies and the Americans—extensive use of the convoy system, attack on the submarines by depth bombs, constant anti-submarine patrols, and development of small, fast "sub-chasers." But we might wonder what would have happened in 1916-1917 (and again in 1942-1943) if the Germans had contented themselves with holding actions on land and had put all their productive fighting energies into the submarine. This they did not do in either war.

The navy of surface vessels that the Germans had built up since the 1890's—and that, as we have seen, was so important in the growth of Anglo-German hostility—never played a really decisive part in the war itself. German surface-raiders caused severe damage in the first year, but they were finally swept off the seas. Once, however, the main German fleet threw a very bad scare into the British. This was the famous Battle of Jutland, which has been re-fought over and over again by naval historians. Fought in the North Sea on May 31 and June 1, 1916, this running battle resulted in the sinking of twice as much British as German tonnage, and showed how good the German navy was. But the German admiral, Scheer, was forced to run into port before the British capital ships, for which he was no match. Although Jutland was a tactical victory for the Germans, the strategic victory remained with the British, for never again did the German

Destroyer sighting Zeppelin during World War I.

surface navy seriously threaten British command of the sea in European waters. At the war's end the German high command attempted to get the fleet out in a heroic last stand. It was the German sailors' refusal to take the ships out—their mutiny, in fact—that gave a critical push to the German revolution which led to the Armistice of 1918.

The Western Front: Allied Victory

This war also saw the beginnings of air warfare. German lighter-than-air machines, the Zeppelins, raided London many times in 1916-1917, and both sides made airplane bombing raids on nearby towns. But the total damage was relatively light, and

"Big Bertha."

had no decisive effect on the final result. The airplane was of more importance in scouting, and especially in spotting for artillery; in spite of its short range in those days, it also proved useful as a means of locating submarines. The fighter plane was greatly improved during the war, and the base was laid for the development of the air forces we now know. Indeed, the airplane made greater strides in these four years of war than it had made since the Wrights first flew at Kittyhawk in 1903.

Although the war was by no means decided in the air, a new type of warfare was developed, especially on the great Western Front. The machine gun, the repeating rifle, and fast-firing artillery, with the guidance of spotter planes, could pour in such deadly fire that it was almost impossible for either side to break through the opposing trench systems on a wide front. Both sides tried to break through in the two years after the Marne, and both sides suffered losses of a kind that had never been suffered before.

Two new weapons almost broke the deadlock. The first was poison gas, which was first used by the Germans in shells in October, 1914, with disappointing results. Then in April, 1915, the Germans used chlorine gas discharged from cylinders. The overwhelmed French broke in a line five miles wide, leaving the line completely undefended. But the Germans had not prepared to follow through, and the gap was closed once the gas had dispersed. Meanwhile the experts developed a simple countermeasure, the gas mask, which became part of the equipment of every soldier on both sides. The age-old balance of attack and defense was once again reestablished.

The second new weapon came much nearer to producing decisive success. This was the tank, a sort of armored land battleship for which plans had been made back in the Renaissance by the fertile Leonardo da Vinci. But Da Vinci's tank remained a mere sketch for lack of propulsive power. In the second decade of the twentieth cen-

444

tury, however, the internal-combustion engine was ready to do what horses could not do. The tank was a British invention that had been nursed along in its infancy by the always adventurous Winston Churchill. But the new weapon was used too soon, in inadequate numbers and before adequate mechanical tests had been made, in the British Somme offensive of 1916. Even so, nine tanks led or accompanied the infantry triumphantly through the German lines to the capture of Flers. Had the tanks been withheld for a few more months, and backed up with careful planning, they might have broken the German lines on a wide front. The Germans naturally took up the tank at once, and were soon producing their own.

The Germans also developed a spectacular new weapon that struck the imagination of the world but had no effect on the outcome of the war. This was a gun of incredibly long range, which began throwing an occasional shell into Paris from the nearest point in the German lines, some seventy-five miles away. The Parisians were astounded, and at first quite unable to account for the bombardment, since no hostile planes had appeared. But "Big Bertha," as the Allied soldiers christened the gun, proved to be of no more than nuisance value.

The technique of attack in the west gradually developed over the years, and in the end broke the defensive stalemate. Long and careful artillery preparation, known as a "barrage," literally flattened out a section of the enemy defenses and the "no man's land" in front of them, and forced the enemy to retire to rear trenches. Then, accompanied or preceded by tanks, the infantry edged in while the artillery barrage was lifted and focused on the next enemy line. It was a slow and costly process, which did not work on a wide scale until 1918. Then the Germans, with the

Aerial dogfight during World War I.

Russians out of the fight, made a last and almost successful effort to break through, trying to separate the British from the French. With the failure of the last German push in the summer, Foch ordered a general attack. French, British, and American armies had all broken the German lines by early autumn, and were just gaining freedom of action in the open country when the Germans surrendered.

Morale on the Fighting Fronts

The long narrow battle lines of the four-year trench war were the scene of a concentrated destruction hardly equaled in the war of 1939-1945; at some points in France the top soil was blown completely away, producing a desert that is still visible today. The war, however, was not unique, unprecedented, or unlike all other wars, as many an excited publicist at the time declared. It produced military heroes and military scapegoats, great generals and generals who failed. As with the Confederacy in the American Civil War, the defeated Germans seem to have had the most-praised generals, the Ludendorffs, the Mackensens, the Hoffmanns. The old traditional chivalrous warfare, the warfare of athletic heroes, was continued, and even heightened in the air, where the "aces" of the highly individualistic duels between planes were the Rolands of a machine age. And in many of the fronts on land, and in the war at sea, the age-old melodrama of war lost none of its reality. Lawrence in Arabia was no disgrace to the tradition of Sir Walter Scott or even, in the eyes of good patriotic Englishmen, to the tradition of Homer.

Yet especially on the Western Front, this war seemed to many of its participants an unheroic nightmare of blood and filth. Sensitive young intellectuals, who in earlier times would never have had to fight, survived to write bitterly about their experiences—in war novels like *Under Fire*, by the Frenchman Barbusse, or *All Quiet on the Western Front* by the German Remarque, and in war poems like those of Siegfried Sassoon and Wilfred Owen. But this literature cannot be trusted fully as an accurate reflection of what the millions of common soldiers who were not intellectuals felt about the war. We know simply that they stood it for four years. But for most of them the dullness, the discomforts, and the brief terror of battle must have tested their patriotism and worn out their sense of adventure.

Here is a passage, not by one of the most bitterly radical of the intellectuals, or about the Western Front. John Masefield, the British poet, is writing about Gallipoli, where he took part in the Dardanelles campaign:

Let the reader imagine himself to be facing three miles of any very rough broken sloping ground known to him. . . . Let him say to himself that he and an army of his friends are about to advance up the slope towards the top and that as they will be advancing in a line, along the whole length of the three miles, he will only see the advance of those comparatively near to him, since folds or dips in the ground will hide the others. Let him, before he advances, look earnestly along the line of the hill, as it shows up clear, in blazing sunlight only a mile from him, to see his tactical objective, one little clump of pines, three hundred yards away, across what seem to be fields. Let him see in the whole length of the hill no single human being, nothing but scrub, earth, a few scattered buildings. . . . Let him imagine himself to be more weary than he has ever been in his life before, and dirtier than he has ever believed it possible to be, and parched with thirst, nervous, wild-eyed and rather lousy. Let him think that he has not slept for more than a few minutes together for eleven days and nights, and that in all his waking hours he has been fighting for his life, often hand to hand in the dark with a fierce enemy, and that after each fight he has had to dig himself a hole in the ground, often with his hands, and then walk three or four roadless miles to bring up heavy boxes under fire. Let him think, too, that in all those eleven days he has never for an instant been out of the thunder of cannon, that waking or sleeping their devastating crash has been blasting the air across within a mile or two, and this from an artillery so terrible that each discharge beats as it were a wedge of shock between the skull-bone and the brain. Let him think too that never, for an instant, in all that time, has he been free or even partly free from the peril of death in its most sudden and savage forms, and that hourly in all that time he has seen his friends blown to pieces at his side, or dismembered, or drowned, or driven mad, or stabbed, or sniped by some unseen stalker, or bombed in the dark sap with a handful of dynamite in a beef-tin, till their blood is caked upon his clothes and thick upon his face, and that he knows, as he stares at the hill, that in a few moments, more of that dwindling band, already too few, God knows how many too few, for the task to be done, will be gone the same way, and that he himself may reckon that he has done with life, tasted and spoken and loved his last, and that

446

CHAPTER XXV

The Home Fronts

London air-raid warning during World War I.

in a few minutes more may be blasted dead, or lying bleeding in the scrub, with perhaps his face gone and a leg and an arm broken, unable to move but still alive, unable to drive away the flies or screen the ever-dropping rain, in a place where none will find him, or be able to help him, a place where he will die and rot and shrivel, till nothing is left of him but a few rags and a few remnants and a little identification-disc flapping on his bones in the wind.*

---

* John Masefield, *Gallipoli* (New York, 1916), 96-99.

These soldiers and sailors were, for the most part, not professionals; they were civilians, "drafted," lifted from civilian families unused to the ways of the military. Behind the front, on the production lines, subject to the unheroic but harassing strains of rationing and all sorts of limitations in daily living, subject also to the constant prodding of war propaganda, the families too were part of this great "total war." They too stood it, though in France in 1917, after the bloody failure of a great offensive under General Nivelle, civilian and military discontent, fanned by politicians, came almost to the point of breaking French morale. And in Germany, the collapse that resulted in the armistice of November 11, 1918, though it obviously had many, complex causes, looks like a general failure of morale, a psychological collapse under intolerable spiritual and material pressures.

For the Germans, still influenced by nineteenth-century ideas about the rights of the individual and laissez-faire economics, were slow to organize their society for total war. They failed notably to ensure the proper and equitable distribution of food supplies, so that as 1918 wore on whole sectors of the urban population began to suffer from malnutrition. Nor were finances and war production managed with that perfection of techniques that most of the world had already come to expect of the Germans. Rationing, strict control of production, price control, systematic use of the resources of conquered countries, these and many other measures were employed by the Germans, but not with the care, decisiveness, and long preparation that characterized them in the war of 1939-1945.

All countries engaged in the war, the democratic western Allies as well as the autocratic Central Powers, sooner or later felt obliged to introduce drastic wartime economic planning, which anticipated in some sense the more collectivistic economy of today. Everywhere war appeared, as the American President Madison's dictum has it, as "the mother of executive aggrandizement." Everywhere there was compulsory military service. Even in Britain, proud of its long devotion to the rights of the individual, the famous Defense of the Realm Act—known with wry affection as DORA—clamped down severely on the Englishman's sacred right to say and do what he liked, even if he did not seem to be giving aid and comfort to the enemy. In the United States, all sorts of men, including the famous "dollar-a-year men," business executives who were working for the government for the first time, flocked to Washington and helped build up an enormous new central government, which regulated the economy as it had never been regulated before. And of course all the belligerents engaged in the war of propaganda, or, as it came to be called in the next great war, in psychological warfare.

The Allies won the battle of the production lines, in which the United States played a major if not a decisive part. We have already noted that in material resources the Allies had a marked potential superiority over the Central Powers; this superiority they were eventually able to realize to the full. Had the Germans not given up when they did, and had the Allies staged the all-out offensive in the west they had planned for the spring of 1919, it seems certain that they would have overwhelmed the Germans. Allied production was slow in getting started. The French, in particular, were lamed by the loss in the first few weeks of the war of their most highly developed industrial regions in the north and northeast. The British even maintained for a few months in 1914 the delusive slogan, "Business as usual." There were mistakes, bottlenecks, and experiments like that of the tanks which failed at first because of undue haste. At the beginning the Allies were often at cross-purposes in production as well as in actual military strategy. And not even at the end were all the Allied resources pooled as effectively as they were to be in the Second World War. Nevertheless, by the end of 1917 the Allied military machine was adequately, indeed in some ways wastefully, supplied.

The Role of Propaganda

The Allies also won the most critical phase of the war of propaganda. They sought to convince the neutral world, especially the neutrals of western civilization, the United States, Latin America, and the Swiss, Dutch, Scandinavians, and Spanish, that the Allies were fighting for the right and the Central Powers for the wrong. It was not a complete victory, for important groups in all these countries remained "pro-German" to the end, and Spain on the whole was probably pro-German, or at least anti-French and anti-English. Still, it seems that a majority of the neutral West was early convinced that the cause of the Allies was just. This conviction was strengthened from the very start by the traditional liberalism of France and Britain in contrast with the traditional autocracy of the German and the Austrian empires, though the presence of the autocratic Russian Empire on the Allied side somewhat handicapped Allied propagandists. The conviction was greatly strengthened in the early days of the crisis of 1914 by the intransigence of the Austrians toward the Serbs, and in particular by the blundering phrase of Bethmann-Hollweg, that Britain had gone to war for a mere "scrap of paper."

The sense of Allied rightness was strengthened by early Allied propaganda, which was often one-sided and unfair. Notably, it accused the Germans of frightful atrocities in Belgium. The Germans did indeed impose rigorous military controls on conquered populations, but little in their record was worse than is usual, and perhaps inevitable, in all warfare. Allied propaganda also simplified and falsified the complex chain of causation that produced the war, making it appear that the Germans and the Austrians were wholly responsible for the outbreak of the war, that the predatory "Potsdam gang" had planned the whole thing from the beginning, and that Serbs, French, Russians, and British had been wholly innocent of deed or word that might have brought on the war. This propaganda backfired shortly after the war; revulsion against its unfairness had much to do with the widespread acceptance of the extreme revisionist thesis that on the whole Germany, in particular, had been quite guiltless of starting the war.

Perhaps wartime propaganda has as its main purpose less the weakening of enemy morale or even the conversion of neutral opinion than the strengthening of the morale of one's own country. Here both sides were substantially successful, and those who guided public opinion were able to convince their fellow countrymen that they were fighting for the right. There were defeatist elements in France and in Italy, but they never quite upset the war effort. In France, Britain, and the United States, as well as in Germany and Austria, the publicists, the preachers, and the teachers rallied to the national cause and poured out millions of words of exhortation and encouragement. In Britain, Kipling sounded a characteristic note:

> For all we have and are,
> For all our children's fate,
> Stand up and take the war.
> The Hun is at the gate!
> Our world has passed away

> In wantonness o'erthrown.
> There is nothing left to-day
> But steel and fire and stone!

> • • •

> No easy hope or lies
> Shall bring us to our goal,
> But iron sacrifice
> Of body, will, and soul.
> There is but one task for all—
> One life for each to give.
> What stands if Freedom fall?
> Who dies if England live? *

Only in tsarist Russia, where the war began with a burst of patriotic feeling, did home-grown defeatist propaganda, fed by failure and suffering, finally win the day with the Bolshevik uprising of November, 1917 (see Chapter XXVI).

Political Repercussions

Except, again, in Russia, the four years of war saw no major changes in political structure. The Central Empires retained until their collapse their incompletely responsible parliamentary governments, and the parliaments on the whole were reasonably submissive. And in spite of the inevitable strengthening of the executive in wartime, France, Britain, and the United States carried on their democratic institutions. In the United States the critical presidential election of 1916 came just before American entrance into the war, and resulted by a narrow margin in the return of the incumbent, Woodrow Wilson. In Britain and France the democratic process brought to power in the midst of wartime crisis two strong men—Lloyd George and Clemenceau—who carried through with great vigor the prosecution of the war, and who, though their fame was dimmed in the troubled years after the war, remain in historic memory as great national heroes.

* "For All We Have and Are," from "The Years Between," *Rudyard Kipling's Verse, 1885-1932* (London, 1933), 326-327.

In Britain the skillful but indecisive Liberal leader Asquith proved unable to master events, even though he widened his government into a coalition in May, 1915. In December of that year he was succeeded by another Liberal, Lloyd George, the architect of Britain's social insurance system (see Chapter XXI), who had also proven himself an admirable organizer of war production. Under Lloyd George the coalition really worked, and his position as war leader was to remain unchallenged.

We shall meet him again at the peace negotiations, as we shall meet his French counterpart, Clemenceau. The "Tiger," as Clemenceau was known to his friends and enemies alike, came to power at the end of 1917, at a time when defeatism threatened both the military and the internal strength of France. Clemenceau took firm command of the war effort and disposed of the disaffected politicians with the decisiveness—and disregard for the peacetime "rights of man"—of an old Jacobin.

IV: The Peace

As in Westphalia in 1648, at Utrecht in 1713, and at Vienna in 1815, the warring powers gathered in a great meeting to make the peace settlement. This time they met at Paris—or, rather, in suburban Paris. They met at Versailles to settle with the Germans, at St. Germain to settle with the Austrians, at Neuilly to settle with the Bulgarians, at the Grand Trianon (in the park of Versailles) to settle with the Hungarians, and at Sèvres to settle with the Turks. But peace congresses almost never meet in a world that is really at peace. There are always aftermaths, local wars and disturbances, lesser diseases that follow the great bout of illness. The aftermaths of 1918-1919 were particularly numerous and acute, and conditioned the whole work of the peace congresses. To them we must turn briefly before we consider the actual settlements.

The Aftermath of World War

The sorest spot was Russia, now in the throes of civil war and foreign invasion. No sooner had the Germans been forced to withdraw from the regions they had gained at Brest-Litovsk (see above, p. 440) than the Allies sent detachments to various points along the rim of Russia—on the Black Sea, on the White Sea in the far north, and on the Pacific (for details see Chapter XXVI). The Allies still hoped to restore in Russia, if not the monarchy, at least a moderate democratic republic. Their dread of final Bolshevik success, and of the possible spread of Bolshevism westward, added to the tensions at Versailles and confirmed the conservative position Clemenceau and Lloyd George were taking.

And Bolshevism was indeed spreading westward. The German revolution of November, 1918, had been carried out under socialist auspices. But all through the winter of 1918-1919 there were communist riots and uprisings, and in Bavaria in April a soviet republic was proclaimed. The government of the new republic of Germany put these communist uprisings down, but only by an appeal to the remnants of the old army and to officers thoroughly hostile to the republic. In the break-up of the Austro-Hungarian monarchy in the autumn of 1918 the successor states—Czechoslovakia, Austria, Hungary, Yugoslavia, Rumania—which had been formed in whole or in part out of the former Habsburg lands, were disturbed by all sorts of social and economic troubles. In Hungary, Bela Kun, who had worked with Lenin in Moscow, won power by means of a socialist-communist coalition, and then elbowed out his socialist colleagues and set up a communist dictatorship. (Note how early this familiar pattern of our own time was established: these events took place in the spring of 1919.) In August, a Rumanian army that had invaded Hungary forced Bela Kun to flee. Finally, all through the Germanies groups of ex-soldiers, the *Freikorps*, were roving about, stirring up trouble, and threatening the overthrow of the German Republic (for details, see Chapter XXVII).

In the Near East the Allies had even worse troubles to face. Greece, which had been so hard to drag into the war, was now in full cry against the Turks. Her nationalists had revived the old hope of a restored Byzantine Empire, with the Greeks once more in command of the Straits. Her armies, not without Allied encouragement, landed at Smyrna in Asia Minor in the spring of 1919 and marched off in the track of Alexander the Great. The French and the British, to whom control over different parts of the former Turkish Empire had been assigned, began at once having trouble with their new Arab subjects—or wards. The Jews were already pressing for the establishment of a national home in Palestine in accordance with the Balfour Declaration, and the Arabs were already opposing them.

In India the aftermath of war was bad indeed. The universal epidemic of influenza in 1918 (which most public-health experts believe killed more people than were killed in battle) had been especially disastrous in India. Indians had fought well as professional soldiers during the war on the Allied side; educated Indians thought their country was ripe for much more self-rule. The disorders of 1918-1919 culminated in the Amritsar massacre of April, 1919, in which a British general, reverting to old-time methods, ordered his soldiers to fire on an unarmed crowd, killing or wounding some 1600 people. Amritsar shocked world opinion, added to the odium the Allies were already acquiring among liberals everywhere, and knitted India more closely together in opposition to the British. In China the weakening of Russia had been taken by the Japanese as a signal to renew their ambitious plans in the north of China, and indeed the American troops sent to Vladivostok in Siberia (see Chapter XXVI) were there less to oppose the Bolsheviks than to oppose the Japanese.

So the world was in turmoil and disorder when the Allies, great, small, and middle-sized, assembled in Paris to make the peace. The problems that faced the peacemakers were world-wide, complex, and often insoluble—insoluble in the sense that no decision on a given problem, say the disposition of the Adriatic port of Fiume which was claimed by Italians and Yugoslavs, could possibly satisfy all the major groups concerned, to say nothing of the minorities. Yet the world hoped, and indeed expected, from the peacemakers more than it had in any previous crisis. Public opinion in the eighteenth and nineteenth centuries had built up a tremendous faith in the possibility of a peaceful, just, and happy world. This war had been a war to "make the world safe for democracy," a "war to end war." It had produced in the American President Wilson a man who could phrase skillfully the hopes of men, and who as he journeyed to Paris after the Armistice appeared to be the heroic savior and hope of mankind.

These liberal dreams and expectations

were, however, by no means the sole tenants of men's minds. All men were not Wilsonians. There were, inevitably, the selfish, the disillusioned, the narrow, the jingoists, and the professionals who had made promises to the Italians and the Rumanians, who had planned all sorts of compensations and adjustments. There were, more important, the plain ordinary men and women who wanted peace and security but who also wanted national glory and the punishment of the wicked Germans who, they believed, had put them through those four years of hell. There were, in short, thousands of conflicting hopes and fears, all of them embodied in living human flesh, not just the abstractions they must seem to be on the printed page.

The Fourteen Points

The more generous of these hopes were in 1918 clearly embodied in one man and in one text. Woodrow Wilson, on January 8, 1918, in an address to the American Congress, had announced the famous Fourteen Points, which at once were taken by the people in Allied and even in enemy countries as a firm platform for the peace to come. Here they are:

I. Open covenants of peace, openly arrived at, after which there shall be no private international understandings of any kind but diplomacy shall proceed always frankly and in the public view.

II. Absolute freedom of navigation upon the seas, outside territorial waters, alike in peace and in war, except as the seas may be closed in whole or in part by international action for the enforcement of international covenants.

III. The removal, so far as possible, of all economic barriers and the establishment of an equality of trade conditions among all the nations consenting to the peace and associating themselves for its maintenance.

IV. Adequate guarantees given and taken that national armaments will be reduced to the lowest point consistent with domestic safety.

V. A free, open-minded, and absolutely impartial adjustment of all colonial claims, based upon a strict observance of the principle that in determining all such questions of sovereignty the interests of the populations concerned must have equal weight with the equitable claims of the government whose title is to be determined.

VI. The evacuation of all Russian territory and such a settlement of all questions affecting Russia as will secure the best and freest cooperation of the other nations of the world in obtaining for her an unhampered and unembarrassed opportunity for the independent determination of her own political development and national policy and assure her of a sincere welcome into the society of free nations under institutions of her own choosing; and, more than a welcome, assistance also of every kind that she may need and may herself desire. The treatment accorded Russia by her sister nations in the months to come will be the acid test of their good will, of their comprehension of her needs as distinguished from their own interests, and of their intelligent and unselfish sympathy.

VII. Belgium, the whole world will agree, must be evacuated and restored, without any attempt to limit the sovereignty which she enjoys in common with all other free nations. No other single act will serve as this will serve to restore confidence among the nations in the laws which they have themselves set and determined for the government of their relations with one another. Without this healing act the whole structure and validity of international law is forever impaired.

VIII. All French territory should be freed and the invaded portions restored, and the wrong done to France by Prussia in 1871 in the matter of Alsace-Lorraine, which has unsettled the peace of the world for nearly fifty years, should be righted, in order that peace may once more be made secure in the interest of all.

IX. A readjustment of the frontiers of Italy should be effected along clearly recognizable lines of nationality.

X. The peoples of Austria-Hungary, whose place among the nations we wish to see safeguarded and assured, should be accorded the freest opportunity of autonomous development.

XI. Rumania, Serbia, and Montenegro should be evacuated; occupied territories restored; Serbia accorded free and secure access to the sea; and the relations of the several Balkan states to one another determined by friendly counsel along historically established lines of allegiance and nationality; and international guarantees of the political and economic independence and territorial integrity of the several Balkan states should be entered into.

XII. The Turkish portions of the present Ottoman Empire should be assured a secure sovereignty, but the other nationalities which are now under Turkish rule should be assured an undoubted security of life and an absolutely unmolested opportunity of autonomous development, and the Dardanelles should be permanently opened as a free passage to the ships and commerce of all nations under international guarantees.

XIII. An independent Polish state should be erected which should include the territories inhabited by indisputably Polish populations, which should be assured a free and secure access to the sea, and whose political and economic independence and territorial integrity should be guaranteed by international covenant.

XIV. A general association of nations must be formed under specific covenants for the purpose of affording mutual guarantees of political independence and territorial integrity to great and small states alike.*

The fourteenth point, the germ of the League of Nations, was especially dear to Wilson.

Just how great a part the Fourteen Points played in the final surrender of the Germans is a delicate and much disputed issue. On October 4, 1918, a German government was set up under the liberal Prince Max of Baden; this development provided a sort of antechamber to the real German revolution of a few weeks later. Prince Max's government did indeed announce its own acceptance of the Fourteen Points, and that of its Austrian ally, and began negotiations with Wilson, who stalled them off until the

*Woodrow Wilson, *War and Peace: Presidential Messages, Addresses, and Public Papers*, R. S. Baker and W. E. Dodd, eds. (New York, 1927), I, 159-161.

real revolution of early November. In November, events moved too fast for formal diplomacy, although on November 5 the Allies conceded the Fourteen Points as a basis for negotiation, with some reservations. But it is quite certain that German public opinion, and liberal opinion throughout the world, thought the Allies had promised a peace in accord with the Fourteen Points.

Opposing Hopes and Promises

The hopes and promises that opposed and contradicted the Fourteen Points were not neatly embodied in a single document. We may classify them roughly in three categories: the previous diplomatic commitments made by the Allies; the immediate and widespread popular hopes fanned by Allied propaganda and confirmed at the last moment by some Allied statesmen; and—much more difficult to pin down—the long-established habits and traditions that had become part of the dominant policies and trends of each nation, big and little.

In the first category, the most difficult of the diplomatic commitments was one of which Wilson seems to have been in ignorance for some time. This was the contradictory set of promises made to both Italy and Serbia by the original entente, including Russia, about the disposal of Habsburg lands. And there were other commitments, especially in the Balkans, that were very difficult to sort out. In the second category were the promises, widely believed by the British and French, that Germany would be made to suffer to the full for her war guilt. She would have to pay the whole cost of the war in reparations, her war criminals would be punished, she would be rendered incapable ever again of assuming the role of the aggressor. In some vague way, everything would shortly be much better for everybody. Lloyd George, always the opportunist, had taken advantage of the psychological lift given by the Armistice to hold a general election in Britain. This was the famous "khaki election" of December, 1918, which took its name from soldiers' uniforms, and in which women first enjoyed the franchise. The election resulted in a huge majority for the coalition headed by Lloyd George. Two phrases from the election campaign caught the mood of many voters: the German orange was to be squeezed dry "till the pips [i.e., the seeds] squeak"; and Britain was to be "a land fit for heroes."

Finally, in the third category were the deeply rooted drives of the various nations —French drives for revenge against Germany and for restoration of French hegemony in Europe, the Italian Irredentist drive, the British longing for a Victorian serenity and economic leadership well armored against German commercial competition, and the nationalist aspirations of the new states of Central Europe that had at last been released from long frustration. And by no means the least important was the old and firmly held American tradition that Americans call "isolationism," the desire to be free from European alliances and entanglements and to go their own pioneer way. Many liberals of the time felt that all these drives were ignoble and backward-looking; but these drives were also "natural," embedded in habit and tradition. They were indeed the toughest of the forces that quickly put the Fourteen Points into the background at Versailles.

The Process of Peacemaking

The Peace Conference met formally in Paris on January 18, 1919. Nearly thirty nations involved in the war against the Central Powers sent delegates. Russia was not represented. The defeated nations took no part in the deliberations; they were simply notified of the final terms and asked to sign. The Germans, in particular, were given but the slightest chance to comment on or criticize the terms offered them. Very soon the German publicists coined a term for the treaty—"*Diktat*," the imposed, the dictated peace. The Germans' anger over this failure of the Allies to negotiate with their new and virtuous republic was to play a large part in the ultimate rise of Hitler.

Although a few western liberals were from the first disillusioned by the exclusion of the defeated nations from the Peace Conference, the conference did get off to a good start. Wilson's reception in Europe had been extremely enthusiastic. People everywhere were still rejoicing over the end of the nightmare. The Fourteen Points seemed already a realized peace; and for the future, the proposed association of nations, working together in the freedom of parliamentary discussion, would soon eliminate the costly burdens of armament. Wilson's hopeful phrases sounded in press and pulpit, and none more loudly than his "open covenants openly arrived at." To many a liberal these words meant that the peace would be made in a sort of big, idealized New England town meeting, in which the representatives of all the powers, big and little, would have their free say in public, in which decisions would ultimately be taken by majority vote, in which the caucus, the smoke-filled room, the back-stairs intrigues would all be missing.

These liberals were almost at once disillusioned, for the conference soon fell into the familiar pattern of centuries. The small nations were excluded from the real negotiations; the business of the conference was carried on in private among the political chiefs of the victorious great powers—the Big Four of Wilson, Lloyd George, Clemenceau, and Orlando (it was really a Big

Paris crowd after the Armistice, 1918.

Three, for Italy was not strong enough to impose her Orlando, who was a much less striking character than his colleagues). Decisions were made in the traditional way of diplomacy, with all the pressures, chicanery, intrigues, compromises, and plain horse-trading that go on when leaders get together in private. Public opinion was consulted only indirectly, as each statesman sought to make sure that he had at least a majority of his own nation behind him. This Wilson in particular failed to do; at some point in early 1919 he had clearly lost the support of his own people.

The hopeful members of the general public were by no means the only ones who grew disillusioned as the Paris Conference went the way of the Vienna Congress a hundred years before. The professional diplomatists of the little and middle-sized powers had probably never really expected that they would be treated on equal terms, but the completeness of their exclusion from the real work of the conference annoyed them, and angered their people back home. More important, all the major powers had brought with them large staffs of experts, economists, political scientists, historians, career men in many fields. These bright young men were sure they knew better than their elders how to solve the problems of human relations, were confident that they would do the real work and make the really important decisions. They drew up report after report, some of which went up through devious channels to Clemenceau or Lloyd George or Wilson. But they did not make policy. The disillusion of the young experts was great and long-lived, and since many of them were quite articulate they did much to discredit the work of the conference.

One of them, the English economist John Maynard Keynes, lived to influence his government in the 1930's and '40's as he could not do in 1919. But he took immediate revenge in a book called *The Economic Consequences of the Peace* (1919). To Keynes the peace was a "Carthaginian"

THE FIRST WORLD WAR

Lloyd George, Clemenceau, and Wilson in Paris during the peace negotiations, 1919.

peace, an attempt to destroy Germany as Rome had destroyed Carthage. But since Germany was an essential part of Europe, to attempt to destroy Germany by weakening her economically would inevitably harm all Europe. Germany could not possibly pay the reparations the Allies were asking from her, the new states of Central Europe were already erecting tariff barriers, and nothing had been done at Versailles to bind Europe together. Keynes' book at once became the bible of liberal opponents of the work of Versailles, not only because of its economic arguments, but also because of a series of portraits of the Big Four which are still memorable. Of Clemenceau, Keynes wrote:

He felt about France what Pericles felt of Athens—unique value in her, nothing else mat-

tering; but his theory of politics was Bismarck's. He had one illusion—France; and one disillusion—mankind, including Frenchmen, and his colleagues not least.[*]

Of Wilson:

The President was not a hero or a prophet; he was not even a philosopher; but a generously intentioned man, with many of the weaknesses of other human beings, and lacking that dominating intellectual equipment which would have been necessary to cope with the subtle and dangerous spellbinders whom a tremendous clash of forces and personalities had brought to the top as triumphant masters in the swift game of give and take, face to face in Council, —a game of which he had no experience at all. . . .

But if the President was not the philosopher-king, what was he? After all he was a man who had spent much of his life at a University. He was by no means a business man or an ordinary party politician, but a man of force, personality, and importance. What, then, was his temperament?

The clue once found was illuminating. The President was like a Nonconformist minister, perhaps a Presbyterian. His thought and his temperament were essentially theological not intellectual, with all the strength and the weakness of that manner of thought, feeling, and expression.[†]

And of Wilson in relation to Lloyd George:

What chance could such a man have against Mr. Lloyd George's unerring, almost medium-like, sensibility to every one immediately round him? To see the British Prime Minister watching the company, with six or seven senses not available to ordinary men, judging character, motive, and subconscious impulse, perceiving what each was thinking and even what each was going to say next, and compounding with telepathic instinct the argument or appeal best suited to the vanity, weakness, or self-interest of his immediate auditor, was to realize that the poor President would be playing blind man's buff in that party. Never could a man have stepped into the parlor a more perfect and predestined victim to the finished accom-

[*] J. M. Keynes, *The Economic Consequences of the Peace* (New York, 1920), 32.

[†] *Ibid.*, 39, 41-42.

CHAPTER XXV

plishments of the Prime Minister. The Old World was tough in wickedness anyhow; the Old World's heart of stone might blunt the sharpest blade of the bravest knight-errant. But this blind and deaf Don Quixote was entering a cavern where the swift and glittering blade was in the hands of the adversary.*

Wilson and his experts were gradually badgered into accepting harsher peace terms. The reparations bill against Germany was lengthened; Poland, Italy, and Japan made claims to lands that clearly were not theirs; the victors more and more openly showed that they proposed to behave as victors in war habitually have behaved. Wilson gave way or compromised on a dozen points, and then chose to stand fast against the weakest of the Allies. He would not let the Italians have the Adriatic seaport of Fiume, which had once been the sole seaport of Hungary. They might have neighboring Trieste and their coveted Trentino, where they could rule over German or Slavic-speaking minorities, indeed, in some areas, majorities; but Fiume they might not have. The Italian delegation left the conference in anger, but Wilson was immovable. The fate of Fiume was not settled at the conference; only in 1924, by treaty with Yugoslavia, did the city go to Italy in return for Susak, a port right next door that served the Yugoslavs quite adequately.

But Wilson did get his new international organization, the cornerstone of his plans for a better world. The covenant of the League of Nations was an integral part of the Treaty of Versailles. The League was no true supranational state, but a kind of permanent consultative system composed of the victors and a few neutrals. The way was left open for the Germans and the Russians to join the League, as they later did. But in 1919-1920 Wilson's League looked a lot like Metternich's and Castle-

reagh's old Congress system of 1815, by no means worth the sacrifices Wilson had made to obtain it. The League had an assembly in which each member-state had one vote, and a council in which the five great powers (Britain, France, Italy, the United States, and Japan) had permanent seats, and to which four other member-states were chosen by the assembly for specific terms. A permanent secretariat, to be located at Geneva, was charged with administering the affairs of the League. In its working out, as we shall see (Chapter XXVIII), the League never fulfilled the hopes of the liberals. It did not achieve disarmament, nor did its machinery of peacemaking prove capable of preventing aggression. The great powers simply went on their usual ways, using the League only as their policy-makers—their heads of state rather than their diplomats—saw fit.

The Territorial Settlement

Central to all the work in Paris was the problem of territorial changes. Here the peacemakers were confronted not merely with the claims of the victorious Allies but also with the claims of the new nations that had sprung up from the disintegrating Austrian, Russian, and Turkish empires. They had to try to satisfy the eternal land hunger of those who run nations, without violating too obviously another great Wilsonian principle, the "self-determination of peoples." This principle was hard indeed to apply in much of Central Europe, where peoples of different language and national self-consciousness were mixed together in an incredible mosaic of unassimilated minorities. The result was to multiply the number of "sovereign" nations in this world. Nationalism, which some hopeful people had thought was on the wane, was now fanned to intense new life in a dozen states.

* *Ibid.*, 41.

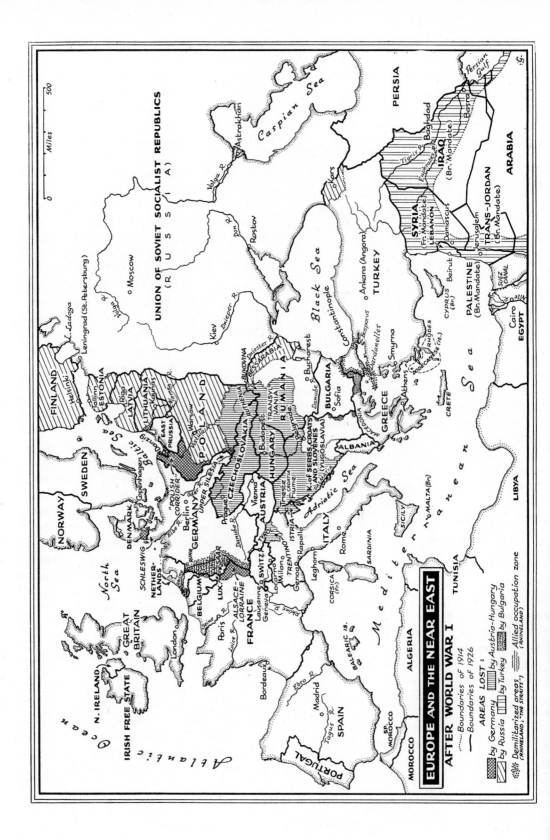

EUROPE AND THE NEAR EAST
AFTER WORLD WAR I

······ Boundaries of 1914
——— Boundaries of 1926

AREAS LOST:
by Germany
by Russia
by Austria-Hungary
by Turkey
by Bulgaria
Allied occupation zone (RHINELAND)
Demilitarized areas (RHINELAND; THE "STRAITS")

France received Alsace-Lorraine back from Germany. Clemenceau also hoped both to annex the small but coal-rich Saar Basin of Germany as compensation for French coal mines destroyed by the Germans during the war, and to detach from Germany the territory on the left (or west) bank of the Rhine, thereby strengthening French security and setting up a Rhineland republic that might become a French satellite. Both French hopes, opposed by Wilson and Lloyd George, went unrealized. The Saar was to be separated from Germany for fifteen years as an international ward supervised by the League of Nations. At the end of the fifteen-year period a plebiscite would determine its future status; meanwhile, its coal output was to go to France. The Rhineland remained part of the German Republic, though it was to be demilitarized and occupied for a time by Allied soldiers.

Belgian was given some small towns on her German border. Italy gained her Irredenta of Trent and Trieste, indeed in generous measure, for thousands of German and Slavic-speaking peoples were included within her new boundaries. Poland, erased from the map as an independent state in 1795, was now restored and given lands that she had had before the partitions of the eighteenth century and that contained important minorities of Germans and other non-Polish peoples. The old Habsburg Empire was entirely dismembered. The heart of its German-speaking area was constituted as the truncated Republic of Austria, which was forbidden to join itself to Germany, and the heart of its Magyar-speaking area became a diminished Kingdom of Hungary. The Czech-inhabited lands of Bohemia and Moravia were joined with Slovakia and the Ruthenian lands of the Carpatho-Ukraine further east in the brand-new "succession state" of Czechoslovakia. On the northwest, the Czechoslovak Republic extended to the mountain ranges separating Bohemia from Germany, but on the Czech side of this "natural" frontier there lived many Sudeten Germans. From the first, therefore, the new republic faced the problem of a large and discontented Sudeten minority.

Another "succession state" was Yugoslavia, officially the Kingdom of Serbs, Croats, and Slovenes, which, as its full name suggests, represented a great expansion of pre-war Serbia to include the south Slav territories of the Habsburgs. Rumania, too, profited by the break-up of the old dual monarchy, by receiving the former Hungarian lands of Transylvania. Rewarded also with Bessarabia, a Russian province that the Bolsheviks could not defend, Rumania emerged with doubled territory. In the southern Balkan Peninsula, Greece received all of Thrace, at the expense of Turkey and Bulgaria.

Out of the former tsarist domains held at the end of the war by the Germans there were set up, in addition to Poland, the "Baltic republics" of Estonia, Latvia, and Lithuania. Once Europe had settled down, plebiscites were provided for to determine certain other territorial adjustments, notably whether certain parts of East Prussia and Silesia should go to Poland or remain German. The new Polish state had been granted access to the Baltic Sea through the so-called "Polish corridor," a narrow strip of land which had once been Polish, and which terminated in the almost wholly German city and port of Danzig. The Poles wanted Danzig, but the Allies compromised by setting up a Free City of Danzig and by giving the Poles free trade with the city. Even so, the Polish corridor now separated East Prussia from the rest of Germany, and Germans had to cross it in sealed trains.

Outside Europe, the Near East presented the most acute problems. By the Treaty of Sèvres the Turks were left in Europe with no more than Constantinople and a small strip of land around it, and in Asia with only their homeland of Anatolia. For the rest, the Hejaz, the old, feudal, desert country of Arabia, was recognized as independent and presently became known as Saudi Arabia, after its ruler, Ibn Saud. Mesopotamia and Palestine were given as mandates —a term we shall shortly explain— to Britain, while Syria and Lebanon were given as mandates to France. The Greeks were to hold Smyrna and nearby regions in Asia Minor for five years, and then submit to a plebiscite. But the Treaty of Sèvres never went into effect, though it was duly signed by the Sultan. In Anatolia a group of army officers led by Mustapha Kemal revolted against the government at Constantinople and galvanized the Turkish people into a new national life. The Turks drove the Greek army out of their country and set up a Turkish republic with its capital not at Constantinople but at Ankara in the heart of Anatolia. With this new government the Allies were finally obliged to conclude the Treaty of Lausanne in 1923. The new peace transferred the Smyrna area and eastern Thrace from Greek to Turkish control and was in general much more advantageous to the Turks than the Treaty of Sèvres had been.

The Mandates

For the rest of the world the old straightforward annexing of the overseas territories of defeated powers, as practiced in 1713, 1763, and 1815, seemed no longer possible in 1919. Liberal opinion both in Europe and in America had already been offended to the bursting point, and Wilson himself would never have permitted outright annexations. The consequence was the mandate system, whereby control over a given territory was assigned to a particular power by the League of Nations, which undertook periodic inspections to see that the terms of the mandate were being fulfilled. This system was designed by its proponents as a means of educating and improving colonial peoples, leading them into the ways of democratic self-government, and preparing them for eventual independence. Under it the former German overseas territories and the non-Turkish parts of the Ottoman Empire were now distributed. Of Germany's African possessions East Africa (now called Tanganyika) went to Britain; Southwest Africa went to the Union of South Africa; and both the Cameroons and Togoland were divided between Britain and France. In the Pacific, the German portion of New Guinea was given to Australia, western Samoa to New Zealand, and the Caroline, Marshall, and Mariana island groups to Japan. In the Near East, as we have seen, France thus secured Syria and Lebanon, while Britain took Palestine and Mesopotamia.

The mandate system may seem to have been a way of disguising annexation, the hypocritical tribute of reactionary vice to progressive virtue. And so to a man like Clemenceau it probably was. The Japanese quite openly annexed and fortified their new Pacific islands in defiance of the terms of their mandate. But to many of the men who put through the idea of mandates the system really was what it professed to be, a nursery for eventual nationhood. And for the most part the mandatory powers did make some show at least of treating mandated territories in a way that would prepare them for eventual freedom.

The Punishment of Germany

After land transfers, the most important business of the Peace Conference was reparations, which were imposed on Austria, Hungary, Bulgaria, and Turkey as well as on Germany. It was, however, the German reparations that so long disturbed the peace and the economy of the world. On paper at least, Lloyd George lived up to his campaign promises about "squeezing the orange"; the Germans were made to promise to pay for all the damage done to civilian property during the war, and to pay at the rate of five billion dollars a year until 1921, when the final bill would be presented to them. They would then be given thirty years in which to pay the full amount. The amount was left indefinite at Versailles, for the Allies could not agree on a figure. But the totals suggested were astronomical. It was clear from the first that the payments would ultimately have to be in goods—German goods in competition with the goods of the Allies. A Germany prosperous enough to pay reparations could not be the weak and divided nation that men like Clemenceau really wanted. Thus from the very start the "realists" at Versailles—Lloyd George and Clemenceau—cherished quite inconsistent hopes for the future.

The Versailles settlement also required Germany to hand over many of her merchant ships to the Allies and to make large deliveries of coal to France, Italy, and Belgium for a ten-year period. Furthermore, a whole miscellany of articles in the treaty was directed toward the disarmament of Germany on land, on sea, and in the air. The German army was to be limited in size to 100,000 men, and the western frontier zone, extending to a line 50 kilometers (about 30 miles) east of the Rhine, was to be completely "demilitarized"—that is, to contain neither fortifications nor soldiers. In addition, the Allies could have armies of occupation on the left bank of the Rhine for fifteen years, and perhaps longer. The treaty forbade Germany to have either submarines or military planes and severely limited the number and size of surface vessels in her navy.

Last, and by no means least important, Article 231 of the Treaty of Versailles obliged Germany to admit that the Central Powers bore sole responsibility for starting the war in 1914. Here is the article that was to cause so much history to be written:

The Allied and Associated Governments affirm, and Germany accepts, the responsibility of Germany and her allies for causing all the loss and damage to which the Allied and Associated Governments and their nationals have been subjected as a consequence of the war imposed upon them by the aggression of Germany and her allies.*

The Settlement Evaluated

To the Germans, Versailles was of course a cruel and humiliating peace, the *Diktat*, the great national grievance on which Hitler was to play so skillfully. To liberals of the time and later, it seemed as it did to Keynes an unsound, revengeful peace, above all disastrous in its unrealistic reparations policy. In our present world of cold and hot wars, Versailles almost arouses nostalgia. It was at least a settlement, and one that in the best moments of the 1920's seemed a basis for slow improvement in international relations (see Chapter XXVIII).

The League it set up was potentially a means by which a new generation of international administrators might mitigate the old rivalries of nations. The reparations could be, and indeed were, scaled down to something more reasonable. The new succession states were based on a national consciousness that had been developing for at least a hundred years. Though the theorist might protest at the "Balkanization of Europe," the creation of more weak and discontented little states like those in the Balkans, the fact remains that it would have been hard to deny national independence, or at least autonomy, to the Czechs,

* S. B. Fay, *The Origins of the World War* (New York, 1928), I, 8.

the Poles, the Baltic peoples, and the south Slavs. Germany, though she certainly was not treated generously, was at least not wiped off the map, as Poland had been in the eighteenth century. She was not even actually demoted to a second-rate position in the world. She remained, as she was shortly to prove, a first-rate power. In the long series of settlements under our modern western state-system, which goes back to the Italian wars of the fifteenth century, Versailles looks nowadays like neither the worst nor the best, but like a typical compromise peace.

It was, however, too much for the American people, who were not used to the harsh needs of international compromise. But it is an oversimplification to argue that this was solely a matter of American idealism turning away in disgust from a settlement that was all too spotted with unpleasant realities. The final American refusal to ratify the Treaty of Versailles, like all great collective decisions, was the result of many forces. Politics certainly played an important part, for the Republicans had won control of both the Senate and the House of Representatives in the congressional elections of November, 1918. The President of course was still Wilson, a Democrat, and Wilson made no concessions to the Republicans either by taking a bipartisan delegation of Democrats and Republicans to Paris with him or by accepting modifications in the treaty which would have satisfied some of his Republican opponents. The Senate thereupon refused to ratify the treaty.

Those who like to conjecture about what history might have been can have a field day here: *if* Wilson had taken a few influential Republicans with him to Paris, *if* he had not gone to Paris at all but had stayed at home as tradition bade and had sent a bipartisan delegation of Democrats and Republicans to Paris, *if* he had been willing to compromise by accepting early and with

good grace reservations proposed by Republican senators favorable to a League; *if*, in short, he had not been Woodrow Wilson, the United States might have entered the League and signed the treaty. As it was, peace was finally made with Germany by a joint resolution of Congress, which was signed by President Harding in July, 1921.

It is, however, extremely unlikely that even a much more pliable and diplomatic American president than Wilson could have secured from the Senate ratification of another treaty. This was the project of a defensive alliance among France, Britain, and the United States into which Wilson had been pushed as the penalty for refusing to accept French proposals for a separate Rhineland republic and for annexation of the Saar. With the United States out, Britain refused a mere dual alliance with France against a German attack. France, still seeking to bolster her security, patched up a series of alliances with the new nations to the east and south of Germany—Poland, and the "Little Entente" of Yugoslavia, Czechoslovakia, and Rumania.

The peace thus left France with an uneasy hegemony in Europe, a hegemony dependent on the continued disarmament and economic weakening of Germany, on the continued isolation of Russia, and on the uncertain support of her new allies. Moreover, France had been disastrously weakened by the human and material losses of the war, and her position of leadership, though it alarmed the British with their long memories of French rivalry in the past, was an unreal thing. In reality, Germany was the strongest nation in Europe, and the Great War had checked, but not halted, her bid to dominate the Continent and indeed the world. The next German attempt was to draw both Britain and America back from the isolation into which they attempted to withdraw after the collapse of the system planned at Paris in 1919.

CHAPTER XXV

Reading Suggestions
on the First World War

The Background: General Accounts

A. J. P. Taylor, *The Struggle for Mastery in Europe, 1848-1918* (Oxford: The Clarendon Press, 1954). A crisp and provocative survey.

S. B. Fay, *The Origins of the World War*, 2nd ed. (New York: The Macmillan Company, 1932). A fully documented account by an American scholar; somewhat sympathetic to Germany.

B. E. Schmitt, *The Coming of the War, 1914*, 2 vols. (New York: Charles Scribner's Sons, 1930). Another well-documented scholarly account; somewhat sympathetic to Britain.

H. E. Barnes, *The Genesis of the World War: An Introduction to the Problem of War Guilt* (New York: Alfred A. Knopf, Inc., 1926). An extreme statement of the "revisionist" position on war guilt.

M. von Montgelas, *The Case for the Central Powers, An Impeachment of the Versailles Verdict* (New York: Alfred A. Knopf, Inc., 1925). Representative of the German "revisionist" school.

L. Albertini, *The Origins of the War of 1914*, 2 vols. (New York: Oxford University Press, 1952-1953). By an Italian scholar; stresses the role of Italy.

The Background: Special Studies

W. L. Langer, *European Alliances and Alignments, 1871-1890*, 2nd ed. (New York: Alfred A. Knopf, Inc., 1950). A detailed scholarly survey, favorable to Bismarckian diplomacy.

W. L. Langer, *The Diplomacy of Imperialism, 1890-1902*, 2nd ed. (New York: Alfred A. Knopf, Inc., 1951). Includes much material pertaining to the shifting alliances of the European powers.

E. M. Carroll, *French Public Opinion and Foreign Affairs, 1870-1914* (New York: The Century Co., 1931) and *Germany and the Great Powers, 1866-1914: A Study in Public Opinion and Foreign Policy* (New York: Prentice-Hall, Inc., 1938). Scholarly studies in a significant and difficult area of research.

R. J. S. Hoffman, *Great Britain and the German Trade Rivalry, 1875-1914* (Philadelphia: University of Pennsylvania Press, 1933). A helpful monograph.

E. L. Woodward, *Great Britain and the German Navy* (Oxford: The Clarendon Press, 1935); A. J. Marder, *The Anatomy of British Sea Power* (New York: Alfred A. Knopf, Inc., 1940); and B. Brodie, *Sea Power in the Machine Age* (Princeton: Princeton University Press, 1943). Three useful studies of the important question of naval power.

E. N. Anderson, *The First Moroccan Crisis, 1904-1906* (Chicago: University of Chicago Press, 1930) and I. C. Barlow, *The Agadir Crisis* (Chapel Hill: University of North Carolina Press, 1940). Two useful monographs on the issue of Morocco in pre-war diplomacy.

E. M. Earle, *Turkey, The Great Powers, and the Bagdad Railway* (New York: The Macmillan Company, 1923). Scholarly account of another major issue of pre-war diplomacy.

A. F. Pribram, *Austrian Foreign Policy, 1908-1918* (London: G. Allen and Unwin, 1923). Balanced statement from the Austrian standpoint.

P. Renouvin, *The Immediate Origins of the War* (New Haven: Yale University Press, 1928). Scholarly account from the French point of view.

G. P. Gooch and H. Temperley, eds., *British Documents on the Origins of the War, 1898-1914,* 12 vols. (London: His Majesty's Stationery Office, 1926-1938). Representative of the great collections of diplomatic documents published by the governments of the major belligerents after World War I.

Outbreak of the World War: German Documents Collected by Karl Kautsky (New York: Oxford University Press, 1924) and *German Diplomatic Documents, 1871-1914,* 4 vols. (London: Methuen & Co., 1928-1931). English translations of some of the vast number of German diplomatic documents.

The Background of the War: American Policy

T. A. Bailey, *A Diplomatic History of the American People,* 4th ed. (New York: Appleton-Century-Crofts, 1950) and S. F. Bemis, *A Diplomatic History of the United States,* 3rd ed. (New York: Henry Holt & Co., 1950). Two standard surveys.

W. Millis, *The Road to War: America, 1914-1917* (Boston: Houghton Mifflin Company, 1935). Readable journalistic account, highly critical of Wilson's policy.

C. C. Tansill, *America Goes to War* (Boston: Little, Brown & Co., 1938). Scholarly treatment, also critical of Wilson's policy.

C. Seymour, *American Diplomacy during the World War,* 2nd ed. (Baltimore: Johns Hopkins University Press, 1942). Sympathetic toward Wilson's policy.

The War

W. L. S. Churchill, *The World Crisis,* 6 vols. (New York: Charles Scribner's Sons, 1923-1931). Detailed survey by the famous British statesman.

C. R. M. Cruttwell, *History of the Great War* (Oxford: The Clarendon Press, 1934). Perhaps the best one-volume history.

Note: There are many detailed military histories of World War I; the general reader, however, will probably find the works listed below under Historical Fiction the best introduction to the subject of the fighting fronts. The problems that arose on the home front have been the subject of a large number of special studies published under the auspices of the Carnegie Endowment for International Peace, with the general title, "The Economic and Social History of the World War," edited by J. T. Shotwell. The list of these studies is very long; some idea of their scope may be had by consulting *Economic and Social History of the World War: Outline of Plan, European Series* (Washington, D.C.: Carnegie Endowment for International Peace, 1924). Another useful collection of special studies has been published by the Hoover Library of War, Revolution, and Peace at Stanford University.

The Peace

H. W. V. Temperley, *A History of the Peace Conference of Paris,* 6 vols. (London: H. Frowde, Hodder and Stoughton, 1920-1924). The standard detailed account; by a British scholar.

H. G. Nicolson, *Peacemaking, 1919* (London: Constable & Co., 1933). A good shorter account; by a British expert on diplomacy.

P. Birdsall, *Versailles Twenty Years After* (New York: Reynal and Hitchcock, 1941). Balanced reappraisal by an American scholar.

T. A. Bailey, *Wilson and the Peacemakers* (New York: The Macmillan Company, 1947). Sound study of America's role.

J. M. Keynes, *The Economic Consequences of the Peace* (New York: Harcourt, Brace & Co., 1920) and E. Mantoux, *The Carthaginian Peace; or, the Economic Consequences of Mr. Keynes* (New York: Charles Scribner's Sons, 1952). Respectively, the most famous attack on the Versailles settlement and a thoughtful study of the results of that attack.

Historical Fiction

E. Childers, *The Riddle of the Sands* (London: T. Nelson, 1913) and H. H. Munro ("Saki"), *When William Came* (New York: John Lane, 1914). Two unusual novels, written before the outbreak of the war and predicting what it might be like. Childers' is a story of intrigue and adventure, and "Saki's" is a forecast of the German occupation of Britain.

J. Romains, *Verdun* (New York: Alfred A. Knopf, Inc., 1939). Excellent and balanced novel about French troops on the western front, 1914-1916; its history and insights are unusually sound.

H. Barbusse, *Under Fire* (New York: E. P. Dutton and Co., 1917) and E. M. Remarque, *All Quiet on the Western Front* (Boston: Little, Brown & Co., 1929). Two famous novels, by a Frenchman and a German, respectively; reflect the horror aroused in intellectuals by trench warfare.

J. Dos Passos, *Three Soldiers* (New York: Modern Library, 1941) and E. Hemingway, *A Farewell to Arms* (many editions). Two American novels about the war, indicative of the post-war disillusionment of the "lost generation."

e. e. cummings, *The Enormous Room* (New York: Modern Library, 1941) and A. Zweig, *The Case of Sergeant Grischa* (New York: Viking Press, 1928). Novels about prisoners of war and the eastern front, respectively.

C. S. Forester, *The General* (Boston: Little, Brown & Co., 1947). Astringent novel about the "brass" in World War I.

J. Buchan, *Greenmantle* (London: T. Nelson, no date). A novel of espionage that indicates that the war contained its ingredient of high adventure in addition to blood and guts.

What Price Glory, in M. Anderson and L. Stallings, *Three American Plays* (New York: Harcourt, Brace & Co., 1926). A famous play showing that the war had its rowdy side.

Communist

Russia

1917-1941

CHAPTER XXVI

I: Introduction

ON JUNE 22, 1941, Adolf Hitler's German armies poured over the frontier of his Russian ally and began a rapid advance toward Moscow, toward the major Russian industrial centers, and toward the most productive Russian agricultural centers. The Russia Hitler invaded was no longer the Russia into which Napoleon had sent the *grande armée* a hundred and twenty-nine years before or the Russia whose millions of embattled soldiers had perished in the First World War against the Germany of William II and his Habsburg allies. It was no longer the Russia of the tsars. Since 1917 it had been the Russia of the Bolsheviks. Yet it was still Russia.

Along with the tsars, the nobility and the bourgeoisie had gone down to ruin after the communist revolution of 1917, and the clergy as a class had suffered almost as much. A small, tightly knit, conspiratorial group of fanatical Marxist revolutionaries had seized power and for the next twenty-four years had striven to make Russia over. Drawn mostly from the peculiarly Russian class of the intelligentsia, and declaring themselves to be the representatives of the industrial proletariat, the Bolsheviks had worked gigantic changes, especially in the years after 1928. Industry, proceeding under forced draft, had expanded enormously, and the proportion of the population employed in industry had risen to almost 50 per cent; the proportion engaged in agriculture had fallen correspondingly.

The peasant had been a victim of serfdom until 1861, had been subject to the initiative-destroying domination of the commune until 1906, and had then been encouraged by Stolypin to make himself a free farmer (see Chapter XXII). Now, under the Bolsheviks, he found himself subjected to new and grievous pressure. Agriculture had been collectivized and the age-old longing of the peasant for private property in land had been ruthlessly suppressed.

These staggering social and economic changes had not been accomplished without internal friction. Inside the government, personal rivalries, plots, counter-plots, fake plots, and charges of plots had produced repeated purges extending down through the ranks of the population. The choking conspiratorial atmosphere which the Bolshevik rulers had breathed during their long years of underground preparation for a seizure of power now enveloped the citadels of power. Personal rivalries for domination of the machinery of the state were cloaked beneath the Byzantine theological language of doctrinal controversy over fine points in the sacred writings of Marx and Lenin. Yet the controversies had immediate significance in the formulation and choice of government policies. The Communist party, the secret police, and the army had become the interlocking agencies which ran the state at the bidding of the dictator. The dictator himself, Stalin, had made his own career possible chiefly through the ruthless use of his position as Secretary of the Communist party.

The foreign policy of the communist state had passed through a brief period in which ideological considerations had seemed occasionally to outweigh national interest in the old sense. It had then returned to the pursuit of traditional Russian ends, coupled with the objective of promoting eventual world-revolution. But in furthering Russian aims abroad the Bolshevik leaders were now in possession of an instrument more flexible than any the tsars had ever commanded. This was the Communist International, or Comintern, a federation of the Communist parties in the individual countries of the world. These parties could often be used as promoters of purely Russian ends rather than strictly communist ends.

Sometimes Russian failure to mask the Russian national aims rather than the revolutionary international aims of a given policy caused trouble inside a given Communist party. On the whole, however, the glitter of Russian Bolshevik achievement at home gave Moscow the status of a world-capital of revolution, whose aims and policies must not be questioned, but merely followed subserviently by communists in countries where the Revolution had not yet been brought to power. With the shifting stresses and strains of international politics during the late 1920's and 1930's, the "line" of the Comintern shifted often and bewilderingly, but always in accordance with the aims of the Soviet foreign office. Usually the majority of communists elsewhere in the world fell meekly into position, and loudly proclaimed when necessary the opposite of what they had proclaimed the day before.

Yet the changes during the first twenty-four years of the Soviet period, vast though they were, could not conceal the continuities between the new Russian system and the old. The dictator of 1941, the revered leader of his people, for whom his followers made increasingly grandiose claims, was not unlike the tsar of 1917 in his assumption of autocratic power. The individual Russian

CHAPTER XXVI

of 1941, despite his sufferings under the new system, had remained deeply patriotic, ready to sacrifice himself for his country, even under a government he hated. The peasant of 1941 still yearned hopelessly for his land; the worker struggled for economic advancement and social security. Bureaucrats, managers, intellectuals, and artists, all in the service of the state, formed in 1941 a new élite which replaced but did not differ greatly from the old privileged class. A police force superior in efficiency to those of Ivan the Terrible, Peter the Great, and Nicholas I, but not different in kind, in 1941 exercised thought control over all citizens, and terrorized even prominent members of the system itself.

More and more, Stalinist communism had taken on the trappings of a religion, with its sacred books, its heresies, its places of pilgrimage, its doctrinal quarrels. Thus the old Russian orthodoxy had by 1941 not been replaced but rather modified. Russian nationalism, too, asserted itself ever more insistently and crudely, until finally, in the war that Hitler began, the government encouraged the cult of traditional heroes of earlier times, and even glorified Ivan the Terrible himself, no longer a symbol of "feudal" domination but a symbol of the Russian national spirit. The early revolutionary departures from accepted standards in Russian marriage, family life, and education, had by 1941 all been abandoned in favor of a return to conventional bourgeois behavior. The first twenty-four years of Soviet domination, 1917-1941, are the subject of this chapter, which will trace in some detail the vast changes here summarized and will attempt to demonstrate the survival of the old Russia beneath the veneer of the new.

II: The Russian Revolution of 1917

The Immediate Background

Ridden by domestic crisis though Russia was in 1914 (see Chapter XXII), the country greeted the outbreak of World War I with demonstrations of national patriotism. The Duma supported the war, and did yeoman service in organizing Red Cross activities. The left-wing parties—the radical agrarian SRs (Social Revolutionaries) and the Marxist SDs (Social Democrats)—though they abstained from voting war credits, offered to assist the national defense. By 1917 more than 15,000,000 Russians had been drafted into the armies. Losses in battle were staggering from the first; the Russians suffered more than 3,800,000 casualties during the first year of war. On the home front, criticism was aroused by the inadequate handling of the supply of munitions, and by mid-1915 the Center and Left groups in the Duma were urging moderate reforms, such as the end of discrimination against minority nationalities and an increase in the powers of the zemstvos, the local assemblies. The Empress Alexandra took the lead in opposing all such measures, and kept urging her weak husband, Tsar Nicholas II, to act more autocratically. When Nicholas took personal command of the armies in the field and prorogued the Duma (autumn, 1915), she became virtually supreme at home. The supremacy of the Empress meant also the supremacy of her favorite, the unscrupulous adventurer Rasputin.

With the Empress and Rasputin in control, a gang of shady adventurers, blackmailers, and profiteers bought and sold offices, speculated in military supplies, put in their own puppets as ministers, and created a series of shocking scandals. Confusion, strikes, and defeatism mounted at home during 1916, while the armies slowly bled to death at the front. Even the conservatives had begun to denounce Rasputin publicly, and in December, 1916, he was poisoned, shot several times, and ultimately drowned, all in one nightmare evening, by a group of conspirators closely related to the imperial family. Despite repeated warnings from moderates in the Duma that the government itself was preparing a revolution by its failure to create a responsible ministry and to clean up the mess, the Tsar remained apathetic. Relatives of the imperial family and members of the Duma began independently to plot for his abdication. In the early months of 1917 all conditions favored a revolution, but the revolutionaries were not prepared.

The March Revolution

On March 8, strikes and bread-riots broke out in the capital, and four days later Romanov rule, which had governed Russia since 1613, was doomed. Yet this revolution of March, 1917, has been well called leaderless, spontaneous, and anonymous. SRs and both Bolshevik and Menshevik factions of SDs (see above, p. 322) were genuinely surprised at what happened. Indeed, the Bolshevik leaders were either abroad in exile, or under arrest in Siberia. The determining factor in the overthrow of the Tsar was the disloyalty of the garrison of Petrograd (the new Russian name given to St. Petersburg during the war). Inefficiency had led to a food shortage in the capital, though actual starvation had not set

in. When the Tsar ordered troops to fire on striking workers, only a few obeyed, and on March 12, in revulsion against the order, the troops joined the strikers, broke into the arsenals, and began to hunt the police, who quickly disappeared from the scene. The Duma lagged behind the revolting troops and workers in estimating the situation, and the Tsar lagged behind the Duma. By March 14, when the Tsar had finally decided to appoint a responsible ministry, it was too late; the cabinet had vanished. Troops ordered to put down the revolt simply melted away and joined the rebels.

A Soviet of workers and soldiers, modeled on the 1905 Soviet of workers (see above, p. 325), but now including soldiers as well, was formed by leftists released from prison by the enthusiastic mobs. The Soviet proceeded to organize a workers' militia, to create a food-supply commission, and to issue newspapers. Its fifteen-man executive committee became the policy-makers of the revolution. The Soviet located its headquarters across the hall from the Duma, which had not dissolved as ordered, but remained in session. The Marxists among the Soviet leaders still believed in the necessity of a preliminary bourgeois revolution, and did not yet regard the Soviet itself as an organ of power. They favored the creation of a provisional government, in which they would not participate, but to which they would offer limited support. They put themselves at the disposition of the Duma, and asked for its leadership. Thus the Duma, a limited assembly elected by a restricted franchise, was literally forced by the Soviet into the position of leading the revolution.

Negotiations between the Soviet and a Duma committee brought a provisional government into existence. Despite the widely differing social and economic aims of Soviet and Duma, both agreed to grant political liberties immediately and to sum-

Russia in revolution. Workers and soldiers invade the Duma.

mon a constituent assembly, which was to establish the future form of government by giving Russia a constitution. The provisional government was composed mainly of Kadets (Constitutional Democrats) and other moderates and was headed by the liberal Prince Lvov, chairman of the union of *zemstvos* and of the Red Cross. It included also one radical member of the Soviet, Alexander Kerensky, Minister of Justice, a clever labor lawyer and member of the Duma also, who accepted office despite the understanding that members of the Soviet would not do so.

After some abortive efforts to save the dynasty in the person of the Tsar's brother, Nicholas finally abdicated, and his brother refused the throne because of the popular hatred of the family. Under pressure from the Soviet, the provisional government arrested Nicholas II and the Empress on March 20. The Duma had thus accepted the mandate given it by the revolutionaries. Had it accepted instead its dismissal at the hands of the Tsar and gone home, it seems probable that the monarchy would have been preserved at the cost of some liberal concessions. But moderate reformers were now in power, and Russia embarked

on the troubled months between March and October, 1917.

The Provisional Government

The provisional government is usually regarded as having been a total failure. Measured by the final results, such a view is perhaps justified. But the judgment of history must take into consideration the dreadful difficulties that faced the provisional government. These were not only immediate and specific, but general and underlying. Russian moderates had had no experience of authority. They were separated by a great cultural gulf from the lower classes. Their opportunity to rule now came to them in the midst of a fearful war, which they felt they had to pursue while reconstructing and democratizing the enormous and unwieldy Russian Empire.

Moreover, the Soviet possessed many of the instruments of power, yet refused to accept any responsibility. Workers and soldiers in the capital supported the Soviet, while in the provinces the new governors appointed by the provisional government had no weapon except persuasion to employ against the local peasant-elected soviets, which multiplied rapidly. Present-day critics of the provisional government often denounce its failure to suppress its revolutionary opponents, but they overlook the fact that the provisional government did not possess the tools of suppression. The Petrograd garrison, for instance, by agreement with the Soviet, could not be removed or disarmed. The support given by the Soviet to the provisional government has been compared to the kind of support that is given by a hangman's noose.

The two great specific issues facing the provisional government were agrarian discontent and the continuation of the war. The peasants wanted land, and they wanted it immediately. The provisional government, however, made up as it was of responsible liberals, believed in acting with deliberation and according to law. It could not countenance irregular or violent actions, and refused to sanction peasant seizure of land, despite increasing disorder in the countryside. Instead, it appointed a commission to collect material on which future agrarian legislation was to be based—an act totally inadequate to the emergency.

As to the war, the members of the government felt in honor bound to their allies not to make a separate peace. Moreover, most of them still unrealistically hoped that Russia might win, and gain the territories which the Allies had promised. But the Soviet subverted discipline in the armies at the front by issuing a "declaration of the rights of soldiers," which virtually put an end to the authority of officers over enlisted men. Although the Soviet made it as hard as possible for the government to pursue the war, it did not sponsor a separate peace. Even the Bolshevik members of the Soviet, who now began to return from exile, supported only Russian participation in general peace negotiations, which they hoped would begin immediately.

Lenin and Bolshevism

The most important of the returning Bolshevik exiles was Lenin. His real name was Vladimir Ilyich Ulianov, but in his writings he used the pen-name Lenin, to which he sometimes prefixed the initial N., a Russian abbreviation for "nobody," in order to tell his readers that he was using a pseudonym. This "N." has given rise to the mistaken but still widely held idea that Lenin's first name was Nikolai (Nicholas). Son of a provincial official and intellectual, Lenin became a revolutionary in the late 1880's and, as we have already seen (p. 322), took a chief role in the early years of the SDs as the leader of the party's Bolshevik wing. He had returned to Russia from abroad for the Revolution of 1905, but he left Russia once more in 1908, and stayed abroad until 1917.

When the news of the March Revolution reached Lenin in Switzerland, he made desperate efforts to get back home. Finally, through the Swiss Social Democrats, he made contact with the German general staff, which felt that it would be a good investment to see that Lenin reached Russia, where he might disrupt the Russian war effort against Germany. Thus it was that the German military transported Lenin across Germany from Switzerland to the Baltic in the famous sealed railroad car. He arrived at the Finland Station in Petrograd on April 16, 1917, a little more than a month after the March Revolution.

Most Russian Social Democrats had long regarded a bourgeois parliamentary republic as a necessary preliminary to an eventual socialist revolution and socialist society. For this reason they were prepared to help in transforming Russia into a capitalist society, though not without grave doubts that the bourgeois capitalists might be as bad as the tsar and the landlords, or that the masses might be "deluded" into accepting the new system. They favored the creation of a democratic republic, at the same time believing that complete political freedom was absolutely essential for their own future rise to power. Despite the Marxist emphasis upon the industrial laboring class as the only proper vehicle for revolution, Lenin early realized that in Russia, where the "proletariat" embraced only about 1 per cent of the population, the SDs must seek other allies. At the time of the Revolution of 1905 he began to preach the need for limited alliances for tactical purposes between the Bolsheviks and the SRs, who commanded the support of the peasantry. When the alliance had served its purpose, the SDs were to turn on their allies and destroy them. Then would come the socialist triumph.

Instead of a preliminary bourgeois democratic republic, Lenin called in 1905 and later for an immediate "revolutionary-democratic dictatorship of the proletariat and the peasantry," a concept that seems to us self-contradictory, and is surely vague. Lenin's view, however, was not adopted by most Bolsheviks. Together with the Mensheviks they continued to believe and urge that a bourgeois revolution and a parliamentary democracy were necessary first steps.

Because Lenin did not trust the masses to make a revolution (by themselves, he felt, they were capable only of "trade-union consciousness"), he favored a dictatorship of the Bolshevik party over the working class. Because he did not trust the rank and file of Bolshevik party workers, he favored a dictatorship of a small élite over the Bolshevik party. And in the end, because he really trusted nobody's views but his own, he favored, though never explicitly, his own dictatorship over this élite. Another future Russian leader, the brilliant intellectual Leon Trotsky, early warned that in Lenin's views one-man dictatorship was implicit.

Trotsky, for his part, voiced an opinion of

Lenin.

his own, held by neither Mensheviks nor Bolsheviks. The bourgeoisie in Russia, he argued, was so weak that the working class could telescope the bourgeois and socialist revolutions into one continuous movement. After the proletariat had helped the bourgeoisie achieve its revolution, he felt that the workers could move immediately to power. They could nationalize industry and collectivize agriculture, and, although foreign intervention and civil war were doubtless to be expected, the Russian proletariat would soon be joined by the proletariats of other countries, which would make their own revolutions. Except for this last point, Trotsky's analysis accurately forecast the course of events. Between 1905 and 1917, Lenin himself accepted Trotsky's view from time to time, but warned that it endangered political democracy.

COMMUNIST RUSSIA

Thus each of the leaders propounded views that the other felt would lead to dictatorship, and each felt that his own views were the more democratic. In fact, each was amply justified in warning the other. In 1917, Trotsky was to accept Lenin's party machine with its dictatorial implications, and Lenin was to accept Trotsky's belief that the proletariat could win power immediately, and, as a minority, exercise dictatorial power.

Trotsky.

Lenin had been deeply depressed by the failure of 1905, and by the threat posed by Stolypin's agrarian reforms. He almost despaired when the socialist parties of Europe went along with their governments in 1914 and supported the war. To him this meant the end of the second socialist International, for the Social Democrats had failed to recognize the war as the "bourgeois-imperialist" venture that it appeared to Lenin to be. He preached defeatism as the only possible view for a Russian SD to follow.

Lenin's greatest talent was not as an original thinker but as a skillful tactician.

He often seemed able to judge with accuracy just what was politically possible in a given situation, and he was not afraid to gamble. Thus, even before he returned to Russia in April, 1917, he had assessed some of the difficulties facing the provisional government, and had determined that the masses could take over. Immediately upon his arrival, he hailed the world-wide revolution, proclaiming that the end of imperialism, "the last stage of capitalism," was at hand. Ignoring the positions previously taken by Bolsheviks and Mensheviks alike, he demanded now that all power immediately be given to the soviets. His speeches sounded to the SDs themselves like the ravings of a madman.

Almost nobody but Lenin felt that the loosely organized soviets could govern the country, or that the war would bring down the capitalist world in chaos. In April, 1917, Lenin called not only for the abandonment of the provisional government and the establishment of a republic of soviets but for the confiscation of estates, the nationalization of land, and the abolition of the army, of government officials, and of the police. These demands fitted the mood of the people far better than the cautious and well-meant efforts of the provisional government to bring about reform by legal means. Dogmatic, furiously impatient of compromise, entirely convinced that he alone had the truth, Lenin galvanized the Bolsheviks into a truly revolutionary group waiting only the moment to seize power.

The Coming of the November Revolution

The months from March to November, 1917, before the Bolsheviks came to power, can be divided into a period between March and July, during which revolution deepened, a feeble reaction from July

474

to September, and a new quickening of the revolutionary current from September to the final uprising in November. In the first period, the government faced a crisis, because the Kadet ministers wished to maintain the Russian war aim of annexing the Straits, while the Soviet wanted a peace "without annexations or indemnities." Out of the crisis Kerensky, the war minister, emerged as the dominant leader. He failed to realize that it was no longer possible to restore the morale of the armies, which were dissolving under the impact of Bolshevik propaganda. A new offensive ordered on July 1 collapsed, as soldiers refused to obey orders, deserted their units, and rushed home to their native villages, eager to seize the land. Ukrainian separatism also plagued the officials of the government. The soviets became gradually more and more Bolshevik, as Lenin and Trotsky worked tirelessly at recruitment and organization. Although the June congress of soviets in Petrograd was less than 10 per cent Bolshevik in make-up, the Bolshevik slogans of peace, bread, and freedom won overwhelming support.

Yet an armed outbreak by troops, who had accepted the Bolshevik slogans, found the Petrograd Soviet unwilling and unable to assume power. While the mob roared outside, the Soviet voted to discuss the matter two weeks later and meanwhile to keep the provisional government in power. A regiment loyal to the Soviet protected it against the working class. The government declared that Lenin was a German agent, and, as his supporters wavered, raided the newspaper offices of *Pravda* ("Truth," the Bolshevik paper); Lenin had to go into hiding to avoid arrest. This episode of mid-July is what is known among Bolsheviks as "playing at insurrection." Though shots had been exchanged and overt action had been embarked upon, there had been no revolutionary follow-through. Power had not been seized, probably because Lenin felt that the Bolsheviks did not have enough support in the provinces.

Now Kerensky became premier. The government hardened its attitude toward the Ukrainians, but could not come to a popular decision on either land or peace. General Kornilov, chosen by Kerensky as the new commander-in-chief of the armies, quickly became the white hope of all conservative groups, and in August plotted a *coup*, intended to disperse the Soviet. His attitude toward the provisional government was uncertain, but, had he succeeded, he would probably have demanded a purge of its more radical elements. The plot, however, was a failure, because railroad and telegraph workers sabotaged Kornilov's movements, and because his troops simply would not obey him. The Bolsheviks, adopting the slogan "We will fight against Kornilov, but will not support Kerensky," threw themselves into preparations for the defense of Petrograd, which proved to be unnecessary. By September 14, Kornilov had been arrested, and the affair ended without bloodshed. The threat from the Right helped the Bolsheviks greatly, and sentiment in the Petrograd and Moscow soviets now for the first time became predominantly Bolshevik.

The Kornilov affair turned the army mutiny into a widespread revolt. Instances of violence multiplied. As peasants refused to pay rent, pastured their animals on the landlords' pasture land, and often burned the manor house and killed its owner, so the soldiers moved from disobedience to the murder of their officers. Orderly and legal reform had attracted nobody. The peasants could not be convinced that the nobility owned less than a quarter as much land as the peasants, and that rash action only retarded progress. As disorder mounted in the countryside, the Bolsheviks tightened their hold over the soviets in the cities.

Lenin returned to Petrograd on October

20; soon thereafter the Bolsheviks got control over a Military Revolutionary Committee, originally chosen to help defend Petrograd against the advancing Germans, and now transformed, under the guidance of Trotsky, into a general staff for the revolution. It sent commissars to the units in the capital, replacing officers of the provisional government. It virtually declared war on the government by urging the soldiers to "defend revolutionary order" against the "counter-revolution of the government," and by declaring that all orders, to be valid, had to be signed by its authorities. Beginning on November 4, huge demonstrations and mass meetings were addressed by Trotsky, and on November 7 the insurrection broke out.

In Petrograd, the revolution had been well prepared and proceeded with little bloodshed. Kerensky escaped in a car of the American Embassy. The Military Revolutionary Committee, as an organ of the Petrograd Soviet, simply took over. The Bolsheviks called a second congress of soviets, and when the Mensheviks and right-wing SRs walked out, Trotsky called them the refuse that would be swept into the garbage-can of history. Co-operating with the left-wing SRs and adopting their land program, Lenin abolished all property rights of landlords and transferred the land thus affected to local land committees and soviets of peasant deputies. Though Lenin did not in the least approve of the system of individual small holdings which this decree put into effect, he recognized the psychological advantage which the adoption of the SR program would gain him. He also urged an immediate peace without annexations or indemnities, and appealed to the workers of Germany, France, and England to support him in this demand. Finally, a new cabinet, called a Council of People's Commissars, was chosen, with Lenin as President, and Trotsky as Foreign Commissar.

As Commissar of Nationalities the Bolsheviks installed a younger man, a Georgian, named Joseph Stalin, who had been a successful organizer of bank robberies in the days when the party treasury was filled in this way, but whose role had otherwise been relatively obscure. Under Lenin's coaching, Stalin had also become the party authority on minority questions and had published a pamphlet on the subject in

CHAPTER XXVI

1913. Lenin had studied and disapproved of the Austrian Social Democrats' writings on the subject (see above, p. 308), which favored only cultural autonomy for the nationalities. He looked forward instead to the disruption of the Russian Empire, and the granting to each nationality of the right to secede, govern its own territory, and enjoy its own political autonomy. Ironically enough, of course, it was the nationalities of the Habsburg Empire that after 1918 obtained the right to secede; the nationalities of the Russian Empire eventually had applied to them by Stalin himself the Austrian doctrine of cultural autonomy, subject to political domination by the central government.

Outside Petrograd, the revolution moved more slowly. In Moscow there was a week of street-fighting between Bolshevik Reds and Whites, as anti-Bolshevik forces were already known. Elsewhere, in factory towns, the procedure was usually fast, in non-industrial centers usually slower. Most of Siberia and of Central Asia came over, but Tiflis, the capital of Georgia, went Men-shevik and passed resolutions calling for a constituent assembly and the continuation of the war. The reason for the rapid and smooth success of the Bolsheviks was that the provincial garrisons opposed the war and willingly allied themselves with the workers. Local Military Revolutionary Committees were created in most places and held elections for new local soviets. Naturally there was much confusion at first, but surprisingly little resistance to the consolidation of the authority of the new regime. The chief centers of opposition were Mogilev, west of Moscow, where the army general staff was located; Kiev, in the western Ukraine, where the Ukrainian separatists had set up a republic of their own; and the Cossack regions of the Don and elsewhere. Gradually the town of Rostov-on-Don, near the Sea of Azov, became the main center of resistance, as Kornilov and other generals, together with a number of the leading politicians of the Duma, made their way there.

This initial triumph of the revolution did not mean that the population of Russia had

Russian troops surrendering to the Germans during World War I.

been converted to Bolshevism. By cleverly sensing the mood of the people, Lenin had opportunistically given the Bolsheviks a set of slogans around which the people could rally, although some of the slogans did not at all correspond with the true Bolshevik views. As we shall shortly see, the Russian people was in fact strongly anti-Bolshevik. But the Bolsheviks had triumphed, and the democratic hopes for freedom of the press and other freedoms were now doomed to disappointment.

Deprived of competent civil servants, the new regime worried along through an atmosphere of continued crisis. Late in November, 1917, an agreement was reached with the Left-Wing SRs, three of whom entered the government, and peace negotiations were begun with the Germans. The revolution proper was over. Lenin was in power. His program is well summarized as follows:

> The immediate objective was to establish a republic of soviets based on the proletariat and the poor sections of the peasantry, and to abolish the police, the army, and the bureaucracy. In the economic field, Leninist doctrine demanded the replacement of the existing managerial groups with a centralized system of control by the industrial workers, together with a sharp reduction of inequalities in pay and the eventual introduction of full equality. In agriculture, Lenin proposed the introduction of cooperative farming only on the large landed estates, while the disposal of the rest of the land was left up to the local population. At the same time, he wanted to avoid, if possible, the transformation of Russia into a land of small peasant proprietors. In the international field, he expected that a successful revolution in Russia would set afire the socialist revolution in Europe, with the result that the Western proletariat would come to the aid of the hard-pressed workers of Russia. Nearly every one of these hopes and expectations was disappointed.*

---

* Barrington Moore, Jr., *Soviet Politics* (Cambridge, Mass., 1950), 57-58.

The Constituent Assembly

It is of great interest to record that the Bolsheviks now permitted elections for a constituent assembly. Lenin had no use for this sort of democratically chosen parliament, which he considered "inferior" to the soviet. Yet, probably because he had so long taunted the provisional government with delaying the elections, he seems to have felt compelled to hold them. The Russians for the first and last time in their history had a completely free election, under universal suffrage. Lenin himself accepted as accurate figures showing that the Bolsheviks polled about one-quarter of the vote. The other socialist parties, chiefly the SRs, polled 62 per cent. As was to be expected, the Bolshevik vote was heaviest in the cities, especially Moscow and Petrograd, while the SR vote was largely rural.

Disregarding the majority cast for his opponents, Lenin maintained that "the most advanced" elements had voted for him. It was of course only his opinion that made those who had voted Bolshevik more "advanced" than those who had voted SR or Kadet. He allowed the constituent assembly to meet only once, on January 18, 1918. Lenin dissolved it the next day by decree, and sent guards with rifles to prevent its ever meeting again. The anti-Bolshevik majority was naturally deeply indignant at this pure act of force against the popular will, but there was no public outburst, and the delegates disbanded. In part, this was because the Bolsheviks had already taken action on the things that interested the people most—peace and land—and in part because of the lack of a democratic parliamentary tradition among the masses of the Russian people.

In spite of the many years of agitation by intellectuals and liberals for just such a popular assembly, Russia did not have the large middle class, the widespread literacy, the tradition of debate, and the respect for the rights of the individual which seem to be an essential part of constitutionalism. Yet it is surely extreme to decide that there was no chance for constitutional government in Russia in 1917-1918. Was the constituent assembly "an attempt to transplant an alien concept of government to a soil where it could never flourish"? Or was it "a noble experiment incorporating a sound principle but doomed by the crisis into which it was born"? The fact that Lenin had the rifles to prevent the constituent assembly from fulfilling the function which the popular will had assigned to it does not answer the question either way.

III: War Communism and NEP, 1917-1928

War Communism

The first period of Soviet history, which runs from the end of 1917 to the end of 1920, is usually called the period of "war communism," or "military communism." The term itself of course implies that the main features of the period were determined by military events. Civil war raged, and foreign powers intervened on Russia soil. But the term is also somewhat misleading. This was a period of militant as well as military communism, symbolized early in 1918 by the change of the party's name from Bolshevik to Communist. At the same time the capital was shifted from Petrograd, with its exposed location on the western fringe of Russia, to the greater security of Moscow, in the heart of the country.

Flushed with victory in Russia, the Bolsheviks firmly believed that world-revolution was about to begin, probably first in Germany, but surely spreading to Britain and even to the United States. The next three to five years were expected to see this global upheaval well under way. This view led the Bolsheviks to hasten the construction of a socialist state in Russia, and to take a casual attitude toward their international affairs, since they expected that relations with capitalist states would be very temporary. Although the actions of the Russian government during this period were later described almost apologetically as emergency measures, this is only partly true. Many of the decisions that were taken in part under the spur of military pressure were also regarded as leading to a new society.

A supreme economic council directed the gradual nationalization of industry. Sugar and petroleum came first, and then in June, 1918, a large group including mines, metallurgy, and textiles was nationalized. By 1920, all enterprises employing more than ten workers (more than five, if motor power was used) had been taken over by the state. The state organized a system of barter, which replaced the free market. Internal trade was illegal; only the government food commissary could buy and sell; money disappeared as the state took over distribution as well as production. It appropriated the banks, repudiated the tsarist foreign debt, and in effect wiped out savings. Church and State were separated by decree, and judges were removed from office and replaced by appointees of the local soviets.

The government subjected the peasantry to ever more arbitrary and severe requisitioning. It mobilized the poorer peasants against those who were better off, called *kulaks* (from the word meaning "fist" and used to apply to usurers, as if to say "hard-fisted"). By calling for a union of the hungry against the well-fed, the regime deliberately, and not for the last time, sowed class hatred in the villages and stimulated civil war in the countryside. It should be remembered that by western European standards even a Russian *kulak* was often wretchedly poor. The decree forming the first secret police, the "Cheka" (from the initials of the words meaning "extraordinary commission"), was issued in December, 1917, only a few weeks after the revolution and long before any intervention from abroad. Terror became a weapon in the civil war.

Before the Communist government could function at all, peace was necessary, as the army had virtually ceased to exist. Negotiations between the Russians and the Germans and Austro-Hungarians at Brest-Litovsk dragged on into 1918, the Russians hoping that revolution would break out in Germany, and the Germans demanding enormous territorial cessions, which they increased as the Russians delayed. Finally, on March 3, 1918, the Russians signed the Peace of Brest-Litovsk, which deprived them of the entire Ukraine, the Baltic provinces, Finland, and some Caucasian lands. It cost Russia one-third of its population, 80 per cent of its iron, and 90 per cent of its coal. Many communists resigned rather than accept the peace, and the Left SRs quit the government. The Germans overran the Ukraine and the Crimea, and installed a highly authoritarian landlord regime, against which the communists continued to agitate. The Whites, with German help, put down the Reds in Finland. It is, however, hard to see how the Bolsheviks could have avoided signing the Peace of Brest-Litovsk, despite its savagery.

Civil War

During the months following Brest-Litovsk, disorder in the countryside as a result of requisitioning and class warfare was swelled by the outbreak of open civil war. During the war a brigade had been formed inside Russia of Czechs resident in the country and of deserters from the Habsburg armies. When Russia withdrew from the war, it was decided to send the Czech brigade across Siberia by rail, and then by ship across the Pacific, through the Panama Canal, and across the Atlantic to France, to fight the Germans there. On the rail trip across Siberia, the Czechs got into a brawl with a trainload of Hungarian prisoners, and one of the Hungarians was killed. This obscure quarrel on a Siberian railway siding between members of the unfriendly races of the Habsburg Empire precipitated civil war in Russia. When the Soviet government tried to take reprisals against the Czechs, who numbered fewer than 35,000 men, the Czechs seized a number of the towns of western Siberia. The local soviets were unprepared, and the SRs were sympathetic to the Czechs. Local anti-Bolshevik armies came into being. It was under threat from one of them in July, 1918, that a local soviet decided to execute the Tsar and his entire family rather than lose possession of them. All were murdered.

By late June, 1918, the Allies had decided to intervene in Russia on behalf of the opponents of Bolshevism. The withdrawal of Russia from the war had been a heavy blow to them, and they hoped to re-create a second front against the Germans in the east. The idea of a capitalist "crusade" against Bolshevism, popularized by Soviet and pro-Soviet historians as the sole motive for the intervention, was in fact a far less impelling motive. Moreover, the Allies had been at war a long time, and their populations were war-weary. So it is perhaps not to be wondered at if they viewed with disfavor communist efforts to stimulate revolution in all the capitalist nations of the world.

Out at the eastern end of the Trans-Siberian Railroad in Vladivostok, the Czechs overthrew the local soviet in June, and by early August, 1918, British, French, Japanese, and American forces had landed. The assignment of the Americans was to occupy Vladivostok and to safeguard railroad communications in the rear of the Czechs. Of the Allies, only the Japanese had long-range territorial ambitions in the area. In effect, the Bolshevik regime had now been displaced in Siberia; the SRs disbanded the soviets and re-established the *zemstvos*, calling for "all power to the constituent assembly." There were three anti-Red governments of varying complexions in three different Siberian centers. Elsewhere, in August, 1918, a small British and American force landed at the White Sea port of Archangel. An SR assassin killed the chief of the Petrograd Cheka, and Lenin himself was wounded.

The regime now sped its military preparations. As Minister of War, Trotsky imposed conscription, and, by a mixture of cajolery and threats of reprisals against their families, secured the services of about 50,000 tsarist officers. The Red Army, which was Trotsky's creation, grew to over 3,000,000 strong by 1920. Its recapture of Kazan and Samara on the Volga in the autumn of 1918 temporarily turned the tide in the crisis that seemed about to engulf the Soviet state.

The German collapse on the Western Front permitted the Bolsheviks to repudiate the Treaty of Brest-Litovsk, and to move back into parts of the Ukraine, where they faced the opposition of a variety of local forces. Elsewhere, the opposition consisted of three main armies. General Denikin led an army of Whites, which moved from Rostov-on-Don south across the Caucasus and received French and British aid. Ad-

Tsar Nicholas II and his family, 1917.

miral Kolchak's forces in western Siberia overthrew the SR regime in Omsk, and Kolchak became a virtual dictator. General Yudenich's army, including many former members of the German forces, operated in the Baltic region, and threatened Petrograd from the west. Allied unwillingness to negotiate with the Bolsheviks was heightened by the successful Red *coup* of Bela Kun in Hungary (see Chapter XXV), which seemed to foreshadow further spread of revolution.

In the spring of 1919, the Reds defeated Kolchak, and by winter took Omsk. In 1920, the Admiral was arrested and executed. Though the Reds also reconquered the Ukraine, mutinies in their own forces prevented them from consolidating their victories and from moving, as they had hoped to do, across the Russian frontiers and linking up with Bela Kun in Hungary. Instead, disorder in their armies was accompanied by the rise of local insurgents, some of whom were violent anti-Semites in an old Ukrainian tradition, and others of whom were anarchist and agrarian in sympathy, fighting both Reds and Whites, and calling themselves Greens. In the summer of 1919, Denikin took Kiev and struck north, advancing to within two hundred and fifty miles of Moscow itself. But his position was weakened by the repressive character of the regime he brought with him and by his recognition of Kolchak as his superior officer, together with the poor discipline of his troops and his own rivalry with one of his generals, Baron Wrangel. Yudenich advanced to the suburbs of Petrograd, but the Reds by the end of 1919 were able to defeat the White threat everywhere, though Wrangel retained an army in the Crimea. Trotsky now called for the militarization of labor to reconstruct the ravaged country; labor battalions were formed, but recovery was long delayed.

In any case, even after the defeat of the Whites, the Reds in 1920 had to face a new war with the Poles, who hoped to keep Russia weak and to create an independent Ukraine. After an initial retreat, the Red armies nearly took Warsaw, from which they were repelled only because the French chief of staff, General Weygand, assisted the Poles. The Reds, eager to finish off the Whites, and persuaded that there was after all no hope for the establishment of a communist regime in Poland, concluded peace in October, 1920. The Poles obtained a large area of territory in White Russia and the western Ukraine. This area was not inhabited by Poles but had been controlled by Poland down to the eighteenth-century partitions. It lay far to the east of the "Curzon line," the ethnic frontier earlier proposed by the British foreign minister, Lord Curzon. The Reds then turned on Wrangel, who had erupted from the Crimea and had established a moderate regime in the territory he occupied. He was forced to evacuate, assisted by a French fleet, in November, 1920. The White movement had virtually come to an end.

Why the Counter-revolution Failed

Many factors accounted for the Whites' failure and the Reds' victory. The Whites could not get together on any political program beyond the mere overthrow of the Reds. They adopted a policy of "non-anticipation," which meant that some future constituent assembly would settle the governmental structure of Russia. Their numbers included everybody from extreme tsarists to SRs, and they disagreed so violently on the proper course for Russia to follow that they could agree only to postpone discussion of these critical problems.

Moreover, their movement was located on the geographical periphery of Russia— in Siberia, in the Crimea, in the Ukraine, in the Caucasus, and in the Baltic. But the Whites never reached an understanding with the non-Russian minorities who lived in these regions. Thus they ignored the highly developed separatist sentiments of the Ukrainians and others, to which the Bolsheviks were temporarily willing to cater. Clinging to their slogan of "Russia one and indivisible," the Whites lost a great deal of the support they might otherwise have commanded. Meanwhile Lenin, opportunist and realist as usual, was saying in effect, "Go ahead and secede if you like," all the time gambling that in the long run the Ukrainians and others would have no alternative but to return to Russia.

Further, the Whites could not command the support of the peasantry. Instead of guaranteeing the results of the land division already carried out with Bolshevik sanction, which they could at least in theory have done, the Whites often restored the landlords and undid the land division. During the war the peasantry on the whole grew sick of both sides. This attitude explains the appearance of anarchist bands, especially in the south. Then too, the Whites simply did not command as much military strength as the Reds, who outnumbered them in manpower and who had inherited much of the equipment manufactured for the tsarist armies. Holding the central position, the Reds had a unified and skillful command, which could use the railroad network to shift troops rapidly. The Whites, moving in from the periphery, were divided into at least four main groups, and were denied effective use of the railroads.

Finally, the intervention of the Allies on the side of the Whites was ineffectual and amateurish. It may even have harmed the White cause, since the Reds could pose as the national defenders of the country and could portray the Whites as the hirelings of foreigners. In the light of hindsight, it seems safe to say that either the Allies should have mounted a full-fledged military operation against the Reds, or, if this was impossible (as it probably was, in view of the condition of their own armies after the end of the First World War), they should have stayed out of Russia and allowed the civil war to burn itself out. It is still sometimes argued, however, that, although the Reds won the civil war, the Allied intervention helped keep them so heavily engaged inside Russia that they could not sponsor successful revolutions in other countries. This point of view may well have some justification.

NEP ("The New Economic Policy")

Since 1914, Russia had been deeply involved in fighting and crises. By early 1921, with the end of the civil war, famine was raging and sanitation had broken down. Family ties were disrupted, human beings were brutalized, and class hatreds were released on an unparalleled scale. Industry was producing at a level of about one-eighth of its pre-war output, and agricultural output had decreased by at least 30 per cent. Distribution approached a breakdown. The communist regime appeared to be facing its most serious trial of all: the loss of support in Russia.

A large-scale anarchist peasant revolt broke out in early 1921, and lasted until mid-1922. Lenin remarked that this revolt frightened him more than all the Whites' resistance. But the decisive factor in bringing about a change in policy was the mutiny at the Kronstadt naval base near Petrograd in March, 1921. Formerly a stronghold of Bolshevism, Kronstadt now produced a movement of rebellious anarchists who called for "soviets without communists" to be chosen by universal suffrage and secret ballot, for free speech and free assembly, for the liberation of political prisoners, and for the abolition of requisitioning. Except for the last item and for the phraseology of the first, the program was ironically similar to that of all liberals and socialists in tsarist Russia. The Kronstadt movement seems to have expressed the sentiments of most Russian workers and peasants. Had the government been conciliatory, there might have been no bloodshed; but Trotsky went to war against the rebels, and defeated them after a bloody fight.

This episode led directly to the adoption of the "New Economic Policy," always referred to by its initials as NEP. But the underlying reason for the shift was the need for reconstruction, which seemed attainable only if militant communism were at least temporarily abandoned. Lenin himself referred to "premature" attempts at socialization. It was also necessary to appease the peasants, and to ward off any further major uprisings. Finally, the expected world revolution had not come off, and the resources of capitalist states were badly needed to assist Russian reconstruction. Concessions to foreign capitalists were now possible; indeed, the adoption of NEP coincided with the conclusion of an Anglo-

Red Cross soup-kitchen in Russia during the economic collapse following World War I.

Russian trade treaty. Abroad, NEP was hailed as the beginning of a Russian "Thermidor," a return to normality like that following the end of the Terror in the French Revolution (see Chapter XIX).

Under NEP the government stopped requisitioning the whole of the peasant's crop above a minimum necessary for subsistence. The peasant had still to pay a very heavy tax in kind, but he was allowed to sell the remainder of his crop and keep the money. Thus the freedom of private trade and the right to sell on local markets had been restored. The peasant could sell his surplus to the state if he wished, but he could also choose to sell it to a private purchaser. Peasant agriculture became in essence capitalist once more, and the profit motive had reappeared. Lenin imitated Stolypin by guaranteeing the peasant permanency of tenure. The whole system tended to help the *kulak* grow richer, and to transform the poor peasant into a hired, landless laborer.

Elsewhere in the economy under NEP the state retained what Lenin called "the commanding heights"—heavy industry, banking, transportation, and foreign trade.

In domestic trade and in light industry, however, private enterprise was once more permitted. This was the so-called "private capital sector" of the economy, in which workers could be paid according to their output, and factory managers could swap some of their products in return for raw materials.

Lenin himself described NEP as a partial return to capitalism, and urged the communists to become good businessmen. Yet NEP was never intended as more than a temporary expedient. Lenin believed that it would take a couple of decades before the Russian peasant could be convinced that co-operative agriculture would be the most efficient. He also argued that a temporary relaxation of government intervention would increase industrial production and give the Russians a useful lesson in entrepreneurship.

Economic recovery was indeed obtained. By 1926-1927, industrial production was back at pre-war levels, although agriculture had not kept pace. But NEP was bitterly disliked by leading communists, who were shocked at the reversal of all the doctrines they believed in. By 1924, private business accounted for 40 per cent of Russian domestic trade, but thereafter the figure fell off. Those who took advantage of the opportunities presented by the NEP were known as NEPmen. They were often persecuted in a petty way by hostile officials, who tried to limit their profits, tax them heavily, and drag them into court on charges of speculation. A NEPman's life, though often profitable, was often harassed, and his career was one long gambling effort to stay out of the clutches of the bureaucracy. The *kulak* had essentially the same experience. Thus the government often seemed to be encouraging private enterprise for economic reasons and simultaneously to be discouraging it for political reasons.

CHAPTER XXVI

Within the Communist party, one group favored the increase of the private sector and the extension of NEP, as a new road toward the socialist goal. These were the so-called "Right deviationists." Their opponents favored the ending of concessions, the liquidation of NEPmen and *kulaks,* and a return to Marxist principles at home and the fostering of world revolution abroad—in short, the pressing of the "socialist offensive." These were the "Left deviationists," who included Trotsky. In the Center stood men who attacked both deviations, the Right as an abandonment of communism, the Left as likely to lead to a disruption of the worker-peasant alliance.

The Struggle for Power: Stalin versus Trotsky

But the big question of NEP was not the only one to agitate the communist leaders in the early twenties. Lenin suffered two strokes in 1922, and another in 1923, and finally died in January, 1924. During the last two years of his life he played an ever lessening role. Involved in the controversy over NEP and the other controversies was the question of the succession to Lenin. Thus an individual communist's answer to the question of how to organize industry, what role to give organized labor, and what relations to maintain with the capitalist world depended not only upon his estimate of the actual situation but also upon his guess as to what answer was likely to be politically advantageous. From this maneuvering the Secretary of the Communist party, Joseph Stalin, was to emerge victorious by 1928.

The years between 1922 and 1928, especially after Lenin's death, were years of a desperate struggle for power between Stalin and Trotsky. Lenin foresaw this struggle with great anxiety. He felt that Trotsky was

abler, but feared that he was overconfident, and inclined to make decisions of his own. He felt that Stalin had concentrated enormous power in his hands, in his role as party secretary, and feared that he did not know how to use it. When he learned that Stalin had gone counter to his orders in smashing the Menshevik Republic of Georgia instead of reaching an accommodation with its leaders, he wrote angrily in his testament that Stalin was too rude, and that his fellows should remove him from his post as general secretary. At the moment of his death, Lenin had published a scathing attack on Stalin, had broken off relations with him, and was about to try to relegate him to the scrapheap. Trotsky's suggestion that Stalin poisoned Lenin is not based on any evidence, but it is clear that Lenin's death rescued Stalin's career, and that, far from being the chosen heir, as he later claimed, he did not enjoy Lenin's confidence at the end.

During these years Trotsky argued for a more highly trained managerial force in industry, and for economic planning as an instrument that the state could use to control and direct social change. He favored the mechanization of agriculture and the weakening of peasant individualism by encouraging rural co-operatives, with even a hint of the collective farms where groups of peasants, in theory, would own everything collectively, rather than individually. As Trotsky progressively lost power, he championed the right of individual communists to criticize the regime. He referred to the policies of Stalin and his other increasingly powerful enemies as "bureaucratic degeneration," and came to the conclusion that only through the outbreak of revolutions in other countries could the Russian socialist revolution be carried to its proper conclusion. Only if the industrial output and technical skills of the advanced western countries could be put at the disposal of communism could Russia hope to achieve its own socialist revolution. This is the famous theory that socialism cannot succeed within the boundaries of one country: either world revolution must break out, or Russian socialism is doomed to inevitable failure.

The opponents of Trotsky's "left deviation" found their chief spokesman in Nikolai Bukharin. A man who never held such responsible administrative posts as Lenin or Trotsky or Stalin, and who had often shifted his position on major questions, Bukharin none the less took a consistent line during these years; as editor of *Pravda* he was extremely influential. A strong defender of NEP, Bukharin softened the rigorous Marxist doctrine of the class struggle by arguing that since the proletarian state controlled the commanding heights of big capital, and since big capital would win, socialism was sure of success. This view is not unlike the "gradualist" position taken by western European Social Democrats. Bukharin did not believe in an ambitious program of rapid industrialization; he favored co-operatives, but opposed collectives. In foreign affairs he was eager to co-operate abroad with non-communist groups who might be useful to Russia. Thus he sponsored Soviet collaboration with Chiang Kai-shek in China and with the German Social Democrats.

In his rise to power, Stalin used Bukharin's arguments to discredit Trotsky and to eliminate him. Then, partly because Bukharin's policies were failing, Stalin adopted many of Trotsky's policies, and eliminated Bukharin. Original Stalinist ideas, however, developed during this process. Stalin was not basically an intellectual or a theoretician; he was a party organization stalwart. He adopted theoretical positions partly because they seemed to him the ones most likely to work, and partly because he was charting his own course to supreme power. He came to favor rapid industrialization, and to understand that this meant an unprecedentedly heavy capital investment. At the end of 1927, he suddenly shifted from his previous position on the peasantry, and openly sponsored collectivization. This shift arose because of his concern that agricultural production was not keeping pace with industry. He declared that the balance could be redressed only if agriculture, like industry, was transformed into a series of large-scale unified enterprises.

In answer to Trotsky's argument that socialism in one country was impossible, Stalin maintained that an independent socialist state could exist. This view did not at all imply the abandonment of the goal of world revolution, as has often been thought. Stalin always maintained that the socialist state (Russia) should be the center of inspiration and assistance to communist movements everywhere; Russia would help them and they would help Russia. But, in his view, during the interim period before the communists had won elsewhere it was perfectly possible for Russia to exist as the only socialist state, and indeed to grow more socialist all the time. In international relations this doctrine of Stalin made it possible for the Soviet Union to pursue either a policy of "peaceful coexistence" with capitalist states, when that seemed most profitable, or a policy of militant support of communist revolution everywhere, when that seemed most profitable. Stalin's "socialism in one country" also struck a responsive chord in the rank and file of Russian communists, who were disappointed in the failure of revolutions elsewhere. It also meant that Russia, not the West, was to be the center of the new society. Stalin's doctrine reflected his own Russian nationalism rather than the more cosmopolitan and more western views of Trotsky.

CHAPTER XXVI

The Struggle for Power: Stalin's Victory

Analysis of the rival theories competing for acceptance in Russia in the twenties helps explain the alternatives before the communist leadership. It does not explain how Stalin won. To understand this we must move from the realm of theory and political platforms to the realm of practice and political power. At the end of the civil war, Stalin was Commissar of Nationalities. In this post he dealt with the affairs of 65,000,000 of the 140,000,000 inhabitants of the new Russian Soviet Republic. He managed the destiny of the Asiatics, whom he, as one of them, understood. Their local Bolshevik leaders became his men; where they did not, as in his native Georgia, he ruthlessly crushed them. Though a Georgian, he identified himself with Russian nationalism in the interests of a centralized Bolshevik state.

It was Stalin who took charge of creating the new Asiatic "republics" which enjoyed the appearance of local self-government, programs of economic and educational improvement, and a chance to use their local languages and develop their own cultures. It was he who in 1922 proposed and guided the adoption of a new Union of Socialist Soviet Republics as a substitute for the existing federation of republics. In the U.S.S.R., Moscow would control war, foreign policy, trade, and transport, and would co-ordinate finance, economy, food, and labor. And on paper it would leave to the republics home affairs, justice, education, and agriculture. A Council of Nationalities, with an equal number of delegates from each ethnic group, would join the Supreme Soviet as a second chamber, thus forming the Central Executive Committee, which would appoint the Council of Peoples' Commissars —the Government. To this constitutional reform Stalin pointed as an achievement equal to Trotsky's military organizational work during the civil war.

Stalin was also Commissar of the Workers' and Peasants' Inspectorate. Here his duties were to eliminate inefficiency and corruption from every branch of the civil service, and to train a new corps of civil servants. His teams moved freely through all the offices of the government, observing and recommending changes, inspecting and criticizing. In creating this post Lenin had hoped to clean house, but the ignorance and the lack of tradition that rendered the tsarist and Bolshevik civil service incompetent and corrupt operated in Stalin's inspectorate as well. Indeed many tsarist civil servants entered the Bolshevik service in the 1920's. Although the Inspectorate could not do what it was established to do, it did perform another role. It gave Stalin control over the machinery of government. Lenin attacked Stalin's work in the Inspectorate just before he died, but by then it was too late.

Stalin was also a member of the Politbureau, the tight little group of party bosses elected by the Central Committee, which included only five men throughout the civil war. Here his job was day-to-day management of the party. He was the only permanent liaison officer between the Politbureau and the Orgbureau, which allocated party personnel to their various duties, in factory, office, or army unit. In addition to these posts, Stalin became general secretary of the party's Central Committee in 1922. Here he prepared the agenda for Politbureau meetings, supplied the documentation for points under debate, and passed the decisions down to the lower levels. He controlled party patronage—that is to say, all party appointments, promotions, and demotions. He saw to it that local trade unions, co-operatives, and army units were put under communist bosses responsible to him. He had files on the loyalty and achievement of all managers of industry and other party members. In 1921, a Central Control Commission, which could expel party members for unsatisfactory conduct, was created; Stalin, as liaison between this commission and the Central Committee, now virtually controlled the purges, which were designed to keep the party pure.

In a centralized one-party state, a man of Stalin's ambitions who held so many key positions had an enormous advantage in the struggle for power. Yet the state was so new, the positions were so much less conspicuous and so much more humdrum than the Ministry of War, for instance, held by Trotsky, and Stalin's manner was so generally conciliatory, that the likelihood of Stalin's success did not become evident until it was too late to stop him. Inside the Politbureau he formed a three-man team with two other prominent Bolshevik leaders, the demagogue Zinoviev and the expert on doctrine, Kamenev. Zinoviev was chairman of the Petrograd Soviet and boss of the Communist International; Kamenev was Lenin's deputy and president of the Moscow Soviet. All three were old Bolsheviks, in contrast to Trotsky, who had been a Menshevik and an independent.

The combination of Stalin, Zinoviev, and Kamenev proved unbeatable. The three put down all real and imagined plots against them by the use of the secret police. They resisted Trotsky's demands for "reform," which would have democratized the party to some degree and strengthened his position while weakening Stalin's. They initiated the cult of Lenin immediately before his death, and kept it burning fiercely thereafter, so that any suggestion for change coming from Trotsky seemed almost an act of impiety. They dispersed Trotsky's fol-

lowers by sending them to posts abroad. They prevented the publication of Lenin's "testament," so that the rank and file of the party would not know about Lenin's doubts concerning Stalin. They publicized all Trotsky's earlier statements in opposition to Lenin, and did not hesitate to "revise" history in order to belittle Trotsky. They were confident, and rightly so, that Trotsky was too good a communist to rally around him such anti-Bolshevik groups as old Mensheviks, SRs, and NEPmen.

Early in 1925, Stalin and his allies were able to force the resignation of Trotsky as Minister of War. Soon thereafter the three-man team dissolved; Stalin moved into alliance with Bukharin and other right-wing members of the Politbureau, to which he began to appoint some of his own followers. Using all his accumulated power, he beat his former allies on all questions of policy, and in 1926 they moved into a new but powerless alliance with Trotsky. Stalin now (1926) deposed Zinoviev from the Politbureau, charging him with intriguing in the army. Trotsky was the next one to be expelled from the Politbureau, and Zinoviev was ousted as president of the Comintern.

In 1927, differences of opinion over Stalin's foreign policy in England and in China (see below, p. 504) led to public protests by the opposition. And these in turn led to the expulsion of the opposition from the party itself. Refusing to renounce his views, Trotsky was deported to Siberia, the first stage in a long exile that took him to Turkey, Norway, and Mexico, where he died in 1940 at the hands of an assassin armed with an ice-pick. The others recanted and obtained a new lease on life. Stalin's victory was virtually complete.

CHAPTER XXVI

IV: Stalin's Supremacy: Russian Internal Affairs, 1928-1941

The Communist party congress that expelled Trotsky in December, 1927, also brought NEP to an end and proclaimed that the new "socialist offensive" would begin in 1928. The thirteen years between 1928 and 1941 were to see almost incredible changes in the domestic life of Russia—collectivized agriculture, speedy industrialization, forced labor, the great purges and the extermination of all political opposition, the building of an authoritarian state apparatus, and a "retreat" to bourgeois standards in almost every department of social and intellectual life.

Collectivized Agriculture

In 1928, the failure of the peasants to deliver to the cities as much grain as had been required seemed to underline the dangers inherent in the land divisions of 1917 and in the concessions of NEP. Farm productivity on the small individual holdings was not high enough to feed the city population. Food prices for the workers were high, yet the *kulaks* wanted further concessions. Grain was hoarded. Stalin had often inveighed against "fanning the class struggle in the countryside," and had denied the intention of collectivizing agriculture rapidly or on a mass scale. The government economic plan issued during 1928 set a figure of 20 per cent of Russian farms as the *maximum* to be collectivized by 1933. Yet during 1929, Stalin embarked on immediate full-scale collectivization, declared war on the *kulaks*, and virtually put an end to individual farming in Russia.

The government did not have the money or the credit to import food. Further, no

governmental machinery is adequate to force peasants to disgorge crops that they are hiding. Therefore, the government enlisted on its side the small peasants; in exchange for their assistance in locating and turning over the *kulaks'* crops, they would be promised a place on a collective farm, to be made up of the *kulaks'* land and equipped with their implements. Probably a good many of the subsistence farmers (about 20 per cent of the number of private farms, possibly 5,000,000 households) more or less welcomed this opportunity. Initial encouraging reports led Stalin to go full speed ahead. The *kulaks*, he declared in late 1929, were to be liquidated as a class. There were about 2,000,000 households of them, perhaps as many as 10,000,000 people in all. They were now to be totally expropriated, and at the same time barred from the new collectives. Since no provision was made for them, this move turned collectivization into a nightmare.

Peasants now were machine-gunned into submission; *kulaks* were deported to forced labor camps or to desolate regions in Siberia. In desperate revolt against the command to join collectives, the peasants burned crops, broke plows, and killed their cattle rather than turn them over to the state. More than half the horses in all Russia, 45 per cent of the cattle, and two-thirds of the sheep and goats were slaughtered. Russian livestock has never since caught up with the losses it suffered because of the excesses of collectivization. Land lay uncultivated, and over the next few years famine took a toll of millions of lives. As early as March, 1930, Stalin showed that he was aware of the ghastly mistakes he had made. In a famous statement on "dizziness

Village housing members of a collective farm in the Moscow region.

with success" he put the blame on local officials who had been too eager to rush through the program. By contradicting his own orders of a few months before he managed to escape some of the hatred that would otherwise have been directed at him. As usual, many Russian peasants disliked the man they could see, the local official, and were willing to exculpate the "little father" in the capital.

Fifty per cent of Russian farms had been hastily thrown together into collectives during this frightful year. Only an additional 10 per cent were added during the next three years, so that by 1933 60 per cent in all had been collectivized. The number rose again later in the 1930's, until by 1939 more than 96 per cent of Russian farms were collectivized. In 1941, there were 250,000 collectives, 900,000,000 acres in extent, supporting 19,000,000 families. Yet the excesses of the early "dizziness with success" were never repeated.

The 1930's also brought a modification of the original rules governing collectives.

Originally collectives had been of two main types: there was the *sovkhoz,* or soviet farm, not strictly a collective at all but a state-owned enterprise, operated by the government and worked by hired laborers who were government employees; and there was the *kolkhoz,* or collective farm proper. The *sovkhozes* were designed as centers of government research and development in agriculture, and were often very large in size. But they were mostly brought to an end by Stalin in the 1930's, when he ordered some forty million acres originally allotted to them to be distributed among the *kolkhozes.* As of 1941, the *sovkhozes* occupied no significant area of land.

The *kolkhoz* itself was also originally of two types: the commune, in which all the resources of the members without exception were owned together, and the *artel,* or co-operative, in which a certain amount of private property was permitted to the members. After Stalin's modifications of the system in the thirties, the *artel* became the overwhelmingly predominant form of col-

CHAPTER XXVI

A "Hero of Socialist Labor" at home with his mother on a collective farm.

lective farm. In an *artel* each family owns its homestead, some livestock, and minor implements; these can be left by will to the owner's descendants. But most of the work is done on the collectively operated land. Each collective has its own managing board, responsible to the government, which oversees the work of the peasants, who are organized in brigades, each under a brigadier. Like factory laborers paid on a "piece-work" basis, peasants are remunerated according to their output, which is measured by the artificial unit of the "labor day." One day's work in managing a farm may be, for example, assessed at three labor days, while one day's work weeding a vegetable patch may be assessed at only half a labor day.

Each *kolkhoz* must turn over to the government a fixed amount of produce at fixed rates, and the total of all these amounts is designed to guarantee the feeding of the urban population, especially workers in heavy industry and members of the Red Army. In addition, the *kolkhoz* pays further taxes to cover government expenses for local construction and education. Any surplus beyond what must be delivered to meet these obligations may be sold by the peasant directly to the consumer, without the participation of any middleman. Private resale is regarded as speculation and is subject to punishment. After 1934, the government obtained at least two-thirds of its revenue by the resale on the markets at a large profit of farm produce bought at low fixed prices from the *kolkhoz*. This government profit is known as the "turnover tax."

The government assists and controls the *kolkhoz* through the supply of mechanical equipment furnished by the machine tractor stations. The collectives cannot own their own tractors, but must rent them from the stations, paying in exchange a fee ranging up to perhaps 20 per cent of the crop. The stations are important centers for political surveillance, and include staff members who are agents of the regime. By the decision when and to whom to allot tractors and how many tractors to allot, administrators of the machine tractor stations can directly affect the success of a collective; their good will is therefore of the utmost importance to the management.

In general, the aim of collectivization was to reorganize farming so as to ensure food for the industrial labor force, which was being increased by recruitment from the farms themselves. The result of collectivization has certainly been to increase the total food supplies at the disposal of the government and to release farmers for work in industry. But it seems certain that the over-all rise in production has been small, and that in many cases the yield per unit has decreased.

Industrialization

Intimately related to the drive in agriculture was the drive in industry. Here, too, Stalin had viewed with scorn the grandiose plans of the "superindustrializers" and as late as 1927 had proposed an annual increase rate in industrial production of only 15 per cent. But just as he shifted to the frantic pace of collectivizing agriculture, so he first gradually, then suddenly, shifted to forced draft in industry also.

In 1928 began the era of the Five-Year Plans, each setting incredibly ambitious goals for production over the next five years. In 1929 and 1930, Stalin appropriated ever higher sums for capital investment, and in June, 1930, he declared that industrial production must rise by 50 per cent in the current year, a fantastic and impossible figure. Under the First Five-Year Plan, adopted in 1928, annual pig-iron production was scheduled to rise from 3,500,000 tons to 10,000,000 tons by 1932, but in that year Stalin demanded 17,000,000 tons instead. It was not forthcoming, of course, but Stalin's demand for it is symptomatic of the pace at which he was striving

to transform Russia from an agricultural to an industrial country.

Part of the reason for this rapid pace lay precisely in the collectivization drive itself. Large-scale farming, to which Stalin was committing Russia, must be mechanized farming. Yet there were only 7,000 tractors in all Russia at the end of 1928. Stalin secured 30,000 more during 1929, but this was nowhere near a beginning. Industry had to produce millions of machines, and the gasoline to run them. Since the countryside had to be electrified, power stations were needed by the thousands. And literally millions and millions of peasants had to be taught how to handle machinery. But there was nobody to teach them, and no factories to produce the machinery. The output of raw materials was inadequate, and the plants to process them were not there.

Another part of the reason for the drive to industrialize lay in the tenets of Marxism itself. Russia had defied all Marx's predictions by staging a proletarian revolution in a country almost without a proletariat. Yet despite the communists' initial political successes, Stalin felt that "capitalism had a firmer basis than communism in Russia, so long as it remained a country of small peasants." The communists felt that the world proletariat expected them to industrialize Russia, but even more they were determined to create as a support for themselves the massive Russian proletariat which as yet did not exist. Further, Stalin was determined to make Russia as nearly self-sufficient as possible, in line with his theory of socialism in one country. Underlying this was a motive at least as intense as any dictated by Marxist doctrine—Russian nationalism.

The strength of this motive is revealed in a speech that Stalin made in 1931:

To slacken the pace means to lag behind, and those who lag behind are beaten. We do not want to be beaten. No, we don't want to. . . . Old Russia . . . was ceaselessly beaten for her backwardness. She was beaten by the Mongol Khans, she was beaten by Turkish Beys, she was beaten by Swedish feudal lords, she was beaten by Polish-Lithuanian gentry, she was beaten by Anglo-French capitalists, she was beaten by Japanese barons; she was beaten by all—for her backwardness. For military backwardness, for cultural backwardness, for political backwardness, for industrial backwardness, for agricultural backwardness. She was beaten because to beat her was profitable and went unpunished. . . . We are fifty or a hundred years behind the advanced countries. We must make good this lag in ten years. Either we do it or they crush us.[*]

Whatever one may think of this quotation as history (and it omits all Russia's *victorious* wars), it reveals that Russian national self-interest as interpreted by Stalin required the most rapid possible industrialization. And it is of interest that ten years afterward the Germans did attack, something Stalin could of course not have predicted so accurately, but something that he seems to have sensed.

Stalin seems also to have felt that he had only to keep a fierce pressure on the management of industry, and the desired commodities and finished goods would be forthcoming in the desired quantities. Just as he became "dizzy from success" in the agricultural field, so he did in the industrial. Instead of a 50 per cent increase in iron and coal during 1930, he got an increase ranging only from 6 to 10 per cent. The goals of the First Five-Year Plan were not attained, although fulfillment was announced in 1932. Immediately, the second plan, prepared by the state planning commission, went into effect, and ran until 1937; the third was interrupted only by Hitler's invasion. Each time the emphasis was on the elements of heavy industry—steel, electric power, cement, coal, oil. Be-

[*] Quoted in Isaac Deutsher, *Stalin* (New York, 1950), 328.

tween 1928 and 1940 steel production was multiplied by four and one-half, electric power by eight, cement by more than two, coal by four, and oil by almost three. Similar developments took place in chemicals and in machine production. Railroad construction was greatly increased, and the volume of freight carried quadrupled with the production of new rolling stock.

By 1940, Russian output was approaching that of Germany, although Russian efficiency and the Russian standard of living were far lower. What the rest of Europe had done in about seventy-five years Russia had done in about twelve. Enthusiasm was artificially whipped up by wide publicizing of the high output of individual workers called "Stakhanovites," after a coal miner who had set production records. "Stakhanovites" and "heroes of labor" were richly rewarded, and the others were urged to imitate them in "socialist competition."

All this was achieved at the expense of dreadful hardships, yet eyewitnesses report that many of the workers were as enthusiastic as if they had been soldiers in battle, as indeed in a sense they were. Valuable machinery was often damaged or destroyed by inexperienced workers right off the farm. Such high production goals were often set that the management of a plant wore out the equipment in a desperate attempt to do the impossible. The problems of repair, of replacement, of achieving balance between the output and consumption of raw materials, of housing workers in the new centers, of moving entire industries thousands of miles into the Ural region and Siberia, were unending and cost untold numbers of lives. An American eyewitness estimates that Russia's "battle of ferrous metallurgy alone involved more casualties than the battle of the Marne."

Administratively, the Russian economy is directly run by the state. The Gosplan, or state planning commission, draws up the

A new Soviet industrial center: Magnitogorsk in the Urals.

Five-Year Plans, and supervises their fulfillment at the management level. The Gosbank, or state bank, regulates the investment of capital. An economic council is in charge of the work of various agencies, a partial listing of which will point up the immensity of its undertakings. Its major divisions are metallurgy and chemistry (iron and steel, non-ferrous metals, chemicals, rubber, alcohol); defense (aviation, armaments, munitions, tanks, ships); machinery (heavy machines, medium machines, machine tools, electrical industry); fuel and power (coal, oil, electric power); agriculture and procurement; and consumer's goods (grain, meat and dairy products, fisheries, textiles, light industry). Under iron and steel, for example, there function the production trusts controlling their own mines as well as blast furnaces and rolling mills. These are the so-called "combinats," or great production complexes

like that at Magnitogorsk in the Urals. In each plant, as in each collective, the manager is responsible for producing the quota set for him within the maximum cost allowed him. He is consulted on production targets, and has considerable leeway in selecting his staff and allocating labor and raw materials. He is bound to render a rigid accounting to the government, which of course fixes the price he must pay for his raw materials.

The Social Impact

The social effects of the economic program have been dramatic. Urban population rose from about 18 per cent in 1926 to about 33 per cent in 1940. The number of cities with a population between 50,000 and 100,000 doubled, and the number of cities with a population exceeding 100,000 more than quadrupled. The largest cities, Moscow and Leningrad (the new name for Petersburg-Petrograd after the death of Lenin), almost doubled in size, and among smaller cities, to take just one example, Alma Ata in Siberia grew from 45,000 to 230,000 between 1928 and 1939. The entire social picture was radically altered.

The relative freedom to choose one's job which had characterized the NEP period naturally disappeared. Individual industrial enterprises signed labor contracts with the *kolkhozes* by which the *kolkhoz* was obliged to send a given number of farm workers to the factories, often against their will. Peasants who had resisted collectivization were simply drafted into labor camps. The old Bolshevik conception of imprisonment as an opportunity for re-education disappeared and was replaced by slave labor, pure and simple. In the factories, the trade unions became simply another organ of the state. The chief role of the unions is to achieve maximum production and efficiency, to discourage absenteeism and poor work. Trade unions may not strike, or engage in conflict with management. All they can do is administer the social insurance laws, and seek improvements in workers' living conditions by negotiation.

Thus in the U.S.S.R. the old privileged classes of noble landlords, already weak at the time of the revolution, ceased to exist. The industrial, commercial, and financial bourgeoisie, which was just coming into its own at the time of the revolution, was destroyed after 1928, despite the temporary reprieve it had experienced under NEP. Most of the old intelligentsia, who had favored a revolution, could not in the end stomach Stalin's dictatorship, and many of them emigrated. Of the million and a half émigrés from Russia after the revolution, only a very small number (contrary to the general view in the West) were cousins of the Tsar. Those of the old intelligentsia who

remained were forced into line with the new Soviet intelligentsia, which Stalin felt to be a very important class. All were compelled to accept the new Stalinist dogma and to drop their interest in the outside world. The new intelligentsia was expected to concentrate on technical advance, and on new administrative devices for speeding up the transformation of the country.

Although the effect of these social changes would presumably have been to level all ranks, Stalin set himself against the old Bolshevik principles of equality. The Marxist slogan, "From each according to his capacity, to each according to his needs," was shelved in favor of a new one, "From each according to his capacity, to each according to his work." Where Lenin had allowed none of the members of the government to earn more than a skilled laborer, Stalin set up a new system of incentives. A small minority of bureaucrats and skilled laborers, factory managers, and successful *kolkhoz* bosses earned vastly more than the great majority of unskilled laborers and peasants. Together with the writers, artists, musicians, and entertainers who were willing to lend their talents to the services of the regime, these men became a new élite, separated by a wide economic and social gulf from the toiling masses. They had a vested interest in furthering a regime to which they owed everything, and without which they would be nothing.

One is told by Soviet propagandists that this is a temporary situation. The present society in the Soviet Union is described as "socialist," while "communism," not yet achieved, is regarded as the goal toward which the U.S.S.R. is still moving. Yet, just as the "withering away" of the state, which the Marxists predicted, was instead replaced under Stalin by the enormous swelling of state power and state machinery, so the equality predicted by the Marxists was replaced by a new caste system. The means of production are publicly owned in the Soviet Union, as the Marxists urged. But the power of the state, the birth of a new élite, the brutalization of millions of human beings, and the ruthless use of force after the revolution had been achieved have all been the contributions of Stalin.

The Purge Trials

Stalin's program was not achieved without opposition. The crisis of 1931 and 1932, when industrial goals were not being met and the countryside was being swept by starvation, created discontent inside the regime as well as outside. A small number of officials circulated memoranda advocating Stalin's deposition as General Secretary, an act which the party had every right to perform. Stalin jailed them for conspiracy, and one leading Bolshevik committed suicide. It is widely believed that Stalin's own wife reproached him at this time with the ravages that the terror was working, and that she too committed suicide. At one moment, but only at one, we are told, Stalin's self-confidence wavered and he offered to resign, but nobody in the Politbureau dared accept the offer, and the moment quickly passed. His attack against those he believed to be his enemies took the form of the famous purges, which began in 1934 and continued at intervals until 1938.

These purges remain the most mysterious episode in Soviet history. They are often compared with the Jacobin Terror of the French Revolution, when the revolution "devoured its children." But, in contrast to the rapid appearance of the Terror in France, the purges did not begin for seventeen years after the Russian Revolution. Members of the opposition had been demoted, expelled from the party, and even exiled, as in the case of Trotsky; but nobody had been executed. There is an entirely credible story that the Bolshevik leaders had agreed among themselves early in their career never to start guillotining each other. Yet, when the terror began in Russia, it was even more drastic than it had been in France. Moreover, unlike Robespierre, Stalin managed to survive.

From exile, Trotsky continued to attack Stalin in a journal called *The Bulletin of the Opposition*. Clever as always, he scored telling points against Stalin, and his words were carefully read by Soviet officials. Yet the older generation of communists, though they may have hated Stalin, made no move against him. A younger group, however, seemingly more restless and convinced that Stalin had abandoned Lenin's program, found the model for conspiracy in the heroes of the terrorist movement who had assassinated Alexander II (see Chapter XXII). They were apparently prepared to use terrorism against Stalin and his henchmen. Even within the Politbureau men loyal to Stalin grew restless at his ruthlessness, and urged him to relax the pressure; Sergei Kirov, boss of Leningrad, took the lead.

Stalin at times seemed to yield to this urging, as when he ordered more gentle treatment for rebellious *kulaks* in June, 1932, and limited the powers of the political police. But at other times he seemed to be taking the opposite course, as when he issued a decree making an entire family responsible for the treason of any of its members. On the whole, however, tension relaxed during 1932-1934. Kirov proclaimed a new era of lenience at a party conference, and former leaders of the opposition, including Bukharin, were appointed to help draft a new and liberal constitution.

Then on December 1, 1934, Kirov was assassinated by a young terrorist communist in Leningrad. Although the story that Stalin himself had plotted the assassination cannot be confirmed, it is clear that Stalin now determined to strike at the opposition. The assassin was executed. Accused of complicity, Zinoviev and Kamenev were jailed, and forced to admit that they had plotted to restore capitalism. Yet the drafting of the new "democratic" constitution went on. Stalin became ever more withdrawn, ever more autocratic, ever more resolved to destroy the old Bolsheviks, as Ivan the Terrible had destroyed the old nobility. After an interlude during 1935 and early 1936, during which Stalin said that "life had become more joyous," the purges proper began.

The official story was that Trotskyite agitation abroad was linked with the murder of Kirov, and the alleged plans for the murder of Stalin. A series of public political trials took place. In the first (1936), Zinoviev, Kamenev, and fourteen others admitted these charges and were executed. In the second (1937) seventeen other leading Bolsheviks declared that they had knowledge of a conspiracy between Trotsky and the German and Japanese intelligence service, by which Russian territory was to be transferred to Germany and Japan. All were executed. Then (June, 1937) came the secret liquidation of the top commanders in the Red Army, who were accused of conspiring with "an unfriendly foreign power" (Germany) with a view to sabotage. All were executed after an announcement that they had confessed. The last of the public trials took place in March, 1938, as twenty-one leading Bolsheviks, including Bukharin, confessed to similar charges and were executed.

But these public trials and the secret trial of the generals give only a faint idea of the extent of the purge. Every member of Lenin's Politbureau except Stalin and Trotsky was either killed or committed suicide to avoid execution. Two vice-commissars of foreign affairs and most of the

Vishinsky at the time he was government prosecutor during the purge trials, 1938.

ambassadors of the diplomatic corps, fifty of the seventy-one members of the Central Committee of the Communist party, almost all the military judges who had sat in judgment and had condemned the generals, two successive heads of the secret police, themselves the leaders in the previous purges, the prime ministers and chief officials of all the non-Russian Soviet Republics—all were killed or vanished. A list of those who disappeared reads like a "who's who" of high officialdom in state and party throughout the twenties and thirties. Literally thousands were executed or disappeared without a trace. The public trials probably included only those who were willing to confess, whether guilty or not. The rest were condemned privately.

Although it is clear that many of those who were executed opposed Stalin, the charges against them were certainly not true. Had they been true, the great conspiracy involving almost everybody but Stalin himself would surely have accomplished more than the assassination of Kirov. It is altogether unlikely that any of the top communists conspired with Hitler, little though they loved Stalin. Some who confessed may have felt so great a loyalty to the cause of communism, however perverted, that they sacrificed themselves for Stalin's soviet state. Some doubtless hoped to save their families, or even themselves, and a few leaders were spared the death penalty to encourage confessions from the others. Many may have hoped that the confessions were so ridiculous that nobody could believe them.

What Stalin apparently wanted was to destroy utterly all possibility of future conspiracies. So he trumped up charges against anybody who conceivably could become a member of a regime that might replace his own. One partial explanation of his action is that he felt sure that war with Germany was inevitable, and he did not trust anybody but himself to meet it. Despite the enormous upheaval of the purges, no breakdown took place in the state. New bureaucrats were found to take the places of the old. The new Stalin-trained officials, uncultivated but competent, boorish and without experience in the western world, now manned all top-level positions.

The Authoritarian State

In the midst of the purges, in 1936, Stalin proclaimed the new constitution, the "most democratic in the world." By its provisions nobody was disfranchised, as priests and members of the former nobility and bourgeoisie had previously been. Civil liberties were extended, but even on paper these have never been more than a sham, since the constitution provides that they can be modified in the "interest of the toilers." The fact that the U.S.S.R. is a one-party state prevents elections from being anything but an expression of unanimity. The right to nominate candidates for the Supreme Soviet belongs to Communist party organizations, trade unions, co-operatives, youth groups, and cultural societies; but all are completely dominated by the party. The party picks the candidates, and no more than one for each post is ever presented to the voters. The party controls the soviets, and the party hierarchy and government hierarchy overlap and interlock.

Every citizen is eligible for membership in the party on application to a local branch which votes on his application after a year of trial. Communist children's organizations feed the youth groups, which in turn feed the party. The party is organized both territorially and functionally in pyramidal form, with organizations at the bottom level in factory, farm, and government office. These are grouped together by rural or urban local units, and these in turn by regional and territorial conferences and congresses. The party organizations elect the All-Union party congress, which selects the Central Committee of the party, and which is in theory the highest policy-making organ, though actually no party congress was held between 1939 and 1954. The Central Committee selects the Politbureau. At each level of the party pyramid there are organizations for agitation and propaganda, for organization and instruction, for military and political training. The party exercises full control over the government, which simply enacts formally what the party has decided upon. The Five-Year Plans, for example, were party programs that went into effect even before they were formally adopted by the government.

The highest organ of the government is the Supreme Soviet, made up of two houses —a Soviet of the Union, based on population, and a Soviet of Nationalities, elected according to national administrative divisions. In theory, the Supreme Soviet is elected for a term of four years. The Su preme Soviet itself does little; it appoints a presidium which issues the decrees and carries on the work of the Supreme Soviet between sessions. It also appoints the Council of Ministers (long called the Council of People's Commissars). This cabinet, rather than the Supreme Soviet or its presidium, enacts most of the legislation, and is thus the legislative as well as the executive organ of the Russian state. The chairmanship of the Council of People's Commissars, the chairmanship of the Polit-bureau, and the General Secretariat of the Communist party were all posts held by Stalin, who in addition served as Commissar of Defense, chief of the State Defense Council, which ran the country during war-time, and Generalissimo. Similar overlapping of party and government posts has been the regular practice.

In 1924, Stalin's constitutional reform (mentioned earlier) had created the new Union of Soviet Socialist Republics, including the enormously large Russian Federative Republic, the Ukraine, White Russia, Georgia, Armenia, and Azerbaidjan, and three central Asiatic Soviet Socialist republics: Uzbekistan, Turkmenistan, and Tadjikistan. In 1936, Kazakh and Kirghiz republics were added, making a total of eleven. As a result of the annexations of the Baltic states and of Finnish and Rumanian territory in 1940, five more republics were created: Lithuania, Latvia, Estonia, Karelia, and Moldavia. These sixteen "Union" republics range in population from the Russian, with about 114,000,000 people, and including most of Siberia, through the Ukrainian, with more than 40,000,000, down to the Karelian, with about 800,000. Within the Russian republic are fifteen "autonomous" republics, and numerous other subdivisions, all called "autonomous." The larger SSR's have similar subdivisions.

Each of the sixteen Union republics and nineteen autonomous republics has a gov-ernment patterned exactly on that of the Soviet Union, except that the supreme soviet of each republic is unicameral and not bicameral, since it lacks a chamber of nationalities. Many complaints have been heard in recent years about the way in which "Great-Russian chauvinism" has permeated official policy toward the individual minority republics. Although this soviet descendant of tsarist Russification policy has always been a menace, it is widely believed that in the years before World War II, the chief objective was not to try to Russify the nationalities but to communize them. With this end in view, the party permitted and encouraged local nationalities to revive their culture, study their past traditions, and use their own language. Like every other cultural manifestation permitted in the U.S.S.R., these national cultural achievements were "managed." Not only was it impossible for anti-Soviet or anti-communist material to appear in print or in any of the plastic arts, but, as everywhere, all artistic effort was closely supervised and had to serve the regime positively. The value of "cultural autonomy" under these circumstances is of course highly debatable.

Although the Stalin constitution specifically gives each republic the right to secede, this provision is pure window-dressing. The central government is overpoweringly stronger than the government of any one republic, which in any case is often not even made up of natives. Although each of the sixteen republics was in 1944 given its own foreign office by an amendment to the constitution, this amendment was never intended to give them autonomy in this critically important field. Actually, it seems simply to have been a device for securing representation of the Ukraine and White Russia in the United Nations. The representatives of these two republics to the United Nations have never been anything but extra Soviet delegates; the first Ukrainian delegate to the U.N. was not even a Ukrainian, but a Russian who was once Soviet ambassador to the independent Ukraine of the revolutionary era.

The Russian Thermidor?

The period between 1934 and 1941, notable for the purges and for the constitutional development of Stalin's one-party state, is also called by many shrewd observers of revolutions the true Russian "Thermidor," as distinct from NEP. The term "Thermidor" has come to mean a period in which a revolution has burnt itself out, and the prevailing mood shifts from messianic enthusiasm to one of desire for normality. In revolutionary France, the shift was signalized by the fall of Robespierre and the Jacobin regime and the advent of the Directory, a different government with different objectives, policies, and personnel, which was in turn succeeded by Napoleon's dictatorship (see Chapter XIX). In the U.S.S.R. the striking fact was that Stalin stayed in office throughout: he was in effect the Russian Robespierre, Directory, and Napoleon all rolled into one. If we accept the parallel, the Russian Thermidor was a managed and manipulated Thermidor, involving no real liberalization of the regime or relaxation of controls. Yet perhaps the parallel is not entirely valid, since Stalin resembled Napoleon far more than he did the weak Directory.

In any case, the period of the late 1930's saw a wholesale retreat from many ideas of the revolution. Simultaneously with the purges and the new constitution, the bread ration was raised, the *kolkhoz* was reformed to permit the individual farmer to own his homestead, new medals and titles were awarded to leading workers in plants and to scientists, engineers, and military men. In the Red Army traditional tsarist distinctions between officers and men were restored, and marshals were named for the first time. Thus, without relaxing political control, Stalin introduced an element of relaxation into the daily life of the rank and file, at the very height of his Terror. The standard of living went up as the production of consumer's goods was encouraged, and as workers were invited to spend their earnings on little luxuries previously unavailable.

Simultaneously, the state rediscovered Russia's great past. The standard communist teaching had been that proletarians have no fatherland; the very name of Russia had almost been abandoned. Now, in contrast, officially controlled organs of opinion editorialized that one should love one's own country, and hailed the heroes of the tsarist era. Alexander Nevsky, who had defeated the Teutonic knights; Dmitri Donskoi, who had defeated the Tartars; Peter the Great; Kutuzov, who had defeated Napoleon; even Ivan the Terrible—all were praised to the skies. Instead of being denounced, as had been the practice, for having cheated the serfs, Tsar Alexander II was now lauded for having set them free. The reputations of the great literary figures of the nineteenth century underwent a similar rehabilitation. This retreat to Russian nationalism reached its climax during World War II, when the Marxist *Internationale* itself was dropped as the national anthem, and every possible note of nationalism was blatantly sounded by the enormous state propaganda machine.

The old Bolsheviks had attacked the family as the backbone of the old order, had made marriage difficult and divorce easy, had drawn no distinction between legitimate and illegitimate children, and had encouraged promiscuity and abortions. Stalin's state now rehabilitated the sanctity of marriage, denounced the seducer, made divorces very hard to get, declared the

500   CHAPTER XXVI

family essential to the state, and encouraged children to obey their parents. Doubtless the shift came in part as a result of the falling birthrate and increasing juvenile delinquency, but it was none the less part of the abandonment of radicalism.

The early Bolsheviks had destroyed the old school system, abolished homework and examinations, and allowed children to administer the schools collectively with their teachers. Attendance fell off, the schools became revolutionary clubs of youngsters, and the training of teachers was neglected. The universities deteriorated, since anybody aged sixteen could enroll in them. Degrees were abolished, and technical training was stressed to the exclusion of other subjects. Under NEP, this chaotic situation was modified, and the basic problem of increasing literacy was seriously tackled. But the subjects of ordinary school curricula were replaced by the so-called "project" system, with heavy emphasis on labor problems and Marxist theory. The teachers had little to do except memorize texts, and quiz the children to test their mastery of them. The Communist party itself took over the universities, purged the faculties, and compelled the students to spend one week in three at work in factories—a system that helped neither the student nor the university, and cannot have increased industrial production by very much.

The "thermidorean reaction," as might have been expected, changed this system drastically. Training of teachers improved, their salaries were raised, and regular ranks in the civil service were established for them. The old pre-revolutionary system of admissions and degrees in the universities was restored, as was the pre-revolutionary school curriculum. Examinations and homework re-appeared; discipline was enforced on school children. The emphasis on political education was reduced, and co-educa-

tion was abandoned. Fees for tuition were restored for secondary schools, the Russian counterpart of the American high school or the French *lycée*. These tuition fees make higher education difficult to obtain except for children of the new élite or unusually talented students who are able to win state scholarships. Literacy has risen to about 90 per cent, if we may believe Soviet figures.

The educational reforms have certainly made books, theaters, museums, and libraries available to many more Russians than ever before. Newspapers and periodicals have multiplied, and the regime's respect for science and learning seems genuine. But the regime's attitude is narrowly utilitarian and thoroughly intolerant. All cultural activities are measured by their positive contribution to the state. Education has become indoctrination. Systems of ideas that might rival communism are not allowed to compete, since the government can always silence those who might be their spokesmen. In this respect the Soviet regime is even more authoritarian than that of a ruler like Tsar Nicholas I (see Chapter XXII).

Under Nicholas I, censorship prevented the writer from saying certain things, but it did not positively prescribe what he must say. It was a negative, not a positive censorship, and it left a margin of personal freedom that permitted some of the greatest works of all literature to be written in Russia. The Soviet censorship, on the other hand, is positive, and requires of all artists that they constantly praise the new system, and devote their talents to publicizing its merits. The party line has extended into all cultural fields, even music, where talented composers have to apologize abjectly for failing to produce communist symphonies, whatever they may be. A lyric poetess, previously in high favor, was severely reprimanded in 1946 for writing poems telling of her loneliness: apparently nobody in the

U.S.S.R. has the right to feel lonesome. The creative artist does not know from day to day whether his efforts will win him a Stalin prize or a sentence to a Siberian labor camp.

Neither does the scientist or scholar. Sciences like physics and genetics involve philosophical presuppositions. Soviet biologists, for example, have been punished for accepting standard western scientific principles that simply cast doubt on the possibility of creating a new biological race in one generation. The defenders of the "new Soviet man" stoutly proclaim that it *is* possible. In the humanities even the students of word-roots and early linguistic development have been victimized, and historians and social scientists steer a particularly perilous course.

The Russian Thermidor came last of all, and doubtless very reluctantly, to modify the traditional communist position on religion. Here militant atheism had been the policy of the early Bolsheviks. They jailed and sometimes executed bishops and priests; they sponsored an atheist society and a museum of anti-religious propaganda. Behind this attitude lay more than the standard Marxist feeling that religion was the opium of the masses; in Russia, the Orthodox Church had always been a pillar of tsarism, and had held back the intellectual advance of the country. Many years of attacks on religion, however, failed to eradicate Orthodoxy from among the people. When in 1937 Hitler built a Russian church in Berlin, and took every occasion to speak kindly of the Orthodox Church, Stalin moved in the religious field also. Declaring that Christianity had contributed to past Russian progress, the government called off its anti-religious propaganda and enlisted its own atheist society to rehabilitate the Church. Church-going became respectable once more, although members of the party were not encouraged to profess religion. As a result, when war came, the leading church dignitaries supported the regime enthusiastically, although Hitler won a number of Ukrainian clerics to his side. In 1943, Stalin received high churchmen; the government lowered taxes on church property, lifted the curfew for Easter, and appointed a new Patriarch, on whose subservience the regime could count.

Viewed together, the changes of the Thermidor period seem to have had a double purpose. They were designed in part to retain popular loyalty during a period when the party itself was being disrupted by the purges. But they were also designed in part to strengthen the country to meet an expected attack from Germany. However far the return to old and popular forms and ideas was carried, it was always the regime that took the lead. And never at any moment did Stalin relax his firm control over all departments of national life.

V: Soviet Foreign Policy, 1918-1941

Foreign Office and Comintern, 1918-1928

During the period of "war communism," the Bolsheviks had a chance to reflect upon their previously firm conviction that the world revolution was to be expected in the immediate future. The communist states in Bavaria and in Hungary proved to be short-lived (see Chapter XXVII); everywhere the moderates triumphed. As the civil war drew to a close,

Lenin and his followers realized that to re-build a shattered Russia it would be necessary to deal with the capitalist world. In the Foreign Office they had two competent men: Chicherin, a learned aristocrat turned Bolshevik, and Litvinov, his shrewd and able chief assistant. These two and their staff now became diplomats in the service of the Soviet state, like diplomats in the service of other states.

But the idea of world revolution was of course not abandoned. Lenin in 1919 founded the Third International, known thereafter as the Comintern. It issued what amounted almost to a new Communist Manifesto, summoning communists all over the world to unite against the "bourgeois cannibals" of capitalism. Zinoviev was put in charge, and his chief assistants were also Russians. Labor, socialist, and anarchist parties in Bulgaria, Norway, Italy, and Spain began to adhere to the new organization, although many withdrew in disgust when it became clear that the Bolsheviks were establishing a dictatorship in Russia with secret police and an army. Yet the Comintern continued to operate side by side with the Foreign Office, and during the next few years often in seeming contradiction to it. This duality gave Russian foreign policy a unique aspect. The maintenance of the Comintern aroused suspicion abroad, and made capitalist states reluctant even to recognize the new Russia.

The Foreign Office concluded a trade treaty with England in 1921, at the beginning of the NEP period, which bound Russia not to stir up the peoples of the British Empire by any means, and re-opened trade between the two countries. Similar treaties were concluded between Russia and Poland, the Baltic States, Scandinavia, Germany, and Italy. A truce had been arranged between the communist and capitalist worlds. In 1922, the Russians were invited to an international economic conference at Genoa. The British and French were convinced that NEP meant a return to capitalism, and had worked out a scheme for investment in Russia as part of a program for the postwar economic reconstruction of Europe. Not only did the Russians reject this plan, but they signed with defeated Germany the Treaty of Rapallo (April, 1922), which provided for the renunciation of all claims for reparations and implied a German willingness to recognize Bolshevik nationalizations. This recognition the other powers, especially France, were unwilling to grant because of the large amounts of capital they had invested in Russia before the revolution. Rapallo relieved Russian isolation, and brought German technical knowledge to the service of the Bolsheviks. They permitted the Germans to build and operate armament and aircraft factories on Russian soil in defiance of the Treaty of Versailles.

In 1923, at Lausanne, Russia lost a dispute with Britain over international regulation of the Straits, and further friction with Britain arose over Afghanistan. But Britain recognized the Soviet regime in 1924, despite Trotsky's description of the mild Laborite Ramsay MacDonald as a "Christian Menshevik" whose country was full of cockroaches—a comment that illustrates some of Russia's difficulty in getting along with the rest of the world. Later in the same year, 1924, the so-called "Zinoviev letter" was published in England. It purported to instruct the British Communist party in the techniques of revolution, and it may or may not have been genuine; but the "Zinoviev letter" influenced the British voters to return a Conservative government, which denounced the treaties with Russia. In 1927, a raid on the offices of a Russian firm doing business in London produced further evidence of communist agitation in England, and the government now broke relations with Russia altogether. The Anglo-

Russian council of trade unions set up by the communists collapsed when the Russians criticized British moderation in the general strike of 1926. Meantime, the United States had no diplomatic relations with the Soviet regime, and did not recognize it until 1933.

During the years 1918-1927, the Comintern compiled a record of failure. First, the Russians failed to keep in line the leaders of the Italian Left in a conference at Leghorn in 1921, and thus contributed handsomely to the success of Mussolini in the next year. They failed in Bulgaria to collaborate with a liberal agrarian regime, and allowed the triumph of a fascist group in 1923. Most important, they failed in Germany, where a revolution actually threatened during 1923 as a result of French occupation of the Ruhr (for details of these events, see Chapters XXVII and XXVIII). After Lenin's death, the feud between Stalin and Trotsky was reflected in the Communist parties of other countries and cost the Comintern heavily.

The Russians failed in Poland, where they helped Pilsudski to dictatorial power in 1926, after which he turned against them. They failed in the Moslem and colonial world. But their greatest failure came in China (see also Chapter XXIX), where in 1923 the Chinese nationalist revolutionary leader, Sun Yat-sen, agreed to take communist advice and received one of the Comintern's best men, Borodin. Borodin helped Sun re-organize his political party, the Kuomintang, and admitted communists to it, although this alienated the right-wing supporters of the national party. In March, 1926, Sun having died, his brother-in-law Chiang Kai-shek led a *coup* against the government, and began to arrest communists. It is often argued that, had Stalin at that moment broken with Chiang and proceeded to sponsor a Chinese communist revolution, he might well have won China.

Indeed Trotsky analyzed the situation that way at the time. But Stalin in his own analysis went back to a theory that the Bolsheviks had not espoused since Lenin's return to Russia in April, 1917: the theory that a bourgeois revolution must precede a socialist revolution, and that all the communists could and should do in China was to help Chiang achieve this first revolution. The eventual result was a series of massacres of Chinese communists by Chiang, and a loss of prestige for Stalin and for Russia.

Indeed Stalin had apparently never really believed in the effectiveness of the Comintern as an instrument of world revolution. When he came to sole power, he could not abandon it, however, because of the criticism he would have aroused, and because he sought to dilute and eventually to eradicate the largely Trotskyite sentiments of communists in other countries. He therefore applied to the Comintern the same techniques he had used against the party at home, and established full control over it through use of the Russian delegation. This delegation was responsible to the Politbureau, and as the representative of the only successful revolutionary country it enjoyed great prestige. Successively, the Comintern was influenced to denounce the enemies of Stalin: Trotsky and the Left in 1924, Bukharin and the Right in 1928. Thereafter there was no divergence between the Comintern and the Foreign Office.

Stalin and the West, 1928-1939

Simultaneously with the adoption of the "new socialist offensive" at home, Stalin swung the Comintern leftward into a new period of militant revolutionary activity. The Social Democrats of western countries were denounced now as social fascists and as the most dangerous enemies of communism. The communists were going to bring about revolutions by themselves. Yet Stalin's personal belief in the possibilty of revolution elsewhere seems to have been small. "One Soviet tractor is worth more than ten good foreign communists" is a remark quoted as typical of the views of Stalin's entourage in the days of the First Five-Year Plan; it reflects his real contempt for the rest of the world and his deep-rooted Russian nationalism.

This lack of real interest in the behavior of communists abroad and the failure to understand the true play of forces inside other countries led directly to the triumph of Hitler in Germany in 1933 (see Chapter XXVII). The communists in Germany, who had been instructed by the Comintern that the Social Democrats and not the Nazis were their worst enemies, fought the Nazis in the streets, but allied themselves with them in the Reichstag. They believed that a Nazi triumph would very soon be followed by a communist revolution. Thus even after Hitler came to power, the Russians renewed their nonaggression pact with Germany.

Yet the shock of realization that Hitler had meant precisely what he said about liquidating communists, and the fear that the U.S.S.R. itself might be in danger, soon led Stalin to modify Russian policy in the direction of collective security. After Hitler had refused to guarantee the Baltic states jointly with Stalin, Russia entered the League of Nations in September, 1934. The Soviet delegate, Litvinov, now became the most eloquent defender of universal disarmament and punishment for aggressors. Soon afterwards, the Russians began to negotiate for an "eastern Locarno" security pact to balance the agreement reached by the western European nations at Locarno in 1925 (see below, p. 589). Although no such structure could be created because of Polish and German hostility to the U.S.S.R.,

Russia did sign pacts with France and Czechoslovakia in 1935 providing for consultation, under the terms of the League, in the event of aggression, and for mutual aid, if the League certified that aggression had occurred. Soviet aid to Czechoslovakia, if the Czechs became victims of aggression, was to be delivered only if the French, who were bound to the Czechs by a long-standing alliance, honored their obligations first.

In view of the shift in Soviet foreign policy, the Comintern also shifted its line. In 1935 the recent deadly enemies, the Social Democrats and bourgeois liberals of the West, were to be warmly embraced as allies against the fascist menace. Communists were to take the lead in forming "popular fronts" against fascism, and might properly welcome anybody, no matter how conservative in other ways, who would stand together with them on this principle. Revolutionary propaganda and anti-capitalist agitation were to be soft-pedaled. The communists in all the countries of the world led the fight for the defense budgets that they had previously sabotaged. Georgi Dimitrov, the Bulgarian communist, hero of the Reichstag fire trial (see below, p. 543) and a symbol of antifascist courage and wit, was made boss of the Comintern. Inside the Soviet Union the adoption of the "popular front" strategy was probably not unrelated to the purges, since the "Right deviationists" were anxious to reach an accommodation with the fascist states, and the "Left deviationists" insisted on the steady pursuit of world revolution.

This was the period when popular front governments came to power in France and Spain, and when many young men and women in the West with bright hopes and little knowledge of the Soviet Union accepted the communists as their true brothers in arms against the menace of Hitler. However effective the "popular front" may have been as a tactic with western individuals, the purges inside Russia disillusioned western governments. A state that had to exterminate its top civil and military personnel for the crime of collaborating with the enemy did not make an attractive ally. If one believed the purge charges, one regarded a Soviet alliance as of doubtful value; if one did not believe them, how could one trust Stalin? On Stalin's side, western appeasement of Hitler and Mussolini (see Chapter XXVIII) doubtless disillusioned him with the West.

Russia and the western European bloc each assumed that the chief purpose of the other was to turn the full force of Hitler's forthcoming attack away from itself and in the opposite direction. That Hitler intended to attack, nobody could doubt. On September 12, 1936, in a speech at Nuremberg, he specifically declared once more that

if I had the Ural mountains with their incalculable store of treasures in raw materials, Siberia with its vast forests, and the Ukraine with its tremendous wheatfields, Germany under National Socialist leadership would swim in plenty.*

There was, then, much reason for the West to hope that the attack would be directed against the U.S.S.R.; this Stalin was determined to avert.

Soviet intervention in the Spanish Civil War (see below, Chapter XXVII) is an interesting demonstration of Stalin's real position. General Francisco Franco, who led an army revolt against the republican government of Spain in 1936, soon obtained aid from Mussolini and Hitler. The Russians, though reluctant to intervene in Spain at all because of their anxiety to prove their respectability to the western powers, realized that a failure to help the Spanish republic would cost them support all over the

world. But their aid was too little and came too late, and consisted largely of police agents who devoted themselves to fighting Spanish anarchists and Trotskyites. The Russians hoped that the western powers would intervene also, feeling that if they did so they would be irrevocably committed to continue the fight against Hitler on other battlefields. But western neutrality in Spain helped convince Stalin that a western alliance could not be counted upon.

A still more important factor here was the western appeasement of Hitler, which reached its climax in the Munich agreement of Britain, France, Germany, and Italy in September, 1938 (see also Chapter XXVIII). From the Russian point of view, the Munich cession of Czech lands to Hitler, and the French failure to support Czechoslovakia and thus make operative the Russo-Czech alliance, could have only one purpose—to drive Hitler east. Stalin was apparently ready to support the Czechs if the French did too; when they did not, he seems to have decided that he had better sound out Hitler for an understanding. Thus a truly operative alliance between Stalin and the West proved impossible between 1935 and 1939.

When the British and French realized that appeasement had failed to stop Hitler, they sought reluctantly for a firmer alliance with the U.S.S.R. From March to August, 1939, Stalin kept open both his negotiations with the West and his slowly ripening negotiations with the Germans, which at first seemed to be concerned only with a trade agreement. The British and French mission, when it finally arrived in Moscow, was not composed of sufficiently high-ranking men to inspire Russian confidence. Moreover, the western powers naturally refused to turn over to Stalin the territories that he wanted as a bulwark against Germany—Finland and the Baltic republics of Estonia, Latvia, and Lithuania.

---

* A. Hitler, *My New Order*, R. de Sales, ed. (New York, 1941), 400.

506

The growing eagerness of the Germans to secure a nonaggression pact gave Stalin the opportunity he sought to divert the war from Russia. In May, 1939, Litvinov was dismissed as foreign minister because he was Jewish and could therefore not negotiate with Germans; he was replaced by Molotov. In the pact Molotov eventually reached with Hitler late in August, 1939, both powers undertook to remain neutral toward each other in the event of war. A secret additional protocol provided for a division between Germany and Russia of Poland, which Hitler was about to attack. At worst, this put Russia's frontier farther west in the event of a subsequent German attack. The Russians lived up to the economic clauses of the agreement to the letter, although the Germans did not. The publication of the Hitler-Stalin pact necessitated an abrupt shift in the world communist line, which had remained staunchly "popular front." Now it was once more necessary for puzzled communists to denounce liberals and Social Democrats as enemies. They had to call the war that Hitler launched against Poland within a few days an "imperialist war," in which there was no difference between the two sides and in which communists should not get involved.

Stalin and the Second World War

Stalin overrated the military power of the Poles to resist Hitler, and thus miscalculated the course of the first weeks of war. Faced with the complete collapse of Poland, he marched into the eastern portion. Disturbed by the lull ("the phony war") on the western fronts, he probably feared that Hitler would turn against him at once. This might well have happened had Hitler been able to secure peace with France and England, as he strove to do.

During the lull, in December, 1939, came Stalin's attack on Finland, which, unlike the Baltic states, had refused to grant him strategic bases. The attack on the Finns by Stalin aroused a storm of anti-Russian sentiment in the West. Both Britain and France supported the recruitment of armies of volunteers, and considered air-raids against Russian targets in support of the Finns. The League of Nations expelled Russia. Despite severe setbacks to the Russian troops, the war against the Finns was won by the spring of 1940 before the western allies had been able to give them effective aid.

And in the spring of 1940, Stalin's second major calculation went awry. Like many observers, he apparently expected France to hold out a long time and had believed that, even if Hitler eventually defeated the French, Germany would be greatly weakened. Now instead came the lightning German operations in the west, and the war on the Continent was over. Only the British held out (see Chapter XXX). Preoccupied with the security of his western frontiers, Stalin simply seized the three Baltic republics and staged rigged plebiscites in which the Latvians, Estonians, and Lithuanians asked to be included in the Soviet Union. He demanded of Rumania in June, 1940, the province of Bessarabia, whose loss after World War I the U.S.S.R. had never recognized, and also northern Bukovina, which had formerly been Habsburg, not Russian, territory, but which had a large Ukrainian population and was strategically valuable. Parts of these territories were annexed to existing SSRs and parts were incorporated into the new Moldavian SSR. The Germans had expected Russian seizure of Bessarabia, but not of Bukovina; they permitted the seizure, however, telling the Rumanians that they could expect no help from Hitler. But that was as far as Hitler's co-operation with Stalin in eastern Europe went. The re-annexation of Bessarabia had given the U.S.S.R. the mouths of the Danube, controlling an important artery. The Russians seemed to be moving into southeast Europe, a region in which the Germans were not prepared to let them operate alone.

Only a few weeks after the Russian seizure of Rumanian territory, Hitler asserted his own southeastern interests by forcing the Rumanians to cede territory to Hungary (August, 1940) and then guaranteeing the new Rumanian frontiers, a guarantee that could apply only against the U.S.S.R. Soon afterwards, German troops appeared in Finland, "to reinforce the German armies in Norway," Hitler explained. And in the autumn of 1940 German troops entered Rumania proper, "to guard the Rumanian oil-fields against British sabotage." These maneuvers on his new frontiers deeply disquieted Stalin, as well they might have.

In October, 1940, Italy attacked Greece, and open war had spread to the Balkans. In November, when Molotov went to Berlin, Hitler tried to dazzle him with grandiose offers of an enormous future Soviet sphere of influence extending through Persia to the Persian Gulf and Indian Ocean, and including India, after the British Empire was destroyed. Each time this luscious bait was held out, Molotov tried to bring the discussion back to southeast Europe and Finland, and to establish Russia's sole rights in this sphere. This the Germans would not allow. After the failure of the conversations, Hitler ordered preparations for an attack on the U.S.S.R.

In the spring of 1941, the Germans had to rescue the Italians from the Greek campaign, which had bogged down in Albania. This rescue was preceded by the movement of German troops into Bulgaria, which the U.S.S.R. regarded as essential to its own defense. Then came an unsuccessful German effort to win Yugoslavia without war, and swift victorious German campaigns in Yugoslavia and Greece (March-May, 1941). Germany alone ruled supreme in the Balkan region, and, though the Yugoslav and Greek resistance had delayed the German timetable, Hitler was able to launch the invasion of the U.S.S.R. on June 22, 1941. Stalin must have known it was coming; indeed the western powers had warned him. But he seems to have hoped against hope to the end. A few weeks before it came, Stalin, proudly calling himself an Asiatic, had secured a neutrality pact with Japan, Hitler's ally. The Japanese, deeply engaged in China, and intending to go to war with the United States, wished as much as did the Russians for insurance against a war on two fronts.

VI: Conclusion

Karl Marx, who scorned and disliked Russia, would have been utterly dumbfounded had he lived to see that backward agricultural land, almost without a proletariat, produce the only successful European communist revolution. Although much ink has been spilled in an effort to discover why a Marxist revolution took place in the country where, in theory, the conditions were least favorable, the problem is not really so difficult. Two possible general solutions suggest themselves: either Marx was wrong, or what happened in Russia was not a Marxist revolution at all. Or perhaps both these answers are partly right. It seems clear that Marx did not correctly estimate the revolutionary force latent in the Russian peasantry; since Marx died in 1883, he could not foresee the full inadequacy of the tsarist regime, the extent of tensions created by World War I, or the feebleness of the provisional government of 1917. But it also seems clear that to bring the Bolsheviks to power it took Lenin's appreciation of the importance of the peasantry, his grasp of the immediate situation, his willingness to risk everything, and his luck at being in the right place at the right time with the right weapons.

On the other hand, the revolution was not wholly Marxist. Once the Bolsheviks were in power, of course, it was inevitable that the succession of real situations they faced should modify their Marxist-Leninist theories. Thus civil war and foreign intervention brought chaos from which NEP provided a necessary respite. And in Stalin there came to power an amalgam of Marxist, Russian nationalist, and power-hungry politician such as nobody could have foreseen. Moved by a combination of motives, Stalin pro-ceeded hastily and brutally to make over Russia in a decade. Although he fell short of his goal, his program had created an industrial state not totally unprepared for the blows that Hitler was to deal it. Slaves of the state though they were, collectivized by force, industrialized by force, purged, terrorized, and struggling by the million to exist in forced labor camps, the Russians in World War II succeeded, with much help from the United States, in defeating Hitler and his allies.

How much the loyalty of Russians to Stalin was due to the failure of the German invaders to treat them well, and how far Hitler with a different policy might have won their support are questions with which we cannot deal here. The Russians were facing a coalition of fascist states—Germany, Italy, Hungary, Rumania, and others grouped together in an alliance called "the Axis powers" (from the German-Italian "Axis"), a coalition pledged to the utter destruction of communism. It is to the history of these powers and of the fascist doctrine that they pursued that we now turn.

Reading Suggestions on Communist Russia

General Accounts

E. H. Carr, *A History of Soviet Russia*. Four volumes of this work, still in progress, have so far appeared (New York: The Macmillan Company, 1950-1954). The only attempt at a complete history of the Soviet Union from original sources; Carr is a somewhat uncritical admirer of Lenin, and his work must be used with care.

B. Moore, Jr., *Soviet Politics: The Dilemma of Power* (Cambridge, Mass.: Harvard University Press, 1950). An illuminating analysis of the relationship between communist ideology and Soviet practice.

R. N. Carew Hunt, *The Theory and Practice of Communism* (New York: The Macmillan Company, 1951). An excellent introduction to the subject.

M. Fainsod, *How Russia Is Ruled* (Cambridge, Mass.: Harvard University Press, 1953). An analysis of the Soviet system in 1953, firmly rooted in the historical background.

W. W. Rostow and others, *The Dynamics of Soviet Society* (New York: New American Library, 1954. A Mentor Book). Attempt by a group of scholars to determine why the Russians behave as they do.

Special Studies

W. H. Chamberlin, *The Russian Revolution, 1917-1921*, 2 vols. (New York: The Macmillan Company, 1935). Still the standard work on the subject.

L. Trotsky, *The History of the Russian Revolution*, 3 vols. (New York: Simon and Schuster, 1932). A brilliant and biased study by one of the leading participants.

B. D. Wolfe, *Three Who Made a Revolution* (New York: Dial Press, 1948). Excellent triple study of Lenin, Trotsky, and Stalin.

D. Shub, *Lenin* (New York: Doubleday, Inc., 1948. Abridgment available as a Mentor Book: New York, New American Library). The best biography of Lenin in English.

I. Deutscher, *The Prophet Armed* (New York: Oxford University Press, 1954). A good biography of Trotsky, by a sympathetic hand.

I. Deutscher, *Stalin: A Political Biography* (New York: Oxford University Press, 1949). The most complete account in English.

J. Maynard, *Russia in Flux* (New York: The Macmillan Company, 1948). Enlightening though sometimes far-fetched attempts to show basic continuities between the old and new regimes; by a British civil servant in India who made Russian studies his avocation.

C. Brinton, *The Anatomy of Revolution*, 2nd ed. (New York: Prentice-Hall, Inc., 1952). Comparison of the Russian revolution with the French revolution of 1789 and the English seventeenth-century revolution.

H. Schwartz, *Russia's Soviet Economy*, 2nd ed. (New York: Prentice-Hall, Inc., 1954). Good introduction to the subject.

N. Timasheff, *The Great Retreat* (New York: E. P. Dutton & Co., 1946). An account of the social changes in Russia during the Soviet period.

R. Pipes, *The Formation of the Soviet Union* (Cambridge, Mass.: Harvard University Press, 1954). Excellent monograph on the question of national minorities in Russia, 1917-1923.

J. W. Wheeler-Bennett, *Brest-Litovsk, The Forgotten Peace* (London: Macmillan & Co., Ltd., 1938). Excellent monograph on the Peace of Brest-Litovsk.

CHAPTER XXVI

L. Fischer, *The Soviets in World Affairs,* 2nd ed. (Princeton: Princeton University Press, 1951). The only study of Soviet foreign policies up to 1929.

M. Beloff, *The Foreign Policy of Soviet Russia,* 2 vols. (New York: Oxford University Press, 1947, 1952). A solid study covering the years 1929-1941.

F. C. Barghoorn, *The Soviet Image of the United States* (New York: Harcourt, Brace & Co., 1950). How the U.S.S.R. looks at the U.S.A.; by a former representative of the American Department of State.

E. Lyons, *Assignment in Utopia* (New York: Harcourt, Brace & Co., 1937). An American journalist records his disillusionment with Soviet communism.

R. H. Crossman, ed., *The God That Failed* (New York: Harper and Brothers, 1950). Brief statements by Arthur Koestler, Stephen Spender, Ignazio Silone, and other intellectuals recording their disenchantment with communism.

V. A. Kravchenko, *I Chose Freedom* (New York: Charles Scribner's Sons, 1946). The most celebrated of many works by ex-Soviet officials and citizens who preferred the West to the U.S.S.R.

Historical Fiction

A. Koestler, *Darkness at Noon* (New York: Modern Library, 1946). A famous novel, presenting in fictional form a keen analysis of the attitudes of the Old Bolsheviks whom Stalin purged.

V. Serge, *The Case of Comrade Tulayev* (New York: Doubleday, Inc., 1950). Another excellent novel of the purges.

G. Blunden, *The Room on the Route* (Philadelphia: J. B. Lippincott Company, 1947). Perhaps the most vivid fictional portrayal of the impact of terror on the ordinary person.

A. Tolstoy, *Road to Calvary* (New York: Alfred A. Knopf, Inc., 1946). Translation of a Stalin Prize Novel about the revolution and civil war.

The Rise of Fascism: 1918-1939

CHAPTER XXVII

Hitler and his entourage driving through Hildesheim,

I: Introduction

IN THIS CHAPTER we shall deal with the rise of fascism in Europe in the period between the two great wars. By 1939, authoritarian governments of the Right were in firm control of Italy, Germany, Spain, and all the countries of eastern and southeastern Europe except Russia. The process by which these regimes came to power differed widely from country to country, as did some of the external features of the regimes. At first glance, fascism is more complex and more difficult to understand than communism, a doctrine whose development can be traced from Marx through Lenin before its followers were able to put it, or something like it, into practice in Russia. Unlike communism, fascism has no such line of theoretical development. Its proponents often seem to have acted first and worried about doctrine later, devising theories to meet the needs of the moment.

Fascism has been called the revolution of the classes of order. Political parties on the Continent have often represented the interests of the various social classes; when those interests have seemed to be about evenly balanced in a parliamentary state, a long and indecisive political tug-of-war has often ensued. For example, let us assume that a revolution from the Left threatens or can be made to seem to threaten. Then the middle classes, so the theory runs, seize power and take refuge in their own form of extremism—fascism, that is, nationalism tricked out with a few radical phrases to win mass support, and draped in mystical garments. This formula can be applied to Mussolini's rise to power in Italy in 1922, to Hitler's rise to power in Germany in 1933, to Franco's rise to power in Spain in 1936-1939, and to many of the eastern European dictators. Yet the formula takes us only so far. Only a study of the different circumstances in each of the different countries can give it body and meaning.

Economic depressions played a role in the rise of almost every dictator: the post-war depression in Italy, and elsewhere the world-wide depression of 1929 and later. We notice, moreover, a certain similarity in the externals of fascism everywhere—colored shirts, private armies, mass hypnotism, special salutes, special war cries and ceremonies, mystical glorification of the nation, and a vast program of conquest. The dictator's program is justified by references to "have" and "have-not" nations; his own nation is always a "have-not," always oppressed.

Fascism is just as violent in its hatred of democracy, liberalism, and parliamentary institutions as in its professed dislike of communism. Indeed fascism shares communism's abhorrence of constitutional procedure, its disregard of the individual human being, and its insistence that the state is supreme. Fascism persecutes its enemies, both real and fancied, with the same ruthlessness we have observed in Stalin's Russia. Censorship, political police, concentration camps, the rule of the bludgeon, the end of legal protection—all these practices are common to both fascism and communism.

When Mussolini ruled in Rome, public buildings everywhere carried the admonition to loyal Italians, "Believe, fight, obey" (*Credere, combattere, obbedire*). Presumably this was intended to be inspiring. Yet all it really means is: Believe (what Mussolini tells you), fight (for Mussolini and his backers), obey (Mussolini). When put this way, the formula is seen to subvert all religion and all human decency, and to express only a nihilist creed, a belief in nothing but opportunism. Yet many an idealist was taken in by it, under the stress of the unbearable pressures on individuals generated by the tension of the years between the wars.

II: Italy and Fascism

The Setting

Although Italy was a member of the victorious Allied coalition, she finished the First World War with a sense of defeat. Six hundred and fifty thousand of her men had been killed and one million wounded. Industry slumped immediately after the war, and within a few months 10 per cent of the industrial workers were unemployed. Prices rose rapidly, and wages failed to keep up. The promised pensions for wounded veterans and families of the killed were long delayed. Strikes and disorders became frequent. Many of the young men released from the armies with no trade but war and no job to go to drifted restlessly and discontentedly, fit prey for leaders with glittering promises.

Perhaps most important, the government itself began almost at once to spread propaganda among the Italian people to the effect that their wartime allies were robbing them of the territories that had been promised them in exchange for their entry into the war. The government hoped to engender a wave of public opinion so violent that it would influence the negotiations for the peace. Although the Allied leaders at the Paris Peace Conference remained unaffected by the storms of protest arising from Italy, the Italian people did come to believe that they had shed their blood in vain. The territories of which they felt themselves deprived were the Slavic lands in Dalmatia, across the Adriatic, promised to Italy by the Secret Treaty of London (see above, Chapter XXV). This arrangement the Americans had never agreed to, and now would not accept. Popular sentiment in Italy, especially in the army, swung away from the government and toward extremists of one sort or another.

Some Italians hysterically supported Gabriele d'Annunzio, a short, totally bald poet and romantic novelist who formed a band of volunteers. They seized the city of Fiume, the Adriatic seaport over which Croatians and Hungarians had long disagreed (see above, p. 304). Referring to the "stench of peace," and denouncing Woodrow Wilson, d'Annunzio declared that the time for heroic individual action was at hand. Fiume had actually not been awarded to Italy even by the Secret Treaty of London, but d'Annunzio felt that Italy must have it, and that was enough. He ran his own government in Fiume until the end of 1920.

D'Annunzio patterned his regime there upon that of an imaginary medieval commune in a poem by Italy's romantic poet Carducci (1835-1907). Modeling himself consciously upon the governor of the commune in the poem, d'Annunzio would appear on the balcony of the city hall, address an inspirational harangue to the crowd, and ask for its unanimous consent for whatever he wished to do. This his listeners would grant, raising their right hands high, as the imaginary citizens of Carducci's commune had done. They also had a cry, which they chanted or shouted rhythmically: *Eya, Eya, Alalà*. Some of d'Annunzio's followers wore black shirts. When d'Annunzio asked them to whom Fiume belonged they would shout *A noi*, "to us," and when he asked them to whom Italy belonged, they would give the same answer. Indeed, he planned to lead his followers from Fiume to Rome, and thence out into the world to conquer it, presumably with daggers, which he preferred to mechanized weapons. He drafted the Statutes of Fiume, a constitution in which he made a conscious attempt to organize society along the lines he imagined to have existed in the guilds and artisans' corporations of the Middle Ages.

In November, 1920, the Italian government signed the Treaty of Rapallo with Yugoslavia, by which Fiume was to become a free city. Italian forces drove d'Annunzio out, and into retirement in a villa on the Italian lakes. But the techniques of force, the haranguing of the mob from the balcony, the straight-arm salute, the black shirts, the rhythmic cries, the plans for conquest, and the "corporative" scheme of the Statutes of Fiume served as precedent and inspiration for Benito Mussolini, founder of Italian fascism.

In the first four years after the end of the war, Mussolini created and brought to power a new political force in Italy. In October, 1922, he was summoned to office by King Victor Emmanuel III (1900-1947); from then on he gradually created a totalitarian state of which he was the sole, un-disputed ruler. Suppressing all opposition at home, and threatening the peace abroad, the fascist state in Italy served in some degree as model for the Nazis in Germany, for the Falangists in Spain, and for totali-tarian regimes in virtually all the European successor states of the Habsburg and Otto-man empires. Eventually, Mussolini was forced, largely by his own propaganda, into an alliance with Hitler. In 1940, this alli-ance took Italy into World War II, and in 1945 it brought Mussolini himself to an ignominious death, upside down on a com-munist partisan gallows, with his mistress beside him.

To understand what really happened, we must first consider Mussolini's career be-fore the foundation of fascism; second, the steps by which he came to Rome; third, the development of the fascist state until the moment of its involvement in World War II; and, finally, the place of earlier thinkers in the history of Italian fascism.

Mussolini: Early Career

Mussolini was born in 1883, in the Romagna, a province of central Italy fa-mous for its political extremists, and for the violence with which they express them-selves. His father was an ardent socialist who had begun his career as an anarchist under the influence of Bakunin (see above, p. 318). Trained as an elementary-school teacher, Mussolini was already a passionate socialist by the time he was eighteen. He spent some time as an agitator among Italian emigrant laborers in Switzerland (1902-1904), but was twice expelled by the police. He taught school in Italy (1906-1908), then went as socialist journalist and labor leader to Trent, an important center of the Italian minority in Austria, from which he was expelled in 1909. Back in Italy, he

was imprisoned for opposing the war against Turkey over Tripoli (1911). In 1912, he became editor of the most impor-tant Italian socialist newspaper, *Forward* (*Avanti*).

When World War I began, Mussolini was at first vigorously opposed to Italy's entry. But then, during 1914, he changed his mind. First he favored "relative neutral-ity," meaning that socialists should leave themselves free to support Italian entry if such a course seemed likely to prove favor-able to them. When the Italian Socialist party refused to follow this idea, he re-signed as editor of *Avanti*. Soon afterward (November, 1914), he founded his own newspaper, *The People of Italy* (*Il Popolo d'Italia*) in Milan, and began to advocate an immediate Italian declaration of war on the side of the Allies. For this the Socialist party expelled him.

But these bare bones of a biography reveal only the externals. As a socialist, Mussolini before 1914 was a passionate left-winger. He was an apostle of violent social revolution and a bitter opponent of milder evolutionary and reformist doctrine. He urged that a small, well-knit armed minority should seize power and establish a dictatorship. He loathed militarism, was himself a draft-dodger, and urged soldiers to desert the army. He hated monarchy, and savagely attacked in his writings all the crowned heads of Europe, especially the Italian House of Savoy. He was a vigorous atheist, urged workers to stay away from church, and scorned the teachings of Christ. As an international revolutionary he opposed nationalism, and even referred to the Italian flag as "a rag to be planted on a dunghill."

Yet he was to repudiate each and every one of these positions, and as fascist chief-tain to substitute almost the exact oppo-sites. As a fascist, he attacked bolshevism and all left-wing movements; he made his peace with the monarchy and the Church; he became a militant nationalist, a mystic patriot, and a rabid militarist. The repudiation of the views he had held so long and advocated so skillfully is not nearly so astonishing as it seems. From the first, Mussolini did not care for programs; what he wanted was to rule.

A complete opportunist, he could shift his line on any question at a moment's notice if it seemed advantageous. For example, after the war, though he was now a fascist, he at first supported a radical program of social change, indistinguishable from the program he would have advocated had he still been a socialist. He favored the action of the Italian workers in the fall of 1920, when they occupied the factories in a kind of sit-down strike. Yet, within a year, he was using the fears which this strike had aroused in the middle classes to argue that he was the only possible bulwark against "bolshevism." About certain matters, however, he was consistent: he always hated parliaments and he always loved violence.

Mussolini's switch from isolationism to interventionism in the war in 1914 was the first of his important shifts. It may be that as a revolutionary socialist he had come to feel that only war could produce in Italy the conditions necessary to a revolution. It may be that his affection for violence got the better of his socialist doctrines, and that he pleaded for action simply for the sake of action. After his expulsion from the Socialist party, he agitated furiously for war, speaking to groups of similarly minded young men called *fasci* or groups (the image is of a bundle of rods, a symbol of office in the Roman Republic of antiquity). Soon after Italy did enter the war in 1915, Mussolini was conscripted and sent to the front. He was badly wounded in 1917 by an Italian mortar shell that exploded during practice, and he spent several months in the hospital. When he got out, he continued to edit his newspaper, now no longer as a socialist but still as a revolutionary, spewing forth a mixture of extreme revolutionary and extreme nationalist propaganda.

Mussolini: Rise to Power

In March, 1919, Mussolini founded the first *fasci di combattimento* ("groups for combat"). These were not unlike similar groups that urged the seizure of Dalmatia, of which d'Annunzio's was the most important. Mussolini's movement was still very small. There was nothing in March, 1919, to indicate that by October, 1922, the leader of the *fasci di combattimento* would become the most powerful man in Italy. In 1919, he called for every kind of revolutionary violence—seizure of the land, attacks on the factories, shooting of storekeepers who charged high prices, expropriation of mines and transports, and war by the vanquished "proletarian" nations against the victorious capitalists who had kept Italy from annexing Dalmatia. He now maintained that socialism was too conservative; his movement, far from setting itself against a revolution, was in the vanguard of those who were crying for one.

Yet in Italy a revolution along Bolshevik patterns was most unlikely, if not impossible. The peasants were not very revolutionary, for they already held much of the land except in the extreme south. And the industrial workers, though often discontented, knew that a revolution could be starved out because the country needed to import most of its raw materials. The Socialist party was overwhelmingly in the hands of moderates, and in 1919 Catholics founded the Popular party (*Partito Populare Italiano*), designed to compete with the Socialists for the votes of the lower classes, who now had universal suffrage.

In the postwar disorders the peasants seized without consent of the landowners less than one-tenth of 1 per cent of the arable land in Italy. The leaders of the Socialist party and the General Confederation of Labor voted down the proposals of anarchist and communist extremists to turn the workers' occupation of the factories into a revolution. The government waited for the workers to grow tired. This they did in less than a month (September, 1920); then they left the occupied factories and went home.

Yet the actual state of affairs is often less important than what influential sections of society persuade themselves to believe is the actual state of affairs. Although the danger of revolution was small, the fear of revolution was great. Thus, during 1920 and 1921 the industrialists and landowners, squeezed by taxation and inflation, became bitter. Shopkeepers and tradesmen wanted street disorders to end, food prices to be regulated, and the co-operative food stores of the socialists and Catholic party to be put out of business as competitors. Professional men and others with fixed incomes suffered even more than others as prices and wages went up and salaries lagged behind. The police grew tired of suppressing local disorders and of being repaid with insults. Ex-servicemen, insulted by anarchists and communists for their war records, naturally grew more patriotic.

All these groups identified the forces they did not like as Bolshevik, and accepted as an article of faith the myth of an impending Bolshevik revolution. After a series of fascist-socialist street fights and riots, these "anti-Bolsheviks" began to look to Mussolini's fascist bands as the defenders of their interests. D'Annunzio's defeat left Mussolini as his natural heir. The Left opposition to Mussolini was weakened when the communists split off from the Socialist party in 1921. The *fasci* grew enormously, from 30,000 in May, 1920, to 100,000 in February, 1921, to more than 300,000 at the time of the "March on Rome" in October, 1922. No longer were they merely squads of discontented and idle youths with vaguely revolutionary and nationalist ideas. Now, says one fascist of the period, "the sons and hangers-on of the bigwigs" poured into the organization:

They had come into the Fascio for their own ends. . . . If they met men in working clothes, they fell on them and began beating them. Their mentality was on a par with that of the Communists, who had beaten and murdered anybody who was decently dressed. One saw . . . the well-known surly and rapacious faces of war profiteers . . . and we were obliged to accept their money because we needed it to stifle an evil worse than they.*

The liberal parliamentary leaders of Italy shared the anti-Bolshevik fears. Instead of attempting to restore order and holding new elections, they felt that the fascist bands were teaching the Left a useful lesson. They encouraged the commanding officers of the army to issue rifles and army trucks and gasoline to the fascists and even assigned army officers to command their operations. The police were encouraged to look the other way during disorders started by the fascists, and local judges were urged to help by releasing arrested fascists. Mussolini's newspaper was circulated free to the soldiers in the army as a "patriotic" sheet.

A genuine campaign of terror now began against the socialists and Christian Democrats, as the fascist squadrons cruised around Italy in trucks, burning down labor-union offices, newspaper offices, and local Socialist party headquarters, and beating up and sometimes murdering labor leaders

_____
* Umberto Banchelli, *Memorie di un Fascista,* quoted by G. Salvemini in *The Fascist Dictatorship* (New York, 1927), 67-68.

CHAPTER XXVII

Mussolini and fascisti during the "march" on Rome, October, 1922.

or local anti-fascist politicians. The *fasci* forced duly elected officials to resign. The torch, the cudgel, and the famous castor-oil treatment were all characteristic weapons. It is estimated that 2,000 people, anti-fascist and fascist, policemen and innocent by-standers, died by violence between October, 1920, and October, 1922.

The "March" on Rome

In the elections of May, 1921, Mussolini and thirty-four other fascists were elected to Parliament, along with ten Nationalists, their political allies. The momentum of the fascist movement was now too great to be slowed down. Mussolini abandoned his anti-monarchical views, and fascism became a political party (November, 1921) as a necessary step in the drive for power. Too late, the government became alarmed and tried to take measures against the fascists, but the squads were too strong, the police too accustomed to

collaborating with them, and the politicians themselves as yet unaware that a tightly directed armed mob could really take over the state. Inside the royal family, the King's cousin, the Duke of Aosta, had become a fascist sympathizer, as had many army generals, the entire Nationalist party, and the leading industrialists.

In the fall of 1922 it was clear that the army would not resist a fascist *coup* in Rome itself. Late in October, the cabinet proclaimed martial law, but the military authorities allowed the fascists to seize railway stations, postal and telegraph offices, newspaper offices, public buildings, and arsenals. When the decree of martial law was presented to the King, he refused to sign it, probably influenced by his knowledge that the army would not fight the fascists and that the Duke of Aosta would gladly take his crown. The refusal of the King to declare martial law greatly heartened the fascists. Now, as the fascists "marched" on Rome, mostly by storming railroad trains and stealing free rides, the

King (October 29, 1922) telegraphed Mussolini in Milan to come to Rome and form a cabinet. Mussolini arrived by sleeping-car the next morning.

Fascism, which had begun as a patriotic anti-Bolshevik movement, and had then turned into an anti-labor movement in the service of the industrialists and landowners, had finally come to power as a conspiracy against parliamentary government in the service of a military clique. Just before taking office, Mussolini announced:

Our program is simple: we wish to govern Italy. They ask us for programs, but there are already too many. It is not programs that are wanting for the salvation of Italy but men and will-power.*

The Fascist Dictatorship

Mussolini now moved gradually to turn his premiership into a dictatorship. A month after coming to office, he obtained dictatorial powers that were to last only until the end of 1923. Although the constitution theoretically remained in force, Mussolini proceeded to take over the administration. He created a Fascist Militia almost 200,000 strong, which owed complete allegiance to him. He enlarged the regular army, and required its members to take an oath of personal loyalty to him. Before his dictatorial powers expired, he secured from Parliament by pressure a new electoral law. This law provided that the political party which received the largest number of votes in a general election, if that number amounted to at least one-quarter of the vote, should automatically receive two-thirds of the seats in Parliament. The rest of the seats would be divided proportionately. This law made

---

* Quoted by H. Finer, *Mussolini's Italy* (New York, 1935), 152.

certain the fascists' domination of future parliaments. Indeed, in the election of April, 1924, the fascists actually polled 65 per cent of the vote cast; but this figure reflects a widespread use of intimidation and terrorism at the polls. The first all-fascist cabinet was now appointed. Meanwhile, local administration was made secure by the appointment of fascist prefects and subprefects in the provinces; these officials pursued the enemies of fascism with the same weapons of murder and mayhem that had been used before Mussolini's March on Rome.

Early in 1924, the leader of the opposition to Mussolini, the socialist Giacomo Matteotti, published a book called *The Fascists Exposed,* in which he detailed many of the outrages the fascists had committed on their way to power. It seemed probable that further revelations were in store, exposing some of Mussolini's cabinet members as corrupt. On June 10, 1924, Matteotti was "taken for a ride" in true gangster style and murdered. The crime was traced to members of Mussolini's immediate circle. This scandal rocked Italy, and for a moment it even seemed possible that Mussolini would fall. But he dismissed from office those who were involved, and pledged to restore law and order. Actually, he delayed trying the guilty men until March, 1926, and even then they all got off lightly.

What really helped Mussolini over the crisis, ironically enough, was the departure of most of the opposition deputies from Parliament. They declared that they would not return until the Matteotti murder had been solved and the government had been shown to be innocent. Far from making things harder for Mussolini, as they had intended, their departure actually made things easier. Mussolini simply denied his own guilt, imposed a rigid press censorship, and forbade the opposition to meet. Most of the deputies never did return to Parliament, and in 1926 their seats were declared forfeit.

Though the Matteotti crisis continued into 1925, Mussolini simply tightened the screws. A series of laws called the "most fascist laws" (*legge fascistissime*) tightened control over the press, forbade secret societies like the Freemasons, whom Mussolini had loathed ever since his socialist youth, and extended the control of the central government to all the cities and towns by depriving them of their elected officials, who were replaced by officials appointed from Rome. Opponents of the regime were arrested and transported into exile on desolate islands off the Italian coast. Early in 1926, Mussolini was empowered to govern by decree. Three attempts on his life led to a new law providing the death penalty for action against the King, the Queen, or Mussolini. All opposition political parties were abolished in the same year, and the Fascist party was left as the only legal political party in Italy.

More and more the Italian state and the Fascist party were brought into co-ordination. Mussolini was both the *Duce* of the fascists and the *capo di governo*, the chief of state. At one moment he also held eight cabinet posts simultaneously. The members of the Fascist Grand Council, a "politbureau" numbering roughly twenty of the highest party functionaries, all appointed by Mussolini, held all the important posts in the administration not held by Mussolini himself. In 1928, the Grand Council was given important constitutional duties: preparing the lists of candidates for election to the Chamber, advising Mussolini, and proposing changes in the constitution or the succession to the throne. The Grand Council thus became a kind of third house, above the other two houses of Parliament, the Senate and the Chamber.

Il Duce.

The Corporative State

Indeed, Mussolini planned to change the principles of the western parliamentary system. He believed that the interests of labor and capital could and must be made to harmonize with the over-riding interests of the state. Instead of a political system as we understand it, he accepted the idea that representation should be based on economic interests organized in "syndicates." Such an idea was not new: the French syndicalist, Georges Sorel (see below, p. 525) had already argued in this vein. But Sorel believed in class warfare, and in government by syndicates of workers only. Mussolini, following the Italian nationalist syndicalist, Rossoni, believed in capitalism, class-collaboration, and producers' syndicates as well as workers' syndicates.

In 1925, fascist labor unions were recognized by employers as having the sole right to negotiate labor contracts. Then, in April, 1926, the state officially recognized producers' and workers' syndicates in each of six areas—industry, agriculture, commerce, sea and air transport, land and inland waterway transport, and banking—plus a syndicate of intellectuals, making thirteen syndicates in all. Each syndicate could bargain and reach contracts, and could assess dues upon everyone engaged in its own economic field, irrespective of membership in the syndicate. Strikes and lockouts were both forbidden. When labor conditions did not improve, a "charter of labor," promising insurance and other benefits, was issued in 1927. In 1926, the syndicates were put under the control of a special Ministry of Corporations; Mussolini was the minister.

In 1928, the system of parliamentary representation was changed in accordance with fascist syndicalism. A new electoral law provided for a new Chamber of Deputies (400 instead of 560 members). The national councils of the thirteen syndicates could nominate a total of 800 candidates. Each syndicate had a quota, half to be selected by the employers and half by the employees. Cultural and charitable foundations could nominate 200 more candidates. When the total list of 1,000 was completed, the Fascist Grand Council could either select 400 of them, or strike out names and add names of its own, or even substitute an entire new list. The voters would then vote in answer to the question: "Do you approve of the list of deputies selected by the Fascist Grand Council?" They could vote "Yes" or "No" on the entire list, but they could not choose from among the candidates. If a majority voted "Yes," the list was elected; if not, the procedure was to be repeated. Despite the highly touted role of the syndicate, all the power obviously lay with the Fascist Grand Council. Universal suffrage was abolished even for this very limited form of election. Payment of a minimum tax or dues to a syndicate was required of each voter; women could not vote. In 1929, the elections under this system produced a "yes" vote of 8,519,559 and a "no" vote of 137,761.

Between 1930 and 1938 several constitutional steps were taken which seemed to move the syndicates into the center of the stage. Representatives from the syndicates and the government were now formed into a Council of Corporations, which was to act as a co-ordinating committee, settle disputes between syndicates, assist production, and establish the fascist corporations themselves, which had not yet been created. The Council was divided into seven sections corresponding to the seven syndicate areas, and in 1931 each of these sections of the Council was simply declared to be a corporation. In 1933, it was announced that the whole corporate system would be revised; and in 1934 the new elections (which of course returned the Fascist Grand Council's list of candidates) produced a "suicide" Chamber of Deputies, which was expected eventually to put an end to its own existence. Its replacement was to be a new "revolutionary assembly," which Mussolini called into existence in the fall of 1934. The assembly, also called the Central Committee of Corporations, contained 824 members, representing twenty-two newly created corporations. The Fascist party, as well as employers and employees, was represented on each corporation.

But it was not until 1938 that the last step was taken, when the "suicide chamber" ended its existence and replaced itself with the Central Committee of Corporations, which was now called the Chamber of Fasces and Corporations. There was nothing left of the old parliamentary constitution that had been set up by Cavour except the Senate, nominally appointed by the King but actually subservient to Mussolini, who on one occasion had the King appoint forty fascist senators all at once. This new structure, the corporative state, was influenced by d'Annunzio's strange medieval ideas, and by Mussolini's own wish to produce new political and economic forms. The Central Committee of Corporations and its successor body, the Chamber of Fasces and Corporations, were designed to advise the government, to settle labor disputes, and to plan and regulate production. In spite of much oratory by fascist sympathizers about the corporative state and its virtues, the corporations were scarcely the modern counterparts of medieval guilds. It does not appear that they ever had very much to do with running the economic or political life of Italy, which remained firmly under the direction of the fascist bureaucracy.

Other Fascist Domestic Policies

During the thirties, the fascist version of the planned economy made its appearance in Italy. The government issued or withheld permits for factory construction. In agriculture, a concerted effort was launched to make Italy more nearly self-sufficient. This effort was dramatized with the "Battle of Wheat," in which the Italians were treated to contests, prizes, personal appearances by Mussolini, and similar trappings. In 1932, official figures reported that wheat production had risen to a point where it could supply 92 per cent of the nation's normal needs, and the drive was enlarged to include other cereal products. The government subsidized steamship and air lines, encouraged the tourist trade, and protected Italian industries by means of high tariffs on foreign products. Marshes were drained and land was reclaimed; the incidence of malaria was reduced. Enormous sums were spent on public works, and great strides were made in the development of hydroelectric power. The trains, at least so thousands of naive American tourists reported, ran on time; as a result, the tour-

ists returned home insisting that "there must be something in this man Mussolini." Yet Italy's weakness in essential raw materials proved to be insuperable.

The state reached into the life of the individual at almost every point. Though Italy was overpopulated, and had for decades relieved the situation only by mass emigration, Mussolini made emigration a crime. He encouraged people to marry and have the largest possible families: he reduced their taxes, extended special loans, taxed bachelors, and extended legal equality to illegitimate children. He hoped in this way to swell the ranks of his armies, and to strengthen his claim that Italy must expand abroad. Children, the future party members, were enrolled in a series of youth movements, beginning at the age of six. The textbooks in the schools, the books in the libraries, the professors in the universities, the plays on the stage and the movies on the screen were all made vehicles of fascist propaganda. The secret police, OVRA (from the initials of the Italian words for "Vigilance Organization against Anti-Fascist Crimes"), endeavored to discover and suppress all opposition movements.

In 1929, Mussolini settled the Roman question (see Chapter XXI) by entering into the Lateran Treaty with the papacy. This treaty recognized the independent state of Vatican City and thus restored the temporal power of the pope, though on a greatly reduced scale. Mussolini also recognized Catholicism as the state religion, and promised to halt anti-papal propaganda. He gave up the right to tax contributions to the Church or the salaries of the clergy, and paid $105,000,000 to compensate the papacy for the Italian occupation of papal territories since 1870. A concordat further regulated the relations between Church and State. Religious marriages were legalized, and religious instruction was extended in schools. The Church agreed not to engage in politics in its newspapers and periodicals.

Yet, despite the fact that many church officials viewed the fascist movement sympathetically, difficulties arose after these agreements had been concluded. In an encyclical, Pope Pius XI (1922-1939) indicated his disapproval of Mussolini's "relentless" economic policies and of the corporations as "serving special political aims rather than contributing to the initiation of a better social order." Mussolini now charged that the Church's "Catholic Action" clubs were engaged in politics, and dissolved them. The Pope denied the charges, and denounced the Fascist party's practice of monopolizing the time and education of the young. In 1931, however, a further agreement was reached, and the clubs were re-opened.

Fascist Foreign Policy and Its Consequences

Since Mussolini's foreign policies form an integral part of the international relations leading up to World War II, we shall discuss them more fully in Chapter XXVIII. Here we may simply point out that his extreme nationalism, his love of panoply and parades, and his militarism were the logical extensions of his domestic ideas and accomplishments. Mussolini's wish to re-create the glories of ancient Rome impelled him to undertake a policy of adventure in the Mediterranean, which he called *Mare Nostrum* (Latin for "our sea") as a sign that he was the heir to the Caesars. This policy began with the Corfu incident in 1923. Five Italians working for the League of Nations were assassinated as they marked out the new frontier between Albania and Greece. This incident led Mussolini to bombard and occupy the

Greek island of Corfu. When the Greeks appealed to the League, Mussolini refused to recognize the League's right to intervene, and threatened to withdraw from the new international body. It was only British pressure that led to a settlement of the matter. The Greeks paid an indemnity, and Mussolini withdrew from Corfu.

But the entire episode, coming early in the history of fascism and the League, showed that the fascists would not be bound by international authority. Later, Mussolini's policy of adventure led him to military aggression in Ethiopia, in Spain, and in Albania (which he dominated during the 1920's and occupied in April, 1939). It drove him into an alliance with his fellow-fascist, Hitler, and led him to voice loud claims against the French for Corsica, Tunisia, Nice, and Savoy. And it alienated Italy from her natural allies, France and Britain. Thus, Mussolini's grandiose fascist ideology first spurred Italy to win self-sufficiency, to rebuild her seaports, and to create a merchant fleet and navy. But the same ideology ultimately separated her from the only powers who might have saved her from the disaster toward which Mussolini was driving.

The German alliance was also responsible for a striking new departure in fascist domestic policy. This was the official adoption of anti-Semitism, which took place in 1938. With only 70,000 Jews, most of whom had long been resident, Italy had no "Jewish problem." Italian Jews were entirely Italian in their language and sentiments, and could be distinguished from other Italians only by their religion. Just like the non-Jews of Italy, many of them were prominent in the fascist movement, and many were anti-fascist. There was no widespread sympathy in Italy for the government's adoption of Hitler's racial policies. Yet Hitler's dominating influence led Mussolini to expel Jews from the Fascist party, and to forbid them to teach or attend school, to intermarry with non-Jews, and to obtain new licenses to conduct businesses. The object was to drive the Jews from the economic, cultural, and political life of Italy.

The Forerunners of Fascism

This analysis of fascism in action leads us to our final question: What role did earlier thinkers play in the creation of Mussolini's system? The names of Machiavelli, William James, Schopenhauer, and other philosophers are often mentioned as precursors of fascism. But it seems probable that Mussolini used their works to explain to himself or to justify to others actions that he had already taken. More significant in the list of alleged fascist forerunners are three nineteenth-century rebels against reason—Nietzsche, Georges Sorel, and Pareto (for further details on Nietzsche and Pareto, see Chapter XXIII).

Nietzsche's distaste for Christianity and democracy, his picture of a heroic Superman with an outsize Will to Power, and his gospel of action and glorification of violence deeply impressed Mussolini, who, while still a socialist, wrote an essay on Nietzsche in 1908. After Mussolini had come to power, Nietzsche's sister, who was the leader of a Nietzsche cult which distorted many of her dead brother's actual thoughts, proclaimed that the Duce was her brother's ideal Superman. Certainly Nietzsche provided convenient rationalizations for Mussolini's actions. Yet Nietzsche disliked the state, and could not have provided the Superman-Duce with any of the inspiration for the actual work of governing Italy.

Georges Sorel (1847-1922) was a French exponent of anarcho-syndicalism (see Chapter XX) and author of *Reflections on Vio-*lence. Loathing the middle classes, and denouncing parliamentary socialists and moderates, Sorel turned to the trade unions as the source of revolutionary spirit. He invented the theory of the general strike as the weapon that would produce revolution. He expected that the general strike would bring to a climax all the noble sentiments that had been aroused in the workers by their experience in past strikes, and that they would be inspired to follow their leaders devotedly. Sorel felt that violence was absolutely essential, but that it must be directed against the system and not against individuals. Here Sorel was probably trying to warn against physical brutality and to define violence in an almost spiritual sense; but such distinctions in times of political and social crisis are unworkable, as he was himself to admit in his horror over the behavior of the Bolsheviks.

Mussolini was intimately familiar with Sorel's works, and in 1909 reviewed the *Reflections on Violence.* But he did not need Sorel to teach him violence. Violence was in the tradition of his birthplace, his family, and the revolutionary socialist doctrines in which he had been bred.

In 1910, Sorel turned away from syndicalism and toward the reactionary nationalism represented by the monarchists and clericals of the extreme Right in France; later he returned to Marx and Lenin. But his temporary interest in reactionary nationalism was a portent. Other revolutionary syndicalists, including some Italians, went through a similar phase. It was natural that groups which despised the middle classes and parliaments and put their faith in small minorities or élites would have much in common. Heroes—hard, tough Supermen—this was what both groups wanted. Thus both the nationalists and the revolutionary syndicalists were among the ancestors of fascism. Although Mussolini bitterly attacked Sorel for his swing to the Right, he himself later followed precisely the same course, with the difference that, whereas Sorel was an intellectual, Mussolini was a man of action and gained power.

Pareto (1848-1923), an engineer and sociologist, emphasized the importance of "myths" in government, as we have already seen. For a ruler to accomplish his ends, he must play upon sentiment, and arouse enthusiasm by means of fables and myths, not by mere reason and argument. Yet this is only an intellectualizing of what successful politicians have always known by instinct and experience. Pareto also believed that societies are governed by élites, which under normal circumstances slowly and continually recruit new members from below. However, under abnormal circumstances élites may be roughly ousted from power when there are too many weaklings at the top and too many strong and able men below. Mussolini knew these theories in his youth; he used the idea of the élite to support his own contention that the proletariat would oust the bourgeoisie. Later, he used the élite theory to support his fascist doctrine. Yet this concept, too, is not specifically fascist, but rather an idea useful to almost any politician anywhere. Pareto also discussed at length the use of force in society, concluding that force is always used in crises by those who wish to preserve the existing order or by those who wish to overthrow it.

Of the so-called forebears of Italian fascism, d'Annunzio was probably the most important. Mussolini knew the others and was influenced by them all to some degree, even by those who merely struck responsive chords in him or shared common views. But his system did not fully reflect the ideas of any one thinker or any combination of thinkers. A quotation from an article that

Mussolini wrote in 1920 to denounce Lenin has been brilliantly used to show, in Mussolini's own words, what his own fascist system was like. In reading it, substitute Mussolini for Lenin, Italy for Russia, fascist for communist, and you will have a clear idea of fascism:

Russia is a state ... composed of men who exercise power, imposing an iron discipline upon individuals and groups and practicing 'reaction' whenever necessary. . . . In the Russia of Lenin there is only one authority: his authority. There is only one liberty: his liberty. There is only one opinion: his opinion. There is only one law: his law. One must either submit or perish. . . . Russia . . . swallows up and crushes the individual and governs his entire life. It is understood that those who love the 'strong' or Prussian or iron-fisted state find that their ideal has been realized there. . . . The army of the Soviets is formidable, and as for the police, it has nothing to envy in the Okhrana [secret police] of the time of the Romanovs. Whoever says state necessarily says the army, the police, the judiciary, and the bureaucracy. The Russian state is the state *par excellence*. . . . It has *statized* economic life . . . and formed a huge army of bureaucrats. At the base of this pyramid, on the summit of which stands a handful of men, there is the multitude; there is the proletariat which, as in the old bourgeois regimes, obeys, works, and eats little or allows itself to be massacred. . . . In Russia there exists indeed a dictatorship of the proletariat exercised not by the proletariat but . . . by the communist party, which . . . represents a very small minority of the total population. In reality it is a few men of this party who govern Russia. Their republic . . . is a genuine and veritable autocracy. . . . Lenin is an artist who has molded men, as other artists have molded marble or metals. But men are stronger than stone and less malleable than iron. There is no masterpiece. The artist has failed. The task was superior to his capacities.[*]

---

[*] Mussolini on Lenin in 1920, quoted by G. Megaro, *Mussolini in the Making* (Boston, 1938), 325-326.

CHAPTER XXVII

III: Germany and the Weimar Republic, 1918-1933

In Germany, where Hitler was eventually to acquire power far greater than Mussolini's, the advent of fascism came later than in Italy. The German experiment with democracy lasted fifteen years after the end of World War I. Two days before the armistice of November 11, 1918, the Social Democrats proclaimed a republic in Germany. On July 31, 1919, this republic adopted a constitution drawn up by a national assembly at Weimar; it is therefore known as the "Weimar Republic." The Weimar Constitution was never formally abandoned, but after Adolf Hitler became chancellor on January 30, 1933, Germany was in fact a dictatorship.

It is convenient to divide the history of Germany between World Wars I and II at 1933, at the moment when Hitler took office as chancellor. Between 1918 and 1933, there are three shorter periods: the period of political threats from Left and Right and of mounting economic chaos, from 1918 to the end of 1923; the period of political stability, fulfillment of the Versailles Treaty requirements, and seeming economic prosperity, from 1924 to late 1929; and the period of economic depression and mounting right-wing power, from late 1929 to January, 1933.

The Impact of Defeat

For the overwhelming majority of the German people, defeat in 1918 came as a great surprise. The military authorities who ran the German Empire during the last years of the war had failed to report to the public German reverses on the battlefield. No fighting had ever taken place on German soil, and the Germans had got used to thinking of their armies as in firm possession of the foreign territories they had overrun. Now these armies came home intact. It is often argued that the Allies committed a grave blunder by their failure to march to Berlin and demonstrate to the German people that they had actually been defeated. Schooled in reverence for their military forces, the Germans could not grasp the fact that their armies had lost the war. Moreover, the Allies, under the leadership of Wilson, simply refused to deal with the Supreme Command of the German armies. Field Marshal von Hindenburg, as supreme commander, was never required to hand over his sword to Marshal Foch, or to sign the armistice. Rather, it was the civilian politicians who had to bear the odium. In this way the Allies unintentionally did the German military caste a great favor.

Before the ink was dry on the armistice agreement, the generals, led by Hindenburg himself, were explaining that the German armies had never really been defeated. This was exactly what the public wanted to believe, and the harsh facts—that Ludendorff and Hindenburg had insisted on surrender because the armies could no longer fight—were never effectively publicized. So the legend that Germany had somehow been "stabbed in the back" by civilians, by liberals, socialists, communists, and Jews, took deep root and became almost an article of faith among many Germans. This legend was widely disseminated by politicians, especially by those who had a stake in the old Prussian system—the monarchists, agrarians, industrialists, and militarists, in short, the nationalist right wing, which still believed in an aggressive Germany. All through the period of the Weimar Republic, these groups remained hostile toward it; their hostility ranged from political opposition to conspiracies to overthrow the government.

The Allies, having made things easier for the worst enemies of peace and democracy in Germany, added another error by including the celebrated "war-guilt" clause in the Treaty of Versailles. The German signatories were obliged to acknowledge what none of them believed, and what subsequent historians would disprove: that Germany alone had been responsible for the outbreak of the war. The war-guilt clause made it harder for the German public to acknowledge defeat and the evils of the past system, to sweep away the militarists, and to bend to the task of creating a virile republic. Instead, it led the Germans to dissipate their energies in denying war-guilt, in hating the enemies who had saddled them with the charge, in bewailing the sellout of their noble generals, and in waiting for a chance to show by force that they had been right all the time.

Postwar Political Alignments and Activities

This strengthening of the anti-republican forces of the Right was further increased by the threat to stability from the Left. Responsibility for launching the republic and for preventing disorder fell upon the "majority socialists," made up of Social Democrats and right-wing Independent Socialists, and led by the Social Democrat, Ebert. The Social Democrats were a moderate group. For example, they made no attack on agrarian property, and they allowed the Junkers to maintain intact their estates and the social and political position that went with them. The Social Democrats, true to their reformist tradition, concluded with the industrialists collective bargaining agreements that guaranteed the eight-hour day, rather than trying to launch a serious movement for nationalizing German industry.

But to the left of the Social Democrats agitation for a proletarian revolution on the Russian pattern was carried on by the left wing of the Independent Socialists and the "Spartacists" (named for Spartacus, the leader of a slave revolt in ancient Rome). In a congress of workers and soldiers councils (the German equivalent of soviets), the Left was defeated in its attempt to perpetuate these councils. In the winter of 1918-1919, the Left tried to stage its revolution, but Ebert called in the army to stop it. The generals used not only regular units but also newly formed volunteer units, or "Free Corps," made up for the most part of professional soldiers, who were embittered by Germany's recent military defeat and were violently opposed to democracy.

After the bloodshed of December, 1918, even the right wing of the Independent Socialists felt unable to remain in a government which used against the workers soldiers under the command of old-line generals. So they withdrew, and sole responsibility thenceforth rested with the Social Democrats, who put their man Noske into the war ministry. As the civil strife continued, the Spartacists took on the appropriate name of the Communist Party of Germany. In January, 1919, they attempted a *coup*, which Ebert, Noske, and the troops put down. Cavalry officers murdered the two chief leaders of the communists after peace had been restored, at the cost of more than a thousand casualties. Meanwhile, in Catholic Bavaria, disorders led to the brief emergence of a Soviet republic, which was liquidated in May, leaving behind in the middle-class Bavarian population a pathological fear of the Left, and making Bavaria the home of a sort of permanent red-scare. The Bavarian local authorities, throughout the entire life of the Weimar Republic, encouraged the intrigues of monarchists, militarists, and nationalists. It was in Bavaria that Free Corps assassinations were planned, and it was there that Hitler got his start.

In this way the forces of the German Right, ostensibly crushed by the war, were given a powerful new lease on life by the very powers that should have been their most determined enemies—the Allies, who allowed the myth of the stab-in-the-back to grow and who insisted on the war-guilt clause; and the Social Democrats, who made an alliance with the generals and put down the communists and their allies. Meantime, Germany still had an army, the *Reichswehr,* under the able direction of General von Seeckt. Though limited in size to 100,000 men, it consisted chiefly of officer cadres, magnificently trained and able to take over the command of far larger numbers if and when troops became available.

The political constellation of the new Germany did not consist solely of Social Democrats and extremists of Right and Left. The old parties of imperial Germany (see Chapter XXII) reappeared, often with new labels. The right wing of the old Liberals now emerged as the People's party, including the more moderate industrialists, with a platform of private property and opposition to socialism. Its leader was Gustav Stresemann, who had been a chauvinist during the war but had been taught a good deal by Germany's defeat. Former Progressives and left-wing Liberals now formed the new Democratic party, a genuine middle-class republican and democratic group, including many of Germany's most distinguished intellectuals. The Catholic Center partly re-emerged with its name and program unchanged. It accepted the Republic, rejected socialism, and favored social legislation under pressure from its left wing of trade-union members, but it opposed far-reaching reform under pressure from its right wing of aristocrats and industrialists. The Social Democrats, the Democrats, the Center, and the People's party represented those groups which, though not all enthusiastic, were willing to try to make the new state work. On the Right, the former Conservatives re-emerged as the National People's party or Nationalists, dominated by the Junkers as before. The Nationalists had the support of some great industrialists, of most of the bureaucrats, and of a substantial section of the lower middle class, which hoped to return to the good old days of the monarchy. The Nationalists did not accept the Republic.

The Weimar Constitution, 1919

When the Germans voted for a national constituent assembly in January, 1919, the parties supporting the Republic won more than 75 per cent of the votes (see table on p. 530), with the Social Democrats alone obtaining nearly 40 per cent. The assembly met in Weimar, elected Ebert to be President of Germany, and formed a government that reluctantly signed the Treaty of Versailles after a delay of some months. The assembly then adopted the new constitution. The new Germany was still a federative state, but the central government had great authority to legislate for the entire country. The president might use armed force to coerce any of the states which failed to obey the constitution or national laws. The cabinet was responsible to the lower house, or *Reichstag,* which was to be chosen by universal suffrage of all citizens (including women) over twenty.

The president, who was to be elected every seven years by the entire people, was given considerable authority. He was empowered to make treaties, appoint and remove the cabinet, command the armed forces and appoint or remove all officers, dissolve the Reichstag, and call new elections. Further, he could take any measure he deemed necessary to restore order when

(Number of seats obtained by the major parties, arranged with the Left at the top, the Right at the bottom)

	Jan. 1919	June 1920	May 1924	Dec. 1924	May 1928	Sept. 1930	July 1932	Nov. 1932	Mar. 1933
Communists	— a	2	62	45	54	77	89	100	81
Independent Socialists	22	81	— b						
Social Democrats	163	112	100	131	152	143	133	121	125
Democrats	74	45	28	32	25	14	4	2	5
Center	71	68	65	69	61	68	75	70	74
People's party	22	62	44	51	45	30	7	11	2
Nationalists	42	66	96	103	78	41	40	51	52
Nazis			38	20	12	107	230	196	288

a The Communist party boycotted the elections to the Weimar constituent assembly.

b In these and succeeding elections the Independent Socialists had merged with the Social Democrats.

it was threatened, and might temporarily suspend the civil liberties that the constitution granted. Yet the Reichstag could order such measures repealed. Inside the cabinet, the chancellor was a real prime minister, with responsibility for planning policy. The constitution also provided for popular initiative: one-tenth of the electorate could bring in a bill or propose an amendment to the constitution. On the economic side, the constitution provided that the government might socialize suitable enterprises, but guaranteed private property and the right of inheritance.

Several other contradictions reflected the conflict of interest between the Social Democrats and the middle-class parties. But the powers of the president and the introduction of proportional representation were perhaps the two chief weaknesses. The powers of the president made dictatorship a real possibility. Proportional representation required that votes be cast for entire party lists of candidates, and thus prevented independent voters from "splitting the ticket," and independent politicians from obtaining office. This system encouraged small splinter parties to multiply.

Right and Left Extremism, 1920-1922

In 1920, pressure from the Right loomed as the most serious threat to the Republic. In March, 1920, a *coup* (in German, *putsch*) was attempted by a group headed by the commander of the troops in the Berlin district and other officers. They wanted to capitalize on military resentment over the disarmament clauses of the treaty, and hoped to bring into power an East Prussian reactionary official named Kapp. Ludendorff and the Free Corps leaders fully supported the movement, which drove the government out of Berlin for several days. Ebert managed to defeat this "Kapp *putsch*" by calling a general strike that paralyzed Germany. It was a measure of the continuity of the old monarchical judicial system that the men arrested and tried for the Kapp *putsch* all got off with extremely light sentences, whereas left-wingers brought before the courts were very harshly punished. Under cover of the Kapp *putsch,* a right-wing government came to power in Bavaria and gave shelter to the Free Corps leaders,

CHAPTER XXVII

who went underground rather than obey the government's efforts to disband their formations.

Moreover, as an immediate outgrowth of the strike called by the government, a communist revolt took place in the Ruhr. In pursuit of the communists, German troops entered the area, which had been demilitarized by the Versailles Treaty; this action in turn led to French military intervention and a brief occupation of the Ruhr and Frankfurt (April-May, 1920). In the elections of June, 1920, the electorate began to support the extremists. The Democrats and Social Democrats lost strength. On the Right, the Nationalists and People's party gained, and on the Left the Independent Socialists gained. But the latter group now split; the left-wingers joined the communists, and the right-wingers came back into the Social Democratic party.

In April, 1921, when the Allies presented the bill for reparations, which totaled 132 billion gold marks, the politicians of the Right favored simple rejection of the terms, while the Weimar parties realistically decided that the threat of invasion made this course impossible. Again, the moderates had to take responsibility for a necessary decision that was sure to prove unpopular, and that they themselves did not approve. The minister for reconstruction, Walter Rathenau, a Democrat and a successful industrialist, hoped that a policy of "fulfillment" might convince the Allies that Germany was acting in good faith, and might in the long run lead to concessions. An intensely patriotic German, Rathenau was also a Jew, and drew the particular venom of the anti-Semitic nationalist orators.

The secret terrorist groups of the Right began a campaign of assassination. The first important figure to be murdered (August, 1921) was Matthias Erzberger, the Catholic Center politician who had signed the armistice, and a leading moderate. His assassins

escaped through Bavaria. When one of them was caught, the courts acquitted him. Next, after some hesitation, the League of Nations awarded to Poland a substantial area of the province of Upper Silesia, containing much wealth and many German inhabitants, which all Germans felt to be rightly theirs. This action aroused the Right still further. Rathenau now became the target, first of a political and press attack, and then in June, 1922, of bullets. His assassins were devout believers in the "stab-in-the-back" theory, and thought that by murdering a Jew they could somehow avenge the "betrayal" of the German army.

Hitler: Early Career

During the months between the assassination of Erzberger and that of Rathenau a new and ominous element had emerged among the welter of right-wing organizations in Bavaria. This was the "National Socialist Party of the German Workers" founded by Adolf Hitler, the son of an obscure, illegitimate Austrian customs official, whose real name had been Schicklgruber. Born in 1889, Hitler early quarreled with his father, and seems always to have felt bitter and frustrated. In 1907, he was rejected by the Vienna Academy of Fine Arts, where he wished to study painting. He became an odd-job man, selling an occasional water-color, but always hovering on the edge of starvation. It was during these years that his hatred of the Jews began. As we know (see Chapter XXII), lower-middle-class Vienna at the time was deeply devoted to its anti-Semitic demagogue, Mayor Lueger, whom Hitler admired. Because Karl Marx himself had been of Jewish origin and because many Viennese Jews were socialists, Hitler associated socialism with the Jews, and lumped both together as somehow responsible for his own personal troubles and for the ills of the world.

There were plenty of nineteenth-century theorists, German and others, from whose works Hitler drew support for his anti-Semitism. In the *Essay on the Inequality of Human Races,* the French Count Joseph Arthur de Gobineau (1816-1882) had laid the pseudo-scientific foundation for modern anti-Semitism, and for theories of "Nordic" and "Aryan" supremacy. One of Gobineau's most influential readers was the great German composer, Richard Wagner (see Chapter XXIII), who thought of the Germans alone as creative, and who felt that the Jews stood for all that was base, and that they should be wiped off the face of the earth. Wagner's son-in-law, the Englishman Houston Stewart Chamberlain (1855-1927), a distant cousin of Joseph Chamberlain (see p. 249), wrote a long and turgid book called *The Foundations of the Nineteenth Century,* which was published in German in 1899. This too glorified the Germans and assailed the Jews; for example, one section was devoted to a "demonstration" that Christ himself had not been of Jewish origin. Chamberlain was furiously opposed to democratic government and, interestingly enough, to capitalism. Thus he provided Hitler with a congenial mixture of racism, nationalism, anti-democratic thought, and radicalism. Hitler was deeply influenced by Chamberlain, and Chamberlain lived to see and hail the foundations of the Hitler movement.

As for German nationalism, we have already encountered it in virulent form in Hohenzollern Germany. Especially articulate had been Heinrich von Treitschke (1834-1896), a learned historian and a popular university professor who had blasted Jews, socialists, capitalists, and the typically English ideas of liberal democracy. He had called for a German state that would act solely in its own interests,

that would be exempt from weak moral precepts, and that would devote itself to the ideal of power, which it should use in military expansion. A whole generation of young nationalists grew up imbued with Treitschke's ideas. These were the men who had been most deeply hurt by the loss of the war, and who were ready in the 1920's to engage in an adventure to restore Germany to what they believed to be her proper pinnacle.

Although Hitler owed much to earlier nationalists and racists, he worked out a twentieth-century adaptation of their nineteenth-century ideas. After he had read their books, he came to hate Vienna as a cosmopolitan and Jewish community, and moved to Munich in 1913. In 1914, he enlisted in the army and fought through the war as a corporal. He won the iron cross for bravery, but was regarded by his commanding officer as too "hysterical" to deserve a commission. After the war, he had come back to Munich, where, as might have been expected, he loathed the new republic and the "Bolsheviks," admired the Free Corps, and decided to become a politician.

Beginnings of the Nazi Party

When the government put down the revolution from the Left, in 1919 and 1920, the Bavarian military authorities supported the Free Corps. Ludendorff moved to Munich, and became the center of the reaction. Hitler was employed as a political education officer for the troops. While engaged in this work, he discovered a small political group that called itself the "German Workers' Party." This group combined nationalism and militarism with a generous amount of imitation-socialist radicalism. Hitler consequently believed that the party might be able to recruit a mass following. He joined the party in 1919 and soon proved himself to be a far abler politician than any of his colleagues. He stressed as basic the need for intensive propaganda, arguing that all Germans should be united in a greater Germany. He supported the elimination of all Jews from political life, a state guarantee of full employment, the confiscation of war profits, the nationalization of trusts, the encouragement of small business, and a land-grant to the peasantry. The seemingly radical character of his program caused many who were otherwise sympathetic to hesitate before giving Hitler money. As early as 1920, he began to reassure them by saying he opposed not "industrial capital" but only "Jewish international loan capital," a clear sign that the nationalization plank in his platform had been abandoned.

Hitler was an extremely successful orator, with almost hypnotic gifts of capturing a crowd. By 1921, he had made himself the absolute leader, the *fuehrer* (compare with *duce*), of the party, and in the same year he strengthened himself by founding the SA (*Sturmabteilung*, or storm-troops), brown-shirted units largely recruited from the Free Corps. The storm-troopers wore armbands with the swastika emblem, patrolled mass meetings, and performed other services for the leader. Their commander was a notorious pervert, Captain Roehm, who was also political adviser to the commander of the infantry stationed in Bavaria. Like the Italian fascists, the German Nazis (so-called from the first four letters of the German word *Nazional*, National, the first word of the party's name) thus had illegal and unofficial access to government supplies of arms through army sympathizers. Besides Roehm, Hitler's closest collaborators included Hermann Goering, a wartime aviator who had shot down twenty Allied planes, but who found himself restless in peacetime, and took on the job of giving the SA a military polish; Rudolf Hess, an Egyptian-born lieutenant and private secretary; and Alfred Rosenberg, a Baltic German dis-

tinguished for fanatical hatred of Jews and Bolsheviks, and first editor of the party newspaper.

Hitler and his Nazis were still a very minor political force in 1922 when the middle-of-the-road parties attempted to strengthen the Republic. After the assassination of Rathenau, Stresemann's People's party moved away from the Nationalists, who were now tainted by murder, and entered into a collaboration with Center and Democrats. So tense was the political situation that the scheduled presidential elections were postponed to 1925.

The Inflation, 1922-1923

Political maneuvers to meet the increasing threat from the Right, however, were largely nullified by the increasing economic problem posed by steadily growing inflation, which in 1922 and 1923 reached unheard-of extremes. Inflation is a complicated economic phenomenon, and no mere list or description of its causes can really tell the full story. But the single chief cause for the runaway inflation in Germany after 1921 was probably the failure of the German government to levy taxes with which to pay the expenses of the war. The imperial regime had expected to win, and to make the losers pay Germany's expenses by imposing huge indemnities. So it paid for only about 4 per cent of the war costs by means of taxation. As defeat neared, the government borrowed more and more money from the banks. When the loans came due, the government repaid them with paper money that was not backed by gold. Each time this happened, more paper money was put into circulation, and prices rose; each rise in prices naturally led to a demand for a rise in wages, which had to be paid with more paper money. The inflationary spiral was under way. Instead of cutting purchasing power by imposing heavy taxes, the government permitted buyers to compete with each other for goods in short supply, thus speeding up the whole process of inflation.

Many other forces helped inflation along. The German gold shortage, which deprived the government of the gold with which to back its currency, was itself due to several factors. Since Germany had had to pay in gold for goods bought abroad during the war, she had stripped herself of her gold supply; the rich sent great sums out of Germany for fear that the government would attach them to pay reparations. Raw materials were in short supply; industry was disorganized; and credit was curtailed. The armies of occupation had to be maintained at German expense, and reparation payments had to be made. Nationalist Germans maintained that these expenses, especially reparations, were the cause of inflation; but, though reparations certainly helped the process, they were by no means solely responsible for it. The total sums involved in reparations were never great enough to affect the German currency until long after the inflation was under way. Indeed, the inflation was partly due to the industrialists' wish to avoid paying reparations, and to clear their own indebtedness by letting the currency become worthless.

The following timetable shows how bad the situation had become by the end of 1922. When the war was over, the mark, normally valued at 4.2 to a dollar, had fallen to 8.4. In January, 1921, it was 45; by December, 160. By September, 1922, it was 1,303, and at the end of the year it was 7,000. In these months, the government begged for a moratorium on reparations payments and for a foreign loan. But the French were unwilling. They had already paid billions for the rebuilding of areas that the Germans had devastated during the war, and they wanted the Germans to pay the bill. As a guarantee, the French demanded the vitally important German industrial region of the Ruhr. Despite British opposition, the French occupied the Ruhr in January, 1923, after the Germans had defaulted on their reparations payments. The French intended to run the mines and factories for their own benefit, and thus make up for the German failure to pay reparations.

The Germans could not resist with force, but they declared the occupation of the Ruhr illegal, and ordered the inhabitants to embark on passive resistance—to refuse to work the mines and factories or to deliver goods to the French. This order the people of the Ruhr obeyed. Local tension in the occupied area became serious when the French took measures against German police and workers, and when German Free Corps members undertook guerrilla operations against the French. In Berlin, the government became afraid that the crisis might lead to war, and authorized illegal military units above the limit set by Versailles.

But the most striking result of the French occupation of the Ruhr was its effect upon the already desperate German economy. Not only was the rest of Germany cut off from badly needed goods from the occupied area, but the Ruhr inhabitants were idle at the order of the German government and had to be supported at government expense. The printing press struck off ever-increasing amounts of ever-more-worthless marks. Now the exchange went from thousands of marks to the dollar to millions, to billions, and, by December, 1923, well up into the trillions.

The Consequences of Inflation

Such astronomical figures are meaningless except in terms of the personal and social consequences. A student set off one afternoon for the university with his father's check in his pocket to cover a year's tuition, room, board, and entertainment. When he arrived the next morning after an overnight journey, he discovered that the money he got for the check would pay for one short streetcar ride! Life-time savings were rendered valueless; people trundled wheelbarrows full of marks through the street in an effort to buy a loaf of bread. Those who lived on fixed incomes were utterly ruined, and the savings of the investing middle classes were wiped out. Real property took on fantastic value. The story is told of two brothers, one frugal and the other spendthrift, who had shared equally in a fortune inherited from their father. The frugal one had invested his money; the spendthrift had bought a fine wine-cellar, which he had proceeded to drink up. When inflation came, all the frugal brother's investments would not buy him a haircut, but the spendthrift found that the empty bottles in his cellar were worth billions on billions of marks apiece, and that he was rich again. Under such circumstances speculation in real estate flourished, and skillful speculators made immense fortunes.

For the German worker inflation did not mean the liquidation of his savings, because he usually had none. It did mean a great drop in the purchasing power of his wages, so great that he could no longer afford the necessities of life. His family suffered from hunger and cold. Since the financial position of the labor unions was destroyed, they were no longer able to help the workers, who gave up their membership in droves. The great industrialists, however, gained from the inflation, in part just because it did cripple the labor unions, but still more because it wiped out their indebtedness, and enabled them to absorb small competitors and build giant business combines.

Politically, inflation greatly strengthened the extremists of both Right and Left. The middle classes, although pushed down to the economic level of the proletariat, still possessed the middle-class psychology. In status-conscious Germany, they would not adhere to the working-class parties of Social Democrats or Communists. Disillusioned, they would not adhere to the moderate parties that supported the Republic—the People's party, the Center, and the Democrats. So the Nationalists, and Hitler's Nazis above all, reaped a rich harvest. The hardships of the working class led many workers to turn away from the Social Democrats to the Communists. But Soviet Russian restraint on the leaders of the German party prevented any concerted revolutionary drive until the fall of 1923, by which time poor organization and strong governmental repressive measures had doomed their efforts.

Inflation in Germany. A banknote for 2,000,000,000 marks.

With the country seething in crisis, Stresemann as chancellor in the fall of 1923 proclaimed that because of the economic dislocation Germany could not keep up passive resistance in the Ruhr. He ordered work to be resumed and reparations to be delivered once again. Political troubles multiplied when the Right refused to ac-

Hitler at the time of the beer-hall putsch, Munich, November 1923.

cept the new policy. At the height of the agitation in Bavaria, Hitler in early November, 1923, broke into a right-wing political meeting in a Munich beer-hall, and announced that the "national revolution" had begun. At gun-point he tried to get other local leaders to support him in a march on Berlin. They agreed, but let him down when they learned that the national government was prepared to deal with the Nazis. Although Ludendorff himself joined the Nazi demonstration in Munich, as he had joined the Kapp *putsch* of 1920, troops broke up the demonstration with only a few casualties.

Ludendorff and Hitler were tried in proceedings that have become famous as the most striking example of the Weimar judicial system's partiality for men of the Right. Ludendorff was respectfully acquitted. Hitler was allowed to use the dock as a propaganda platform for his ideas, and was sentenced to the minimum term for high treason: five years. He actually spent eight months in comfortable confinement, during which time he wrote large portions of *Mein Kampf* (*My Battle*), the famous bible of the Nazis. Although the law said that Hitler should be deported, he never was. Goering escaped abroad, became a dope addict, and did not return to Germany until 1927, when he rejoined the Nazis.

The End of Inflation, 1923-1924

Communist disorders and the Nazi beer-hall *putsch* marked the last phase of the inflation period. A couple of weeks before Hitler's effort, the government had given extaordinary financial powers to Hans Luther, minister of finance, and Hjalmar Schacht, banker and fiscal expert. All printing of the old currency was stopped. A new bank was opened to issue new marks, which were simply assigned the value of the pre-war mark (4.2 to the dollar). The new currency was backed not by gold but by an imaginary "mortgage" on all Germany's agricultural and industrial

CHAPTER XXVII

wealth, a psychological gesture that won public confidence. It took one trillion of the old marks to equal one of the new. Simultaneously, rigorous economy was put into effect in every branch of the government, and taxes were increased. The public protested loudly, but the measures remained in force until they had accomplished the intended effect. The cure for inflation produced serious hardships too. Prices fell, and over-expanded businesses collapsed. Unemployment rose sharply, wages stayed low, and workers labored long hours.

During 1924, the Allies contributed to the ending of the crisis in Germany by formulating the Dawes Plan, named for Charles G. Dawes, the American financier and later vice-president under Calvin Coolidge. The plan recommended the evacuation of the Ruhr by the French, the establishment of a special bank to receive reparations payments, gradually rising annual payments for the first five years, and an international loan of 800,000 gold marks to finance the German deliveries in the first year. The Nationalists violently attacked the proposals as a sinister scheme to enslave Germany to foreign masters. In the Reichstag elections of May, 1924, the Nationalists scored impressive gains, as did the Nazis and the Communists, while the moderate parties all suffered (see table on p. 530). But a coalition managed to win acceptance of the Dawes Plan in August, 1924, by the device of promising the Nationalists representation in the cabinet. When new elections were held in December, the Nazis and Communists suffered losses, and the Social Democrats and moderates gained. A Center-People's party–Nationalist coalition took office early in 1925 and governed Germany. One wing of the Nationalists, however, led by the enormously rich industrial press and film magnate, Alfred Hugenberg, who had made a fortune during the inflation, opposed all co-operation with the

Republic. Though Germany had moved appreciably to the Right, foreign policy remained in the conciliatory hands of Stresemann, who remained foreign minister through all governments between November, 1923, and his death in October, 1929.

Recovery at Home, 1924-1929

During these less-troubled middle years of the Weimar Republic economic recovery proceeded steadily, until, in 1929, German industrial output exceeded that of 1913. First-rate German equipment, coupled with superb technical skill and a systematic adoption of American methods of mass production, added up to a highly efficient industrial machine. This "rationalization" of industry increased production but brought with it over-borrowing and some unemployment. "Vertical trusts," which brought together in one great corporation all the parts of an industrial process from coal and iron mining to the output of the finished product; and cartels, associations of independent enterprises that controlled sales and prices for their own benefit, were characteristic of the German system. The emphasis was always on heavy industry, which meant that continued prosperity would depend upon a big armaments program.

All through this period, reparations were paid faithfully, with no damage to the German economy. Indeed, the money that flowed out in reparations was greatly exceeded by the money that flowed into Germany from foreign, especially American, investors. Dependence on foreign capital, however, which would cease to flow in time of depression, made German prosperity artificial.

In 1925, after President Ebert died, a presidential election was held in which three candidates competed. The Catholic

Center, the Democrats, and the Social Democrats supported the Center leader, Wilhelm Marx. The Nationalists, People's party, and other right-wingers joined in support of Field Marshal Hindenburg, then seventy-seven years old. The Communists ran their own candidate, and thus contributed to the election of Hindenburg, who won by a small plurality. Abroad, the choice of a man so intimately connected with imperial militarist Germany created dismay; but until 1930 Hindenburg acted entirely in accordance with the constitution, to the distress of most of the nationalist groups.

The domestic issues of this period—whether the old imperial flag should be flown together with that of the Republic, whether the properties of the former princely houses should be expropriated, whether the army should be subjected to civilian control—all aroused great heat, but were settled by democratic process. In 1927, labor won a new system of unemployment insurance. The Junkers gave Hindenburg as a present an estate in East Prussia that had once belonged to his ancestors, and thus ensured his opposition to all land-reform schemes. Indeed the Reichstag voted vast sums in annual subsidies to the Junkers; this scheme, which was called *Osthilfe* ("east-help"), paid the landowners' debts at the taxpayers' expense. In the elections of 1928, the Social Democrats were returned to power, and the Nationalists and Nazis were hard hit (see table on p. 530). All in all, prosperity encouraged moderation and a return to support of the republic.

"Fulfillment" Abroad, 1925-1930

In foreign affairs, this middle period of the Weimar Republic was one of gradually increasing German participation in the system of collective security. Thus in 1925 Germany signed the Locarno treaties, which

President Hindenburg.

took the French armies out of the Rhineland, substituted a neutral zone and a frontier guaranteed by Britain and Italy, and set up machinery for the arbitration of disputes between Germany and her neighbors. These treaties did not, however, guarantee to Poland and Czechoslovakia the eastern frontiers of Germany. In 1926, Germany was admitted to the League of Nations, with a permanent seat on the League's Council. Thus Germany gained full equality of status with the Allies. In 1929, Germany accepted the Kellogg-Briand Pact, which outlawed aggressive war (see below, p. 583).

In 1929, a new reparations plan named after the American, Owen D. Young, chairman of the committee which drew it up, substantially reduced the total originally demanded by the Allies. The Young Plan also established lower rates of payments than those under the Dawes Plan and allowed the Germans a greater part in their collection. Before June, 1930, the Rhine-

CHAPTER XXVII

Soup-kitchen for the un-employed, Berlin, 1931.

land was evacuated by the Allies, four years ahead of the date set by the Treaty of Versailles. Although many of these gains for Germany were accomplished only with so much preliminary difficulty that they were robbed of their sweetness, and although the German Nationalists, Nazis, and Communists thoroughly opposed them all, still German foreign policy was generally calculated to reassure the rest of the world.

The Impact of the Depression, 1929-1931

But even before the last achievements of this "period of fulfillment," the depression had set in to knock the foundations out from under prosperity and moderation. Unemployment rose during 1929. After the American stock-market crash in October, foreign credits, on which prosperity had so largely depended, were no longer available to Germany. Short-term loans were not renewed, or else were recalled. Tariff barriers were hurting foreign trade. Hunger and want reappeared.

Although unemployment insurance cushioned the first shock for the workers, the lower middle classes, painfully recovering from the inflation, had no such barrier between them and destitution. Their desperation helped Hitler, whose fortunes during the years of fulfillment had fallen very low, although he had attracted a number of new followers who were later to be important in his movement. Paul Joseph Goebbels, publicist and journalist, proved to be a master of mob psychology and an effective orator. Heinrich Himmler, a mild-mannered but ruthless chicken-farmer, took charge of the élite black-shirted SS (*Schutzstaffel*, defense corps), which was formed as a special guard of honor. The SS, with a higher standing than the SA, and with special membership requirements of "racial purity," was later to become the nucleus for the Gestapo, or secret police. Hitler also recruited Joachim von Ribbentrop, champagne salesman and party ambassador to the German upper classes.

The government fell in 1930 over a disagreement on a question of unemployment insurance benefits. Hindenburg appointed to the chancellorship Heinrich Bruening, a member of the Catholic Center party. Bruening would have liked to support parliamentary institutions and to continue Stresemann's policies of fulfillment, but he was to find it impossible to do either. President Hindenburg, now eighty-two, had come more and more under the influence of General Kurt von Schleicher, an ambitious political soldier who had intrigued himself into the President's favor. Hindenburg was now itching to rule by decree, as the constitution authorized him to in an emergency. By failing to pass Bruening's economic program, the Reichstag gave Hindenburg the opportunity he wanted. Bruening went along, partly because he felt that a genuine emergency existed, but partly because he was determined to keep his bitter political rivals, the Social Democrats, from replacing him in office.

The budget was declared in effect by presidential decree; when the Reichstag demanded that the decree be abrogated, the Reichstag was dissolved and new elections were called. The electoral campaign was notable for a running series of street fights between Communists and Nazis. When the votes were counted (September, 1930), these two extreme parties made great gains at the expense of all the moderates (see table on p. 530). The Nazis' Reichstag representation rose from 12 to 107, and the Communists' from 54 to 77. Bruening had to carry on against the wishes of the electorate; supported only by Hindenburg, he now turned authoritarian.

In order to avoid a new government in which Nazis would participate, the Social Democrats decided to support Bruening. When the Reichstag met, Nazis and Communists created disorder on the floor, but they voted together in opposition to government measures. These measures passed only because the Social Democrats voted for them. In 1931, Bruening made an effort to arrange an Austro-German customs union which would co-ordinate the tariff policies of the two countries and help them both fight the depression without affecting their political sovereignty. Whether such an arrangement between two countries that were both suffering from unemployment would actually have succeeded cannot be decided; nor can we be sure whether the impulse for Germany and Austria to unite politically might not have proved overpoweringly strong. At any rate, the whole project raised in the minds of the Allies, especially the French, the specter of a "greater Germany," and the scheme was vetoed by the World Court (see Chapter XXVIII). The collapse of the great Austrian bank, the *Kredit-An-stalt*, deepened the depression, despite a British loan to Austria in 1931, and despite the one-year moratorium on reparations payment procured for Germany by President Herbert Hoover.

The Republic in Danger, 1931-1932

After the failure of the Austrian customs union scheme, a right-wing political coalition was formed against the Bruening government. It included Nazis, Nationalists, the veterans organization of the Steel Helmets (*Stahlhelm*), the Junkers' Agrarian League, industrialists, and representatives of the former princely houses. This coalition had great financial resources, and a mass backing, chiefly Nazi. It had its private armies in the SA, in the *Stahlhelm*, and in other semi-military organizations. Because the Left was split, and the Communists in effect acted as political allies of the Right, nothing stood between this new right-wing coalition and a political victory except the person of Hindenburg. The President controlled the army, and by virtue of the Weimar Constitution was able to keep Bruening in office, although the Chancellor was deeply unpopular.

540

The coalition was further strengthened in early 1932, when Hitler was invited by the great industrialist, Fritz Thyssen, to address a meeting of coal and steel magnates. Hitler warned them against Bolshevism, inveighed against the principles of democratic government, reassured them of his own respect for private property, and won their financial support by convincing them that if he came to power he would be their man. Some of Hitler's followers were now impatient for a new *putsch*, which they were sure would be successful. But Hitler curbed them, believing that the Nazis could come to power legally.

With new presidential elections scheduled for 1932, Bruening tried to avoid the excitement and expense of a campaign by obtaining from the Reichstag an extension of Hindenburg's term. Hitler refused, and the elections were held in March, with Hitler as the candidate of the Nazis. Hindenburg ran as the candidate of the Center, Social Democrats, and other moderate parties. The Nationalists nominated a *Stahlhelm* man, and the Communists of course ran their own candidate. Hitler polled 11,338,571 votes, and Hindenburg polled 18,661,736, only four-tenths of 1 per cent short of the required majority. In the run-off election, the Nationalists backed Hitler, whose total rose to 13,400,000 as against Hindenburg's 19,360,000. The eighty-four-year-old Marshal, re-elected as the candidate of the moderates, was, however, no longer a moderate himself, but the tool of the Junkers and the military.

Although the government now ordered the Nazi SA and SS disbanded, the decree was not enforced. In April, 1932, the Nazis scored impressive victories in local elections, especially in all-important Prussia. Bruening was unable to procure in time either an Allied promise to extend the moratorium on reparations payments or permission for Germany to have "parity" (i.e., equality)

in armaments with France. Schleicher, who was now deeply involved in intrigue against Bruening, worked on Hindenburg to demand Bruening's resignation. This Hindenburg did on May 29, 1932, the first time a president had dismissed a chancellor simply because he had lost personal confidence in him. Bruening's successor was Franz von Papen, a rich Catholic nobleman and a member of the extreme right wing of the Center, who installed a cabinet composed of nobles. Papen was Schleicher's man—or so Schleicher thought.

The Center disavowed Papen, who had the real support of no political party or group, but whom the Nazis temporarily tolerated because he agreed to remove the ban on the SA and SS. Papen called new Reichstag elections, on the theory that the Nazis had passed their peak, that they would obtain a decreased vote, and that then they could be chastened and would co-operate in the government. In foreign policy Papen succeeded where Bruening had failed, as the Allies scrapped the Young Plan and required Germany to pay only three billion gold marks into a fund earmarked for general European reconstruction. Instead of being bound for many decades to pay reparations, Germany was now freed from all such obligations. But the Nazis, for electioneering purposes, attacked even this settlement as a "new tribute pact," and launched a violent pre-election campaign marked by many murders.

The election of July 31, 1932, gave the Nazis 230 seats and made them the biggest single party in the Reichstag; the Communists gained also, chiefly at the expense of the Social Democrats. The Democrats and the People's party almost disappeared, while the Nationalists suffered, and the Center scored a slight gain (see table on p. 530). Papen had gained no support in the new Reichstag. He wanted to take some

Nazis into the government, but the Nazis demanded the chancellorship, which Hindenburg was determined not to hand over to Hitler. Papen now planned to dissolve the Reichstag and to call new elections. By repeating this process, he hoped to wear down Hitler's strength each time, until he brought Hitler to support him and accept a subordinate place. And Papen put pressure on the industrialists who had been supporting Hitler; the Nazi funds began to dry up, leaving Hitler seriously embarrassed. The elections of November 6, 1932, demonstrated the soundness of Papen's theories. The Nazis fell off from 230 seats to 196; and, although the Communists gained substantially and ominously, Papen too won some support (see table on p. 530). Now the Nazis were really desperate. Goebbels wrote in his diary:

Received a report on the financial situation of the Berlin organization. It is hopeless. Nothing but debts and obligations, together with the complete impossibility of obtaining any reasonable sum of money after this defeat.*

Hitler:
Rise to Power, 1932-1933

Had Papen been permitted to continue his tactics, it is possible that Hitler might have been kept from power. But Papen resigned as a matter of form because he could not count on majority support in the Reichstag. It was generally expected that Hindenburg would reappoint him, but Schleicher, who was jealous of Papen, intrigued against the reappointment. Angry with Schleicher and sorry to lose Papen, Hindenburg forced Schleicher himself to take the office on December 3, 1932. Now the backstairs general was chancellor, but he had no political support whatever, and had alienated even Hindenburg. He lasted

in office only about eight weeks before Hitler was appointed chancellor.

Schleicher did score a great diplomatic success by winning a five-power declaration that recognized in principle Germany's right to parity in armaments. At home, he made every effort to appeal to all shades of opinion, except the extreme Left. But this attempt in itself alienated the implacably anti-labor industrialists and the Junkers. The Junkers also opposed a land-settlement scheme in East Prussia that Schleicher had backed, and feared that he would expose their corrupt use of *Osthilfe* funds. The tortuous Papen, eager for revenge, intrigued with these enemies of Schleicher. Early in January, 1933, Papen met Hitler at the house of the Cologne banker, Baron Kurt von Schroeder. The industrialists, who had temporarily abandoned Hitler, now agreed to pay the Nazis' debts. Hitler, in turn, no longer insisted on the chancellorship for himself, thus leading Papen to hope that he would come back into office with Hitler's backing. Hindenburg, too, was enlisted. When the President refused to give Schleicher the authority to dissolve the Reichstag at its first new session, which would surely have voted him down, Schleicher had no choice but to resign (January 28, 1933).

But Hitler had now raised the ante and demanded the chancellorship for himself. Papen consented, provided Hitler undertook to govern in strict accordance with parliamentary procedure. Papen was to be vice-chancellor, and still thought he could dominate the government, since only three of its eleven ministers would be Nazis. He therefore persuaded Hindenburg to take Hitler as chancellor. But Papen underestimated Hitler. Though Hitler swore to Hindenburg that he would maintain the constitution, the Weimar Republic was doomed from the moment Hitler came to the chancellor's office on January 30, 1933.

* Quoted by S. William Halperin, *Germany Tried Democracy* (New York, 1946), 511-512.

CHAPTER XXVII

IV: Germany under Hitler, 1933-1939

The Nazi Dictatorship

Hitler's first weeks in power were devoted to transforming his chancellorship into a dictatorship. He dissolved the Reichstag and called for new elections. During the campaign, opponents of the Nazis were intimidated by violence and threats, and were denied radio time and free use of the press. Yet a Nazi victory in the election still did not seem sure. On February 27, 1933, fire opportunely broke out in the Reichstag building, and Hitler could point to it as a sample of the disorders that the Communists were likely to instigate. Hindenburg issued emergency decrees suspending free speech and the free press, and thus made it even easier for the storm-troops to use terror against their political opponents. It is now generally supposed that the Nazis themselves set the Reichstag fire, but in a later trial they convicted and condemned to death a Dutch communist named Vanderlubbe, who apparently was mentally deficient. Other communists, German and Bulgarian, including the Bulgarian Georgi Dimitrov, who was later to become boss of the Comintern (see above, p. 505), were acquitted.

Despite their campaign the Nazis won only 44 per cent of the votes, which gave them 288 seats in the Reichstag (see table on p. 530). Using the SA as a constant threat, Hitler bullied the Reichstag. Except for 94 Social Democrats (the Communists were denied their seats), its members voted for the famous Enabling Act (March 23, 1933). This act conferred dictatorial powers upon the government, and suspended the constitution. The act was renewed in 1937 by a subservient Reichstag, and again in 1943.

Now Hitler could act as he chose, unimpeded by the laws. He instituted a Ministry of Propaganda under Goebbels. He stripped the state governments of the powers they had had under Weimar, and made Germany a strongly centralized state (April, 1933) by appointing governors from Berlin who had the power to override the state legislatures. When President Hindenburg died in August, 1934, at the age of eighty-seven, Hitler assumed the office of president as well as that of chancellor, but he preferred to use the title *Der Fuehrer* (the leader) to describe himself. This new move was approved by a plebiscite, in which Hitler obtained 88 per cent of the votes cast.

Political parties which opposed Hitler were forced to dissolve. The government banned Communists and Socialists (May, 1933); the Nationalists dissolved themselves (June, 1933); the government put an end to the Catholic parties (July, 1933), and all monarchist groups (February, 1934). The *Stahlhelm* was incorporated into the Nazi party (June, 1933) and was deprived of its identity (November, 1935). As early as July, 1933, the Nazis were declared to be the only legal political party in Germany.

The appeal of the Nazis to the German people lay in part in their denunciation and repudiation of the "disorderly" parliamentary system. The replacement of the parliamentary bickerings in the Reichstag by a strong man who got things done struck a responsive chord in the public. In the last elections, November, 1933, there were no opposition candidates, 92 per cent of the electorate voted Nazi, and there were only two non-Nazi deputies in the chamber of 661. As in fascist Italy and communist Russia, youth groups fed the party, which soon had a powerful regional organization all over Germany.

Hitler and Schacht, 1936.

The "Blood Purge" of 1934

Within the Nazi party itself, however, a difficult situation was created by those who had believed Hitler's more radical pronouncements on social and economic questions. Many of these Nazis were concentrated in the SA. SA men, most of them from the lower middle classes, were also distressed by the way in which Hitler had treated their organization. The SA had made possible his rise to power, but now it was rather an embarrassment to him, no longer quite respectable, and certainly not in favor, as were the SS and especially the army.

On June 30, 1934, Hitler ordered and personally participated in the celebrated "blood purge," or, as he himself called it, "the night of the long knives." Roehm himself, founder and leader of the SA, was shot, and so were, by Hitler's own admission, seventy-three others, including Schleicher and his wife. The slippery Papen was arrested, but lived to serve Hitler well as a diplomat. Other estimates of the casualties run as high as 1,000. Among the victims were prominent Catholics and a number of generals, all of whom, Hitler charged, were united in a plot on his life. In any case, after June, 1934, there was no further opposition to Hitler inside the Nazi party or out. Annual "party-days" at Nuremberg were the occasions for spectacular shows of Nazi loyalty: massed swastika banners, military music, roars of approval as Hitler shrieked his vituperations hour after hour.

Racism

Within a few days after the passage of the enabling law, Hitler struck the first of his many blows against the Jews, whom he had so long denounced. In a country of approximately 60,000,000 people, the Jews counted less than 1 per cent of the population (something under 600,000), not including part-Jewish Germans. The Jews had become leading members of the professions and the arts, and had made outstanding contributions to German culture. Since most Jews were assimilated and deeply patriotic Germans, many of them would probably have become Nazis if they had been permitted. They would have supported Hitler in everything but anti-Semitism. Instead, anti-Semitic doctrines required their ruthless elimination.

The businesses and professions of the Jews were boycotted; they were forbidden to hold office (April, 1933), although a temporary exception was made for veterans of World War I. In the "Nuremberg laws"

CHAPTER XXVII

of September 15, 1935, a Jew was defined as any person with one Jewish grandparent. All such persons were deprived of German citizenship. Intermarriage between Jews and non-Jews was forbidden as "racial pollution." Jews might not fly the national flag, write or publish, act on stage or screen, teach in any educational institution, work in a bank, exhibit paintings or give concerts, work in a hospital, enter any of the government's labor or professional bodies, or sell books or antiques. They were not eligible for unemployment insurance or charity; and the names of Jews who had died for Germany in World War I were erased from war memorials. Many towns and villages, under the spur of government-sponsored propaganda, refused to permit Jews to live inside their precincts.

In November, 1938, a Jewish boy of seventeen, driven to desperation by the persecution of his parents, shot and killed a secretary of the German embassy in Paris. Two days later, organized German mobs looted and pillaged Jewish shops all over Germany, burned and dynamited synagogues, and invaded Jewish homes to beat up the occupants and steal their possessions. The state then compelled the Jews to restore the damaged properties, and to pay an enormous fine. Jews were forced to take special names, to wear yellow stars of David, and to belong to a Reich "Union of Jews." Although some Jews managed to leave Germany, it was usually at the cost of abandoning all their possessions; yet they were the lucky ones. All these measures and many others (for example, "cows purchased from Jews may not be serviced by the communal bull") designed to drive the Jews into ghettos and starvation were but the prelude to the physical extermination in gas-ovens to which they were to be subjected by the Nazis during World War II. What distressed many horrified western observers almost more than the actions themselves was the failure of any substantial number of highly educated and "civilized" non-Jewish Germans to register any form of protest.

Enthusiasm for "racial purity" had its positive as well as its negative side. The blond, blue-eyed ideal "Nordic types" were urged to mate with each other early and to have many children. German motherhood was made the object of paeans of praise. And, to keep the race pure, sterilization was introduced, supposedly for the prevention of the inheritance of disease. A "court of eugenics," including a judge, a doctor, and a specialist in hereditary disease, had to pass on each case. Although this enactment was accepted as an advanced social step even in some non-German quarters, the proper functioning of such a law depended upon the condition of the medical and legal professions. In Germany, both law and medicine soon fell into the hands of charlatans whose chief asset was that they were ardent Nazis. Medical experimentation of horrifying cruelty and of no conceivable scientific value was practiced during the war on human beings of "inferior" races—Jews, Poles and other Slavs, and gypsies. These practices were the direct outcome of Nazi "eugenic" legislation.

Legal and Economic Policies

Hitler entirely revamped the judicial system of Germany, abandoning traditional legal principles, and substituting "folk" justice, which, Hitler said, subordinated the individual totally to the people (Volk). So mystic a doctrine meant in practice that whatever Hitler wanted was German law. People's Courts (May, 1934) were established to try all cases of treason, a crime that was now extended to include a wide variety of lesser offenses, such as circulating banned newspapers. Hitler appointed all the judges of the People's Courts. Concentration camps were established for enemies of the regime, who could be immured or executed by the headsman's axe, without appeal. In fact, they could not even have defense counsel of their choice, but had to accept counsel approved by the courts. The Gestapo (*Geheime Staatspolizei*, Secret State Police) was established in April, 1933, in Prussia, and a year later was extended to all of Germany. It had a free hand in opening private correspondence, tapping wires, and spying on individual citizens.

All economic life was brought under the regime. In agriculture, the Nazis aimed at the largest possible measure of self-sufficiency, and, of course, at political control over the peasantry. The Junkers were protected, and no effort was made to divide their vast estates. In 1933, a special law protected farms of less than 312 acres against forced sale and attachment for debt, an act that won the small farmer to Hitler. But the government determined the production required of farms, and fixed farm prices and wages, and fees for distributing farm products. Unused land was put under cultivation, and private citizens were required to grow vegetables in greenhouses. This was part of Hitler's preparation for war. By 1937, Germany was 83 per cent self-sufficient in agriculture, a rise of 8 per cent since the Nazis had come to power. Fats and coffee were perhaps the two most important deficiencies remaining.

In industry, taking a leaf out of Stalin's book, Hitler proclaimed a Four-Year Plan in 1933 and a second one in 1936. The first was aimed chiefly at economic recovery and at ending unemployment. Labor camps for men and women helped decrease unemployment, as did rearmament and a program of public works. By 1936, unemployment had dropped from about 7,000,000 to less than 1,500,000. The second plan was designed to prepare for war, and especially to make Germany blockade-proof. Output of raw materials was increased and the materials were distributed first and foremost to armament and other war industries; labor was allocated with similar ends in view; and prices and foreign exchange were controlled. Goering was made boss of the plan.

Under his direction fell the new Goering Iron Works, designed to make up for the loss of the rich iron resources of Alsace-Lorraine, which had yielded three quarters of Germany's iron. To this end, low-content ores were worked, and the government absorbed the higher costs. Output went up in two years more than 50 per cent. Germany's gifted scientists were enlisted to make up for other deficiencies by devising successful but expensive synthetic products. Important in this field were the distillation of motor fuel from coal, and the production of synthetic rubber. The state also built strategic highways, the *Autobahnen*.

The Nazis abolished all labor unions in 1933, and employers' associations in 1934. To replace them, a "Labor Front" was established under Dr. Robert Ley, including all wage-earners, salaried persons, professionals, and employers. Strikes and lockouts had been forbidden. Each plant had its own council made up of employees chosen on the recommendation of the employer and of the local Nazi party boss. This council made recommendations for improvements within the plant. All Germany was divided into thirteen districts, each under a "trustee of labor," who fixed wages, settled disputes, and ousted anyone, whether employer or worker, whom he felt to be hindering the operation of the Labor Front. Such decisions were liable to review by "Social Honor Courts." Workers were assured of jobs so long as they quietly accepted the entire system. The Labor Front in one of its aspects was a huge spy organization constantly on the alert for

CHAPTER XXVII

anti-Nazis in the factories; it could reduce their pay, fire them, or put them in jail. An adjunct to the Labor Front was the "Strength through Joy" organization, which provided paid vacation trips for German workers to resorts or tourist centers, and which sponsored concerts and other entertainments.

As the second Four-Year Plan went into effect, the worker found himself increasingly immobile. He had a work-book, detailing his past training and positions held, and he could not get a new job unless the state decided it would be more suitable for him. All graduates of secondary schools had to register with the employment authorities. Men and women of working age were liable to conscription for labor. Just before the war, all agricultural and mining and certain industrial workers were frozen in their jobs. On the side of capital, the big cartel became the all-pervasive feature of German industrial organization—a system of profitable monopoly under state control. The interlocking directorate made the system even tighter than it looked. Six industrialists, for example, held among them one hundred and twenty-seven directorates in the largest corporations, were presidents of thirty-two, and all held government posts besides. The Minister of Economics sat at the top of the economic pyramid, authorizing plant expansion, controlling imports and exports, fixing prices, establishing costs, and allocating raw materials.

Religion and Culture

The Christian churches, both Protestant and Catholic, posed a problem for the Nazis. Extremists among Hitler's followers had always been in favor of a return to paganism and the old German gods celebrated by Wagner's operas. Hitler himself, born a Catholic, had once declared that Germany was his only God. Yet office brought sobering second thoughts, since Germany was after all nominally a Christian country. In the hope of avoiding state domination, the Lutheran ministry in 1933 organized a national synod, which the Nazis almost immediately took over by appointing their own bishop. The efforts of extreme Nazis to purge the Bible and to abandon the crucifix led to discontent. The dissidents, led by Pastor Martin Niemoeller, objected to Nazi theology and efforts at control. But Niemoeller also pledged his loyalty to Hitler, made no objections to Nazi racism, and went to a concentration camp solely out of determination to resist dictation over the Lutheran Church. When war came, he petitioned to be allowed to command a submarine. The "confessional" movement he led probably did not extend beyond about 15 per cent of the Protestant clergy. The rest were able to swallow the regime whole without gagging.

In July, 1933, Hitler and the German Catholics reached a concordat guaranteeing freedom of worship and permitting religious instruction in the schools. Catholics were to be allowed to form youth groups, and to appoint professors of theology. But the Nazis did not live up to these terms. They interfered with the circulation of Catholic magazines, persecuted the youth groups, and insulted Catholic priests in their press as members of the "black international." On the other hand, the Catholic Church found much to oppose in the teachings to which Catholic children were exposed in the Hitler youth groups. Cardinal Faulhaber of Munich denounced the Nazi violation of the concordat in 1933, but his action only intensified the struggle. In 1937, a large number of priests was arrested and tried for a variety of alleged crimes. Many were sentenced to concentration camps. Thus in the case of the Protestants, a national church sponsored by the Nazis met with some opposition, while in the case of the Catholics, the Nazis acted as Bismarck once had done and conducted a genuine *Kulturkampf* (see Chapter XXII). Not that millions of Catholics, both clerical and lay, did not support the regime wholeheartedly, persecutions of the Jews and all. They did; and no voice was raised from among the clergy of either major Christian sect to protest against Nazi racism or militarism.

The Nazi process of *Gleichschaltung* (coordination) was applied in every portion of the national life, including education and the arts. One of the leading Nazi officials once remarked, "When I hear the word culture, I reach for my revolver," a revealing and not untypical reflection of the extreme Nazi attitude. Hitler's own artistic views were simple in the extreme: he preferred nudes, the more luscious and Germanic the better, and this taste he strove to impose on the nation, denouncing most modern and experimental trends in art as non-Aryan. The school curriculum, especially history, could no longer be taught with that "objectivity" which was a "fallacy of liberalism," but had to be presented to the student in accordance with the Nazi doctrine of "blood and soil." Nazi racial doctrines, the great past achievements of Germany, the development of the military spirit, and physical culture—these were the cornerstones of the new education. The great emperors of medieval Germany, Frederick the Great, and Bismarck now were joined as national heroes by Horst Wessel, a party member and pimp who had been killed in a street brawl in 1930, and who had composed the Nazi song.

The Bases of Foreign Policy

Hitler's foreign policy is discussed in detail in Chapter XXVIII. But because so much of his domestic policy was geared for war, and because so much of his popular support rested upon his announced aim of restoring Germany's military prestige by expansion abroad, we shall examine some of the theories on which that policy was based. German racism justified the incorporation of all territory inhabited by Germans, including Austria, the western borderlands (Sudetenland) of Czechoslovakia, Danzig, the Polish corridor, and other less important places. And the doctrine of "living-space" (*Lebensraum*) justified the incorporation of non-German areas—the rest of Czechoslovakia, Poland, and all southeastern Europe, as well as large areas of Russia. Hitler felt that what the Germans needed, they were entitled to take, since they were a superior people.

The notion of *Lebensraum* stems in part from twentieth-century German intellectuals who looked back with longing upon the Holy Roman Empire of the Middle Ages, the first *Reich*, and hoped, after the war had ended the second *Reich* of William II, to behold a third one, incorporating the old territories, no matter who now lived in them. This is the meaning of Hitler's use of the term "Third Reich," to describe the Nazi state, which he proclaimed would last a thousand years. A "scientific" basis for the *Lebensraum* theory was supplied by the teachers of "geopolitics," chief among whom was Karl Haushofer, professor of geography, retired major-general, and teacher of Hitler's close friend, Rudolf Hess. The geopoliticians supplied a respectable front for Nazi territorial ambitions. Haushofer declared that Britain and France were decadent, that small powers must disappear (except for Switzerland and the Vatican City), that Germany, preserving its master-race pure, must possess the will to power, and expand ruthlessly, occupying the "heart land" of Eurasia, from which the world could be dominated. In support of his claims to more space, Hitler often maintained that Germany was overcrowded. Yet he himself made every effort to increase the overcrowding by subsidizing bigger and bigger families. Like Haushofer's arguments, this argument was one more justification for Hitler to do what he had all along intended to do anyhow.

Finally, we may point to a school of thought in Germany that is often neglected. An examination of this school will give us a better understanding of the Hitler-Stalin pact of 1939, and also of Hitler's success at home. At one level, this was simply a pro-Russian school. The military members had a theory that Germany's future lay in an alliance with Russia in which Russia's inexhaustible manpower would be joined with Germany's industrial output and military techniques for purposes of conquest. This notion had been strong in German army circles in tsarist days, and continued to exist after the Bolshevik Revolution, especially after the Treaty of Rapallo (see above, p. 503), concluded between Germany and the Soviet Union in 1922. Outside the purely military circles, there persisted also the Bismarckian attitudes of hostility to the West and to Poland and of friendship toward Russia, whatever the color of her regime.

Now that Russia was Bolshevik and the active sponsor of the German Communist party, many German nationalists tried to find some common ground between their nationalism and the ideas of the new Russia. This task was made easier for them by the fact that they had always been violently anti-liberal and anti-parliamentarian in any case, and so were the Stalinists. Thus, during the Weimar Republic, and even after Hitler's triumph, there existed a whole school of extreme German nationalists who were not unsympathetic to communism. Moreover, there also existed among the German Marxists, communists included, a strong nationalistic feeling, which, at its most extreme, brought them quite close to the nationalists. The way in which hundreds of thousands of voters in the last years of the Weimar Republic shifted back and forth between the Nazi and Communist parties is in some measure an evidence of this feeling.

Yet such views were officially combatted both by communists, who penalized nationalism among their followers, and among those nationalists who were essentially conservative. It was Hitler who "presented nationalism in a proletarian disguise and captured the imagination of his followers." Where neither communists nor nationalists could attract the support of the all-important lower middle class, Hitler's national socialism succeeded. It succeeded in large part because of its leader's skill in tricking nationalism out in the Marxist phrases that had become part of the general German vocabulary.

V: The Failure of Parliamentarism in Spain and Eastern Europe, 1918-1939

In the troubled years between the wars, non-democratic authoritarian governments emerged not only in Germany and Italy. They also emerged in Spain, in the succession-states to the Habsburg Empire (with the exception of Czechoslovakia), and in the other states of eastern and southeastern Europe.

Spain: The Background

Spain is so different from the other countries of Europe, and its politics are so complicated, that foreigners are tempted to draw dangerously misleading parallels. The developments leading to the establishment of the Franco regime are meaningless unless we keep in mind the special geographic, economic, cultural, and social background against which they took place. In Spain, local feeling in town and village and province is intense; only occasionally has some common cause united the Spanish people. Politically, this has meant that separatism is often an issue, particularly in Catalonia and in the Basque provinces of the north.

Second, religion, as the driving force that united Spaniards against the Moslems in the Middle Ages, and against the Protestants in the sixteenth and seventeenth centuries, has played an extraordinarily large part in the national life. But early in the nineteenth century, the Catholic Church in Spain decided to lead against liberalism the same kind of struggle it had led against its earlier enemies, instead of identifying itself with popular causes. So in most parts of Spain the Church became identified with the landowners. Loss of faith became very widespread. Catholic sources report that by the 1930's only minute fractions of the population attended Mass. With the same devotion and passion they had once shown for the Church, the lower classes in Spain adopted one or another of the modern revolutionary doctrines.

Third, though Spain approaches economic self-sufficiency in both agriculture and industrial raw materials, the soil is poor, the system of farming is backward, and the rural areas are heavily overpopulated. Poverty is endemic, which means that discontent is everywhere. Yet the Spanish poor cared less for a higher standard of living for themselves than for freedom from outside interference. Agrarian reform, however, based on expropriation of large estates and the institution of some sort of cooperative farming, has long seemed an essential factor in overcoming poverty.

Fourth, when the Spaniards turned to revolutionary doctrine, it was chiefly in Bakunin's anarchist beliefs and later in Sorel's syndicalism that they found ideas they could cling to. Anarchism (and anarcho-syndicalism) really took hold in Spain, and in Spain alone. The industrial workers of Catalonia and the miserable peasants of Andalusia were anarchist; they wanted to destroy the state utterly rather than conquer and use it. Despite a long history in Spain, anarchism, which at its peak numbered a million to a million and a half adherents, could do no more than create a wish for revolution. It could harass governments but could not overthrow them, and its positive achievements were limited to securing by means of strikes an occasional increase in wages. It was deeply puritanical in tone, and fanatically anti-Catholic. Shrewd observers have likened it to a Christian heresy that takes all too seriously the social teachings of the New Testament. Its adherents turned against the Church with all the fanaticism with which they had once supported it, because they felt that the Church had let them down. The burning of churches and the killing of priests, with which Spanish revolutions have always been marked, have been the work chiefly of anarchists, who "aim at reaching by violence a state from which even the mildest form of compulsion is to be excluded." Anarchist ranks included many professional criminals, drawn only by their love of violence.

But Spanish revolutionary ideas were not confined to the anarchists. Spain also had an increasingly substantial Marxist Socialist party, with its own federation of trade unions parallel to that of the anarchists. The socialists drew their first strength from the urban workers of Castile and from the mining and steel-producing centers of the north. When Spain became a republic in 1931 (see below), the socialists added many rural supporters and the party numbered a million and a quarter in 1934. The socialists were moderates who had refused to adhere to the Comintern in 1920, but who had joined the revived Second International a few years later. Dissidents founded a small Communist party, from which there were soon Trotskyite deviations. Catalonians had their own socialist formation, and the Church also supported labor unions of its own in the north, where it had not become identified with the landlords. The socialist doctrine that each should be rewarded according to his needs fits with the traditional Spanish contempt for success and property. In fact, Spain is essentially a country that has never accepted the capitalist system or the industrial revolution any more than it has accepted the Protestant Reformation.

Carlism, the doctrine of the extreme Right, is another vivid illustration of Spanish maladjustment to the outside contemporary world. Founded in the nineteenth century as a movement supporting Carlos, a pretender to the throne, Carlism is more interesting as a sweeping repudiation of modern society. It calls for the restoration of the Inquisition, regards the railroad and the telegraph literally as inventions of the devil, and rejects the Copernican theory of the universe. Carlism has its lower-class devotees, too, especially among the rebellious farmers of Navarre in the north.

Birth of the Spanish Republic

Over this country there ruled until 1923 King Alfonso XIII, a constitutional monarch strongly ambitious for absolute power. He was supported by a government based entirely on electoral corruption and intimidation, in which "liberals" and "conservatives" took orderly turns at office, and in which the real power rested with the local political bosses. Not having participated in World War I, Spain was spared much of the ensuing anguish. Yet wartime trade with the combatants had built up Spanish industry and had increased the tension between rich and poor. In Morocco, the army proved incompetent to deal with rebellion, and many Spaniards were killed there in a military disaster in 1921. Catalonian separatism, as always, harassed the government.

In this situation a *coup* took place in 1923 led by General Primo de Rivera, acting with the approval of Alfonso. Primo de Rivera proclaimed martial law, imposed censorship, and persecuted political opponents. His dictatorship lasted until 1930, but lost its popularity after 1926. Both its success and its failure are comprehensible in the light of world economic conditions. The regime spent too much on public works, and was caught in the depression. Moreover, it did not fulfill its promises for a constituent assembly and political reform. Rivera did at last succeed in pacifying Morocco, however. He also got the socialists to participate in his regime, and put through appropriate labor legislation in the hope of weakening the anarchists. But, since he depended on the army and the landowners, he could not institute agrarian reform. He also alienated the Catalonians, and his repressive measures deprived him of middle-class support.

After Rivera's resignation and death in 1930, King Alfonso soon restored the constitution. Municipal elections (April, 1931) resulted in a victory for the republicans, representing the lower middle classes of the towns, small tradesmen, intellectuals, teachers, and journalists. The King left the country without abdicating. Elections to a constituent assembly in June, 1931, brought in a great republican-socialist majority, and in November the assembly forbade the King's return and confiscated his property. Spain was a republic. The monarchy, having stood only for clergy, army, and aristocracy, had failed.

The assembly went ahead to adopt a new constitution in December. This provided for a single-chamber parliament, a president to be chosen by an electoral college consisting of parliament and an equal number of electors chosen by popular vote, and a responsible ministry. It was clear that the army would rise against the Republic whenever the opportunity was presented, and that the army would have the support of the Church and the large landowners. Moreover, although the Republic temporarily had socialist support, it did not have the support of the anarchists. Thus it was from the first in danger both from the Right and from the Left; its task was to steer between the many extremists of both sides while striving to build up a republican Center.

Crisis of the Spanish Republic, 1933-1936

The first crisis arose over a new constitutional statute defining the position of the Church. The assembly rejected a moderate proposal which would have preserved the Church as a special corporation with its own schools, and which might have proved acceptable to most Catholics, even though the Cardinal-Primate of Spain had already denounced the Republic. Instead, a measure was passed that closed church schools and ended state grants to the Church after two years. This hurt education badly, and lost the republicans many supporters, especially among the lower

clergy itself. Although the Republic secured much Catalan support by a grant of autonomy, it failed to act decisively on agrarian reform. This failure was in part due to the depression, which raised rural unemployment and caused the landowners to permit land to go out of cultivation; but it was due even more to the disagreement between the republicans and the socialists on what to do with expropriated property. The socialists wanted collectivization; the republicans, like Stolypin in tsarist Russia and for the same political reasons (see above, p. 327), wanted individual small holdings, which would probably not be practical in Spain. The agrarian law as passed satisfied nobody.

The anarchists expressed their dissatisfaction by major risings (1933), which the government put down by force. The jails were full, and unemployment was as high as ever. Repression of the anarchists lost the Republic much Left support, but of course failed to gain it that of the Right, which came back strongly in the elections of November, 1933, as the largest party in parliament. Now the government helplessly swung to the Right, and much of its previous legislation, especially legislation affecting the Church and the working classes, remained a dead letter. The Church and monarchists put forward a young man named Gil Robles as their leader. His views were strongly fascist, and he especially admired Dollfuss, the Austrian chancellor (see below).

On the Left, the socialists no longer collaborated with the government. Grown more revolutionary, they now engaged in strenuous competition with the anarchists for the loyalty of the Spanish workers. Strikes and disorders multiplied. In October, 1934, the socialists called a general strike in protest against the inclusion of three of Robles' followers in the government. Catalonia declared itself a republic, and was deprived of its autonomy. The coal-miners of the Asturias in the north staged a revolt, joined in by both anarchists and socialists, which was put down with the loss of more than 3,000 lives. The government's use of Moors (Moslems from North Africa) against Spaniards was deeply resented; the Moors had been dispatched by the new minister of war, General Francisco Franco.

Thus the Right in turn lost its public support; and now the Left, under the impact of the Asturias uprising, and influenced by the line of the Comintern (see above, p. 505), united in a "Popular Front" for the elections of February, 1936. For the first time, anarcho-syndicalists went to the polls and voted for a common list with republicans, socialists, and communists. The Left won a considerable victory, perhaps largely because it promised an amnesty for men involved in past outbreaks. Catalan autonomy, land reform, and anticlerical measures were of course the first order of business. The moderate Republican, Azaña, was elected president.

But moderation was now out of fashion on the Left. The Popular Front was a coalition *for election purposes only.* Instead of entering Azaña's cabinet, Largo Caballero, leader of the left wing of the socialists, now "played at revolution." He was hailed by *Pravda* as a new Lenin, and acted as if he intended to seize power. Yet he could not have made good this threat, since he had no force with which to back it up. The route to power for left-wing revolutionaries would open up only if the Right attempted a military *coup,* if the government then armed the workers to fight it, and if the workers then won.

On the Left also, and for the first time, the Spanish Communist party in 1936 emerged as a considerable element. Under Primo de Rivera's dictatorship the communists had been so insignificant that he

had not even taken the trouble to suppress their newspaper. But their participation in the Asturian uprising and the Popular Front gained them political strength despite their numerical weakness (3,000 members). Oddly enough, they were more moderate in their immediate aims than the socialists, because they felt the need for a long preliminary period of Popular Front co-operation to increase their own power, and because this was Stalin's "respectable" period.

Simultaneously in 1936, on the Right, there emerged, also for the first time, the *Falange* (phalanx), a party founded in 1932 by the son of Primo de Rivera. The founder was an orthodox fascist on the Italian pattern ("harmony of all classes and professions in one destiny") but was not opposed to agrarian reform or other socialist programs. The Falange had the usual paraphernalia. Its symbol was a bunch of arrows; its slogan was *Arriba España;* its program called for national expansion in Africa, the annexation of Portugal, the building of an empire in South America; it had youth groups and a private army. Although the Falange polled relatively few votes in the election of 1936, most of Gil Robles' right-wing support went over to it after the Popular Front victory. Through the spring of 1936 the Falange worked for a counter-revolution with army, monarchist, clerical, and Carlist groups. Everybody knew a military *coup* against the government was in the offing. In July it came, under the military leadership of General Franco.

The Spanish Civil War, 1936-1939

The international significance of the Spanish Civil War (1936-1939) as the first act in the conflict that was to ripen into

World War II will be considered in Chapter XXVIII. Decisively aided by Germany and Italy, Franco's forces pushed on to victory, which culminated in their capture of the republican strongholds of Madrid and Barcelona in 1939. During the war, the functions of the weak republican government were usurped by a series of workers' committees, and then a Popular Front regime under Caballero came to office in September, 1936. Franco's forces named him chief of state in November. In government territory, terror reigned. At first the terror was the work of anarchists, but they were suppressed. Their terror was replaced by police terror, the work of the communists, who, with Russia behind them, ruthlessly worked against their rival leftist parties in the regime. On the Franco side, terror also took its toll, as men of all sorts connected with the Republic were killed. After the Franco triumph, the prisons were filled and the executioner was kept busy.

With all its fascist trappings, the Franco regime, the only fascist regime to survive World War II, still depended after the war upon the same classes that had supported the Spanish monarchy—the landowners, the army, and the Church. It was presumably opposed by the poor in city and country alike. But the fear of a new civil war, which lay heavily on all classes, prevented open opposition.

Eastern Europe

The triumph of the Right in one form or another in eastern Europe is explained partly by the lack of a firm parliamentary tradition; partly by the failure to solve grievous economic problems, especially after the great worldwide depression of 1929; and partly by a popular fear of Bolshevism, often quite out of proportion to any serious threat, but skillfully played

upon by unscrupulous leaders. Perhaps as important as all the other factors put together was the initial impression created by the successes of Mussolini and Hitler. The way to get ahead in the world, at least after 1935, seemed to be to put on a uniform, proclaim a doctrine of extreme nationalism, and launch a war of nerves against your neighbors by loudly voicing your claims, whatever they might happen to be, and by threatening to make them good by means of the sword.

But it was not only the political example set by the dictators that turned the unstable states of eastern and southeastern Europe toward dictatorship. After the depression, the economic pressures exerted by Germany, whose industrial economy complemented the agrarian economy of these states, enabled her to dominate their foreign trade, especially in the Balkan area. To show how these factors operated, we shall now examine three case-histories—Austria, Hungary, and Yugoslavia—and then indicate briefly the course of developments elsewhere.

Austria

The Austria that was left at the end of World War I had an almost purely German population of about 8,000,000, about 2,000,000 of whom lived in the former imperial capital of Vienna. Long the great market for an enormous hinterland and the supplier of industrial finished goods to the agricultural provinces, Vienna was now cut off from its former territories by political boundaries and tariff walls. Between 1922 and 1925, Austrian finances were under direct League of Nations supervision; a League loan and reconstruction policies brought a measure of recovery. But what might have represented one road to economic salvation—union of Austria with Germany—though voted by the assembly of the new Austrian republic in March, 1919, was forbidden on political grounds by the Allies in the Treaty of St. Germain (September, 1919). These two problems, economic survival and union with Germany, were complicated by the continuation in even more violent form of the basic political struggle of imperial Austria: Social Democrats against Christian Socialists (see Chapter XXII). The Social Democrats were a gradualist reformist, but Marxist, party with strong urban support, especially in Vienna itself. The Christian Socialists were a conservative clerical party with a mass following in the countryside and among the urban lower middle classes, and counted many priests among their leaders.

In the mid-twenties, the two hostile parties, usually almost evenly balanced in the parliament, organized private armies. The Christian Socialists organized the *Heimwehr* (home guard), and the Social Democrats organized the *Schutzbund* (defense league). Their mutual hostility was increased by the relief and workers' housing measures undertaken by the Social Democratic municipal government of Vienna. These measures were financed by taxing the rich. After 1930, when a treaty was signed with Italy, Mussolini more or less overtly supported the Christian Socialists, who grew more and more fascistic in their outlook. The failure of Bruening's plan for a customs union with Germany and the related collapse of the Vienna *Kredit-Anstalt* bank (see above, p. 540) increased tension in 1931, and in September, 1931, the *Heimwehr* tried its first fascist *coup,* which failed. Efforts in 1932 to organize a Danubian economic co-operation scheme—an alternative to Austrian union with Germany, and favored by France—were rendered futile by Italian and German opposition. After Hitler came to power in early 1933, many Christian Socialists became openly Nazi.

The Christian Socialist chancellor, Engelbert Dollfuss, however, strove to curb the Nazis. To this end he suspended parliamentary government in March, 1933, and in effect ended parliamentary democracy. He forbade the wearing of uniforms by political groups, and tried to expel Nazi agitators. In retaliation, Hitler made it prohibitively expensive for German tourists to visit Austria, and thus destroyed one of the most lucrative sources of Austrian income. In the face of Nazi-inspired disorder, Dollfuss banned the Nazi party (June, 1933). But, instead of burying the hatchet and uniting with the Social Democrats against Hitler, Dollfuss pursued them too. He banned all parties except his own "Fatherland Front," a union of all right-wing groups except the Nazis, and raided Social Democratic headquarters, precipitating a workers' riot. The government then bombarded with artillery the workers' new apartment houses, in which the Social Democratic leaders had taken refuge (February, 1934). The Social Democratic party was broken, but the Vienna workmen were permanently alienated and were united in opposition to the regime. Dollfuss had to depend more and more upon Italy to support him against the threat from Hitler. He established himself as a fascist dictator (April 30, 1934), but was assassinated in July by the Nazis. It was only Italian troop concentrations on the frontier that led Hitler to disavow this attempted *coup.*

Dollfuss' successor, Schuschnigg, was committed to the same policies. But Mussolini's desire to win Hitler's support for Italian aggression in the Mediterranean weakened Schuschnigg. The Austrian Chancellor made plans looking toward a Habsburg restoration, tried to concentrate armed power in his own hands rather than those of the *Heimwehr,* and strove to create an understanding with France and her allies to replace the one with Italy. But he failed

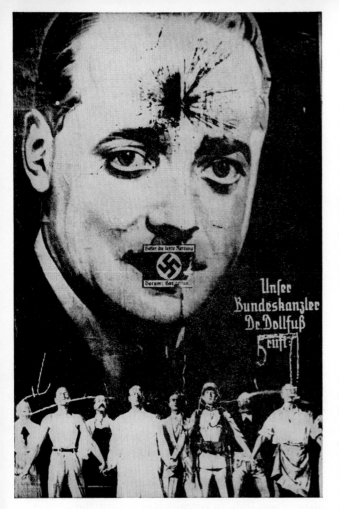

Poster of Chancellor Dollfuss and representative Austrians defaced by Nazis, 1933.

nigg's announcement that a plebiscite would be held on the question of Austrian independence. Hitler marched in, installed a Nazi chancellor, put Schuschnigg in jail, and began the extension of the Nazi system to Austria by allowing storm-troopers to force elderly Viennese Jews to clean the sidewalks with acid under a hail of abuse and blows. In April, 1938, he held the plebiscite on the question of Austrian union with Germany and obtained a 99.75 per cent vote of *Ja*. Mussolini had to bow in 1938 to what he had prevented in 1934, and Austria, increasingly fascist since 1930, had become a mere province of Nazi Germany.

Hungary

In Hungary, the most overwhelmingly important political issue between the wars was "revisionism," the effort to revise the peace treaties that had deprived the Magyars of all territories predominantly populated by Slavic and Rumanian minorities. The Treaty of Trianon (June, 1920) confirmed the loss of a small strip of land to Austria, of Transylvania to Rumania, of Slovakia to Czechoslovakia, and of Croatia and other Serb and Croat territories to Yugoslavia. No tourist who visited Budapest thereafter could escape the huge statue of Hungary mourning the lost provinces, north, east, south, and west, or the great map laid out in flowerbeds in the public park, showing in different colored blossoms the far-flung territories relinquished but still claimed by the Magyars. The national motto was now "*Nem, nem, soha*" (No, no, never). Revisionist propaganda made a considerable impression in those circles where the Hungarian aristocracy had always had sympathizers, especially among the English upper classes, who had often failed to grasp the great difference in political tradition between themselves and

in the face of German aggression. In February and March, 1938, Hitler increased the pressure on Schuschnigg, who was subjected to the first of the famous series of grim interviews between Hitler and statesmen of lesser countries. The Fuehrer demanded and obtained privileges for the Nazis in Austria. When the predictable Nazi disorders broke out, Schuschnigg desperately tried to win working-class support, but it was too late.

The final move that precipitated armed German invasion of Austria was Schusch-

their cultivated and tweedy horsey Magyar friends, and who were usually quite ignorant of Hungary's black record in governing her minorities.

The rank and file of Hungarians were relatively indifferent to revisionism as an issue, as they had always been indifferent to the chauvinist questions which agitated their rulers, the great aristocrats and the gentry (see Chapter XXII). This unreal and sterile issue continued to dominate Hungarian life after 1920 because the aristocrats and the gentry were able to keep their dominant position. Hungary was one of the few countries of eastern Europe not to experience an effective land reform between the wars. The enormous estates of the great magnates and the smaller properties of the gentry remained almost intact. Behind a thin screen of parliamentary government, an authoritarian dictatorship governed the country on behalf of the old ruling groups. It was helped by a greatly swollen bureaucracy, and it became more and more fascist in character as the years went on. In the troubled days immediately after the war, the Allies paved the way for this triumph of the Right by their failure to support the efforts of Hungarian moderates to create a stable democratic regime. They also permitted a bloody-handed Bolshevik dictatorship to take power briefly. In the reaction against this communist regime, moderation and reform lost out in Hungary and fascism won.

The brief opportunity (if it really was an opportunity) for a moderate regime in Hungary began on October 31, 1918, twelve days before the Armistice, when Count Michael Karolyi became prime minister, after the country had already severed its ties with Austria. Karolyi was one of the richest of the great magnates, but a democrat on the western pattern. He had always been pro-Allied, and was deeply imbued with Wilsonian ideas. Though not a socialist, Karolyi favored social reform. He proved his sincerity by handing over the 50,000 acres of his own estate to be divided among the peasants, and by preparing a land-reform law. He made every effort to reach a compromise with the national minorities, but these groups would no longer trust any Magyar. The French commander of Allied troops did not assist Karolyi, and demanded a retreat of Hungarian forces from Slovakia. Karolyi resigned in March, 1919, in protest over the loss of Transylvania.

National sentiment and growing radicalism, stimulated by the news of Bolshevik activities brought by Hungarian prisoners returning from Russia, now made possible a left-wing government more and more dominated by Lenin's agent, Bela Kun, a Hungarian-born Jew. Revolutionary nationalization decrees were at once passed and a soviet political system was installed, but land reform was delayed—a delay that alienated the peasants. The Reds used terror in the countryside to overcome opposition. If Hungary had been as large as Russia or as far from the main theater of Allied operations, Kun might have gained time enough to compensate for his lack of trained men, a handicap that it had taken all the genius of Lenin and Trotsky to overcome in Russia.

But the Allies were determined not to let a Bolshevik government rule Hungary. The Rumanians invaded and drove Kun out; they occupied the country during 1919 and part of 1920, and stripped it of everything they could move. Meanwhile, a counter-revolutionary government had been formed under French protection and had returned to Budapest, where Admiral Horthy, a member of the gentry, became regent and chief of state (March 1, 1920). Hungary was now a kingdom without a king, Horthy an admiral without a fleet. Two efforts of the Habsburg King Charles to regain the

Hungarian throne were frustrated, largely because of the opposition of the neighboring states. The Hungarian counter-revolution gave free rein to a "White Terror" directed largely against the Jews, but also against Magyar workers and peasants.

For ten years (1921-1931) Count Bethlen as prime minister was the real power in the country, which he ran as if nothing had changed since 1914. The peasants were effectively disfranchised as they had always been; the Social Democrats were tolerated as a trade-union party; and the upper house of magnates was re-established. The League of Nations helped economic recovery by a loan and a reconstruction plan (1923-1926), and in 1927 a treaty with Italy began an intimate relationship between Hungary and Mussolini. The depression and the financial crisis of 1931 drove Bethlen from office. He was succeeded by the strongly nationalist and fascist-minded Gömbös, who was pro-German as well as pro-Italian, and who permitted the first Nazi-like organizations to form. Of these the Arrow Cross was the strongest, but it remained on the fringes of power until almost the end of World War II, largely because Hitler got what he wanted in Hungary without it.

Following Gömbös' death in 1936, his successors were all men of the same stripe. The Italians supplied arms to the Hungarians; Hitler favored their revisionism along with his own. After Austria had fallen to Hitler, he had Hungary in his pocket, and when he broke up Czechoslovakia in March, 1939, the Hungarians seized the extreme eastern portion, Ruthenia, and a small part of Slovakia. To pursue revisionism, the Hungarians had to follow Hitler, since he alone offered the opportunity to re-draw the map as they felt it should be drawn. So, before war broke out, they had withdrawn from the League, and had enacted anti-Semitic laws in the Nazi pattern. But because Hitler needed Rumania too,

he would not give the Magyars all of Transylvania. Ironically enough, the price they paid for espousal of revisionism between the wars was the Soviet-dominated regime installed in Hungary after World War II.

Yugoslavia

In the new "Kingdom of the Serbs, Croats, and Slovenes," proclaimed in December, 1918, there came together for the first time in one state the former south-Slav subjects of Austria and Hungary and those of the former independent Kingdom of Serbia. This was in most respects a satisfied state from the territorial point of view; revisionism therefore was not an issue. But, as the name of the new state shows, it faced the serious problem of creating a governmental system that would satisfy the aspirations of each of its nationality groups. Over this problem democracy broke down and a dictatorship was established. The dictatorship was in many respects not of the fascist type, although, as German power waxed, important politicians in the country became convinced that the future lay in Hitler's hands, and responded accordingly. The rank and file of the population, by and large, were peasants deeply devoted to freedom, although unskilled in western forms of parliamentarism. They opposed fascism, and, when they got the chance, ousted the politicians who sought to align them with it.

Serbian political ambitions had helped to start the war. The Serbs were more numerous than Croats and Slovenes together (approximately six million to three and a quarter million Croats and a few over one million Slovenes in 1931). Many Serbs felt that the new kingdom, which their Serbian king ruled from his Serbian capital of Belgrade, should be that "greater Serbia" of which they had so long dreamed. Orthodox in religion, using the Cyrillic alphabet,

*Assassination of King
Alexander of Yugoslavia
at Marseilles, 1934.*

and having experienced and overthrown
Ottoman domination, many Serbs tended
to look upon the Croats as effete subjects
of the Habsburgs who were lucky to get the
chance to live in the same state with them.
Roman Catholic in religion, using the Latin
alphabet, and having opposed Germans and
Magyars for centuries, many Croats felt
that the Serbs were crude easterners who
ought to give them a full measure of autonomy within the new state. Thus the
issue was posed: Serb-sponsored centralism
against Croat-sponsored federalism. The
Slovenes, more conciliatory and less numerous, sometimes acted as balance wheel to
keep the political machinery moving. But
the Serbs forced the acceptance of their
answer to the constitutional question. This
brought about dictatorship, alienated large
numbers of Croats, bred extremism among
them, and contributed greatly to the benefit
of the country's enemies and to its own sufferings during the second war.

The Croats, under their peasant leader
Radich, boycotted the constituent assembly
of 1920, and the Serbs put through a constitution providing for a strongly centralized
state. In the 1920's both sides generally refused to compromise, although occasionally
temporary understandings were reached, as
when Radich joined the cabinet briefly in
1925-26. When a Serb deputy shot Radich
dead on the floor of parliament in June,
1928, a crisis arose that terminated only
when King Alexander proclaimed a dictatorship in January, 1929. Alexander made
every effort to settle the problem by wiping
out all vestiges of old provincial loyalties.
There was to be no more Serbia or Croatia,
but new artificially created administrative
units named after the chief rivers that ran
through them. The whole country was renamed Yugoslavia, as a sign that there were
to be no more Serbs and Croats. But it was
still a Serbian government, and the Croats
could not be made to forget it. Elections
were rigged by the government, and all
political parties were dissolved. Croat leaders spent much time in jails, which, like
most Balkan jails, were highly uncomfortable. This dictatorship of King Alexander
passed no racial laws, elevated no one poli-

tical party to exclusive power, and had no colored shirts, special songs, or other fascist paraphernalia. But it was unmistakably authoritarian and anti-democratic.

One result was the strengthening of Croat extremists, who had wanted an independent Croatia in the days of the Habsburgs, and who now combined this program with terrorism, supported from abroad by the enemies of Yugoslavia—Italy and Hungary. The Croat extremists were called *Ustashi* (rebels), and their leader, Ante Pavelich, was subsidized by Mussolini. He was deeply involved in the assassination of Alexander at Marseilles in October, 1934. Under the regency of Prince Paul (Alexander's cousin) the dictatorship continued. As German economic power in the Balkans grew, leading politicians grew enamored of Germany, and some efforts were made to bring Yugoslav policies into line with those of the Axis. But these policies met with such unconcealed popular opposition that they were never pursued very far. In the summer of 1939, on the very eve of war in Europe, an agreement was finally reached with the Croats that established an autonomous Croatia. But by then it was too late, since the Croats were not satisfied with the boundaries of their own province.

Though the Yugoslavs in 1941 bravely resisted German invasion, they did not have the military power to hold Hitler's armies back. When the conquering Germans and Italians split the country up, they turned Croatia over to the extremist Croat Pavelich, head of the Ustashi, who carried out horrifying massacres of Serbs and Jews. The innocent men, women, and children suffering death and torture at the hands of Pavelich's forces owed some of their anguish to the short-sightedness of Serbian politicians who had failed to solve the problem of Croat autonomy within a peaceful Yugoslavia, and who had thus stimulated the extremists.

Other Authoritarian Regimes

The case-histories we have been considering are unique in detail, yet they furnish interesting parallels to developments elsewhere in eastern Europe. Thus in Poland, Pilsudski led a military *coup* against the democratic government in 1926, and exercised a military dictatorship that became ever more authoritarian, especially after the depression. This *coup* was made possible largely because of the government's failure to grant concessions to Lithuanians and other national minorities, and to deal with the economic problems left by the years of war and occupation. Tension was heightened when Germany denounced a trade treaty and precipitated a crisis in the Polish coal industry. The violent hatreds that divided the political parties made it even easier. Once he had won power, Pilsudski turned to the great landowners and big industrialists, and built his government on their support and on that of his military clique.

In Rumania it was the deep entrenchment of corruption in political life, an inheritance from Ottoman and Phanariot Greek rule, that initially jeopardized the parliamentary system, as the party in power usually rigged elections without shame. In addition, there was widespread anti-Semitism, which was adopted as the chief program of the "Iron Guard," a Rumanian Nazi party not unlike the Hungarian Arrow Cross, but more popular with university students, unemployed intellectuals, and, in the end, the peasants. Green-shirted and wearing bags of Rumanian soil around their necks, the Guard began a program of assassinating moderate politicians early in the 1930's. Economic dislocation and peasant misery brought about by the worldwide agricultural depression strengthened the Guard and other fascist groups. To head off a Guardist *coup*, King Carol of Rumania installed his own fascist dictatorship in 1938. Although the Guardist leaders were "shot while trying to escape," Rumania could not avoid German pressure. After Hitler had acceded to Russian seizure of Bessarabia and Northern Bukovina, and had given Hungary northern Transylvania (August, 1940), Carol had to leave the country, and Hitler's man, Marshal Antonescu, took over, with Iron Guard support. It should be noted that the one source of hope in Rumanian politics, the reformist leader of the Peasant party, Maniu, had disappointed his supporters when he was in power in the late 1920's by his failure to accomplish anything for the peasants whom he claimed to represent.

In Bulgaria, always a strongly pro-Russian country, the genuine threat of communism was a serious problem between the wars, and gave a more or less valid excuse to those who sought dictatorial power. Moreover, Bulgaria, like Hungary, was revisionist because of her failure to gain the Macedonian territory given by the peace treaties to Yugoslavia and Greece. The issue was exacerbated by the presence in the country of thousands of Macedonian refugees, who tended to join revolutionary terrorist societies. Bulgaria, an equalitarian country with no minorities problem, no rich landowners, no aristocracy, and no great industries, none the less produced political cleavages even more violent than those in countries where economic inequality prevailed. Unparalleled ferocity has marked its political life. In the early twenties, a remarkable agrarian political leader, Stamboliisky, a staunch believer in peasant democracy and in good relations between Bulgaria and Yugoslavia, gave the country a period (1920-1923) of reasonably popular government. But even he curbed the press and interfered with intellectual freedom, as he strove to curb the Macedonian terrorists and the communists both.

His imposition of high income taxes alienated the bourgeoisie, and his conciliatory policies toward Yugoslavia infuriated the army.

In 1923, a plot to oust Stamboliisky succeeded, and was followed by his murder and the installation of a strongly authoritarian regime. From then on, communist plots and bomb outrages and Macedonian terrorist strife racked the country. After 1930, the Italian marriage of King Boris led to a rapprochement with Mussolini. In 1934, a military *coup* brought a group of army officers to power; they dissolved the political parties and tried their hands at a dictatorship of their own. But this development was successfully countered in 1936 by King Boris himself, who, like Alexander of Yugoslavia and Carol of Rumania, imposed a royal dictatorship, which lasted from then until his mysterious death during World War II.

In Greece between the wars, the main issues were whether the country should be a monarchy or a republic, and how to overcome the economic difficulties consequent on the transfer of 1,250,000 Greeks from Turkey. On the constitutional question, the population wavered, voting for a monarchy in 1920, for a republic in 1924, and for a monarchy again in 1935, always by enormous majorities. Economic dislocation brought strength to communism among the refugees and in labor groups. The political exuberance for which Greece is celebrated made the regular conduct of parliamentary government impossible. The inter-war period was punctuated by a whole series of *coups* by generals, some republican, some monarchist, all more or less authoritarian, but most of them ineffective and none especially bloodthirsty. The last of these was the most fascist, General John Metaxas, who became dictator in August, 1936. Metaxas abolished political parties, instituted censorship and political persecution

Fascism in Rumania.
Iron Guard rally, 1940.

of his opponents, launched a program of public works, and imitated the Nazis in other ways. But when the Italian invasion came from Albania in October, 1940, Metaxas ordered resistance, which was the beginning of Greece's heroic showing in World War II.

Fascism in Review

None of these regimes in eastern Europe was fascist in the full sense of the term. In Italy and Germany the regimes rested, at least initially, upon the popular support of a substantial proportion of the people, even though that support was kept alive by the technique of artificial stimulation. In eastern Europe, on the other hand, the dictatorships rested on the police, the bureaucracy, and the army, and not on the support of the peasant masses. To an eastern European politician of almost any complexion an election was an occasion for bribery, intimidation, and totally absurd promises that he had no intention of trying to fulfill. The hope placed by some western liberals in peasant parties like those of Radich, Maniu, and Stamboliisky proved in the end illusory, either because the original peasant leaders allowed the party to fall under middle-class urban control, as did Radich and Maniu, or because the Right crushed them, as in Bulgaria and Poland.

Thus the growth of anti-democratic governments of the Right in Europe during the period between the wars strikingly reveals the difficulties in the way of moderate parliamentary regimes in countries without parliamentary traditions. This is not to say that the western liberal tradition is not for export, but only to emphasize that a liberal constitution on paper and a liberal franchise are in themselves no guarantee that a regime on western models can become stabilized. The postwar economic agony had scarcely disappeared before the depression of the late twenties and early thirties struck. Under these circumstances men turned to extremists of the Left and Right. But the fear of communism, combined with the seductive nationalist propaganda of the Right, brought about fascist victories in Italy and Germany. Thereafter, the triumph of the Right elsewhere was assured, and a new world war was inevitable.

562

CHAPTER XXVII

Reading Suggestions
on the Rise of Fascism

The Roots of Fascism

A. Cobban, *Dictatorship: Its History and Theory* (New York: Charles Scribner's Sons, 1939). Highly suggestive survey, reaching well back into history.

P. Viereck, *Metapolitics: From the Romantics to Hitler* (New York: Alfred A. Knopf, Inc., 1941). A survey of the background in German political thought.

C. J. Hayes, *A Generation of Materialism, 1871-1900* (New York: Harper and Brothers, 1941). Contains a concise and corrosive section on the seedtime of fascism.

Note: The titles listed above present differing views on the origins of fascism, a subject still much debated by historians. Further titles bearing on the subject may be found in the reading suggestions for Chapter XXIII.

Italy

G. Megaro, *Mussolini in the Making* (Boston: Houghton Mifflin Company, 1938). An unequaled study of Mussolini's early career.

H. Finer, *Mussolini's Italy* (New York: Henry Holt & Co., 1935) and H. A. Steiner, *Government in Fascist Italy* (New York: McGraw-Hill Book Co., 1938). Two very solid studies by expert political scientists.

G. A. Borgese, *Goliath: The March of Fascism* (New York: Viking Press, 1938) and G. Salvemini, *Under the Axe of Fascism* (New York: Viking Press, 1936). Lively works by important anti-fascist Italians.

G. Salvemini, *Prelude to World War II* (New York: Doubleday Inc., 1954). A survey of Mussolini's foreign policy, by one of his most implacable enemies.

Germany

A. Hitler, *Mein Kampf* (New York: Reynal and Hitchcock, 1939). A complete English translation of the Nazi bible, the basic work to be read for an understanding of the movement.

A. Hitler, *My New Order*, R. de Sales, ed. (New York: Reynal and Hitchcock, 1941). Speeches after the Führer's coming to power.

A. L. C. Bullock, *Hitler: A Study in Tyranny* (London: Oxham's, 1952). The best biography.

S. W. Halperin, *Germany Tried Democracy* (New York: Thomas Y. Crowell, 1946). A reliable history of the Weimar Republic, 1918-1933.

R. G. L. Waite, *Vanguard of Nazism* (Cambridge, Mass.: Harvard University Press, 1952). A good study of the "Free Corps" movement.

J. W. Wheeler-Bennett, *Wooden Titan* (New York: William Morrow & Co., 1936) and *Nemesis of Power* (New York: St. Martin's Press, 1954). Two first-rate studies, the first dealing with Hindenburg, and the second with the role of the German army in politics from 1918 to 1945.

F. L. Neumann, *Behemoth: The Structure and Practice of National Socialism* (New York: Oxford University Press, 1944). The best work on the subject.

K. Heiden, *History of National Socialism* (New York: Alfred A. Knopf, Inc., 1935) and S. H. Roberts, *The House That Hitler Built* (New York: Harper and Brothers, 1938). Two older and still useful studies of the Nazis.

F. von Papen, *Memoirs* (New York: E. P. Dutton & Co., 1953). An apologetic autobiography by the scheming right-wing politician.

E. Wiskemann, *The Rome-Berlin Axis* (London: Oxford University Press, 1949). A study of the formation and history of the Hitler-Mussolini partnership.

R. Fischer, *Stalin and German Communism* (Cambridge, Mass.: Harvard University Press, 1948). A study of the role played by the communist movement in the history of Germany between the wars.

Note: Some of the titles listed under the reading suggestions for Chapter XXVIII deal with international relations during the inter-war period and will illuminate Nazi foreign policy.

Other Countries

G. Brenan, *The Spanish Labyrinth* (New York: The Macmillan Company, 1943). A useful study of the Spanish Civil War against its historical and economic background.

C. Bowers, *My Mission to Spain* (New York: Simon and Schuster, 1954); C. J. Hayes, *Wartime Mission to Spain, 1942-1945* (New York: The Macmillan Company, 1945); and Lord Templewood (Sir Samuel Hoare), *Complacent Dictator* (New York: Alfred A. Knopf, Inc., 1947). Three differing views of Franco and the Spanish problem, by three ambassadors, the first two American, the last British.

G. E. R. Gedye, *Betrayal in Central Europe* (New York: Harper and Brothers, 1939). A careful journalist's account of Austria and Czechoslovakia.

H. Seton-Watson, *Eastern Europe between the Wars, 1918-1941* (Cambridge, England: The University Press, 1946). A useful account dealing with all the eastern European countries except Greece and Albania.

R. L. Buell, *Poland: Key to Europe* (New York: Alfred A. Knopf, Inc., 1939). A helpful survey.

R. West, *Black Lamb and Grey Falcon* (New York: Viking Press, 1941). A highly subjective account of Yugoslavia, loaded with political bias, but fascinating and informative reading.

Historical Fiction

I. Silone, *Bread and Wine* (Harmondsworth, Middlesex: Penguin Books, 1946) and *Fontamara* (New York: Smith and Haas, 1934). Two good novels on rural Italy under fascism; by a distinguished anti-fascist writer.

C. Levi, *Christ Stopped at Eboli* (New York: Farrar, Straus, 1947). An anti-fascist Italian doctor and painter writes movingly of his exile in a remote and poverty-stricken southern Italian village.

H. Fallada, *Little Man What Now?* (New York: Simon and Schuster, 1933) and E. Remarque, *Three Comrades* (Boston: Little, Brown & Co., 1937). Two touching novels of depression-ridden Germany.

E. von Salomon, *"Der Fragebogen"* (*The Questionnaire*) (New York: Doubleday, Inc., 1955). One of the plotters against Rathenau, a strong sympathizer with authoritarian movements, tells his life story satirically, against the background of American military government in post-1945 Germany.

E. Hemingway, *For Whom the Bell Tolls* (New York: Charles Scribner's Sons, 1940). A characteristic Hemingway novel, set in the Spain of the Civil War.

The Atlantic Democracies

I: Introduction

During the Twenty Years' Truce

CHAPTER XXVIII

THE CENTRAL FACT—or irony— of politics between the two world wars is that the war "to make the world safe for democracy" seemed to have made it in effect a difficult and dangerous place for democracy. Idealists like President Wilson had expected that the collapse of the old Romanov, Habsburg, and Hohenzollern empires would automatically insure an increase in the number of democratic states. But instead, as we have just seen in the last two chapters, much of Europe came under totalitarian or partly authoritarian regimes that were hostile to liberal democracy. Even Italy, which had long seemed to be evolving toward a democratic constitutional monarchy like that of Britain, turned fascist. In the 1920's and 1930's, then, the core of democracy remained in the North Atlantic community (see Chapter XXI), that is, in Britain, France, and the United States.

The very fact of the upsurge of communism and fascism created grave problems in international relations for the three great democracies. At times in the 1920's it looked as if they might successfully overcome these problems and bring the world back to peaceful habits. But in the 1930's the great world-wide depression, the advent of Hitler, and the aggressions of fascist states in the West and of an expansionist Japan in the Far East rapidly darkened the international scene. With the outbreak of another general war in 1939, it was clear that the two decades since 1919 had been at best a twenty years' truce, a truce broken with increasing frequency by international trouble-makers.

Certainly the totalitarian aggressors bore the major responsibility for the unleashing of a second world war. Yet a far from minor factor in the deterioration of the twenty years' truce was the relative weakness of the great peaceful democracies themselves. In the 1920's Britain, France, and the United States each became preoccupied to some degree with its own domestic problems. In the early 1930's this preoccupation increased as a result of the urgent crisis of the depression. But this was the very time when international problems demanded equally urgent attention. International trade was steadily shrinking in the face of the

depression and of mounting tariff barriers; the prospects for peace were steadily fading before the saber-rattling and actual saber-wielding of the enemies of democracy. Faced with two equally urgent sets of problems, the democracies turned first to the domestic ones, and then discovered that the international situation was rapidly moving toward war.

The two sets of problems, foreign and domestic, could not really be separated. They were interconnected and interrelated in countless ways. Our survey here will underline some of these interrelations, in the same manner in which we have shown the links between the internal and external policies of the communist and fascist states. But, in order to point up the main issues, we shall sometimes separate national from international problems in a fashion that may oversimplify the complexities of real life. Our survey of the Atlantic democracies during the twenty years' truce begins with the chief domestic problems faced by each of the major states. We start with Britain.

II: Great Britain

The Postwar Depression

Save for trifling losses from German Zeppelin raids and coastal bombardments, the British Isles suffered no direct material damage in World War I. But the British armed forces lost about seven hundred and fifty thousand men killed in action, and about a million and a half wounded. The losses of the Empire and the Commonwealth as a whole came to nearly a million killed and over two million wounded. The economic losses of the mother country had been grave indeed—the almost incalculable

difference between the actual cost of destructive war and what might otherwise have been productive effort.

The national debt after the war was ten times that of 1914. Many British investments abroad, returns on which had been a great factor in Victorian prosperity, had had to be liquidated. The great British merchant fleet, the income from which had been another major factor in balancing Britain's international accounts and paying for her imports, had been damaged by enemy action. The whole fabric of international trade on which Britain depended was torn in a thousand places in 1918, and could not be rapidly restored in the unsettled conditions that prevailed in the world, especially in central and eastern Europe. And, finally, to supplement the war production of Britain and France, the industrial plants of the United States, of Canada, and even of India had been called on, and had received a stimulus that made them in peacetime more effective competitors of the British. In the 1920's, the war-damaged French industrial plant was restored to new efficiency, and that of the Germans, nourished in part by loans from newly enriched America, once more took up the rivalry that had so alarmed the British before the war.

In short, victorious Britain faced in the postwar years and in an aggravated form the basic economic difficulty that we analyzed in Chapter XXI. The land that had been in Victorian days the "workshop of the world" had now hopelessly lost its great head start and could no longer give full employment to its millions of workers. And yet those workers were in no mood to accept a lower standard of living. They had made great gains in social security before the war, and they had fought the war in the hope and promise of still better things to come. In the "khaki election" held just after the Armistice of 1918 they had been promised a "land fit for heroes"; they had, indeed, been promised that the defeated enemy would through war reparations pay the costs of the war, and give Britain a new start.

This hope was very early disappointed. No substantial reparations came through, and after a first flush of prosperity resulting from postponed orders from abroad and from new work at home economic difficulties began to accumulate. By 1921 there were already almost a million unemployed. In that same year the British government, faced with the rising cost of living, increased unemployment payments for both men and women. These payments, soon christened with the derogatory name of the "dole," were strictly speaking not old-fashioned poor relief, but payments on unemployment insurance policies that had been part of Lloyd George's social legislation of prewar days (see Chapter XXI). However, large-scale unemployment continued, and some young workers never acquired employment status. Unemployment insurance could not be maintained on a sound actuarial basis, and the payments became in fact a form of poor relief.

The Great Britain of the 1920's experienced no equivalent of the "Coolidge prosperity" that the United States was to enjoy. We must not exaggerate: the British economic decline was not catastrophic. London, Manchester, and Liverpool did not become ghost cities, though some of the gravely depressed areas, like the coal-mining regions of South Wales, did begin to show real signs of decay. What happened was rather a *relative* decline, the comparative slowing up of an economy geared to dynamic growth, with a working population conditioned psychologically to a slowly rising standard of living and a middle class similarly conditioned to traditional comforts. The British economy simply did not produce enough to realize traditional expectations. Moreover, this was the twentieth century, the century of the newspaper, the movie, the radio. The British were well aware, for instance, that Americans had automobiles, radios, and a lot else; they, too, wanted those things.

Textiles and Coal

Britain was, then, suffering from ills characteristic of economic old age in an era of intense international competition. American readers can best realize the British plight if they think of the textile industry in New England. New England's textile plant, which had a great head start in the early nineteenth century, is now obsolescent; her workers, long well organized in unions, are firmly determined to get high wages; the New England states have had a long social and political development that has produced a closer approximation to the "welfare state"—and the high taxes needed to support it—than is common in the South; New England itself produces neither raw cotton nor wool. Much of her textile industry has therefore migrated southward, to brand-new, efficient plants, a more docile labor supply, lower state and local taxes, and other competitive advantages. Similarly, the English textile industry found itself unable to compete, especially in the cheaper grades of cloth, with the newer factories in India, the United States, and many other parts of the world. But here the parallel stops. For New England remains a part of the United States and has full legal access to this important area of free trade in a world of increasing trade restrictions; old England enjoys no such privilege.

The coal industry is an even more concrete illustration of the plight of Britain since World War I. There was still a lot of coal in Britain; but it was difficult and costly to mine, since the most easily and cheaply worked seams were being exhausted. The industry was badly organized, with many small and inefficient mines running at a loss, and with machinery and methods that were antiquated in comparison with American and the best continental standards. Productivity per man-hour over the whole industry was low. Worst of all, perhaps, the 1920's saw the rapid rise all over the industrialized world of major competitors to coal—oil, and electricity based on water power. The British Isles had no petroleum and, in comparison with many other countries, no very great potential in hydroelectric power. Yet coal, the historic basis

of British industrial power, simply had to be mined. The workers were unionized and were in no mood to accept cuts in wages; the owners were naturally indisposed to run their business at a loss. A strike in March, 1921, after the government had rejected Labor party proposals for making permanent the wartime nationalization of the industry, focused national attention on this critical problem. The strike was settled in July, but only by the government's consenting to pay subsidies to cover increased wages.

The Conservative Program

British domestic politics during the twenty years' truce display, therefore, a fairly clear class basis. The first casualty in the struggle between the Labor party and the Conservatives was the old Liberal party, which was ground to a mere husk between the two contending groups. The Conservatives, who had won the lion's share of seats in the "khaki election," decided in 1922 to withdraw their support from the coalition government headed by the Liberal Lloyd George. In the ensuing elections the Conservatives won, and the Liberals, split between the followers of Lloyd George and those of the more orthodox Asquith, lost heavily. Labor won 142 seats—more than the Liberals did—and became for the first time His Majesty's Opposition.

Both Conservatives and Labor realized the underlying difficulties of Britain's position. Both were fully aware that twentieth-century Britain had to sell enough goods and services abroad—enough manufactured goods and shipping, insurance, banking, and tourist services—so that the return on them would buy food for her people and much of the raw materials for her factories. But the parties were not agreed on how to achieve this necessary task. Broadly speaking, the Conservatives wanted to retain private industry, with government and other technical experts helping to make it efficient. But they were thwarted by high tariffs in the United States and elsewhere, by the drive to economic self-sufficiency all over the world, and by the difficulties of trade with the vast area under Russian communist control.

The state of world trade drove the Conservatives more and more to the solution Joseph Chamberlain (see Chapter XXI) had advocated earlier: protective tariffs against competing foreign goods, and the knitting of the Empire and Commonwealth, with their vast variety of resources, into a largely self-sufficient trade area by "imperial preference" agreements. Such agreements would give raw materials from the colonies and dominions preferred treatment in the British market in return for preferred treatment of British manufactures in the colonial and dominion markets. In theory, at least, the scheme could have worked, for the Commonwealth and Empire of the twenties—one-quarter of the world's land and people—had the natural resources and offered a potential market capable of supporting the British Isles in the style to which they were accustomed.

The great snag, of course, was the unwillingness of the constituent parts of the Empire and Commonwealth to accept for themselves the role of producers of raw materials in exchange for British manufactured goods and British services. The self-governing dominions, loyal though they had been during the war, were in no mood to assume a role essentially like that of colonies in the old mercantilistic days. As we shall shortly see, they were looking toward independent nationhood, and they wanted what seems to go with nationhood in our world—their own industries. This was also true of what was potentially the richest unit in the Empire, India.

The Labor Program

The Labor solution was nationalization—that is, government purchase and operation of key industries with just compensation to their private owners, rather than outright seizure without compensation as in Soviet Russia. The key industries were transportation, power, coal, steel, perhaps even textiles, cutlery, pottery, machine tools—all the industries that seem in these days to thrive best on large-scale organization. A good many Laborites wanted nationalization simply because, as socialists, they had been brought up to believe that profits, rent, and interest paid to "capitalist" private owners were forms of worker-exploitation, and that under nationalization these forms of exploitation would cease. But many of their leaders were fully aware that even nationalized industries would still have to face the fundamental problem of selling enough goods abroad to keep the economy going. They argued, therefore, that nationalization would enable British industries to produce more cheaply and efficiently. It would do away with wasteful competition and with the inefficient firms so conspicuous in the coal industry, for instance. It would force into productive work both unnecessary managerial and selling staffs, and stockholders and other investors who lived without working.

Moreover, the Laborites believed that, once socialist nationalization had been achieved, the British workmen would experience a transformed attitude toward their work. Knowing that they were now the *real* owners of their own industries, they would put their hearts into their work, abstain from feather-bedding, absenteeism, and similar practices, and raise their production to a point where the goods of Britain could undersell those of her capitalist rivals in world markets. This belief was reinforced by the somewhat paradoxical faith in free trade that the Laborites had inherited from the Liberals, and by their high hopes for improved international relations. Consequently, the Laborites were hostile to the Conservative policies of protective tariffs and imperial preference.

British writings of the period are full of discussions of the economic policies that were needed to lift Britain out of her depression. An old-fashioned individualist, Sir Ernest Benn, could write this in a book entitled *This Soft Age:*

The damage done to immense masses of good human material is reflected in the economic crisis now troubling the world. Millions of God-made human beings, who in a better governed world would be full of the desire to *do,* have been degraded to the mere desire to *get.* Powerful governments are chiefly occupied in telling people that they ought to *have* more and on the other hand that everybody must *do* less. This soft, safety-first philosophy spreads like an epidemic disease. The work of deception, now the chief occupation of official government, is backed up by a host of unofficial minor governments, committees, trade unions, trade associations. No man may work or trade until some sort of authority has granted him permission to do so. . . . These changing world theorists suggest that there must be no competition, no effort above the common level, no desire to do better. So far as these madnesses have found acceptance there has of course been change. Hundreds of Acts of Parliament witness the strength of the effort to alter the course of nature. . . .

No change, however, can or ever will be imposed upon the spirit of man. The alterations which occur in the soul, the spirit, in good and evil are beyond the reach even of the anthropologists. The desire to master the mysteries of the here and hereafter is a priceless personal possession outside the jurisdiction of political power. The urge to reproduce, the satisfaction of work and play, the desire to excel, the yearning for experience, and the discovery that all is vanity—no change is discernible in any of these things. Neither is there any change in the true aims and purposes of government. Liberty is the first and last thing to be said about it. All this talk of change is concerned with the varying degrees of understanding which succeeding generations possess of the meaning and quality of liberty. When the aim of government has been in the direction of liberty, life has been better; when in the opposite direction, as in recent years, life has been more difficult. The error of this changing world theory can be traced back to the false idea that to take the powers of suppressing the individual out of the hands of one tyrant and give it to thirty million electoral tyrants is good.

Democracy was conceived as a way of destroying tyranny, not of extending it, and democracy will only survive if it returns to its original purpose.*

Yet the believers in collectivism were quite unregenerate. Here is an outspoken collectivist, the late Olaf Stapledon, better known as a writer of science-fiction:

Financial reward, which means reward in the form of power to command the labour of others for one's personal service, must be strictly limited. And unearned financial benefit in the form of dividends from joint-stock companies must be at once restricted, and subsequently, as soon as possible without dislocating the national economy with too rapid change, it must be abolished. The citizen must, of course, be assured of an adequate minimum of earnings, and may be encouraged by the prospect of considerable increase of wages in reward for outstanding skill or devotion; but he must not be allowed to amass a great fortune either by his own skill or by manipulation of stocks and shares or by the luck of inheritance. The notion that the prospect of vast financial gain is needed to call out the best in man is a delusion, peculiar to an age which is obsessed with the economic side of life. Other forms of prestige and power are equally effective incentives.

It may be politic to allow the citizen to save, up to a point, and to lend his savings to the state, so that in his old age he may reap benefit from work done in his prime. It may be politic also to allow him to bequeath a modicum to his children to ensure them the best possible start in life. But the amassing of fortunes and the inheritance of fortunes must be stopped. On the other hand, the married

---

* E. J. P. Benn, *This Soft Age* (London, 1933), 180-182.

572

Volunteers lining up for government service during British general strike, 1926.

couple must know that when they are too old to work, even if they have saved nothing, they will be assured of a reasonable degree of comfort without being a burden on their children, and that even if they die young their children will be adequately cared for and equipped.*

Postwar Politics

In the twenty years between the wars neither Conservatives nor Laborites were able to carry out their full platform. Labor itself, though it came to power briefly in 1924 and in 1929, with its leader Ramsay MacDonald as prime minister, never had a parliamentary position firm enough to nationalize any industry. The Conservatives, by no means unanimous on the degree of economic self-sufficiency they wanted for the Empire, were decisively held up by the unwillingness of the Commonwealth countries to go much further than to accept certain limited imperial preferences that were set up at the Ottawa Economic Conference in 1932.

Underneath the play of British party politics in these years there lay a deep class division over the degree of government intervention that should be permitted in economic matters. Yet on the surface British politics still retained many of the amenities of Victorian parliamentary life. The House of Commons, even though it now included workingmen and others who by no means spoke with an "Oxford accent," was still one of the best clubs in the world. For a few weeks in 1926 some 2,500,000 trade-union members attempted a general strike in support of the coal-miners, who were already on strike in protest against a cut in their wages. The general strike failed, but during its brief course fundamental British attitudes were revealed. Thousands of men from the middle and upper classes volunteered to keep essential services operating,

---

* Olaf Stapledon, *New Hope for Britain* (London, 1939), 174-175.

and in Plymouth a soccer team of strikers played a team of police. Britain, despite mounting tensions, remained a land of general law-abidingness, where the class struggle that the Marxists talked so much about seemed to have come rather thoroughly under the control of the parliamentary decencies.

In 1928, almost unnoticed, the last step was taken in the political democratization of Britain that had begun in 1832. In 1918, in preparation for the "khaki election," the government had put through a Fourth Reform Bill, which eliminated all the old exceptions to universal male suffrage and gave the vote to all men over twenty-one. Culminating a long and spectacular campaign in which "suffragettes" had demonstrated, marched, orated, and written in behalf of women's rights, the bill also gave the vote to women. But, with almost a caricature of British caution, it set the voting age for women at thirty years, thus insuring that there would always be more male than female voters. The distinction was too irrational to stand up, especially after experience had demonstrated—as it also did in the United States—that women divide politically about the way men do. In 1928, a bill known irreverently as the "bill for flapper suffrage" gave women the vote at twenty-one.

Although the dole, depressed industries, and other signs of economic ill-health persisted, Britain did experience a measure of economic recovery in the late 1920's. But then the great depression, the signal for which was given by the New York stockmarket crash in October, 1929, began its spread around the world. Britain, already weakened, was one of the first to be engulfed. Faced by a serious deficit, and unwilling to try to meet it by cutting the dole and other social services, the second Labor government of Ramsay MacDonald resigned in August, 1931.

It gave way to a coalition of Conservatives, Liberals, and right-wing Laborites headed by the same MacDonald. This coalition cabinet put through reductions in the dole and the social services that the outgoing government had refused to enact. Late in 1931 it took the decisive step, a hard one in view of Britain's traditional financial leadership and devotion to the gold standard, of going off the gold standard and letting the pound fall in value. In 1932, it took the first step away from free trade by enacting protective tariffs, and in the same year Britain ceased payment on her war debts to the United States, except for a few "token" payments that were unacceptable to the American Congress. These measures did little to help the unemployed or to strike at the root causes of British economic troubles. But they did stem the depression sufficiently to enable the coalition to win two general elections in 1931 and 1935.

Yet the coalition government was in fact dominated by Conservatives, and after the 1935 election the Conservative leader, Stanley Baldwin, took over the post of prime minister. Gradually the British economy pulled out of the worst of the depression, although—some economic theorists might say *because*—Baldwin did nothing beyond keeping the budget in balance. By 1936, however, Mussolini's and Hitler's aggressions were beginning to demand British attention. The economic question and the social question, by no means solved, faded before the threat of another war.

Settlement of the Irish Question

The years between the wars were of great importance for Ireland. The outbreak of war in 1914 put off the threatened revolt against Home Rule in Ulster (see Chapter XXI), but the Irish were hardly reliable partners in the war. In 1916, the faction at the political pole furthest removed from the Ulster rebels, the Irish nationalists, got German aid and staged an armed rising in Dublin. The British put down this "Easter rebellion," but not before they had created a fresh and effective set of Irish political martyrs. The British government did not dare attempt to extend conscription to Ireland until April, 1918, and the attempt made then led the Irish nationalists to boycott the British Parliament and to cease attending its sessions.

In 1919, Home Rule as decreed in 1914 was not enough for the nationalists of Ireland. The Home Rulers of prewar days had yielded to more extreme rebels, the Sinn Fein (meaning in Gaelic, "ourselves alone"), who wanted complete independence. The years 1919-1921 were filled with violence, ambushes, arson, and guerrilla warfare; the Irish, who now had their own illegal parliament, the Dail Eireann, moved into full revolution. The British, tired from their long war, were not in a state of mind to use force effectively; the Irish, on the other hand, were admirably organized and full of fight.

Yet the immediate upshot of the violent phase of the revolution was a compromise, for the Sinn Fein split in two. A moderate wing, led by Arthur Griffith and Michael Collins, was willing to accept a compromise in which Protestant Ulster would remain under direct British rule and the Catholic counties would be given dominion status. A radical wing, led by Eamon de Valera— exceedingly Irish in spite of his Spanish name—insisted that the whole island achieve complete independence as a republic. The moderates negotiated with the British, and in 1921 obtained for the twenty-six counties of southern Ireland dominion status under the name of the Irish Free State. The Free State had its own parliament, the Dail, and was completely self-

governing; it merely accepted the British Crown as symbolic head. The six Protestant counties of Ulster maintained their old relationship with Great Britain, which now became officially the United Kingdom of Great Britain and Northern Ireland.

This settlement was unacceptable to De Valera and the republicans, and the Irish revolution now became a civil war between partisans of the Free State and partisans of a republic, with the old round of burning, ambush, and murder. But the Irish, too, were beginning to tire of violence. When the moderate leader, Michael Collins, a man much closer to earth than De Valera, was assassinated by a republican, public opinion turned away from the extremists. Meantime the Free State was gradually settling down; it acquired international recognition when it was accepted into the League of Nations in 1923. De Valera, after refusing to sit in the Dail because he would have had to take an oath of loyalty to the king, changed his mind and decided to bring his fellow republicans into the national parliament in 1927.

From then on, almost in the manner of illogical and compromise-loving England, the Irish Free State gradually and peacefully got what the extremists had been killing and burning for. De Valera's party won a plurality in the Dail in 1932, and a majority in 1933; thereupon it proceeded to abolish the oath of loyalty to the Crown and to cut most of the slender threads that still tied the Free State to England. In 1939, Catholic Ireland was so free from British domination that she could declare and maintain her neutrality throughout World War II. In 1949, the final step was taken when Britain recognized her as the Republic of Eire (Gaelic for "Ireland"). Eire now enjoys an independence even more complete than the title "Free State," with its connotation of dominion status, had suggested.

The British Commonwealth of Nations

No such secession took place elsewhere among the British possessions in the years between the two world wars. On the contrary, definite constitutional recognition of the essential independence of the dominions seemed to make them more secure and loyal, though at the cost of any central British authority over their economic policies, and, at least in law, over their foreign policies. The capstone of a long process that had begun with the Durham Report nearly a century before (see Chapter XXIV) was the Statue of Westminster of 1931. This legislation spelled out the new relations between the dominions and the mother country that had been worked out in an imperial conference five years earlier. The new status of the dominions was symbolized by a change in terminology. Henceforward they were no longer to be considered parts of the Empire but free members of the British Commonwealth of Nations (see also Chapter XXIX).

In this new relationship Britain would have to *negotiate* with Canada or Australia about tariffs, trade conditions, immigration, and the like, just as if they were foreign countries. And, although Britain was unable during the twenty years' truce to build a self-sufficient economic unity out of her dominions, still in 1939, as in 1914, the dominions all came into the war on Britain's side. They made this decision even though they had the legal right to follow the example of Eire and remain neutral.

The Abdication Episode

Final evidence that the British Crown is the creature of Parliament came in the mid-1930's in an incident that attracted more attention than did the more important but less dramatic course of British social and political development. This was the abdication of Edward VIII in 1936, the year of his accession to the throne. Edward had had a long and successful career as Prince of Wales, appearing indefatigably and effectively in public all over the world. He fell in love with an American divorcee, Mrs. Wallis Simpson, and wanted to marry her. His own family, the cabinet, and most of the British people opposed him, and he quietly abdicated in favor of his brother, who became King George VI. Some of the opposition to Edward's marriage stemmed from dislike for America (always endemic in Britain, but never with the depth and intensity of American dislike for Britain). But much more of it stemmed from strong feeling against having a divorcee on the throne and a vaguer feeling that Mrs. Simpson's background as a member of what Americans call "café society" made her unfit for ceremonial functions. The episode—for it deserves no stronger name—left no great mark on British history.

III: France

The Impact of the War

In France, both World War I and the postwar difficulties caused more serious dislocation than they did in Britain. In the war itself, France lost proportionately more in human lives and in material damage than did any other belligerent. Two million Frenchmen in the prime of life were either killed or so seriously mutilated as to be incapable of normal living. In a land of only 39,000,000, and with an already low birth rate, it is likely that this human loss directly injured the collective French potentiality for achievement in all phases of civilization. Many of the men who would have been statesmen, industrialists, scientists, and artists in the 1930's were killed off in 1914-1918. Three hundred thousand houses and twenty thousand factories or shops were destroyed. In a land of conservative economic organization, where work was done slowly and without large-scale automatic machinery, this material setback would be long felt. Psychologically, the feeling of victory by no means compensated for the traumatic losses of the four years of struggle.

France, under the leadership of Clemenceau, almost inevitably set as her goal the laming of her recent enemy, Germany, in every possible way. She tried to extract reparations to the last possible sum, undeterred by the arguments of economic theorists that Germany could not pay. But she insisted even more on keeping Germany down, isolated in international relations, and without the physical means of warfare. In a pinch, most Frenchmen would probably have been willing to forego reparations in order to keep Germany poor, deprived of the economic plant necessary for modern war. They would have preferred this to collecting reparations from a rich and productive Germany that had once more built up its war plant.

In the postwar years, however, French statesmen attempted to follow both policies; they naturally failed in the attempt. The culmination came in January, 1923, under the premiership of the conservative Raymond Poincaré, when French and Belgian troops occupied the great German industrial region of the Ruhr in an effort to make Germany pay full reparations. The Germans replied by passive resistance (see Chapter XXVII). By 1925, it was clear that the Ruhr occupation had brought no gains to France, and the new French government, chosen after the failure of Poincaré's policy, withdrew the troops.

Meanwhile, the French were undergoing inflation. The inflation resulted in part from the cost of rebuilding their devastated areas —a cost that drained government finances and that was only partly covered by German payments. Inflation resulted also from the high cost of maintaining armed forces— for the French dared not disarm—from the general disorder of international trade, and from the staggering debts piled up during the war by the French government. By the mid-1920's the franc had slipped from its prewar value of 20 cents to a dangerous low of about 2 cents. In the crisis, Poincaré was recalled to power to "save the franc," and in 1926 he headed a coalition ministry of "national union." Poincaré initiated new taxes and stern measures of economy which, with the gradual restoration of international trade after the French withdrawal from the Ruhr, stemmed the decline of the franc. In 1928, it was officially revalued at 3.92 cents.

The French inflation, though mild compared with the German (see Chapter XXVII), nevertheless caused economic and social dislocation. Frenchmen who had lent their government francs worth 20 cents now found themselves deprived of four-fifths of what they had lent. This very considerable degree of repudiation fell severely on the monied classes, disastrously on the small investor. It added to the social tensions that form the central theme of French domestic history in the period between the two world wars.

Social and Political Tensions

During World War I, the French had temporarily put aside the great political and social conflict that they had inherited from the great revolution of 1789 and that they had never quite resolved (see Chapter XXI). After the war, the "sacred union" of political parties that had carried France through the struggle soon dissolved, and the traditional conflict was resumed. This is sometimes termed the conflict between the "two Frances"—the republican France of the Left, and the royalist, or fascist, France of the Right. The conflict was not quite a simple Marxian class struggle between rich and poor, capitalist and proletarian, though it was certainly in part such a struggle. On the Right were the wealthier classes, many of them openly hostile to the very existence of the parliamentary state. They were reinforced by conservative peasants, especially in the west, and by small businessmen and investors, who were not hostile to the Third Republic as such but who were determined to resist any attempt to extend the social services of the "welfare state." As a result of this right-wing resistance, France lagged behind Britain, Germany, Sweden, and other European states in providing measures of social security.

On the Left were the champions of the welfare state, the Socialists and the Communists, backed by the more radical workers and by many white-collar people, especially in the government service, and by some intellectuals. The effectiveness of the Left was hampered by the postwar split between the Communists, who followed the Moscow line, and the Socialists, who did not, and by a considerable schism within the major trade-union organization, the C.G.T. (*Confédération Générale du Travail* —General Confederation of Labor). Still nominally part of the Left, but actually in the political middle and not anxious to go far toward the welfare state, was the misnamed Radical-Socialist Party, long the political bulwark of the Third Republic. The Radicals were strong among peasants in the south, and among white-collar workers and smaller professional men.

Religious difficulties further embittered French politics. French Leftists, including the Radical-Socialists, were firmly anticlerical by tradition. After the war they rashly attempted to introduce anticlerical measures into strongly Catholic Alsace. Alsace, since it had then belonged to Germany, had not been affected by the separation of Church and State carried through in France after the republican victory in the Dreyfus crisis (see Chapter XXI). In the long run, the government had to make compromises on the Alsatian question and on other clerical issues. After bitter public debate, diplomatic relations with the Vatican, which had been broken off in 1904, were resumed in 1921. They were broken off again in 1925 under the Leftist government that followed Poincaré's failure in the Ruhr, and were resumed again a few months later.

In the late 1920's, the years of economic upswing and increased prosperity that followed the revaluation of the franc and the Locarno agreements, the Third Republic seemed to be getting the better of its internal difficulties. Indeed, the world economic crisis that began in 1929 was late in striking France, and for a while in 1930 it looked as though the French economy, less devoted to large-scale industry than that of the United States, Britain, or Germany, might weather the crisis much more easily. But France, too, depended on international trade, particularly on the export of perfumes, wines and brandies, Paris gowns, and other luxuries. By 1932, the depression had struck, and the government was in serious difficulties.

The Stavisky Case and the Popular Front

The political crisis came to a head in February, 1934, as a result of the Stavisky case, a financial scandal reminiscent of the

Demonstrators in the Stavisky riots, Paris, February, 1934.

Panama scandal of the 1890's. Stavisky, a shady promoter who had all sorts of connections with important men in the affairs of the Third Republic, was caught at last in a fraudulent bond issue of the municipal pawnshop of Bayonne. The full details have never emerged, but Stavisky's suicide—or murder—in December, 1933, rocked France. Royalists, enjoying the freedom of a democratic society, had long been organized, notably in a pressure group known as the *Action Française,* and were gaining recruits among upper-class youth. They had a terrorist wing, which went about beating up Communists and other radicals, who in turn responded by violence. There were also fascist groups, such as the *Croix de Feu*

("fiery cross") organized by a war veteran, Colonel de la Rocque. Serious riots, unleashed by the Right in the agitation against the government following the Stavisky case, broke out in Paris in February, 1934; they were countered on the Left by a brief general strike. France seemed on the eve of revolution.

Once more, however, as in the time of Dreyfus, the republican forces rallied to meet the threat, and once more after the crisis had been surmounted France moved to the Left. The February crisis itself was overcome by a coalition of all parties save Royalists, Socialists, and Communists. But the franc was once more falling, and the conservative premier, Flandin, attempted to retrench government expenditures with measures similar to those that had worked a decade earlier under Poincaré. The forces of the Left joined in the so-called Popular Front, made up of the Radical-Socialist, Socialist, and Communist parties, and backed by the C.G.T., which had temporarily healed the schism between Communists and non-Communists. Their victory in a general election in May, 1936, led to the formation of a Popular Front ministry under the leadership of the Socialist Léon Blum.

The Popular Front came into power in part certainly as a kind of French equivalent of the American New Deal. The workers, the white-collar men, the government employees, even many of the peasants and shopkeepers, were now convinced that the classical formulas of economic retrenchment were not the remedy for the ills of France. They wanted a frontal attack on the stronghold of retrenchment, the Bank of France, still a private institution and, in a substantially correct popular belief, the creature of the "two hundred families" alleged to control the French economy. They wanted more equal distribution of wealth by government spending; in short, they wanted the "welfare state."

Other factors entered into the Leftist victory. Hitler and Mussolini were now in power; Mussolini had begun his Ethiopian adventure, and Hitler his rearmament. Many a Frenchman in 1936 voted Left as a protest against the compromises with the dictators that French politicians had been making. Finally, these were the years when Russia, just admitted to the League of Nations, seemed to be pursuing a course of collaboration with the West against the threat of Nazi Germany (see Chapter XXVI). Moscow therefore urged the French Communists to give up their old policy of constant opposition—which had in many votes in the Chamber of Deputies lined them up with the Royalists—and to co-operate with their hated enemies, the Socialists.

It was a bad time for a French New Deal. The nation was bitterly divided between partisans and enemies of the Popular Front; business and farming classes were traditionally reluctant to pay income taxes, which would have to be raised to meet the costs of social services; the economy was not geared to labor-saving devices. The Blum cabinet had an ambitious program—a maximum work week of 40 hours; partial nationalization of the Bank of France, the railroads, and the munitions industry; compulsory arbitration of labor disputes; and other measures of social welfare. Although Blum enacted most of this program, everything conspired to block its successful execution. The Communists did not really co-operate, for they refused to participate in the Blum cabinet and they sniped at it from the sidelines in the Chamber and in the press. Businessmen took fright at the mushrooming membership of the C.G.T. and at the "sit-down" or "stay-in" strikes of French industrial workers in June, 1936—the first use of this dramatic weapon that was to be successfully imported by American automobile workers in 1937.

Moreover, as the anti-democratic regimes in Germany, Italy, and Spain went on to new victories, France was driven to expensive rearmament. Capital, however, was rapidly leaving the country, and the monied class would not subscribe to the huge defense loans that were essential if the French armed forces were to be put in shape to face the war that began to seem inevitable. Blum was obliged to call a halt in March, 1937. The Popular Front now disintegrated, and the C.G.T. lost millions of its newly recruited members and suffered a new schism between Communists and anti-Communists.

CHAPTER XXVIII

Divided France

A period of great ministerial instability followed on the collapse of the Popular Front in 1937. Under the mounting tensions of 1938 and 1939, the Radical-Socialist premier, Daladier, kept France on the side of Britain in opposition to the Rome-Berlin axis, and various measures of retrenchment—including virtual abandonment of the 40-hour week—kept the French economy from collapse. But the workers took very badly the failure of the Popular Front, and as late as November, 1938, a general strike almost came off, and had to be combatted by putting the railway workers under military orders. The possessing classes, on the other hand, were outraged by the fact that Blum's experiment had been made at all; many of them were convinced that their salvation lay in a French totalitarian state—"better Hitler than Blum," as their despairing slogan went. The France that was confronted with war in 1939 was not only inadequately prepared in terms of materials; it was psychologically and spiritually divided, uncertain of what it was fighting for.

An American historian of France, commenting on this failure of the French spirit in the 1930's, summarized:

It is a tragedy when a great man loses his strength and his personality; it is a catastrophe when a nation loses its assurance. To me the tragic pathos of the French problem can be summed up in a remark made by my hostess in a Parisian pension in 1937 when she called my attention to the notice about the air-raid shelter for the neighborhood. 'Over there [in Germany],' she said with a choke in her voice, 'the shelters will be safe; ours will be faulty.' She wanted to be proud of the nation for which her husband had given up his life in 1916; she wanted to believe in the community that had given her nurture, but she had lost faith and with it her nerve. These simple words are dramatic evidence of the failure of the *élan vital* of a great people.[*]

---

[*] J. B. Wolf, "The Elan Vital of France: A Problem in Historical Perspective," *Modern France*, E. M. Earle, ed. (Princeton, 1951), 31.

IV: The United States

The Impact of the War

Neither the human nor the material losses of the United States in World War I were at all comparable with those of Britain and France. Except for some enemy sabotage in munitions plants, America suffered no direct material damage. American casualties were 115,000 dead and 206,000 wounded; the comparable French figures were 1,385,000 dead and 3,044,000 wounded *in a population one-third as large.* Moreover, in purely material terms, the United States almost gained from the war. Heavy industries, in particular, were greatly stimulated by Allied war orders; the war put the growing financial center of New York at least on equal terms with that of London; the dollar had begun to dethrone the monarch of the nineteenth century, the pound sterling. It is true that the Allies had borrowed from the American government; but until 1933 some interest came in on these loans. Moreover, it is now clear that the stimulation of industry resulting from these loans exceeded the loss from the final repudiation of war debts in the early 1930's. The United States, then, came out of the war almost unscathed, victorious, and prosperous.

Isolationism

Yet in some senses the American revulsion against the war in 1919 and the years following was as marked as that of Britain, France, and defeated Germany. In the United States that revulsion took the form of *isolationism,* the desire to withdraw from international politics. This isolationism was by no means universal among Americans. In spite of the best modern techniques of the social scientist, much uncertainty remains about the range and variety of "public opinion" in great modern states. Certainly the United States of 1919 had a whole spectrum of opinions on the specific issue of American membership in the League of Nations; this spectrum ranged from those who would have the United States join under any and all conditions to those who would have her join under no conditions.

Historians are divided on just what determined the American withdrawal from *direct* participation in international politics in 1919. Some feel that the drives and attitudes of millions of men had already made isolationism certain. Others feel that a slight shift in the words and deeds of men in high places could have changed the final decision and could have brought America into the League. If the Democratic President Wilson had been willing to meet Republican opposition in the Senate by a few concessions, or even by a little tactful flattery of opponents like Senator Lodge, then perhaps the Treaty of Versailles, League of Nations and all, might have achieved the two-thirds majority in the Senate the Constitution requires for treaties. Or if someone on the Republican side, with skill and prestige, had been able to put through the notion of a bipartisan foreign policy, then with patience and good will the United States might have been brought into the League with no more than face-saving reservations. Public

opinion, say those who take this view, was not against our carrying on the task we had begun in 1917; only a noisy minority in the country as a whole, and the little group of obstinate senators at the top, wanted us to withdraw.

On the other hand, the very fact that the Republicans won the off-year congressional elections in November, 1918—when news from the front was excellent—seems to many a sign that Wilson's known internationalism had begun to turn many voters against him. Those who remember the years right after 1918 find it hard to deny that the country was swept by a wave of desire to get back to "normalcy," as President Harding later termed it, ungrammatically. A great many Americans felt that they had done all they needed to do in beating the Germans, that further direct participation in the complexities of European politics would simply involve American innocence and virtue that much more disastrously in European sophistication and vice. The not uncommon American reaction against its "strong" presidents took the form of repudiating all of Wilson's work at Paris as that of an un-American tyrant. Furthermore, as the months of negotiation went on with no final decisions reached, Americans, always an impatient people, began to feel that sheer withdrawal was about the only effective action they could take.

The Treaty of Versailles, containing at Wilson's insistence the League of Nations, was finally rejected in the Senate on March 19, 1920. Since Wilson had vetoed a joint resolution of House and Senate making separate peace with Germany, the United States remained technically at war with Germany until July, 1921, when a similar resolution was passed and signed under the presidency of Harding. American isolationism was expressed in these years in other concrete measures. The Fordney-McCumber Tariff of 1922 and the Smoot-

Hawley Tariff of 1930 set successively higher protective tariffs against foreign goods, and emphasized America's belief that her high wage scales needed to be protected from cheap foreign labor.

Yet the United States continued all through the 1920's to insist that the debts owed to her by the Allied powers be repaid. It is true that these were refunded in a series of agreements, and that in the closely related problem of German reparations Americans on the whole cast their weight on the side of a general scaling-down of German obligations. But Congress paid little heed to the argument, so convincing to most economists, that European nations could not repay save through dollars gained by sales of their goods in the American market, and that American tariffs continued to make such payment impossible, at least in the large amounts needed. Congressmen tended to reduce the complexities of international debts to President Coolidge's simple dictum: "They hired the money, didn't they?"

The spirit of isolationism also lay behind the immigration restrictions of the 1920's, which reversed the former American policy of almost free immigration. The act of 1924 set an annual quota limit for each country of 2 per cent of the number of nationals from that country resident in the United States in 1890. Since the heavy immigration from eastern and southern Europe had come after 1890, the choice of that date reduced the flow from these areas to a mere trickle.

The Road to International Leadership

Yet during this era of supposed isolationism the United States by no means withdrew entirely from international politics. Rather, as an independent without formal alliances, she continued to pursue policies that seemed to most Americans traditional, but that in their totality gradually lined her up against the chief perturbing nations of the years between the two world wars. Even before the drift of her commitments against Germany, Italy, and Japan became clear in the 1930's, Americans had in fact engaged themselves. At what seems to some hardboiled thinkers the level of abstract and meaningless general declarations, they had gone far before the Democratic administration of Franklin Roosevelt in 1933.

In 1928, the Republican Secretary of State Kellogg submitted to the great European powers a proposal for a renunciation of war. Incorporated with similar proposals from the French Foreign Minister Briand, it was formally adopted in August of that year as the Pact of Paris, commonly known as the Kellogg-Briand Pact. It was eventually signed by twenty-three nations, including the United States. It is now the fashion to decry the Pact as futile, another piece of "sublime mysticism and nonsense," like the Holy Alliance of Alexander I; and it is certainly true that it did not prevent World War II. And yet by this action the United States expressed a concrete concern over the peace of the world.

In a hundred ways the United States was at work laying the foundations for the position of world leadership it reached after World War II. American businessmen were everywhere; American loans were making possible the revival of German industrial greatness; American motors, refrigerators, typewriters, telephones, and a dozen other products of the assembly line were being sold everywhere. In the Far East, the United States as early as 1922 took the lead in the Nine-Power Treaty that committed her and the other great powers, including Japan, to respect the sovereignty and integrity of China. If President Roosevelt in 1941 resisted the Japanese attempt to swallow China and other Far Eastern territory, he was simply following a line laid down under President Harding. Finally, in 1930—still before the "Roosevelt Revolution"—President Hoover's State Department issued the so-called "Clark Memorandum," specifically stating that the Monroe Doctrine does not concern itself with inter-American relations. The United States was no longer to land the Marines in Latin America at the drop of a hat, but was trying to build up hemispheric solidarity.

Boom—and Bust

In domestic affairs, the Coolidge era (1923-1929) has now become legendary. These were years of frantic prosperity; many people played the stock market and the value of stocks rose to fantastic heights. They were the years of prohibition, the speak-easy, the bootlegger. They were the years of the short skirt—the shortest, probably, in all western history—of sex appeal, the Charleston, and other forms of sin. They were years which, like the "naughty nineties" of the nineteenth century, we look back on now with a sort of reproving envy, years that somehow now look colorful, romantic.

But the Coolidge era was by no means completely summed up in novels of the jazz age, like *The Great Gatsby* of F. Scott Fitzgerald, or even in Sinclair Lewis' half-satirical *Babbitt* and *Main Street*. It was an era of marked industrial progress, of solid advancement of the national plant and productive capabilities—a fact that is often overshadowed by the breaking of the speculative boom that accompanied this concrete work. It was an era of the steady spreading in the United States of standards of living heretofore limited to the relatively few, standards of living that seemed to intellectuals vulgar and inadequate, but that were nevertheless a new thing in the world. These were the years when, if you had a servant, you could no longer take her for granted, but had to take some pains to keep her satisfied. They were years for which, at their best, the right symbol is no Hollywood character, no intellectual, no great pioneer of industry, nor even a gangster, but President Coolidge himself, sober, plodding, unimaginative.

At its most glamorous, however, the era ended with the onset of the great depression in the autumn of 1929. During the preceding year, Wall Street had enjoyed an unprecedented boom; the value of stocks had almost doubled. Speculators by the millions were playing the market in the hope of quick resale of stocks at huge profits; they bought shares "on margin," paying only a fraction of their cost in cash, and often borrowing the money to pay that small fraction. Not only stocks but many other purchases were financed on borrowed money. Credit had swollen to the point where it was no longer on a sound basis in a largely unregulated economy. Eventually, shrewd investors began to sell their holdings in the belief that the bubble soon would burst. The result was a disastrous drop in stock values, beginning in October, 1929, and continuing almost without let-up to 1933. Both the speculators and the lenders from whom they had borrowed money were ruined.

The immediate cause of the depression, then, was the stock-market crash. About the more deep-seated causes the economic physicians are not even today wholly agreed. Some of them believe that a capitalist society inevitably produces business cycles oscillating from the highs of prosperity to the lows of depression; that these cycles are of various lengths, short, medium, and long; and that an unusual number of cyclical lows coincided in the late 1920's to make the depression particularly serious.

Others, not uninfluenced by Marx, hold that under American capitalism the troughs of a depression are bound to be deeper each time, if only because of the great scale of the American economy.

This much seems certain: Coolidge prosperity, even at its most dazzling, was very unevenly distributed among the various parts of the American economy and American society. Agriculture, notably, suffered a kind of permanent depression throughout the 1920's. At the close of World War I, farmers commanded very high prices for their produce and enjoyed an apparently insatiable market at home and abroad. They expanded their production—and borrowed to finance the expansion—often at a reckless rate. Then, as "normalcy" returned in the early 1920's, the foreign market dried up, the home market shrank, farm prices fell rapidly, and the inevitable foreclosure of farm mortgages began. Wage-earning workers, though not hard hit like the farmers, gained but little increase in their purchasing power during the 1920's. The worker did often raise his standard of living, by purchasing a house or a car, but he did it on credit, by assuming the burden of a heavy mortgage or by financing a purchase on installments to be paid over a long period. The "big money" of the Coolidge era went chiefly to business, above all to big business.

The great depression was very severe in many countries throughout the world, but nowhere was it worse than in the United States. Its effects may be measured by the round figure of 16,000,000 Americans unemployed at the low point in the early 1930's—something like one-third of the national labor force. In terms of what economists call the "gross national product" the United States Department of Commerce sets for 1929 the figure of $103,828,000,000; for 1933, the figure set is $55,760,000,000, a little more than half that for 1929.

The most remarkable thing about this grave crisis in the American economy is that it produced almost no organized movements of revolt, no threat of revolution. The intellectuals of the 1930's did indeed turn to "social consciousness," and Marxism made some converts among writers and artists. But the bulk of the population showed no serious signs of abandoning for any revolutionary creed their fundamental belief that the way out lay through the legal means provided by existing American institutions. Even before the election of Franklin D. Roosevelt in 1932, local authorities and private charities, helped out by the establishment early in 1932 of the federal R.F.C. (Reconstruction Finance Corporation) to release frozen assets, did a good deal to soften the worst sufferings of the unemployed.

The New Deal

The Republican administration of President Hoover (1929-1933), however, was generally committed to the philosophy of laissez-faire; aside from the R.F.C., it did little to cushion the effects of the depression. The victory of the Democrats in the election of 1932, therefore, seemed to give them a clear mandate to do something more fundamental. The Democratic president, Franklin Roosevelt (1933-1945), took office on March 4, 1933, in the midst of a financial crisis that had closed the banks all over the country. He at once summoned Congress to an emergency session, and declared a bank holiday. Congress convened on March 9, and legalized the President's actions. Gradually the sound banks reopened, and the New Deal began its course. During its subsequent convalescence, much of the American business community under better conditions turned with great bitterness against Roosevelt and all his works.

But in those early months of 1933 the mere fact that a national administration was trying to do something about the situation was a powerful restorative to national morale. The nation emerged from the bank holiday with a new confidence, echoing the phrase from Roosevelt's inaugural address that there was nothing to fear "but fear itself."

The New Deal was in part a series of measures aimed at immediate difficulties and in part a series of measures aimed at permanent changes in the structure of American society. The distinction between its short-term and its long-term measures is in a sense arbitrary, for the men who carried it through were never quite clear in their own minds exactly what they were trying to do. What must chiefly interest us is the long-run implications of their work. In the perspective of western history, the New Deal is the coming to the United States, under the special pressures of the great depression, of those measures—"socialist" to some of their opponents—that we have already seen in European countries like Britain and Germany. They are best summed up in that value-charged term, the "welfare state."

The short-term measures of the New Deal aimed to lower the price of American goods in a world that was abandoning the gold standard by releasing the dollar from its tie with gold. They aimed to thaw out credit by extending the activities of the R.F.C. and by creating such new governmental lending agencies as the Home Owners' Loan Corporation. They aimed to relieve unemployment by public works on a large scale, to safeguard bank deposits by the Federal Deposit Insurance Corporation, and to regulate speculation and other stock-market activities by the Securities and Exchange Commission. The historical significance of many of these measures rested above all in the fact that they were undertaken not by private business or by state or local authorities but by the federal government.

The long-term measures were, of course, more important. The Social Security Act of 1935 introduced to the United States on a national scale the unemployment, sickness, and retirement allowances of the kind that Bismarck had brought into Germany and that Lloyd George had brought into Britain. Federal taxation, especially income taxes on individual and corporate income, was used to secure a more equal distribution of the national product. Congress passed a whole series of acts on labor relations, the net effect of which has been to strengthen and extend the role of organized labor in American economic life. A series of acts on agriculture, though leaving the business of farming still in the hands of several million individual farmers producing for sale in a cash market, nevertheless regulated crops and prices to a degree that would have been incomprehensible to a nineteenth-century farmer. And finally—the showpiece of the New Deal—a great regional planning board, the Tennessee Valley Authority, has used government power to make over the economic and social life of a relatively backward area by checking the erosion of farmlands, by instituting flood control, and by providing cheap electric power generated at government-built dams.

The New Deal in Perspective

More than twenty years after the bank holiday of 1933, Americans were still debating the New Deal. It unquestionably left the United States of the mid-twentieth century a society very different from that pictured by the classical economists. No real society, indeed, has ever quite corresponded to the theoretical extreme of free enterprise, in which every man sells and buys what he wants to—or can—and in which the man who cannot "earn" a living quite simply dies. But in the sense in which the United States of, say, 1870 was close to such a society, the United States of the New Deal and after is quite far from such a society.

The rush of free competition has been tempered by collective action and by government regulation, because it has become clear that in such competition much that men prize would in fact be competed out of existence. If everyone today were free to catch all the trout he wanted to and could, there would soon be no trout left at all. But most Americans accept, and with some help from game wardens observe, the fish and game laws. And in general they have come to see the need for government regulation in the field broadly known as the conservation of natural resources. Even here, however, when it comes to the overgrazing of pasture lands or the farming methods that lead to soil erosion, many Americans are still reluctant to have the government interfere with their "rights."

When the question at stake is the distribution of wealth, rather than its actual exhaustion, Americans are still often unwilling to accept limitations on free enterprise. On this issue, even after the New Deal, the champions of government regulation and private initiative still do battle. The Marxist indictment of a competitive society, that under it the rich tend to become richer and the poor to become poorer, is not wholly true. But the last two hundred years of western history suggest that without some government interference the modern scramble for wealth tends to produce a society pyramidal in structure. With a few men of great wealth at the top, the pyramid spreads out through the well-to-do to a broad base of human beings just able to scrape along. In our western society, however, the political power democracy gives to that numerous broad base has over the years been used to alter the very shape of the social pyramid. "Soak-the-rich" taxation and government aid to the poor have flattened it out, cutting it down at the top and pushing it up from the bottom. Indeed, the figure may no longer be a pyramid, but somewhat diamond-shaped, widest in the middle. It is not yet in any human society a straight line, representing absolute social and economic equality.

There is, then, in modern America a leveling, both up and down. The great baronial mansions of the Hudson Valley, of Newport, even of California, are too expensive to maintain, and are being turned into museums or put to institutional use. The worst of the urban slums are being slowly cleaned up to make way for modern housing projects. The very rich still exist, at least in Texas, but the number of the very poor is diminishing. Meanwhile, the total national product has increased. It is not merely that a fixed national income is being more evenly distributed; despite the complaints of conservatives that the leveling process is destroying incentives to hard work and invention, the real national income has increased greatly since the depth of the depression in 1932-1933. There is more to be shared.

It must, however, be noted that the American society that emerged from the New Deal was by no means collectivist; it can by no means be accurately described as "socialistic." The United States of the mid-twentieth century is rather a "mixed economy," in which individual economic activity—that of the worker as well as that of the entrepreneur or manager—is indeed regulated and restricted, but not entirely controlled, by government. The United States still displays an extraordinary range of economic activity, from the "socialistic" Post Office to enormous private industries that are themselves societies, almost governments, with administrative problems and bureaucracies of their own, and on down to small independent businessmen.

Confident America

Although Americans still battle over the New Deal, it seems evident that the measures taken by the Roosevelt administration, combined with the natural strength of American institutions and culture, pulled the United States at least part way out of the depression. They also restored a high degree of confidence to Americans. The intellectuals, whose role in modern America has generally been in opposition to the men of business, in the 1920's had found the United States a hopelessly crass and vulgar society. But in the 1930's, though some intellectuals flirted with Marxism, many turned to support the new American way of the New Deal.

The onset of war in Europe found Americans, as we shall see in the last section of this chapter, anxious not to jeopardize in war their still precarious prosperity, anxious to remain neutral if Europe should persist in going to war. But the United States was not, like the France of 1940, a tired, skeptical land, divided fundamentally into mutually hostile classes. Roosevelt and his Republican opponents had been for some time exchanging insults: the "economic royalists" fought back at "that man in the White House." Yet in the pinch of the international crisis of 1939-1941 it became clear that, although the nation was not completely united, at any rate it was not pathologically divided. As so often in American history, the violence of verbal politics masks a very basic unity. When the war came to the United States in 1941, Americans were largely ready for it psychologically and—what is really remarkable in a western democracy—not too unready for it militarily.

V: International Politics, 1919-1932

During the twenty years' truce, international leadership of the democratic world rested with Britain and France. Though supported in principle and often in practice by the United States, they were increasingly unable to stem the rise of powers hostile to liberal democracy—Italy, Germany, Spain, Russia, Japan. In the end, the beaten perturber of 1918, Germany, once more waged aggressive warfare against the major Allies of 1918. This time Germany allied with two of its former enemies, Italy and Japan, each disappointed with its share of the spoils of victory in 1918. World War II is thus intimately related to World War I.

In both, a German perturber challenged a precarious balance of power, of which the North Atlantic democracies were the chief protectors.

Why was the peace settlement of 1919 followed in twenty years by a second great war? Why was it so unlike the last great settlement, that of 1815 following the Napoleonic wars, which had inaugurated a long period of general peace, interrupted only by localized wars? Nazi Germany maintained that the second war was the direct and inevitable result of the *Diktat,* the dictated peace of Versailles that ended the first war. Supported by most Germans and many German sympathizers, the Nazis claimed that Germany was humiliated by the war-guilt clause, stripped of territories and colonies that were rightfully hers, saddled with an astronomical and unpayable reparations bill, denied the normal rights of a sovereign state in armaments—in short, so badly treated that simple human dignity made revolt against the *Diktat* and its makers a necessity. Now something of this is true. The settlement of Versailles did saddle the new German Republic with a heavy burden in part dictated by revenge and fear toward the old German Empire. A wiser Allied policy would perhaps have tried to start the new government off without too great a burden, as the Allies in 1815 did with the France of Louis XVIII (see Chapter XIX).

The "Era of Fulfillment"

But the *Diktat* thesis is very far from containing the whole truth. What breaks down the argument that the iniquities of Versailles *alone* explain the second war is the "era of fulfillment." As we have already seen (in Chapter XXVII), there were many signs in the late 1920's that the Weimar Republic would "fulfill" faithfully the terms of the 1919 settlement, once those terms had been revised and moderated. Together, Germany and her former enemies undertook the gradual, peaceful negotiations that softened some of the harshest features of the Versailles Treaty. Reparations, for instance, were scaled down to manageable proportions in the Dawes Plan of 1924 and the Young Plan of 1929.

The great landmark of the "era of fulfillment" was the Locarno Treaty negotiated in October, 1925. At Locarno in Switzerland, Germany agreed with France and Belgium on a mutual guarantee of their common frontiers; Britain and Italy agreed to act as guarantors, that is, to provide military aid against the violator if a violation of the frontiers occurred. These agreements made a substantial contribution to the reconciliation of Germany and the Allies. Germany affirmed her acceptance of the western frontier drawn for her at Versailles, and France, for her part, affirmed the new moderate direction that her German policy had taken since the failure of her occupation of the Ruhr.

The "Locarno spirit" of reconciliation endured for the next several years. It was nourished by the general prosperity of both the French and the Germans and by the constructive policies of their respective foreign ministers, Briand and Stresemann. In 1926 Germany was admitted to the League of Nations, an event that seemed to signify not only the restoration of Germany to international respectability but also German acceptance of the peaceful purposes and duties of League membership. These hopeful impressions received confirmation when Germany signed the Kellogg-Briand Peace Pact of 1928 (see above, p. 583). In 1929, the French consented to withdraw the last of their occupation troops from the Rhineland during the forthcoming year, thus ending the Allied occupation of Germany at a date considerably in advance of the one stipulated in the Versailles Treaty.

The League of Nations

Meantime, other international developments were bolstering the "Locarno spirit." The great world-wide organization planned by Wilson, the League of Nations, began its operations in 1920. We shall soon see that the League was never able to impose its will on a determined and defiant aggressor. Yet the record of the League during the 1920's was by no means one of unmitigated failure. In the first place, the

League became a going concern. Its Council, dominated by the great powers, and its Assembly, representing all its members, met regularly at the League's "capital," the Swiss city of Geneva. Second, the League played a direct part in the peaceful resolution of two crises that, had they not been resolved, might well have led to little wars—in 1920 a dispute between Sweden and Finland over some Baltic islands, and in 1925 a frontier incident in the Balkans involving Greece and Bulgaria.

Third, a host of other activities supplemented the basic work of the League. The "World Court" (formally, the Permanent Court of International Justice) held regular sessions at The Hague, in the Netherlands, to settle litigation between nations. The International Labor Office, sponsored by the League, organized conferences on labor problems and sought to improve the status of workmen in economically backward countries. Under League auspices international economic meetings were arranged, statistics on epidemics and other health hazards were compiled, and a beginning was made in the regulation of the international traffic in opium and prostitutes. In a dozen different ways the League was laying the foundations for the more ambitious economic and social programs to be launched later on by its successor, the United Nations.

Attempts at Disarmament, 1922-1932

The failure of the United States to join the League dealt a hard blow to the organization's effectiveness; the parent had in effect denied the child. But the blow was softened by the major role that the United States took in furthering one of the League's chief objectives—disarmament. Soon after the first war the United States invited the other principal sea powers to consider the limitation of naval armaments. Meeting in Washington during the winter of 1921-1922, the naval conference achieved an agreement establishing a ten-year "holiday" in the construction of capital ships (battleships and heavy cruisers). The agreement also set the allowed tonnages of capital ships at a ratio of 5 for the United States, 5 for Britain, 3 for Japan, and 1.67 each for France and Italy.

In 1930, five of the parties to the Washington agreement met at London to extend their arrangements to the smaller, "noncapital" ships. This time they had less success. They did reach an understanding regulating submarine warfare, but mistrust between France and Mussolini's Italy made it impossible to reach an effective five-power accord on small ships in general. In the end, the United States, Britain, and Japan undertook to limit their tonnages of such vessels, but an "escalator" clause provided that, if one power, say France or Italy, increased its tonnages, the others might do likewise.

The partial failure of the London naval conference was a portent. Two years later, after long preparation, the League itself convoked a meeting to address the still more pressing problem of limiting military armaments. Not only the League members, but also the United States and the Soviet Union, sent representatives to Geneva. The Geneva conference of 1932, however, accomplished nothing. It was wrecked above all by a renewal of Franco-German antagonism, by the German demand for equality in armaments with France, and by the French refusal to grant the demand.

In 1932, then, the "Locarno spirit" was dead, and the "era of fulfillment" had ended. In the West, Germany, with Italy following suit, was about to abandon negotiation as a way of revising the Versailles Treaty and was about to take Hitler's way

CHAPTER XXVIII

of denunciation and defiance. In the Far East, Japan had already upset the balance in 1931 by seizing Manchuria from China. The postwar period had ended; the prewar period was beginning. Thus the genesis of World War II involved many factors in addition to the Treaty of Versailles; we may explore some of them by asking why the promise of "fulfillment" faded so rapidly in the early 1930's.

Why "Fulfillment" Faded

There is one very obvious explanation for the failure of the hopes aroused in the 1920's—the world depression that began in 1929. In Germany itself the depression was a last straw, a decisive factor in putting Hitler into power. In the democracies, too, it had heavy consequences for the peace of the world. In France, in particular, as we have just seen, the depression deepened social and political cleavages to the verge of civil war. It helped turn the sympathies of the possessing classes in part toward active sympathy with fascist regimes, even in hated Germany, and sharpened their distrust for Great Britain and the United States. Furthermore, in a phrase that sounds vague but that is very real, the economic difficulties of the thirties sapped French national morale and made the French more anxious for peace at any price. In Britain, where the whole twenty years' truce was one long economic depression, the added difficulties of the 1930's made her people also more anxious for peace, a fact that came out in Chamberlain's tragic concessions to Hitler in the Czechoslovak crisis of 1938. In short, the democracies, already inclined as beneficiaries of the Peace of Versailles toward the defensive, were pushed further in that direction by the depression.

Another factor that was unsettling to international politics was Soviet Russia. In the eyes of the western nations, Russia was a revolutionary power that could not really be trusted, that could not be fully integrated into the international state-system. The doctrine of legitimacy and the restoration of the Bourbons had made revolutionary France respectable after 1815. But after 1917 Russia remained, in a sense, illegitimate and very far from respectable. The Soviet Union was a center of revolutionary faith that was hated and distrusted by the politicians of the West, who feared, by no means without justification, communist agitation among their own peoples. An "eastern Locarno," the acceptance by Russia, Germany, and the lesser states of eastern Europe of the territorial settlements made after World War I, was long talked about and hoped for. The "eastern Locarno," however, never came to fruition. Russia was admitted to the League of Nations in 1934, but the Soviet Union remained an uncertain factor in the balance of power; she was no clear and satisfactory counterweight to the growing power of Nazi Germany.

Still another basic factor that led to the second war was the continuing failure of the three great western democracies, Britain, France, and the United States, to present anything like a united front. Americans of internationalist sympathies have probably exaggerated the results of the sudden American withdrawal into isolationism in 1919. It is hard to believe, especially in light of the rivalry and cross-purposes that Britain and France displayed *within* the League of Nations, that formal American membership in the League would have helped the situation greatly. Still, the isolation of the United States undoubtedly exacerbated French fears and the French sense of weakness, and pushed France toward the sort of intransigence that was illustrated by her disastrous intervention in the Ruhr in the mid-1920's.

The Halting Partnership
of France and Britain

More serious was the failure of France and Britain to work together effectively. France, exhausted and underpopulated, endeavoring to play the part of a first-rate power but supported only by second-rate resources, lived in perpetual fear of a revived Germany. She sought not only to carry out to the full the economic and political measures of the Versailles Treaty that aimed at weakening Germany and keeping Germany weak. She sought also to make up for Russia's defection as her eastern ally against Germany. This she did by making alliances, beginning in 1921, with the smaller states to the east of Germany—Poland, Czechoslovakia, Rumania, and Yugoslavia. All of them wanted French protection against the possible restoration of the Habsburg Empire, from which they had gained so much territory, and all of them except Poland were informally linked together as the "Little Entente."

To a Britain whose statesmen knew well the long story of Anglo-French conflicts from the Hundred Years' War to Napoleon, the France of the 1920's seemed once more aiming at European supremacy, seemed once more an active threat to the traditional British policy of preventing any such supremacy. Although it is now plain that the French were animated rather by fear than by ambition, and that they could never again be aggressors, it is true enough that many of their statesmen seemed to be falling into old ways. The mistaken British diagnosis was at least understandable. Moreover, Britain was physically undamaged, and by no means as apprehensive about German recovery as were the French. Indeed, from an economic point of view the restoration of a healthy Germany seemed to British statesmen desirable both as a market for British exports and as an element in the general restoration of international trade. Therefore, as against the French, the British early adopted a "soft" policy toward Germany, and openly condemned the Ruhr adventure.

Finally, something of the old British isolationism had survived the war, and made the British—and especially their dominions—unwilling to commit themselves too firmly to guarantees in continental Europe. Britain did indeed accept Locarno, but in the previous year the dominions had played a large part in her rejection of the more sweeping "Geneva protocol" urged upon her by France. The Geneva protocol aimed to fortify the League by an agreement forcing the submission of international disputes to arbitration and binding its signatories to take reprisals against any state that refused to accept arbitration. It would have restored, without American participation, something like the unrealized alliance system against German aggression that Clemenceau had tried to wring from Wilson and Lloyd George in 1919. Although relations between France and Britain improved after Locarno, and although the Nazi and fascist menace of the late 1930's pulled the two states closer together, the damage had been done. Germany profited by these divisions between the democracies, and revived under a government more unprincipled and more aggressive than that of William II.

The difficulties of the Anglo-French partnership also go far to explain the weaknesses of the League of Nations. The effectiveness of any piece of machinery is bound to hinge on the skill and co-ordination of the mechanics who operate it. The machinery of the League had flaws. It was badly deficient in "teeth," so to speak, in methods of enforcing its decisions against recalcitrant states. And it was a somewhat top-heavy instrument, since the fully representative Assembly counted for less than did the smaller Council, where Britain and France took a preponderant role. When these two mechanics disagreed, therefore, the machinery scarcely operated at all. One example of the way in which the grand purposes of the League suffered from Anglo-French friction is the rejection of the Geneva protocol. Another is the Corfu incident of 1923, when Mussolini for a time defied the League and set a sinister precedent for the later use of gangster tactics by the dictators (see Chapter XXVII for details). In the midst of the Corfu crisis the League was crippled by Anglo-French discord over the Ruhr policy of France.

The Aggressors

The Corfu incident underlines the presence of one more element, the most important of all, in the rapid deterioration of the twenty years' truce. This, of course, was the fact of aggressions by Italy, Germany, and Japan. In Chapter XXVII we saw how the ruthlessly ambitious programs of fascism and Nazism steadily led Mussolini and Hitler to a foreign policy of adventure and disruption. Here we must sketch in the background of the aggressions of their Japanese ally in World War II.

In the settlement after the first war Japan had been obliged to content herself with mandates over the smaller German islands

in the Pacific. Her ambitions for a territorial foothold in China were thwarted in 1919 and thwarted again by the Nine-Power Treaty of 1922, which bound her to respect Chinese territorial integrity. But Japanese statesmen continued to nourish these ambitions, the more so since China remained weak and divided in the aftermath of her political revolution of 1912 (for details on China, see Chapter XXIX). Moreover, Japan was fast becoming a great industrial state, with a dense population, in need of raw materials and trade outlets. Her leaders, following a pattern that one must admit had been set by the West, sought outlets in imperialist expansion. The general disruptions of the world depression affected Japan also. All these factors impelled her toward that seizure of the Chinese province of Manchuria in 1931 that was the first great step on the road to World War II.

With this background of underlying tensions—the punitive features of the Versailles settlement, the disastrous effects of the depression on the Locarno spirit, the continuance of the revolutionary focus in Russia, the defensive attitude of the western democracies and their mutual distrust, the new aggressive faiths of fascism and Nazism, and the rise of imperialist Japan—we may proceed to the actual steps along the road to a second world war.

VI: The Road to War, 1931-1939

The First Step:
Manchuria, 1931

Manchuria was a particularly attractive field for Japanese aggression. It had good resources of coal and iron; it adjoined

Korea, which had been annexed by Japan in 1910; and it was an outlying northern province of China that had never been fully integrated into the structure of Chinese government. Japan had driven Russia from Manchuria in the Russo-Japanese War of

"Rule Japannia. Very nice, yes!—so long as honourable foreign ladies continue to sit apart." Cartoonist Low comments on Japan's profiting by British and American failure to pursue a co-ordinated Far Eastern policy during the 1930's.

1904-1905, and her imperialists regarded themselves as the natural successors of the Russians there. Under western protection Chinese rights over Manchuria were confirmed, but the inability of China to establish a firm national government in the 1920's made Manchuria appear a precariously held province, which the Japanese believed could easily be pried loose. In September, 1931, the Japanese acted on their belief. Their troops seized the Manchurian city of Kirin, and soon spread over other areas.

The Chinese responded to Japan's aggression by a very effective boycott of Japanese goods, to which the Japanese countered by landing troops at the great Chinese port of Shanghai. Stimson, President Hoover's Secretary of State, at once announced that the United States would recognize no gains made by armed force. The League of Nations sent out a commission headed by the British Earl of Lytton, and the subsequent Lytton Report condemned the Japanese act as aggression. But neither the United States nor the League fortified its verbal protests by effective action; force was not met by force. The Japanese succeeded in setting up in Manchuria a puppet ruler, Pu-Yi, the

last Emperor of China, and a puppet state, to which they gave the name of Manchukuo. The new state was not granted international recognition, and constant tension persisted between the Japanese and the Chinese. Japan, refusing to accept the Lytton Report, withdrew from the League of Nations in March, 1933, the first formal breach in the League's structure.

The Second Step: German Rearmament, 1935-1936

The next breach in the League's structure, and the next step toward war, were made by Germany. In October, 1933, Hitler withdrew from the League, thereby virtually serving notice on the world of his aggressive intentions. The purge of 1934 (see Chapter XXVII) now consolidated his power at home, and on March 16, 1935, Hitler denounced the clauses of the Treaty of Versailles that limited German armaments. He set about the open rebuilding of the German armed forces.

The response to this unilateral and hence illegal act set the pattern for the next few years. On April 17, 1935, the League of

CHAPTER XXVIII

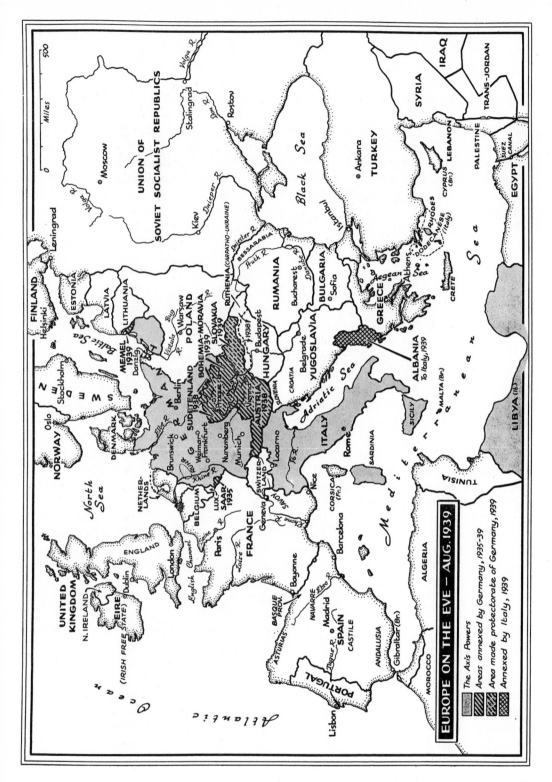

EUROPE ON THE EVE — AUG. 1939

The Axis Powers

Areas annexed by Germany, 1935-39

Area made protectorate of Germany, 1939

Annexed by Italy, 1939

595.

Nations formally condemned Germany's repudiation of treaty obligations—and Germany continued to rearm. In May, 1935, France hastily concluded with Russia a treaty of alliance against German aggression—and Germany continued to rearm. In June, 1935, the British, realistically and short-sightedly—for their action seemed like desertion to the French—signed with rearming Germany a naval agreement limiting Germany to 35 per cent of British ships of war, including submarines.

It is hardly surprising that Hitler's next act drew no more than the customary protests from the signatories of Locarno. This was the "reoccupation" of the Rhineland in March, 1936—that is, the sending of German troops into the western German zone that had been demilitarized by the Treaty of Versailles. The reoccupation of the Rhineland raises one of the nicer problems of history-in-the-conditional. If Britain and France had taken action and had countered by marching their own troops into the Rhineland, could the Hitlerian aggression have been nipped in the bud? Military experts incline to the belief that in 1936 the rearmament of the Germans was not advanced enough to withstand what the French and British could have thrown against them, and it is clear that Hitler's own military advisers were against the reoccupation. But Hitler so far was a better psychologist than they, and he won the gamble.

The Third Step: Ethiopia, 1935

Meanwhile the Italians struck in Ethiopia. In that pocket of old Africa, relatively isolated on its mountains and tablelands, a "sovereign" state had precariously maintained itself, largely because its imperial neighbors, Britain, France, and Italy, would neither agree to divide it nor let any one of the three swallow it. The Italians, who wanted it most, had lost the disastrous battle of Adowa to the native Ethiopians in 1896. This humiliation rankled with the fascists, who felt they had to show the world that there was more than rhetoric in their talk about a revived Roman Empire.

In 1934, a frontier incident at Ualual in desert Italian Somaliland—or in Ethiopia, for both sides claimed the place—put the matter before the international politicians. France and Britain were characteristically quite ready for appeasement of Italy, partly because they hoped to align Mussolini with them against Hitler. They offered him almost everything in Ethiopia, including those concrete economic concessions naive people think are the essence of imperialism. But since Ethiopia was a member of the League, the French and the British insisted that its formal independence be observed. This Mussolini would not accept, and in October, 1935, his troops began the invasion of Ethiopia. Airplanes, artillery, and tanks made the difference between 1896 and 1935. This time the underdog was not the winner. Poison gas finished the task early in 1936, and the King of Italy acquired the coveted title of Emperor of Ethiopia.

The League of Nations had already formally condemned the Japanese aggression in Manchuria and the German denunciation of the disarmament clauses of the Treaty of Versailles. In 1935, it at once declared that Italy by invading Ethiopia, a League member, had violated her obligations under the Covenant of the League. Now the League made the momentous decision to test its power to move from words to deeds. In this it had the full and hearty accord of most of its members, and was urged on by the British, and less vocally by the French, and by Haile Selassie, the rightful Emperor of Ethiopia. Haile Selassie made a dramatic appeal in Geneva itself, where Italian diplomats perpetrated the supreme insult of hissing him. On October 11, 1935, fifty-one member nations of the League voted to invoke against Italy the famous Article 16 of the League Covenant:

1. Should any Member of the League resort to war in disregard of its covenants under Articles 12, 13 or 15, it shall *ipso facto* be deemed to have committed an act of war against all other Members of the League, which hereby undertake immediately to subject it to the severance of all trade or financial relations, the prohibition of all intercourse between their nationals and the nationals of the covenant-breaking State, and the prevention of all financial, commercial or personal intercourse between the nationals of the covenant-breaking State and the nationals of any other State, whether a Member of the League or not.
2. It shall be the duty of the Council in such case to recommend to the several Governments concerned what effective military, naval or air force the Members of the League shall severally contribute to the armed forces to be used to protect the covenants of the League.
3. The Members of the League agree, further, that they will mutually support one another in the financial and economic measures which are taken under this Article, in order to minimise the loss and inconvenience resulting from the above measures, and that they will mutually support one another in resisting any special measures aimed at one of their number by the covenant-breaking State, and that they will take the necessary steps to afford passage through their territory to the forces of any of the Members of the League which are co-operating to protect the covenants of the League.
4. Any Member of the League which has violated any covenant of the League may be declared to be no longer a Member of the League by a vote of the Council concurred in by the Representatives of all the other Members of the League represented thereon.

The economic sanctions—that is, "the severance of all trade and financial relations"—invoked against Italy under Paragraph 1 of Article 16 failed. There were loopholes; oil, for instance, was not included in the list of articles barred from commerce with Italy, which had only meager stockpiles of this vital war material. There was much mutual recrimination among members of the League over what articles should be placed on the prohibited list and over the fact that Britain and France did nothing to check Italian movements of troops and munitions through the Suez Canal. Germany was no longer in the League, and was wholly unbound by its decision. Indeed, in the tension and confusion of the Ethiopian crisis, she found a favorable opportunity to reoccupy the Rhineland in March, 1936.

The Ethiopian fiasco sounded the death knell of the League, which from now on was helpless in high international politics. Its special services as a group of trained international bureaucrats persisted, however, to be absorbed after World War II by the United Nations. But for the rest of the 1930's the League was hardly even a formal factor in the increasing tensions. No one was surprised or greatly concerned when Italy, belatedly copying Japan and Germany, withdrew from the League in December, 1937.

The Fourth Step: The Spanish Civil War, 1936-1939

The next step after Ethiopia on the road to war is of great psychological interest. No doubt the later direct aggressions of Hitler in Czechoslovakia and Poland were the politically decisive steps. But the Spanish Civil War (for details, see Chapter XXVII), which broke out in July, 1936, was the emotional catalyst that divided millions of men and women all over the western world. It is still a kind of great collective Dreyfus case, a test of conscience and loyalty for our time.

The Spanish Civil War was fought with

"Honest, Mister, there's nobody here but us Spaniards." Franco's explanation to Chamberlain and Daladier.

the great violence and with the consecrated devotion that mark wars of principle. No one can say for sure how the struggle would have ended if it had remained a purely Spanish one, as the American Civil War had remained a purely American one. Franco's insurgents had the initial advantage of attack and of a professional army led by trained officers. But the Loyalists controlled perhaps greater assets—the richest industrial sections and the capital of Madrid—and they had the nucleus of an army and adequate manpower eager to fight. Such speculation, however, is useless. Almost from the very start the Spanish Civil War engaged, not merely the vicarious emotional participation of the West, not merely individual foreign enlistments, but the active though never wholly open intervention of other nations. This intervention was decisive and effective on the part of the fascist powers, Italy and Germany; it was less determined on the part of communist Russia, and feeblest of all on the part of Britain and France.

Britain, indeed, took the lead in organizing a committee to supervise a policy of nonintervention, a committee on which nearly thirty nations were represented at one time or another. But the committee

achieved very little. Even the "anti-piracy patrol" that the British sponsored in the Mediterranean had to cope with mysterious submarine attacks. On land, the Italians, increasingly emboldened, sent masses of "volunteers," perhaps 75,000 in all, to aid Franco; the Germans also sent "volunteers," and help in the air war. Russia took the opposite side, and though distant from the scene and not too well prepared herself she did send supplies to the Loyalists. She also sent communist politicians and secret police agents who devoted most of their energy not to fighting Franco but to combatting Trotskyites, anarchists, and other non-Stalinists on the Loyalist side.

The French government remained officially aloof from the Spanish Civil War and did little directly to help the Loyalists. But these were the years of the Popular Front in France, and sympathies with the Loyalists were strong. The long frontier of the Pyrenees was not well guarded. From men of principle to adventurers, soldiers of fortune, and communist dupes, individuals flocked to Spain; there was even an American Loyalist group, the Abraham Lincoln Brigade, fighting against Franco. But the interventionists on the side of Franco had the arms, the special skills, and the supplies.

CHAPTER XXVIII

Early in 1939, with the fall of Barcelona, the Civil War was in effect over. Once more a fascist group had won.

Meantime, dizzy with success, Mussolini was going on to other adventures. In October, 1936, he signed a pact with Hitler, thereby formally establishing the Rome-Berlin "Axis" and committing fascist Italy to alliance with Nazi Germany. Mussolini gave strong support to Franco's rebellion in Spain. And, late in 1938, he orchestrated a public outcry in Italy for the French to hand over certain territories. He wanted not only Nice and Savoy, which had been ceded to Napoleon III during Italian unification negotiations almost a century earlier, but also the Mediterranean island of Corsica, which had been French since the days of Louis XV in the eighteenth century, and Tunisia, which had never been under Italian rule and had been French since 1881. These outrageous demands came to nothing, but they did not exactly improve relations between France and Italy. Finally, on Good Friday (April 7), 1939, Mussolini attacked Albania, long coveted by the Italians, and quickly subjugated this backward little Balkan state. For a few years, Victor Emmanuel was to be King of Albania as well as Emperor of Ethiopia.

The Fifth Step: "Anschluss," 1938

The immediate origins of World War II lie, however, neither in Italian nor in Spanish fascist aggression, but in the mounting series of German aggressions. Hitler had begun the open rebuilding of German armed forces in 1935. Three years later, he felt strong enough to undertake the first enterprise of expansion, an enterprise which, like all he undertook, he insisted was no more than a restoration to Germany of what the *Diktat* of Versailles had de-prived her of. Austria, German in language and tradition, had been left a mere fragment by the disruption of the Habsburg Empire. Ever since 1918 there had been a strong movement among Austrians for annexation (*"Anschluss"*) to Germany proper. This movement had been strenuously opposed by the victors of the first war, who blocked the 1931 project for an economic *Anschluss* in the form of an Austro-German customs union. A year after the Nazis came to power in Germany, they attempted a full *Anschluss*. Their 1934 *putsch* in Austria, though it claimed Chancellor Dollfuss as a victim, failed because of inadequate preparations and because of the hostility of Mussolini's Italy (for details, see Chapter XXVII).

Hitler carefully laid the ground for the success of the next Nazi attempt. The pact with Italy that formally established the Rome-Berlin "Axis" (October, 1936) disarmed Mussolini's opposition to *Anschluss*. Early in 1938 Hitler began what turned out to be his standard technique of softening his victims for the final blow. He unleashed a violent propaganda campaign by press, radio, and platform against the alleged misdeeds of the government of independent Austria. In February, 1938, he summoned the Austrian Chancellor Schuschnigg to his Bavarian retreat at Berchtesgaden, where he let loose a bullying tirade against the hapless Schuschnigg. In March, Hitler moved his troops into Austria and made *Anschluss* a fact. The Nazis met no effective opposition from native Austrian anti-fascists, by no means a negligible group, nor any serious international resistance. There was not even a blast from the League of Nations.

Hitler now had six million more German-speaking nationals in the fold; and in the union of Austria and Germany he had achieved something that no Habsburg and no Hohenzollern had been able to do in modern times. But he showed no signs at all of taking the Bismarckian position of being content with what he had gained. Almost at once he went to work on the acquisition of the Sudeten Germans of Czechoslovakia.

The Sixth Step: Czechoslovakia Dismembered, 1938-1939

The Czechoslovak republic was the only state in central or eastern Europe where parliamentary democracy had achieved a resounding success after World War I. The republic faced a difficult problem of national minorities. It had a large minority of Sudeten Germans (about 3,250,000), most of whom lived on the rim of its territory, and who were included within its boundaries because they fell on the Czech side of the natural frontier, the Sudeten Mountains, separating Bohemia from Germany. There was also a smaller minority of Magyars (about 700,000). Moreover, the Slavic majority of the republic's population was divided into three groups—Czechs (almost 7,000,000), Slovaks (over 2,000,000), and Ruthenes (about 500,000)—with widely different political, economic, and cultural traditions.

But Czechoslovakia had the good fortune to inherit most of the best and most highly developed industrial regions of the old Habsburg Empire. Its economy, consequently, was far better balanced between industry and agriculture than was that of the other states of eastern Europe. This healthy economy was mirrored in the social structure, where a working balance was maintained among peasants, middle classes, and industrial workers. The period immediately after the war and the great depression, times of great suffering elsewhere, affected Czechoslovakia very lightly. Yet these advantages could hardly have preserved de-

mocracy in the republic had it not been for the enlightened policies of Thomas Masaryk, liberator and president of his country until his resignation at the age of 85 in 1935.

Even the enlightened Czech regime, however, could not keep the country from ultimately being smashed by outside pressures working on its sensitive minorities. The Sudetens formed the great problem. Anti-Czech since Habsburg days, they resisted the new republic at every turn, even when the Prague government made concessions to satisfy their just grievances. Sudeten extremists early turned to Hitler, but even moderates and socialists among the Sudetens were more or less pan-German in their views. From 1933 on, Nazi agitation, supported by Hitler with men and money, became increasingly serious in Czechoslovakia. Early in 1938, having secured Austria, Hitler decided to push the Czech affair next. Henlein, his Sudeten agent, made demands on the Prague government for what amounted to complete Sudeten autonomy. The summer of 1938 was spent in negotiations and in mutual propaganda blasts. The Czechs relied heavily on their allies, the British and the French. Whereas British statesmen now for the first time began to announce publicly that Germany had gone far enough, the British sent out a mediator, Lord Runciman, who seemed inclined to meet Hitler at least halfway.

By the autumn of 1938, Hitler was ready for action. On September 12 he made a violent speech at Nuremberg, insisting on self-determination for the Sudeten Germans. This was the signal for widespread disorders in Czechoslovakia and for the proclamation of martial law by its government. The situation was now a full-fledged European crisis that called for the personal intervention of men at the very top of their states. The British Prime Minister, Neville Chamberlain, made two preliminary visits to Hitler in Germany in an effort to moder-

600

Chamberlain, Daladier, Hitler, Mussolini, and Ciano (Mussolini's son-in-law) at Munich, September, 1938.

ate German demands, and finally persuaded Hitler—with the help of Mussolini—to call a full conference of the four great western powers. This conference—Hitler, Mussolini, Chamberlain, and Daladier for France— met in Munich on September 29, 1938. Russia was not invited; her exclusion was to complete her abandonment of the "Popular Front" policy (see Chapter XXVI).

Munich was a sweeping victory for Hitler. Czechoslovakia was partially dismembered; her Sudeten rim-lands were turned over to Germany; her whole economy and transportation system were lamed; and the defense of her frontiers was made impossible by the loss of the border mountains and their fortifications. The Czech leaders had felt it impossible to resist the Germans without the aid of their French and British allies; their people acquiesced bitterly in the settlement of Munich. The Germans had played fully on the differences between the more industrialized Czechs and the still largely agricultural Slovaks. But even had the country been strongly united, the laming blow of Munich would have ruined its morale. Hitler acted quickly. In the very next spring, before the final lines of demarcation set at Munich had actually been drawn, he summoned the Czech President, Hacha, to Germany for another of those ghastly interviews in which he announced that the fate of the Czech people "must be placed trustingly in the hands of the *Fuehrer.*" In March, 1939, Hitler marched his army into the remaining fragments of Czechoslovakia, meeting no real resistance.

The dismemberment of the Czechoslovak republic was now completed. Bohemia and Moravia, the Czech areas, became a German "protectorate"; the status of the remaining minority areas was also changed. In Slovakia, the conservative Catholic population had long been at odds with the Czechs, and Hlinka's separatist movement (see above, Chapter XXII) had put down deep roots. The province proved a fertile field for the Nazis, who forced the creation of an autonomous Slovakia after the Munich settlement and allowed Hlinka's successor, Father Tiso, to become its premier. After March, 1939, Slovakia became nominally independent; actually, it was the first of the German satellite states that were to be set up on the outer fringes of German expansion. Finally, after Munich, Ruthenia was also awarded a brief autonomy; its name was changed to the Carpatho-Ukraine. This remote province at the eastern extremity of Czechoslovakia, backward economically and culturally, had been ruled by the Magyars in Habsburg days. In the spring of 1939, Hungary invaded and re-annexed the Carpatho-Ukraine.

The most respectable defense that can be made of Munich and appeasement rests on the argument that the West was buying time to prepare for a war which it knew to be inevitable but for which it was not yet ready. But it also seems likely that Chamberlain and Daladier, as well as millions all over the world, believed, or hoped, that the acquisition of the Sudeten Germans would satisfy Hitler, that after Munich he would behave as Bismarck had behaved after Sedan, and that he would settle down and try to preserve the balance of power. Some westerners even hoped that Hitler would perhaps ally with them against communist Russia or obligingly get himself so entangled in eastern Europe that he would bring on a Russo-German war. Hitler's words and deeds, however, had given no real foundation for the belief that he would now "play ball" with the West. More fundamentally, this was a belief to which the last

four hundred years of the European state-system gave no support. Hitler resembled Napoleon far more than he resembled Bismarck; no such strong aggressor had ever been stopped without a general war. History, psychology, sociology, and perhaps even common sense all pointed to the prospect that Hitler would actually be *encouraged* in aggression by Munich, that he would try again soon.

The actual absorption of more Czech lands by Germany seems not to have surprised anyone. Indeed the curious mixture of resignation, condemnation, and resolution with which this action was greeted in the West marks a turning point. The days of appeasement were over. Hitler's next aggression would not lead to a Munich. We can never be quite sure whether Hitler and his aides thought they could take their next step without bringing on a general war. In public and semi-public, Hitler, Goering, and the other leaders made no secret of their feeling that the British and French were decadent, spineless, inefficient societies, quite unable to summon the courage needed to resist an inspired and rejuvenated Germany. Yet there is good evidence that Hitler expected at least a local war with Poland this time, and that he was quite prepared to face involvement with the French and the British.

The Final Step: Poland, 1939

Poland was almost inexorably his next victim. The Polish corridor dividing East Prussia from the rest of Germany was an affront to great-power psychology. So, too, was the separation from Germany of the Free City of Danzig, on the edge of the Polish corridor. Danzig was thoroughly German in language and tradition. The western regions of the Polish republic, which Hitler now also wanted, had been Prussian for over a hundred years when Poland was set up after World War I. Germans, even quite enlightened Germans, thought of the Poles as inferior people who would benefit from capable German supervision. Hitler began his Baltic adventure in March, 1939, when he took the port town of Memel from Poland's northern neighbor, Lithuania.

The critical issue in the tense half-year that led up to the outbreak of war on September 1, 1939, was not the possibility that Poland, unsupported by Britain and France, would undergo the same fate as Czechoslovakia. The British government publicly supported Poland by signing a pact of mutual assistance with her in April. Indeed, in the midst of the final week of crisis, Chamberlain's foreign minister, Lord Halifax, sent a telegram to Hitler himself in which he made a rather pathetic appeal to the lessons of history:

It has been alleged that if His Majesty's Government had made their position more clear in 1914 the great catastrophe would have been avoided. Whether or not there is any force in that allegation, His Majesty's Government are resolved that on this occasion there shall be no such tragic misunderstanding. If the need should arise, they are resolved and prepared to employ without delay all the forces at their command. . . . I trust that Your Excellency will weigh with the utmost deliberation the considerations which I have put before you.*

The real critical point was the attitude of Russia. Hitler had an almost obsessive fear of a war on two fronts, a war against major powers to the east and to the west of the kind on which Germany had embarked in 1914. He was in fact drawn within

two years into just such a war. Even if he had been faced in 1939 by the united front of Britain, France, and Russia in support of Poland, it is perfectly possible that he could not have restrained himself and his followers. One is tempted to see the Nazi top command as driven on by some abnormal and obsessive motivation and quite oblivious to ordinary considerations of self-interest. Hitler perhaps could no more keep his hands off Poland than an alcoholic can keep his hands off liquor. But, as events developed, Hitler was able to seize Poland without fear of Russian intervention. Indeed, he was able to arrange with Stalin a partition of Poland quite recognizably on the model of the eighteenth-century partitions.

We are still too near these events to assess them with the detachment that men will one day attain. Hitler, in *Mein Kampf*, had made ample theoretical preparation and justification for this sort of deal. The Russians, however, had joined the League, had talked much about collective security and international organization, and, on the plane of action, had shown clear evidence that they felt more danger from Hitler than from the western powers. Yet in the summer of 1939 they faced about and came to terms with their mortal enemy. The public utterances of Germans about Russians, and of Russians about Germans, changed rapidly from abuse to a somewhat awkward praise, and faithful communists throughout the world took unnatural leaps to follow this change in the party line.

Why did the Russians make their about-face? They had been deeply hurt by their exclusion from the negotiations over the Czechoslovakian crisis of the year before, an exclusion that they blamed primarily on the British and the French. From the failure of the western powers to stand up to German violations of the Versailles Treaty ever since 1934, the Russians had drawn con-

---

* *Documents on British Foreign Policy, 1919-1939*, E. L. Woodward and R. Butler, eds. (London, 1954), 3rd series, Vol. II, No. 145.

After the Hitler-Stalin pact, August, 1939.

clusions at least as disparaging to the western will to fight as those drawn by Hitler. In particular, they deeply distrusted the British Tories under Neville Chamberlain, for they believed that in many ways Tory Britain was more fundamentally hostile to communist Russia than even Nazi Germany was.

The Russians' mistrust of the West was not dispelled by the diplomatic mission that Britain and France sent, belatedly and grudgingly, to negotiate with Russia in the summer of 1939. The western powers proposed a mutual assistance pact, but the efforts of their negotiators were inept and halfhearted. Moreover, Chamberlain's government made a tactless choice of negotiators. One of them, Ironside, had been involved in the British intervention against the Reds at Archangel in the early days of the Bolshevik state; another was a mere functionary of the Foreign Office. The Russians like to deal with top people; they like to be made to feel important. Significantly, Hitler, who was also negotiating with Russia at the time, put Foreign Minister Ribbentrop himself on the job. So the

Anglo-French overture to Moscow came to nothing. The Russian leaders had reached the conclusion that the West was a broken reed, that if they themselves did not come to terms with Hitler he would attack them anyway.

Finally, the Russians were quite as distrustful of the Polish government as of anyone else. The western, especially the French, policy of encouraging the smaller powers of eastern Europe to act as counterweights to *both* Germany and Russia now bore its natural fruit. The Poles would not accept Russia as protector; they would not, in these hectic months of negotiation, consent to the passage of Russian troops in case of war with Germany. The Russians were tempted by the opportunity to recover lands in eastern Poland that they had lost in World War I and its aftermath. To the horror of the West, they signed at Moscow on August 23, 1939, a nonaggression pact with Germany; a week later, the German army marched into Poland. On September 3, Britain and France honored their obligations, and declared war on Germany. The twenty years' truce was at an end.

CHAPTER XXVIII

Democratic Policy in Review

Intellectuals—the men who write and teach and preach—in the western world have been harsh in their judgment of the foreign policies of the democracies. They have condemned not only France and Britain in these two decades between the wars, but also the smaller states of Europe and the United States. The democracies seem to have stood by in impotence and frustration while in Italy, in Japan, in Germany, and in Spain societies formed and grew strong with the overt intention of destroying democracy on this earth. The democracies were committed by their most fundamental beliefs to the protection of independent nations from aggression. Yet from the Japanese invasion of Manchuria in 1931 to the German invasion of the rump of Czechoslovakia in 1939 there was a steady series of unmistakable aggressions in complete defiance of the existing fabric of international law. No democracy—and this includes the United States, with its long historic interest in the independence of China—did more than protest. By the time the democracies were stung into action, their foes were strong and confident.

Yet it is not really difficult to understand why the democracies behaved as they did in these years. Britain, France, and the United States were the victors of 1918, and by the very fact of their victory they were on the defensive. Wisdom and luck might have made their defense more effective than it was, but nothing could have altered the fact that they were on the defensive. In the long past of our state-system, the defensive has always proved a difficult position, has always been—perhaps from the very nature of western culture with its drives toward change—at a disadvantage against aggression. This disadvantage seems by no means associated with democracies as such. Absolute monarchies have suffered quite as

much from the difficulties of the defensive, as the failure of Metternich shows (see Chapter XIX).

In the years between the two world wars, the normal tendency of the victors to relax was increased by some of the facts of democratic life. The western democracies were committed to an effort to secure for every citizen some minimum of material comforts; they were committed to the pursuit of happiness. Their normal tendency was to produce butter rather than guns. Their totalitarian opponents may well have been quite as "materialistic" as they, but for them the butter was to be attained in the future, and by means of the guns. In short, the German, Japanese, and Italian governments were able to get their societies to tighten their belts in order to make military preparation possible. It was exceedingly difficult for democratic governments to get such sacrifices until war actually broke out.

Moreover, the democratic societies held optimistic beliefs about human nature and human societies. They found it hard to measure the true depths of totalitarian aggression. Especially to Americans, but also to the man in the street in France and Britain, World War I still seemed a freakish interlude in the steady rise of a society based on reason and decency. To many, particularly among the British, the vengeful phases of the Versailles settlement seemed to justify a great deal of German policy; they were indeed ashamed of having helped impose this wicked settlement. But important though this feeling of guilt over Versailles may have been, democratic moral values and democratic feeling about the kind of world we live in served in a much more general way to blind the West to the dangers it was running. To many decent democrats it seemed that Hitler could not be as bad as he sounded; he must be putting on an act for some strange reasons of showmanship; underneath he must be reasonable and willing to compromise. He could not really intend to bring on another world war, a war that would perhaps destroy the West, and that would leave even the victor defeated. Hitler, these democrats reasoned, was surely no madman; if he were, the Germans would not follow him to self-destruction.

They did indeed follow him to the worse-than-Wagnerian frenzy of the last days of Berlin. Hitler, and the millions who fol- lowed him, did not behave as those west- erners who took their views from the eighteenth-century Enlightenment believed men were bound to behave. The West has now perhaps learned its lessons; it does not—or at least many of its responsible leaders do not—expect the enemies of the western democracies to share their habits of mind and heart. But we should not hold it too much against the men of the twenty years' truce that they found it hard to learn that lesson.

Reading Suggestions on the Atlantic Democracies

Britain and France

R. Graves and A. Hodge, *The Long Weekend* (London: Faber and Faber, Ltd., 1940). A lively social history of Britain during the inter-war years.

G. E. Elton, *The Life of James Ramsay Macdonald* (London: William Collins Sons, 1939); G. M. Young, *Stanley Baldwin* (London: R. Hart-Davis, 1952); and K. Feiling, *The Life of Neville Chamberlain* (London: Macmillan & Co., Ltd., 1946). Biographies of three important British statesmen.

C. R. Attlee, *The Labour Party in Perspective*, 2nd ed. (London: Victor Gollancz, Ltd., 1949). A review of the period by the British Labor leader.

D. Brogan, *France under the Republic* (New York: Harper and Brothers, 1940) and D. Thomson, *Democracy in France*, 2nd ed. (London: Oxford University Press, 1952). These general studies provide an excellent introduction to French problems in the inter-war years.

E. J. Knapton, *France since Versailles* (New York: Henry Holt & Co., 1952. A Berkshire Study). Handy little manual.

A. Werth, *The Twilight of France, 1933-1940* (New York: Harper and Brothers, 1942). Condensation of several longer studies by an able foreign correspondent.

M. Bloch, *Strange Defeat* (London: Oxford University Press, 1949). Very per·· ceptive analysis of modern French problems by an eminent medieval scholar.

The United States

Four volumes in the "Chronicles of America Series" (New Haven: Yale University Press) provide good coverage of the period: H. U. Faulkner, *From Versailles to the New Deal* (1950); D. Brogan, *The Era of Franklin D. Roosevelt* (1951); A. Nevins, *The United States in a Chaotic World* (1950); and A. Nevins, *The New Deal and World Affairs* (1950).

F. L. Allen, *Only Yesterday* (New York: Bantam Books) and *Since Yesterday* (New York: Harper and Brothers, 1940). Lively social histories of the 1920's and 1930's, respectively.

F. Perkins, *The Roosevelt I Knew* (New York: Viking Press, 1946). One of the most illuminating memoirs of Franklin Roosevelt; by his Secretary of Labor.

R. E. Sherwood, *Roosevelt and Hopkins*, 2 vols. (New York: Bantam Books). One of the most informative studies of the Roosevelt presidency.

Economic Developments

P. Einzig, *The World Economic Crisis, 1929-1932* (London: Macmillan & Co., Ltd., 1932); H. V. Hodson, *Slump and Recovery, 1929-1937* (New York: Oxford University Press, 1938); and H. W. Arndt, *The Economic Lessons of the Nineteen-Thirties* (London: Oxford University Press, 1944). Useful books on the great depression.

J. Schumpeter, *Capitalism, Socialism, and Democracy*, 3rd ed. (New York: Harper and Brothers, 1950); J. M. Keynes, *The End of Laissez-Faire* (London: L. and V. Woolf, 1926). Thoughtful essays by two major economic thinkers.

International Developments

E. H. Carr, *The Twenty Years' Crisis* (London: Macmillan & Co., Ltd., 1946). A stimulating and somewhat opinionated survey of inter-war diplomacy.

F. Gilbert and G. A. Craig, eds., *The Diplomats, 1919-1939* (Princeton: Princeton University Press, 1953). A useful symposium.

A. Wolfers, *Britain and France between Two Wars* (New York: Harcourt, Brace & Co., 1940). A solid analysis of the foreign policies of the two powers.

S. R. Smith, *The Manchurian Crisis, 1931-1932* (New York: Columbia University Press, 1948). Monograph on the crisis that marked the turning point from the post-war to the pre-war period.

J. W. Wheeler-Bennett, *Munich: Prologue to Tragedy* (London: Macmillan & Co., Ltd., 1948); and L. B. Namier, *Diplomatic Prelude, 1938-1939* (London: Macmillan & Co., Ltd., 1948). Good studies of the last international crises of the 1930's.

Historical Fiction

E. Waugh, *A Handful of Dust* (Norfolk, Conn.: New Directions, 1945). Corrosive novel satirizing English society in the inter-war years.

H. Spring, *Fame Is the Spur* (New York: Viking Press, 1940). A politician is corrupted by ambition; largely parallels the career of Ramsay Macdonald.

W. Holtby, *South Riding* (New York: The Macmillan Company, 1936). Good social novel of industrial England.

A. Gide, *The Counterfeiters* (New York: Alfred A. Knopf, Inc., 1927). Mordant study of the French middle class by an eminent novelist.

F. Scott Fitzgerald, *The Great Gatsby* (many editions). A celebrated picture of "flaming youth" in the American Jazz Age.

J. Steinbeck, *The Grapes of Wrath* (many editions). The famous novel about exiles from the Oklahoma "dust bowl" of the 1930's.

The Loosening of Imperial Ties

CHAPTER XXIX

Sir Stafford Cripps, the British negotiator, receiving Gandhi in New Delhi before India gained her independence.

I: Introduction

THERE WERE SIGNS even before 1914, especially in Egypt, French North Africa, the Philippines, China, and India, that the more advanced "colonial" peoples were already chafing under imperialism. World War I itself speeded up the process of rousing national consciousness among these peoples, and at its end there was no doubt that the hold of the West had been loosened. For one thing, defeated Germany was eliminated from the imperial scramble. Her colonies passed to Britain, to some of the dominions, and to France and Japan, but under the mandate system of the League of Nations and not under absolute annexation (for details, see Chapter XXV). The Arab states formed out of the old Ottoman Empire had raised armies of their own, and had fought with European aid for their own freedom from Turkey. French North African and Negro troops, and British Indian troops, had all taken part in the conflict, sometimes in Europe itself. The British had made great use of native troops in subduing the German colonies in Africa.

Psychologically, it seems evident that the mere experience of the war gave a lift to non-western peoples; they had been

609

United States forces in China at the time of the action against the Boxer Rebellion, 1900-1901.

of importance to their white masters, and their own leaders had widened their knowledge of the world of the West. The very spectacle of the masters quarreling among themselves did something to lower the prestige of the West among subject peoples. Moreover, the Allies had fought the war in the name of democratic ideals of self-determination for all peoples, and in their propaganda against the Central Powers they had stressed heavily their opposition to imperialism. It is true that they did not give up any of their territories in 1919, and did indeed add to them under the mandate system. To many of the subject races, as to liberals in the West itself, the mandate was simply a disguise for the old imperialism; but it is surely significant that a disguise seemed necessary to the imperialist powers. The West was committed now in some sense officially to a process of at least gradual emancipation of the colonial dependencies.

II: The Far East

Before 1914, the revolt against the West had made an important beginning in China. This decaying empire, ruled by the Manchu dynasty, remained nominally independent, but its effective sovereignty was much impaired by extensive concessions of naval bases and economic and political privileges to the western imperialist powers and to Japan. Following China's defeat by Japan in 1895 (see Chapter XXIV), the western powers engaged in a hectic scramble for further concessions in the late 1890's. The results in China were the formation of the Boxers, a nationalist and anti-foreign secret society, and the Boxer Rebellion of 1900, in which more than 200

CHAPTER XXIX

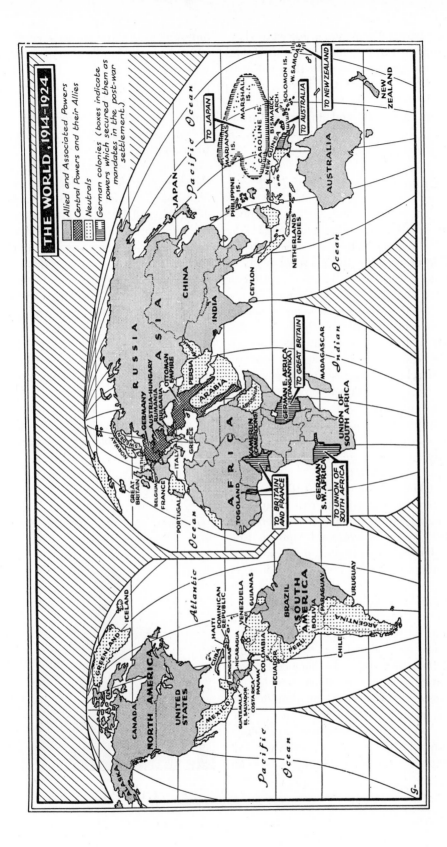

THE WORLD, 1914-1924

Allied and Associated Powers
Central Powers and their Allies
Neutrals
German colonies (boxes indicate
powers which secured them as
mandates in the post-war
settlement.)

TO JAPAN
TO AUSTRALIA
TO NEW ZEALAND
MARIANAS IS.
CAROLINE IS.
MARSHALL IS.
NEW GUINEA
BISMARCK ARCH.
SOLOMON IS.
W. SAMOA
PHILIPPINE IS.
NETHERLANDS INDIES
AUSTRALIA
NEW ZEALAND

JAPAN
CHINA
INDIA
CEYLON
RUSSIA
ASIA
GERMANY
AUSTRIA-HUNGARY
RUMANIA
BULGARIA
OTTOMAN EMPIRE
PERSIA
ARABIA
GREECE
ITALY
NORWAY
SWEDEN
NETH.
GREAT BRITAIN
BELGIUM
FRANCE
PORTUGAL

Pacific Ocean
Indian Ocean

MADAGASCAR
GERMAN E. AFRICA (TANGANYIKA)
TO GREAT BRITAIN
UNION OF SOUTH AFRICA
CAMERUN (CAMEROONS)
TOGOLAND
TO BRITAIN AND FRANCE
GERMAN S.W. AFRICA
TO UNION OF SOUTH AFRICA

AFRICA

Atlantic Ocean

ICELAND
GREENLAND
NORTH AMERICA
CANADA
UNITED STATES
MEXICO
GUATEMALA
EL SALVADOR
COSTA RICA
PANAMA
HONDURAS
NICARAGUA
CUBA
HAITI
DOMINICAN REPUBLIC
COLOMBIA
ECUADOR
VENEZUELA
GUIANAS
BRAZIL
SOUTH AMERICA
PERU
BOLIVIA
PARAGUAY
CHILE
ARGENTINA
URUGUAY

Pacific Ocean

611

foreigners, mainly missionaries, were slain. The foreign powers, including the United States, used troops to protect their nationals and property against the Boxers, and in 1901 obliged the Manchu government to pay an indemnity and to grant further rights.

The Chinese Revolution of 1911

The next Chinese rebellion, the revolution of 1911, was directed against the Manchu regime that had proved so incapable of resisting the encroachments of imperialist states. In this revolution a factor operated that can be found more or less clearly in the whole process of loosening western controls with which we are concerned in this chapter. The movement is directed against the West—against westerners themselves or against native governors who seem to the rebels to be the agents of the West, or against both. But it is a movement inspired at least in part by western ideas and examples, a movement that could scarcely have come into being without the influence of the West.

The Chinese revolution of 1911 was comparatively bloodless in its early stages. It was sealed by the abdication on February 12, 1912, of the six-year-old Manchu Emperor, Pu-yi. From the start, it was inspired by two groups with conflicting ideas of the new society that the revolution was aiming to create. One group soon formed the Nationalist party, the Kuomintang, led by Sun Yat-sen and many young intellectuals who had studied and traveled in the West. Its leaders wanted a democratic parliamentary republic of China modeled on the western political system, though preserving as far as possible the basic Chinese family and village structure, on which western industrial society was to be grafted. The other group, whose leader was Yuan Shih-k'ai, wanted a strong central government basically authoritarian in structure, with authority not in the hands of an emperor and the traditional and highly conservative Chinese mandarin bureaucracy, but in the hands of strong men capable of achieving the modernization of China from above.

A struggle for power broke out between the assembly elected after 1911 and Yuan Shih-k'ai. The party of Sun Yat-sen was defeated, and by 1914, after a "purge" of the Kuomintang members of the assembly, Yuan Shih-k'ai issued a constitutional compact that put him in the presidential office for ten years. Sun Yat-sen and his followers had failed to turn China into a western parliamentary democracy. Sun was, however, a gifted leader, and the ideas for which he stood, though they have never got firmly rooted in China, have never quite disappeared. Sun remains somewhat paradoxically the great hero of the Chinese revolution.

Yuan's subsequent career bears some resemblance to that of another military

Sun Yat-sen.

CHAPTER XXIX

reformer, Oliver Cromwell. Faced with continuing opposition, not only from the republicans of the Kuomintang but also from the monarchists, Yuan decided to follow the age-old Chinese pattern and set himself up as the first of a new dynasty of emperors to follow the Manchus. A revolt caused him to revoke his plans, and early in 1916 he reorganized the republic with a military cabinet. He died on June 6, 1916, leaving the new republic enmeshed in another age-old Chinese political pattern—the dissolution of all but the shadow of central control and the assumption of real power by regional strong men. A new era of provincial "war-lords" had begun.

Japan's Attempted Aggression, 1915-1922

In the years of crisis following 1911, China faced not only the serious internal difficulties brought about by the attempt to introduce western parliamentary democracy too rapidly into a land unprepared for it. She also faced the aggressive attempts of Japan to take over the Far Eastern imperial interests of European powers now at war among themselves. Early in 1915, the Japanese presented in secrecy to the Chinese government the "Twenty-One Demands," which amounted to a demand for something close to a protectorate over China and for all sorts of concrete concessions. The Chinese republic, now at the nadir of its strength, countered by declaring war against the Central Powers, thus securing at least the nominal protection of two of the Allies, Britain and France.

Had the Japanese felt able to defy western objections and undertake an all-out military invasion of China, they might conceivably have got so strongly established there that they could not have been dislodged. But they contented themselves with

taking over the German concessions in ·the Shantung peninsula. At the end of the war, the victorious Allies, with the United States in the lead, acted to check the ambitions of their recent military partner, Japan. At the Washington Conference of 1922 (see Chapter XXVIII) Japan was forced to sign the Nine-Power Treaty guaranteeing the independence of China. This rebuff to Japan is one of the first events in the long chain that aggravated the hostility of Japan toward the United States and ended, nineteen years later, in the attack on Pearl Harbor.

Main Elements of Recent Chinese History

The details of Chinese history between the end of World War I and the consolidation of the Chinese Communists' power are extraordinarily confused and complex. The main elements during this thirty-year period were the Kuomintang, the Communists, and the Japanese invaders. To the parts played by the last two of these we shall turn in a moment. The Kuomintang, after the death of Sun Yat-sen in 1925, came under the leadership of Chiang K'ai-shek, an army officer trained in Japan. The Nationalists of the Kuomintang were engaged in a constant and often very unsuccessful struggle to set up an effective central government against the power of provincial "war-lords." They were also often locked in battle with the Communists and the Japanese.

All three of the main forces fought in word and deed for the allegiance—or at any rate for the passive acceptance—of nearly five hundred million Chinese, for the most part peasants, and for the most part illiterate. For the most part, too, the masses of China were so far from sharing western attitudes toward the state that it is hardly an exaggeration to say that they

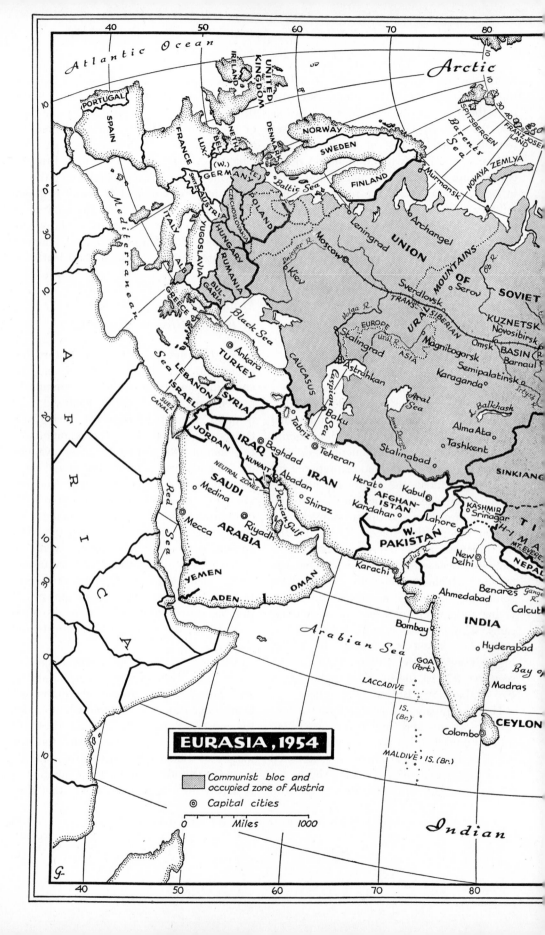

EURASIA, 1954

Communist bloc and
occupied zone of Austria

◎ Capital cities

0   Miles   1000

felt toward politics as we westerners feel toward the weather—that it is something beyond human control, beyond the participation of ordinary human beings. In transforming the Chinese into a nation in the western sense, the indispensable step was something more than building railroads and factories or promoting the study of modern science instead of the Chinese classics. It was getting the Chinese peasant to feel himself an individual Chinese citizen.

This indispensable process was beginning during the twenty years' truce between the two world wars. It goes far to explain why the Japanese, when they renewed their aggression in 1931, were virtually beaten from the start in the attempt to make themselves the true masters of China. In an earlier age one can readily imagine the Japanese as military conquerors in China setting up a new dynasty, foreign in origin, but very soon thoroughly absorbed by the Chinese. That this age-old pattern was not followed in the 1930's shows that China herself was changing, that here too the modern expansion of the West was radically altering her traditional way of life.

Japan's Aggressions, 1931-1945

In a purely military way the Japanese did very well, starting with their occupation of Manchuria in 1931 (see Chapter XXVIII). Having consolidated their hold in this northern Chinese territory, which was rechristened Manchukuo, the Japanese attempted to absorb all the rest of China. The invasion came in July, 1937, without a formal declaration of war. By October, when the key southern Chinese city of Canton fell, the Japanese had taken the strategic points of the coastal area and the thickly peopled lower river valleys. Chiang K'ai-shek took refuge with his army and his fellow politicians of the Kuomin-

tang in the interior province of Szechwan. There he set up his capital at Chungking; and there, protected by distance and a ring of mountains, receiving western aid through India by the Burma Road and, when that was closed, by air, the Nationalist government held out until the end of World War II. In 1945, the Japanese, acknowledging defeat by the Allies, were obliged to withdraw their armies from the whole mainland of Asia.

Yet even at the height of their success, the Japanese had achieved no more than the stretching across China of a string of garrisons, and the control of great cities like Shanghai and Peiping. They held the railroads, subject to guerrilla attacks; they could put their puppets into place in the more important centers; and they could make shift to run the country. But away from the relatively sparse lines of modern communication they were helpless. Many a Chinese village in the area nominally Japanese never changed its ways during the occupation. Nowhere did the Japanese win over the acquiescence, to say nothing of the loyalty, of the Chinese people.

Nationalists and Communists

The Nationalists had from the early 1930's led the resistance to the Japanese. And in the most crucial moments of the long war of resistance, before World War II involved the Japanese elsewhere, Chiang K'ai-shek could count on the help of even the Communists in resisting the invader. Yet Chiang's armies were never able to stand upon equal terms with the Japanese. They lacked a good base in modern industrial society, and as the Japanese early seized the few industrial cities of China, Chiang was always relatively badly off in terms of logistics.

In the long exile in Szechwan, moreover,

something faltered in the morale of the Nationalists. The ordeal, far from purifying and strengthening them, emphasized their alienation from the masses of the Chinese, their corruption and intrigue, their inability to live up to the early promise of Sun Yat-sen and the Kuomintang. For it was not the Nationalists, but the Communists, who succeeded in capturing and harnessing the human emotions and aspirations, the binding power that will hold men together in society with the tightness modern material culture needs. The Communists, not the Nationalists, came to stand to most Chinese for what made them Chinese, for their "nationalism."

The Chinese Communist movement began in the early 1920's. It was inspired by direct contacts with the Comintern in Moscow, guided by Soviet agents like the famous Michael Borodin, and encouraged at first by leaders of the Kuomintang. Sun Yat-sen hoped that the example and advice of the successful Russian party might help to strengthen his own faltering party organization. For a time, then, the Chinese Communists were no more than a left-wing, fellow-traveling tail to the Kuomintang. Soon, however, the inevitable breach occurred between them and the more conservative elements among the Nationalists, led by Chiang K'ai-shek.

The Communists lost out badly in this early struggle for power. In 1926, Chiang's forces began a campaign of persecution and assassination against the Communists; in 1927, the Communists were expelled from the Kuomintang and obliged to set up their own separate party organization. An important reason for this setback sustained by the Chinese Communists was their failure to get effective support or help from Moscow. The years 1926 and 1927 were the years of the Trotsky-Stalin feud in Russia, and the conflict between these two titans was intensified by their differences over the "correct" Chinese policy of the Soviet Union (see above, p. 504). Stalin, who was rapidly gaining the ascendancy, believed that China was not ripe for a proletarian revolution; therefore, he did nothing to succor his Chinese comrades.

The Road to Communist Success in China

During the next two decades, down to the end of World War II, the relative strength of Communists and Nationalists underwent a gradual and decisive shift. Both parties, it should be noted, were in a sense totalitarian. Both were organized on the pattern of the one-party political system, which left no place for an opposition party; neither of them was geared to the give-and-take of western party politics. The Communists, driven about over much of China during the 1930's, ended up with a base in the region of Yenan in the north; their strategic position somewhat resembled that of Chiang in his southern base of Szechwan. But there was an important difference. In the long years of Japanese occupation, Chiang remained in Chungking with his army and his bureaucracy. The Communists, on the other hand, managed to string their network of organized armies and local councils in and around the Japanese in the north; they extended their apparatus right down to the sea and up through Manchuria.

Thus the Communists profited by the long struggle against Japan to broaden their base of operations and to widen their popular appeal. One great reason why they were able to do so is clear. They made a successful effort to bring their soldiers into good relations with the peasants, and to make soldiers and peasants alike aware that they could act together. China was a land where the soldier was traditionally regarded as

Communist China: measuring out the land for redistribution.

the lowest of human beings, a destructive force like a flood or a typhoon, natural but most unpleasant. Against such a traditional view the Communist slogan—"the soldiers are fish and the people water"—came as a really revolutionary stroke. This characteristic Chinese aphorism was at once understood to mean that the army rested on popular support and confidence.

Again, the Communists were able to bridge the traditional gap in China between the intellectual and the ordinary person. Communist success here was facilitated in the 1940's by the uprooted state of mind of Chinese intellectuals, who were searching for new beliefs and seeking fresh hope. They seemed to find what they sought in the program of the Communists. An American expert on China, Professor Fairbank,

writing soon after the close of World War II, concluded that the struggle with Japan revolutionized the outlook of the Chinese intellectual:

The encouragement of popular participation in cultural, economic, and political programs, according to most observers, created a new psychological atmosphere or morale in those wartime areas where the Communist program became effective. Participants in the new order have been moved by a new creed, a humanitarian love of the peasant masses. This religion of the common man embraces the revolutionary ideal that modern technology and a new social organization may be used to remake and enrich the life of the peasant. This cult of the common people, the *lao-pai-hsing*, animates the cadres of party workers and the military forces. In order that the revolution may draw perpetual sustenance from the masses, the party workers must live in the villages, work

CHAPTER XXIX

with the peasant, eat his food, lead his life, think his thoughts. Only thus can the party cadres lead the peasant masses in their regeneration.

This almost religious concept of liberation is the most dynamic spiritual element in the modern Chinese scene; and by a seemingly inexorable logic of events it has become the sanction for a new party dictatorship.*

The Communist Victory in China

American policy-makers during World War II had been most eager to maintain China as an ally and as an important member of the United Nations. The United States had backed up the Nationalists in Chungking and, when the war ended, hoped to be able to reconcile the Nationalists and the Communists and make China a democratic, pro-American parliamentary state. In such a state the Communists would have been a legal party and a large one, as in France or Italy, but not a majority group. In 1946, the American negotiator, General Marshall, however, failed in his attempt to bring the two parties to a working agreement.

After Marshall's return to the United States in January, 1947, the result of the renewed Chinese civil war was never seriously in doubt. The Communists now received very effective support from the Soviet Union, including war material that the Japanese had surrendered to the Russians in Manchuria. The Kuomintang government of Chiang K'ai-shek was weakened by its own ebbing morale, by its dwindling popular support, and by an ever-mounting inflation that had gathered force during the war and further ravaged an economy already ruined by the long Japanese occupation. Late in 1949, the Nationalists, driven

from the mainland, transferred their government to the island of Formosa, which Japan had relinquished in 1945. The Communists, lacking naval strength, could not pursue Chiang and the Nationalists.

China, then, by 1950 had gone Communist and formed part of the great Soviet bloc. Americans, in the face of the total failure of their China policy, began a bitter debate over the reasons why the Communists had been able to unite China under their control. This controversial question is clearly not yet a historical question, since no one can command all the documents or the partial detachment necessary to achieve a fair appraisal of the situation. The historian can, however, warn here as elsewhere against any explanation of the Communists' success that rests on the notion that a few conspirators, a few wicked men, with perhaps a few misled ones, brought about the Communist victory. Wicked men and conspirators were indeed active in China, but they were powerless to accomplish anything on the scale here involved without the assistance of what we call "social forces," "economic needs," and "morale." These may be vague terms, but they represent millions upon millions of human beings; in the preceding paragraphs we have tried to spell out their meaning in China.

The historian, of course, cannot predict with any confidence what will come of the Communist experiment in China. It is pretty clear that China has achieved complete independence from the West. Many of the old colonial concessions enjoyed by the western powers went rapidly after World War I. And after World War II all legal traces of subjection went by the boards, notably extraterritoriality— the right of certain European states to try their own nationals in China by their own courts and their own law. The old ties between China and the West have been replaced by new ties with Soviet Russia. One reason for this

---

* J. K. Fairbank, *The United States and China* (Cambridge, Mass., 1948), 268-269.

certainly lies in the Chinese belief that Russia can supply modern western technology without imposing western imperial controls. We can only speculate on the degree of disillusion this belief may lead to in China, as we can only speculate about the chances for a permanent close tie between China and Russia.

The Communist regime in China, in its brief existence, has both paralleled and diverged from the path of development followed by Russia in the 1920's and 1930's. Down to 1954, the parallels outnumbered the divergences. In political structure, the similarities have been striking. In China, as in Russia, there is the same emphasis on Spartan service to the state, the same interlocking of the party hierarchy and the administrative hierarchy, and the same concentration of real authority in the hands of the dictatorial few at the top. A major difference has existed in social and economic policy, where the Chinese Communists have focused on the peasantry and on the meeting of peasant hopes for the breakup of large private holdings and for an end to landlordism. This focus is at odds not only with Marxian theories of the industrial proletariat as the major revolutionary class, but also with many of the actual policies practiced by Lenin and Stalin (see Chapter XXVI).

On the other hand, there are signs that the Communist leaders in China are adjusting their social and economic policies to the tradition of Marx, Lenin, and Stalin. Certainly they are more than simple agrarian reformers, for they have launched the equivalent of the Russian Five-Year Plans for industrialization. To release manpower from farms for industrial jobs and at the same time to maintain agricultural production will be a formidable undertaking indeed. Here we should bear in mind that the Soviet Union accomplished a similar undertaking, but only at a very high price

in human misery and under conditions relatively more advantageous than those prevailing in China. By 1928, at the onset of the first Five-Year Plan, the economy of Russia was relatively more modern than that of China in 1949, and her population was relatively better educated and more familiar with at least the rudiments of the economic revolution of modern times.

The Political Development of Japan, 1919-1941

Alone among non-western peoples, the Japanese experienced the industrial revolution and were able to maintain themselves as a fully independent and major political entity during the great age of imperialism down to 1914 (see Chapter XXIV). More than that, as the twentieth century opened, it was clear that Japan was a great power, a full but somewhat unwelcome member of the nations engaged in the struggle for imperial position. As we have seen, the Japanese made these impressive accomplishments without radically altering their traditional oligarchical and absolutist political structure.

In the decade after World War I, it looked as though Japan might at last undergo a gradual political revolution. The cabinets of the 1920's included many men from the business class who favored vigorous expansion abroad but who also granted some measures of cautious liberalism at home. The originally very limited suffrage was gradually extended, and in 1925 all men received the right to vote. For the first time, political parties, western-style, began to put down roots, especially in the urban population, and seemed likely to give new vitality to the Diet, the not very powerful central representative assembly of Japan. Trade unions also took shape and began to win a following.

Japan, however, did not evolve into a parliamentary democracy on the western model during the twenty years' truce. By the early 1930's, political power was falling more and more into the hands of army and navy officers, many of them descended from the feudal *samurai* class (see above, p. 400). This military clique hated the prospect of liberal civilian government and envied and mistrusted the business class. They found a potent political weapon in the office of the emperor, who was supposed to be the descendant of a god and to possess the kind of political infallibility that westerners associate with a divine-right monarch. Putting their own words into the emperor's mouth, the admirals and generals used his pronouncements to further their own ends. And, to make doubly sure, they assassinated or terrorized the chief spokesmen of nascent Japanese liberalism.

The consequence was the progressive clamping of a military dictatorship on Japan during the 1930's. The Diet lost the relatively little real power that it had once possessed. Popular elections were held and their results were then disregarded. Businessmen supported the new regime out of fear or out of anticipation of the huge profits to be secured from its adventures abroad. A cult of emperor-worship, known as state Shinto, was concocted out of an innocuous traditional Japanese religion in order to focus popular loyalties on the divine mission of the emperor and to insure popular submission to the will of the men who ruled in his name. A corps of ruthless agents, picturesquely named "thought police," hounded anyone suspected of harboring "dangerous thoughts." In short, Japan now had a government that, while exploiting many uniquely Japanese traditions, in its operations showed a striking resemblance to the totalitarian governments of Europe.

Communist China. Shanghai Electrical Machinery Works.

Japanese Imperialism, 1931-1945

Nowhere was the resemblance to European totalitarianism more marked than in the foreign and imperial policy of Japan in the 1930's and early 1940's. Like Hitler's Nazis or Mussolini's fascists, the Japanese claimed to be a "have-not" nation. They, too, pointed to their steadily growing population—and did all they could to encourage its further growth. They, too, harped on the overcrowding of the homeland, its inadequate resources, and its restricted markets. Behind this lay real economic problems of sustaining the Japanese economy in the face of the depression and the world-wide disruption of international trade, problems of providing food and work for the 60,000,000 Japanese of 1930. In seeking to solve the problems by imperial expansion, the military clique of the 1930's was following the path already marked out by the Japanese officers and politicians who had secured Formosa in 1895, annexed Korea in 1910, and then sought to subjugate China.

We have just been concerned with Japan's adventure in China, and in Chapter XXVIII we saw how her Manchurian aggression in 1931 was the first step along the road to World War II. China, however, though it was the most important of Japan's imperial aims, was only part of her truly grandiose ambition. During World War II, she briefly managed to build up "The Greater East-Asia Co-Prosperity Sphere." As we shall see in more detail when we come to World War II (Chapter XXX), Japanese expansion at its height took in most of China, French Indo-China, the Dutch East Indies, Siam and most of Burma, the Philippines, and many other Pacific islands, not to mention Korea and Formosa.

This "co-prosperity sphere" had many very obvious analogies with Napoleon's system of satellite states and even more with that of Hitler. Save in Korea and Formosa, which were administered as a part of Japan, the Japanese did not have time to organize their suddenly acquired empire. Their methods, however, seem to have been strikingly unoriginal, directly patterned on western precedent. They relied chiefly on the time-honored device of setting up puppet or satellite native governments, and exploiting for their own benefit the economic resources of the conquered lands. Their empire disintegrated in the atomic blast of Hiroshima. It was never cemented by the loyalty of its component parts.

Yet the Japanese started with at least one very great asset: they were an Asian people, a colored people, not westerners with the burden of white supremacy to carry. They could come as the emancipators of Asians and Pacific islanders, and in their propaganda they did indeed sound this note

vigorously. And they made converts, but only a minority in each conquered land. Asians though they were, they did not endear themselves to their fellow Asians. Their armies looted and committed atrocities on a scale hard to measure objectively, perhaps no worse than the average of atrocities in the West, but certainly no better. What is more, the Japanese abroad, again on an average, behaved like any other master race; they showed that they felt superior to the natives, even in the China from whose culture they had historically taken so much. Time might have taught the Japanese a lesson in social psychology, and they might have been able with time to consolidate their grandiloquently named "co-prosperity sphere"; but time they did not have.

Occupied Japan, 1945-1954

The end of World War II saw Japan reduced to her own islands, stripped of her overseas possessions. The overwhelming extent to which the military defeat of Japan was due to American efforts insured that the occupation and indeed the peace terms would be almost wholly an American concern. Though there was a strong current in American opinion that demanded the deposition of the Emperor and the establishment of a formal republic of Japan, less radical counsels prevailed. The Emperor was left on his throne, deprived of his divine status, and subjected to the close control of General MacArthur and the forces of occupation. Americans found to their astonishment that on the surface at least the Japanese people, far from taking the occupation with hostility, far from behaving as the Chinese had behaved toward them, seemed almost to admire their occupiers. They seemed not to understand what democracy meant—apart from baseball and some other

American folkways—but they seemed very anxious to learn. Their behavior roused a good deal of rather loose speculation about national group psychology, some of which appealed to the rigorous early toilet-training of Japanese children to explain the national willingness to obey a master. The old western distrust of the wily Oriental appeared in the theory that it was all a vast piece of national double-dealing: the Japanese were smothering their hatred of America for a time, cloaking it in apparent subservience in order to knife their occupiers later.

The fact is that here as in contemporary China we are dealing not only with history, but also with a very problematic and uncertain present. The Japanese have certainly not had a democratic society or a democratic political organization in the past, and it is unlikely that they can set up a democracy of the western type in short order. If a well-developed industrial economy is an indispensable base for the development of democracy, the Japanese have already a great start over all other non-western peoples, including even the East Indians. We must, however, beware of the simple conclusion that, because Japan took over industrialism from the West, she will automatically become thoroughly westernized. Sir George Sansom, a wise western observer who knows Japan well, writes:

Thus, while it may be said that the introduction of power-driven machinery brought to bear upon Japanese life a strong influence of Western origin, this is true only with qualifications. If we take separate instances we can see that modern inventions may well be used to counter foreign influence in other directions. Printing and binding machinery, for example, increases the number and circulation of books and newspapers, of which the contents may well be such as to spread ideas critical of foreign countries. . . . It might even be regarded as characteristic of Western influence upon Eastern peoples that it carries the germ of its own destruction. Of this the most striking and tremendous example is probably to be found in the modern history of India, where English political teaching created the spirit of revolt against English political authority, and the record of English constitutional growth provided precedents for rebellion. . . .

It is true that Western clothing, food, transport, and communications, as well as Western ideas, have enlarged and diversified Japanese life, but they have not necessarily changed its essential character. The cumulative effect of industrialization upon a people whose material culture is simple must destroy much of what is indigenous; but the impact of an advanced Western culture upon an advanced Eastern culture may, despite far-reaching superficial changes, succeed in producing resistance, or even hostile reactions in matters of vital import —in the totality of a people's feelings about life and society.*

Poor though the Japanese peasant and laboring classes are by American standards, they are far ahead of other non-western peoples. And grave though the population problem is, with 85,000,000 people living in 147,000 square miles, it is not as desperate as it is in the crowded farmlands of India or Java. Japan must, however, find foreign markets for her industrial production if she is to maintain and improve her national standard of living. Her position is singularly like that of Britain: she must export or die.

Finally, the growth of the tension between the United States and Russia has made Japan an American ally, an island outpost off the eastern edge of the Communist land-mass, somewhat as Britain is an island outpost off the western edge. If Japan is to be an effective ally, the United States must find a way to help her obtain in the free world the markets she needs. But, when the Japanese have recovered their strength, they may well renew their imperial aspirations and try once more to build up possessions outside their own

* G. B. Sansom, *The Western World and Japan* (New York, 1949), 497-498.

Republic of Indonesia. The President hands the Holy Flag to an honor guard celebrating independence day.

islands. It may be that old imperial powers like France and Britain are cured of imperialism, though to date they have given up overseas lands only with great reluctance. But it would seem most improbable that a country like Japan, new at the imperial game and in the early part of the first round most successful at it, should naturally give it up.

Southeast Asia

As in the rest of the Far East, spectacular changes took place in Southeast Asia after World War II. In this area, reaching east from India and south from China through the islands of the East Indies, the first war and the twenty years' truce of the 1920's and 1930's witnessed few conspicuous changes. But good observers noted the slow growth of nationalist opposition to the French in Indo-China and to the Dutch in the East Indies. They saw that the British-controlled Malayan Peninsula, with its characteristic colonial economy of rubber and tin production, was peculiarly dependent on the economic health of the western world.

Then came World War II, attendant occupation by the Japanese, and a really major political explosion. The white masters had been beaten by Asians; their magic invulnerability was gone. The Japanese themselves, though behaving like a new master race, had to set up native puppet governments, at least for political purposes. The natives were broken in to governing. When the Japanese were beaten, the western powers were by no means able to pick up where they had left off. Moreover, American influence against the perpetuation of European colonialism was particularly strong in this region. American emotions and interests had been engaged in the Far East since the days of the clipper ships; now the United States was in the process of granting independence to its own imperial wards, the Filipinos. In the years after World War II, consequently, the Netherlands East Indies obliged the Dutch to give them independence; they became the Republic of Indonesia. Britain gave Burma independence and in Malaya made conces-

624

sions toward eventual self-government. The French made similar concessions to the constituent states of Indo-China, but they did not go far enough or fast enough to prevent a chronic Indo-Chinese war, in which the native rebels got Chinese Communist support.

This major political revolution has by no means solved the problems of Southeast Asia. One great problem is economic. This area, so long cast in the colonial role of producing raw materials, will find it hard to achieve economic independence without western assistance. Politically, it is natural that many of these peoples should suspect the aid offered by their former masters; yet if they do not take it, they may simply drift into economic chaos and facilitate their own capture by another set of imperialists, the Communists.

This takes us to the second great problem, which is of course political. In 1954 it was not yet clear that the new nations of Southeast Asia could establish stable governments and maintain themselves in the face of Communist infiltration. Moreover, in the summer of 1954 the French, increasingly hard pressed in Indo-China, agreed to partition Viet Nam, the chief Indo-Chinese state; the northern half went Communist, and the southern half came under a weak native government. Thus the possibility of Communist expansion into Southeast Asia, which had already threatened Burma, Malaya, and the Philippines, became a reality.

III: The Indian Subcontinent

In India, World War I was a very crucial turning point. India made important contributions to the British armies; indeed the British victory over the Turks could not have been achieved without the Indian army. Her educated classes, growing in numbers, and by now exposed for more than a century to the kind of ideas we may call liberal, progressive, democratic, got the full impact of Allied propaganda in favor of the war to save the world for democracy; monetary inflation and other war dislocations favored the growing agitation for self-government. Already in the war period the British Viceroy, Lord Chelmsford, and his experts, both British and Indian, were working toward a plan for reform. Public opinion not only in India but throughout the world was sharpened in favor of the Indians by what seemed to be a throw-back to the crude days of imperial force when, in April, 1919, at Amritsar, the British General Dyer ordered his troops to fire on unarmed Indians during a mass demonstration, killing nearly four hundred of them.

One basic fact about India, then, was the long and relatively serene British rule, with its attendant slow but steady acclimatization of Indians to western material things like railroads and hospitals and to western ideas like progress and equality. In addition, there were three other striking factors in the situation of the Indian subcontinent. These were Hindu-Moslem tension, the unique Hindu way of life, and the immense problem created by a large and increasing population.

Hindu-Moslem Tensions

A large Moslem minority had grown up in the seven hundred years since the first invasion of India by Moslem peoples. In the Indus Basin and part of the Punjab in the northwest, and in part of Bengal in the east, the Moslems were actually a majority; elsewhere they lived scattered among the Hindus and other non-Moslems. In India, though some of the native rulers and their aristocracies are Moslems, the bulk are peasants, and on the whole the Moslems have been outstripped industrially and financially by the Hindu community. Although some Moslems, especially in the upper classes, are proud descendants of conquering tribes, for the most part the Moslems and the Hindus are roughly of the same racial mixtures, both really native Indians indistinguishable by any clear ethnological sign.

Yet Moslems and Hindus feel—we are talking in terms of average members of the two communities—toward each other in a way exceedingly difficult for most westerners to understand. A friendly British observer has summed it up in this manner:

What are the things which keep Muslims and Hindus apart, which make them feel that they are different races and nations, which keep them permanently potentially on edge with each other? The first perhaps is the doctrinal issue of idolatry. The Muslim has borrowed from the Semitic races both his passionate rejection of polytheism and his passionate hatred of idolatry. A Muslim has not only an opinion about idolatry, but a deep-seated feeling, an instinct which affects his whole outlook on life. The worship of many gods, the portrayal of the divine in human form, is something to him which is less than human, the mark of the beast. It has, I think, no counterpart in the West; for it is far stronger than our ideas of good form or fair play or the behaviour of a gentleman. The nearest analogy in Western experience, is, perhaps, that of obscenity. The ramifications of these emotions are widespread through the whole realm of Hindu-Muslim relations because of the ubiquitous working of the Hindu doctrine of incarnation. So much in Hinduism is divine. The Muslim does not mind a Hindu not eating beef, for example, but he does object to his worshipping the cow. In times of irritation there is consequently a strong urge to kill a cow out of sheer bravado.

On the side of social custom the chief irritant among Muslims is the caste system in general and the claims of the Brahmins in particular. These claims offend the strong Muslim sense of equality and repel by their exclusiveness. The Muslim taboo of pork is another sore point in social relations, for though it is not a food of caste Hindus any more than of Muslims, its defiling effect makes it an easy subject for provocation. So, too, does the Muslim prohibition of music in worship. Pork in the mosque or music outside are certain ways of provoking a Hindu-Muslim riot.

But the mental anguish of mutual relations is not all on the Muslim side. Hindus suffer acutely in the ceremonial sphere. Hindu feelings about the cow are as untranslatable into Western terms as are Muslim feelings about idolatry, and they are no less strong. A Hindu may literally turn sick at the sight or smell of beef. Muslim practice in the matter of food seems to the typical Hindu to be impure, dirty, and degraded, something beneath the level of man. He cannot understand, on the other hand, what he calls Muslim fanaticism on the subject of idolatry. Orthodox Hindu and Muslim individuals can be, and often are, very good friends, but they usually take good care that their intercourse avoids these danger areas. The mined waters of the Indian social ocean are numerous and intricate and by no means clearly buoyed, and it is no wonder that not only the oblivious European, but sometimes Indians themselves suffer sudden shipwreck therein.[*]

It is not surprising, therefore, that after serious attempts to bring Hindu and Moslem into a unified resistance movement against the British, two separate bodies grew up in the twentieth century—the Indian National Congress and the All-India

---

[*] Percival Spear, *India, Pakistan, and the West* (London, 1949), 89-91.

CHAPTER XXIX

Indian village. Boys' school in background, village elders sitting in the center.

Moslem League. Immediately after World War I the two bodies collaborated to the extent of assigning each other quotas in the constituent assembly for which they were agitating. They did often succeed in presenting a common front against the British, but as time went on their mutual opposition, indeed their irreconcilability, tended to increase rather than diminish.

The Hindu Way of Life

A second unique element in the situation in India was—and is—Hinduism, the immensely complex, millennially old way of life for which the word "religion," in its western sense at least, is not ade-quate. Hinduism has no church organization in the Christian sense, no clear-cut theology, no established Bible. Of the three major developed ways of life or cultures that the West has encountered in its expansion over the world, Hinduism is furthest from ours, and the hardest for us to come to working relations with. In comparison, Islam is actually a relative of Christianity, for both have common Hebrew and Greek origins. And Chinese society, in spite of its quite un-western family structure, has affinities with what one may call the utilitarian or worldly strain in the West.

In this book we cannot even scratch the surface of the subject. We can only note that for Hinduism this world of sense-experience is an illusion, but an illusion that

Indian farmers.

has somehow to be overcome. Death is essential to the overcoming, but death is not enough. Each living man, indeed each living thing, is a soul alienated by the very fact of living from the ultimate, universal soul which is peace, absence of struggle and desire, ineffable non-being. The holiest of men by turning away entirely from the world, by living without desire—but not by any such simple solution as suicide—can perhaps attain this non-being in the end. But most human beings are now living out in this world the consequences of a sinful life as another personality in the past. Indeed, the most sinful of men who have lived in the past have been punished by reincarnation as animals or even as insects (which is why the most orthodox of Hindus will harm no living thing). And even among men, their sins in past incarnations are reflected by their status, their *caste*. The poor, the humblest, are such because their sins have been greater; they cannot improve their lot in the western sense, for they can only slowly in subsequent incarnations re-

deem their wickedness by living as holy a life as possible.

Hindu society, with its caste system, its lack of any basis for belief in material progress and in what we call "welfare," its innumerable tabus, found grave difficulties in the way of adopting western culture. That the Hindus have adopted as much as they have is another proof of the penetrating power of the West. For instance, it is quite impossible to preserve literal untouchability in modern India. The lowest Hindu group, actually below and outside the caste system, were called "untouchables" because even their shadow would corrupt a caste-Hindu. No one can keep untouchable in an Indian railroad car. Many Hindu intellectuals have indeed been so far westernized that they have no real intellectual basis for calling themselves Hindus; but even for westernized intellectuals, and much more for the uneducated, the long accumulation of habits, feelings, and ingrained attitudes cannot be quickly altered.

CHAPTER XXIX

The Population Problem

A third and most important factor, though not unique to India, has there reached perhaps its most acute and most important manifestation. This is the pressure of population. Already noticeable in the nineteenth century, this increase of population has continued in our time. The population has doubled in the last seventy years; there are now over 350,000,000 people in India (excluding Pakistan). The law and order the British rule did achieve, the improvements in agriculture, the growth of an Indian industry, have made it possible for this population to exist, though it is often threatened by famines and by actual death through starvation. It is clear that if the Indian masses are to attain the standards of human welfare that westernization seems to make people want, India will have to solve—and not by starvation or war—her problem of population. Her citizens will have to interfere with "nature" and institute birth control, something abhorrent to the basic ways of Hinduism.

Self-Government—and Partition

In spite of all these difficulties, the Indian drive for self-government and indeed for independence went on steadily from the end of World War I to a triumphant conclusion in 1947. For the Hindus, the effective political organization of the Congress party was held together and given extraordinary influence over the masses by one of the great leaders of the twentieth century, Mahatma Gandhi (1869-1948). Gandhi was not a Brahmin (a member of the highest Hindu caste) but a member of the *bania* or shopkeeping caste. Educated as a lawyer at Oxford and therefore familiar with the West, trained during his youth in politics in South Africa with its Indian minority, Gandhi was admirably equipped

India on the brink of independence: Gandhi and crowd, 1945.

to deal with both British and Hindus. Among his own people he appealed by his simple and austere personal life, his fasts, and his exiguous native costume. He worked out the technique of insurrection called "non-violent non-coöperation," which appealed to the fundamental Hindu belief that force is illusory and therefore ineffective. Characteristic measures sponsored by Gandhi were the organized Indian boycott of British goods and the Mahatma's own resistance through hunger-strikes.

Other Congress leaders, especially at the local level, were not unwilling to use more clearly western methods of agitation, propaganda, and, it must be admitted, rather violent non-violence. Concession after concession was wrung from the British, and as the Indians gained political experience in provincial self-government and in the civil service, dominion status appeared to be just around the corner. In 1945, the election victory in Britain of the Labor party, pledged to grant India self-government, seemed to make it certain.

The hitch came when the Congress party and its Moslem counterpart, the All-India Moslem League under the able leadership of Mohammed Ali Jinnah, faced the need to make a working constitution for the new self-governing India. They found themselves up against a blank wall of complete disagreement. The Moslems had long been working for a partition into separate Hindu and Moslem states, and this was in the end reluctantly accepted by the Hindus. In 1947, Hindu India and Moslem Pakistan were set up as self-governing dominions within the British Commonwealth.

Pakistan is a state divided into two parts, widely separated by the intervening Hindu territory—the larger, West Pakistan, in the northwest, and the smaller, East Pakistan, in East Bengal (the great city of Calcutta, in West Bengal, went to India). The rest of the former British Indian Empire became by its constitution of 1950 the Republic of India. Pakistan, with its 75,000,000 people and its relatively poorly developed industry, is weaker than India with its over 350,000,000, and at first kept closer political ties with the British Commonwealth. Even India has not, however, sought like Eire to break all such ties. With an apparent lack of logic which suggests that perhaps the Indians have taken lessons from Britain, the independent Republic of India is still a part of what it calls the "Commonwealth of Nations"—without that adjective "British." Indeed, with independence a reality, Indian-British relations seem to have entered on an era of good feeling that would have been unthinkable before 1940.

The partition was not achieved without violence. In view of the way races and religions are geographically mingled in the subcontinent, it could not result in a complete separation of Hindus in one state and Moslems in another. The line of partition as drawn through the Punjab evoked bitter fighting between members of the two communities, and thousands of lives were lost. It resulted in a wholesale transfer of populations as Hindus moved from Pakistanian territory into India and Moslems moved from Indian territory into Pakistan. The refugee problem became acute in both countries, but after a few years it was reasonably well solved in both. Still a source of trouble between India and Pakistan is the mountainous region of Kashmir, which is ruled by a Hindu reigning house but has a population in the majority Moslem. The Indian army is holding it in occupation, to the great economic disadvantage of Pakistan, a nation still struggling to balance its budget. Down to 1954 efforts to arrive at a decision by plebiscite conducted under the United Nations had failed to secure the necessary approval from both parties.

India and Pakistan have at least got a start as independent nations. The radical step of partition, which in 1947 threatened to result in an immediate war between the new-born states, has at least been accepted, reluctantly by India, joyfully by Pakistan. Both have undergone some difficulties as a result of the political inexperience of their leaders, but, thanks to their British training, not on the scale apparent in some of the new nations of Southeast Asia. Both are getting down to the hard task of solving their pressing internal problems, and both have done very well in the business of international politics, where their diplomats have been busy and effective. India in particular, led by Nehru, seems to have undertaken the difficult and risky task of setting up as mediator not only between East and West, but between Communism and the democratic world. It is a task flattering to the national sense of self-esteem, and has already given the new Indian ruling class a great feeling of importance.

IV: The Near East

The European powers had a long history of trying to get an imperial stake in the Near East or Middle East—essentially Persia and the Asiatic and African portions of the decaying old Ottoman Empire. This had been true in the nineteenth century, when these lands were for the most part poverty-stricken. In the twentieth century, a new source of great wealth, petroleum, was discovered along a zone roughly corresponding to the old Mesopotamian river valley and its borderlands. The proved reserves of this region have actually been constantly increased as oil geologists have explored further, until today it is potentially the successor to the North American-Caribbean area as the richest such area on earth. Naturally this new wealth did not lessen the interest of the European powers in the region. And in the 1930's, as American experts began to worry about the exhaustion of the oil reserves of their own continent, the United States entered the Near East in something more than its older role of benevolent educator at the American colleges in Beirut (Lebanon) and Constantinople.

Political Changes Since 1918

Even before the outbreak of World War II, it was quite clear that no western state could actually hold any part of this region in crude annexation. At the end of World War I, Turkey itself, pushed back into its own national domain in Asia Minor, began under Mustapha Kemal (1881-1938) an ardent nationalist revival, greatly extending the "Young Turk" revolution initiated shortly before 1914 (see above, p. 429). The old Ottoman Empire was abolished in 1922, and in its stead the Republic of Turkey was proclaimed, which subsequently developed along true parliamentary lines. To point up the new orientation of the republic, Kemal moved the capital from Istanbul, now on the western edge of Turkish territory, to Ankara in the heart of Asia Minor. To make the population of the republic more homogeneous, arrangements were made for the emigration of the most discontented minority group, the Greeks of Asia Minor, in exchange for the transfer of Turks living under Greek rule. Kemal followed these initial steps by imposing rapid, wholesale, and sometimes ruthless measures of westernization. Women were emancipated from traditional Moslem restraints; the whole fabric of social and political life was largely removed from the age-old and highly conservative influence of Islam; even the Turkish language was modernized and written in western letters instead of the traditional Arabic script. Kemal, in short, revolutionized his country and insured its independence from the West.

The example of Turkey has been followed, though less rapidly and less effectively, by the other traditionally independent major state of the Middle East—Persia. Beginning in 1906, Persia's medieval political structure was gradually altered into the shape of a constitutional monarchy, with an elected parliament and the Shah as monarch. In 1935, to stress the break with the past, the name of the state became officially Iran. The political transition, however, was far from smooth, and the country did not adapt easily to modern western political institutions. The history of twentieth-century Iran, consequently, has been marked by political instability and violence. It has also been marked by a continuation of British and Russian competition for spheres of influence and concessions. Yet Iran has gradually managed to free herself from the most obvious forms of European imperial control.

The "succession states" of the old Ottoman Empire—Syria, Lebanon, Iraq (Mesopotamia), Arabia, Palestine, and Palestine's eastern Arab neighbor Transjordan—did not fare so well as Turkey during the years immediately following World War I. The French held mandates over Syria and Lebanon; the British, in addition to their older protectorate over Egypt, now secured as mandates Iraq, Palestine, and Transjordan (see also Chapter XXV). Only Saudi Arabia, established by Ibn Saud in the 1920's, at first enjoyed a status approaching true independence. And Saudi Arabia was essentially a medieval state, covering most of the Arabian Peninsula; Ibn Saud (1880-1953) was the patriarchal leader of the puritanical Moslem group that was known as the Wahabis.

In most of the Near East, then, during the twenty years' truce the western states had sufficient control to make possible the orderly exploitation of the oil and to keep the Arab states from fighting excessively among themselves. But all the "succession states" had political lives of their own. They all developed nationalist movements in which the usual ingredients—hatred of westerners, desire to emulate them, western education—were mixed with a common adherence to Islam and a faint but real feeling of belonging to some kind of common "Arabic" world. Palestine, of course, with its Jewish population, was an exception and a growing source of conflict with the surrounding Arab states.

The Arab states gradually won at least partial independence. In Syria and Lebanon, all through the twenty years' truce, the French clung to their mandate in the face of growing and bitter native opposition. Then in 1946, badly weakened by World War II, the French agreed to terminate their rule and to recognize the full sovereignty of both their former wards. The British followed a different policy, granting nominal independence but often retaining special military and economic rights for some time thereafter. Egypt, for example, achieved official independence in 1922, but it was not until 1954, and then after prolonged and stormy negotiations, that arrangements were finally worked out to end the strategic British privilege of maintaining troops in the Suez Canal zone. Events followed a somewhat similar course in the Kingdom of Iraq, officially freed from the tutelage of the mandate system in 1932, and in Transjordan, recognized in 1946 as the Hashimite Kingdom of the Jordan (Hashimite, from its ruling dynasty).

This rapid political survey shows that the imperial ties binding the Near East to the West have been decidedly, albeit somewhat unevenly, loosened. It points up Arab aspirations to independence as one of the most important problems confronting the Near Eastern world in the twentieth century. We may now investigate other major Near Eastern issues, all connected to some degree with the central political problem. These issues are oil, communism, the divergences among the Arabs themselves, and their hostility to the new Jewish national state of Israel.

Oil and Communism

In the last thirty years the oil resources of the Middle East have been developed by joint-stock companies with European or American capital, or both, operating under the close supervision and protection of their national diplomatic services. Westerners have not simply taken the oil, as the Spaniards took the precious metals from the New World. They have paid for it, perhaps not what they would have paid at home, but still they have paid, and at mounting rates. But as might be expected, the money that has flowed into the Middle East for oil has gone primarily to the upper or ruling classes; very little, even when it has been paid to Near Eastern governments, has gone to the masses. Native labor has certainly been paid at least at current local rates, and the western companies have maintained various social services. Still the basic fact is that oil in the Near East has enriched the few and has left the many where they were—but with the spectacle of new wealth there for all to see.

Into this situation the Russians, carrying on the old tsarist drive in the Near East, have brought communist propaganda. In spite of the general resistance that the religion of Islam seems to make to Marxist ideas, communism sometimes finds fertile soil for development. It is aided by the fact that throughout the Near East the western powers are identified as backing the ruling class, the "effendi" class. This effendi class has been most reluctant to accept the kind of gradual extension of political and economic equality, the "welfare state," that has done so much to protect the West up to now from the spread of communism and social revolution. Yet social revolution, with or without Russian inspiration, seems no more than a rather remote threat in the Middle East. In dealings with Iran since World War II, for example, the Russians have proved to have as heavy a hand with the natives, to be as crude imperialists, as any of the western nations.

Differences among the Arabs

A much more immediate danger in this region appears to be the possibility of renewed hostilities between some or all of the Arab nations and the new state of Israel. Here the Arab states, despite their much larger population, suffer from the handicap of their disunity. In 1945, Lebanon, Syria, Jordan, Iraq, Saudi Arabia, and Egypt formed the Arab League. This league does give its members some sense of common purpose, and many Arab intellectuals nurse Pan-Arabic schemes and dream of a great Arab nation united from Morocco to the Black Sea, the Caspian, and the Persian Gulf.

Realization of this Pan-Arabic dream seems a long way off. "Arabic" is a multipurpose word, clear and exact perhaps only in reference to a language; and even there it applies both to a classic written language and to many differing local dialects. Arabic may also be used to refer to a "race," or at least to a group once localized in the Arabian Peninsula. Yet the inhabitants of the "succession states" in the Near East are by no means all racially Arabic, but an extraordinary mixture developed over thousands of years of history in this racial melting pot. Finally, Arabic is not completely coincidental with Islam in the Near East. For example, about half of the population of Lebanon is Christian, though the main language spoken by the Lebanese is Arabic.

In cultural and economic life, and in political and religious attitudes, the Arabic world covers a wide range, from Saudi Arabia, where twentieth-century oil flows in a medieval land, on up to Egypt, richest and most advanced of the Arab states. In Christian Lebanon, for example, the French, now that they are gone, are fairly popular; in neighboring Moslem Syria, the departed French are considered worse than ever, if only to spite the Lebanese. In terms of religious differences, there is a great gap between the ardent Wahabis of Saudi Arabia and the relatively mild devotion of urban Egyptians, to say nothing of the decidedly modernized outlook of Turkish Moslems.

Israel

The Arab states are truly united only in their hatred of the Jews established in Israel. In 1917, Britain made the Balfour Declaration, promising to promote the establishment of "a national home for the Jewish people" in Palestine. Under the British mandate Jews from all over the world, many of them poor, but many of them with capital, came to Palestine. They built a big new city at Tel-Aviv, and with the advantage of their western capital and background they began to create new industries. Hitler's persecutions and World War II made the problem of increased Jewish immigration to Palestine critical. Britain, the mandatory power, felt obliged to protect its great interest in the Near East by cultivating the friendship of the Arab states. But within Palestine itself the flooding Jewish tide was submerging the Arabs, who had been long settled there and felt that this was *their* homeland. After the war, British troops refused entrance to shiploads of Jewish immigrants, thus further embittering the situation.

Worn out with fruitless efforts to secure a compromise, the British withdrew in 1948 and the Republic of Israel was at once proclaimed, and recognized by the United Nations. The Israelis now had to fight to maintain their new state. In the ensuing war, the total resources in manpower of the Arab states were far greater than those of Israel, but the inability of the Arabs to put a united army in the field, their military inefficiency, and the better technical equipment and morale of the Israelis resulted in victory for the Jews. A truce, but not a formal peace, was then patched up under the auspices of the United Nations. The Republic of Israel was given somewhat irrational frontiers, not including the whole of Palestine. Israel is a long, narrow strip of land along the Mediterranean coast, touching the Red Sea at the apex of a triangle, with an eastward projection taking in part of Jerusalem, the great spiritual capital of Judaism. The "old city" of Jerusalem, however, remains in the hands of Jordan and thus under the control of the Arab enemy.

In the course of the Arab-Jewish struggle, some million Arabs fled from Israel into the surrounding Arab states, which were scarcely able to absorb the refugees. This problem of the dispossessed Palestinian Arabs has, of course, sharpened the age-old hostility of Arab and Jew. Moreover, within Israel there is still a sizable minority of Moslem Arabs; their existence sets up all the problems of an unreconciled minority within the state. The partitioned city of Jerusalem has also been a bone of contention. The upshot since 1948 has been a most uneasy truce, in which a border incident might at any moment lead to another shooting war.

The Republic of Israel faces not only a grave problem in external relations but also grave internal issues, quite apart from those of the remaining Arab minority. Independent Israel has naturally continued to admit as many Jewish immigrants as possible, some of them of advanced western culture, but others, from North Africa and Arabia, still largely living in the Middle Ages. The forging of these disparate human elements into a single nationality is a formidable task. Furthermore, even with the loss of the evicted Arabs, immigration has greatly swollen the population of Israel, which now contains about a million more people than it did before World War II and in an area not much bigger than the American state of Connecticut. Much of that area is mountainous, with a thin rocky soil and inadequate rainfall, and some of it is sheer desert. The Israelis have applied talents and training derived from the West to make the best use of their limited resources, but they have not been able to attain a balanced budget and the balanced economy that would make such a budget possible. They must still depend on outside aid, especially from their many sympathizers in the United States.

V: Africa and Elsewhere

Other Non-western Peoples

Outside the Near East, India, and the Far East, there are many other areas in the world where non-western peoples are struggling with the kinds of problems that we have been considering in this chapter. On the mainland of the Americas south of the Rio Grande most of the Latin-American republics face the problem of lifting the cultures of their Indian and mixed populations to the modern western level. The Caribbean remains a problem area, beset with overcrowded islands like Britain's Jamaica and the United States' Puerto Rico. Americans, British, Dutch, and French are trying to solve the difficulties of their Caribbean possessions in a generally co-operative and democratic spirit. Since World War II the British, for instance, have made political concessions to their West Indian islands that may eventually secure them something like dominion status. Though still economically depressed, the Caribbean is by no means one of the areas where internal and external troubles are so serious that they threaten the peace of the world.

In the islands of the Pacific, the decline of the native Polynesian peoples (see Chapter XXIV) has by no means been arrested. A bright spot exists in the Hawaiian Islands, where the American melting pot seems to be working to assimilate mixed peoples into a common western culture. It is working not just among peoples of European and Negro stock, as on the American continent, but among a most extraordinary mixture of Chinese, Japanese, Polynesians, and whites. Further, the completeness of the American victory in World War II has meant that in terms of global strategy the Central and South Pacific no longer seem an immediate danger zone.

Nor in this survey of the non-western world must the U.S.S.R. be forgotten. All along the Asiatic fringes of the great land empire the Russians have to deal with non-European peoples. There are indeed some 25,000,000 Moslems in the Soviet Union. The Iron Curtain keeps us from anything like adequate knowledge of how far the Russians, too, are faced with "colonial" problems. According to Marxist theory there should indeed be no such problems, for a Marxist society by definition cannot be an imperialist society. Uzbeks, Turkmens, and the rest of Russia's Asian subjects may be perfectly contented members of the Soviet Union, feeling no hostility toward their Great Russian fellow countrymen, while the Great Russians in turn feel in no sense superior to them. But the historian is bound to express his doubts, reinforced by what we know of Russian behavior in eastern Europe since 1939, as to whether their Marxist principles have in fact given them a master key to the reconciliation of peoples once in a clearly "colonial" status.

"Black" Africa

There remains Africa. Here, too, events since 1918 have made old-fashioned imperialism, based on comfortable notions of white supremacy, very outdated. Negro Africa at the beginning of European expansion was everywhere at a far lower stage of culture, as culture is conventionally rated, than were the Chinese, East Indians, and the peoples of the Near East. It was also at a far less efficient level of economic and political organization. Yet so fast have events moved that all over Negro Africa since World War II there has been a demand for increased self-government and for fairly rapid attainment of independence.

In the mid-twentieth century the Nigeria we studied in Chapter XXIV, for instance, has reached a stage where Lugard's formula of "indirect rule" or "dual control" no longer fits. Nineteenth-century indirect rule meant that at bottom the natives would rule in those matters where traditional tribal customs still held, while whites would apply the rules of the modern world, the complex techniques of sanitation, engineering, western law, and the other western instruments. What has happened in no more than two generations is that the natives—at least the considerable minority of natives educated in western schools—now want to apply the western rules themselves. What is known as the "Africanization" of the civil service has already gone far in British West Africa, and there are already Negroes appointed to the important administrative posts of Assistant District Commissioner.

The policy does not stop with the civil service. It involves also the adoption of western parliamentary government, with elected legislatures, freedom of the press and of assembly, all the apparatus of western democracy. In the early 1950's one British possession in West Africa, the Gold Coast, obtained sizable grants of self-gov-

ernment that may eventually make it the first "black" dominion in the British Commonwealth.

The road to political emancipation in tropical Africa, however, is by no means completely smooth. The other imperial powers with colonies there—the French, the Belgians, and the Portuguese—have lagged behind the British in the matter of political concessions. And even in the Gold Coast, where the advance has been rapid, a native publicist asserted in 1950 that the prospect of dominion status was "outmoded" and that his people were "clamouring for complete national independence now. Now. Now." Furthermore, tensions have arisen in "black" Africa between the educated natives of town and city and their fellows of the tribal villages. To the villagers the Negro civil servant who has risen in the service is often a most objectionable character, a man who is blocking the advancement of his fellows.

Finally, in a society still economically colonial—that is, with raw materials still produced by a labor force barely emancipated from slavery or something like it, still uneducated and with very low standards of living—there is a real danger that political reform will get ahead of economic growth. The politically emancipated masses under these conditions then become ripe for agitation that is bound to look communistic, and indeed often is communistic. Since World War II the British have met this experience not only in West Africa but in the rather comparable colony of British Guiana in South America. Naturally it has led the home government to slow up the process of political emancipation and sometimes to withdraw concessions already made.

The possessions of the European powers in tropical Africa, it should be remembered, are not colonies of settlement. The whites are there in a tiny minority as administrators, missionaries, plantation owners, entre-

Self-government in British Africa. Opening of the legislative assembly in the Gold Coast, 1954.

preneurs in the export-import business. Few of them have settled as farmers or set up in small businesses or the professions. It is hard to conceive that in our time the whites will voluntarily withdraw entirely from tropical Africa. But it is quite conceivable that they and their home governments will have to consent to the establishment of Negro republics which will have in the community of nations something like the status of present-day republics in Central America.

"White" Africa

Over the past century or so, the whites in Africa have pushed northward from the Cape of Good Hope for several thousand miles as true settlers. On the plateaus and highlands of South and Central Africa they live—or try to live—as their more fortunate fellow Europeans who settled the relatively empty continents of North America and Australia live. They have tried to make new homes as farmers, grazers, businessmen, professional men. But there is this great difference: in South and Central Africa they have not been able to push aside the natives, as Americans pushed aside the Red Indians, and as the Australians pushed aside the Blackfellows.

Everywhere the whites are in a minority. Everywhere, though in a few regions they have adopted the nineteenth-century

American method of putting the natives in "reservations," they have for the most part used the natives also as a cheap labor force on farms and in mines. The living conditions of the black masses were and are bad, as in the fearful Negro slums around the South African metropolis of Johannesburg. But what happened everywhere else, except among the Polynesians, happened in South and Central Africa: the native population has increased substantially in numbers.

Kenya. Young Kikuyu suspected of Mau Mau terrorism.

Kenya

We may take as one example a region very much in the public eye in the mid-twentieth century. This is Kenya, a British crown colony in East Central Africa. Kenya is on the Equator, and is therefore at first sight a tropical area and should not be a colony of settlement. But through it runs the mountain spine of Africa, and though at lower altitudes Kenya is quite unsuited to white settlement, there are in the interior thousands of square miles of rolling grass and forest lands with an excellent climate for Europeans. As late as the 1890's, this was still explorers' country, dan-gerous country. But slowly the British penetrated, army first, engineers and railway builders right behind. Realizing this was white-man's country, the British government followed ample imperial precedent and decided to reserve some five million acres for European settlement. The Europeans have come, a few tens of thousands of them, and largely with native labor have developed big farms.

There remain something over five million natives in Kenya. Some of them are in the regions unsuited to white settlement; there the problems are basically those of the rest of tropical Africa. The natives in the highlands, however, were pushed aside into native reserves that they have now outgrown. The lands that they sold to the British they could not have realized they were alienating forever, for their whole land system was quite unlike the white man's. (This is a familiar pattern in American dealings with Red Indians, too.) The natives have made extraordinary progress in fifty years. Now they too want *tyledees* (title deeds); they want the land back.

The main native tribe in the highland regions, the Kikuyu, has responded to the growing pressure in a way that has struck fear into the hearts of Europeans everywhere in Africa. They have developed a secret society known as the Mau Mau into an instrument of terror directed not only at the whites but at the more peaceful and conservative of their own fellow tribesmen. There is no doubt that the Mau Mau are a minority among the Kikuyu, a daring and fanatical minority capable of the most cruel deeds, and their goal is the extermination or at least expulsion of the whites. There is no doubt that some Kikuyu are honestly opposed to the methods and ends of the Mau Mau. But, though precise information is lacking, it may well be that the Mau Mau are working toward a nationalistic goal approved by many of their fellow countrymen.

It must be added that some white observers believe the Kikuyu majority opposes the Mau Mau, and is held down only by fear.

Among uneducated tribesmen the Mau Mau cannot use the methods of direct propaganda familiar among pressure groups in the West. What they do is spread terror by murder, not only of occasional isolated white farmers, but of their own tribesmen who stand against them. Here we may see the great difficulty of eliminating in a few years customs and folkways of old standing. The Mau Mau forces reluctant fellow tribesmen to take an oath backed by full tribal fear of the gods of the oath; if a man goes back on the oath, the Kikuyu believe, the gods will take vengeance not only on the foreswearer himself but also on those closest to him, his family. Many moderate Kikuyu have indeed been emancipated on the surface from the tribal religion, but not enough at heart to risk the Anglo-Saxon procedure of reporting to the police an oath extracted from them by force. A few really convinced Christian Kikuyu have held out against Mau Mau at the risk of their lives; a few still loyal to the old pagan religion have held out quite as courageously, for they, too, are morally outraged by the unscrupulousness of the Mau Mau campaign.

Caught in the Mau Mau net, however, is the great mass of the tribe. These are the Kikuyu who are torn between the old and the new, no longer secure in the complex institutions of the tribe (primitive people have complicated, not simple, institutions), and yet by no means secure in the competitive individualistic life of the West, and indeed fundamentally handicapped in that life by the lack of economic opportunity. It is the "average" Kikuyu who supports the Mau Mau. It is the young Kikuyu who needs but cannot afford a motor bike with a seat behind for the girl whom he is courting (they did not court that way in the old days); it is the tenant Kikuyu who, lacking land of his own, sees no possibility of surviving in old age; it is the Kikuyu who wants his children to be educated but cannot afford the school fees.

A British expert who knows the Kikuyu well sums up their troubles this way:

Under conditions as they are today among the Kikuyu, young boys and girls get little of the education in behaviour, native law and custom, and character training that were all part of the organized tribal educational system. The vast majority of the boys and girls go to school; to mission schools, to government schools, and to independent schools. In all of these, owing to the shortage of fully trained teachers, and of teachers for whom their profession is a real vocation, the classes are very large. The emphasis is placed on the pupils acquiring enough book knowledge to pass examinations, so that there is all too little real education in preparation for becoming adult members of the community.

It should perhaps be stressed that the Kikuyu thirst for 'education' is insatiable. For them, the key to better salaries, a higher earning capacity, and a better chance to satisfy their needs, lies in education.

Among ourselves, a large part of the character and moral training of our children is considered to be among the normal duties of the parents—and long may it remain so. There are, too, many Kikuyu parents, especially among the genuine Christians and among those who still retain faith in their ancient beliefs, who try to train their children to become fit members of the adult community. But there are countless other Kikuyu children today for whom 'education' means only book learning and who are growing up without any real preparation for good citizenship and the responsibilities of modern life. On this failure of the education system that we have introduced, in place of the old tribal one, a heavy responsibility for the troubles of today must rest.*

Late in 1952, the Kenya government declared a state of emergency. Local police and troops were called out, and help was flown from Britain. Yet two years later order was by no means fully restored, for

* L. S. B. Leakey, *Mau Mau and the Kikuyu* (London, 1952), 76-77.

the Mau Mau terror feeds on underground methods. The immediate crisis was, however, surmounted, and the Kenyans were once more calling attention to the tourist attractions of this temperate zone on the Equator and to its economic opportunities.

South Africa: Racial and National Tensions

In the long run, what happens in Kenya, and in the regions to its south and west—Tanganyika (old German East Africa), Uganda, and Rhodesia—will be powerfully affected by what happens in the Union of South Africa. The Union, the oldest seat of true white settlement in Africa, is technically a self-governing, indeed independent, member of the British Commonwealth of Nations. It could therefore be included in the subsequent section of this chapter dealing with that Commonwealth. But actually South Africa is, as we have seen in Chapter XXIV, by no means the kind of colony of settlement that the other dominions, the United States, and even the republics of Latin America are. The Union is today the most dramatic center of race conflict, the place where the old, unregenerate feeling of white supremacy comes up most clearly against subject peoples already stirred by western institutions, western machines, western ideas and ideals.

According to the census of 1951, there were in the Union of South Africa over 10,000,000 non-Europeans and a little over 2,500,000 Europeans, a ratio for the whole Union of four non-Europeans to one European. The non-Europeans include eight and a half million Bantu Negroes, nearly a million and a half "Colored" persons—that is, of mixed European and non-European blood—and 365,000 Asians, mostly Indians. The census, no doubt for reasons of political tact, does not break "Europeans" down into

"British" and "Afrikaners" (the older term for these descendants of the Dutch and Huguenots was "Boers"). Political parties in South Africa, however, are organized by nationality, and to judge by party votes the Afrikaners outnumber the British everywhere in the Union except Natal.

These five elements—Afrikaner, British, Bantu, Asian, Colored—exist as quite self-conscious, propaganda-making groups, sometimes mutually exclusive in their aims. Their practice is not quite so extreme as their claims. They do indeed live in some sense together; to date, at least, life goes on in South Africa without actual civil war or revolution. Not even the Afrikaners, the most ardent believers in racial superiority, can bring themselves to undertake the extermination of Bantus and Colored. The cynic might add that the Afrikaners without the blacks would have to do a lot of unpleasant work that the blacks now do for them. But the difficulties of South Africa go deeper into the human heart than economics can ever go.

Events moved fast in South Africa after World War I. South African nationalism was flattered by the mandate for the former German Southwest Africa, entrusted by the League of Nations to the Union. This barren and semi-desert land was annexed to the Union in 1949 after the South African government refused to transfer its League of Nations mandate into a United Nations trusteeship. Politically, Southwest Africa supports the Nationalist Afrikaner party, since it has attracted Afrikaner rather than British immigrants.

During the 1930's, as Hitler gained ground in Europe, Afrikaners seized upon Nazism as a consolation for themselves and as a welcome stick to beat the British with. In World War II, the Union came close to declaring its neutrality, as many Afrikaners would have wished; and its actual participation was comparatively limited. After the

Top. *Slums near Johannesburg, Union of South Africa.* Bottom. *Adderley St., Capetown, Union of South Africa.*

641

war, the gap between British and Afrikaner increased; in the province of Natal, the only one where the British are in a majority among the whites, there were vigorous threats of secession from the Union.

This Afrikaner-British hostility, this return after the hopeful first years of the Union to the emotions that made the Boer War, is puzzling. If ever two groups "ought" to get together against a threat to their common position, if ever adages like "in union there is strength" should have persuasive force, it is among the outnumbered Europeans facing the great mass of non-Europeans in South Africa. Yet the fact is that in the mid-twentieth century Afrikaner and British are mutually hostile. To the Afrikaner majority, the British are not sufficiently firm toward the blacks, are too soft and "liberal." Yet the average Britisher is by no means without his sense of what he calls the "color bar," by no means anxious to turn the Union over to a black majority.

The Negroes now do not have the vote, though by the Cape Colony Constitution of 1853 they once could vote for three representatives to the colonial legislature, who had to be white. The voting rights of the colored, that is, those of mixed blood, are still debated, but the defenders of "white supremacy" are against any colored participation in politics. The Afrikaner majority is frankly segregationist.

South Africa: "Apartheid"

The developed native policy of the Afrikaners is known as *Apartheid*, literally apartness, separation. Behind *Apartheid* there is simple race prejudice of a kind quite familiar to any honest American. Yet the Afrikaners also believe, as some Americans believe, that whites and blacks can develop in separate but adjacent groups, intertwining but never mingling. They believe that the whites can dominate political life, while the blacks get some of the benefits of modern economic and technological progress, and develop their own professional classes, their own schools and hospitals, their separate quarters in the cities to which all but Negro domestic servants for whites will retire at night.

All this is quite familiar to anyone who knows the history of race relations in the United States. But in South Africa the policy of *Apartheid* is more rigorously separatist than the corresponding policy of segregation in the United States. It seems at the moment to be tightening, whereas segregation in the United States has appreciably loosened in the course of the twentieth century. Above all, *Apartheid* is set as an aim in a land where, unlike the United States, the blacks outnumber the whites at least four to one.

It is quite clear that the South African non-Europeans, and especially the great Bantu majority, do not accept *Apartheid* as a blueprint for the future. Their extremist leaders, like the Mau Mau in Kenya, would like to get rid of the whites, and of Asians too, would like to sweep them out of South Africa altogether. Again, we cannot be sure what the ordinary South African Negro wants. The Negroes are by no means a unified group in terms of sociological analysis. Some of them are still on reservations, still living under tribal law and custom, though not beyond the penetrative power of western gadgets and western ways. Some very few of them, under missionary influence, have acquired an education and substantially middle-class status. The great majority are little better than slaves; they are farm workers and domestic help in rural regions, or are gathered into great slum compounds from which they emerge to work for business and industry.

642

VI: The British Commonwealth

Within the British Commonwealth, aside from South Africa, domestic history has produced no striking novelties since World War I. In New Zealand, smallest of the dominions, the advance of social legislation has continued, capped as early as 1941 by a national scheme for socialized medicine, anticipating that of the mother country by several years. New Zealand still has a partly colonial economy, exporting wool, frozen meat, and other raw materials, and importing finished goods, still for the most part from Britain itself. But it has enough home industry to preserve its self-respect. Its original native population of Maoris is no longer declining in size, and has risen from a low point of 40,000 in the 1890's to over 100,000. The islands with their 100,000 square miles are not yet crowded by their 2,000,000 total population, and the Maoris are by no means in the position of straitened peoples like the Kikuyu in Kenya, or the Navahos in the United States. They have produced military and political leaders and professional men, and seem to be in the midst of as successful a process of peaceful and dignified westernization as has yet been recorded.

Canada

Canada is in the mid-twentieth century in the midst of an economic boom exceeding even that of the United States, and supported to a large extent by American capital. She has enjoyed extraordinary political stability, chiefly under the Liberal party, but with a solid and unembittered Conservative opposition. The "Americanization" her United Empire Loyalists have so long worried about has certainly gone on apace. No American traveler in Canada really feels himself in a foreign land, unless he hunts down a very remote French-Canadian village. Yet there are subtle and important differences between the United States and Canada. A gifted Canadian novelist has his American businessman, Lassiter, attend a lunch with Canadians in a small Ontario town:

When he reached the hotel for lunch he found the hall crowded with local business men, and then he remembered he was supposed to be an honored guest at the Rotary Club that day. He went upstairs to his room and washed. When he came down he heard the buzz of conversation, and listening to some of it he gathered that the news in the papers that morning had been worse than usual, for they were all talking about Hitler. They were so similar in appearance to Rotarians in any old-fashioned town in New England that he was somewhat startled to hear one of them remark to another that in politics the Americans were children and always would be, and that there was no point in anyone expecting Roosevelt to make them internationally responsible over night.

Lassiter grinned and turned to a man he knew. 'I wish you'd hurry up and join the States,' he said. 'Then maybe a guy like me could know where he stands. Right now I feel as if I were looking at a state of the Union just enough out of focus to make me feel cross-eyed.' *

Economically, Canada is pretty well integrated into the American system, and is a part of the "dollar bloc," not of the "sterling bloc." It is, contrary to an opinion not still wholly rooted out of the American mind, in no sense "ruled" by Great Britain. Canada is, in short, an independent state tied to Great Britain by no juridical bonds, though an active and loyal member of the British Commonwealth of Nations. Those who determine her national consciousness by no means feel themselves a mere ap-

---

* Hugh Maclennan, *The Precipice* (New York, 1948), 88-89.

pendage of the United States, but think of themselves rather as an influential and independent mediator between the United States and Great Britain.

It is true that Canada is not all of one piece. The French Canadians, who are increasing in numbers slightly but not overwhelmingly faster than the rest of the Canadians, still speak their own language, and still in their Province of Quebec possess special privileges for which the United States has no parallel. There are French Canadians who have the kind of irredentist nationalist feelings that elsewhere cause so much trouble. To judge by the extremist French-Canadian periodical press and by some campaign speeches, one might well believe that in Canada the problem of nationality is as acute as it is between Afrikaners and British in South Africa, or between Ulstermen and the men of Eire in Ireland. In neither world war have the French Canadians been exactly enthusiastic for the Allied cause, and in both they have had to be very carefully managed by the federal government. But the majority of French Canadians are loyal to the existing government, and anxious to work with the English-speaking majority. They cannot sensibly hope to make all Canada French; as devout Catholics, they cannot want reunion with a France that since 1789 has had so strong a republican and anticlerical cast; and from a possible partition of Canada into separate English-speaking and French-speaking nations they are held back by a fear of absorption into the United States, which they know would make an end to their special group privileges.

Australia

In Australia, there are no minority problems. The Commonwealth has had to overcome some provincial separatism, but Australian states are hardly more basically differentiated than are, say, those of the American West. Twentieth-century Australia too is in a large degree a welfare state. Organized labor has worked, as it did in England, through a political Labor party which has had its terms of power in the federal as well as in state governments. But Australia today is well short of full socialism, as might be expected from a society that was so recently a frontier society with all the individualism of the frontier.

Australia, a society even newer than the United States, has still a greater touch of frontier boisterousness. In both world wars, American troops seemed to neutral observers positively quiet and disciplined, positively devoted to spit-and-polish, in comparison with their Australian allies. The historian with a touch of irony will enjoy noting that one American trait gets quite reversed in the Antipodes. All Americans who can possibly do so like to find at least one ancestor who came to Jamestown or Plymouth or Philadelphia with the first settlers; and the extraordinary crowding of the *Mayflower* has become a national joke. The Australians, however, have no desire to go back to their first settlers, who were convicted criminals deported to what was in origin a penal settlement. It is seriously maintained in Australia that in fact these criminals did not perpetuate their stock; they all died out without progeny.

Modern Australia shares with New Zealand, however, a very serious problem indeed. The two together are but a handful of whites on the edge of a Far East with a rapidly growing population for whom there are no good lands left at home. Both have maintained rigorous policies of excluding all save white immigration. Both are relatively thinly settled, having together a population but little over 10,000,000. Both fear the rise of a power in Asia that might reach out and overwhelm them. The decisive defeat of Japan in World War II has quieted their worst fears, but the threat remains a very real one, never far from the back of their minds. In terms of international relations, this means that both must rely on the United States as ultimate defender. But this by no means implies that they will cut themselves off from Britain, a step for which emotionally and even economically they are not prepared.

The Nature of the Commonwealth

The British Commonwealth as a whole has had a very important development since 1914. Its constitutional structure was fixed in 1931 by the Statute of Westminster. And its membership was in 1947 and 1948 formally enlarged by the addition of India, Pakistan, and Ceylon, lands that are certainly not "British" or "Anglo-Saxon" in any ordinary sense of the words. In fact, India saw fit in its formal adhesion in 1950 to omit the word "British" and to join simply the Commonwealth of Nations.

The gist of the Statute of Westminster is in a preparatory report of 1926 declaring that Britain and the dominions

... are autonomous communities within the British Empire, equal in status, in no way subordinate one to another in any aspect of their domestic or external affairs, though united by a common allegiance to the crown and freely associated as members of the British Commonwealth of Nations.

That phrase "freely associated" means also "able to choose to be freely dis-associated." In other words, the right of a state to secede, which Americans fought a great civil war to decide is *not* a part of the United States Constitution, *is* a part of the constitution of the British Commonwealth of Nations. And the twenty-six counties of

Democracy in Canada. Explaining voting procedure to Eskimos in Labrador.

Southern Ireland have in effect taken advantage of this right to set up their Republic of Eire quite outside the Commonwealth.

A member of the British Commonwealth can set up tariffs against other members, regulate immigration by citizens of other states in the Commonwealth, have its own diplomatic services, make treaties with states both inside and outside the Commonwealth, raise and use its own armed forces, have its own flag, and much else. Most have in fact done these things. In short, the statement in the Statute of Westminster that these are "autonomous communities" is not mere rhetoric.

Yet surely the Commonwealth itself is not mere rhetoric, not just an imaginary entity? In juridical language, the "Crown" remains as a stated link among the dominions. But this term is an extraordinary rarefied abstraction. Canadians may dutifully put the Queen on their postage stamps. They do indeed cheer visiting British royalty; but in these days so do Americans. The Canadians now legally, and very carefully, call themselves "Canadian citizens" and not "British subjects." In India, the Crown seems to be nothing as flesh-and-blood as a Queen, but a complete abstraction.

Yet the Commonwealth has held together in two great wars, and has to date managed to retain India with its past of bitter rebellion. Perhaps nothing more than convenience and habit holds the Commonwealth together. These are, however, powerful forces, especially when they take the form of economic and strategic convenience and democratic habits. Certainly the Commonwealth rests in part on the solid foundation of mutual consent among its peoples and their practice of mutual give-and-take.

The Institutions
of the Commonwealth

The Commonwealth nations have expressed their democratic habits and traditions in the shape of actual institutions. They have a solid backlog in law, in the practice of parliamentary and party government, in education and in political ideas, in the unspoken assumptions and folkways of their peoples. This obviously applies to the older dominions, the white ones. On the surface, especially in terms of folkways, it might appear obviously *not* to apply to a country like India. Yet British ways have sunk deep roots into Indian life, especially among the new ruling classes. In this complex land, with its anarchy of tongues, English is still the common language. And the deep rooting of British ways is visible in other details. To take one example from recent history: the Indian commander of the forces supervising the repatriation of prisoners under the terms of the 1953 truce in Korea looked, to judge from the press

photographs, very much like a well-tanned English general, who might be named Cholmondely or Massingham.

The British Commonwealth has no common federal organ of government. "Imperial Federation"—a scheme for the establishment of a true federal government with executive, legislative, and judicial branches —was much talked and written about in the late nineteenth and early twentieth centuries. Nowadays Imperial Federation is hardly even seriously considered. It came to grief over many details, but at bottom over a central difficulty that was evident as long ago as the eighteenth century when moderate reformers sought a way to get the American colonists represented in the British Parliament. Equal representation of each dominion in federal organs would not do, for the power thus given the smaller ones would be intolerable to the larger. Representation on the basis of population would not do, for until 1947 it would have given too much power to Great Britain, and after that it would have given too much power to India.

The business of the British Commonwealth, however, does get done, despite the lack of formal central institutions. Regular imperial conferences among British and dominion prime ministers and their staffs, and among administrators and experts of all sorts, have become the established procedure. Such conferences are the meetings, not of mere diplomats, but of conscious political partners. Hopeful men, especially in the Commonwealth, like to believe that this rather infomal type of association not only has proved its strength but also can be expanded to include such colonies as Malaya and Nigeria when they are ready for self-government. And there are some who believe that the British Commonwealth can set a better pattern for a possible world federation than can any other scheme yet devised.

CHAPTER XXIX

VII: Conclusions

The Shrinking of Empires

In the half-century since 1900, the status of colonial peoples has altered more than in any period of comparable length since the modern expansion of Europe began in the fifteenth century. Since the end of World War II, in particular, the size of western colonial empires has shrunk dramatically. The British have given up Burma and Palestine, have emancipated India, Pakistan, and Ceylon, and have started to grant concessions elsewhere. The Dutch have given up Indonesia reluctantly, the Americans have liberated the Philippines voluntarily, and the Italians have seen the liquidation of Mussolini's African empire.

The French, next to the British the most important of colonial powers, have lost Syria, Lebanon, and part of Indo-China. But they still retain the bulk of their old imperial possessions, chiefly in Africa. Whether they will continue to do so is a question impossible to answer. Only two facts are clear. One is that native nationalist movements are growing, especially in the French North African possessions of Morocco, Algeria, and Tunisia, all influenced by the example of Egypt and by the political ferment of the Arab world. The second fact is the apparent shift of French colonial policy signalized by the announcement at the close of World War II that a "French Union" was being created to associate the mother country and her territories overseas.

For a time after 1945 it looked as though the French Union were largely window-dressing, a new term for the old French colonial policy of assimilation (see Chapter XXIV). It looked as though the French would make few real concessions to native nationalists. In 1954, however, shaken by the debacle in Indo-China, the French government indicated its willingness to consider a new status for Tunisia and Morocco, something approaching, at least part way, dominion status. For the first time it seemed possible, though not necessarily probable, that the French Union might develop along lines roughly paralleling those of the British Commonwealth.

The Near-Equality of East and West

In Asia, developments since 1900 have driven home to colonial peoples everywhere—and to the more worrying leaders of the old imperial peoples—the fact that the Japanese and the Chinese are in warfare virtually the equals of western powers, with almost equal chances of success. Witness the Japanese victory over Russia in 1905 and the damage inflicted by the Japanese on American warships at Pearl Harbor in 1941. The long centuries of European expansion since Cortés and Pizarro had indeed seen natives victorious in raids and ambushes, had occasionally witnessed defeats like that of the Italians by the dark-skinned Ethiopians at Adowa in 1896. But the rule was clear: when a western power really went to work and used its full military and economic power for the task, it could crush even the abundant manpower of the Hindus or the Chinese. Now in the mid-twentieth century, on the other hand, it is evident that non-whites can stand up in something like equal battle to whites. And the West has also experienced such effective types of resistance as the non-violence of Gandhi, the savage terror of the Mau Mau, and the guerrilla tactics of

Communist-led rebels in Indo-China and Malaya.

This dramatic equalizing, or near-equalizing, of westerner and non-westerner in the test of physical force had been long preparing. The forces that brought it about were cumulative, and go far back for their origins in the five-hundred-year record of the expansion of Europe. Most fundamental of these factors has been the education, both formal and informal, of the natives. This education gathered speed and depth as the nineteenth century wore on. It owed a great deal to the efforts of Christian missions, though toward the end of the century it became rather a secular education inspired by the deliberate efforts of the governing power. It was a most uneven process, varying with the different countries and with different social classes. Broadly speaking, however, formal education at least was almost everywhere limited to a comparatively small class among the natives. Just who should be so educated was decided by no simple formula. In India the sons of rajahs went to Oxford, but so too did bright boys from the slowly rising middle classes; and by the twentieth century western education in India itself had begun to take on something of the form of the western "career open to talents." In China, too, a somewhat similar process went on. The highly educated Sun Yat-sen used to remark with a kind of pride that sounds almost American, "I am a coolie and the son of a coolie."

Some non-Europeans turned against this western education and took refuge in a reaffirmation of the old values of their cultures. But for the most part the educated natives came to feel that their native lands could have true independence only by imitating the West, by learning from the West its industrial, technological, and military skills. The new educated classes throughout the world of western imperialism emphatically wanted independence. They were by the twentieth century revolutionists, often very well acquainted with the long tradition of revolution in the West itself, skilled technicians in the ways of revolution.

The Spread of Nationalism

The unreconstructed advocates of white supremacy made the great mistake of assuming that these nationalist revolutionaries were a totally unrepresentative minority of the native population; that the great masses, uneducated and poor, did not really follow their own native educated class but asked nothing better than to be ruled by the kindly whites. Of course the subject races have always had their quota of "Uncle Toms" (a term used as one of scorn by American Negroes for those of their number who appear too submissive toward the whites). But the "Uncle Toms" have not given the stamp to great non-western populations. The masses of people might not speak a word of their master's tongue, they might be quite illiterate in their own tongue, they might be poor indeed. Yet the urban masses, and slowly after them the peasant masses, began to share the feelings of nationalism. They began to feel that the foreigner did not belong in their country; they began to feel that, though their own educated classes might put on airs, they were on the right track. The foreigner must go.

The ripening of nationalism was greatly aided by the imperialist powers themselves. Almost everywhere they penetrated they brought enough sanitary engineering, enough medicine, enough law and order to lower the death rate and to enable the native population to grow as it had never grown before. But that very growth made more mouths to feed, and the fact of population pressure became obvious to educated and uneducated alike. Though the westerners might not in fact be numerous enough to consume a very appreciable portion of the total food supply, they were natural objects of attack from many points of view. In Kenya, for example, it was quite obvious that the whites did hold land that might otherwise feed Negroes.

Furthermore, education gave the natives some of the white man's special magic, his control over material things and over the elaborate machines of the modern world. The natives learned to handle railroad engines and automobiles, airplanes and automatic machinery. They began to learn something of the scientific knowledge and engineering skills that made these things possible. By the very acquisition of these skills, they came to feel more and more the white man's equal, less and less willing to take the subordinate position in matters of the spirit now that, in matters of the body, they were drawing even.

The Role of the West

Finally, we must again point out that the mainsprings of western culture— Christianity and the secular faiths of progress, democracy, and nationalism—provided little nourishment for imperialist policies. The West could not conceal from the educated natives its own great ethical and political writings. Indeed, it often laid before them with pride the Christian Bible, the American Declaration of Independence, the French Declaration of the Rights of Man, even the Communist Manifesto. It was hardly possible to keep on telling the natives indefinitely that "all men are created equal" really meant that "white men are created the superiors of colored men." To this great body of western democratic thought the work of the Social Darwinists and the other defenders of white supremacy was a very poor antidote indeed. In terms

of ideals and ideology, western imperialism carried within itself the seeds of its own ultimate failure.

This conclusion, however, must now be tempered a bit. In the mid-twentieth century western imperialism, though certainly in retreat, is not finished or dead. We have entitled this chapter "The Loosening of Imperial Ties," not "The Destruction of Imperial Ties." Even in terms of old-fashioned imperialism—that is, the colony in which ultimate decisions are made by the imperial home government—the British, French, Belgians, and Portuguese have great territories, notably in Africa, that are still in varying degrees of tutelage. The United States has a few Pacific outposts, Guam and the islands taken from the Japanese in World War II, that are still colonies in the old sense; and America has not yet fully solved the problem of the status of Puerto Rico. Spain and Holland have their fragments of empire.

Most colonies, and some of the newly self-governing territories, still have essentially colonial economic status; they still supply raw materials and receive finished goods. Finally, it is by no means clear that the great experiments in a new kind of tie between the western homeland and former dependencies, the British Commonwealth and the French Union, are foredoomed to failure. The loose tie that binds these groups together is not much like the old imperial tie, but it may still be sufficient to keep them together as a going concern.

In any case, it is evident that western imperialism has already profoundly changed the non-western states. Even the former imperial preserves that have won full independence have been shaped anew by the expansion of the West, the wide movements of western men, western things, and western ideas. The West will not inherit the earth; but it has already set its stamp upon the future.

Reading Suggestions
on the Loosening of Imperial Ties

Note: Some of the titles suggested for Chapter XXIV will be useful here also.

General Accounts

R. Linton, ed., *Most of the World* (New York: Columbia University Press, 1949). A good survey of the peoples of Africa, Latin America, and Asia.

E. Fischer, *The Passing of the European Age* (Cambridge, Mass.: Harvard University Press, 1943). Advances the thesis that leadership in western civilization has passed from Europe to other continents.

H. J. Morgenthau, *Politics among Nations: The Struggle for Power and Peace,* 2nd ed. (New York: Alfred A. Knopf, Inc., 1954). An excellent survey from a tough-minded, realistic standpoint.

F. S. C. Northrup, *The Meeting of East and West* (New York: The Macmillan Company, 1946). A philosophic discussion of the problems of One World.

A. J. Toynbee, *Civilization on Trial* (New York: Oxford University Press, 1948). Essays dealing with the contacts between civilizations.

Special Studies

W. M. Hailey, *African Survey,* 2nd ed. (London: Oxford University Press, 1945). Scholarly work treating the continent south of the Sahara.

A. Campbell, *The Heart of Africa* (New York: Alfred A. Knopf, Inc., 1954). The native problem as seen by a competent journalist.

R. Wright, *Black Power* (New York: Harper and Brothers, 1954). Self-government in the Gold Coast viewed by an American Negro intellectual.

L. S. B. Leakey, *Mau Mau and the Kikuyu* (New York: The John Day Company, 1954). The indispensable book on the subject.

J. H. Hofmeyr and J. P. Cope, *South Africa,* 2nd ed. (New York: McGraw-Hill Book Co., 1952); L. Marquard, *The Peoples and Policies of South Africa* (New York: Oxford University Press, 1952); G. H. Calpin, ed., *The South African Way of Life: Values and Ideals in a Multi-Racial Society* (New York: Columbia University Press, 1953). Three useful introductions to the South African problem.

G. Wint, *The British in Asia,* rev. ed. (New York: Institute of Pacific Relations, 1954). A scholarly survey.

T. G. Spear, *India, Pakistan, and the West,* 2nd ed. (New York: Oxford University Press, 1952. Home University Library); R. Symonds, *The Making of Pakistan,* 3rd ed. (London: Faber and Faber, 1951). Useful introductions to the new states of the Indian subcontinent.

W. N. Brown, *The United States and India and Pakistan* (Cambridge, Mass.: Harvard University Press, 1953). Another good introduction, with stress on the relations between the new states and the U.S.

L. Fischer, *Gandhi* (New York: New American Library, 1954. A Signet Book). A sympathetic biography.

J. K. Fairbank, *The United States and China* (Cambridge, Mass.: Harvard University Press, 1948). A most instructive introduction.

K. S. Latourette, *The American Record in the Far East, 1945-1951* (New York: The Macmillan Company, 1952); H. Feis, *The China Tangle* (Princeton: Princeton University Press, 1953). Two admirable attempts at a balanced approach to the vexed problem of U.S. policy toward China during and after World War II.

W. W. Rostow and others, *The Prospects for Communist China* (Cambridge, Mass.: Technology Press of M.I.T., 1954). An ambitious and suggestive survey of the potentialities of Red China.

E. O. Reischauer, *Japan, Past and Present* (New York: Alfred A. Knopf, Inc., 1946). A good introductory manual.

R. I. Crane, *Aspects of Economic Development in South Asia* (New York: Institute of Pacific Relations, 1954); C. Dubois, *Social Forces in South East Asia* (Minneapolis: University of Minnesota, 1949). Two good works laying the foundation for an understanding of a little-known area.

C. Wolf, *The Indonesian Story* (New York: The John Day Company, 1948) and G. McT. Kahin, *Nationalism and Revolution in Indonesia* (Ithaca, N.Y.: Cornell University Press, 1952). Two useful accounts of the young republic.

The Middle East: A Political and Economic Survey, 2nd ed. (London: Royal Institute of International Affairs, 1954). A most useful reference book.

E. A. Speiser, *The United States and the Near East*, rev. ed. (Cambridge, Mass.: Harvard University Press, 1949); and L. V. Thomas and R. N. Frye, *The United States and Turkey and Iran* (Cambridge, Mass.: Harvard University Press, 1951). Two useful introductory accounts, with stress on the relations between the Near Eastern states and the U.S.

G. Lenczowski, *The Middle East in World Affairs* (Ithaca, N.Y.: Cornell University Press, 1952). An informative survey.

H. A. R. Gibb, *Islamic Society and the West* (New York: Oxford University Press, 1951). A study of the western impact on the Moslem civilization of the Near East; by a great authority on the subject.

E. A. Walker, *The British Empire: Its Structure and Spirit* (New York: Oxford University Press, 1943); and W. K. Hancock, *Empire in the Changing World* (New York: Penguin Books, 1943). Two good older accounts.

G. Grady, *Democracy in the Dominions*, 2nd ed. (Toronto: University of Toronto Press, 1952). Attacks an important subject seldom treated: the comparative institutional history of the various dominions.

M. Wade, *The French-Canadian Outlook* (New York: Viking Press, 1946). Perceptive study of a point of view generally ignored, even in North America.

Historical Fiction

A. Malraux, *Man's Fate* (New York: Modern Library, 1936). Excellent novel about Chinese Communist revolutionaries in the 1920's.

A. Paton, *Cry, the Beloved Country* (New York: Charles Scribner's Sons, 1948). The famous novel about the plight of the South African Negroes.

R. Godden, *Breakfast with the Nikolides* (Boston: Little, Brown & Co., 1942) and *The River* (Boston: Little, Brown & Co., 1946). Two sensitive novels about India by an Englishwoman.

Nayantara Saghal, *Prison and Chocolate Cake* (New York: Alfred A. Knopf, Inc., 1954). Informative novel about India by an Indian.

The
Second
World War
and After

CHAPTER XXX

*Hiroshima, a year
after the atomic
bomb hit.*

I: Introduction:
The Nature of the War

THE FIRST WORLD WAR of our
century had, in its main theater, the Western Front, been one long siege. Since even
the military experts tended to fight it over
and over again, both France and Germany
in the 1930's built two confronting lines of
fortifications on their common frontier.
The Maginot Line, on the French side, and
the Siegfried Line, on the German, were
far more formidable than the improvised
trenches of the war of 1914-1918. So it is
not surprising that on the outbreak of hostilities in September, 1939, most people
expected first, that the war would be
decided primarily in the area between
France and Germany, and second, that it
would be a closely confined war of siege in
the West, with at most diversional activity
in other parts of the world.

But the war itself showed once more the
perils of prediction in great human affairs.
As Germany was joined by her Axis
partners, Italy and Japan, this second world
war became much more truly a world war
than the first had been. It was decided in
Russia, in the Pacific, even in the Mediterranean, quite as much as in the West. And
it turned out to be one of the most extraor-

653

dinarily open wars of movement in history.

It was also a war in which for the first time the airplane played a major role, a role foreshadowed in the fighting waged in Ethiopia and Spain during the 1930's. Over the water, the airplane, both land-based and carrier-based, soon established itself as a central factor in naval warfare; in the opinion of many experts, it had made the great warship obsolete. Over the land, the airplane soon established itself as an essential arm of the fire power of land armies, an arm that needed and in the end got careful integration with the ground forces. But even in this war the airplane did not live up to the advanced billing given it by its more imaginative proponents; it did not become the sole means of warfare, superseding all others. Air power by itself proved inadequate in the great test of 1940, when the Germans tried to reduce Britain from the air.

Aerial bombardment—toward the end of the war carried on by German pilotless aircraft and rocket missiles—did indeed bring the horrors of warfare back to the civilians of the cities. Military experts had been inclined to believe that civilians could not possibly stand aerial bombardment, and that any country whose cities were subject to a few such bombardments would be obliged to sue for peace. Yet European and Asian civilian populations proved able to stand up to months of bombardment. German civilian deaths from air bombardment have been estimated at about 500,000. Organized systems of shelter, partial dispersal of populations, the obvious but not previously noted fact that much of the space of modern cities is made up of streets, parks, gardens, churches, and other public buildings not used at night (when much of the bombing was done)—all combined to make it possible for the people of heavily bombed cities like Berlin and Tokyo to endure what were in effect front-line conditions.

Yet at the very end of the war a technical innovation was introduced that may indeed have altered radically the character of war, may indeed make any future war so unendurably destructive that it will at least be brief. This was the atomic bomb, developed in secrecy by American and British experts, and first used on the Japanese city of Hiroshima on August 6, 1945. A single bomb destroyed something over half the city. Somewhat less material damage was done by a second and somewhat different bomb dropped on Nagasaki, a hilly city, three days later. But over a hundred thousand people were killed in the two cities by the two bombs, an incidence of death that seems to justify fully the fears that the atomic bomb and its still more frightful successors have roused in our generation.

II: Early Successes of the Axis

Polish and Finnish Campaigns

The first campaign of World War II reached a by no means unexpected conclusion. No one had seriously supposed that isolated Poland could possibly stand up for long against the German armed forces, or that Britain and France could possibly get into action rapidly enough to help their Polish ally decisively. Yet the speed of the German conquest surprised almost everyone. The German air force, the *Luftwaffe*,

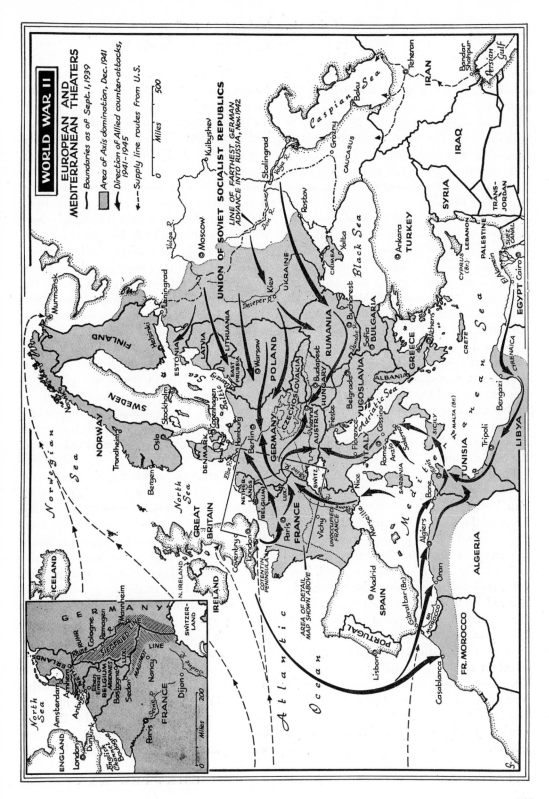

soon gained absolute command of the air, and used it to disrupt Polish communications and to spread terror with its dive bombers. Special German task forces, fully motorized, swept through and around the more primitively armed Poles. This was what the Germans called a *Blitzkrieg,* or lightning war. The German word was later simplified by the English into "blitz," and was used by them to apply to the German air bombardment of Britain in the years 1940-1941.

So rapid and successful was the German conquest of Poland—it lasted less than four weeks—that Hitler's new collaborator, Stalin, seems to have taken alarm. Stalin hastened to push the Russian armies in from the east on the helpless Poles. He also established Russian military bases in the Baltic republics of Estonia, Latvia, and Lithuania, which had been created out of Russian provinces at the close of World War I. "Mutual assistance" pacts between giant Russia and the tiny Baltic states were to be the entering wedge for their full occupation by Russia in 1940 and their amalgamation, as constituent republics, into the Soviet Union.

Fear of Germany, or an imperialistic desire to expand, or both, also drove the Russian leaders into a war with Finland for bases in the Baltic (November, 1939). The Russians, who had perhaps miscalculated the strength of their little opponent, did rather badly at first. By March, 1940, however, they had worn down the Finns; they secured their bases and annexed Finnish lands very close to the great Russian city of Leningrad. It seems quite possible that this "winter war" with Finland had a major effect in encouraging Hitler to his fateful decision of 1941 to make war on Russia. The German military experts drew from Russian difficulties in this war conclusions extremely disparaging to Russian capabilities.

"Phoney War" and Blitzkrieg in the West

Meanwhile in the west what the British called the "phoney war" was pursuing its uneventful course. The French and the British duly mobilized as in 1914, and as in 1914 the British sent a few divisions to the Continent. But the Germans refused to repeat the pattern of 1914. Occupied in Poland, they did nothing in the west. Occasionally a French patrol from the Maginot Line would exchange shots with a German patrol, but for the most part the troops ate, slept, and went on leave as though they were merely in training. French and British cities, ready for the enemy air attacks, waited tensely for the first few weeks, and then relaxed. War production was indeed speeded up in both countries, and in Great Britain it is quite possible—so close was the Royal Air Force to the exhaustion of its fighter planes in the summer of 1940—that these months of opportunity to go ahead at full speed with the production of airplanes made the ultimate difference between defeat and victory.

The Germans, however, had no intention of sitting out a defensive war in the west. But not even modern warfare is wholly emancipated from the weather. The German general staff was not prepared to begin a decisive campaign in the west with the winter ahead. They waited until spring, and in April they made sure, as they had not in 1914, of their northern flank by making a sudden sea and air invasion of Denmark and Norway. Denmark, totally unprepared, was occupied almost without resistance. Norway, also unprepared, made a brave showing. But neither the British nor the French were able to help her with more than token forces, and by the end of April important Norwegian resistance was broken. The Germans now had ad-

Churchill at a steel plant.

mirable bases for air and submarine action against the British.

The great blow was struck, without warning, on May 10, 1940, when the German armies, brilliantly supported in the air, invaded the Low Countries. Holland, spared in 1914, was this time invaded so that the Germans might make doubly sure of their northern flank. A carefully planned attack on the key Belgian fort of Eben Emael, an attack that had been carefully rehearsed on a dummy of the fort set up inside Germany, was at once successful, and opened the way into the Low Countries. In the era of weakness in the 1930's, both the Belgians and the Dutch had been extremely anxious to avoid compromising themselves by planning for joint resistance with Britain and France against a possible German attack.

The failure of Britain and France to secure effectively this northern flank was a major factor in the German success. Indeed, though much has since been written against the "Maginot mentality," it is a fact that the Germans did not take the Maginot Line by frontal assault, but outflanked it at the critical point where it tapered off along the Franco-Belgian border in the hilly region of the Ardennes. Through the Ardennes the Germans poured their best motorized troops into France. In a Blitzkrieg that once more capitalized on the "lessons of 1914," the Germans resisted the temptation to turn at once on the prize of Paris, but instead drove straight through northern France to the Channel, where the port of Boulogne fell on May 26, a little over two weeks after the start of the campaign. By this stroke the Germans separated the British, Belgian, and part of the French troops from the bulk of the French armies to the south. The British had reacted at once to the German attack by replacing Neville Chamberlain with Winston Churchill as prime minister, and shortly afterward the French replaced General Gamelin with General Weygand as commander-in-chief.

The new leaders, in a desperate last moment, attempted to work out a plan for pinching off the adventurous German motor-

Hitler's elation after the armistice with France, 1940.

ized thrust by a concerted attack from north and south. But the Belgians, badly disorganized, decided to capitulate, and neither the French nor the British could rally themselves to carry out the movement. In the last days of May and the first days of June the British did indeed achieve the miracle of the successful withdrawal of some 215,000 British and 120,000 French soldiers by sea from the beaches around Dunkirk at the northern tip of France. With useful protection from the Royal Air Force, an extraordinary flotilla of all sorts of vessels, including private yachts and motorboats, got the men off, though almost all their equipment had to be abandoned. Dunkirk was a courageous action, and one that did much to help British morale. But from German documents that fell to the Allies after the final defeat of Germany it is pretty clear that the miracle of Dunkirk was possible only because Hitler himself decided not to press home the destruction of the British forces penned on the coast, on the ground that Britain was no longer a real

threat. At the last moment, Hitler too gave in to the lure of Paris, and decided to push the attack on the French homeland at once. Here he was wholly and rapidly successful. The French under Weygand could not rally, and the Germans marched southward almost unopposed. The clear signal to the world that the rally of 1914 at the Marne would not be repeated was given on June 13, when the French declared Paris an "open city" and evacuated it without fighting.

"The Fall of France"

The battle of France was thus decided by mid-June. But the French might yet try to defend the south, or, failing that, use their navy and merchant marine to get as many men as possible across the Mediterranean into French North Africa. There, based on their great empire overseas, they might have continued with British aid the fight against the Germans. Some of the French leaders wished to do this, and in the crisis Winston Churchill made to the French the extraordinary offer of a complete governmental union of the two countries to continue the struggle. His offer was not accepted.

On June 16, Reynaud was supplanted by Marshal Pétain as prime minister, in what amounted to a kind of *coup d'état*. Pétain and his colleagues were determined on peace at any price, and this they got. On June 22, 1940, an armistice was signed at Compiègne at the spot where the armistice of November 11, 1918, had been signed. By this armistice the French withdrew from the war, handed over three-fifths of France, including the whole Atlantic and Channel coasts, to German occupation, and retained under strict German supervision no more than the central and Mediterranean regions. This "unoccupied France" was ruled from the little resort city of Vichy, where Pétain set up a French form of authoritarian, anti-

CHAPTER XXX

democratic state of which he was "chief." History has labeled his government simply "Vichy France."

Some few of Pétain's collaborators were undoubtedly pro-German, convinced that the German form of totalitarianism was the "wave of the future." But it is now clear that for most of them, even for men like the "collaborator" Laval, a dominant figure at Vichy, and indeed for Pétain himself, the dominant motive in those bewildering June days of 1940 was simply a desire to make terms with the inevitable. They were absolutely sure that Hitler had won the war. They did not believe that Britain had any chance of successfully resisting the German war machine that had crushed France. In this belief they were followed at first by the great majority of Frenchmen.

A few, led by General Charles de Gaulle, refused to give up. De Gaulle was flown out to London, where he set up a French National Committee of exiles, and broke off relations with Vichy. A nucleus of French soldiers who had been saved at Dunkirk and a stream of refugees who gradually assembled in England formed the "Free French" forces. In the next few months these Free French managed to obtain control of some of the French colonial empire, though not of its strongest areas in North Africa. Weak as the Free French were in these early days, they were at least a rallying point, and they were able to set up an effective radio center in England from which they conducted a propaganda offensive against the Germans and against Vichy that ultimately prepared the way for the return of France to the fight.

As with all such complex problems of historical causation, the reasons for the "fall of France" in 1940 will probably never be fully understood. We have, however, already sufficient perspective to discount somewhat the impression so prevalent in 1940 that France had really been rotten to the core, defeatist from the start, hopelessly old-fashioned in her reliance on the methods of 1914. France was indeed ill-prepared for the kind of war she got, weak especially in mechanized warfare and in the air. She was a deeply divided country, with a privileged class not really convinced that the war was necessary, and with an active communist minority which, according to the party line of 1940 after the Hitler-Stalin pact, was treasonously opposed to the war. She had been drained of strength, physical and spiritual, in the previous war. Still, the campaign of May and June, 1940, was not quite hopelessly one-sided. The defection of the Belgians, the weakness of the northern end of the Maginot Line, the failure of the French Ninth Army directly opposed to the German drive through the Ardennes, the thousand accidents of specific engagements in the fatal three weeks, must all be taken into account in explaining the military defeat of 1940.

On June 10, Hitler's ally Mussolini had brought the Italians into the war against France and Britain, too late to affect the outcome of the battle of France. But this "stab in the back" further outraged American opinion, already alarmed by the Nazi successes. And Italy was now irrevocably engaged in the struggle, anxious to secure some kind of success that would offset the great gains of her German ally. The war, until now confined to northern and western Europe, now spread to the Mediterranean.

The Battle of Britain

The Germans, for all their miracles of planning and execution, had not really worked out a way to deal with Britain. Hitler seems to have believed that with France out of the war Britain would see the light and make a separate peace, a peace of compromise in which Germany would dominate the continent of Europe

London during the "blitz."

and Britain would continue satisfied with her overseas empire. This division of the spoils, Hitler reiterated in public and private, should be eminently satisfactory; he did not threaten the British Empire. Yet for over four centuries Britain had gone to war rather than accept the kind of one-power domination over western and central Europe that Hitler exercised after the fall of France. The British, therefore, paid no attention at all to his peace feelers.

Hitler was counting heavily on the possibility that German submarines could eventually cut off British supplies of food and raw materials from overseas, and thus starve her into submission. But at best this must take a long time, and Hitler was impatient. The obvious thing to do was to attempt a landing in England. But the Germans had made no real preparation for amphibious warfare; they had no specially designed landing craft. Moreover, the German air force and the German navy were at odds over the best way of combining for an invasion across the Channel. A hastily assembled flotilla of miscellaneous vessels was badly damaged by British aircraft, and early in August, 1940, Hitler and Goering,

his air marshal, made the fateful decision to try to do the job from the air.

The Battle of Britain that followed had two main phases. First, in August and September the Luftwaffe attempted in daylight bombing attacks to wipe out British airports and fighter planes. The Royal Air Force, admirably organized and directed, and using the detection apparatus called radar to spot the attackers early, proved just barely strong enough to check the Germans. In the critical actions of September 16, some 185 German planes were brought down, a rate of loss that Goering felt the Germans could not stand. In one of his imperishable phrases, Churchill said of the British fighter pilots, "Never have so many owed so much to so few."

The second phase began in the autumn of 1940. The Germans sought by night bombing of major British industrial centers to destroy British production and to terrify the civilian population so that the government would be obliged to sue for peace. Neither aim was successful. Even at Coventry, an important center of the automotive industry, though grave damage was done, the industry was by no means knocked out.

CHAPTER XXX

As for civilian morale, it is clear that these bombings strengthened the British will to resist. Civilian defense measures proved adequate to protect both persons and property from that extreme of destruction which might indeed have broken the will to resist. By winter, when the weather gave the British some respite, the Battle of Britain had been won.

Mediterranean and Balkan Campaigns

Hitler now faced the possibility of a long stalemate, something that conquerors like Napoleon in the past have rarely been able to face. Like Napoleon, Hitler turned at first to the obvious strategy of getting at Britain through her Mediterranean lifeline to India and the East. His ally Mussolini, already itching to expand in the Mediterranean, in October, 1940, invaded Greece from Albania—with no success. Just how far Hitler himself wanted to invest in action in this theater is not clear. Certainly he toyed with the idea of a campaign against the British fortress of Gibraltar through Spain, to be co-ordinated with Axis attacks in the eastern Mediterranean to clear that sea of the British. But the Spanish dictator Franco wanted too high a price from the French for his consent to a German march through Spain, and Hitler was unwilling to risk driving Vichy France, which still controlled French North Africa, too far. In the upshot, the Germans had to be content with backing up Mussolini in Greece and with an attack on Egypt from the Italian colony of Libya. Efforts to rouse native action against the British and French in the Near East were suppressed without grave difficulty by British and Free French action, and Turkey stood obstinately neutral.

Nevertheless, the German commitment to help the Italians in Greece took valuable German divisions away from another task in the spring of 1941, and as the Germans attempted to move overland through Yugoslavia they were involved in a costly guerrilla war. The British did their best to back up their Greek allies, but once more they were not strong enough. German air power crippled British naval power in the waters around Crete, and by June the Axis had conquered the Greek mainland and the islands.

The Invasion of Russia

The other task for which the German forces were to be used in the spring of 1941 was the conquest of Russia. Hitler had firmly resolved not to repeat what he thought was the fateful mistake of Germany in 1914; he would not engage in a war on two fronts. Yet by his invasion of Russia in June, 1941—an invasion delayed for a perhaps decisive two months by the Balkan adventure—he committed himself to just such a war. Russia was indeed a tempting goal. The Nazi plan had always looked to the fertile areas of Poland and South Russia as the natural goal of German expansion, the *Lebensraum* (space for living) of German destiny. With the precedents of successful Blitzkrieg in Poland, western Europe, and now Greece, Hitler and his military experts believed that they could beat the Russians in a single campaign before winter set in. It was quite clear that Britain was incapable of any offensive action in 1941. Although the United States was already helping the British with arms and other supplies, raising an army by conscription and strengthening its navy, it was equally clear that America could not fight effectively in Europe in 1941. An attack on Russia, then, Hitler seems to have told himself, would not really create two fronts. Indeed, once Russia was conquered, as in Hitler's mind it was sure to be, the Germans would have no trouble disposing of Britain, not even were the United States to come to her aid in a shooting war.

Russia was not conquered in 1941. But it was a very close thing, closer perhaps than the Battle of Britain. Hitler's plan almost worked. There really was a successful Blitzkrieg. Within two months the Germans were at the gates of Leningrad, and in the south they had conquered the Ukraine by the end of October. Hundreds of thousands of Russian troops had been killed or taken prisoner. In sheer distance, the German armies had pushed more than twice as far as they had in France.

Yet, as the Russian winter closed in, the Germans had taken neither Moscow nor Leningrad. Russian heavy industry had been in part transferred to the remote Urals, and existing plants there and in Siberia had been strengthened. The United States was beginning to send in supplies. The vast resources of Russian manpower were still adequate for Russian needs. The government had not collapsed, and national spirit was high. Moreover, the Germans had shown once more, as they had in the Battle of Britain, that their boasted planning was far from perfect. Their troops were not equipped to stand the rigors of a Russian winter. Confident that one summer and autumn would be enough to finish the business, the German planners had left the winter to take care of itself. Indeed, between December, 1941, and May, 1942, the Russians regained much useful ground.

American Policy

Meanwhile, the Germans had fallen into a second fatal involvement. Obsessed with what he thought were the disastrous failures of German policy in World War I, Hitler had sought to keep out of war with the United States. Although the United States had a strong isolationist party, and even a handful of Axis sympathizers, American opinion had from the very beginning of the attack on Poland in 1939 been far more nearly unanimous against the Germans and Italians than it had been against the Central Powers in 1914. With the fall of France in 1940, anti-Axis sentiment grew stronger, reinforced by a feeling that if Hitler had his way in Europe the United States would be marked out as his next victim.

Between June, 1940, and December, 1941, the Roosevelt administration, with the consent of the Congress and with the general—though not unanimous—backing of public opinion, took a series of steps "short of war" in aid of Britain and later Russia. By conventional nineteenth-century standards of international relations, these steps were far from being in accord with America's technical status as a neutral; they would have given Hitler ample justification for declaring war against the United States. The American government transferred to the British fifty "over-age" destroyers in exchange for Atlantic naval bases in British colonies, supplied the British with all sorts of arms, and used the American navy to help get these supplies across the Atlantic. Above all, in March, 1941, by the so-called "Lend-Lease Act" the United States agreed to supply materials needed for defense, including foodstuffs, to "any country whose defense the President deems vital to the defense of the United States." Supplies at once began rolling into England, and later to other allies in the struggle against the Axis, without the unfortunate complications produced by the war-debt methods of World War I.

Yet Hitler still did not let himself get involved in war against the United States.

CHAPTER XXX

He had, however, firm commitments to aid Japan. And Japan, controlled by a militarist group, had taken advantage of the fall of France and the Netherlands and the weakness of Britain to speed up vastly the policy of expansion in Asia that she had begun in Manchuria as far back as 1931. She early took advantage of the fall of France to penetrate into French Indo-China. She continued to press her campaign on the mainland of China. The American government, which had never in the days of technical peace in the 1930's been willing to accept Japanese conquests in China, did not now abandon its policy of opposition to what it considered Japanese aggression. It is indeed highly likely that had the American government been willing to allow Japan a free hand to do what she liked in the Far East there would have been no Pearl Harbor. But short of such complete abandonment of the previous American policy in the Far East, it is unlikely that the United States could have kept out of war with Japan.

Pearl Harbor and After

In the summer and autumn of 1941, the American government took steps to freeze Japanese credits in the United States, to close Japanese access to raw materials, and to get the Japanese to withdraw from China and Indo-China. Negotiations toward these ends were going on between the Japanese and the Americans when on December 7, 1941, the Japanese without warning struck with carrier-based airplanes at the American naval base at Pearl Harbor in Hawaii. Grave damage was done to ships and installations, but American power in the Pacific was by no means destroyed. And the consequence was the immediate declaration of war against Japan by the United States. Germany and Italy honored their obligations to their Axis partner by declaring war against the United States on December 11. The war was now literally a world war.

Although the United States was incomparably better prepared than she had been in 1917, she was still at a disadvantage. Against Germany she could for the moment do no more than continue, indeed increase, aid to Britain and Russia by Lend-Lease and take full part in the struggle against the German submarines. Against Japan she was almost as powerless. Her Pacific outposts of Guam, Wake Island, and the Philippines fell in rapid succession to Japanese arms. Nor could the British and the exiled Dutch governments protect their colonies in Southeast Asia. By the spring of 1942, the Japanese had taken Malaya from the British and Indonesia from the Dutch, and had virtual control of Siam and Burma. They seemed poised for an attack on Australia.

In population, resources, and actual industrial strength, Britain, the British Commonwealth and Empire, Russia, China, the United States, and the other lands of what were soon to be the "United Nations" were vastly superior to the combined forces of Germany, Italy, and Japan, even if the lands occupied by these Axis powers in the summer of 1942 are included in Axis strength. Yet the Axis seemed at that time everywhere triumphant. A wise observer, however, must have seen even then that if the coalition against the Axis could hold together, its total resources would ultimately wear the Axis down. The coalition did hold together, on the whole rather better than most such coalitions in the past few centuries of our western state-system. In three years—three short years in terms of the coalitions against such aggressors as Louis XIV and Napoleon—the Axis powers had been beaten into "unconditional surrender."

III: The Victory of the United Nations

The Turning Points

There were several turning points in the struggle. The earliest was a series of naval actions in which Japanese expansion was stopped. In these actions, carrier-based airplanes played a decisive role. On May 7, 1942, in the battle of the Coral Sea in the southwest Pacific, Allied sea and air power halted a possible Japanese invasion of Australia and its protecting islands. In June, American sea and air power dispersed a Japanese fleet that was aiming at the conquest of Midway Island. Although the Japanese landed on American territory in the Aleutians, they never seriously threatened Hawaii or Alaska.

In the West, the Americans and the British were as yet unwilling to respond to Russian pressure for a "second front" on the European mainland. But they were able in November, 1942, to effect a series of landings in French North Africa. Secret negotiations with anti-Axis elements among the French in North Africa were not completely successful, and the landings in Morocco were sharply though briefly resisted by the Vichy French. None the less, the Allies were rapidly established in force in Morocco and Algeria.

The Libyan segment of the long North African coast had been held by the Germans and their Italian allies since the beginning of the war in the Mediterranean, and there had been seesaw campaigns in these desert areas. At the time of the North African landings, the British under General Montgomery were holding a defensive line inside the Egyptian frontier, but on October 23, 1942, the British started on an offensive which was planned to co-ordinate with that of General Eisenhower, commander of the Allied forces in French North Africa,

in the classic maneuver of catching the enemy in a vise. The Germans responded quickly to the threat, and succeeded in reinforcing their African armies through Tunis, which was delivered to them by the Vichy authorities. The planned expulsion of the Germans and Italians from North Africa was thus delayed, but the vise closed slowly. In May, 1943, Free French, British, and American troops took the last Axis strongholds of Tunis and Bizerte, and accepted the surrender of some three hundred thousand Axis troops.

The North African campaign had clearly been a turning point. The Allies had successfully made large-scale amphibious landings, and they had annihilated one of the most renowned of Axis forces, commanded by one of the few German generals to strike the imagination of the world, Rommel, the "desert fox." North Africa was by no means a great central operation, but it was nevertheless a major campaign in which the Allies gained confidence and prestige.

The great turning point on land was, however, the successful Russian defense of Stalingrad, a defense that turned into an attack in the same month (November, 1942) that saw the Allied landing in North Africa. After their check in the winter of 1941-42, the Germans had turned their Russian summer offensive of 1942 away from Leningrad and Moscow, and toward the oil-rich regions of southeastern European Russia. The Germans were already beginning to suffer oil shortages, partly because of Allied bombing, but even more because, though they held the oil fields of Rumania, they simply did not have oil enough for the ravenous demands of mechanical warfare. This push toward the Russian oil fields carried the Germans a prodigious distance inside Russia, over a

Stalingrad.

thousand miles from their original starting point. But again it failed, falling just short of the really rich oil fields of Grozny and Baku. Russian distance and Russian manpower, and the Russian ability to take punishment, were too much for these over-extended Germans. Their armies were pinched off at Stalingrad, and early in 1943 the Russians started the long march that was to take them to Berlin two years later.

The Battle of Supply

A much less spectacular turning point than the engagements in the Coral Sea, in North Africa, and at Stalingrad was the Allied victory in the battle of supply. Yet this victory was of even greater importance, since naval and military successes ultimately depend on supplies. Even for Russia, an important source of supplies was the United States. But the United States was separated from its allies—and its enemies—by water, and all but the most precious and least bulky supplies, which could go by air, had to move across the seas. If the Germans could stop this movement, or even reduce it greatly, they might still be able to win in spite of the overwhelming resources of the Allies. They made important improvements in their submarines, notably the schnorkel, a device that enabled submarines to travel submerged for great distances. Submarine crews and commanders were well trained and resourceful. But there were not enough submarines, and the countermeasures of the Allies—radar, co-ordination of naval vessels and aircraft, the convoy system, and others—slowly reduced the proportion of sinkings.

Early in 1942, after Pearl Harbor, the rate of sinkings had been really dangerous, and German submarines had operated close to the Atlantic coast of the United States.

But by the end of 1942 the statistics showed a turn of the tide, and in the summer of 1943 the Allies were confident enough to announce publicly that the number of sinkings from U-boat action in the first half of 1943 was only a quarter of what it had been in the first half of 1942. Here an interesting conjecture arises: What would have happened if Hitler had had the courage, after June, 1940, to do no more than hold on with other arms, and invest all the German productive capacity in U-boats? As it turned out, the critical battle of supply was also won by the summer of 1943.

The Axis on the Defensive

In the last two years of the war, the Axis powers were on the defensive. Both in Europe and in Asia the coalition forces attacked with land forces along definite lines of march; these were "campaigns" of the traditional kind. But the way for these armies was made easier by two new factors in warfare, air power and modern propaganda, or "psychological warfare." These new methods did not "win" the war by themselves, but they were useful adjuncts, and they undoubtedly hastened the process. Air bombardment, at least until the atomic bomb at Hiroshima, was never quite the perfect annihilation that the prophets of air power had preached. The Germans put some of their key production underground. Allied "precision" bombing rarely reached perfection. But as the superior Allied air power grew, as it was used systematically to destroy enemy capabilities in critical things like ball bearings and the oil industry, and as American airplanes dropped incendiary bombs on the relatively flimsy Japanese cities, it did much to destroy the Axis will and power to resist.

On Germany and Italy the attack by land was pressed in three directions—by the Russians from the east, and by the British, French, Americans, and the smaller Allies from the south and from the west. In the south the Allies moved over to Sicily in a successful amphibious operation (July, 1943) within two months of their final victory in North Africa, and from Sicily they moved in another six weeks across the Straits of Messina to the mainland of Italy. Yet the Italian campaign was never quite the great success the Allies hoped it would be in these earlier days, and its continued prosecution was, as we shall see shortly, one of the serious sources of policy dispute between Americans and British. The Allied successes of the summer of 1943 were, however, sufficient to put Italy itself for the most part out of the war. High officers of the Italian army and others close to the king engineered a *coup* in July which brought about the fall and imprisonment of Mussolini and the beginnings of negotiations between the Allies and the new government headed by Marshal Badoglio.

But the Germans were quite unwilling to abandon the peninsula, as much for reasons of prestige as for military reasons. A detachment of German troops rescued Mussolini from his Apennine prison (September, 1943), and set him up as the head of a "Fascist Republic." The former *Duce* continued in this post until he was executed by partisans in April, 1945. Meantime, Italy had a civil as well as a foreign war on her hands. Her people were for the most part worn out and anxious for peace, but the two minorities, the Fascist-Axis group and the anti-Fascist pro-Allied group, fought on. In June, 1944, the Allies succeeded, after particularly severe fighting around Cassino, in breaking through to Rome, and by August they were in Florence. They did not really penetrate any farther until the final collapse of the Germans in the early months of 1945.

CHAPTER XXX

The Defeat of Germany

The great Allied push in the west, it was finally decided at the Teheran conference of Churchill, Roosevelt, and Stalin (December, 1943), would be in France. After meticulous preparation, the long-awaited landings in France began on June 6, 1944. The Allies had chosen the Norman coast east and west of the curve of the Cotentin (Cherbourg) peninsula near Carentan, and seem thereby to have gained some initial advantage of surprise, for the German high command believed the landings would come farther north and east along the Channel coast. The Germans had in their four years of occupancy fortified the French coastline with great thoroughness. But the Allies had also had those four years for study, invention, and planning. In the test, Allied landing craft, amphibious trucks, naval and air support—by now the Luftwaffe had almost been driven from the skies—artificial harbors, and a well-organized supply system proved sufficient to gain a beachhead for the land forces. From this beachhead, a little over a month after "D-Day," they were able to break out and sweep the Germans back across the Seine in a great flanking movement led by the American General Patton's Third Army.

A long-planned auxiliary landing on the French Mediterranean coast and a march north up the Rhone-Saône valleys was launched on August 15, 1944, and met very little resistance. Everywhere the French, by now well organized for resistance, welcomed the liberating forces, some of whom were French and French colonials fighting as heirs of the Free French of 1940. Paris, a symbol rather than a mere place, was liberated toward the end of August after its inhabitants had staged an uprising, barricades and all, against the German garrison.

The Germans were beaten, but not disorganized. In July, 1944, an attempt to assassinate Hitler and to pave the way for negotiations was made by conservative elements, both military and civilian. But Hitler survived the bomb intended for him, and the Nazis retained their firm grip on the German state. The Allies were encouraged by their rapid successes in July and August to try to destroy the German armies before winter, or to cut them off from their homeland. Patton's mechanized troops ran out of fuel, however; the new German pilotless planes and rockets delayed the full use of Antwerp as a port of supply; and by late autumn it was clear that the Germans had retired in good order to their own Siegfried Line.

From the east, the Russians had been pushing on relentlessly ever since the turning of the tide at Stalingrad. In the campaign of 1943, while the western Allies were busy in Italy, the Russians won back most of their own territories that had been lost in 1941 and 1942. On November 6, they announced the recapture of the great city of the south, one of the symbols of Russian power, Kiev. They kept up the pressure during the winter, and started an early spring campaign in the south. By the autumn of 1944, the Russians had been able to sweep through half-hearted resistance from Hitler's Balkan satellite governments to a juncture with the Yugoslav communist guerrillas under Tito, and were ready for the attack on Hungary. In the center and north, they had recovered all their own territory, and were ready to attack Germany itself from the east.

The year 1945 saw the rapid conclusion of the Battle of Germany. In the west, the Germans made a last effort to regain the offensive in December, 1944. They pushed a salient out from the Ardennes toward Antwerp, isolating the American garrison of Bastogne. But, though the "Battle of the

Bulge" alarmed an Allied public—and even military—opinion that had grown used to unbroken victory, it was never a real threat to the now overpowering Allied military power. The Russians had not stopped for winter, but had pressed on through Poland to menace Berlin early in March. The western Allies broke through the Siegfried Line in February, crossed the Rhine, and entered the heart of Germany.

Early in February, 1945, the leaders of the three great Allied powers, Stalin, Churchill, and Roosevelt, met at Yalta in the Crimea and confirmed final plans for the conquest of Germany. It was plain that the Germans, whose key industries had been so riddled from the air that they no

longer could support their armies adequately, and whose manpower had been reduced to the very bottom, could not hold out for long. But the Allied planners were anxious to prevent, or at least to check, the race to be the first to arrive in Germany; and they wanted to arrange peacefully for demarcations between the parts of Germany that each ally was to occupy. The decision to give the Russians the honor of taking Berlin is one that, with many other decisions reached in the conference at Yalta, has since been severely criticized in the West. At the time, however, it seemed a natural decision, a legitimate recognition that during the two years of successful offensive against the Germans the Russians had worn

Nordhausen concentration camp. Bodies of Gestapo victims.

CHAPTER XXX

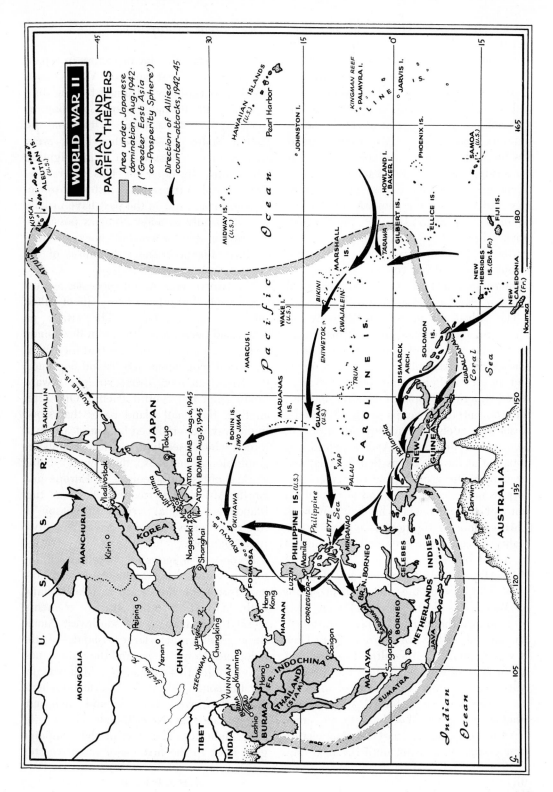

WORLD WAR II

ASIAN AND
PACIFIC THEATERS

Area under Japanese
domination, Aug.1942.
("Greater East Asia
co-Prosperity Sphere")

Direction of Allied
counter-attacks, 1942-45

down many more German divisions than had the western Allies.

The Russians fought their way into a Berlin already pulverized by the air power of the western Allies. Hitler went down to his death, as he had long promised, in a Germanic funeral pyre at his Berlin headquarters. Though his body was never found and identified, there can be no serious doubt concerning his fate. But legends do grow up under such circumstances, and the future may find Hitler in the company of the lost dauphin ("Louis XVII"), of the English princes in the Tower, perhaps even of the medieval emperor Frederick Barbarossa, whom the ballad has still alive in his subterranean castle awaiting the day of final German glory.

The Allied advance into Germany revealed for the first time the full ghastliness of Nazi treatment of slave laborers from conquered lands, of political opponents, and of Jews, Poles, and other German-styled "inferior" peoples. One after another, the concentration camps were liberated—Auschwitz, Belsen, Buchenwald, Dachau, Nordhausen, and others. And the world was appalled at the gas ovens that had claimed so many victims, at the piles of emaciated corpses not yet cremated, and at the pitiful state of the prisoners who had survived. This was one of the horrors of war whose reality exceeded the grimmest expectations of Allied opinion.

By May 8, 1945, Churchill and Truman (who had become the American president on Roosevelt's death in April) were able to announce the end of German resistance, the day of victory in Europe, V-E Day. It was symbolic of difficulties to come that Stalin was offended because the western Allies had accepted from some of the German army leaders a formal surrender at Rheims in France. He chose to announce separately, on Russia's part, the final victory over Germany, and not until the next day.

The Defeat of Japan

V-J Day, the day of victory in Japan, was now the great goal of Allied effort. Russia had carefully refrained from adding Japan to its formal enemies as long as Germany was still a threat. Britain and the United States, on the other hand, were anxious to win Russia as a formal fighting ally against the Japanese. This natural desire—natural in the sense of historical precedent, for coalitions in the past have usually sought to rally as many allies as possible—was responsible for many of the concessions made to Russia in the last months of the German war.

The two years of Allied successes against Germany had also been two years of Allied successes against Japan. The attack on Japan had been pressed home in three main directions. First, in a process that the American press soon christened "island-hopping," the American navy drove straight toward Japan from the central Pacific. One after another, the small island bases that stood in the way were reduced by American naval forces, which used both air support and the amphibious methods that were being worked out simultaneously in Europe and North Africa. The names of these tiny islands are now a part of the litany of American arms—Tarawa, Kwajalein, Iwo Jima, Okinawa.

Second, in a series of operations calling for the close co-operation of air, sea, and land forces the Americans and Australians, with help from other British elements, worked their way up the southwest Pacific through the much larger islands of the Solomons, New Guinea, and the Philippines. The base for this campaign, which was under the command of the American General MacArthur, was Australia and such outlying islands as New Caledonia and the New Hebrides. The start of the campaign goes back to the first major offensive step in the Far East, the dramatic and difficult seizure of Guadalcanal in the Solomons by the United States Marines on August 7, 1942. These campaigns involved jungle fighting of the hardest sort, slow and painful work. But by October, 1944, the sea forces had won the great battle of the Philippine Sea and had made possible the successful landing of MacArthur's troops on Leyte and the reconquest of the Philippine Islands themselves from the Japanese.

The third attack on the "Greater East Asia Co-Prosperity Sphere" of Japanese expansion came from the south, in the "CBI"— the China-Burma-India Theater. No brief narrative can do justice to the complex interweaving of events in this theater, where the main effort of the Allies was to get material support in to Chiang Kai-shek and the Chinese Nationalists at Chungking (see Chapter XXIX) and, if possible, to damage the Japanese position in Burma, Thailand (Siam), and Indo-China. After Pearl Harbor, when the Japanese seized and shut the famous "Burma Road," the only way for the Allies to communicate with Chiang's Nationalists was by air. It is perhaps true that the western Allies did not invest an overwhelming proportion of their resources in this CBI Theater, but they did help keep the Chinese formally in the fight. And, as the final campaign of 1945 drew on, the British, with Chinese and American aid, were fighting three Japanese field armies in this CBI Theater.

The end came in Japan with a suddenness that the Allied peoples, perhaps even the Allied governments, hardly expected. From the Pacific island bases, American airplanes inflicted crippling damage on Japanese industry in the spring and summer of 1945; the first atomic bomb fell on Hiroshima on August 6; and on August 8 the Russians, who had agreed to come into the war against Japan once Germany was beaten, began an invasion of Manchuria in full force. Faced with what they felt was certain defeat, the Japanese government, unlike the German, decided not to make a last-ditch stand in their own country. On September 2, after brief negotiations, the Japanese made formal surrender at Tokyo. Japan gave up its conquests abroad, and submitted to American military occupation. Contrary to the desires of part of Allied opinion, however, the Emperor of Japan was not dethroned. Purged of the most conspicuous militarists, the Japanese government continued under Allied—actually American— supervision to do the work of ruling.

Nature of the Allied Coalition

The "Grand Alliance," known in its last years as the "United Nations" (see p. 689), had mustered overpowering strength against Germany, Japan, Italy, and such collaborators as the Axis powers could secure in the Balkans, Southeast Asia, and western Europe. Britain, Russia, and the United States were the heart of the Allied coalition. But Nationalist China, for all its inefficiencies, had occupied the attention of hundreds of thousands of Japanese soldiers, and the resources of the French Empire and the French resistance movements at home and abroad had been most useful. The United Nations had been able to count on the resources of Latin America, and Brazil had been an active member of the alliance. In this truly global war, Brazilian troops had fought in Italy, which at the end had been the most cosmopolitan of theaters. There American (including Japanese-American, or Nisei), French imperial, British imperial, Polish, and other troops had fought, in addition to the Brazilians. At the very end of the war, even Argentina was brought into the United Nations coalition, when she declared war on Germany and Japan on March 27, 1945.

In the years since V-J Day, some of the steps taken during the war to hold the United Nations together, and especially those taken to secure Russia as a firm ally, have come under severe criticism. It is well to remember, however, that modern western history has frequently demonstrated the weaknesses of coalitions, and that the Allied wartime leaders were determined to profit by the lessons of history. One of the arguments frequently used by Hitler to hold his subordinates to his policy of resisting to the bitter end was the example of the break-up of coalitions in the past, particularly Russia's defection from the alliance against Prussia in the Seven Years' War, which unquestionably saved Frederick the Great in 1762 (see Chapter XVI).

The instruments of continuing Allied union were the conferences of the "Big Three"—Churchill, Roosevelt, and Stalin—with their political and military advisers and experts, and the more frequent Anglo-American conferences. Even before the United States entered the shooting war, Roosevelt and Churchill met off Newfoundland and issued the Atlantic Charter, on August 14, 1941, in which they declared for the freedom of the seas, equality of access to economic opportunity, abandonment of aggression, and the restoration of rights to conquered peoples. The Atlantic Charter has been attacked as no more than another empty assertion of impossible ideals, but the true realist sees in it an important step in rallying world opinion against the Axis. Later, formal conferences—between Roosevelt and Churchill at Casablanca (January, 1943) and Quebec (August, 1943), and among the "Big Three" at Teheran (December, 1943) and Yalta (February, 1945) —brought to a head consultations that had been steadily carried on at lower political and military levels.

There were always grave military and political matters to be ironed out. It was not easy to maintain even the Anglo-American collaboration, which was perhaps the closest military collaboration between two major sovereign powers ever achieved. For the actual direction of operations in the field, the British and Americans decided to set up, not just the sort of supreme command the Allies painfully achieved late in World War I under Foch (see p. 435), but a complete intermeshing of staffs. All down the line, an American in command always had a Britisher as his second, and a Britisher in command always had an American as his second. In the pinch, and in spite of normal national jealousies, the arrangement worked. An anecdote about General Eisenhower from North African days relates that he sent an American officer home, not because he called his immediate superior a so-and-so, but because he called him an *English* so-and-so. At the highest level, the Combined Chiefs of Staff, in close touch with top American and British government officials, did the over-all planning. The Russians were never brought into such close military co-operation, and in the field the Russians always fought on their own.

Strategic Disagreements

The major source of disagreement in grand strategy between British and Americans was the problem suggested by Churchill's famous phrase, "the soft under-belly of the Axis." Churchill himself and many of his commanders were convinced that the best way to get at the Germans was not a major, head-on landing in France. Instead, there should be a series of strikes at the "soft under-belly" from the south, through the gap at the head of the Adriatic into the Danubian plain, and through a similar gap at the head of the Aegean. The

CHAPTER XXX

Teheran, 1943: Stalin, Roosevelt, Churchill.

British brought out even then the consideration that, if this operation proved successful, the Allies would not only get at Germany effectively, but would also liberate the Balkan and Danubian regions *ahead of the Russians* and thus would forestall any plans the Russians might have for controlling those areas.

Against these arguments, the Americans insisted that the supply problem in the Mediterranean would be difficult, that the terrain involved was mountainous and poorly supplied with roads, at least until the Danubian plain had been reached, and that Germany had to be beaten where she was strongest, in the west. In favor of the attack from the west, they added the strength and convenience of "the unsinkable aircraft carrier," Britain, the shortness of the sea and air passage across the English Channel, the gains to be enjoyed from French assistance, and the propaganda value of a successful landing on the French coast, where the Germans had proclaimed their "Atlantic Wall" impregnable. The

Americans prevailed, and the main push of the Allies was made in northern France, supplemented by the push from southern France with troops drawn from the Italian theater.

The British and the Americans of course had to meet many other difficulties in working out their joint military policy. After the break-through in Normandy, the British would have preferred to concentrate all the Allied troops in a straight line across northern France and Belgium in a drive aimed at the Ruhr. The speed with which Patton's Third Army was able to move toward southern Germany led the Americans to back this drive as well as the Canadian-British drive farther north; the result was that neither one reached Germany before the winter set in. But the whole problem of supply, particularly the supply of oil and gasoline for mechanized troops, was so difficult that no one can say for sure that the single co-ordinated drive desired by the British would in fact have broken the Germans in the west in 1944.

Political Issues

A political issue that bulks large in retrospect seems not to have seriously divided the Allies during the war itself. This is the issue of "unconditional surrender." Here recent history had an overpowering influence on the policy adopted. Hitler had simply followed widespread German opinion in insisting that in World War I Germany had not really been defeated in the field, but had been betrayed by the false promises of Wilson's Fourteen Points into surrendering while still undefeated. This time the Allied leaders were determined to give the Germans no excuse for a future rallying point of this sort. The Germans must be beaten unmistakably, and Allied troops must enter Berlin as conquerors. There must be no political negotiation at all, simply unconditional military surrender. There was some opposition to this policy during the war, at least in lands of free political expression like Britain and the United States. This opposition rested partly on humanitarian grounds, but also on the belief that the prospect of unconditional surrender would inevitably stiffen the German will to resist, and would unite the nation behind Hitler instead of allowing Allied psychological warfare its full effect by promising anti-Nazi elements some reward for deserting the Nazi cause.

Another political problem made a much clearer rift between the British and the Americans. The underlying issue was just how far anti-German elements in France, Italy, and other occupied lands must go in proving that they were good honest democrats in order to secure the backing of the democratic western powers. Here the difference in the underlying tone of American and British policies was evident in the views of Roosevelt and Churchill. Roosevelt was convinced that if the Allies did not interfere to support scheming right-wingers in the occupied lands, but instead allowed their peoples to choose their form of government freely, then they would choose democracy. Churchill was much less idealistic. He was eager to use any elements that were hostile to the Germans, even if their hostility was quite recent, and he had little faith in the capacity or desire of peoples like the Italians for Anglo-Saxon democracy. Therefore he was quite willing to back Badoglio and the monarchists in Italy; Roosevelt kept insisting that the Italians wanted and needed a republic.

In French politics the issue was further complicated by Roosevelt's suspicions of De Gaulle, whose firm resistance in June, 1940, had made him the inevitable leader of the French movement for liberation. To Roosevelt, De Gaulle seemed a potential man on horseback, no better than Boulanger or Napoleon III. To Churchill, De Gaulle seemed indeed difficult, a man obsessed with the need to restore the greatness of France, but an indispensable ally. As it turned out, the Gaullists, in collaboration with the organized French resistance in the homeland, did take over the civilian administration of French territory as it was liberated, and France by free popular vote restored in the Fourth Republic a form of government essentially like that of the Third. In Italy, the liberated people voted the establishment of a republic. What had threatened at one time to be a serious difficulty between the idealistic American policy and the realistic British policy was resolved by the action of the liberated people themselves.

But the political issue that has bulked largest since World War II was by no means so clear an issue during the war itself. This is the problem of Russian domination in eastern and southeastern Europe. It is easy to say that at Yalta the western powers took much too soft a line with the Russians, allowed them to push their armies much too far westward, and relied foolishly on Russian promises to permit free elections in Poland, Hungary, Czechoslovakia, and the Balkans. This criticism may be supplemented by the old British motif of the "soft under-belly," by maintaining that the western powers should have struck as soon as possible, perhaps in 1943, from the Mediterranean into the Danube Valley in order to have arrived there ahead of the Russians. Proponents of these criticisms present us with an Iron Curtain drawn far to the east of where it now is, with an eastern and a southeastern Europe on the side of the West rather than on the side of the Russians.

The chief trouble with this argument is that it fails to take into account two basic facts. First, most of the small eastern European countries had no real tradition of western-style democracy; most of them had moved toward fascist totalitarianism before World War II (see Chapter XXVII). Second, during the war itself it was by no means clear to western leaders, or to western public opinion, that the Germans and the Japanese would be beaten so readily.

Even leaders like Churchill, who seems never really to have trusted the Russians and who was to coin the phrase "the Iron Curtain" soon after the war, did not dare risk losing the aid of Russian manpower and material resources during the war itself. Even in 1945, at Yalta, with Japan still very much in the fight, appeasement of the Russians seemed absolutely essential.

In the Far East, political problems seemed less serious—at least in wartime. There was general agreement that the Chinese Nationalists, however corrupt and inefficient their government was, had to be supported against the Japanese. Nor did the final decision to accept the continuance on the throne of the Japanese emperor arouse serious opposition in the West. The critical decisions on the Far East were rather the work of the troubled period after V-E and V-J days, when to the bitter disappointment of most western peoples it became clear that the peace was likely for some time to be no more than a continuation of war. To these years we now turn.

IV: The "Cold War"—The International Aftermath

By now it is clear to the reader that the great ills of general war take many years to clear up, that they are never neatly cured by a formal peace. As we have seen in earlier chapters, it took a long time to repair the damage done to European nations by World War I. In France, for instance, the human losses were so great that full recovery was impossible. The damage of World War II greatly exceeded that of the earlier war because of its farflung battle-grounds, the mass executions in Nazi concentration camps, the casualties suffered by civilians through air attacks, starvation, and disease. The total number of human deaths resulting from the war has been estimated at 22,000,000, more than half of them civilians, a total at least double that of World War I. The property losses have been judged in excess of $2,000,000,000,000, many times that of World War I. These tragic, gigantic losses can never be fully

EUROPE AND THE NEAR EAST

1954

A   NATO countries { North Atlantic Treaty Organization

▨   Communist bloc and occupied zone of Austria

◎   Capital cities

repaired. But they were at least offset in many countries during the decade following 1945 by a high birth rate and by brisk programs of economic reconstruction and modernization.

Of all the problems created by modern wars, perhaps the knottiest is that of reconstructing international politics. As we have already seen in Chapter XXIX, after 1945 a widespread revolution swept the colonies and dependencies of the European states. Imperial ties were loosened, and new independent states appeared in areas like India and Indonesia, which were once western colonies. In the world as a whole, a new international alignment developed after the defeat of the Axis aggressors. The rival states of the United States and Russia faced each other in a struggle that has been called the "cold war."

These troubles are not unprecedented. An aftermath of political turbulence followed World War I and the Versailles Treaty of 1919. Even the Vienna settlement of 1815, which seems in retrospect a generally satisfactory peace, was not without its aftermath, the revolutions of 1820-21 that Metternich tried so hard to suppress (see Chapter XIX). It may be, however, that the aftermath of World War II will seem even to future historians, with more perspective than we now have, to have been more than usually severe.

New Elements and Old
in the International Situation

New elements of course entered into the post-war situation. The atomic bomb, guided missiles, the very real possibility of bacteriological warfare and other horrible weapons for the first time made concrete and plausible the threat that a new general war might wipe out the human race—or at the very least might destroy the physical and the moral bases of civilization, and reduce what is left of mankind to something like another Stone Age. This amounts to the statement that the age-old balance between attack and defense, and, more important, between human ability to destroy and human ability to build and repair, has in fact been so altered that attack and destruction will be paramount. Still, this statement has not been empirically verified, and for all the horrors of the last two world wars there are today more human beings and more wealth on this earth than ever before.

Further, the existence of only one system of states related in international politics—the existence of One World—was new. Ever since Columbus, civilization had been building up to this One World, which was clearly foreshadowed in World War I. But after 1945 what had once been rhetoric became fact. There were still out-of-the-way pockets on the earth where the inhabitants had no direct concern with international politics, but by and large all organized political units were either in the western camp or in the Russian, or else they were wavering between the two.

The actual leaders of the rival camps were new to that position. In the world wars of Napoleon and the Kaiser, Britain and either France or Germany had been the centers of the opposition groups. Now the United States and Russia became the unquestioned focal points of world power. Although Russia had been an important element in international politics since Peter the Great, and although the United States had been active in international politics in spite of isolationist theories ever since it was founded, neither state assumed leadership until the 1940's.

But it is a grave mistake to simplify the situation, as some publicists do, into one where only the United States and Russia count as superpowers, and where all the rest of the world can be neglected. Great as these two states are in manpower and in production, actual and potential, the two together have no more than an eighth of the total population of the globe. And, although, thanks especially to the extraordinary productive capacity of the United States, the two together have a much greater proportion of the world's productive capacity, they still have less than the potential of the rest of the world combined. Neither state is, in fact, materially autarkic, self-sufficient. The leaders of both have shown by their actions that they do not regard their rivalry as a simple duel of rival autarkic units, but rather as a competition for the active allegiance of the rest of the world.

Indeed, if their rivalry breaks into a general war, that war will probably be decided in favor of the side that does win the allegiance of the strongest combination of countries. In short, any such war will be a war of coalitions. In the past, the successful coalitions have always been directed against a combination of powers that seemed to those resisting it as the aggressor, the perturber. In a sense, then, the future of the world depends on whether those who are neither Russian nor American decide that the Soviet Union or the United States is in fact the aggressor. The present rivalry between these two states is indeed a rivalry for the heart and soul of mankind.

This kind of rivalry, we repeat, is not new. It has in its current form, however, a depth and intensity attributable to a new combination of elements. Eighteenth-century wars, for instance, were largely struggles for sheer power, sheer territorial and other material gains, with perhaps a touch of emotional nationalism as an added incentive. With the wars of the French Revolution and the nineteenth century, nationalism entered in more forcefully, and remains, along with the struggle for power,

a major element in the present situation, never to be neglected. But now the opposition between the United States and Russia has taken on an aspect of genuine religious struggle. We need to go back for a parallel, not so much to the confused struggles of early modern times between Protestants and Catholics, as to the older struggle between Christianity and Islam. Communism and western democracy, as symbolized and focused in the struggle between Russia and the United States, stand opposed as rival and mutually intolerant interpretations of man's destiny on earth, as religions that cannot accept a world divided between them. Yet Christianity and Islam have for several centuries accepted just such a division.

The Communist Bloc in Europe

Concretely, the years following the end of the war in Germany and Japan saw the alignment of most of the world either on Russia's side or on that of the United States. After Yalta, the Russians disregarded what western statesmen believed were firm commitments to allow the countries of eastern Europe and the Balkans to choose freely their own form of government—and presumably to align themselves with the West if they wished. The Russians built up, by familiar methods of one-party politics, with rigged elections, proscriptions, pressures of all sorts, the solid bloc of satellite lands that we know as the Iron Curtain countries. To their immediate west, beginning early in World War II, the Russians simply absorbed, as constituent republics of the U.S.S.R., part of Finland, the whole of Estonia, Latvia, and Lithuania, and part of Poland and Rumania. They also annexed part of East Prussia, so that Königsberg, sacred to Germans as the home of the great philosopher Kant, was now Kaliningrad,

Top. *The center of Rotterdam, after 1940.* Bottom. *Rotterdam rebuilt.* (*The building at the upper right here may be found in the lower right of the top picture.*)

renamed for a high Soviet official. In eastern and southeastern Europe they organized "people's republics," dependent states with communist governments, in Poland, Czechoslovakia, Rumania, Hungary, Bulgaria, and Albania.

Their troops formally occupied about one-third of Germany, roughly between the Elbe and the Oder rivers, where they also organized a satellite East German Republic. The parts of Germany lying east of the Oder, save for the sections of East Prussia directly annexed to the U.S.S.R., they handed over to their Polish satellite. Here apparently a wholesale transfer of population removed the Germans into either East Germany or exile, and the Germans were replaced with Poles. Finland became part of the Russian system, but has subsequently enjoyed rather more autonomy than the other satellites. Austria, divided between the occupying forces of East and West, was detached from Germany, and Hitler's first major territorial gain, the *Anschluss,* was undone.

Berlin, to the east of the dividing line between the Soviet and the Allied zones in Germany, was occupied in separate zones by Russia, the United States, Great Britain, and France. Here on April 1, 1948, the Russians began one of the most bitter phases of the "cold war." By shutting off the land routes from the west into Berlin, they attempted to force the western allies to turn Berlin wholly over to them. The Allies stood firm, however, and achieved the almost incredible feat of supplying a great metropolitan area wholly by air. In the six months of the blockade, Allied aircraft flew over 2,300,000 tons of coal, food, and other necessities into western Berlin. They also set up their own counterblockade of eastern Berlin. On September 1, the Russians gave up, and Berlin returned to its sufficiently abnormal status of joint occupation.

Yugoslavia

One anomaly developed in this great bloc of Russian satellites in eastern Europe. Yugoslavia, which had refused to go over to the Germans in 1941, remained throughout the war a theater of intense guerrilla action. There were two main groups, the Chetniks, led by General Mikhailovich, representing the conservative Serb domination of the south Slav kingdom, and the Partisans, led by Joseph Broz, better known by his underground communist name of Tito. As the war went on, the communist-inspired Partisans gained ground against the Chetniks, who seem to have preferred to compromise with the Germans and Italians rather than continue a war on the communist side. By 1943, the western Allies, their eyes fixed on the paramount need of beating Hitler, decided to support Tito with supplies; when the Russians entered Belgrade in October, 1944, they found their fellow communist Tito in control.

Yugoslavia seemed a natural satellite. Yet in June, 1948, the world learned with some surprise that the Tito regime had been expelled from the propaganda union of communist states known as the Cominform (Communist Information Bureau), successor to the Comintern (see Chapter XXVI). Soon relations between Yugoslavia and the Russian satellite system were terminated amid mutual recrimination. Yugoslavia remained a communist state, though after 1948 Tito slowed down the process of land collectivization and sought to gain support from the West. In our present perspective, Yugoslavian nationalism seems to have proved stronger than communism. The break between Tito and Stalin, though furthered by the unwillingness of a strong personality like Tito to take orders from Moscow, seems to have been at bottom an expression of the strength of Yugoslav national feeling.

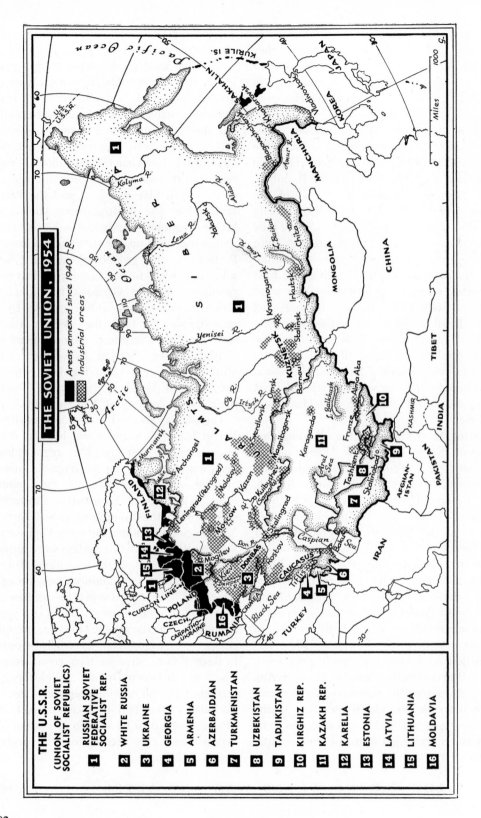

THE SOVIET UNION, 1954

Areas annexed since 1940
Industrial areas

THE U.S.S.R.
(UNION OF SOVIET
SOCIALIST REPUBLICS)

1 RUSSIAN SOVIET
FEDERATIVE
SOCIALIST REP.

2 WHITE RUSSIA

3 UKRAINE

4 GEORGIA

5 ARMENIA

6 AZERBAIDJAN

7 TURKMENISTAN

8 UZBEKISTAN

9 TADJIKISTAN

10 KIRGHIZ REP.

11 KAZAKH REP.

12 KARELIA

13 ESTONIA

14 LATVIA

15 LITHUANIA

16 MOLDAVIA

682

China

To the east, the Russians at the end of the war added to their bloc the most populous nation on earth, China with its half-billion inhabitants (for details, see Chapter XXIX). A land with which the United States in the past had had most friendly relations, a land she had for years sought to protect from European and Japanese aggression through her policy of the "Open Door," was now formally enrolled among America's enemies. Inevitably, this turn of events aroused great bitterness in the United States. The bitterness was expressed not only in the refusal of the United States to recognize Communist China, but also in the reproach that the American government, and particularly the Department of State, had so bungled relations with China that the Reds won by default—if not by the positive encouragement of fellow-traveling Americans.

These events are so recent that it is foolish to hope that they can be judged with detachment. But this much can be affirmed: once the negotiations of General Marshall had failed after the close of World War II, the Chinese Nationalist government could have been maintained on the mainland of China only by all-out American support, including almost certainly the use of American troops. It is most unlikely that in 1948-1949 any American government would have felt it had the support of American public opinion in committing the country to an active war in China.

Stresses within the Communist Bloc

The communist bloc is a vast area, a set of contiguous states occupying the "heartland" of the great Eurasian continent, from Leipzig to Vladivostok and Peiping. How solid a bloc it will prove to be is one of the great unsolved problems of our time.

It apparently survived intact an event that some observers believed might bring on a major internal crisis—the death of Stalin. After Stalin died, early in 1953, there were at first few signs of the kind of public struggle for power that had followed the death of Lenin three decades earlier.

Yet the communist bloc since World War II has been subject to two interrelated stresses. First, all its constituent states, including the two giants, Russia and China, have faced the internal problems set by the communist revolutions of which they are the children. The study of revolutions in the past suggests that, after the initial enthusiasm of the great common effort to establish the new society, there is a period of stress and adjustment. Russia may already have weathered successfully the Soviet equivalent of Thermidor (see Chapter XXVI). But communism also makes very great promises to men—promises of peace, material abundance, the good life for all, not in another world after death, but right here, now, or at least very soon. In the communist states these promises have not yet been fulfilled. Perhaps they can be partially fulfilled, enough to maintain the populations in a reasonable state of content; perhaps they can be softened and compromised; perhaps the populations can be made to accept such substitutes as the absurd nationalistic claims that the Russians were the first to invent virtually everything worth inventing. And perhaps not. It is significant that, though the Soviet Union continued after the war the pre-war Five-Year Plans, some emphasis was placed on consumers' goods, the sort of things that the ordinary person purchases for his own use.

We may be somewhat more certain of a second possible weakness in the communist bloc. The units of the bloc are after all nation-states, some of them with long histories as self-conscious, independent states and societies. Publicists who take the word for the deed have sometimes echoed the Marxist word that communism has now destroyed entirely the sentiment and fact of nationalism. But the historian will be very cautious here. He will incline to believe that not even the magic of communism can at once master the nationalistic forces that in the past prevented the merging of such self-conscious states and societies into perfectly unified blocs. It would be absurd to predict that Poland, Czechoslovakia, or China will go "Titoist" and follow the Yugoslav example of breaking with Moscow. But it would be simple historical common sense to assert that the present Russian communist coalition is by no means immune from the stresses and strains that have always made coalitions hard to hold together.

Communists outside the Russian Bloc

Beyond the U.S.S.R. itself and its bloc of communist countries, communism under Russian inspiration has been at work, in varying degrees of strength, all over the world. That strength is hard to measure country by country for the period since 1945. In some parts of the world, such as Malaya and Indo-China, the communists soon became organized fighting groups with partisan armies in the field; in 1954, indeed, they won control of northern Indo-China (see Chapter XXIX). In other parts, such as Spain, the communists have been outlawed, but they most certainly exist as an active underground movement. In still other areas, as in France and Italy, they are a legally organized party taking part in elections for legislative bodies. Here a yardstick of their strength is the popular vote and the number of seats they have obtained in the national legislatures. The yardstick, however, may often be misleading. In France, for example, the communists secured a bit more than a quarter of the popular vote in the national elections of 1946 and 1951. Yet students of the French scene believe that of the communist votes only a small fraction represented party militants; the bulk formed a "protest" vote, workers protesting the high cost of living, intellectuals and others protesting the do-nothing policies of post-war French cabinets and the alleged American threat to French cultural and political independence.

Broadly speaking, communism as an internal movement in the non-communist world can be divided for convenience into two broad categories. There are the communists in lands of darker-skinned people who have until recently, or who are still, in a colonial relation to the West; and there are the communists in the western states themselves. In the first group—Southeast Asia, India, Africa, the Near East—communism has appealed not only to class and economic resentments among the underprivileged, but also to the national and racial resentments that developed in long years of colonial contacts with the West. In the second group, the communists, though willing for propaganda purposes to appeal to nationalism in a way that would have shocked Marx himself, have in the main relied on discontented proletarians and their sympathizers among intellectuals.

The "Free World"

After World War II, the United States succeeded to the leadership of the "free world," the coalition opposed to the great Russian coalition. On this western side are the British Commonwealth and Empire, France and the French Union, western Europe generally, West Germany, Greece, Turkey, the Near East, Latin America, and the recent enemy Japan. In organized productive activity, in potential material resources, even in actual population, this coalition is stronger than the Russian bloc. Even in geopolitical terms, though the solid land mass of the communists may at first glance seem to have the advantage over the scattered lands of the free world, modern sea and air power has helped to knit the free world together in a military sense.

Soon after 1945, in fact, the United States took the lead in developing measures to strengthen the non-communist states, particularly in Europe, against possible communist aggression from without or subversion from within. Notably, in 1947 America sponsored the Marshall Plan (named for the Secretary of State, General Marshall) to accelerate economic recovery from the damage and disruption of World War II and thus to rectify conditions on which communists might otherwise have thrived. In 1949, the United States sponsored the North Atlantic Treaty Organization, "NATO," a defensive alliance including not only the states on the European and American shores of the North Atlantic but also Italy, Greece, and Turkey.

The central problem of the free world since 1945, however, has been not so much military as political: whether the free world really is united against the communist bloc, whether it has the political and moral resources to hold together. The "free world" is by no means uniformly free. Doctrinaire liberals in the West complain that some of the states lined up with them—Franco's Spain, Portugal under the milder dictatorship of Salazar—are totalitarian and anti-democratic; that the Argentine Republic under Perón is not only a dictatorship but is not even on the western side; that many other Latin-American countries are very far from being democracies; that throughout the Near East it is not the miserably oppressed people, but only the exploiting "effendi," who support the West; that throughout Africa America's allies, the

British, French, Portuguese, and Belgians, still hold the Negroes in colonial subjection; that semi-feudal Ethiopia is a caricature of a free country. To this liberal indictment the candid observer has to reply that it is in large measure true. If he is content to take a simple realistic position, the observer can remark that in an international crisis like the "cold war" the enemy of your enemy is in fact your friend. The important thing is that Franco, Salazar, Perón, and other dictators are at least bitterly opposed to the communists.

All but the most confirmed idealists would have to accept something of this last argument. But a profounder analyst of the world situation would add that gradually and over the long run one may hope that the western states may be able to use their influence, not to interfere directly, say, to overthrow Franco, but to promote conditions under which the Spanish people themselves can build a more democratic society. Or, to put the matter another way, we must not expect that the whole world will be able suddenly, or perhaps at all, to adopt the full way of life we call democratic.

This brings us to another central aspect of the problem of international relations since World War II. The war thrust the United States into a position of leadership. How well equipped has she shown herself for that position? Events since 1945 have shown that Americans lack the kind of experience that peoples like the Romans and the British acquired over the long years of their leadership. Americans are idealistic, impatient, anxious for quick results; they could learn much wisdom from the old French proverb—"The best is often the enemy of the good." But events have also shown the assets of Americans. Though they have continued to have difficulty with the color line in the United States, they have also done much since World War II toward ending the segregation of Negroes in schooling, in the armed services, and elsewhere. In relations with peoples of darker skin overseas, further, the Americans seem to be rather less overbearing than their British predecessors. They are not, like the Germans, burdened with a belief in crude racist theories. Though they find it hard to understand the religious views of people like the Hindus, for instance, they are used to the practice of religious toleration.

The enemies of the United States, for obvious reasons, paint Americans as simply another aggressive conquering nation, out to dominate just as conquerors have always dominated. Americans do not recognize themselves as so painted. Their success in helping make the world a better place will depend on whether they can convince the rest of the human race that they are not the usual sort of conquerors.

The democratic coalition led by the United States of course has been subject to nationalistic stresses and strains—the pride, the economic interests, the long traditions that make Englishmen or Frenchmen or Germans or Luxemburgers want some things that other members of the coalition do not want. But we have already seen that the Russian bloc suffers from comparable stresses. Communist difficulties, however, cannot really come out into the open, save for such an exceptional instance as the break between Tito and Stalin. Western difficulties can and do come out into the open.

In most of the free world it is possible for ordinary interested citizens to consider in public, in the schools, in the press, in political meetings, the problems that confront them. They can attempt to assess their weaknesses objectively, in the firm democratic conviction that they can understand and overcome these weaknesses. This, it is clear even from our incomplete knowledge of what goes on behind the Iron Curtain,

the communists cannot do. Rigorously controlled from above, they cannot learn the truth about the West—or about themselves. The experience of two world wars has shown that, in spite of the inconvenience and dangers of such openness of disagreement, in the long run full and fair discussion leads to better results than does suppression. The freedom of the free world is an asset, not a liability.

Old international tensions and disputes involving free nations have been settled, or at least eased, by difficult and sometimes painful negotiations. For one example, in 1954 the Italian Republic and Tito's Yugoslavia agreed to partition the area of Trieste, so long disputed between Italians and Yugoslavs (see above, p. 266). Another strategic and hotly disputed territory came a bit closer to having its status defined in 1954. This was the Saar (see also Chapter XXV); it was tentatively agreed that its economy should be integrated with that of France, but that its preponderantly German population should enjoy a large measure of political autonomy. The Saar settlement of 1954, though not definitive, marked a step toward the easing of traditional Franco-German bitterness, a bitterness that had only recently been exacerbated by the brutal Nazi conquest of France in the early 1940's.

In some ways, however, the West is handicapped by the fact that the Russians have a new, aggressive, revolutionary faith with special appeal to underdog groups everywhere. They have something of the proselyting strength that helped Napoleon as the heir of the great French Revolution. They can and do promise the downtrodden something new. All this need not mean that the West should be driven into a kind of conservative defensiveness, like Metternich after 1815 or the western democracies after 1918. It does mean that the western nations must be constantly aware of such a danger, that they must not let themselves appear, especially in the less advanced countries of Asia and Africa, to be backing up the established order at all costs, to be resisting all social and economic changes. Under-developed countries have applauded statements like that of President Truman in his inaugural address in 1949, when he promised backward areas help in the task of raising their standard of living. Since 1945, the western states have begun to understand that they must make their own democratic faith in reality what it has always been in ideal, a gospel of advance all along the line.

The Korean War

So far in this discussion of post-war international politics we have fixed our attention on the division of One World into two, the opposing camps headed by the United States and the U.S.S.R. Their opposition was open enough in the first few years after the defeat of Germany and Japan, the years of a cold war of propaganda and jockeying and the communist siege of Berlin. In June, 1950, the tension broke out openly into a real, though localized, war in Korea. The Japanese had annexed this once independent kingdom on the Asiatic mainland in 1910 (see Chapter XXIV). In 1945, Russian troops moved into the northern part, and Americans moved into the southern part. The country was divided in the middle by a line along the 38th parallel of latitude; a communist-inspired North Korean People's Republic was set up on one side, and an American-inspired South Korean Republic on the other. When all American forces except for a few specialists were withdrawn from South Korea, the North Koreans marched in to unite the nation under communist control.

In June, 1950, the United States did not follow the pattern that England and France had followed when Hitler and the other totalitarian leaders made their aggressions in the 1930's (see Chapter XXVIII). Instead of appeasing, America at once moved troops into Korea. It was a close call, but American troops got there soon enough to halt the North Korean drive and then to push them back well north of the 38th parallel. At this point, the Chinese communist government entered the war, and once more began a push southward. By 1951, the line of battle had been roughly stabilized along the old boundary between North and South Korea. To end the stalemate, negotiations were begun; they dragged on for two years, but an armistice was finally concluded in July, 1953.

The government of the United States had acted firmly to resist with military force the attempted communist aggression in South Korea. It carried on its defense of South Korea in the name of the United Nations, and received small but valuable detachments of troops from some of its allies. The American government was equally firm in its effort to limit the war to resistance to aggression at a given spot. The United Nations commander in Korea, the American General MacArthur, concluded that it was necessary to press the war into Communist China. But American officials, and in particular America's allies, feared that such a step would bring Russia actively in on the Chinese side, and would unleash the much-dreaded World War III. In consequence, General MacArthur was recalled by order of President Truman in April, 1951.

The United Nations

In spite of this open clash between communists and the free world in Korea, in spite of guerrilla warfare elsewhere in the

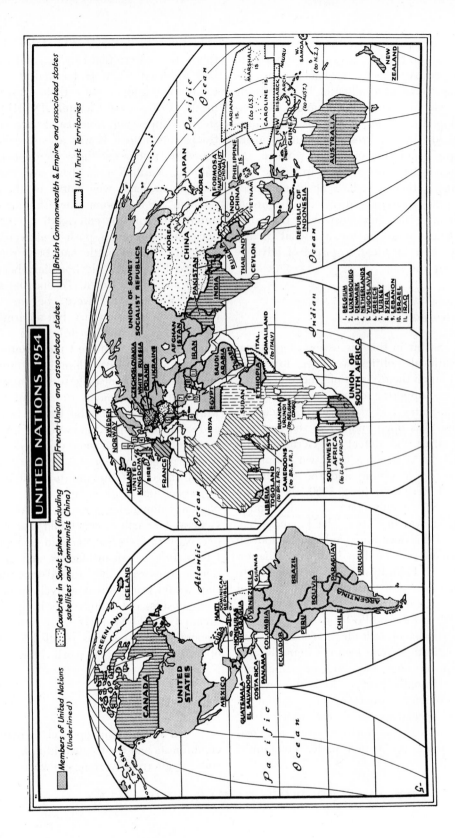

UNITED NATIONS, 1954

Members of United Nations (Underlined)

Countries in Soviet sphere (including satellites and Communist China)

French Union and associated states

British Commonwealth & Empire and associated states

U.N. Trust Territories

1. BELGIUM
2. LUXEMBOURG
3. DENMARK
4. NETHERLANDS
5. YUGOSLAVIA
6. GREECE
7. TURKEY
8. SYRIA
9. LEBANON
10. ISRAEL
11. IRAQ

688

East, there has existed since World War II an international organization in which both communist and non-communist countries meet in at least nominally peaceful discussion. This is the United Nations. Formed of active opponents of the Axis during World War II, the United Nations was broadened and endowed with a charter in a great general meeting at San Francisco in 1945. By 1950, it had sixty member-nations, including Russia (with extra votes for the Ukrainian and White Russian republics of the U.S.S.R.), the Soviet satellites of Poland and Czechoslovakia, and the maverick communist state of Yugoslavia. The former enemy nations were denied entrance, as were Rumania, Bulgaria, Albania, Spain, and Eire, since either American or Russian opposition prevented their admission.

The United Nations is the direct successor of the League of Nations, and its structure is almost the same as that of the League. Like the League, the U.N. represents a conference of sovereign states, a meeting of diplomats, not a world government in any way. The U.N. has a General Assembly, which can make recommendations on many issues of international interest; here each member-state has an equal voice. And it has a Security Council to deal primarily with threats to the security of states. This council has eleven members, five of whom—Nationalist China, France, Great Britain, the U.S.S.R., and the U.S.A.—are permanent members; the other six are elected for two-year terms by the General Assembly.

The key fact about the organization of the U.N., the fact that has made it for the most part simply a great international forum, is the veto power of the permanent members of the Security Council. For all save matters of procedure, the five permanent members must be unanimous if a vote is to pass the Security Council. Thus any one of the "Big Five" has the right of absolute

Secretariat Building, United Nations, New York.

veto in the Council. This veto was incorporated in the charter of the U.N. primarily in deference to the U.S.A. and the U.S.S.R., both of whom sought to safeguard their independence of action and to avoid being forced by the U.N. to follow policies of which they did not approve. The veto, however, was employed almost exclusively by Russia. The result was to cripple the effectiveness of the Security Council, but a by-product was the increased significance of the General Assembly, which became, in the phrase of the late Senator Vandenberg, "the town meeting of the world."

Like the League of Nations, the U.N. has special functional councils and agencies. The list of these agencies is very long and includes, among many others, the Trusteeship Council to supervise former mandated colonial territories, the Economic and Social Council, the International Court of Justice or "World Court," UNESCO (the U.N. Educational, Scientific, and Cultural Organization), the World Health Organization, the Food and Agriculture Organization, and the International Bank for Reconstruction and Development (the World Bank). The U.N. has its own permanent staff of civil servants, and has its headquarters in a dramatic new building on the East River in New York City. Many critics hold that this transfer of the world capital from neutral Switzerland, the home of the League, to the greatest city of the most powerful member-state was a mistake. It gives color, they hold, to the accusation that the U.N. is simply a device to further American imperialism.

The Record of the United Nations

It is still far too early to appraise the value of the U.N. Impatient advocates of a world-state are fond of pointing out that the U.N. is no more than a diplomatic gathering, that it has no "teeth" of its own, that it had to borrow the American army in the Korean crisis, that it must be transformed into a real government with the power to act directly on individuals, not just on states. These advocates of world government make much of the parallel with the United States Articles of Confederation from 1781 to 1789, in which the thirteen states were loosely organized under a Congress that had no taxing power, no police power, and no judicial power over the member-states. They call for an international duplicate of the American Constitution of 1789, which set up a federal government with these direct powers over citizens of the United States. In 1789, however, the thirteen former colonies had a common language, common political institutions and traditions, obvious common

Security Council of the U.N. in action.

interests of many kinds. The sixty nations of the U.N. today have hardly the beginnings of such things in common. It looks as if a world government today may be quite impossible unless it is imposed by force.

But the United Nations does exist, and its very existence is for all but the most impatient idealist a promise of something

U.N. promotes world health: disinfecting Arab refugees.

better. In its first decade of operations, the U.N. was not able to solve big problems like the "cold war" or the international control of atomic weapons. But it did arrange the partition of Palestine and keep the Israeli-Arab "little war" from becoming a major conflict (see Chapter XXIX). It did act forcefully, with United States help, against the aggression of North Korea in 1950—a single achievement quite surpassing any achievements of the League of Nations.

Finally—a major accomplishment of the U.N. too often overlooked—some of its special agencies have made a most promising start in aiding the underdeveloped, disease-ridden, famine-threatened countries of the globe. The World Bank gave them loans to finance basic projects like electric generating stations. The World Health Organization mobilized the medical resources of the world to nip in the bud a cholera epidemic menacing Egypt. And W.H.O. also launched campaigns to immunize European and Asian children against tuberculosis and to curb malaria in Italy, Greece, and many other lands. Experts from the Food and Agriculture Organization have gone to overcrowded states like Italy and India to advise farmers in ways to increase their output and make more food available. In these and dozens of other ways the U.N. has executed its charter's pledge "to promote social progress and better standards of living."

V: Other Post-war Problems

After 1945 the problems of international order, the threat of a third world war, atomic and bacteriological, seized the attention of the world. Yet each country was also confronted by its own domestic problems. Indeed, it may be maintained that if each country could reach better solutions to its own pressing internal problems, the world would probably be on its way to a better solution of the great question of international order. In the past, discontented, unstable nations have been a threat to international order, if only because their leaders have been tempted to try to mend domestic quarrels by getting their peoples united in war against a foreign foe. It is sometimes argued, for example, that the men in the Kremlin have exaggerated the threat of the "capitalist democracies" in order to distract the Russian people from the issue of their own relatively low standard of living.

The concrete domestic problems of post-war nations vary from state to state and are so numerous that it is quite impossible to list them all in our summary. We may start with a reminder that men have always faced problems of the kind that the post-war world has faced. Modern prophets of doom assert that the troubles of the mid-twentieth century are unprecedented, that we have got to find a complete solution for them or perish. But sensible men with the slightest knowledge of the past know that there have always been troubles, that this is what being human and alive means. With some human problems, like that of disease, no perfect solution has hitherto been possible, and it is most unlikely that physicians will ever be able to eliminate all disease. We should not expect more from our political, economic, and moral doctors than we expect from our medical doctors.

Economic Problems

Economically, the peoples of the post-war world have faced the problem of how to organize themselves to get the material things they want. This is the problem that our fathers knew in the simple form of Capital *versus* Labor. It has now assumed significant social, political, and moral overtones. Few men nowadays, even in the United States, defend the full theo-

retical implications of nineteenth-century laissez-faire, a society in which each man makes, buys, and sells whatever he can, becomes a millionaire if he can, or starves to death if he cannot earn enough money to live on. The practical issue in the modern West is not really individualism (laissez-faire) *versus* socialism or communism (collectivism). It is, rather, what degree and what kind of controls on economic activity there shall be, and who shall enforce them.

Broadly speaking, the western nations in their recent history have solved the problem by adopting some kind of "mixed economy." In this economy the government regulates industry, fixes minimum wages, enforces a host of other measures of social security, levies taxes increasing in amount with the taxpayer's ability to pay, and in many other ways determines in part what is produced and how it is distributed. But in these "mixed economies" it is still possible, within limits of course, for individuals to choose what they shall make or what services they shall provide, what prices they shall offer their goods and services for.

Within the "mixed economies" of the West the relative importance of the governmental or "public" sector and of the "private" sector has varied considerably. The United States has retained a relatively large "private" sector. Yet in the post-war years the widening of the "public" sector accomplished by the New Deal before the war was also maintained. Both the "Fair Deal" Democratic administration of President Truman (1945-1953) and the succeeding Republican administration of President Eisenhower widened and deepened the benefits of the federal social security system. The two American parties, despite the violence of their verbal disagreement on many issues, appeared to accept this central element of the welfare state and the mixed economy required to support it.

In Britain, to take only one of many

possible examples, the "public" sector of economic life broadened very rapidly after World War II. The Labor party, which controlled the government from 1945 to 1951 with its leader, Attlee, as prime minister, introduced an ambitious and largely successful program of socialized medicine. Labor also nationalized the Bank of England, the coal mines, iron and steel, the railroads, civil aviation, and a few other key enterprises. In every case—and in contrast to the confiscatory nationalizations of the Bolsheviks in Russia after 1917—the former private owners received due financial compensation. The nationalizations in Britain were partly a matter of doctrine, the belief of Labor in the moral desirability of a moderate democratic socialism. But they were in part a matter of economic imperatives; it was generally agreed in Britain that a sick but essential industry like coal could be rehabilitated, not by private enterprise, but only by national planning and financing. In 1951, when the Conservatives came into power under Churchill, they retained most of the innovations introduced by Labor. In Britain, as in the United States, there seemed to be large area of agreement between the two major parties on what kind of mixed economy they should have.

In all the mixed economies of the West there is still freedom of competition, in which the successful gain concrete monetary rewards and the unsuccessful lose their money. In Russia and in communist countries generally, by contrast, the ideal, certainly, is a society in which a few top "planners" lay out in advance all decisions on just who is to make what and what it will sell for. The individual has no more freedom or initiative than has the soldier in an army. But even in these communist countries there is a money economy, and the farmer or the worker has at least some consumer's choice. He can at least decide whether he will buy a pair of shoes or a piece of furniture for the house.

But so far as we can tell from news behind the Iron Curtain, the farmer or the worker can hardly hope to buy an automobile or even a television set. Perhaps it is just the head start the western nations enjoyed in the industrial revolution, but since World War II westerners have continued to produce far more, and to enjoy a higher standard of living, than the nations under communism. One of the marks that have come to distinguish westerners from communists is a belief that some economic freedom must be preserved, that total collectivization of economic life is, as our fathers held, a deadening and a stifling of something in human beings that makes them work hard, and, above all, imaginatively, inventively, efficiently. For that something there is perhaps still no better phrase than the one our fathers used— freedom of competition.

Political Problems

Politically, the western democracies have continued to face hundreds of problems at all levels, from that of the best way to run a city—whether by appointed city manager or by elected officials—up to the role of judicial bodies like the American Supreme Court, the relation between legislative and executive, the handling of foreign policy. In the immediate post-war period some states faced a decision on their basic form of government. In Italy, a referendum in 1946 abolished the monarchy that had at least theoretically reigned over the country since its unification in the nineteenth century. And in 1948 a constitution, providing a parliamentary, democratic republic with a two-chamber parliament, went into effect. In France, during World War II, both De Gaulle and the Free French outside the country and the resistance movement inside expressed disgust with the weaknesses of the Third Republic. They projected a Fourth Republic that would have a stronger executive, more stable governments, and less parliamentary maneuvering, and that would thus recapture the glories of France. But the new French Constitution of 1946 was most marked by its basic similarity to the Third Republic's Constitution of 1875 (see Chapter XXI). France continued to be a parliamentary state, to have a largely ornamental president and an executive cabinet responsible to the lower house of the legislature (now termed the National Assembly instead of the Chamber of Deputies). The new upper house, the Council of the Republic, retained few of the powers of the old upper house, the Senate. But in general the Fourth Republic in operation has been much like the Third. Coalitions of the numerous political parties have been formed and have broken up with great frequency, parties themselves have been splintered into discordant factions, and cabinets have gained and lost office at the usual rapid French rate. And, also as usual, underneath the turbulent surface the corps of permanent officials in the various ministries has given a good deal of continuity to basic French policies.

The French Fourth Republic shows one aspect of a central political problem faced all over the West. This may be stated as the question of the degree of power in political matters to be assigned to the permanent appointed expert—the bureaucrat, the professional—compared with the temporary elected official—the politician, in a sense the amateur. All the western nations, including the United States, seem to have been moving since 1945 toward a greater degree of government by experts at all levels from the local city or town manager to the national official. The sheer technological complications of modern civilization have made the use of these technicians imperative. Special skills are needed to make out a national budget or to be a public health officer or to report to a government on the complex maneuverings of French political parties. Yet the democracies have also sensed that some limit must be put on this trust in the expert if democracy is to persist. They have continued to believe that the great decisions of policy, even in local government, must be taken by men and women elected by their fellows to carry out general lines of action desired by the majority. Democracy is inevitably in part government by amateurs.

Civil Rights

Another closely related balance is essential in a true democracy. This is the balance between the rights of the individual, his "civil" rights, and the powers of government. Here there has never been an absolute unvarying balance. Freedom of speech, for instance, one of the most treasured of these rights in the democratic tradition, has never been absolute; libel, perjury, and treason have always been illegal forms of public utterance. In times of trouble, no doubt freedom of speech has to be somewhat curtailed. But if it is ever wholly curtailed, if in a given country it is ever forbidden for the individual citizen to criticize in any way in speech or writing the acts of public officials, then that country has ceased to be a democracy.

In modern democracies these civil rights have often been claimed by and for groups of individuals rather than for isolated individuals. These groups may be organized religious groups; they may be fraternal orders, service clubs, professional associations, colleges or universities. They may be groups organized to achieve by democratic discussion and election certain specific ends or sets of ends. Such groups range from major and minor political parties to such "pressure groups" as the Anti-Saloon League, the Society for the Prevention of Cruelty to Animals, and, in some phases of activity, labor unions and the National Association of Manufacturers. They may be groups of men and women singled out as "minorities," groups strongly marked out by race, nationality, or religion as distinct from the majority of a given state, like Negroes or Jews in the United States, or French-Canadians in Canada.

Here once more the truest democracies have sought to strike a balance. No state can let any and all minority groups within its boundaries do just as they please. A simple instance from American history is that of the religious group of the Latter-Day Saints, commonly known as Mormons. One of the original tenets of the Mormons was polygamy—or, more precisely, polygyny, plurality of wives. Polygamy is forbidden by our Common Law, and yet the Mormons claimed it as a religious right. American public opinion was strongly against the practice, and the price the Mormons had to pay for their inclusion in the United States and for the eventual admission of Utah as a state (1896) was the abandonment of that particular tenet of their faith.

On the other hand, a state and a society without a rich group life, without broad toleration of all sorts of group differences, would not be a true democracy. Many of the critics of democracy, such as John Stuart Mill in the nineteenth century (see Chapter XX), insisted that one of the great dangers of a democratic society was the "tyranny of the majority." The majority, they asserted, tended to use political measures and social and educational pressures to stifle the rich variety of group life, to make everybody conform to common patterns of belief and behavior, to produce a kind of mass uniformity. In the United States, Britain, France, or indeed any western society, the worst fears of men like Mill have by no means been confirmed in the last hundred years. Very modern artists like Picasso and traditional artists, antivivisectionists and vivisectionists, believers in birth control and opponents of birth control, nudists and legions of decency, and hundreds of other groups of all sorts continue to flourish in the free world, to quarrel among themselves, and yet somehow to live in common.

Yet the dangers of a deadening uniformity have constantly threatened modern democracies. The balance between variety and conformity is never an easy one to maintain, and in times of crisis like the "cold war" and the Korean War the balance is all too easily tipped toward the elimination of healthy group differences. In a democracy, groups seeking to change political, economic, and social institutions have the right to advocate such changes by peaceful means. But suppose the changes they advocate mean in fact the destruction of democracy? Should a democracy allow groups to promote anti-democratic measures, particularly when they seem to be in fact conspirators rather than advocates of peaceful change by open discussion? The United States in particular, and the other western states to a certain extent, have decided since World War II that it is necessary to curtail the usual civil rights of any such group, fascist or communist. The democracies have concluded that they cannot fully tolerate intolerance, cannot leave free those who intend to destroy all forms of freedom.

VI: Conclusion: The Prospect before Us

The Prophets of Doom

Underlying all these concrete difficulties of the twentieth-century world there has been a spiritual pessimism, a kind of fatigue. This attitude comes out most clearly in the writing of those intellectuals who may be called the prophets of doom. Among them are the French existentialist philosopher, Sartre, and in particular the philosophers of history, from the German Spengler, who died in 1936, down to the Englishman Toynbee and the American Sorokin. The philosophers of history feel bound to compare our fate with that of previous civilizations, and in particular with that of the Greco-Roman world. They do not agree on just how far down the road to final destruction we have come, and indeed on whether the direction we seem to be taking is irreversible. Many of them seem to feel that even though our western civilization is doomed, the human race as a whole is not. Our descendants may win their way through to a new dawn, a new civilization.

Now in the few thousands years for which written historical records are available, it is quite clear that man—biological man, *homo sapiens*—has as a species maintained himself, and indeed in the last few centuries has markedly increased in numbers. But the various groups he has formed, most strikingly the political groups, have lived and died. The Assyrian state, the Athenian *polis*, the Roman Empire, the Inca Empire, no longer exist, though something of their culture may survive. The German philosopher of history Spengler claimed that the higher cultures have a normal life-cycle of about a thousand years. This span he maintained is an objective fact, just as the seventy-year life span is an objective fact for *homo sapiens*. Since Spengler had conveniently decided that our own western culture was "born" about 1000 A.D., he was able to decide automatically that in the late twentieth century we should be very near our inevitable end. But most historians would maintain that western culture was "born" somewhere around the fourth or fifth century A.D., with the triumph of Christianity in the West, the fall of Rome, the beginnings of the German succession states. If this really is our birth date, then our culture has lived 1700 years, the equivalent for *homo sapiens* of an impossible life-span of 160 years.

Actually, we cannot prove scientifically that a given political and cultural group is dying; we do not understand what determines the life-cycles of these groups. We have a reasonably clear historical knowledge, however, of the growth and decay in the Mediterranean of a great culture, the Greco-Roman, and especially of its culmination in the Roman Empire. It is from this classic cycle that most of our modern philosophers draw their conclusions about our approaching end. Toynbee has brought out the comparisons between the dying classical world and our own—an art and literature over-elaborated, imitative, and lacking freshness, very great centralization in government, perhaps even a new proletarian religion over against the established one, then Christianity against paganism, now communism against Christianity. But no natural scientist would dare make prophecies on the strength of one case. And there are obvious differences between the world of declining Rome and our own, most conspicuous of which is our modern science and technology and our command over the material things they give us. Besides, to

Picasso, "The Three Musicians," 1921.

take a modern painting like that by Picasso, illustrated above: this art is perhaps strange, and it is experimental, building on the new theories of late-nineteenth-century painters (see Chapter XXIII); but it can scarcely be called over-elaborate, imitative, or stale.

The cautious historian looking at the world today will content himself with saying that the twentieth-century West has lost some of the Victorian faith in progress, shows a tendency toward pessimism about the immediate future of civilization, shows a feeling of insecurity. But even in making this statement, the historian will add qualifications. First, prophecies of doom are nothing new in the West. The notion of the end of the world and the second coming of Christ in a Day of Judgment goes back to the beginnings of Christianity, and keeps returning. In recent centuries the pessi-

mistic view has often taken the form of belief in the badness of the times, the rottenness of civilization, the need and therefore the inevitability of destruction and rebirth. Rousseau himself (see Chapter XVII) was a prophet of doom two hundred years ago.

Second, the historian will ask himself whether or not, especially today, these prophets of doom are good mirrors of ordinary men and women. It seems pretty clear, for instance, that in the United States since World War II there has been a gap between the pessimism of the intellectuals and the optimism of the people. Most Americans still believe in progress, and even in western European nations like France, where there is a kind of national fatigue, one may doubt whether the man in the street is in fine existentialist despair. Still, it would be absurd to maintain that even in the United States the two world wars, the great depression, and the threat of a third world war have left men in the optimistic frame of mind of their fathers.

The Optimism of the Enlightenment

As we have pointed out, there grew up among western men in the early modern centuries, and there came to full bloom in the eighteenth and nineteenth centuries, a view of man's fate here on earth which was essentially new. This is the view that all men may rightly expect to be happy here on earth. As St.-Just, the youthful colleague of Robespierre in the French Revolution, put it, "Happiness is a new idea in Europe"; or as Jefferson, with his gift for phrasing, put it, one of the rights of man is the "pursuit of happiness." Of course men have presumably always sought happiness here on earth. In historic Christianity, however, they did not really expect it here, but only in an afterlife in heaven; indeed, Christianity had an overtone of belief that happiness in heaven was in part at least a reward for suffering here on earth.

The *philosophes*, the eighteenth-century thinkers who set the broad terms of this modern optimistic world-view (see Chapter XVII), meant by happiness a condition or state in which each man had at any given moment what he wanted, a state in which each man—each woman, and, incredibly, even each baby—was not aware of being thwarted. To the inner state of this happiness there would conform an outer state of material plenty in which everyone would have what he wanted to eat, would be well-housed, would have a satisfactory sex life, and would of course enjoy good health, both mental and physical. The matter may indeed be put in terms of modern psychology. Men can rightfully expect in this world a life of perfect adjustment, a life without conflict, aggression, insecurity.

Broadly speaking, the *philosophes* held that such perfect happiness had not yet been attained on earth—an obvious fact—because there had grown up a whole set of institutions, habits, and beliefs that had brought evil into human life. Men in 1750 were not following the *natural laws* that would make them happy, but the *unnatural laws* that made them unhappy. The formulators of the new idea of happiness believed that the unhappy state of the world could be traced to a combination of the privileges unnaturally acquired over the centuries by the few rich and powerful together with the unnatural ignorance and prejudices the few had imposed on the many. They therefore concluded that the solution lay first in depriving the few of their unnatural privileges and, second, in disclosing to the many by a natural system of education and government the key to their own happiness. In short, they believed that men are by nature good not evil, reasonable not foolish, intelligent not stupid.

This, then, though put oversimply, is the essence of what may be called the democratic dream of the eighteenth-century philosophers, the dream of a heavenly city here on earth. But two hundred years later the dream has not come true. Some men still persist in it, holding that we have not yet conquered the privileged classes, not yet opened men's minds, not yet really tried full democracy. But the failure of the dream has caused many more men to question its very basis, the doctrine of the natural goodness and reasonableness of man. Such men hold that something profoundly rooted in human nature, and not merely in man's institutions or in his environment, makes a measure of unhappiness the natural lot of mankind. The modern western world, in consequence, has witnessed a process of reaction and adjustment to the contrast between the high hopes of the Enlightenment and the continuing evils of the world.

We may distinguish three broad classifications of these reactions and adjustments.

Repudiation and Revision of the Enlightenment

First, there is the reaction of complete repudiation of all the Enlightenment stood for. This reaction takes many forms. One of them, limited largely to some emotional intellectuals, is the sense of doom we have just discussed, the feeling that in trying to make this earth a heaven man has in fact made it a hell. More commonly, this reaction takes the form of denying all the premises of democracy. It is maintained that most men are wicked or stupid or foolish, that they need to be ruled by their betters, who are always few in number, and that therefore we must return to divine-right monarchy or to the feudal-clerical aristocracy of the Middle Ages, or else devise some new authoritarianism.

Second, there is the Christian view that men must return to the basic Christian concept of a mixture of good and evil in humanity. In this view, life on earth must always demonstrate the conflict between the divine and the animal in man, a conflict tragic and profound, not mean and vile as the mere pessimist sees it. For some of these Christians the desirable earthly society is indeed rather an aristocracy than a democracy. But many of them, like the American theologian and moralist, Reinhold Niebuhr, may be described as moderate democrats. Though they believe that the democratic dream in its radical eighteenth-century form is impious nonsense, they none the less hold that a balanced democratic society is the best way of attaining justice on earth, the best earthly reflection of man's dual nature.

Third, there are those who accept the aims of the *philosophes* and even in part the eighteenth-century estimate of human nature. But they find that the Enlightenment went wrong in its time-sense, wrong in its hope that its claims could be attained in a generation or two. These thinkers are essentially chastened children of the Enlightenment. They share the view that men are made to be happy, but are convinced by the events of the last two generations that wickedness and unreason are not, as the *philosophes* believed, rooted shallowly in a few bad institutions. On the contrary, evil and prejudice are deeply rooted in very complex institutions, in tradition, and perhaps even in man as a biological organism.

These thinkers have been much influenced by the emphasis that modern psychology has put on the irrational character of the human personality, on the subconscious and the unconscious, and on the consequent difficulty of the actual task of "enlightenment." They now think the task of making the world better will be long and difficult. But it is a task they believe can and must be continued. And they differ basically from the Christians in that they refuse to accept the Christian tension between this world and the next. They hold that man is a product of nature, and that the supernatural does not exist.

The important thing for us to note at the end of this long historic record is that between the second and the third groups we have been discussing, between the Christians and the chastened children of the Enlightenment, a practical accord is possible. It is indeed being worked out in the West. In this accord is the possibility that the men of the first group, the enemies of democracy, may be defeated, and that democracy may live on to give the lie to the prophets of doom. In such an accord we may preserve the willingness to put up with restraints, with imperfections, and with suffering without losing the hope, the dream, that is still alive for us in "liberty, equality, fraternity."

Reading Suggestions
on the Second World War and After

World War II

J. F. C. Fuller, *The Second World War* (New York: Duell, Sloane and Pearce, 1949). A useful military history.

W. L. S. Churchill, *The Second World War*, 6 vols. (Boston: Houghton Mifflin Company, 1948-1953). Magisterial account by a chief architect of Allied victory.

C. Wilmot, *The Struggle for Europe* (New York: Harper and Brothers, 1952). Important statement of the thesis that the Allies should have struck at the soft under-belly of Axis Europe, thereby saving eastern Europe from communism.

H. F. Armstrong, *Chronology of Failure* (New York: The Macmillan Company, 1940); "Pertinax" (André Géraud), *The Gravediggers of France* (Garden City, N.Y.: Doubleday, 1944); M. Bloch, *Strange Defeat* (New York: Oxford University Press, 1949). Three perceptive studies of the French defeat in 1940.

A. J. Liebling, ed., *The Republic of Silence* (New York: Harcourt, Brace & Co., 1947). Excellent collection of materials relating to the French resistance movement.

Many detailed histories of special aspects of World War II have been published, as have the memoirs of some of the leading participants. We may cite as examples of particular interest to American readers: in the first category, S. E. Morison's multi-volumed *History of United States Naval Operations in World War II* (Boston: Little, Brown & Co., 1947—); in the second category, D. D. Eisenhower, *Crusade in Europe* (New York: Doubleday, 1948).

Post-War Politics and the Cold War

C. Brinton, *The Temper of Western Europe* (Cambridge, Mass.: Harvard University Press, 1953). A cautiously optimistic evaluation.

F. Williams, *Socialist Britain* (New York: Viking Press, 1949). Sympathetic account by a socialist.

C. Palmer, *The British Socialist Ill-Fare State* (Caldwell, Idaho: Caxton Press, 1952). The title reveals the point of view.

C. Brinton, *The United States and Britain,* 2nd ed. (Cambridge, Mass.: Harvard University Press, 1948). General survey of the British scene, with particular attention to the economic problems of post-war Britain and to British-American relations.

E. M. Earle, ed., *Modern France* (Princeton: Princeton University Press, 1951); D. C. McKay, *The United States and France* (Cambridge, Mass.: Harvard University Press, 1951). Two good general introductory works on the problems of post-war France.

CHAPTER XXX

G. Wright, *The Reshaping of French Democracy* (New York: Reynal and Hitchcock, 1948); P. Williams, *Politics in Post-War France* (New York: Longmans, Green & Co., 1954). Valuable studies of practical politics.

M. Einaudi and others, *Communism in Western Europe* (Ithaca, N.Y.: Cornell University Press, 1951); M. Einaudi and F. Goguel, *Christian Democracy in Italy and France* (Notre Dame, Indiana: University of Notre Dame Press, 1952). Illuminating works on two important political movements in France and Italy.

H. S. Hughes, *The United States and Italy* (Cambridge, Mass.: Harvard University Press, 1953). A useful brief introduction to post-war Italy.

J. P. Warburg, *Germany: Key to Peace* (Cambridge, Mass.: Harvard University Press, 1953). Helpful survey of post-war Germany.

F. L. Allen, *The Big Change* (New York: Harper and Brothers, 1952). Perceptive essay on American social history during the first half of the twentieth century.

G. Kennan, *Realities of American Policy* (Princeton: Princeton University Press, 1954). Thoughtful work by an exponent of a realistic policy.

A. B. Ulam, *Titoism and the Cominform* (Cambridge, Mass.: Harvard University Press, 1952). A study of the communist heresy.

D. J. Dallin, *The New Soviet Empire* (New Haven: Yale University Press, 1951). Survey from an anti-Soviet standpoint.

G. A. Almond, ed., *The Appeals of Communism* (Princeton: Princeton University Press, 1954). An interesting symposium.

The Prospect before Us

C. T. Chase, *The Evolution of Modern Physics* (New York: D. Van Nostrand Co., 1947) and L. Barnett, *The Universe and Dr. Einstein* (New York: New American Library, 1952. A Mentor Book). Two helpful popular accounts of a difficult and most important subject.

C. G. Darwin, *The Next Million Years* (Garden City, N.Y.: Doubleday, 1953); R. Seidenberg, *Posthistoric Man* (Chapel Hill: University of North Carolina Press, 1950). Two stimulating attempts to chart the future of the human race.

P. Geyl, *From Ranke to Toynbee* (Northampton, Mass., 1952. *Smith College Studies in History*, Vol. 39). Lectures on Spengler and other important philosophers of history.

S. Hughes, *Oswald Spengler: A Critical Estimate* (New York: Charles Scribner's Sons, 1952). On a characteristic prophet of gloom.

A. C. Valentine, *The Age of Conformity* (Chicago: Henry Regnery, 1954). A representative work of the school of writers who fear that democracy may contain more peril than promise.

R. Niebuhr, *The Children of Light and the Children of Darkness* (New York: Charles Scribner's Sons, 1944) and *The Irony of American History* (New York: Charles Scribner's Sons, 1952). Characteristic works by an important American theologian and philosopher, who argues that Christian pessimism provides a good working basis for practical democracy.

K. R. Popper, *The Open Society and Its Enemies* (Princeton: Princeton University Press, 1950). A major work on the problems of modern democracy.

C. Kluckhohn, *Mirror for Man* (New York: McGraw-Hill Book Co., 1949). Modern problems seen from the perspective of an anthropologist and sociologist.

S. Chase, *The Tyranny of Words* (New York: Harcourt, Brace & Co., 1938). A popular introduction to semantics and the theory that words themselves are the cause of much misunderstanding in the world.

D. Riesman, *Individualism Reconsidered* (Glencoe, Ill.: Free Press, 1954). Essays on modern problems by a social psychologist.

Fiction

N. Mailer, *The Naked and the Dead* (New York: Bantam Books, 1954); I. Shaw, *The Young Lions* (New York: New American Library. A Signet Book). Characteristic examples of the American novel of World War II.

H. P. M. Brown, *A Walk in the Sun* (New York: Alfred A. Knopf, Inc., 1944). Unusually good novel about the Italian campaign.

N. Monsarrat, *The Cruel Sea* (New York: Pocket Books); H. Wouk, *The Caine Mutiny* (New York: Doubleday). Two justly popular novels about the naval aspects of World War II.

A. J. Guérard, *Maquisard* (New York: Longmans, Green & Co., 1948). Good novel about the French resistance.

A. Camus, *The Plague* (New York: Alfred A. Knopf, Inc., 1948). A novel about the human predicament, with important political overtones; by a talented member of the post-war generation of French writers.

L. Trilling, *The Middle of the Journey* (New York: Viking Press, 1947). Enlightening novel about an American ex-communist.

A. Huxley, *Brave New World* (New York: Bantam Books, 1953) and G. Orwell, *1984* (New York: New American Library. A Signet Book). Two celebrated tales of nightmarish utopias.

Illustrations

ILLUSTRATIONS

705

Index

A

Abstractionism, 351
Adowa, battle, 268, 596, 647
Adrianople, Treaty of (1829), 169
Aehrenthal, Count von, 306, 429
Aerial bombardment, 654, 666, 667; *illus.*, 660
Africa, Belgian imperialism in, 397; "Black," 636-637; British imperialism in, 384-389; French imperialism in, 393-397; German imperialism in, 397; imperialist rivalry in, 380-381; Italian imperialism in, 397; 1914, *map*, 385; slave trade, 38, 42; South, British imperialism in, 384-386; South, racial and national tensions, 640-642; "White," 637-638
Agrarian crisis (1848), 178
Agrarian League, 292
Agricultural revolution, 7, 11-14, 201-202; in France, 100; science and, 12; spread of, 12-14
Agriculture, collectivized, 489-492
"Aide-toi, le ciel t'aidera!," 173
Aix-la-Chapelle, Treaty of, 38
Alaska, 379
Albania, 599
Alberoni, Giulio, 22
Aleutian Islands, 664
Alexander, King of Yugoslavia, 559, 560; *illus.*, 559
Alexander I, Tsar of Russia, 136, 141, 142, 160, 161, 164-165, 170-171, 175; *illus.*, 170
Alexander II, Tsar of Russia, 312, 320, 500; foreign policy under, 320-321; reforms, 315-317
Alexander III, Tsar of Russia, 312, 320, 321, 322
Alexandra, Empress of Russia, 469-470; *illus.*, 481
Alexis, son of Peter the Great, 30
Alfonso XIII, King of Spain, 551-552
Algeciras Conference (1906), 429
Algeria, 394-395, 664
Algiers, capture by French (1830), 173
All-India Moslem League, 626-627, 630
All Quiet on the Western Front (Remarque), 446
Alsace-Lorraine, 258, 263, 288, 459
Alton Locke (Kingsley), 229
Alvensleben convention, 284

America, Anglo-French struggle in, 38-39, 42; sugar-rum-slave trade, 39
American Anti-Saloon League, 244
American colonies, British, 16; French, 20; Spanish, 22
American Indians, uprising under Pontiac, 77
American War of Independence, 16, 20, 43, 76-82, 276; background of, 76-79; Boston Tea Party, 78; Burgoyne's surrender, 79-80; Declaration of Independence, 76-81; Declaratory Act and, 78; effect on Britain, 79-80; European states and, 80; first bloodshed, 78-79; France and, 79, 80; French aid in, 104; George III, 76; Intolerable Acts and, 78; Loyalists, 80; Quebec Act and, 78; revolutionaries, 80-81; Stamp Act and, 77-78; Sugar Act and, 77; Townshend duties and, 78
Amiens, Peace of, 131
Amritsar massacre, 451, 625
Amsterdam, commercial capital, 9, 10
Amundsen, Roald, 376
Anabaptists, 84
Anarchists, 227
Angell, Norman, 418, 434
Anglo-American War of 1812, 139, 271
Anglo-Austrian alliance, 37
Anglo-French Entente, 427
Anglo-Prussian alliance (1756), 39, 42
Anglo-Russian treaty (1755), 39
Anne, Queen, 17
Anticlericalism, of Joseph II, 71; of Voltaire, 57-58
Anti-Corn Law League, 202, 244
Anti-imperialists, arguments, 404-405
Anti-rationalism, 358-359, 360-361
Anti-semitism, Dreyfus affair in France, 261-262; Fascism, 523-524; Frederick the Great, 40, 64; Hitler, Adolf, 531-532, 544-545; in Austria, 307; in Hungary, 309, 558
Antonescu, Marshal, 561
Aosta, Duke of, 519
Arab League, 633
Arabs, differences among, 633-634
Arakcheev, Aleksei, 171
Architecture, 352-354; classical revival, 87; of Enlightenment, 87; Gothic revival, 88, 155-156

Arnold, Matthew, 245, 344, 348
Artois, Count of, *see* Charles X, King of France
Asbury, Francis, 85
Asiento privilege, 10, 36, 38
Asia, British imperialism in, 390-393; French imperialism in, 396-397; *map*, 382-383; status in twentieth century, 610-630
Assembly-line methods, 195-196, 201
Atlantic Charter, 672
Atomic bomb, 622, 654, 666, 671
Auerstädt, battle of, 133
Augustus the Strong, Elector of Saxony, 33-35
Ausgleich, 296, 298, 302, 303, 310, 311
Austerlitz, battle of, 132, 133
Australia, 407, 410, 412, 644-645; commonwealth founded, 248
Australian Colonies Government Act of 1850, 410
Austria, 24; annexation by Hitler, 599-600; constitution of 1867, 297; dual monarchy, 296-298; entry into World War I, 433; Fascism in, 554-556; Habsburg Empire, *see* Habsburg Empire; Joseph II, 71-74; Lombardy and, 23; Maria Theresa, 69-70; Napoleon and, 140; Napoleon attacks, 131; partition of Poland and, 69, 70; society and politics (1867-1914), 306-309; Third Coalition, 132; Vienna settlement, 161; war with revolutionary France, 122-124; war with Germany (1866), 285-286; war with Prussia, 73
Austrian Succession, War of the, 17, 36-38
Autobiography (Mill), 214
Aviation, World War I, 444; World War II, 654-656, 660
Azov, 33, 34

B

Babbitt (Lewis), 348, 584
Babeuf, Gracchus, 121
Bach, Johann Sebastian, 89, 91
Bach system (Austria), 295
Bacon, Francis, 368
Baden, 131, 286
Badoglio, Marshal, 666, 674
Bagehot, Walter, 243, 369
Bahamas, 389
Bakewell, Robert, 12
Bakunin, Michael, 227, 318, 319, 516

Hundred Years' War, Second, 36

Hungary, 24, 73, 186-187, 296; aftermath of World War I, 451; dual monarchy, 296-298; fascism in, 556-558; independent republic, 189; minorities in, 302-303; Revolution of 1848, 188; society and politics, 1867-1914, 309-311

Huxley, T. H., 334

"Hymn of Hate" (Lissauer), 423

I

Ibsen, Henrik, 236, 346

Idealism, 357

Idyls of the King (Tennyson), 348

Illyrian Provinces, 140, 141

Immigration, United States, 274-275

Imperialism, anti-imperialists' argument, 404-405; areas involved, 380-381; Belgian, 379, 397; British, 247-248, 379, 381-393; colonies of settlement, 407; debate over, 401-405; defense argument, 404; economic aspect, 376-377; French, 379, 393-397; German, 379, 397; Italian, 379, 397; Japanese, 381, 399-401; migration, 377-379; movement in general, 375-381; new and old, 375-376; nineteenth-century, 375-412; powers involved, 379-380; results, 405-412; Social Darwinism argument, 401-402; United States, 380, 397-399; "White Man's Burden" argument, 402-404

Imperialism (Hobson), 376

Imperialism as the Latest Stage of Capitalism (Lenin), 376

Impressionists, 349-350

India, 645; aftermath of World War I, 451; Black Hole of Calcutta, 41, 42; British, *map,* 382; British ascendancy in, 43; British imperialism in, 390-393; East India companies, 38; Hindu-Moslem tensions, 626-627; Hindu way of life, 627-628; "Meeting of East and West," 391-393; partition, 629-630; political organization, 390-391; population, 392, 629; self-government, 629-630

India Office, 390, 391

Indian Civil Service, 392

Indian National Congress, 626

Indians, American, *see* American Indians

Indo-China, 624-625

Indonesia, Republic of, 624, 663; *illus.,* 624

Industrialism, 194-195; economic and social consequences, 201-208; middle-class aspirations, 203-204; Russian, 492-494; timetable, 199-201; working-class grievances, 204-208

Industrial Revolution, 7, 14-15, 193, 196-201; background, 196; banking, 198-199; beginnings of, 14-15; British leadership, 199; capital, 198-199; coal, 197; communication, 197-198; iron, 197; machine, the, 196-197; timetable, 199-201; transportation, 197-198

Inflation, Germany, 533-534; consequences, 534-536; end of, 536-537

Influence of Sea Power upon History (Mahan), 276

In Memoriam (Tennyson), 348

Inness, George, 349

"Insular Cases" (1901), 399

Insurance, houses, 7; marine, 38

Intellectual revolution, 333-370; Darwinism, 333-343; literature and the arts, 343-356; philosophy, 357-361; political thought, 365-370; psychology, 361-365; social thought, 365-369

International Labor Office, 590

International politics, 1919-32, 588-593

Intolerable Acts (1774), 78

Invention, 196-197, 198

Iran, 631-632

Iraq, 632, 633

Ireland, 99; home rule, 248-250, 574-575

Irish Home Rule Bill, 249-250

Irish Land Act of 1870, 249

Iron, revolution in manufacture, 197; smelting, 14-15

Isolation, myth, 275-276; United States, 582-583, 591

Israel, 634-635

Italia Irredenta, 301, 303

Italo-Turkish War, 397

Italy, assets and liabilities of united, 266-268; corporative state, 521-523; disunited, 23; Ethiopian conquest, 596-597; fascism in, 514-526; fascist domestic policies, 523-524; fascist foreign policy, 524-525; imperialism, 379, 397; in 1700's, 23; "march" on Rome (1922), 519-520; Mussolini, *see* Mussolini; Napoleon and, 136; Revolution of 1820, 166; Revolution of 1830, 175-176; Revolution of 1848, 182-183, 188; unification, 264-266, *map,* 265; Vienna settlement, 164; World War I, 440

Ivanhoe (Scott), 152

Ivan the Terrible, 500

Iwo Jima, 670

Izvolski, 429

J

Jacobin Club, revival of, 125

Jacobins, 111-113, 115, 116, 117, 118, 119, 120, 143, 144

Jacobite activities, 17, 18, 38

Jacquard loom, invention, 200

Jamaica, 635

James, William, 357, 358, 359, 525

James II, King of England, 17, 38

Jameson Raid, 293, 385-386

Japan, aggression, 1915-45, 593, 613, 616; defeat in World War II, 670-671; imperialism, 381, 399-401, 621-622; Manchuria seized by, 590, 593-594; occupation, 1945-54, 622-624; Pearl Harbor attack, 613, 647, 663; political development, 1919-41, 620-621; Russo-Japanese War, 322-324; World War II, 622, 663-664, 670-671

Jefferson, Thomas, 50, 269; in France, 103; neoclassical architect, 155

Jellachich, Joseph, 188

Jena, Battle of, 133

Jenkins' Ear, War of, 36, 41, 44

Jesuit Order, dissolution of, 57; expulsion from Spain, 75; in France, 172; in Prussia, 64; re-establishment, 157; refugees, 59

Jesus, Society of, *see* Jesuit Order

Jews, *see also* Anti-Semitism; in Austria, under Joseph II, 71; Polish, in Prussia, 26; Polish persecution of, 32; under Napoleon, 129

Jinnah, Ali, 630

Joffre, Joseph J. C., 438

Johnson, Dr. Samuel, 80, 87; *illus.,* 87

Joint-stock companies, 7, 9

Jonathan's Coffee House, 7

Joseph II, Emperor of Austria, 71-74, 75; *illus.,* 72

July Monarchy, in France, 179, 194, 204, 205

July Ordinances, 173

July Revolution, France, 172-174

June Days in Paris, 181, 190, 203

Junkers, 27, 28, 32, 44, 65, 75, 141, 280, 283, 292, 528, 538, 542, 546

Justice, in Age of Enlightenment, 55-56

K

Kadets, Russian, 322, 324, 326-327

Kallay, Baron, 305-306

M

Mably, Abbé, 83
Macadam, John Loudon, 197
MacArthur, General Douglas, 622, 670, 671
MacDonald, Ramsay, 503, 573, 574
Machiavelli, 525
Machine, development, 196-197
MacMahon, Marshal, 258, 259
Madagascar, 395
Madame Bovary (Flaubert), 344
Madison, James, 81-82, 448
Madras, 38
Maeterlinck, Maurice, 236
Maginot Line, 653, 656, 657, 659
Magyars, 186-187, 188, 295-296, 298, 302-303, 309-311, 556-557
Mahan, Alfred T., 276
Maillol, Aristide, 352; *illus.*, 353
Maine, U.S.S., 398
Main Street (Lewis), 348, 584
Malaya, 390, 624, 663
Mallarmé, Stéphane, 349
Malta, 131, 164
Malthus, Thomas, 209-210, 211, 219, 334
Man and Superman (Shaw), 346
Manchester, England, 8
Manchukuo, 616
Manchuria, 401; seizure by Japan, 590, 593-594
Mandates, World War I, 460-461
Manet, Edouard, 350; *illus.*, 351
Maniu, Iuliu, 561, 562
Maoris, 411-412
March Laws, 188
"March" on Rome, 519-520
Mariana Islands, 460
Marie-Antoinette, 96-97, 102, 111, 113; execution of, 116; story concerning, 107; *illus.*, 96, 117
Maria Theresa, 24, 35, 36, 38, 96, 107; reforms of, 69-70
Marie-Louise, wife of Napoleon, 137
Marine insurance, 7, 38
Marne, battle, 438
Marshall, George C., 619
Marshall Islands, 460
Marx, Karl, 158, 190, 195, 221-226, 227-228, 320, 334, 369, 508-509, 531; *Communist Manifesto*, 223-225; later career, 225-226; principles, basic, 221-223
Marx, Wilhelm, 538
Masaryk, Thomas, 300, 302, 304
Masefield, John, 446-447
"Massacre of Scio, The" (Delacroix), 146, 154, 169
Matteotti, Giacomo, 520

Mau Mau terrorists, 638-640, 647
Maupassant, Guy de, 346
Mauretania, 394
Max, Prince of Baden, 453
Maximilian, Prince, 256
Mazzini, Giuseppe, 165, 177, 182, 183, 189-190; *illus.*, 183
McCormick, Cyrus, 200
McKinley, William, 227
Mediterranean, diminished importance of, 23
Mediterranean campaign, World War II, 661
Mehemet Ali, 169, 314
Mein Kampf, 308, 536, 603
Melville, Herman, 343
Mendel, Gregor, 335
Mensheviks, 322, 470, 474
Mercantilism, 7, 9, 16; of Frederick the Great, 64; Physiocrats' attack on, 53-55
Meredith, George, 419
Mesopotamia, 460
Metallurgy, pioneers in, 15
Metaxas, John, 561-562
Methodism, 85
Metric system, 119
Metternich, Prince Clement, 159, 161, 167, 169, 176, 177, 184, 187, 188; *illus.*, 160, 189
Mexico, Maximilian in, 256
Midway Island, 664
Migration, 377-379
Milan Decree, 138, 139
Mill, John Stuart, 177-178, 214-215, 216, 320, 369
Mind and Society, The (Pareto), 367
Minorca, 41, 80
Mirabeau, Comte de, 104
Mississippi Bubble, 9-10; consequences of, 11
Mississippi Company, 10, 11
Modena, Duchy of, 183
Molière, Jean Baptiste, 82
Molotov, Vyacheslav, 507, 508
Moltke, Helmuth von, 437
Monet, Claude, 350; *illus.*, 350
Money, 8-11; *assignats*, 108
Monroe, James, 167-168
Monroe Doctrine, 168, 256, 276, 380, 584
Montagu, Lady Mary, 21
Montesquieu, 50, 52, 59-60, 83, 98, 181; American Constitution and, 81; political concepts, 59-60
Montgomery, General, 664
Moravian Brethren, 84, 85, 161
Morocco, 394, 395, 664
Morris, William, 356
Morse, Samuel, 200
Mosca, Gaetano, 366-367
Moscow, 29; Napoleon in, 142; siege of, 662, 664
Moussorgsky, Modeste, 354
Mozart, Wolfgang Amadeus, 90-91

Munich Agreement, 506, 601; *illus.*, 601
Murat, Joachim, 136
Music, Enlightenment, 89-91; in later nineteenth century, 354-356; Romantic movement in, 152-153
Mussolini, Benito, 267, 504, 506, 514, 515-516, 555, 558, 560, 561, 593, 596, 599, 659, 661, 666; *illus.*, 519, 521, 601; corporative state, 521-523; domestic policies, 523-524; early career, 516-517; fascist dictatorship, 520-521; foreign policy, 524-525; "march" on Rome, 519-520; rise to power, 517-519

N

Nagasaki, 399, 654
Nanking, Treaty of (1842), 390
Naples, Revolution of 1820, 166, 167
Napoleon III, Emperor of France, 181-182, 253-257, 258, 264, 266, 282, 283, 285, 286-287, 288, 314
Napoleon Bonaparte, 36, 96; abdication of, 142; attack on Austrians, 131; background of, 123; "Battle of the Nations," 142; Britain and, 131-132; Brumaire, *coup d'état* of, 125-126; *Code Napoléon*, 127, 143, 172, 175; Continental System, 138-139; death of, 142; economic program, 130; education and, 129-130; Emperor, 126; Empire (1807-12), 136-138; escape from Elba, 142, 164; Europe and, 130-144; First Consul, for life, 126; French army under, 133, 136; Germany and, 131, 140-141; government of, 126-128; in Russia, 142; Italian campaign, 124; Josephine and, 123, 127, 137; law and justice under, 127-128; legend, 143; meeting with Tsar Alexander I, 136; Prussia and, 132-133; relatives of, as rulers, 136, 137; religion and, 128-129; rise of, 123-125; saint of nationalism, 254; son of, 137; Spain and, 139-140
Narva, battle of, 34
Nassau, Germany, 285
Natal, 386
National Assembly, French, of 1789-1791, 103-104, 107-111; of 1848, 181; of 1871-1875, 253, 257-258
National Insurance Act of 1911, 245
Nationalism, Czech, 188, 300; Germany, 140-141, 184, 532; Habsburg Empire, 187; Italy,

INDEX

Tilsit settlement, 136, 141
Tirpitz, Admiral, 293
Tiso, Father, 602
Tisza, Coloman, 310
Tisza, Stephen, 311
Tito of Yugoslavia, 226, 667
Tkachev, 319
Tocqueville, Alexis de, 144, 179
Togoland, 397, 460
Tokyo, 399
Tolerance of Enlightenment, 57, 58; Voltaire on, 59
Tolls, river, 8
Tories, American, 80
Toulon, recapture of, 123
Toussaint L'Ouverture, 131
Townshend, General, 442
Townshend, Viscount, 12
Townshend duties, 78
Toynbee, Arnold, 237, 391, 696
Trade, in 1700's, 7-12; under Continental System, 138-139
Trafalgar, battle of, 132; *illus.*, 133
Transjordan, 632
Transportation, in 1700's, 8; revolution in, 197-198
Transvaal, 384
Treitschke, Heinrich von, 532
Trent, 266, 457
Triangle trade, 39
Trianon, Treaty of, 556
Trieste, 266, 301, 457
Triple Alliance, 301, 425, 433; *map*, 426
Triple Entente, 433; *map*, 426; formation, 425-429
Tripoli, 397, 429
Tristan and Isolde (Wagner), 355
Trollope, Anthony, 344, 356
Troppau Protocol, 167, 177
Trotsky, Leon, 473-474, 475, 476, 481, 483, 487, 488, 496, 497, 503, 504; *illus.*, 474; Stalin versus, 485-486
Tschaikovsky, 354
Tsushima, battle, 323; *illus.*, 324
Tull, Jethro, 12
Tunisia, 394-395
Turgenev, Ivan, 319-344
Turgot, 52, 97, 102
Turkey, Catherine the Great and, 68-70; entry into World War I, 433; Greek War of Independence, 168-169; in 1700's, 33; political changes since 1918, 631; "Sick Man of Europe," 32; wars with Russia, 43, 69-70, 305, 320-321; World War I, 440-442
Turkish Wars, 34, 43, 69-70, 425
Turnpikes, construction of, 8
Tuscany, Grand Duchy of, 23
"Twenty-One Demands," 613
Two-party system, British, 240-243
Two Sicilies, 23, 182

U

Ukraine, 175
Ultras, French reactionary group, 172, 173
Under Fire (Barbusse), 446
Union Act of 1840, 409
Union of South Africa, 247, 248, 386, 412, 640-642
United Nations, 597, 619, 630, 634, 640, 687-691; *illus.*, 689, 690
United States, agricultural revolution, 201; boom-and-bust, 584-585; Civil War, 271-272; commerce, 276; confident America, 588; Constitution, 60, 270-271; continental growth, *map*, 270; economic development, 273-274; entry into World War I, 433-434; federal union, 269-271; French Revolution and, 123; immigration, 274-275; impact of World War I, 581; imperialism, 276, 380, 397-399; industrialization, 200; international leadership, road to, 583-584; isolationism, 275-276, 582-583, 591; Louisiana Purchase, 131; Napoleon's Continental System and, 139; navy, 276; New Deal, 585-588; occupation of Japan, 622-624; population, 269; reconstruction, 272-273; social development, 274-275; Spanish-American War, 276; transportation, 269-270; War of 1812, 271; World War II, 662-666, 667-675
Unkiar Skelessi, Treaty of, 314
Utilitarianism, 83, 212-214; reforms, 243-244
Utrecht, Peace of, 3, 6, 22, 26, 36
Utopians, 216-221
Uvarov, 313

V

Vaihinger, Hans, 358
Valmy, 113, 122
Van Gogh, Vincent, 351
Vatican City, 267
Veblen, Thorstein, 347
Venetia, 124, 266, 285; Revolution of 1848, 188
Vendée, revolt in, 127
Venizelos, 441
Ventôse, Laws of, 117, 118
Verdi, Giuseppe, 354
Versailles, 103; march of women to, 107; *illus.*, 106
Versailles Treaty of 1919, 419, 457-462, 528, 529, 531, 539, 582, 589, 593
Victor Emmanuel, King of Italy, 265; *illus.*, 266

Victor Emmanuel III, King of Italy, 268, 515, 519-520, 599
Victoria, Queen of England, 193, 247, 390
Vienna, Congress of, 142, 148, 159-164; evaluation of settlement, 164; Revolution of 1848, 182, 187-189
Villeneuve, Admiral, 132
Vishinsky, Andrei, *illus.*, 497
Voltaire, 21, 41, 50, 52, 86; *illus.*, 46; anticlericalism, 157; *Candide*, 58; deism, 57; Frederick the Great and, 63, 65; in England, 57-58; letter to Catherine the Great, 66; pensioner of Frederick the Great, 63

W

Wagner, Richard, 354, 355, 532; *illus.*, 356
Wake Island, 663
Wallas, Graham, 359-360
Walloons, in Belgium, 174
Walpole, Horace, 88
Walpole, Robert, 11, 17, 18-19, 36, 42; *illus.*, 18
Warsaw, Grand Duchy of, 136, 137, 140
Washington, George, 39, 80, 87
Washington Disarmament Conference (1921-22), 590, 613
Water Babies, The (Kingsley), 229
Watt, James, 15, 196
Watts, George Frederic, 349
Way of All Flesh, The (Butler), 347
Wealth of Nations, The (Smith), 54
Webb, Sydney and Beatrice, 252
Weber, Karl M. von, 153
Wedgwood, Josiah, 88
Weights and measures, 8, 119
Weimar Republic, 527-542, 589; constitution, 529-530; depression, 1929-31, 539-540; extremists, right and left, 530-531; foreign policy, 538-539; impact of defeat, 527-528; in danger, 1931-32, 540-542; inflation, 1922-23, 533-537; Nazi party, 532-533; political alignments, 528-529; recovery, 1924-29, 537-538
Wei-hai-wei, 390
Wellington, Duke of, 139, 140, 142, 239
Wells, H. G., 252, 347
Wesley, Charles, 85
Wesley, John, 84-85
Wessel, Horst, 548
West Indies, 635; American trade with, 39
Westphalia, Kingdom of, 137; Peace of, 24

1870   Outbreak of Franco-Prussian War: leads to completion of Italian and German unification and to Third Republic in France

1882   Triple Alliance of Germany, Austria, Italy

1891   *Rerum Novarum*, encyclical by Pope Leo XIII: basic document of modern Catholic social philosophy

1898   Zola's *J'Accuse:* agitation over Dreyfus case in France
Spanish-American War: U.S. emerging as world power

1899   Outbreak of Boer War in South Africa

1904   *Entente Cordiale* between Britain and France: Triple Entente being formed

1905   Japanese victory in Russo-Japanese War, leading to partly successful revolution in Russia

1909   Budget in Britain: "soak-the-rich" taxation to finance social security measures

1911   Revolution in China begins: start of long period of political turbulence

1914   (June 28) Assassination of Archduke Francis Ferdinand at Sarajevo leads to World War I

1917   (March 8) Riots in Petrograd usher in Russian Revolution

1919   Peace conference at Paris following World War I; Treaty of Versailles

1922   (October 30) Fascist "march" on Rome: Mussolini in power in Italy